CW00918801

ENCYCLOPEDIA MADONNICA 20

RICHARD CORMAN

ENCYCLOPEDIA MADONNICA 20

MATTHEW RETTENMUND

ENCYCLOPEDIA MADONNICA
& ENCYCLOPEDIA MADONNICA:
20TH ANNIVERSARY EDITION

Copyright © 1995, © 2015 & © 2016 by Matthew Rettenmund.
All rights reserved.
No part of this book may be used or reproduced in any manner
whatsoever without written permission, except in the case
of brief quotations embodied in critical articles or reviews.

For information, address
matthewrettenmund@gmail.com or
Matthew Rettenmund
529 W. 42nd St., #6M
New York, NY 10036, USA

Design and layout by Anthony Coombs.
anthonycoombs@mac.com

Cover courtesy of Alejandro Mogollo.
Visit Facebook.com/AlejandroMogolloArt.

Back cover by Kiri Teshigahara.

ISBN: 978-0-692-51557-0

THIS BOOK IS DEDICATED TO MY MOTHER,
WHO TAUGHT ME HOW TO PREY.

©GEORGE-DUBOSE.COM

"It's endlessly entertaining to me how people grab on to things and turn them inside out and endlessly scrutinize them and make them mean what they want to make them mean. I think that's funny. Y'know? And it's funny to see, it's funny to hear how people analyze the work I do from my songs to my videos … in a way, it's great that they derive their own meanings from it, but I sometimes laugh and say, 'I never thought that for a second,' y'know? But I like it. It's good. That's what it's all about. It's about making people think."–MADONNA (1990)

ENCYCLOPEDIA MADONNICA:
20TH ANNIVERSARY EDITION ACKNOWLEDGMENTS

First and foremost, though this work is unofficial and affiliated in no way with Madonna directly,
I would like to thank Madonna for her work; for creating art and causing commotions
that transcend what they appear to be on the surface; and for secretly caring what people think,
but never letting that stop her from doing *exactly* what she wants.

**I am grateful to the following people for speaking with me,
facilitating interviews with subjects and/or providing or pointing me to valuable resources:**

Linda Alaniz-Hornsby, Nadia Ali, Gregory Antis, Joey Arias, Michael Ausiello, Kevin Aviance, Don Bachardy, Bruce Baron, BenDeLaCreme, Andre Betts, James Bidgood, John Blair, Mickey Boardman, Lisa Bohart, Pandora Boxx, Troy Bronstein, Betty Buckley, Carol Burnett, Charles Busch, Robin Byrd, Carmen Cacciatore, Michael Caprio, Keith Caulfield, Margaret Cho, Andy Cohen, Anthony Coombs, Wyn Cooper, Richard Corman, Shannon Cosgrove, Buddy Daher, Jesse Daly, Thomas De Pascale, Colman deKay, George DuBose, Chip Duckett, Jancee Dunn, Billy Eichner, Denis Ferrara, Karen Finley, Larry Flick, David Frank, Jordan Frazes, Nadya Ginsburg, Jess Glynne, Carin Goldberg, Brad Gooch, Gorgon City, Steve Grand, Tony Hadley, Darren Hayes, Paul Heller, Dennis Hensley, Coati Mundi Hernandez, Perez Hilton, Joe Jervis, Robert Joy, Kiesza, Mike Killmon, Evelyn "Champagne" King, Steve Kmetko, Curtis Knapp, Mitchell Kozuchowski, Bruce LaBruce, Chi Chi LaRue, Mary Lambert, Cyndi Lauper, Amanda Lepore, Sharon Maczko, Maripol, Angie Martinez, Maureen McGovern, Nick Mendoros, Michael Michaud, Liza Minnelli, Jerry Mitchell, Alejandro Mogollo, Jinkx Monsoon, Susan Morabito, Esai Morales, Haviland Morris, Michael Musto, Mýa, Ne-Yo, John Norris, Olivia Newton-John, Pegasus Street Artist, Pierre et Gilles, Sarah Pillsbury, Missi Pyle, Tim Ransom, Judith Regan, Debbie Reynolds, Nathaniel Rogers, Reid Rosefelt, Midge Sanford, Kenny Scharf, Fred Schneider, Andy Schwartz, Susan Seidelman, Don Shewey, Brooke Shields, Michelangelo Signorile, Liz Smith, Marlene Stewart, Jeff Timmons, Michael Urie, Kimberly Van Pinxteren, Louis Virtel, Michelle Visage, Tatiana von Furstenberg and Tony Ward.

I would like to thank the following people for their support and input:

Steve Berman, Anthony Coombs, Tim Hamilton, Melissa Hasan, Shaun Martz, Giulio Mazzoleni, Gregory Pace, Linda Rettenmund, Marvin Rettenmund, Lavinel Savu, Jason Viers and Gordon Wallace.

I would like to give extra-special thanks to my Kickstarter supporters:

Patrick A., AdamMaleBlog.com, Shaun A. Airey, Ray Allen, Marie Amadis a.k.a. Amber Flynn, Chris America, Tasos Anastasis, Anna-Clare, Robbie Antonio, Mark Aquilino, Neil Aristy, Nicolas Arroyo, Joe Artz, Ernie Ashby, Rafael Augustto, Kenneth Averett, George Avgouleas, Arturo Avina, Fil Baloca, Andrea Balocco, Joseph Barco, Renato Barreto, Dustin Basco, Chad Belicena, Emily Bell, Kristina Bell, Sandro Bellini, Andrew Geoffrey Beres, Shannon Berkstresser, Margit Berner, Nina Bialowons, Chris Bigham, Joe Bilodeau, Mark Blane, Michael Bourret, Todd Bowers, Anthony Branch, William Branch, Clayton Brandão, Sean Brennan, John Breslawski, Allan Brocka, Olaf Brodersen, Dean Brydges, Castro Burger, Bradley Burleson, Harry Burton, Jeannie Buxo, Paul A. Cabral, Jr., Christopher Calix, Steven Cameron, Donald Campbell, James Anthony Capelonga, Johnny Caps, Amanda Carr, Lucas Casanova, Simon Caskey, Trey Cauley, Keith Caulfield, Dwight Chambers, Chris Chandar, Eric Rico Antonio Chavez, Michael Chia, Bryan Chin, Matthew Chojnacki, Eduardo Cisneros, Ruben Cloetens, Sean Conwell, Anthony Coombs, Adam Cooper, Giulio Mazzoleni Corti, Richard Cotzabuyucas, Corey Creekmur, Mike Cronin, Houston Cropp, Dan Crowley, Dan Cullinan, Rob Curry, Nicholas Cyr, Edsel D'Souza, Buddy Daher, Jaime Danehey, Frederick S. Davidson, George Davillas, Cali Day, Jeff Dayton, Maurizio de Cillis, Qraig De Groot, Daniel Dean, Stephen Decker, Michael Delaney, Jessica DeRemer, Olivier Despouys, Bob Deutsch, Viktor Devonne, Geoffrey Dicker, Alejandro Mogollo Díez, Mark Doctrow, Jeff Dorion, Reed Drake, John Duff, Mario Alvaro Durand, Steve Eck, Mathew Edwards, Wendy Edwards, Gehrett Ellis, Sylvia Emmens, Sandra Engle, Marlon Esco, Abdi Estrella, Thomas Evans, Danny Falcione, Marsena Farris, Louis Feder, Taunya Ferguson, Pablo Vinicius Cardoso Fernandes, Jordi Betrián Fernández, Angel Love Figueroa, Kurt Fleagle, Santiago Fouz-Hernandez, Greg Fowler, Michael Allan Fox, Hector Martin Frias, Bobby French, Paul Fusco, Raymond A. Galazzo, Matthew Galley, Ian Garatt, Alex R. Garcia, Curtis Garca, Denny Garbuio, Wallace Gibbs, Jamie Gibson, Todd Giese,

Winston Gieseke, Stephen Gil, Melissa Gilson Schneider, Annmarie Giovanniello, Diego Giuliarini, Jerome Gonzales, Pedro Gonzalez, Eugenio Gorrasi, the Gottlock Family, David Goulart, Jason Govier, Steve Grand, Travis Gray, Joe Greene, Mark Greeno, Joe Gregori, Haavard Grimstad, Camilo Gutierrez, Rick Guzman, Delvin Gzz, Jason Hageman, Bonnie Hall, Scott M. Ham, Tim Hamilton, Jihyuk Han, Philip Hannan, Jennifer Hanson, Tim Harris, Melissa Hasan, Jason Haun, Mark Heck, Anthony Hello, David Henrik, Bob Henson, Donn Hestand, Antoine Higginbottom, Mike Hisey, Trina Histon, Rachel Hoffrichter, Mike Howerton, Brandon Hughitt, William Hyde, Massimo Iafrati, Alan Ilagan, Norman Jackson, Chris Jambor, Adam Michael James, Robert Javorsky, Lesley Anne Jeavons, Robert Jeffrey, Delray Johnson, Farrell Johnson, H. Scott Jolley, Jonathan Jones, Peter Jones III, Stevie Journey, Rich Juzwiak, Kosta Kalogerogiannis, Neerav Kapadia, Rajas Karnik, Craig Karpel, Stephanie Karten, Tracy Kendall, Adam Kennedy, Richard Kennedy, Joe Kirkendall, Sergio Kletnoy, David Kline, Lucas Koolschijn, Nick Koperski, Christopher Krakora, Kevin Kuzma, Ryan Labay, Phillip Lane, Chris Le, Hong Van Le, Shane Lear, Tom Legan, David LeMaire, Craig Lenti, Robert Levy, Ron Linssen, Kevin Lismore, Richard Littler, John Logsdon, Vincent Long, Scott Lyon, Craig Mackintosh, Jared Mackley, Madonna-Charts.com, Michelle Mama, Garrett Manry, Robert Marano, Peter Michael Marino, Powell Marshall, David Marshburn, Amanda Martin, Sheli Martin, Shaun Martz, Philip Matusavage, Ross McAlpine, Jordan McAuley, Walter McManamay, Matthew McPeck, Jason Menendez, Edi Menhart, Christopher Miele, David Miller, Matthew Mills, Andrew Miranda, Craig Moody, Sonya Moreno, David Morgan, Debbie Mostoller, Silvio Mühlheim, Jorge López Muñoz, Ricardo Nardelli, Abdi Nazemian, Sean Neary, Alexander Nesbitt, Andrew Nestler, Christopher Neu, Kelly Norris, Sean O'Connell, Jason O'Malley, Eric P. Olson, Jenni Olson, Frank Orlik, Eric Osborn, Gregory Pace, Aldo Parise, Wayne Parker, David Pasteelnick, Marc Patlan, Robert Patterson, Jason Pearl, Alex Pearlman, David Pearson, Michael Polimeno, Anthony Porto, Marek Bang Poulsen, Kerry John Poynter, Holly Cara Price, Mat Probert, Kuloko Quando, Chuck Raffoni, Denae Ramos-Pachucki, Layth Raoof, Vladimir Ratnikov, William Shane Ready, Dominick Recine, Linda Rettenmund, David Rios, Angela Rivera, Ruben Robles, Harry Rodriguez, Nathaniel Rogers, Scott Rogers, Patricia Rogler, Michal Rosenn, Gabriel Roy, Jeremy Rueger, Henry Ruiz, Michele L. Ruiz, Justin Russ, Patrizio Russo, Peter St. Eloi, Alexandra Sakason, Guido Alexander Sanchez, Rob Sanders, Adnilton Santos, Luigi Saturnino, Lavinel Savu, Chris Saxon, Erik Schut, Jeffrey Schwarz, Heather J. Shane, Jennifer Shapiro, Brian Sheperd, Joao Simoes, Jim Simpson, Marc Sinoway, Mark Slone, Todd Smee, Nina Smith Brannon, David Sockol, Miguel Sotelo, Toby Sowers, Michael Stabile, Yann Steininger, Michael Stern, Peter Stickles, Rachelle Stoller, Michael Stolper, Casey Strachan, Rob Stuart, Neil Symons, Chris Tackett, Duane Talley, Marguerita Tan, Antonio Samar Thomas, Juan Tovar, Robb Toyra, Ryan Turrin, Nick Tyrovolas, GertJan van Schuppen, Veronica Vasquez, Tomas Vazquez, Lammert Veendorp, Simon Venekeo, Venfield 8, Dirk Verbeeck, Nicola Vesco, Jason Viers, Gordon Wallace, Willie Wanker, Ian Webster, Brian Williams, Curtis Wong, Darren Wood, Steven Yany, James Yoke, Matt Zakosek and Stan Zeto.

ENCYCLOPEDIA MADONNICA ACKNOWLEDGMENTS

**Special thanks to the following people for their support and invaluable contributions to the first edition
(and, in many cases, to this edition) of this book:**

Christine Aebi, Chris America, Reagan Arthur, Ana Aulina, Mariam Ayub, Nancy Barr-Brandon, Glen Bassett, Staffan Berg, Michel Birnbaum, Paolo Bonanni, Paul Borysewicz, Mauro Bramati, Sandra J. Brant, Jane Jordan Browne, Nancy Burson, Cynthia A. Cannell, Stephen Caraco, Robbie Charrier, José Luis Cordoba, The Council of Fashion Designers of America, Charles Criscuolo, Eric Colmet Daage, Viney Daley, Keith Davies, Antonio de Felipe, A. Degenhard, Daryl Deino, Francesco De Vincentis, Lori DeVito, Delory Didier, Karen J. Dolan, Sebastien Dolidon, Kate Duffy, Thomas L. Dunne, David Dunton, Rodney Dyksman, Danielle Egan-Miller, Steve Eichner, Brad Elterman, Sandra Engle, Alex Escarano, Alex Eulen, Twisne Fan, J.J. Fenza, Miranda Ford, Laurie Fox, Peter Fressola, Evan Gaffney, Andrew D. Gans, Matthew Garcia, Teresa Gibson, Allen Ginsberg, Julie Grahame, Romain Grandveaud, André Grossmann, Peter Hale, E.B. Hallett, Matt Hanna, Eryk Hanut, Mike Hardwick, Joe Harris, Melissa Hasan, Nancy Hirsch, Nicole C. Hughes, Suzohito Imai, JEFFOTO, Harry M. Johnston III, Jill Jones, Terry Jones, Derek Kay, Marguerite Kramer, Yasuko Kuse, Joseph A. Lawrence, Sauro Legramandi, Olivier Le Guinguis, Martine Leoni, Robert H. Levine, Barbara Lewis, Greg Lugliani, Howard Mandelbaum, Chris Marquez, Brad Masoni, Moto Matsushita, Luca Mautone, Zafar Mawani, Giulio Mazzoleni, J.V. McAuley, Brian McCloud, Patrick McMullan, Elizabeth McNamara, Roberta Meenahan, Michael Mendelsohn, Steve Meyers, Bill Miller, Robert A. Moon, Robin Muir, Dean Mullaney, Laura Mullen, John Murphy, Michael Musto, Christopher Noble, Linda O'Brien, Mick O'Reilly, Lisa B. Overton, Panos Pitsillides, John Radziewicz, Juan Ramos, Monica Rebosio, Eric Renet, Linda Rettenmund, Marvin Rettenmund, Ken Riel, Amy Routman, Patrizio Russo, Ramon Santos, Yastaka Sasaki, Oliviu Savu, Julius F. Scott, Ava Seave, Fred Seidman, Richard Settes, Michael Shulman, Louise Smith, Cynthia Tebbel, Gloria Ubardelli, Thorsten Ungefronen, Giuseppe Videtti, Denise Vlasis, Katie Webb, Pete and Linda Weinzettl, Peter Wolverton, Kelly Worts, Tim Wright, Denis Xamin, Andreas Zeffer, Karen J. Ziffra and Jaye Zimet.

RICHARD CORMAN

ABDUL, PAULA
SPONSORED BY
PATRICK ALFICH

ACTING
SPONSORED BY
JENNIFER SHAPIRO

ART
SPONSORED BY
EDI MENHART

BEDTIME STORIES
SPONSORED BY
JUAN TOVAR

"BITCH I'M
MADONNA" (SONG)
SPONSORED BY
MICHELE L. RUIZ

*BLOND AMBITION
WORLD TOUR*
SPONSORED BY
RAJAS KARNIK

CONFESSIONS TOUR
SPONSORED BY
JASON VIERS

DANCETERIA
SPONSORED BY
DAVID RIOS

FUCK
SPONSORED BY
IAN GARRATT

GAY
SPONSORED BY
RICHARD
COTZABUYUCAS

GUITAR
SPONSORED BY
EMILY BELL

HARING, KEITH
SPONSORED BY
WENDY EDWARDS

HARRY, DEBBIE
SPONSORED BY
JASON HAGEMAN

HATE
SPONSORED BY
STEVE GRAND

"HUNG UP"
(VIDEO)
SPONSORED BY
RUBEN CLOETENS

INTERVIEW
SPONSORED BY
DUSTIN BASCO

"INTO THE
GROOVE" (SONG)
SPONSORED BY
ERIC P. OLSON

JONES, GRACE
SPONSORED BY
ALEX PEARLMAN

JOSE & LUIS
SPONSORED BY
JOE GREGORI

KAMINS, MARK
SPONSORED BY
CASEY STRACHAN

"LA ISLA BONITA"
(SONG)
SPONSORED BY
ANDREW
GEOFFREY BERES

LAMBERT, MARY
(DIRECTOR)
SPONSORED BY
MATTHEW MCPECK

LIKE A PRAYER
(ALBUM)
SPONSORED BY
SERGIO KLETNOY

MARIPOL
SPONSORED BY
NINA SMITH
BRANNON

MINOGUE, KYLIE
SPONSORED BY
HARRY BURTON

NEW YORK
SPONSORED BY
JAMES YOKE

OBAMA, BARACK
SPONSORED BY
KEVIN LISMORE

PENN, SEAN
SPONSORED BY
TOMAS VAZQUEZ

RITTS, HERB
SPONSORED BY
ROBBIE ANTONIO

SEX (BOOK)
SPONSORED BY
JIHYUK HAN

"SORRY" (VIDEO)
SPONSORED BY
JOE GREENE

STUDIO 54
SPONSORED BY
SCOTT M. HAM

TRUE BLUE
(ALBUM)
SPONSORED BY
VERONICA VASQUEZ

WARD, TONY
SPONSORED BY
ANTHONY PORTO

"WASH ALL OVER ME"
SPONSORED BY
LUIGI SATURNINO

MARIPOL

NOTES

Bold words within entries are cross-references to other entries within the book. Within each entry, only the initial use of each cross-reference appears in **bold**. Variations of a common word are sometimes chosen as cross-references in cases where confusion is minimal; for example: "danced" will lead to "dance" and "sexy" will lead to "sex" (ain't that the truth). When two consecutive words are potential cross-references, one or the other is chosen so as not to create the impression that the phrase itself is an entry; for example, "drag mother" may appear as "**drag** mother" or "drag **mother**," but not as "**drag mother**," since there is no entry for "drag mother," while there are entries for both "drag" and "mother." Still, no mothers were dragged in the creation of this book.

All release dates are US, except for cases where a product had no US release date. In those cases, the release date is for its first release anywhere else in the world, usually the UK or Japan.

All *Rebel Heart* album credits were pulled from the most up-to-date information available at the time of publication and may not be 100% correct. It is possible Madonna herself would flunk a pop quiz on who wrote and produced those dozens of songs.

For a complete list of resources (books, magazine articles, newspaper articles, blog posts, TV interviews, eavesdropped morsels) used in compiling this book, please visit encyclopediamadonnica.com.

A good-faith effort was made to determine the correct copyright holders of images used in this book in cases not covered by fair use. Please advise the author of any errors, which will be corrected.

If you find any factual errors, please write a nice note (why rip a new asshole when there are so many perfectly good ones already in existence?), have any interesting information to add, have rare memorabilia to share or sell or have any other comments, please do not hesitate to write:

matthewrettenmund@gmail.com

I am also at:

Facebook @matthewrettenmund and @boycultureblog
Twitter @mattrett
YouTube @ boyculturedotcom

Visit encyclopediamadonnica.com for corrections and updates.

©CURTIS KNAPP

ABDUL, PAULA: *b. June 19, 1962.* Pop star who was first a dancing **cheerleader**, then **Janet Jackson**'s choreographer, then an A-lister and eventually an *American Idol* (2002–2016) judge from 2002–2009. From early on, Abdul was a Madonna **fan**, saying in a late '80s interview, "I think Madonna is a true superstar. I really admire her drive. If I could—I mean, I really, really admire her hard **work** and her, uh, ability to not be afraid to make changes, because I really think she's writing the **book** on how to do it ..."

It's incredible to imagine now, considering the many female singers who have provided credible threats to Madonna's throne, but from late 1988 through 1991, Abdul was a serious contender. Perhaps feeling the heat, Madonna offered some tart advice to her rival on the eve of Abdul's first tour (1991): "If she's really trying to sing for real for the first time, then she should stand still, y'know? 'Cause it's really difficult unless you're in amazing shape."

Translation: *You can't sing and you're fat.* Meow.

When Abdul was slapped with an unsuccessful **lawsuit** by a backup singer claiming she had ghosted Abdul's vocals, cold-hearted Madonna couldn't resist mocking the situation. On **MTV**'s 10th anniversary special, Madonna mimicked a sobbing Abdul (without naming her), whining, "I *did* sing on that record ... I'll prove it to you," then launched into a comically strained vocal exercise.

Abdul should've been used to the abuse—Madonna had already embarrassed her by quizzing **Arsenio Hall** about their relationship, intimating that Hall had left Abdul's tights askew backstage at the **MTV Video Music Awards**.

There were apparently no lingering hard feelings on Abdul's part after Madonna's teasing. Abdul tweeted of Madonna's **Super Bowl** performance, "O. M. G. #Madonna #killedit BRILLIANT #HalfTime show!!!!!!!!!!!!! SUPERB choreography & Madonna was FLAWLESS!"

ABORTION: The first true Madonna scandal™ had to do with abortion. In the song **"Papa Don't Preach,"** the singer's desire to "keep my baby" *could* refer to keeping her lover, but it more likely referred to carrying her **pregnancy** to term. Even if the singer was keeping it, keeping it meant there had been a decision, which meant abortion had been in the mix.

In the video, there is no question that the singer is nixing abortion—Madonna grasps her abdomen protectively.

In her personal life, Madonna confirmed in the October 1994 issue of *The Face* **magazine** that she'd had "several abortions," though backpedaled a bit during a subsequent Scandinavian **TV** interview, saying, "Well, some people think that two is several ..."

Barbara Victor's 2001 biography *Goddess* made headlines by asserting that Madonna had had 11 abortions from the time she was 18 until the time she was 40, including while she was with the artist **Jean-Michel Basquiat** in the '80s, a claim Madonna's UK publicist dismissed as "completely untrue." Film runner **Andy Bird** publicly confirmed a 1998 abortion.

From what is known, it seems likely that Madonna had at least one abortion while she was seeing **Jellybean Benitez**, which occurred just before *The Virgin Tour* kicked off. She was reportedly pregnant when **Sean Penn** proposed to her in 1985, but decided the timing was off and had an abortion even though Penn wanted them to keep the baby. She also reportedly ended a pregnancy by **Tony Ward** in December 1990.

During two separate *Truth or Dare*-era interviews, Madonna said of her lack of **privacy** that she sometimes feels like the whole world even knows "when I have an abortion." Around that time, Madonna is said to have approached a taxi full of **fans** outside her apartment in **New York** to expressly tell them not to follow her. "Not today," she implored. Her request was ignored, and so they witnessed her journey to an ob-gyn.

Before a *Girlie Show World Tour* performance, **feminist** icon Gloria Steinem presented Madonna with two bracelets, one inscribed with the names of women who died as a result of botched illegal abortions and one engraved, "Because of you, there will be fewer of these." Madonna contributed her song **"Goodbye to Innocence"** to the pro-choice album *Just Say Roe* in 1994.

A woman's right to have an abortion falls well within Madonna's message of self-determination. Her inability to avail herself of the procedure privately speaks to the slippery slope that is **fame**.

> "It's common to have abortions. Many people have them and it's nothing to be ashamed of."—MADONNA (1994)

ACADEMIA: With the rise of pop culture as a social science, Madonna crept into college curricula and scholarly writing beginning in the late '80s. The University of Colorado at Boulder (Boulder, CO) started the ball rolling with a course called "Madonna Undressed," dealing with issues of body language, costuming, gender, spectator response, post-modernism and **gay** imagery.

Institutions as far-flung as Harvard (Cambridge, MA), Florida State University (600 W. College Ave., Tallahassee, FL), the University of Chicago (5801 S. Ellis Ave., Chicago, IL) and Wayne State University (42 W. Warren Ave., Detroit, MI) have offered courses devoted to Madonna's influence on the culture. Any complete course on pop culture or **feminism** since the early '90s has touched on Madonna's music and videos.

The concept seems to amuse Madonna, though she's made it clear that many of the abstract intentions laid at her **feet** by scholars are figments of their imaginations. But Madonna scholarship is a field that does not require her input or her express intent to validate its theories.

In November 1992, *The Madonna Connection* [SEE: **bibliography (about Madonna)**], an entire **book** on

Madonna scholarship edited by Cathy Schwichtenberg, was published. Six months later, Cleis Press published Lisa Frank's book of essays on **sex** and popular culture, *Madonnarama*, featuring the opinions of Susie Bright, Pat Califia, Simon Frith and others.

ACCENT: Madonna's short-A-dominated Midwest accent has been her most consistent, though starting around 1995, many listeners have perceived from her an affected British accent.

At the **VH1 Fashion Awards**, it was noted by *Entertainment Weekly* that Madonna was "enunciating every long O and trilling every R." A dialect coach said it was a case of Classical or Elevated American English, while **Liz Rosenberg** said, "She's been undergoing rigorous vocal coaching to strengthen her singing voice for the *Evita* soundtrack, and it may have affected her speech ..." (That training also left Madonna using a hard R, such as in the word "narcissist" in her 2015 song **"Rebel Heart."**)

Madonna's so-called British accent only intensifies when she's around British people, for example throughout *The Next Best Thing* opposite **Rupert Everett**. It was at its most prominent during the period in which she lived in **England** and was married to **Guy Ritchie**. Not so strange for an American to unconsciously adapt a slight accent when surrounded by Brits, but something else is also often at play when Madonna's accent switches up—Madonna, when discussing serious or sensitive subjects, seems to trade "and" for "ahnd," speaking in a more clipped way that can sound British. In short, if she is on the defensive, the **Queen of Pop** can sound like the **Queen of England**.

This might be attributable to her adoration of teacher **Christopher Flynn**, who spoke with a long A; after all, while Madonna's accent got more British in the '90s, hints of it can be heard in some of her earliest recorded interviews.

Madonna has put on a variety of accents intentionally for fun and profit, including the tough-girl talk she frequently slips into for comedic effect. In the film *Who's That Girl*, she arguably upstages her own otherwise sparkling performance with a daffy Outer Boroughs accent, but a sorta-Queens, New Yawk, accent has **worked** on her cover of **"Santa Baby,"** in sketches on her *Blond Ambition World Tour* and in the songs **"Cry Baby"** and **"Now I'm Following You (Part II)"** on *I'm Breathless: Music from and Inspired by the Film Dick Tracy*.

Madonna attempted a straight-up British accent on purpose in an ill-advised sketch about **Princess Diana** on her first *Saturday Night Live* appearance, but more

Madonna flaunts accessories to die for in this rare print ad for a *Tatler* cover story.

bizarre is her histrionic Spanish accent, unveiled during that same episode in a skit as fictitious Latin American singer "Marika." The latter accent followed her, showing up again on her instant **camp** classic **"I'm Going Bananas."**

By far, Madonna's most impressive use of accent was on the "Coffee Talk with Linda Richman" sketch from *SNL*, in which her Lawn Guyland accent as "Liz Rosenberg" (not that one!) killed.

> "I can say what I wanna say in the inflection and accent that I wanna say it in."
> —MADONNA, *THE ROSIE O'DONNELL SHOW* (2000)

> "Just getting [Wallis Simpson's] accent right was tough. The way she speaks is so odd. She had this, y'know, what they call a transcontinental accent. It's the way the movie stars in Hollywood spoke—Americans trying to sound like they're English. And it happens to a lot of Americans that move to England, you start to speak half and half, which is a little bit bizarre."
> —MADONNA ON DIRECTING *W.E.* (2012)

ACCESS HOLLYWOOD: *Airdates: September 9, 1996–.* Long-running syndicated entertainment show that features Madonna regularly and, as per its celeb-friendly policy, respectfully.

She has been interviewed on the show many times, including a 2003 Nancy O'Dell interview in Beverly Hills about the *American Life* album. Madonna said, "Since, y'know, **9/11**, it feels like danger and, and suffering is creeping closer and closer to us." She described her state of mind about the Iraq War as "haunted."

In her sit-downs with Madonna, O'Dell always looks like she's prepared to bolt from the room at a moment's notice in case Madonna suddenly tries to snatch her wig ... which admittedly would be terrifying since O'Dell doesn't wear one.

ACCESSORIES: In 1985, Madonna was speaking about her reliance on stylist **Maripol** when she said, "I feel naked without accessories."

ACCOMMODATIONS: Where to stay when one is the world's biggest star? Crash with friends? Au contraire, Madonna always stays at world-class establishments when she's traveling, unless she is a short flight away from one of her homes, in which case she's been known to fly **back** and forth rather than cool her heels in a hotel.

When Madonna visits her **father** and **stepmother** in **Michigan**, she stays with them, at times sleeping on the floor.

When on tour in Detroit, she has stayed at the Hotel St. Regis (3071 W. Grand Blvd., Detroit, MI). In the Windy City, she's graced both the Ritz-Carlton Chicago (160 E.

Pearson St., Chicago, IL) and the Four Seasons (120 E. Delaware Pl., Chicago, IL) with her presence.

During her *A League of Their Own* shoot, Madonna spent time in **Evansville**, Indiana, where she and other cast members took over separate private houses. Madonna wasn't thrilled with hers, publicly complaining about the cable and saying she missed her **MTV**. The home's realtor, Geri Garrison, disputed that complaint.

In **England**, Madonna has stayed at the exclusive Lanesborough **London** (Hyde Park Corner, London, England, UK), usually in the Royal Suite.

When in **Paris**, she's often at the Ritz Paris (15, place Vendôme, Paris, France), though she opted for the Royal Monceau (37 av. Hoche, Paris, France) while shooting her **"Justify My Love"** video. The Hôtel de Crillon (10, place de la Concorde, Paris, France) is a historical luxury hotel Madonna has also frequented in the City of Light.

In Italy, Madonna has stayed at the Principe di Savoia (Piazza della Repubblica 17, Milan, Italy), a landmark luxury hotel in Milan. She has also darkened the doorstep of the St. Regis Rome (Via Vittorio Emanuele Orlando, 3, Rome, Italy).

While on her *Girlie Show World Tour* in Brazil, Madonna checked into the Caesar Park Rio de Janeiro Ipanema (Av. Vieira Souto, 460, Ipanema, Rio de Janeiro, State of Rio de Janeiro, Brazil), described as the best hotel in the country.

Madonna has put **Malawi** on the map. When she visits every year or so, she stays at the Kumbali Country Lodge (Capital Hill Dairy Farm, Plot 9 & 11, Area 44, Lilongwe, Malawi), a folksy, family-owned establishment.

Madonna has expensive and exacting tastes in lodgings, but she won't overpay; she is known to personally inspect every hotel bill in search of illegitimate add-ons.

"ACT OF CONTRITION": Written and produced by Madonna and **Patrick Leonard**, this is one of the strangest songs Madonna has ever committed to record. This track makes use of a reverse sample from the song **"Like a Prayer"** and appears on her *Like a Prayer* album. The lyrics are a prayer that end with a play on the word "reservation." Madonna's angry, "What do you mean it's not in the computer???" is an all-too-familiar restaurant query used by those of us who are not (yet) famous, but it shows that even Madonna is sometimes not on the list.

ACT UP (AIDS COALITION TO UNLEASH POWER): Radical **AIDS**-awareness group formed in March 1987 whose by-the-**balls** tactics—including disrupting mass at St. Patrick's Cathedral (Fifth Ave., NY, NY) in 1989—definitely jibe with Madonna's own modi operandi. In her 1991 interview with *The Advocate*, when asked if she was for ACT UP or against them, she replied, "I'm for 'em." She also issued a joint press release with the group, urging **condom** distribution in **New York** City public **schools**.

ACTING: In spite of being an actor whose performances are often mentioned in the same breath as those of **Sofia Coppola** and "Citizen Kane"'s wife, Madonna has been a thespian far longer than she's been a singer, and it's also obvious she enjoys the theatrical aspect of her musical career more than the actual belting.

"Acting is just another kind of performing," she said in 1984. "It's just an expression, it's just being honest with your audience. So to me, it's just an extension of what I do already."

Madonna starred in **plays** in high **school**, and from her earliest interviews referred to herself as an actor. She is not a singer who tried her hand at acting (like **Michael Jackson**, **Elvis Presley**, **Prince**, **Rihanna** or **Diana Ross**), but an actor whose singing career (rightfully) superseded her acting career.

Madonna's first agent, **Camille Barbone**, sent her off to acting lessons with coach Mira Rostova, who instantly **hated** Madonna's guts. After only one session, their association was dissolved. "This girl will never be an actress," Rostova reportedly spat. "She is too vulgar and she thinks she knows it all. Besides, I do not like her." The reviews are in!

Madonna acted in *A Certain Sacrifice* before she had a record deal and appeared in films regularly from *Vision Quest* (1985) through *Die Another Day* (2002), the last feature film (so far) in which she has acted, not counting **voice** work.

But ... can she act?

Madonna's acting tends to match her surroundings. If the script's lousy or the direction weak, her performance suffers accordingly. Give her good material and she usually delivers. The ultimate chameleon! Unfortunately, she has had mostly terrible taste in choosing vehicles.

Madonna's most credible acting is in her music videos, the best of which are short films in which she plays a variety of parts. Standout acting performances in her videos include **"Papa Don't Preach"** (extremely convincing as a **pregnant** teen, though she was nearing 30), **"Bad Girl"** (mopping up the screen as a **sex**-addicted career woman) and especially **"I Want You"** (emoting in a hotel with only a rotary phone as a witness). Of the latter, Madonna's director Earle Sebastian said, "I've read negative reports of Madonna's acting, but I must say she's phenomenal in this."

In films, Madonna's most winning performances are as femmes fatales in *Desperately Seeking Susan* and *Dick Tracy*, her most layered is as femme banale "Sarah Jennings" in *Dangerous Game* and her most conventionally convincing are in *A League of Their Own* and as Eva Perón in *Evita*, for which she won a dang **Golden Globe**.

A crackling comic actor in the past, Madonna's celebrated *Saturday Night Live* appearances have ranged from WTF? to OMG! Her stabs at live theater—in *Speed-the-Plow* on Broadway and in the West End dramedy *Up for Grabs*—generated mostly pans, though it could be argued that she was perfectly used by **David Mamet** in the former and many who saw it thought she was completely effective in the latter.

—CAROL BURNETT

"What's a 'trained' actress? I think that in living the life I've paid my dues."—MADONNA (1986)

The worst? Well, she was dreadful in *Shanghai Surprise* and *Body of Evidence*, was virtually asleep in *The Next Best Thing* and turned in her most self-conscious performance in her husband's ill-advised remake of *Swept Away*. As iconic as her **"Like a Prayer"** video is, Madonna's broadly mouthed, "He didn't do it!" is about as subtle as a cross afire.

In spite of positive reviews from the likes of Vincent Canby, Pauline Kael and Leonard Maltin ("I think she has the potential to be a great movie star and she even has the potential to become a really good actress. She's not a bad actress now," Maltin said in 1993), acting is Madonna's Achilles' heel.

Madonna told *Out* **magazine** in 2006, "You know ... I have sort of let [movie stardom] go. There is too much resistance. What film can survive people saying it's going to be a bomb from the second it's announced to the day it is released?"

It ain't over till it's over. Though with each passing year it seems less and less likely that Madonna will jump **back** into film acting, one tantalizing possibility is the movie version of the Broadway musical *Sunset Boulevard*; who can deny Madonna was born ready for that close-up?

In August 2016, Metrograph (7 Ludlow, NYC, NY) hosted a series of Madonna's best films, organized by Joe Berger, perhaps signaling a reassessment of her contributions to film acting.

"ACTRESS HASN'T LEARNED THE LINES (YOU'D LIKE TO HEAR), THE": Cutting song from *Evita: The Complete Motion Picture Music Soundtrack*, in which the snarktastic movers and shakers of Argentina put Evita down, only to have her—viper-like—remove and replace them. It's a great piece of singing by Madonna that would make an interesting choice as aural connective tissue on a tour.

"ADDICTED": Hot, twangy **love** song with fangs from the Super Deluxe Edition of *Rebel Heart*, written by Madonna, **Avicii**, Ash Pournouri, Carl Falk, Rami and Savan Kotecha and produced by Madonna, Avicii and Falk. It boasts an arresting chorus that sounds like Madonna from her **Breakfast Club** days. Effortlessly entertaining, '80s-inspired song that will sound great live. **Roger Friedman** creams every time he hears this one.

ADDICTED TO SWEAT: *Director: Darren Capik. Release date: 2012.* Four-disc video workout branded to Madonna and her **Hard Candy Fitness** venture hosted by **Nicole Winhoffer**, who was at the time Madonna's personal trainer.

ADELE: *b. May 5, 1988.* Powerhouse British singer whose first two albums were worldwide sensations, including the US #1 hits "Rolling in the Deep" (2010), "Someone Like You" (2011) and "Hello" (2015).

In 2012, Madonna defended Adele when **Karl Lagerfeld** criticized her **weight**, saying, "That's horrible. That's ridiculous, that's just the most ridiculous thing I've ever heard ... The thing for Adele to remember is at the end of the day,

> "I WANTED TO BE A MOVIE STAR, BUT WHEN YOU GROW UP IN SOME HICK TOWN IN MICHIGAN, THERE'S NOTHING YOU CAN DO THAT WILL MAKE YOU FEEL LIKE YOU'RE GOING TO BE A MOVIE STAR."—MADONNA (1985)

> "TO ME, A SCRIPT IS A SKELETON THAT I HAVE LIKED ENOUGH TO HANG MY SKIN ON." —MADONNA (1985)

> "SHE HAS NO REAL SENSE OF HERSELF YET, SO SHE CAN'T BE A REALLY GOOD ACTRESS." —SHELLEY WINTERS (1989)

> "THE WHOLE PROCESS OF BEING A BRUSHSTROKE IN SOMEONE ELSE'S PAINTING IS A LITTLE DIFFICULT." —MADONNA OF HER *SHADOWS AND FOG* EXPERIENCE (1992)

> "I'M NOT PARTICULARLY INTERESTED IN BECOMING A GREAT BIG MOVIE STAR. I *AM* INTERESTED IN BECOMING A GOOD ACTRESS. IF ONE COMES WITH THE OTHER, THAT'S FINE. BUT I DON'T SPEND MY LIFE MOURNING MY FLOPS."—MADONNA (1996)

> "ACTING HAS ALWAYS TAKEN A BACKSEAT TO MUSIC. I DON'T THINK I WAS AS SCRUPULOUS IN MY CHOICES. I'VE MADE 10 MOVIES NOW. I THINK HALF OF THEM HAVE BEEN GOOD AND HALF OF THEM HAVE BEEN SHIT."—MADONNA (2000)

> "EVEN 'BAD' IS GOOD, BECAUSE 'BAD' IS THERE TO HELP YOU RESIST IT ... SO IS THERE 'BAD?'"—MADONNA (2008)

whether you rise or fall, it has so much to do with how you sustain yourself and keep your integrity and your inner strength."

It was reported that Madonna met with Adele in 2014, leading to rumors of a collaboration. They almost collaborated at Madonna's **Super Bowl** halftime show—Adele was invited to join Madonna on **"Like a Prayer,"** but had to turn it down due to her impending throat operation.

ADVOCATE, THE: *Publication dates: 1967-.* The world's longest-running **gay**-interest **magazine**, initially characterized by its political content and eventually a broad lifestyle publication that helped to push policy and dissect trends.

In 1991, Madonna granted the magazine one of the best interviews she's ever given, to promote *Truth or Dare*. Don Shewey, who wrote that the gay community "gets Madonna in a big way," asked Madonna anything and everything, including one of the best questions she's ever been asked: "Do you enjoy playing that role of castrating **bitch**?" See her answer at DonShewey.com.

Madonna covered her personal history with gay men (accidentally **outing** her brother **Christopher Ciccone** in the same interview in which she declares outing to be unproductive) and discussed her fascination with **Marilyn Monroe**, being aroused by seeing guys kiss, her reputation as a **size queen**, whether **Warren Beatty** has "a gay bone in his body," her early **sexual** experiences with girls, her take on religion and her desire to make an *Evita* movie.

The interview was so juicy and long (almost as big as **Sandra Bernhard**'s dick), it had to be split between two issues.

Pathetically, *The Advocate* did an about-face and branded Madonna its "Sissy of the Year" in 1995 for confirming that she is not a lesbian. Sissy or no, she has worked with the publication since, including granting a 2012 cover story.

AFRICA: SEE: Malawi.

AGEISM: When Madonna was a new phenomenon, she was largely engaged in pushing **back** at society's preconceived notions about **sexuality**, religion, gender and **fashion**. This **powerful** mix of pressure points has made Madonna's **work** not only initially sensational but also culturally resonant, its effects long-lasting.

As Madonna has gone from twentysomething to fiftysomething, she has been able to continue needling the world on those core issues, helping to nudge it into change, all the while embodying an entirely new debate on age.

Not that Madonna has always been a warrior against ageism. "Pop music is the **voice** of youth," she told *Seventeen* **magazine** in 1985. "I don't want to be a pop star when I'm 45, but I might want to be a great actress."

As recently as 1998, she told **Rupert Everett**, in response to his question about whether she intended to "stomp around" **Madison Square Garden** at age 50 like **Mick Jagger**, "No ... I do not ... I don't think there's a stop date, but I don't envision myself making pop records and videos when I'm 50 years old."

Madonna's work has almost never dealt explicitly with age. Rather, Madonna's challenge of society's ideas on how older women should look and how they should behave is represented by her actions. In other words, we haven't seen Madonna dressed in a gray wig while pumping iron in a music video as a statement. Instead, we have simply seen Madonna being herself and carrying on with her music and her other work, refusing to allow her age to define her—a far more radical statement.

Madonna has done many things well worth criticizing, but it is an embarrassing reflection of the culture when some of the harshest criticism she receives is so frequently intertwined with unapologetically ageist commentary.

She's the #1 solo touring act on the planet, every move she makes still sparks debate in the media and she is a decade from the age at which workers typically consider retiring, yet a common thread in the public complaints she's received for the past several years has been the suggestion—the *insistence*—that she is too old to be doing, well, *anything*.

Asked if Madonna, then 53 and about to slay (is this writer too old for that term?) at the **Super Bowl**, should retire, Gilles Marini, then 36, said, "There's a time when you should do something else and let the youth take the spot." To this day, Marini is used in most of his roles as a shirtless piece of ass. Should there be an expiration date on that if he continues, as he does, to look the part?

"I mean, the thing is, I do think that what I do is **art**," Madonna asserted to *Arena* magazine in 1999, age 40. "And does an artist, does the creative, you know, mind turn off at 40? Did Picasso stop painting at 40 ...?"

The reaction to Madonna has always been the most interesting thing about her (she would probably agree), and has always been the best way to tell that she is indeed an important artist. So what does the reaction mean when it has moved on from a multi-pronged attack on her **talent** and values, crystallizing into a resounding contempt for her age? Male artists Madonna's age and beyond are not subjected to the same level of ageist comments, and when their ages do come up, it's usually in jest. Is it the fact that Madonna's a woman that brings out the ageist commentary? If so, it's worth noting that she has just as many women engaging in bashing her for her age as she does men, women who seem to have bought into the rules of how their gender should behave, as dictated by men. This should come as no surprise; Madonna has been hounded by women from the beginning in the arena of sexuality, also due to constructs put in place by men.

Madonna herself has said, "You can be sexy, but you can't be smart. You can be smart, but you can't be sexy. You can be sexy, but you can't be 50 ... And, I feel like a lot of my biggest critics are women."

Also of interest is the fact that many people Madonna's age and older engage in ageist commentary at her expense. What could be inspiring is instead threatening, and we know Madonna enjoys it when her threat is felt.

Madonna has often been the target of ridicule for her age even when her age has nothing to do with the topic at hand. Celebrity stylist Robert Verdi, who disliked Madonna's (c'mon, spectacular!) **Dietrich** look from 2013, wrote in *Life & Style*: "Madonna isn't pushing boundaries anymore, but someone should be pushing her wheelchair." At the time, Madonna was all of 54 years old. Verdi was about to turn 45. Whatever happened to saying an outfit looks bad or good and offering an opinion why? He went on to say her outfit looked costumey ... okay, but where does the wheelchair come in?

"Yeah, fuck you, I'm 50. That's what I'm gonna say when I turn 50."–MADONNA (2008)

The idea that Madonna's age has become a lightning rod for pushback only works *for* her because while she may seem old to some people now, she'll only get older, and as long as she's alive and is interested in releasing music or creating art, she certainly has the means by which to make that happen. Maybe people aren't used to seeing older people do the things Madonna is doing and behave in the way Madonna is behaving because society largely removes opportunities from us as we age, but all of Madonna's banked power from her youth is allowing her to override that barrier.

In 2012, Madonna told **Naomi Wolf**, "I find whenever someone writes anything about me, my age is right after my name. It's almost like they're saying, 'Here she is, but remember she's this age, so she's not that relevant anymore.'

"HOPEFULLY, I'LL BE INCREDIBLY MELLOW AND WISE WITH AGE. NOT MELLOW, BUT VERY WISE AND STILL JUST AS MISCHIEVOUS, CHILD-LIKE AND WONDERING AS I AM NOW."
-MADONNA ON HOW SHE SAW HERSELF IN HER MID-50S (CIRCA 1987)

"TIME MAY BE RUNNING OUT FOR MADONNA … UNLESS SHE CAN ADMIT TO HERSELF THAT WHAT SHE DOES ONSTAGE IN HER THIRTIES MIGHT SEEM GROTESQUELY INAPPROPRIATE FOR A WOMAN IN HER FIFTIES."
-CHRISTOPHER ANDERSEN, A MAN THEN IN HIS FORTIES (1991)

"… I THINK, ULTIMATELY, PROBABLY WHEN I'M A VERY OLD WOMAN, PEOPLE WON'T BE THREATENED BY ME … AND THEY WILL UNDERSTAND WHAT IT IS THAT I'M TRYING TO SAY."-MADONNA, 7 SUR 7 (1992)

"BEING A POP GODDESS IS A YOUNG WOMAN'S GAME, AND MADONNA IS 35. NOW, 35 ISN'T ALL THAT OLD IN HUMAN YEARS. MADONNA'S AGE, HOWEVER, MUST BE MEASURED IN CELEBRITY YEARS, WHICH, LIKE DOG YEARS, MOUNT UP IN A SHORT TIME. AND AS SHE AGES, HER OPTIONS CLOSE IN … AND NOT ONLY IS MADONNA OLD, BUT THE IMAGE SHE HAS CULTIVATED—THAT OF AMERICA'S LEADING BAD GIRL—HAS BEEN CHALLENGED BY SHARON STONE, DREW BARRYMORE AND OTHERS."
-JAMIE MALANOWSKI, US (1993)

"I'M NOT A TEENAGER ANYMORE, AND I WON'T PRETEND TO BE ONE TO SELL RECORDS. HOW RIDICULOUS WOULD THAT BE?"
-MADONNA, BILLBOARD (2000)

… To have fun, that's the main issue. To continue to be a provocateur, to do what we perceive as the realm of young people, to provoke, to be rebellious, to start a revolution."

In 2015, a report suggested that the UK's Radio 1 had banned Madonna for being too old. They denied the allegation, saying it was not that she was too old, just **irrelevant** to their young listeners. That is some serious equivocation.

"It's still the one area where you can totally discriminate against somebody and talk shit. Because of their age. Only females, though. Not males. So in that respect we still live in a very sexist society," Madonna said in a lively ***Rolling Stone*** cover story in 2015. "… [W]hy is that accepted? What's the difference between that and racism, or any discrimination? … I don't follow the rules. I never did, and I'm not going to start."

"ISN'T 47 A BIT OLD FOR AN ENFANT TERRIBLE?"
-CHURCH OF ENGLAND OFFICIAL STATEMENT (2006)

"I LOVE THIS PHRASE, I JUST LEARNED IT THE OTHER DAY: COUGAR."
-MADONNA TO DAVID LETTERMAN (2009)

"MADONNA, MADONNA, MADONNA, WHY DO YOU KEEP FLASHING YOUR BITS ONSTAGE? YOU JUST LOOK DESPERATE, AND IT'S AN EMBARRASSMENT TO YOUR ENTIRE AGE GROUP! … IT'S TIME TO GROW UP!"-WENDY WILLIAMS, LIFE & STYLE (2012)

"MADONNA AND LMFAO DANCING DURING #SUPERBOWL HALFTIME FELT LIKE PARENTS TRYING TO EMBARRASS THEIR KID IN FRONT OF THEIR FRIENDS."-TYLER OAKLEY (2012)

"IDIOTIC PEOPLE HAVING A DIG @MADONNA ABOUT AGE. YOU'RE SHITTING IN YOUR OWN BED. UNLESS OF COURSE YOUR CLOCK IS GOING BACKWARDS?"-ALISON MOYET (2015)

"I AM ACTING MY AGE. THIS IS ME, THIS IS HOW I WANNA BE. I CAN DO WHAT I WANT. THERE'S NO RULES AND, Y'KNOW, PEOPLE SHOULD JUST LEAVE ME ALONE. LET ME DO WHAT I WANNA DO. I SHOULDN'T BE LIMITED BY MY AGE OR BY A NUMBER. SHOULD I?"-MADONNA (2015)

"A NEW MADONNA ALBUM, A FRESH REMINDER THAT WE'RE ALL GOING TO DIE."
-CHRIS RICHARDS, WASHINGTON POST (2015)

RICHARD CORMAN

Her kiss with **Drake** at **Coachella** that year did absolutely nothing to tamp down concerns that she was too old for our culture's own good.

Madonna's ultimate commentary on age will be what she's accomplished, what wisdom she's imparted, the sex she's had, the children she's raised and the people she's loved, not when she stops working, but when she stops aging.

And as for those who criticize Madonna's age not in relation to her work but just because she is, *no shit*, older than Nefertiti, Madonna is guaranteed the last laugh; if they're lucky, they'll get to be her age one day, too, at which time they will have some serious self-loathing to sort out.

AGENT CODY BANKS: *Director: Harald Zwart. Release date: March 14, 2003.* Kiddie spy flick starring Frankie Muniz and Hilary Duff that was produced by MGM, Splendid Pictures and Madonna's **Maverick Films**. Madonna was executive producer for this and its 2004 sequel.

AGUILERA, CHRISTINA: *b. December 18, 1980.* Along with **Britney Spears**, this is the other person who kissed Madonna at the **MTV Video Music Awards**.

AHMADZAÏ, MIRWAIS: SEE: **Mirwais.**

Can Madonna ever be too old to be Madonna?

TOP: Madonna's *Who's That Girl World Tour* stop raised cash for AIDS.

MIDDLE: AIDS trading card

BOTTOM: Rare fundraising letter for AIDS

AIDS: Madonna has lost a host of friends to the disease, including **Howard Brookner**, **Martin Burgoyne**, **Christopher Flynn**, **Keith Haring** and **Haoui Montaug**. She was a prominent **voice** in the fight against AIDS, particularly in the '80s and '90s. Her June 25, 1990, *Blond Ambition World Tour* show at the Brendan Byrne Arena (now the Izod Center, 50 New Jersey 120, East Rutherford, NJ) raised $300,000+ for amfAR, The Foundation for AIDS Research, in the name of Haring. She has made several **PSA**s on the topic and was the most famous person to attend the fund-raising AIDS **Dance**-A-Thons.

In the '80s, Madonna was fearless when it came to doing the right thing regarding AIDS. Brad Gooch says that when her director Howard Brookner, his partner, was very sick, Madonna was there for him: "Madonna was very brave, coming up to St. Vincent's, visiting Howard, kissing him on the lips, visiting the other patients."

On September 7, 1990, along with David Hockney, Ian McKellen and Rep. Henry Waxman (D-California), Madonna received a Commitment to Life **Award** from AIDS Project Los Angeles at the Commitment to Life IV benefit. She performed her **MTV Video Music Awards** rendition of **"Vogue."** In accepting her award, in a pinstriped suit, Madonna said: "I'm very honored to receive this award. In the **back** of my mind I feel that I don't really deserve it. In fact, I feel a little guilty because it's very easy to lend your name to a celebrity fundraiser if you're famous, and it's very easy to donate **money** to AIDS research if you're **rich**. What isn't easy is changing the way people think. While the AIDS epidemic is wreaking havoc on this planet, it's also released a wave of homophobia that is truly frightening."

On December 10, 1991, Madonna was honored with an Award of Courage from amfAR at a time when rumors had started that Madonna was herself about to announce that she was HIV positive. In accepting her award, Madonna said, "Now, I'm *not* HIV positive ... but what if I were? I would be more afraid of how society would treat me for having the disease than the actual disease itself." Madonna's **work** for amfAR has continued; she coheadlined amfAR's Cinema Against AIDS event alongside **Sharon Stone** in 2008.

Madonna's AIDS-warrior status has been taken for granted since the '80s, and was immortalized by Eclipse

"YOU KNOW, AIDS IS A POWERFUL AND MYSTERIOUS DISEASE THAT CONTINUES TO ELUDE US, BUT WE ARE MORE POWERFUL BECAUSE WE CAN STOP IT FROM SPREADING ANY FURTHER BY EDUCATING OURSELVES AND FINDING OUT THE FACTS." -MADONNA (1987)

"IT TAKES A LOT OF COURAGE THESE DAYS TO COME OUT AND SAY, 'I'M GAY,' BUT IT TAKES A FUCKING WARRIOR TO COME OUT AND SAY, 'I HAVE AIDS.' THESE ARE THE PEOPLE WHO DESERVE AWARDS SO MUCH MORE THAN ME ... YOU ARE MY HEROES." -MADONNA (1990)

"FOR SOMEONE WHO'S AS BIG AS SHE IS TO CARE SO MUCH ABOUT SOMETHING LIKE THAT AND TO REALLY DO AS MUCH AS SHE CAN, I THINK IS ABSOLUTELY AMAZING." -LISA STANSFIELD (1991)

"TODAY, TOO MANY PEOPLE SHUN THOSE WITH AIDS. PEOPLE WITH AIDS ARE OFTEN VICTIMS OF DISCRIMINATION AND EVEN VIOLENCE. PUTTING THAT KIND OF STIGMA ON PEOPLE IS WRONG. THIS IS THE 21ST CENTURY; THERE'S NO EXCUSE FOR FAILING TO TREAT THOSE WHO ARE SICK, AND THERE'S NO EXCUSE FOR TREATING PEOPLE BADLY, WHO HAVE AIDS. THE CHOICE IS OURS TO MAKE. LET'S BE SMART, AND LET'S BE COMPASSIONATE. AND REMEMBER, IT'S NEVER TOO LATE TO DO THE RIGHT THING." -MADONNA, AIDS PSA (2003)

"I WAS EXTREMELY AFFECTED BY IT. I REMEMBER LYING ON A BED WITH A FRIEND OF MINE WHO WAS A MUSICIAN, AND HE HAD BEEN DIAGNOSED WITH THIS KIND OF CANCER, BUT NOBODY KNEW WHAT IT WAS. HE WAS THIS BEAUTIFUL MAN, AND I WATCHED HIM KIND OF WASTE AWAY, AND THEN ANOTHER GAY FRIEND, AND THEN ANOTHER GAY FRIEND, AND THEN ANOTHER GAY FRIEND. THEY WERE ALL ARTISTS AND ALL TRULY SPECIAL TO ME." -MADONNA (2012)

Enterprises, a Forestville, California, novelty-card company that caught flak for introducing mass-murderer trading cards and that in 1993 launched a series of 100 AIDS trading cards designed to promote awareness. The cards feature watercolors of "AIDS stars," men and women whose activism and/or infection qualified them as icons in the history of the disease. Sure enough, there was a Madonna card.

ART © 1993 GREG LOUDEN FROM 'AIDS AWARENESS TRADING CARDS'/ECLIPSE CARDS

Full-page ad in *Billboard* raising awareness of AIDS

Madonna posed for the cover of *Esquire*'s March 1999 issue alongside a number of AIDS stars—**Tom Hanks**, Grant Hill, Lauryn Hill, Dr. Mathilde Krim, **Chris Rock**, Natasha Richardson and Sharon Stone. The cover was meant to help remind readers that AIDS was not a problem resolved in the '80s.

Madonna had long worried about AIDS prevention becoming passé. In 1992, she told a French **TV** interviewer, "I think it's still a big problem ... It's not a trendy thing right now, so people are sort of ignoring it. And I think that there's a lot of homophobia in the country and a lot of these people, they hate **gays**, and they use [AIDS] as something to point their finger at them and say, 'AIDS is because of you.' I think the Bush Administration isn't doing what they should be doing."

On a personal level, it has been widely reported that Madonna refused to get tested for HIV in the '80s, even when it became a bone of contention in her marriage to **Sean Penn**. But in spite of her personal aversion to getting tested back then, she has been a good friend to many suffering from the disease, including Burgoyne (whose medical expenses she covered, and who died in her arms) and Howard Brookner. Madonna donated $5,000 to Brookner's hospital fund when he was dying of AIDS right after shooting *Bloodhounds of Broadway*.

The personal toll AIDS has had on Madonna is well documented. In 2010, she told *Interview*, "After going to **New York** and being a dancer when the whole AIDS epidemic started and nobody knew what it was ... all these beautiful men around me were dying—just one after the next ..."

During the **Lady Gaga**/Madonna stan wars, a group of Gaga boosters, including self-styled journalist **Angela Cheng**, asserted that Madonna had been in some ways responsible for AIDS because she supported **sexual** promiscuity. Cheng later apologized and a letter from Little Monsters to **GLAAD** that slammed Madonna as being responsible for the spread of HIV was yanked from the Internet. To this day, trolls posting under such names as "Madonna Aids Flop" continue to smear Madonna in this unthinkable way.

AIELLO, DANNY: *b. June 20, 1933.* Italian-American character actor who played Madonna's papa in her **"Papa Don't Preach"** video. Aiello later claimed he had no idea who Madonna was when he was called for the gig, but his daughter did, and she begged him to take the **job** and to be allowed to come with him and take pictures on the set. This was a very odd thing to request (unless he was claiming his daughter just wanted a quick photo op with Madonna), but apparently his daughter made it to set, where she was denied access. "Madonna sort of backed up and told her representative that, 'I don't do that.' My daughter has **hated** her ever since ... I'm a movie actor doing this piece of crap!"

Aiello was not one to let go of his anger. Rather, he teamed up with fellow conservative Arthur Schroeck on an answer song and video called "Papa Wants the Best for You." Aiello claimed he made the video because "Papa Don't Preach" ignored the problem of communication between parents and teens.

Aiello delusionally thought Madonna would appear in the video to his answer song. He contacted "Papa Don't Preach" director **James Foley** to ask, saying, "She owes me this."

To quote from Madonna's **original** song, *"Pleeease!"*

"AIN'T NO BIG DEAL": One of her earliest recorded songs, written by **Stephen Bray** and recorded by Madonna in 1981, it was one of the songs on the demo that DJ **Mark Kamins** played at **Danceteria** and that was given by **Michael Rosenblatt** to **Sire Records** honcho **Seymour Stein** in 1982. The song was everyone's favorite of the bunch, so it was scheduled to be Madonna's first-ever release, a 12" **dance** single backed with a ditty called **"Everybody."** When the final mixes were in, Stein ditched "Ain't No Big Deal," securing a place in music history for "Everybody" as Madonna's first official release of any kind.

After the release of both "Everybody" and **"Burning Up"** as singles, Madonna hoped to use "Ain't No Big Deal" to promote the arrival of her *Madonna* album, but Bray had licensed it to July Fourth Music, and it was recorded and released by a group called Barracuda. So when Madonna's first album was finished, "Ain't No Big Deal" had to be replaced; the inarguably superior **"Holiday"** filled the slot.

The prophetically titled "Ain't No Big Deal" was unceremoniously released on the Japanese 12" of **"Dress You Up"** in 1985, as the B-side of Madonna's **"True Blue"** 7" and 12" singles in 1986 and on the **Warner Bros.** compilation album *Revenge of the Killer B's* (1984). The song finally got some serious **love** when Bray released Madonna's demos without her permission (bold!) in 1997; *Pre-Madonna* contains the song in its **original** form, a '97 Edit and a '97 Extended version.

ÅKERLUND, B.: Swedish stylist and wife of director **Jonas Åkerlund** who has styled **Beyoncé**, **Lady Gaga**, **Britney Spears** and—most famously—Madonna. She has **worked** with Madonna since 2006, when she styled the video for **"Sorry,"** and her handiwork was on display during Madonna's **Super Bowl** performance and in her **"Living for Love"** video.

She said in 2012: "I don't get **nervous** working for anybody, more so she gets my blood pumping to be better at my **job**."

ÅKERLUND, JONAS: *b. November 10, 1965.* Swedish director whose hip vision and edgy-glam aesthetic have delivered for Madonna in the form of some of her best (**"Ray of Light," "American Life"**), most famous (**"Music"**), most resourceful (**"Jump"**) and well, some of her other (**"Celebration"**) music videos. Most recently, he was chosen to direct

STRIKE A POSE: MEETING LINDA ALANIZ, MADONNA'S FIRST PHOTOGRAPHER

Madonna's first real photo shoot was in 1977, and it came about when her friend Linda Alaniz suggested she do some poses for fun. For Madonna and the camera, it was love at first sight—she connected with the lens immediately, surprising her friend with her "provocative" poses. Yes, she went topless.

Alaniz has also captured exquisite early images of Madonna in her dancer's leotard, and contributed her thoughts to Andrew Morton's Madonna biography.

Alaniz took time out from her many projects (including a book called *Les Pompiers Dévoilées*, written to raise money for children with special needs) to reminisce about her times with a future superstar.

EM2O: Do you remember the very first time you met Madonna?

LINDA ALANIZ: The first time I saw Madonna was in Christopher Flynn's ballet class. I think it was in the fall of 1977. I remember her as being very thin, very attractive and very eager to please Christopher and anyone else who might be watching. Whitley [Setrakian] introduced her to me after class and we kind of hit it off and became friends.

EM2O: As a fellow dancer in the same class, were you impressed with Madonna's skill?

LA: Yes, she was impressive to watch. She was quick to catch on and danced beautifully. She definitely had something about her that was alluring.

EM2O: Did Madonna strike you as a great beauty?

LA: Yes, she was a dark-haired, striking beauty and fun to look at.

EM2O: I'm from Michigan, and I can't imagine a woman with unshaved underarms (I was graduating high school in 1987) being accepted. Was it something that struck people as out-there?

LA: I don't know … it didn't seem all that strange to me at the time. Keep in mind this was in the '70s, after all. The hippie movement was in its heyday!

EM2O: Did you socialize much with Madonna and Whitley? What kinds of things did you do for fun, and do you remember the places in Ann Arbor you would hang out at?

LA: Yes, we hung out a lot. We would sometimes go to the Blue Frogge to dance, but our favorite place was the Rubaiyat. It was a gay bar and we didn't have to worry about guys trying to hit on us and we could be as outrageous as we wanted.

EM2O: Aside from Whitley, were there other friends of Madonna's you remember well?

LA: I don't really remember any others except Stephen Bray and Mark Dolengowski.

EM2O: When Madonna left for NYC, did you keep in touch via letters or phone calls? You must've been fairly tight if you went to NYC expressly to visit her? (Or maybe you were going and made sure to see her as part of the trip?)

EM2O: What was it like the first time you shot her?

LA: The first time I shot Madonna was in my apartment in Ann Arbor. I had no photographic lights at the time, so I used a bare tungsten light bulb. I asked her if I could photograph her and she didn't hesitate to say yes. Even then she was very comfortable in her skin, I don't recall if it was me or Madonna who suggested she take off her shirt.

EM2O: How many shots did you take the first time you shot her?

LA: I didn't take many photos … 13, to be exact.

EM2O: How did Madonna act while being photographed?

LA: I think we kind of worked together, but like I said before, she was very at ease in front of the camera. She knew how to work it. Even then she was quite provocative; like parting her lips, sticking her tongue out just enough while looking directly into the camera.

EM2O: Did Madonna talk at all about her future?

LA: Yes, the year before she left she talked about going to New York all the time. She always had a part-time job—modeling for art classes, scooping ice cream at Baskin-Robbins or serving drinks at Dooley's Bar. I remember she used to stash her money in a big book of New York City ballet dancers.

EM2O: When Madonna left for NYC, did you keep in touch via letters or phone calls? You must've been fairly tight if you went to NYC expressly to visit her? (Or maybe you were going and made sure to see her as part of the trip?)

LA: I don't recall any letters or phone calls. I think I stayed in touch with her via Christopher Flynn. I didn't go to NYC expressly to visit her. I went with Whitley to check out the dance and photography scene in order to move there after graduating. We did catch a subway out to Queens where she was rehearsing with a band. I remember not being overly impressed at the time.

EM2O: Did you hang out much with Madonna in NYC?

LA: After I moved to NY we saw each other occasionally, but she was on her way to making her name known in the music industry. She would often call to tell me where she was playing. She played at places like CBGB, the Cat Club and Studio 54. Just before her gig at Studio 54, she did ask me to take some photos for her "Like a Virgin" single, but once she performed at Studio 54, her career

started to skyrocket. That was pretty much the last I heard from her. I would sometimes see her at clubs and we would dance together, but that's all.

EM2O: Madonna confided in you about her rape. Many years later, when she referred to it publicly, a lot of Internet commenters felt it was a fake story just to get attention. Why do you think someone like Madonna would be less likely to be believed?

LA: I sympathized with her. She was obviously very traumatized by it. I don't know why people would be less likely to believe a victim like Madonna.

EM2O: What are your thoughts on Madonna's career?

LA: I always felt Madonna would be successful. However, I never dreamed she would be world-famous! Then again, you don't get to be at the top without unrelenting discipline, motivation and desire. Madonna had all of these even back when I knew her.

LINDA ALANIZ

the videos for **"Ghosttown"** and **"Bitch I'm Madonna,"** making him the video director who's **worked** for Madonna over the longest span of time.

In 2014, he said, "She's really the one that I learned so much from when I started. She's amazing and still has that impact. It's an obvious thing, but she really changed my life."

Madonna has placed a lot of trust in Åkerlund, returning to him for video direction over a stretch of nearly 20 years, enlisting him to direct both her personally revelatory *I'm Going to Tell You a Secret* and documentary special *The Confessions Tour: Live from London.*

ALANIZ, LINDA: Madonna's friend and a fellow student in **Christopher Flynn**'s **dance** class at the **University of Michigan.** Alaniz photographed Madonna twice, including a brief 1977 shoot that was Madonna's first posed shoot outside of goofing off with friends. Alaniz became a successful photographer, yachtswoman and chef, and currently lives in the South of France.

Jimmy, Jimmy

"If you were in the middle of a big box of chocolates, I would pick you out, pop you in my mouth and savor every tasty morsel, let you melt on my tongue and then swallow you whole."–MADONNA LOVE NOTE TO JIMMY ALBRIGHT (1993)

ALBRIGHT, JIMMY: The late **Whitney Houston** isn't the only singer who knew a thing or two about bodyguards; Madonna had a lengthy fling in 1992/1993 with Jimmy Albright, one of hers. Albright cashed in on the affair, selling gushing **love letters**, an outtake from *Dangerous Game* on video and phone messages from his smitten client/lover to a private collector in 2007, who wound up **auctioning** them off publicly two years later.

Albright replaced **Vanilla Ice** and was replaced by **John Enos** in Madonna's heart. He told Madonna's biographer **Andrew Morton**, "She can stand before 80,000 people in a stadium and hold them in the palm of her hand. Yet off the stage she is the most insecure woman I have ever met."

ALCOHOL: Madonna seemed to rarely touch the stuff for much of her early career, at least publicly. She did admit to being

roaring drunk on New Year's Eve 1990/1991, when she threw up and passed out (thankfully, Bill Cosby was nowhere near). There were also some drunken snaps of Madonna at **New York**'s Club USA (formerly 218 W. 47th St., NY, NY) in 1992, but it's rare to see Madonna under the influence of anything stronger than her own determination.

Madonna's relative teetotaling could be a reaction to the **memory** of her **father**'s alcoholic parents and other alcoholics on her **mother**'s side, or to the booze troubles faced by some of her siblings, but she has noticeably loosened up and now enjoys social drinking. It must be the Tanqueray.

These days, if Madonna's coming to your place for drinks, just have a dirty martini waiting or perhaps a Lemon Drop (shot of vodka and lemon juice in a sugar-rimmed glass). As she sings in a **Pharrell Williams** collaboration from the *Rebel Heart* sessions, the **unreleased** "Back That Up (Do It)": "I'll be drinking Krug Rosé/And sometimes Lemon Drops."

ALFRED, DOUG: *b. 1958.* In 1992, hot on the heels of an unflattering biography on Madonna, this junior-high boyfriend of hers came forward to tell the world that she'd been "... the sweetest, most devout **Catholic** girl you could ever meet." Madonna is reported to have "screamed" with laughter at his description of her as a good girl.

Alfred, who described himself as "a 'Johnny jock,' big man on campus," told the *Detroit News* that they'd been sweethearts and described her as "a good-looking girl, with long, curly, brunette **hair**. And she had that little mole on the side of her face that was just devastating to guys." He said her body was "a little chubby, maybe. She always did have baby fat on her, although she wasn't chunky."

ALIASES: Madonna can't always use her own name when registering at a hotel or leaving a message, so she has employed more dodgy monikers than a **rich** person's baby-naming **book**. She used "Daisy Miller" (after the 1879 Henry James novella) while married to **Sean Penn**, "Melissa" when calling for **Debi Mazar**, "Lulu" (a tribute to silent-movie star **Louise** Brooks) during her *Who's That Girl World Tour* and "Kit Moresby" (the heroine from the 1949 novel *The Sheltering Sky*) during her *Blond Ambition World Tour* travels. Using **"Dita Parlo"** to check in

led to Madonna using the name far more publicly, on **"Erotica"** and in *Sex*. When giving birth to **Lola** in 1996, she checked into the hospital as "Victoria Fernandez."

Professionally, Madonna thought she fooled 'em all as "Lulu Smith" while providing backing vocals for **Peter Cetera**'s "Scheherazade" (a gig she took because **Patrick Leonard** worked on the record), but she is not, contrary to popular belief, the "Mystery Girl" deep within **Michael Jackson**'s "In the Closet."

OLIVIU SAVU

"Her breasts were very large for a seventh-grade girl ..."
–DOUG ALFRED, MADONNA'S JUNIOR-HIGH BEAU (1992)

AMERICAN LIFE

①
"American Life"
(Madonna/Mirwais)
-4:58, produced by
Madonna/Mirwais

②
"Hollywood"
(Madonna/Mirwais)
-4:24, produced by
Madonna/Mirwais

③
"I'm So Stupid"
(Madonna/Mirwais)
-4:09, produced by
Madonna/Mirwais
(additional pro-
duction by Mark
"Spike" Stent)

④
"Love Profusion"
(Madonna/Mirwais)
-3:38, produced by
Madonna/Mirwais

⑤
"Nobody Knows Me"
(Madonna/Mirwais)
-4:39, produced by
Madonna/Mirwais

⑥
"Nothing Fails"
(Madonna/Guy
Sigsworth/Jem
Griffiths)-4:49,
produced by
Madonna/Mirwais
(additional pro-
duction by Mark
"Spike" Stent)

⑦
"Intervention"
(Madonna/Mirwais)
-4:54, produced by
Madonna/Mirwais

⑧
"X-Static Process"
(Madonna/Stuart
Price)-3:50,
produced by
Madonna/Mirwais

⑨
"Mother and Father"
(Madonna/Mirwais)
-4:33, produced by
Madonna/Mirwais

⑩
"Die Another Day"
(Madonna/Mirwais)
-4:38, produced by
Madonna/Mirwais

⑪
"Easy Ride"
(Madonna/Monte
Pittman)-5:05,
produced by
Madonna/Mirwais

ALL ABOUT MADONNA: *Airdates: November 1993–January 1994.* This four-part cable-access series that ran in the LA market was hostessed by perky Laurie Pike. Series highlights include chats with **Queerdonna**, with one of Madonna's former **dance** compatriots, with a **wannabe** who prostituted himself for a *Blond Ambition World Tour* ticket (what's wrong with that?) and with a shrink who psychoanalyzed Madonna, plus the airing of an **unreleased** song called "We Live in a House."

ALLEN, STEVE: *December 26, 1921–October 30, 2000.* The early **TV** pioneer, humorist, composer and creator of the first late-night talk show became a high-profile scold who campaigned against racy content. As such, he was not a big Madonna **fan.** Allen wrote an 11-page takedown of Madonna in the *Journal of Popular Culture* (summer 1993), in which he dismissed her **talent** entirely, blasted her for her sacrilegious stage name (oops!) and decided, "She has succeeded for a reason that reflects no credit upon the rest of us. She has succeeded because of her neurosis, her moral weaknesses, her willingness to prostitute herself for **fame** and **money,** to shame her family."

ALLEN, WOODY: *b. December 1, 1935.* One of the most (in)famous directors of all time. Madonna jumped at the chance to appear in the pint-sized genius's *Shadows and Fog,* and was defended by him when rumors surfaced that her part had been left on the cutting-room floor. The tabloid *News Extra* fabricated a story that Madonna had an affair with Allen, apocryphally quoting him as saying, "From all the things I heard about you, I thought you'd be just another bimbo with a bust size higher than your **IQ**," which is definitely a great way to get a lady wet and ready.

ALTER, ADAM: Madonna's early-'80s comanager, in conjunction with **Camille Barbone.** Madonna met Alter in **The Music Building** and told him he looked like John Lennon before asking if he might have any music-biz connections. He referred Madonna to Barbone, the woman who would later be described by **Stephen Bray** as her "knight in shining armor" and her "Svengali." Alter noted that Madonna was a "spoiled brat" during this period, but that they **loved** seeing her blossom as a musician.

"I never got a thank-you from Madonna. Nor did I expect it." -ADAM ALTER (2001)

"AMAZING": A **love** song from *Music* that shares a similar vibe with **"Beautiful Stranger"**; both songs were written and produced by Madonna with **William Orbit.**

AMERICAN BANDSTAND: *Airdates: September 1952–October 7, 1989.* Madonna's national **TV** debut was on this music show, a longstanding fave of youngsters, on January

14, 1984, performing her #1 **dance** single **"Holiday."** She had an instantly arresting exchange with host and "America's oldest teenager" Dick Clark, who used the crowd's extended cheers as an **excuse** to hug Madonna, then asked, "We are a couple of weeks into the New Year. What do you hope will happen, not only in 1984, but for the rest of your professional life? What are your **dreams**? What's left?" Madonna replied, "Mm—to rule the world."

Madonna always had a soft spot for Clark. For his December 31, 2004, *New Year's Rockin' Eve* special, after Clark had suffered a debilitating stroke, Madonna contributed a video message imploring him, "Get well soon. Come **back.** We need ya in Times Square."

AMERICAN DANCE FESTIVAL: Six-week **dance** program held at **Duke University** that Madonna attended in July 1978. She is pictured in the yearbook sipping what one might guess to be tea as Pearl Lang instructs her.

AMERICAN GOTHIC: **Sean Penn**'s brother Michael, later a rock/folk musician, drew a takeoff of this world-famous, 1930 Grant Wood painting to adorn the Penns' 1985 **wedding** invitation. The barely humanoid figures in his illustration possess such malevolent grins it could hardly have been seen as a mitzvah. Even "George Costanza's" wedding announcements were less toxic.

AMERICAN LIFE (ALBUM): *Release date: April 21, 2003. Billboard 200 peak: #1.* Madonna has often had controversial albums, but with *American Life,* she presented her first album whose controversial element—a perceived antiwar message—actually affected its sales negatively.

With her ninth studio album, Madonna, not content with the critical fawning she'd received on her last two journeys into an increasingly electronic sound, decided to tackle the entire American Way. Or did she? Certainly, the album's title single, which preceded its release, trumpeted a more political Madonna. Then there was that cover portrait by **Craig McDean**, which looked like a blend of Che Guevara and Patty Hearst. The unwelcoming image seemed to scream, "Steal this album," but in due time it was discovered she couldn't give the thing away.

Why the shift?

Promoting the album in an *Access Hollywood* sitdown, Madonna explained of her far-left turn, "I don't wanna keep saying the same thing, singing about the same subject ... I don't even wanna have the same color **hair,** as you can see." (She had gone *Like a Prayer* brunette for this one, letting us know she was getting real.)

But what would be more accurate to ask is why Madonna felt it was essential to name her album after its explicitly political lead single when the rest of the album is almost devoid of similar content. Aside from **"American Life,"** *American Life* is a folkier *Music,* and contains a raft of sumptuous, introspective pop; the closest thing to a second protest song is one that complains about the uniformity of radio, hardly the stuff of insurrection.

The album had its genesis as a *Music* sequel; Madonna, happy with the **work** she'd done with **Mirwais**, chose him as her collaborator for this follow-up and work began in 2001. Still distracted by **acting**, she shot the film *Swept Away* and starred in *Up for Grabs* in **London** before work began again in earnest, leading to a time span of over a year between her first sessions with Mirwais and the album's completion.

The final product is a solid, philosophical album whose direct, at times child-like, lyrics have often been dismissed as corny. It's about the ability to absorb lines like, "And I know I can feel bad/When I get in a bad mood/And the world can look so sad/Only you make me feel good," and hear the **beauty** and truth in their simplicity as opposed to deciding that because the words aren't more complicated, they're idiotic.

American Life opens with its title track, an almost universally maligned song that actually crackles with a freshness and a bracing sense of dissent—the world's biggest pop star casting aspersions on the current state of popular culture even as she continues to be its greatest product. Riding uncomfortably atop an erratic bass line, the song starts out working like poison, unfolds in its beautiful choruses, then is killed out of nowhere by a brave but unsuccessful rap. Because Madonna's critics found it unpalatable that a middle-aged white lady would attempt rapping, and because as executed the rap is unpleasant to listen to and beyond self-referential, it not only sank the song (it was a minor hit), it also unfairly painted the album as an exercise in ridiculousness. Madonna had almost 20 years of stewing in the world's inability to grasp the **irony** of **"Material Girl,"** so it's anyone's guess why she thought people would grasp the irony of a super-duper rap about soy lattes and nannies.

"Hollywood" follows, sounding like a cowed **disco** song after that knock-down, drag-out intro rather than the fairly haunted "Hotel California" (1977) it has the potential to be. There's a pleasantly spooky vibe in this song; it paints a landscape with its electro malevolence. As much of an indictment as "American Life," it's not sweepingly political so is far less intimidating. Also, it's catchy as hell.

Never let it be said that Madonna doesn't participate in her own critical mauling. Next up is a song called **"I'm So Stupid"** that, in spite of some beautiful lower-register vocals, is somewhat torpedoed by its preachy message, at once deep and inarticulate. Madonna's hard R is on a Cialis drip herrre.

As a break in mood, **"Love Profusion"** flutters by next, a sort of synth **Joni Mitchell** song. It's a good cushion between "I'm So Stupid" and **"Nobody Knows Me,"** which becomes the album's **"Human Nature"**—a song about Madonna that still functions as an anthem for the generic fed-ups.

Madonna's most heartfelt vocal is on **"Nothing Fails,"** a gorgeous song clearly influenced by **Karen Carpenter.**

It's a big, thoughtful, modern ballad, and it's worth taking a moment to ponder what the final sales tally would have been for *American Life* had it been called *Nothing Fails* and been represented by this song as its lead single. A continuation of the thought process begun with **"Nothing Really Matters,"** the song is also thematically similar to **"Like a Prayer."**

"Intervention" is another of the album's unapologetic folk numbers that represents the kind of "age-appropriate," cerebral music her critics are always demanding of Madonna, but that they seldom enjoy when they get it.

Sounding like a track from *Evita* being sung in a coffeehouse, **"X-Static Process"** is Madonna at her most naked. This is the girl who bawled her **eyes** out when she moved to **New York** and it almost beat her. The overlapping vocals effectively create a duet between Madonna and herself, clever in a song in which she candidly admits, "I don't know who I am."

After that experiment in split personality, a (bi)polarizing song follows, **"Mother and Father"** features Madonna singing in a high register that renders her **voice** almost unrecognizable. (**Cyndi Lauper**, is that you?) This time, she's shrilly picking apart one more element of American life—the family unit, and how hers was a cheat. "I've got to give it up," she sings over and over, and it's here where a chunk of this album's listeners were cattily agreeing. Yet it's an extremely thought-out song, playing on the childhood theme with Madonna's vocals and hopscotch-ready lyrics. It's filler, but like beef is in a pasty.

Next up is **"Die Another Day,"** a rattled-off Bond theme that was added to the record to ensure it had at least one guaranteed hit (since it had already gone Top 10). Its orchestral background calls to mind **"Papa Don't Preach,"** the awkward Freudian quip would have been at home on *Erotica* and it's a club stomper. It's the most "Madonna!" of all the songs here.

For this writer's **money**, everything Madonna's been saying on the rest of *American Life* is perfectly distilled in its final track, making for the best ending of any Madonna album: **"Easy Ride."** In a leisurely manner, Madonna sings of her shortcomings and her long-term goals. In 1984, she said she wanted to rule the world, but in 2003, all she wanted was to "live forever, not defined by time and space."

Though considered a stiff within moments of its release, *American Life* debuted at #1 thanks to Madonna's momentum as the **Queen of Pop**. Its first-week sales of 241,000 were her lowest since 1994, and it quickly sank from the charts. **Matt Drudge** proclaimed it the "end of an era," presumably meaning Madonna's career had gone abs up.

The album underperformed, but Madonna *performed* and *performed*—she sang "Mother and Father" live for Matt Lauer as part of a *Dateline NBC* special, did a live set for **MTV** called *Madonna: On Stage & on the Record* and even did an April 23, 2003, in-store appearance at Tower

—LIZ SMITH

Records (formerly 692 Broadway, NY, NY), in which she indulged the crowd with a taste of **"Like a Virgin."** When she forgot the lyrics, Madonna relied on her **fans** to assist. She told them, "Thank you for making me feel like a star … a star in the real sense. I feel really **loved.**"

• •

"… [Y]OU CAN TRY SWEEPING HER AWAY WITH DISMISSALS OF IRRELEVANCE IN A 50 CENT WORLD, BUT YOU CAN'T COUNT HER OUT. AT ITS BEST, HER NEW ALBUM OFFERS BLUNT, DISQUIETING, DECISIVE MUSIC AT A CHAOTIC TIME. AT ITS WEAKEST, SHE SOUNDS LIKE A GAL WHO'S GROWN CONTENT WITH HUBBY AND KIDS AND THE HARD-EARNED PRIVILEGE OF HIRING THE HELP TO KEEP HERSELF AT TIP-TOP TAUTNESS …"-KEN TUCKER, *ENTERTAINMENT WEEKLY* (2003)

• •

"MADONNA WAS ONCE THE DEFINITIVE POP AUTEUR, CRAFTILY CULTIVATING AN ENTIRE IMAGE FOR MASS CONSUMPTION WHILE REMAINING TRUE TO HER OWN UNIQUE ARTISTIC VISIONS. SHE'S OFTEN BEEN INSCRUTABLE, OCCASIONALLY IRRITATING, AND MOST OF THE TIME SHE'S BALANCING ON THE VERY LIMITS OF GOOD TASTE (IF NOT COMPLETELY IGNORING THEM), BUT AT LEAST SHE'S ALWAYS BEEN INTERESTING AND (MORE IMPORTANTLY FOR POP MUSIC) ENTERTAINING. FOR ONCE, MADONNA HAS STUMBLED NOT BECAUSE SHE REACHED TOO FAR, BUT BECAUSE SHE DIDN'T REACH FAR ENOUGH."-ED HOWARD, *STYLUS* (2003)

• •

"DRAWN WITH DARK, INTROSPECTIVE HUES, *AMERICAN LIFE* IS THE FLIP SIDE TO … *MUSIC*, WHICH WAS INTENTIONALLY AIMED TO BE EASY ON THE BRAIN AND HEAVY ON THE HIPS."
-LARRY FLICK, *THE ADVOCATE* (2003)

• •

"LIKE LAURENCE FISHBURNE'S ODDBALL 'MORPHEUS' IN *THE MATRIX*, MADONNA TRIES TO ACCENTUATE THE PLIGHT OF HUMANITY BY ENUNCIATING LIKE A ROBOT."
-JOSH TYRANGIEL, *TIME* (2003)

• •

"MADONNA SPENDS MUCH OF *AMERICAN LIFE* BEMOANING THE EMPTINESS OF CELEBRITY CULTURE. IT'S A DRAMATIC GESTURE FROM AN ARTIST WHO'S SYNONYMOUS WITH AMERICAN GLAMOUR, BUT INSTEAD OF LASHING OUT AT THE SYSTEM THAT CREATED HER, SHE CASTIGATES HERSELF."-JAMES HANNAHAM, *SPIN* (2003)

• •

She also promoted the album with her **Re-Invention World Tour**, even as that show also offered up plenty of oldies mixed in with the rejected newcomers.

American Life—derisively **nicknamed** by some her "mid-life crisis album"—is the album where Madonna stopped singing about **sex** and parties, where she offered a stripped-down version of herself that didn't involve nipples, where she made herself as lyrically vulnerable as any pop star ever has … and it was resoundingly rejected by the public, her career declared over. Don't complain that she went **back** to chasing the ideal club sound—you might do the same.

In 2006, Madonna said of the drubbing her album received: "It's not good for you to always be well received. [A negative response] makes you try harder and gives you a strength and conviction to go against the grain and stand up for what you believe in—and it's fuel for my fire because I like being a rebel."

American Life went on to sell 5 million copies worldwide.

"AMERICAN LIFE" (SONG): *Release date: April 8, 2003. Billboard Hot 100 peak: #37.* Cowritten and coproduced by Madonna and **Mirwais**, this song from *American Life* was surely Madonna's most daring single ever. This uncategorizable diatribe became forever unfondly remembered for its **rich**-lady rap. It's an undervalued song, one that made for great live entertainment on the **Re-Invention World Tour**, on **Madonna: On Stage & on the Record** and at 2003 in-store gigs at Tower Records (formerly 692 Broadway, NY, NY) and HMV (formerly 363 Oxford St., London, England, UK).

The song was given to HBO to promote its edgy dramas, including *The Sopranos* (January 10, 1999–June 10, 2007) and *Six Feet Under* (June 3, 2001–August 21, 2005).

"After two decades of nimble Zeitgeist-surfing, Madonna nearly wipes out with the title song from her coming album."
-JON PARELES, *THE NEW YORK TIMES* (2003)

"AMERICAN LIFE" (VIDEO): *Director: Jonas Åkerlund, 2003.* Madonna's most controversial video is the only one so offensive to a swath of the American public that she actually pulled it from circulation, a huge decision for a super expensive, incredibly detailed and—let's say it—brilliantly, blackly, bleakly effective piece of **work**. Not only was it a total loss on a major creative statement, it was a rare example of Madonna flinching under a barrage of criticism.

Madonna and director **Jonas Åkerlund** conceived the clip as anti-war. It also savages the citizens of any society that blithely accepts war as anything less than the final alternative, and who enjoy their freedoms—many mind-numbingly superficial—while blood is being spilled a world away. It was storyboarded in November 2002 and shot in February 2003 at a rumored expense of approximately $600,000 ahead of a proposed April 2003 release.

In the genuinely shocking clip, Madonna is shown singing in an intentionally frivolous **sexy**-dictator outfit from behind the scenes (in the john, actually) of a massive **fashion** show with a glib combat theme. The show takes an ominous turn when small Jewish and Muslim children, representing the human price of an endless cycle of conflict like the one in the Middle East, join the mix, much to the amusement of the crowd (among them a **Sophia Loren** look-alike and figures representing recognizable fashion-world figures).

Before anyone had seen more than clips from the video, Madonna told *Access Hollywood*, "I'm trying to portray the fragility of human life with the children, with the soldiers, and I'm trying to say this is not a show, this is not a fashion show, this is not entertainment … this is real, and we have to recognize it."

Next, Madonna, in full camouflage, leads her troupe of female soldier-**dancers** into a Mini Cooper, literally crashing the show. Madonna hoses down the audience as the models on the runway are suddenly blown to bits, graphically; the frothy war theme has turned real. Most disturbingly, real footage of adults and children injured during war flash as one "model" screams down the runway, on fire. Throughout, those in the crowd become progressively more tickled by what they're seeing.

The video's **original**, incendiary ending portrayed Madonna tossing a grenade at a George W. Bush look-alike, only to have him jovially crack it open, revealing it to be a novelty lighter. He lights his stogie and puffs away, unperturbed by any of the events going on around him. (This ending was edited out even before the entire video was pulled, but Madonna denied **Warner Bros.** compelled the edit. "No one forced me to change anything," she insisted.)

Because the video's release was slated for April, which would have meant a debut within weeks of the beginning of the US-led ground invasion of Iraq, an anti-war video suddenly took on an anti-American feel. Madonna said on *Madonna: On Stage & on the Record* that there were "about 10" versions of the video floating around, but none that she felt comfortable releasing.

Madonna pulled it and released a ridiculous version, showing only takes of her singing against a backdrop of world **flags**. Caving to the pressure, instead of presenting her most daring video, one of her best, she presented a timid video, one of her worst.

To be fair, Madonna was being called a traitor at a time when her country's citizens had gone from being thoroughly unimpressed with the likes of Bush to handing him a 92% approval rating in the wake of **9/11** and had set aside misgivings about the Iraq invasion once Bush gave the go-ahead. Artists like the Dixie Chicks were being excoriated for voicing disapproval.

> "… [I]t was conceived and created long before the war in Iraq ever started and it was meant to wake people up to the horrors of war. By the time it was finished we were at war and it felt like releasing it was the wrong thing to do. I am not sorry I did it, but timing is everything and sometimes you can have the most amount of influence by taking a step back."
> —MADONNA ON PULLING HER "AMERICAN LIFE" VIDEO (2003)

Just check out this hawkish assessment by Ethan Brown in *New York* **magazine** at the time: "When Dresden-like civilian casualties failed to materialize during the war with Iraq, Madonna pulled the album's Bush-taunting, blood-and-guts title video. Civilian casualties and quagmires—they're just *so* March. Liberation is totally April. Pop stars like Madonna always cast their most critical **eye** on the easiest of targets: America. Too bad we're not as evil as they'd hoped." Someone spoke too soon!

American Life: The revolution of Madonna.

ALEJANDRO MOGOLLO

'85

'87

BRAD ELTERMAN ('85)

MLC at the AMAs

Madonna said of the criticism she faced, "You know, it's ironic that we're fighting for democracy in Iraq, because we ultimately aren't celebrating democracy here, because anybody who has anything to say against the war or against, um, you know, the president or whatever is punished—and that's not democracy."

In 2005, Madonna said she had no **regrets** about pulling the video. "I did it because I didn't want people throwing rocks at my children on the way to school. I did it for them, not me. There's a lynch-mob mentality that goes on."

AMERICAN MUSIC AWARDS: *Dates presented: 1973–.* Popular **awards** show founded by **Dick Clark** that rewards musicians based on polling of the public.

On January 28, 1985, Madonna and Huey Lewis presented the award for Favorite Black Album to **Prince** for *Purple Rain*, which beat **Michael Jackson**'s *Thriller* and **Lionel Richie**'s *Can't Slow Down*. This was the show after which many of the stars recorded "We Are the World"; not so Madonna, whose **"Crazy for You"** would eventually dislodge the **charity** single from #1.

Between 1985 and 2003, Madonna was nominated 17 times for American Music Awards, winning three: Favorite Pop/Rock Female Video Artist (January 26, 1987), Favorite **Dance** Single: **"Vogue"** (January 28, 1991) and the Michael Jackson International Artist of the Year Award (January 14, 2003).

Her 1987 award came during her *Who's That Girl* look. Presented her award by Richard Page of Mr. Mister and Robert Bell of Kool and the Gang, she noted the inappropriate height of her mic, saying, "I think I have to be a midget to speak into this."

On January 30, 1995, Madonna and **Babyface** (introduced by Tom Jones) performed their smash-hit duet **"Take a Bow"** on the telecast, accompanied by a live orchestra. Madonna was decked out in a red kimono, echoing the song's Oriental flair. It was her only live performance of her longest-running #1 hit.

"AMERICAN PIE" (SONG): *Release date: March 3, 2000, Billboard Hot 100 peak: #29.* While **cooking** up revisions to Tom Ropelewski's *The Next Best Thing* script, Madonna's costar **Rupert Everett** suggested that she record a version of this 1971 Don McLean song, **working** it into the story. It appeared as a singing break during an otherwise bleak funeral scene.

Madonna's version, which she coproduced with **William Orbit** relatively soon after their outta-this-world *Ray of Light* collaboration, lost some lyrics and converted the folk-rocky number into a spare, electronic, aural wave. Everett sings some of the backing vocals.

The **original** is so ubiquitous in the culture it's considered a bit cheesy, and so Madonna's remake is not looked on too kindly in most quarters. Musical snobbery aside, it's a pleasing, if minor, addition to her catalogue, one that garnered some airplay stateside and became a #1 hit overseas.

McLean, who wrote the song as well as performed it (wanna try to estimate how much moolah he raked in for it?), graciously said, "Madonna is a colossus in the music industry and she is going to be considered an important historical figure as well. She is a fine singer, a fine songwriter and record producer, and she has the **power** to guarantee success with any song she chooses to record. It is a **gift** for her to have recorded 'American Pie'. I have heard her version and I think it is sensual and mystical. I hope it will cause people to ask what's happening to music in America. I have received many gifts from **God** but this is the first time I have ever received a gift from a goddess."

Guess he liked it!

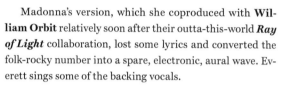

"There are certain songs that do get under your skin, there is something inexplicable about them—they remind you of your past, or your innocence, and as a singer you are drawn to do them but you can't explain why."—MADONNA ON "AMERICAN PIE" (2000)

"AMERICAN PIE" (VIDEO): *Director: Philipp Stölzl, 2000.* If Madonna's cover of the Don McLean song for the film *The Next Best Thing* came off as unnecessary to some rock critics, the video—no-muss, no-fuss on Madonna's part since it was just ad-libbed **dance** moves filmed against an American **flag** backdrop in **London** with costar **Rupert Everett**—became far more interesting when its director made use of stark video portraits of regular Americans juxtaposed with Madonna's performance clips. The citizens used are posed unnaturally, stiffly, creating arresting images that seem to be a hat tip to photographer Diane Arbus. The people chosen to appear in the video represent types who would probably never hang out together—**gun**-toters, Goth kids, an obese woman in a wheelchair, muscle boys, kissing **gay** couples. The video is a simple, sneakily provocative statement on the diversity of the country.

Wimping out in the end a bit, it closes with Madonna goofily pulling up her jeans, then sitting as a tearing sound effect breaks the spell.

AMOS, TORI: *b. August 22, 1963.* The American singer told *Details* **magazine** in 1994, "She's the shadow of the Christian Madonna. So while the Christian Madonna was pure and sanctified, Madonna has become the **sexuality** of it incarnated. But I don't think Madonna's been very nurtured as a human being. I said a few years ago that I'd make her a plate of spaghetti, and I mean that."

In 2015, Amos came to Madonna's defense over **ageist** comments: "I think people want her to be shamed into a role that they find acceptable for her age. It makes me sad that we can't embrace Madonna and say, 'Wow, this is an artist who's expressing herself in a certain way.'"

Amos has performed some memorable covers of Madonna songs: **"Like a Prayer"** on her *Original Sinsuality* Tour (2005); **"Live to Tell"** on her *Night of Hunters Tour* (2011) and both "Like a Prayer" (mashed up with **Bon Jovi**'s 1986 tune "Livin' on a Prayer") and **"Frozen"** during the "Lizard Lounge" section of her *Unrepentant Geraldines Tour* (2014).

"AND THE MONEY KEPT ROLLING IN (AND OUT)": Song sung by **Antonio Banderas** on *Evita: The Complete Motion Picture Music Soundtrack.* In the film, the song plays while Madonna as Evita is shown sucking up to her husband's constituents.

ANDERSEN, CHRISTOPHER: *b. May 26, 1949.* Christina Crawford's **excuse** was the wire hangers, but why does *this* author try so hard to vilify his subject? Scandal and conflict sell.

Andersen's *Madonna: Unauthorized* (1991) was the first serious, international Madonna biography. It became a #9 bestseller, largely on the hype that it contained salacious secrets. The worst it had to offer was that Madonna was sometimes rude to her **fans**, that she had a penchant for cruising Alphabet City in **New York** in a limo to pick up Latino boys for **sex** (who doesn't?), that she participated in group sex and is **bisexual**, that she can be ruthless, that she's a penny pincher, that she's had more than one **abortion** and that she's a serial **love** cheat.

Andersen's revelations don't always pack the punch they might, relying on unnamed interviewees and stretching the limits of the imagination—do we really believe Madonna and **Michael Jackson** stripped and explored each other's **nude** bodies after the **Oscars**?

Also, Andersen's uptight attitudes hang over the **book**. Look for phrases like "devoutly homosexual" to pass the time and smile as Andersen views every aspect of Madonna's existence as yet another indication that she is a psychological time bomb waiting to explode—*tick-tock, tick-tock, tick-tock.*

In the end, the book is a lot of *tsk-tsk*ing over Madonna's "sexually promiscuous lifestyle" and "exploiting" of religious icons. (Let's talk about exploiting icons, Chris.) Andersen humorlessly tries to invoke the pathos behind his vision of a geriatric Madonna shimmying to **"Like a Virgin"** before a crowed of blue-haired **wannabes**, having been unsuccessful in imagining what actually came to pass: a sleek, fortysomething Madonna selling that song majestically on stage during her *Confessions Tour.*

Andersen *did* assemble a lot of exacting details regarding Madonna's journey to stardom, including an extensive genealogy that was crafted before the Mormons invented Ancestry.com, and he presents some enlightening interviews, notably one with **Christopher Flynn**. The book is occasionally witty and always readable. The best thing about it, though, is its **original** dust jacket—a sizzling shot of Madonna's ass, which Andersen would be well advised to kiss.

Andersen went on to write over a dozen more high-profile biographies, not all of them quite so negative. Unfortunately, this negative one was turned into *Madonna: Innocence Lost*, a **TV** movie for Fox.

ANDERSON, TRACY: *b. March 3, 1975.* The most independently famous personal trainer with whom Madonna has ever **worked**, the tiny terror with a carapace of steel was credited with keeping Madonna rock-hard in her late forties and very early fifties. They worked together from about 2006 to fall of 2009, when Madonna left Anderson for Anderson's assistant, **Nicole Winhoffer**. The exit was acrimonious. Officially, Anderson wanted to spend more time with her son, but she had also begun a relationship with Philippe van den Bossche, the executive director of **Raising Malawi**, who quit his LA **job** with the foundation to move to **NYC** to be with Anderson. It's been said that Madonna isn't wild about employees fraternizing.

In 2013, someone close to Anderson (maybe *very* close) spoke to the media to sniff that Winhoffer had been an overweight beneficiary of Anderson's knowledge, words that were timed to coincide with Madonna and Winhoffer's release of their *Addicted to Sweat* line of workout videos.

"ANDROGYNY CABARET": One of Madonna's early live solo engagements in **New York** was at a small show organized by entrepreneur/artist **Michael McKenzie** in 1981. The performers included people McKenzie had photographed for his *Androgyny* series (John **Sex** was one), so Madonna, still a member of the band **Emmy**, appeared with short, dark **hair** and in little-boy PJs.

"ANGEL": *Release date: April 10, 1985. Billboard Hot 100 peak: #4.* Up-tempo pop song in the classic early Madonna mold. The song is a collaboration between Madonna and **Stephen Bray**, and was produced by **Nile Rodgers** for *Like a Virgin.* One of the first songs finished for the album, "Angel" inhabited the upper reaches of the **Billboard** Hot

100 simultaneously with her ballad **"Crazy for You"** in 1985. Because **Sire** wanted to push "Angel" and the album from which it was taken, the much more popular **"Into the Groove"** was denied a proper single release in the US, though it was the B-side of "Angel"'s 12" single. The "Angel" Extended **Dance** Mix is characterized by a crowd of **fans** chanting her name and Madonna's wickedly naughty laugh.

"Angel" has only ever been performed live on ***The Virgin Tour***, something she needs to address—stat!

ANGIE: *Director: Martha Coolidge. Release date: March 4, 1994.* Doomed **Geena Davis** starrer that screenwriter Todd Graff had originally adapted from the well-regarded 1991 novel *Angie, I Says* by Avra Wing with Madonna in mind.

Graff felt Madonna's motherless youth and street smarts would make her a natural for the titular part of a **pregnant** Brooklyn woman who decides not to marry the **father** of her baby. Jonathan Kaplan [*The Accused* (1988)] was Madonna's director of choice, and things seemed locked and loaded to roll at Twentieth Century Fox. Then, Fox's Joe Roth left for Disney and *Angie* went into limbo. The film's proposed producer, Larry Brezner, was allowed to pitch the project to others, and the project was greenlit by ... Roth at Disney.

Madonna was set to shoot a film called *Snake **Eyes*** (later retitled ***Dangerous Game***) from February to March 1993, which conflicted with Brezner's schedule. Brezner reportedly already resented what he perceived as Madonna's overconfidence, and her hypersexual image at the time made him queasy. The scheduling conflict was as good an **excuse** as any, and Madonna was out, clearing the way for **Oscar** winner and recent Madonna costar Geena Davis.

Rosanna Arquette at a 25th-anniversary screening of *Desperately Seeking Susan* in NYC

Madonna was enraged. Her reaction was scathingly sarcastic, arriving in the form of a faxed diatribe to Roth. The missive's industry-wide leak (via copy machine) was an analog precursor to the 2014 Sony hacking scandal:

"After directing *Coupe de Ville* [1990] and *Revenge of the Nerds* [II (1987)] ... you are certainly qualified to speak about the **art** of **acting** and great filmmaking. I can understand why you had reservations about my ability. I can see why you think Geena Davis the better actress for the part. After all, she's Italian and she has an edge. How foolish of me to think I had the ability to play a vulnerable character unlike anything I've done to date. I should just stay in the gutter where I belong, **working** with lowlifes like **Abel Ferrara** and being **hated** by the general public."

"ANOTHER SUITCASE IN ANOTHER HALL": *Release date: March 24, 1997. Billboard Hot 100 peak: NA.* Beautiful ballad from ***Evita: The Complete Motion Picture Music Soundtrack***. In the stage version of the story, the song was sung by Juan Perón's mistress, but it was given

to Madonna to sing in the movie version of ***Evita***, one of the few flashes of humanity in her unnervingly conniving character. The song was a single, but only outside the US.

ARMITAGE, KAROLE: *b. March 3, 1954.* Known as the "punk ballerina," the acclaimed choreographer was hired by Madonna for her **"Vogue"** video. They did not collaborate again. Armitage has described Madonna as being all about "marketing," and even entered into a charged conversation about **cultural appropriation** in a 2013 chat with **famed** voguer Benny Ninja. While Ninja said he wasn't "mad" at someone like Madonna for bringing vogueing to the masses, Armitage sharply disagreed, in spite of her own complicity in what she called "theft."

"I choreographed 'Vogue', so I was in on this. Madonna had friends who were going to the **balls**, and she knew I was at the balls, and she knew my **work**. And I really felt like it was theft, I have to say, and, um, what has been disturbing to me is, well, okay, she has a genius for pi—for picking the thing at the right moment that she knew, that somehow the culture was ready for it, so it wasn't like she was pushing *any* boundaries *ever*; it was already pre-digested and it was ready to be a product of cons-, you know, to be consumed. I mean, that is a certain kind of genius. It's not the kind I'm interested in ..."

Armitage's assertion that America was totally ready to consume vogueing in 1990 sounds like something a member of the **art**-world elite might believe, but while Madonna did not provide a deep history of vogueing when she sprang it on the malls, its status as something queer was very much noticed and was very much a threat, as much as **Boy George**'s genderfucking had been years earlier.

It's probably also worth pointing out that if vogueing should never have been Madonna's to co-opt, is it Armitage's to defend?

ARQUETTE, ROSANNA: *b. August 10, 1959.* Incandescently beautiful actor who starred in the acclaimed films *Baby, It's You* (1983), *After Hours* (1985) and many more, part of a Hollywood **acting** dynasty that started with her grandfather Cliff Arquette and most definitely *not* the inspiration for Toto's 1982 song "Rosanna," Arquette was Madonna's costar in ***Desperately Seeking Susan***.

Arquette gives a note-perfect performance in *Susan* that completely holds the film's disparate elements together, one that led to a **Golden Globe** nomination. And yet, as reflected by her win of a BAFTA (British Academy Film **Award**) as "Best Actress in a Supporting Role," Arquette suffered the indignity of being overshadowed by Madonna's rising star. Adding insult to injury, Arquette was shipped to **New York** to promote the film on ***Good Morning America*** while Madonna was left in LA to attend its premiere!

Though Arquette was not happy, understandably so, when the film evolved into "the Madonna movie" and the

MATTHEW RETTENMUND

women shared very little screen time, she nonetheless became a pal of Madonna's during shooting. The two posed together memorably for **Herb Ritts** one Saturday off, and the images were so spectacular that they were used to promote the film and have become iconic in their own right; one became a shared cover of ***Rolling Stone***.

In 1985, Arquette attended Madonna's **wedding** to **Sean Penn** all in white (shade!) and with a peace-symbol belt buckle. Arquette was one of the celebrities on hand for the premiere of ***Truth or Dare***.

Arquette has said of her old castmate, "Madonna goes right for it and gets what she wants. I admire that a lot. But I think behind all that is a little, tiny girl inside." She has expressed continuing affection for Madonna despite their drift over the past 30 years, and told an interviewer in 2011 that she looked forward to seeing ***W.E.***—both "Susan" and "Roberta" have become directors. Good goin', strangers!

> "She was becoming the biggest thing in the world as we were doing the film. So she wasn't that big, but she was this presence on MTV, so I kept seeing the 'Lucky Star' video and just being obsessed with how gorgeous she was. She has that star quality. She really does. It's like Angelina Jolie, where she walks in and you just go, 'Wow …' She has it."—ROSANNA ARQUETTE ON MADONNA (2011)

ARSENIO HALL SHOW, THE: *Airdates: January 3, 1989– May 27, 1994.* At the time, Arsenio Hall was the most exciting thing to happen to late night since mutual **masturbation**.

Madonna graced Hall's show three times, first appearing in a no-holds-barred ***Blond Ambition World Tour*** interview that made for legendary TV. At the top of the show, Madonna—all in white with dramatic stage makeup—appeared in Hall's stead, a funny gag that set the tone. They talked about Madonna's **dance** moves, **La Toya Jackson**'s presumed **plastic surgery**, Madonna's topless shot in ***Vanity Fair***, ***Dick Tracy***, the relative threat posed by **Joan Collins**, her **Catholic** upbringing, Hall's long fingers and Madonna's childhood desire to be black (she thought black kids had more fun).

After Hall had questioned her for a while about her relationship with Warren Beatty and about things like her supposed passion for spanking, Madonna turned the tables on her host, razzing him endlessly about his fling with **Paula Abdul,** even bringing up rumors about Hall's alleged affair with Eddie Murphy. Hall countered with the rumors about Madonna and **Sandra Bernhard**, which wasn't a very effective tactic since Madonna had started them.

Madonna cut to the quick by asking about Abdul's bed: "I mean, is it a king-size, or is it a queen-size?" She even had the gall to insult Hall's "tired" hairstyle. Hall later griped to *Ebony* **magazine** that a bleached-**blonde** white girl

had no **business** dictating black hairstyles, but in spite of being a seasoned stand-up comic, he maintained his cool and was extremely gracious to Madonna during their sparring. Madonna's appearance on the show was his highest-rated episode ever, attracting almost 6.5 million households.

Another Hall

Madonna next appeared on the show in the company of **Rosie O'Donnell** to promote *A League of Their Own*. Madonna had her **hair** up, almost no **eyebrows** and wore a sheer black top with a black bra underneath, offset by the most obnoxious gold necklace with a giant dollar sign hanging off of it. O'Donnell performed a **parody** of **"Vogue"** that poked fun at Madonna's **exhibitionism**, told stories about **Evansville** and expressed interest in doing a movie called *White Girls Can't Rap* costarring Queen Latifah that led to an intentionally bad rap duet between O'Donnell and Madonna. The raunchy exchange ("You're hurting people!" O'Donnell scolded Madonna in jest) was cut short when Hall craftily brought out Madonna's father, **Silvio "Tony" Ciccone**. "Now I have to be good! … I mean, Dad, I'm glad to see you but now I can't say anything," Madonna moaned. The show's highlight came when Hall asked Mr. Ciccone what Madonna had been like as a child. "She was very, a very nice young lady," he replied with a straight face.

The interview was re-enacted verbatim by Alison Brie, Adam Pally and Paul Scheer in 2013 for the Web series *ArScheerio Paul.*

Hall's 1,000th-episode special at the Hollywood Bowl (2301 Highland Ave., LA, CA) brought Madonna **back** one last time. She opened with a traditional version of **"Fever,"** her auburn hair curled under à la Barbara Stanwyck, clad in a sleek gown and stiltlike platforms. She kept her footing and sounded great but starting singing out of place at one point, admitting, "I'm sorry, baby. I screwed up, didn't I? We all make mistakes, don't we?" She muddled through, dramatically snubbed out a cigarette and got seriously leggy before slinking offstage. She showed up later in an inspired duet with Red Hot Chili Pepper **Anthony Kiedis** (in **drag**). Both wore horned hats, duetting on "The Lady is a Tramp" (1937).

Hall is a **fan** of Madonna's **AIDS** work (his 1,000th-episode show raised $250,000 for the Magic Johnson Foundation), but is turned off by her sex activism.

> "… The crazy thing about me and Madonna is we always left there and got along. It was one of those, uh, one of those cool relationships where you throw barbs and then you go to a Laker game, y'know? She's a good girl."—ARSENIO HALL (2014)

"I am my own painting. I am my own experiment. So, I am my own work of art."—MADONNA (1991)

ART: In 1996, Madonna said if she weren't a singer, she'd be "an art dealer or patron of the arts." Instead, she became an avid collector, especially in the '80s and '90s.

Madonna has made the *Art & Antiques* **magazine** list of Top 100 Collectors of art in the world. She owns hundreds of photography **books**, attends exhibits (including the acclaimed showing of Nazi-confiscated "Degenerate Art") and routinely peppers her music videos and photo shoots with imagery directly or indirectly reminiscent of the **work** of prominent artists. She even played an art dealer in *Up for Grabs* on stage in **London**.

Madonna's natural interest in acquiring art was enhanced beginning in 1986 via a collaboration with advisor Darlene Lutz, with whom she contentiously parted ways a dozen or so years later.

The first piece Madonna ever purchased as a collector—not counting the many objects she acquired from friends and lovers in the '80s who went on to become some of the most collected artists in history—was a "beautiful, sort of abstract" Robert Smithson painting that used to hang over her bed and that Madonna called "my guardian angel." Since then, her homes have become little Guggenheims.

Madonna's former apartment on **New York's Central Park West** was designed as an artistic as well as comfortable space by Stephen Wang of Procter & Wang, and was decorated by her brother **Christopher Ciccone** in the space of a few weeks. The result was an art deco showcase housing such important works as *Nude* (1930) by Laure Albin Guillot; Salvador Dalí's *The Veiled Heart* (1932); Pierre Dubreuil's *Les Gants de Boxe* (1930); *Nude* (1929) by André Kertész; Fernand Léger's *Trois Femmes à la Table Rouge* (1921, sold at **auction** by Madonna in May 2013 for $7.2 million to benefit her **Ray of Light Foundation**) and *Les Deux Bicyclettes* (1944, bought in 1987 for just $1 million); Maxfield Parrish's *The Young King of the Black Isles* (1906); Pablo Picasso's *Portrait of Dora Maar* (1937) and *Buste de Femme à la Frange* (1938) and Claggett Wilson's *Portrait of a Boxer* (1945). Special places were reserved for works by one of Madonna's favorites, **Tamara de Lempicka**: *Andromeda* (1929), *Nana de Herrera* (1928/9) and *Nude with Dove* (1930). Among her many **Keith Haring** holdings is a heart-stopping mixed-media collage that used to hang in her kitchen.

Madonna's California mansion in the '90s was far more eclectically decorated, featuring everything from a Kertész of a nude woman searching for her rolls of fat to a working radio designed by Rhonda Zwillinger. This was the home where one would find one of Madonna's most famous acquisitions, **Frida Kahlo**'s *My Birth* (1932), a harrowing depiction of the painter giving birth to herself. Madonna told *Vanity Fair* that if someone couldn't relate to that painting, "then I know they can't be my friend." Madonna also owns Kahlo's *Self-Portrait with Monkey* (1938), contemporary artist John Kirby's *Family Ties* and Léger's *Composition* (1932), the latter of which dressed up her foyer.

"My interest in art started as a child because several members of my family could paint and draw and I couldn't, so I was living vicariously through them. And from going to the Detroit Institute of Arts, which is how I got into Diego Rivera, which is how I found out about Frida Kahlo and started reading about her," she told *Aperture* magazine in 1999.

Madonna owns photography by František Dtrikol and George Platt Lynes as well as Jacques Henri Lartigue's *The Famous Rowe Twins of the Casino de Paris* (1929). She has, at various times, displayed the work of photographers **Guy Bourdin**, Martín Chambi, **Patrick Demarchelier**, Sean Ellis, Nan Goldin, Matt Mahurin, **Steven Meisel**, **Tina Modotti**, **Herb Ritts**, Mario Sorrenti, **Mario Testino**, **Inez van Lamsweerde & Vinoodh Matadin**, Weegee and Edward Weston, but once said she most prized an Ilse Bing photograph given to her by **Warren Beatty** on her 31st **birthday** and a shot of Detroit-born **boxing** champ Joe Louis (you can take the girl out of Michigan ...) by Irving Penn. The one photographer Madonna most wishes had shot her? Man Ray. She owns his *Kiki de Montparnasse* (1932).

Her furniture is also art, including a 19th-century Pompeiian-style klismos chair, a Jean Pascaud ebony table, a Eugene Printz armchair and a copy of a sofa from Coco Chanel's studio.

Aside from paintings, photos and price-ful furniture, Madonna owns an Elie Nadelman **statue**. Two of many drawings in Madonna's collection include a 1924 pencil drawing of a reclining nude by Jean Despujols that was presented to her by **Warner Bros. Records** and a David Salle that was a **wedding** gift to the Penns from the artist and **Karole Armitage**.

The most jaw-dropping piece of art Madonna owns may be a ceiling-mounted Jean-Charles Langlois painting originally created for Versailles, showing Cupid, Diana and Endymion. It's said to be so soothing that Madonna would spend hours on her **back** looking up at it.

You don't want to bid against Madonna in an auction. In 1992 at Sotheby's, she plunked down $814,000 for a 14th-century panel by a painter known mysteriously only as The Master of 1310. The painting portrays the life of a saint, complete with serpents, bears, an executioner and an all-girl version of *The Last Supper*.

Madonna has incorporated her taste in art into her work. In her *Sticky & Sweet Tour,* she used artist **Marilyn** Minter's video *Green Pink Caviar* (2008).

In recent years, Madonna's interest in acquiring art has seemed to recede.

The artistic merits of Madonna's own output are often debated. To save time, tell any naysayers that Madonna's work *is* art, but give him or her the prerogative of deciding whether it's any good.

ART FOR FREEDOM: Since September 2013, *Vice* **magazine** and Madonna have partnered on this project, a global initiative that pushes for creative expression and that underscores human rights violations. Aspiring artists are encouraged to share their work, which is judged by Madonna and celebrity guest curators (**Miley Cyrus**, **Anthony Kiedis** and **Katy Perry** among them). Winners have their work shared, and choose a non-profit organization to receive a $10,000 donation. For more info, visit ArtforFreedom.com.

ARTHUR AND THE INVISIBLES: *Director: Luc Besson. Release date: December 13, 2006.* Known abroad as *Arthur and the Minimoys*, this children's fantasy flick involves a little boy (Freddie Highmore) who discovers his missing grandfather (Ron Crawford) has left a trail of clues leading him to a secret world of tiny, warring critters. In what to date is her most recent **work** in a feature, Madonna **voiced** the character of "Princess Selenia."

Even in animation, Madonna has a tough time at the box office; writer/director Luc Besson—who had previously worked with Madonna on her **"Love Profusion"** video—received withering reviews for the film, and the box office in the US was abysmal, just $15,132,763 for a film that cost $86 million. Happily, the movie was a phenomenon overseas, making another $92,811,473.

It contains a marijuana-inspired scene featuring the voice of Snoop Dogg that must be seen to be believed.

ARTIFACTS: Items touched, used, signed, worn or even kissed by Madonna are highly prized by collectors, as if owning something that has been in her presence draws the collector that much closer to her being.

Costumes worn by Madonna are especially valuable. Her **"Express Yourself"** video suit, complete with slits for her **cone bra**, sold for $10,000 and a brown-and-purple **Gaultier** bra seen in *Truth or Dare* went for over $11,000. One of Madonna's gold *Blond Ambition World Tour* basques fetched $15,000, and a corset from the same tour achieved $18,150 in 1994 dollars. These amounts would increase by several multiples if the same items were sold today.

Madonna maintains a meticulously organized archive of her clothing, but has been generous in **gifting** some. One of her donated bustiers achieved $1,200 (to benefit a rehab center), and residents of Mount Clemens, **Michigan**, had the rare opportunity to bid on the blue hanky she waves in the non-US version of her **"True Blue"** music video to benefit the city's local Rotary Club. (It went for the bargain-basement price of $714.) The hanky is on display at Mon Jin Lau (1515 East Maple Rd., Troy, MI), an Asian fusion restaurant. Her unsigned high **school** yearbook sold for $770 and one of her Rockford Peaches uniforms from *A League of Their Own* sold for $2,100—unwashed. Most intimately, an Evian bottle Madonna fellated at a *Truth or Dare* publicity party sold for $1,100.

That is some expensive head.

Since Madonna artifacts are so valuable, they sometimes sprout legs. Madonna's powder blue "True Blue" dress took a walk from a display case in a Detroit mall,

reappearing safely weeks later. During the LA riots, when most looters were going for electronics, someone liberated Madonna's **"Open Your Heart"** video bustier from Frederick's of Hollywood (6751 Hollywood Blvd., Hollywood, CA). It, too, was recovered.

By 2014, Madonna's **auction** market had blown up—one of the *Desperately Seeking Susan* pyramid jackets used in the film sold for over a quarter of a of a million dollars, though there was a problem with the sale and it was re-auctioned for $87,500 in 2016.

Madonna artifacts have infiltrated major museums. Most famously, one of her *Blond Ambition* basques resides at **New York**'s Museum of Modern Art (11 W. 53rd St., NY, NY) in its Costume Division.

ASSAULT: On December 28, 1988, Madonna allegedly drove from her **Malibu** mansion to the sheriff's office to file charges of "corporal injury and traumatic conditions" and "battery" against her husband **Sean Penn** following an incident that sparked her decision to begin **divorce** proceedings on January 4, 1989, and to officially file on January 25, 1989.

Rumors vary about what Sean did to Madonna, but most of them involve Madonna being bound and gagged, verbally abused and roughed up. *Star*'s cover screamed: "SEAN PENN BOUND AND GAGGED MADONNA FOR 9 HOURS!" The tabloid claimed Penn tied Madonna to a chair, threatened to cut off her **hair** and attempted to shove her head in a gas oven. Madonna later dropped all charges against Penn. In 2015, Penn sued filmmaker Lee Daniels for remarks Daniels made implying that Penn beat Madonna. As part of the suit, Madonna swore in an affidavit that Penn had never abused her.

AT CLOSE RANGE: *Director: James Foley. Release date: April 18, 1986.* **Sean Penn**'s paternal drama was the film he was shooting in Mexico in May 1985 while Madonna blazed across the US on her *Virgin Tour*. Just a couple of months after his return to the States, they married.

The Penns attended the film's world premiere at the Berlin Film Festival in February 1986, blowing off press. (They were shooting *Shanghai Surprise* at the time and feeling smothered by paparazzi.) They were much more sociable at the film's LA premiere at the Bruin (948 Broxton Ave., LA, CA), where Madonna debuted the gamine look that would be immortalized in her **"Papa Don't Preach"** video.

A highlight of the film is the song Madonna wrote for it, **"Live to Tell."**

AUCTIONS: Madonna has long been a hot ticket at pop culture auctions at every major house, with **autographs**, handwritten lyrics and **artifacts** from her movies and music videos commanding impressive prices.

AUDUBON BALLROOM: *Formerly 3940 Broadway, NY, NY.* The abandoned structure at Broadway and W. 165th St. in Washington Heights that became The Magic Club

—FRED SCHNEIDER

GIRL MATERIAL:
INSIGHTS INTO THE MADONNA-RELATED AUCTION MARKET

Julien's Auctions (9665 Wilshire Blvd., Ste. 150, Beverly Hills, CA), "the auction house to the stars," is an LA-based business known for selling artifacts related to (and sometimes previously owned by) stars like Marilyn Monroe and Michael Jackson. Over the years, Julien's has made its name by working directly with stars (its 2006 auction on behalf of Cher is the stuff of legend) and by offering impossible-to-find items that make fans' hearts flutter to a stop.

EM20 went to CEO Darren Julien to get the lowdown on the auction market as it pertains to the Marilyn Monroe of her time: Madonna.

EM20: How would you rate Madonna as a collectible icon in relation to some of the other greats, such as Marilyn Monroe, Elvis Presley and Michael Jackson?

DARREN JULIEN: Well, Madonna has the fortunate collectability of being highly collectible and still alive. The other above artists never got to see how highly collectible they were during their lives. Madonna will only continue to grow in value because she has proven herself to be a true icon.

EM20: What types of Madonna items are your most reliable sellers?

DJ: Items from her career are the most sought after. The more iconic or memorable, the higher the value.

EM20: What's been the #1 most amazing Madonna item you've ever auctioned?

DJ: The most amazing and highest price was the jacket from *Desperately Seeking Susan*.

EM20: Why do you think the bidding went so crazy over the jacket more so than any other item of clothing or jewelry associated with Madonna?

DJ: Because this was early Madonna before she ever was really famous. Collectors like iconic items that were worn by someone early in their career that first helped launch them.

EM20: Who are your best customers?

DJ: It's a combination: About one third are fans, one third are investors and one third are museums. It used to be just fans, but the investor side of this business has really made Madonna's values skyrocket.

EM20: Have you had to refuse items that seemed too good to be true?

DJ: Yes, all the time. We also work with Madonna's archivists sometimes to make sure something is right or authentic. We had someone who submitted the wedding dress she supposedly wore in the "Like a Virgin" video. This would be a major piece, but when comparing it to the video there were inconsistencies. In addition, the provenance or history was not solid.

EM20: What's the weirdest Madonna item anyone's ever tried to consign with you—and did you sell it?

DJ: The strangest was someone tried to sell us her dishes from a restaurant she ate at. They were dirty and had not been washed. No, we did not sell them.

EM20: Can you think of any Madonna items you have heard exist that you would love to be able to auction?

DJ: Yes, we have some clients who have some pretty amazing things. There are very few items from *The Virgin Tour* available, and anything from that tour would be highly sought after. I have also wanted to do a major auction for her, like we have done for Cher and Barbra Streisand.

set for *Desperately Seeking Susan*. The facility, erected in 1912, is where Malcolm X was assassinated on February 21, 1965. In 1996, it was demolished—except for the better part of its façade, which was restored—to make way for Columbia University development.

AUSTIN, DALLAS: *b. December 29, 1970.* R&B songwriter and producer who has **worked** with **Janet Jackson**, **Michael Jackson**, **Lady Gaga**, **P!nk**, TLC and many more. Austin was a huge part of the success of ***Bedtime Stories***, contributing work on the smash single **"Secret"** as well as the standout album tracks **"Survival," "Don't Stop"** and the epic **"Sanctuary."**

AUTOGRAPHS: Madonna's autograph can sell for thousands, depending on its provenance. Over 100 examples exist on eBay at any given time, but most are ridiculously fake. Things to watch out for: She probably didn't sign those ***Playboy*** photos and she definitely didn't sign that portrait of a convincing impersonator.

Historically, Madonna's been alternately generous and stingy with her siggy. She signed zero at the ***Speed-the-Plow*** stage door in 1988, but following her interview with Harry Crews that same year, she signed for the whole kitchen staff at **Trump** Plaza (formerly 2500 Boardwalk, Atlantic City, NJ). She told Crews it is the "impertinence" of most autograph hounds that usually turns her off. She reportedly signed a stack of 8"×10"s for a **fan** at **Martha Graham**'s swan-song **dance** recital.

She signed some dude's passport aboard **David Bowie**'s yacht in **Cannes** (asking him, "Isn't this illegal?") and overruled security at a 1994 **basketball** game when they tried to dissuade a man from getting her autograph for his pops.

Currently, Madonna *does* sign for **business** contacts (graciously signing the first edition of this **book** and of the **magazine** edited by the author), and in the 2010s began to sign quickly for fans at public events. Unfortunately, Madonna's signature when in a rush is little more than a scrawl. If you're thinking of camping out near one of her homes, you're more likely to get an angry, **"Fuck** off!" than an autograph.

An expert once told *Smash Hits* magazine that her handwriting indicates sincerity, intelligence, sensuality, flamboyance and joie de vivre. "Her looped-rightward D formation shows peace, fulfillment and understanding."

"AUTO-TUNE BABY": Never let it be said that Madonna has no sense of humor; that can't be true when she recorded a song with this particular title, in light of criticism of her natural singing abilities. This sweet ditty, written by Madonna, **Diplo**, Mike Dean, **Kanye West** and TB, and produced

$875K

ANDY SCHWARTZ

by Madonna, Kanye West, Mike Dean and Charlie Heat, is found on the Media Markt Deluxe Edition of *Rebel Heart*, complete with an extremely annoying crying-baby sample.

AVICII: *b. September 8, 1989.* Born Tim Bergling, this Swedish DJ and producer has become one of the biggest hitmakers on the **dance**-music scene. In March 2014, Madonna used social media to announce that she and Avicii—who had appeared onstage with her at the **Ultra Music Festival** in **Miami** in 2012—were **working** on new music together. By November, two Avicii tracks had **leaked**, "**Rebel Heart**" and "**Wash All Over Me.**" When many more demos from Madonna's *Rebel Heart* album followed, she released six songs on iTunes, including the Avicii collaboration "**Devil Pray.**"

"... It's been obviously such an honor to be able to do anything with her, y'know, she's such a, y'know, musical icon. It's someone that everyone has grown up with almost, it's such a legend."–AVICII (2012)

AWARDS: In spite of being the ultimate female pop star of all time, Madonna has rarely won major awards. She has won a total of seven **Grammys**, but only one for Best Pop Album (1998's *Ray of Light*) and only one songwriting award, for "**Beautiful Stranger**," a song she wrote for a movie soundtrack. She's received 28 Grammy nominations total.

The Academy of Motion Picture Arts & Sciences **hates** Madonna. True, she's only ever given one dramatic performance that had a real shot at being nominated and wasn't; she was seen by some, including herself, as a shoo-in to get a nomination as Best Actress in a Leading Role for *Evita*, but failed to get the nod in the same year the Academy also blew off **Courtney Love** and Debbie Reynolds. But why wasn't *Truth or Dare* nominated for Best Documentary? The year it was released, it drew critical raves and was the #1 documentary of all time at the box office. (It's still #15.)

Acting (and acting bratty) aside, Madonna has written some exceedingly fine songs for movies, none of which has ever earned her so much as a nomination: "**Into the Groove**" from *Desperately Seeking Susan*, "**Live to Tell**" from *At Close Range*, the title song and/or "**Causing a Commotion**" and/or "**The Look of Love**" from *Who's That Girl*, "**This Used to Be My Playground**" from *A League of Their Own* (1992), "**I'll Remember**" from *With Honors*, "**Beautiful Stranger**" from *Austin Powers: The Spy Who Shagged Me* and "**Masterpiece**" from *W.E.*, the latter of which was disqualified on the technicality that the song wasn't the first heard over the film's closing credits. Instead, Madonna helped win **Oscars** for songwriters **Stephen Sondheim** for "**Sooner or**

MEGA-FAN SPOTLIGHT:
ARTURO AVIÑA

As a kindergarten teacher and mega-fan, I decided to replace nursery rhymes with Madonna songs in my classroom. In 2012, my kindergarteners had their first moment in the spotlight when their performance of "Vogue" became a viral hit. Since then, I have continued to blend Madonna's music into the curriculum, earning my students recognition from *The Huffington Post*, *Queerty* and Buzzfeed for their Madonnalicious productions. Their magnum opus thus far is "Like an Alphabet," a collection of 26 mini-music videos inspired by Madonna's oeuvre, which was lauded as "ambitious" and "innovative" by the *Los Angeles Times*. To check out these Ciccone youths, visit their "Kindergarten Vogue" channel on YouTube or follow them on Twitter @artavina.

Later (I Always Get My Man)" from *Dick Tracy* and **Tim Rice** and **Andrew Lloyd Webber** for "**You Must Love Me**" from *Evita* by doing two things: (1) singing the songs, and (2) not cowriting them.

The only conclusion to draw is that the film industry's perception of Madonna's acting keeps her at (muscled) arm's length from Oscar.

To date, Madonna's only acting award of note is her **Golden Globe** for *Evita*. Grammys are hard to come by, but the Globes did recognize her for "Masterpiece," and she has won **American Music Awards**, songwriting awards from ASCAP and Ivor Novello, a couple dozen *Billboard Awards*, two **Brits**, two Junos, a pair of **Nickelodeon Kids' Choice Awards**, one **People's Choice Award**, some impressive **Guinness** world records focusing on sales and a raft of **MTV Video Music Awards** ... though nothin' from **MTV** since the '90s.

For her **AIDS** work, Madonna proudly accepted amfAR's Award of Courage, and she was honored with an Excellence in Media Award from **GLAAD** (**Gay** & Lesbian Alliance Against Defamation) that same year, both in 1991. GLAAD had Madonna hand their Vito Russo Award to **Anderson Cooper** in 2013, but she is ripe for another award of her own from the organization.

Dubious honors Madonna has won include the Sour Apple Award from The Women's Press Club in 1992, for being uncooperative with the media and *Variety*'s "I'd Rather Have a Pulitzer Than an Oscar" Award for refusing to allow *Body of Evidence* to be released the same week as *Sex*. She is a sure bet when it comes to the **Razzies**.

MATTHEW RETTENMUND

B12: When **Justin Timberlake** was under the weather during his *Hard Candy* sessions with Madonna, he reports that she whipped out a B12 syringe from her purse and demanded that he bare his butt to her: "She gave me a shot in my ass!" Gerard Butler said Madonna also gave him a B12 shot, which happened while he was filming her husband **Guy Ritchie**'s *RocknRolla* (2008). "She just said, 'Drop your pants.' I stood there with my little bottom out, and she gave me a shot in the bum!"

BABY SHOWER: Madonna's baby shower when she was expecting **Lourdes** was held in July 1996 in LA. **Debi Mazar**, **Rosie O'Donnell**, **Sharon Stone** and Donatella **Versace** attended, playing games such as guessing Madonna's waist measurement. After the event, the gender of the baby and Madonna's desire to call her **Lola**—her eventual **nickname**—were leaked in *USA Today*.

BABYFACE: *b. April 10, 1959.* Kenneth "Babyface" Edmonds is one of the most acclaimed R&B musicians, songwriters and producers of the past 25 years. At the arguable peak of his **powers**, Babyface—a renowned creator of **love** songs—cowrote the album track **"Forbidden Love"** and the single **"Take a Bow"** from *Bedtime Stories*, both of which he coproduced with Madonna.

When "Take a Bow" became a #1 hit with stamina (following a career slump for Madonna), Babyface performed a live version of the song with her on the **American Music Awards**. He also gamely lip-synched the song alongside Madonna at the 1995 **Sanremo** festival in Italy.

BACHELOR PARTY: **Sean Penn**'s bachelor party was thrown by his brother, Chris Penn. The guests included *Fast Times at Ridgemont High* (1982) scribe Cameron Crowe, **Tom Cruise**, Robert Duvall, David Keith and Harry Dean Stanton, with entertainment provided by Kitten Natividad, the impossibly busty star of Russ Meyer films. Kitten stripped to **"Material Girl"** while the groom-to-be rubbed Stanton's face in her cleavage.

BACHELORETTE PARTY: What's good for the goosed ... Madonna's own pre-nup celebration before she made it legal with **Sean Penn** took place at the Hollywood Tropicana (formerly 1250 N. Western, Hollywood, CA), at which Madonna and her gal pals watched a raucous evening of lady mud-wrestling. Check out HollywoodTropicana.net for a *flesh-back*. Like the marriage, the club ceased to exist in 1989.

BACK: Madonna considers her back to be the most sensitive, yet the most **powerful**, part of her body ... which is a major snub of those biceps.

"BACK IN BUSINESS": A Madonna/**Patrick Leonard** composition from *I'm Breathless: Music from and Inspired by the Film Dick Tracy* that nearly matches that album's contributions from musical-theater maestro **Stephen Sondheim**. It starts with a breathy threat and swings into celebratory mode, later incorporating the first half of Madonna's most famous line from the film, "You don't know if you wanna hit me or kiss me ... I get a lot of that." As the song progresses, witty, sassy female backing vocals provide Madonna a perfect opportunity to break into some confident semi-scatting and to bust out her most authoritative lower-register vocals.

"BAD GIRL" (SONG): *Release date: February 22, 1993. Billboard Hot 100 peak: #36.* Written by Madonna, **Shep Pettibone** and **Tony Shimkin**, and produced by Madonna and Pettibone, the third single release from *Erotica* became her least successful single since **"Burning Up."** The problem wasn't the song's merits, but the timing—it was released during the *Sex* and *Body of Evidence* backlash—and with the fact that introspective, mid-tempo downers rarely sail on Top 40 radio.

Record buyers rejected what was perceived as Madonna's attempt at atonement for her wicked, wicked ways, but the song did become a #1-selling **dance** single thanks to the **"Fever"** remixes on the B-side. She sang it beautifully on *Saturday Night Live* (its only live performance to date).

In 2014, **drag** personality Pandora Boxx chose "Bad Girl" as one of Madonna's Top 10 most underrated songs.

"BAD GIRL" (VIDEO): *Director: David Fincher, 1993.* One of Madonna's most cinematic videos, "Bad Girl" marries the storyline of *Looking for Mr. Goodbar* (1977) with the visual style of *Wings of Desire* (1987) in its depiction of a smoldering but miserable businesswoman—"**Louise Oriole**"—who degrades herself with sleazy sexcapades, too much liquor and chain-**smoking**.

Though she is watched over throughout by a chic guardian angel (**Christopher Walken**) who nudges her away from dangerous games and toward a date with a respectably nebbishy guy played by James Rebhorn, he slacks off while protecting her, creating an opening for a murderous thief. Her guardian angel now assuming the role of the Grim Reaper, Louise is strangled with one of her own stockings by a one-night stand (Rob Campbell), appearing elated to slip the surly bonds of earth. Her spirit is shown looking carefree once she's by the angel's side. It's surprising to see Madonna "die" in a music video, but not too; after all, we are shown the discovery of her character's corpse in the beginning.

The message in the video is simple, but it's Madonna's layered silent performance that makes the video sing.

"Bad Girl" is noteworthy for Fincher's masterful direction. It's just as well that planned directors like Tim Burton and **Ellen von Unwerth** never panned out. It provides an early peek at Walken's dancing 10 years before his fancy footwork in Fatboy Slim's "Weapon of Choice." Watch for character actor Mark Margolis as a bartender and Tomas Arana as one of Louise's **boy toys**. Contrary to urban legend, Matt Dillon does *not* appear.

While making the video, Madonna developed an ear infection, causing her to push back her European ***Body of Evidence*** promo tour by a couple of days. She received press while lying in bed in a black bathrobe, her body very much in evidence.

BAGGIO, ROBERTO: *b. February 18, 1967.* During a ***Blond Ambition World Tour*** performance at Flaminio Stadium (Piazza Maresciallo Pilsudski, Rome, Italy), Madonna surprised **fans** by appearing in the #15 game jersey of this now-retired Italian World Cup soccer star. It endeared her to fans even as the nearby **Catholic** press was denouncing her show as blasphemous.

BAKER, ARTHUR: *b. April 22, 1955.* Longtime hip-hop and pop music producer. Baker was friendly with DJ **Mark Kamins** when Kamins first heard Madonna's demo and scored her and himself a record deal. Kamins, having no idea how to produce a record, leaned heavily on Baker for advice, resulting in Madonna's first single, **"Everybody."**

BALDWIN, WILLIAM "BILLY": *b. February 21, 1963.* The most boyishly cute Baldwin allegedly had a fling with Madonna in late 1991 during a temporary lull in his relationship with Chynna Phillips of Wilson Phillips, whom he went on to marry. When Baldwin was photographed leaving Madonna's apartment after the sun went down, he promptly punched out the offending paparazzo, Mitchell Gerber, smashing his camera. The shutterbug sued and received a reported $2,000 in damages.

BALLS: Nuts, rocks, jellybeans, jawbreakers, joy beans, dick dumplings, scrotum mice. We're talking about testicles.

In 1989, Madonna asked choreographer **Vincent Paterson** if he were the one "who had **Michael Jackson** grab his balls." Paterson couldn't claim that honor, but she was inspired nonetheless, and took his suggestion, resulting in her infamous **"Express Yourself"** video crotch-grab.

Madonna's later crotch-grab on the ***Interview*** (May 1990) cover was so controversial, some stores decided not to display it. She told ***The Advocate*** in 1991 that though ***Truth or Dare*** director **Alek Keshishian** had fairly large balls for locking horns with her, she felt she had the larger balls for allowing her life to be "splayed" on the screen.

To the frustration of **feminists**, Madonna has always used the term "balls" to connate strength and bravado.

BANDA, DAVID: *b. September 24, 2005.* Full name reportedly David Banda Mwale **Ciccone** Ritchie. With **Guy Ritchie**, Madonna's adoptive son from **Malawi**.

Following several years of unsuccessful fertility treatments, Madonna and Ritchie decided to adopt, making the decision on Christmas in 2005. Sometime in 2006, the couple—spurred by Madonna's research into Malawi's needs as she prepared a charitable commitment to the African nation—further decided that the child they would adopt would come from Malawi.

Ritchie visited Malawi first, then the couple announced a joint visit. They did not publicly confirm they were looking to adopt, but an official in the Malawian government told the media of their plans, asking for their **privacy** to be respected. Um, yeah, *no*.

Though the Ritchies denied they were adopting, the truth is that officials in the government had already scouted possible children for them. Madonna and Guy visited orphanages, one of which, Home of Hope (HomeofHope-Malawi.org), housed David Banda Mwale. That's where Madonna and her husband met David, who was just a year old.

Madonna told ***New York*** in 2008 that when she first encountered David, "He was basically going to the bathroom on himself. Of course, next day you come back with a truckload of Pampers. It sounds corny, but he just has these big, bright, intelligent, so-aware **eyes**, and I felt a connection to him."

Banda Mwale's **mother**, Marita, had died six days after giving birth to him, and his **father** Yohane Banda, from the village of Lipunga, had been unable to take care of his son. Still, Yohane Banda had visited David twice a week. In spite of their bond, he was receptive when a government official broached the subject of adoption by a foreign couple.

"My interest is in the child's best chance for health and education. It was a hard choice to make, but when it seemed likely that David would have a better life with a new family, I could not say no."

The Ritchies met David's father for the first time at a hearing at which the country's residency law (requiring prospective parents to live in Malawi for 18 months before adoption could be granted) was waived. Yohane Banda and his family slaughtered a goat to celebrate the adoption. "She is such a lovely lady. She asked me questions about me, David, and my family."

When Madonna and Guy removed David from Malawi, the international press asked whether they'd just "stolen" a child.

Advocacy group Eye of the Child objected to what was perceived as a bending of the rules, and many other child-welfare figures **voiced** concern about making foreign adoption so easy. Heartless comparisons were made between the adoption and the purchasing of an **accessory**; cynicism about Madonna's motives ran rampant.

Rafiq Hajat, an executive director at the Institute for Policy Interaction in Malawi suggested Madonna might be adopting David to "sell more records." Internet commenters were even less likely to mince words.

Was it because Madonna was wealthy, white or because she was Madonna? Angelina Jolie and **Brad Pitt** had

ALEJANDRO MOGOLLO

successfully adopted in Africa without as much (though not without some) negative attention, yet Madonna was branded a human trafficker.

In July 2008, Madonna and Guy's adoption of David was approved.

Unfortunately, Yohane Banda changed his tune, giving agonized interviews to the media, claiming Madonna had broken a promise to educate his son about his roots, and to allow visitation. By 2009, when David visited his biological father, the Ritchies were no longer a couple, a development Yohane Banda found tragic. But the elder Banda had returned to being on good terms with Madonna, praising her parenting. Madonna, a glutton for punishment, was in Malawi that time regarding a second adoption, this time of her eventual daughter, **Mercy James**.

Over the years, David Banda has made many appearances on Madonna's **Instagram**, showing off what appear to be rapidly progressing **dance** skills. Unlike his mama, he is not shy around paparazzi.

> "This was an eye-opening experience. A real low point in my life. I could get my head around people giving me a hard time for simulating masturbation onstage or publishing my *Sex* book, even kissing Britney Spears at an awards show, but trying to save a child's life was not something I thought I would be punished for."–MADONNA (2013)

BANDERAS, ANTONIO: *b. August 10, 1960. Paper* **magazine** summed him up as "THE MAN MADONNA COULDN'T GET." As the lead hunk of a series of Pedro Almodóvar films, he was one of Spain's biggest stars, but it wasn't until Madonna went (you should pardon the expression) gaga over him at a party thrown for her by his maverick director that he caught Hollywood's **eye**. At the party, seen in ***Truth or Dare***, Madonna confides to her backup singers that she has the hugest **crush** on Banderas, getting all dolled up in a Pucci top, short-shorts and fishnets for the occasion of their introduction, only to discover that he's happily married to actor Ana Leza. Madonna kicks herself in the bathroom, Leza mugs for director **Alek Keshishian**'s camera and Banderas does a slow burn across the screen.

Sexy, Latin, down with playing **gay** on screen and straight, he would seem to have been the perfect mate for Madonna. Though their would-be romance was supposedly stillborn, paparazzi snapped photos of Madonna and Banderas driving around together sans his wife. Keshishian must have blinked.

But Banderas—who has admitted that he didn't understand "shit" of what Madonna was saying to him when they first met due to his poor English—has stated firmly that they never had an affair. "I was afraid of it at the time, because she was a very **powerful** woman. I didn't want to be Madonna's boy. For good or bad, I just wanted to have my own career."

Banderas was always Madonna's first choice to play Che in a movie adaptation of the Broadway musical ***Evita***, and once she persuaded director **Alan Parker** to cast her in the title role, she got her way. Madonna and Banderas have incredible chemistry in the movie, but were again kept apart by marriage—he'd dumped his first wife in order to marry his **pregnant** girlfriend Melanie Griffith mere months before filming on *Evita* commenced. Griffith haunted the set, but needn't have worried; Madonna was too busy getting pregnant by **Carlos Leon**, re-learning how to sing and focusing on what would be the most important role of her career to have time to seduce Banderas. Griffith was one of the women who had lost the title role in ***Desperately Seeking Susan*** to Madonna back in 1984, but she did *not* lose Banderas until the couple filed for **divorce** in 2014.

> "We had dinner. We had rehearsals. We talked about the movie. And I sort of became his friend. I mean, he was married and I got to know his wife. I respected the fact that he was married."–MADONNA ON ANTONIO BANDERAS (1996)

BARBONE, CAMILLE: *b. August 16, 1950*. Madonna's first manager, her Gotham Records (run with **business** partner **Adam Alter**) offered its services to the newcomer in 1981 after meeting Madonna at **The Music Building** and then seeing her perform with the band **Emmy** at Max's Kansas City (formerly 213 Park Ave. S., NY, NY). Forsaking a record deal with Emmy, Madonna instead signed her Gotham Records deal on March 17, 1981, with an extension signed on July 22.

Barbone paid Madonna $100 a week (with $250 for **unreleased** masters and $500 plus a 3% royalty for anything released commercially), helped her secure an apartment, financed a demo and pitched her to record labels while Madonna played gigs around **New York**. The two became inseparable, Madonna looking up to Barbone while Barbone began falling for her client. The duo (along with Barbone's female lover and Madonna's boyfriend **Ken Compton**) even summered on Fire Island together.

Madonna recorded her Gotham demo in August 1981 under the auspices of John Roberts and Susan Planer at their Media Sound Studios on W. 57th. The songs recorded were "Take Me (I Want You)," "Love on the Run," "Get Up," "High Society (Society's Boy)," "Remembering Your Touch," and "Are You Ready for It?"; the first four were used for Madonna's demo, the last two discarded.

Backed by a seasoned band (including **Stephen Bray**), Madonna appeared in her first solo gig at **Chase Park** on October 8, 1981, and at showcases on October 16 and 17, 1981, at **U.S. Blues**. She also played at Max's and Cartoon Alley, The Underground Club and opened for **David Johansen** of the New York Dolls at My **Father**'s Place (formerly 19 Bryant Ave., Roslyn, NY).

Around this time, manager Bill Lomuscio took over from Adam Alter as Madonna's comanager, pumping more money into the project to make Madonna a star, but tensions between Madonna and Barbone (who was battling personal problems) were boiling over, and Madonna's rising star was attracting more **powerful** players.

In February 1982, Barbone and Lomuscio were fired, not by Madonna but by Jay Kramer, a music-biz lawyer for Billy Joel who had taken on Madonna as a client at the behest of William Morris agent Rob Prince, who hoped to do the same. (Prince never did officially sign on.) Madonna still had a contract with Gotham; a decade later, everything was settled with Barbone.

Performers change representation all the time, but one can't blame Barbone for feeling scorned, getting kicked to the curb so close to Madonna's career blowing up. She filed suit against Madonna for breach of contract, getting very little compared to the 15% of half a billion dollars she couldn't have known she stood to make.

In 1993, Barbone appeared on **Robin Leach**'s *Madonna Exposed* **TV** special, lamenting her estrangement from Madonna. Barbone shares Madonna's **birthday** (different years), but she wanted to share a lot more than that; in 1994, she marketed a melancholic proposal for a memoir called *Making Madonna* in which she confessed that she'd been in **love** with her former client, a complicating factor that hastened their rift.

Barbone wanted Madonna to do rock 'n' roll, steering clear of **disco**. If that's true, we can only thank Barbone for discovering Madonna, and thank Madonna for leaving Barbone.

"She wanted me to do Pat Benatar-like rock. I was crying for a more funky sound, black stuff. She told me that I couldn't do that because I was a little white girl. I refused to listen. You can't have a manager who wants to exploit your identity if you have a different idea of what your identity is going to be. We split, not too amiably."—MADONNA (1984)

BARKLEY, CHARLES: *b. February 20, 1963.* One of the all-time **basketball** greats, Barkley was rumored to have had a brief fling with Madonna the weekend of May 22, 1993. The pair met at a Suns-Lakers game in LA on May 5, 1993, and her sudden appearance in Phoenix at the time Barkley was playing for the Suns seemed to coincide with a rendezvous. But did they do it? You know they did it.

The **power** forward and the power bottom ate out at Tomaso's (3225 E. Camelback Rd., Phoenix, AZ), then spent some alone time in Madonna's Ritz-Carlton (2401 E. Camelback Rd., Phoenix, AZ) suite. Barkley, estranged from his wife Maureen at the time, soon moved on. When asked directly by a reporter why he'd slept with her, the chronically outspoken Barkley became flustered and shot

back, "Because I think Madonna is a great person," before back-pedaling with, "No, I did *not*."

The media and others were pretty merciless in razzing Barkley about the rumors. In June, Barkley claimed the stress had contributed to his **mother**-in-law's heart attack: "She has had a lot of stress from the jokes about me and Madonna and has been harassed with people calling the house. She's not doing well right now and that's a major concern. I only met [Madonna] one time when she was in Phoenix. We don't date. We don't have a relationship. They should leave my wife and daughter alone. When my wife goes out, they play Madonna songs, they're calling my in-laws. This stuff is ridiculous, unbelievable. Nothing happened. I'm trying to concentrate on the finals, but this is harassment of me and my family."

As for Madonna, she dropped Barkley's name repeatedly during an interview she conducted with her friend **Rosie O'Donnell** for *Mademoiselle*, calling him, "**God**." Ever fickle, she told **David Letterman** in 1994 that Barkley "doesn't know the meaning of the word ['friendship']."

BARNEY'S: Upscale department store (106 Seventh Ave., NY, NY, since relocated to 660 Madison Ave., NY, NY) where Madonna made a runway appearance on November 10, 1986, modeling designer denim jackets at an **auction** to benefit **AIDS**. One of the jackets was a **Martin Burgoyne** original, #54 on the agenda. Under the jacket, Madonna wore a black Lycra outfit from her *Who's That Girl* movie, which was then in production. Among the more than 80 other artists/designers represented were **Jean Paul Gaultier** and **Andy Warhol**. The star models included Peter Allen (who would later die of AIDS), **Debbie Harry** and Iman.

The benefit directly enriched the HIV center of St. Vincent's Hospital Manhattan (formerly 170 W. 12th St., NY, NY), which closed in 2010 after serving **NYC** for 161 years.

BARON, FABIEN: *b. July 5, 1959.* A lauded creative director, editorial director of *Interview* magazine and the **art** director of *Sex*, Baron is a gifted image junkie who has elevated his field. Just as it took until the late '50s for film directors to be considered "auteurs," so it took until Baron's emergence in the '80s for graphic designers and art directors to be seen as artists in their own right.

Baron soared to **fame** as the visionary behind those erotically chilly, PG-13 Calvin Klein ads (including **Mark Wahlberg** vs. Kate Moss), Issey Miyake's fragrance boxes, and as the force behind *GQ*, *Harper's Bazaar*, *French Vogue*, *Italian Vogue* and *New York* Woman before his **reinvention** of *Interview*.

Baron's style is shot through *Sex*: the stacked lettering, the superimposition, the collage ... they're all signature Baron. Madonna thanked him in the **book**'s acknowledgments for his "complete disdain for organization and utter disregard for detail."

Some of Baron's **work** on the much-maligned *Sex* is underrated—the "My **pussy** has nine lives" pages, the urinal juxtapositions, the most angular of the collages, the sizzling "I'll teach you how to **fuck**" spread—but Madonna should have cracked the whip to keep some of her most **eye**-popping poses from being jammed together in ways that led to them being overlooked.

As of 2008, Baron was working on a secret photo book for Team Madonna that was said to compile all of her greatest shoots and that would include the kinds of outtakes that make **fans** tingle *down there*. Rumor had it that photographers were being asked to submit all their goodies, but that Madonna didn't want to pay—the honor of inclusion would have been payment. The book never happened, but it was around then that countless previously unseen Madonna images began to **leak** on the Internet, many of them from the '80s and '90s. One theory as to the origin of all the leaks could be that once all these previously analog archives were scanned for submission, a weak link (or many!) along the way began sharing with friends, who began sharing, and so on.

At any rate, any fan in his or her right mind would agree to go hitchhiking **nude** if promised a new Madonna photo book designed by Baron. Thumbs up!

> "I admit to one error there. I allowed the book to be designed by somebody who did magazine layouts. And what looks great in a magazine doesn't always translate as a book. The text—yes, there *was* text!—was difficult to read. It was supposed to be ironic. People didn't get it. But if you're waiting for me to say I regret doing it, you'll be waiting a very long time."
>
> —MADONNA ON SEX (1996)

BARR, ROSEANNE: *b. November 3, 1952.* Pioneering female stand-up comic and **TV** icon who flopped in movies, became one of the weirder celebrities to deal with on **Twitter** and ran a crackpot presidential campaign in 2012.

In 1990, when Barr cheekily sang the national anthem badly, grabbing her crotch (like a baseball player) at the end, many in the US flipped out, accusing her of being unpatriotic. While touring with her ***Blond Ambition World Tour*** in France, Madonna took a moment to say, "And speakin' of grabbin' crotches. Roseanne Barr, baby—thumbs up, okay? I know you was payin' tribute to me, I know it was a joke, and I'm honored to be honored. So **fuck** what all those people say. You know what I have to say to America? Get a fuckin' sense of humor, okay? Lighten up!"

Barr and Tom Arnold were the hosts of ***Saturday Night Live*** in 1992 when both Madonna and **Barbra Streisand** made surprise appearances in the classic "Coffee Talk with Linda Richman" sketch, in which Barr was the unexpected weakest link.

Years later, Barr criticized Madonna (and everyone else) fairly regularly. In 2008, she snapped of Madonna, "Please lay off the Botox. You are scaring the children! Act your age!" This from a woman whose own surgical interventions have rendered her almost unrecognizable—in a good way!

In a who-asked-ya? screed in *Newsweek* 2011, Barr wrote at length about how Madonna—for whom she now feels sorry—doesn't yet realize that "life will even the score, and it will go against you. Despite the Botox, spas and youthful boyfriends, and about the same time you acquire gray pubes, a clothing line not with **Dolce & Gabbana** but at Macy's, will be all the haute couture your dusty old brand can muster ... Being 53 and having **sex** with folks in their early 20s is just so 'Norma Desmond.' There, I said it. I can dig the dead writer in the pool thing, though."

It's a shame that Barr, who in the article was trying to write unsparingly of her personal experience with menopause in such a **feminist** way, resorted to criticizing Madonna's choices in life in terms more bitter than wise.

A broken record on the topic of Madonna, after Madonna's **Super Bowl** performance, Barr tweeted, "Madonna kicked ass 4 **gays** kabbalists and Botox."

BARRON, STEVE: *b. May 4, 1956.* This director of the beloved '80s comedy *Electric* ***Dreams*** (1984) and the massively successful *Teenage Mutant Ninja Turtles* (1990) also directed two of the most famous, most celebrated music videos of all time: "Billie Jean" by **Michael Jackson** (1983) and "Take on Me" by a-ha (1985).

In 1983, Barron became the director of Madonna's first studio music video, the kitschily stylish **"Burning Up,"** which presented Madonna to great advantage.

"I hadn't heard of her, and I didn't like the song very much," Barron said in 2012. "I was on vacation, and I was being told that I had to meet her because she's going to be this huge star. I met her and she was cheeky, and I saw her play a gig at **Danceteria**. She did a few tracks there, and she had a lot of character. When we actually met, we were talking and she was sitting at a table and kept putting her head onto the table, first down onto one side, then the other, and I thought, 'You know, that's what we'll do in the video.'"

BASKETBALL: Madonna used to like watching basketball in the '90s.

"It reminds me of **dancing**," she said. "**I love** the action ... You can see the guys' legs and arms and faces. They're so graceful. And it's so in-your-face intimate." She has cited Horace Grant, Michael Jordan, **Dennis Rodman** (whose rebellious nature made him, in Madonna's words, "the Madonna of the NBA"), Brian Shaw and John Starks as her favorites, going so far as to say she hoped to be **reincarnated** as Jordan. Her preferred teams were the Knicks and the Lakers.

Madonna has been romantically linked with basketballers **Charles Barkley**, Anthony Mason, Rodman and Rony Seikaly.

She once joked that she would like to own a team and then said she'd be "hands-on. Definitely. My hands would be all over the place."

BASQUIAT, JEAN-MICHEL: *December 22, 1960–August 12, 1988.* Massively influential, Brooklyn-born artist of Puerto Rican–Haitian descent with whom Madonna was fleetingly involved romantically for about 90 days in 1982–1983 after an introduction by **Ed Steinberg** at Lucky Strike Club (formerly 9th St. & Third Ave., 2nd Fl., NY, NY). Images of the couple shot by Basquiat's assistant Stephen Torton memorialized their time together, showing a paint-splattered Basquiat with a hypnotized-looking Madonna. Artichokes are involved.

Basquiat was the most troubled of Madonna's lovers, a heroin addict with a self-destructive streak a mile wide. He shot to **fame** along with **Keith Haring**; was affiliated with gallerist Larry Gagosian, with whom Basquiat and Madonna stayed in late 1982 (Gagosian recalled that over the holidays, "Madonna had the yellow pages in her lap and she was feverishly looking for a pharmacy that could deliver **condoms** to **Malibu** on Christmas Day. Most of them were closed. I think they had to buy about $200 worth."); and collaborated closely with **Andy Warhol**, selling his Primitivist canvases for thousands of dollars while still in his early twenties.

Madonna remembered that she, Basquiat, **Futura 2000**, Keith Haring and Warhol were at a Japanese restaurant on 2nd Ave. and 7th St. in 1982 when her single **"Everybody"** came on the radio. She told *Rolling Stone* that Basquiat expressed jealousy that her **art** would get mass attention, but Warhol told him to stop complaining.

Like Madonna, Basquiat would come to feel used by some of his friends from the time before he found fame, who sold **works** he'd **gifted** them, turning a profit on their friendship. Basquiat's meteoric rise in a nutshell: He was once ejected from the Whitney Museum (then 945 Madison Ave., NY, NY; now 99 Gansevoort St., NY, NY) for vandalism, but before long, his work was displayed there.

When they broke up, Basquiat made Madonna give back all of the paintings he'd given her, save one, which she now sees as one of her most **prized possessions**. She later found out he'd painted over the ones she'd returned.

Basquiat died of a heroin overdose at his **NYC** studio.

BAY CITY: Madonna called this, her birthplace, a "little smelly town in northern **Michigan**," but her maternal grandmother **Elsie Fortin** told biographer **Barbara Victor** that the town's mayor, Timothy Sullivan, who decided Madonna was unworthy of being offered a key to the city after her **nude** photo scandal of 1985, called her "seven or eight times a day" to see if she could get Madonna to do a free concert to benefit the town.

In 2014, amateur Bay City music historian Gary Johnson tried to persuade townsfolk to embrace the idea of promoting the city as Madonna's birthplace, but many locals are still pissed off at being called "smelly" and see Madonna as someone who thinks of herself as better than them.

Madonna may not fully embrace Bay City and vice versa, but she has more of a history there than simply being born within its city limits. She has spoken of her "great affection" for the town, has said she enjoyed spending time in Bay City State Park and chose Tony's Amusement Park (formerly Euclid Ave. and Beaver Rd., Bay City, MI) as her favorite Bay City spot.

Madonna's **mother** is buried in Calvary Cemetery (2977 Old Kawkawlin Rd., Bay City, MI); her 1990 visit to the site was filmed for use in *Truth or Dare*.

BBC CHILDREN IN NEED: *Airdates: 1980–.* Telethon held annually by the BBC in the UK to benefit at-risk youth and the disabled.

On November 18, 2005, the telecast featured performances by Girls Aloud, Liberty X, Rod Stewart and—oh, yeah!—Madonna. Madonna, in the same sequin-tastic '70s-style dress she'd worn on France's *Star Academy* and rocking her "Valerie Cherish" 'do, performed what host **Terry Wogan** characterized as a "storming" performance of her smash **"Hung Up"** and an unembellished, giddy version of **"Get Together,"** accompanied by **Stuart Price** on keyboard.

Wogan later confessed that even though he'd interviewed Madonna before, she "completely blanked" (deliberately ignored) him when appearing on this **charity** show.

"B-DAY SONG": A widely derided '60s-style song from the Deluxe Edition of *MDNA* written by Madonna, **M.I.A.** and **Martin Solveig**, produced by Madonna and Solveig, that features M.I.A. singing with Madonna. The song, which maintains a cloying juvenile tone throughout, opens with a lyrical reference to "The Beat Goes On" (1967) by Sonny & **Cher**. Musically, it could be described as a stunted take on reggae.

"BE CAREFUL WITH MY HEART (CUIDADO CON MI CORAZÓN)" PERF. BY RICKY MARTIN AND MADONNA: This somewhat limp ballad performed by **Ricky Martin** and Madonna (written and produced by Madonna and **William Orbit**) was added to Martin's self-titled 1999 English-language solo debut after the artists embraced at the **Grammys**. Less than three months elapsed between their first meeting and the album's release. Both singers' vocals are subdued, underscoring the song's theme of emotional fragility. Madonna sings some of her part in Spanish.

"BEAST WITHIN, THE": Disturbing remix of **"Justify My Love"** from late 1990 that appeared on the B-side of the **dance** single of that song.

Over a pounding bass line and interspersed with the song's bluntly **sexual** lyrics, Madonna chants from Revelation. The "they are not Jews" passage is one often used

—BILLY EICHNER

by anti-Semites to justify their **hate**, so Madonna (not a Christian girl, not yet a Jewish woman) was criticized by the Simon Weisenthal Center and the Anti-Defamation League of B'nai B'rith

She apologized for having accidentally created an anti-Semitic song with a good beat that you could dance to, but she wound up using the same song (minus offending lyrics) in a militaristic **gay** dance break on *The Girlie Show World Tour* and as the opening song of her *Re-Invention World Tour*, where it played over a series of hella raw images filmed by **Steven Klein** during their collaborative *X-STaTIC PRO=CeSS* shoot.

BEASTIE BOYS: Consisting of Michael "Mike D" Diamond, Adam "Ad-Rock" Horovitz and Adam "MCA" Yauch, they were the young, bombastic Jewish punk-rap group chosen to open for Madonna on *The Virgin Tour*. The logic behind the pairing was that (1) Madonna **fans** didn't care who was opening, they were just desperate to see their idol; and (2) after sitting through the antics of the Beasties, her fans would be even more desperate. Ad-Rock recalled, "... Madonna, the thing is that, like, she—also besides she's awesome and great and all that stuff—but she realized, like, they **hated** us so much that by the time she got on stage it was, like, the greatest thing ..."

Who knew they'd go on to become musical legends? Who knew Madonna would?

Their manager, Russell Simmons, had first offered Run-DMC as a support act, but wanted $50,000 per night. The next possibility was the Fat Boys. Finally, Simmons told Madonna's manager **Freddy DeMann** that he had this Beastie Boys group who'd do it for $200.

Upon hearing of Yauch's **death** in 2012, Madonna called him "one of a kind" and said that the Beastie Boys were "integral to the musical revolution that was happening at the time."

"They don't wanna see rap music, they don't wanna see the Beastie Boys, they don't care what we're doing, they want one thing and one thing only, and that's to see Madonna come on stage. But then, we go out there, work hard, win 'em over, and then they get real happy. It's really kinda cool."

—BEASTIE BOYS ON OPENING FOR MADONNA (1985)

"BEAT GOES ON" FEAT. KANYE WEST: Perhaps the most underrated track from Madonna's *Hard Candy*, written by Madonna, **Pharrell Williams** and **Kanye West**, the latter of whom is featured on the song in a snappy rap. Produced by the **Neptunes** and Madonna, this house-inflected fist-pumper recalls **"Into the Groove"** overall, has a **"True Blue"**-esque "Hey!" and also exhibits Donna Summer "Hot Stuff" (1979) echoes. A dramatically

different version **leaked** in demo form in advance of its official release. Lyrically, "Beat Goes On" is not Madonna's most adventurous effort, however—Madonna has sung about beats going on and about waiting/anticipating quite enough for one career.

"Beat Goes On" was performed on her *Sticky & Sweet Tour*.

BEATLES: The most successful pop entity of all time, they started as pop stars and became poets. Madonna **worked** with George Harrison, is friendly with Paul McCartney (due to a close friendship with his daughter, **Stella McCartney**), remade John Lennon's **"Imagine"** and ... wait, was there a fourth guy?

In 1992, Madonna identified her favorite Beatles song as "If I Fell" (1964) and sang a snippet of it on the French TV show *7 sur 7*.

BEATTY, WARREN: *b. March 30, 1937*. That's **"Pussy Man"** to you.

Madonna lovingly called her most independently famous lover by that pet name in *Truth or Dare*, then wondered why they seemed to spar all the time.

Beatty was the world's most legendary lothario and 21 years older than Madonna at the time of their affair, which lasted for about a year from the spring of 1989. Beatty had first shown interest in Madonna in 1985, when he watched the dailies of *Desperately Seeking Susan* with director **Susan Seidelman**, telling her he liked the enigmatic tough chick he saw therein. Madonna and Beatty even met briefly on Madonna's first date with **Sean Penn**, the same evening she first met **Sandra Bernhard**, Jack Nicholson and Mickey Rourke—what a night!

In 1989, when Beatty was casting *Dick Tracy*, a film he'd been trying to get made since Madonna's senior year in high **school**, she agreed to play villainous chanteuse "Breathless Mahoney" at scale wages ($1,440 per week). Manager **Freddy DeMann** resisted Madonna's participation at first, which makes sense. Was it really a sterling idea for Madonna to play a comic-strip character? But Beatty promised to photograph her beautifully, so DeMann relented.

As soon as filming started, the actor and her director began their tempestuous affair, which eclipsed the buzz about the movie itself.

Beatty has rarely spoken of his relationship with Madonna, of whom his **mother** Kathlyn reportedly did not approve. Madonna later said Beatty had confided his **regret** at not having explored **gay** sex when he was younger. She also indiscreetly told **Arsenio Hall** that, contrary to popular belief, Beatty is definitely satiable in the sack, and when asked if the couple had practiced safe **sex** quipped, "If I have to give Warren Beatty safe-sex lessons, what is this world coming to?"

On May 16, 1990, Beatty allegedly proposed to Madonna, giving her a six-carat, diamond-and-sapphire ring; she accepted the ring, though their engagement was not publicly announced. By that August, after seeing an early cut of *Truth or Dare*, Beatty had his lawyer serve Madonna notice that she would be sued if certain of his private phone conversations with her were in the final cut. They weren't.

Not long after, Madonna and Beatty were history. Their relationship ended on cool but friendly terms shortly after the film's premiere. So effective was their liaison in generating free PR that some observers felt it had all been a showmance. But like so many things in Madonna World, it was another example of an organic thing that Madonna played to her advantage.

After it was all over, Madonna moved on to **Tony Ward**, while Beatty bounced briefly to model Stephanie Seymour before landing in wedded bliss and experiencing parenthood with acclaimed actor Annette Bening. Think of Madonna as his extended **bachelor party**.

> "She's a big, beautiful, hilarious, touching, brilliant fact of life. And I think we should all just relax and enjoy it."
> —WARREN BEATTY ON MADONNA (1990)

"BEAUTIFUL KILLER": Song from the Deluxe Edition of *MDNA*, written by Madonna, **Martin Solveig** and Michael Tordjman, and produced by Madonna and Solveig. With its traditional pop meets electronica sound, it would have sounded right at home on *Music*. The song's title is whispered for emphasis within the melodic confection, but the real drama comes at the end, when things are wrapped up with the sound of a gunshot. In the lyrics, Madonna puts forth French actor Alain Delon as the kind of man you'll never be.

"Beautiful Killer" was performed live only once, at her **Olympia Hall** show, mashed up with **"Die Another Day."**

"BEAUTIFUL SCARS": Perky, house-infused track from the Super Deluxe Edition of *Rebel Heart* that continues Madonna's ongoing advocacy for unconditional **love**. The song was written by Madonna, **Rick Nowels**, DJ Dahi and Blood Diamonds. Madonna produced it with the latter two musicians.

"BEAUTIFUL STRANGER" (SONG): *Release date: May 29, 1999. Billboard Hot 100 peak: #19.* High on their success with *Ray of Light*, Madonna and **William Orbit** immediately teamed up again for this song, created for the soundtrack of *Austin Powers: The Spy Who Shagged Me*. Madonna was game for the project because she was both friendly with Mike Myers and her **Maverick** label was releasing the soundtrack commercially.

With a *Ray of Light* sound but without a shred of seriousness, the song recalls '60s psychedelica. It was embraced by **fans** (it was a #19 hit in the US based on airplay alone and was a sweeping smash abroad) and critics (it won the 2000 **Grammy** for Best Song Written for a Motion Picture, **Television** or Other Visual Media). Confoundingly, it did not receive an **Oscar** nomination.

Madonna performed the song live on her ***Drowned World Tour*** and as a bonus on her ***Rebel Heart Tour.***

"BEAUTIFUL STRANGER" (VIDEO): *Director: Brett Ratner, 1999.* Filmed May 1, 1999, the video for Madonna's *Austin Powers: The Spy Who Shagged Me* hit song is a simple affair, beginning with Mike Myers in character as "Austin Powers" being given an assignment to stop a spy (Madonna) who has been (literally) charming the pants off of agents. Michael York, as "Basil Exposition," enlists Austin's aid in a short intro:

"Someone is seducing our top agents. As you can see, she's a master of disguise." Images of Madonna throughout her career flash on the screen. "But Austin, whatever you do, don't fall in **love**. We've already lost 007 and 008."

Next, Austin is watching Madonna executing saucy **dance** moves in a club. Right away, he begins fantasizing about dancing with this beautiful stranger, leading to scenes of the pair jumping for joy on a psychedelic swirl background and driving around what's supposed to be **London**, plus a shot of Madonna rubbing her butt right on Austin's face. Yeah, baby! (It needed to be said.)

In spite of the video being a couple of steps above a clips compilation, a video to which Madonna probably gave very little thought, it won her an **MTV Video Music Award**.

BEAUTY: Madonna may not be a model, but she is a great beauty and always has been, a combination of classical features (her **eyes**) and beguiling imperfections (that **gap** in her teeth), with **sexual** charisma as the pop-my-cherry on the top.

In its July 18, 1991, 50 Most Beautiful People issue, *People* included Madonna as one of its lauded lookers.

As the epoch's most visible woman and a sex symbol to boot, her beauty has always been a major issue in any discussion of Madonna, whether used in a complimentary way, or to belittle her artistically.

Peers Joan Baez and **Joni Mitchell** have warned that Madonna shouldn't rely too heavily on her looks, which is all very, "Beauty fades!"

Of note: The more sexually transgressive Madonna became in her **work**, the more derided her looks were in the media, whether it was noticing the arrival of crow's-feet or downy facial **hair** or—international gasp—her muscular arms. Don't even *talk about* the commentary swirling around her apparent adventures in **plastic surgery**.

On December 6, 2014, as controversy swirled around 56-year-old Madonna's decision to pose topless for **Mert and Marcus**, tabloid writer Liz Jones published a perverse exercise in **ageism** in the UK's *Daily Mail*, in which she allegedly tried to show, by posing like Madonna, how difficult it is for

RICHARD CORMAN

an average woman Madonna's age to look as good as she does. Jones's photos are deliberately botched—she makes awkward faces and apes Madonna's exact poses instead of creating some that might work better for her, all so that she could write that Madonna should be "ashamed" as "a woman who places physical perfection above all else" (guess she missed Madonna's motherhood, **charity** work and prolific artistic output) and whose appearance is "surely adding to figures that show half of 17- to 21-year-old women feel ashamed about the way they look." Jones's ridiculously naked gambit for clicks is a perfect example of how Madonna's looks—while presumably giving her a leg up from the beginning—can be used in sexist, ageist, illogical ways to tear her down.

But if having narrow-minded and/or jealous people begrudging you for your beauty is the worst of the problems that come with being a knock-out, you might as well just be a knock-out and enjoy your **haters'** melt-do

BEAUTY MARK: Madonna's is under her right nostril, just above her lips. It's real, though she conceals or darkens it, and it's not as prominent as it seemed in the '80s.

BECKER, ANGELA: Madonna's assistant, praised to high heaven in *I'm Going to Tell You a Secret*. Following the tenure of **Caresse Henry**, Becker briefly comanaged Madonna with **Guy Oseary** before she was succeeded by Oseary, solo. Becker was **pregnant** with **Stuart Price**'s child at the time she left Madonna's employ, leading to rumors as to why the women parted ways. Becker, a veteran of the industry, has managed **Pet Shop Boys** since 2009.

"MADONNA'S MOST RECENT ANTECEDENT, DEBBIE HARRY, WAS FAR TOO STUNNING AND BEATIFIC TO APPEAL TO MOST WOMEN. AFTER ALL, SHE WAS IMPOSSIBLE TO IMITATE WITHOUT THE AID OF A COSTLY SURGICAL OVERHAUL. MADONNA, HOWEVER, IS HARDLY GOD'S GIFT TO BEAUTY. SHE'S PLAIN-LOOKING, HAS LEGS LIKE A SYCAMORE TREE, BUT MAKES THE BEST OF MAKEUP AND USES HER RECENTLY EXPOSED ASSETS WITH GUSTO."

—TED MICO, *MELODY MAKER* (1985)

"… MADONNA HAS MADE HERSELF THE MIRRORED BALL OF POP CULTURE, REFLECTING AND FRACTURING OUR OBSESSIONS WITH POWER, SEX AND FAME. BUT IS SHE REALLY BEAUTIFUL? OF COURSE SHE'S BEAUTIFUL! THAT COMES WITH THE TERRITORY, WITH THE POWER."—*PEOPLE* (1991)

"… I THINK PASSIVE BEAUTIES HAVE THEIR PLACE IN THE WORLD. IT'S HARD FOR ME TO RELATE TO THAT BECAUSE I'VE NEVER BEEN A VERY PASSIVE PERSON. PHYSICALITY, FEELING STRONG, FEELING EMPOWERED WAS MY TICKET OUT OF MIDDLE-CLASS MIDWEST CULTURE. SO I EQUATE MOVEMENT AND STRENGTH WITH FREEDOM."—*MADONNA* (2006)

BEDTIME STORIES: *Release date: October 25, 1994. Billboard 200 peak: #3. The theme: It's lonely at the top. Funky, too.*

Her sixth studio album launched a virtual creative resurrection of Madonna in the **eyes** of the media. With its fuddy duddy–friendly softness, out-there trance experiments and street-hip R&B, the album has something for everyone. The fact that the cover was released first with Madonna's face upside down and then right-side up (marketers feared consumers wouldn't recognize her) serves as a metaphor for how much Madonna shook things up here.

Featuring collaborations with **Dave Hall** (cowriter of **Mariah Carey**'s 1993 song "Dreamlover"), Atlanta songwriter **Dallas Austin**, **Björk** buddy **Nellee Hooper** and hitmaker **Babyface**, *Bedtime Stories* has a sound that shotgunmarries new jill swing to Enigma. (What to call this sound? Madonna Culpa? Benedictine Funk?) It's no shock that Madonna would get around to trying her hand at hip-hop, but plenty of listeners were blown away by the trip-hop, and by the fact that the album is not a pose, but an inspiration. The styles explored on the record sound like second nature to Madonna, and *Bedtime Stories* serves as an argument against rigid categorization of black vs. white music, a pet peeve of Madonna's from her earliest interviews.

All that said, she received no **Grammy** nominations in R&B categories; *Bedtime Stories* was nominated for Best Pop Album.

The mix of styles was a challenge, but no more than **working** with so many producers. Madonna admitted in 1998, "Yeah, that was a really hard record for me to make, 'cause it was the first time that I had ever, um, worked with four producers on one record … [I]t was really hard for me to sort of glue the sound together and make one kind of theme happen through the music, sonically and lyrically."

The alchemy pays off with an album of 11 breathy, intoxicating tunes cozily nestled in shimmering instrumentation. The songs distinguish themselves not only from most of Madonna's previous efforts, but also from each other.

Paradoxically, another secret of the album's success is its clever self-reflexivity. In **"Survival,"** Madonna concedes that she's no **"Angel,"** but that she plans to **"Live to Tell."** Both **"I'd Rather Be Your Lover"** and **"Secret"** assert that happiness lies in your own hand and the former sports a run-down of relations Madonna would rather *not* be (your sister, **mother**, friend, brother), echoing *Erotica*'s **"Where Life Begins,"** which is also hinted at on the album's **"Inside of Me."** Two lines from **"Don't Stop"** are almost identical to lines in Madonna's first single, **"Everybody,"** and Madonna's plea to "get up on the **dance** floor" harkens back to 1990's **"Vogue."** Most effective is Madonna's repeated command to **"Express Yourself"** on **"Human Nature."** It's one of Madonna's definitive statements of purpose, and here it's an acidic counter-attack on her legions of critics.

BEDTIME STORIES

① "Survival" (Madonna/Dallas Austin) –3:31, produced by Dallas Austin/Nellee Hooper/Madonna

② "Secret" (Madonna/Dallas Austin/Shep Pettibone)–5:05, produced by Madonna/Dave Hall

③ "I'd Rather Be Your Lover" feat. Meshell Ndegeocello (Madonna/Dave Hall/Isley Brothers/Christopher Jasper)–4:39, produced by Madonna/Dave Hall

④ "Don't Stop" (Madonna/Dallas Austin/Colin Wolfe)–4:38, produced by Madonna/Dallas Austin (additional production/remix by Daniel Abraham)

⑤ "Inside of Me" (Madonna/Dave Hall/Nellee Hooper)–4:11, produced by Nellee Hooper/Madonna

⑥ "Human Nature" (Madonna/Dave Hall/Shawn McKenzie/Kevin McKenzie/Michael Deering) –4:54, produced by Madonna/Dave Hall

⑦ "Forbidden Love" (Babyface/Madonna) –4:08, produced by Babyface/Nellee Hooper/Madonna

⑧ "Love Tried to Welcome Me" (Madonna/Dave Hall) –5:21, produced by Madonna/Dave Hall

⑨ "Sanctuary" (Madonna/Dallas Austin/Anne Preven/Scott Cutler/Herbie Hancock) –5:02, produced by Madonna/Dallas Austin (remix by Nellee Hooper)

⑩ "Bedtime Story" (Nellee Hooper/Björk/Marius de Vries)–4:53, produced by Nellee Hooper/Madonna

⑪ "Take a Bow" (Babyface/Madonna) –5:21, produced by Babyface/Madonna

ALEJANDRO MOGOLLO

nonetheless nearly as subdued as the rest of the batch, but it's a more-than-credible re-creation of '70s soul with a **disco** bump-and-grind.

Vulnerability is another defining characteristic of *Bedtime Stories*; "Inside of Me" is the musical embodiment of the moment in ***Truth or Dare*** when Madonna confesses that **Sean Penn** is the **love** of her life. Perhaps because Madonna has said she was singing about her mother, the song, in spite of its relative obscurity, stands alongside "Live to Tell" and **"Oh Father"** as among her most poignant musical statements. It's touching for its optimism in the face of loss.

"I think people are starting to think of me as a songwriter as a result of this record," Madonna said in 1995 of the album. "People are listening to these songs and reflecting over the last twelve years and saying, 'You know what? She's a good songwriter!'"

"Human Nature" is Madonna at her most defensive, and a rare example of an answer song that actually works. It's petty to talk back, but enough is enough, and here, Madonna's sass is a hoot, an unbridled bitchfest. **"Forbidden Love"** could be about an interracial relationship, **gay** love or anything that anyone might consider to be taboo, or simply about wanting him to say yes when he has steadfastly said no thanks, creating considerable sexual tension with Madonna's charged delivery over the music's erotic thump. **"Love Tried to Welcome Me"**—an extremely poetic sentiment from the woman most reviewers to this day insist on referring to as "the **Material Girl**"—finds the singer listing her useless body parts and disclosing her penchant for sadness.

One of the album's standouts is the 10-plus-minute suite created by the run-on songs **"Sanctuary"** and **"Bedtime Story,"** both of which rank among Madonna's most deliciously uncharacteristic songs. The former is a meditative self-eraser that bleeds into Madonna's choked whimper at the onset of "Bedtime Story," the only song on the album she had no hand in writing. It makes no difference that Björk, Hooper and **Marius de Vries** put the words in Madonna's mouth, "Bedtime Story" is a hypnotic, almost hallucinogenic, ride through an idealized-consciousness state of mind in which words (elevated by **"Words"** on *Erotica*) are rendered useless. **"Dress You Up"**? No, thanks. We're just gonna pass **fucking** *out*.

The whole throbbing ordeal simmers to an end with **"Take a Bow,"** Madonna's take on "Superstar" by the Carpenters, featuring her full vocal range on a song about love between a **fan** and "one lonely star." The song's references to the cessation of a masquerade and to a sense of finale evoke images of ***The Girlie Show World Tour***, playing up the sadness of the solitary Pierrot in platforms.

Listening to *Bedtime Stories* is a beautiful kind of lonely. There is romance in yearning, and Madonna captures it here perfectly.

It hit the spot, selling over 7 million copies worldwide, an improvement over *Erotica*.

Adding to the air of familiarity are inspired samples from Lou Donaldson's "It's Your Thing" (1969), Aaliyah's "Back and Forth" (1994), the Gap Band's "Outstanding" (1982), The Gutter Snypes' "The Trials of Life" (1994), Main Source's "What You Need" (1994), Grant Green's "Down Here on the Ground" (1970) and Herbie Hancock's "Watermelon Man" (1962).

Even the album **art** reminds: Take off that nose ring and squint at that platinum **hair**, and you're left with what could pass for a still from her **"Like a Virgin"** video. Madonna's even wearing lace, and this **Patrick Demarchelier** portrait screams, "Get yer classic Madonna here, step right up!"

Buyer beware: The album may be a classic to some, but it has little to do with the Madonna of *Like a Virgin* or *Like a Prayer*. *Bedtime Stories* is a step in a different direction from where she'd previously been—and it's a direction in which she's never really gone again.

"Survival" kicks things off, establishing the jazzy tone and surprising with Madonna's girlish delivery, in contrast with the defiant lyrics. "Secret," the indelible first single, is next, leading into "I'd Rather Be Your Lover," an understated **sex** anthem the likes of which **"Justify My Love"** invented. The album's sole dance track, "Don't Stop," is

"THIS TIME, S&M MEANS SILKY AND MELLOW … AN APPEALING HYBRID OF STREET HIP-HOP AND LUSH BALLADRY …"-EDNA GUNDERSEN, *USA TODAY* (1994)

"AFTER SO MUCH CIGAR-SMOKING, LATE-NIGHT BULL WACKY, AMERICA'S BITCHY BLONDE SWEET-TART IS BACK WITH A FELINE FOLLOW-UP TO *EROTICA*. *BEDTIME STORIES* LAYS HEAVY ON THE TINY ICON'S LOWER VOCALS AND KICKS DANCE PUSSY WITH LANGUID HIPFUNK FLOOR-WRECKERS. WITH HOLES IN ALL THE RIGHT PLACES, AND A VERY HARLOW POWDER-PALE ELEGANCE, THE VIRGIN IS BACK AND SHE'S READY TO DANCE."-*NEXT* (1994)

"[T]HERE'S NO DENYING THAT MADONNA KEEPS MOVING FORWARD AND CROSSING BARRIERS— THIS TIME, HELPING ANOTHER KIND OF BLACK MUSIC FURTHER PENETRATE INTO THE MAINSTREAM. APPARENTLY, POP'S MOST SHAMELESS EXHIBITIONIST STILL HAS SOMETHING TO REVEAL."
-JIM FARBER, *ENTERTAINMENT WEEKLY* (1994)

"FOR MONTHS LEADING UP TO ITS RELEASE, IT WAS MARKETED AS AN APOLOGY FOR HER SEXUAL BEHAVIOR, AND CRITICS HOPED IT WOULD BE HER RETURN TO INNOCENCE. INSTEAD, SHE OFFERED A LYRICAL #SORRYNOTSORRY AND A RESPONSE TO THE PROBLEM OF FEMALE MUSICIANS BEING SCRUTINIZED FOR THEIR SEXUALITY RATHER THAN THEIR MUSIC."-MARY VON AUE, *NOISEY* (2014)

"BEDTIME STORY" (SONG): *Release date: February 13, 1995. Billboard Hot 100 peak: #42.* Madonna's trip-notic performance of a song written by **Björk, Nellee Hooper** and **Marius de Vries** (from a demo entitled "Let's Get Unconscious"), produced by Madonna and Hooper, was a total curveball at the time of its inclusion on the *Bedtime Stories* album. Beginning with a parched moan, not necessarily of the **sexual** variety, it quickly spins into a trance track that urges the listener to join Madonna in getting "unconscious" and that slurs words (especially sentences, those bastards) as essentially meaningless. It's beyond cool, but was probably too cool for the room, missing the Top 40, thus making "Bedtime Story" her first single to do so since **"Burning Up."**

One reason for the single's failure could also be its position as the next song released after **"Take a Bow,"** a massive radio hit; songs as long-lived as that have a tendency to quash whatever comes next.

Madonna performed the song live at the **Brit Awards**, and used a remix for an interlude on her *Re-Invention World Tour.*

As for Björk, she revealed before the song's release, "… I've never met her … Well, basically, she asked my friend for a song, and my friend asked me to help him, and I did it in a way as a, like, a favor to him, really. Not, you know—no offense to Madonna, but I was kinda more doing it as a present to my friend."

She later said that Madonna had gotten her lyrics wrong, but there is confusion as to exactly how; apparently, the **original** lyric was "learning logic and reason," whereas Madonna opted for "leaving" it. Björk reworked her initial song entirely and released the results on her own. Her "Sweet Intuition" shares very little (outside of one matching lyric) with Madonna's "Bedtime Story."

"It's going to be a kind of futuristic, surreal dreamscape. Does that make sense? Don't worry, I don't get it either, but Mark Romanek … knows what he's doing so I feel safe."-MADONNA (1995)

"BEDTIME STORY" (VIDEO): *Director: Mark Romanek, 1995.* Madonna's second and final video with visionary director **Mark Romanek**, "Bedtime Story" took six days to shoot and is a tour de force by any measure. A sprawling view of one's outer and inner space, the video shows Madonna awakening as if in a spacecraft. Soon thereafter, the events of the video, seemingly a **dream**, begin.

Madonna, her **hair** knotted and her gaze fixed, mouths the song's lyrics as a giant sunflower sensually **flirts** with engulfing her from behind. An elaborate scene involving other—male, female, adult and child—figures (and a levitating cube containing Madonna's image in full Bettie Page mode), unfolds, becoming more and more surreal. Alarmingly, a **pregnant** Madonna "gives birth" to a flock of white doves just before she flies down a chamber unaided as computer-generated whirling dervishes inexorably spin. Just before her character wakes up, Madonna is shown with mouths for **eyes** and an eye for a mouth—all reality has broken down.

Rife with mystical, Sufi and **art**-world allusions, the video is a singular creation in Madonna's oeuvre. Reported to cost a cool $5 million, it is a damn impressive achievement, enough so that it is a part of the collection of **New York**'s Museum of Modern Art (11 W. 53rd St., NY, NY). It played on movie screens before feature presentations in some markets, including Chicago, New York and Santa Monica.

BEGO, MARK: *b. September 23, 1952.* Best-selling biographer who wrote one of the first **books** on Madonna, entitled simply *Madonna!*—which sold a million copies. That feat would be impossible in today's publishing climate minus vampires or bondage, the latter of which Madonna hadn't gotten to yet in 1985. The book was celebrated at a launch party on May 16, 1985, at The Red Parrot (formerly 617 W. 57th St., NY, NY).

Bego interviewed Madonna on the set of *Desperately Seeking Susan* and funneled material to various teen publications, which actually meant something in the '80s—the teen mags made and broke careers back then, boy.

Bego went back to the well a couple of times on Madonna, publishing two versions of *Madonna: Blonde Ambition* (1992 and 2001) and hosting *Madonna: The Name of the Game.*

BEHAR, JOY: *b. October 7, 1942.* This longtime cohost of *The View* (1997–2013), *The Joy Behar Show* (2009–2011) and *Joy Behar: Say Anything!* (2012–2013) is also a longtime Madonna skeptic, often skewering M for her behavior.

When Madonna intentionally flashed a breast while on her *MDNA Tour*, Behar made a crack about the roadies having to pick them up and opined, "I mean, she's 50 now … it's a bit of a desperate plea, don't you think?"

On *Joy Behar: Say Anything!*, both Howard Bragman and **Michelangelo Signorile** endorsed Madonna flashing her audience, while Behar insisted it was a case of "desperately seeking attention."

It would be great if Behar were a **fan**—both women are progressive, outspoken **feminists**. But like does not always attract like, and there are quite a few personality traits they don't share (for a **TV** star, Behar is actually quite camera-shy).

BELLE, ERIKA: A bosom buddy from Madonna's early days in **New York** who **worked** at Lucky Strike (formerly 9th St. & Third Ave., 2nd Fl., NY, NY), the striking Belle remembers first meeting Madonna when the future superstar was dressed all in white. She has said that the third sentence out of Madonna's mouth was, "I wanna be the most famous woman in the world."

Belle and Madonna started going out every night dancing, yet when Madonna landed a singles deal with **Sire** and mused aloud that she needed to audition **dancers**, Belle was no shoo-in. "… I said to her, 'I'll dance for you!' and then she said, 'You can *audition* for me.'" The audition went well, securing Belle's position as one of Madonna's back-up dancers at early club dates, along with Madonna's brother **Christopher Ciccone** (who presumably also had to audition … *burn!*) and **Bags Rilez**, as well as dancing with Madonna on international **TV** appearances. She appears in four of Madonna's official music videos: **"Everybody," "Lucky Star," "Papa Don't Preach"** and **"True Blue."** **Maripol** told MadonnaTribe .com in 2007, "Erika Belle used to make a lot of [Madonna's] clothes." Perhaps Belle's most high-profile contribution in that regard was conceptualizing the entire look of the "Lucky Star" video, for which she made all of the costumes.

Madonna and Belle shared an intense friendship (biographer **Barbara Victor** claimed it was **sexual**), which Belle told author **Christopher Andersen** included making out, and while his story that Madonna used to be a limo-riding cruiser of Latino boys in Alphabet City in the early years of her **fame** is sourced to Belle, Belle later clarified to **Andrew Morton** that it was more **flirtatious** and less **pornographic** than Andersen made it out to be.

"Sure, those were the days when girls were having sex on the floor of The Pyramid, but Madonna never wanted to be known for that. She was always self-aware, in control."-ERIKA BELLE (2001)

BELLY BUTTON: As hard as it is to believe now, Madonna's penchant for flashing her navel was kind of a big deal when she first starting making videos. It is most prominently on display in her **"Lucky Star"** video.

In 1985, Madonna said, "The most erogenous part of my body is my belly button. I have the most perfect belly button—an innie, and there's no fluff in it. When I stick a finger in my belly button, I feel a nerve in the center of my body shoot up my spine. If one hundred belly buttons were lined up against a wall, I would definitely pick out which one was mine."

When confronted with this quote in 1990, she said, "Well, that's a damn lie. I just said that to be, you know … that's in the very beginning. I don't really care about my belly button so much right now."

When she had it pierced in the '90s, Madonna said she nearly passed out in agony. She debuted her pierced innie at the premiere of **Alek Keshishian**'s film *With Honors* on April 26, 1994.

BENASSI, BENNY: *b. July 13, 1967.* Italian music producer who provided memorable remixes of Madonna's single **"Celebration"** (and opened for her on some *Sticky & Sweet Tour* and *MDNA Tour* dates), and **worked** with

erika belle

Madonna on her most potent **dance** tracks for *MDNA*: "**Girl Gone Wild,**" "**I'm Addicted**" and the Deluxe Edition track "**Best Friend,**" with his cousin Alle Benassi.

Benassi said working with Madonna was "an honor and very stimulating."

BENATAR, PAT: *b. January 10, 1953.* One of Madonna's direct predecessors, though far more rock than Madonna wanted to be; she was pushed in the Benatar direction early on and resisted.

Madonna's onetime physical similarity to Benatar may have inspired Benatar's 1985 quote to *Spin*: "I taught her how to wear **fucking** tights, man. Let her have a good time. Now maybe they won't look at the color of my panties, and they can concentrate on my singing."

BENITEZ, JELLYBEAN: *b. November 7, 1957.* John "Jellybean" Benitez was a hot DJ at **The Fun House**, the Paradise Garage (formerly 84 King St., NY, NY), **Studio 54** and Xenon (formerly 124 W. 43rd St., NY, NY) clubs. He became a top remixer of the '80s. Madonna was in love with Jellybean, and maybe both were a little in love with themselves ... with good reason.

Madonna met the influential DJ and remixer in the fall of 1982 at The Fun House while she was out promoting her debut single "**Everybody**" with **Sire Records** promoter Bobby Shaw. Benitez was DJing and promised to give the song some spins, but wound up giving the artist some play as well.

The pair was hot and heavy, appearing at public events and partying together—they were even shot by **Andy Warhol** at the *Like a Virgin* release party. The two were virtually engaged, though both played the field (and surrounding environs). Their last date was on January 28, 1985, to the **American Music Awards**; Madonna lost.

Professionally, the Latin cutie produced Madonna's "**Holiday**" and did some remixing on the rest of the *Madonna* album. His GF also wrote "**Sidewalk Talk,**" an irresistible '80s track from his 1984 *Wotupski!?!* album, and provided her distinctive backing vocals, ensuring the song Top 40 success. Most interestingly, Madonna did backing vocals on Jellybean's 7" and 12" Mixes of the Naked **Eyes** hit "Promises, Promises" (1983), but his mixes were not released commercially at the time and the vocals weren't heard until a 2001 best-of compilation. Other Madonna songs he's remixed include "**Borderline,**" "**Dress You Up,**" "**Like a Virgin,**" "**Lucky Star**" and "**Material Girl.**" His **work** on *You Can Dance* really makes that album's title convincing.

"Definitely, Jellybean was the man for her. She was crazy about him. I think the reason she started playing around behind his back was to get his attention. She would do anything to get him to treat her the way she wanted to be treated, even if that meant inciting his jealousy."

—MELINDA COOPER, FORMER ASSISTANT TO FREDDY DEMANN (2001)

BENNETT, TONY: *b. August 3, 1926.* Class-act crooner whose first #1 song was in 1951 and who is still going strong as of 2015, **reinvented** as **Lady Gaga's** duet partner.

On the occasion of Bennett's fiftieth anniversary in showbiz in 1998, Madonna filmed a short video of congratulations, playfully reminding him that his songs had babysat her as a child. "That's the reason I got into the music **business,**" she cooed, blowing him a kiss. Bennett's reaction when it was aired on *Tony Bennett Live by Request: An All-Star Tribute* (1998) was, "She's so beautiful."

Bennett has always had kind words for Madonna, and has expressed an interest in recording with her.

BERG, PETER: *b. March 11, 1962.* Famous as an F-able doctor on the **TV** series *Chicago Hope* (1994–2000), Berg also had movie cred for his performance in 1992's *A Midnight Clear*. But what he really wanted to do was direct, which resulted in the successful film *Friday Night Lights* (2003) and epic action flick *Battleship* (2012).

Madonna dated Berg briefly, in August 1998, making him another director (or future director) amongst her romances.

BERGMANN, ELIZABETH: Madonna's **dance** professor at the **University of Michigan**. She went to meet **Christopher Flynn** in 1974 to interview him for a teaching position at the U of M (which he eventually landed). During her meeting with Flynn, she met 16-year-old Madonna. She recalled to **VH1**, "She was so beautiful and so lithe and so small and her lines were gorgeous ... She has the soul of an artist."

Later, when Madonna attended the U of M and studied under Bergmann, she impressed her teacher by being a front-row student who landed roles in major productions that would not normally have cast underclassmen. Bergmann choreographed a "kind of male/female confrontation" dance between Madonna and Joshua Cabot that was filmed, footage of which exists on the Internet.

BERNHARD, SANDRA: *b. June 6, 1955.* "Laverne" had "Shirley," "Wilma" had "Betty" and "Nancy Drew" had "George." But the real question in 1988 was: Did Madonna *have* Sandra Bernhard?

The answer turned out to be no.

Madonna remembered first laying **eyes** on the outrageous, funny-faced comedian on the night of her first date with **Sean Penn** in 1985 at a party in **Warren Beatty's** home, three years after Bernhard had wowed critics in Martin Scorsese's neo-classic *The King of Comedy* (1982). Bernhard has said she found Madonna quiet and observant that evening.

The two didn't meet again until 1988, when both were in shows in **New York**—Madonna on Broadway in **David Mamet's** *Speed-the-Plow* and Bernhard in her inspired Off-Broadway one-woman show *Without You I'm Nothing*. Madonna saw the latter, having a **pizza** delivered to her table during the performance. As part of

OLIVIU SAVU

Bernhard's pop-heavy (some people consider Madonna to be a pop heavy), hysterically **camp** monologue in her show, she related a nuclear holocaust **dream** in which she and Madonna were the last two people left alive. (**Cher** was probably living underground as a mole person.) In the fantasy, Madonna was upset that her hubby had been nuked—"Don't tell me they got Sean!" Bernhard wept sarcastically. Madonna thought the script was hilarious and was going to appear in director John Boskovich's 1990 film version as a Madonna **wannabe** called "Shoshanna," but noted Madonna **tribute artist** Denise Bella Vlasis stepped in when she reconsidered.

Upon their reintroduction, Bernhard said, "I can't imagine being you." Madonna replied, "I can't imagine being *you*." Madonna and Bernhard attracted a small group of rowdy female artists (including actor Jennifer Grey), who caroused at hot spots like short-lived dinner club M.K. (formerly 204 Fifth Ave., NY, NY) between shows, igniting rumors that the two were having a lesbonic convergence.

Adding fuel to the fire, Madonna tagged along on one of Bernhard's regular appearances on **David Letterman**'s talk show. They were dressed in matching cut-off jean shorts and white tees, joking that they frequented the **Cubby Hole** (a vadge-ically delicious lesbian bar still operating at 281 W. 12th St., NY, NY). Bernhard boasted to Letterman that she'd slept with both of the Penns, and when Madonna alluded to having a big secret, all her **gay** fans lunged toward their **TVs**, hoping against hope that their fave star might come out of the closet. Didn't happen.

As rumors of an affair peaked, the terrible twosome did a bump-and-grind version of the 1965 Sonny & Cher smash "I Got You Babe" at **Don't Bungle the Jungle**. Intimate girl talk with Sandra made for a genuinely funny, selves-effacing scene in *Truth or Dare*, the premiere of which Bernhard attended. Bernhard was gobsmacked by the attention Madonna's received. "Every time Madonna farts, [the press] picks up on it. They want to see how it smells. I **hate** to break the news, but it smells like everybody else's farts."

Madonna apparently never slept with Bernhard, and has caught flak for "exploiting" gay people, but it's to her credit that she was willing to allow the public to believe she was a lesbian in 1988, something most of Hollywood's *lesbians* still are not willing to allow the public to think of themselves in 2015.

So how did it end? Badly. Madonna's fast friendship (some said it was more) with Bernhard's ex **Ingrid Casares** enraged Bernhard, which is understandable, but Bernhard has had many unkind things to say about Madonna over the years (Jesus, Madonna, try not to alienate comedians because they are articulate in their verbal vivisection skills), including an assertion that Madonna "will steal your friends and anything she can get her grubby little hands on." It makes one wonder if *anything* Madonna could've done should've provoked so public an outcry.

—BROOKE SHIELDS

Years later, when both were studying **Kabbalah**, they interacted again and have apparently buried all hatchets ... but they're not friends. Remember, Madonna—when you stop being friends with a stand-up comic, you become material, girl.

"I have long legs, Madonna has short legs. They're stubby, like a midget. She looks stupid without makeup and her broom."
—SANDRA BERNHARD (1994)

"Oh, we're totally fine with each other ... She's a part of our cultural landscape. So it's not so much personal at this point if I do talk about her, and I don't talk about her anymore, really."—SANDRA BERNHARD (2008)

"BEST FRIEND": Staccato *MDNA* Deluxe Edition bonus track written by Madonna and the **Benassi** brothers, and produced by those parties along with the Demolition Crew. This breakup song from her so-called breakup album isn't on speaking terms with the English language (sample lyric: "I miss the countryside where we used to lay"). Though it comes off as filler, Madonna thought enough of it to use it with a dose of **"Heartbeat"** as a video interlude on *The MDNA Tour*.

"BEST NIGHT": Madonna says, "You can call me 'M' tonight ..." as this meandering, atmospheric mid-tempo tune unwinds. It sounds like a missing track from *Hard Candy*. In reality, it's a track from *Rebel Heart* written by Madonna, **Diplo**, MoZella, Toby Gad, Jimmy Napes, and Andrew Swanson, and produced by Madonna and Diplo. It's another of that record's **sex** songs, but one by a woman in **love**, not just a woman in heat. The song incorporates the "wanting ... waiting ... for you ..." from **"Justify My Love."**

BETTS, ANDRE: Beat-guru record producer and songwriter with whom Madonna collaborated on **"Justify My Love"** and then *Erotica*. Betts shares writing and producing credit with Madonna on the songs **"Did You Do It?,"** **"Secret Garden"** (his best **work**), **"Waiting"** and **"Where Life Begins."**

Betts actually sued Lenny Kravitz in order to get paid for his work on "Justify My Love," claiming he'd been given an associate producer's credit and no **money** for helping "develop the rhythm track" on the song, which itself was a riff on **Public Enemy**'s work.

BEYONCÉ: *b. September 4, 1981.* Famous first as the **Diana Ross**–style leader of phenomenally successful girl group Destiny's Child, Beyoncé Knowles has become one of the most popular and talked about solo female singers (and songwriters) of all time, with massive pop/R&B crossover singles like "Crazy in **Love**" (2003) and "Single Ladies (Put a Ring on It)" (2008), to name just two of her #1 hits.

Madonna and Beyoncé shared the stage for **Oprah Winfrey**'s final show in 2011. In 2012, Madonna raved to

Ellen DeGeneres that Beyoncé has an "incredible **voice**." The following year, Beyoncé kissed Madonna's daughter at one of her concerts, leading to Madonna posting a snap of it on **Instagram** with the caption, "**Mercy James** gets a big fat one from the Queen. B!" The women had also partied together at that year's **Met Ball**.

In 2015, Madonna joked that she would probably be invited to meet **Barack Obama** in the White House if she were not so shocking, and "if I was just married to Jay Z. Hey, if Jay would only take me as his second wife, then I'd score an invitation." Shortly thereafter, Madonna and Beyoncé appeared and posed playfully together at the launch of the **TIDAL** project, and Beyoncé made a cameo in the "Bitch I'm Madonna" music video.

BIEBER, JUSTIN: *b. March 1, 1994.* SEE: **DeGeneres, Ellen**.

BIEL, JESSICA: *b. March 3, 1982.* **TV** teen star turned leading lady of the movies who married **Justin Timberlake** in October 2012. As seen in a famous pap snap, Madonna accidentally stepped on the train of Biel's Ellie Saab dress at the January 15, 2012, **Golden Globes**. Madonna looked shocked and apologized; Biel waved it off.

BILLBOARD: Trade **magazine** founded in 1894 whose music charts are the final word on the relative successes and failures of albums and singles of every genre. Though its methodology changes with the times, much of its sales info comes from the Nielsen SoundScan system since 1991. It has in recent years moved to incorporate social media impact and streaming into its rankings.

Madonna is one of the most successful female artists in the history of *Billboard*'s charts. Some of her more important achievements include being the artist with the most Top 10 singles on the *Billboard* Hot 100, with 38 (the **Beatles** are second, with 34); having a streak of 17 consecutive Top 10 hits from **"Borderline"** through **"Cherish"**; having seven Hot 100 #1 hits in the 1980s, tying her with **Whitney Houston** among women during that decade (12 #1 hits in all, tying her with the Supremes at fifth among all artists in the category); and releasing a mind-boggling 46 songs that have hit #1 on *Billboard*'s **Dance** Club Songs chart.

Madonna has also had 21 Top 10 albums on the *Billboard* 200 ... and counting.

Throughout her career, many of Madonna's songs have been among the most successful on the *Billboard* charts in their respective years of release. For example, Madonna's **"Like a Virgin"** was #2 on the *Billboard* Year-End Hot 100 Singles of 1985, while **"Crazy for You"** came in at #9 that same year; **"Like a Prayer"** was #25 for 1989; **"Vogue"** was #5 for 1990; and **"Take a Bow"** was #8 for 1995. **"4 Minutes"** was #23 in 2008, the last time she had a song on the year-end list.

Madonna has granted *Billboard* exclusive interviews, and has also been honored at the **Billboard Music Awards**.

BILLBOARD MUSIC AWARDS: *Dates presented: 1990–2007; 2011–.* Trade **awards** show that rewards artists based on chart supremacy, as determined by *Billboard* magazine.

Madonna made her first public appearance after the birth of **Lola** at this event in Las Vegas at the Aladdin Resort & Casino (formerly 3667 Las Vegas Blvd. S., Las Vegas, NV) in 1996, receiving the first-ever Artist Achievement Award (since then, only **Cher**, Destiny's Child and **Janet Jackson** have received the same honor). **Tony Bennett** presented the award, leading the new mommy, wrapped in a demure floral housecoat-style dress, to joke, "They said Tony Bennett was going to give it to me, and I said, 'All right, [Lola] won't miss me for a few more hours.'" On the flight back to LA, Madonna and Bennett reportedly sang Dean Martin songs to each other.

In 2013, Madonna was awarded the *Billboard* for Top Touring Artist from will.i.am. Madonna absolutely killed on the carpet and onstage in one of her trademark no-pants ensembles. Custom Givenchy Couture, it was made up of a short, fur-collared black bomber and a fishnet skirt over gartered stockings. It was outrageously costumey, in step with receiving an award for a stage show, but it also revealed her hot bod, making it a classic instance of Madonna being simultaneously funny (*Can ya believe I'm wearin' this?*) and dead-serious (*But really, my legs, right?*). Don't think Madonna ever has no idea what she's wearing or the reaction it will generate; this was no **Mae West** moment, kids.

On May 22, 2016, Madonna closed the show with a respectful tribute to **Prince**, who had died a month earlier. Clad in a metallic-brocade suit with a lilac-paisley print by Gucci's Alessandro Michele and clutching a cane, she sang a beautifully controlled, somber "Nothing Compares 2 U" (written by Prince, taken to #1 by **Sinéad O'Connor** in 1990) before leading Stevie Wonder onstage for a truncated "Purple Rain" duet. In spite of Madonna's technically sound, teary and clearly humble performance, and in stark contrast with rave reviews from entertainment media (even TMZ!), **Twitter** collectively decided "let's go crazy!" and rejected the homage, trashing her voice, her song choice, her right to salute Prince, her **age** (yawn). Madonna was probably receiving major resentment for the perception that she is a lesser musician than Prince, yet one who is still alive, knew him and slept with him. Whatever. **Céline Dion** liked it.

BIRD, ANDY: *b. circa 1970.* Struggling filmmaker and doorman who met Madonna in September 1997. They remained romantically involved for over a year. Twelve years her junior, the 6'2" Bird was also impossibly naïve about dealing with the attention their relationship engendered, finding himself shocked when UK radio stations posted his picture and invited callers who knew him to phone in and spill their guts. Bird rather idiotically spoke to the media about being with Madonna, even referencing his fondness for **Lola**.

On and off, they were back on when Madonna told him she was **pregnant** in 1998. They decided not to keep it, and Bird confirmed to the press that she'd had an **abortion**.

"Without you, I wouldn't have a show to do, and a showgirl needs her fans ..."
—MADONNA AT THE BILLBOARD MUSIC AWARDS (2013)

REBEL CHART:
AN INTERVIEW WITH *BILLBOARD*'S
KEITH CAULFIELD

Keith Caulfield, the Co-Director of Charts at *Billboard*, has a byline familiar to many Madonna fans—he not only covers the Madonna beat, he authentically admires her.

In an *EM2O* exclusive interview, Caulfield—who has interviewed Madonna twice—opens his heart about Madonna's dizzying success on the *Billboard* charts.

EM2O: You're a big Madonna fan. What's your history with her and how has she inspired you?

KEITH CAULFIELD: I think I became aware of her around the time of the *True Blue* album. I didn't start to really become interested in her music until the *Like a Prayer* album. I recall watching the premiere of the Pepsi commercial during *The Cosby Show* and talking about it the following day at school. I also remember an interview she did with MTV where she talked about how involved she was with the "Express Yourself" video, including casting the male models. Since then, I've followed her music career.

EM2O: What are your favorite Madonna singles and albums?

KC: Some of my favorite singles are "Into the Groove," "Express Yourself," "Like a Prayer," "Music,"
"Ray of Light" and "Burning Up." The albums that I generally recommend to people—as introductory sets to her career—are *True Blue*, *Like a Prayer* and *Ray of Light*.

EM2O: What do you think is Madonna's most impressive *Billboard* achievement?

KC: Definitely her record of having the most Top 10 singles on the *Billboard* Hot 100 chart. She's had 38—four more than the Beatles.

EM2O: Do you think Madonna, all things considered, will ever have another #1 Hot 100 hit?

KC: Anything is possible.

EM2O: You've interviewed Madonna a couple of times for *Billboard*. How did you find her to be in person, and is there a moment from your chats that stands out as being the most memorable or exciting?

KC: I've interviewed her twice for *Billboard*; once very briefly, on-camera at the Billboard Music Awards a few years ago, and then in December 2014 over the phone shortly after she released the first six songs from *Rebel Heart* to iTunes.

Both interviews were memorable for different reasons. The on-camera one was funny because she had just come off stage where she had been wearing
a pair of sunglasses for most of her acceptance speech. When she came and spoke to me, she said, "Want me to put my sunglasses back on?"—in a jokey way. And I said, "Only if you want to, babe." I don't know what came over me where I thought I could say "babe" to her, but she didn't seem to mind.

Then, before we could even get started with the interview—which was live, by the way—she complained that we didn't have enough light on her. "Where's the flattering light, you guys?" she said. Of course, in my head I'm like, "Do whatever it takes not to lose Madonna," so I say, "It's all over. It emanates from you," as our lights started to illuminate her face. Then, happy with the situation—and the lighting—she said with a smile, "Really? K." And then we started the actual interview.

The phone interview was better in terms of actual reporting, since I spoke to her for a significant amount of time and got to ask her more substantial questions. We broke the news that she was probably going to be performing on the Grammy Awards from that interview.

EM2O: What do you think is Madonna's most underrated (by chart performance) song?

KC: One of her most enduring singles, "Holiday," never made the Top 10 of the *Billboard* Hot 100. It peaked at #16, but spent 21 weeks on the chart. It's still an incredible shame that "Into the Groove" was never released as a commercial single in the US, thus it never charted on the *Billboard* Hot 100.

EM2O: Some fans dislike it when Madonna teams up with younger acts, but I wonder what you, as a chart manager, think about this strategy?

KC: As we've seen, multi-artist singles can attract more attention from radio programmers and consumers. Madonna herself essentially had a feature on "Take a Bow," but just didn't give him artist credit: Babyface. A collaboration can help draw attention, yes, but if the song is a clunker—then it's a clunker.

EM2O: Do you think Madonna cares about chart positions anymore?

KC: I hope she cares about chart positions, but I doubt she's losing sleep over questions like, "Will this song make the Top 10?"

EM2O: Some of today's up-and-coming pop princesses are around the age Madonna was when she first started her career, yet they're already rivaling her in chart accomplishment due to the changes in how positions are assigned (pre-SoundScan era, SoundScan, social media
impressions). Do you think it's meaningful to directly compare chart records of someone like Nicki Minaj or Taylor Swift to someone like Madonna?

KC: Everything has to be put in perspective, and we try to do that. Especially with regards to artists who have achieved a lot of hits as a result of featured billing, collaborations or earning brief hits as a result of momentary download sales or viral videos.

EM2O: Pundits have forever wanted to dub each new girl singer "the new Madonna." Even if there can never be a duplicate since Madonna existed in a temporal, social context that can't be repeated, which singer would you say is closest to being the Madonna of now?

KC: No one will ever been "the new Madonna." She is singular in her success and relevance.

Bay City Mercy Hospital, where Madonna Fortin Ciccone opened for Madonna

"I wasn't sure I should be allowed to **father** a child. I was in a tumultuous state, but trying my hardest to be calm. It was a really awful time for us." His words were reported in such tasteful articles as *Popdirt*'s "Last Aborted Madonna Baby Details Revealed."

The abortion and Bird's flapping gums proved too much for Madonna, who'd dumped him for good by early 1999, while she was seeing **Guy Ritchie**. In April 1999, it was reported that Ritchie slugged Bird at the Met Bar (Old Park Ln., London, England, UK). The fact that Madonna's involvement with the two men overlapped can't have helped.

BIRTHDAY: Madonna blows out her candles on August 16. She was born that day at 7:05 a.m. at **Bay City** Mercy Hospital (now Bradley House, 100 15th St., Bay City, MI) in 1958. She was delivered by Dr. Abraham H. Jacoby, who had also delivered her mom. Coincidentally, the King, **Elvis Presley**, left the building for good on the **Queen of Pop**'s birthday in 1977.

It's not known how Madonna has spent *all* of her birthdays, but here are a few highlights:

Madonna made a classic blunder by getting married on her birthday in 1985, meaning she will forever think about her first **divorce** on the same day she turns one year older.

When Madonna turned 29, she did it with a party while on her *Who's That Girl World Tour* in **London**. **Sean Penn** couldn't be there because he was in the slammer, which was the **original** title of her *Who's That Girl* movie.

Madonna turned 30 in 1988 with a fab bash on a boat with her hubby, **Sandra Bernhard**, **Debi Mazar**, her *Speed-the-Plow* costar Ron Silver and others in attendance. **Warner Bros.** employees made her a surprise video wishing her a happy birthday, which you just *know* Madonna kept somewhere safe and retains to this day. (Not.)

She turned 31 with **Warren Beatty** and his jet-setting crowd in LA, a big change from the year before, but so go the dirty thirties.

When Madonna turned 32, it was apocryphally said her birthday **gift** from **Herb Ritts** was **Tony Ward**. Guess what? He fit perfectly! She was back with him again at the following birthday. That gift kept on giving.

She turned 35 ensconced in her **Castillo del Lago** palace, munching on homemade **snacks** with close buddies only.

Her 36th in **Miami** was poolside, featuring **drag** entertainment. She wore a clingy sapphire satin slip and took a dip in the pool. Guests included the Estefans, **Gerardo**, Adam "Ad-Rock" Horovitz of the **Beastie Boys**, Theresa Randle, **Nile Rodgers**, Mickey Rourke and the **Versaces**.

Madonna's 37th was odd! She basically threw a mini-presser outside in her clingy pink Versace dress, publicly introducing **Carlos Leon** on August 17, 1995, with the Estefans and others waiting inside for her to finish up.

Turning 39, Madonna had a Hindu-themed bash in LA, at which Jackie Beat and Justin Bond performed in drag. "It was a nightmare. They just wanted to party, not see a show ... Madonna was completely ignoring the show," Beat later

fumed. D'Angelo allegedly kicked Bond for putting a drink on one of the front tables. Bond then toasted Madonna with a bottle of whiskey, saying, "This helped me get through the twilight years of my career, Madonna, and I hope it'll help you do the same." Pissed, Madonna heckled her performers, asking them to sing a happy song. Beat said Madonna looked "like a housewife dressed like **Gwen Stefani** for Halloween."

The week Madonna turned 40, she hung out at Chez Es Saada (formerly 42 E. 1st St., NY, NY) in the **East Village**, singing along to '80s hits like Soft Cell's "Tainted **Love**" (1982).

Madonna had a geisha-themed party when she turned 44. What to get the girl who has everything? **Cultural appropriation**!

The day Madonna hit 45, **Britney Spears** and **Jennifer Lopez** both dropped by her LA mansion. They were there to discuss Madonna's plan to kiss them on **MTV**, but J.Lo begged off, opening the door for **Christina Aguilera**. Madonna held a party for herself the following day with family and friends.

Madonna celebrated a rather unhappy fiftieth (she was about to make public a separation from hubby **Guy Ritchie**) with a $200,000 bash at the club Volstead (formerly 9 Swallow St., St. James's, London, England, UK) on August 16, 2008. **Lola** sang "Never Alone" (1980) from *Fame* for her mom from a piano, David Blaine did card tricks and Ritchie toasted Madonna to the 60 or so guests by saying, "She looks better now than ever. I'm so proud. I love her so much." He gave his wife a $100,000 Rolex Masterpiece 18k gold watch encrusted with 42 brilliant-cut baguette diamonds. Wonder who paid for it ...? Madonna looked fantastic in Givenchy, long **hair** and long gold chains.

Madonna turned 51 with **Jesus Luz**, a guy young enough to be her former husband's son, renting out a whole floor of the Belmond Hotel Splendido (Salita Baratta 16, Portofino, Italy). She and her intimate group inhaled a huge dinner and spent time hanging out on the **Dolce & Gabbana** yacht.

She celebrated turning 52 with a party at the Shoreditch House (Ebor St., London, England, UK) with Luz on August 13, 2010. She wore a tight gray satin D&G dress with a diamond cross necklace.

Madonna celebrated her 53rd in the Hamptons with **Brahim Zaibat**. So many men, such little boyfriends. The trick is for them to get younger as you get older.

On August 17, 2013, Madonna toasted herself turning 55 with a decadent party in France, themed to the French Revolution. Madonna's Marie Antoinette (with **eye** patch) look was enhanced by her **original** lavender *Re-Invention World Tour* (European leg) corset.

In 2014, Madonna partied hearty in **Cannes** at a '20s-themed gathering that found her own kids dressing the part. Madonna's flapper look choked her **Instagram** feed, as did shots of guests like DSQUARED² designers Dean and Dan Caten, **Mert and Marcus**, Kate Moss and designer **Riccardo Tisci**.

At the rate she's going, she looks to be planning many happy returns for herself.

BISEXUALITY: True bisexuality is having a **sexual** and emotional attraction to both genders, not necessarily equally.

Some of Madonna's early intimates, like **Bobby Martinez**, claim that she is straight-up bi, but lacking corroborating tattletales, there is room for doubt.

Madonna has recalled sexual experiences with girls when she was little ... Moira McPharlin, anyone? When she was gal-palling around with **Sandra Bernhard**, the press labeled them lesbian lovers, but both denied it. Madonna has pooh-poohed later speculation that she had an affair with **Ingrid Casares**, even if her brother **Christopher Ciccone**—perhaps getting some revenge for her outing him—said he thought Madonna and Casares were more than pals in his **book**.

When *Sex* came out, chock-full o' girl-on-girl action, including Madonna being pushed around by two dykes to watch out for, simulating oral sex with **Naomi Campbell** and beachcombing with Casares, **Isabella Rossellini** and Tatiana von Furstenberg—the public began to see Madonna as bisexual.

In spite of all this, Madonna does not identify as bi. She has conceded that she gets aroused by the idea of making **love** to another woman, but says she is fulfilled by men.

When Mim Udovitch quizzed her for *The Village Voice* in November 1992, Madonna's responses on the subject of lesbianism were at first completely circular. Madonna claimed her sex life is **irrelevant** (**God** forbid), then, under duress, responded with a "yes" to a direct question as to whether she'd ever slept with a woman.

> "I'll never have mainstream acceptance, never. I mean, I'm an unwed mother. I've kissed girls in public."-MADONNA, *SPIN* (1998)

BISHOP, LIONEL: Dancer who is alleged by biographer **Barbara Victor** to have been the stranger Madonna connected with in 1978 upon her arrival in **New York**. Bishop was supposedly charmed by her open nature and naked desperation for a place to stay, so offered her his couch. He lived at Manhattan Plaza (misidentified as "Manhattan Towers" in Victor's **book**) at 484 W. 43rd St. in NYC, where numerous famous entertainers lived.

According to Victor, Bishop would soon after **dance** in the **original** stage production of the musical *Evita*, ironic considering what was in store for his young couch-surfer. Bishop has never been quoted anywhere else on his experience hosting Madonna.

BITCH: Madonna has used the word in several songs, including "**Thief of Hearts**," "**Human Nature**" and "**Holy Water**." Speaking of *Rebel Heart*, on which the latter appears, that album boasted two songs with "bitch" in the title ("**Bitch I'm Madonna**" and "**Unapologetic Bitch**") and a third from the sessions that remains **unreleased** ("Trust No Bitch," which is a high-drama, bad-karma song that embarrassingly rhymes "besties" with "testes"). In a 2015 interview with *Billboard*, she was asked about the idea that the word "bitch" is misogynist and should be banned.

"I think that's bullshit," Madonna seethed. "The word police can **fuck** off. I don't want to be policed! I'm not interested in political correctness ... If I say to you, 'I'm a badass bitch,' I'm owning myself, I'm saying, 'I'm strong, I'm tough and don't mess with me.'"

Just days before the interview was published, Madonna was introduced at the **Grammys** by **Miley Cyrus** and **Nicki Minaj**. Cyrus called Madonna "our bitch" and quickly added, "She made me call her that."

"**BITCH I'M MADONNA**" **FEAT. NICKI MINAJ (SONG):** One of the first six songs released to iTunes from *Rebel Heart*, this noisy earworm of a club track sells partying more effectively than any Madonna song since "**Where's the Party**" and its "Who do you think you are?" echoes "**Act of Contrition**"'s "What do you mean it's not in the computer?" Effortlessly of-the-moment, the song with the title that made it seem a surefire candidate for worst

MATTHEW RETTENMUND

song ever actually wound up selling better than the five other songs with which it was released, no doubt boosted by a committed **Nicki Minaj** rap.

As lyrically simple as it is, it took MoZella, Madonna, **Diplo**, Toby Gad, Ariel Rechtshaid, Sophie and Nicki Minaj to write it, and was produced by Madonna and Diplo.

Critic Adam Markovitz wrote in *Entertainment Weekly*, "... 'Bitch I'm Madonna' ... I honestly don't know what that means anymore." Jamieson Cox wrote in *Time* that the song is "... a glorious mess, a whirlwind of unexpected texture and silly sound."

Madonna has said, "I feel like I've earned the right to say, 'Bitch, I'm Madonna. Don't fuck with me.' I'm allowed to do this now. I've earned my stripes." This is her children's favorite song from *Rebel Heart*, which makes sense because I've always **loved** my mom's song "Bitch I'm Linda."

Madonna's first live take on the song was on *The Tonight Show* on April 9, 2015. It became her third *Rebel Heart* single and was performed on her *Rebel Heart Tour*.

"BITCH I'M MADONNA" FEAT. NICKI MINAJ (VIDEO): *Director: Jonas Åkerlund, 2015.* Her *Rebel Heart* had long since stopped beating on the charts when this garish, loud, tacky glob of pure fun was released, a snottily joyous explosion of color, iPhoned-in cameos and nepotism (Madonna's son **David** tries hard to **dance** away with the whole thing). In the maximalist messterpiece, Madonna barely-wears a Moschino leopard dress reminiscent of that one-piece swimsuit she wore for a famous **Herb Ritts** poster, a custom leather jacket by Discount Universe, a Chanel whistle and—yes—a **grill** as she traipses through a party scene reminiscent of her performance of the song for **Jimmy Fallon**.

Dotted with appearances by **Miley Cyrus**, **Katy Perry**, **Beyoncé** (**vogueing**, no less), **Chris Rock**, **Kanye West** and **Nicki Minaj** (who really should've shown up in person to do her bit rather than sending footage), the video was a red cape to **ageist** embryos, who sneered that Madonna was thirsty and desperate and several other words they saw hashtagged on **Twitter**.

You know what's more depressing than a 60-year-old acting like a 20-year-old? A whole bunch of 20-year-olds acting like 60-year-olds. Loosen up, kids, you've got plenty of time to shrivel up and be angry at life.

The video marked the third exceptional clip from *Rebel Heart*, but it also continued a trend of botched releases by coming out a day later than expected on **Tidal**. Upon release, it crapped out around the three-minute mark until the beleaguered service could fix it.

Glitch, I'm Madonna.

"BITTERSWEET": Verse written by 13th-century Persian poet Rumi and edited by Deepak Chopra that was given a hypnotic reading by Madonna in 1998 on the album *A Gift of Love: Deepak & Friends Present Music Inspired by the Love Poems of Rumi.*

BJÖRK: SEE "Bedtime Story" (song).

BLACK-AND-WHITE: Madonna's fondness for black-and-white film in her video **work** started with the opening and closing scenes of **"Lucky Star"** and continued with half of **"Borderline,"** which employs a *The Wizard of Oz* (1939)-like shift from B&W to color photography to tell its story.

Her first all-B&W video was **"Cherish,"** which paved the way for **"Oh Father," "Vogue," "Justify My Love"** (including a *Saturday Night Live* spoof and an *MDNA Tour* video interlude that recalls the **original** and in which Madonna looks more stunning than ever 22 years later), most of **"Erotica," "Secret," "I Want You"** and—17 years after her last B&W music video—**"Girl Gone Wild."** Both *Truth or Dare* and *I'm Going to Tell You a Secret* are mostly in stylish B&W, and some **TV** appearances Madonna made to plug the former were also B&W, including sit-downs with **Kurt Loder** for **MTV** and with **Regis Philbin**.

B&W photography flatters Madonna and conjures up images of Old Hollywood and/or **art** films. It's also particularly appropriate for Madonna, whose very reception could be called black or white, **love** or **hate**.

BLACKFACE: Madonna told *Rolling Stone* that *Hard Candy*—which was being presented as one of her excursions into R&B—was almost entitled *Black Madonna*. She even posed with her face painted black for shooter **Steven Klein**. "Then I thought, 'Twenty-five percent of the world might get this, probably less. It's not worth it.'" Good call.

Incredibly, in spite of the wholesale leak of hundreds (if not thousands) of images of Madonna by Klein, this one has never reared its ugly head. Considering the uproar over her **Instagram** re-posts from the *Rebel Heart* era, it's not hard to predict how the public would react.

BLACKWELL, MR. (RICHARD): *August 29, 1922-October 19, 2008.* A former juvenile actor and successful designer, the **überbitchy fashion** critic always included Madonna on his Worst-Dressed List, prompting her to

Take note, Drake—this is how one properly receives a kiss from Madonna.

ALEJANDRO MOGOLLO

quip that he was on her list of "men whose opinions I'm least affected by."

In 1993, Mr. Blackwell seemed to have had a change-of-heartless about Madonna, naming her to his Best-Tressed List for her admirable "shock appeal" in hairstyling. My stars, if an interesting monster can't have an interesting hairdo, then I don't know *what* things are coming to.

BLAST 'EM: *Directors: Joseph Blasioli & Egidio Coccimiglio. Release date: 1992.* Shoestring documentary cobbled together between 1990 and 1991. The well-reviewed film is about the animalistic competition between paparazzi vying for "the shot" of various celebrities, following mad-**dog** shooter Victor Malafronte as he pursues his prey. Mega-**fan**/stalker/impersonator **Queerdonna** appears, and Madonna is singled out as one of the most desirable subjects. It's a must-see.

BLOND AMBITION: JAPAN TOUR 90: *Release date: July 25, 1990.* One of only two official releases—in the world, ever—containing an entire **Blond Ambition World Tour** performance (April 26, 1990, from Yokohama, Japan), this version came out on VHS and **laserdisc** only in Japan.

BLOND AMBITION WORLD TOUR: *Show dates: April 13, 1990–August 5, 1990.* The pinnacle of the lady's achievements as an artist in the first decade of her career, this tour was the perfect combination of all things Madonna: top-notch pop, brazenly **sexual** contemporary **dance**, a fixation on **Catholic** iconography and a title that was truly pun of a kind.

Announced in November 1989 and on the road for just under four months in 1990 with Technotronic as the opening act for all dates, *Blond Ambition* was the first mega-tour of the '90s and in **Rolling Stone**'s estimation the best of the entire decade, its unique structure instantly becoming a blueprint for all other pop concert tours to follow. It was Madonna's biggest trek up to that time, and felt like a star communing with her audience at the peak of her **powers**. The greatest thorn in her side? Italy, where for weeks prior to the shows powerful Catholics had called for an altar-boycott; Madonna cancelled one of her three planned appearances in the country, for **God**'s sake, though locals have pointed out that a far bigger problem was the fact that everyone had spent their lire on a worldwide football championship—**Prince** and the Rolling Stones had a rough time selling tickets that summer, too.

It was a behemoth. There were 1,500 spotlights and four sets that completely covered an 80'×70' stage, all of which was transported from town to town in 18 trucks. Over 100 crewmembers spent two full days assembling a monstrous stage at each new venue, generating catering bills of $15,000+ per gig.

Codirected by Madonna and her choreographer **Vincent Paterson**, the show's artistic director was her brother **Christopher Ciccone**, with musical direction by Jai Winding (who also played keyboards). Madonna's most famous backup singers, **Niki Haris** and **Donna De Lory**, were on board, as were a troupe of male dancers—Luis Camacho and Jose Gutierez (**Jose & Luis**), **Oliver Crumes**, **Salim "Slam" Gauwloos**, **Kevin Stea**, **Gabriel Trupin** and **Carlton Wilborn**—whose personal stories would later become entertainment for the masses when the behind-the-scenes documentary **Truth or Dare** was released.

Madonna's look for *Blond Ambition* stymied her **wannabes** ... after all, it's difficult to ape **Gaultier** on Contempo Casuals wages, and since the designer had costumed most of the show (with some pieces by **Marlene Stewart**), anyone trying to mimic Madonna's style mostly stuck to the lengthy **blonde** ponytail hairpiece she wore for the Asian and North American stops. By the time she set foot in Europe, Madonna had grown tired of the ponytail's desire to entangle itself in her headset, so she went with curls instead.

The show was a taut 100-minute roller coaster ride that reviewers (and Madonna herself) consistently likened to musical theater, but *Blond Ambition* was not *like* musical theater, it *was* musical theater and should one day be restaged by another artist as such. It offered sets as elaborate as anything from an **Andrew Lloyd Webber** spectacle, choreography more inventive than had ever been seen in a rock concert and a performance as inspired and evocative as any Tony winner's.

Paterson reports that Madonna wanted to "break every rule we can ... She wanted to make statements about sexuality, cross-sexuality, the church ... But the hardest thing we tried to do is change the shape of concerts. Instead of just presenting songs, we wanted to combine **fashion**, Broadway, rock and performance **art**."

They succeeded.

Blond Ambition was made up of five sets:

First was an irrepressible dance set known as *Metropolis*, named for the 1927 silent-film classic. The opening tableau was straight out of her "**Express Yourself**" video, with half-naked musclemen standing subserviently at all points across the stage. Following a snippet from her first single, "**Everybody**," Madonna appeared at the top of a staircase, center stage, greeting her audience and asking (in whatever tongue was appropriate to the venue), "Do you believe in **love**?" She knew we

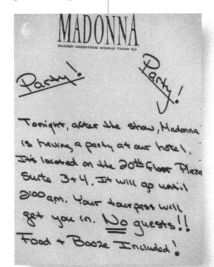

BLOND AMBITION WORLD TOUR SET LIST

① "Express Yourself" (snippets of "Everybody")

② "Open Your Heart"

③ "Causing a Commotion"

④ "Where's the Party"

⑤ "Like a Virgin"

⑥ "Like a Prayer"/ "Act of Contrition"

⑦ "Live to Tell"/ "Oh Father"

⑧ "Papa Don't Preach"

⑨ "Sooner or Later (I Always Get My Man)"

①⓪ "Hanky Panky"

①① "Now I'm Following You (Part 1)"/ "Now I'm Following You (Part II)"

①② "Material Girl"

①③ "Cherish"

①④ "Into the Groove" [snippets of "Ain't Nobody Better" by Inner City (1989)]

①⑤ "Vogue"

①⑥ "Holiday" [snippets of "(Are You Ready) Do the Bus Stop" by Fatback Band (1975)]

①⑦ "Keep It Together" [snippets of "Family Affair" by Sly and the Family Stone (1971)]

Rare note, posted backstage during the tour

MONICA REBOSIO

Madonna slays on tour decades before "slaying" was invented.

"AS I LEFT AMIDST SCORES OF OVERLY
COIFFED MALL QUEENS AND THEIR DELICIOUSLY
MUSCLE-BOUND ESCORTS, I COULDN'T HELP BUT
THINK THAT WHAT I HAD JUST WITNESSED
WAS THE VERY EMBODIMENT OF WAGNER'S
CONCEPT OF THE *GESAMTKUNSTWERK*–THE TOTAL,
ORGANIC, MULTISENSUAL WORK OF ART."

—MAYER RUS, *OUTWEEK* (1990)

"MADONNA IS A LEAN, MEAN DANCING MACHINE …
DURING HER FIRST TOUR SINCE 1987, NO
ONE WILL MISTAKE MADONNA FOR AN EASYGOING
PARTY GIRL OR PLIANT FANTASY OBJECT;
SHE IS IN FULL CONTROL, CASTING HERSELF
AS VICIOUS OR COY OR DEVOUT IN VIGNETTES
THAT ARE ALL READY FOR VIDEOTAPE."

—JON PARELES, *THE NEW YORK TIMES* (1990)

"FOR THREE GENERATIONS IN ROCK, WE HAVE
BEEN USED TO PERFORMERS CAPTIVATING US
WITH THEIR VOICE AND SONGS. MADONNA CAN'T
COMPETE, ARTISTICALLY, WITH THE GIANTS
OF THAT TRADITION. SHE IS MORE A
CONCEPTUAL POP ARTIST THAN A PURELY
MUSICAL ONE. CREDITABLE ON RECORD,
SHE COMES ALIVE ON VIDEO AND ON STAGE."

—ROBERT HILBURN, *LOS ANGELES TIMES* (1990)

"THE GYMNASTIC DANCE PRODUCTIONS IN
SONGS SUCH AS 'WHERE'S THE PARTY' AND
'LIKE A PRAYER' ARE ASTONISHING,
AND THE THEATRICAL EXTRAVAGANCE OF
'LIKE A VIRGIN' PLAYS AS VEGAS SCHMALTZ
GONE HILARIOUSLY KINKY."

—TY BURR, *ENTERTAINMENT WEEKLY* (1991)

did. We also believed in her **cone-bra** Gaultier corset, which debuted here (and which sold for $52,000 at **auction** in 2012).

The rest of *Metropolis* was comprised of similar crowd-pleasers: a duet-dance with Crumes on **"Open Your Heart,"** a good-natured girl party with Haris and De Lory in Tour de France–ready gear on **"Causing a Commotion"**; and, following a bizarre skit in which Madonna pretended to *beat* up her *back* ups, a carefree **"Where's the Party."**

Next up was a passion **play** called *Religious* and defined by one of Madonna's most important performances, a Middle Eastern-flavored **"Like a Virgin,"** in which she shocked the world with graphic mock **masturbation** on a crimson-sheathed bed while Jose & Luis attended. This performance provoked an outcry from the decency police and nearly led to Madonna's arrest in Toronto.

From sins of the flesh to absolution, Madonna segued into the religious ecstasy of **"Like a Prayer,"** her whole troupe in matching black robes of devotion. Dramatic, but stripped-down renditions of **"Live to Tell"** and **"Oh Father,"** with Wilborn serving as **father** confessor, continued the set's Catholic fantasia. The reverence came to a halt with a candlelit workout version of **"Papa Don't Preach."** Rarely have Madonna's well-known concert sequences been as perfectly chosen thematically as they were here.

The film was current, so Madonna dutifully included a cabaret segment of *I'm Breathless: Music from and Inspired by the Film Dick Tracy* numbers in her *Dick Tracy* segment: a husky **"Sooner or Later (I Always Get My Man)"** performed *Fabulous Baker Boys* (1989)–style atop a piano, the bouncy burlesque of **"Hanky Panky"** and **"Now I'm Following You (Parts I & II)."** Knowing critics would dislike her lip-synched dance routine set to the latter, Madonna joked onstage to "Dick Tracy" stand-in Gauwloos, "You can't sing? That's all right—neither can I and lookit how far I've gone!" (Yokohama, Japan) or, "Lots of people who can't sing make records today!" (Houston, Texas).

Art Deco was lighthearted, running from a silly send-up of **"Material Girl"** (performed as a squeaky-**voiced** housewife under a row of hairdryers to show that Madonna, indeed, has a sense of humor) to a sugar-sweet version of **"Cherish"** (complete with mermen) to an **"Into the Groove"** remix brought to life with *West Side Story* (1957) flair. The sequence ended with a minimalist rendering of her then-current super smash **"Vogue."** Of all her live performances of this number, this one comes closest to capturing the **original** form of the dance.

And for *Encore*, Madonna danced gaily in discofied **black-and-white** polka dots to **"Holiday"** and ended cerebrally with a meticulous *A Clockwork Orange* (1971) version of **"Keep It Together,"** wickedly performing Fosse-caliber dance moves in a black-hearted interpretation of the song's notion of "family."

Critics generally embraced the show, calling it ambitious, rigorous and entertaining. *USA Today* and other papers complained about Madonna's reliance on lip-synching, but the star defended her right to employ backing tracks as part of her spectacle.

For the record, Madonna sang audibly over her own pre-recorded vocals on some songs ("Express Yourself") and barely audibly over them on others ("Where's the Party," "Vogue"). Madonna can sing, okay, you guys? However, her fragile voice deserts her after long hauls and her concerts are full-body workouts, so vocal sweetening is a necessity, and is now a staple of every pop star's tours. *All* of 'em do it. Yes, even *her.*

The show ran afoul of prudes in the UK, where her BBC Radio 1 broadcast made for a great drinking game every time you heard her say the word "**fuck**." (**Alcohol** poisoning is real.)

Blond Ambition, which grossed $62.7 million, was a major triumph, proving Madonna to be a stage performer with no parallels, a physical presence of seeming invincibility (despite having to cancel four shows due to a persistent throat infection), and the world's most popular live entertainer. "This tour really pushed her over the top. It was Madonna—there was nobody else," Paterson declared in 2013.

The final performance—in Nice, France—was aired live on HBO on August 5, 1990, and the concert was further preserved in *Truth or Dare*. It was released by tour sponsor Pioneer on the now relatively moribund **laserdisc** format, but has never been sold on VHS, DVD, or Blu-ray in the US, and is probably #1 on most **fans**' wish lists among past gems they wish Madonna's management would guide to the marketplace.

Asked when fans could expect an official release, Madonna wrote—on Reddit.com in 2013—that one would occur "when i can find the tapes in the archives."

P.S. A Ben & Jerry's flavor called Blondie Ambition (brown sugar ice cream with blonde brownies and butterscotch toffee flakes) was made exclusively available at Target in 2015.

BLOND AMBITION WORLD TOUR LIVE: *Release date: December 13, 1990.* The only official US release of Madonna's most famous tour was restricted to this **laserdisc**-only presentation. It contains the final show from the tour. In 1992, the laserdisc won Madonna a **Grammy** for Best Music Video, Long Form.

BLONDE: Madonna has said in the past that when she went brunette, it was because she liked to match her pubic **hair** sometimes. She also believes blonde is better for live performances because it's easier to see. Also, women will tell you that going blonde as you get older is a lot easier to maintain and more flattering than clinging to brunette hair.

In one of her last teen-entertainment **magazine** interviews in 1987, Madonna was asked if she'd ever go back to brunette. "Oh, **God**! *No.*" Why? "I looked like a mouse!"

As **Norman Mailer** wrote in his 1984 novel *Tough Guys Don't Dance*, "Any lady who chooses to become a blonde is truly blonde."

BLOND AMBITION
WORLD TOUR
PERFORMANCES

April 13-15, 1990:
Chiba, Japan
(Chiba Marine Stadium)

April 20-21, 1990:
Nishinomiya, Japan
(Hankyu Nishinomiya
Stadium)

April 25-27, 1990:
Yokohama, Japan
(Yokohama Stadium)

May 4-5, 1990:
Houston, Texas, US
(The Summit)

May 7-8, 1990:
Dallas, Texas, US
(Reunion Arena)

May 11-13, May 15-16,
1990: Los Angeles,
California, US
(Los Angeles Memorial
Sports Arena)

May 18-20, 1990:
Oakland, California, US
(Oakland Coliseum Arena)

May 23-24, 1990:
Rosemont, Illinois, US
(Rosemont Horizon)

May 27-29, 1990:
Toronto, Canada
(SkyDome)

May 31-June 1, 1990:
Auburn Hills, Michigan,
US (The Palace of Auburn
Hills)

June 4-5, 1990:
Worcester, Massachu-
setts, US (The Centrum)

June 8-9, 1990:
Landover, Maryland, US
(Capital Centre)

June 11-13, 1990:
Uniondale, New York, US
(Nassau Veterans
Memorial Coliseum)

June 16-17, 1990:
Philadelphia, Pennsyl-
vania, US (The Spectrum)

June 20-21, June 24-25,
1990: East Rutherford,
New Jersey, US
(Brendan Byrne Arena)

June 30, 1990:
Gothenburg, Sweden
(Eriksberg)

July 3-4, July 6, 1990:
Paris, France
(Palais Omnisports de
Paris-Bercy)

July 10, 1990:
Rome, Italy
(Stadio Flaminio)

July 13, 1990:
Turin, Italy
(Stadio della Alpi)

July 15, 1990:
Munich, West Germany
(Olympia-Reitstadion
Riem)

July 17, 1990:
Dortmund, West Germany
(Westfalenhalle)

July 20-22, 1990:
London, England, UK
(Wembley Stadium)

July 24, 1990:
Rotterdam, The Neth-
erlands (Feijenoord
Stadion)

July 27, 1990:
Madrid, Spain (Estadio
Vicente Calderón)

July 29, 1990:
Vigo, Spain (Estadio
Municipal de Balaídos)

August 1, 1990:
Barcelona, Spain
(Estadi Olímpic de
Montjuïc)

August 5, 1990:
Nice, France
(Stade de l'Ouest)

The finale of Madonna's first epic tour

MONICA REBOSIO

PHOTOFEST

Vamping it up
Theda Bara-style

BLOODHOUNDS OF BROADWAY: *Director: Howard Brookner. Release date: November 3, 1989.* Madonna costarred in this gangster film set in the '20s, contributing a delicately amusing performance as "Hortense Hathaway," a Prohibition pre-Madonna with bang-up **Louise** Brooks bangs.

Madonna got involved with the project after being pitched by director/cowriter **Howard Brookner**. Brad Gooch, Brookner's partner at the time, writes in his memoir *Smash Cut: A Memoir of Howard & Art & the '70s & the '80s*, "A meeting took place at Madonna's apartment on **Central Park West**. She lay on her bed, while he convinced her not only to play a Broadway showgirl, but to **dance** and swing and sing a swanning period duet with Jennifer Grey, getting her to commit to perform the indie-style role in the fall when she would be back from her 1987 **Who's That Girl World Tour.**" He goes on to say that Madonna always seemed to Brookner "like his collaborator on the film, not just an actor."

The movie, which Brookner wrote with Colman deKay, is based on four stories by Damon Runyon—"Bloodhounds of Broadway," "A Very Honorable Guy," "Social Error" and "The Brain Goes Home." Runyon was the originator of phrases like "guys and dolls," "monkey **business**" and "put up your

dukes," and was pretty great with colorful character names, with people called "Crunch Sweeney," "Missouri Martin" and "Handsome Jack" making appearances in his **work**.

Madonna gets to play a character who connives at the expense of her charming oaf of a boyfriend "**Feet** Samuels" (her old **Saturday Night Live** scene partner Randy Quaid), sings the 1931 (oops, the film's set a coupla years earlier) Bing Crosby tune **"I Surrender Dear"** with **Snatch Batch**-er Grey and does a mesmerizing shimmy in a Theda Bara beaded bra. The press notes sum up Hortense as the prototypical misunderstood material girl: "Hathaway **dreams** of more important things than the jeweled trinkets that Samuels believes she desires."

The film was made in Union City, Newark and Jersey City, New Jersey, on a ruthlessly limited budget. Cast dressing rooms in a Knights of Columbus Hall were separated by shower curtains with names inscribed in Magic Marker. Along with Madonna, Grey and Quaid, those names included Steve Buscemi, Matt Dillon, Julie Hagerty, Rutger Hauer, Dinah Manoff, Esai Morales, Anita Morris, Ethan Phillips, Alan Ruck, Fisher Stevens and even author **Williams S. Burroughs**.

. . . .

"COMPARED TO *THE COTTON CLUB*,
IT'S PASTE TO A TIFFANY DIAMOND."
—LORIEN HAYNES, *RADIO TIMES* (1989)

. . . .

"THIS IS A YARN ABOUT DAMES AND CRAP
GAMES, FLOOZIES AND BOOZE, STIFFS AND
SUCKERS, GUYS WITH GATS IN THEIR POCKETS
AND HOOKERS WITH HEARTS THAT WOULD
CHILL A MARTINI. IT'S A LOVE STORY. THE
RESPECTED PBS *AMERICAN PLAYHOUSE* SERIES
WILL PRESENT ONE OF THE MOST THOROUGHLY
ENTERTAINING, SPIRITED PRODUCTIONS
IN ITS HISTORY WHEN *BLOODHOUNDS
OF BROADWAY* AIRS …"
—DANIEL RUTH, *CHICAGO SUN-TIMES* (1990)

. . . .

"IT'S A SHAME THE STENCH OF FAILURE
STILL SURROUNDS *BLOODHOUNDS OF BROADWAY*,
BECAUSE I THINK IT'S THE BEST
ADAPTATION OF DAMON RUNYON'S WRITING TO
DATE … THE TWO WRITERS HAVE MANAGED TO
CREATE A COHERENT, WELL-WRITTEN STORY
FROM A PATCHWORK WITHOUT COMPROMISING THE
FLAVOR OF RUNYON'S WORK. MOREOVER, THE
VISUAL LOOK OF THE FILM IS ASTONISHING …
[I]T'S A MINOR MIRACLE TO SEE MADONNA
DOING CAREER-BEST WORK."
—BILL TREADWAY, *DVD VERDICT* (2004)

. . . .

The final film, cut without Brookner's approval (he was dying of **AIDS**) is episodic enough that during its arthouse run in **New York**, a reel was accidentally omitted and no one noticed until the second week in spite of the fact that a narrator based on Walter Winchell had been added to help connect the plot's dots.

Unfairly dismissed by film critics, *Bloodhounds of Broadway*'s theatrical run grossed $43,671 in five theaters, and aired on PBS (it had been produced by *American Playhouse* in conjunction with Columbia Pictures), where it scored solid ratings.

Bloodhounds of Broadway is a treat that should definitely be considered, along with ***Desperately Seeking Susan***, before Madonna's taste in film projects in the '80s is condemned.

BLOWJOBS: Regardless of any impression created by *Truth or Dare*, sexpot Madonna doesn't like giving BJs. She has joked that there is some sort of misogynist conspiracy behind the submissive aspect of a woman having to choke in order to give men head, as opposed to the relative ease of man-to-woman or woman-to-woman oral **sex**. And you wondered why she has such a hard time keeping a man.

BLUE FROGGE: *Formerly 611 Church St., Ann Arbor, MI.* The student pub where Madonna met lover and future band mate/collaborator **Stephen Bray**, who was waiting tables there. Madonna claims it was the first time she ever bought a guy a drink, but Bray remembers buying *her* a gin and tonic. The pub later became a raunchy rock bar called Rick's American Café, about which a recent LocalWiki.org review notes, "The men's toilets have no doors, so plan ahead."

BLUE IN THE FACE: *Director: Wayne Wang. Release date: October 13, 1995.* One of Madonna's most obscure, seldom-seen movie appearances is as a singing telegram chick in this sequel to the director's *Smoke* (1995). Shot in just five days, the film is essentially a series of ad-libbed sequences by actors from *Smoke* (plus fun add-ons, like Madonna, Lou Reed and RuPaul).

In a two-minute scene, Madonna—in a revealing **orange**-and-yellow costume with a musical note at the breast—sings (including sound effects) a message to frequent costar **Harvey Keitel** that a deal is off, bumping and grinding along the way. She ain't impressed with his tip: "Five dollars? Thanks a lot, Mister. I'll finally be able to buy that hearing aid my **mother** always wanted."

Rare, auctioned test Polaroid from *Body of Evidence* … would have made a great Oscar ad for the trades.

BELOW: Receiving direction from Uli Edel during the filming of *Body of Evidence*

BODY OF EVIDENCE: *Director: Uli Edel. Release date: January 15, 1993.* For this film, Madonna was paid $2.5 million for her services in a contract that guaranteed her top billing, approval of stunt/body doubles and foreign **voice** dubs, that no promo photos would be distributed to supermarket tabloids and that she could keep her wardrobe (which she largely didn't do, as examples have appeared at **auction**). The best part of the whole deal was that the filming took just 43 days on location in Portland, Oregon, and at Culver Studios (9336 W. Washington Blvd.) in Culver City, California.

On her shortlist of major career missteps, this $30 million **sex** thriller ranks right up there. Opening on over 2,000 screens, it made $7,365,429 its opening week for a #5 debut, which wasn't too bad, but then plunged on terrible reviews and word of mouth, winding up with a total of $13,273,595 at the US box office ($37,938,251 worldwide). In spite of inestimable advance press, it ranked as only the #85 film of 1993, behind such fare as *Super Mario Bros.*, *Untamed Heart* and *Jason Goes to Hell: The Final Friday*.

Madonna read the script and **hated** it, as did its director Uli Edel ("We knew the film could be really, really junky. It was a thin line," he said), but because she'd admired Edel's **work** in *Last Exit to Brooklyn* (1989), she believed he could elevate the material.

I SURRENDER, DEAR:
AN INTERVIEW WITH
BLOODHOUNDS OF BROADWAY
SCREENWRITER COLMAN DEKAY

Many Madonna fans have already discovered that the rarely-seen *Bloodhounds of Broadway* holds more pleasures than its reputation suggests, not least of which is a cute performance by Madonna that holds up just as well as her other takes on vintage showgirls in *Dick Tracy* and *Evita*. If you have yet to figure this out, get your ever-lovin' ass in gear and watch it–it's more than somewhat good.

But as sweetly entertaining as the final product is, intrigue surrounds what might have been. The film's first cut, finished by director Howard Brookner just before AIDS claimed his sight and, soon after, his life, suffered drastic edits mandated by Columbia Pictures that left the film in a state that its creators loathed and despised.

Like so many silent movies from the era it attempts to evoke, the original cut of *Bloodhounds* no longer exists, creating a dead end to the mystery of not only what might have been, but what once was.

Equally intriguing is the story of how a small indie period piece attracted one of the most stellar casts of the 1980s. *EM2O* is grateful to screenwriter Colman deKay for taking the time to fill in some of the blanks on how the movie was conceived, written and filmed.

EM2O: Thanks for agreeing to share some of your memories of Madonna from the *Bloodhounds of Broadway* period.

COLMAN DEKAY: We had a little encounter for a coupla months back in the '8Os when she was kind of at her peak. I remember the first time I met her, we were rehearsing in a basement studio in lower Broadway, New York, and she was a bit late for rehearsal and ... the door to the studio came crashing open and she came tearing in, *screaming* at people behind her–I guess she'd been stalked by paparazzi, this whole gang of paparazzi that were always around. She was yelling up the stairs, "Go fuck yourself!" [Laughs]

EM2O: Did you think, "What have we gotten ourselves into?"

CDK: Li'l bit. But it calmed down. It was really strange walking down the street with her or being anywhere with her because at the time, the *New York Post* had three photographers on eight-hour shifts around the clock. There was this constant gang of paparazzi following her like pilot fish. We would walk down the street and she'd go, "Don't touch me, look straight forward and smile." [Laughs] "Don't protect me. If you feel the need to protect me because these guys are getting too intense, don't bother, because then they'll get a picture of that."

We would be standing at a street corner waiting for a light to change and they'd be like [makes incessant camera clicks] and she would bear it patiently and then finally go, "Okay, guys, I think you got enough–whaddaya say?" and one turned to another and said, "She asked nice–we should go," and the other one said,

"Fuck her!" and just kept on taking pictures.

EM2O: To backpedal some: How did you know Howard Brookner, and how did the movie come about?

CDK: Howard and I went to high school together at Exeter and we kinda lost touch with each other until one day he was out here [in LA] taking meetings and stuff and we met at a mutual friend's house and he said, "*American Playhouse* wants me to make a movie for them and I keep on striking out with my pitches and I figure I've got one more good pitch before they think I'm completely insane."

I said, "Well, read this, read this, read this, and while we're at it, we should take a look at some Damon Runyon stories." So we just sort of decided to take four stories that could be condensed into one night and sort of interlock the stories. We pitched them to Lindsay Law (head of *American Playhouse*) and he said, "Go."

We had to wait about seven months to get the rights. The agent for the rights was this Damon Runyon character himself. We would move forward and feel like we were about to close it and he'd have some kind of psychotic break and we'd have to go back to square one! I remember one of the last big fights was he was gonna pull the rights because we cast a black man [Graham Brown] as a doctor and he said, "Back in those days, *nobody* would go to a black guy! 'Brain' would never go to a black guy." And I said, "He's been to everyone else; this is sort of a last straw if

you really wanna look at it *that* way." And he was like, "Oh, okay." [Laughs]

We wrote it in like a week, and made a pick-up deal with Columbia to do the thing, and we figured at the time, "Okay, this is a small movie, so if we're lucky, we'll get one person who's been in a movie before and the rest will be unknown." We were paying scale and favored nations, so everyone was getting the same money, and it was gonna be a hard shoot-outdoors at night in New Jersey in January. But all of a sudden, it became the movie that everybody wanted to be in that season.

EM2O: When you were writing the role of "Hortense Hathaway," did you have anyone specific in mind?

CDK: No, and we originally cast Karen Allen, and she begged off to go do *Scrooged* [1988] with Bill Murray, so she left us this long, apologetic message and our casting director said, "If you wanna give her the Hollywood treatment, do not call her back."

EM2O: How did Madonna get involved?

CDK: Out of the blue. Probably we went to CAA and said, "Who've you got?" and Howard was on a Scout in a van and he got a page saying, "Call CAA, Madonna wants to talk to you." So they pulled over at a gas station and he called from a payphone in the middle of bleak New Jersey and Madonna was in her agent's office, got on the phone and said, "If you want me, I'm in." And Howard said, "Oh, you're in to consider the role?" and she said, "No, I'm in–I wanna do it." [SEE: *Bloodhounds of Broadway* entry for Brad Gooch's memory of how Madonna said yes.]

So I called Randy Quaid and I said, "You know, we lost Karen, so we sorta had

to cast somebody and I'm really sorry to give you this news, but we did cast somebody–I don't know if you'll be happy with it." He said, "Well ... who ya got?" And I said, "Madonna." [Laughs] And he just flipped out. It was completely out of nowhere.

EM2O: Did Madonna have a lot of input on her role?

CDK: She came in for that first rehearsal and she had already decided what she was going to look like–she'd already changed her look with no input from us. She came in with short black bangs. She'd been looking at Louise Brooks movies, decided that was what this character should look like and did it. That was all her doing.

You know the movie was released in New York with a reel missing?

EM2O: I always wondered if that was true.

CDK: It was made through three regimes at Columbia, so nobody had ownership of it; it was such a tiny movie, and they had really no particular interest in it by the time it came down to Dawn Steel releasing it–oh, no, it was [Peter] Guber/[Jon] Peters.

But they weren't gonna release it in New York. I said, "C'mon, guys, it's not called the *Bloodhounds of Biloxi*–it's *Bloodhounds of Broadway*, so it should be in New York." So they released it and the reviews came out and the *Post* said, "How could these guys be so stupid as to cast Madonna as a showgirl and not give her a number?" And I said, "Well ... there *is* one." My brother was going to see the movie, so I said, "Keep your eye out to see if there's that production number." I'm thinking.

"They can't have spent more money to recut it and screw it up more than they already have." So he went and he came back and said, "No, there wasn't one."

It turns out there was this one *pivotal* reel missing. There's four stories, right? And all of the characters in those stories had third-act reversals that happened in that reel, so without that reel, all of a sudden they're acting in contradiction to everything they've said in the movie and there's no explanation why!

EM2O: How much was missing?

CDK: Ten key minutes where everyone changes their mind, and without that information, you're just going, "Whaaat?" [Laughs] Also missing was the little number ["I Surrender Dear"] with Jenny Grey.

EM2O: How did Madonna behave on set?

CDK: She was great! We were shooting under the harshest of conditions in this Knights of Columbus hall, so while we're shooting, there were all these Knights of Columbus guys playing cards in our green room. But the dressing room was one big room with plastic sheets dividing people's dressing areas. It was really about as Spartan as it could be, and she was just totally game—she was really great.

We were shooting in Union City, New Jersey, and the reason that we could shoot there without worrying about the Teamsters was that they were under indictment. [Laughs] Union City is a very corrupt city. The mayor was a big Madonna fan. He wanted to give her a key to the city, he wanted her to come down to City Hall and have this big event where he'd give her a key to the city and the location manager was pitching this to me really

hard. And I'm going, like, "We don't have time! We're on a tight schedule, we have no money, we can't stop production just to do this." Besides, everyone was on favored nations, so if we did it for her, we'd have to do it for everybody else. And he said, "Do you want the streets to be plowed? Do you wanna be able to bring the trucks into our location? Because you won't be able to if you don't do this for the mayor."

So we brought the mayor to our Knights of Columbus hall and we had the mayor and his staff, during the lunch hour, give us this plaque that said, "To the entire cast and crew of *Bloodhounds of Broadway*." Which I still have. She was there; that's all he cared about.

EM2O: Working on the film must have been so hard for Howard.

CDK: Howard was really sick [with AIDS] during shooting, and the only medication during those days was AZT. I didn't know he was sick—nobody knew, because he didn't want the bonding company to know—and he took himself off the AZT because it fuzzied up his brain. He probably lost six months to a year of his life just for this movie; because of that and shooting outdoors at night in freezing weather, he got really sick.

One of the things he wanted to do—he went legally blind—was his lover [Brad Gooch] had written a book [*Scary Kisses*] that he couldn't read. So he had all his friends and the people from the movie come in and read a chapter each of the book on video. He was out in LA in a bungalow at the Sunset Marquis finishing it up and Madonna came in with Sean Penn to do their

chapter. She wanted to direct Sean, so they set up the camera and Sean goes, "Okay, whaddaya want me to do?" and Madonna goes, "I want you to get down on your knees and bark like a dog!" [Laughs] So Sean Penn got down on his knees and barked like a dog! It was her vision of how that chapter should start.

EM2O: *Bloodhounds* was cut so much beyond your control; when you first saw the final product, did you hate it?

CDK: I was really sad. We had a conference call set up with our executive. The disease hit Howard in the brain first, which was really frustrating for him. So we're setting up for this conference call and we're in a room with Camilla Toniolo, our editor, and I'm sitting across from Howard in the living room and I go, "Okay, when he asks a question where the answer is yes, I'll nod my head like this, and when he asks a question where the answer is no, I'll shake my head like this, and you just answer." And he goes, "Okay!" And the exec gets on the phone, and the first question he asks is a yes question, so I nod my head and Howard looks at me and says into the phone, "Ab-so-lute-ly NOT!" He had it backwards! [Laughs]

We said, "Please—these cuts are character cuts, they're plot cuts, they're continuity cuts, they're atmosphere cuts ... you're cutting the first reel so tight the audience won't be able to breathe." The exec said, "We're out of time, we're out of money. Make these cuts, cut the negative—we're done."

And so the movie screened at a test screening ... and we screened the studio's cut of the movie and it was bad. I'm standing out in the lobby afterwards, just destroyed, and the exec comes out, claps me on the shoulder and goes, "Welp! You were right!" and walks out.

It was as close as I've been to murder.

ALEJANDRO MOGOLLO

Madonna should've known better. The part, which she described as the best lead she'd been offered—not a good reason to take a part when you're **rich** anyway and hoping to make your mark as an actor—is a one-dimensional sexpot role of the variety **Sharon Stone** had only the year before taken to new levels of insipidity in the smash hit *Basic Instinct* (1992).

The plot is a joke: "Rebecca Carlson," a sex-driven sex sire/gallery owner sexily has sex with a sex-crazed sex maniac, who later dies from afterglow. Did she do it on purpose? Her *pubic* defender is "Frank" (**Willem Dafoe**), a family man who finds himself falling prey to Rebecca's wiles, and to his secret attraction to kink. The high concept here is: Can sex be a deadly weapon?

Interesting potential **AIDS** metaphors are overlooked, and the film stagnates as a straight courtroom drama. *Body of Evidence* asks us to suspend disbelief at every turn: Rebecca's coke addiction is shown to be a silly misunderstanding—that's actually **healthy** Chinese peony powder she's been snorting (yeah, and Vanessa Hudgens was lick-

....

"IT'S HOLLYWOOD'S VERSION OF AMATEUR NIGHT AT A TOPLESS BAR, WHERE SOME BLONDE HAS JUST CLIMBED ONSTAGE AND TAKEN EVERYTHING OFF BUT DOESN'T KNOW HOW TO DANCE. SO, EVERYONE JUST SITS THERE DUMBFOUNDED, EQUALLY EMBARRASSED BY HER AUDACITY AND HER INCOMPETENCE."

–JACK MATHEWS, *NEW YORK NEWSDAY* (1993)

....

"A SLICK THRILLER THAT EMBODIES ELEMENTS OF *WITNESS FOR THE PROSECUTION*, *THE STORY OF O* AND *BASIC INSTINCT*."

–DAVID ANSEN, *NEWSWEEK* (1993)

....

"WHAT TO DO ABOUT POOR MADONNA? … AS A MOVIE, IT LOOKS AS IF IT WANTED TO BE *BASIC INSTINCT*, THOUGH IT WINDS UP MORE LIKE *ILSA, SHE-WOLF OF THE SS*."

–VINCENT CANBY, *THE NEW YORK TIMES* (1993)

....

"I'VE SEEN COMEDIES WITH FEWER LAUGHS THAN *BODY OF EVIDENCE* … THE MOVIE STARS MADONNA … THE QUEEN OF MOVIES THAT WERE BAD IDEAS RIGHT FROM THE BEGINNING."

–ROGER EBERT (1993)

....

"TRY NOT TO WORK WITH A DIRECTOR WHO HATES WOMEN. IN MY CASE, THAT USUALLY MEANS I'LL BE PHOTOGRAPHED BADLY AND END UP DEAD IN THE END."

–MADONNA ON ADVICE TO FEMALE ACTORS, *COSMOPOLITAN* (1996)

....

ing white chocolate at **Coachella**)—and we are supposed to believe that Frank's wife (**Julianne Moore**) doesn't notice his torn, bloody shirt after he lies on broken glass *en flagrante*. The sex, apart from the film's weirdly cute candle wax-dripping scene, is mechanical, not erotic.

Also, either Edel filmed his actors unflatteringly or that wind in Portland ages people a dozen years.

The **acting** is competent, even Madonna's, but her performance was universally panned, as if she were generating all of the other things *more* wrong with the film. "If everyone says it's horrible, I'll slit my wrists," she had joked before the reviews came in. Thankfully, she went back on her word.

Madonna cited actors Kim Novak, Lana Turner and Alida Valli as influences for her portrayal. When you're studying Lana Turner's acting technique, it's time to make a record. And try to imagine Novak husking, "I fucked you, I fucked Andrew, I fucked Frank. That's what I do; I **fuck**." Madonna and Dafoe had gone to an actual murder trial for research. Dafoe told John Waters that mid-way through, the judge stopped the proceedings to gush to Madonna, "I *love* your movies!"

The worst thing about the film is that it's a blatant cautionary tale that vilifies sex, not exactly a credible belief for Madonna to help espouse. The "it's only a movie" defense doesn't cut it, not from the woman who can take something as ordinary as **hair** color and charge it with symbolic meaning.

Over 20 years after it bombed, *Body of Evidence* can safely be placed in the **camp** camp. So ridiculous is the dialogue and so vampy is Madonna, that it *could* be used to argue that in the realm of film, when Madonna's good, she's very good, and when she's bad, she's better.

"BODY SHOP": *Rebel Heart* track with more "heart" than "rebel" in it, meaning it's got a bouncy **guitar** feel more than a club thump. Madonna's girlish vocal is a **flirty** flashback to tunes like **"True Blue"** and **"Cherish."** Because the lyrics (by Madonna, MoZella, Toby Gad, S1, DJ Dahi and Blood Diamonds) compare parts of Madonna's body to the parts of a car, the song (produced by Madonna, Toby Gad, DJ Dahi and Blood Diamonds) is the same make and model as **"Candy Shop."**

The song received its live-performance debut on the *Rebel Heart Tour*.

BON JOVI, JON: *b. March 2, 1962.* Lead singer of the rock band that bears his last name. Very much a contemporary of Madonna's (the band Bon Jovi also hit the Top 40 for the first time in 1983) and a fellow musician parent, the rocker has called Madonna out on her mothering. Bon Jovi took exception to Madonna's children being seen at public events, saying in 2005, "These kids have done nothing and yet we all know what they look like. It's crazy … I've been in this industry for 22 years and no one has any idea what my four kids look like."

–ANDY COHEN

GREGORY PACE

BOOKS: Like **Marilyn Monroe** before her, Madonna flaunts her **love** of reading to counter any notion that she's dumb. Unlike Monroe, Madonna seems to genuinely love reading, and always has. Wyn Cooper, a high **school** classmate/beau of Madonna's and director of **The Egg Film**, tells *EM20*, "Madonna liked that I was a reader and writer, and I loaned her books and we discussed them, including *Lady Chatterly's Lover* [1928]."

When Madonna first moved to **NYC** and entered a club for the first time, she brought ... a book. She recalls reading F. Scott Fitzgerald's *Tales of the Jazz Age* (1922) at Pete's Place because she didn't know anybody.

In 1984, **Susan Seidelman** happened upon Madonna hunched over a collection of Sam Shepard's **plays**, and in 1986 **Bruce Weber** shot her reading the bio *The Dark Side of Genius: The Life of Alfred Hitchcock* (1983).

Aside from frequently citing favorite writers like most stars name-drop each other, she frequently insinuates books into interviews. Interviewers meeting her at one of her homes have noted the books she "happens" to have on view. *Us* **magazine** spotted *The **Andy Warhol** Diaries* (1991), in which Madonna appears numerous times, available as bathroom reading. She **hated** the 1990 film adaptation, but adored Paul Bowles's *The Sheltering Sky* (1949), even taking its heroine's name as a temporary **alias**. Madonna found *Giovanni's Room* (1956) by James Baldwin sufficiently compelling to recommend it to one interviewer and to consider optioning it as a film project.

Madonna loves a love story, calling *Corelli's Mandolin* by Louis De Bernieres (1994) "so romantic." But after love comes ... well, you know. Unsurprisingly, Madonna praised the controversial book *L'Amant* (1984) by Marguerite Duras, the story of a Chinese teacher and his pubescent conquest. She's said the book that best describes her life is the 1869 classic *War and Peace* by Leo Tolstoy, and that the author whose writing most reflects her own sensibilities was J.D. Salinger. "That's how I would write," she said in 1990, though *Sex* ain't exactly *Franny and Zooey* (1961).

When **Rolling Stone** visited her **Upper East Side** apartment in 2015, *Gay New York* by George Chauncey (1995), Luc Sante's *Low Life: Lures and Snares of Old New York* (1991) and Curtis Sittenfeld's *Sisterland* (2013) were in plain view, as was a biography of **John F. Kennedy Jr.** She told *Us* that *The Glass Castle* by Jeanette Walls (2005) is "so good."

Writers Madonna has read include: Charles Bukowski, Raymond Carver, Jung Chang, Honoré de Balzac, Guy de Maupassant, Lawrence Durrell, Bret Easton Ellis, Louise Erdrich, Ernest Hemingway, Henry James, James Joyce, Jack Kerouac, Milan Kundera, D.H. Lawrence, Thomas Mann, V. S. Naipaul, Sylvia Plath, Françoise Sagan, **Anne Sexton**, Anne Tyler, Kurt Vonnegut Jr. and Alice Walker.

Madonna became a writer of books herself, an entire line of children's tales that sought to teach moral lessons echoing the sentiments of **Kabbalah**. [SEE: **bibliography (by Madonna)**.] Madonna, in a matronly floral dress, attended a tea party to promote her first children's book, **The English Roses**, in **London** on September 14, 2003. At this and other events for her kids' books, Madonna read to lucky little ones and handed out free books. On September 29, 2003, she repeated the process in the US at Barnes & Noble (555 Fifth Ave., NY, NY), reading to the assembled tots and paying special attention to curly-haired cutie Jeremy Zorek. On June 7, 2005, Madonna read her *Lotsa de Casha* book to children at the Time Warner Center Borders (formerly 10 Columbus Circ., NY, NY), followed by a party at Bergdorf Goodman (745 Fifth Ave., NY, NY) attended by **Rosie O'Donnell** and other kids at heart.

Madonna's *The English Roses* was a #1 *New York Times* bestseller for kids, moving 57,369 copies in its first week alone. All of her children's books enriched her Spirituality for Kids Foundation (now called **Success for Kids**), a branch of the Los Angeles Kabbalah Center.

"BORDERLINE" (SONG): *Release date: February 15, 1984. Billboard Hot 100 peak: #10.* Madonna's second Top 10 hit was the fifth and final single from her first album, **Madonna**, a **flirty**, confectionery complaint from one lover to another.

In spite of being Madonna's first Top 10 hit in the U.S. and a classic just about everybody can get behind, frequently turning up on lists of the best songs of the '80s, "Borderline" has been performed by Madonna very few times. Madonna lip-synched the song on Joe Bingo's The **Dance Show** (1984), offered truncated versions during **The Virgin Tour** and the first leg of her **Sticky & Sweet Tour**, and delivered a faithful version at her **Tears of a Clown** show.

In 2016, she was joined by the Roots in performing a chill version of the song on **The Tonight Show**. It marked the first time she'd ever sung "Borderline" in full on TV. She is thought to have performed the song at host **Jimmy Fallon**'s request, and mainly in order to finally meet fellow guest **President Barack Obama**.

> "Is 'Borderline' not the sweetest song ever recorded about an orgasm?"
> —ADAM SEXTON, *DESPERATELY SEEKING MADONNA* (1990)

"BORDERLINE" (VIDEO): *Director: Mary Lambert, 1984.* Madonna's first iconic video was shot from January 30–February 2, 1984, in Los Angeles by film director **Mary Lambert**, who would go on to direct a number of

"It amazes me when I talk to people in their early twenties and they've never read the classics, things we read as children." —MADONNA (1996)

Madonna's best clips: **"Like a Virgin," "Material Girl," "La Isla Bonita"** and **"Like a Prayer."**

In "Borderline," Madonna plays an aspiring model who breaks up with her macho boyfriend (convincingly played by singer Louie Louie) in favor of concentrating on her budding career. She screws up big-time by absent-mindedly spray-painting her photographer/Svengali's car during a graffiti-themed shoot. Lambert described the video in 1997 to ***Rolling Stone*** as "boy and girl enjoy simple pleasures of barrio **love**." It's the video's and the song's simplicity and authenticity—Madonna was very much of that downtown world—that make it captivating.

The video uses color footage for the scenes involving the Madonna character's romance, and **black-and-white** scenes for its extended modeling sequences.

In one scene, "Borderline" predicts what would become a mainstay of the Madonna myth by featuring a **magazine** with Madonna on the cover. The cover image of that prop publication as well as several others seen in the video were all shot by Andy Caulfield. The images still exist, but Caulfield has decided to keep them private. For now.

John Leguizamo was an extra in the video. He said in 2010, "I mean, she was—she was superfine, but I didn't get any time because I was an extra. I'm subliminal and you have to really freeze-frame it. And, you know, they gave you a sandwich and a pat on the back."

"Borderline" was Madonna's first smash music video. According to **MTV**'s Gale Sparrow, Madonna asked the network to play her **"Everybody"** video as a favor, late at night, so she could watch herself. It wasn't considered to be in their wheelhouse. The network found **"Burning Up"** to be "night-and-day better." Then, 'Borderline' was next and Madonna was a star. That was when everything started changing … It was a little more pop. This image became as important as the music."

BORING: Madonna said in 1991, "If you take everything I do at face value, you're going to be horrified. Or intimidated. Or insulted. Or bored."

As a provocateuse, Madonna's greatest enemy is boredom, and it becomes the greatest weapon for her critics.

Calling Madonna boring removes the need to discuss her **work** in any meaningful way, a naked attempt to seem cool. The trend started in earnest in 1991, when a *Time* **magazine** poll concluded that 73% of Americans were "uninterested" in Madonna. She was rated #1 on The Boring Institute's Most Boring Celebrity list that same year, though was such a yawn she'd slid to #10 by 1992. (Wait, that's a chart on which one *wants* to fall. Guess she was actually #10 with a bullet.)

"BORROWED TIME": This ***Rebel Heart*** Super Deluxe Edition mid-tempo tune about the importance of seizing the moment continues a vaguely political suite on the album. "Is it all worth dyin' for?" Madonna asks, invoking the disparity of prosperity that plagues the planet. The song was written by Madonna, **Avicii**, Arash Pournouri, Carl Falk, Rami, Savan Kotecha, DJ Dahi and Blood Diamonds, with production by Madonna, Avicii, Carl Falk, DJ Dahi and Blood Diamonds.

BOURDIN, GUY: *December 2, 1928–March 29, 1991.* Late French **fashion** photographer who created radically **sexualized** images that approached surrealism. His representations of women have been the source of much debate—are they objectifying, or playfully liberating? Post-**feminist**? Male chauvinist?

Circa 1998, Madonna had at least two of his prints in her bedroom.

In 2003, Madonna's **"Hollywood"** video contained numerous exact references to some of Bourdin's most famous images, uncredited, which is fairly standard practice for music videos—appreciation bleeds into appropriation. His son, Samuel Bourdin, filed suit against Madonna on September 29, 2003, arguing in part, "It's one thing to draw inspiration; it's quite another to simply plagiarize the heart and soul of my **father**'s work." In 2004, Madonna settled with the younger Bourdin in a deal that required no admission of wrongdoing. Bourdin is not allowed to say how much **money** he won, but it was called a "very, very successful settlement."

MTV had withdrawn the video during litigation, but seems to have forgotten to add it back; it hasn't been seen on any MTV specials worldwide since.

BOWIE, DAVID: *January 8, 1947–January 10, 2016.* Enduring English rock innovator whose adoption of various personae during his 50-plus-year career and whose flamboyance in the '70s has made him one of the most avantgarde of all pop icons.

The first concert Madonna ever attended was David Bowie at Cobo Hall (now Cobo Center, 1 Washington Blvd., Detroit, MI). She was "punished severely" for going without her **father**'s permission.

Wyn Cooper (***The Egg Film***), a high **school** BF of Madonna's, recalled driving around in his '73 Capri listening to the 8-track of Bowie's *The Rise and Fall of Ziggy Stardust and the Spiders of Mars* (1972).

Madonna referenced Bowie's Aladdin Sane in this '70s letter to pal Sharon Maczko.

Ms. Sharon Maczko
1211 Van Nuys
San Diego, Cal 92109

Who will love Madonna Sane ?!?

Madonna the artist was compared to Bowie as early as 1986, when Robert Hilburn of the *Los Angeles Times* wrote, "Like David Bowie, Madonna *visualizes* music so that her best **work** seems equally designed with the stage or screen in mind—not just the jukebox."

Madonna also caught Bowie on his *Glass Spider Tour* in LA in October 1987. She went backstage and wound up posing for one of her strangest group photos ever with Bowie, **Billy Idol** and Sam Kinison. Bowie later said he thought the critically maligned tour had been inspirational to other artists, including Madonna, **Prince** and the Stones.

A lifelong **fan** of Bowie's, Madonna was excited to accept on his behalf when he was inducted into the **Rock and Roll Hall of Fame** in 1996, saying, "His image was an amazing influence on me. He is so **fucking** gorgeous."

In 1998, Madonna unabashedly chose Bowie as her favorite male artist of all time as well as the masculine ideal. "... I still think he's an amazing human being. He keeps pushing the envelope in his way. I can think of a lot of male artists that I admire, but every time I start to think about them, and how they behaved, they were all real shits. Fuckfaces."

On January 12, 2016, two days after Bowie's death, Madonna performed a spirited rendition of his 1974 song "Rebel Rebel" on her *Rebel Heart Tour* stop in Houston.

"It would be my guess that Madonna is not a very happy woman. From my own experience, having gone through persona changes like that, that kind of clawing need to be the center of attention is not a pleasant place to be."–DAVID BOWIE (1992)

BOXING: She may not like violence, but she digs boxing.

At a June 1, 1995, ceremony at which Muhammad Ali was being honored by the Parkinson's Disease Foundation, **award** presenter Madonna proudly announced, "I have more photos of Muhammad Ali hanging in my home than anyone else, including my family, and my favorite is the one that he **autographed** to me. It's a picture of Ali standing in the ring in Lewiston, Maine, after he knocked out Sonny Liston, and it says, 'To Madonna, we are the greatest' ... and I have to agree! Because, you see, we are both arrogant."

There was an extensive boxing tableau in *The Girlie Show World Tour*, that Chinese **hopping ghost** in the "**Erotica**" video really knew how to put up its dukes and Madonna's *Hard Candy* packaging shoot with **Steven Klein** made use of boxing imagery, as did her *Sticky & Sweet Tour* program **work** with **Tom Munro**. Video footage from the latter shoot played during a pre-taped "**Die Another Day**" interlude on the same tour, in which male **dancers** sparred, dodged, weaved and danced in a boxing ring. She's also a longtime casual friend of **Mike Tyson**, whom she invited to appear on her song "**Iconic**."

BOY GEORGE: *b. June 14, 1961.* An '80s New Romantic singer par excellence, first in Culture Club and then solo. Culture Club's chart success coincided with Madonna's, but she was already familiar with George—she'd met him on her first trip to **England** with **Martin Burgoyne** in 1982. In 2005, Madonna remembered that when she and Burgoyne went to a club, they encountered George at his most flamboyant. She recalled him as an intimidating "force to be reckoned with." She also remembered, "He was really mean to me ... he's still mean to me!"

Perhaps still smarting from the encounter, Madonna was mean back in '84. When she was asked to comment on Boy George's style, Madonna sniffed, "Yuck! That makes me sick ..."

Over the years, George has expressed everything from admiration to contempt for Madonna. His opinion of her took a dive when a spoof of "**Vogue**" that appeared in his musical *Taboo* (based on George's life, first produced in **London** and later on Broadway by Madonna's pal **Rosie O'Donnell**) caught the notice of Madonna's lawyers, leading to a cease-and-desist order.

"I used to think she was an icon but she's more eyesore to me now," George said.

He once argued **Kabbalah** was homophobic, which Madonna diagnosed as an unholy case of him having "a bee in his bonnet."

In 2008, George sang backup on a cover of Madonna's "**Bad Girl**" recorded by his friend Amanda Ghost.

By 2014, though he reserved the right to be critical of her, George had had a change of heart. "I mean, I've said awful things about Madonna and I'm not proud of that at all. I'm really not proud of that because I don't know her. And like everyone, I've always secretly kind of been into her ... I can't see us ever being friends now, but she's going to be at this event that I'm going to ... I said to my friend, if you can get a picture of me and Madonna, you'll get a medal. Can you imagine? I'd be really happy! It would be great just to have a photo with her and to **fucking** put this shit to bed. I don't **hate** her at all!"

The picture has yet to happen.

BOY SCOUTS: On March 16, 2013, Madonna presented **Anderson Cooper** with the Vito Russo **Award** at the **GLAAD** Media Awards in **NYC**. Playing off of the national debate as to whether the Boy Scouts should allow **gay** people as members and scoutmasters, Madonna took to the stage dressed as the most glamorous scout ever, wearing a uniform she obtained by lying to the BSA, saying she needed it for **Rocco**.

Madonna's opening remarks were, "Howdy! So happy to be here. I wanted to be a Boy Scout, but they wouldn't let me join. I think that's **fucked** up, um, I can build a fire. I know how to pitch a tent. I have a very good sense of direction. I can rescue kittens from trees. Mm-hm. Listen, I wanna do good for the community. But most importantly,

I know how to scout for boys. So I think that I should be allowed to be a Boy Scout. And I think they should change their stupid rules, don't you?"

The crowd roared its approval.

You cock-socker!
あんかつ、くそくらえ!

BOY TOY: On her *Like a Virgin* album cover, Madonna wears a silver belt buckle that reads BOY TOY. She wore that belt often in 1984 and 1985. End of story, right? Wrong. "Boy toy" has become one of the phrases most associated with Madonna.

Reproductions of her BOY TOY belt were sold in a short-lived 1985 line of clothing called Madonna by **Wazoo**. In 2003, **Britney Spears** and **Christina Aguilera** wore matching "BOY TOY" belt buckles during the **"Like a Virgin"** portion of their infamous **MTV Video Music Awards** performance. Madonna's official merchandise was marketed by her company Boy Toy, Inc.

Originally, the phrase was Madonna's street tag of the variety used by graffiti artists **Keith Haring** and **Futura 2000**. She even confessed to having spray-painted the name around **NYC**. Wonder if any examples still exist?

"It also has a kind of ... *humorous* meaning to it, if you know what I mean." —MADONNA ON "BOY TOY" (1984)

ABOVE: Bizarre Japanese photo insert with sucky text illustrates her BOY TOY look.

BELOW: Bootleg Madonna soap not recommended by Dr. Brandt

BRANDT, FREDRIC: *June 26, 1949–April 5, 2015.* Dermatologist to the stars who was known for his unnervingly ageless visage and winning personality. Among many other boldface names trying to avoid being oldface names, Madonna was a client. "If I have nice skin, I owe a lot to him," she said by way of endorsement. Brandt was lampooned by guest star Martin Short in an episode of *Unbreakable Kimmy Schmidt* (2015–). Shortly thereafter, the doctor, suffering from depression, hanged himself in his home.

FOR A CLEAR HEALTHY SKIN

Grace

MADONNA®

SOAP

ANTISEPTIC + MEDICATED

BRAY, STEPHEN: *b. December 23, 1956.* Aspiring musician Bray met Madonna in 1977 at a Hustle lesson at the **Blue Frogge** during her days in Ann Arbor, **Michigan**. Sources say they were lovers, but Bray defines it as a "social friendship." Bray was one of the first people with whom she explored music, as he and his band played glam gigs in the local Holiday Inn and Howard Johnson's.

After any romantic overtones had fizzled and Madonna had moved, she was looking for a third band mate to join her and Gary Burke, so she invited Bray to **New York**. They went to a Talking Heads concert in Central Park the moment he arrived in 1980, but otherwise got right to **work** trying to sort out a new band. "I was excited to find that she had written some solid songs," Bray said in 2001.

Bray said his Christianity meant that the band's name **Madonna and the Sky** was "sacrilegious," so they went with the Millionaires, then Modern **Dance**, then Emmenon/Emanon ("no name" spelled backwards), Emmy and the Emmys, and finally just **Emmy**—which was Madonna's **nickname**.

Madonna and Bray were also in the band the **Breakfast Club**, though not at the same time; Madonna had left before forming Emmy, Bray eventually left Emmy to join the Breakfast Club.

Bray played with Madonna and Emmy on a demo produced on November 30, 1980, that included four songs to be sent to music industry decision-makers: "(I Like) **Love** for Tender," "Bells Ringing," "Drowning" and "No Time (For Love)."

When Madonna went solo under the management of **Camille Barbone** and **Adam Alter**, Bray was brought along to be the **drummer** in her band.

In 1982, Bray also collaborated with Madonna on the songs—"Burning Up," "Everybody," "Ain't No Big Deal" and "Don't You Know" (later re-invented as "Stay")—that secured her a recording contract with **Sire**, but was denied the opportunity to produce her first single in favor of **Mark Kamins** when Bray's composition "Ain't No Big Deal" was sold to another artist and disqualified from appearing on Madonna's debut album; both lost out to **Reggie Lucas** when it came to producing the album as a whole.

Though Bray is sometimes counted as one of the guys Madonna used on her way up, he was the first to say, "It seems like you're leaving people behind or you're stepping on them, and the fact is that you're moving and they're not."

Bray went on to cowrite the music for and/or coproduce **"Angel," "Can't Stop," "Causing a Commotion," "Express Yourself," "Into the Groove," "Jimmy Jimmy," "Keep It Together," "Over and Over," "Papa Don't Preach," "Pretender," "Spotlight,"** "Stay," **"True Blue"** and **"Where's the Party,"** making him a millionaire and, along with **Patrick Leonard**, **William Orbit** and **Stuart Price**, among Madonna's most frequent and important musical collaborators.

"I've always kind of made the rib cage and the skeleton [music] of the song already—she's there for the last things like the **eyebrows** and the haircut [lyrics]. She writes in a stream of mood, really," Bray said in 1999.

He also worked on several Madonna tracks which remain **unreleased**, including an alleged title track from the film ***Desperately Seeking Susan***, "First Is a Kiss," "Love Attack," "Pipeline," "Warning Signs" and "Working My Fingers to the Bone." In 1997, Bray capitalized on his ownership of Madonna's pre-Sire master recordings by releasing an album filled with them called ***Pre-Madonna***. According to **Liz Rosenberg**, Madonna was "surprised and not particularly enthusiastic" about this product.

Bray's related Madonna work includes the **Nick Kamen** single "Each Time You Break My Heart" and **Nick Scotti**'s "Get Over" (both of which feature Madonna on backing vocals), and the tune "Baby Love" by Madonna's vocal clone, **Regina**.

BREAKFAST CLUB: Madonna's first-ever band, from 1979–1980, in which she initially played **drums** and fidgeted with a **guitar** before persuading the guys to let her sing.

The band had a fluid roster, but during Madonna's era was made up of brothers Ed Gilroy (guitar) and **Dan Gilroy** (drums and Madonna ... he was a beau) and **Angie Smit** (the first lead singer). The group took their name from frequent early-morning conferences at the local IHOP or an Italian diner called Army's.

Madonna says the first songs she wrote for the band were about pain and loneliness and **love**.

Following extensive guidance by Dan Gilroy, Madonna the drummer made her debut with the band on a nine-song set at UK Club in Manhattan. She sang lead on the first song she'd ever written, which she remembers as being "Tell the Truth," and also on "Born to Be a **Dancer**."

Their next gig was at CBGB (formerly 315 Bowery, NY, NY), where Madonna's singing led to a good response—until she burped loudly. Madonna was booed off the stage at the Our Lady of Mt. Carmel Feast in Corona, Queens, which was a case of the wrong band for the wrong event if ever there was one.

But the bored reaction the Breakfast Club received at Bachelors 3 (a bar owned by ex-baseball player Phil Linz) so infuriated Madonna that Dan Gilroy later identified it as the major reason the band's lineup changed; Angie was out and Madonna in as lead singer and keyboard player, Gary "the Bear" Burke joined as bass guitarist, and Mike Monahan came aboard as the drummer. Both men have said they developed **crushes** on Madonna.

When the bandmates fought over whether Madonna should front the band (with the Gilroys no longer singing at all), Madonna split from both band and brother in 1980 to form **Emmy** with **Stephen Bray**.

The Madonna-free Breakfast Club went on to some success with the #7 US hit "Right on Track" (1987).

BRIDAL SHOWER: Madonna's shower before she married **Sean Penn** was thrown by Nancy Huang, then a girlfriend and musical collaborator of **Nile Rodgers**, in Huang's **Upper East Side** apartment. Twenty-five of their closest pals attended, including **Erika Belle**, Thompson Twin Alannah Currie, Mariel Hemingway, **Maripol** and **Debi Mazar**. The party was supposed to be all-girl, but **Martin Burgoyne** and **Jellybean Benitez** made loopholes of themselves, crashing in **drag**.

At the party, Huang later told *New York* **magazine**, the late socialite Sandy Marsh gave Madonna a pair of antique berry spoons from James Robinson. Huang remembers, "Madonna opened the package and said, 'So what is *this*?'"

BRIT AWARDS: *Dates presented: 1977–*. British **awards** show honoring excellence in music.

On February 20, 1995, Madonna made one of her most exciting one-off appearances, performing her single **"Bedtime Story"** with a live band and two **sexy**-as-hell male **dancers**. Sounding great and singing in her lower register, Madonna's flowing **blonde** hair, debuted in the music video for the song, was blown wildly about by strategically placed **fans**. Speaking of fans, the audience was filled with them, going nuts as Madonna strolled past, hand-slapping some lucky music lovers while exhorting everyone to get unconscious. She lost Best International Female to **k.d. lang**.

Backstage, Madonna posed playfully with future frenemy **Elton John**, both tearing their tops open for the photographers. (John showed his nipples, Madonna merely her bra.)

She would not perform at the show for another 20 years, and considering what happened, she might've waited 25. Madonna, in a heavily hyped appearance, closed the Brits on February 25, 2015, with a performance of **"Living for Love."** Entering in a cape by Armani, she ascended three steps, paused, tried to untie the cape and then was dramatically yanked backwards and onto the floor when the cape failed to totally disengage. It was a stunning fall. Madonna stood back up and calmly resumed her performance, picking back up with the lines, "Took me to heaven/Let me fall down/Now that it's over/I'm gonna carry on." The **irony** was *thick*.

But as disastrous as the fall itself was—Madonna thankfully was unharmed—her true mettle was shown; she simply continued, and gave what many still felt was the best performance of the evening. The fall also demonstrated the extent to which Madonna was singing live, as only a faint guide vocal continued on.

She spoke at length about her spill on an episode of ***The Jonathan Ross Show***, taped February 26, 2015, and aired the following March 14 to incredible ratings.

Celebrities who took to social media to express support and admiration for Madonna in the aftermath of her accident included **Boy George**, **Cher**, Elvira, Ronan Farrow, Juliette Lewis, **Lindsay Lohan**, Mario Lopez, **Bette Midler**, Liza Minnelli, J.K. Rowling, Nancy Sinatra and **Michelle Visage**.

As far as Brit Award nominations, Madonna has nabbed 12 of them, two resulting in wins. In 2001, she was a no-show

"Thank you, Stephen Bray. It always starts with the bass line and the beat."–MADONNA (2009)

when she won a *Music*-driven Best International Female trophy, but sent a video in which **Guy Ritchie** accepted the award while Madonna flitted in the background doing housework, speaking in a prissy British **accent**. In 2006, she showed up in a smart red dress, **worked** the carpet, kibitzed with Ritchie in the audience and picked up an award for International Female Solo Artist on the strength of *Confessions on a Dance Floor.*

> "Madonna falls over, giving the evening its longed-for news angle. Seated only yards from the stage I hear the crash as she goes down, most shocking of all being the heavy ker-THUMP of her mic hitting the floor. 'Golly,' I think, 'that mic's actually on.' Not a given nowadays–and quite a thrill. What is most remarkable, though, and confirms everything I've ever thought about the indestructible will-to-power of Stars, is her recovery. Have you ever fallen flat on your back? I have once, on the slippery decking outside my back door, and on landing whiplashed and winded did what you would do, and burst into tears of self-pity. Which is why I'm not a global superstar with a decades-spanning career, and neither are you."-TRACEY THORN, *NEW STATESMAN* (2015)

> "It's ironic because even though I'm an American recording artist, it is British recording artists who have influenced my work the most: From David Bowie to Elvis Costello, Portishead to Radiohead, the Pet Shop Boys to Goldfrapp …"-MADONNA, *THE BRITS* (2006)

BRITISH COMEDY AWARDS: *Dates presented: 1990–.* Annual **awards** show that bestows trophies upon the funniest performances and performers of the year. Taking her life into her own hands, Madonna appeared in 2006 to give the Writer's Guild Ronnie Barker Award to **Sacha Baron Cohen**, immediately receiving congrats from **Jonathan Ross** on her "lovely little black baby, **David** … I went to **Africa**, all I came back with is a wallet." Madonna's retort: "Well, you might go home with a black **eye**."

BRIXTON ACADEMY: *211 Stockwell Rd., Brixton, London, England, UK.* On November 29, 2000, just over three weeks after a similar show at **NYC's Roseland Ballroom**, Madonna played a promo concert in support of her *Music* album at this venue. Recycling the set (with one surprise), look and performers from the Roseland show (she wore a "**Rocco**" tank for the cowgirl-themed performance), Madonna sang **"Impressive Instant," "Runaway Lover," "Don't Tell Me," "What It Feels**

Like for a Girl," "Holiday" and **"Music."** As a webcast on MSN.co.uk, it reached an audience of approximately 9 million. She had not toured in the UK since 1993. She got rave reviews, pardners.

> "… [S]he dances fantastically, and she sings. She sings very well. Her voice has changed from its Minnie Mouse origins: it's bright and clear, a good strong experienced pop voice."-MIRANDA SAWYER, *THE GUARDIAN* (2000)

"BROKEN": Synth-pop stomper recorded during the *Celebration* sessions but left off the album, it was offered in 2010 as a premium to members of Madonna's **fan** club but was not actually available until 2012. The song (which has echoes of **"Sorry"**) was pressed on hot-pink vinyl and included in a strictly limited, lavishly produced edition with a **boxing**-themed cover by **Tom Munro**. The **Original** Extended Mix (remixed by Paul Oakenfold) and Instrumental Version were included. The collectible has sold for over $200 on eBay.

BROOKNER, HOWARD: *April 30, 1942–April 27, 1989.* The director of the acclaimed documentaries *Burroughs: The Movie* (1983) and *Robert Wilson and the Civil Wars* (1986), Brookner undertook the feature *Bloodhounds of Broadway*, in which Madonna had a memorable supporting role, when he was very ill with **AIDS**. Brookner shot over 8,000 feet of celluloid and delivered an edit to Columbia, but his version was rejected; a studio-cut version of the film left it disjointed, deeply disappointing Brookner and his cowriter, Colman deKay.

When being courted to star in the movie, Madonna was impressed by two things: Brookner's film about **William S. Burroughs** and that "he didn't try to flatter me."

Madonna became one of Brookner's confidantes during the making of their movie and the unraveling of his life. She was sympathetic, having recently cared for her friend **Martin Burgoyne** until his own **death** from AIDS. "When he phoned and said, 'I have to tell you something,' he couldn't get it out. I said, 'I already know.' I think it was kind of a relief that I knew and that my feelings about him weren't going to change."

In April 2015, Brookner's partner Brad Gooch published the memoir *Smash Cut: A Memoir of Howard & Art & the '70s & the '80s* in which he notes that Brookner and Madonna had "a connection of the heart … that broke through the barriers of celebrity."

For *Bloodhounds of Broadway*, Brookner assembled one of the most **talented** casts of the '80s to make a small film, solely on the merits of his dedication, the script and his **power** of persuasion.

Brookner's wry epitaph, taped to his refrigerator at the time of his death, was, "There's so much **beauty** in the world. I suppose that's what got me into trouble in the first place."

In 2012, Brookner's nephew, Aaron Brookner discovered his uncle's film archives and successfully Kickstarted a restoration and re-release of *Burroughs: The Movie*. In 2014, Aaron Brookner completed *Uncle Howard*, a documentary about Howard Brookner, which contains footage of Madonna. He said he was inspired by a line his uncle wrote in the last year of his life: "If I live on, it is in your **memories** and the films I made."

BROSNAN, PIERCE: *b. May 16, 1953.* The suave star of **TV**'s *Remington Steele* (1982–1987) and the cinema's fifth "James Bond" (1995–2002), Brosnan said to *Us* **magazine** in 1985 of Madonna—who was its #10 **sexiest** star of the year—"Any girl who jives on stage in her undies can't be all bad. And she has a great pair of, uh, vocal cords."

In *Die Another Day*, Brosnan's final appearance as Bond, he shared a fetching fencing scene with Madonna.

BROTHERS, DR. JOYCE: *October 20, 1927–May 13, 2013. The* famous-for-being-famous shrink had a split personality when it came to analyzing Madonna. In the early '90s, she said, "Madonna is a **sexy** person for our time. She's independent and on her own two **feet**." Yet in summing up *Sex*, she bemoaned the state of the world when impressionable kids choose to emulate "a **rich** slut."

BROWN, BOBBY: *b. February 5, 1969.* **Gay** guys used to **love** icons who were tragic, but maybe now we just relate to those with tragic taste in men. Brown, the **talented** breakout star of boy band New Edition and later a solo sensation, became best known as Mr. **Whitney Houston**, but Madonna allegedly bedded him as well. This tidbit comes to us via a **book** called *Bobby Brown: The Truth, The Whole Truth and Nothing But ...* by Derrick Handspike.

Could it be true? Madonna said herself at her 2000 **Roseland Ballroom** promo concert, "The last time I played Roseland was 18 years ago. I was the opening act for New Edition." How literally did she mean it?

BROWN, JULIE: *b. August 31, 1958.* Hysterically funny comic whose obnoxious Valley Girl stage persona and penchant for singing offbeat tunes like the now uncomfortably accurate "The Homecoming Queen's Got a **Gun**" (1984) made her the perfect girl to rib Madonna.

Brown's December 1991 *Truth or Dare* send-up for Showtime, *Medusa: Dare to Be Truthful* is the funniest Madonna **parody** ever, featuring a **"Vogue"** satire called "Vague." Brown said of Madonna at the time, "In my fantasy, she's like the toughest chick in high **school** who throws you up against a locker and says, 'I'm gonna beat you up!'"

"BUENOS AIRES": Buoyant track from *Evita: The Complete Motion Picture Music Soundtrack,* and the song in the film *Evita* that illustrates 15-year-old Eva's arrival in the city of her **dreams.** She really wants to "be a part of B.A.—Buenos Aires—Big Apple." (Never mind that nobody but **Tim Rice** ever called Buenos Aires the Big Apple.) Some of Madonna's best singing is on this song, which, while not an official single, was released promotionally to plug the movie and the soundtrack. Also, some of her best dancing is in the film sequence, including a turn with her former backup **dancer** Luca Tommassini. The song features percussion by Emilio Estefan, who was brought in at Madonna's request.

BURGOYNE, MARTIN: *Circa 1963–November 30, 1986.* Madonna's best friend, roommate and occasional backup **dancer** from her early years in **NYC** who died of **AIDS** at 23. Burgoyne and Madonna were inseparable as they tore through the downtown scene with the energy of two transplants, she from the Midwest, he from **England** via New York state and Florida.

Madonna **dreamed** of being a famous dancer and actor, or maybe a singer, biding her time **working** at the **Russian Tea Room.** Burgoyne was a **talented** designer struggling to make his mark while still having as much fun as possible, going through the motions as a **Studio 54** bartender. When Madonna's career took off, her friendship with Burgoyne remained strong. She remembered in 2005 that their bartending **jobs** at Lucky Strike (formerly 9th St. & Third Ave., 2nd Fl., NY, NY) funded her first trip to the UK with him. "We used to rob the cash register blind!"

Burgoyne was well liked by all; when he became ill, it affected people deeply. When he learned he had AIDS, Madonna supported him completely, both by paying his bills (reportedly over $100,000) and by subletting for him a 12th St. apartment near St. Vincent's Hospital Manhattan (formerly 170 W. 12th St., NY, NY). Madonna sent **Sean Penn**—who at the time was known to be quite AIDSphobic

Martin Burgoyne as shot by Richard Corman in the East Village in 1983

RICHARD CORMAN

—MARGARET CHO

HE WAS ONLY 23:
AN INTERVIEW WITH MARTIN BURGOYNE'S
HIGH SCHOOL FRIEND LISA BOHART

Lisa Bohart has something in common with Madonna that very few other people on earth have in common with the superstar—Martin Burgoyne was one of her best friends. Before he arrived in NYC to study at the Pratt Institute, Burgoyne had been a misfit in Tampa, Florida, an artsy party boy with a penchant for doing his female buddy's hair and makeup, and an unquenchable desire to be creative.

Once he hit NYC and met Madonna, the two were inseparable. Many images of Madonna and Burgoyne together exist, revealing them to be kindred spirits. Burgoyne has also long been a source of fascination for the first wave of Madonna's gay fans—he was the mystery boy who made it so easy for us to imagine being best friends with Madonna, and also the one who convinced us her affinity with the gay community was no pose.

Madonna has referred to Burgoyne many times over the course of her career, and decades after his untimely death, he is similarly rarely far from his old friend Lisa Bohart's thoughts.

EM2O: How did you first meet Martin?

LISA BOHART: He came to Seminole High School [2701 Ridgewood Ave., Sanford, FL] about the same time of our junior year that I did. I was sitting in art class and everybody was looking at him strange and just being jerks. I called him over and said, "Hey, I'd love to see your portfolio," and we just started talking. That's how our friendship started—I defended him in the face of a bunch of *stupid* people. They were judging him without having a clue of who he was.

EM2O: What was he like to talk to?

LB: He had a strong [British] accent—his parents did, too—mannerisms, lifestyle, he was very European.

EM2O: As you became friends, what would you do together?

**LB: We used to go on Clearwater Beach and sit out there with our sketchbooks and draw. We used to lay on his living room floor—his mom would sit in there—and do projects. We'd come up with the craziest things to do, just he and I. We'd go to thrift shops and pick up cigar boxes and do cut-outs and collages and shellac over them and make our own little cool boxes.

EM2O: Why do you think he made such a strong impression on you?

**LB: He was fearless and the best person in the world you could ever meet. I have to thank him for who I became and the strengths I gained, because I was a very shy person when I met him.

EM2O: Martin was very into the downtown party scene in NYC. Was he like that when you knew him?

**LB: We would go out—probably too much! We'd start early. He would do my hair, then we'd stop at Dillard's and he would do my makeup, then we'd stop at a store that still is in Ybor City called La France [1612 E. 7th Ave., Tampa, FL] and buy old, cool jackets and stuff and go out together and we would stay out until three and four in the morning.

We would go to El Goya [formerly 1430 E. 7th Ave., Ybor City, Tampa, FL]. They had female impersonators.

And we would go to Rene's, another bar in town. Martin's funnest thing to do was to tell the guys that I was really a guy and they would go, "Let's go in the bathroom and check it out."

He's just such a good dancer! He loved Grace Jones and all the pop dance music. Some of it, he knew before Tampa because of his New York exposure.

EM2O: What did he tell you about his ambitions?

**LB: He just wanted to go to New York City. Florida was very boring to him. I have a piece of paper that he drew, we were sitting drawing together, and I think it was crayons, and it said, "Off to New York!" or "I love New York!" and he signed it—he signed everything he drew.

He tried to talk me into going with him—he was going to Pratt and I wasn't sure I wanted to go to New York City at that time. I ended up going down to Sarasota and he went to Pratt. That was fine … it was kinda sad when he left. He kept trying to get me to come up. I kept all his letters; he drew cool stuff on them. He would always write me letters and tell me all the wild stuff that he witnessed! [Laughs]

EM2O: What did he tell you of his life in NYC?

**LB: He was the assistant to the head maître d' at Windows on the World in the World Trade Center and he worked at the Parachute store. He used to pick out clothes for … think he said Cher one time. One of our favorite things to do was take Polaroid pictures of each other in odd places. There's one of me on a gas tank at a Mobil station. Crazy, fun stuff like that—self-expression.

I kept trying to get together in New York with him. He kept telling me I had to come up and be a soap opera star and change my name to Lisa Minova … and I *loved* that name.

EM2O: Did he ever mention Madonna?

**LB: He came to visit me one day and he brought a little cassette and popped it in and said, "Listen to this girl, she's gonna make it really big, she's really good." Well, it was Madonna singing ["Lucky Star"] and I'm like, "Yeah, that's a really cool song!" And we were talking about her, so at that point I knew he'd already met her and was hanging out with her.

What he did with me, I know he did with her. We didn't have scanners and computers then, so we had photocopy machines. When *W* magazine was a newspaper, we'd collect those and all these old photos of famous stars in really avant-garde poses and beautiful photographs and photocopy them, blow them up and do art on top of it. We always did photo booth pictures, too. Everything was really hands-on back then. Madonna's record cover that he did for her, I can *so* see his style of art.

EM2O: But you didn't stay in touch with him right up until he died?

**LB: We did lose touch with each other. I ended up moving to Toronto. I think that's when he got really busy with Studio 54. I got married and I was sitting in Toronto in a graphics department and I was really thinking about him, and it was really weird … I had called Mom and I said, "Mom, have you heard anything on Martin?" and she told me that he had died of AIDS. At almost the same time, I picked up this paper and saw an article on him, too. It was just like … *darn.*

EM2O: When you see pictures and videos of him in NYC after you'd lost touch, how do you feel?

**LB: I couldn't see anything more fitting for him. I know Andy Warhol made a jacket for him. I've seen pictures of him with Madonna just before he died … it's an extremely great loss, of course, but in his short life, he did *so much* and experienced so much. It's almost like nothing could hold him back from what he truly felt inside in his heart and mind, what he wanted to do and experience. I think he accomplished quite a bit.

I'm fond of Madonna because I think she's a great role model. She's a kick-ass woman and gets it done. Also because I know how close she was to Martin, and I loved Martin.

martin burgoyne

RHONDA CORTE

(he'd changed a lot by the time he was winning an **Oscar** for *Milk* [2008])—to Mexico to buy an experimental **drug** for Burgoyne. She remained physically and emotionally close to her friend as his illness rapidly progressed.

"He called me up, and I have total recollection of that devastating moment because by then I knew it was something you didn't recover from," Madonna remembered after his **death**. "And he said, 'I have something.' It was something you get before full-blown AIDS, and I remember he told me and I was like, 'Okay, so that's it, that's it.' I just felt incredibly enraged and of course did everything I could to save him …"

She was in the room when Burgoyne died, telling **Carrie Fisher** in *Rolling Stone* that his rage at dying haunted her. She memorialized those moments in her *Erotica* song **"In This Life."**

The loss of Burgoyne, in part, inspired Madonna to funnel millions into AIDS organizations. Her *Who's That Girl World Tour* date at **Madison Square Garden** in NYC on July 13, 1987, was in his honor, with all proceeds going to amfAR. She dedicated that evening's performance of **"Live to Tell"** to his **memory**.

Burgoyne collaborated with Madonna artistically. He is one of the dancers behind her at her **"No Entiendes!"** performance of **"Everybody,"** and he designed her bold **"Burning Up"** b/w **"Physical Attraction"** 12" sleeve. He also designed **Michael McKenzie**'s early **book** on Madonna, *Lucky Star*.

In 2014, Burgoyne's elderly parents commissioned Myers Fine Art & Antiques **Auction** Gallery (1600 4th St. N., St. Petersburg, FL) to auction off 16 lots of their son's earthly possessions. These included the **original** photo booth images used for the "Burning Up" b/w "Physical Attraction" art, Madonna's personal gold record for **"Holiday,"** a platinum record for *Madonna* given to Burgoyne, an **Andy Warhol** graphite drawing of Burgoyne, photography of Madonna and Burgoyne and his original portfolio of color pencil and ink drawings, which sold for many times its estimate.

"BURNING UP" (SONG): *Release date: March 9, 1983. Billboard Hot 100 peak: NA.* Madonna's second single in 1983 was the 12" for this **disco**-rock song b/w **"Physical Attraction,"** featuring sleeve **art** by her good buddy **Martin Burgoyne**. The illustrations and the photo booth images upon which they were based were sold for thousands of dollars at **auction** in 2014.

Madonna has solo writing credit on "Burning Up." It has a similar-sounding chorus to the **unreleased** track credited to the **Breakfast Club** called "On the Ground." In demo form, it was one of the tunes that landed her a record deal with **Sire**. The released version was produced by **Reggie Lucas** with additional remixing done by **Jellybean Benitez** when Madonna objected to the changes Lucas had made to the **Stephen Bray** original.

"Burning Up" was not a big hit, failing to chart on the *Billboard* Hot 100, but it is a quintessential Madonna song for its forthright take on **sex**, featuring her most directly sexual lyrics until **"Justify My Love."**

In 1984, the song was on the soundtrack of *The Wild Life*, a rare instance of a Madonna tune being licensed to a non-Madonna project in the '80s.

She performed "Burning Up" on *The Tube* and at a large but indeterminate number of **NYC** and UK clubs (also at **The Metro Club** in Boston) while promoting it, and three times on tour—on *The Virgin Tour*, on her *Re-Invention World Tour* and on her *Rebel Heart Tour*. She chose **Iggy Pop** and the Stooges to play her into the **Rock and Roll Hall of Fame** in 2008, signing off on their performing "Burning Up" in their set.

Artists as diverse as Jonathan Groff (for *Glee* in 2010) and **Britney Spears** (on her *Femme Fatale Tour* in 2011) have covered "Burning Up." It happens to be **Guy Oseary**'s fave classic Madonna tune.

"BURNING UP" (VIDEO): *Director: Steve Barron, 1983.* Madonna's first studio music video was an auspicious debut, featuring her as a siren in white, writhing in the middle of the road, pulling a chain across her throat, floating serenely on a raft and dancing with gusto in a barrage of typically early-'80s surreal settings. The video was directed by Irish filmmaker **Steve Barron** and costars Madonna's real-life lover boy **Ken Compton**. We see the character played by Compton driving toward a vulnerable Madonna as she squirms on the pavement, but in the end, it is the singer who winds up in the driver's seat. The video's four-wheel drive **feminism** is vintage Madonna.

In 2014, Barron self-published the must-read memoir *Egg n Chips & Billie Jean: A Trip Through the Eighties*, in which he described meeting Madonna for the first time in her apartment, where he found her stretching in white boxers and nothing else. She did cover up, but talk about a great way to audition directors! Barron writes of his first impression of Madonna, "And there's something captivating and compelling that's beyond **sexy**. There's some vibe that comes from her that's hard to put my finger on. It's hard to describe. It's a kind of light within her that gives her a quality that you don't come across very often. She's oozing it right now. What is that? Is there a word for that? What do you call that? Duh! Star. Inevitable."

Barron later admitted to almost killing Madonna on this shoot when a crane filming her from above (you know the shot) nearly fell on her. "… [W]hen it got directly over her, I look back, and the wheels had left the ground. We're on the tipping point with this thing that's basically eight tons of metal that's 16 feet above her face, and I yelled, 'Stop! Stop!' It stopped, it wobbled, and we slowly inched backward. Another move forward and it would have come crashing down. It definitely would have killed her."

Barron reports that **working** with Madonna was a pleasure. He says she was "a hugely ambitious and determined young girl learning and acquiring the **talent** she needed to get to where she wanted to go," calling her fun and saying he wished he'd been able to direct a video for one of her better songs. (Steve … you got to direct the video to one of her all-time *best*.)

"The episode ends in romantic death rather than sexual encounter, a more fitting conclusion since Madonna's desirous frenzy could scarcely be fulfilled within the pop visual medium in a simply sexual manner."
—STEVE NEUMANN ON "BURNING UP," ISLAND (1983)

BURROUGHS, NORRIS W.: *b. July 1952*. Artist Burroughs became Madonna's lover for three months in 1978 after meeting her at a party at **Pearl Lang**'s. He actually introduced Madonna to his romantic successor, **Dan Gilroy**.

Burroughs was a part of the **NYC** downtown **art** scene, a graffiti and T-shirt entrepreneur. He said in 1993, "Madonna was definitely a **sexual** being, but not in the same sense of wearing lace panties and torpedo bras. It was just kind of an animal sexuality. She called me up one day and said, 'Get your gorgeous Brando body over here.'"

According to Burroughs, Madonna would sing songs by Blondie, the Pretenders and Donna Summer. She also liked to sing Nancy Sinatra's "These Boots Are Made for Walkin'" (1966) around his apartment, as well as her favorite **disco** tune, Gloria Gaynor's "I Will Survive" (1978).

In 2012, Burroughs published the 125-page digital **book** *My Madonna: My Intimate Friendship with the Blue Eyed Girl on Her Arrival in New York*, in which he details his affair with Madonna.

Burroughs's description of Madonna as a "goddess" may well have inspired the title for biographer **Barbara Victor**'s biography of the diva. In that book, Burroughs is quoted saying, "Goddesses make mistakes, but they go on. I believe that to the extent that I believe in life energy. What separates a **god** from a mortal? Why does Madonna have a divine spark that lifts her above the average person? Because people embody ideas and energy, and because we make people out of myths."

BURROUGHS, WILLIAM S. *February 5, 1914–August 2, 1997*. Beat figure, essayist, novelist and painter who drunkenly shot and killed his second wife while playing William Tell.

After being introduced to him by **Allen Ginsberg**, Madonna partied with the literary icon on December 19, 1987, at Canal Bar (formerly 511 Greenwich St., NY, NY) after a Burroughs show at Tony Shafrazi Gallery (formerly 163 Mercer St., NY, NY), as captured in a photo by wowe (a.k.a. Wolfgang Wesener).

BUSINESS: If Madonna is a **sex** icon, she's also a business icon, the one woman about whom every misogynist businessman will admit, "She's shrewd." She takes that kind of reaction as a compliment, but Madonna doesn't like having her business affairs scrutinized, and actively dissuaded friends and associates from commenting for a 1990 *Forbes* cover story.

She is the corporate head of all her companies, and is hands-on involved in the business side of her career. David Salidor, a publicist who's **worked** closely with her, said, "She used to walk into meetings with a legal pad and a written agenda. She was very much in charge."

This image conflicts with Madonna's stories of glibly eating **popcorn** during meetings, letting a piece fall into her cleavage, then fishing it out to eat it. "I used to worry

©CURTIS KNAPP

about surviving, what I was going to do. Now I have to worry about being ripped off. If my lawyer is making the right deals, if my accountant is paying me. **Boring** stuff like that," she said in 1986.

In recent years, Madonna's been criticized by fans for being more about making **money** than making music, including launching multiple business ventures in the areas of **fitness**, fragrance and **fashion**. But as **Nicki Minaj** raps on **"I Don't Give A"**: "Yo, I ain't a businesswoman/ I'm a business, woman/And I'm known for giving **bitches** the business, woman."

"BYE BYE BABY": *Release date: November 15, 1993. Billboard Hot 100 peak: NA.* Written by

"My business sense isn't very good. If someone says, 'You're getting a half-million dollar advance,' I go, 'Big deal.' I don't care. I'm not interested, as long as I have enough money to pay the rent and buy all my rubber bracelets and stuff."—MADONNA, *GRAFFITI* (1985)

Madonna, **Shep Pettibone** and **Tony Shimkin**, this acidic anti-**love** song from *Erotica* became the final single from that album when it was released (abroad only). On "Bye Bye Baby," Madonna's vocal is distorted to sound tinny and mechanical. The same effect was employed when she performed it in male **drag** on the **MTV Video Music Awards** and on *The Girlie Show World Tour,* which made it a breeze to sing—that vocoder is forgiving.

RICHARD CORMAN

CALDEIRÃO DO HUCK: *Airdates: 2000-.* Hosted by Luciano Huck, this *wildly* popular Brazilian talk show nabbed Madonna for one of the most relaxed interviews of her career, conducted on November 19, 2012, after an *MDNA Tour* stop in **Miami**. Huck quizzed Madonna right on the floor of her hotel bathroom, leading to its **nickname** "In the Bathroom with Madonna."

"Sometimes I just lay down on the floor and I can't get up," Madonna said of the bathroom, which goes a long way toward explaining some of her **Instagram** photos.

The casual chat was interrupted by **Rocco**, leading to some cute moments between **mother** and son ("I like my children clean," she noted, asking him if he'd brushed his teeth and showered).

Huck's chemistry with Madonna was rare among interviewers, leading to unguarded chatter about the tour, her **fans**, her dislike of performing in the rain and her special affection for Brazil, which she described as having "a lot of heart" as well as unique music and **talent**.

Mid-way through, Madonna took a soup break courtesy of her chef Marco, demonstrated her facial steamer and showed off how she does her vocal cool-down, using ... a gigantic vintage tape recorder. ("If I put it on an iPod, it doesn't **work**!")

CAMACHO (XTRAVAGANZA), LUIS: SEE: Jose & Luis.

CAMDEN PALACE: *Now KOKO, 1A Camden High St., London, England, UK.* The site of Madonna's British debut in spring 1983. Club manager David Chipping said he gave her the equivalent of about $16 to cover her expenses for her first gig. She made a second appearance on October 13, 1983.

Robin Denselow wrote in *The Guardian* at the time of Madonna's second Camden Palace gig, "Given a full set and a live band behind her, Madonna would seem to have the makings of a major star." He described her look as "Holocaust chic."

Madonna returned to Camden Palace on November 15, 2005, by which time the venue had been renamed KOKO, for a promo date in support of *Confessions on a Dance Floor*. She popped out of a glitter ball and tore through **"Hung Up,"** **"Get Together," "I Love New York," "Let It Will Be"** and **"Everybody."** This time, Madonna—in purple from head to toe—had a full troupe of **dancers** and sang live. Progress!

On Madonna's earliest trips to the UK, she also appeared at the Beatroot Club, the Hacienda and Heaven (Under the Arches, Villiers St., London, England, UK).

CAMP: Trying to define "camp" is like trying to define **pornography**—ya know it when ya see it. Camp is when something dead serious has no idea that it's also screamingly hilarious. It's a soap opera from the '50s; it's Ethel Merman singing **disco**; it's *The Brady Bunch Variety Hour* (1976–1977).

Though the wickedest camp is accidental, since the '70s it's become more common for camp to be on purpose. Madonna has used camp both intentionally and not.

On the one hand, Madonna is a lover of good camp, which she sometimes files under "**irony.**" There is a knowingness to Madonna, just like the knowingness that emanated from **Mae West** (the first camp icon to recognize her status as such). Madonna knows what's funny to see Madonna doing and saying. Witness *Truth or Dare*, made not because she was so desperate to invite us into her personal life, but because there is no denying the ridiculous fact that we're *dying* to take a peek. Or screen her **"Fever"** video, where her subtle smile as she parades in outrageous costumes and red pigtails screams, "Can you believe this?"

Camp moments in Madonna's career are endless, but any list must include the stage-wiping antics of the **MTV Video Music Awards** performance of **"Like a Virgin"**; interviews she gave on Japanese **TV** in 1985, wearing full **boy toy** regalia and blankly, impatiently waiting as the questions and her answers were methodically translated back and forth; and stage costumes like **cone bras** (especially on men), phony ponies, paisley jackets with purple lace tights, **blonde** afro wigs and bustiers with tassels.

Madonna is also a fertile source of unintentional camp because she is one of those people who believes so strongly in everything she does that she sometimes has blinders on. Her movies *Shanghai Surprise*, *Body of Evidence* and *Swept Away* certainly qualify as bad/good camp, and there's no doubt that she entered into them with the serious intention of creating solid cinema, not snark-a-thons.

Liz Smith tried to save her some face by saying that *Body of Evidence* was *supposed* to be campy, but Madonna (ignoring the swift kick under the table) denied that the film was supposed to be any such thing. (But ya *are* campy, Madonna, ya are!) And whenever Madonna says she is an avenger for self-expression and **sexual** freedom, the camp-meter gets a **hernia**. She actually *is*, but hearing her *say* it ...!

CAMP FIRE GIRLS OF AMERICA: As a little girlie, Madonna joined the Camp Fire Girls (now known simply as Camp Fire), a nonsectarian alternative to the Girl Scouts of America that's been in operation since 1910. She could have been a Brownie, but she went with their rivals because "they had the cooler uniforms." Too bad—imagine the amounts of cookies that kid could've sold. (In 2013, Madonna joked that she used to eat all the cookies ... were those the last cookies she ever tasted?)

CAMPBELL, NAOMI: *b. May 22, 1970.* Volatile British supermodel who posed in *Sex*. Madonna and Campbell had socialized prior to the *Sex* shoot, having been introduced by **Steven Meisel**. Campbell appears in shots with Madonna and rapper **Big Daddy Kane** in and around a pool, and a naked Campbell simulates oral sex on a partially clothed Madonna in one pose. It is Naomi's toe that Madonna is **shrimping** in *Sex* and on the back cover of *Erotica*.

At the time of the **book**'s publication, Campbell apparently couldn't take the heat surrounding *Sex*, so she meticulously avoided the subject. Asked why she posed for the book, she allowed, "I did that for the photographer, Steven Meisel, who is a great friend of mine. I did what Steven told me to do. I don't know if she had any fantasies for me because I was just directed by Steven." Campbell's ultra-religious **mother** denounced the poses, claiming that she, too, had been asked to pose, but had declined.

In 2002, Campbell was forced to answer for the poses during an invasion-of-**privacy** lawsuit she was waging against the UK tabloid *The Mirror*. When her participation in the book was brought up, she testified, "My **grandmother**, who's older, said she did not think it was pleasing to her, but I didn't think it was vulgar ... I have a lot of respect for Madonna being bold enough to come out and do a book on **sex**. I've never reneged on that."

CAMPOS, DANIEL "CLOUD": *b. May 6, 1983*. Smooth, sleek, nimble guy who **danced** for Madonna on her *Re-Invention World Tour* and *Confessions Tour*, and stood out in her **"Hung Up"** and **"Sorry"** music videos. In *I'm Going to Tell You a Secret*, Madonna **gifts** Cloud with a **guitar**, which visibly moves him.

Cloud posted a dazzlingly edited montage of footage from the road in celebration of Madonna's 48th **birthday**, perhaps a sneak peek of his future vocation as a music video director.

CANCER: Madonna's **mother** died at 30 after battling breast cancer, so Madonna herself is very cancer-conscious, going for mammograms every six months.

The *National Enquirer* reported that she found small lumps in her right breast in late 1987, saw LA specialist Jerrold H. Steiner, and then postponed follow-up visits for months before having a biopsy done, which proved that the lumps were benign cysts. She has never commented on the veracity of that story.

Her sugar is raw.

CANDY: The *Hard Candy* diva has a sweet tooth. "Our favorite thing to do," **Sandra Bernhard** said, back when it was still *cool* to be Madonna's friend in 1989, "is to go to 7-Eleven and buy junk candy late at night."

Madonna's favorite kind of candy is a long-lasting **lollipop**, and her sucker of choice is a Charms Blow-Pop.

"CANDY PERFUME GIRL": Unique, '60s-style rock track on *Ray of Light*. The song was produced by Madonna and **William Orbit**, and its lyrics are credited to Madonna, William Orbit and Susannah Melvoin (the twin sister of Wendy Melvoin of Wendy & Lisa).

In spite of the wallop the song packs, its lyrics are trippy to the point of nonsensical. A Minnesota-based company called Magnetic Poetry that manufactured sets of magnetized words meant to be arranged on your fridge to create poetry claimed the song may have been written using its Magnetic Poetry Sequel Kit, pointing out that only 3.2% of the words in Madonna's song do not appear in that kit. The kit contained the words "**candy**," "devour," "ghost," "girl," "perfume," "poison," "porcelain," "throb," "velvet" and "window."

Madonna denied using the product.

"CANDY SHOP": Madonna's favorite song on her *Hard Candy* album was not only the first song on the album, it was the first **leak** from that project, many months (summer 2007) ahead of its official release. Written by Madonna and **Pharrell Williams**, the track was produced by the **Neptunes** and Madonna. Its lyric "sticky and sweet" became the title of her wildly successful *Sticky & Sweet Tour*, and the song its opening number.

Prior to that world tour, Madonna had premiered the song live at a **Roseland Ballroom** promo gig. She has subsequently performed the song on her *MDNA Tour* and *Rebel Heart Tour*.

The song is characterized by **candy** as a metaphor for **sex**, leading to an awkward picturing of what exactly Madonna is equating with Turkish delight.

CANNES INTERNATIONAL FILM FESTIVAL: *Dates presented: 1946–*. The 10-day Festival International du Film de Cannes, got its start as an alternative to 1939's Fascist-dominated **Venice Film Festival**, and was officially launched in 1946. Since then, it has been the premier film festival in the world, a place where movies and careers have been toasted and booed.

Films are screened at the annual festival from morning to midnight, leaving precious little time to flaunt one's fabulousness to the assembled world media. And who wants to spend all day in a dark movie theater when you're on the French Riviera? Madonna didn't.

She blew into the 44th annual festival on May 13, 1991, to promote *Truth or Dare* (actually, *In Bed With Madonna*, the non-US title), which was shown out of competition at a midnight screening at Palais des Festivals et des Congrès

MATTHEW RETTENMUND

(Boulevard de la Croisette, Cannes, France). It was chaos, with stars like **Spike Lee** and Eddie Murphy in the half-empty theater—the crush to get in had been so overwhelming that even though it had been one of the fest's must-sees, many ticket-holders had given up or been turned away. No matter. The film got great word of mouth and Madonna had already created an iconic moment: When she ascended the stairs out front (with **Alek Keshishian** as her date) and turned, **eyes** gleaming, gums exposed with glee, the world sank to its knees as Madonna threw open her hot-pink cape to reveal an ivory **Gaultier** bullet-bra and girdle.

In explaining why Madonna's appearance at the fest was the most anticipated since Brigitte Bardot's, **Harvey Weinstein** explained, "Madonna is honest. She says what she feels, doesn't **censor** herself and has an adventurous spirit."

Three days later, Madonna showed up to the screening of Lee's *Jungle Fever* in one of her most awkward looks ever—her dark **hair** slicked down and pulled back, she wore a double-breasted gray suit top and matching gray tutu with white knee socks, rendering her a film-festival short.

Films in competition that year included *Barton Fink*, *Guilty by Suspicion*, *Jungle Fever*, *Miller's Crossing*, *A Rage in Harlem* and Akira Kurosawa's *Rhapsody in August*. Other stars at Cannes in 1991 included **Rosanna Arquette**, Geraldine Chaplin, **Rupert Everett**, Robert De Niro, Terry Gilliam, Whoopi Goldberg, Gina Lollobrigida, Robert Mitchum, Arnold Schwarzenegger and Donald Sutherland. She avoided her ex, **Sean Penn**, who was in town to promote his directorial debut, *The Indian Runner*.

Madonna was in her element at Cannes: a **sex** goddess by everyone's estimation, the world's biggest star, the brains, bucks and bod behind the year's most talked-about cinéma vérité doc and the biggest dose of glamour to hit the festival in decades.

In 2005, *I'm Going to Tell You a Secret* was rejected by Cannes, but by 2008, Madonna returned to present her film *I Am Because We Are*, wearing a sheer '20s ball gown, **Guy Ritchie** at her side.

In 2011, the fest passed on screening Madonna's *W.E.*, which instead premiered at the Venice Film Festival.

"Was I a good shayna maidel?"
—MADONNA TO HARVEY WEINSTEIN AFTER DISROBING AT CANNES (1991)

CANONERO, MILENA: *b. 1946.* Italian costume designer behind Madonna's elaborate "Breathless Mahoney" wardrobe for *Dick Tracy*. Her **Oscar**-nominated designs formed the basis of an entire line of clothing for which stores were urged to establish Breathless Mahoney departments. The short-lived collection, bolstered by over 60 licensees, consisted of black-sequined gowns, fake diamond **accessories**, **blonde** wigs, fire-engine red lipstick, hosiery, shoes and sunglasses.

In *Dick Tracy*, director **Warren Beatty** wanted vain Breathless to have eight costume changes, humble "Tess Trueheart" to have half that and everyone else to stick to one, easily identifiable signature outfit.

Of her experience fitting Madonna, Canonero has positive **memories**: "She just wanted the clothes to fit well and to be able to feel the tightness of the dress on her body."

CANSECO, JOSE: *b. July 2, 1964.* Former Major League baseballer for the Oakland Athletics and seven other teams, with whom Madonna reportedly had a fling in mid-1991. In preparation for her role in *A League of Their Own*, she met with several pros, and when she had a one-on-one with Canseco—then estranged from his wife Esther—from 11 p.m. until 1 a.m. in her apartment, tongues wagged. Earlier in the evening, she had attended Liza Minnelli's *Stepping Out* show with a ticket provided by **John F. Kennedy Jr.,** and fortified herself with a salad.

Madonna didn't comment on the supposed affair, though Canseco said, "We're just friends. She's a nice lady." When a spectator heckled Canseco by taunting him on the subject, the dude received a string of obscenities in response. Later in the year, a pair of satirical Madonna/Jose Canseco baseball cards was issued by a private company.

The press was left assuming he got a walk after only one ball.

In 2008, Canseco told *Us* that he and Madonna "were not intimate," but claimed she had come on to him and wanted his Cuban baby. "I then told her I was trying to **work** things out with my wife. That if I left her, I would lose a lot of **money** and she said, 'I have lots of money. Don't worry about that.'"

"CAN'T STOP": Aerobics-ready song from the *Who's That Girl: Original Motion Picture Soundtrack* that was written and produced by Madonna and **Stephen Bray**. Peppy as hell, it would make an interesting mash-up with **Miley Cyrus**'s 2013 super smash "We Can't Stop." Otherwise, it has the distinct sound of filler.

CAR: Madonna's first car established her expensive taste in automobiles, and was also a **gift**: a 1968 red Mustang for her sweet 16 from her **father** in 1974. She let her license lapse after high **school** and in 1985 had to take driver's ed to receive a license immediately prior to *The Virgin Tour*. Once, when asked (not by Barbara Walters, amazingly) what kind of car she would be, she chose a gold Mercedes sedan, though she has answered that same question elsewhere by selecting an Aston Martin.

Madonna has purred around town in a blue-black Mercedes 560SL when not chauffeured in a limo. She graduated to those wheels after growing tired of **Sean Penn**'s **wedding** gift: a coral Thunderbird. The T-bird, which can be seen in the non-US **"True Blue"** video, was given away for a Ronald McDonald House **auction**. (Hey, Sean had peeled out of their marriage, why keep it?). It brought in $60,000 for the **charity**.

In 1995, she also allowed her **black-and-white** 1961 Mercedes Benz 280SE convertible to be auctioned off, raising $46,350 to the Philadelphia Museum of **Art** (2600 Benjamin Franklin Pkwy., Philadelphia, PA) to fund a **Tina Modotti** exhibit.

Madonna's not big on flashy cars. If you spot her in a vehicle these days, it's likely to be a black SUV.

CAREY, MARIAH: *b. March 27, 1969.* Mega-diva with a five-octave range who has been a *Billboard* chart phenom, racking up records since her debut in 1990. According to Carey's own press releases, she considers herself the #1-selling female artist of all time, though **Guinness** sides with Madonna.

Their memberships in each other's **fan** clubs lapsed long ago.

In 1995, Madonna told **Bob Guccione Jr.** for *Spin*'s January 1996 issue, "I don't want to get into slagging off other artists, but we were talking about [**k.d. lang**'s] record versus someone like Mariah Carey's—and I think she's a very **talented** singer—but we have to realize that the same country that acquitted O.J. is the same country that makes a complete piece of shit movie #1, that buys Mariah Carey records. It's this homogeneity. But it's got nothing to do with **art**." She later joked that she'd kill herself if she were like Carey, singing what Guccione termed "silly pop songs."

Pretty hard to defend *that* as being out of context.

At a December 7, 1995, **London** in-store appearance, Carey served Madonna her own ass by responding, "I really haven't paid attention to Madonna since I was in, like, seventh or eighth grade when she used to be popular ..."

Over the years, Carey has had a vision of **hate**, often seeming to throw shade Madonna's way without naming her. She told *W* **magazine** in June 1996, "I don't want the **fashion** to outshine the music. I'm not one of those people who feels I need to change my look every five minutes, because I'm overcompensating for, uh, other areas."

Twice on London **TV** shows, Carey has pointed out that she has disdain for Americans who put on English **accents**, something for which Madonna is bloody well known.

During a sit-down at *The View* on November 17, 1998, Carey responded to criticism that she was dressing too provocatively saying, "... Aren't there people out there that are a *little* more extreme than I am? Especially some of the [air-quotes] *singers* that we know?"

In 2005, the long-simmering feud was alleged to have boiled over, with Madonna telling her people to keep Carey "far away" from her when both performed at **Live 8**. This rumor was denied, but a year later, rumors emerged that Carey was livid when she was not allowed to open the **Grammys**, which were instead opened by Madonna and **Gorillaz**.

By 2008, there was a little glasnost, with Carey diplomatically deeming Madonna's upcoming foray into R&B (*Hard Candy*) to be "very interesting." Which, come to think of it, sounds like a hollow compliment you'd give a terrible actor about the terrible **play** that she's in.

But perhaps the two women have other things to worry about (or other feuds to manage). In a phoner with *Papel Pop* in 2014, Carey was asked to pick Madonna or **Beyoncé**. While she raved about Beyoncé as a good person, friend

and talent, she did say, "Madonna is a trailblazer, she, she really helped the music industry in a lot of ways."

So ... choose your sides. Or like both to really piss them off.

CARLISLE, BELINDA: *b. August 17, 1958.* Lead singer of the all-girl rock band the Go-Go's, and a solo star in her own right, with pop hits like "Mad About You" (1986) and "Heaven Is a Place on Earth" (1987).

In a 1988 interview, Carlisle reported seeing Madonna often at her **gym**. "She's a real athlete. She was doing advanced classes with weights on her ankles and wrists. She's heavy-duty."

Madonna gently mocked Belinda's vibrato in a *Truth or Dare* scene.

CARPENTER, KAREN: *March 2, 1950–February 4, 1983.* One half of the singing duo the Carpenters, her rich, heartfelt vocals elevated all-time classic pop hits like "Superstar" (1971), "Top of the World" (1973) and many more. Carpenter died after battling anorexia nervosa.

Liz Rosenberg confirmed that both **"Angel"** and **"Rain"** are "tributes" to Carpenter. You can hear it in the vocal style of "Rain" ... but *"Angel"*? Maybe because Karen *is* one? Madonna cites Carpenter as an influence, which is apparent in many of her ballads, not least of which **"Ghosttown."**

On the second night of the **New York** stop of *The Girlie Show World Tour*, Madonna made her dancer **Carlton Wilborn** sing the Carpenters hit "(They Long to Be) Close to You" (1970) to his **mother**, who was in the audience.

CARRAMBA! CHE FORTUNA: *Airdates: 1998–2000, 2008.* Madonna made a rootin', tootin' appearance on this Italian **TV** show on December 2, 2000, lip-synching her hit **"Don't Tell Me."**

CARSON, JOHNNY: SEE: *Tonight Show, The.*

CASARES, INGRID: *b. May 1964.* One of Madonna's closest friends, Casares is a chic Cuban-American mover y shaker born in **Miami** who has **worked** as a model, agent, image consultant and club owner. She is also an inveterate starfucker, according to her ex, **k.d. lang**, who told *New York* in 1998, "... [O]ne of the things I **love** most about Ingrid is that she has definitely said to me, 'I'm a starfucker.' To me, that's more respectful than someone who is and denies it. She knows she's a socialite."

Madonna met Casares in 1991 at Madonna's **birthday** party, to which Casares arrived as **Sandra Bernhard**'s date. They would get better acquainted at Madonna's New Year's Eve party (1991/1992), which featured many female guests dancing bare-breasted. The women had instant chemistry, with Casares impressed by how attentive Madonna was to her, and how interested the superstar was in her opinions.

When Bernhard and Casares called it quits, Madonna gravitated to Casares, which outraged Bernhard, who was quoted as characterizing the situation as Madonna having

STEVEN CHRISTEN

"run off with a girlfriend." Casares saw it as fate. "I've always had a theory that you meet people to meet other people. I met Sandra because I was supposed to meet M."

Rumors were rampant that Madonna and Casares, who rejects labels but has had high-profile affairs with women, were an item (they lived together for a spell). Their raunchy poses in Madonna's *Sex* did little to dispel that notion. If the women ever played doctor, they're preserving doctor-patient confidentiality.

Madonna and Casares have remained tight for over 20 years, attending events together (the White Party in Miami, 1992, as just one example) and socializing privately. She has been described by Madonna, **Liz Rosenberg** and others close to Madonna as a true-blue friend who never ass-kisses.

Yet in spite of the incredible devotion Casares has shown to Madonna over the decades, she's one of those people who engenders cynical assessments. Responding to the suggestion that Casares is sweet, gossip Cindy Adams once replied, "Yeah—sweet like diabetes." Madonna's brother **Christopher Ciccone** wrote in his memoir that Ingrid is a total yes-woman: "At the time of Madonna's first meeting with Ingrid, the woman in Madonna's life was Sandra [Bernhard], but—whether or not their relationship was physical—Madonna couldn't **control** Sandra. A woman with her own career, a definite personality and opinions, Sandra has never been Madonna's puppy **dog**. Ingrid, however, is quite another story."

In 1998, for Casares's birthday, Madonna threw a massive party at "the Kit Kat Klub" (Studio 54, 254 W. 54th St,, NY, NY) where a revival of *Cabaret* was playing. Stars in attendance included Kevin Aucoin, David Barton, Susanne Bartsch, Brian and Ed Burns, D'Angelo, Robert De Niro, Stephen Dorff, Michael Douglas, Jennifer Grey, Calvin & Kelly Klein, **David LaChapelle**, lang, Donovan Leitch, **Kurt Loder**, Cameron Mathison, Tommy Mottola, Billie Myers, **Chris Paciello** & (then-unknown) Sofia Vergara, Joe Pesci, Ian Schrager, Jon Secada, Ione Skye, Ivana Trump, Amber Valetta and Mark Vanderloo, among others.

Casares had past **drug** problems that found her in and out of rehab, for which she has had Madonna's support; Madonna reportedly even staged an intervention at one point. She also had to endure scrutiny when her **business** partner, Paciello, with whom she operated the successful Miami Beach club Liquid (formerly 1439 Washington Ave., Miami Beach, FL), was revealed to have mob ties, was convicted of murder and did time in prison. Madonna was allegedly romantically involved with Paciello, so remember that when you cringe over the likes of **Andy Bird**—it gets worse!

It would seem that whatever bond exists between Madonna and Casares, it is genuine and sturdy.

"Ingrid looks at life with innocent eyes. She is like 'Puck' in *A Midsummer Night's Dream*."-MADONNA (1998)

CASTILLO DEL LAGO: *6342 Mulholland Dr., W. Hollywood, CA.* Madonna paid $5 million for this Hollywood Hills mansion in 1993, a landmark designed by John De Lario for oil tycoon Patrick Longdon that was built in 1926. Its other famous resident was mobster Bugsy Siegel, who lived there in the late '30s.

With a fantastic 300-degree view, it seemed an ideal palace for a queen. Madonna hired her brother **Christopher Ciccone** to spruce it up as part of a $3 million-dollar renovation, which resulted in its most famous alteration—cream and blood-red horizontal stripes that **Ciccone** said were inspired by a Portofino church but which also inspired the anger of all the neighbors. Of their complaints, Ciccone sniffed, "I don't hold their bad taste against them."

Even if the paint **job** wasn't to your liking, the castle itself, a treasure, was a sight to behold, with its giant tower, a spiral staircase, nine bedrooms, six baths, a game room, library, wine cellar and separate offices and servants' quarters.

Madonna sold the luxurious home for just $5.3 million in 1997 to director/restaurateur Joe Pytka, which may or may not have had to do with persistent rumors that it is haunted.

CATHOLIC: "Once a Catholic, always a Catholic," says Madonna and every other adult survivor of what she once called this "really mean," "incredibly hypocritical" religion.

Madonna rejected Catholicism for its restrictive attitudes toward women and its even stricter outlook on human **sexuality**, but could never fall out of **love** with its artifice, high drama and symbolism.

Catholicism is the Broadway of religions, spectacular both in scale and the degree to which it takes itself seriously. Its rituals—so like a pop concert—seek to draw its participants into a mass perception of divinity exuding from its center (in the case of the church, the **Pope;** in the case of a pop concert, **Beyoncé** or **Justin Bieber** or ... Madonna).

Though Madonna used to describe herself as agnostic and since the '90s has been a spiritually hungry devotee of **Kabbalah**, she has constantly returned to the iconography of Catholicism in her **work** and in her look.

Our earliest **memories** of Madonna are dressed in marital lace and draped with rosaries and **crucifixes**. Her crosses caused a stir, primarily because she projects 100% sex. By merely wearing Catholic accoutrements, she was a walking billboard for lost sheep. Her image was Catholic in its bounce between the two components of the great

A castle of a different stripe

"I did a lot of bad things and I didn't feel guilty about it because I knew I could go to confession at the end of the week and all would be forgiven …"—MADONNA (1990)

dichotomy in the Church: the Virgin (Mary, **Mother** of **God**) and the Whore (Mary Magdalene, who, Madonna has theorized, probably nailed Jesus once or twice). In her **"Like A Virgin"** video, she is both the virginal bride, swathed in white, and the sexual huntress, barely clad in black lace. The mix is thought-provoking and intoxicating, and it got the world talking about Madonna in religious terms.

On the **Who's That Girl World Tour**, the Pope's image was flashed as one example of "Papa," but the real embodiment of the struggles between humanism and Catholicism, between flesh and spirit, was Madonna's **Blond Ambition World Tour**. Madonna cavorted through dens of iniquity, defying Catholic stances against **masturbation**, **homosexuality**, adultery, sodomy, **nudity** and sex for pleasure— only to wind up at an altar, praying to **God**, confessing to a priest she cannot help seducing.

Unsurprisingly, the church does not see the value in deconstructing its tenets, and found Madonna's frank discovery of sex at its roots tantamount to blasphemy. But you can't be a heretic if you don't care, merely a disrespectful outsider. Her rebuke of the church's rebuke of *Blond Ambition* stands as a rarity in the Modern Age—a mainstream pop star dressing down the frickin' Catholic Church for attempting to rule the minds of its believers.

Of course, if you don't believe in Catholicism, that leaves room for belief in Madonnaism. For proof, watch **Truth or Dare** and listen to her vigorously humanistic prayers to "God," or, more probably, to herself and her own reserves of strength. Is it an accident (you know she had to take it there) that Madonna herself wound up physically on a cross, singing **"Live to Tell"** during her **Confessions Tour**?

Madonna's name was her initiation into the fun to be had in toying with religion. Aside from that assigned reference, she has *chosen* references to Catholicism throughout her career: "Like a Virgin," as above; *Like a Prayer*, with its praying theme, its rosary-laden packaging, songs like **"Spanish Eyes"** and **"Oh Father,"** with its paternal/Paternal metaphor; the cleverly-named *The Immaculate Collection*, fresh on the heels of *Blond Ambition*, and a further play on Madonna's own status as a "goddess" of pop; her use of crosses in photo shoots from the beginning of her career right through the *Rebel Heart* era; and her entire fascination with sadomasochism (which has its roots in punishment-driven belief systems like Catholicism), as expressed in everything from the back cover of *Madonna* to the **"Burning Up"** and **"Express Yourself"** videos, from **"Hanky Panky"** to **Jean-Baptiste Mondino**'s bondage-esque **"Justify My Love,"** to the pleasure-pain of *Sex* and *Erotica*.

Is Madonna anti-God? No. Is she anti-Catholicism? Probably, but rather than state it so baldly, she chooses to use its own symbols as convincing arguments against its place in a modern world.

"CAUSING A COMMOTION": *Release date: August 25, 1987. Billboard Hot 100 peak: #2.* One of Madonna's many #2 hits and one of her biggest hits that she seems not to care for, "Causing a Commotion" was the second single from the **Who's That Girl: Original Motion Picture Soundtrack**. In the film, it was introduced to **fans** during the opening cartoon sequence. The song—written and produced by Madonna and **Stephen Bray**—was performed on the **Who's That Girl World Tour** before most audiences had ever heard it, in advance of the film's release, and was received as enthusiastically as a greatest hit. It was then performed on the **Blond Ambition World Tour**—and never again. An early example of a Madonna song that quotes from another Madonna song (in this case, **"Into the Groove"**), "Causing a Commotion" was directly inspired by **Sean Penn**'s physical altercation with a paparazzo.

CAVIAR: Madonna adores the food most commonly associated with luxury—fish eggs. She has Beluga, Sevruga and/or Ossetra caviar at all her parties

CD:UK: *Airdates: 1998–2006.* In 2003, Madonna sat for an interview with this British music-countdown **TV** show to promote **American Life**. She playfully demanded that a Cosmo be readied for her, but got serious when asked if the album reflected the most honest version of herself that the public had seen, saying, "Honestly? Yes. To thine own self be true." She also expressed skepticism for the *Pop Idol* phenomenon and got feisty when asked if she felt she needed to step up to the rising stars of 2003: "No, I think *they* might have to step up to *me*."

CELEBRATION (ALBUM): *Release date: September 18, 2009. Billboard 200 peak: #3.* Madonna's fourth compilation of greatest hits, following **The Immaculate Collection**, **Something to Remember** and **GHV2**, this two-disc set somewhat haphazardly (tracks were laid out in a mysteriously creative rather than chronological manner) gathers 34 of Madonna's hits and shoulda-been hits along with three new songs, presenting them as a definitive aural portrait of her musical career.

Somewhat fittingly, this was Madonna's last album for **Warner Bros.**

Audiophiles were unhappy with mastering errors in some of the tracks, some critics were left scratching their heads by the sequencing, but the set received positive reviews, selling 4 million worldwide.

The unique cover is a Mr. Brainwash (Thierry Guetta) commission. Brainwash is a prominent street artist and protégé of Banksy, known for his pop-**art** style. To create the cover, he merged a 1987 portrait of Madonna by Alberto Tolot (the **hair**) with a 1990 portrait of Madonna by **Jean-Baptiste Mondino** (the face), winding up with an image strikingly similar to **Andy Warhol**'s *Marilyn Diptych* (1962) and Warhol's other **Marilyn Monroe** works.

CELEBRATION
(Disc One & Disc Two)

Standard Edition
(Track listing is 1-9
from Disc One, then 3, 9,
2, 4, 5 from Disc Two,
then Disc One tracks 12,
13 and 1, and finally
Disc Two track 18.)

Digital Deluxe Version
(Disc One & Disc Two + A)

Amazon MP3 Deluxe
Version (Disc One
& Disc Two + A, B)

iTunes Store Deluxe
Video Edition (Disc One
& Disc Two + A, C + D)

DISC ONE

①
"Hung Up"
(Madonna/Stuart Price/
Benny Andersson/Björn
Ulvaeus)-5:38, produced
by Madonna/Stuart Price

②
"Music"
(Madonna/Mirwais)
-3:45, produced by
Madonna/Mirwais

③
"Vogue"
(Madonna/Shep Pettibone)
-5:16, produced by
Madonna/Shep Pettibone

④
"4 Minutes"
feat. Justin Timberlake
and Timbaland
(Madonna/Justin Timber-
lake/Timothy Mosley/
Nate Hills)-3:09,
produced by Timbaland/
Justin Timberlake/Danja

⑤
"Holiday"
(Curtis Hudson/Lisa Ste-
vens)-6:08, produced by
Jellybean Benitez

⑥
"Everybody"
(Madonna)-4:10,
produced by Mark Kamins

⑦
"Like a Virgin"
(Thomas Kelly/William
Steinberg)-3:09,
produced by Nile Rodgers

⑧
"Into the Groove"
(Madonna/Stephen Bray)
-4:45, produced by
Madonna/Stephen Bray

⑨
"Like a Prayer"
(Madonna/Patrick Leonard)
-5:42, produced by
Madonna/Patrick Leonard

⑩
"Ray of Light"
(Madonna/David Atkins/
Christine Leach/Clive
Skinner/William Orbit),
-4:33, produced by
Madonna/William Orbit

⑪
"Sorry"
(Madonna/Stuart Price)
-3:58, produced by
Madonna/Stuart Price

⑫
"Express Yourself"
(Madonna/Stephen Bray),
-4:00, produced by
Madonna/Stephen Bray

⑬
"Open Your Heart"
(Madonna/Gardner Cole/
Peter Rafelson)-3:49,
produced by Madonna/
Patrick Leonard

⑭
"Borderline"
(Reggie Lucas)-3:59,
produced by Reggie Lucas

⑮
"Secret"
(Madonna/Dallas Austin)
-4:28, produced by
Madonna/Dallas Austin

⑯
"Erotica"
(Madonna/Shep Pettibone/
Anthony Shimkin)-
4:30, produced by
Madonna/Shep Pettibone

⑰
"Justify My Love"
(Madonna/Ingrid Chavez/
Lenny Kravitz)-4:54,
produced by Lenny Kravitz

⑱
"Revolver"
feat. Lil Wayne
(Madonna/Dwayne Carter/
Justin Franks/Carlos
Centel Battey/Steven
Andre Battey/Brandon
Kitchen)-3:40, produced
by Madonna/Frank E

DISC TWO

①
"Dress You Up"
(Andrea La Russo/Mar-
garet Stanziale)-4:02,
produced by Nile Rodgers

②
"Material Girl"
(Peter Brown/Robert Rans)
-4:00, produced by
Nile Rodgers

③
"La Isla Bonita"
(Madonna/Patrick Leonard/
Bruce Gaitsch)-4:03,
produced by Madonna/
Patrick Leonard

④
"Papa Don't Preach"
(Brian Elliot/Madonna)
-4:29, produced by
Madonna/Stephen Bray

⑤
"Lucky Star"
(Madonna)-3:38, produced
by Reggie Lucas

⑥
"Burning Up"
(Madonna)-3:44, produced
by Reggie Lucas

⑦
"Crazy for You"
(John Bettis/Jon Lind)
-3:44, produced by
Jellybean Benitez

⑧
"Who's That Girl"
(Madonna/Patrick Leonard)
-4:00, produced by
Madonna/Patrick Leonard

⑨
"Frozen"
(Madonna/Patrick Leonard)
-6:18, produced by
Madonna/William Orbit/
Patrick Leonard

⑩
"Miles Away"
(Madonna/Justin Timber-
lake/Timothy Mosley/
Nate Hills)-3:45,
produced by Timbaland/
Justin Timberlake/Danja

⑪
"Take a Bow"
(Madonna/Babyface)
-5:20, produced by
Babyface/Madonna

⑫
"Live to Tell"
(Madonna/Patrick Leonard)
-5:51, produced by
Madonna/Patrick Leonard

⑬
"Beautiful Stranger"
(Madonna/William Orbit)
-4:22, produced by
Madonna/William Orbit

⑭
"Hollywood"
(Madonna/Mirwais)
-4:23, produced by
Madonna/Mirwais

⑮
"Die Another Day"
(Madonna/Mirwais)
-4:36, produced by
Madonna/Mirwais

⑯
"Don't Tell Me"
(Madonna/Mirwais/Joe
Henry)-4:11, produced by
Madonna/Mirwais

⑰
"Cherish"
(Madonna/Patrick Leonard)
-3:51, produced by
Madonna/Patrick Leonard

⑱
"Celebration"
(Madonna/Paul Oakenfold/
Ian Green/Ciaran Gribbin)
-3:34, produced by
Madonna/Paul Oakenfold/
Ian Green

Ⓐ
"Celebration"
Benny Benassi Remix Edit
(Madonna/Paul Oakenfold/
Ian Green/Ciaran Gribbin)
-3:58, produced by
Madonna/Paul Oakenfold/
Ian Green, remixed by
Benny Benassi

Ⓑ
"Celebration"
Felguk Love Remix
(Madonna/Paul Oakenfold/
Ian Green/Ciaran Gribbin)
-3:58, produced by
Madonna/Paul Oakenfold/
Ian Green, remixed
by Felguk

Ⓒ
"It's So Cool"
(Madonna/Mirwais/
Monte Pittman)-3:26,
produced by Madonna/
Paul Oakenfold

Ⓓ
Videos:
"Lucky Star," "Border-
line," "Like a Virgin,"
"Material Girl," "Crazy
for You," "Papa Don't
Preach," "Open Your
Heart," "La Isla Bonita,"
"Like a Prayer," "Ex-
press Yourself," "Cher-
ish," "Vogue," "Justify
My Love," "Erotica,"
"Rain," "Take a Bow,"
"You'll See," "Frozen,"
"Ray of Light," "The
Power of Good-Bye,"
"Music," "Don't Tell Me,"
"What It Feels Like
for a Girl," "Hung Up,"
"Sorry," "Get Together,"
"Jump," "4 Minutes,"
"Give It 2 Me,"
"Celebration"

—MÝA

"THIS COMPILATION IS HEAVILY WEIGHTED
TO HER GLORY DAYS—EVERYTHING ON *THE
IMMACULATE COLLECTION* OF 1990 IS ALSO
HERE EXCEPT, WEIRDLY, 'RESCUE ME.'
BUT THE SELECTION FROM THE REST OF HER
CAREER REVEALS JUST HOW CONSISTENTLY
SHE HAS DELIVERED THE GOODS …"

—SARAH CROMPTON, *THE TELEGRAPH* (2009)

"… [F]ROM THE OPENING ONE-TWO OF
'HUNG UP' AND 'MUSIC', TWO OF HER
BEST EVER, *CELEBRATION* KICKS OFF WITH
PUREBLISS AND NEVER LETS UP."

—ROB SHEFFIELD, *ROLLING STONE* (2009)

"AND SO, MADONNA: A DODDERING, OBSOLETE
GOAT WHO HASN'T BEEN CURSED WITH
ILLNESS LIKE THE FORMER CASSIUS CLAY
BUT WHO WROTE HERSELF OUT OF CONTENTION
BY RELEASING SOME OF THE WORST MUSIC
HUMANITY EVER HEARD. *CELEBRATION* …
IS THE PERFECT DOCUMENT OF WHAT HAPPENS
WHEN GENIUS, INTELLIGENCE AND INSPIRATION
FADE AWAY TO BE REPLACED WITH SAD
DESPERATION AND THE ECHOING NAUSEA
OF MAMMON-LIKE CASH-HUNTING."

—STEPHEN BURKETT, *THE QUIETUS* (2009)

"CELEBRATION" (SONG): *Release date: July 31, 2009. Billboard Hot 100 peak: #71.* The title song and first of two new songs on Madonna's career-retrospective package *Celebration*, "Celebration" was written by Madonna, **Paul Oakenfold**, Ian Green and Ciaran Gribbin, and was produced by the same team minus Gribbin. It is an enthusiastic if slightly throwaway club throbber that, with its European sound, did very well there and tanked in the US, where it failed to hit the Top 40 in spite of becoming a #1 **dance** hit. Whether someone **loves** or **hates** this song can be a good litmus test to separate Madonna **fans** who see her as a genius from those who see her as a former genius.

The song begins with one of Madonna's familiar **sexual** come-ons, spoken as the music revs up, "Haven't I seen you somewhere before? You look familiar …" a train of thought completed much later in the tune with, "I guess I just don't recognize you with your clothes on." **Mae West**, eat your *self* out.

As fun as it is, the song does not compare to some of the greatest hits of Madonna's career on *Celebration* (in particular **"Holiday,"** to which it seemingly owes its inspiration, or any of her many "hesitation"-based contributions to pop music). Strains of "Celebration" can be heard in the "Holiday"

Sticky & Sweet Tour performances from 2009, and the song made for a truly cathartic finale for *The MDNA Tour.*

"CELEBRATION" (VIDEO): *Director: Jonas Åkerlund, 2009.* The usually brill **Jonas Åkerlund** was **"Ray of Light"**-years away from his best **work** with Madonna when he directed the phoned-in clip for "Celebration." But considering he crafted the instant classic "Paparazzi" for **Lady Gaga** in the same year, it was probably the fault of Madonna, whom one maybe can't blame for not being totally into her umpteenth music video, this time for a song from an album put out to fulfill her **Warner Bros.** contract.

In the clip, shot at **Dolce & Gabbana**'s Metropol theater (Viale Piave, 24, Milan, Italy) Madonna vamps with and kisses her real-life romeo **Jesus Luz,** who is playing a DJ, then **dances** with abandon on a sound stage. Dressed in a short, tight, studded Christophe Decarnin dress and sporting **Joan Rivers** *What Becomes a Semi-Legend Most* (1983) **hair**, Madonna's choreography proved incontrovertibly that the 50-plus-year-old had the moves of a teenager (as a handy comparison, her own teenager, **Lola**, appeared in the video), but due to the sped-up camera effects and randomness of her boob-and-crotch-grabbing thrusts, Madonna at times seems a self-**parody**, something of which her critics often accuse her, almost always inaccurately.

A remix video using footage of Madonna **fans** from Barcelona and Milan that was shot during her *Sticky & Sweet Tour* is way cuter because it seems to take itself less seriously. If you wanna live vicariously, watch as Lola plays dress-up in Mommy's *Like a Virgin* album-cover duds … imagine raiding that closet???

CELEBRATION: THE VIDEO COLLECTION: *Release date: September 26, 2009.* Madonna's most comprehensive collection of any kind, this DVD release rounds up 40 of her most memorable music videos, many of whose songs were not represented on the companion album *Celebration.* The videos included, in order, are:

First DVD: **"Burning Up," "Lucky Star," "Borderline," "Like a Virgin," "Material Girl," "Crazy for You," "Into the Groove," "Live to Tell," "Papa Don't Preach," "True Blue," "Open Your Heart," "La Isla Bonita," "Who's That Girl," "Like a Prayer," "Express Yourself," "Cherish," "Vogue," "Justify My Love," "Erotica," "Deeper and Deeper," "Rain"** and **"I'll Remember."**

Second DVD: **"Secret," "Take a Bow," "Bedtime Story," "Human Nature," "I Want You," "You'll See," "Frozen," "Ray of Light," "The Power of Good-Bye," "Beautiful Stranger," "American Pie," "Music," "Don't Tell Me," "What It Feels Like for a Girl," "Die Another Day," "Hollywood," "Love Profusion," "Hung Up," "Sorry," "Get Together," "Jump," "4 Minutes," "Give It 2 Me," "Miles Away"** and **"Celebration."**

The DVD collection was successful, though criticism emerged regarding image quality on many of the earlier videos.

ANDRÉ GROSSMANN

LAVINEL SAVU

CELEBRITY CLUB: *Formerly 35 E. 125th St., NY, NY.* Long-lived club in Harlem that hosted the fine queens of the '30s and '40s, and that went strong into the '80s, when it became a happening part of the hip-hop scene. Madonna performed there on June 17, 1983, where she was captured backstage and in action by photographer **André Grossmann**.

CENSORSHIP: Madonna hasn't been censored, per se, in the United States, but she *has* had rules imposed on her by corporations, which have affected her artistic output.

During the Golden Age of Music Video, **MTV** had standards as fluid as those of the Motion Picture Association of America (MPAA). It banned **nudity,** gore, product endorsements and other elements it found gratuitous, from any music videos it played. This is not censorship, but a private code of acceptability.

MTV asked Madonna to delete scenes in which she is chained to a bed from **"Express Yourself,"** a scene from **"Oh Father"** in which the lips of a corpse are obviously sewn together and the scenes in **"Vogue"** in which her breasts are clearly visible through a lace blouse. In each case, Madonna refused and MTV relented.

But when she submitted **"Justify My Love,"** MTV banned it outright, citing the video's overwhelming **sexual** content. In the end, she did not alter the video, but released it as a video single—a first. Two years later, MTV would play the heavily edited final cut of **"Erotica"** only three times, and in 2001, MTV and **VH1** rejected **"What It Feels Like for a Girl"** due to violence. The latter was played just once on each of the networks.

MTV and VH1 aren't the only companies that have tried to **control** Madonna—she has said that for *I'm Breathless: Music from and Inspired by the Film Dick Tracy*, Disney demanded that she delete references to "sodomy," which could refer to a toning down of the spankfest **"Hanky Panky."**

The video for **"Like a Prayer"** so angered **Catholics** and other religious conservatives that it destroyed Madonna's **commercial** deal to endorse **Pepsi**, and was *truly* censored—banned by the government—in Italy for almost a month after its release.

Real censorship also occurred when Japanese copies of *Sex* were graphically smeared by order of the government to obscure a visible penis and shots of pubic **hair**.

> "MTV has found the video 'Like a Prayer' to be acceptable for air. Ultimately, MTV supports an artist's right to interpret his or her music."—MTV PRESS RELEASE A YEAR AND A HALF BEFORE BANNING "JUSTIFY MY LOVE" (1989)

Throughout her career, Madonna has aligned herself with the plight of those whose **voices** have been stifled, either by corporate dicta or actual censorship (**Pussy Riot**).

CENTRAL PARK WEST: *1 W. 64th St./41 Central Park W., NY, NY.* Madonna bought her longtime **NYC** apartment in the Neo-Italian Renaissance Harperley Hall in 1985, closing for $850,000 after being rejected in her bid to buy a place in the **San Remo**. Over the years, she expanded it until it was a 6,000-square-foot unit on the fifth and sixth floors that was fit for a … you know the rest.

During extensive renovations, Madonna and fam stayed at the Lowell Hotel (28 E. 63rd St., NY, NY).

Her time at Harperley was not without some bumps. One of her neighbors sued her over a noise complaint and Madonna sued her co-op board when it tried to block her from buying an extra apartment in the building—Madonna won.

Originally listed for $23.5 million, reduced to $19.995 million and sold to Deepak Narula for "considerably less," the luxurious digs changed hands in 2013. Perhaps the fact that Madonna made such a tidy profit on the home was due to its eight bathrooms, its seven bedrooms, its views of Central Park, its roof deck or its fully contained private **gym**, but it probably didn't hurt that the place could also boast, "Madonna Slept Here."

> "You have to expect a certain amount of invasion … but then you have to draw the line. I draw the line when I get to my house. Wherever I live, that should be sacred."—MADONNA (1987)

CERTAIN SACRIFICE, A: *Director: Stephen Jon Lewicki. Video release date: 1985.* Madonna's first feature film. Madonna answered an ad that ran in both *Backstage* and *Show Business* in August 1979 seeking "a dark, fiery young woman, dominant, with lots of energy, who can **dance** and is willing to **work** for no pay." She sent a three-page, handwritten letter (shades of *Evita*) and a Polaroid. Her effort nabbed her a meeting with this experimental film's director, Stephen Jon Lewicki, in **NYC**'s Washington Square Park.

Lewicki has said of meeting Madonna, "I thought my fantasies were being realized." Madonna said, "Look, I'll do your movie. But there'll be no screwing." She was *perfect* for the part of an uninhibited dominatrix in the $20,000 production, which in spite of a pretentiously arty tone contains some of the elements of a classic exploitation film, including **nudity**, a creepily lingering **rape** scene and devil worship. Madonna plays "Bruna," a raven-haired downtown

girl carrying on an intense relationship with "Dashiel" (Jeremy Pattnosh), a Midwest outcast. When she is raped by the villainous "Raymond Hall" (Charles Kurtz) in the bathroom of a diner, Bruna enlists her gang of **sex** slaves to help perform a Satanic human sacrifice on her rapist.

The film was shot in October 1979 and November 1981. Lewicki was smitten with Madonna, later raving about her sex appeal and describing her as easy to work with, "very direct-able." Madonna's acquiescence might have been because she was the only paid participant—she'd put her foot down, demanding all of $100.

A Certain Sacrifice didn't emerge from post-production until 1984, and only because Madonna's participation had become an obvious selling point. In 1985, when Lewicki was shopping rights to the film, Madonna's manager **Freddy DeMann** had a chance to suppress it. Madonna's camp had offered to buy the film out for a mere $5,000 or $10,000 and had been rejected because Lewicki already had 60,000 pre-orders. But DeMann opted to see all buzz as good buzz, so he stood aside and let the film go on sale. Madonna *did* halfheartedly sue to block the flick, but her insistence on being paid $100 for her services had resulted in a simple but iron-clad signed release; it has been theorized that her lawsuit was as much to generate press as it was to actually squelch the film.

Lewicki's lucky that Madonna didn't have her sex slaves sacrifice him—he's also lucky because his unwatchable film, sold on video for $59.95 a pop, made him (at minimum) hundreds of thousands of dollars. A true material boy.

Madonna's awful in the movie, though mesmerizing in the modern **dance** sequences. Even she knows she sucked in it, saying she wanted it suppressed because her performance was "second-rate."

Lewicki does claim that he gave Madonna a chance to see the movie first, screening it for her privately. When she left, she said, "**Fuck** you," which was about the best review it has ever received.

The film's song/chant "Certain Sacrifice (Raymond Hall Must Die Tonight)" and a short outtake of Madonna singing the 1969 song "Let the Sunshine In" with costar **Angie Smit** distinguish the film for bearing two of the earliest known recordings of Madonna singing.

A Certain Sacrifice—which was retitled *Rape* for the Japanese market—was never given an official release in theaters, but in 1986 it did play as a **camp** midnight movie.

Pattnosh now calls Madonna "a young, beautiful, brave, inventive, compelling songstress, passionate **artist** and brilliant cultural icon!"

••

"IT WAS SICK IN A CHILDISH KIND OF WAY, ABOUT THIS GIRL WHO'S LIKE A DOMINATRIX—ME, OF COURSE. THERE'S HARDLY ANY, LIKE, SEX SCENES OR ANYTHING LIKE THAT, IT'S JUST IMPLIED ALL THE TIME."-MADONNA (1983)

••

"MADONNA HAD AN INTERESTING ALOOFNESS, A KIND OF CLINT EASTWOOD COOLNESS, BUT SHE WAS ALWAYS VERY PROFESSIONAL."

-JEREMY PATTNOSH (1985)

••

"A TRUE ENDURANCE TEST, IT'S AS ACCURATE NOW AS IT WAS THEN TO SAY THAT THIS SHOULD SOLELY BE VIEWED BY THE DIEHARD MADONNA FANS, AND EVEN THEY WILL BE DISAPPOINTED."

-GRAEME CLARK, *THE SPINNING IMAGE* (2005)

••

CHARITY: In addition to her high-profile **AIDS** activism in the '80s and '90s, Madonna has lent her name, time and services to a variety of causes.

Her earliest charitable effort may have been involvement in Help-a-Kid, a Big Sisters–like program in which she participated in high **school**. Somewhere out there is a woman whose "Big Sister" turned out to be *Madonna*.

In 1985, Mr. and Mrs. **Sean Penn**—insisting on a "no publicity" policy—visited Cornell Medical Center at **New York** Hospital's pediatric wing (525 E. 68th St., NY, NY), where they played Santa and Mrs. Claus for terminally ill children. She also did "a little show" for the kids at Memorial Sloan-Kettering **Cancer** Center (1275 York Ave., NY, NY) on June 5, 1985. She brought a huge ghetto blaster and lip-synched along with the kids to **"Angel," "Into the Groove"** and **"Burning Up."** After, she passed out tambourines, lace gloves, **crucifixes** and balloons stamped: **"Dreams come true."** Madonna said she would never complain again after visiting with the struggling children.

She spoke at a Sport Aid press conference in 1988 to combat world hunger. In 1989, friends convinced her to perform at **Don't Bungle the Jungle** to raise awareness of the depletion of the rainforest.

Madonna has donated dozens of personal objects to charity **auctions**, including a chair that she once sat on (Greater Chicago Food Depository); her ***Blond Ambition World Tour*** masturbatory bed (UNICEF); a ***Who's That Girl World Tour*** bustier (Project Children ... maybe she was thinking "Tits for Tots"); a leather bomber jacket (New York's LGBT community center) and an **autographed** blouse (Tappan Zee Playhouse, formerly 20 S. Broadway, Nyack, NY).

"CHARITY CONCERT/THE ART OF THE POSSIBLE": From ***Evita: The Complete Motion Picture Music Soundtrack***, a melding of songs blending an introductory lead vocal by **Jimmy Nail** (and ensuing testy exchange between his character and Madonna's) with a brief, utilitarian piece of music sung by **Jonathan Pryce** and **Antonio Banderas**. Not exactly the kind of song you'll find yourself dancing to on a tabletop.

CHARLES, PRINCE OF WALES: *b. November 14, 1948.* The heir apparent to the throne in **England** and the man whose stormy marriage to **Diana** made royal-watching all the rage in the '80s and '90s.

Though Madonna had once counseled Diana from afar to "dump him," when she actually dined with Charles, she seemingly changed her mind. She observed him stealing lettuce off of her plate and decided, "He was quite fun."

CHARLIE HEBDO: *Dates of publication: 1970–1981; 1992–.* French satirical **magazine** known for its provocative cartoons. On January 7, 2015, two terrorists forced their way into the magazine's offices in **Paris** and killed 12, injuring 11 more. Madonna, like millions of other supporters, posted the slogan "JE SUIS CHARLIE" on her **Instagram** account. Because she hashtagged it #rebelhearts, the media jumped down her throat, accusing her of using the tragedy to promote her ***Rebel Heart*** album.

In the first issue after the murders, the magazine ran a cartoon listing plusses and minuses of the attack; Madonna (throwing her panties in support) was a plus, while German Chancellor Angela Merkel doing the same was a minus.

On the March 2, 2015, edition of ***Le Grand Journal***, Madonna was surprise-introduced to *Charlie Hebdo* massacre survivor Luz (real name Rénald

Luzier), a cartoonist who had been celebrating his **birthday** with his wife and narrowly missed being executed. The two embraced warmly for 12 seconds, to a standing ovation from the audience. Luz thanked Madonna for her support, and she replied, "Thank you so much for being a freedom fighter."

CHASE PARK: *Formerly 599 Broadway, NY, NY.* After leaving the **Breakfast Club** and **Emmy**, Madonna's first solo gig was billed as being Thursday, October 8, 1981, at this rock venue.

CHE TEMPO CHE FA: *Airdates: September 2003–.* Italian talk show hosted by Fabio Fazio for which Madonna did an in-studio taping on March 1, 2015. In a blazing-red corset, she tore through live renditions of **"Devil Pray"** (that song's first public performance) and **"Ghosttown."** The show aired March 8, 2015.

CHEERLEADER: The ultimate rebel of the '80s and premier **sexual** revolutionary of the '90s was a high **school** cheerleader in the '70s.

Madonna said of NBA cheerleaders, "I **hate** those **nude** pantyhose and those big hairdos. They're trapped in a time warp."

CHENG, ANGELA: Pseudonym of a former Examiner.com writer who presented herself as a young Asian female (complete with bizarrely **Photoshopped** picture suggesting a random image snatched off the Internet, which it turned out to be) who was "a recent Communication Media Studies graduate of the University of Oklahoma," a field in which the college does not offer degrees. Oh, and no one named Angela Cheng graduated from that university.

Cheng distinguished herself as a poor speller who stanned for **Lady Gaga** and gunned for Madonna in many click-bait "articles" for the site, which pays its writers based on Web traffic. On April 25, 2013, Cheng published her top reasons to dislike Madonna, one of which declared, "Madonna is almost a senior citizen. She should be baking cookies or knitting." Madonna was 54 at the time.

Cheng also repeated a libelous (and scientifically absurd) claim made by a small number of Gaga's "Little Monsters," the concept that Madonna "helped

An ad for Madonna's first solo gig, illustrated by a Fred Seidman head shot

encourage the spread of **AIDS** by glorifying **sexual** promiscuity. It ranks as the worst thing anyone's ever said about Madonna. The article eventually disappeared, but only after it had tens of thousands of views.

By 2013, Cheng had flipped, and began viciously attacking Gaga, claiming that **Interscope** had lost $25 million promoting her underperforming *Artpop*, a figure that was repeated in the media. She published a ridiculous piece attempting to trace how Gaga deliberately set out to destroy Madonna's legacy, including a claim that Gaga and her since-fired manager Troy Carter would quiz each other on Madonna trivia using *Encyclopedia Madonnica*.

Perez Hilton, famously on the outs with Gaga, cheekily tweeted Cheng in December 2013, "Thank you for all the amazing **work** you did this year! xoxo"

On January 1, 2014, Cheng wrote that *Billboard* editorial director Bill Werde would soon be fired. Werde had earned the ire of the anti-Gaga movement because of its perception that Gaga's 2013 song "Applause" was semi-successful on the **magazine**'s charts thanks only to his intervention. When Werde was replaced by longtime magazine-industry EIC Janice Min, Cheng declared victory ... except Werde wasn't actually fired, just reassigned. When Buzzfeed wrote a bombshell post investigating the real identity of both Cheng and sound-alike "reporter" Sabrina O'Connor, Examiner.com pulled every article under both bylines.

Cheng soldiered on, posting at her new site, PopMusic-Gadfly. ("Gadfly?" This is not a youngster making this shit up.) The site folded quickly, and Cheng's **Twitter** account has been silent since October 22, 2014.

Werde, who has moved on from *Billboard*, posted an excellent meditation on "the culpability of media," pointing out the demonstrable falsity of Cheng's ID and assertions. He was resentful of the fact that he had been contacted by Buzzfeed to comment on their post about her. His realization: "The only real lesson I can take away from this is that it's better to be the platform than the person trusting the platform ... [Truth is sometimes] stranger than fiction. You just need to be very, very careful about where you choose to read it."

CHER: *b. May 20, 1946.* This **camp** superstar started her 15 minutes of **fame** as a hippie singer alongside hubby Sonny Bono over five decades ago, then became known for her delightfully tacky and revealing Bob Mackie next-to-nothings on **TV** and in Vegas, then shocked everyone by becoming an effective film lead. Winning an **Oscar**, she delved back into **singing** (this time Top 40-seductive pop/rock), hosted a widely mocked **infomercial**, became passé, became Topic A again in the wake of her ex-husband's **death** and has continued to be a popular, if reluctant, concert draw.

Cher knew **Sean Penn** before she met Madonna, which guaranteed her an invite to their **wedding**. Characteristically, she wore a spiked purple fright wig. Madonna asked Cher for cake-cutting advice: "Hey, you've done this before. Do you just cut one piece or do you have to slice up the whole thing?"

The world's oldest living cheerleader tells all.

Described as either disliking Madonna or simply desperate to collaborate with her at the time, Cher's feelings toward Madonna have been all over the map since, but take heart—they've steadily improved.

When **MTV** sentenced her "If I Could Turn Back Time" video to late-night-only airings in 1989 because of her rear-endy outfit, Cher pulled Madonna in front of her to take the bullet, saying that at least she didn't do the "tasteless" things Madonna did in her **"Express Yourself"** video. "What about Madonna? She's naked on a bed with chains."

In 1991, Cher was asked by Steve Kmetko about Madonna on *CBS This Morning*. She said, "There's something about [Madonna] that I don't like. She's mean." In her opinion at that time, Madonna "could afford to be a little more magnanimous and a little less of a cunt."

Soon after, during an interview on the UK show *Wogan*, hosted by **Terry Wogan**, Cher was giggling about the controversy between herself and "my *best friend* Madonna." She explained, "Someone said to me, 'What do you think about her?' and I said, '... in my day, I was pretty good at doing the same thing she's doing, but she does it so much better. But, I mean, she's unbelievably creative because she's not unbelievably **talented**, she's not beautiful, but she's kind of, she's rude, and so this man said, 'How do you feel about her?' I said, 'Well, she's nice, but I mean, she's creative, but she's rude.' And then I used another word and they bleeped me."

This looks like something Cher would wear to vote in.

In Madonna's second **Rock the Vote** appearance the following year, she humorously rejected an outfit being offered to her in a dressing-room sketch: *"Please—Cher votes in stuff like that."*

When Cher was asked if she felt Madonna had gone too far with *Sex*, she was semi-complimentary: "**Art** is art and thank **God** I don't have the responsibility of deciding what's

MATTHEW RETTENMUND

"Actually, I think Madge might be one of the most amazing artists I've known."—CHER (2013)

too far and what's art. I mean, I've seen her **book** and I thought some of the pictures were interesting and really beautiful, and I thought some of the pictures were silly."

One not-so-silly picture taken in 1997 shows Cher, **k.d. lang**, Madonna and **Joni Mitchell** at a Gianni **Versace** tribute. Cher and Madonna sat a seat apart that evening, at the same table with **Jon Bon Jovi**. Perhaps they buried their stage-hatchets for good, because by the time Cher was riding high on the success of her *Believe* album in 1999, she had seemingly snapped out of it. In fact, Madonna told *Entertainment Tonight* she had wanted to direct Cher's "Dov'è l'amore" music video—which would've been her directorial debut. (In 2013, Cher confirmed to *Billboard* that she'd still like Madonna to direct one of her videos because, "Madge has got some great ideas.")

Flash forward to 2012, when Cher—one of **Twitter**'s most entertaining users—innocently asked, "Wtf is **mdna**" because she'd seen it all over social media. Some took it as a dig, but Cher—who's shared a publicist, **Liz Rosenberg**, with Madonna for years—just laughed it off. She also tickled her own funnybone by tweeting that she'd celebrated Madonna's **birthday** by getting a colonic. Even the colonic was just a joke. "I'm totally good with Madonna. Madge and I have gone through our things, but I'm totally good with her."

Someone needs to get Cher to interview Madonna and vice versa. That would be far more entertaining than even a musical collaboration.

"I think she's very creative and I think that she does a lot with the talent that she has … She's a major, major star and she's not really a great, great singer, she's not really a great, great actress, but, I mean, she's one of the biggest stars in the world, so that's a special art to be able to turn whatever you have into—it's like spinning straw into gold …"—CHER ON MADONNA (1991)

"CHERISH" (SONG): *Release date: August 1, 1989. Billboard Hot 100 peak: #2.* Not a remake of the Association's 1966 song of the same name, and not related to an **unreleased** Madonna song from 1981, "Cherish." "Cherish" was written and produced by Madonna and **Patrick Leonard**, Madonna's third single from *Like a Prayer*, and a welcome respite from all things controversial. The sugary **love** song was just one of the singles that helped Madonna emerge as the #1 adult contemporary singles artist of 1989, even as critics at the time considered her audience (and Madonna) to be strictly juvenile.

Amidst the sweetness and light, "Cherish" manages a well-disguised lyrical zinger—Madonna cheerily forbids listeners to underestimate her point of view.

"The songs that I think are the most retarded songs I've written, like 'Cherish' and 'Sorry'… end up being the biggest hits. 'Into the Groove' is another song I feel retarded singing, but everybody seems to like it."—MADONNA (2009)

"CHERISH" (VIDEO): *Director: Herb Ritts, 1989.* Madonna's favorite photographer **Herb Ritts** directed this **black-and-white** clip, but he didn't think he was up to the challenge at first.

"She kept asking me, and I said I really didn't know the first thing about moving imagery," Ritts said in a 1999 François Quintin interview. "Finally, I practiced with a little Super 8 camera when I was on a **job** in Hawaii, and came back and said I could do it. Two weeks later, I was filming 'Cherish'. I directed it and did the camera **work** as well. It was invigorating."

In the final video, Madonna—who is clearly more voluptuous for her role in *Dick Tracy*—splashes in low tide in a black button-up dress. She flexes her **muscles**, poses playfully and cavorts with a little merchild, who seems to have lost his way from a **school** of nearby mermen (note future lover **Tony Ward** in the school).

Ritts wisely avoided the pitfall of trying to one-up "Cherish"'s immediate predecessors, the crowded, busy, impactful **"Like a Prayer"** and **"Express Yourself."**

"Cherish" plays as an idyllic Ritts photograph come to life, smoldering as it shows us Madonna reclining in the surf. Ritts's greatest achievement here was perfectly capturing Madonna's free spirit.

CHICAGO: *Director: Rob Marshall. Release date: December 27, 2002.* Even if you **loved** the final film, which won the **Oscar** for Best Picture, wouldn't it have been more fun to watch with Goldie Hawn and Madonna than with Renée Zellweger and Catherine Zeta-Jones?

Almost immediately after the classic 1975 John Kander/Fred Ebb/Bob Fosse musical was revived successfully on Broadway in 1996, talk about a movie version was reignited. Madonna, a hit in *Evita*, seemed a natural to play the all-singing, all-dancing murderess "Velma Kelly" (a part originated by Chita Rivera and revived by Bebe Neuwirth) and Hawn was considered a front-runner to play daffy "Roxie Hart" (a part originated by Gwen Verdon and revived by Ann Reinking), a chorus girl who's also got blood on her hands.

As of January 15, 1997, **Harvey Weinstein** of Miramax had veteran theater producer Marty Richards on board as producer, Herbert Ross of *Footloose* (1984) **fame** as director, Larry Gelbart from the **TV** show *M*A*S*H* (1972–1983) to adapt it, Madonna and Hawn to star, plus **Rosie O'Donnell** as prison matron "Mama Morton" and John Travolta as slick lawyer "Billy Flynn." At that time, Richards said, "It's obviously our **dream** cast and we have our fingers crossed."

Madonna confidently told her **fan** club members that she was "definitely filming *Chicago* with Goldie Hawn … sometime in the new year. That should be a lot of fun."

In June 1998, Madonna's brother **Christopher Cic-cone** was reportedly "weekending" with Richards in East Hampton. Couldn't hoit.

By late 1998, Madonna and Goldie—who'd been photographed dining together to discuss the all-but-done deal and who were seated together at the December 9, 1998, Fire & Ice Ball—were still in place, but Nicholas Hytner of *The Crucible* (1996) was now directing with a rewrite of Gelbart's script by playwright Wendy Wasserstein; Hytner and Wasserstein had just done *The Object of My Affection* together (1998). It was reported that *Chicago* would film in February 1999, but that was also the start date for Madonna's bomb-in-the-making with **Rupert Everett**, *The Next Best Thing*.

Next, ominously, Madonna used the same fan-club forum to mention the fact that *Chicago* was "kind of on hold," saying, "*Evita* took ten years to get made." She was quoted by **Liz Smith** as saying of the film's long, long delay, "Who knows? They never tell me anything. I'm just a chorus girl."

The problem was that Hytner felt Hawn, 53, was too old; she was fired. Then, Miramax felt uneasy about the script and the entire direction of the project. One day, Rob Marshall, a successful choreographer, took a meeting with the company and spoke of how *he* would do *Chicago* as a film. By now, Madonna had moved on to other things (a *Ray of Light* tour one casualty of her waiting around) and Marshall recast and reconceived the entire picture.

After rejecting minor participation by **Britney Spears** and **Janet Jackson**, Marshall created a film that won six Oscars, the first musical to win Best Picture in over 30 years. Zeta-Jones won an Oscar for the part Madonna would have played.

CHINA: China's Ministry of Culture asked Madonna to perform *The Girlie Show World Tour* at the 12,000-seat Beijing Workers **Gymnasium** (Workers' Stadium West Road, Beijing, China) on the condition that she stick to cheesecake without **nudity** or vulgarity.

The Girlie Show World Tour never made it to China (she played Taiwan, Hong Kong and Macau in 2016), though she was ranked the #4 most popular act of 1993 there, behind the Red Hot Chili Peppers, Nirvana and **Michael Jackson**. Madonna said in 2015 her favorite thing about China was "the food."

CHIRAC, JACQUES: *b. November 29, 1932.* Conservative French prime minister and future president of France whose then 24-year-old daughter Claude convinced him in 1987 to overrule the mayor of Sceaux's decision to disallow the *Who's That Girl World Tour* to be performed in that town's Parc de Sceaux (Communes de Sceaux et Antony, Sceaux, France), a scenic 17th-century park.

After listening to her music and watching her videos, Chirac embraced Madonna as a "genius" and received her like a fin de siecle Venus passing through at a public forum. Worth noting: Claude became her dad's personal advisor in 1994.

Madonna presented Chirac with an $83,000 check for **AIDS** research and played before 130,000 **fans**—the largest concert in French history.

It was an election year.

CHO, MARGARET: *b. December 5, 1968.* Comic actor and Kim Jong-il impersonator who once reported to *Detour* **magazine** that after a meeting at **Maverick** in LA, she was allowed to roam around Madonna's office. She said it was small, that it reminded her of the **"Express Yourself"** video**,** and that it had a really "tacky'" magnetic paper-clip holder. "I twirled around and picked up the phone. It was weird, because I had been very businesslike through the whole meeting, and then when I got in the office, I all but peed on the carpet because I was so excited."

In 2003, Cho ranted on her website about a charge leveled against her and other female stars, including Madonna: "I heard about an article that was written in some newspaper that said that Madonna, **Megan Mullally** and me, being **gay** icons, are hypocrites because we be married and that we have no credibility when we talk about how it is wrong that gay marriage isn't acknowledged in the government ... I am not Madonna, nor am I Megan Mullally. They are famous and out of my league ... Madonna is in a different universe, untouchable and otherworldly. Madonna is like **God**, but she does **yoga** ... Lumping me in with Madonna and Megan just makes me look like a shithead, which I am, but I don't like it when you say it ... Why do I **work** intensely for the queer community, demonstrate, protest, endure being called a hypocrite, not give a shit and keep going like the Energizer Bunny? Because **love** is love. Love is love. Love is love. Love is love. Motherfucker."

CIAO ITALIA: LIVE FROM ITALY: *Release date: May 24, 1988.* Also referred to as *Madonna: Ciao Italia: Live from Italy.* A loving video record of Madonna's ***Who's That Girl World Tour*** that was chiefly shot in two Italian cities (mainly Turin but also Florence), and that contains some elements from her Tokyo stop on that same tour. Fantastic video that finds Madonna's skills as a stadium-worthy showwoman expanding exponentially. Contains every performance from the tour.

SEE: ***Who's That Girl: Live in Japan***.

CICCONE: Madonna's surname. Madonna briefly used "Cicconi" in her early days in **New York**, such as in the credits of the experimental film ***In Artificial Light***.

CICCONE, ANTHONY: *b. May 3, 1956.* The eldest **Ciccone** child, who used to be known as "T.G.," Ciccone is Madonna's older brother. He has made unfortunate news for being a homeless alcoholic. Living under a bridge while

—KENNY SCHARF

ANDRÉ GROSSMANN

Madonna's brother
Christopher in 1983

CICCONE, CHRISTOPHER: *b. November 22, 1960.* Madonna's **gay** brother, the one to whom she was closest from childhood through her forties. He was **nicknamed** "Mr. Cynic" in his family.

Ciccone, a **talented** and expressive painter (his Primitivist portrait of his sister adorns her **"Like a Prayer"** 12" sleeve), has **worked** with Madonna numerous times. He was one of her backup **dancers** on track dates and appeared in her **"Lucky Star"** video, graduating to designing the stage for her *Blond Ambition World Tour* and directing one of her most entertaining tours, *The Girlie Show World Tour.*

Before their **father** had come to terms with Ciccone's **sexuality**, Madonna casually referred to him as gay in her 1991 interview with *The Advocate*; Ciccone complained that she had outed him. Hard feelings over that aside, he shopped for and decorated her homes and for years socialized with her at public events. There is no underestimating his influence on his sister at the time.

In 2008, Ciccone released a shocking memoir entitled *Life With My Sister Madonna*, which could be described as 342 pages of unbridled passive aggression that begins by identifying itself as a "catharsis," a classic Madonna word from *Blond Ambition* onward. Madonna must've bent that page in the Ciccone Family thesaurus.

In the **book**, instead of purging all his pent-up emotions, Ciccone seems to teeter from dispassionate assessments of his sister's good qualities (her work ethic, her post-1995 **voice**, her instincts on stage, her **memory**, her charm) to seething examples of her bad qualities (a lack of empathy and humor, an obsession with **money**, an unbreakable no-**smoking** rule in her house, a desire for people to put their dirty dishes in the dishwasher).

In childhood passages, Madonna is painted as her father's pet thanks to being the spitting image of their **mother** and sharing her name. Taking advantage of her special status, Madonna is petulant, demanding and self-absorbed—the oft-repeated story of a provocative talent-show performance covered in Day-Glo paint here has the effect of revealing how oblivious she can be to embarrassing her dad.

One of the most disappointing aspects of Ciccone's book is that even though he is the LGBT guy in the family, he seems so clutch-the-pearls over Madonna's free-wheeling ways. When Madonna weathers her **nude**-photo scandal in 1985, Ciccone is overly worried about his father and **grandmother**'s reactions. He's icked out by seeing her naked, embarrassed by her **"Like A Virgin"** number in *Blond Ambition* ... Madonna may be provocative to a fault, but Ciccone comes off as distressingly milquetoast.

Ciccone dispels the myth of his sister's "$35 in my pocket in Times Square" story at least four times in the book, but does have to admit she was brave to head to NYC. After having been turned on to dance by Madonna, who had invited him to her classes with mentor

his sister approaches billionaire status made for great headlines, as did Ciccone's rancor for his sister and **father**: "Madonna doesn't give a shit if I'm dead or alive. She lives in her own world. I never **loved** her in the first place, she never loved me."

"I got the best grades, straight As ... and all my brothers and sisters **hated** me!" Madonna told *Teen* in 1984, without realizing some actually did.

Ciccone has been arrested several times for offenses like driving drunk and swearing in front of children (it's a thing in **Michigan**), spending a month in jail as recently as 2013.

Their brother **Martin Ciccone**, in recovery himself, defended Madonna against Anthony's negative comments, saying, "She wants to help him, but he doesn't help himself." His own parents turned Ciccone away after a short-lived **job** helping at their vineyard which, all things considered, would seem to have been not a good fit.

In April 2013, Ciccone was arrested and physically restrained when he refused to leave a bathroom at the Traverse City Civic Center (1213 W. Civic Center Dr., Traverse City, MI). He required nine stitches after this run-in.

Christopher Flynn, Ciccone wound up working as a dancer. This is when Madonna called him out of the blue, inviting him to live with her in Manhattan and then callously informed her jobless brother he couldn't stay with her when he arrived.

The book gives a detailed account of the torturous filming of *Shanghai Surprise* in Hong Kong and has an interestingly iconoclastic take on *Truth Or Dare*, which he calls mostly staged and whose emotional centerpiece—Madonna visiting their mother's grave—seems to have been the moment when he began to seriously resent his sister.

Madonna's husband **Guy Ritchie** is depicted as a **wannabe**-thug. Thanks to some homo-unfriendly toasts at his **wedding** to Madonna and to a firm directive not to make the home Ciccone was designing too "twee," Ritchie is branded a homophobe (he sure doesn't sound like a friend of the friends of Dorothy) and blamed for the rift between brother and sister.

The straw that broke the brother's back seems to have been money—Madonna has a lot of it and is apparently ridiculously tight with it. He says she was only giving her grandmother $500 plus living expenses a month, never helped out her father and dramatically underpaid her brother. As her decorator, Ciccone made way less than he felt he was worth, and then was often denied part of his fee. Their relationship seemed to terminate after she stuck him with $65,000 in **art** he bought for her but that she decided against.

In one of the book's final recounted fights, Ciccone berates his sister for her "mediocre **talent**," only to end the book by saying, "She hasn't forgotten how little faith many people once had in her, and I'm proud never to have been one of them ... I don't hold any grudges against her, nor do I bear her any ill will."

Ciccone closed this book on Madonna with a promise to her kids: "I want them to know that, as their uncle, I will always be there for them—because that, when all is said and done, is the nature of family." After the preceding book, this could be read as a threat!

For good measure, while promoting the book, Ciccone said it seemed "obvious" that Madonna had had a **face-lift**, saying, "They probably shouldn't have pulled it so tight." Even Chelsea Handler seemed fazed by his willingness to go there.

Bizarre rumors that Madonna ghostwrote the book to generate publicity were swatted down by **Liz Rosenberg**: "If she had anything to do with that book, it would have been better written."

Since the book's release, Ciccone has commented publicly on his sister many times. While promoting his own lifestyle brand in 2012, he said of Madonna's kids, "Frankly, nobody sees them. My parents barely see them." But in the same interview, he asserted he and his sister were "on a perfectly personable level right now. As far as I'm concerned, we're good. We are in contact with each other, although I haven't seen her for a long time. We're back to being brother and sister."

He also summed her up as "a force to be reckoned with. Does she have **Barbra Streisand**'s voice? No. Can she dance like **Martha Graham**? Probably not. But the combination of her abilities has made her great, and left a huge legacy for her, and through her, for me. So yeah, **God** bless her."

In 2015, Madonna told **Jonathan Ross** that she has forgiven her brother for writing the book and that they're in a good place again. "... I would say we're, we're speaking again, we're friends again. It took a while. It really hurt me ... that really hurt me. Um, and it took a while. There was many years of silence, but I do believe in forgiveness. So, and I think that he feels bad that he did it."

P.S. Apparently, all of Madonna's brothers have the same middle name: Gerard.

CICCONE, JENNIFER: *b. May 22, 1968.* Madonna's half sister, known as "Bunny" when she was younger, according to a 1986 *Life* piece on Madonna. Jennifer has kept the lowest profile of all Madonna's siblings, but did appear at the Detroit *MDNA Tour* show, watching with her half sister **Paula Ciccone** and her mom, Madonna's **stepmother**.

CICCONE, JOAN CLARE GUSTAFSON: *b. July 1, 1943.* Stern **blonde** lady who started as a housekeeper for the Ciccone family following the **death** of Madonna's **mother**, and who eventually became the second Mrs. **Ciccone** in 1966– and a second mother to **Silvio Ciccone**'s kids. In 2003, Madonna claimed Joan and Silvio had a baby who died. In her 2015 **Howard Stern** interview, Madonna let slip a piece of the puzzle never previously known: Gustafson had left the Ciccone employ to have another man's baby, then she came back to marry Silvio, surprising the children. No mention was made of what became of this child, who due to the timeline does not appear to be any of the kids thought of as Madonna's blood or half siblings. Intrigue!

Growing up, Madonna resented her stepmom, rebelling against her strict rules, the uniformlike outfits she sewed for the Ciccone kids and what Madonna perceived as her attempt to take the place of her late mom.

In 1985, Madonna admitted to seeing herself as a "Cinderella" figure because of the existence of her **stepmother**. She claimed that her stepmother once bloodied her nose, but she was happy for it since it enabled her to skip mass. Madonna also said that her stepmother wouldn't allow her to use tampons when she began **menstruation**, warning that Madonna shouldn't wear such things until she was married. Mrs. Ciccone has denied all the outrage-inducing stories.

Seen in *Truth or Dare* and in some brief on-camera interviews about life as a famous stepmom, Ciccone always seems calm but resolved, making it easy to envision she and Madonna battling like spiders in a terrarium. Footage showing Ciccone disapprovingly watching Madonna writhe onstage during her *MDNA Tour* is priceless.

"My sister is her own masterpiece. Is there any other way to do it right?"—CHRISTOPHER CICCONE (1991)

Some people who knew Madonna as a kid and teen side with her, some with her stepmother. Madonna's cheerleading coach recalled Ciccone as a wicked stepmother figure, but Madonna's pal from elementary **school**, Ruth Dupack Young, has said, "For all the grief she put up with, Mrs. Ciccone was a real **cheerleader** for Madonna. She was desperate to be a **dancer** and if she didn't win a competition she was very disappointed. Mrs. Ciccone was always there to lift her spirits."

"She was a smart girl, always motivated. Brilliant. Manipulative, I guess so. Yes. But you knew she would survive. You knew she would never be weak. And you were glad about that."—JOAN CICCONE TO J. RANDY TARABORRELLI (2001)

CICCONE, MADONNA FORTIN: *July 11, 1933–December 1, 1963.* Madonna's mother, who died of breast **cancer** when Madonna was only five years old. Madonna Fortin's parents were Willard and **Elsie Fortin**. Her brother Dale was good friends with **Silvio "Tony" Ciccone**, the man whom "Big Madonna" would marry.

Madonna, called "Little Nonni," remembers her mother as beautiful and kind, even putting up with her children's naïve lack of respect for the gravity of her illness in the final year of her life.

"I have a **memory** of my mother in the kitchen scrubbing the floor," she told *Time* in 1985. "She did all the housecleaning, and she was always picking up after us. We were really messy, awful kids. I remember having these mixed feelings. I have a lot of feelings of **love** and warmth for her but sometimes I think I tortured her. I think little kids do that to people who are really good to them." Her mother was a homemaker and also a hardworking radiation technologist; Madonna has wondered whether her **job** led to the cancer that killed her.

Madonna's **school** guidance counselor, **Nancy Ryan Mitchell**, said on VH1's *Driven: Madonna* that at the time of Madonna's mom's **death**, her school records bore a touching note from the women running her **Catholic** kindergarten class: "The **nuns** wrote, 'Madonna needs a lot of extra love at this time.'"

Madonna and her sisters thought their mom looked like **Anne Sexton**, so became obsessed with her poetry. Their image of their mother took on a mythical character.

Sometime in 1988, Madonna's father sent to his adult kids copies of letters Madonna Sr. had written, revealing her to have been fervently religious. These letters may have in part inspired Madonna's relentless exploration of Catholicism and religion in her **work**.

Madonna's lovely mom in a school photo

Madonna has said of her namesake, "It's extremely rare that a religious Italian woman would name a child after her. My mother wanted to be a singer. So it was like I have a mission to live up to this name." Or at least to *try,* and the song **"Promise to Try"** on *Like a Prayer* is Madonna's most maternal statement, focusing on a girl's pledge to her mother to forgive her for dying, and to never forget her. That album is "dedicated to my mother, who taught me how to pray."

Madonna told *60 Minutes II* that losing her mother was "like having your heart ripped out of your chest. Like a limb missing. The ultimate abandonment. And it was such a great mystery to me where she went." And life *is* a mystery.

Asked by *Ladies' Home Journal* in 2005 if she felt any connection to her mom spiritually, Madonna paused before saying, "I don't know. My mother was a religious zealot, a Catholic—there were always nuns and priests in my house growing up. I don't know how curious my mother was, how much she pushed to know what was going on behind the curtain, and that's my personality ..."

Madonna has identified a photo of her mom on a **horse** as her most treasured possession; she admits she stole it from her dad when she moved to **New York**.

"I went through a lot of pain when I was a very young girl and the only way to get through it was to tell myself that this was an education: this was a test for me. If I could get through this, then I would be rewarded in the end. When I'm older, I would get the things I wanted."—MADONNA, *MOVIE SCENE* (1985)

CICCONE, MARIO: *b. 1969.* Madonna's youngest sibling is her half brother Mario. Madonna helped him out in his youth (he had a coke habit and was arrested), and he followed her on tour to see what her **job** was really like. A songwriter, he picked up a **guitar** and thought he would follow her into the music industry on the creative side. Instead, "Mar" went to **work** for Madonna as the national director of merchandising for her **Maverick Records**. He said in a 2003 interview, "My parents have always placed a high value on working and working hard ... It is that mindset that I bring to work each day."

He now works at the family vineyard.

CICCONE, MARTIN: *b. August 9, 1957.* Madonna's big lug of a brother who has had bouts with alcoholism and **drug** abuse, and to whom Madonna refers lovingly as a "con artist" who "cracks me up." He cracked up the entire planet in *Truth or Dare* with his charming hustler antics, showing up hours late to see his sister after a performance. With drinking buddies in tow, he arrived at her hotel only to be unceremoniously turned away. Martin has struggled to make it as a white rapper ("MC Ciccone" released a pretty challenging-to-listen-to rap CD in 1994 called *Judgment*

Day with juvenile cover **art** depicting prison **rape**), and as a Detroit DJ, and made his national singing debut on *The Jane Whitney Show* (1992–1994) in 1993.

In 1994, Ciccone was bitter toward Madonna: "This is not the sister I grew up with, who **mothered** me, who was so full of compassion. I guess **fame** really changes people."

By 1999, he was trying to clean up his act, so Madonna helped him get into rehab, causing him to miss her 2000 **wedding** to **Guy Ritchie**. In 2003, he was in recovery at Royal Palms Recovery Home (360 S. Westlake Ave., LA, CA) to the tune of $450/month (free to the unemployed). Asked about his famous (and **rich**) sis, he said, "Even though I am doing the recovery here on my own, my sister Madonna is very supportive of me. But she's got her own life and is very busy."

By 2013, Madonna was buying "Mard" a new set of teeth as a reward for a year of sobriety. He **works** at a rehab center and seems to be happy, at peace and proud of his work. He has also sought work as a **voice** artist.

Martin's rare rap record

"My two older brothers were jazz musicians, and that sort of had a reverse influence on me, because they would tell me pop music was a pile of shit, they'd scratch my records so that I couldn't play them. It only made me love pop more."–MADONNA (1983)

CICCONE (HENRY), MELANIE: *b. July 1, 1962.* The sibling to whom Madonna is closest is her younger sister, Mel a.k.a. "Smells." Melanie Maria Ciccone, a former music-industry publicist who also once **worked** at **Warner Bros.** in the **art** department, married the musician **Joe Henry**.

She was with Madonna in the delivery room when **Lola** was born, and was described by her sister as "a very good **mother**" to *Redbook* in 1997. "She's very calm, she's very patient—a good person for me to learn from," Madonna said.

Their mother was **pregnant** with Melanie when she was diagnosed with the **cancer** that would kill her less than 18 months after giving birth.

CICCONE, PAULA: *b. 1959.* Madonna's younger sister, Paula Mae, made a go of it as a high-**fashion** model in the late '80s. Her career with the Richard Ferrari Agency never really took off, but she struck an impressive pose on the cover of **England's** *The Face* **magazine** in 1987.

A go-go **dancer**, then a singer with the Downtown Dukes and Divas, her performance at the Limelight (formerly 656 Ave. of the Americas, NY, NY) made the front page of the ***New York*** *Post*.

Unflattering stories used to circulate regarding "P's" jealousy of "M's" **fame**, including a report of her behavior during Madonna's **wedding** to **Sean Penn**.

There were some hard feelings when Madonna refused to pay her sister's way to her 2000 wedding to **Guy Ritchie**, but Paula has said, "[W]hen Madonna became famous, I wasn't shocked, I wasn't surprised. I always thought of her in those terms, as being really popular. She just got a bigger apartment and came home less, that's all."

They're said to be on great terms now. Paula, who **works** at their father's vineyard and has in the past worked for Madonna at her production company (O Pictures), attended Madonna's ***MDNA Tour*** in Detroit.

CICCONE, SILVIO "TONY": *b. June 6, 1931.* Madonna's first-generation Italian dad never wanted to be that way, but he was the **original** papa who preached to her. He's the legendarily strict disciplinarian whose outrage Madonna has spent her life provoking, even while courting his respect.

Ciccone's **father** and **mother**, Gaetano Ciccone and Michelina née di Ulio arrived in the US on the *Presidente Wilson* from Italy. The family settled near Pittsburgh, Pennsylvania, and raised six boys, of which Silvio was the youngest. Ciccone's parents didn't speak English, and he became the only one of their children to attend college. He was also in the Air Force.

Armed with an engineering degree, Ciccone moved to **Michigan**, where he **worked** for Chrysler/General Dynamics on defense projects (including tank design) and optics. His best friend happened to have a younger sister who was beautiful and a devout **Catholic** with the unusual name of Madonna Fortin—Ciccone married her and raised a little family in **Pontiac**, including her namesake. Little Madonna was deeply affected by Big Madonna's **death** from breast **cancer**, bonding all the more tightly with her father. She told him, "If you ever die, I'm going to get buried in the casket with you."

Much to Madonna's dismay, Ciccone became engaged to a lady she recalls as a "Natalie Wood look-alike." And to Madonna's eternal discomfort, he later ended up marrying the family's housekeeper, **Joan (Gustafson) Ciccone.**

Mr. Ciccone is a quiet guy who in spite of his disapproval of some (okay, *most*) of Madonna's work, has good-naturedly shown up onstage with her at the climaxes of many of her Detroit tour stops, including for his **birthday** during the ***Blond Ambition World Tour***. Madonna has said she tones down her show when he's in the audience, but she doesn't cower from him anymore. (In ***Truth or Dare***, she sounds like a Ticketmaster agent while discussing how many free tickets he'll need for her show.) He also surprised his daughter as a fellow guest on ***The Arsenio Hall Show***, which drove Madonna crazy.

"All my brothers and sisters were artistic, too, but I was the most manipulative and scheming."–MADONNA (1983)

Ciccone, a George W. Bush voter who nonetheless became friendly with **Michael Moore** after being introduced to him by Madonna, may not always see **eye** to eye with his her, but as Madonna told *Time* in 1985, "My father was very strong. I don't agree with some of his values, but he did have integrity … He believed that making **love** to someone is a very sacred thing and it shouldn't happen until after you are married. He stuck by those beliefs, and that represented a very strong person to me. He was my **role model**."

In the late '90s, Ciccone said, "Madonna has said her piece over the years, but I have never spoken, because, in truth, what is the point? I was not an easy father. But I did the best I could and I believe I was a good father. I always raised my children to believe women are equal to men and can do anything they set out to do."

Ciccone, a member of the Christian Family Movement, never makes a fuss about Madonna's **fame**. He has only ever expressed satisfaction with a handful of her performances. Madonna told *Rolling Stone* in 2005 that he was especially proud of *I'm Going to Tell You a Secret* and that he'd liked *Dick Tracy*, *Evita*, her *Re-Invention World Tour* "and a couple of my ballads." Madonna said she was "in shock" when he left a message on her machine to say her 1991 **Oscars** performance was "great."

The meanest thing a **fan** has ever done to Madonna? Someone called her entourage in Japan in 1985 during her promo tour and pretended to break the news of her father's sudden death … just to hear Madonna's **voice**. It destroyed her.

Now retired and a survivor of prostate cancer, Ciccone has run Ciccone Vineyard & Winery (10343 E. Hilltop Rd., Suttons Bay, MI) since October 1995, with the help of his wife and some of his adult kids. Madonna is said to be a fan of the vineyard's output, and signed off on a series of 2005 vintage wines branded to her *Confessions Tour*.

"I wouldn't have turned out the way I [am] if I didn't have all those old-fashioned values to rebel against."-MADONNA (1987)

CICCONE YOUTH: From 1986 to 1988, this out-there side project of alt-rockers Sonic Youth released experimental rock themed to Madonna … it was very *My Strange Obsession: Downtown Edition*.

Made up of Kim Gordon, Thurston Moore, Lee Ranaldo, Steve Shelley and Mike Wyatt, **Ciccone** Youth—the moniker is a tribute to Madonna's legal surname—the group first released a 12" single with the tracks "Into the Groove(y)" (a take on **"Into the Groove"**), "Tuff Titty Rap" and "Burnin' Up" (their version of **"Burning Up"**). The cover was a blue-and-white silkscreened image of the famous headline "MADONNA ON **NUDE** PIX: SO WHAT!" The sound could best be described as anti-pop.

Their 1988 *The Whitey Album* was a full LP, including 13 non-Madonna tracks characterized by sampling, **guitar** riffs and non-traditional forms, along with the three from the single. This time, the cover was an enlargement of a **Herb Ritts** portrait of Madonna (focusing on her **beauty mark**). The band had no right to use the image, but Madonna had said she was cool with it.

Wyatt, alongside **Iggy Pop**, helped play Madonna into the **Rock and Roll Hall of Fame** in 2008.

"CINEMA IN BUENOS AIRES, 26 JULY 1952, A": A short piece of dialogue (with no participation by Madonna) set to music, it takes place in a movie theater. The track, which is found on *Evita: The Complete Motion Picture Music Soundtrack*, ends with the following announcement by the theater manager to a restless audience that (spoiler alert!) Evita has died: "It is my sad duty to inform you that Eva Perón, spiritual leader of the nation, entered immortality at 8:25 this evening."

CLARK, DICK: *November 30, 1929–April 18, 2012.* SEE: *American Bandstand*.

CLARK, GEN. WESLEY: *b. December 23, 1944.* Decorated retired general of the US Army who in 2004 ran for president as a Democrat.

In an unexpected move, Madonna endorsed Clark, saying in a statement on Madonna.com, "I've looked at all the Democratic candidates. I respect them all for their dedication and patriotism. But I'm supporting Wes Clark because in him I see the qualifications, character and vision we so desperately need. I've never done this before. I've never aligned myself with a presidential candidate during the primary season. But this time, the stakes are too high, we have too much to lose, and there is so much **work** to be done." Madonna warned, "Our greatest risk is not terrorism and it's not Iraq or the 'Axis of Evil.' Our greatest risk is a lack of leadership, a lack of honesty and a complete lack of consciousness." (In other words, taking the lyrics of **"Bedtime Story"** literally is not advisable.)

Madonna was introduced to Gen. Clark by **Michael Moore**, and she became another of his many celebrity endorsers, including Aaron Sorkin and **Barbra Streisand**.

CLEO FROM 5 TO 7: On December 9, 1986, Madonna signed an agreement to star in *Cleo from 5 to 7*, a remake of the French film *Cléo de 5 à 7* (1962), to be produced in conjunction with Paul Heller—who'd produced *First Monday in October* (1981) and would go on to produce *Withnail & I* (1987)—for Universal Pictures. The agreement was renewed a year later, on December 7, 1987, but the film became a **lost project**.

Speaking to *EM20* in 2014, Heller recalls that his friendship with the **original** film's writer/director, French legend Agnès Varda, began at the **Venice Film Festival**, where *Cléo de 5 à 7* was playing on the same bill on the same day as a film he produced, *David and Lisa* (1962).

In the '80s, he conceived of a modern-day remake of the story of a not-quite-famous rocker who's waiting to find out whether she has **cancer**, a call that will come sometime between the hours of 5 and 7. He thought Madonna would be perfect for the part.

"It would have been a fabulous role for her," Heller asserts. "It would not have taxed her **talent** beyond her capabilities." He recalls Madonna as being "contained" during their superficial face-to-face meetings on the project.

"She was beginning her career and she was looking to do movies, but she was a pop singer, and she didn't know much about it. I gave her credit for more insight into seeing that that was a brilliant role for her. But I just think that it got caught up in a whole whirlwind of possible projects. It happens at studios all the time—they give someone a development deal with a lot of **money**."

Heller, a former **Warner Bros.** executive, concedes that he put himself in a vulnerable position and soon found himself pushed out by events beyond his **control**. "I mean, she was surrounded by idiots, y'know, little sycophants who didn't have any idea how to make a movie ... I wouldn't have minded if there was somebody brilliant pushing me out, but there were a bunch of young kids who thought they knew everything about movies ..." Varda was *not* impressed with Heller's chosen star.

"Agnès came over to meet with her and there was a disaster and Agnès said, 'No, I'm not gonna let you do it. I want my rights back.' And she got 'em back. She got mad at me for putting her in that spot. Not *mad*, but it was professional disappointment and I felt shitty."

Regardless of what caused the project to falter, consider Madonna as the star of a dramatic remake of a French New Wave classic in 1987 instead of Madonna as the star of *Who's That Girl*; the course of pop history would have been radically altered.

CLINTON, BILL: *b. August 19, 1946*. Democratic president of the United States (January 1993–January 2001) and the first candidate for whom Madonna ever voted, in 1992. She defended Clinton immediately prior to his election, telling the French **TV** show *7 sur 7* that she was "glad" he had evaded the draft during the Vietnam Era, and adding of the controversy over his inhalation of weed, "So he experimented with marijuana ... who cares?"

Clinton sat for an interview in Madonna's *I Am Because We Are*.

CLINTON, HILLARY: *b. October 26, 1947*. Former US First Lady (January 1993–January 2001), Senator from **New York** (January 2001–January 2009), Secretary of State (January 2009–February 2013) and 2016 Democratic presidential candidate. Madonna has seemed ready for Hillary for some time, stating in 2005, "In Europe and Asia, women have ruled over millions. But in America, men are still afraid of women. And women, I don't think,

Madonna has been my closest friend for over 30 years. I mean, we have never met in person, nor is she aware of my existence but I have always felt our relationship goes beyond that of a pop star and her fan. Yes, as many other gay men, I've been a longtime admirer of her chutzpah, and have used her words as mantras of self-empowerment. But since long before I decided to pursue an artistic career, I have also admired her ability to push people's buttons and to take creative chances. I have followed her career over the years, not only to enjoy her creations, but to pay attention to her way of taking charge of her body of work. With her example, she has made me realize it's possible to entertain people while breaking down artistic barriers and spreading a message of love and kindness. She's gotten me through personal heartbreak, and also pushed me to become a better artist. I look forward to many more years of friendship.

MEGA-FAN SPOTLIGHT: EDUARDO CISNEROS

trust women. I find that amazing. Hillary should go for it. You've got to start somewhere in terms of women leading the US."

On International Women's Day (March 8) in 2015, Madonna—like many others—dutifully reposted a meme with this quote:

"You may not agree with a woman, but to criticize her appearance - as opposed to her idea or actions - isn't doing anyone any favors, least of all you. Insulting a woman's looks when they have nothing to do with the issue at hand implies a lack of comprehension on your part, an inability to engage with high level thinking. You may think she's ugly, but everyone thinks you're an idiot.—Hilary Clinton"

Aside from misspelling Clinton's first name, the meme is a misattribution; the quote was written *about* Clinton by Erin Gloria Ryan. Ryan, in letting Madonna know her mistake, and in objecting to the fact that Madonna hashtagged her **Rebel Heart** album in posting the meme, wrote in an unnecessarily venomous piece for the **feminist** site Jezebel:

"Maybe it's because Madonna has built her entire career on passing off other people's innovations as her own and making sure the **original** authors of things don't get as much credit for their **work** as she does. Maybe it's because Madonna's social media campaign to promote her new album has been among one of the most irritating in modern internet history. I don't have the platform to correct her myself and hope to be noticed, so, Madonna, consider this my correction: I am not 'Hilary Clinton.' And please stop using something I wrote to promote your goddamn album."

A quote that applies to Ms. Ryan: "Get the **fuck** over yourself."—Santa Claus.

CLOONEY, GEORGE: *b. May 6, 1961.* Handsome devil and **Oscar** winner who seems to pretty much run Hollywood. In 1996, Clooney launched a boycott against *Entertainment Tonight* as a protest against its sister show, *Hard Copy* (1989–1999), which had bought and aired invasive footage of himself with his French girlfriend Céline Balitran. Madonna, who had been outraged to discover stalkerazzi images taken of her with her new baby, **Lola**, joined Clooney's boycott. It was resolved, and *Hard Copy* went off the air within three years.

Prior to this, Clooney had presented Madonna with the **MTV Video Music Award** in 1995 for Best Female Video ("**Take a Bow**"). Oddly, Clooney seemed to go in for a kiss then pulled away. "I guess this is the closest I'll get to George Clooney," Madonna joked.

In 2008, Clooney remarked on Madonna, "She's probably everybody's, uh, high-water mark when it comes to learning how to reinvent yourself every few years and continue to stay alive ... And she's nice, I like her, she's a friend, and she seems to handle things, you know, really well all the way through. People can be tough on you on and off at times, and she seems to be very good at handling it."

CLOSE, GLENN: *b. March 19, 1947.* Though this acclaimed movie, **TV** and stage actor did attend the premiere of *Evita* in LA (at which she said, "Madonna has an incredible gift for reinventing herself."), it would appear that several quotes attributed to Close in which she gushes over Madonna's stage shows were made up—Close has never attended a single Madonna concert.

Close's closest connection to the **Queen of Pop**? Well, Madonna wore a dress from Close's hit movie *Dangerous Liaisons* (1988) during her 18th-century take on "**Vogue**" at the **MTV Video Music Awards** ... but it was Michelle Pfeiffer's. Oh, and Madonna has been talked about as a candidate to take over Close's role as "Norma Desmond" in a movie version of the musical version of the movie (phew!) ***Sunset Boulevard***.

CLUB MADONNA: *1527 Washington Ave., Miami Beach, FL.* All-nude **Miami** strip joint owned by producer/nightclub owner Leroy Griffith since the '60s. In 1994, the club was the target of Madonna's lawyers over its clever use of her name. Or wait, wasn't it the other way around? "The name 'Madonna' has been around for hundreds of years. She has no lock on it," Griffith griped to the press as Madonna threatened a lawsuit. He prevailed.

COACHELLA: The Coachella Valley Music and Arts Festival, staged every year since 1999 (except 2000) in Indio, California, is a three-day music and arts fest characterized by a variety of hip music on multiple stages and lots of **drug** use.

On April 30, 2006, Madonna made her debut at the fest, performing "**Hung Up**," "**Get Together**," "**I Love New York**," "**Ray of Light**," "**Let It Will Be**" and "**Everybody**." She wore a snazzy purple $30,000+ "M" pendant by Neil Lane with 10 karats of sapphires, hardly the normal gear for the alt-rockin' get-together.

She threw some attitude when her stage got wet, but otherwise, her 30-minute set in the scorching-hot Sahara **dance** tent was a crowd-pleaser. She even took a moment to ask everyone if her ass looked okay. It did.

Billboard named it the sixth best Coachella performance of all time.

On April 12, 2015, Madonna made a surprise appearance during **Drake**'s set. She sang a short, *meh*-dley of "**Human Nature**" and "Hung Up," then pulled Drake's head back and engaged him in what appeared to be a planned kiss. After the 10-second aggressive smooch, during which Madonna swatted his hand away when he went to grab her head (not the **hair**!), she declared, "**Bitch**, I'm Madonna!" and triumphantly stalked off the stage. Unfortunately, Drake wiped his mouth after and made a face, exclaiming, "Oh, shit! What the **fuck** just happened?" The optics made it seem like he wasn't so into the kiss, leading to one of the busiest days Madonna's name has ever had on **Twitter**, mostly focusing on her being too old to be allowed to continue living.

Consensus was that the kiss was gross and unwelcome, even though Drake posted a picture of it on **Instagram** with the caption, "Moments to write home about" and emoticons for tears and applause. Rumor had it any face he'd made was due to her lipstick tasting bad. He later clarified on Instagram, "Don't misinterpret my shock!! I got to make out with the queen Madonna and I feel [100] about that forever. Thank you @madonna." Still, many Internet denizens and some commentators seized on it to discuss issues of sexual **assault** and **race**. Even many of Madonna's **fans** weren't wild about the appearance, which is fair, though concern-trolling about what it would mean to her legacy was aggressively passive-aggressive.

Michael Jackson was accused of having **sex** with children and **Elvis Presley** died on the toilet, yet both of their legacies are intact. It's safe to say that Madonna kissing a nearly 30-year-old man while daring to look hot in her fifties is survivable.

Madonna's best response to the pounding backlash she received was to post the following quote on Instagram: "If you don't like me and still watch everything I do. Bitch, You're a fan."

COHEN, ANDY: *b. June 2, 1968.* Bravo **TV** executive, producer and on-air **talent** as host of his nightly series *Watch What Happens: Live* (2009–). A buddy of **Anderson**

Cooper, who also **loves** Madonna, Cohen is one of Madonna's biggest **fans** and staunchest defenders in the media.

Following Madonna's **Grammys** appearance in 2015, Cohen became a crusader for her right to bare her butt. "I like that Madonna puts on a show every time she comes out ... when I'm 56, if my ass looks like that, I'll wear fishnets and a matador outfit and show my ass." He also got personal with some women who were complaining that Madonna was too old to be showing her body, tweeting back, "Look, I'm looking at your avatar, and with all due respect, honey, you have a situation happening yourself."

Madonna has come to parties Cohen has thrown, including one for Cooper. At one of his house parties, Madonna wanted to drink either a Cosmo or Krug Rose champagne, because all other champagne "is for losers."

COHEN, SACHA BARON: *b. October 13, 1971.* Outrageous English prankster comic whose mockumentaries *Borat* (2006) and *Brüno* (2009) were hits and controversy-magnets.

Madonna was an early **fan** of Cohen's idiotic poseur "Ali G" character, inviting him to play a chauffeur in her **"Music"** video. In the video, which he promptly stole from her, Ali G is starstruck when Madonna, in white fur and cowgirl hat, greets him. "Is you Madonna? Is you Madonna? Your babylons look less big than they do on the telly, but I still *definitely* would." He sticks around, driving Madonna, **Niki Haris** and **Debi Mazar** on a club crawl, performing cheesy **dance** moves and also appearing in the animated sequence. Three-quarters of the way through, the driver attempts to pitch Madonna on his rap career, freestyling some **"Like a Virgin"**-inspired verses. He mutters, "Respek ..." (respect) when she shuts him down. In the end, he's seen attempting to persuade some bimbos to check out his Big Ben.

When Madonna performed "Music" live at the **MTV Europe Music Awards** (EMAs), Cohen (as Ali G) introduced "Maradona" as someone who has "consistently produced **work** that is worthy of **masturbation**." When Madonna kicked ass at the same show's 2005 edition, debuting **"Hung Up,"** Cohen quipped, "It was very courageous of **MTV** to start the show with a genuine transvestite."

In 2006, Madonna presented Cohen with a prize at the **British Comedy Awards**.

COLLAGEN: In September 1990, Madonna had her lips injected with collagen, giving her a temporarily swollen pout for a mere $500. The 10-minute procedure produced a bee-stung effect for three months. Madonna tried it due to her well-documented dissatisfaction with her "thin" lips.

Madonna abandoned the look after one treatment at the time, not that other needles with other payloads have never touched her in that region since. (SEE: **plastic surgery**.)

Screen legend Catherine Deneuve said at the time, "Because the mouth expresses so much, I'm amazed that she could take the risk to change her lips. She has a very different expression."

The hypersexy pout, which **Liz Rosenberg** jokingly referred to as Madonna's "Lucille Ball tribute," is immortalized in the **Patrick DeMarchelier** photos used on the sleeve of the **"Justify My Love"** single as well as in the video, and on the cover of *Glamour* **magazine**'s 1990 year-end issue.

COLLINS, DAVID: *March 1, 1955–July 17, 2013.* Irish architect whose **work** on restaurants and bars made him an A-list designer of spaces in **London**. Madonna struck up a close friendship with Collins when he designed her London pad and redesigned her longtime **NYC** apartment. So close were they and so much faith did Madonna have in his **talent** that she used a poem he wrote when constructing her deeply personal song **"Drowned World/Substitute for Love"**—Collins was credited and made a large amount of cash for the contribution. He kept a massive 6'×8' portrait of Madonna outside the boardroom of his office suite.

Madonna attended several public events with Collins, including the *GQ* **Awards** on September 4, 2007, and Diane von Furstenberg and Claridge's launch party at Claridge's (49 Brook St., London, England, UK) on June 23, 2010.

Sadly, Collins was diagnosed with melanoma in 2013, dying less than a month after it was found. Madonna was said to be devastated, and attended his **funeral** in Dublin, Ireland.

She posted a tribute on her **Instagram** that read: "In **memory** of David Collins. He was a great talent and a good and loyal friend for 17 years! **God** bless him and may he RIP."

COLLINS, JOAN: *b. May 23, 1933.* (Kindly imagine the *Dynasty* theme song trumpeting as you read.) A B-movie queen of the '50s and '60s who provided a little class to Z-movies of the '70s before becoming an AAA-list **TV** star as "Alexis Morell Carrington Colby Dexter Rowan" on *Dynasty* in the '80s. In real life, the conservative Collins has been married five times, has followed her sis Jackie into writing as a serial memoirist and novelist and is these days agreeably, glamorously accessible on the **autograph**-show circuit.

Collins kissed and told about her former fiancé **Warren Beatty**, who had her heart from 1959 to 1961, writing of Beatty's ability to have **sex** while fielding phone calls. This trait may shed some light on why Beatty was so adamant that Madonna edit his secretly taped calls from *Truth or Dare*.

When Madonna was dating Beatty, she seemingly savaged Collins on *The Arsenio Hall Show* on May 1, 1990. Hall asked Madonna, "Like, does the name 'Joan Collins' make you jealous?" Madonna immediately replied, "No," then added, "Have you seen her lately?" The interpretation was that Collins, about to turn 57 at the time, was no match for fresh, young Madonna. But it seems quite possible Madonna initially meant that Collins was no threat to her, having broken up with Beatty decades earlier. Still, she laughed wickedly and allowed the former, unkinder interpretation to stand. "Damn, Muh!" Hall exclaimed (using his **nickname** for Madonna).

"She's Madonna. Let her keep being Madonna. Don't take that away." —ANDY COHEN (2015)

In 1992, Collins attended the star-packed Spago (formerly 8795 Sunset Blvd., LA, CA) **Oscars** party and found herself at a table with a place card that read "**Ciccone.**" She wondered aloud who that might be. Imagine her surprise when Madonna, escorted by **Alek Keshishian**, plopped down one seat away. **Rosie O'Donnell** said on a 1992 episode of *The Arsenio Hall Show* that Madonna and Collins talked the whole night. Wouldn't you **love** to know what they chatted about?

In 2008, Collins wrote a special column for the UK's *Daily Mail*, commenting at length on Madonna's **divorce** from **Guy Ritchie**. She was of the opinion that Madonna shouldn't have to give Ritchie a dime. "Even though Madonna has zillions, I didn't think she should give half to Guy—she made it all herself, as I did my **money** ... I despise men who think they deserve money from women." Collins apparently got bad information when writing her **book** *The World According to Joan*, however, because she had by then heard Ritchie took zero from Madonna. She wrote, "For example, Guy Ritchie, eschewing Madonna's fortune and instead wanting only as much time with his sons as possible, has become a total hero to many of my female friends ..."

"While 'Alexis [Carrington]' is a parodic Thatcherine in drag, Madonna at her best is a smarter kind of clown; and in times like these there are worse kinds of sinners to wish you could be like."-DAVE HILL, DESIGNER BOYS & MATERIAL GIRLS: MANUFACTURING THE '80S POP DREAM (1986)

COMMERCIALS: Madonna's most famous commercial endorsement was her short-lived **Pepsi** spot in 1989, but it's not the only time she's pranced to promote a product on **TV.**

In 1985, Madonna joined other **MTV** artists like **Pat Benatar**, **Billy Idol** and **Cyndi Lauper** as part of George Lois's iconic "I want my MTV!" ads. For hers, Madonna angrily demands her MTV, kissing the network's cartoon logo.

On October 6, 1985, Madonna joined **Rosanna Arquette** in filming a brief appearance in a TV spot for the Great Peace March for Global Nuclear Disarmament, a demonstration conceived by **gay** politico David Mixner. The march took place from March 1, 1986, through November 15, 1986. In the ad, filmed at a pro-peace rally, the women are marching along with a large group of other protesters, including Malcolm McDowell, whose *A Clockwork Orange* (1971) character Madonna *kindasorta* played in the "**Keep It Together**" finale of her *Blond Ambition World Tour*. Madonna wears the same jacket she wore at **Live Aid.**

Less idealistically, Madonna had a long-running deal to promote the **Mitsubishi** Electric Company's stereo products in Japan. One 1987 commercial for them (shot in '86) featured her dancing and spinning in the toreador outfit from her "**La Isla Bonita**" single sleeve as the song plays; another, more conceptual, shows Madonna inserting

a glowing "M" into a VCR as "**True Blue**" plays. "Beautiful," Madonna intones at the end. Still another (shot in June 1987) features Madonna in a red *Who's That Girl World Tour* costume dancing to "**Spotlight.**"

One of the **sexiest** ads Madonna ever filmed was in 1991 for Elephant, a Japanese brand. Dressed in a revealing showgirl outfit, she undulates on an elephant, actually riding one in another variation; her song "**Rescue Me**" livens things up.

Also in Japan, a unique 1990 Madonna portrait was used to plug Elleseine, a company offering "aesthetic treatments" for the terminally chubby, a gig later plucked away by Brooke Shields.

In 1995, Madonna starred in an elaborate spot for Takara Legend sake, dressed as a samurai who slays a dragon. The ad was directed by Pierre et Gilles, who photographed her at the time of the filming in their inimitable hyper-real style.

Madonna's April 1999 **Alek Keshishian**–directed Max Factor ads played up her sarcastic sense of humor, showing her (with mid-length reddish **hair**) at a table with her makeup artist (Sarah Monzani, who beautified her for *Evita* and *The Next Best Thing*) getting ready to shoot the ad. In various quick edits, she seems on the verge of hysteria, joking about being smitten ("That man is so gorgeous! ... Dishy? More like a full-course meal. And I'm starving.") with her handsome costar (Raoul Bova).

Madonna's most creative "commercial" was her 2001 performance in a film short entitled *Star*.

In 2003, Madonna did one of her most high-profile spots, teaming with **Missy Elliott** for a massive **Gap** campaign. In the TV ads, Madonna and Elliott perform "**Into the Hollywood Groove**," a mash-up of "**Into the Groove**" and "**Hollywood**," along with an **original** Elliott rap (sample lyric: "Hollywood and **New York**/Madonna is the queen"). The ad shows Madonna and Elliott in their Gap denim, strolling through a movie studio with fake backdrops, winding up in a soundstage, where they and a group of **dancers** strut their stuff, including some deep squats (by Madonna) and splits (by both).

As part of her deal with Motorola, Madonna became one of a dozen music names who are filmed (through trick photography) piling into a phone booth in a 2005 ad for the MotoROKR. Madonna shot the ad for this Motorola phone with iTunes in a shoot near **London** on August 31, 2005, just over two weeks after a bone-breaking **horse**-riding accident. Still wearing an arm sling, she appears in a phone booth, and through the magic of **Photoshop** is squished by fellow personalities Amerie, Michelle Branch, Bootsy Collins, Common, Little Richard, **Alanis Morissette**, Mýa, **Iggy Pop** and ?uestlove. Once all are inside, a Biggie Smalls look-alike lumbers toward the door. Closeup on Madonna, squished, pleading, "Biggie ... no!" Odd.

In a pair of 2007 Japanese commercials on behalf of Brillia Mare Ariake, Madonna looks stunning, and stunningly different from ad to ad. In the first, she wears a shiny vinyl gown, her **hair** looking like a throwback to *Ray of Light*—long, reddish and lightly curled. As she sensuously feels her own arms, she whispers, "Family is everything. Family comes first. It's not what I expected it to be … nothing ever is. Just … perfect." The other variation shows Madonna in her short white-**blonde "Jump"** video wig, a similarly shiny black gown and bracing herself with a **guitar** (barely visible in the shot). In this one, Madonna speaks firmly: "Beyond **race**, beyond gender, beyond religion, beyond culture, beyond tomorrow … just perfect," she says in the spot. The 2007 ads were plugging a new luxury condo.

At the same time, Madonna entered into a deal with **H&M**, designing a line called M by Madonna. The cheap duds were hawked in part by her most hilarious TV spot, a 1:30 tour de force that clearly references *The Devil Wears Prada* (2006). Madonna plays a domineering **fashion**-brand honcho, ruling over an army of skinnygirls with an iron fist, using a riding crop to punctuate important points in her boardroom speeches, smacking an employee, shredding résumés willy-nilly and eventually waltzing off with an underling whose glam transformation she's just directed. The ad has it, it, it, it, it.

In 2012, Madonna's **black-and-white** spot for her own **Truth or Dare** fragrance (with **"Girl Gone Wild"** pulsing) finds her vamping abstractly, including a shot of some cleavage no fiftysomething **mother** should still posses. Her 2014 Japanese-only **MDNA** Skin product earned a spot that was similar in style but far more conceptual. Madonna says dead-seriously, "Having good skin is important to me … *Having good skin* … but so are other things. Creation. Your body smells of honey from the comb. Essence. Your amber-silken skin smells of your mind. *Aishiteimasu*. Alchemy. I've spent hours on it. *Touch my skin*. Months on it. *Touch me*. Years on it. *My skin*. MDNA. Transformation. *Love*. Enigmatic. *Touch my skin*. Substance. *Substance*. Connection. Revolution. Spirit. Intuition. *Skin*. Radical. *Magic*. Mystical. Ambition. Infinity. *Infinity*. *Immortal*. MDNA Skin Care Line from MTG. *Chrome clay mask*. Serum. Skin rejuvenator. Can you feel it? *Beautiful. Skin*. Je t'aime. Shhh! The future. *Love*. Now."

Madonna's music has occasionally been used in TV commercials. **"Open Your Heart"** was used as the theme for a British ad for Peugeot, and became so popular it was rereleased as the B-side of her British **"Rain"** single in 1993. More lucratively, **"Ray of Light"** was used by Bill Gates in 2001 for a Windows XP spot that saturated the airwaves. Michael McLaren, a veep at McCann-Erickson, the ad company behind the song's inclusion, noted, "The product is all about empowerment, and we wanted a song that really brought that spirit to life. It's a very positive track that speaks to the human potential."

As her career moves along and as the realities of the music biz change, Madonna has become more open to doing commercials in the US. There is every indication the trend will continue.

COMPTON, KEN: Painter and musician with whom Madonna was involved in 1983. He plays her boyfriend in the music video for **"Burning Up."**

CONDOMS: "Hey, you!/Don't be silly/Put a rubber/On your willy!" With that demure verse, Madonna endorsed condoms all around the globe on her *Blond Ambition World Tour*. In February 1991, she one-upped herself by issuing a joint statement with **ACT UP**, calling for the distribution of condoms in **New York** public high **schools**, a notion that was approved by the city at the time.

Condoms seem to follow Madonna like obsessed **fans**: When *The Girlie Show World Tour* cruised into São Paulo, Brazil, in November 1993, the Bahia **Gay** Group sent her 100 condoms of assorted colors, urging her to promote safe **sex** during her show. Rumor has it the latex never made it out of South America.

Photographer **Martin H.M. Schreiber** sold the right to reproduce his 1979 images of Madonna to a company called VDM, which in turn licensed to Condomania the right to use one on a Madonna-branded box of condoms. Madonna, the least litigious of major stars, sent Condomania a cease-and-desist letter, but the company was unrepentant, claiming she'd signed away all rights at the time of their shoot. Condomania gave away tens of thousands of the condoms to safer-sex programs. Madonna condoms are no longer in production, and Condomania's NYC brick-and-mortar location closed in 2007.

CONE BRA: From her **"Open Your Heart"** video's pointy corset, to the exaggerated black cone bra she sports in the **"Vogue"** video, to her iconic *Blond Ambition World Tour* bullet-bra basque and its **reinvention** via exaggerated, structural torpedo tits on her *MDNA Tour* performance, where Madonna goes, pointy boobies follow.

Or, rather, they *lead*.

"It was her idea to put the cone bras on the men in her show," **Jean Paul Gaultier** confided. He should know—he designed the costumes for *Blond Ambition*. "I would have put them on their penises!" Gaultier first designed a cone bra for his teddy bear as a child, because it was the easiest way to fold the paper to make a bra for his furry little supermodel.

CONFESSIONS ON A DANCE FLOOR: *Release date: November 11, 2005. Billboard 200 peak: #1.* Each time Madonna releases an album, there seems to be a feeling that she has something to prove, as if whatever has come before has not been enough to resolve doubts about her **talent** and staying **power**. In most cases, that perception is absurd; Madonna has weathered many storms in her career, and a poorly received album here or there has not stopped her. But it would be tough to underestimate how important this transitional album was to Madonna's career longevity when it arrived in 2005; in short, with *Confessions on a Dance Floor*, a DJ (**Stuart Price**) may have saved her creative life.

"Being a superstar can be so incredibly tedious and superficial…superficial is nice."
—MADONNA, MAX FACTOR COMMERCIAL (1999)

CONFESSIONS
ON A
DANCE FLOOR

Standard Edition
(1-12)

Special Edition Box Set
(1-12, A)

Fan Club Download
Bonus (B)

① "Hung Up"
(Madonna/Stuart Price/
Benny Andersson/
Björn Ulvaeus)-5:36,
produced by Madonna/
Stuart Price

② "Get Together"
(Madonna/Anders Bagge/
Peer Åström/Stuart
Price)-5:30, produced by
Madonna/Stuart Price

③ "Sorry"
(Madonna/Stuart Price)
-4:43, produced by
Madonna/Stuart Price

④ "Future Lovers"
(Madonna/Mirwais)
-4:51, produced
by Madonna/Mirwais

⑤ "I Love New York"
(Madonna/Stuart Price)
-4:11, produced by
Madonna/Stuart Price

⑥ "Let It Will be"
(Madonna/Mirwais/Stuart
Price)-4:18, produced by
Madonna/Stuart Price

⑦ "Forbidden Love"
(Madonna/Stuart Price)
-4:22, produced by
Madonna/Stuart Price

⑧ "Jump"
(Madonna/Joe Henry/
Stuart Price)-3:46,
produced by Madonna/
Stuart Price

⑨ "How High"
(Madonna/Christian
Karlsson/Pontus Winnberg/
Henrik Jonback)-4:40,
produced by Madonna/
Bloodshy & Avant/
Stuart Price

⑩ "Isaac"
(Madonna/Stuart Price)
-6:03, produced by
Madonna/Stuart Price

⑪ "Push"
(Madonna/Stuart Price)
-3:57, produced by
Madonna/Stuart Price

⑫ "Like It or Not"
(Madonna/Christian
Karlsson/Pontus Winnberg/
Henrik Jonback)-4:31,
produced by Madonna/
Bloodshy & Avant

Ⓐ "Fighting Spirit"
(Madonna/Mirwais)
-3:32, produced
by Madonna/Mirwais

Ⓑ "Super Pop"
(Madonna/Mirwais)
-3:42, produced
by Madonna/Mirwais

In the wake of negative reviews and public indifference toward her highly personal *American Life* in 2003, Madonna seemingly set about to create a follow-up that would return her to her roots, yet would do so in a way she could find palatable. She had already enlisted the aid of British producer and musican Price to **work** on a potential film score (*Hello, Suckers!*), on which she'd been collaborating with **Patrick Leonard** and **Mirwais**. Price had started working with Madonna when he mixed some of her *Music* music, then became musical director of her *Drowned World Tour*. He continued as musical director of her *Re-Invention World Tour*, which directly led to his collaborating with Madonna in a bigger way.

When Madonna nixed doing *Hello, Suckers!*, she decided to incorporate some of the music into her new studio album, which would be **dance**-oriented, but with a European edge. It would be the opposite of *American Life*. It would also be informed by her immersion in the documentary *I'm Going to Tell You a Secret*. Madonna later told *Attitude* **magazine** that *Confessions* was in part "a reaction to the torment that I went through" editing that film.

Madonna has described the recording of *Confessions* as being "like going back. It was so liberating. I want to be in the shit holes. I want to be in a small place with no furniture. I want to keep it the way it was when I started, sitting on the floor and scribbling in my notebook. I work best under those circumstances." She spent a lot of time in Price's apartment, which led to tabloid rumors they were having an affair. (No confessions were forthcoming.)

As she wrote the album, it became clear that while it would be dance music, it would still reflect her changing world view. It wouldn't come off as preachy as *American Life* had, but it wouldn't be mindless.

"Most people equate dance music with being fluffy and superficial; it's just about having fun. That's fine, but I can't write 12 songs about nothing. My feelings or point of view inevitably sneaks in," Madonna told *USA Today*. Once she settled on the **disco** theme, Madonna watched *Saturday Night Fever* 20 times to "soak up all of John Travolta's coolness." That coolness was reflected in the album cover, a **Steven Klein** salute to disco offering a red-headed Madonna, her back to the camera. Her style inspiration can only have been *Saturday Night Fever*'s Karen Lynn Gorney.

Confessions is Madonna's most stylistically consistent album, so much so that all the songs are seamlessly joined in a continuous mix. "I wanted a record with no ballads. I wanted there to be no breaks, with one song segueing into the next—just like in a disco," she told ***Billboard***.

The album opens with the ticking of a clock, **ballsy** for a 47-year-old woman in a field where her rivals were in their teens and twenties. Though she claims that "time goes by so slowly," the exact opposite impression is conveyed, a sense that if you don't seize the moment, it will pass you by. This feeling is helped along by the legendary call to action that is ABBA's bassline from the 1979 hit "Gimme! Gimme! Gimme! (A Man After Midnight)" sampled here to the point of saturation. In the **original**, it was "half past twelve," while in **"Hung Up"** it's "a quarter to two"—maybe time really does go slowly, since in the 26 years from ABBA's invention to Madonna's addictive **reinvention**, only an hour and 15 minutes has elapsed. The song is an irresistible pop perfect storm with a stop-start quality that manipulates the listener as easily as the tide toying with driftwood. It's musical crack. At one point in "Hung Up," Madonna sings with conviction, "I don't know what to do." It's a lie. She knows.

Madonna's most perfect club song, **"Get Together,"** arrives next, dripping with a **sexuality** so open it's innocent. It begins with a ringing bell that could either be a neat outro providing closure to "Hung Up"'s *60 Minutes* intro or a **school** bell indicating class is in session/let recess begin. Sampling Stardust's "Music Sounds Better With You" (1998), "Get Together" exudes optimism, boiling down club-hopping to **love**-seeking. The song is a fantastic example of Madonna's subtle but honest songwriting abilities.

The chorus communicates what we all seek in the darkness of a club—and in life.

"Sorry" is, ironically, another unapologetic vacation for the mind and draft notice for the **feet**. Opening with Madonna murmuring "I'm sorry" (or close to it) in several different languages, the song zips along aerobically, as if a long-lost cut from *Flashdance: Original Soundtrack from the Motion Picture* (1983). It's a vastly improved take on her admittedly pleasing *Erotica* tracks **"Thief of Hearts"** and **"Words."** Madonna has held out a long time without a classic woman-scorned kiss-off song (**"You'll See"** came close). If she was waiting for a worthy cut, her patience pays off with a grade-A entry in the genre.

"Future Lovers" is a fabulous—in both the **gay** and non-gay ways—concoction, which finally commits to the psychedelic grandiosity Madonna has occasionally toyed with, notably on **"Up Down Suite," "Bedtime Story,"** parts of *Ray of Light* and the enjoyable but somewhat stunted **"Impressive Instant."** "Future Lovers" washes over a soundalike bassline from Giorgio Moroder's "I Feel Love" (1977), managing to rekindle the excitement generated by Donna Summer's orgasmic vocal with a completely different, revelatory narrative. Here, Madonna speak-sings, "I'm gonna tell you about love" (a dozen years after teaching us "how to **fuck**") like a sexy HAL—let's agree to call this song's feminine narrator SAL. When Madonna sings "in the evidence of its brilliance" with the shrill, almost tinny urgency first heard on **"Mother and Father,"** the effect is very different—it's not gut-level intimacy, it's the opposite, a proclamation of the connectedness of the cosmos. **Andy Warhol** said, "In the future, everybody will be world-famous for 15 minutes." Instead, perhaps in the future everybody will be lovers for 15 minutes.

The easy ride through the first four tracks is interrupted by **"I Love New York."** Early pro reviews raved about this tribute to the city that never sleeps, while consumer reaction was more mixed, running from ranking it a ways down the list of fave songs on the CD to being embarrassed for Madonna over this clunky *American Life* reject. The deftly spare lyrical quality that shines on other songs is supplanted here by a clumsy approach that gives birth to some you'll-never-live-this-one-down lines. The song is saved from becoming the next **"I'm So Stupid"** with a killer chorus, an exhilarating demand to "get off my street," the Cure-ish **guitars** and a '60s instrumental wash that evokes images of a beautiful stranger dancing the Pony. Is it enough to win you over? Love it or **hate** it, mad, sad or glad, "I Love **New York**" definitely stops traffic—and that's no good when the rest of your CD is a runaway train.

"Let It Will Be" is an odd duck, and not only for the title. It has an opening that mimics **"Papa Don't Preach"** or even **"Dear Jessie"** and a vocal with a palpable sense of narrative urgency growled by Madonna, as if she's relieved to have the good times of the previous tracks behind her as

a synthesized cowbell clangs somewhere in the mix. "The place that I belong/It won't last long" she predicts, like a disco Nostradamus. Though she could easily launch into a sermon, she's saved by the music and has never sounded more righteous than when she spits, "Just watch me burn!" Our own little Joan of Arc, aflame at the stake of criticism.

"Forbidden Love" is a charming electro *Romeo & Juliet* guaranteed to give you fever—it could be the promise of "Future Lovers" realized, yet also continues Madonna's more old-fashioned appreciation for a boy and girl in love as stated in **"La Isla Bonita."** One Madonna song it sounds nothing like is her own 1994 tune "Forbidden Love"—but don't count this as self-reflexivity because she probably forgot she was recycling.

"Jump" is a kinetic construction that's universal and yet fresh. After a raspy spoken-word introduction, the song becomes a semi-remake of **"Keep It Together"** with its high praise for family and paraphrasing of Sister Sledge's "We Are Family" (1979).

A song called **"How High"** is a natural progression from a song called "Jump," though "How High" is infinitely more pensive. Madonna again returns to questioning **fame** and fortune. Of achieving her goal of notoriety, she bitterly wonders if it was a worthy pursuit.

Before the album was released, **"Isaac"** pissed off Israeli Kabbalists who felt she was blaspheming by using the name of 16th-century mystic Yitzhak Luria. Madonna blew them off as "naughty rabbis" who hadn't even heard the song. She denied the mystic was her inspiration. Regardless, it's a gorgeous masterpiece of a song, a lush Middle Eastern–flavored gem that's the spawn of **"Frozen"** and **Sting**'s "Desert Rose" (1999) with the moaning from **"Secret"** thrown in for good measure.

Madonna announced that **"Push"** was meant as a love song to her special **Guy** (**Ritchie**). There is a slave-galley rhythm, and both the delivery and content of the lyrics communicate effort. Words fall across one another in a jumble. Progress is made, which is good since the song definitely feels like climbing a mountain in 3:45. Quoting the Police's "Every Breath You Take" (1983) and perhaps some Tom Tom Club, the song is certainly not as inaccessible as a mountain aerie.

Confessions closes with **"Like It or Not,"** an anthem for those who live their lives with no regard for the small minds around them, and for those who wish to **God** they could. A flash of **"Die Another Day"** at the beginning winds down into an almost exact regurgitation of the opening of "Frozen" before completely about-facing into a giddy declaration of independence set to a clapping percussive beat—close your **eyes** and picture Madonna snapping her fingers to this and dancing like a Shark or a Jet.

Fan club members received a special bonus track, the frenetic **"Super Pop,"** and fans who sprang for the Special Box Set got **"Fighting Spirit."** Both Madonna/Mirwais compositions are great added value to an already priceless set.

—JIMMY SOMERVILLE

"Believe the hype, this is even better than *Ray of Light*."—*NME* (2005)

The album received extremely positive reviews and, buoyed by the worldwide success of "Hung Up," made it okay to love (and respect) Madonna again. Written off in 2003, she had been reborn. "[2005] was a very tumultuous year. I felt I came out of my disco ball like most people get shot out of a cannon," Madonna said, flush with success.

In the US, the album sold 349,500 copies in its first week, besting a release by *American Idol*'s young country star Carrie Underwood. Worldwide, it has sold 12 million copies.

••

"… MADONNA GETS BACK TO GIVING THE PEOPLE WHAT THEY WANT ON HER BODY-ROCKING LATEST. SHE DOESN'T MAKE LIKE A FOLKIE. SHE DOESN'T RAP ABOUT DOING PILATES. SHE DOESN'T STRIKE A MILITANT POSE. SHE SIMPLY GETS INTO THE GROOVE …"
—CHUCK ARNOLD, *PEOPLE* (2005)

••

"FOR MADONNA, THE QUEST FOR TRANSCENDENCE HAS ALWAYS BEEN CLOSELY LINKED TO THE ECSTATIC RELEASE OF DANCING. BUT WHERE HER PREVIOUS EFFORTS AT CLAIMING DANCE-FLOOR SUPREMACY HAVE USUALLY REVOLVED AROUND THE SUBJECT OF MUSIC ITSELF (THINK 'EVERYBODY' OR 'VOGUE' OR 'MUSIC'), ON *CONFESSIONS* SHE SHIFTS HER FOCUS TO EMPOWERMENT AND SELF-SUFFICIENCY."
—ALAN LIGHT, *ROLLING STONE* (2005)

••

"[STUART] PRICE PLAINLY LACKS THE ELEGANT MUSICIANSHIP OF A TRUE TECHNO ARTIST LIKE PAUL VAN DYK. DISCO IS VISCERAL—A QUALITY MISSING HERE. IN MY OPINION, THERE ARE ONLY TWO TRULY STRONG SONGS, 'HUNG UP' AND 'JUMP'—ESPECIALLY THE LATTER, WITH ITS MAGNIFICENT, HYMNLIKE ASCENSIONS."
—CAMILLE PAGLIA, *SALON* (2005)

••

"I LIKED IT. I THINK SHE'S DOPE, AND SHE LOOKS GREAT FOR 47."—JC CHASEZ, *OK!* (2006)

••

CONFESSIONS TOUR: *Show dates: May 21, 2006–September 21, 2006.* **Jamie King**-directed tour that has been called Madonna's most consistently entertaining, less about flash and more about Madonna's performance … well, if you never mind that **crucifix** centerpiece. It was one of her tours with few old hits on the set list—she performed almost every track from the album it was supporting, ***Confessions on a Dance Floor.*** It was no coincidence that the album's producer, **Stuart Price**, was the tour's musical director.

Fans will also remember *Confessions Tour* as the first to introduce **Nicki Richards** on backing vocals and the last to feature **Donna De Lory** in the same capacity. Madonna had a new slate of **dancers**, most prominently beautiful **Daniel "Cloud" Campos**, who had caught many **eyes** in the "Hung Up" video and who has gone on to be a high-profile dancer in other capacities outside of his Madonna **work**.

Along with the aforementioned crucifixion set piece, the show was characterized by its massive **disco** ball—perfect, because Madonna was back to performing disco and she was clearly having a ball—and by an innovative catwalk that allowed her to perform in the midst of her diehard fans.

As is now standard for every Madonna outing, *Confessions Tour* was divided into distinct parts, this time *Equestrian, Urban Bedouin, Glam-Punk* and *Disco Fever.*

The opening of the show and the *Equestrian* section, **"Future Lovers,"** was as heart-stopping as fans had come to demand from Madonna. Popping out of a mirrored disco ball in riding gear, Madonna looked 30 from the neck up and 18 from the neck down. All the sheep injections in the world couldn't give **Marlene Dietrich** a body like that, and it's essential that our rock stars look young. Why? Because we have too much of our selves invested in them to embrace their getting older. Sure, Madonna's loyal fans will rightfully and righteously **bitch** about all the **ageist** bullshit propagated by the media, but would we as a culture be able to take watching a fattish Madonna huffing through her golden oldies with gray roots? For better or worse, that she looked not only good but supernaturally so only added to her star **power**.

Next up was **"Get Together,"** an entrancing segue that personified the communal aspect of loving Madonna, and of loving escapist club music. Some people think dance music is vapid, but there is, by definition, depth in a sea of bodies pressed tightly together—and it's not **candy**-ass metaphorical depth, it's **fucking** individual souls plugged into each other like the most expansive Internet you've ever surfed.

The third song in the set was the first old-**school** jam, **"Like A Virgin."** Madonna could never top her *Blond Ambition World Tour* sequence or *The Girlie Show World Tour* "Like A Wirgin" … but she came close, riding a carousel **horse** (it let her get on top) and showing off some rather insurance-worthy moves that might make even the daring young man on the flying trapeze blanch.

Madonna then hopped into **"Jump,"** memorable for some in-the-moment-shocking leaps accomplished by her dancers, less so for a slightly walked-through feeling by Madonna.

A dance interlude followed in which the dancers confessed their personal stories via choreography, an artsy way to accomplish what sneaky behind-the-scenes footage tried to do with ***Truth or Dare.***

After this sequence came the much-ballyhooed *Urban Bedouin* segment, featuring a haunting Madonna vocal on **"Live To Tell,"** one of her most underperformed #1 hits. Finally given another airing, the song's layers of meaning were ignored by the media, which simply could not get over the sight of Madonna strapped to a mirrored cross, J.C.-style, complete with a crown of thorns. Sure, it's controversial and audacious. But if Evangelical Christians can get behind buying mass-marketed *The Passion of the Christ* (2004) cross-shaped ballpoint pens, surely more open-minded types in the "liberal" media could've taken a sec to give Madonna the benefit of the doubt. Was it a stunt? No. A stunt is done simply for its own sake and with no deeper meaning or purpose. Madonna rarely indulges in stunts, though her critics would have us believe she is one gigantic stunt. When Madonna creates controversy, it's almost always to highlight a hypocrisy in society. There is a method to her megalomania. It isn't very taxing to read this performance as a critique of so-called Christian values, which are supposed to be about **love**, and every individual's

confession to himself that he is not perfect. That footage of starving and **AIDS**-orphaned **African** children playing in the background only magnified the message: Put your **money** where your mouth is, or "walk the walk, don't just talk the talk," as Madonna barked.

"Forbidden Love" was executed with a stunning arm-dance between men, representing intolerance of homosexuality. When Madonna wedged herself between the men, engaging in the arm-dance herself, it felt like a dramatization of her career for many of her fans—she has probably helped more gay people come to accept themselves than any ex-gay ministry could ever un-recruit: Madonna Wins Out.

"Isaac," a song that brings to mind the superior **"Secret"** or **"Frozen,"** and whose staging was similarly good but not as good as the **originals'** have been live, paired Madonna with a Middle Eastern vocal, making for a haunting duet. Perhaps she will do an album of duets at some point. Maybe pencil it in for May of When Hell Freezes Over. The visuals in the background were of a vast desert; seeing Madonna in an inverted cage while birds flew free was one of the only times that the images on the screens truly seemed to distract, momentarily, from what was happening on stage.

For a straightforward **"Sorry,"** the audience maniacally shouted every word of the song, more evidence that (1) her fans were more than happy to attend a concert heavy on the fresh stuff and that (2) "Sorry" was criminally underserved by radio, at least in the US.

Madonna's chanteusey **"Like It Or Not"**—her love-me-or-leave-me anthem—was convincingly, if unimaginatively, recreated live. It was an example of how the *Confessions Tour* was neither overthought, nor overwrought.

One of the most effective parts of the show happened with Madonna offstage, and it's a shame because the following video interlude of "Sorry," with outtakes from the video and merciless, big-screen manipulations of the images of such bullshit peddlers as George W. Bush, Condoleeza Rice (she got the loudest, "Exactly!!!" anti-cheer) and Saddam Hussein really should have been the main performance of the song with Madonna singing it live.

The *Glam-Punk* segment was the part where old-school fans might've tuned out, and yet it's also the one where Madonna shone as a musician and vocalist. **"I Love New York"** was predictably momentous when performed in **New York**, and **"Let It Will Be"** felt like an early-'80s downtown punk excursion, though the New Order chords kept it on the New Wave side of punk. She sang her heart out on these two songs. Critics are sick of Madonna's finger-wagging over the high price of **fame**, but the chick believes it. Every inch of her body and every ounce of her **voice** were called upon to make the point.

"Ray of Light" was a welcome flashback and enthusiastically gobbled up, and while **"Drowned World/Substitute For Love"** was given a far more muscular, memorable performance on her *Drowned World Tour*, that song and especially the ensuing **"Paradise (Not For Me)"** were beautifully sung. *The New York Times* dippily stated that Madonna always rose above her weak material, blithely ignoring that without such superb material, Madonna would have been fighting with other club artists to be the grand marshal of some local pride parade by 2006.

The *Disco Fever* segment was a highlight—that mashup of **"Music"** and "Disco Inferno" (1976) turned the beat around. For once, all the imagery on the screens served to rouse the crowd; the musical build-up was almost unbearable, and the eventual performance unforgettable.

Hardcore fans were rewarded with an absolutely bangin' airing of the previously **unreleased** original version of **"Erotica,"** the arguably superior "You Thrill Me." It was a lot to digest, but Madonna's ABBA wardrobe at this point was yet another fun distraction.

"La Isla Bonita," one of Madonna's silliest hits and yet a song she seems to be dead-set on doing live at every opportunity, was reimagined in a fun, frothy remix that eclipsed the more musically serious *Drowned World Tour* version. (It was a last-second replacement for **"Everybody,"** which had been rehearsed.)

The final number was a long blending of **"Lucky Star"** (complete with light-up cape) and the night's finale, "Hung Up." It was a terrific marriage, even if "Hung Up" would have made a better opener than closer.

Time went by so quickly, and two hours later, Madonna was history and "Have you confessed?" was glowing at the crowd from the stage, a parting thought similar to her previous tour's final words: "Re-Invent Yourself."

The tour received positive reviews but negative press for that crucifix and for Madonna's well-advertised insistence that no air conditioning be used. It became the highest-grossing tour by a female solo artist, raking in $194.7 million. It was aired on **TV** in the US on NBC on November 22, 2006, as *Madonna: The Confessions Tour Live from* **London** and was also released as a top-selling live album/DVD. The LA leg attracted celebrity fanboys 'n' girls **Ellen DeGeneres**, Salma Hayek, Ashton Kutcher, **Lindsay Lohan**, **Demi Moore**, **Rosie O'Donnell** and Nicole Richie, as well as **Kabbalah** heavyweight Rabbi Yehuda Berg.

Madonna's final word on the show: "It's very rewarding to have the fans appreciate and love this show ... so much blood, sweat and tears went into it."

CONFESSIONS TOUR, THE (ALBUM): *Release date: January 26, 2007.* CD/DVD combo created from *Madonna: The Confessions Tour Live from* **London** TV special. The album skips **"Get Together," "Live to Tell," "Forbidden Love," "Like It or Not," "Ray of Light," "Drowned World/Substitute for Love," "Paradise (Not for Me)"** and **"La Isla Bonita,"** while the DVD contains the whole show.

> "... [W]HEN MADONNA CELEBRATED HER GIFT FOR SUBSTANTIAL GLITZ, SHE SEEMED NEARLY AS YOUTHFUL AS WHEN HER LUCKY STAR BEGAN RISING A LONG, LONG TIME AGO."
> —BARRY WALTERS, *ROLLING STONE* (2006)

> "WHY WOULD SOMEONE WITH SO MUCH TALENT SEEM TO FEEL THE NEED TO PROMOTE HERSELF BY OFFENDING SO MANY PEOPLE?"
> —CHURCH OF ENGLAND OFFICIAL STATEMENT ON *CONFESSIONS TOUR* (2006)

> "THIS IS HER MOST ENTHRALLING TOUR, NOT BECAUSE THERE'S DRASTICALLY LESS SENSATIONALISM OR HYDRAULICS, BUT BECAUSE YOU'LL FINALLY RECALL THOSE SPECTACULAR SET PIECES A LOT LESS THAN YOU REMEMBER MADONNA HERSELF ..."
> —CHRIS WILLMAN, *ENTERTAINMENT WEEKLY* (2006)

> "... MADONNA SINGS ... 'HUNG UP', A SONG ABOUT A WOMAN WHO MIGRATES BETWEEN BOREDOM AND AGONY AS SHE WAITS FOR A MAN TO CALL. BUT WHO COULD THIS MAN POSSIBLY BE? UNLESS MADONNA IS EXPECTING A CALL FROM WLADIMIR KLITSCHKO ABOUT MEETING HIM IN THE RING, THE SIGHT OF HER SINGING A SONG LIKE THIS, IN A LEOTARD NO LESS, LEAVES YOU FEELING AS YOU MIGHT IF YOU WERE FORCED TO WATCH ETHEL MERMAN TRYING TO IMPERSONATE CHET BAKER."
> —GINIA BELLANATE, *THE NEW YORK TIMES* (2006)

CONTROL: "I like to have control over most of the things," Madonna admitted in 1986, "but I'm not a tyrant. I don't have to have it on my album that it's written, arranged, produced, directed and stars Madonna. To me, to have total control means you can lose objectivity." Since that statement, Madonna's name does, in fact, show up more and more on every credit for every song on every album. However, she is still a big believer in **working** with other great **talents**, and does enjoy giving them their chance to shine.

COOKING: Guess who isn't a very good cook? Madonna says she can make only four things—**popcorn, Krispy Marshmallow Treats,** French toast and scrambled eggs. That's okay; it wouldn't be any fun worshiping a woman with a prize-winning recipe for Yankee Pot Roast.

COOPER, ANDERSON: *b. June 3, 1967.* Deadpan anchor of *Anderson Cooper 360°* on CNN. His prematurely

MATTHEW RETTENMUND

gray **hair** and uppercrust demeanor (he is the son of so-cialite/writer/one-woman brand Gloria Vanderbilt) give him gravitas, while his team-ups with Kathy Griffin have shown he has a sense of humor.

In 2011, Cooper hosted Madonna on his daytime show, *Anderson* (2011–2013). His excitement while interviewing her was evident, as was his cute **nervousness** when Madonna proclaimed his question about her five-year plan to be "mundane." On the same episode, Madonna, clad in a squeaky black leather dress that kept interfering with her mic, confessed she was worried about having to "put on the greatest show on earth in the middle of the greatest show on earth" (the **Super Bowl**) and spoke about all the research she did while prepping to direct *W.E.* Interestingly, Cooper's great-aunt, Lady Thelma (played by Katie McGrath), was depicted in the movie.

Cooper is a self-professed Madonna **fan** who has seen her in concert on numerous occasions, often with friends like **Kelly Ripa** in tow.

In 2012, Cooper shot his own video of *The MDNA Tour*, which he saw three times, and played it on his daytime show, re-branded for a second season as *Anderson Live*. "I'm like the world's oldest groupie. I'm too old, I think," he admitted sheepishly. But still, he had to observe, "Her butt is amazing!"

On March 16, 2013, Madonna showed up to the **GLAAD** Media Awards to present Cooper with a Vito Russo Award.

Her 12-minute speech included lavish praise for Cooper: "... I do **love** that word, 'brave.' I don't fling it around very often. I don't know a lot of brave people. In the song you just heard, I sing the line, 'It's so hard to find someone to admire,' and that is the reason I am here, to give an award to someone I admire, to acknowledge someone who is brave, someone who has made a difference in the world by promoting equality and giving a **voice** to the LGBT community. I am here to honor you, Anderson Cooper."

In calling Cooper to the stage, Madonna continued, "All hail the king ... Anderson Cooper! Please, come and get your ... GLAAD Award ... and let me have a reason to grab your ass." Madonna's playfulness seemed to embolden Cooper, who gave her a lingering hug, then, out of nowhere, zeroed in for a kiss on the lips that took Madonna by not-unpleasant surprise.

Cooper said it was hard to follow Madonna, then thanked her for being there and "for her entire career" as "an extraordinary ally, and I'm so thankful for her artistry and for her friendship."

On September 24, 2013, Cooper was one of a number of celebrities who attended Madonna's **#secretprojectrevolution** premiere in **NYC**, spending several charmingly starstruck minutes chatting with her. On October 3, 2013, Cooper conducted an interview with Madonna about the film, also speaking with her about parenting, about their GLAAD lovefest and about her message. "I believe we are at a very low level of consciousness, and we do not know how to treat each other as human beings," a relaxed Madonna

> "If you don't wanna give up things, then don't love. And if you don't wanna love, don't live."
> —MADONNA, *ANDERSON* (2011)

Hangin' with Mr. Cooper, the ultimate unapologetic bitch

told Cooper. "We are caught up in our own lives, our own needs, our own ego gratifications. I feel a strong sense of responsibility in delivering that message."

COOPER, MELINDA: Freddy DeMann's former assistant. Cooper told biographer **Christopher Andersen** that their **work** with Madonna encompassed *all* aspects of her life, including arranging for an **abortion** when she became **pregnant** by longtime boyfriend **Jellybean Benitez**.

Cooper told another biographer, **J. Randy Taraborrelli**, that she recalled telling Madonna while en route to the set of her **"Material Girl"** music video that her whole world was going to change after the video came out. Madonna allegedly replied, "I know that, Melinda. Now can we please just get there?"

COPPOLA, SOFIA: *b. May 14, 1971.* Longhaired and possessing the soulful, dazed look of a flower child, she was hamburger to sharks when she took over from an exhausted Winona Ryder in her **father** Francis Ford Coppola's film *The Godfather Part III* (1990).

As a one-time pal of Madonna's (who can probably relate to disproportionate criticism, and who herself had been discussed for the same *Godfather* role), Coppola appeared in Madonna's **"Deeper and Deeper"** video, and in 1993 **Maverick** and Zoetrope (Coppola's dad's production company) produced a pilot for a Sofia-driven talk show called *Hi Octane*, sort of a *House of Style* (1989–2000; 2012; 2014) on wheels. The project went to series, airing briefly on Comedy Central. The celebrity-saturated series was the first ever to be filmed entirely on digital video.

All's well that ends well for Coppola, who found her calling as the admired director of such films as *The Virgin Suicides* (1999), *Lost in Translation* (2003) and *Marie Antoinette* (2006); the latter film clearly influenced an intentionally anachronistic rock-'n'-roll sequence in Madonna's *W.E.*

CORMAN, CIS: One of **Barbra Streisand**'s best friends, her partner in her Barwood production company and a noted producer and casting director, Corman auditioned Madonna in the early '80s for the role of Mary, **Mother of God**, in Martin Scorsese's *The Last Temptation of Christ* (1988). She recalled to biographer **Barbara Victor** that Madonna showed up with a ghetto blaster, in torn jeans with her **hair** tied up in a rag, "but she looked absolutely gorgeous."

Corman urged her son **Richard Corman**, an aspiring photographer, to meet and shoot Madonna. Those images became artful records of Madonna's downtown, pre-**fame** existence when they were widely published 30 years after their creation.

So taken was Corman with Madonna's life story that she and Rusty Lemeron worked on a film or TV adaptation of it. She also saw Madonna as the potential lead in a film she conceived with Jack DePalma that in treatment form was described as an urban take on *Cinderella* called *Midnight: A Rock Fable*. A series of Polaroids by Richard Corman was shot to show Madonna cleaning (in denim) and radiating beauty (on her roof) as "Cinderella." Neither project went anywhere.

Corman sent Madonna's audition tape to Jon Peters, which directly led to Peters casting her in a small singing role in *Vision Quest*.

CORMAN, RICHARD: Well-known, **New York**–based **fashion** photographer who has shot everyone of note you can think of, and who as an aspiring photographer twice shot Madonna in, on top of and around her **East Village** digs in 1983 at the suggestion of his casting-director **mother, Cis Corman**. Corman's **work** with Madonna also includes shooting her in a series of **eye**-popping '80s sweaters for the Italian fashion **magazine** *Per Lei*, on the Washington set of *Vision Quest* and as part of the cast of *Desperately Seeking Susan* for *Vogue*, the latter under the watchful eye of Anna Wintour.

Most of Corman's images of Madonna at home as well as most of his sweater series remained unpublished and unseen until he began exhibiting them in 2010, culminating with a traveling exhibition around his **book** *Madonna NYC 83* (Damiani, 2013).

COSTNER, KEVIN: *b. January 18, 1955.* **Oscar**-winning director and actor most famous for his baby *Dances with Wolves* (1990) and *The Bodyguard* (1992).

In Madonna's *Truth or Dare*, Costner is shown going backstage after a performance of the *Blond Ambition World Tour* and telling Madonna the show was "neat," to which Madonna says, "No one's ever described it quite that way." Once Costner's back is turned, Madonna makes a gagging motion with her finger, saying aloud, "'Neat'? Anybody who says my show is 'neat' has to go."

Burn. End. Right? No.

RICHARD CORMAN

SIDEWALK TALK:
RICHARD CORMAN ON SHOOTING
PRE-MADONNA

Turned on to her by his mother, an accomplished casting agent, photographer Richard Corman recalls meeting Madonna for the first time at her 232 E. 4th St. apartment building after calling her via pay phone to alert her that he'd arrived. Why did he have to call?

"It was a rough building. That's why Madonna told me to call from across the street. I could see a group of people around the building, protecting their turf. When Madonna let me know that it was cool to come over, the seas kind of parted. I walked to the back staircase and looked up and saw this girl I'd never met with those cat-like eyes. I knew right then that this was somebody to be reckoned with, that there was real charisma. I could tell from four floors up."

The perfect hostess, Madonna served Corman a cup of coffee on a silver tray with three pieces of Bazooka bubblegum.

Corman shot her that day with a group of boys who were in Madonna's thrall at that time. "She was like the Pied Piper of the neighborhood," Corman recalls. She described them as her family, and would share pizza with them in her apartment, where they'd all dance and sing. One of them, Lamont Clarke, later told the *New York Post* that the kids used to call her "Flaca" and that they viewed her as a big sister.

"I am happy for her because she is a beautiful person," Clarke said in 2014. "She didn't judge or discriminate and helped all the people she could. She had a lot of heart, and she'll always be my older sister."

Corman was moved hearing from the grown-up Clarke 30 years after his shoot. Unfortunately, Clarke was in prison for robbery, but he impressed the photographer with his sincerity. "I always knew there was something very hard-edged about that kid, that he was 13 going on 30. They were called the TFKs, the Tough Fucking Kids. They were a gang, but they weren't out hurting people, and they definitely kept an eye on Madonna."

His next time shooting Madonna was to get some photographs to help flesh out a pitch for a movie. "My mother was trying to produce a film—my mother had written a proposal and brought it to Jon Peters to do a modern *Cinderella* with Madonna. The cast was everyone from Aretha Franklin as one of the sisters to you name it."

Corman says he shot Madonna in her brother Christopher's small apartment for about 30 minutes, then she said, "Let's go up to the roof."

Madonna had styled herself with care. "She was dressed down in denim, cleaning, and then she put on that vintage dress she found for $6 someplace to pose as Cinderella."

"The tragedy is that somewhere there is a book of Polaroids showing Madonna with a broom, sweeping, and transforming into Cinderella." The film was never made.

That same year, when Madonna was performing at Studio 54, Corman, his best friend, his mother, Martin Scorsese and the head of Armani went "because everyone wanted to actually see her perform. Madonna was due on at 11 p.m., but started closer to 4 a.m. –Corman and his friend stayed, but the others had left.

When Corman was assigned to shoot Madonna for *Per Lei*, she was frustrated by the quirky, oversized sweaters. "This was absolutely not her look, but she made it her look. Betweeen the jewelry and the attitude and the swag and the humor, she turned it around. She brought some of her own props—the boombox, some of her own accessories—but it was totally her intelligence and sense of humor that made that shoot. Otherwise, it could have looked like a catalogue shoot."

Also in 1983, Corman brought Madonna to Café Central (formerly 384 Columbus Ave., NY, NY), where all the stars hung out, to meet with his parents. "Madonna walked in and they were all there, De Niro and Chris Walken, that whole crew. De Niro's best friend was the manager of this bar/restaurant. I remember she introduced herself to my father with, 'Hey, Dad.' When the dinner was over, Madonna asked De Niro to put her in a taxi to Harlem, where she had a show. "He said, 'I really can't do that, I can't be seen with you.' He was very shy and introverted. But she just forced his hand and made him put her into a cab."

"She was so cocky in the best way and so confident," Corman says.

Test Polaroids from Corman's "Cinderella" shoot, plus the program from his 2010 Madonna exhibition

RICHARD CORMAN

"She was so cocky in the best way and so confident." — Richard Corman

On February 12, 2015, Costner said on SiriusXM radio that Madonna made up for the incident at a *Re-Invention World Tour* performance he'd taken his daughters to:

" ... I bought the tickets myself and took my daughters to see Madonna and we didn't get any special seat, we're off to the right, and lights were on and the show started and I could just see how happy my daughters were, watching her show and she was just blazing, she was going really strong and then the lights dipped the second time as the show was mid-way through and also she goes: 'I want to apologize to somebody.' And the audience got really quiet and she said: 'I want to apologize to Kevin Costner.' And I had no idea that she even knew that I was in the audience. And it was a very big thing and my daughters turned and looked at me like: 'What was that?' And I was so glad, #1, to hear that ... I just thought it was a really nice thing for her to do."

CRAVEN, KAREN: Madonna's high **school** cheerleading coach. In the **TV** documentary ***Driven: Madonna***, she recalled Madonna as being very resentful of her **stepmother**: "I don't wanna say about the evil stepmother ..." When Madonna was supposed to be home babysitting her brother **Mario Ciccone**, Craven admitted she would run interference, calling Madonna's stepmom and saying that all **cheerleaders** were required to attend school dances.

"CRAZY FOR YOU" (SONG): *Release date: March 2, 1985. Billboard Hot 100 peak: #1.* Madonna's first big ballad was so popular in 1985 it dethroned "We Are the World" at the top of the charts (maybe they should've made sure Madonna participated in the charity single?) and managed to chart concurrently with her other Top 5 smash, **"Angel,"** even though the film whose soundtrack it graced, ***Vision Quest***, was a box-office letdown. **Fans** were pleasantly surprised by Madonna's deep **voice** on this record after a string of upper-register **disco** tunes.

The song had been written by John Bettis and Jon Lind as the *Vision Quest* theme after they watched the film. The movie's producer, Jon Peters, knew of Madonna via casting director **Cis Corman**, leading to him hiring her as a vocalist and to make a short cameo in the movie.

She performed "Crazy for You" live on ***The Virgin Tour***, her ***Re-Invention World Tour*** and her ***Rebel Heart Tour***.

"I'd like to dedicate this next song to all of my fans! Thank you for sticking by me through all these years!"–MADONNA INTRODUCING "CRAZY FOR YOU" ON HER RE-INVENTION WORLD TOUR (2004)

"CRAZY FOR YOU" (VIDEO): *Director: Harold Becker, 1985.* The music video for Madonna's second #1 hit in the US made use of footage shot by Harold Becker for her cameo in the movie ***Vision Quest***, along with scenes from the rest of the movie. Madonna's popularity was such at the time that a makeshift video filled with clips was an offer **MTV** could not refuse, even if it was little more than a free **commercial** for the film. The same was true of the videos for **"Gambler"** from the same film and **"Into the Groove"** from ***Desperately Seeking Susan***.

CREATIVITY: Madonna's belief that she can summon hers at will is strikingly reminiscent of **Marilyn Monroe's** conviction that she could turn on and turn off her **"Marilyn"** persona.

"CRIMES OF PASSION": Super sweet song that was written by Madonna and produced by **Stephen Bray** in 1981, but left off her first album, ***Madonna***. It would have been a terrific addition. Musically reminiscent of a low-metabolism **"Love** Sensation" (1980) by Loleatta Holloway, this gem was saved from oblivion when Bray made it the second track on ***Pre-Madonna***.

The inspiration for this song (or at least for the title) came from David Frank, who was a friend of Madonna's and Bray's and who **worked** with them casually during her days in **The Music Building**. Frank remembered in 2005 being encouraged to cut a 12" record using a female singer, so he approached Madonna to collaborate. Madonna provided lyrics and a melody, but when she wanted to pull Bray in, Frank balked; he wanted to keep the song very synth-based, and knew Bray would add **guitars**.

Once Madonna exited, Frank instead called up Mic Murphy and they changed the song completely, winding up with "It's Passion" (1982). Madonna and Bray apparently kept their own version of the **original** song, and recorded it.

Frank and Murphy wound up becoming the duo the System, who hit #4 on the ***Billboard*** Hot 100 with "Don't Disturb This Groove." Frank also eventually cowrote "Genie in a Bottle," the song that put **Christina Aguilera** on the map.

CROSS, CHRISTOPHER: *b. May 3, 1951.* The onetime **Grammy**-attracting hitmaker has spoken highly of Madonna. In 1995, he told a **gay** magazine, "Even Madonna has been very gracious when we have come in touch with each other. She understands how tough it is to be on top and takes the time to acknowledge me and says hi. I feel proud, and I've only ever seen her behave like a lady."

CROW, MELISSA: Madonna's personal assistant from the '80s until 1992 came directly from Madonna's manager **Freddy DeMann,** for whom Crow had **worked.**

In ***Truth or Dare***, Madonna recites a special dirty, dishy **birthday** limerick to her right-hand girl. Crow was known throughout Madonnadom as "Baby M" and as being legendarily sweet and industrious.

According to **Christopher Ciccone**, following Crow's resignation, Madonna forbade him from remaining friends with her.

On April 25, 2010, a man bought the contents of a Chatsworth, California, storage unit for just $150 at a

RICHARD CORMAN

blind **auction**. The unit turned out to have been rented by Crow, who'd fallen behind on her monthly payments. Legally, everything in the unit belonged to the bidder, who auctioned it on eBay throughout the rest of April and May 2010 over Crow's vehement protestations.

The episode allowed a rare peek at some of the inner-workings of Madonna's creative process and day-to-day **business** activities for the years 1987 to 1992, including a handwritten tour diary, "to-do" lists for Crow to execute, **autogaphs** intended for **fans**, stacks of never-before-seen Paula Court, **Patrick Demarchelier, Steven Meisel** and **Herb Ritts** images, one-of-a-kind Polaroids showing Madonna behind the scenes at famous photo shoots (and one of Madonna, **Liz Rosenberg** and **Debi Mazar** with a phal-

lic squirt **gun**), a video of **Warner Bros.** employees wishing Madonna a happy 30th birthday, rare ***Blond Ambition World Tour*** booklets and dozens of personal snapshots.

Even that **original**, handwritten limerick Madonna recited to Crow in *Truth or Dare* was in the stash.

In the end, the seller made tens of thousands of dollars on his $150 investment (he even sold off Crow's personal belongings, including her high **school** yearbook).

CRUCIFIXES: Madonna burst onto the scene wearing elaborate crucifixes. One of her most oft-repeated quotes is: "Crucifixes are **sexy** because there's a naked man on them." She has explained, "Everything I do is sort of tongue-in-cheek. It's a strange blend—a beautiful sort of

In her *Vision Quest* trailer, as captured by Richard Corman symbolism, the idea of someone suffering, which is what Jesus Christ on a crucifix stands for, and then not taking it seriously." She's also joked about only attending church to steal crucifixes.

She started a trend that has yet to run its course, as crosses and crucifixes continue to find their way into nearly every new **look**, years after their peak as staples of Madonna's wardrobe. She even *became* one on her ***Confessions Tour.***

CRUISE, TOM: *b. July 3, 1962.* One of the biggest box-office draws in Hollywood history, the star of hits like *Risky **Business*** (1983), *Top **Gun*** (1986), *Mission Impossible* (1996) and *Tropic Thunder* (2008) became friendly with Madonna thanks to his **working** relationship with costar **Sean Penn** from *Taps* (1981). He attended their 1985 **wedding.** (SEE: **Maripol** interview.)

On February 6, 2008, Cruise attended Madonna's star-studded **Raising Malawi** benefit in **NYC**. At that time, Madonna defended Cruise's faith in Scientology to *New York* **magazine**: "I don't care if people worship turtles or frogs—if they're good people, that's all that I care about, and he is a good person. I think he gets a raw deal, just as I think the orphans in **Malawi** get a raw deal, just as I think a lot of marginalized people get a raw deal."

Madonna was obviously speaking as a student of **Kabbalah**, which she probably also thinks gets a raw deal. In 2005, she had said she felt that she and Cruise were "both in the take-a-lot-of-shit club together."

In 2010, producer Irwin Winkler let slip that Cruise and Madonna had both been talked about to star in *Goodfellas* (1990), and that director Martin Scorsese had gone to see Madonna in ***Speed-the-Plow*** before going in a different direction.

Madonna and Cruise were onstage together in May 2011 for the taping of the **Oprah Winfrey** Surprise Spectacular finale.

CRUMES, OLIVER: *b. 1972.* **Dancer** on the ***Blond Ambition World Tour*** whom Madonna seemed to take under her wing as her favorite. He was the only dancer with her when she shot a dressing-room shout-out for the German **TV** show ***Wetten, dass ...?*** Mid-way through her appearance, she grabbed Crumes into the frame and said, "This is Oliver. Oliver's the fiercest dancer. He's dancing in my show."

As captured in ***Truth or Dare***, Crumes fears for his manhood as the only straight dancer on the tour, a tension made worse by tabloid reports that he was Madonna's lover. Crumes's personal story is given ample screen time in the film—we sit through his reunion with his disapproving **father**, watch him talking to himself and listen to his opinions on his employer as he sits in a well-lighted chair.

After the film's release, Crumes, **Kevin Stea** and **Gabriel Trupin** sued Madonna, alleging they had been misled regarding how footage shot while they were on tour would be used.

In 1993, Crumes claimed to ***Entertainment Tonight*** that he had "refused" to dance on ***The Girlie Show World Tour*** (unlikely he was asked since he'd sued her) because, "I don't think kids should be watching it. I think it's just too much. She went out. She went kinda over."

Crumes appears in the 2016 documentary ***Strike a Pose.***

CRUSH: Madonna's first crush was on Ronny Howard (no relation) in the fifth grade, who had "white-blond **hair** and sky-blue **eyes.**" She wrote his name on her sneakers. "I used to take off the top part of my [**school**] uniform and chase him around."

"CRY BABY": A brassy Madonna/**Patrick Leonard** composition from the ***Dick Tracy***–inspired album ***I'm Breathless: Music from and Inspired by the Film Dick Tracy*** that is reminiscent of her **"Santa Baby"** cover. Perfect for the period it is recalling (the '30s), it hilariously descends into a cacophony of tears before Madonna squeakily tells herself to "knock if off, please." Elements are repurposed on the same album's **"Now I'm Following You (Part II)."**

CUBBY HOLE: *281 W. 12th St., NY, NY.* **New York** dyke bar that Madonna jokingly told **David Letterman** in 1988 she frequented with **Sandra Bernhard.** In 1989, Madonna confirmed to ***Rolling Stone*** that the whole thing had been an "inside joke" and that, "I've never been inside." As of 1994, the place goes by "Cubbyhole" and advertises itself as "lesbian, **gay** and straight friendly."

CULTURAL APPROPRIATION: On many occasions, and across several decades, Madonna (and plenty of other white artists, starting with **Elvis Presley**) has been accused of "stealing" ideas from cultures other than her own. The allegations began with her usurping of so-called black **music** and has continued with commentary about Madonna's use of **vogueing** (a black and Latin **gay** tradition) and elements of Japanese culture.

Race is always in the mix, to be sure, but should race dictate **art**? Or is it only a problem when that art is commercial?

The cultural appropriation argument is particularly frustrating for Madonna because she acknowledges her appreciation and respect for the origins of the items she is incorporating into her **work.**

In 1999, Madonna spoke of the reason why she felt a kinship with geishas, which was expressed in photo shoots and in her **"Nothing Really Matters"** video and **Grammy** performance: "Sometimes I think that what I do is like being a modern-day geisha. On the one hand, geishas were trapped; on the other, they had a lot more freedom in traditional Japanese society than, say, a married woman. And they lived in a community of other women who were all educated and trained and cultured and they came in contact with some pretty amazing, **powerful** people." This is hardly a superficial, trendy appreciation.

Cultural appropriation is a valid concern, but what are its boundaries? Is it only bad when the race in question has been disenfranchised? If an artist is only allowed to express and reflect aspects of his or her own culture, does it begin and end with race, or are men disallowed from taking inspiration from women? Was it okay for Madonna's *Confessions on a Dance Floor* to be European in flavor because her ancestors were European, or is it wrong for Americans to use anything non-American? What, exactly, *is* Madonna's (or any fiftysomething American white woman's) culture, if not an impossible-to-deconstruct melding of many other cultures, some of which will inspire her to be creative, others of which will not?

In 2014, Nesrine Malik, writing for TheGuardian.com, said, "Whether it is usurping religion—**crucifixes** and **nun** habits are passé now; it's niqabs on naked bodies—keep up—homosexuality or now minority rights, Madonna is a manifestation of how privilege feeds off the authenticity of 'struggle.' This is a double plundering that leads to further marginalization: the dominant narrative will oppress you, then co-opt you, and then weave you into your own tiny little section of the tapestry." This was in response to the fact that Madonna expressed admiration for Martin Luther King Jr. and Nelson Mandela; it is apparently now offensive to support the struggle for equality if you are not a member of the group doing the struggling.

In 2015, *Hunger Games* (2012) star Amandla Stenberg made a Tumblr video entitled "Don't Cash Crop My Cornrows" on the subject of cultural appropriation. Because she used stars like Madonna, **Taylor Swift**, **Miley Cyrus** and **Katy Perry** to make her point, the media covered this as an "attack" against such artists. In reality, she was asking why white people **love** black *culture* but don't seem to love black *people*. As the media coverage of her video demonstrated, it's easy to vilify the white artists, which leads to white people defending their icons (and themselves), a far easier thing to do than to have a more nuanced conversation.

Cultural appropriation is a messy topic, but it should never boil down to, "Stop wearing **grills**, **bitch**." The argument should be rooted in an artist's grasp of the culture he or she is incorporating into his or her art, and also in how it affects the culture it is using.

CURFEW: Madonna's was 9:30 p.m. until the day she left **home**. When **Johnny Carson** asked her what one could possibly do with such an early curfew, she replied, "Nothing—or a lot, fast."

CUSTOMS: French customs detained Madonna for hours when she arrived in **Cannes** in 1991, apparently **acting** on a tip that she would be smuggling **drugs**. She wasn't, and she later accused officials of searching her bags simply for the pleasure of having trudged through her unmentionables.

A repeat performance occurred with US customs in 1993. Officials demanded to inspect **Liz Rosenberg**'s bag (all press clippings), refusing to believe that Madonna & Co. had not bought anything while in Europe. "It was a **business** trip!" Rosenberg scolded, but Madonna wrapped things up by saying, "I know you just want to look through *my* luggage, so why don't you just *do it* and get it over with!"

"CYBER-RAGA": Sanskrit chant set to music that served as a bonus track on the Japanese and Australian CDs of *Ray of Light*. It reappeared as the B-side of her **"Music"** single and portions were used in Madonna's *MDNA Tour* performance of **"I'm a Sinner."**

CYRUS, MILEY: *b. November 23, 1992.* Disney Channel superstar who parlayed her **TV** fame on kiddie series *Hannah Montana* (2006–2011) into brief movie success and a massive music career.

Despite her country roots (she is the daughter of "Achy Breaky Heart"-throb Billy Ray Cyrus), Cyrus has long exhibited affection for Madonna. In 2008, when **"4 Minutes"** became a radio hit, Cyrus—known for epic **dance**-challenge videos on **YouTube**—created a video starring herself and her **talented** friends dancing to the song.

They first met May 19, 2013, backstage at the **Billboard Music Awards**, where Cyrus and Ke$ha posed for a picture sandwiching Madonna.

Madonna joined Cyrus as a guest on her *Miley Cyrus: MTV Unplugged* special, aired January 29, 2014. The two dueted on a medley of Madonna's **"Don't Tell Me"** and Cyrus's "We Can't Stop" (2013), dressed as outrageously tacky cowgirls. The dancing was kept to suggestive shimmying as Madonna was still suffering from a leg injury. Reviews of the performance were mixed (Madonna-loathing **Rufus Wainwright** called it "one of the most horrifying things I've seen in my life"), but the episode became the highest rated *Unplugged* installment in a decade.

Since then, the women have stayed in touch on social media, with Miley reposting an image of her face on Madonna's *Rebel Heart* cover. Madonna's final word on Cyrus, from 2015: "I see a lot of people getting really pissed off at Miley because she kind of just acts like a dude—but if she *were* a dude, no one would say anything."

"Leave her alone … She's gonna be 16 soon. And then 17, and then 18. And then she might show her knees, and then what's going to happen?"
—MADONNA DEFENDING MILEY CYRUS TO RYAN SEACREST (2008)

"[She's] the real queen."—MILEY ON MADONNA (2013)

Unique

–EVELYN "CHAMPAGNE" KING

FABIO DIENA

D

DAFOE, WILLEM: *b. July 22, 1955.* Gaunt, slightly seedy-looking leading man who shone in films like *Platoon* (1986), *The Last Temptation of Christ* (1988) and *The English Patient* (1996), and who starred as "Frank Dulaney" to Madonna's "Rebecca Carlson" in ***Body of Evidence***.

Dafoe and **Ciccone** *did* have good screen chemistry in the film. Of their initially **NC-17**-rated **sex** scenes, Dafoe said at the time, "They were great fun to do. Whether they're erotic or not, or whether they have to be erotic or not, I'm not sure."

He got along with Madonna **swimmingly**: "I like her a lot, and I think she gives a good performance. You can't **control** what baggage and expectations people bring into a movie about who this person is."

At a 2011 *John Carter* press event, Dafoe told the author what he was thinking at the time the film was made: "I was thinking a lot—before, during and after that movie! I think that movie would have done well if it had come out another time. I think maybe Madonna was overexposed at the time; it was too much." He also said that he didn't feel the movie was a *Basic Instinct* (1992) rip-off. Dafoe clarified that it had started as a much artier endeavor, and stressed how much he liked that the roles were flipped in the film, with Madonna in the traditionally male role and Dafoe in the traditionally female role.

"You know, I can't do an interview in **England** without being teased for *Body of Evidence*. It's like, 'Come on, guys—what's it been, 20 years?'"

"Gracious as a man, generous as an actor and absolutely the best pretend fuck I ever had."–MADONNA ON WILLEM DAFOE (1993)

DANCE: To dance is to be free, to take the chance of making a fool of yourself, to be so in touch with your body that you are able to express how you're feeling not with words but with actions.

Madonna and dancing are virtually synonymous.

Our girl's own first ambitions were **acting** and dancing—singing didn't come into the picture until much later. She taught herself to dance, then taught the other neighbor kids. At 12, she taught a boy to dance using "Honky Tonk Woman" (1969) by the Rolling Stones as the soundtrack, and this moment was so **powerful** it became an early association with **sexuality**. She would eventually go to dance classes of the jazz, tap, baton-twirling and gymnastics variety, calling it "a place to send hyperactive girls, basically."

In tenth grade, Madonna performed a dance she choreographed for a **talent** assembly in high **school**. Her guidance counselor, **Nancy Ryan Mitchell,** remembered to **VH1** in 2001 that Madonna "was a phenomenally great dancer, strutted her stuff, a little risqué, but her dance quality in the **art** took over and she was the hit of the talent assembly." Mitchell felt Madonna had star quality, thanks

Busting a move at an AIDS Dance-A-Thon

in large part to her diligence. "The thing I believe that set Madonna apart from many of the other talented kids in school is that she **worked** longer and harder at her dance."

The most influential person in her life was **Christopher Flynn,** 30 years older and her ballet teacher from her teens. Aside from continually encouraging her to pursue dance as a career, he took her to **gay** discos in the early '70s, where she first witnessed the sheer ecstasy of moving around in front of other people in a place where gay men could express themselves, providing her with a strong image of the sexual energy in dancing.

"Dancing is sexually provocative," she said in 1984. "It's moving to music, only you're by yourself. It's masturbatory. You're just moving your body to music ... Dancing and music and sex—they're all the same thing. It comes from your soul, ultimately."

©NANCY BARR-BRANDON

That image must've stuck, because it compelled Madonna to dance her way into a scholarship to the **University of Michigan**. Fellow dancer and roomie **Whitley Setrakian** said to **J. Randy Taraborrelli** of Madonna's technique, "Her front extensions were very high, which meant a lot at the time ... She took chances. She was raw, but we were all raw then."

Later, Madonna secured an impressive position under **Pearl Lang**, but realized that dancing would not be her best shot at achieving success as a performer. "When you're a dancer, you act, you perform with your body, and I think I had a lot of things to say in other ways besides movement," she said in 1984. Still, her music always had a danceability to it, whether hip-hop or **disco**. That danceability has never deserted the tunes, even as her lyrical content has evolved and her musicianship improved.

Madonna has always asked us to dance, beginning with **"Everybody"** and its plea to "dance and sing." She made dance a metaphor for sex and **love** with **"Into the Groove,"** perhaps her all-time best dance song, urging us to dance for "inspiration," preferably not all alone.

By 2005, Madonna had cooked a borderline concept album organized around dancing, ***Confessions on a Dance Floor***.

The extended dance mixes of her songs are sometimes the versions she executes onstage. Her contribution to the disco demimonde was immortalized on ***You Can Dance***, the first retrospective remix album.

Madonna's dance background has held her in good stead. Her dance-saturated videos like the ones for **"Lucky Star"** and **"Human Nature"** captivated enough imaginations to firmly cement her image in the minds of a wide audience. Her moves in her videos are often artistic as opposed to slick executions of current styles.

One way to separate Madonna's most irrational **fans** from her most irrational anti-fans is to play a record, ask them to dance and see who *can*.

"DANCE 2NIGHT" FEAT. JUSTIN TIMBERLAKE: Song featuring **Justin Timberlake**, written by him, Madonna, **Timbaland** and Hannon Lane. **"Dance** 2night" is a ***Hard Candy*** track produced by Timbaland, Timberlake, Lane and Demo Castellon. An underrated slice of '70s funk that re-states some of the same assertions found in **"American Life,"** but in a more palatable way, the song sounds like a lost track from **Michael Jackson**'s *Off the Wall* (1979).

DANCETERIA: *Formerly 30 W. 21st. St., NY, NY.* Legendary **NYC** club that existed in different locations throughout its seven-year (1979–1986) existence. Madonna was a frequent and enthusiastic patron as an aspiring musician, dancing her ass off many nights.

Most importantly to Madonna's career, this was the club where her demo was played by DJ **Mark Kamins**, getting such a great reaction that it led to Madonna's first record deal.

Madonna played Danceteria as a solo artist numerous

"THE THING ABOUT DANCING—WHAT IT TAUGHT ME ALL THOSE YEARS—IS IT GIVES YOU AN AMAZING SENSE OF DISCIPLINE IN FORCING YOURSELF TO DO THINGS THAT YOU KNOW ARE GOOD FOR YOU BUT YOU DON'T REALLY WANT TO DO. IT'S SELF-PRESERVATION."-MADONNA, *FLEXIPOP* (1983)

"SOMETIMES, I SING AND DANCE AROUND THE HOUSE IN MY UNDERWEAR. DOESN'T MAKE ME MADONNA. NEVER WILL."
-JOAN CUSACK AS "CYNTHIA," WORKING GIRL (1987)

"I DON'T LIKE OTHER PEOPLE'S IDEAS FOR HOW I SHOULD MOVE. I'M MY BEST CHOREOGRAPHER."-MADONNA (1999)

times, booked by Ruth Polsky, who was known for her keen ear for the emerging New Wave music scene. Madonna's full-price rate for a performance shortly after her record deal was $2,000. She played there on December 16, 1982, at good friend (and club doorman) **Haoui Montaug**'s **"No Entiendes!"** night, among many other gigs.

In 1984, Madonna was filmed dancing here as "Susan" and encountering costar Mark Blum as "Gary Glass" for a key ***Desperately Seeking Susan*** scene. Seventy-five authentic East Village punkers were employed to fill out Danceteria for the scene. When a frisky cameraman asked a pretty brunette punker what her name was, he was taken aback by "her" response: "It's *Clark*."

Because of its use in *Desperately Seeking Susan*, Danceteria also became immortalized in the makeshift video for Madonna's song from the film, **"Into the Groove."**

On the roof at Danceteria in 1983

"When Madonna danced, there was always a group of people that would surround her and watch her, her moves."-MARK KAMINS ON MADONNA'S DANCETERIA DAYS (2001)

© GEORGE-DUBOSE.COM

DANCIN' ON AIR: *Airdates: October 12, 1981–December 31, 1987.* Madonna appeared on this local Philadelphia music show lip-synching along to **"Everybody"** in 1982 with backup dancing by **Erika Belle** and **Bags Rilez**. The three made use of folding chairs and performed while the studio audience swayed directly behind them. Madonna's look was androgynous-light for what was surely one of her first **TV** appearances.

Michael Nise, who was an executive producer on the show, told *Star* **magazine** years later that Madonna "had something special."

DANGEROUS GAME: *Director: Abel Ferrara. Release date: November 19, 1993.* Gut-wrenching arthouse film starring Madonna, **Harvey Keitel** and James Russo that has been described as *Scenes from a Marriage* (1973) meets *The Player* (1992).

Madonna wanted to **work** with **Abel Ferrara** ever since seeing his acclaimed *Ms. 45* (1981), and **loved** his *Bad Lieutenant* (1992). With *Dangerous Game*, she got her chance to do so as actor *and* de facto producer: The film was produced by **Maverick**, with her manager **Freddy DeMann** also listed as a producer.

Be careful what you wish for.

Financially, *Dangerous Game* was disastrous. As a gritty

Madonna's *Dangerous Game* persona and performance were far more effective than she herself believed.

film made for less than $10 million, it was never going to make much, but its French run was only so-so, and in America it only made $56,798, winning 334th place (of 345) on the highest-grossing films of 1993 list. Even though *Dangerous Game* sold out its first two weeks in release, bringing in more per screen than the average Top 10 film, it had no staying **power**. Ferrara **fans** were turned off by Madonna and general audiences were turned off by Ferrara.

Maverick's first production was originally titled *The Last Pimp* and later called *Snake Eyes* for its European debut. It premiered in competition at the 50th Annual **Venice Film Festival**, garnering impressive reviews for film, director and actors. Its general release in France soon followed to an even more enthusiastic critical reception and a highly favorable cover story in the lofty *Cahiers du Cinema*.

But the French like Jerry Lewis, so American fans weren't sure what to expect when *Snake Eyes* became *Dangerous Game* (as the result of a suit by an adult-film director) and bowed at only one theater in **New York** City. Reaction was *wildly* mixed, running from raves to two-fisted attacks. When a film engenders such a passionate response, it is well worth seeing.

Dangerous Game is a film within a film, making use of conventional scenes and video shot with cameras in plain sight (Ferrara reportedly used rehearsal footage that the

actors never **dreamed** would be commercialized). The plot follows gonzo director "Eddie Israel" (Keitel) and his struggle to make a movie. He perceives his film, *Mother of Mirrors*, to be hard-hitting high art, but we the audience see it to be a shallow statement made by a director devoid of humanity, the result of the Hollywoodization of his vision.

Mother of Mirrors is the cautionary tale of a high-strung white-collar exec ("Francis Burns"/Russo) and his sexpot wife ("Sarah Jennings'"/Madonna), who gets religion. He becomes obsessed with reclaiming the whore that was displaced by this unwelcome virgin, and their relationship turns into one long shouting match-cum-**rape** scene. For a comparison in tone, note that Madonna's part had been conceived by writer Nicholas St. John and Ferrara as being like "Martha" in *Who's Afraid of Virginia Woolf?* (1966).

As both *Mother of Mirrors* and *Dangerous Game* progress, they trade places, so that the director's tawdry existence becomes ridiculously warped, and his film becomes disturbingly powerful.

Israel is directly based on Ferrara—his wife is played by Ferrara's real-life wife—and Sarah Jennings became a stand-in for Madonna herself, a popular star who wants to be taken seriously. Madonna didn't see how referential the film was, not even when her ex-husband **Sean Penn**'s best friend Russo was cast.

She has never given a richer, more interesting performance. She is utterly convincing as a shallow **TV-movie** queen with an unfulfilled ambition to break into serious film **acting**. Sarah is flashy, the kind of woman who will smoke a cigarette in key lighting while telling cobwebby dumb-**blonde** jokes, unaware of the **irony** that her own **hair** is as blonde as it comes.

"... [Madonna] plays an actress who's so bad, the director commits suicide. Who else would be better for the part?" Ferrara snarked in 2002.

Madonna as Sarah was completely fluid for the first time in any film; she moved about unselfconsciously, delivered her lines conversationally, effortlessly exuding **sexiness**. The effect was startling—she was almost like a young Jeanne Moreau, sophisticated and finally, finally put to good use on the big screen. Most deliciously, and probably accidentally, the performance that Sarah gives in *Mother of Mirrors*—which is supposed to be stiff and melodramatic—is the performance that Madonna gave in *Body of Evidence*. A plug for recycling.

"Madonna's good, but she has chosen the wrong projects and worked with a lot of idiots," Russo said. "She's pissing in the wind because everybody wants to see her fail."

Dangerous Game is a credible effort at meaningful cinema, but Madonna loathed the film, sending Ferrara a melt-down via fax in which she accused him of destroying her career.

Ferrara said in 2002 that he blamed the film's failure on Madonna, because she betrayed the film by badmouthing

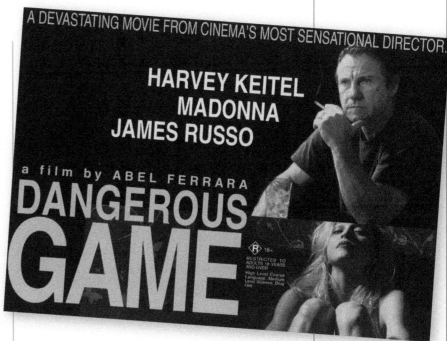

it. "And she actually got good reviews. She never got a good review from **The [Village] Voice** or *The New York Times* in her life, but she got good reviews for this movie, which she came out and trashed. I'll never forgive her for it."

• •

"THE TURKEY OF THE YEAR HAS ARRIVED JUST IN TIME FOR THANKSGIVING. *DANGEROUS GAME*, ABEL FERRARA'S NEW FILM, STARRING AMERICA'S FAVORITE FEMALE IMPERSONATOR, MADONNA, IS DANGEROUSLY DULL … HER ACTING STYLE IS MORE INDICATIVE THAN METHOD; SHE INDICATES EMOTIONS RATHER THAN EMBODYING THEM. SHE ISN'T SEXUAL; SHE'S ABOUT SEXUALITY. SHE ISN'T EROTIC; SHE'S ABOUT EROTICISM. WATCHING HER ACT IS A COLD EXPERIENCE."*-NEW YORK POST (1993)*

• •

"THE ROLE, WHICH ISN'T GLAMOROUS, IS FREE OF ARTIFICE IN A WAY THAT MADONNA'S SCREEN ROLES SELDOM ARE. VIEWERS MAY ACTUALLY HAVE TO REMIND THEMSELVES THAT THEY'VE SEEN THIS ACTRESS SOMEWHERE BEFORE."*-JANET MASLIN, THE NEW YORK TIMES (1993)*

• •

"MADONNA HAS EITHER LEARNED HOW TO ACT OR FINALLY FOUND A CHARACTER NOT SO DIFFERENT FROM HERSELF, WHOM SHE CAN SIMPLY *BE* FOR THE CAMERA. IN EITHER CASE, SHE'S TERRIFIC, EXACTLY WHAT THE ROLE REQUIRES … THOSE BRAVE ENOUGH TO BREATHE *DANGEROUS GAME'S* POISONOUS ATMOSPHERE SHOULD BRACE THEMSELVES FOR A CORROSIVE BUT REWARDING EXPERIENCE." *-NEW YORK PRESS (1993)*

• •

DANJA: *b. February 22, 1982.* Nate "Danja" Hills is a record producer known for his association with **Timbaland**. Along with hits like "Promiscuous" by Nelly Furtado (2006), "SexyBack" by **Justin Timberlake** (2006) and "Gimme More" by **Britney Spears** (2007), Danja has writing and producing credits on the *Hard* **Candy** songs **"4 Minutes," "Devil Wouldn't Recognize You," "Miles Away"** and **"Voices."**

According to a *Wall Street Journal* article from the mid-2000s, Danja was at the time charging $50,000–$100,000 per song for his services.

DARLING, CANDY: *November 24, 1944–March 21, 1974.* One of **Andy Warhol**'s most famous-for-being-famous Superstars was this trans woman who appeared in movies like Warhol's *Flesh* (1968).

In 2005, rumor had it that Madonna would play Darling for no pay in *Factory Girl* (2006), starring Sienna Miller as Edie Sedgwick. Considering the fact that Madonna was 47 at the time and Darling died of lymphoma at 29, the preposterous rumor did not come to pass.

DATELINE NBC: *Airdates: 1992–.* In 2003, Madonna sat for a series of interviews with **Matt Lauer** for this American news show. The footage became an hour-long special called *Madonna: An American Life*, originally aired April 29, 2003. Lauer and **Ciccone** sparred congenially but exhibited great chemistry on topics of her marriages and relationships (Madonna noted she either destroyed her good relationships or was just "a magnet for A-holes"), parenting, **Kabbalah**, *Swept Away*, *Will & Grace* and *American Life*. Madonna sang **"Mother and Father"** for Lauer, accompanying herself on the **guitar**, footage that was used exclusively for Lauer's morning show-gig, *Today*.

When asked by Lauer why she was still famous, Madonna reacted incredulously. "Once famous, always famous!" she exclaimed, citing the fact that **Marilyn Monroe** was still famous 40 years after her **death**. When pressed as to why people who started in the **business** alongside her were nowhere to be seen, Madonna said, "I don't know. Go ask them ... I'm not here to comment on other people. I mean, I still have things I wanna do and things I wanna say, and, y'know, if people wanna hear it, then that's great."

On the subject of **acting**, Lauer pointedly asked Madonna if she thinks she can act. She replied, "Yeah, I do."

The show then aired exclusive footage of her live Tower Records performances of **"American Life," "Hollywood"** and **"Like a Virgin."** Preparing to take the stage, Madonna admitted she's blanked on stage in the past and is often **nervous** about "doing a good **job**."

She returned to the show's November 1, 2006, episode for a lengthy chat with Meredith Vieira, granting the show her first primetime interview since her adoption of **David Banda**. "I didn't expect to be demonized," Madonna told Vieira, still reeling from the beating the media had been doling out.

DATES: Madonna's first date was with a boy named Colin McGregor in the sixth grade, with whom she went to see a movie called *House of Dark Shadows* (1970), based on the freaky soap opera. Hand-holding ensued.

Asked in 1984 whom she would rather date, **Simon Le Bon**, **Lionel Richie**, David Lee Roth or Rick Springfield—she replied, "Ugh. UGH. Yeeeuch! C'mon. I wouldn't go out with any of them if you want to know the truth. If I had to choose, I'd go out with David Lee Roth, but I wouldn't dress up for him."

In the '90s, Madonna described her perfect date as being comprised of dinner, a movie and a conversation over margaritas. Presumably, the hand-holding would **work** just as well now, so long as it isn't Le Bon's hand.

DAVID: SEE: **Banda, David.**

DAVIS, GEENA: *b. January 21, 1956.* An **Oscar**-winning supporting actress for *The Accidental Tourist* (1988) and leading lady of numerous '80s and '90s films.

Madonna shared the screen with Davis in *A League of Their Own*. Not long after, Madonna wrote bitterly of Davis nabbing the lead in *Angie*, a project close to Madonna's heart. Their first mutual project was actually in 1982, when both appeared as models in the **book** *Harriet Love's Guide to Vintage Chic*. Madonna, in an image by Fred Seidman originally shot for *The Village Voice*, wears an Adrian black gabardine suit jacket over a vintage tweed suit skirt. As stunning as she looked, Madonna was upstaged—Davis got the cover. There's no crying in vintage **fashion**, just icy stares and incredible lines.

DAYBREAK: *Airdates: September 6, 2010–April 25, 2014.* To promote *MDNA*, Madonna granted a sit-down interview to Dan Wootton for the April 20, 2012, episode of this British **TV** show and sister show *Lorraine*. In the interview, strung out across the entire morning, Wootton excitedly pumped Madonna for lots of pop culture reactions and goss. When he brought up **Adele**, Madonna gushed, "I would **love** to meet her. I think she's brilliant." She also revealed that Adele had been on her shortlist to join her musically at the **Super Bowl** halftime show.

Wootton asked Madonna if she ever makes mistakes. She copped to doing so, as close as she'll ever get to owning actual **regrets**. "I still make mistakes and I have to say I'm sorry to people."

DE BECKER, GAVIN: *b. October 26, 1954.* Safety/security expert employed by Madonna (and, at various times, the likes of **Michael Jackson, Olivia Newton-John**, Robert Redford and **Tina Turner**). He and his team kept records of dangerous fanatics who were a threat to Madonna's security, monitoring their whereabouts as closely as possible. De Becker was also charged with keeping her projects under wraps: He called in the **FBI** when photos from *Sex* were stolen.

–DON BACHARDY

DE LEMPICKA, TAMARA: *May 16, 1898–March 18, 1980.* Polish **art** deco painter whose **work**, especially that from the '20s and '30s, presented male and female figures with sleek, cold, knowing looks and uncompromising glamour. Art-lover Madonna has long been a great **fan** of de Lempicka's; she owns several examples of her work.

De Lempicka's stylized renderings heavily influenced the look of the **"Express Yourself"** video, and her work has been shown on the *Who's That Girl World Tour* and in the videos for **"Open Your Heart"** and **"Vogue."**

DE LORY, DONNA: *b. September 10, 1964.* Along with **Niki Haris**, Madonna's most famous backing vocalist, and one of the creative partners with whom Madonna **worked** over the longest span of time—20 solid years.

De Lory's first association with Madonna came when she did the vocals on a demo for **"Open Your Heart,"** written by her boyfriend, Gardner Cole. Madonna snapped up the track for *True Blue*.

When the *Who's That Girl World Tour* came up, De Lory heard Madonna "only wanted black girls," but when one person was fired last-second, De Lory got the call to audition. She wound up a primary backup singer/dancer on every Madonna tour from the *Who's That Girl World Tour* through the *Confessions Tour*. One of the reasons was how compatible and complementary her **voice** is to Madonna's. During *Who's That Girl World Tour* rehearsals, Madonna at one point asked De Lory why she wasn't singing. When it was pointed out that she *was* singing, but that Madonna couldn't hear it because their voices blended so seamlessly, Madonna was blown away.

While on the *Drowned World Tour*, De Lory said, "It's great, but you know, we're not curing **cancer** here. It's show **business**; we're making people feel good. But I'm still grateful that I'm here. I still feel proud. What keeps me here is a respect for what Madonna's doing."

De Lory provided backing vocals on all of Madonna's albums from *Like a Prayer* through *Ray of Light* and joined Madonna and Haris in performing **"Express Yourself"** on the **MTV Video Music Awards** in 1989.

The women stopped working together at least in part due to what De Lory perceived as pressure to embrace **Kabbalah**. "Kabbalah, all of a sudden, was mandatory. I thought it couldn't hurt, but it wasn't my belief system per se. However, two times the teacher tied on the [Kabbalah symbol of the] red string, and two times I watched it untie and come off me. They tie these things and knot them and they aren't supposed to come off for a long time. After it came off two times on its own, I figured that I didn't need that to protect me."

De Lory's presence has been sorely missed by **fans**, many of whom would gladly trade Kabbalah for her.

She has a solo recording career of her own that was launched with 1992's *Praying for **Love*** album. The second single from that album, **"Just a Dream,"** was cowritten and coproduced by Madonna and **Patrick Leonard** and had been recorded by Madonna for *Like a Prayer*. De Lory's version (a **dance** hit) features Madonna backing *her* for a change. Her later work is devotional in nature. In other words, very *much* like a prayer.

In 2013, De Lory reteamed with Haris on the track "Kinder" from her *The Unchanging* album. If it could be likened to anything in Madonna's catalogue, it could be called an a cappella number from *American Life*. De Lory and Haris released a cover of **"Rain"** in 2015.

> "I had a French boyfriend I met on the first tour. We were going to break up, but we were holding off. So I was off with Madonna in London and they asked me if I had ever messed around on my boyfriend and I told the truth. Sitting in the screening, I was so afraid, even though I was breaking up with my boyfriend, that he would see this … Luckily, none of that about me ended up in there."—DONNA DE LORY ON *TRUTH OR DARE* (2013)

DE VRIES, MARIUS: *b. 1961.* Accomplished British producer and songwriter who played keyboards for the Blow Monkeys, whose "Digging Your Scene" was a #14 hit in the US back in 1986. Madonna collaborated with him on her *Ray of Light* album, resulting in his coproduction credits on **"Little Star," "Skin"** and the single **"Nothing Really Matters."** Madonna had previously recorded **"Bedtime Story,"** a song cowritten by de Vries with **Nellee Hooper** and **Björk**, that appeared on *Bedtime Stories*.

DEADMAU5: SEE: Ultra Music Festival.

DEAN, KILEY: *b. April 12, 1982.* Glam **blonde** backup singer for Madonna since her *Sticky & Sweet Tour*. Dean previously toured as an opening act for **Britney Spears**. In 2011, she told YouKnowIGotSoul.com that in spite of her aspirations as a solo artist, she didn't hesitate when asked to sing with Madonna. "It's very humbling because what Madonna is doing is what I want to be doing ultimately. To work for somebody like her who is an icon … I know a lot of people think they're too proud or too good. Well, I'm not too proud. I want to win."

MATTHEW RETTENMUND

Kiley Dean and Nicki Richards in 2013

"DEAR JESSIE" (SONG): *Release date: December 10, 1989. Billboard Hot 100 peak: NA.* **Beatles**-esque song from *Like a Prayer* that was a Top 10 hit abroad, though not released as a single in the US. The song, written and produced by Madonna and **Patrick Leonard**, is named for his daughter, Jessie, with whom Madonna once shared a very close, godmotherlike relationship.

"At Madonna's **birthday** party," Leonard said in 1989, "they **danced** for about two hours together. In fact, Madonna got her drunk on champagne—I could *kill* her."

"DEAR JESSIE" (VIDEO): *Director: Derek Hayes, 1989.* With no participation from Madonna forthcoming, the video for her final non-US single from *Like a Prayer* was commissioned by **Warner Bros.** from Animation City in the UK. The whimsical video features Madonna as "Tinker Bell," in a rendering strongly reminiscent of the animated "Nikki Finn" seen in the credits of *Who's That Girl*. In the live-action portion, a sleeping little girl is shown **dreaming** of fantastical scenes reflective of the song's lyrics, done in a variety of animation styles. Yes, there is a pink elephant.

"Dear Jessie" has been ignored when it comes to Madonna's official video compilations.

DEATH: Asked how she wants to die, Madonna in 1999 told *Arena* **magazine**, "I'd like to die ready." She references **yoga** as a way to learn about how to prepare for death.

The public and the media are equally enthralled by the concept of Madonna's death, as exemplified by the **rumors** that swept Europe in August 1987 that Madonna had died in a California car crash and that US officials were covering it up.

Madonna has died on-screen—we're talking her characters, not her performances—several times. If her melodramatic death scene in *Dick Tracy* was an impressive dramatic stretch, her deathbed scene at the end of *Evita* probably got her to within an inch of getting an **Oscar** nomination.

Madonna's shot to the head in *Dangerous Game* was a tense edge-of-your-seater, and her murder at the hands of Mr. Wrong in the **"Bad Girl"** video was effectively a **PSA** against one-night stands. Probably her worst death scene was at the end of *Body of Evidence*, if only because it felt like a creative decision meant to punish a character unrepentant in her adoration of getting horizontal.

When Madonna dies in real life (ages from now!), look for a mind-boggling critical reassessment of her **work** ... and expect your phone to blow up.

"DEEPER AND DEEPER" (SONG): *Release date: December 8, 1992. Billboard Hot 100 peak: #7.* Cowritten by Madonna, **Shep Pettibone** and **Tony Shimkin** and produced by Madonna and Pettibone in late 1991, the second single off *Erotica* was a return to **dance**-floor form for Madonna.

It's a purely **disco** song about **love**, a happy marriage of **"Express Yourself"** and **"Vogue,"** the **lyrics** of which "Deeper and Deeper" actually incorporates at its climactic finish. "Deeper and Deeper" is Madonna's "I Will Survive" (1978), tapping into that song's determination and drive, and also evoking **gay** love with its repeated, heady exclamations that the singer will never hide her love again. How gay is it? So gay it quotes *The Sound of Music* (1959). So, it's not only gay, it's a **power** bottom.

Performed live on *The Girlie Show World Tour*, the song's roots and subtext were brought to the fore: It was performed in full '70s gear—complete with afros, glitterball, sequined shorts and a stageful of androgynes. It was transformed into jazz for her *Re-Invention World Tour* and nearly made the cut for her *Confessions Tour*. A faithful rendition of the song was one highlight of her *Rebel Heart Tour*.

"DEEPER AND DEEPER" (VIDEO): *Director: Bobby Woods, 1992.* Even as she was facing indifference or outright hostility during her *Erotica* and *Sex* era, Madonna was still pouring lots of energy into her music videos, as is evidenced by the creatively costumed, conceptually tight and energetic clip for "Deeper and Deeper," shot at The Roxbury (formerly 8225 W. Sunset Blvd., W. Hollywood, CA).

The self-referential video offers Madonna driving (very reminiscent of her **"Burning Up"** video), has strobe-lit **black-and-white** segments that echo the video for **"Erotica"** and brought to life a song with explicit references to her **"Vogue"** single.

"Deeper and Deeper" begins with a heavy quote about letting go of one's demons, and then loosely tells the tale of a Madonna-like star, clad in a sheer gown and boa, who goes back to her roots in a club to see if any of her old friends—and her old Svengali-like flame, played by creeptastic **Udo Kier**—are still around. The **Andy Warhol** vibe is strengthened by Madonna's momentary **love** interest, a Joe Dallessandro look-alike. (Not played by **Joey Stefano**, contrary to what is reported by some sources.)

Fashion-wise, Madonna got to dress up in '70s gear, including bellbottoms and platforms. So taken was she with the **look** that she inserted an entire breakaway to a photo shoot where her character parades in more period fashions (used in a **Steven Meisel** *Italian Vogue* layout), sans **eyebrows**.

There are lots of delish cameos, including **Ingrid Casares, porn** director Chi Chi LaRue, former Warhol Superstars Maria and Geraldine Smith and Holly Woodlawn, Sims Ellison of the rock group Pariah (he committed suicide in 1995), her future manager **Guy Oseary**, the man who signed her to **Sire Records, Seymour Stein**, and more.

Freshest are the scenes involving an all-girl slumber party featuring **Debi Mazar, Sofia Coppola** and Madonna, who sports a **blonde** afro à la **Marlene Dietrich** in *Blonde Venus* (1932). The women nonchalantly peel and eat bananas while watching a male friend strike beefcake poses in his **underwear**, listening to a record bearing the **Maverick** label. Their at first zombie-like reaction is reminiscent of those infamous Popsicle-licking twins from *The Gong Show* (1977–1980).

Ending like *Cinderella*, the video shows Madonna's character frantically abandoning the **disco** (the past?) ... or at least trying.

Negative reactions to the video might have to be reassessed in light of its unique position as one of the only unabashedly **nostalgia**-courting things in Madonna's oeuvre.

"... [T]hey called me over for another shot—and Madonna acted like she didn't know me. She said, 'What's your name again?' and when I said Larry, she turned to the director and said, 'I want *Chi Chi* to pretend that she's buying drugs from those guys.'"

—CHI CHI LARUE ON "DEEPER AND DEEPER" (1996)

"The dance sequences in the video are 100% spontaneous. We loaded a dance floor with people, put her record on, and the dancing began. I have danced with Madonna many times, so I can understand why those people wanted to dance with her as well. It's a thrill."—BOBBY WOODS ON "DEEPER AND DEEPER" (2008)

DEGENERES, ELLEN: *b. January 26, 1958.* Emmy-winning talk show host whose *The Ellen DeGeneres Show* (September 8, 2003–) is a daytime powerhouse on American **TV**. The host, one of the first major stars to come out as a lesbian, has advocated on behalf of LGBT issues, animal rights and disadvantaged kids. Her humor is cheeky, but for the most part is characterized by wholesomeness. She opens each episode by dancing, occasionally to Madonna music.

DeGeneres is a big Madonna **fan**, and has hosted her on her show several times.

Madonna's 2006 sit-down with DeGeneres—her first—happened immediately after the **Grammys**, with Madonna still tricked out in her glittering costume. Madonna reiterated that she rarely watches TV (not even Ellen's show!), but liked the **original** British version of *The Office* (2001–2003). She also denied rumors that she and **Guy Ritchie** had split up. In speaking about Ritchie's less enthusiastic approach to **Kabbalah**, she noted that "Brits are sort of allergic" to religion. At the end of the segment, the women **danced** to "Sorry."

In 2010, with the issue of bullying in the news, Madonna did a remote interview with DeGeneres to say, "I just feel like it would be incredibly remiss of me to not say

something. I am incredibly disturbed and saddened by the overwhelming number of teen suicides that have been reported lately, um, because of bullying. I mean, suicide in general is disturbing, teenagers committing suicide is extremely disturbing, but to hear that children, teenagers are taking their lives because they're being bullied in **schools**, dormitories, what have you, is kind of unfathomable ..."

In 2012, Madonna appeared on the show in her **"Vogue"** outfit from *The MDNA Tour*, DeGeneres wearing her own version of the **cone-bra** look. To raise $10,000 for breast **cancer**, Madonna brought her son **Rocco** out and let Ellen douse him in water. Rocco, 12, was begrudgingly interviewed by DeGeneres, saying Madonna "is a good **mother**" and confessing that he didn't see those parts of the tour during which Madonna flashed her breasts.

During this appearance, DeGeneres confirmed that Madonna had called to offer words of encouragement before she came out as **gay**: "It's Madonna, and I just wanna say that I'm behind you, I'm with you, I support you."

Madonna appeared on every episode the week of March 16–20, 2015. On the 16th, she was shown in a pre-taped video demanding that DeGeneres wear fishnets in order to get Madonna on the show. The host called Madonna's tone in the video "scary."

On the 17th, Madonna was shown giving DeGeneres a wide-ranging interview, which touched on her **Brit Awards** disaster, her appreciation for **Kanye West**'s un-PC mouth, her affection for dating youngsters and her desire for more, not less, attention. Madonna performed a remix of **"Living for Love"** on the show, her first daytime TV performance since *The Oprah Winfrey Show* in 1998.

On the 18th, Madonna played "Never Have I Ever" with DeGeneres and fellow guest Justin Bieber. In the game, the three had to hold up paddles indicating whether or not they had ever or had never participated in a variety of scenarios. Madonna copped to having phone **sex**, using someone's toothbrush without telling them, fooling around in a bathroom during a party, dating someone and their sibling, fooling around while someone else was in the room and forgetting the name of the person with whom she was fooling around. She denied ever having gotten kicked out of a bar. Invited to create her own question, Madonna asked about "having sex with more than two different people in one day." Only Madonna admitted doing that. In contrast to the game, she contributed a sweet and sensitive performance of **"Joan of Arc."** Madonna wore a dramatic Schiaparelli dress with a distinctive arrows-through-the-heart design that eagle-**eyed** fashionistas recognized as being directly inspired by a Howard Greer dress worn by Ginger Rogers in the 1938 film *Carefree*.

For her March 19, 2015, appearance, a previously taped performance of **"Ghosttown"** aired. It was her first live take of the song in the US market. Somehow, virtually no one noticed that Madonna's background video used footage from **9/11** of the Twin Towers collapsing;

"Things come to you when you let go and you don't care and need the validation anymore."
—MADONNA TO A THEN-CLOSETED ELLEN DEGENERES (1997)

it was a non-issue on social media, where Madonna received positive feedback for the performance the same week *Rebel Heart* nonetheless tumbled in sales.

DeGeneres revived her "Bathroom Concert Series" on the 20th, airing a pre-taped performance of **"Dress You Up"** that she and Madonna did as a funny duet. Funny or not, Madonna sang the song perfectly, whetting appetites for a proper airing in concert.

Madonna and DeGeneres are allegedly 11th cousins, depending how much faith one places in deep-geneaology.

DEMANN, FREDDY: The former manager of **Michael Jackson,** axed after Michael's **father** Joe ignited a racial war of words with the man he claimed to have hired "when I felt I needed white help in dealing with the corporate structure at CBS."

Madonna pursued DeMann for management, mistakenly believing he still represented Jackson, the kind of all-around entertainer she aspired to be. **Seymour Stein** introduced them.

After meeting with her in July 1983, DeMann was compelled to scout her out at a **Studio 54**. He was floored and inked her posthaste.

Madonna remembers DeMann as being "white as a ghost" after her 1st Annual **MTV Video Music Awards** performance, telling her he was "very disappointed" in her.

DeMann's star turn came in *Truth or Dare*—he's the charmingly exasperated hustler who bets the Canadian cops that not only would his client refuse to tone down her act to avoid arrest, she'd make it even racier.

It was just as well that Jackson wasn't on DeMann's roster when he took on Madonna: He still managed other acts, but managing Madonna kept his plate full and his pockets noisy (he got 10 percent of *everything* she grossed). He managed her from 1983 until 1998, when an acrimonious split proved sticky indeed, since DeMann was intricately involved with Madonna's **Maverick** venture. She reportedly had to buy him out for at least $20 million.

DEMARCHELIER, PATRICK: *b. August 21, 1943.* French **fashion** photographer whose **work** with all the top **magazines** put him on a collision course with Madonna.

Demarchelier first shot Madonna for the May 1989 issue of American *Vogue*, eating **popcorn** and enjoying a dip in her pool. He soon after shot her in character as "Breathless Mahoney" in *Dick Tracy* promo photos, two of which adorned the front and back covers of *I'm Breathless: Music from and Inspired by the Film Dick Tracy.*

Demarchelier also captured Madonna for the cover of *Glamour* (December 1990). Another look from that shoot, of Madonna in Marlon Brando gear, was the one that

Unseen original cover of all-M publication *Madonna! Superstar of the Century* (1996)

became the cover of her **"Justify My Love"** single. He did the *Bedtime Stories* packaging shoot and shot her 1999 *Harper's Bazaar* geisha-themed cover story.

DESPERATELY SEEKING SUSAN: *Director: Susan Seidelman. Release date: March 29, 1985.* Just as **Marlene Dietrich** had *The Blue Angel* (1930)—not her first film but her early, iconic breakthrough—so Madonna had *Desperately Seeking Susan*, the best film in which she's ever appeared, and the one featuring her most likable, most indelible screen performance. It is one of the reasons she had a very, very good 1985, along with the massive success of her *Like a Virgin* album and her on-the-road thriller, *The Virgin Tour*.

"I can't postulate what kind of response the film would have gotten had Madonna's star not risen so fantastically in such a short period of time," director **Susan Seidelman** told *The New York Times* in 2010, "... [S]he had this movie, and had the movie not been well-received, it wouldn't have mattered. But the fact that she's good in the movie, people seemed to like the movie and she suddenly had this meteoric album—all that converged. So much about what makes something happen or not happen has to do with having the right stuff at the right time."

Even as her debut album *Madonna* was kicking out pop singles, Madonna was pursuing a film career. She told Aussie writer **Ian "Molly" Meldrum**, "I arrived in **New York** a **dancer**, got involved in music, but I've always been interested in film ... whether it be a musical film with me singing or without music. Film to me is the ultimate visual."

She knew immediately that "Susan" was a role she could handle. "When I read the script to *Desperately Seeking Susan*," she said in the '80s, "I felt immediately that I could play the part. Susan is the quintessential femme fatale. Everyone wants to know her. Everyone wants to be like her. She has no roots, she represents freedom and adventure and all the things that normal people think they can't do."

In order to secure the supporting (but title) role in Seidelman's follow-up to *Smithereens* (1982), produced by Midge Sanford and **Sarah Pillsbury**, Madonna first had to beat out a host of other actors who had read for or been considered for the role, including Ellen Barkin, Melanie Griffith, Jennifer Jason Leigh, Kelly McGillis and Lori Singer. (Before the part had been retooled into that of a downtown diva, Goldie Hawn and **Diane Keaton** had been possibilities.) Nearly a cinematic virgin (she'd done "**art**" films and played a singer in *Vision Quest*), Madonna was not the producers' first choice, but Seidelman felt her Soho neighbor *was* Susan, so she pushed hard. "So much in life depends on timing ... luck and timing ..." Seidelman said in 2015, yet she left out a third factor in the case of *Desperately Seeking Susan*: vision.

"Most comedy is geared to 12-year-olds, so you have a lot of throwing-up jokes. *Smithereens* and *Susan* are not youth films," Seidelman asserted in *The Video Age*. "I think my style is young and the look is young, but *Smithereens* is a tough film. *Susan* is a happier film, but they both have **irony** and humor."

Madonna shot an audition reel with Seidelman and DP Ed Lachman in Union Square, where Seidelman heard someone say, "That's **Cyndi Lauper!**" She then did a screen test with Tim Ransom, who would later appear in the film as a bellhop in the last scene of the entire shoot. Madonna wasn't great in her tests, so she was sent to **acting** lessons for a month. Her final screen test, while still imperfect, showed enough improvement that the **powers** that be signed off on her, with reservations.

Madonna later explained her desire to play the part trumped the hoops she had to jump through: "I chose the film because I really **loved** the character and identified with her." She drew explicit parallels between herself and Susan in 1985: "People would say, 'You don't have a **job**, how do you live? How are you paying your rent? Where'd you get what you're wearing?' People couldn't understand how I could get away with those things. But I did ... I thought I shared a lot with 'Susan' ... She charms her way into every situation, gets guys to take her out to dinner and girlfriends to let her stay at their apartments, and she borrows their clothes, and trades, swaps and barters. She's a clever con artist and she doesn't let you know when you're being conned."

Indeed, Susan is the closest Madonna's ever come to playing herself, including appearances on talk shows.

Having survived the audition process, Madonna was officially cast in July 1984 and negotiated a salary of $80,000, the entire budget of Seidelman's previous film, but still five times less than her winsome costar **Rosanna Arquette**. Arquette was something of an "It" girl, so she did not have to beat out a slate of other actors for her part—Keaton (again) had been a real possibility, **Barbra Streisand**'s name had been mentioned in passing and Jennifer Tilly was floated as an alternate. (In 1999, Tilly chose Madonna's Susan as her favorite film character because, "She has an unstructured way of life, a free spirit and, of course, fabulous clothes and jewelry.")

Shooting in various NYC locations, *Susan* had no problems ... at first. In 1986, Seidelman told *The Video Age*, "On Madonna's first day, we were shooting in the street. She wasn't mobbed; she could still walk down the street and hang out. One month into filming, her album *Like a Virgin* came out. By the time of the opening in Los Angeles, she had an entourage of three huge bodyguards. It became quite apparent that this person couldn't go out without causing a major riot. She is unbelievably famous."

Photographing Madonna and the cast during filming was a challenge, too, but one that still photographer **Andy Schwartz** tells *EM20* was memorable, "Madonna was great to **work** with on *Desperately Seeking Susan*. She certainly had a distinct static electricity about her ... To me, she was smart, approachable and a genuinely happy person with a purpose."

Madonna remembered the filming of *Susan* as an example of being pulled in every direction at once. "I was working on the set every day and people were calling me up to do interviews or photo sessions—you start to feel like you've got a split personality," she said the year the film was released. "It was confusing, but if everything is timed right you can work it out. You have to have a pretty clear head on your shoulders, though."

One of the most important off-set things that happened during filming was a photo shoot on a Saturday with **Herb Ritts** that Madonna and Rosanna Arquette did. It was Madonna's first introduction to the man whose work would help define her image, and who would remain a close friend of hers until his **death** 20 years later. Those images became the movie poster and immediately became pop cultural and style touchstones.

Susan is a happy-go-lucky farce, a screwball comedy that plays out in slow motion, giving Seidelman's thirsty camera plenty of time to absorb New York City in all its seedy, scrappy, outlandish, 1984 glory—there's even a glimpse inside **Danceteria**.

Arquette plays "Roberta Glass," a Fort Lee, New Jersey, woman (the **original** desperate housewife) so bored with her marriage to cheesy hot tub salesman "Gary Glass" (Mark Blum) that she gets off on following a series of romantic personal ads placed in the fictitious tabloid *The Mirror* by a man named "Jimmy" (**Robert Joy**, who beat out **Bruce Willis** for the part) for the benefit of a mysterious woman called "Susan" (Madonna). When the ad "DESPERATELY SEEKING SUSAN" appears, Roberta knows (and romantically hopes) that trouble may be brewing, so she goes to the bench in Battery Park where the **lovers** are set to meet, hoping to catch a glimpse.

ALEJANDRO MOGOLLO

She voyeuristically observes Susan and Jimmy passionately kissing good-bye as his rock band departs (in the coolest van ever) for a gig in Buffalo, then follows Susan around the Lower East Side. When Susan trades her far-out jacket for a pair of killer boots at Love Saves the Day (formerly 119 Second Ave., NY, NY; it closed in January 2009, and the building was destroyed in a freak gas explosion in 2015), Roberta buys the jacket and takes it home, obsessing over the Polaroid selfie of Susan inside and worrying that the key she finds in one of the pockets may be important to the woman through whom she's living vicariously.

Deciding the time may be right for a meet-up, Roberta places an ad for Susan to meet in Battery Park, offering the key as bait, but Susan gets arrested for bailing on cab fare, leaving Roberta to deal with a shady character (Will Patton) who thinks Roberta is Susan. He gets rough, causing Roberta to suffer a konk on the head that leaves *her* thinking she's Susan, too. What she hadn't bargained for was the fact that Susan has gotten herself mixed up in an international smuggling operation and is unknowingly in possession of some priceless earrings that belonged to Nefertiti … *no shit!*

Now functioning as Susan, Roberta relies on Jimmy's blue-**eyed** hunk of a best buddy, "Dez" (Aidan Quinn), who carts her around the city in an effort to clear her amnesia

Therein lies the rub … Madonna with Tim Ransom on the *Susan* set

and reluctantly allows her to crash in his dank loft after they use the key to retrieve Susan's personal belongings from a Port Authority (W. 42nd St. & Eighth Ave., NY, NY) locker. In the meantime, Susan and Gary—along with his obnoxious sister "Leslie" (Laurie Metcalf)—team up to find Roberta. Both parties want their possessions back—Susan wants her pilfered silverware, mesh tanks and Polaroids, Gary wants his wife.

Arriving at The Magic Club (SEE: **Audobon Ballroom**) courtesy of a postcard found amongst Susan's things, Roberta takes over as the lovely assistant of a low-rent magician named "Ian" (Peter Maloney), but is eventually stalked by the man who previously **assaulted** her and when caught, konks her head again— this time, the blow reverses her amnesia, leaving her with the difficult decision of whether to continue a budding romance with Dez, who believes he is stabbing his pal Jimmy in the back by sleeping with the girl he believes to be Susan. *Whew!*

Roberta confesses her identity, but Dez isn't buying what he figures is another mindfuck by the wily girl Jimmy's warned him all about.

In the end, all roads lead to The Magic Club, where Roberta and Susan finally meet and team up to defeat the murderous thief after their earrings, and Roberta works up the courage to dump Gary. The film ends with Roberta and Dez in love, Susan and Jimmy reunited and Nefertiti's earrings returned … good goin', strangers!

Madonna shines in the role, coming off as a siren for the ages, and Rosanna Arquette is so wonderful that she won not only strong reviews but a British Academy **Award** (inexplicably, for *supporting* actress).

Casting directors Risa Bramon and Billy Hopkins, known for their work in the theater, made their film debuts with *Desperately Seeking Susan*, hitting a homerun with their uncannily spot-on selection of actors at every level. Metcalf steals every scene she's in thanks to her genius timing and hysterical one-liners (courtesy of screenwriter Leora Barish) and the incredible ensemble cast includes the likes of Richard Edson, Giancarlo Esposito, Annie Golden, Anna Levine, Ann Magnuson, John Turturro and Steven Wright in small but effective roles.

Esposito, who had a tiny part as a street vendor whose table is disrupted by a distracted

ANDY SCHWARTZ

Madonna's "Susan" eats junk food and models bras.

Roberta, tells *EM20*, "I had a great time on that. It's a great movie. I really got along with the director."

Two aspects of the film that also help elevate it from a typical multiplex comedy are its production design (characterized by surrealist color gels) and costume design, both by Santo Loquasto, who would go on to become one of the most acclaimed production designers in the industry, including his work on many **Woody Allen** films. Though Madonna resisted some of his costuming, incorporating some of her own **Maripol**-fueled style, the pyramid jacket ("It was black and gold and it had a sort of a pyramid thing on it, like on a dollar bill") became iconic.

Then there is the fact that the real star of the film—not to dismiss the dazzling work of Arquette—is New York City. Ransom sums it up by telling *EM20*, "All I would say is that being a (small) part of making that movie remains and always will be among my fondest of **memories**, and my affection for [Madonna] back then was deeply felt. I truly enjoyed my time around her in the NYC of a bygone era, which she was such a pure product of. What fun we had shooting all over that incredible city, a place that no longer exists except in memory, unfortunately." (At the end of filming, Madonna gave all of her coworkers a signed *Like a Virgin* poster or album. To Ransom, she wrote, "You can be my second husband after therapy.")

It's important to note that the movie's **feminist** message was made manifest by its creation. "It was kind of interesting and in actual point amazing that in ... 1984 ... Orion Pictures financed *Desperately Seeking Susan*, which was directed by a, well, I was a second-time director, having made this other small, independent film, with two first-time female producers, a female screenwriter and two female stars. To me, that was really kind of a breakthrough," Seidelman said in 2015.

"A female-driven movie about females? It just didn't happen like that. You didn't see films with women running them in every way, shape, or form," Arquette said in 2011.

In spite of the many female hands that made *Desperately Seeking* Susan a great film—*The New York Times* selected it as one of the 10 best of 1985—Madonna's lighting-fast ascension from little-known pop singer to superstar that occurred during filming led it to take on the unofficial moniker "The Madonna Movie," a phrase Orion actually used to sell it when it hit the home video market.

Susan garnered positive reviews and was a sensation at the box office, raking in $27,398,584, making it the 31st highest-grossing film of the year.

Speaking at a 2015 presentation of the film at NYC's Museum of Modern Art (11 W. 53rd St., NY, NY), Seidelman said, "You know, when you make a movie you never know—you kinda hope it will do okay opening week at the box office, then you hope it will stick around a couple of weeks...or if you're lucky a month or two, but you never really think that people are gonna be watching it up on a big screen 30 years later ..."

EVERYBODY I KNOW IS DESPERATE:
AN INTERVIEW WITH
DESPERATELY SEEKING SUSAN'S
PUBLICIST

Reid Rosefelt was the man in charge of publicizing *Desperately Seeking Susan*, a smalltime movie with one rising star (Rosanna Arquette) and lots of unknowns, including a pop singer with the preposterous name of "Madonna." What started as simply his first job as unit publicist on a feature film turned into an '80s adventure in an impossibly short span of time as the singer became one of the most famous women on the planet and the smalltime movie became one of the buzzed-about hits of 1985.

Rosefelt was there many days that *Susan* filmed, worked with still photographer Andy Schwartz, attended Madonna and Arquette's Herb Ritts shoot and then set about sending images to countless publications.

He would also wind up escorting Madonna to a party for the film *Amadeus*, at which she was famously snapped by Patrick McMullan.

Rosefelt is a born storyteller, as is evidenced by his informative blog at ReidRosefelt.com, and by his sharp recollections of his time working on *Susan*. In some ways, he's still working on the movie, connecting *EM2O* with several players from the film and taking time out to help get the story all down, and get it all down right.

EM2O: Do you remember the first scene shot for *Desperately Seeking Susan*?

REID ROSEFELT: The very first shot was on St. Mark's Place–it was Richard Edson from *Stranger Than Paradise* [1984] going into the outside newspaper thing.

In order to shoot that shot, we had to move everybody away, block it off, then bring in *our* extras who were dressed just *like* everybody. [Laughs] We had to hire people who were dressed the same because we were trying to capture that. So it was fantasy.

People did care a lot about what they looked like. Is there a Klaus Nomi today? We had a whole town full of 'em. People were inventing themselves by the way they looked. For example, the scene in Danceteria, that was just a leafletting for extras: Do you wanna be part of a movie? I doubt many people were in that scene who weren't wearing their own clothes.

EM2O: How did the film come to you?

RR: I'd always dreamed of doing a production publicity job. I really wanted that job, in spite of all the stuff I'd done, but it never worked out because in order to get your first shot, and not *be* somebody, you have to *know* somebody. [Executive producer] Michael Peyser had tried to get me on *Arthur* [1981], there were people who had tried to get me on jobs and failed, because there was always somebody who would say, "I know this [other] person."

Desperately Seeking Susan is defined as a film of people doing something for the first time. Pretty much everyone, in some way. Susan Seidelman hadn't made a film for a studio, Aidan Quinn had done a film that had not come out yet called *Reckless* [1984]. Only

Rosanna was hot–you can't believe how hot she was because of *Executioner's Song* [1982] and *Baby It's You* [1983]–these were big deals. She was just at the point where ... I mean, in the production office, down the hall was the *After Hours* [1985] production office. She had just worked with Scorsese, for Christ's sake.

How did I get the job? I knew Susan [Seidelman]. I had done some work on *Smithereens* [1982], so I knew her. So she called me and we went out to breakfast and she said, "I'm doing this movie," and I was excited about that because I thought she would probably get me on it and I was happy for her, too. I lived on Center Market Place. Madonna lived a few blocks away. Jim Jarmusch–with whom I was working on *Stranger Than Paradise* at the time–lived a few blocks away in the other direction. Everybody lived a few blocks away.

EM2O: What did she say about Madonna?

RR: She said, "I want this singer Madonna to play Susan–the studio does not want her. They really don't want her." If you think of it from the perspective of Mike Medavoy and Orion and people like that, they have no idea who she was, and it would be just sensible on their part to want a trained actress, a name actress ... and there were less famous people who just had training. They thought, "This is a really important part, how can you give it to someone who has no acting training at all?" The script was really much more suburban in the beginning, and Susan's vision of the film

was to bring out that whole downtown vibe. She knew if you're making cinema, you're taking pictures, and suburbia isn't as interesting as what that downtown world looked like. If that's the way your mind is going from the script, then you're gonna think about the way somebody like Madonna looks, and what she embodies; it's not about whether she can play "Lady Macbeth," it's about whether just by taking one glance at her, she's going to give you that feeling of, "This is 1984."

She said she wanted to cast Madonna and I said, "Can she act?" and she said, "I think she can pull it off ..." and she talked about the moon face. She said that Madonna reminded her of movie stars from the old days because her face was so round. Which is kind of interesting because later on Madonna would adopt images of old stars in her music vides and Susan saw that in just the shape of her face. Susan had this spectacular sense of the visual.

EM2O: Did you have a clue who Madonna was?

RR: I'd just seen videos. I knew who she was. I wasn't, like, buying her record.

EM2O: When did you meet Madonna?

RR: Shortly before Labor Day 1984, I went to the production office and was introducing myself to everybody and they said, "Oh, y'know Madonna, Rosanna, they're in this room here," so I went in and they were both sitting on the floor and I said, "Hi, I'm the publicist on the film," and Madonna said, "So?" [Laughs] That was my introduction to Madonna.

And then John Clifford [Seidelman's boyfriend at the time, later a successful still photographer] and I took Madonna and Rosanna out into a park, I don't know which one, and

we were followed by little kids who said, "That's not Madonna!" It's not like we were saying, "This is Madonna!"–they were just telling us. They were also the only ones who recognized her. Her fame was really big with these young kids. So we took these pictures, I think I even had Polaroids and stuff when I headed off to Telluride to show people about the new project I was working on.

My relationship with Madonna, if you could call it that, there were numerous ways that we, that she related to me. It was kind of like high school. I was not cool. In high school, it's okay to talk to certain people if no one sees you talking to them. You know? In public, she didn't really hang with me on the set. In private, we had very interesting conversations.

Rudeness was very much a part of my relationship with Madonna. She's not a *nice* person. [Laughs] But I really liked her enormously and was impressed with her and after the film shoot, because so many people knew me in the media, I often got asked by all these people, y'know, whether I thought she'd last more than a few months.

Orion pushed the production–they had to do this crazy-fast turnaround and the reason for this crazy-fast turnaround was because they thought Madonna's career would be over, completely over.

Madonna was not a person that was aspiring, Madonna was a person that was already there. Madonna wasn't even a person who didn't know *when* it was gonna happen, she said, "1985 is gonna be my year –you watch."

EM2O: What happened on the set after she'd performed "Like a Virgin" at the MTV Video Music Awards?

RR: It's just so weird to me that the day after she rolled around on that stage, she came to work and we talked about it. Those are kind of like musical history moments in my mind, but it was just, "This is what happened last night." She said that Cyndi Lauper was really mean to her and that bothered her.

EM2O: Did Madonna think she was good on the show?

RR: I think she didn't give a fuck if she was or not. I don't think she came like you or I would with, "I wonder if I did well?" Obviously, it was a very divisive moment, kind of like Miley Cyrus's moment [2013], and I think people respond to it in the same colossally stupid way they responded to Miley Cyrus, not understanding that that was going to be one of the many things that she was going to be doing and how perfect and planned it was. People just said, "Oh, that poor girl!" Who's selling five trillion records the next day. "Oh, she's out of control." [Laughs]

EM2O: Can you talk a little about the look of *Susan*? It's incredibly colorful and stylized. Nothing feels accidental.

RR: Santo Loquasto was Woody Allen's production designer—he brought in an image. It's interesting, about the clothes: Madonna hated that pyramid thrift-shop jacket, which she would never have worn.

There was a lot of stuff that he was dressing her in that she despised, so she was always sneaking in her baubles.

EM2O: How did Madonna and Rosanna Arquette get along?

RR: Remember that this was a Rosanna Arquette movie and people watching us film would ask Rosanna who was in the film and she would say, "Madonna." She was extremely insecure. She loved Madonna, they hung out together, but Madonna had kind of invaded her movie and taken over and Madonna didn't even work much. But her being in the movie made it "the Madonna movie" and if Madonna rolls around on that stage on MTV and the next day they see her dressed exactly like that filming a movie, they're gonna get excited about it. That was the dynamic. Rosanna looked up to Madonna, admired her.

Rosanna was not happy with Susan [Seidelman]. I don't think that it's an exaggeration to say that Susan was not an actor's director. Somebody like Madonna does not need a director to tell her how to play the character that she has invented. She's got that one down. She knows who the [airquotes] Madonna character is and she can come out and

play her. Rosanna, on the other hand, really needs to be treated like someone understands her method.

EM2O: As the publicist, did you get floods of teen-magazine requests?

RR: It wasn't anything like that. Madonna was extremely sophisticated about the media. She knew who Mark Bego was. You didn't have to tell her that. She knew how that whole game was played. Because I had to do a lot of international publicity, Madonna said, "Here's a list of where I'm popular: Japan, boom, boom, boom." She went down the list. You might have to say that Madonna ran the job for me for international. I told the international department to get me somebody from every country that Madonna was already successful in.

With Mark Bego, knowing the deal, I wouldn't be surprised if I learned more about the way it worked with him from her. I went to Bego and negotiated what we could do in terms of how many pictures I could give him and I was astonished by what he offered, which was all these covers … it was essentially, if I could bring her in for an hour, and they'd have all these people there, we could be in all these teen magaiznes for, I don't know, a year! It was crazy.

EM2O: Was Madonna okay with that sort of thing, or did she resist?

RR: In all my dealings with her, I always said, "Look, you have to do this now so you won't have to do it later, and you'll have a point in your career where you won't have to do this shit, but you have to do it now."

EM2O: Did Madonna have a diva reputation on the set?

RR: No. None. She's just a hardworking person who takes things seriously and she did her job. Rosanna was difficult. Madonna was easy.

EM2O: Is there a lot from the Herb Ritts poster shoot we have yet to see?

RR: It's *possible* that some of that he sat on and then it got published years later, and I forgot. But he shot a shitload. I kept Mark Bego busy for a long time with the shots I got in 10 minutes in costume, so that should give you a suggestion of the talent and the eye of Herb Ritts and how fast he could work. He had all these things set up for her and was just taking her from one to the other.

EM2O: Is the reason *Playboy* wasn't sued for its *Susan* cover of Madonna that the Ritts photos were technically handout photos?

RR: They all were! Correct. I came to work with the slides, with the big [transparencies], the whole thing, as you do to show it to the actors so they can cross

out stuff. So we were at The Magic Club set, which was the Audubon Ballroom, and it was like a ruin, a total mess, but somehow we could shoot The Magic Club and the dressing room. Peyser really had this whole thing about going to a location and building lots of stuff there. So we were there for quite a while and there were big tables where we all ate together: Madonna, Rosanna, we all ate at the same table, and you know, Ann Magnuson, and all the cool people. Tom DiCillo was one of the extras who came, the cinematographer from *Stranger Than Paradise* [1984]– everyone was in the movie.

I came in with the transparencies, and they were large—I don't think there were any slides. And I sat down with Madonna and Rosanna, and there were no kills. They loved them all. Herb sorted through it and we went through a few pages of the stuff and they were nuts about every single frame. So I went back, I was working out of my apartment, and I made a lot of slides, copies out of them. And I just let anybody have 'em. I obviously decided where each one was gonna go, but Mark Bego got his set and I retained exclusive stuff because I believed in the film and I knew I would want to have them. It was pretty free and easy, it wasn't like later where you had to sign deals and contracts about pictures

ANDY SCHWARTZ

and stuff like that. Orion wasn't the kind of studio that really cared that much about what I was up to. I wanted a lot of publicity on the film, and I didn't care if it was *Playboy* or *High Times*. I just wanted a lot of press, I thought that would be good and I liked the film.

I'm not gonna say that the *crew* believed in the film. This is a film with amnesia. How many people do you know who get konked on the head and get amnesia? It's a really bad plot device. But it worked! So a lot of people thought it was really stupid, even people very high up on the totem pole thought it was dumb.

When we were shooting outside people would ask, "Well, what's the name of the movie?" and I'd say, "*Desperately Seeking Susan*," and they'd say, "That sounds like a porno film."

EM2O: And then the title became a staple of the English language.

RR: Everybody went for that. The day I went to the production office, I saw the ad that was placed for *Susan* so I took that home and I Xeroxed it and I made it the cover of the provisional press book—that ad was on it.

I promoted it every which way but loose. I promoted Susan Seidelman as a new star woman director— think how big a deal that was. I worked with Rosanna everywhere I could—her publicist was not easy.

EM2O: What about Madonna's publicist, Liz Rosenberg?

RR: So easy to work with. She was smart. She was like about as great as great can be. And that was another reason Madonna did well: No prob with Freddy, no problem with Liz. I'd say, "This is what I wanna do," and they'd go, "Yes."

EM2O: What do you make of the *Susan* jacket being auctioned for so much money?

RR: That's a real weird thing, isn't it? Somebody wants to have something that she absolutely hated and didn't wanna wear. That's fetishism. There was one for Rosanna and one for Madonna, and there were maybe duplicates? I would say it would be insane not to have at least two of both or even three of both. I'm sure there were many of both—there were probably six of them at least.

And the crew jacket had a similar pyramid design, and I threw it away. I kept it but I had a girlfriend who had it at her house and when we broke up I didn't wanna get it back.

EM2O: Did you have any alone-time with Madonna?

RR: Yes, I went to her apartment all the time. We did our photo approvals. She lived a few blocks away from me, so if I had pictures of her, I went to her apartment. Many, many times. And obviously you talk when you do that.

When it comes to the still photography, she killed some, I guess ... actors kill stuff. And Andy was in a rage at me when the Herb Ritts thing happened because he wanted to do the special photography, he wanted the poster, but y'know, while Andy shot some of the most iconic images of *Susan*— he really did, they're famous images—and he has captured some of the most famous images in cinema, Herb Ritts was Herb Ritts. And it wasn't my decision. Ann Lander of Orion told me that was what was happening. I would've been fine to have Andy do it—I loved Andy.

EM2O: What was her apartment like then?

RR: It was like an empty loft space, mirrored at the end for practicing dance, and, I mean, it looked like some place that you just moved into because there was nothing there. The thing that impressed me— because I'm into synthesizers—she had this really great Roland synthesizer. It was a Roland Juno-60 or Juno-106. Her stuff was rough, analog, and she had the synthesizer that made that sound, so as a music fan I was very jealous that she had this great synthesizer. I'm sure there was a bedroom somewhere.

EM2O: Is it true that one time she threw your stills down into the street rather than bother coming down?

RR: Into the fuckin' street! It wasn't like it went onto the sidewalk, it went into the fucking street. I was literally clambering, as cars would come by, to grab them. And those pictures, if a car goes over it, they're lost forever, there's no other copy.

EM2O: Hm, that sounds kind of rude.

RR: Really? You think so? [Laughs] Kind of rude? Madonna? I remember I did an interview with her and David Edelstein was on the set from the *Voice*, and she said, "Reid! I can smell you approaching!" [Laughs] So she was on the one hand really rude and not nice and on the other hand about as easy to work with as you could ever find, because if you made a deal with her, she did it. I did an interview with David Keeps—it was a big booking for *Smash Hits* for Dave—and she put the whole costume on. She didn't wake up in the morning dressed like that. She put on Madonna drag. Doesn't that speak of professionalism?

The Keeps interview was at Planet Hollywood [formerly 221 W. 57th St.; now 1501 Broadway, NY, NY]. They tried to clear us off the table until I told them, "The lady is Madonna."

EM2O: What types of stuff would you talk about privately?

RR: She had done a song "Sidewalk Talk" for a compilation thing that Jelly was doing, and she played it for me and I loved it, so there was enough respect for her to be really happy that I liked the song. Everyone was telling me she couldn't sing, but she *could* sing. She sang a lot. There'd be something playing and she would sing along with it and you know, she wasn't an opera star, but she sang exactly the way she sung on the record. There was no processing. The woman could sing and that was something everybody told me wasn't true and I'd heard it.

I'm sure from that point on she took every voice lesson there was so she could sing better. When she wasn't working on *Susan* and I tried to make plans with her and called her, she would be swimming; she was never *not* working out. She was building up her body. She wasn't going swimming for fun. She was always at work. She was not leaving any minute unused. I'm sure she was writing songs and practicing dancing and working out moves.

I loved the way she looked then, where she was fleshy. That's my favorite Madonna look of all. There was this really louche way she had about her that was really sexy as hell, I thought.

EM2O: You've said that Madonna taught you a lot about PR. How so?

RR: Well, first there was a sense that she began with the idea of who was the biggest star? Michael Jackson. "All right, so I'm gonna go to Michael Jackson's manager because I'm this nobody dancing to backing tracks and of course he'll sign me." And that was the first thing that she taught me—there's no reason to be afraid of the things that people would laugh at you for trying. So, #1: Aim high. And #2: Don't give a fucking shit whether you're wrong.

EM2O: Why was there no NYC premiere?

RR: There was no premiere for the public, just a first showing for the crew … who were stunned by how good it was. If you're on a set and you're watching things being done for a lot of times, you're gonna just feel like, "God, that was a long night!" and you won't realize there was that one thing that happened—boom, and that thing happens there and that thing happens there and that thing happens there and it all comes together. I saw a few cuts and there was really a big difference from a week away until when it had to come out.

EM2O: Was there much unused footage?

RR: I'm sure there are things … There was that scene—what's the woman from *Liquid Sky*? [1982; Anne Carlisle]—Aidan had a line. I believe he had a line that was, "Nobody drives a Porsche in Manhattan!" He said that on the set like 400 times, and then it was just not there. There are all kinds of things—the editor [Andrew Mondshein] did a really good job. That whole scene—now that I think about it—that whole scene where she stayed at his apartment had a lot more dialogue, and what he did is he made it silent.

EM2O: I've heard another important '80s film was shooting near the *Susan* set …?

RR: When we were going to dailies at the screening room, there was another film shooting at the same time where the production team was watching dailies, so quite often we would wait while they finished, and it was *Parting Glances* [1986], so that was the first time I saw Steve Buscemi. Of course, I assumed he was gay, he was so convincing. This is a big problem I had in those days. When they were a good enough actor, like Laurie Metcalf, I thought they *were* that person.

Just to give you a sense of how stupid I was in that area, I did a photo shoot after we wrapped for *Vogue*. I invited all the people I thought should be in it for one photo, and Madonna agreed to be in it. So while I was at the photo shoot, co-casting director Risa Bramon turned on me and said, "John Turturro should be here. He's gonna be a big star!" I was like 'What? That guy who was just kinda jerky at The Magic Club? He's a big star?" And afterwards, I was walking around and I saw that he was this huge, well-known theater star.

EM2O: You took Madonna to a Limelight party. How did that come about?

RR: Orion called me and they said, "Well, this is a party for *Amadeus* [1984], and we're gonna have a lot of rock stars there so bring Madonna." I went over to her and said, "Blah-blah-blah, Roger Daltrey's gonna be there, can you come?" and she said, "Sure," so I was gonna take her to the party. I was extremely uncomfortable with that. I just didn't want to be sitting at that party all night with her, so I said, "You can bring Jelly." I think there were some boy toys; that was her boyfriend, but she definitely had some fun while the movie was shooting.

EM2O: The movie is sweet, but it has a lot of sexiness to it, don't you think?

RR: That bellboy scene was *the* last thing we shot. She did a crawl in that scene, so she was literally on her knees with her ass up. My memory is when I saw the film it wasn't as hot and didn't go on as long, that it had been an extremely sexy scene but had been sanitized a bit.

The movie was PG-13. Anna Thompson [a.k.a. Anna Levine] is always trying to take her shirt off in all of her movies because she just feels that's gonna be good for work, so she took her shirt off when they were undressing and stuff, nobody asked her to, and Midge Sanford came running in, "PG-13! PG-13!" and made her put her top back on.

EM2O: How did you leave things with Madonna when the shoot wrapped?

RR: She gave me a nice gift at the end, a signed *Like a Virgin* poster that said, "Reid, you've been a pain in the ass but thank you." And I lost it before I brought it home. It was this huge poster, and I wanted the poster *and* the record, but you could only have either the poster *or* the record, so I had her sign this massive poster of *Like a Virgin*, it was at the hotel, I set it down somewhere and I forgot it.

EM2O: What do you think about Madonna 30 years later?

RR: I don't think about her a lot anymore. I thought about her constantly then and I thought about her a lot for years. I admire her enormously with what she's done with her career. It's a ridiculous thing to say—she's one of the most successful pop stars, human beings—in terms of marketing herself. She had specific plans. She had movies she wanted to do: She wanted to do *The Blue Angel* [1930].

I don't think there's anything she told me that I didn't use. I learned from Harvey Weinstein and I learned from [Robert] Redford and Madonna, these people who actually create something big and maintain something big are better than publicists. Angelina Jolie is better than any publicist—she has no publicist. There are certain people who understand what publicists are supposed to know. But publicists are not Madonna, so they don't know that.

EM2O: Why do you think Madonna skipped the NYC 25th-anniversary reunion of *Susan*?

RR: It's not surprising to me to see people not wanna go back and be reminded of who they were and of the people who helped them at the beginning.

EM2O: And how do you view *Susan* 30 years later?

RR: It was an enchanting experience for me and it changed my life forever. I wanted that spell to continue, it was so wonderful for me. Things like that don't happen very often.

ANDY SCHWARTZ

KIMBERLY VAN PINXTEREN

Sickeningly rare
German standee

"THE CHARACTER I PLAY IS SORT OF A
COMBINATION BETWEEN JUDY HOLLIDAY AND
CAROLE LOMBARD, YOU KNOW,
FROM A LONG TIME AGO."-MADONNA (1984)

"MADONNA BRINGS A CERTAIN AURA OF
INNOCENCE AND COQUETTISHNESS TO 'SUSAN.'
SHE HAS AN INCREDIBLE FACE, ALMOST LIKE
VINTAGE MOVIE STARS LIKE GARBO AND
DIETRICH. A FACE YOU WOULD LIKE TO LOOK AT
BLOWN UP 50 FEET HIGH AND 30 FEET WIDE."

–SUSAN SEIDELMAN, *HIGH TIMES* (1985)

"… MADONNA LOOKS CONFIDENT ENOUGH TO
CRUNCH BOULDERS…A COARSE EROTIC OBJECT,
MADONNA IS A CARICATURE OF THE MOVIE
FEMMES FATALES OF THE PAST. BUT SHE
WANTS TO PLAY THAT ROLE SO BADLY–SHE'S
SO DEMANDING OF YOUR ADORATION–THAT
YOU WOULD HAVE TO BE A PERFECT BEAR TO
RESIST."-DAVID DENBY, *NEW YORK* (1985)

"… [T]HIS PICTURE IS, TECHNICALLY
SPEAKING, A COMEDY, AND SO THE CHARACTER
[OF 'SUSAN'] DOESN'T HAVE TO PAY FOR HER
NARCISSISM. AND MADONNA DOESN'T LOOK AS IF
SHE'S ABOUT TO, EVEN IF THE SCRIPT CALLED
FOR IT. SHE HAS DUMB-FOUNDING APLOMB."

–PAULINE KAEL, *NEW YORKER* (1985)

"MADONNA HAS ENORMOUS AUTHORITY.
WITH HER MEATY LITTLE BODY, FLARED
NOSTRILS AND LEWDLY PUCKERED LIPS,
SHE'S IMPERIOUSLY TRAMPY–JUST WALKING
DOWN THE STREET SHE SEEMS X-RATED."

–DAVID EDELSTEIN, *THE VILLAGE VOICE* (1985)

"SOON ENOUGH, MADONNA'S GRUNGY
DOWNTOWNNESS WOULD BE BUFFED TO A
MAINSTREAM SHEEN. BUT HERE IT IS,
CAPTURED FOR ALL ETERNITY."

–*TIME OUT NEW YORK* (2012)

DESSERTS: As of 2013, Madonna said her fave indulgences were lemon tarts and a rose petal cake from Ladurée (864 Madison Ave., NY, NY).

"DEVIL PRAY": Electrifying track on *Rebel Heart* that was among the first six sold on iTunes following an unprecedented wholesale **leak** of dozens of that album's demos. Written by **Avicii**, Rami, Savan Kotecha, Carl Falk, DJ Dahi, Blood Diamonds and Madonna, and produced by Madonna, Avicii, Blood Diamonds and DJ Dahi, it's a messy acoustic number with great drama and a surprisingly frank chorus about taking **drugs** that's actually about the opposite.

Madonna's first public performance of "Devil Pray" was filmed March 1, 2015, for the Italian TV show *Che tempo che fa,* and she included it on her *Rebel Heart Tour.*

"DEVIL WOULDN'T RECOGNIZE YOU": This *Hard Candy* song took an awful lot of people to write it: Madonna, **Timbaland**, **Justin Timberlake**, **Danja** and **Joe Henry** all had a hand in it. The reason is that it was written years before by Madonna and Henry for her aborted movie musical *Hello, Suckers!* It was almost performed on the *Re-Invention World Tour* as a torch song, but instead it was saved, and Madonna's *Hard Candy* collaborators reworked it into a more contemporary number. Alas, in spite of its delicious lyrics and sustained tension, it was never a single. Reflective of Madonna's regard for the song, its final form was part of her *Sticky & Sweet Tour*—and her own daughter, **Lola**, was the pianist for the last performance in Israel.

D&G: SEE: **Dolce & Gabbana.**

DIANA, PRINCESS OF WALES: *July 1, 1961–August 31, 1997.* One of the most famous women to ever live, and she never even saw her 40th **birthday**. The former Lady Diana Spencer married **Prince Charles**, in a mind-bogglingly elaborate formal royal **wedding** in 1981 that reignited worldwide interest in the British royal family. When Diana split from her husband, it was equally headline-grabbing, as was her relationship with department-store heir and movie producer Dodi Fayed. When Diana and Fayed died in a car crash in **Paris** while being pursued by paparazzi, it sparked a backlash against invasive media tactics.

Madonna (who had played Diana on *Saturday Night Live*) was distraught at the initial news of the princess's car crash, recalling she cried out, "Please, **God**, let her live!" She'd met Diana at a **London** party hosted by Sarah Ferguson in 1995. "I said I had always sympathized with her position and made some joke about how the only person who seemed to get more attention than me was her." Diana reportedly replied that Madonna handled the press better.

Madonna went on to say she sensed desperation from Diana. "The bravest and most dignified thing about Diana was that while she exposed herself to the public, she also said, 'I'm not perfect. I have my problems.'" Madonna's comments about Diana in 1997 ticked off **Elton John**, who felt the concern was insincere. Madonna shared a ***Rebel Heart***–ized image of Diana on **Instagram** in 2015.

> "I was at, um, Gloria Estefan's birthday party in Miami. I was devastated, like everyone, I guess. In shock, in denial, you know, just enraged … and really sad."
>
> —MADONNA ON HEARING OF PRINCESS DIANA'S DEATH (1998)

DICK TRACY: *Director: Warren Beatty. Release date: June 15, 1990.* The film that almost made us believe our favorite bad seed had become a reliably solid film star you could bring home to Mom and Dad's VCR.

Madonna campaigned hard to win the role of "Breathless Mahoney" in the larger-than-life adaptation of Chester Gould's comic strip. Virtually every leading lady in Hollywood had been tested for the role, and director/producer/star **Warren Beatty** especially wanted **Kathleen Turner**, who was fresh from providing the vampy **voice** of "Jessica Rabbit" for *Who Framed Roger Rabbit?* (1988), or Kim Basinger, who was fresh from screaming nonstop through *Batman* (1989) as "Vicky Vale."

In the end, Turner just wasn't drawn that way and Basinger became un-a-Vale-able, leaving the door wide open for Beatty to cast old acquaintance—and new **lover**—Madonna in the role.

"I chose to do *Dick Tracy* because I **love** the character of Breathless Mahoney and no one else could play her part but me," Madonna said. "Breathless wears a lot of tight dresses … those are her redeeming qualities."

Madonna's offer to accept Screen Actor's Guild scale wages helped Beatty feel even better about his decision; with a final production budget of around $47 million, getting Madonna for $35K was a bargain too good to resist. (Rumors that the overall cost of the film was closer to $100 million have not been substantiated, and were mocked by Beatty himself in **"Now I'm Following You: Part II."**)

Having been written off as an actor after the back-to-back disasters ***Shanghai Surprise*** and ***Who's That Girl***, Madonna promptly stole *Dick Tracy* right out from under its impressive cast, including Beatty in the title role, Al Pacino (**Oscar**-nominated for his "Big Boy Caprice"), Glenne Headly ("Tess Trueheart"), Mandy Patinkin ("88 Keys"), Dustin Hoffman ("Mumbles"), Charlie Korsmo ("The Kid") and Beatty cronies Dick Van Dyke, Charles Durning and James Caan strewn about in cameos. It wasn't hard for Madonna to excel in the film—she played not only a glamorous femme fatale, but one who got to sing, **dance** and vamp it up outrageously. If the film's striking primary-color palette and inventive latex masks were its main drawing points, Madonna's was the performance

that drew it together and made it worth watching. She had the unfair advantage of getting all the best lines ("Aren't you gonna frisk me?" "I'm wearing black **underwear**." "I sweat a lot better in the dark." "I was beginning to wonder what a girl had to do to get arrested."), and of turning out to be the mysterious villain, "The Blank," in the end. Spoiler alerts were not invented in 1990.

Madonna's sumptuous musical numbers—she croons **original** songs by **Stephen Sondheim**—are sensational. She knocks 'em dead at every turn, dancing, slinking, bumping and grinding, delivering **"Sooner or Later (I Always Get My Man)"** so powerfully that Sondheim was guaranteed his Best Original Song Oscar well in advance of the ceremony. The only thing wrong with the numbers, choreographed by **Jeffrey Hornaday**, is Beatty's aggressive editing; he splices up her scenes haphazardly, which pissed Madonna off greatly when she saw the final version. Perhaps he feared *Dick Tracy* would be seen as another "Madonna movie," or perhaps he just didn't know any better.

When she is provoking Beatty/Tracy, Madonna underplays, but that telltale stiffness **works** well in a film with glacial pacing, making Breathless seem a sensual time bomb.

Dick Tracy gave Madonna a decent mainstream success and a much-needed critical boost in Hollywood. It showed that given the right part in the right movie, she was capable of a credible performance, and also of helping to attract a large audience—though **"Vogue"** does not appear in the film, it was sneakily used as the soundtrack for an all-Madonna trailer that played on **MTV**. That sort of box-office drawing **power** was fairly short-lived.

The film did reasonably well at the box office, winning $103,738,726 after a boffo $22,543,911 opening weekend, the highest opening for any Disney film up to that point. Worldwide, *Dick Tracy* nabbed $162,738,726. Still, it is often referred to as a bomb because its performance was far off the mark set by *Batman*, which pulled in three times as much moolah and spawned sequels … and reboots to boot!

Including the statuettes it won for Best Original Song, Best Makeup and Best **Art** Direction, *Dick Tracy* received seven Oscar nominations total.

Dick Tracy was only one part of Madonna's multimedia **assault** in 1990: She wrote an entire album of original music "from and inspired by" the film (***I'm Breathless: Music from and Inspired by the Film Dick Tracy***) and launched her ***Blond Ambition World Tour***, which featured a *Dick Tracy* sequence. Together, the three projects made 1990 one of the most critically and commercially successful years of Madonna's career.

For once, when it came to summing up the wisdom of doing a film, Madonna was right on the **money** when she explained why doing the film had been a net positive: "[Warren Beatty is] a real artist and he's a real perfectionist and he's in charge of everything that he does, from the way the scenery looks to the way that the costumes are to the way the scene's lit to the, y'know, writing of the script

—KEVIN AVIANCE

and it was a real inspiration, a real learning experience to work with someone like that, because I like to be in charge of everything that I do, too. So I sort of got to be an apprentice with the master in a way."

Unfortunately, the film's static quality and the excessive marketing that accompanied it left a bad taste; it's nearly impossible to find **fans** of the film today. In spite of a lush *Dick Tracy* Blu-ray release over 20 years after

•••••••••••••••••••••••••••••••••••••••

"[MADONNA] LOOKS LIKE A SWEETLY LICENTIOUS KEWPIE DOLL AND HANDLES HER LINES WITH SUITABLY MOCK SUGGESTIVENESS … MADONNA DOES RIGHT BY THE SONGS, TWO OF WHICH, 'MORE' AND 'SOONER OR LATER', ARE VINTAGE SONDHEIM. THEY, IN TURN, GIVE HER A KIND OF CLASS SHE'S NEVER SHOWN ON SCREEN BEFORE."-VINCENT CANBY, *THE NEW YORK TIMES* (1990)

•••••••••••••••••••••••••••••••••••••••

"QUIVERING WITH LUST, DOUBLE ENTENDRES AND BAD INTENTIONS, MADONNA IS SMASHINGLY UNSUBTLE AS THE FEMME FATALE. LIT LIKE A '30S GLAMOUR QUEEN, SHE STRIKES ARCHETYPAL VAMP POSES: PART MONROE, PART DIETRICH, AND WHEN SHE SINGS, MORE THAN A LITTLE BERNADETTE PETERS."-DAVID ANSEN, *NEWSWEEK* (1990)

•••••••••••••••••••••••••••••••••••••••

"IT'S MADONNA'S BEST WORK EVER-SHE REDEFINES THE PHRASE 'BLONDE BOMBSHELL' FOR A WHOLE NEW GENERATION."
-JOEL SIEGEL, *GOOD MORNING AMERICA* (1990)

•••••••••••••••••••••••••••••••••••••••

"I FORGOT YOU CAN SEE MADONNA'S BREASTS IN *DICK TRACY*. I WISH THAT WEREN'T THE CASE BECAUSE IT'S A FUN MOVIE AND I WANT TO SHOW IT TO MY KIDS."
-DANIEL PELFREY, *POST POST MODERN DAD* (2012)

•••••••••••••••••••••••••••••••••••••••

"MADONNA, AT THE HEIGHT OF HER FAME AND THEORETICALLY A NATURAL FIT AS THE FEMME FATALE, DELIVERS LINE READINGS THAT CONTINUALLY LAND ON THE WRONG SIDE OF THE LINE BETWEEN SUGGESTIVE AND VULGAR."
-KEITH PHIPPS, *SLATE* (2013)

•••••••••••••••••••••••••••••••••••••••

"RATHER THAN AGING AS BADLY AS ITS STAR MADONNA, IT'S QUITE POSSIBLE THAT TWO DECADES ON *DICK TRACY* CAN FINALLY FIND ITS AUDIENCE, AND WITH THE QUALITY OF THIS BLU-RAY RELEASE, THERE'S NO REASON IT CAN'T."-BEN GOURLAY, *TWEAKTOWN* (2013)

•••••••••••••••••••••••••••••••••••••••

the film first came out, young critics reassessing it almost always go against all the great reviews Madonna received at the time, unfairly categorizing her performance in *Dick Tracy* as just another of her many missteps in the movies, perhaps influenced by their opinions of the work (and play!) Madonna has done since.

In 2011, Beatty won a lawsuit brought against him by the property's rights-holder (the *Chicago Tribune*), which had wanted the rights to the series to return to them since he had not pursued any sequels. To get around the stipulation that he continue using the character in order to retain the rights, as outlined in his 1985 contract, Beatty made a **TV** special that aired one time in 2010 in which he is interviewed in character as Tracy … but nothing else seems to be on the horizon.

"DID YOU DO IT?": Written and produced by Madonna and **Andre Betts**, this *Erotica* track gets the author's vote for the least amazing song Madonna has released commercially (hey, we all have our un-favorites). It is a reworking of the same album's **"Waiting,"** but is dominated by a moronic rap by Mark Goodman and Dave Murphy that Sir Mix-a-Lot would find distasteful. Betts (who did far better stuff with Madonna) has said this song started out as a joke. It ended up as one, too.

Following a **wedding** reception Madonna attended with her manager **Freddy DeMann**, she brought him to the studio for Betts to play him "Waiting." Betts played "Did You Do It?" Imagine DeMann's face …!

DIE ANOTHER DAY (MOVIE): *Director: Lee Tamahori. Release date: November 22, 2002.* So-so "James Bond" flick that marked **Pierce Brosnan**'s last as the world's most famous spy, featuring performances by John Cleese, **Oscar** winners Halle Berry and Judi Dench and future Oscar nominee Rosamund Pike, and a plot revolving around the infiltration of a sensitive North Korean site. The North Koreans and also some South Koreans found the film offensive, citing a **sex** scene photobombed by a Buddha **statue** and another in which an American appears to direct South Korean soldiers.

Madonna provided the title song, much to the chagrin of **Elton John**, and appeared in a cameo as "Verity," a fencing instructor whose sexuality is hinted at when she exits a tense confrontation between Bond and a rival by announcing, "I don't like cockfights." Though her part is about as substantial as something that could have been the result of a winning Charitybuzz bid, she's photographed beautifully (her closeup shimmers with CGI), in stark contrast to how she was shot in *Swept Away*, released just a month earlier, and she does well—she even gets to be there for the moment when Bond says, "Bond. James Bond."

Madonna won a **Razzie** in spite of barely being in the movie.

The premiere of the film afforded Madonna her first chance to meet **Queen Elizabeth II**, and was filmed as part of the UK **TV** documentary *Premiere Bond: Die Another Day* (2002).

Die Another Day was criticized for overuse of special effects, but it wound up making more **money** than any other Bond movie up to that time, raking in $160,942,139 in the US, $431,971,116 worldwide. As such, it is by far the most successful film in which Madonna has ever shown her face. As of 2015, it is also the final, live-action feature film in which Madonna has been seen. Thanks, **Obama**.

"DIE ANOTHER DAY" (SONG): *Release date: October 22, 2002. Billboard Hot 100 peak: #8.* The only truly successful single from Madonna's *American Life*, it was actually a theme for the "James Bond" film of the same name that was tacked onto the album after it had been a Top 10 hit. A polarizing tune to be sure, this ultra-modern techno number (written and produced by Madonna and **Mirwais**) was a club-pleaser that thoroughly disappointed Bond purists and music critics.

Billboard's Chuck Taylor wrote, "It's an odd number, somewhat disjointed, a bit nonsensical, and not so much melodic as a highly stylized jam ..." **Elton John** has called the song "the worst Bond tune ever." To be sure, no other Bond theme carries the stamp of its performer as strongly as this one, with its weird **Sigmund Freud** take-down line and its Kabbalistic exhortation to destroy the ego.

Still, it was a high-profile release (the biggest Bond hit in almost 20 years), one that nabbed a **Golden Globe** nomination for Best **Original** Song and **Grammy** nominations in the Best Short Form Music Video and Best **Dance** Recording categories.

Madonna is fond of this song; she has performed it on her *Re-Invention World Tour*, it was an interlude on her *Sticky & Sweet Tour* and, outta nowhere, she semi-revived it in 2012 for her show at the **Olympia Hall** merging it with **"Beautiful Killer."**

"... [Not] just the worst James Bond theme of all time (and no, I haven't forgotten Sheena Easton's) but also the most soulless song of Madonna's career."-JOSH TYRANGIEL, *TIME* (2003)

"DIE ANOTHER DAY" (VIDEO): *Director: Traktor, 2002.* Directed by a team of Swedes, the video for "Die Another Day" has an impressive filmic feel; it's a "James Bond" theme and it looks almost as expensive as the movie in which the song appeared.

Madonna approached Traktor (a creative group that directed videos and **commercials**) with a handwritten letter (her M.O.) detailing what she was looking for, and the video was shot over the course of five days in August 2002 in Hollywood with a budget north of $6 million.

Critics of the technofied Bond theme would be hard-pressed to criticize the music video's quality; it wound up being far more entertaining than *Die Another Day*, the film. In the video, which is rife with digital effects, Madonna is brutally interrogated and tortured by villainous government figures (the movie's baddies are the North Koreans), intercut with scenes of a white-clad Madonna and a black-clad Madonna fencing each other—she's really kicking her own ass! Mid-song, Madonna, somewhat of a female Bond, tries to orchestrate her escape (with time for a quick **yoga** pose) as her alter egos turn from fencing to battle-axes. In the end, good Madonna kills bad Madonna and our heroine has somehow slipped away after being strapped into an electric chair, possibly thanks to the Hebrew letters that mysteriously appear on site, which translated mean "freedom." Madonna's use of the phrase and other Jewish religious objects in the video led to outrage among some conservative Jewish scholars.

Because Madonna.

DIETRICH, MARLENE: *December 27, 1901–May 6, 1992.* German film actor and early perfecter of the cult of personality whose glamour helped define the Golden Age of Hollywood, in films like *The Blue Angel* (1930), *Dishonored* (1931), *Shanghai Express* (1932), **Blonde** *Venus* (1982), *The Devil Is a Woman* (1935) and *Destry Rides Again* (1939). Always a singer, she later **reinvented** herself as a dazzling chanteuse who toured the globe in her signature "**nude**" sequined gowns and swan coat. Dietrich was outspoken against the Nazis, had a freewheeling attitude toward **sex** with men or women and had a singleminded self-absorption that was meticulously analyzed—along with her incredible career—in a memoir by her daughter Maria Riva published in 1992.

Almost as often as she has with **Marilyn Monroe**, Madonna has drawn inspiration from the icy, androgynous sex icon, many of whose films were panned upon release but revered by the time of her **death**.

In spite of many similarities, there are noteworthy differences between **Ciccone** and Dietrich. Both were outspoken, but Dietrich never consciously promoted sexual liberation, she *embodied* it. She didn't care if others caught on—if they didn't, that was *their* problem. Dietrich was a less self-conscious force of nature compared to Madonna, who prefers to force nature.

Dietrich viewed the difference between Madonna and herself in an interesting way. "I *played* vulgar," she was quoted as saying in reference to her role in *The Blue Angel* (1930), "she *is* vulgar." When Madonna was contemplating a remake of the film in the mid-'80s, rumors flew that the stars were going to meet to discuss the role. Dietrich, by then a cranky shut-in, issued a frigid statement that must have tickled Madonna: "I have no intention, nor have I been contacted, to meet this Miss Madonna."

Even their egos differ crucially: Dietrich's self-involvement

"Of course not! Dietrich never retired."
—MADONNA ON RETIREMENT (2006)

GREGORY PACE

vest and pants by **Tom Ford** and a Jacob & Co. diamond glove, she was the picture of Dietrich—even though Dietrich had been nearly half Madonna's age in the movie the look referenced.

Madonna immortalized Dietrich in her roster of yesteryear **"Vogue"** (and recreated one of her poses in the accompanying video), and in 1991, shortly before the elder entertainer died at 90, Madonna told interviewer **Carrie Fisher** that she wished she had slept with Dietrich. (To which one might apply Dietrich's 1961 observation, "Americans are ambitious by nature.") It's debatable whether Madonna desired Dietrich simply for the pleasure that sleeping with a sexy woman brings, or as a hands-on approach to iconic assimilation. Or it could have been like how most **gay** men would sleep with Madonna given half a chance just because ... how could they *not*?

"Since Princess Stephanie of Monaco has taken to singing, it's become the fashion to have as little voice as possible! Madonna at least is above that! She sings badly and is very vulgar, but her show is impeccable! The public never makes a mistake!"-MARLENE DIETRICH, *I WISH YOU LOVE: CONVERSATIONS WITH MARLENE DIETRICH BY ERYK HANUT (1996)*

DI-GEI MUSICA: Acting a little high (even though we *know* she rarely used **drugs!**) and sporting some seriously crimped **hair**, Madonna delivered juicy lip-synched performances (solo, no **dancers**) of **"Holiday"** and **"Everybody"** on this Italian show that aired on Rai 1 on October 23, 1983, and that was filmed at a club called Le Rotonde Di Garlasco. It was her first appearance on Italian **TV**. In-between songs, Madonna said she was from **New York** and introduced "Everybody" in a pronounced British-sounding **accent**. She must've been pleased with her performance—Madonna's official **YouTube** account uploaded the "Everybody" portion on October 6, 2012, to celebrate the song's thirtieth anniversary.

During this 1983 promo stop in Italy, Madonna had a day off, so asked to see some of Milan's **art**, culture and music. She was sent to a Lucio Dalla concert at Teatro Lirico (Via Largo, 16, Milano, Italy). She also had dinner with Elio **Fiorucci**.

DILDOS: Penis-shaped rubber things you stick inside yourself to simulate **sex**. "I'm not really interested in dildos," Madonna said in 1991. In fact, Missy Sexpert dislikes sex toys in general: "I don't see how anyone could look at them with a straight face." She didn't say anything about looking at them with gayface.

DIPLO: *b. November 10, 1978.* Born Thomas Wesley Pentz in **Elvis Presley**'s hometown of Tupelo, Mississippi, this DJ and producer really hit his stride in the 2010s, **working**

Madonna's been falling in love again and again with Marlene for decades.

was that of a singular woman with no need for other human beings except to applaud for, or to amuse, her. Madonna likes the sound of hands clapping, too, but her need is more from the self-involvement of a determined, visionary artist *motivated by* other people, by the lust to provoke, enrage, please and change them.

Physically, the icons share a razor-browed, blonde-mannequin quality. Madonna has posed convincingly as Dietrich more than once. In 1986, she mirrored the elder icon for Matthew Rolston in *Rolling Stone*, has frequently utilized Dietrich's menswear approach (the beret, the suits), directly imitated her (complete with an **accent** straight out of the parodic 1974 film *Blazing Saddles*) during her performance of **"Like a Virgin"** on *The Girlie Show World Tour* and donned full Dietrich *Morocco* (1930) **drag** for the premiere of her *MDNA Tour* Blu-ray on June 18, 2013. Decked out in a **Dolce & Gabbana** bowtie and tux shirt, with a jacket, with **Beyoncé**, **M.I.A.**, **Britney Spears** and more. "It was kind of stupid," Diplo said of his ex-girlfriend M.I.A.'s behavior during Madonna's **Super Bowl** halftime show. "I think her being on that Madonna song is kind of lame, and she was trying to make up for that. That song is such a flop." Note: **"Give Me All Your Luvin'"** hit #10 in the US, **"Living for Love"** hit # nothin'.

Madonna decided she wanted to work with him on *Rebel Heart*, telling *Rolling Stone* she was drawn to his worldly quality. He told *Time Out New York*, "She's actually kind of hard-core. You can't get away. I'll be glad when we're all wrapped up. It's been a lot of work."

"She was the first person to really bring in different sounds and co-opt things for her own sound, and I've always loved her for that."-DIPLO ON MADONNA, *TIME OUT NEW YORK* (2014)

DISCO: In the September 1983 issue of the British **magazine** *The Face*, Madonna said, "Most **dance** records now are just sounds, they're not songs that go with the group that go with the feeling that go with the **fashion**. I think that was the whole downfall of disco—that it didn't represent anything to anyone."

DISCORING: *Airdates: 1977-1989.* Immediately after her Italian **TV** debut on *Di-Gei Musica*, Madonna was taken to a **disco** (she has recalled it being called something like "Quasar") in Sardinia that took hours to get to, where she performed **"Holiday"** on this TV show, broadcast on Rai 1.

#DISNIGGA: Madonna was castigated far and wide for having the temerity to use this common hashtag along with an **Instagram** image she posted on January 17, 2014. Playfully using it in reference to her white son **Rocco Ritchie** ("No one messes with Dirty Soap! Mama said knock you out! #disnigga" on an image of him **boxing**), she was immediately handed her white ass because (1) white people can't use the word and (2) she has black children.

Called a racist and a bad **mother**—and many unrelated things, by people who **hate** Madonna and seize on any misstep as an opportunity to slam her—Madonna was at first defiant. Then, she re-posted the image with a new message: "Ok let me start this again. #get off of my dick haters!" The new message could easily have been a total do-over, a fresh (if similarly juvenile) message to match the image, but it was immediately taken as Madonna telling everyone who'd reacted badly to her use of #disnigga to **fuck** off.

Madonna delights in poking fun at stupidity, but as much as she hates the policing of speech, she also seemed to have waded into this brouhaha unwittingly. She gave up and released the following statement on January 18:

"I am sorry if I offended anyone with my use of the N word on Instagram. It was not meant as a racist slur. I am not a racist. There's no way to defend the use of the word. It was all about intention.. It was used as a term of endearment toward my son who is white. I appreciate that it's a provocative word and I apologize if it gave people the wrong impression. Forgive me."

Of course, anyone willing to dump Madonna entirely over using not the N-word but "nigga"—which is at least arguably contextually different—in a hashtag used routinely by black and white people is unlikely to accept any apology offered.

In a transparent follow-up move, Madonna appeared on a red carpet for the first time ever with her black son **David Banda** (in matching Ralph Lauren) at the **Grammys** on January 26, 2014.

The use of the actual N-word casually by a non-black person is impossible to **excuse**, but the use of "nigga" by non-black people is hard to get behind as being a sign of **racism** even if it's pretty insensitive. Black artists lace it into their music liberally—are white people who buy the music supposed to sing along and then stop when "nigga" comes up? Is buying the song a racist act?

On the other hand, would Madonna really have casually used that hashtag on an image of her black son?

DITA: SEE: **Parlo, Dita.**

DIVORCE: Madonna first filed for divorce from **Sean Penn** on grounds of "irreconcilable differences" on December 4, 1987. The divorce spawned a *People* "Diary of a Mad Marriage" cover story that most of its subscribers didn't even have time to read before she withdrew her petition on the 16th. The suit was dismissed "without prejudice," leaving the door open for her to re-file, which is exactly what she did on January 25, 1989, after having lived apart from Penn since New Year's Eve 1988. The second filing was incorrectly rumored to have been caused by a bizarre **assault** on Madonna at the hands of Penn. The details are known only to the former Penns, but Madonna filed a formal complaint that she withdrew before filing for divorce. In 2015, Madonna swore in an affidavit that Penn never abused her.

Their marriage was just over four years old by the time the divorce was finalized on September 14, 1989. Respondent Sean's middle initial was incorrectly identified as "T." on petitioner Madonna's papers (it's "J" for Justin). He consoled himself with his loot from the marriage: full ownership of their **Malibu** mansion, reimbursement of his investment (about $500,000) in their **New York** apartment (which went to Madonna) and about $20,000 connected with their joint account. Otherwise, since the Penns had signed a prenuptial agreement, they kept their own possessions and earnings. As part of the divorce, Madonna's former name, Madonna **Ciccone,** was restored.

Madonna's divorce from **Guy Ritchie** was more contentious. The story of their split broke on October 15, 2008. Madonna's lawyer accused Ritchie of "verbal abuse," citing instances in which he allegedly called Madonna "past it," a

"If your joy is derived from what society thinks of you, you're always going to be disappointed."
—MADONNA, *VANITY FAIR* (2008)

"granny" and a subpar actor. It was also alleged that they hadn't had **sex** in the previous year and a half. It should go without saying that it's probably pretty tough to live with Madonna and to live by her rules (comments made by Ritchie "to a friend" focused on Madonna being all about showbiz, angry and on a mission to save the world), but if those comments happened, she did the right thing. Her big-mouthed **father**-in-law, who'd often spoken out of turn in the press, called her "beastly" for bad-mouthing his son; he was especially incensed when Madonna said at a concert that she knew "emotionally retarded" people, a shot taken to have been at Ritchie.

Interestingly, rumors congealed around the story that Mr. and Mrs. Ritchie first began to drift after Madonna's serious **horse**-riding accident.

Madonna hired Fiona Shackleton, Paul McCartney's attorney, while Ritchie used Lady Helen Ward, known for her ability to win big settlements.

By December 15, 2008, **Liz Rosenberg** issued a statement that the parties had come to a settlement, with Ritchie getting between $76 million and $92 million, their pub and their home in Wiltshire. Shared custody of their natural son **Rocco** and adoptive son **David** was easily agreed upon. Once news of the settlement hit, Madonna and Ritchie denied it, calling the monetary figure "inaccurate" and saying that all details would remain private. (Not counting song lyrics.)

Madonna's second divorce was finalized in January 2009.

> "I enjoyed my first marriage. It's definitely not something I regret."-GUY RITCHIE ON DIVORCING MADONNA (2011)

> "Because when you start off, everything's great and lovely, and the person you've married is flawless, and you're flawless. Then time goes by, and you share a life, you have children, and there are cracks in the veneer. It's not as romantic as it used to be. You think, 'This isn't what I thought it was going to be,' and, 'How much am I willing to sacrifice?'"
> —MADONNA ON DIVORCING GUY RITCHIE (2012)

DOGS: Madonna's first dog was apparently the hapless half-wolf, half-Akita named Hank that she bought for herself and **Sean Penn** in December 1986, only to leave him behind when the marriage went sour.

In 1994, Madonna received three Chihuahuas—Evita, Rosita and Chiquita—from **Ingrid Casares**. Madonna was seen carrying the dogs around in public, and even cast Chiquita in her **"Human Nature"** video. Some time after *Evita* (the movie, not the dog) went into production

Eyes wide shut

GREGORY PACE

and Madonna became **pregnant**, she realized she was not spending time with the dogs and placed them in what she thought would be a caring home. Years later, it was reported that Evita (the dog, not the movie) died of injuries sustained while under the care of someone irresponsible, and that Chiquita and Rosita were rescued and raised by a woman named Patricia Wrightfield.

It's kinda scary to wonder what happened to her cute, white pit bull pup Pepito, whom Madonna was given in August of 1994 by Arlyne Brickman, a **Miami**-based Mafia informer connected to one of her **lost projects**. He was only ever seen in photos taken to promote *Bedtime Stories*, though reference was made to him being in Madonna's home as late as 1996, as per an interview.

Madonna currently owns Boston terriers named Olga and Gypsy Rosa Lee.

DOLCE & GABBANA: Italian **fashion** house run by Stefano Gabbana (b. November 14, 1962) and Domenico Dolce (August 13, 1958), founded in 1985.

Madonna has had many associations with D&G over the years. She is a **fan** of their artistry, close-fitting Baroque dandy-suits, **Beatles**-mania send-ups, sumptuous '70s prints and attention-grabbing showmanship.

STEVEN CHRISTEN

Former lovers and **Madonna queens** themselves, they became great friends with the star they once believed to be the "ideal Mediterranean woman."

Speaking of their first meeting with Madonna, the design team said, "She arrived in this restaurant in **New York** all dressed up as a young man. She was affable, seductive. And there was a positive feeling right away, a positive feeling."

In Italy to promote *Sex* in October 1992, Madonna attended the D&G show and was the guest of honor at a party they threw, to which 300 members of the fashion press were invited. The duo was later accused of paying her to attend. Dolce said, "She's a friend. Better not to have a friend than to pay a friend. In Italy all the designers have starlets, not stars. Starlets they pay to come to the show."

When D&G appeared in the audience of *Partita Doppia*, an Italian talk show Madonna was doing, her face lit up and the interview ended with D&G&M strolling off the **Fellini**-esque stage together.

D&G later designed the heady frocks she paraded around in during *The Girlie Show World Tour*. She wears D&G on her *Ray of Light* and *Confessions on a Dance Floor* album covers.

In 2009 and 2010, Madonna shot a formal campaign for D&G, an inspired **Steven Klein** shoot showing Madonna as a hardworking, yet **sex**-kittenish Italian mama (think: Anna Magnani with Vaseline on the lens). At the scene of the April 21, 2010, Harlem shoot, Madonna gamely posed for a paparazzo with her Vita Coco in hand. (**Guy Oseary** was an investor.) The campaign started running July 13, 2010.

Her son in the photos was played by model/actor Max Schneider, who later appeared on the short-lived Nickelodeon series *How to Rock* (2012). Schneider revealed in 2014 that the shot of him walking arm in arm with Madonna was her idea. She announced, "I wanna do a shot on the street right now." Everyone moved outside for the chaotic shot, giving the paps a chance to get photos of her with a cute, 17-year-old boy. "She knew exactly what she was doing ... that was totally intentional, what a brilliant media move," he said admiringly.

Also in 2010, Madonna and D&G teamed up for MDG sunglasses, a line personally designed by Madonna. Its **commercial** showed a high-glam, blown-out Madonna sensually moving in a confined space with a hot, horny boy, looking very Sylvia Miles, circa *Midnight Cowboy* (1969).

Both D&G ad campaigns were criticized for being overly retouched when many of the raw images **leaked**. Madonna looked good without the excessive retouching, but as usual, she was damned if she did (get retouched) and damned if she didn't (get retouched).

Although they are openly **gay**, D&G hold some retrograde views. In 2013, Dolce said he never would've married his partner because he's a "practicing **Catholic**." He said, "I don't believe in gay marriage." In 2015, the former

couple granted an interview to *Panorama* in which they dismissed IVF (creating "synthetic" children) and gay parenting: "The only family is the traditional one. No chemical offsprings and rented uterus: Life has a natural flow, there are things that should not be changed."

Gay people who think Madonna hasn't done enough for our cause should first look within.

Elton John called for a D&G boycott, and Madonna chimed in, writing a passionate defense of IVF and surrogacy that ended with, "Think before you speak ..." When Madonna is telling you to watch what you say, you are definitely speaking out of turn, girl.

"It's not easy to say what our favorite Madonna era is. What we love is her way of expressing feelings, her way of being [a] woman—she is not afraid of saying what she thinks."-D&G (2008)

DOMESTICITY: In 1989, Madonna said, "I liked folding Sean's **underwear**. I liked mating socks. You know what I **love**? I love taking the lint out of the screen."

DON'T BUNGLE THE JUNGLE: A May 24, 1989, benefit for the rainforest cohosted by Madonna and artist **Kenny Scharf**, held at the Brooklyn Academy of Music (30 Lafayette Ave., Brooklyn, NY).

After **Sandra Bernhard** sang the **Joni Mitchell** song "Woodstock" (1970) and the Patrick Crowley/Sylvester banger "Do Ya Wanna Funk" (1982), Madonna came onstage to make a short speech against rainforest depletion. Bernhard hollered, "Who the **fuck** do you think you are? Tracy Chapman?" Madonna replied, "No, I don't **work** in a convenience store. But I do like to sneak off to 7-Eleven at night for some jawbreakers."

Then the pair, wearing matching halters, **drag** makeup and brightly handpainted, vintage Levi 501 cutoff jeans by Leslie Hamel, sang a notoriously lascivious, booty-bumping rendition of Sonny & Cher's "I Got You Babe" (1965). Referring to the rampant rumors that they were rubbing rugs (women had rugs back then, but bare linoleum is de rigueur these days), Madonna cautioned the crowd, "Don't believe those stories." Sandra embraced her saucy comrade and retorted, *"Believe* those stories." Madonna, who did the Sonny part, forgot the words halfway through.

At the end, Madonna and Bernhard were joined in a triumphant, fist-pumping post-event photo by **Keith Haring**, **Debi Mazar**, Scharf, Rob Wasserman and Bob Weir.

The celeb-soaked crowd (**Glenn Close**, Billy Joel and Christie Brinkley, Calvin Klein, Tatum O'Neal and Meryl Streep) later grazed at an after-party at the French-Vietnamese restaurant Indochine (430 Lafayette St., NY, NY).

The event raised $250,000—and 10 times as many **eyebrows**.

"DON'T CRY FOR ME ARGENTINA": *Release date: January 10, 1997. Billboard Hot 100 peak: #8.* Though Madonna had proved her vocal chops on **Stephen Sondheim**'s tricky *Dick Tracy* songs, in many ways, her ability to sing the most famous song from the musical *Evita* represented a huge accomplishment in her career—she had tackled a song (and movie) she'd been circling for many years, and most critics (not all) found her version to be anywhere from credible to a revelation. (Not everyone **loved** it: *People*'s Jeremy Helligar likened it to "sucking in her tummy and balancing a stack of **books** on her head.")

There is no comparing Madonna's version to that (from 1980) of the song's most famous singer, **Patti LuPone**—their **voices** could not be more different. But Madonna's version is very much in keeping with the first version ever recorded, an upper-register, fragile take by Julie Covington (1976). That Madonna was able to bring something new to the **Andrew Lloyd Webber/Tim Rice** song and to make her version one of the best ever recorded was a herculean task—everyone from Sarah Brightman to **Olivia Newton-John** to Elaine Paige to Donna Summer had already given it a spin.

In the film version of *Evita*, Madonna's delivery of this song makes the entire movie and her entire performance; surely Madonna must consider it among her proudest achievements.

As a single, the song was somewhat disrespectfully given a **Miami** Mix uptempo treatment by Pablo Flores and Javier Garza. It feels a bit like smacking a lady on the ass and getting her to boogie-oogie-oogie in her ballgown. It is also an undeniably fun mix, but the cheese factor is upped by a million, calling to mind Festival's 1979 **disco** take on many of the songs from the stage version of *Evita*. But hey—it never would've had radio airplay in its **original** form.

For better or for worse, Madonna's singing changed forever once she'd gone through vocal training for *Evita*. She had to nail this and other difficult songs, and the process changed her phrasing permanently. To check out her progress, search for Madonna's tentative singing of a few lines from "Don't Cry for Me Argentina" on *The Girlie Show World Tour* when she was in Argentina and compare that to the recorded version. She is a diamond, but was a diamond in the *rough* until she got serious with the song.

Madonna sang the song on her *Sticky & Sweet Tour* in Argentina (a version that is preserved on the show's Blu-ray), revisited it again in Argentina on her *MDNA Tour* and sang it in Miami on her *Rebel Heart Tour*.

> "Easily one of Madonna's greatest vocal performances to date, the singer's dramatic interpretation of *Evita*'s unofficial theme song was both loyal and bizarrely autobiographical."-SAL CINQUEMANI, SLANT (2001)

"DON'T STOP": Written by Madonna, **Dallas Austin** and Colin Wolfe, and produced by Madonna and Austin, this breezy *Bedtime Stories* track is an early '70s pre-**disco** shuffler. It typifies the R&B half of the album.

"DON'T TELL ME" (SONG): *Release date: November 14, 2000. Billboard Hot 100 peak: #4.* One of the best-written songs (it is lyrically almost 100% by her bro-in-law **Joe Henry**, with tweaks by Madonna and **Mirwais**, who produced it) Madonna has released as a single, "Don't Tell Me" is a kinder, gentler **"Human Nature"**; it draws a clear line in the sand for her detractors to see and provided a pre-emptive reply to critics who would later exasperatedly ask when Madonna was ever gonna give it up: Never.

Madonna told *Interview*'s Ingrid Sischy the inspiration for the song "came from my brother-in-law, Joe Henry, who's married to my sister. He's one of my all-time favorite people in the whole world, and a true poet ..."

The countrified shuffler gave Madonna one of her biggest radio hits in ages and won her critical raves. **"Music"**—its immediate predecessor on the charts—had been a smash, yet had turned off some older listeners with its of-the-moment flash; not so "Don't Tell Me."

On November 3, 2000, Madonna performed an acoustic version of the song with **Monte Pittman** (both strumming their **guitars**) on *Late Show with David Letterman*. She lip-synched it for the UK's *Top of the Pops*, Germany's *Wetten, dass ...?* and Italy's *Carramba! Che fortuna*, but went all-live for France's *Nulle part ailleurs*. The song was on the setlists of both the *Drowned World Tour* and *Re-Invention World Tour*, and was a *Rebel Heart Tour* bonus. It was sung as a duet with **Miley Cyrus** and at the Melbourne *Tears of a Clown* show.

> "Suffice it to say that, yet again, Madonna has found a way to mesh the often disparate elements of art and mass-appeal music. ['Don't Tell Me'] is at once a toe-tapping, easy-on-the-ears hit, and an inner sanctum far from the faux rhythms of much of today's assembly-line pop fodder."-CHUCK TAYLOR, BILLBOARD (2000)

"DON'T TELL ME" (VIDEO): *Director: Jean-Baptiste Mondino, 2000.* One of Madonna's best-executed music videos, **Jean-Baptiste Mondino**'s artful clip casts her as a quasi-cowgirl in distressed jeans and plaid shirt, showing off line-dancing moves before a series of projections. The use of the projections and of a billboard-come-to-life stylishly plays with the concept of authenticity; here, Madonna seems to acknowledge the pose she is inhabiting.

With help from four hot male **dancers** (yee-haw!), she also displays her return to fine-fillydom following the birth of her son **Rocco**. Madonna has never looked more casually **sexy**, nor has her body ever been as judiciously displayed and *not* displayed.

It is a pop **art** masterpiece about which *New York Post* writer Kristina Feliciano commented, "... [W]ith the video, this little **love** ditty wrangles up feelings of the eternal struggle of romance and, um, wild **horses** that just can't be tamed."

"DON'T YOU KNOW": Early version of the song **"Stay"** that was released on *Pre-Madonna*. It was written by Madonna and produced by Stephen Bray.

DOUGLAS, SEAN: *b. May 27, 1983.* The songwriter son of actor Michael Keaton achieved instant **fame** when his dad incorporated him into his heartfelt **Golden Globes** speech on January 13, 2015, but Madonna already knew all about him—he'd **worked** with her on *Rebel Heart*'s **"Ghosttown,"** one of the first six songs from the album that she released on iTunes, and **"Inside Out."** Madonna had liked his previous work with Jason Derulo and personally requested him.

"She liked 'Talk Dirty' [2013], actually, and so they put me and [cowriters] Jason Evigan and Evan Bogart in with her and we had this great session. I was incredibly **nervous** for obvious reasons, but she showed up, was super personable and was ready to work." The killer "Ghosttown" was created in just three days.

> "I basically checked it off my life bucket list."—SEAN DOUGAS ON WORKING WITH MADONNA (2015)

DRAG: Drag queens around the world breathed a collective sigh of relief when Madonna burst onto the scene. "Now *there*," they thought, "is someone young who I can *do*."

She became a favorite subject of drag performers because she herself is so androgynous—those biceps!—and because her costumes/wardrobe are so extreme they're easy to ape.

Madonna has done male drag. She posed as James Dean for photographer **Bruce Weber**'s lens in *Life* in 1986, and has since often appeared in men's clothing. She wore a navy blue men's Commes des Garçons suit to meet with **Warner Bros.** executives to discuss her interest in doing the film *Who's That Girl*, and *The Girlie Show World Tour* audiences found her not only *looking* like a man (that tuxedo!), but *behaving* like one, too. It could even be argued that she often does *female* drag—her *Blond Ambition World Tour* look was so severe and arched she appeared to be either a beautiful woman or a beautiful drag queen.

Karlene Faith, in 1997's *Bawdy & Soul*, wrote, "Madonna doesn't seem to be saying, when in male drag, that she wants to be a man, any more than she seems to be saying, when dressed like **Marilyn Monroe**, that she wants to be that woman."

There are some legendary drag queens in Madonna's **"Deeper and Deeper"** video, but you'll find a lot more of them on the 1999 **MTV Video Music Awards** telecast, on which a slew of drag queens appeared in Madonna's honor, representing her looks for: **"Like a Virgin," "Open Your Heart,"** her *Blond Ambiton World Tour*, the MTV Video Music **Awards** rendition of **"Vogue," "Deeper and Deeper," "Take a Bow," "Bedtime Story," "Human Nature," "Frozen," "Ray of Light"** and **"Nothing Really Matters."**

In her personal life, several of her **birthday** parties have had drag entertainment.

DRAKE: *b. October 24, 1986.* In 2015, the Canadian rapper **flirted** with Madonna via **Twitter** and added a song called "Madonna" to his mixtape *If You're Reading This It's Too Late*. The song is from the perspective of a hustler picking up a girl with the line that she could "be big as Madonna" if she would "just get in the car." Drake tweeted, "I wanna ride with you" and Madonna proclaimed it to be the best song on his album, telling Drake so in the tweet: "@champagnepapi i **love** your new song about me! It's my favorite!"

In an interview with *Complex* to promote *Rebel Heart*, Madonna firmly asserted that she was going to get into Drake's metaphorical car in the future, promising a collaboration one day. She also told an interviewer she **dreamed** of going on a date with Drake, then kissing him—just kissing him.

The kiss happened, at **Coachella**, but the word "just" didn't apply.

DREAM: Madonna's earliest **memory** of a dream is from the sixth grade in which she kissed Robert Redford. As an adult, she has said her dreams are usually really violent, mostly about being chased by obsessed lunatics.

As an omnipresent and symbolically charged figure, Madonna turns up in *our* dreams frequently. In fact, the **book** *I Dream of Madonna: Women's Dreams of the Goddess of Pop* is the result of editor Kay Turner's interviews with 91 women aged 13–61, from France, Canada, the UK and the US. The book, which is cleverly illustrated to play off the theme, is a straightforward recounting of the women's dreams involving Madonna, including **sexual** encounters, friendly exchanges, bull sessions, pats on the back—you name it, and some woman has probably dreamed it.

As Turner notes, the dream motif pervades Madonna's **work,** from her recurring slogan **"Dreams Come True"** to songs like **"Justify My Love"** and **"Waiting."** In **"La Isla Bonita,"** Madonna recalls dreaming of San Pedro, **"Like a Prayer"** is "just like a dream" and **"American Life"** refers to the American dream.

DREAM DIRECTORS: "I'm ready for my close-up ..."

Despite being a **control** freak, Madonna has submitted to the visions of many directors. Madonna's wish list of directors she'd **love** to **work** with (circa 1985) included the now-deceased Rainer Werner Fassbinder, Bob Fosse, Mike Nichols and George Stevens, as well as still-living auteurs Francis Ford Coppola, Roman Polanski and Martin Scorsese. That's a pretty tony list of **dream** directors for a young singer to cough up so early in her career.

—DARREN HAYES

Examples of Madonna's catchphrase litter Japanese promo items.

"DREAMS COME TRUE": The phrase at the center of (especially) the early part of Madonna's career. She signed open letters to her **fan** club with this slogan, which was also printed on balloons dropped on *The Virgin Tour* audiences.

Dreams Come True is also the name of a British organization that helps to fulfill the wishes of desperately ill children. Madonna visited with five such kids in August 1987 while in **London** for her *Who's That Girl World Tour*, on the condition that no members of the press be notified.

The phrase "Dreams Come True" illustrates Madonna's appeal. She's the world's biggest star, and yet she steadfastly maintains—in songs like **"Spotlight"** and in her self-penned May 1994 *Harper's Bazaar* article (which ends with, "Inspiration is inspiration—go for yours")—that what she has achieved is not out of reach, that ambition and hard **work** can make things happen and that even in a **dog**-eat-dog world, dreams come true.

"I went to New York, I had a dream, I wanted to be a big star, I didn't know anybody, I wanted to dance, I wanted to sing, I wanted to do all those things, I wanted to make people happy, I wanted to be famous, I wanted everybody to love me, I wanted to be a star, I worked really hard and my dream came true."—MADONNA, MADONNA LIVE: THE VIRGIN TOUR (1985)

"DRESS YOU UP" (SONG): *Release date: July 24, 1985. Billboard Hot 100 peak: #5.* Breakneck **dance** song from *Like a Virgin* that makes use of an extended metaphor between **fashion** and **sex**. Written by Andrea LaRusso and Peggy Stanziale and produced by **Nile Rodgers** (who brought the song to Madonna's attention), the song is about the fancy duds she'd like to drape over her man, obviously for the pleasure of having her hands all over his body. Madonna also sings that she'll create a "look" for her lover, prefiguring a concept (rapid-fire look renovations) that would become unique to Madonna's own **fame**. Despite **Tipper Gore**'s protests, "Dress You Up" was an easy Top 5 in 1985.

The song's writers were—for real—housewives of New Jersey, LaRusso (music) from Caldwell and Stanziale (lyrics) from Llewellyn Park. The women were introduced by their husbands. They toiled for four years before taking the bull by the horns. Stanziale told a local news program in 1985, "... [W]e just called the record company and, um, said, y'know, 'Would you listen to a song? We think we've got something really good for Madonna.'" La Russo said the phone rang on a Friday afternoon shortly thereafter and when she asked who it was, the **voice** on the other end of the line said, "This is Madonna." **Dreams come true**.

The song was featured on *The Virgin Tour* and the *Who's That Girl World Tour*, then not again until the 2009 leg of her *Sticky & Sweet Tour*, though the latter was a rock version. In 2015, she sang the song as a humorous duet with **Ellen DeGeneres**, and it anchored a medley on her *Rebel Heart Tour*.

"DRESS YOU UP" (VIDEO): *Director: Daniel Kleinman, 1985.* This music video was pulled straight from Madonna's first concert home video, *Madonna Live: The Virgin Tour*. It was nominated for a 1986 **MTV Video Music Award** for Best Choreography.

DRIVEN: MADONNA: *Producer: James Bolosh. Air date: 2001.* Extremely thorough **MTV** special about Madonna's early life, which contained interviews with many of the people who knew her when she was in high **school**, college and during her downtown **NYC** days. Madonna did not sit for an interview.

"DROWNED WORLD/SUBSTITUTE FOR LOVE" (SONG): *Release date: August 24, 1998. Billboard Hot 100 peak: NA.* Written by Madonna and **William Orbit**, with contributions by Rod McKuen, Anita Kerr and **David Collins** and produced by Madonna and Orbit, this contemplative ballad about the emptiness of **fame** became the third single from *Ray of Light* outside the US.

The song features the **voice** of Jesse Pearson (famous as "Conrad Birdie" in the 1963 movie version of *Bye Bye Birdie*) saying "you see" from a beatnik song by McKuen and Kerr called "Why I Follow the Tigers" (1969). McKuen, a celebrated songwriter who died in 2015, has said that Madonna's song follows his closely, but that seems dubious; good for him for getting that paycheck, though. Madonna had a thing for Mr. McKuen—her **unreleased** "If You Go Away" was McKuen's English adaptation of a Jacques Brel song.

"Drowned World/Substitute for Love" is a moody masterpiece she performed on her *Drowned World Tour* (of course!), *Confessions Tour* and at her Melbourne *Tears of a Clown* gig. It was a one-off bonus on her *Rebel Heart Tour*.

**"DROWNED WORLD/SUBSTITUTE FOR LOVE"
(VIDEO):** *Director: Walter Stern, 1998.* The intimate, atmospheric video for one of Madonna's most personal singles begins with her character having to rush through a crush of paparazzi. As she is driven away in her car, they pursue her, their flashes illuminating her in the back seat. The scene, so soon after the **death of Princess Diana**, was clearly intended to remind viewers of that tragedy, though Madonna had experienced the same sort of scene many times in her own life. She was point-blank accused of "exploiting" Diana's death.

As the singer makes her way to a public event and then into a hotel, the faces of the people clamoring around her become horrendously distorted, strangers snap her picture rather than say hello, touch her, even steal her sunglasses. In the end, Madonna is running (for her life?) from the press again, winding up at home with a little girl in her arms.

Just another day in the life of a superstar not unlike Madonna.

DROWNED WORLD TOUR: *Show dates: June 9, 2001–September 15, 2001.* Madonna had not toured in any capacity since the end of 1993 when she finally hit the road with what was heralded as a major comeback tour. At the time, it almost felt like had she waited any longer, she may never have returned to touring at all. "... Madonna's first [tour] in eight years ... could well be the last time she presents a show on such a large scale," Sharon O'Connell wrote in *Time Out **London***. How wrong she was!

What *Drowned World Tour* did was not merely extend Madonna's reputation as a dynamic live performer and refresh her own interest in touring as a central aspect of her career, it confirmed her status as an of-the-moment, forward-looking, uncompromising artist.

It also pissed off some people hoping to hear **"Like a Virgin."**

Madonna had not toured with *Bedtime Stories* (a successful album) or *Ray of Light* (a global smash), instead opting to make *Evita* and, gulp, *The Next Best Thing*. Once she decided to launch her fifth tour, she poured everything she had into it, aware that any signs of appearing rusty would diminish her draw in the future.

"You need a minute to make things just right," Madonna told ***Billboard*** in 2000. "I can't just go out there half-assed. It has to be right. I'll spend a lot of the first part of 2001 preparing for it." And she did, **working** with **Jamie King** as her creative director, choreographer Alex Magno, future *Confessions on a Dance Floor* collaborator **Stuart Price** as her musical director and investing $200,000 in the clothes alone. (Chief wardrobe coordinator Rob Seduski said four copies of each costume existed, mostly with Velcro and snaps.)

The run-up to the show was not without its rough patches. Mike McKnight, who ran all the aspects of the show via computer, had to be poached from U2. He'd been given some of Madonna's songs to prep for a *possible* tour, including some analog tapes, but was assured she wasn't really touring. Then she suddenly was.

More drastically, Madonna fired her longtime musical director Michael Bearden (who has been recruited recently by **Lady Gaga**) when things weren't clicking. Price noted that Madonna simply fired anyone who got in her way of putting on the show she wanted, while Bearden said that he was "glad" not to be there.

All the work and all the drama paid off with a handsomely, darkly visual machine of a show with a true rock star at its center. It functioned as an audition for the **Rock and Roll Hall of Fame**, and it was also a great example of Madonna's skill as a cultural aggregator. It is alarming to watch this Madonna and compare her with the Madonna of the *Rebel Heart* era, not because one or the other is superior, but because the two seem to be complete opposites.

Asked to describe the show for prospective audience members, Madonna stated, "It's a theatrical presentation of my music. I've taken my inspiration from many things: martial arts, flamenco, country & western, punk rock, Butoh **dance** and the circus. If [**fans**] want to know specifics, they can come and see the show."

As it turned out, *everyone* wanted to know specifics.

At the show's opening night in Barcelona, Spain, 18,000 people were in the crowd. The whole tour was sold out before she'd even finalized the set list. **Mick Jagger**, **Elton John**, **Angelina Jolie**, Claudia Schiffer and members of Oasis and Steps watched her at her six sold-out **London** shows.

"I have moments where I feel incredibly invincible and know that I have the audience in my hand—I know that everything is absolutely perfect ... and then I have panic attacks, where I feel like everyone is breathing my air and I cannot live up to everybody's expectations, and I might just die on stage,"—Madonna told *Dazed & Confused* in 2008. Longtime backup singer **Niki Haris** said of Madonna's state after each performance, "Madonna was very, very happy. And tired."

No wonder.

The show's first section, *Neo-Punk*, opened with Price, **Monte Pittman**, Mohawked dancers (including backup singers **Donna De Lory** and Haris) rising to the stage to the sound of a swirl of fragments from some of Madonna's recent hits, the overhead lights resembling something out of *Close Encounters of the Third Kind* (1977), except with a bank of **TV** screens in place of the **mother** ship. In her simplest opening ever, Madonna appeared out of the mist in a punk-styled look, very much the **Pat Benatar** that **Camille Barbone** had once envisioned. Her live vocal of **"Drowned World/Substitute for Love"** was instantly one of her best. No choreography, just Madonna standing there singing. Much was made of her kilt (red in Europe, **black-and-white** in the US), but the **Arianne Phillips**/Michael Schmidt design was really a bum flap, slitted at the sides.

Next, Madonna, at her most gaunt, was surrounded by dancers in gas masks for a spirited rendition of the album

"The good, bad and the very ugly. I like to refer to it as the agony and the ecstasy."
—MADONNA ON "DROWNED WORLD/SUBSTITUTE FOR LOVE" (1998)

track **"Impressive Instant."** She reclined across them like human props, and the dancing—while artful—was reserved, the movements that were abrupt. Her chest pops on the song were razor-sharp. The spinning world of which the song speaks could have been the dystopia of the *Drowned World Tour.* "Mad Max" couldn't have survived this shit.

Continuing to challenge her fans, the third song performed was another edgy album track, **"Candy Perfume Girl."** For the first time ever, audiences of a Madonna tour were treated to her work-in-progress **guitar** playing. She strummed along while she sang, punctuating the song with a finger down the throat, mirrored by a punk dancer, all of it ending in a barrage of guitar licks and a command to, **"Fuck** off, motherfuckers!" Even her guitar strap said "FUCK YOU." (The strap was meant as an homage to **Debbie Harry**, **Chrissie Hynde** and **Patti Smith**.)

Her next spoken words lightened the mood: "Do I make you horny?" Madonna came out doing the Pony to **"Beautiful Stranger,"** complete with a Mike Myers projection (he was the **original** Lil Wayne). Her use of a stripper pole was playful rather than a committed nod to **Demi Moore**'s 1996 *Striptease.* This was the first actual hit of the concert, and it was a recent one at that. Hopefully you enjoyed Madonna in that Donna and Niki sandwich, because this was their last tour as a trio. The song ended with a "crew member" being molested.

Unlike Madonna's future tours, this one contained a lot of straightforward rockin', which continued with an uncomplicated take on **"Ray of Light"** that restaged her **award**-winning music video for the song, now considered one of her signature hits. It ended with a "Drowned World/Substitute for Love" reprise, just like they do in musical theater, you cretins.

The *Geisha-Anime* section was kicked off by a Japanese-themed video interlude, in which Madonna was shown singing **"Paradise (Not for Me)"** while her dancers slowly descended to the stage from above, first in pods and then by threads, spider-like ... or are they aliens?

As the interlude wrapped, Madonna took the stage in a black **Jean Paul Gaultier** kimono, which when unfurled gave her a stage-wide wingspan as she belted **"Frozen."** The tableau was black, red and flesh as the dancers waved the sleeves gently back and forth—one false move and Madonna seemed like she could fall or be rended in half. Instead, she was abruptly de-sleeved and the crouching tiger revealed her hidden dragon lady, launching into some karate moves before elegantly traversing the stage, finally ending in high Kabuki theatrics.

The audience was probably hoping for a full rendition of **"Open Your Heart"** when the opening strains of that song were heard. Instead, Madonna offered a vocodered **"Nobody's Perfect"** opposite an angry samurai warrior.

Unbelievably, Madonna insisted on doing a bit of her most esoteric song of all time, the **powerful** ballad **"Mer Girl,"** continuing the show's maternal theme, but it quickly exploded into **"Sky Fits Heaven,"** kicked off by an aerial

stunt in which she leapt halfway across the stage in one seamless maneuver. It wasn't a hit tune, but it was an uplifting number and it allowed for more stage-jumps and some chopsocky choreography for Madonna and her troupe, ending with a dizzying spiral leap and—in an *MDNA Tour* preview?—Madonna breaking the neck of her foe.

Milking the applause, Madonna ended the section with a seated reprise of "Mer Girl."

Preceded by a violent **"What It Feels Like for a Girl"** anime interlude, the next section, *Country-Western*, brought Madonna back to her early '80s singer-songwriter roots. Madonna, in DSQUARED[2] duds and a modified leather shirt from Fred Segal, sat still to sing **"I Deserve It,"** leaning on nothing but her own **voice**.

"Don't Tell Me" followed, a game re-creation of her **Jean-Baptiste Mondino** music video, complete with line dancing and hunky dance pardners.

"Human Nature"—the least C&W song ever, but one whose theme echoes that of "Don't Tell Me"—followed, finding Madonna stripped to a US **flag** tank (by Catherine Malandrino) and sensually riding a mechanical bull as memorably as John Travolta in *Urban Cowboy* (1980). The mechanical bull was manufactured in Cheyenne, Oklahoma, and had been blessed by a priest—though clearly that didn't take.

Putting on a decent southern twang, Madonna then performed the indecent **"The Funny Song (Oh Dear Daddy),"** a **parody** track.

Madonna's simple take on **"Secret"** contained another of the concert's outstanding vocals, accompanied by a mélange of religious images behind her, including baptisms, followed closely in tone by **"Gone"** (or **"You'll See,"** depending on which US tour date you attended; always "Gone" elsewhere). When Madonna sang in that song that selling out was not her thing, the *Drowned World Tour* was her putting **money** where her mouth was.

A tango between dancers on **"Don't Cry for Me Argentina"** paved the way for the *Latin* section, kicked off by an all-Spanish version of "What It Feels Like for a Girl" on an abstract podium. Madonna's looks for this and the prior Japanese section were described by costumer Gaultier as a mix of "Spanish cliché and '40s lesbian."

"La Isla Bonita," one of Madonna's most performed '80s hits, was one of the only classics revived for the un-**nostalgic** *Drowned World.* Performed by the company, it was finally given an authentic Spanish rendition.

Urban/Ghetto found Madonna, De Lory and Haris pimped out (by **Versace**, **Dolce & Gabbana** and Gaultier) for an exciting mash-up of **"Holiday"** and Stardust's "Music Sounds Better With You" (1998). Madonna's tank said "MOTHER" on the front. *Aw!* And "FUCKER" on the back. *Oh.* A new burgundy beaver fedora had to be made nightly for her to wear and then toss into the crowd. Leaving no stone unturned, the inside of the hat read "PIMP MAMA."

De Lory and Haris had pushed for "Holiday" to be the last song of the show but they were overruled. Still, the whole

—LIZA MINNELLI

FABIO DIENA

thing ended on an upbeat note, with what was then (and is now) her most recent US #1 single, **"Music."** The finale teased the audience with images from throughout Madonna's career, but Madonna really cut loose dancing-wise, owning the stage with more synchronized chaos than had come before.

Madonna's *Drowned World Tour* aired on August 26, 2001 (from Detroit) on HBO as ***Madonna Live!—Drowned World Tour 2001*** (scoring 5.7 million viewers, the third most watched HBO concert in four years) and was released on DVD as ***Drowned World Tour 2001***.

• •

"… [Y]OU'D STRUGGLE TO FIND A BETTER SHOW THAN *DROWNED WORLD*, AND YOU'D FIND IT DIFFICULT TO FIND A MAINSTREAM ARTIST WHO CAN COMMAND NEAR-UNIVERSAL RESPECT FOR ANYTHING LIKE AS LONG AS THIS FINE LADY."

—MICHAEL HUBBARD, *MUSIC OMH* (2001)

• •

"RATHER THAN INDULGING THE FANS WITH A COMBINATION OF NEW AND OLD, WE WERE GIVEN A PU-PU PLATTER GLEANED MOSTLY FROM HER LAST COUPLE OF ALBUMS—1998'S *RAY OF LIGHT* AND LAST YEAR'S *MUSIC*. THE FANS WERE LEFT DESPERATELY SEEKING THE MADONNA WHO RULED THE '80S AND '90S."

—DAN AQUILANTE, *NEW YORK POST* (2001)

• •

"WE HAD BEEN TOUCHED BY POP ROYALTY. THE FEELING WAS ONLY SKIN-DEEP. BUT WHAT OUTLANDISH AND ENDURING STYLE."

—DAVID SINCLAIR, *ROLLING STONE* (2001)

• •

"THE SET LOOKED LIKE SKYLAB MEETS STUDIO 54, WITH, FOR A WHILE, A SEA ANEMONE THROWN IN … NEARLY NAKED DANCERS HUNG UPSIDE DOWN FOR AN UNCOMFORTABLY LONG TIME, AND SEVERAL GUYS DANCED AROUND IN GAS MASKS. FROM THIS THEY MAKE A LIVING?"

—LENORE SKENAZY, *NEW YORK DAILY NEWS* (2001)

• •

DROWNED WORLD TOUR PERFORMANCES

June 9-10, 2001: Barcelona, Spain (Palau Sant Jordi)

June 13-15, 2001: Milan, Italy (FilaForum)

June 19-20, June 22-23, 2001: Berlin, Germany (Max-Schmeling-Halle)

June 26-27, June 29-30, 2001: Paris, France (Palais Omnisports de Paris-Bercy)

July 4, July 6-7, July 9-10, July 12, 2001: London, England, UK (Earls Court)

July 21-22, 2001: Philadelphia, Pennsylvania, US (First Union Center)

July 25-26, July 28, July 30-31, 2001: New York, New York, US (Madison Square Garden)

August 2, 2001: East Rutherford, New Jersey, US (Continental Airlines Arena)

August 7-8, 2001: Boston, Massachusetts, US (Fleet Center)

August 10-11, 2001: Washington, DC, US (MCI Center)

August 14-15, 2001: Sunrise, Florida, US (National Car Rental Center)

August 19-20, 2001: Atlanta, Georgia, US (Philips Arena)

August 25-26, 2001: Auburn Hills, Michigan, US (The Palace of Auburn Hills)

August 28-29, 2001: Chicago, Illinois, US (United Center)

September 1-2, 2001: Paradise, Nevada, US (MGM Grand Garden Arena)

September 5-6, 2001: Oakland, California, US (Oakland Arena)

September 9, September 13-15, 2001: Los Angeles, California, US (Staples Center)

• •

DROWNED WORLD TOUR 2001: *Release date: November 13, 2001.* DVD containing the entire ***Drowned World Tour***, and packaged with images taken by Madonna's good buddy **Rosie O'Donnell**.

DRUDGE, MATT: *b. October 27, 1966.* Firestarting right-wing blogger who assisted **Bill Clinton** in besmirching his legacy and whose blog the Drudge Report is an influential news aggregator.

Drudge, a former Madonna fanatic (according to his enthusiastic participation in online forums in the early days of the Internet) before becoming whatever it is he's become, has reported on Madonna in a uniformly nasty way since at least the early 2000s. In 2003, he called Madonna's **"American Life"** video "antiwar, anti-Bush" and implied it was anti-American. Madonna's response, in *W* **magazine,** was, "Who's Matt Drudge? He's on the Internet? Never believe anything you read on the Internet. I don't want to comment on idiotic people making assumptions."

DRUGS: Madonna doesn't use them, but it would be inaccurate to say she is antidrugs. There is nothing "Just Say No" about her. The reason she avoids drugs is that she didn't get much enjoyment from them when she experimented and she dislikes relinquishing **control** of her mind. "I **hated** the lazy, spaced-out potheads," Madonna told *Seventeen* in 1985 of her peers in high **school.**

"She never touched **alcohol**, she didn't smoke pot, cigarettes—nothing," BFF **Debi Mazar** said in 1998. "And she always was on a natural high."

Madonna has said she never liked cocaine, which makes her even more **nervous** than she is naturally.

Her great friend **Maripol** tells *EM20* that Madonna's experimentation with drugs paled in comparison to what all their friends were doing in the '80s. "Because we did drop something at some point, yes, of course. Smoke, she never liked; coke, maybe a line here or there, maybe just New Year's Eve. And ecstasy, definitely."

Ecstasy is the one drug Madonna admits to having enjoyed. Just like Madonna remixes, ecstasy is a prime club drug. In her **Rock and Roll Hall of Fame** induction speech, Madonna recalled doing ecstasy with **Michael Rosenblatt**, whom she credits with discovering her. In 2012, she got into some drug trouble with deadmau5 at the **Ultra Music Festival**, though it led to her reasserting that she doesn't condone drug use ... in spite of her album being titled *MDNA*.

In her 2014 song **"Devil Pray,"** Madonna sings about the double-edged sword that is our freedom to use drugs. Madonna explained to David Blaine—in a 2015 *Interview* feature—that the song was about "how people take drugs to connect to **God** or to a higher level of consciousness," but it's not necessarily successful. "... [T]hat's the illusion of drugs, because they give you the illusion of getting closer to God, but ultimately, they kill you."

In 2015, she said, "I am not a big **fan** of drugs ... I just ask my daughter to make wise decisions and to do things in moderation and to try not to mix her alcohol. I am not going to say, 'No, don't do it,' because that is just absurd. And it is not fair. Yeah, I did it."

> "I think, ultimately, drugs destroy you. They take away your natural ability to be creative or love yourself, deal with people, communicate, *whatever.*" -MADONNA (1989)

DRUMS: Madonna was first a drummer in the band the **Breakfast Club**, teaching herself to play by listening to Elvis Costello records. "She wasn't a great drummer, but neither was Ringo," bandmate Gary Burke said in 2001. Later, she convinced the other members to let her try singing. "I wanted to be in the front. Who wants to be hidden behind all those drums?" she remembered in 1998.

In 2008, responding to a question coming from Costello himself, Madonna said she no longer has a drum kit but, "It's a very visceral instrument to play. And it makes sense to go from being a **dancer** to being a drummer because it required rhythm and coordination."

DUBOSE, GEORGE: Photographer who specialized in shooting the downtown **NYC** music scene, including numerous punk acts as well as important pop cultural figures the B-52s, Klaus Nomi, R.E.M. and Tom Waits.

DuBose shot Madonna at **U.S. Blues** in Roslyn, New York, in 1981.

"I shot Madonna at Camille's request," he tells *EM20*, referencing Madonna's first manager as a solo artist, **Camille Barbone**. Though the story has been told that Madonna was fronting the **Breakfast Club** that evening, it's more likely that this was in fact the first Madonna solo gig with a backing band, prior even to her first advertised gig at Chase Park. "She told me, 'Only shoot the singer.' I didn't even know the name of the singer when I got to the club."

Barbone was angry when she found out that DuBose had given Madonna verbal notes on her performance ("She seemed a bit nervous about her sexy presentation and I just told her, 'It's working.'"), which included costume changes. Still, he wound up shooting Madonna again, on the roof of **Danceteria** and in Boston.

"By then, she was singing to tapes and had her brother and another woman dancing behind her. I had invited some Boston promoters to see her Danceteria show, and they invited her to come to Boston and perform at **The Metro Club**. There was a three-camera video shoot made that night, but Madonna won't let it be released."

DuBose sells his **work** at George-DuBose.com and RockPaperPhoto.com.

DUKE UNIVERSITY: *1515 Hull Ave., Durham, NC.* Madonna auditioned for **Pearl Lang** and was subsequently invited to attend the **American Dance Festival** at this college in July 1978 at the urging of her mentor, **Christopher Flynn**.

Madonna at her first solo gig, shot by George DuBose.

© GEORGE-DUBOSE.COM

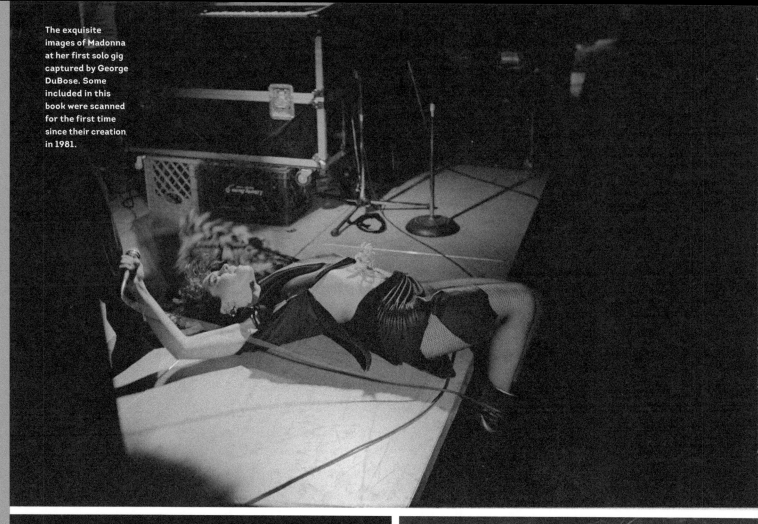

The exquisite images of Madonna at her first solo gig captured by George DuBose. Some included in this book were scanned for the first time since their creation in 1981.

©GEORGE-DUBOSE.COM

©GEORGE-DUBOSE.COM

EAR SAY: *Airdate: 1984.* UK **TV** show that featured a unique interview with Madonna exiting the **NYC** subway on a rainy day and walking with her on-and-off lover **Bobby Martinez**. In the interview, she bragged about torturing her younger neighbors as a kid when she wasn't teaching them to **dance** and also recalled "pantomiming" to the girls on *The Lawrence Welk Show* (1955–1982).

EARLY SHOW, THE: *Airdates: 1999–.* Madonna has twice been interviewed on this CBS morning program, both times by newsman Harry Smith.

On the December 20, 2004, installment, Smith told Madonna he was "blown away" by her foray into writing children's **books.** Madonna expressed that *The English Roses* was about, "… getting people to at least stop and think every once in a while about what they, what they're gonna say and what this might do to someone if they say it." She razzed Smith when he pointed out a tremor in her **voice**, saying she felt like she was talking to her shrink.

For the December 12, 2005, episode, Madonna was interviewed backstage before, and then the day following, her promo show in Tokyo. Madonna, in a great mood, expressed kinship with her **fans** and waxed philosophical about how best to live her life. "I would **love** to get to the end of every one of my days and think, 'Did I do everything I meant to achieve?'" She also talked about being grateful for the fact that when she is perceived to have failed, she is well situated to ride it out. Foreshadowing **"Living for Love,"** she cracked that whenever she was knocked down, her attitude is, "Pick my crown up off the floor, put it back on my head, and keep goin'."

> "There's a rumor going around that I'm a perfectionist—but it's just a rumor."
> —MADONNA, THE EARLY SHOW (2005)

E. 4TH ST.: The first apartment in which Madonna lived on her own in **NYC** was at 232 E. 4th St. and Avenue B in Alphabet City. She reportedly told a neighbor she'd moved there from the Congo, where she was studying apes … before asking for a loan. Shortly thereafter, she also lived at 102 E. 4th St. on the 6th floor, a return address she handwrote on at least one impromptu C.V. she sent to a filmmaker prior to the widely seen letter she wrote to filmmaker Stephen Jon Lewicki to say she was available to **work** on his movie *A Certain Sacrifice.*

> "Once I moved down here, this is when I really started to, like, enjoy myself, started to have a circle of friends … well, things were looking up, and I was about to get a record deal."—MADONNA ON THE LOWER EAST SIDE (1998)

E. 13TH ST.: Madonna told *People* in 1985 that after she'd fled her **E. 4th St.** apartment a few years earlier, she lived for a while in Yippie leader Abbie Hoffman's old apartment, which would have to be 114–116 E. 13th St. There is no indication how long Madonna stayed.

"EASY RIDE": The last track on Madonna's *American Life*, this simple song alternates subtly between vulnerable and tough, featuring Madonna singing that she wants a happy life, but only if she has to "**work** for it." The song is as good an example as any that *American Life* was shamefully undervalued. Written by Madonna with **Monte Pittman** and produced by Madonna and **Mirwais**, "Easy Ride" has only been performed live at *Tears of a Clown* in Melbourne.

Tracy Young's Mixshow Remix of this song is, to this day, *fire.*

EGG FILM, THE: *Director: Wyn Cooper; Filmed: 1974.* This odd, minute-long piece of film makes use of a urinal for its title card (the words were written in grease pencil and partially peed off by classmate Steve Meadows) before cutting to a 16-year-old, bikini-clad Madonna slurping in and spitting out the contents of a raw egg. After Madonna's pre-"Rocky Balboa" egg consumption, we see her sunbathing. Another teenage girl (who wishes to remain uncredited) then cracks open a fresh egg on Madonna's abdomen, salts it and through the magic of a jump-cut eats (with silverware) the fried end-result.

In the 2002 Madonna-themed episode of the **VH1** series *Driven*, the director of *The Egg Film*, Wyn Cooper, said the film wasn't about anything and noted of his leading lady, "It's pretty clear that even at that age she was willing to do quite a bit in front of a camera, including eating a raw egg."

Cooper, a high **school** classmate and boyfriend of Madonna's, made *The Egg Film* for a film class—"I got an A on it," he remembers to *EM20*. It was filmed on the deck of a home at which Madonna was babysitting—the baby was sleeping inside.

As for his recollection of Madonna, Cooper tells *EM20*, "She was fun, smart and a great **dancer**—best in the school by far—though a bit of an outsider. Had only a few really close friends." He definitely figured out a good way to bring her out of her … shell.

EICHNER, BILLY: *b. September 18, 1978.* Comedian known for his outrageous series *Billy on the Street* (2011–), which also aired on *Conan*. His schtick is to approach people on the street and shout offbeat questions at them, often castigating them, in character, for having the wrong opinion even when they play along. His pop culture quizzes are a no-win proposition.

When Madonna provided the **Super Bowl** halftime show, Eichner traveled to Indianapolis, asking if people were excited about seeing her perform. Some were, some were

"Madonna is basically an icon in this business—to everybody."—MISSY ELLIOTT (2005)

not, including a gross old man who confidently declared her to be an "old hag." The **cheerleaders** were all about Madonna, but weren't helpful in scoring Eichner any cocaine.

For a later 2012 episode, Eichner ran around **NYC** asking randos if they were excited that Madonna's *MDNA Tour* was playing Yankee Stadium. Answers ranged from, "I don't like Madonna," to goodnatured support to stunned silence. Eichner then headed to the stadium, where he crashed Madonna's tour rehearsal, dancing on the stage behind her before being thrown out by her in a planned skit. He headed back to confront her and to ask if she would do **"Holiday"** or **"Vogue,"** gushing that he **loved** her in *Dick Tracy*. **Rocco** crashed the interview. After, Eichner and **Ciccone** shared a funny moment, in which Madonna suggested they "get to know each other" after her show.

I'm, like, a huge Madonna fan from way back ... surprise!"—BILLY EICHNER (2012)

EL SEPTIMO DE CABALLERIA: *Airdates 1998–1999.* On the November 23, 1998, episode of this RTVE **TV** show filmed in Spain, Madonna, with her geisha haircut and a tight brown leather jacket, sang a stirring live rendition of **"The Power of Good-Bye."** She was also interviewed by the Spanish actor and musician Miguel Bosé, who heaped praise on her for the song and for her *Ray of Light* album. Madonna confirmed that the album was a true reflection of where she was in her life at that time, saying, "Life is a journey, and hopefully as you get older you get wiser and you get closer to who you are and the truth of who you are ..."

ELIZABETH II, QUEEN: *b. April 21, 1926.* **Queen of Pop** Madonna met Queen of **England** Elizabeth once, on November 18, 2002, at the world premiere of the film *Die Another Day* at Royal Albert Hall in **London**. A series of awkward photos reveals Madonna to be quite **nervous**, making a distressed face before her much-practiced curtsey ("Madonna bowed perfectly," reported the *Daily Mail*). With upswept **hair**, Madonna—in a conservative black dress apparently accessorized with as many diamonds as she could lay her hands on—seemed almost to have coasted below the Queen's radar for 20 years; the Queen reportedly had to be told that Madonna sang the film's title song, to which she replied, "Oh, really—did you?" Madonna shouldn't have felt bad ... the Queen next asked John Cleese, "And what do you do?"

ELLIOTT, MISSY: *b. July 1, 1971.* Groundbreaking female rapper, producer and songwriter whose massive pop hits include "Hot Boyz" (1999), "Get Ur Freak On" (2001), **"Work** It" (2002) and "Lose **Control**" (2005), and who has guested on countless other tracks.

In 2003, Elliott teamed up with Madonna to endorse **Gap**, rapping on a mash-up of Madonna's songs called **"Into the Hollywood Groove."** The collaboration was a big hit for Gap. Madonna then enlisted Elliott to be a part of her **MTV Video Music Awards** performance that year when she kissed **Britney Spears** and **Christina Aguilera**.

Continuing their association, Madonna guest-starred on the "That's Madonna, Right There" episode of Elliott's series *The Road to Stardom with Missy Elliott*, which aired February 16, 2005. Madonna shook hands with and/or hugged a group of aspiring musicians who were under Elliott's wing, allowing them to ask her any questions they wanted about her career and her then upcoming *Re-Invention World Tour*.

Madonna's main advice to them was, "It's all about the right influences around you and, you know, to remember why you're doing it in the first place."

ELVIS: SEE: **Presley, Elvis.**

EMINEM: *b. October 17, 1972.* One of the most successful rappers of all time, the Michigander has engendered and weathered controversies over homophobic and misogynistic lyrics, starred in the smash-hit movie *8 Mile* (2002) and was presented the **Oscar** for Best **Original** Song for "Lose Yourself" (2002). Well, he didn't actually show up, but **Barbra Streisand** read his name.

In 2001, Madonna defended Eminem against critics of his **work,** saying, "What is the big deal about Eminem? Since when is offensive language a reason for being unpopular? I like the fact that Eminem is brash and angry and politically incorrect. At least he has an opinion. He's stirring things up, he's provoking a discussion, he's making peope's blood boil. He's reflecting what's going on in society right now. This is what **art** is supposed to do."

Eminem paid her back by turning his nose up at her *Drowned World Tour*, saying, "I wasn't impressed with her recent live shows. I'd rather sit in a dentist's chair."

At the 2003 **MTV Video Music Awards**, Madonna made sure to say hello to Eminem. Backstage, he did a formal bow and she said, "Get up, boy—we're from the same town!"

Madonna has recently expressed her continuing admiration for Eminem, going so far as to say she had wanted to work with him, "but he didn't seem to want to." Asked on *106 & Park* what famous artists she would have signed to her label if she'd had the chance, Madonna chose **Eminem**, Jay Z and 50 Cent.

EMMY: Madonna's early-'80s rock band following her departure from the **Breakfast Club**, bearing one of her many **nicknames**. (Previous names, none apparently lasting, include the Millionaires, Modern **Dance** and Emmenon or Emanon, the latter of which is "no name" spelled backwards.)

Emmy featured herself, Gary Burke, **Stephen Bray** and a guitarist named Vinny. Vinny was replaced by Mike Monahan, but he became too busy to keep performing, so Brian Symmes joined. The final incarnation of Emmy became roommates while they were **working** as a band.

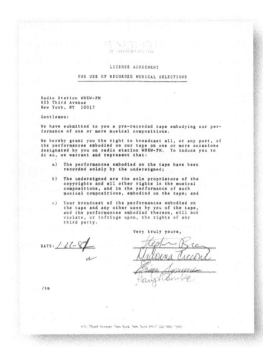

Contract granting
rights to play
Emmy's music on
the radio

Emmy's most high-profile gigs were at **Chase Park** in July 1980, Botany Talk House (formerly 6th Ave. and 27th St., NY, NY) in December 1980, and Max's Kansas City (formerly 213 Park Ave. S., NY, NY) in March 1981. After its Max's Kansas City gig, Madonna took on **Camille Barbone** to manage her as a solo artist.

A sample nine-song Emmy set list was typically "Best Girl," "Hothouse Flower," "Bells Ringing," "Simon Says," "Nobody's Fool," "No Time for **Love**," "Drowning," "Love for Tender," and "Love Express," all officially **unreleased**. The band's December 1980 gig at Botany House was recorded and commercialized as a bootleg called *Emmy & The Emmys: First Time Out of Manhattan* (1994).

"We kinda sucked. I mean, we didn't suck *bad*, but we weren't that good."
—STEPHEN BRAY ON EMMY (2001)

EMPIRE DINER: *210 10th Ave., NY, NY.* Vintage 24-hour diner where scenes from the **"Bad Girl"** video were shot.

ENDO: In 1994, Madonna asked **David Letterman** if he'd ever smoked endo, eliciting a tongue-tied denial that he had any idea what she meant. "You're a goddamned liar," she seethed, and her vehemence seemed to imply that she knew for a fact that Letterman *had*. Since Madonna says she isn't into **smoking** *or* doing **drugs**, she must have spent time in the library researching: Endo is extremely potent marijuana.

ENGLAND: The British press has always been particularly unkind to Madonna. "I'm not interested in preaching to the converted, so basically I'm going to the places where I have the most enemies. That's why I'm starting in London," she said of *The Girlie Show World Tour* itinerary.

Madonna wound up living in a manor in the English countryside for many years when she was married to **Guy**

Ritchie. They lived on a 1,134-acre estate called Ashcombe House in the UK, worth in excess of $20 million. It was formerly owned (and adored) by Cecil Beaton; Madonna found out about it via a relationship she'd struck up with Beaton's biographer Hugo Vickers.

"To me, Ashcombe is a reflection of me and my husband in many ways because it reflects our willingness to make a commitment," she told *Vogue* in 2005.

Madonna has owned and lived in several London properties, including a 10-bedroom Georgian townhouse in Marylebone that she still owns and visits every Christmas while her sons spend time with their dad.

"I long to live in the countryside of England on a sheep farm, and have two children and live this idyllic life. I'd get bored ... That kind of idyllic situation—it's not good for creativity. You need tension. You need friction."—MADONNA, WHO (1999)

ENGLISH ROSES, THE: Madonna's 2003 best-selling children's **book**. (SEE: **bibliography** (**by Madonna**).]

ENOS, JOHN: *b. June 12, 1962.* Hunky actor/model/peripheral celeb/nightclub owner with whom Madonna has been linked romantically. In 1992, they attended a **birthday** bash for Lou Rawls's **mother** at the Los Angeles restaurant Georgia (formerly 7250 Melrose Ave., LA, CA).

Side note: Gossips noted the chumminess between Enos and Mickey Rourke, his real-life best buddy, spurred on by photos of the men holding hands. Rourke threw a birthday party for Enos at Enos's club Roxbury (in West Hollywood) at which they slow-**danced** and carried on in much the same way as Madonna and **Sandra Bernhard** used to. Gender roles can be *so* confusing sometimes!

"I think I'm at the beginning of a very fruitful career."
—MADONNA, *ENTERTAINMENT TONIGHT* (1984)

ENTERTAINMENT TONIGHT: *Airdates: 1981–.* The **TV** show that practically invented entertainment news as a commodity, *ET* (for short) has been covering Madonna, sometimes exclusively, from the very beginning of her career. It would be impossible to catalogue every meaningful appearance Madonna has made on the show because there have been stories on her surrounding every move she's made for over 30 years. But some highlights include:

Madonna's first *ET* appearance seems to have been in 1984, when the show nabbed her for a behind-the-scenes interview during the filming of her **"Borderline"** video for its February 12 episode that year. Madonna, interviewed in a bar near the set, told *ET*, "I'm out to do something and I'm gonna do what I have to [sic] get there ... I have to be calculating, but I also have to be open, I mean, it's both, really."

Also early on, a young reporter named Maria Shriver filed a 1985 report on Madonna mania. In it, Madonna said of career longevity at her *Desperately Seeking Susan* premiere, "I want longevity as a *human being.* I want it to last forever."

At her *Truth or Dare* premiere in 1991, the show's camera caught Madonna explaining that the film was about so much more than just herself: "I think it's about life ... homophobia, um, sexual abuse of women, um, family issues, alcoholism—all kinds of stuff." She also confessed that "the truth makes me uncomfortable, but I can deal with it."

In 1997, Madonna gave herself a good review for her *Evita* performance to *ET*, saying, "I feel...that I have given birth to something beautiful, and I'm very proud of it."

The following year, Madonna granted *ET* a world-exclusive peek at the making of her video for **"The Power of Good-Bye."** She told a bored-looking Bob Goen that she likes to be involved in every aspect of the making of her videos. The show also had an exclusive peek at her next video, **"Nothing Really Matters."** This time, *ET* was invited into Madonna's home, watching her watching herself film the geisha-themed video. Madonna claimed **Lola**—then a toddler—totally got what her mom was going for with the video, showing up on the set with a cheerful, "Hi, Hatsumomo!," a reference to the *Memoirs of a Geisha* character Madonna was unofficially playing.

Madonna plugged *Confessions on a Dance Floor* in a sit-down with **sexy** host Mark Steines, who showed up in his white polyester suit in order to **disco** it up with her.

In 2010, Madonna hyped her **Material Girl** clothing line in a short interview in which she admitted that she's a "mean **mother**" who frowns on fun stuff like TV.

In 2014, Madonna was telling *ET Canada*'s Roz Weston that he needed to **work** out before admitting she has a "**love/hate**" relationship with her body.

During a tidal wave of press for Madonna's *Rebel Heart* release in March 2015, she sat with *ET*'s Jason Dundas (lisping through her **grills**), speaking about **ageism**, **"Living for Love"** ("Matadors have to be really brave. They have to go into a ring and fight a beast, right? So ... that's kinda like life. It's a metaphor.") and the purple lipstick she was wearing during her **"Borderline"** video.

"She's fresh and she's new and she's '85. She's 'it' now."—FAN ON *ENTERTAINMENT TONIGHT* (1985)

EROTICA (ALBUM): *Release date: October 20, 1992. Billboard 200 peak: #2.* Madonna's fifth studio album snuck in the back door in October 1992 while its sister release, *Sex*, stomped in the front door, *naked*. Because the two were released virtually simultaneously in the wake of the **"Erotica"** video, pundits and music consumers had a difficult time focusing on the tunes.

Some commentators with obvious agendas claimed to **hate** the album, railing against its worthlessness as a mere accessory to a **book** and a movie. Others groused that *Erotica* was too dirty, then turned around and called it unsexy—kind of like telling a naked lady she's a whore for not covering up and then critiquing her rack.

Even Madonna's favorable legit reviews—of which there were many—tripped over themselves, qualifying every positive statement with concern that they were somehow being duped. What is the world coming to when an artist's **powers** of persuasion are so potent that rational-minded critics begin to question their own opinions?

The media's paranoia and contempt influenced record-buyers, some of whom avoided the album like the clap, almost as if they expected it to be a series of obscene phone calls and guttural grunts.

What *Erotica* actually is: An almost seamless, edgy joyride through various pop styles, most prominently house and **disco**. It is also an album that was created

GREGORY PACE

erratically—Madonna was busy shooting *Sex* and **Body of Evidence**—but one about which Madonna had concrete ideas from the beginning. She wanted it to be very *now*. For that reason, and no doubt because of their phenomenal success with her previous #1 singles **"Vogue"** and **"This Used to Be My Playground,"** Madonna chose **Shep Pettibone** as her main coproducer and cowriter (with **Tony Shimkin**, who officially received some credit long after the album was released). She also collaborated with **Andre Betts**, who had previously helped to deliver her the format-challenging #1 hit **"Justify My Love."**

There is a **school** of thought in Madonna standom that says *Erotica* is her best album, thanks to its unified **assault** on **sex** and **love**, and its consistency in deconstructing feelings, whether erotic or romantic.

While most critics noted the chill in the album, some invariably failed to see the connection between that frigidity and human sexuality.

Try standing in a hip club**,** hearing throbbing music, glimpsing forms in the flashing lights, overheated yet numb with the cold lack of any kind of connection. Watch the other people there and look for one you're attracted to. Now look for more. In every one of them, there is a story to be played out, a tale of how you two could connect, or fail trying. In the end, there is always the less involving transaction, the coldest—sex without strings. *Erotica* is often about that chill; it doesn't follow through and tie up all its loose ends in one big happy package, but then that would be **boring**. Rather, it leaves you with pleasing music masking the contemplative lyrics underneath, and all the pleasure, and disappointment, of a grand, zipless **fuck**.

For packaging, Madonna is pictured in arctic ecstasy in extreme close-up on the front cover (applause for photog **Steven Meisel**), and she's **shrimping** a famous toe on the back cover (applause slows to silence). Problematically, both are images created during the shooting of *Sex*, adding to the blurred lines between Madonna's record and her book.

The album opens with the scratched-vinyl menace of the title track. The tone is set with Madonna's growling diva turn as **"Dita,"** a jaded soul who walks us through an SM landscape, daring us to question whether a human heart might be found somewhere under her sexual bravado. It is a threatening beginning, putting the listener on the defensive.

After the daring of the first song, Madonna's breathy, submissive **"Fever"**—the last song to make the album—is a deceptively straightforward disco-ization of **Peggy Lee**, though Madonna gets extra credit for lending a fetching insouciance to her minimalist vocals.

"Bye Bye Baby" is, depending on your taste, either an annoyingly mechanized, tinny trifle, or an effectively venomous anti-love song, but it marked an early harbinger of a trend in Madonna's vocals toward using studio gimmicks to help extend her limited range.

Smack dab in the middle of the **AIDS** crisis, **"Deeper and Deeper"** represents the kind of old-school nirvanic

EROTICA

① "Erotica" (Madonna/Shep Pettibone/ Tony Shimkin)–5:20, produced by Madonna/ Shep Pettibone

② "Fever" (John Davenport/Eddie Cooley)–5:00, produced by Madonna/Shep Pettibone

③ "Bye Bye Baby" (Madonna/Shep Pettibone/ Tony Shimkin)–3:56, produced by Madonna/ Shep Pettibone

④ "Deeper and Deeper" (Madonna/Shep Pettibone/ Tony Shimkin)–5:33, produced by Madonna/ Shep Pettibone

⑤ "Where Life Begins" (Madonna/Andre Betts) –5:57, produced by Madonna/Andre Betts

⑥ "Bad Girl" (Madonna/Shep Pettibone/ Tony Shimkin)–5:23, produced by Madonna/ Shep Pettibone

⑦ "Waiting" (Madonna/Andre Betts) –5:46, produced by Madonna/Andre Betts

⑧ "Thief of Hearts" (Madonna/Shep Pettibone/ Tony Shimkin)–4:51, produced by Madonna/ Shep Pettibone

⑨ "Words" (Madonna/Shep Pettibone/ Tony Shimkin)–5:55, produced by Madonna/ Shep Pettibone

⑩ "Rain" (Madonna/Shep Pettibone) –5:25, produced by Madonna/Shep Pettibone

⑪ "Why's It So Hard" (Madonna/Shep Pettibone/ Tony Shimkin)–5:23, produced by Madonna/ Shep Pettibone

⑫ "In This Life" (Madonna/Shep Pettibone) –6:23, produced by Madonna/Shep Pettibone

⑬ "Did You Do It?" feat. Mark Goodman and Dave Murphy (Madonna/ Andre Betts)–4:54, produced by Madonna/ Andre Betts

⑭ "Secret Garden" (Madonna/Andre Betts) –5:32, produced by Madonna/Andre Betts

song that made you wish the **dance** floor hadn't gotten so G.D. crowded all of a sudden, before you realize how long it had been since the disco era, and how good it used to be surrounded by bodies not guided by fear.

"Where Life Begins" has a jazzy style to it, a somewhat cloying oral-sex anthem with an infamous fried-chicken reference. It's pretty revolutionary ... how often have female rockers sung about wanting head? It's a sexually liberated, **feminist** jam.

"Bad Girl" returns Madonna to her unsung forte, the singer of lush, multi-dimensional love songs. Here, her upper register delivers an impressively weary confession with a sweeping sense of space, all of it inner.

What is there to say about **"Waiting,"** which knocks your socks off (unless you'd prefer to keep them on?) with its sheer, unrepentant lust?

Madonna virtually remakes Blondie's "Rip Her to Shreds" (1977) in the more subdued **"Thief of Hearts,"** a hilariously smug song that attacks a cock-blocking **"bitch."** Yes, Madonna is one of those women who calls other women bitches when they cross her, and the kind of woman who makes men her bitch if they let her. It may well have been directed at the woman then in **Sean Penn**'s life, Robin Wright.

"Words" is an important cornerstone of the album—Madonna tears down the concept of language to its most rudimentary component, taking the facade away from speechmaking, a strip-mining much like she attempts to do with sex elsewhere on the record. Her lyrics on this are prescient; how could she have known the extent to which she would be the victim of verbal drive-bys after the release of this album?

Serving as the hopeless romantic that inhabits every club fixture, "Rain" is a gorgeous ballad, one constructed with a dewy attention to sensuality that makes it more erotic than anything else on the record; it's one of the few songs here one could envision making love to, Madonna's Johnny Mathis moment.

"Why's It So Hard," modernized, modified reggae, features Madonna pleading for a sort of tolerance that she herself knows can never be. To her credit, that knowledge doesn't stop her from begging for it.

Madonna is at her most heartsick in her AIDS ballad "In This Life," written about the **deaths** of friend **Martin Burgoyne** and **Christopher Flynn**. Though there is definitely something off-kilter when she accidentally-sexily asks if we've ever seen our best friend die, her sincerity here—not just owing to the fact that we know she *has* seen her best friend die—is unimpeachable.

"Did You Do It?" appeared only on copies of the album with a CONTAINS LANGUAGE THAT SOME PEOPLE MIGHT FIND OFFENSIVE sticker, but it's really just low humor that makes light of the hardcore, sex-bragging songs children were listening to unsupervised every day in 1992 ... and beyond.

The album's denouement is the lush, jazzy "Secret Garden," which reveals Madonna's songwriting skills and imagination to be as fertile as her womb. She has never sounded more convincingly engaged (the song is about a French lover of hers) nor more defiant in enjoying her artistic journey and her womanhood.

Erotica is perfectly titled after all. It doesn't always make you feel the things it is about, but every one of its songs could stand in for a splintered emotion that possesses you as you stand in that club and look for someone with whom to connect: hopefulness, horniness, the rush of **power**, the humiliation of defeat, joy, **flirtation**, fear, the urge to compete, all-consuming need.

Erotica was Madonna's first music release on her own **Maverick** label, and was considered her first "flop" album. It has sold over 6 million copies worldwide.

"EROTICA" (SONG): *Release date: October 13, 1992. Billboard Hot 100 peak: #3.* Her name is **"Dita"** ... and she's *frisky.*

Madonna continued to explore the potency of spoken-word vocals on this first single from *Erotica*, produced by Madonna and **Shep Pettibone** and written primarily by Madonna, Pettibone and **Tony Shimkin**, with further

"FOR SOMEONE WHO THRIVES ON DEMYSTIFYING SEXUAL MORES, MADONNA IS RIGHT ON TARGET. LISTEN TO *EROTICA* AND THEN TAKE A COLD SHOWER!"-KEITH SHARP, *PULSE* (1992)

"WHAT THE ALBUM'S ABOUT IS DISTANCE—BETWEEN IMAGES OF SEX AND SEX, BETWEEN POP STYLIZATIONS OF EMOTION AND THE MESSINESS OF THE REAL THING. LIKE MOST OF US, SHE VALUES BOTH. BUT SHE RECOGNIZES THAT ULTIMATELY THEY'RE OPPOSITES, NOT COMPLEMENTS. AND NEVER, OR ANYWAY FAR TOO SELDOM, THE TWAIN SHALL MEET—WHICH IS THE THEME OF *EROTICA*, THE SUBTEXT OF *SEX*, AND EVER, OR ANYWAY FAR TOO OFTEN, THE STORY OF SEX."-TOM CARSON, *LA WEEKLY* (1992)

"YOU AND SHEP SURE DO A BANG-UP JOB—PUN INTENDED—TRANSFORMING 'FEVER', THAT OLD PEGGY LEE HIT, INTO A TECHNO DRONE, BUT LISTEN TO THE PARCHED SOUND EMITTED FROM YOUR THROAT ON SUCH TRACKS … THERE'S NOTHING EROTIC ABOUT IT, UNLESS ONE FINDS THE IDEA OF A SINGING DEATH MASK SEXY." -DAVID BROWNE, *ENTERTAINMENT WEEKLY* (1992)

"NO MADONNA ALBUM WAS EVER MET WITH A LOUDER BACKLASH OR WAS MORE RAMPANTLY MISREPRESENTED THAN THIS DARK MASTERPIECE, SO YOU KNOW IT WAS DOING SOMETHING RIGHT … UNDERNEATH MADONNA'S BONDAGE GETUP AND SHEP PETTIBONE'S OVERSIZED DRUM TRACKS BEATS A TRULY PAINED HEART."-ERIC HENDERSON, *SLANT* (2011)

"*EROTICA* IS A STRONG CASE FOR MADONNA THE MUSICIAN … THE MUSIC STILL SOUNDS BRACING, COOL, FUNNY AND SAD. IF IT'S BEEN A WHILE SINCE YOU'VE PLAYED THIS … DO IT TONIGHT, LATE. IT'LL HIT YOU LIKE A TRUCK." -STEPHEN SEARS, *IDOLATOR* (2012)

writing credits for Dennis "D.T." Thomas, Donald Boyce, George Brown, Richard Westfield, Robert "Kool" Bell, Robert "Spike" Mickens and Ronald Bell due to sampling. Madonna was hit with a lawsuit for the unauthorized use of the song "El Yom 'Ulliqa 'Ala Khashaba" ("Today, He Is Held to a Cross," 1962) by Fairuz, which was settled out of court. The same song had been used without credit on **"The Beast Withn,"** a version of **"Justify My Love."**

On "Erotica," Madonna assumes the ID of a libidinous dominatrix figure who talks about nothing but **sex,** pointing up the pleasure in pain, the appeal in submission and above all, the **power** of attraction.

Madonna's **voice** is gravelly, but the refrain is a breathy plea to put your hands all over her. Similar to "Justify My Love" for its frankly sexual content, "Erotica" nonetheless distinguishes itself as a unique musical statement, capturing a menacing sexuality that was truly rare coming from a female artist at the time.

Despite a relative lack of airplay due to its controversial content and a bad case of Madonna burn-out, "Erotica" blasted onto the charts at #13 (which meant something in those days) and eventually went gold. When it stalled at #3, it was the first time a kickoff single from a Madonna album had failed to hit #1 since the release of *Madonna*.

Madonna has performed "Erotica" on three of her tours: *The Girlie Show World Tour*, the *Confessions Tour* (on which she performed one of its early demo versions, "You Thrill Me") and *The MDNA Tour* in a mash-up with **"Candy Shop."**

At the same time of the song's release, Madonna included a different, even edgier version called "Erotic" on a CD that came "free" with the purchase of *Sex*.

"EROTICA" (VIDEO): *Director: Fabien Baron, 1992.* Madonna's least linear music video, resembling a Kenneth Anger short meets a burlesque loop. Many critics dismissed the clip as a creative statement because it is a chaotic series of images, but that's the point. The video's style is very much in keeping with the song's presentational lyrics.

Image after image attacks the viewer: Here is Madonna sharing a **lollipop** with another woman, their tongues caressing across a sticky orb; here she is dancing decadently poolside; now she is laughing maniacally as she whips a herd of **nude** men. There is no storyline; the unifying portion of the **video** is a simple scene of **"Dita Parlo"** in a black mask and dominatrix outfit, lip-synching onstage at what appears to be a sleazy erotic theatre. Shot in **black-and-white**, this segment crackles like radio interference, buzzing with the image of sparkly silver strips at the back of the stage, through which she enters and coyly departs, like a penis confidently slipping in and out of an orifice it well and truly owns.

Though we are used to Madonna parading around in a variety of guises, this time she had *really* done it, really made herself look *different*. By wearing a simple mask and pulling her **hair** back, she looked like your worst nightmare, or your most sinister fantasy.

Providing the capper is the scene-stealing Chinese **hopping ghost** doll Madonna produces. In this setting, the doll is diabolical, and when Madonna sucks on its tiny, **boxing**-gloved fist, you either have to shudder with dread or laugh **nervously** out loud. Still more effective is when the doll punches out, its fully extended glove landing precisely at Madonna's angular jaw.

To assemble this *mess*terpiece, accomplished **magazine** designer **Fabien Baron** shot studio and on-the-fly footage of Madonna as she posed for **Steven Meisel** for *Sex*, which Baron was in the process of designing. Baron shot it on Super 8 film, often very old or damaged stock, giving it an authentically distressed, vintage look, in the same way that vinyl surface noise lends the song true grit. Baron filmed the studio bits at the storied performance space The Kitchen (512 W. 19th St., NY, NY), which had been styled to resemble the tackily glittering stage of the **Gaiety**.

Thanks to its raunch factor (despite the little black bars that shakily cover her naughty bits in the nude hitchhiking finale), "Erotica" was banned from a planned broadcast on *Friday Night Videos* (1983–2002) and on the NBC screen in Times Square, which at the time was like a living, breathing "Erotica" video. Sapping interest for a **"Justify My Love"**–like video single, **MTV** did play the video in its entirety after 10 p.m. … albeit only three times. An uncensored version of the video aired in France before, during and after the 10 p.m. hour.

"Erotica" is remembered more than some of the videos for Madonna's bigger hits. **Beyoncé**'s 2013 video "Haunted" pays homage to several Madonna clips, including this one.

ESCAPES: *Formerly Merrick Ln., Merrick, Long Island, NY.* This hot and happenin' Long Island club hosted Madonna for at least two early performances, the first in 1983. Greg Antis, who **worked** from 1979 to 1989 at the club as a DJ and bartender, remembers the place was "packed" and that Madonna performed there about a month before her gig at **Uncle Sam's**, a rival establishment.

Madonna's set list was probably the same as at Uncle Sam's (**"Physical Attraction," "Everybody," "Holiday"** and **"Burning Up,"**) with **Erika Belle, Christopher Ciccone** and **Bags Rilez** as backup **dancers**, and all the music on reel-to-reel tape and live vocals.

"The first time she showed up, I was really excited to see her. I was bartending," Antis tells *EM20*. "John, the waiter, comes up to me and he goes, 'Give me four Hennessy straight up in cognac glasses.' There were no computers then, it was a ticket. He goes, 'For Madonna.' I go, 'Okay.' He comes back 10 minutes later, I give him four more. He comes back 10 mintues *later*, I give him four *more*. Finally, I go, 'John, you know, this is a bar where I can serve Screwdrivers, Alabama Slammers, Screaming Orgasms, Melon **Balls**, Budweiser, Michelob … where the **fuck** are the cognac glasses?' He goes, 'She's keeping them.' I'll never forget that! I said, 'Tell her to go back to France.' I got a bunch of plastic cups and poured the Hennessy in them instead. [Laughs] That was my first impression of her."

Madonna played Escapes after a strip show at the venue, but so did many other top club acts. In fact, even James Brown played Escapes—the Godfather of Soul and the **Queen of Pop.**

Madonna at her 1983 Escapes gig. See never-published images from the evening on the following pages.

GREG ANTIS

MADONNA
ROCKS
ESCAPES
IN 1983!

GREG ANTIS

"Put her in a gay disco, and most of the guys would be very happy to have sex with her."–RUPERT EVERETT ON MADONNA, US (1999)

ESTHER: In 2004, it became known that Madonna had chosen this name as part of her ongoing devotion to **Kabbalah**. Immediately, the press made it seem that Madonna was *changing* her name, and that she expected people to call her by this new one. Not so. Madonna explained to *Tatler* that no one had ever called her Esther, saying, "It is completely metaphysical." She likened it to taking the name of **Veronica** when she was confirmed as a kid, and has said she simply "wanted to attach myself to the energy of a different name."

"EVA AND MAGALDI/EVA BEWARE OF THE CITY": Track from *Evita: The Complete Motion Picture Music Soundtrack* that features references to **"Buenos Aires"** as Che (**Antonio Banderas**) warns Evita's temporary boyfriend "Magaldi" (**Jimmy Nail**) of her true intentions, and Magaldi warns Evita that she may get more than she bargained for in Buenos Aires. The music is the least Spanish-inflected of any in the whole musical, pure '70s rock-opera. Someone needs to create a club track that samples Madonna's, "Screw the middle classes! I will never accept them." Chaotic components aside, the song is an important transitional piece in *Evita*'s story.

EVANSVILLE: Indiana city that was the site of a substantial amount of on-location shooting for *A League of Their Own* in August 1991. Madonna and fellow cast/team members leased private homes for the duration of the shoot, a problem for Madonna's realtor since no one wanted to lease her a furnished home for fear a raunchy rock star would trash the place. She eventually secured a house at 9010 Whetstone Dr. for $7,500 per month.

Though she was warmly embraced by the town at the time of her stay (except for a local pastor, who sent her a missive telling her he was praying for her), she later turned her nose up at the experience.

Offending two cities across the world from each other simultaneously, Madonna sniffed, "I may as well have been in Prague," to **Kurt Loder** in *TV Guide*, complaining about not having access to cable or **MTV**.

Oddly, United Artists Cable billed realtor Jeri Garrison $750 for three cable boxes and remote controls that went missing from the house in which Madonna stayed. "I sure learned something from this: Don't put a bill in your name if you don't even know the last name of the other person," Garrison joked. (**Ciccone.**)

But the population of Evansville wasn't joking about Madonna's snub when it rallied into a human anti-Madonna message (her name with a slash through it) on the parking lot of Roberts Stadium (now The Ford Center, 1 SE Martin Luther King Jr. Blvd., Evansville, IN). "Madonna's probably doing this," offered W.D. "Turk" Walton, president of the Metropolitan Evansville Chamber of Commerce at the time, "because she wants to keep Evansville for her own private getaway place because she likes it so much."

"Evansville, where all the women are called Shanda or Jolene, an evening out is a trip to the seed store and you feel vaguely effeminate if you're not wearing a Desert Storm T-shirt. Live here long enough, and you'd probably buy a Johnny Cash album and marry a close relative."–SIMON BANNER, *YOU* (1992)

"EVA'S FINAL BROADCAST": Mournful **death** ballad Madonna sings on *Evita: The Complete Motion Picture Music Soundtrack*. In the film, the song's reprise of **"Don't Cry for Me Argentina"** contains the final words Evita speaks to her public. This, along with **"Lament,"** was one of the few parts of the film in which the actors sang live.

EVERETT, RUPERT: *b. May 29, 1959.* British dramatic and comedic actor who made seriously **sexy** impressions in films like *Another Country* (1984) and *Dance with a Stranger* (1985) before a mainstream breakthrough as the longtime **gay** pal of Julia Roberts in the hit film *My Best Friend's Wedding* (1997). His career has been seriously damaged by his costarring role in *The Next Best Thing* alongside his longtime straight pal Madonna.

Madonna and Everett first met in 1985, and while never high-profile besties, were known to have hung out and partied together over the years. Explaining their chemistry in 2000, Everett offered, "We're both minorities, and we both **love** to shop."

Everett played **TV** tour guide on **VH1**'s *Madonna Rising*.

Their friendship turned to **business** when Everett became interested in making a film with Madonna that would explore the complicated, at times adversarial bond between straight women and gay men, throwing in the hot-button topic of gay parenting. Nicholas Hytner's *The Object of My Affection* (1998) beat them to the punch, and *The Next Best Thing* became a fiasco, earning Madonna some of her worst-ever reviews (and that is saying a lot) and tainting Everett.

Everett, already a novelist, became a serial memoirist with the well-received *Red Carpets and Other Banana Skins: The Autobiography* (2007) and *Vanished Years* (2013). He referred to Madonna as "an old whiny barmaid" in the former, which instantly made him a former friend of Madonna's.

In 2014, while discussing Madonna's topless *Interview* shots, Everett claimed to the UK's *Daily Mail*, "Contrary to popular belief, we are still friends."

 "EVERYBODY" (SONG): *Release date: October 6, 1982. Billboard Hot 100 peak: NA.* The very first Madonna song ever available commercially has remained one of her enduring classics. "Everybody" actually began life as a demo written solely by Madonna and produced by

Stephen Bray. Madonna had persuaded a reluctant **Mark Kamins** to play the demo at **Danceteria**, where he was the DJ. He fretted, "What if it's terrible? What if everybody stops dancing?" He brought it home to preview it and to calm his **nerves**. He liked it and Madonna's feminine wiles won out (they became a couple). The crowd **loved** "Everybody" and Madonna's other songs, which led Kamins to introduce her to **Michael Rosenblatt** of **Warner Bros.** Rosenblatt asked her what she wanted to do in her career and Madonna told him, "I want to rule the world." Simple as.

When Rosenblatt sent the song to **Sire's Seymour Stein**, who was in the hospital, Stein gave it a listen and fell hard for it. He asked to meet Madonna and reflected 30 years later, "I saw a young woman who was so determined to be a star."

Stein signed Madonna for $5,000 plus $1,000 for each song she wrote, committing to release two 12" singles by Madonna, the second of which turned out to be **"Burning Up"** b/w **"Physical Attraction."** Kamins was allowed to produce "Everybody" over Bray, but as a new producer, he required help from experienced pro **Arthur Baker**. It was not a positive **work** experience for Madonna, who never worked with Kamins again, but who did work with Bray many times.

"I wanted Mark Kamins to direct me, but 'Everybody' was the first record he'd ever done," Madonna told *NME* in 1983. "I have this friend called Steve [Bray] who's doing a version of that song, and it's really full and lush-sounding, which is how it should have been."

"Everybody," which expressed the optimism and the encouragement of self-expression that would characterize most of Madonna's work, immediately established her as a **disco** queen, eventually rising to #3 on the *Billboard* dance chart.

Already successful, the single was reworked in an effort to achieve greater chart glory. In *Dance Music Report* (March 19–April 1, 1983), Robert Ouimet (the DJ known as the Godfather of Montreal Disco) wrote of Sire's 12" import: "Everybody knows this song by now, but they've done it again. The British version is different than the American. I've heard through the grapevine that Rusty Egan has done a strong remix of the tune. The 12" still contains a vocal version b/w a dub but it is entirely remixed. He didn't really improve the record—rather his alternative gives the record another chance for stardom."

The marketing of the single intentionally led many listeners to assume Madonna was black by leaving her image off the sleeve; instead, designer Lou Beach was instructed to create a scene showing "everyday people in the street."

The lack of a public image was memorialized in one of her first mentions in *Billboard* in November 1982—Madonna was described as "a young **New York** duo produced by DJ Mark Kamins."

Not only did "Everybody" become Madonna's first single, it was also her first (albeit low-budget) music video

> "I made a demo, I took it to a nightclub, I gave it to a DJ, he played it, people danced to it, an A&R guy was there, he signed me, I made a record. Then my song—if everyone liked it, fingers crossed—was on the radio. It was just simpler. There wasn't Twitter and Facebook and Snapchat."–MADONNA, *LA TIMES* (2015)

and she performed the song live at many clubs like **The Roxy** while building her name. On **TV**, she performed it on *Dancin' on Air* (US, 1982) and *Di-Gei Musica* (Italy, 1983). Madonna has performed "Everybody" in full on *The Virgin Tour* and *The Girlie Show World Tour*. "**Dance** and sing/Get up and do your thing" from "Everybody" kicked off her *Blond Ambition World Tour* opener performance of **"Express Yourself."** She also performed it at **Coachella**, at her *Confessions on a Dance Floor* promo show at **KOKO** and as a special request on her *Sticky & Sweet Tour*.

On October 6, 2012, when "Everybody" turned 30, Madonna commemorated the occasion at her San Jose, California, *MDNA Tour* stop, saying:

"It is the 30th anniversary of the release of my first single ever, which ... I remember to this day the amazing feeling that I had when I heard this song on the radio for the first time in New York City; I was living like one broke-ass motherfucker ... wondering when and if anything good was ever gonna happen for me. Well, be careful what you wish for, is all I have to say. And I am a perfect example, an illustration that **dreams ... come true.**" She then performed a spirited, abbreviated rendition of the song that started it all.

The song appeared as part of a medley only at the very beginning of her *Rebel Heart Tour*.

"EVERYBODY" (VIDEO): *Director: Ed Steinberg, 1982.* To promote Madonna's first single, **Sire Records** hired videographer **Ed Steinberg** to shoot a straight performance clip of Madonna at **Danceteria**. Instead, Steinberg rented Paradise Garage (formerly 84 King St., NY, NY) in December 1982 and shot a choreographed routine by a butchy Madonna with backup **dancers** extraordinaire **Erika Belle** and **Bags Rilez**.

Steinberg tells *EM20*: "Even back in the beginning, M kept it together. One of her dancers was a no-show for our music video shoot at Paradise Garage. That meant she had to totally reblock her on-stage routine. Without missing a beat, she had Erika and Bags restaged with precision and the show went on."

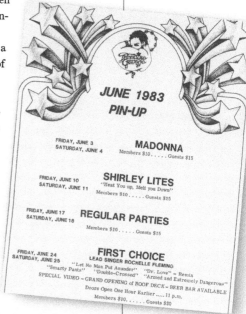

Rare Paradise Garage handbill from the "Everybody" era

Making use of spotlights, backlighting and the club's glittering backdrop, Steinberg captured a stylish, minimalist video postcard of the downtown scene. Madonna's image was already mesmerizing.

Not bad for the $1,000 he received. It was supposed to be $1,500, but the other $500 never arrived. Years later, Steinberg was referring to being stiffed and **Freddy De-Mann** pulled $500 out of his pocket to shut him up. Steinberg refused it, preferring to have the story.

EVITA: *Director: Alan Parker. Release date: December 25, 1996.* The film version of the celebrated (and reviled) stage musical *Evita*, based on the life of the celebrated (and reviled) Argentinean icon, Eva Perón, played by the celebrated (and reviled) Madonna wound up being ... you know the rest.

Narrated by the cynical Che Guevara (**Antonio Banderas**), the film centers on Eva Duarte (Madonna), a poor Argentinian teenager desperate to make something of her life after fleeing her hometown. In Buenos Aires, she is an ingénue, singer and radio host who sleeps her way to the very top, ultimately becoming the wife of Col. Juan Perón (**Jonathan Pryce**), a populist politico on the rise. With her touch of star quality and her perceived affinity for the lower classes, from whence she came, Perón becomes president. Eva—adoringly known as Evita by her subjects—embarks on a goodwill tour of Europe, where she is alternately embraced and rejected. When she returns home, she becomes mortally sick with **cancer**, signs off in an address to her fanatical followers and dies young, becoming an immortal symbol in her homeland.

Flashback to when Madonna was taken semi-seriously as an actor

Though those with short **memories** nowadays sometimes attempt to cast *Evita* as a bomb or as an example of Madonna's poor **acting**, the film was in fact the first successful Hollywood musical in decades. With its $55 million budget, it was a major gamble for Disney's Hollywood Pictures that paid off to the tune of a worldwide gross of $141,047,169. That made it profitable, though less so than the musical adaptations it preceded, such as *Chicago* (2002). Summing up the stakes, *Newsweek* wrote, "If all this hype propels *Evita* to blockbuster status, it will be the first movie musical since 1978's *Grease* to succeed—and it could pave the way for more. How about Travolta and Newton-John in *Rent*?"

As for Madonna, though some critics found her unspecial, most appreciated her surprisingly convincing embodiment of the late First Lady of Argentina; she won a **Golden Globe** for her trouble and generated **Oscar** buzz.

But it was no cakewalk.

First a concept album (1976), then a West End musical (1978) before becoming the toast of Broadway (1979), *Evita*—with a score by **Andrew Lloyd Webber** and a **book** by **Tim Rice**—had long been a **dream** movie project for a series of directors, producers and ambitious actors. The most famous Evita of all, **Patti LuPone**, was considered to recreate the role on film, but many others coveted and were talked about for the part, including **Mariah Carey**, Charo, **Glenn Close**, Gloria Estefan, **Cyndi Lauper**, Ann-Margret, **Bette Midler**, Liza Minnelli, **Olivia Newton-John**, Elaine Page, **Barbra Streisand** and Pia Zadora.

As early as 1987, Oliver Stone had written what *Newsweek* called a "widely admired" script for a sung-through film. Stone had gotten further than previous **directors** mentioned in conjunction with the project, among them Richard Attenborough, Hector Babenco, Francis Ford Coppola, Alan Pakula, Herbert Ross, Ken Russell and Franco Zeffirelli.

In July 1988, gossips reported that Madonna was set for *Evita*, but in reality the project was still in its infancy. With Stone in charge, he spent an evening with Madonna and Andrew Lloyd Webber at Webber's Trump Tower (725 Fifth Ave., NY, NY) apartment. Webber played selections from *Aspects of **Love*** (1989) on the piano as Madonna talked about how she intended to rewrite some of *Evita*'s score, asking for script approval. She also wanted Jeremy Irons cast as Juan Perón and Antonio Banderas cast as Che Guevara.

That's when Madonna was fired, so to speak, by Stone, who kicked her when she was down by saying in the press, "Madonna—she's like toilet paper. She's on every **magazine** cover in the world. Devalued." For her part, Madonna said she'd already decided she couldn't **work** with a misogynist like Stone.

By the end of 1989, Meryl Streep had become the top pick, but the creative process with Stone and dealmaking exhausted her patience. "I was insulted. It was a long, horrible story. It was very disappointing, more than I can say. I prepared for that role for a year."

Madonna confidently proclaimed, "I've decided that if anybody's going to do it, I'm going to do it—I'd kill Meryl Streep. I'm just kidding." Streep kidded back, "I could rip her throat out." Natural born kidders.

In 1991, producer Robert Stigwood made a deal with Disney, where Madonna became attached to a version of the film to be written and directed by Glenn Gordon Caron of *Moonlighting* (1985–1989). The $30 million budget seemed anemic to Madonna and the project languished a few more years, during which time all parties moved on.

Stone circled back in 1994, putting together a deal for a $60 million film to star Michelle Pfeiffer. Stone even scouted locations in Argentina, but was rebuffed by the country's Perónist president; he exited as director once again, and this time **Alan Parker** became the director of choice.

Parker was known for his films *Bugsy Malone* (1976), *Midnight Express* (1978), **Fame** (1980) and *Mississippi Burning* (1988); he would bring to *Evita*'s script (he shared a writing credit with Stone) a sober quality, for better or worse. Under his guidance, the film would not be frivolous, but dark and dramatic.

Parker had all but cast Pfeiffer, who did some fairly catastrophic test vocals, but who lost out because she wanted to shoot the film in Hollywood while Parker favored shooting in Argentina.

Madonna continued lobbying for the part, even though an anonymous Disney executive had been quoted as saying "not if it's the last breath I take" to the question of whether she was still being considered for the role. She wound up sending one of her famous handwritten letters to Parker explaining why she was born to play Evita. Their meetings were fruitful and Parker was sold.

"I know this sounds ridiculously immodest," Madonna told *Cosmopolitan* in 1996, "but I always had a feeling I'd do *Evita*. Not that it was something that occupied my thoughts constantly, and not that I didn't give up several times—after Meryl Streep was supposed to do it, and then Michelle (Pfeiffer). But it always fell through, and I couldn't help feeling that somehow *I* was hexing it; that it was meant for me."

For his part, Parker told *Newsweek*, "Eva Perón is actually Madonna …" This was a sentiment shared by some reviewers, including **Liz Smith**, who said making *Evita* was "… the closest [Madonna will] ever get to filming her own story."

Madonna had decided against touring with her album **Bedtime Stories** so she could make the film. She took vocal lessons and sought advice from Webber, who told *Attitude* in 2007, "I came in and worked with her a bit. We got on fine; it was purely professional. I introduced her to a couple of people to help her through on the musical direction side and that was it. I'd never met her before [sic] and I haven't met her since."

Madonna said, "I felt the movie was a chance for me to challenge all areas of my career—singing, dancing and, above all, acting." Understanding the project's potential, she approached *Evita* with characteristic seriousness, but also with a personal connection to the piece. "People were frightened of the **power** [Evita] had and undermined her accomplishments by calling her a whore. I can certainly relate to that," she told *USA Today* in 1996. She still felt the source material was misogynist, so became determined that the film would be an evolved piece, something she could **control** with her portrayal.

The cast—including Madonna, Pryce as Perón, Banderas as Che and **Jimmy Nail** as Magaldi, arrived in **London** in September 1995 to rehearse. *Evita: The Complete Motion Picture Music Soundtrack* was recorded first, Madonna resting her **voice** in the mornings and laying down vocals in the afternoons. The recording took 400 hours—and that was before any film had been shot.

Though the filming would take place in London, Budapest and Argentina, it was the latter location that mattered more to the film's authenticity. Madonna arrived in Buenos Aires on January 20, 1996, and set about doing last-minute research for her role. She most valued a meeting with Tuco Paz, a diplomat who remembered that Eva had been aggressive as a **nervous** reaction, out of self-doubt.

But as she soon discovered, the troupe's arrival in the country was the beginning of a rocky road. They were met with protests and demeaning graffiti. Marta Rivadera, a deputy in Congress from La Rioja, proposed a decree to declare Madonna and Parker personae non grata. Madonna received **death** threats that led **Freddy DeMann** to tell *Variety* columnist Army Archerd, "I'm one minute away from calling her out of that country." A former secretary to Evita, Clara Marin, told **TV** reporters, "We want Madonna dead or alive. If she does not leave, I will kill her."

Perónistas were enraged that Madonna was daring to portray their sainted spiritual leader, and were all too

ALEJANDRO MOGOLLO

familiar with the source material's cynicism toward her character. Madonna would often have to travel lying down in a van to escape the notice of angry mobs and paparazzi. Her manager **Caresse Henry** got arrested for getting into an altercation with paparazzi while acting as a decoy.

Madonna was also besieged by adoring **fans**, who followed her around as aggressively as her detractors. She said she was "flattered" when fans sang and chanted outside her hotel window, but also reported that it wasn't great for sleeping, a major issue when you're 37 but are playing a 15-year-old in some scenes.

In spite of all the madness, Madonna managed to visit Evita's grave at La Recoleta Cemetery, and she and Parker were finally able to wangle an audience with President Carlos Menem, the first Perónist elected to national office in Argentina back in 1973, who had opposed the production publicly. Madonna's first attempt to meet Menem, via his friend Constancio Vigil, had been rebuffed. Menem had even turned down a chance to greet Madonna when she was on tour with *The Girlie Show World Tour* in 1993 (he'd called it "blasphemous and insulting to women").

This time, with all **eyes** on him, Menem blinked and invited the filmmakers to meet him on February 7, 1996.

"I didn't come all the way to Argentina to sing **'Don't Cry for Me Argentina'** on a soundstage," Madonna would later say; her mission was clear.

Madonna's years of seducing DJs into playing her shit had left her with potent **powers** of persuasion; thanks to an artfully exposed bra strap and Madonna's shocking physical transformation into the very picture of Eva, Menem gave his blessing to the production, even allowing "Don't Cry for Me Argentina" to be filmed on the balcony of the presidential palace, the Casa Rosada.

"President Menem was very charming. I was surprised at how much I liked him," Madonna coyly wrote in a diary of the filming that was published in *Vanity Fair*.

Filming in Argentina began February 13, 1996. The shoot (it took 84 days total) was draining for all involved, even a workhorse like Madonna, who was under more pressure than ever before. Her costar Pryce told *Genre*, "She was everything you'd expect from a committed, professional performer. She worked very hard." Parker admitted that Madonna, who endured 85 costume changes, was a pain in the ass, but noted that she was supremely prepared and therefore above criticism.

Being made up for a scene, Madonna diaried, "People sit around all day scrutinizing you, turning you from left to right, whispering behind the camera, cutting your nose **hairs,** plucking stray **eyebrow** hairs, and patting down your sweat while they fill in the lines on your face with Spackle ... You wonder if you're pretty enough or good enough or attractive enough and you inevitably feel like a slab of beef. Rare, medium, or well done. It doesn't matter as long as people want to eat you."

Midway through, Madonna announced that she was **pregnant** with her first child, a bit of news that made in-

— STEVE GRAND

• •

"I MEAN, A FILM IS JUST A LONG VIDEO OR A VIDEO A SHORT FILM. I DON'T THINK THEY'RE THAT FAR APART."-MADONNA (1985)

• •

"IT'S THE BIGGEST, LOUDEST, MOST EXPENSIVE MUSIC VIDEO EVER MADE."
-ANTHONY LANE, *NEW YORK* (1996)

• •

"BUT LOVE OR HATE MADONNA-EVA, SHE IS A MAGNET FOR ALL EYES. YOU MUST WATCH HER. AND TO FIND THE SOUL OF THE MODERN MUSICAL FOR ONCE ON THE BIG SCREEN, YOU MUST SEE *EVITA*."-RICHARD CORLISS, *TIME* (1996)

• •

"MADONNA GIVES HER ALL TO THE TITLE ROLE AND PULLS IT OFF SUPERBLY. DARK-EYED, INTENT AND SERIOUS, SHE CONQUERS THE CHARACTER AS EVITA CONQUERED EVERY CHALLENGE SHE SET FOR HERSELF, AND IF COMMENTATORS WISH TO MAKE THEIR OWN PARALLELS OF THIS TALENT TO THE SINGER-ACTRESS'S OWN CAREER, SO BE IT."
-TODD MCCARTHY, *VARIETY* (1996)

• •

"ALL BUSINESS AND NO FUN, MADONNA HAS CERTAINLY DONE HER HOMEWORK. ALTHOUGH NEVER ANYTHING OTHER THAN HERSELF, SHE HAS EVA'S GESTURES DOWN AND ... HAS VASTLY IMPROVED ON HER MODEL'S DIOR WARDROBE. IT'S A CHILLY PERFORMANCE IN A MEDIOCRE FILM, BUT IT'S A TRIUMPH OF IMAGE—WHATEVER EVA PERÓN WAS, SHE WILL HENCEFORTH BE MADONNA."
-J. HOBERMAN, *THE VILLAGE VOICE* (1996)

• •

"*EVITA* IS A KIND OF FASCIST PSEUDO-OPERA, AND THERE'S SOMETHING CREEPY, ALMOST PHYSICALLY ALARMING, ABOUT WATCHING IT ... MADONNA HAS GONE FROM SCANDAL TO CANONIZATION WITHOUT PASSING THROUGH ACCOMPLISHMENT. THIS SPECTACLE, AS YOU MAY HAVE GATHERED, IS UNIQUELY NAUSEATING."-DAVID DENBY, *NEW YORK* (1997)

• •

ternational headlines. "Being pregnant should be cheering me up, but it's not," she told *Vanity Fair*. "I keep having this nagging feeling that I'm going to destroy what we've all worked so hard to accomplish."

Filming ended on May 27, 1996, after 299 scenes, 4,000 extras, 6,000 costumes, 20 different costume houses, 320 sets and 24,000 props. Madonna alone had burned through 45 pairs of shoes and 56 pairs of earrings.

Oscar ad for the
Evita music

Even before it was in the can, *Evita* was the most buzzed about movie of 1996—would it be good, or would it suck? A 10-minute teaser shown at **Cannes** in May 1996 won over some film-biz bigshots.

LuPone, commenting on clips before she'd seen the film, said, "It looks like a **boring** piece of shit, frankly. I'm sorry, but that's what it looks like. I'm sure this is not Madonna. Madonna is being directed." Another famous Evita, Elaine Page, told *HX*, "... Madonna is Madonna. She's a huge star with huge charisma. She's **reinvented** herself so many times; she's quite a chameleon. And I think Eva was similar in all those aspects. So I think Madonna is possibly the perfect person for the part." Bob Crowdey of Technicolor said, "This is one of the finest-looking films I've ever seen photographed ..." Madonna's old **dance** mom **Pearl Lang** was effusive in her praise as quoted by **Barbara Victor**: "She was wonderful, really marvelous. If she had to give up dancing, this was the role that came naturally to her. It convinced me that she had enormous innate **talent**. There's no doubt that Madonna is Eva Perón!"

The film's premiere was held on December 14, 1996, at the Shrine Auditorium (665 W. Jefferson Blvd., LA, CA) with a black-tie party after at the Shrine Exposition Center. Madonna wore a slightly bizarre **John Galliano** creation that harkened back to the period of the film, and drank in the good vibes—though the film's reviews were mixed-to-positive, it was overall seen as a prestige project. All involved had done themselves proud.

Evita did well in limited release and made $8.6 million in its opening week on 704 screens, beaten to #1 at the box office only by a genre flick called *The Relic*. Disney marketed the hell out of the film, including authorizing *Evita*-themed boutiques at Bloomingdale's with Elie Tahari suits, Victor Costa tango dresses, Nicole Miller purses, Ferragamo shoes and faux furs from Adrienne Landau. *Evita* was everywhere, and with it, so was Madonna.

One of the most important things Madonna has ever done in—and for—her career, *Evita* survives as an entertaining, cerebral, psychoanalytical biopic that gave Madonna "time off from being myself," erased the backlash she'd endured in the early to mid-'90s and set her up for a massive pop comeback with *Ray of Light*.

EVITA: THE COMPLETE MOTION PICTURE MUSIC SOUNDTRACK: *Release date: November 12, 1996. Billboard 200 peak: #2.* The soundtrack for the film version of *Evita* starring Madonna is about as polarizing as anything she's ever recorded—a revelation to some critics, an abomination to **Patti LuPone** purists, a moving example of the surprising fluidity and fragilty of Madonna's **voice** to some of her **fans**, a cheesy snore to others.

When Madonna listened to the songs she'd have to sing in order to bring the musical *Evita* to the screen, she was intimidated. Even though she was by that point already the most successful female singer of all time, she took voice lessons from acclaimed coach Joan Lader. Lader said, "She had to use her voice in a way she'd never used it before. *Evita* is real musical theater—it's operatic, in a sense. Madonna developed an upper register that she didn't know she had." Madonna surprised herself with the sound she was able to achieve, accessing aspects of her instrument that she'd never touched in over 15 years of singing.

The recording of the soundtrack occurred months before the filming of the movie; the idea was for the performers to achieve musical perfection and then act to the music, lip-synching in most cases. During the **London** recording sessions, costar **Antonio Banderas** recalled that Madonna was "quite ritual in the way she prepared the studio," including candles and flowers and low lighting.

She needed the calming atmosphere, having to record "**Don't Cry for Me Argentina**" with the song's composer **Andrew Lloyd Webber** watching on the first day. She broke down and the venue was changed to further relax Madonna and her new voice.

Madonna for the most part succeeded, turning in a vocal performance different from those of the famous women who'd embodied Evita before her. Madonna offered a more human Evita, a more accessible Evita—but one no less interesting. From her first appearance on the soundtrack—toward the end of the third song—Madonna's voice is pure and sweet, even as she sings, "So share my glory/So share my coffin."

For music lovers not thrown off by the musical's at times nonsensical lyrics, there are many Madonna highlights. "**Buenos Aires**" finds Madonna singing from the

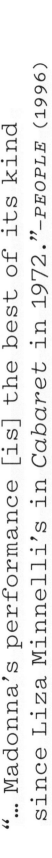

"... Madonna's performance [is] the best of its kind since Liza Minnelli's in *Cabaret* in 1972."—*PEOPLE* (1996)

**EVITA:
THE COMPLETE
MOTION PICTURE
MUSIC SOUNDTRACK**

DISC ONE

① "A Cinema in Buenos Aires, 26 July 1952" (Tim Rice/Andrew Lloyd Webber) performed by John Mauceri-1:20, produced by Nigel Wright/Alan Parker/Andrew Lloyd Webber/David Caddick

② "Requiem for Evita" (Tim Rice/Andrew Lloyd Webber) performed by John Mauceri-4:16, produced by Nigel Wright/Alan Parker/Andrew Lloyd Webber/David Caddick

③ "Oh What a Circus" (Tim Rice/Andrew Lloyd Webber) performed by Madonna/Antonio Banderas-5:44, produced by Nigel Wright/Alan Parker/Andrew Lloyd Webber/David Caddick

④ "On This Night of a Thousand Stars" (Tim Rice/Andrew Lloyd Webber) performed by Jimmy Nail-2:24, produced by Nigel Wright/Alan Parker/Andrew Lloyd Webber/David Caddick

⑤ "Eva and Magaldi/Eva Beware of the City" (Tim Rice/Andrew Lloyd Webber) performed by Madonna/Jimmy Nail/Antonio Banderas-5:20, produced by Nigel Wright/Alan Parker/Andrew Lloyd Webber/David Caddick

⑥ "Buenos Aires" (Tim Rice/Andrew Lloyd Webber) performed by Madonna-4:09, produced by Nigel Wright/Alan Parker/Andrew Lloyd Webber/David Caddick

⑦ "Another Suitcase in Another Hall" (Tim Rice/Andrew Lloyd Webber) performed by Madonna-3:33, produced by Nigel Wright/Alan Parker/Andrew Lloyd Webber/David Caddick

⑧ "Goodnight and Thank You" (Tim Rice/Andrew Lloyd Webber) performed by Madonna/Antonio Banderas-4:18, produced by Nigel Wright/Alan Parker/Andrew Lloyd Webber/David Caddick

⑨ "The Lady's Got Potential" (Tim Rice/Andrew Lloyd Webber) performed by Antonio Banderas-4:24, produced by Nigel Wright/Alan Parker/Andrew Lloyd Webber/David Caddick

①⓪ "Charity Concert/The Art of the Possible" (Tim Rice/Andrew Lloyd Webber) performed by Jimmy Nail/Jonathan Pryce/Antonio Banderas-2:33, produced by Nigel Wright/Alan Parker/Andrew Lloyd Webber/David Caddick

①① "I'd Be Surprisingly Good for You" (Tim Rice/Andrew Lloyd Webber) performed by Madonna/Jonathan Pryce-4:18, produced by Nigel Wright/Alan Parker/Andrew Lloyd Webber/David Caddick

①② "Hello and Goodbye" (Tim Rice/Andrew Lloyd Webber) performed by Madonna/Andrea Corr/Jonathan Pryce-1:46, produced by Nigel Wright/Alan Parker/Andrew Lloyd Webber/David Caddick

①③ "Perón's Latest Flame" (Tim Rice/Andrew Lloyd Webber) performed by Madonna/Antonio Banderas-5:17, produced by Nigel Wright/Alan Parker/Andrew Lloyd Webber/David Caddick

①④ "A New Argentina" (Tim Rice/Andrew Lloyd Webber) performed by Madonna/Jonathan Pryce-8:13, produced by Nigel Wright/Alan Parker/Andrew Lloyd Webber/David Caddick

DISC TWO

① "On the Balcony of the Casa Rosada (Part 1)" (Tim Rice/Andrew Lloyd Webber) performed by Jonathan Pryce-1:28, produced by Nigel Wright/Alan Parker/Andrew Lloyd Webber/David Caddick

② "Don't Cry for Me Argentina" (Tim Rice/Andrew Lloyd Webber) performed by Madonna-5:31, produced by Nigel Wright/Alan Parker/Andrew Lloyd Webber/David Caddick

③ "On the Balcony of the Casa Rosada (Part 2)" (Tim Rice/Andrew Lloyd Webber) performed by Madonna-2:00, produced by Nigel Wright/Alan Parker/Andrew Lloyd Webber/David Caddick

④ "High Flying, Adored" (Tim Rice/Andrew Lloyd Webber) performed by Madonna/Antonio Banderas-3:32, produced by Nigel Wright/Alan Parker/Andrew Lloyd Webber/David Caddick

⑤ "Rainbow High" (Tim Rice/Andrew Lloyd Webber) performed by Madonna-2:26, produced by Nigel Wright/Alan Parker/Andrew Lloyd Webber/David Caddick

⑥ "Rainbow Tour" (Tim Rice/Andrew Lloyd Webber) performed by Antonio Banderas/Gary Brooker/Peter Polycarpou-4:50, produced by Nigel Wright/Alan Parker/Andrew Lloyd Webber/David Caddick

⑦ "The Actress Hasn't Learned the Lines (You'd Like to Hear)" (Tim Rice/Andrew Lloyd Webber) performed by Madonna/Antonio Banderas-2:31, produced by Nigel Wright/Alan Parker/Andrew Lloyd Webber/David Caddick

⑧ "And the Money Kept Rolling In (and Out)" (Tim Rice/Andrew Lloyd Webber) performed by Antonio Banderas-3:53, produced by Nigel Wright/Alan Parker/Andrew Lloyd Webber/David Caddick

⑨ "Partido Feminista" (Tim Rice/Andrew Lloyd Webber) performed by Madonna-1:40, produced by Nigel Wright/Alan Parker/Andrew Lloyd Webber/David Caddick

①⓪ "She Is a Diamond" (Tim Rice/Andrew Lloyd Webber) performed by Jonathan Pryce-1:39, produced by Nigel Wright/Alan Parker/Andrew Lloyd Webber/David Caddick

①① "Santa Evita" (Tim Rice/Andrew Lloyd Webber) performed by John Mauceri-2:30, produced by Nigel Wright/Alan Parker/Andrew Lloyd Webber/David Caddick

①② "Waltz for Eva and Che" (Tim Rice/Andrew Lloyd Webber) performed by Madonna/Antonio Banderas-4:31, produced by Nigel Wright/Alan Parker/Andrew Lloyd Webber/David Caddick

①③ "Your Little Body's Slowly Breaking Down" (Tim Rice/Andrew Lloyd Webber) performed by Madonna/Jonathan Pryce-1:24, produced by Nigel Wright/Alan Parker/Andrew Lloyd Webber/David Caddick

①④ "You Must Love Me" (Tim Rice/Andrew Lloyd Webber) performed by Madonna-2:50, produced by Nigel Wright/Alan Parker/Andrew Lloyd Webber/David Caddick

①⑤ "Eva's Final Broadcast" (Tim Rice/Andrew Lloyd Webber) performed by Madonna-3:05, produced by Nigel Wright/Alan Parker/Andrew Lloyd Webber/David Caddick

①⑥ "Latin Chant" (Tim Rice/Andrew Lloyd Webber) performed by John Mauceri-2:11, produced by Nigel Wright/Alan Parker/Andrew Lloyd Webber/David Caddick

①⑦ "Lament" (Tim Rice/Andrew Lloyd Webber) performed by Madonna/Antonio Banderas-5:17, produced by Nigel Wright/Alan Parker/Andrew Lloyd Webber/David Caddick

uppermost **heights** to lowermost depths of her range with the verve of the 15-year-old she doesn't really resemble on film. It's the entire musical's earthiest and most freewheeling number. Madonna insisted on singing **"Another Suitcase in Another Hall"** (a song originally sung by Perón's mistress) in the film, giving her (and Evita) a chance to express vulnerability before becoming a shark. **"Rainbow High"** gives Madonna a shot to veer into operetta.

"My secret **dream** is to sing Italian **art** songs, so at the end of my lesson my teacher would let me sing Italian operetta. Maybe that affected me unconsciously," Madonna told *Spin* in 1998.

Probably Madonna's three best performances on the soundtrack would have to be her game-changing "Don't Cry for Me Argentina" (which did indeed make one consider crying for a fascist manipulator), her charmingly cheeky **"I'd Be Surprisingly Good for You"** and her absolute best, her chilling, whimperingly half-sung swan song, **"Lament."**

Ultimately, the soundtrack was judged in the court of public opinion: The double-album sold over 2.5 million copies in the US, translating to quintuple platinum status in her home country, with 11 million sold worldwide.

∙∙

"COMPARING THIS ALBUM WITH MADONNA'S SELF-TITLED DEBUT IN 1983 PROVIDES AMPLE EVIDENCE THAT NOT ALL SINGERS WERE BORN TALENTED. SOME NEED TO LEARN, AND MADONNA CERTAINLY HAS. HER EVA PERÓN PUTS HER VOICE IN A CLASS WITH PATTI LUPONE AND ELAINE PAGE."-NEIL STRAUSS, *THE NEW YORK TIMES* (1996)

∙∙

"IS MADONNA UP TO THE TASK? YOU HAVE NO IDEA. THE NEWLY PUMPED-UP THRUSH SINGS THE HELL OUT OF THE MATERIAL AND, JUST AS SIGNIFICANTLY, REDEFINES IT IN WAYS THAT MIGHT MAKE IT HER MOST 'PERSONAL' ALBUM, IF ONLY FOR THE TELLING ADJUSTMENTS SHE'S MADE TO AN EXTREMELY FAMILIAR TEXT."

-CHRIS WILLMAN, *ENTERTAINMENT WEEKLY* (1996)

∙∙

"MADONNA … DOES NOT ALWAYS RISE TO THE OCCASION. SHE IS HINDERED BY THE THIN TONE AND LIMITED RANGE OF HER VOICE AND SEEMS AT TIMES TO BE INTIMIDATED BY HER MATERIAL."

-ELYSA GARDNER, *ROLLING STONE* (1996)

∙∙

"HER ARCHNESS AND IRONY ARE REPLACED WITH SINCERITY. VOCALLY, SHE'S PURGED OF POP MANNERISMS AND SINGS WITH AN ARRAY OF NEW COLORS."

-DAVID PATRICK STEARNS, *USA TODAY* (1996)

∙∙

EXCUSES: In response to her critics, Madonna is fond of making one of three excuses for why she's under attack. They're often accurate, but are also sneaky enough to cover her tracks even in the cases where they're untrue: (1) "I was being ironic." (2) "You just don't *get* me." (3) "I'm being attacked because I'm a woman."

EXHIBITIONISM: The act of shamelessly exposing your body or your private self for your own pleasure—egotistical, **sexual**, manipulative, subversive or otherwise.

Madonna's penchant for baring all in public started in sixth grade, at the St. Andrew's annual **talent** show, when she performed in a little bikini and a lot of fluorescent green body paint ("sort of a flower-**power** thing") doing her Goldie Hawn impression to the strains of the Who's "Baba O'Riley" (1971) in front of an auditorium full of parents. Her **father** was enraged, grounding her for two weeks, but the reaction she received was nectar: The girls in her class refused to talk to her and the boys chased her. This experience demanded an encore that has never ended.

Madonna became involved in school **plays** and performed as a **dancer** ("I think all entertainers are exhibitionists, admitted or not," she said in 1992), and once she turned 18 had no qualms about posing **nude** as an artist's model. Later, when tasteful photos from those sessions emerged in *Playboy* and *Penthouse*, her response to the press was to shrug off any suggestion that she should be ashamed. Indeed, her only real worry was the effect it

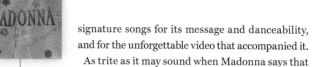

would have on her father (still fuming over that Goldie Hawn number?), and on her career. Her father disapproved, but the photos only enhanced her popularity.

Madonna's wardrobe has always been an exhibitionist's **dream.** Her wearing of bras and boxer shorts and pajamas and bustiers and sheer *everything* has been an arresting way of manipulating attention. As a result, her audiences have become especially conscious of Madonna's clothing, her body and their own expectations of how a person should be viewed. The effect is not dissimilar to Alfred Hitchcock using *Rear Window* (1954) to remind us that we are all voyeurs at heart. Madonna shows us things to make us realize how badly we want to see them.

Madonna has since become increasingly exhibitionistic to the point where she is a symbol of public revelation of self, both corporal and spiritual. *Truth or Dare*, for all its contrivance, remains one of the most personally revelatory pieces of film from a public figure prior to the rise of **Paris** Hilton and Kim Kardashian. She has exposed her body continuously from 1990, culminating with *Sex*, in which she exposed not only her body but (for all intents and purposes) her fantasies, simultaneously tapping into the exhibitionistic thrill of being a sex star, like a stripper who craves the catcalls.

Her exhibitionism is hard to resist. Even if you **hate** someone, or find them unattractive, you are likely to take a look if they flash you, if only to gape at their lack of shame. Put a copy of *Sex* on your coffee table and watch as *everyone* who never saw the **book** gravitates to it and looks to see what she was willing to show.

Her performance of **"Living for Love"** at the **Grammys** in 2015 was widely praised, and yet it was overshadowed by Madonna's revealing je t'oreador look on the red carpet, in particular the moment when she turned around and flashed her ass to the cameras. The danger of this kind of exhibitionism is that it can stifle more substantive activities. But Madonna seems to be challenging us, not to look *past* her exhibitionism, but to see *through* it—she wants us to observe the smutty appetizer, reacting not with misogynist, **ageist** or provincial horror, but with a sense of humor, and then to continue watching for the heartfelt main course.

"I don't think I'd like it if everyone was walking around naked all the time. I like clothes. But I think everybody should run naked through the streets at least once. Or be naked when you're not supposed to be naked. It's very liberating."—MADONNA (1994)

—MARLENE STEWART

"EXPRESS YOURSELF" (SONG): *Release date: May 9, 1989. Billboard Hot 100 peak: #2.* The second single from *Like a Prayer*, this went on to become one of Madonna's signature songs for its message and danceability, and for the unforgettable video that accompanied it.

As trite as it may sound when Madonna says that she is "expressing herself" with her music, it was at the time incredibly uplifting to hear a pop song advocating for individuality. "The ultimate thing behind the song is that if you don't express yourself, if you don't say what you want, then you're not going to get it. And in effect, you are chained down by your inability to say what you feel or go after what you want," she said at the time of the song's release. Though "Express Yourself" also deals with **love** and relationships in a **feminist** way, uncompromising individualism is its primary theme.

The song—which was written and produced by Madonna and her longtime collaborator **Stephen Bray**—grabs everyone's attention with an all-call at the beginning: "Come on, girls!/Do you believe in love?" After being hopelessly hooked, there's no let-up as the singer passionately belts her belief in equality in relationships and mutual fulfillment over a bouncy house beat. It's no coincidence that some of Madonna's rawest vocals came hot on the heels of her **divorce.**

Though the song has been called a take on the Staple Singers hit "Respect Yourself" (1971), the songs sound nothing alike; the **original** is at most a source of inspiration.

In 2011, **Lady Gaga** released the title single from her new album *Born This Way* after **Elton John** had already called it a **gay** anthem that would "obliterate" the 1978 song "I Will Survive." Rather than Gloria Gaynor, the artist most listeners thought of upon hearing Gaga's latest was Madonna—"Born This Way" is melodically very similar to "Express Yourself," shares a chord progression and even has a similar theme. The comparisons trended on **Twitter**, putting Gaga on the defense. Gaga admitted to *NME* that the songs do share "the chord progression. The same one that's been in **disco** music for the last 50 years." Madonna expressed herself by saying she liked "Born This Way," adding, "I'm glad that I helped Gaga write it."

The similarity—and if Tom Petty was able to legally get a piece of **Sam Smith**'s "Stay with Me" (2014), Madonna could easily have done the same with "Born This Way"—clearly rankled Madonna.

Madonna's first-ever live performance of "Express Yourself" occurred at the 1989 **MTV Video Music Awards**, backed by **Donna De Lory** and **Niki Haris**. In a dazzling display of confident singing and aerobic dancing, Madonna incorporated vogueing into her act for the first time.

Madonna has performed "Express Yourself" live on her *Blond Ambition World Tour*, *The Girlie Show World Tour*, her *Re-Invention World Tour*, as a requested oldie on her *Sticky & Sweet Tour* and in a controversial mash-up with "Born This Way" on her *MDNA Tour*, the latter of which was intended to tweak Gaga; she did not seek Gaga's permission to perform "Born This Way," and the mash-up segued into Madonna's bitter *Hard Candy* burn song **"She's Not Me."**

> "To express yourself deep down inside is important. If you didn't, you'd be just like a dead person."—MADONNA (1984)

"EXPRESS YOURSELF" (VIDEO): *Director: David Fincher, 1989.* Before the video for "Express Yourself" premiered in 1989, hot on the heels of the controversial **"Like a Prayer"** video, it seemed impossible that Madonna could follow up such a sensational statement.

She did, in spades, with the help of director **David Fincher**, who went on to become an acclaimed film director, and choreographer **Vincent Paterson**.

"Express Yourself" is one of Madonna's most popular and elaborate videos, one of the most expensive ever made (costing $2 million at the time) and is consistently ranked among the best of all time. Heavily influenced by the aesthetic of **Tamara de Lempicka**, it also manages to give a clever interpretation of the battle-of-the-sexes anthem by polarizing men and women, playing up their traditional **sexualities**, but reversing their stereotypical roles in society.

Madonna's character is the **height** of femininity: glamorous, sexual, untouchable. Yet she is also presented as the **power** figure, an intelligent, cultured woman who single-handedly runs what appears to be an entire futuristic civilization inspired by the Fritz Lang silent classic *Metropolis* (1927). The city is supported by the sweat of a mass of toiling men. And you thought solar was the power of the future.

Her counterpoint among these men (Guess jeans model Cameron Alborzian, who is now an ayurvedic guru known as Yogi Cameron) is the prototypical strong, silent type, but he is completely subservient, a near-anonymous slave.

The two are connected by the feline embodiment of the woman's desire (another archetypal—and some say sexist—reading of femininity) as a slinky, predatory cat that navigates the pipes and ventilation ducts linking ivory tower and pit. Madonna's desire is made even more explicit when she crawls across the floor like a stalking cat, under a table and to a bowl of milk, which she laps up, **back** arched. The point is so clear we half expect to see her raise a leg for a little bath. Missed opportunities ...

"David's idea for the cat and pouring the milk, it's great, and believe me I fought him on that. I didn't want to do that," Madonna said at the time. "It's just so over-the-top and silly and clichéd. Like a film-student kind of trick. But I'm glad that I gave in to him."

"Express Yourself" was Madonna's first video that breathed real sensuality and blistering eroticism, as opposed to **flirtation**. The cat annoyed **feminists**, as did a provocative scene featuring Madonna chained to a bed, but critics avoided addressing the video's message that sexual desire can be animalistic and as confining as a literal chain—or entombment in a solitary tower—if it's repressed.

Fortunately, the Madonna character's, er, *pussycat* is finally able to attract the man of her **dreams**—the hunk lumbers in at video's end, somewhat roughly takes her in his arms, and makes passionate **love** to her, an updating of *Gone with the Wind* (1939).

Madonna took a strong hand when it came to the creation of this video, saying at the time, "I oversaw everything—the building of the sets, everyone's costumes, I had meetings with makeup and **hair** and the cinematographer and, you know, everyone ... casting, finding the right cat ..."

Aside from its artistic impact, "Express Yourself" is notable as the video in which Madonna introduced her version of **Michael Jackson**'s crotch-grab. Wearing a man's suit in a performance segment that alternates with the main storyline, she **dances** enthusiastically and grabs herself with such gusto you're just *sure* she must have a penis after all ... or that she must have something even better.

Choreographer Vincent Paterson takes credit for that bit: "And then when I choreographed the video 'Express Yourself' for Madonna, there was a movement where she's at the top of these steps. She said, 'Well, Vince—' ... she's yelling at me from up there ... 'Vincent, what do I do with my, my other hand?' and I said, "Well, honey, grab your crotch, you know, because you've got bigger **balls** than mostly everybody in this room, so go ahead and grab 'em."

> "Here, as elsewhere, we see that Madonna is much more radical in what she does with gender identity than she is in what she does with either gender or class relations, and this is precisely because, in Madonna's world, someone is either above or below the other; never are they equal."—PROF. LYNNE LAYTON, HARVARD (1992)

> "It's really exciting, and there's a lotta, like, big men and they're all greasy, but they also have bobs ..."—MARGARET CHO ON THE "EXPRESS YOURSELF" VIDEO (2008)

EXTORTION: During the filming of *Shanghai Surprise* in Hong Kong, mobsters reportedly demanded **money** in exchange for allowing the crew to film in particular locales. One mobster even refused to move his car before receiving $50,000 to do so. He wasn't paid, and he apparently responded by having the entire movie bumped off.

EYEBROWS: Initially as famous as Brooke Shields for her lush eyebrows—each one is bigger than Griffin Dunne's whole body on the *Who's That Girl* movie poster—Madonna had tamed them by 1992, when she thanked François Nars in *Sex* for "getting rid of my eyebrows forever." Madonna has referred to plucking them as a favored method of procrastination.

EYES: Madonna's are naturally blue. She has said they're her favorite part of her body.

ANDRÉ GROSSMANN

F

FAB FIVE FREDDY: *b. circa 1959/1960.* Hip-hop musician and visual artist who was one of Madonna's downtown **NYC** pals. He told Madonna's biographer **Andrew Morton,** "She was never some dingy white chick who slept around with the guys; she was smarter than that. All the way through her career, she has been very **sexy,** but take a closer look and she is always in **control.** Like **Sharon Stone** in *Basic Instinct,* she flashed you her **pussy,** but she's in charge."

Freddy is the man responsible for bringing Madonna together with her stylist and pal **Maripol;** he was looking for hot girls to join him onstage and Maripol became his picker, leading her to Madonna, who was both wearing and in possession of a cute top.

FACEBOOK: Madonna's is @madonna. She was late to social media, but has racked up 20 million likes since joining Facebook, or one for each of her looks over the years.

FACE-LIFT: Not that she *needed* **plastic surgery,** but in 1992 one rude reporter inquired as to her feelings on the subject. "A face-lift?" Madonna replied. "That's pretty frightening. "I don't think I could do it. What if they screw up?"

They didn't.

FAIN, ELIOT: According to a note Madonna handwrote when seeking **work** in 1979, she had posed for or worked with this filmmaker (the name is possibly misspelled) at the same time she was doing **nude** modeling to support herself. No details of who he is (or was) have emerged.

"FALLING FREE": The last track on the standard edition of *MDNA,* this melodic, paradoxically plucky dirge defies that album's reputation as a **sexy,** angry fist-pump of a record. Written by Madonna, Laurie Mayer, **William Orbit** and **Joe Henry,** it was produced by Madonna and Orbit.

Orbit, who has publicly expressed his dissatisfaction with *MDNA* and with Madonna, has also sung her praises. Of this collaboration, he said it was "Madonna's favorite. She just sang it. She usually picks holes in everything. Everything gets changed obsessively. That's what we do. She's great to **work** with creatively. But this one, she just **loved** it straight away, sung it, never changed a note. Just enjoyed it. She had a very bad cold, but she wouldn't be put off."

FALLON, JIMMY: *b. September 19, 1974.* On March 24, 2012, Madonna gave a Livestream interview to longtime **fan** Jimmy Fallon (currently host of *The Tonight Show*)

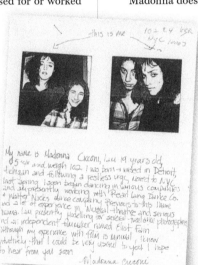

at **Facebook**'s **NYC** offices. Fallon, using some questions from fans, produced a lively Q&A that resulted in Madonna asking Quentin Tarantino to direct a music video for **"Gang Bang"** (gratis), expressing her desire to cover Serge Gainsbourg and explaining that she'd wanted to **work** with **M.I.A.** and **Nicki Minaj** "because they're bad-ass **bitches,** long story short. I think they're both smart, clever; they have strength. They don't just play on their **sexuality** or being cute. They're not ingénues ... I wouldn't mess with them."

Most memorably, Madonna taught Fallon her **"Girl Gone Wild"** moves.

Madonna also joined Fallon and **Justin Timberlake** when they cohosted *Saturday Night Live.* She sent herself up in a *Barry Gibb Talk Show* skit as being able to mesmerize the Gibbs with her **grills.**

FAME: Madonna has a complicated relationship with fame. She left her home state with very little **money** and put herself in danger and in line for some very lean, unsafe years while she pursued it, but almost immediately after attaining it, began to tire of the sacrifice of her anonymity. "It's bigger than anything I could imagine," she said of her fame in 1987, and she seems to have meant it both positively and negatively. In *Tatler,* Julie Burchill cut to the chase in describing Madonna: "She is just very good at being a star: the same way a dwarf is good at being small."

Madonna doesn't revel in her fame so much as she has come to terms with its permanence, learning how to use it to allow herself the freedom to do whatever she likes, whether it be artistically or personally, or for **charity.**

Most of all, Madonna seems to enjoy using her fame to challenge provincial attitudes on a host of issues, from **sex** to parenting to religion.

Even before she'd done anything of note, Madonna was perceived by those around her as some kind of star. According to her old college roomie **Whitley Setrakian,** "If you went into a room, like a party or something like that, you could feel everything in the room kind of changing so that all of a sudden she was the focus of the room."

By 2000, Madonna was telling AOL, "I get **nostalgic** for a time in my life before I was an empire."

Madonna said in 2002 that she was at peace with her notoriety: "Fame is only a desert island if you give it a place of importance in your life." Big of her, though one wonders how she felt when she was mistaken for a secretary by author James Jackson, who arrived for a meeting that same year with **Guy Ritchie** and promptly asked Madonna for a cup of tea. He was mortified later on, but did not get his ass handed to him, so there's that.

Handwritten letter (plus Polaroids) Madonna sent in her early NYC days in search of work

The girl who cheekily admitted in 1985 that at least part of the point of her drive was "to be famous" had, 20 years later, moved on from the concept of fame for fame's sake. In her documentary *I'm Going to Tell You a Secret*, Madonna offered, "... It's not a very good thing to aim for: 'I just wanna be famous.' I mean, it's good to be famous for actually doing something, or, you know, creating something ... We do live in a celebrity-mad culture, for sure, and I don't think it's doing anybody any good."

It should be some comfort that one of the most famous women alive—indeed, one of the most famous persons who's ever lived—cares at least as much about "doing anybody any good" as she does about extending her fame.

> "Being famous has changed a lot, because now there's so many outlets, between magazines, TV shows and the Internet, for people to stalk and follow you. We created the monster."
>
> —MADONNA, *VANITY FAIR* (2008)

FAME (TV SERIES): *Airdates: 1982–1987.* Madonna auditioned for this series in 1982. She was vying for the role of "Danny Amatullo's" (Carlo Imperato) **love** interest, but she blew her audition by being, well, *Madonna.* As casting director Joel Thurm reported 20 years later of her **lost project**, "She was supposed to be a nice, plain, simple, virginal girl next door." Madonna's audition has been released online, and along with being stilted, she comes off as none of the things they were looking for.

FAN SITES: Check out these **fan**-tastic domains when you're surfing for Madonna news, rumors, **nostalgia**, **magazine** scans, animated gifs, copyright infringement and more:

All About Madonna (**allaboutmadonna.com**): Keeps on top of all the latest news, as well as Madonna's **Instagram** statements, in an easy-to-read format.

Divina Madonna (**divinamadonna.com**): Chris Marquez's fan club that started in 1987 has made the jump to the Web with this muy stylish destination.

Drowned Madonna (**drownedmadonna.com**): Dishy resource that seems to have an inside track on the inner **workings** of Madonna, Inc., providing far-in-advance details on **unreleased** projects.

Mad-Eyes (**mad-eyes.net**): An exhaustive catalogue of Madonna's entire career.

Madonna.com (**madonna.com**): Madonna's official site. Join for early-bird access to great seats when she tours!

Madonna Infinity (**madonna-infinity.net**): Fantastic

vintage section as well as an up-to-date blog. Don't miss the colorized images.

Madonna New Era (**madonnanewera.net**): World's oldest Madonna site to publish continually, starting in 1999.

Madonna: On the Cover of a Magazine (**onthecoverofamagazine.blogspot.com**): Insanely thorough collection of **Madonnabilia**, especially—but not limited to—rare magazine covers and articles.

Madonna-tv.com (**madonna-tv.com**): The ultimate place on the Web for new (and rare) video from all phases of Madonna's life and career.

Madonna Underground (**madonnaunderground.com**): Always updated and has outstanding visuals. The team has kept it up since 2006.

Madonna's Tattoos (**facebook.com/groups/MadonnasTattoos**): Adi Bar runs this group of over 6,000 freaks (meant in the good way) obsessed with the combined topics of Madonna and getting inked.

Madonna's World (**madonnasworld.com**): Fan site run by famous fan Jeannie Buxo (a.k.a. "DJ Jene") since 1999. You're always home here.

MadonnaChile (**madonnachile.cl**): One of the Web's most active and scandalous forums, where downloads are often not of the variety that Mama condones.

Madonnalicious (**madonnalicious.com**): One of the most frequently visited all-Madonna sites.

MadonnaNation (**madonnanation.com**): Gotta check out its packed forum, which is "reserved for the queen."

MadonnaOnline (**madonnaonline.com.br**): Premier Brazilian site, and you know how Madonna loves Brazil.

Madonnarama (**madonnarama.com**): Sleek site with dynamic visuals and reliable dish on current affairs.

MadonnaTribe (**madonnatribe.com**): Not Madonna's official site, but perhaps it should be. Massively influential, it provides news and interviews with Madonna's associates.

MadonnaWeb (**madonnaweb.com**): Once *the* Madonna fan site, it was a major loss when this one went bye-bye. As of 2015, it's returning.

News-of-Madonna (**news-of-madonna.com**): Splashy site with good pap shots and quite a few exclusive interviews.

—JOHN NORRIS

Pud Whacker's Madonna Scrapbook (**madonnascrapbook.tumblr.com**): Crazy-good Tumblr with an attitude that started as a Web site in 2008, it's a great resource for rare and random Madonna images and the best place for stealable (with credit!) animated gifs.

Today in Madonna History (**todayinmadonnahistory.com**): Quite simply *the* place to go if you wanna know what Madonna was doing in the past on any particular day, month and year

FANS: On the Italian talk show ***Partita Doppia*** in 1993, Madonna said, "I have a … *passionate* relationship with my fans … Sometimes they **love** me, sometimes they **hate** me, sometimes they're angry with me and—that's love."

She was right. Sort of. There isn't a love-hate thing going on between Madonna and her fans, but between Madonna and the general public, many of whose members love her music but hate her, or vice versa, or who decide to love or hate her with every new project.

But her fans *looooooooove* Madonna. Someone like **Taylor Swift** is better liked by the public, but if Madonna is more intensely *hated*, she is also more intensely *loved*.

One real love-hate aspect of her relationship with the public comes from Madonna herself. As a self-described maverick, she is singular in her quest to make her mark on the world, an individualist whose clearest message has always been **"Express Yourself."** It should be no wonder that she is ambivalent about having fans. On the one hand, she is an artist who wants to affect people, change their minds, entertain them in mass quantities; she considers herself cool, and she wants others to agree with her on that topic. On the other hand, she can't help finding people who camp out by her apartment, follow her around, mimic her, spend all their time and **money** on her and do little else with their lives a little pathetic. "Get a life!" she used to shout at her pursuers in the '80s, and she didn't mean *hers*. (That line was recycled in ***W.E.***)

In ***Truth or Dare***, Madonna wryly observes that her fans want her even when she feels like shit, and stories of Madonna treating her fans like shit are legendary (and often made up), including rumors of pitching **gift** bouquets into a Dumpster outside the theater during her ***Speed-the-Plow*** run. Of Madonna's time in that **play**, Guy Trebay wrote in ***The Village Voice***:

"Head bowed, she walks through the blinding strobe barrage, making the stage door in just under four seconds. She doesn't stop, doesn't sign **autographs,** doesn't pose, even when a photographer shouts, '**Bitch.**'"

It's no fun to have your idol treat you brusquely, but some fans *can* be a pain. In 1988, Madonna was pestered continually by a woman named Darlene, and when Darlene and her little brother got pushy, Madonna was

photographed getting pushy right back. At the **Cannes** party for **Spike Lee**'s *Jungle Fever* (1991), Madonna's **bodyguards** shooed away an overzealous fan who then threw a fit. "Don't **fuckin'** touch me!" the fan screamed at the minders, but Madonna defused the situation by cooing, "Can't I touch you, honey?" She did, and he took off, sated.

Madonna has mellowed regarding her fans, always thanking us at public appearances, occasionally signing autographs and engaging in promo activities that show respect for longtime boosters: intimate gigs, a Reddit chat, a contest to chat with her on **Grindr**.

In general, Madonna has a strong female following, is a virtual goddess among the **gay** community (though there is no requirement to adore her—chill out) and has a fanbase that has aged from our teens to our thirties and older. But Madonna has many fans outside these parameters—her concerts are a melting pot.

In 2005, Madonna was asked how she's managed to bring fans with her through all her **reinventions**. She said, "Kids are so curious and alive. The only way is to take them with you. They'll be able to relate to something."

"I've been a fan since '83. I started Pud Whacker's Madonna Scrapbook because I found that a lot of the diehard fans always held back, and I wanted to share all the high-quality scans of photos and magazines so these new fans could see how fabulous it was for us growing up. There's never been a star like Madonna, and there never will be again."—PUD WHACKER (2015)

OLIVIU SAVU

FASHION: "Madonna is to fashion what the Big Bang theory is to creation," wrote designer Todd Oldham in 1993.

Madonna is held in high esteem by many top designers for her individuality, and for the fact that she is someone who can be counted on to actually *wear* high fashion. Madonna's street-smart siren garb forced haute couture to mimic the looks of the masses instead of vice versa, and designers for many years kept one **eye** on her and the other on their sketch pads. **Karl Lagerfeld** and Christian Lacroix were influenced by her early looks, **Jean Paul Gaultier** and **Dolce & Gabbana** later created entire lines around her tours, and she adores **Versace**.

Madonna's style has directly affected contemporary fashion, though her personal style is no longer spawning **wannabes**. As Madonna has aged, her offstage style has been less studied and is indeed often mocked by young people with careers organized around shading celeb sartorial choices they do not understand. But Madonna has also gotten bored with fashion, or at least with attempting to function within that world; rather than expressing her personality by which of a set number of pieces of clothing she has selected to wear from the trendiest lines, Madonna has gravitated toward dressing down when she's not **working** and dressing in costume when she is, often including on red carpets. For example, who took her **sexy** matador look by Givenchy at the **Grammys** in 2015 seriously?

Even when Madonna checks her sense of humor and shows up looking pretty, her fashion sense is often subjugated by whatever role she is playing at that moment.

As an ancient-history lesson and as an illustration of Madonna's desire not to repeat herself in any medium (music, film, clothes), note Madonna's favorite ensemble circa 1984: her Vivienne Westwood skirt with **Keith Haring** designs, her ripped-up black net shirt and her denim jacket with the phrase **"BOY TOY"** on the **back**. Now she'd be caught dead in anything *but* that outfit.

As much as we all **love** Madonna's '80s and '90s looks, she derided some of her most famous outfits ever for a 2008 *Us* piece, saying of her 1991 **Oscars** Bob Mackie ensemble, "I don't know what to say. It's shocking."

Because Madonna isn't dressing to conform to expectations, and because she can wear outrageous articles with utter confidence, she is one of those people who looks good in just about anything. No matter the outfit, she can pull it off. And often does.

FATHER: SEE: Ciccone, Silvio "Tony."

FAVORITE MOVIES: Madonna's taste in movies runs foreign and old, but she has talked about a wide variety of films as being among her favorites. This list includes, but is by no means limited to: *The Bad Seed* (1956), *The Blue Angel* (1930), *Bonnie and Clyde* (1967), *Brokeback Mountain* (2005), *The Conformist* (1970), *Entre Nous* (1983), ***Farewell My Concubine*** (1993), *Good Will Hunting* (1997), *Goodfellas*

"… [THE LOOK AT THE FUN HOUSE IS] CUTE— I LIKE ATHLETIC SPORTSWEAR. I'VE GONE ALL THROUGH THAT WITH MY PUERTO RICAN BOYFRIENDS. I READ ALL THE FASHION MAGAZINES AND I FOLLOW DESIGNERS LIKE WESTWOOD AND JEAN PAUL GAULTIER. I DON'T HAVE MUCH TIME TO GO SHOPPING, THOUGH, AND HALF THE STUFF I WANT I CAN'T GET IN NEW YORK."—MADONNA (1984)

"FIRST OF ALL, NOTHING MATCHES … I NEVER WEAR THE SAME EARRINGS ON EITHER EAR, AND I LIKE TO WEAR THINGS THAT CLASH."—MADONNA (1985)

"I GUESS YOU COULD CALL MY FASHION STYLE 'SPORTSWEAR FOR SEXPOTS.'"—MADONNA (1985)

"MADONNA IS THE LAST WORD IN ATTITUDE AND FASHION, THE EPITOME OF COOL. MADONNA IS THE VIDEO GENERATION'S BARBIE." —JOYCE MILLMAN, *BOSTON PHOENIX* (1986)

"ONE DAY SHE MIGHT GET SICK OF HER BRACELETS AND RIP THEM ALL OFF." —LIZ ROSENBERG (1987)

"NEVER BE PHOTOGRAPHED IN ANYTHING YOU WOULDN'T WEAR YOURSELF."—MADONNA (1989)

"I'VE LIVED THROUGH THE DANCE-HALL FLOOZY FIASCOS, THE LURID LACE LINGERIE, THE PSEUDO-MARILYN MISHAPS, THE BAWDY BUSTIER BOMBS, THE ICE-CREAM-CONE BRAS, THE SPANDEX RUNNING SHORTS, THE BARRAGE OF BLACK ROOTS. I'VE MANAGED TO SURVIVE THE CLONELIKE ARMY OF FASHION ATROCITIES WHO EMULATED HER EVERY WARDROBE MISTAKE, FROM THE MASS OF CHEAP JUNK JEWELRY CIRCLING HER NECK TO THE BATTERED COMBAT BOOTS COVERING HER FAD-MAD FEET … SHE'S AN INSULT TO AMERICAN MEN."—MR. BLACKWELL, EXPERT ON AMERICAN MEN (1993)

"SHE COULD MAKE ANYTHING LOOK GOOD, LIKE, AN OLD MAN'S SHIRT THAT I DIDN'T WANT ANYMORE AND SHE WOULD, LIKE, RAID IT OUT OF MY CLOSET." — WHITLEY SETRAKIAN, *DRIVEN: MADONNA* (2002)

(1990), *Grey Gardens* (1975), *House of Games* (1987), *In the Mood for* **Love** (2000), ***In the Realm of the Senses*** (1976), *The Lair of the White Worm* (1988), *Le Samourai* (1967), *The Marriage of Maria Braun* (1979), *Ms .45* (1981), ***The Nasty Girl*** (1990), *A Place in the Sun* (1951), *Spike of Bensonhurst* (1988), ***Sunset Boulevard*** (1950), *To Kill a Mockingbird* (1962), *The Tree of Life* (2011) and *Under the Skin* (1998).

> "… I thought I died and went to heaven. I discovered Fellini and Visconti and Pasolini and De Sica and Buñuel."
> —MADONNA ON FINDING THE UNIVERSITY OF MICHIGAN FILM CENTER (2008)

FAVORITE WOMEN: In an interview with the Brazilian magazine *Veja* in 1993, Madonna decided her favorite women of all time were **Marlene Dietrich**, Peggy Guggenheim, Billie Holiday, Grace Kelly and **Marilyn Monroe**.

FBI: In 1992, photo negatives from *Sex* were stolen from the Lexington Labs, allegedly with the assistance of an employee of the company. Madonna's security expert **Gavin de Becker** called the FBI into the investigation. First, they faxed 18 tabloids around the world, promising to sue if the 'bloids published any of the stolen shots.

Then, with the help of the UK scandal rag *News of the World*, the FBI organized a successful sting operation at the Sunset Marquis Hotel (1200 Alta Loma Rd., W. Hollywood, CA) that led to the capture of the culprit, William Stacey Anderson, who was trying to sell the photos for $100,000. *News of the World* ran a story on how they'd been instrumental in catching the thief, complete with amazingly accurate (it would later prove) illustrations of the contraband photos, long before *Sex* was released. Madonna thanked the FBI in the acknowledgments of *Sex* for "rescuing photographs that would make J. Edgar Hoover roll over.'"

Bob Guccione Sr. and his ***Penthouse*** magazine came to the rescue when a couple offered some stolen *Sex* photos to the **magazine**, saying they'd found them on a bench in Central Park. When it became obvious they were in trouble, the couple claimed they were *giving* the photos to Guccione because they had no idea how to return them.

> "I am profoundly grateful to the FBI, the Israeli police investigators and anyone else who helped lead to the arrest of this hacker. Like any citizen, I have the right to privacy. This invasion into my life—creatively, professionally and personally—remains a deeply devastating and hurtful experience, as it must be for all artists who are victims of this type of crime."—MADONNA (2015)

In 2015, Madonna was again thanking the FBI, along with the Israeli authorities, after a suspected hacker based in Israel was arrested on suspicion of stealing dozens of Madonna's demos and breaking into many other celebrities' computers.

FEET: Madonna's least favorite part of her body are her "**dancer**'s feet. They are pretty disgusting."

FELLINI, FEDERICO: *January 20, 1920–October 31, 1993.* Late Italian filmmaker of some of the most hallucinatory, imaginative films in cinema history, including *La Dolce Vita* (1960), *8 1/2 (1963)* and *Satyricon* (1969).

On his deathbed, Fellini received a bouquet from Madonna along with a note saying that she admired him greatly and wanted to **work** with him. Fellini's reaction? "Why not? She's a beautiful girl." He sent her a **love letter** that she framed and displayed in her home.

FELLOWS, MARILYN: Madonna's philosophy and history teacher at Rochester Adams High **School**. In 2001, Fellows recalled to **VH1** that Madonna sat front-and-center in her class as a junior. "I focused completely on her, and she engaged me, and then later, that engagement intensified."

Fellows has been cited by Madonna as one of two people—along with **Christopher Flynn**—most responsible for giving her the confidence she needed to leave **Michigan**: "The two of them, I think they were a conspiracy that **God** sent to me. The conspiracy of angels …"

Upon graduation, Madonna presented Fellows with a photo of herself inscribed: "Mrs. Fellows, I can't begin to tell you how I feel about you, and how I will always treasure your words of encouragement. Sometimes I think you might explode with so much energy inside of you. I think you are crazy, and I am really in **love** with your craziness, and of course, you."

FEMINISM: Have you ever wondered whether **Tina Turner** considers herself a feminist? How about Meghan Trainor? Or have you ever read an article analyzing whether the film **work** of **Angelina Jolie** is feminist? Or whether **Miley Cyrus**'s personal life is a good example for young feminists?

Since at least her *Like a Virgin* days, Madonna has been called everything from the "future of feminism" to a woman who's "set back feminism 30 years."

Because Madonna is so important and influential in our culture, her politics and any perceived message to her madness is important to many groups who would like her to promote their beliefs. Because Madonna is a woman, feminist groups feel she should make feminism a priority, and, depending on how they interpret her actions, some feminists **love** her, while others deplore her. Neither group is necessarily correct in their reading of what Madonna is trying to get across—they're just seizing on contradictory clues to see if Madonna is a good or bad **role model**, when she's far more interested in an agenda of absolute self-expression.

Camille Paglia, whose own brand of feminism is so offbeat it has earned her the enmity of the feminist Old Guard, exclaimed of Madonna in response to her **"Justify My Love"** video, "Finally, a real feminist!" But it's easy to read Madonna as a setback to feminism: She promotes glamour and body perfection, and sometimes embodies traditional gender roles.

So, is she a feminist, or what? The solution is that Madonna is not a feminist in the **original** sense of the word, but is a feminist nouvelle who behaves exactly as she likes, *presuming*, rather than *promoting*, the notion that men and women are equal. Equal, but different: Madonna in her work plays with archetypes like the **flirty** girlie and strong, silent stud; the manipulative vamp and the tough guy; the innocent maiden and the boy wonder. She also deals with the virgin and the whore, tweaking our perceptions of women by making us aware of how we feel when she is submerged in either role.

It could be argued that instead of campaigning to destroy what could be seen as constricting stereotypes, by taking them for granted and twisting them around, Madonna is that much more effective in her deconstruction and exploration of them.

When a **fan** in her *Madonna: On Stage & on the Record* audience asked Madonna if she considered herself a feminist in 2003, she shot back, "No." She then qualified her answer by asserting she is a "humanist," an answer she repeated to *Cosmopolitan* in 2015.

All that said, Madonna frequently speaks on behalf of women's issues, castigating "misogynist" overlords like **David Mamet** and Oliver Stone. Though much of the feminism in her work is of the **"Bitch I'm Madonna"** woman-on-top variety, and though she often sings about "girls" in one form or another (**"Who's That Girl," "Some Girls," "Girl Gone Wild"**), perhaps Madonna's most feminist creation is the song **"What It Feels Like for a Girl."**

FERRARA, ABEL: *b. July 19, 1951.* Director of indie films who is most famous for his twin wallows through the sewers of humanity, *King of New York* (1990) and *Bad Lieutenant* (1992). Madonna pursued Ferrara professionally, starring in his film ***Dangerous Game***.

Being notoriously high-strung, Ferrara was reported to have warred with a willful Madonna throughout filming. He later said he had gotten more out of Madonna onscreen than from most of his other leading ladies, but he was enraged when Madonna decided she **hated** his movie and conveyed those feelings to the press. Madonna had a point; Ferrara wound up using footage in the film that showed her rehearsing, scenes she never knew would be used. Ferrara explained:

"She had no idea we would ever use this footage. Look at her, she's totally on it, she's totally cool. She didn't know the camera was on. She's alive. This chick is really alive."

"SOMETIMES PEOPLE THINK THAT IF YOU'RE A GIRL, YOU'RE GONNA BE A PUSHOVER AND THEY CAN GET AWAY WITH MORE, AND THEY CAN KINDA PULL THE WOOL EVER YOUR EYES … YOU'RE NOT GONNA BE AS STRONG AS A MAN, AND, LIKE, GETTING WHAT YOU WANT, DEMANDING WHAT YOU ASKED FOR. BUT, UM, I JUST SURPRISE THEM, AND THEY SEE THAT THEY'RE WRONG."-MADONNA, *EAR SAY* (1984)

"TO CALL ME ANTIFEMINIST IS LUDICROUS."
 -MADONNA, *TIME* (1985)

"AND THEN THERE IS THE TIME WHEN JIM MORRISON ACTUALLY PULLED HIS PENIS OUT ON STAGE. EVERYBODY REMEMBERS THAT—BUT NO ONE CALLED HIM NAMES."-LYDIA CAROLE DEFRETOS ON THE SLUT-SHAMING OF MADONNA, *ARTS AQUARIAN WEEKLY* (1985)

"MADONNA IS A FEMINIST'S MARILYN."
 -MICHAEL GROSS, *VANITY FAIR* (1986)

"I THINK I'VE HAD ADVANTAGES BECAUSE I'M A GIRL."-MADONNA (1986)

"ALL WOMEN SHOULD BE AS MADONNA AS POSSIBLE."-KAREN FINLEY (1980S)

"I DON'T THINK ABOUT THE WORK I DO IN TERMS OF FEMINISM … I'M CERTAINLY NOT MILITANT ABOUT IT, NOR DO I EXACTLY PREMEDITATE IT."-MADONNA (1987)

"PEOPLE DON'T THINK OF ME AS A PERSON WHO'S NOT IN CHARGE OF MY CAREER OR MY LIFE, OKAY? AND ISN'T THAT WHAT FEMINISM IS ALL ABOUT, YOU KNOW, EQUALITY FOR MEN AND WOMEN? AND AREN'T I IN CHARGE OF MY LIFE, DOING THE THINGS I WANT TO DO?"
 -MADONNA, ON THE "EXPRESS YOURSELF" VIDEO AND HER IMAGE (1990)

"SHE'S A REAL GIRL'S GIRL. USUALLY WOMEN ARE THEIR OWN WORST ENEMIES. SHE'S NOT THREATENED BY OTHER WOMEN."
 -DAWN STEEL ON MADONNA, *THEY CAN KILL YOU … BUT THEY CAN'T EAT YOU: LESSONS FROM THE FRONT* (1993)

"AS A FEMINIST CULTURE HERO, SHE CAN'T MUSTER A CRITIQUE OF SEXISM THAT'S AS COGENT AS THE ONES OFFERED BY THE WOMEN IN BANDS LIKE THE BREEDERS AND BIKINI KILL. FACE IT, MADONNA: RIOT GRRRLS ARE TOUGHER THAN MATERIAL GIRLS."-KEN TUCKER, *ENTERTAINMENT WEEKLY* (1994)

"BEING MISQUOTED, BEING MISUNDERSTOOD, BEING JUDGED UNFAIRLY BECAUSE I AM A WOMAN PEOPLE HAVE A HARD TIME FEELING SORRY FOR. I THINK THAT'S THE KEY—YOU'RE ALLOWED TO BE BAD IF PEOPLE CAN FIND SOMETHING IN YOU THAT THEY CAN PITY."

–MADONNA ON THINGS SHE HATES, *SPIN* (1996)

"A BITCH IS A WEAK PERSON, A BITCH IS A PUSSY, A BITCH IS A COWARD WHO RATS THEIR FRIENDS OUT. I DO BELIEVE THAT PRODIGY ARE USING THIS SLANG TERM IN AN IRONIC WAY. AND I CHOOSE TO ENJOY IT AS SUCH. SO IF YOU'RE GOING TO BE A BORING, HUMORLESS FEMINIST THEN BE ONE—BUT LEAVE ME OUT OF IT."–MADONNA ON PRODIGY'S "SMACK MY BITCH UP" (2000)

"YOU KNOW, THE WOMEN IN *CINDERELLA* OR *SLEEPING BEAUTY* OR *SNOW WHITE* ARE REALLY PASSIVE. THEY DON'T MOVE THE PLOT ALONG AT ALL. THEY JUST SHOW UP, THEY'RE BEAUTIFUL, THEY GET SNAPPED UP BY THE PRINCES, THE PRINCES TELL THEM THEY WANT TO MARRY THEM AND THEN THEY GO OFF AND LIVE HAPPILY EVER AFTER … WELL, WHAT'S A GIRL SUPPOSED TO GET OUT OF THIS? THAT'S SUCH A LOAD OF CRAP."–MADONNA, *SUNDAY TIMES* (2003)

"THE MUSIC BUSINESS WOULD BE, I DON'T THINK IT WOULD BE ANYTHING AS FAR AS FEMALES, WITHOUT MADONNA."–MARY J. BLIGE (2008)

"WOMEN ARE STILL THE MOST MARGINALIZED GROUP. THEY'RE STILL THE GROUP THAT PEOPLE WON'T LET CHANGE."–MADONNA, *OUT* (2015)

"IN OUR SOCIETY, WE HAVE ALWAYS WANTED TO PIT WOMEN AGAINST EACH OTHER. STRONG, POWERFUL WOMEN AREN'T COMFORTABLE IN A ROOM WITH OTHER STRONG, POWERFUL WOMEN—OR THEY'RE TWO BITCHES THAT HAVE TO FIGHT EACH OTHER, OR BE COMPETITIVE WITH ONE ANOTHER."–MADONNA, *REFINERY29* (2015)

"I WAS INFLUENCED BY WRITERS LIKE ANNE SEXTON, SYLVIA PLATH, CARSON MCCULLERS—WOMEN WHO DIDN'T TAKE THE PATH MOST TRAVELED. I WASN'T THINKING, 'OH, THEY'RE FEMINISTS AND I WANT TO BE A FEMINIST.' I WAS JUST THINKING, 'THEY'RE STRONG WOMEN AND I WANT TO BE LIKE THEM.'"

–MADONNA, *COSMOPOLITAN* (2015)

"FEVER" (SONG): *Release date: March 6, 1993. Billboard Hot 100 peak: NA.* As performed by **Peggy Lee**, one of the slinkiest slow-burn songs ever recorded. Madonna slipped into it on a rare cover version for her *Erotica* album. The music for Madonna's "Fever" was originally for a song called **"Goodbye to Innocence,"** which she said goodbye to the second she improvised some of the lyrics to the Eddie Cooley/John Davenport song. **Shep Pettibone** sent out for the lyrics and that was that.

Madonna's take on the song **reinvented** it as whispery gloss, just as hot, but not as up-close-and-personal-like, as Lee's. It became a non-US single and a major **dance** hit.

Madonna thought enough of the song to perform it live on three separate occasions and in three radically different versions within the course of a year: She did a classy, beautifully sung version on *Saturday Night Live* clad in a black halter; a traditional, vampy version (during which she stumbled over the lyrics and improvised an apology) on **Arsenio Hall**'s 1,000th telecast; and a remix version, complete with actual flames for the finale, on *The Girlie Show World Tour*. It was a rare bonus on her *Rebel Heart Tour*.

Ex–gal pal **Sandra Bernhard** had performed a swank cover version of "Fever" in her stage show only a year prior to Madonna's cover.

Other artists who have recorded or performed "Fever" include **Beyoncé**, Boney M., Michael Bublé, Jerry Butler, Ray Charles, Joe Cocker, Rita Coolidge, the Cramps, Ella Fitzgerald, Barry Gibb, Wanda Jackson, the Jam, Little Willie John, Chaka Khan, the Kingsmen, Amanda Lear, Judith Light, La Lupe, Annabella Lwin, Shirley Manson, the McCoys, **Bette Midler**, Rita Moreno, **Elvis Presley**, Suzi Quatro, Nancy Sinatra, Tom Verlaine and Marcia Wallace.

"FEVER" (VIDEO): *Director: Stéphane Sednaoui, 1993.* The song that was never released as a single in the US required a video for other territories, so Madonna threw together an engaging **fashion** video by French photog **Stéphane Sednaoui**. "Fever" is similar to Sednaoui's clips for the Red Hot Chili Peppers and Neneh Cherry, featuring Madonna covered in silver paint (she went for it because she was convinced it projected a "clubbing" vibe that she wanted) against a blood-red backdrop, decked out as a wasp-waisted future-diva, in a short red wig, joyfully shaking her hips like a child straining to **dance** and vamping as an Indian goddess.

"The idea came that I wanted, basically, to burn her," Sednaoui told *Rolling Stone* in 2015. "My concept was that she was kind of Joan of Arc. I wanted her like a provocative saint, somebody that speaks out and tells the truth, and is ready to burn for it."

The clip, which premiered on May 11, 1993, on **MTV**, is **powered** by Madonna's ironic smirk and jerky photography that combine to make it far more re-watchable than it ever needed to be. It is now a sort of time capsule of '90s chic.

"Madonna has taught young women to be fully female and sexual while still exercising total control over their lives."
–CAMILLE PAGLIA, *THE NEW YORK TIMES* (1990)

FIFTY SHADES OF GREY: *Written by E.L. James. Publication date: June 20, 2011.* It started out as *Twilight* **fan** fiction, but this erotic novel wound up outselling even *that* phenomenally successful **book**—over 100 million copies sold ... how's that for a **money** shot? It has the staying **power** of a college boy on Viagra.

When the book was made into a 2015 movie (directed by Sam Taylor-Johnson, released on February 13, 2015), Madonna was asked by *Billboard* what she thought of the source material. The woman who'd had a Top 10 hit called **"Hanky Panky"** about spanking was not impressed: "It's pulp fiction. It's not very **sexy**, maybe for someone who has never had sex before. I kept waiting for something exciting and crazy to happen in that red room thing, and I was like, 'Hmm, a lot of spanking.' I also thought, 'This is so unrealistic because no guy goes down on a girl that much.' I'm sorry, but no one eats **pussy** as much as the guy in that book."

"FIGHTING SPIRIT": Bonus track written and produced by Madonna and **Mirwais** that came with the limited edition box set of *Confessions on a Dance Floor.* The song opens with a tinking of piano keys and slithers along atop a Giorgio Moroder–style beat, with a dash of Blondie's "Rapture" (1980) bells. Madonna's vocal is haunting on this album-worthy song.

"When I die, I am going to go straight to heaven. And you're going to ask me why. Because I told the truth."- EUGENE HÜTZ AS "A.K." IN *FILTH AND WISDOM* (2008)

FILTH AND WISDOM: *Director: Madonna. Release date: February 13, 2008.* Madonna's theatrical directorial debut was not *W.E.*, but this entirely different, decidedly more punk effort. Madonna shot the 81-minute feature in **London** the last two weeks of May 2007.

The romantic dramedy, written by Madonna and Dan Cadan, follows an immigrant (Gogol Bordello singer Eugene Hütz, whom Madonna hired after admiring his **work** in 2005's *Everything Is Illuminated*) from Ukraine who funds his goal of being a rock star by working as **sex** Master (or dominatrix when he's in **drag**). His roomies (Holly Weston and Vicky McClure) are on similarly hardscrabble paths, the former an aspiring ballet **dancer** who reluctantly strips to make rent and the latter a pharmacist's assistant ... hard to decide which of the three has the most embarrassing **job**.

Madonna said she chose to do this film to "explore the paradox of life, really. To show that you can't, you can't ... first of all, you can't make judgments about people and you can't make judgments about the choices people make because ultimately you never know where someone's going to end up. And in many, in many respects, I mean, it is a bit of an insight into my philosophical point of view about life, that, that out of darkness comes light, and that you

can't really reach, um, a level of enlightenment without going through a period of darkness or a period of doubt or a period where you perceive yourself as having less fun."

The film is most interesting when viewed as Madonna's autobiography; all of the elements of her early days in **NYC** are there, even if they're transferred to London. Madonna attracted an interesting cast, including Richard E. Grant as a rather nutty professor (based on **Christopher Flynn**), and created a film with a lot of verve. She has said the film was influenced by her favorite filmmakers, auteurs Jean-Luc Godard, Pier Paolo Pasolini and Luchino Visconti.

Filth and Wisdom had its world premiere at the Berlin International Film Festival on February 13, 2008, where Madonna granted a number of lengthy interviews about the project. Her appearance attracted more attention for what can only have been a round of **plastic surgery**, allegedly after being upset over her appearance in her *Hard Candy* promo shoot.

In spite of the attention paid to Madonna's new look (until things settled in, it looked as if she'd had her *Madonna* removed!), the assembled media focused on her work on the film, not on the work she may have had done. "... I **loved** going to the Berlin Film Festival—it was the first time in my career that no one asked me a personal question. When you're a pop star, everyone feels entitled to know what color your underpants are," Madonna said after returning home.

The movie mostly received negative reviews, taking in only $354,628 at the box office following a microscopically narrow release by IFC Films. It was the first feature film by Madonna's production company, Semtex Films.

"Madonna and movies have never been a good combo."-PETER TRAVERS, *ROLLING STONE* (2008)

"Madonna has done herself proud. Her film has an artistic ambition that has simply bypassed her husband, the film director Guy Ritchie ... Altmanesque would be stretching the compliment too far, but *Filth and Wisdom* shows Madonna has real potential as a director."
—JAMES CHRISTOPHER, *TIMES OF LONDON* (2008)

FINCH, CHRIS: *b. November 20, 1973.* The boy who re-enacted the adolescent role from the **"Open Your Heart"** video on the *Who's That Girl World Tour* when **Felix Howard** failed to obtain a **working** license for the tour. Finch said of the job, "I had the most terrific summer that any kid could ever have," dancing up a storm with Madonna all over the world.

Madonna adored Finch, making faces at him when her **back** was to the audience and planting a grown-up kiss on his lips when she played his hometown of Anaheim, California, just to help him show off to his friends.

"He's the ideal man. He does everything I ask him to do and never complains."
—MADONNA ON CHRIS FINCH (1987)

As part of the gig, Finch appeared in the music video for **"Who's That Girl."**

Since then, Finch has continued **acting**, and is on **Twitter** @thechrisfinch.

FINCHER, DAVID: *b. August 28, 1962*. As one of the founding interests behind Propaganda Films (along with Michael Bay, Nigel Dick, Steve Golin, Dominic Sena and Sigurjón Sighvatsson), Fincher became the go-to music video director for artists like **Paula Abdul**, the Motels and Jody Watley, among many others.

But it is Fincher's **work** with Madonna that makes him one of the medium's most celebrated directors: He's the man behind **"Express Yourself," "Oh Father," "Vogue"** and **"Bad Girl,"** therefore competing with the likes of **Mary Lambert** and **Jean-Baptiste Mondino** for the title of Madonna's #1 video visionary.

Fincher's first big shot at feature-film directing was *Truth or Dare*, but it didn't pan out when he was replaced by **Alek Keshishian**, leaving him to direct the ill-fated *Alien³* (1992) instead. Fincher and Madonna remained cordial, however, and his career has gone nowhere but up. Via films like *Seven* (1995) and *Fight Club* (1999), he became one of Hollywood's coolest, most bankable directors. Carrying on with *The Curious Case of Benjamin Button* (2008), *The Social Network* (2010), *The Girl with the Dragon Tattoo* (2011) and *Gone Girl* (2014), he has amassed a slew of nominations and **awards**; it's only a matter of time before he has his **Oscar.**

FIORUCCI: Madonna performed at a 1983 gig in honor of the 15th (give or take—it was founded in 1967) anniversary of this Italian **fashion** label at **Studio 54**. She landed the gig thanks to her tight bond with **Maripol**, who was **working** with the brand. It was a major boost for Madonna, giving her beaucoup buzz.

Madonna was then invited and flown to France for the Fiorucci **Paris** opening, where she entertained fashion-biz luminaries like Issey Miyake, **Karl Lagerfeld**, Yves Saint Laurent and Hubert de Givenchy. It was Madonna's first introduction to the world of high fashion, and its first to her.

FIRST KISS: Madonna's came at age 11, from a boy named Tommy.

FISHER, CARRIE: *b. October 21, 1956*. "Princess Leia" of the *Star Wars* films, the author of comic novels and a serial memoirist, this daughter of crooner Eddie Fisher and Hollywood sweetheart Debbie Reynolds became friendly with Madonna via **Sean Penn**. She attended the Penns' **wedding** in 1985 and interviewed Madonna for ***Rolling Stone*** in 1991 when **Norman Mailer**'s fee was deemed too stratospheric.

The result was an unaffected interview that featured as much about Fisher as about Madonna. We learned about the **AIDS**-related **death** of Fisher's friend, that she never fucked **Warren Beatty** and her idea of Mr. Right. But the interview also addressed Madonna's interest in making movies about women ("I couldn't do any men."), how wary she was of **Alek Keshishian** as *Truth or Dare* was being filmed and her childhood desire to be a **nun** ("Sister Mary Fellatio").

FITNESS: Madonna is a fit-freak, but her methods of maintaining her body over the years have changed frequently, like a criminal switching cabs to throw the cops off the trail. She swam in the '80s, then ran, lifted weights, practiced **yoga** in the '90s and then graduated to **Pilates**, went back to aerobic workouts and has returned to yoga. Her diet has changed a lot, too, from **vegetarian** to vegan to macrobiotic with indulgences, from teetotalling to drinking socially.

Madonna **works** out for two hours at a stretch, pun intended.

In 2006, *Us* calculated Madonna's yearly fitness expenses at $158,269, counting a thrice-weekly Pilates class with James D'Silva ($477), a private chef ($9,300/month) and seven bottles of **Kabbalah** water a day ($49).

Note: You won't get that body by drinking the water alone.

Party invite to Madonna's Fiorucci gig

"Bruce Springsteen was born to run. I was born to flirt." —MADONNA (1985)

FLAG: A next-to-**nude** Madonna appeared in a **Rock the Vote** ad for **MTV** wrapped in the American flag in 1992. She also used the US flag in *The Girlie Show World Tour* as a backdrop to her rendition of **"Holiday"** and as the lining of her troupe's military broadcoats for that same number. A massive US flag became a backdrop for her **"American Pie"** music video, she wore a flag-print tank on her *Drowned World Tour* and a series of world flags waved behind Madonna in her edited **"American Life"** video.

She's a patriot, but not of the variety that most self-described patriots would embrace.

More shocking to Puerto Ricans was Madonna's impulsive use of the island's flag to dry herself of sweat while on tour there in 1993, as well as a later embrace of the flag ... followed by a quick swipe of it between her legs. Many interpreted these as ultimate acts of disrespect. The "Puerto Rican flag flap" was fueled by the fact that it came only two weeks before citizens were to vote on whether to remain a US commonwealth, seek independence, or become an official state. For the gesture, Madonna was officially condemned by Puerto Rico's congress.

In 2016, Madonna draped herself with the Taiwanese flag while on her *Rebel Heart Tour*, an act that enraged many in mainland **China**.

FLIRT: "I flirt with **grandmothers** and **garbage** men and stuff like that. It's part of my nature." When Madonna defined her rules of flirtation to **Johnny Carson** in 1987, her androgynous nature made it seem only natural that she would favor both men and women with her sly wink—Johnny didn't even blink at her unisex philosophy. Madonna's *Who's That Girl* director **James Foley** has dubbed her "the greatest flirt of all time."

FLOCK OF SEAGULLS, A: Neil Tennant, later one of the **Pet Shop Boys** but at the time a music writer for the **fan** magazine *Smash Hits* (and its US counterpart *Star Hits*) was supposed to interview this '80s band in 1983 ... but they stood him up. Needing to fill his schedule, Tennant called up newcomer Madonna, which led to a large feature in *Star Hits*. He later recalled, "I couldn't stop her talking."

FLYNN, CHRISTOPHER: *Circa 1930–October 27, 1990.* The man Madonna describes as having been her biggest influence. Flynn, a former Joffrey Ballet dancer nearly 30 years her senior, was Madonna's ballet instructor in her teen years at his Christopher Flynn Dance **School** at the **Rochester** School of Ballet (formerly 404 Main St., Rochester, MI). There, Madonna (in classes with her brother **Christopher Ciccone**) developed her skills as a dancer as well as her drive to be perfect.

In 1978, Flynn was appointed to a position at the **University of Michigan**, Ann Arbor, teaching ballet, just in time for Madonna to continue her studies with him while pursuing her higher education. Madonna's grandma **Elsie**

Christopher Flynn, not long before his death

Fortin said of Flynn, "He once said that all the articles about my granddaughter are deceptive because they make her out to be this kook who says things off the top of her head, when in reality, she is the most intelligent and hard-working student he ever had. She never missed a class. Come hell or high water, Madonna was always there."

More than a **dance** teacher, Flynn was the first man to tell her she was beautiful. He was **gay**, and took her to Detroit bars (it was the '70s, IDs weren't checked ... chill out!) where she first experienced gay culture, dance culture and adulation by a crowd as her gyrations elicited the enthusiastic approval of the horny hordes.

"She **loved** it and *God*, was she hot. She just cleared the floor and we just cut loose and everybody loved her," Flynn later told Madonna biographer **Christopher Andersen**. "What fun she was, always that, what fun—and it's the kind of fun I like because it does not deny responsibility, or deny seriousness, or deny classicism, things that the love of what we were doing was all about."

Flynn said Madonna asked him to explain why Judy Garland and **Marilyn Monroe** had such an appeal to gay men. When he explained it was the tragic nature of their lives, Madonna reportedly said, "Well, then forget it. I will never be tragic. If it takes being tragic to have gay **fans**, then **fuck** it. I'll appeal only to straight people, I guess."

His bohemian tastes rubbed off on Madonna, resulting in a major transformation during her time with him. It was Flynn, whom she cryptically called her "imaginative first lover" (she probably meant "imaginary"), who campaigned to get Madonna to move to **New York** and to attend the **Duke University** workshop that put her in the path of **Pearl Lang**.

Flynn was renowned as a *Whiplash* (2014)-level tough instructor who enforced weigh-ins, struck his charges with sticks and placed sharpened pencils between a dancer's chin and throat to teach proper posture. "He was brutal. He was ruthless, and he walked around with a stick and he hit you with it," Madonna has recalled.

But as exacting as Flynn could be, Madonna was the apple of his toned thigh. Fellow student **Peter Kentes** has recalled that Flynn treated her as his favorite and would use her to demonstrate proper technique to his other students.

Barbara Victor's *Goddess* bio claims that Flynn bragged to (anonymous) friends about having **sex** with Madonna in a motel in 1976.

When he became ill with **AIDS**, Madonna helped him financially and supported him in his efforts as an AIDS activist. She appeared with him at an AIDS Dance-A-Thon in 1989, where he introduced her. She said of him that evening, "You know, he's thanking me for being here, but I have to say thank you to him because he's the man responsible for encouraging me to go after my **dreams** ..." She mourned his **death** in private, avoiding his memorial for fear of causing a commotion.

In 2008, Madonna based the character played by Richard E. Grant in her film *Filth and Wisdom* on her old mentor.

"You will understand the depth of my faith in her when I tell you that she was among the first persons I turned to when I was diagnosed [with AIDS]."–CHRISTOPHER FLYNN ON MADONNA (1989)

FOLEY, JAMES: *b. December 28, 1953.* Director of films like *Reckless* (1984), *After Dark, My Sweet* (1990) and *Glengarry Glen Ross* (1992) who became tight with Madonna when he directed **Sean Penn** in *At Close Range* (1986), for which Madonna wrote her classic ballad **"Live to Tell."**

Foley directed Madonna in the film *Who's That Girl*, a vehicle that unfortunately crashed and burned. Madonna made him bend over and kiss her foot in order to reshoot a scene in that film (which turned out not to have been worth it), but she still considered "Jamie" one of her best friends. He was one of Penn's best friends, too, and in fact had served as the best man at the **Ciccone**/Penn **wedding** in 1985.

Foley directed three music videos in a row for Madonna: "Live to Tell," **"Papa Don't Preach"** and the non-US version of **"True Blue."** The only music videos he ever directed, they were all lensed under the pseudonym "Peter Percher."

FOOTLOOSE: *Director: Herbert Ross. Release date: February 17, 1984.* Popular music-driven film about a rebellious kid (Kevin Bacon) who clashes with a small town's uptight minister (John Lithgow) to defeat the antiquated local ordinance banning dancing, and another **lost project** for Madonna.

Madonna auditioned for the part of "Ariel," which was won by Lori Singer. Singer also beat out Madonna for a part on the **TV** series *Fame* (1982–1987). Madonna had won her role in *Desperately Seeking Susan* over several actors, Singer among them.

"FORBIDDEN LOVE" (1994): Suggestive ballad from *Bedtime Stories* written by Madonna and **Babyface** and produced by the writers along with **Nellee Hooper**, and the first of two (so far!) songs with this title in Madonna's catalogue. It is simple, lyrically, almost like a lullaby about the pleasures of rejection.

"FORBIDDEN LOVE" (2005): Found on *Confessions on a Dance Floor*, Madonna's second song with this title is a similarly sensual rumination on taboo **love** and lust, and shares with its 1994 namesake a fairytale-like feel. The music couldn't be more different, a wash of electronic blips and bleeps. It was performed as a **gay**-themed plea for peace in the Middle East using two of Madonna's male **dancers** and elaborate hand choreography on her *Confessions Tour*.

FORD, TOM: *b. August 27, 1961.* Handsome **fashion** designer who revamped Gucci and has become his own luxury brand, and whose foray into film directing with 2009's *A Single Man* was an unqualified success.

Madonna is friendly with Ford. Her *W.E.* shared both *A Single Man*'s preoccupation with style and the composer of its score, Abel Korzeniowski. Madonna attended a special screening of Ford's flick at the Museum of Modern **Art** (11 W. 53rd St., NY, NY) in 2009 along with Kevin Bacon, **Courtney Love**, **Julianne Moore**, Michael Stipe and Anna Wintour. **Naomi Wolf** compared the negative reception of *W.E.* to the positive reception of *A Single Man* to mine them for gender disparity, ignoring the possibility that Ford's film was better.

Ford has dressed Madonna in the past, saying of her style, "If there was ever anybody who knew who they were, it's Madonna. She definitely does, and she does what she wants."

FORTIN, ELSIE MAE: *June 19, 1911–March 9, 2011.* Madonna's maternal grandmother, an indomitable spirit who was a major force in her young life. Madonna stayed with Fortin the summer between junior high and high **school** at her home (1204 Smith St., Bay City, MI) and was the apple of her **eye** at a time when Madonna felt unloved by her **stepmother**.

When Fortin died at 99 in 2011, Madonna had recently visited her grandmother. When various news outlets wondered if Madonna would attend Fortin's **funeral**, **Liz Rosenberg** told the press, "I'm sorry, but Madonna will not be issuing any statements or conversing with the media regarding her grandmother. It is a totally personal matter to her."

Mlive.com reported that while Madonna did not attend Fortin's funeral service on March 12, she was seen with her children attending a memorial service the evening before. Madonna's **London** home was burgled in her absence.

FOSTER, DAVID: *b. November 1, 1949.* Prolific producer of pop smashes by everyone from Toni Braxton to Rod Stewart. For her *Something to Remember* ballads collection, Madonna **worked** with him on the songs **"You'll See," "One More Chance"** and "I Can't Forget," the latter of which remains **unreleased**.

While promoting his humbly titled memoir *Hitman: Forty Years of Making Music, Topping the Charts and Winning Grammys* in 2008, Foster was asked to sum up Madonna in one word but declined, instead saying, "When I met Madonna to decide whether we were gonna work together, she wanted to have dinner in **New York**, and I'd never met her before, I knew her music, and I sat down at dinner—she

—BENDELACREME

MATTHEW RETTENMUND

During "4 Minutes" at *Sticky & Sweet*, she bangs ...

does the **Bill Clinton**, um, the Bill Clinton thing where she breaks the 18-inch rule, right? She will get right up in you, right? But I must tell you that Madonna was so seductive at dinner that night and—she wasn't doin' it, she was not interested in me, it's just who she is, she just, it just *oozes* out of her. And I was like, I was like [mouth open]. I found her to be so seductive, it was, it was hard for me to concentrate ..."

"4 MINUTES" FEAT. JUSTIN TIMBERLAKE AND TIMBALAND (SONG): *Release date: March 17, 2008. Billboard Hot 100 peak: #3.* The lead single from *Hard Candy*, written by **Madonna**, **Timbaland**, **Justin Timberlake** and **Danja**, and produced by Timbaland, Timberlake and Danja, was this sermon delivered in the form of an earworm, a call to action for an age in which world hunger, global warming and global *warring* were of increasing concern. The lyrics and the song's marching-band implacability seem to play on the same concept as the nuclear Doomsday Clock.

Some **fans** disliked Madonna's vocal positioning in the song; for a first single from a Madonna album, her part is more like that of a featured performer. Nonetheless, "4 Minutes" took off at radio, giving Madonna her most recent unqualified hit (as of publication). It went to #1 in many territories and rose to #3 in the US.

Madonna debuted the song live at her 2008 **Roseland Ballroom** gig, performing it with Timberlake. On her *Sticky & Sweet Tour*, she managed to present it without Timberlake in the flesh, though he did team up with her live for her LA show.

"4 MINUTES" FEAT. JUSTIN TIMBERLAKE AND TIMBALAND (VIDEO): *Directors: Jonas Euvremer & François Rousselet, 2008.* For the all-important kick-off video from *Hard Candy*, Madonna and **Justin Timberlake** went with French duo Jonas & François, known for their **work** on **TV** ads and for directing **Kanye West**'s "Good Life" (2007).

To represent the song's panicked warning about the elapsing of time, images are shown being fractured by a black, Blob-like, creeping void, which leaves all in its path fractured and then dissolved. Shockingly, the faces of a kissing couple are shown disintegrating in great anatomical detail.

The video for the high-concept song has a low-concept hipness to it, referencing OK Go's "Here It Goes Again" video (2006) with a winking treadmill sequence, making use of intentionally obvious film sets (randomly parked cars that are just begging to get parkoured, a staged grocery-store scene, a chic light board clock). It almost has an early-**MTV** quality, with its abundance of images included seemingly just 'cuz they're kinda cool-looking.

The choreography, by **Jamie King**, marked an increasingly rare instance of Madonna doing conceptual **dance**

"... [A]n event record between superpowers who not only share equal billing, but sound gangbusters together."-CHUCK TAYLOR, *BILLBOARD* (2008)

moves (as opposed to her favored spontaneous writhing), and heightens the **sexual** chemistry between its stars, though the video is not preoccupied with eroticizing the Madonna/Timberlake union.

The video spawned numerous homemade versions on **YouTube**, most prominently one viewed by millions and uploaded by Disney Channel upstart **Miley Cyrus**.

FOUR ROOMS: *Directors: Allison Anders, Alexandre Rockwell, Robert Rodriguez, Quentin Tarantino. Release date: December 25, 1995.* Anthology comic flick by four superhot young directors, containing four oddball segments joined by a bellhop character (Tim Roth).

In the film, Madonna appears in the Allison Anders segment *Honeymoon Suite: The Missing Ingredient*, which is about a witch coven (rounded out by Sammi Davis, Amanda de Cadenet Valeria Golino, Ione Skye, Lili Taylor, Alicia Witt) seeking semen as the final ingredient of a spell intended to resurrect a fellow sorceress. Madonna's character, "Elspeth," is the lover of Witt's "Kiva."

Madonna took the part because she was interested in **working** with Anders, and because the film was a Miramax project—she had strong ties with the company's overlords the **Weinsteins** ever since their successful distribution of her *Truth or Dare*.

She also noted, "The role of a **gay** witch interested me; I thought it was funny, and I liked the ensemble aspect of the film itself."

Prior to its release, the film had big buzz, thanks to advance testing that was "through the roof." Unfortunately, that test screening was a fluke, as the film's actual reception was more through the basement; it suffered from extremely negative reviews and word of mouth, grossing a scant $4,257,354 at the box office.

FRANCO, JAMES: *b. April 19, 1978.* Actor and filmmaker who started out in teen heartthrob territory with films like *Never Been Kissed* (1999) and *Whatever It Takes* (2000), and who quickly blossomed into an appealing leading man in pieces like the **TV** film *James Dean* (2001), in which he played the title role, and the *Spider-Man* (2002–2007) and *Planet of the Apes* (2011–2014) franchises. **Working** feverishly, he has appeared in close to 100 disparate films and TV projects that cater to audiences who wouldn't seem like they'd even know each other, from a pothead in *Pineapple Express* (2008) to the object of Harvey Milk's affection in *Milk* (2008) opposite **Sean Penn**, and including a series of queer films.

In some ways, Franco is a direct descendant of Madonna for his willingness to make people wonder if he is **gay** and for his unashamed embrace of **art** for art's sake. Also, he is captivated by photos of himself.

Franco is a big Madonna **fan**. They met in 2011 when Madonna was handing a Gucci **award** to Jessica Chastain (another big Madonna fan) in Venice. Chatting with Swide .com in 2013, he said that if he could be **reincarnated** as any of history's great divas, he would choose, "Madonna. She rules." In December 2014, he uploaded to **Instagram** a video of himself lip-synching (badly) to **"Like a Virgin."** It's hard to believe they won't collaborate at some point.

"FREEDOM": Uplifting Madonna/**Dallas Austin** song originally recorded for the *Just Say Yes* album series but that was initially **unreleased** before finding an outlet on the **charity** album *Carnival!*, which raised **money** to fight the depletion of the rainforest. It has a decidedly world-music vibe, and would have been a creditable addition to the album for which it was originally recorded.

FREIRE, RODRIGO: *b. March 27, 1978.* Madonna's "Rubba," except not.

When rumors surfaced in 1993 that Madonna was affairing with this gorgeous young model, her lawyers had a calf, man. He was 15 at the time. Back then, it was called "robbing the cradle," while today it's called "statutory **rape**" and leads to giant settlements and/or prison time.

Madonna's lawyer's response when the *New York Post* implied she was sleeping with Freire was, "Because these statements expressly allege or imply inter alia immoral and illegal conduct on the part of our client, they are libelous per se."

But was the rumor true? It didn't help that Madonna had gushed about having **sex** with a teenager in *Sex* the year before. The tabloid newspapers relied on information that Freire's friends said she had flown him to "be by her side" several times. Regardless, the publicity didn't hurt him—he made the cover of the February 1994 *Interview*.

FRENCH AND SAUNDERS: Gifted British comedy duo made up of Dawn French (b. October 11, 1957) and Jennifer Saunders (b. July 6, 1958) whose *French and Saunders* sketch series has often poked fun at Madonna, including takes on her *Truth or Dare* ("This is chocolate soup. If I don't eat this right, I'm compromising my artistic integrity."), **Gap** ad, **"Hung Up"** video, *English Roses* series and more.

In 2012, the team was duped into doing a reading of **Garry Trudeau**'s **parody** interview, thinking it was real.

Saunders has said she tried for years, in vain, to get Madonna to appear on one of her series, including *Absolutely Fabulous*. In 2008, Saunders told *Attitude*, "I think she's extraordinary, but I don't even think she has ever heard of us, and that's what's excruciatingly hard to bear."

Eventually, Madonna sent Saunders a nice note, but still no collaboration was forthcoming. "It became sort of a joke, actually," Saunders mused, "[that] if she ever did say yes, we'd probably say no!"

FREUD, SIGMUND: *May 6, 1856–September 23, 1939.* German shrink who invented psychoanalysis as a scientific way of saying that we're all obsessed with **sex** and that women would be happier with penises. In a nutshell.

Though Madonna name-dropped Freud in **"Die Another Day,"** it was sarcastic. During a Reddit.com chat in 2013, Madonna noted that she's not a **fan** of his: "i think he was too cerebral and a misogynist. im a fan of carl jung."

#foreverjung

FRIDAY NIGHT WITH JONATHAN ROSS: *Airdates: November 2, 2001–July 16, 2010.* Popular UK chat show on which Madonna appeared on May 2, 2003. Ross's house band, 4 Poofs and a Piano, was her opening act, welcoming her with a medley of **"Express Yourself," "Material Girl," "Music," "Like a Virgin"** and **"Holiday,"** all gussied up in Madonna incarnations.

Madonna had previously spoken to **Jonathan Ross** for his *Jonathan Ross Presents ... Erotica* Madonna in 1992. For her second sit-down with him, she was wearing a beret again, this time in full *American Life* regalia.

For her first performance, Madonna gave a vulnerable read on her single **"American Life"** immediately before sitting to chat about **Guy Ritchie**, moving to **London**, learning to **love** ale, the congestion charge, housework and other scintillating topics. Breaking news: Madonna makes her own bed on the housekeeper's day off.

Her other performance was a pitchy **"Hollywood"** (high notes be damned!), and she closed with an oldie. "How far back do you want me to go?" she joked, before ending with a spot-on **"Don't Tell Me,"** a song that was all of three years old at the time.

In 2015, Madonna appeared on *The Jonathan Ross Show*.

"... career-denting fiasco ..."
—JANET MASLIN ON *FOUR ROOMS*, *THE NEW YORK TIMES* (1995)

FRIEDLANDER, LEE: *b. July 14, 1934.* Respected **art** photographer who had the good fortune to shoot **nudes** of a starving young Madonna at his 35 E. 7th St. studio in 1979. His images had their first exposure to the masses via *Playboy*'s 1985 "last stapled issue."

Friedlander heard Madonna was a good model from his friend **Anthony Panzera**, who had been sketching and painting her in the buff. Once Friedlander went to see *Desperately Seeking Susan* in the spring of 1985, he called Panzera and asked, "Is that the same Madonna?" When told they were one and the same, Friedlander got on the horn to his lawyer, Neale Albert, and then contacted *Playboy* ... and the rest is herstory.

Friedlander referred to the resulting brouhaha as "a media event; this has nothing to do with me. I never have anything to say about my **work**, anyway. Let the pictures stand on their own. Look at them—say anything you want about them."

Madonna admitted in 1998 that at the time Friedlander sold his nudes of her, "I wanted to rip his face off."

FRIEDMAN, ROGER: Former Fox News movie critic who was bounced for reviewing a bootlegged movie and who later founded *Showbiz 411*. Friedman is one of Madonna's staunchest *offenders* in the media, needling her for clicks at every turn.

Friedman wrote in 2008, "I often criticize Madonna in this space for her nutty politics and her membership in **Kabbalah**," by way of introducing a piece noting that her *Sticky & Sweet Tour* was selling well. But in the same article, he made sure to say that *Hard Candy* was light on hit singles, and, "By contrast, **Mariah Carey**—whose sales have outpaced Madonna's considerably—is already on her third single from her contemporaneous release, *E=MC*."

Madonna's **fans** have long alleged that Friedman is in the tank for Carey.

During the *MDNA* era, Friedman—writing for *Forbes*—hit Madonna hard for having the temerity to offer copies of her album along with tickets to her *MDNA Tour*. The strategy guaranteed her a #1 debut on the *Billboard* 200, which meant the latest by **Lionel Richie**—which outsold *MDNA* by a mile in the US over time—was relegated to #2. Friedman sniffed, "I do think that all the people involved in the Madonna ticket-CD deal should apologize to Richie for denying him his rightful place at #1." Are you getting the idea that this guy would have been the most annoying kid in the sandbox? And that he never left it?

In the *Rebel Heart* era, Friedman softened his stance on Madonna, praising her record while still concern-trolling its sales as well as the sales of her *Rebel Heart Tour*. In a piece published the day after *Rebel Heart* dropped, Friedman wrote, "Madonna has not sold a lot of records in a long time ... even though the Material Middle Aged Lady continued to sell concert tickets by the truckload." He went on to point out that she is "the oldest pop star in the Top 40."

You know the type.

"FROZEN" (SONG): *Release date: February 23, 1998. Billboard Hot 100 peak: #2.* Another of Madonna's incredible songs that stopped just short of hitting #1, the *Ray of Light* mid-tempo electro-ballad "Frozen" is her most sonically daring lead single from an album. She wrote it with **Patrick Leonard** after being inspired by *The English Patient* (1996) and produced it with him and **William Orbit**, the latter of whom brought to it his characteristic astral quality.

Sung with great restraint and delicacy, "Frozen" stands out in Madonna's catalogue for its timeless quality and mature lyrics. It was such a sensation that when it was played early on a Singapore radio station, **fans** uploaded a recording on the Internet before its official release, making it Madonna's first **leak**.

Madonna was sued many years after the song's success by Belgian musician Salvatore Acquaviva, who claimed it was stolen from his tune "Ma vie fout le camp" ("My Life's Going Nowhere"). His theory was that Madonna must've heard his song while briefly in Belgium with **Patrick Hernandez**, a ridiculous idea since over 15 years had passed between her trip and the release of "Frozen." Madonna lost the case in 2005, resulting in an effective ban on "Frozen" in the country. In 2014, the case was reversed, because *duh*.

Madonna performed "Frozen" on The *Rosie O'Donnell Show*, for the BBC's *National Lottery* (February 21, 1998), on the German series *Wetten dass ...?*, *Best M of the World* in Japan and at **Sanremo** in Italy, all of which were elaborate performances that were nonetheless lip-synched.

On April 29, 1998, Madonna appeared at the Rainforest Foundation Benefit Concert at Carnegie Hall, where she flawlessly performed the song completely live, accompanied by the East Harlem Violin Project as run by Roberta Guaspari-Tzavaras, a woman Madonna was at that time set to play in the movie *Music of the Heart*. No video from this event has ever surfaced.

Madonna's *National Lottery* performance of "Frozen"

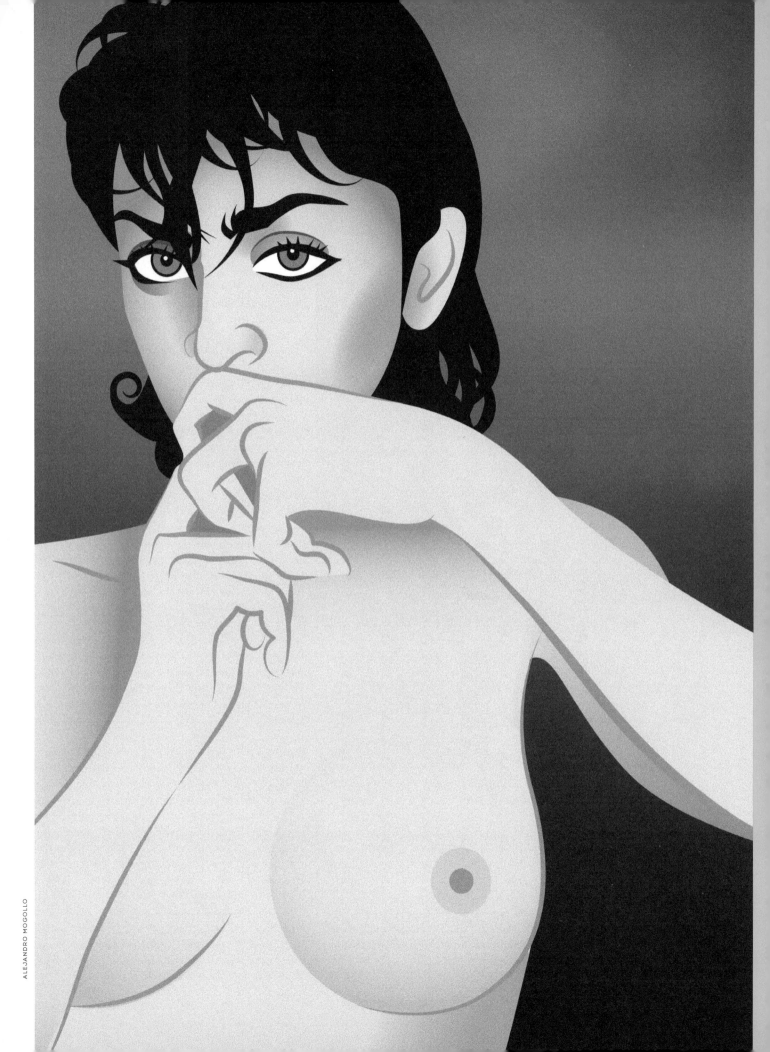

ALEJANDRO MOGOLLO

ALEJANDRO MOGOLLO

also wanted it to carry the look of a **dance** choreographed by **Martha Graham**. It needed sweep, but it needed mystery.

Dressed in a black gown by avant-garde designer Olivier Theyskens (she was just beginning to work with her now longtime stylist **Arianne Phillips**) and in a long black wig, Madonna spent long hours dancing in the Mojave Desert in January 1998, freezing to **death** (it *does* get quite cold in the desert, Madonna).

It was well worth her discomfort, and the discomfort of longtime **fans** surprised not to be getting "**Lucky Star** 2: Electric Boogaloo."

The blue-tinted video opens with the camera traveling across the desolate landscape, finding Madonna—witchy and alone—levitating above the parched earth while the wind wreaks havoc with her long locks and flowing wardrobe. Are you a good Nicks, or a bad Nicks?

"I'm a mystical creature in the desert, and I'm the embodiment of female angst," Madonna told **MTV**'s **Kurt Loder** of her character.

The first of several visually shocking statements occurs when Madonna appears to fall over, shattering into a flock of black birds. Immediately thereafter, Madonna appears in triplicate, singing with herself, a compelling representation of the multiple sides to her personality that have struggled to stay at the fore of her career.

Next, her form morphs into a running **dog**, continuing a theme of transformation, and of a startlingly simple connectivity with the natural world. The illusion that Madonna has extra arms as she performs Hindu movements underscores the video's mystical vibe.

"Frozen" is consistently ranked among Madonna's most innovative music videos.

FRY, STEPHEN: *b. August 24, 1957.* The English comedian and professional atheist wasn't sold on Madonna in 1987, saying, "It is a great injustice that so vain an individual has acquired the reputation for being the best in the world. She does a disservice to womankind." Wonder if he's changed his mind?

FUCK: If you think she was raunchy on *Late Show with David Letterman,* try listening to Madonna's BBC broadcast of her *Blond Ambition World Tour* from **London**; she said the dreaded F-word countless times, none of which was **censored** since it was live. She explained that "'fuck' is the reason we're here" since all our parents did it. Madonna also plugged the word by uttering, "Fuck me," at the end of the Hip Hop Mix of **"Justify My Love."** Since then, the word has popped up in various Madonna songs, including **"American Life," "I Fucked Up"** and **"Unapologetic Bitch."** It is conjured, but not quite uttered, in **"Erotica"** and **"I Don't Give A."**

In 2005, she was played on (instrumental only!) for another Letterman chat with the **unreleased** song "Cook and Fuck" that she wrote with Michael Bearden.

> "'Frozen' is nothing less than a smash hit."—TOMMY MOTTOLA (1998)

> "Fresh from the vocal demands of *Evita*, La M has found a comfy new ground between the theatrical demands of that project and the more casual vibe of her past pop efforts, showcasing a fluid, flexible range that's executed to haunting effect here."—LARRY FLICK, BILLBOARD (1998)

Madonna has included "Frozen" on her *Drowned World Tour, Re-Invention World Tour* and *Sticky & Sweet Tour* (2009 leg). It was a *Rebel Heart Tour* bonus.

"FROZEN" (VIDEO): *Director: Chris Cunningham, 1998.* In the way that there had never been a Madonna song like "Frozen" until there was, the same could be said of the mystical, hypnotic epic created as its music video by Chris Cunningham. Having **worked** under film **god** Stanley Kubrick and being known for creating music videos for alternative artists, Cunningham's dark tableaux appealed to Madonna, who wanted the video to reflect the fact that the song was inspired by *The English Patient* (1996), but

Fun House promo card

FUN HOUSE, THE/FUNHOUSE, THE: *Formerly 526 W. 26th St., NY, NY.* Popular and gigantic (nearly 30,000 square feet) New Wave and hip-hop **dance** club owned by Joe Monk that lasted from 1979 to 1985. Madonna was a regular, in part because her boyfriend **Jellybean Benitez** was its DJ.

Writer Steven Hager, who was **working** on a major piece about The Fun House, first met Madonna there, even though he'd told a mutual friend he didn't think he needed to make her acquaintance.

"That night, Madonna came up behind me and started talking to me like we were old friends. I was wearing a Levi vest that East Village artist Ellen Berkenblit had customized with one of her iconic punk ponies in white marker on leather. Ellen was a very obscure artist, but one Rene Ricard was currently gushing over. Rene was already famous for 'launching' Julian Schnabel and **Jean-Michel Basquiat**. 'Ellen, right?' she said."

Later in the week, Hager saw Madonna perform.

"I got to see Madonna perform on stage at The Fun House with her backup dancers. She was amazing and captured my full respect immediately. She obviously had a gift for choreography and oozed with youthful **sex** appeal. I knew right then she was going to be a star. I suddenly wished I could turn that unfortunate first encounter around, and wondered if that opportunity would ever present itself."

When Hager's article on The Fun House ran as a *The Village Voice* cover story, the club got raided and Madonna and many others associated with the club turned their backs on him. Hager does point out, however, that the next time he saw Madonna, he was with photographer **André Grossmann**, who Madonna invited to photograph her.

FUNERAL: Madonna has said the song that should play at her funeral is **Frank Sinatra**'s "My Way" (1969).

"FUNNY SONG (OH DEAR DADDY), THE": Crude, C&W novelty number Madonna performed on her *Drowned World Tour.* It was definitely a *song*, though how *funny* it was depended on your sense of humor once you realized she was devoting several minutes worth of the concert to

this tune instead of something she recorded in the '80s. The song is sung in a southern **accent**, and is all about an angry daughter who barbecues her murdered daddy because he "brought out the worst" in her. She wrote this one all by herself, probably inspired by the Dixie Chicks single "Goodbye Earl" (2000).

FUTURA 2000: Graffiti artist (real name: Leonard Mc-Gurr) and multi-**talented** designer whose decorating of the walls of Madonna's East Village digs got her evicted in 1982. He and Madonna were an item for a minute during her, um, busiest days in the '80s. Madonna took **Sandra Bernhard** and Jennifer Grey to one of Futura 2000's **art** openings in 1988.

"FUTURE LOVERS": The fourth track on Madonna's *Confessions on a Dance Floor* album, written and produced by Madonna and **Mirwais**, owed more than a little to Giorgio Moroder's Donna Summer classic "I Feel Love" (1977), hijacking its instantly recognizable bassline. Still, the song had plenty of **originality**, including a humorously **sexy**, borderline nonsensical spoken-word intro that sounds like a corny spaceship announcement married with something a coked-up Studio 54 partygoer might be found mumbling in a corner. The song, like its Summer sister song, climaxes with a climax, although Madonna's is rather beatific and restrained compared to Summer's.

"Future Lovers" made for a dazzling opening on the *Confessions Tour,* on which the "I Feel Love" inspiration was made explicit.

Strap-on attitude

FABIO DIENA

MATTHEW RETTENMUND

GAIETY THEATRE: *Formerly 201 W. 46th St., NY, NY.* Seedy **New York** strip-joint catering to **gay** men in which the **dancers** used to go all-**nude** while desperate patrons pondered where to slip their dollar bills. It was actually more of a place to meet the reasonably-priced hustler of your **dreams** than a good venue for dancing; if you wanted high kicks, you had to go across the street to one of the legit Broadway houses within swallow-or-spitting distance.

Madonna (disguised in a baseball cap and pantsuit) first scouted the place in November 1991, with **Alek Keshishian,** designer Marc Jacobs and **Steven Meisel** in tow.

She was recognized and was treated to an X-rated performance as all 12 strippers took to the stage to try their, er, *hands* at **vogueing.**

Madonna later featured the Gaiety and some of its regular dancers, including hustler **Rocky Santiago** and gay **porn** star **Joey Stefano,** in *Sex.* The silvery strips that served as its stage's curtain are recalled in her **"Erotica"** video as well.

In 1993, the Gaiety's DJ was quoted as saying, "Since Madonna's **book** appeared, more women have been coming by to see the show. I'd like to say we have room for that, but the old-timers don't like it."

The Gaiety was in operation for just under 30 years, closing in 2005, prompting blogger Andy Towle to write, "The Gaiety's demise is certainly a milestone in the history of **sex** in New York." The building has since been torn down.

GALLIANO, JOHN: *b. 1960.* The controversial designer who has variously headed up Givenchy, Dior and his own line told *Tatler* of Madonna in 1987, "I just **love** her. In fact, I was the first person in **London** to get into her ... Even when everybody said she was just a slag, I knew she was a star."

Madonna has long been a **fan** of Galliano's **work,** attending his shows (including in 1995 with **Steven Meisel** at her side) and wearing his **eye**-popping creations in her **"Take a Bow"** video and on the red carpet for the world premiere of *Evita.*

In 2008, Galliano declared, "Madonna is a style icon because she is unafraid to lead. She embodies conflict as well as curiosity, and can shock, seduce and speak through her music and style."

After a drunken, explicitly anti-Semitic rant captured on a cellphone in 2011, Galliano was relieved of his duties at Dior. In that same year, Madonna included Galliano (and Nazi propagandist director Leni Riefenstahl) in her *W.E.* acknowledgments, which left many observers scratching their heads; the subjects of *W.E.* have long been thought to be Nazi sympathizers, an image Madonna's film tries to dispel.

GALLOWAY, JANIS: Madonna's early-'80s roommate, with whom she and Joshua Braun wrote the **unreleased** song "We Live in a House" in 1982. Galloway later married **Warner Bros.** exec. **Michael Rosenblatt.**

"GAMBLER" (SONG): *Release date: October 3, 1985. Billboard Hot 100 peak: NA.* The second of Madonna's two *Vision Quest* soundtrack songs, "Gambler" was a non-single hit in 1985. (It did become a Top 10 hit outside the US.) Written by Madonna and produced by **Jellybean Benitez,** the song was held from being a single because of a glut of Madonna product in the marketplace at the time.

Gambling is to "Gambler" as **fashion** is to **"Dress You Up"** as sweets are to **"Candy Shop"** as auto repair is to **"Body Shop."** But while the lyrics are a fairly straightforward metaphor, one line stands out in her oeuvre as a stinger: "You're just jealous 'cause you can't be me."

Along with performing it in *Vision Quest,* Madonna performed the song on *The Virgin Tour.*

"GAMBLER" (VIDEO): *Director: Harold Becker, 1985.* While "Gambler" was not released as a single in the US, it was hot overseas. A music video was assembled using clips from Madonna's performance of the song in *Vision Quest,* framed by clapboard strikes and including some footage not seen in the film. In this way, the video is very similar to **"Crazy for You"** and **"Into the Groove."** "Gambler" received good play on **MTV,** resulting in the mandatory blurring of logos that were visible behind Madonna while she performed the song in the film's bar scene.

"GANG BANG": This thermonuclear breakup song from Madonna's *MDNA* is one that's **loved** and **hated** in equal measure. It started life as the remarkably different demo "Bang Bang Boom" with Priscilla Renae (Hamilton)'s vocal, but was completely transformed into a dubstep-driven revenge song with credits for Madonna, **Mika, William Orbit,** Hamilton, Keith Harris, Jean-Baptiste, Don Juan "Demo" Casanova and Stephen Kozmeniuk, with production credit to Madonna, William Orbit and the Demolition Crew.

Torn apart by the sounds of squealing tires and gunshots, the song features the most aggressively hostile lyrics Madonna's ever sung, including **death** threats and promises to kill **bitches** in hell.

When the **original** demo **leaked,** Orbit said he was "not happy" and that he knew exactly who'd done it.

Mika has said that the song was written in 10 minutes with Renae as an icebreaker after they'd been arguing, and that the lyrics come from his Arab grandfather who immigrated to **New York.** Gramps sounds like one tough customer.

GAP: Madonna is the world's most famous gap-toothed woman. While **eyebrows, hair** color and the visibility of her **beauty mark** all come and go, the gap—though decidedly less pronounced than it once was—is omnipresent. She reportedly threw a fit when *Glamour* **magazine** airbrushed her teeth together for its December 1990 cover.

RICHARD CORMAN

Madonna on the set of *Vision Quest*, in full "Gambler" mode

GAP, INC.: Madonna endorsed Gap and became a pitch-woman for its jeans and cords in spite of not being seen in a pair of jeans for years leading up to the deal. In the aftermath of the commercial failure of her *American Life* album, Madonna signed up along with **Missy Elliott** to plug Gap. She married her classic hit "**Into the Groove**" with her flopping single "**Hollywood**" to create "**Into the Hollywood Groove**" as a theme for the campaign. In a **TV** spot, Madonna was seen strutting through a studio lot and bumping her "Lady M"-stitched denim-clad booty with Elliott, ending with an out-of-nowhere **yoga** pose and then a splits-off between the women.

The ad's stylist, Joe Zee, said, "Madonna and I talked about ways to personalize blue cords, to give them some flavor; the idea of 'Lady M' came from her."

The filming of the **commercial** was not without drama, as Madonna got tired of waiting for Elliott to finish a call but was brushed off by the rapper, who was not in the mood.

The final ad debuted July 28, 2003, on **VH1** and was deemed a great success, bumping up Gap's bottom line and enriching Madonna by up to $10 million. Her *The English Roses* was even granted placement in Baby Gap locations.

GARBAGE: In 1990, two French photographers swiped bags of garbage from outside Madonna's home, laid her trash out neatly, and sold photos of the junk to **magazines** around the world. The contents of Madonna's trash included shredded documents, hemorrhoid suppositories, a prescription for nasal spray that belonged to then boyfriend **Warren Beatty**, **Reebok** labels, **Weight** Watchers dinner boxes, the remnants of a McDonald's feast, Evian and Diet Coke containers and a copy of the *Hollywood Reporter*.

It certainly could have been worse.

GARRETT, SIEDAH: *b. June 24, 1958.* Most famous as the girl with whom **Michael Jackson** sings "I Just Can't Stop Loving

You" (1987) and the cowriter of his 1988 hit "Man in the Mirror," Garrett sang backup on Madonna's *True Blue* and *Who's That Girl: Original Motion Picture Soundtrack* albums.

In 2004, Garrett was reunited with Madonna, singing backup (and getting a featured solo on **"Like a Prayer"**) on the *Re-Invention World Tour*. Garrett said there had been some drama from **Donna De Lory**, who was "through with" Garrett over a step-out that Garrett was afforded.

GASH: Preferred synonym for "vagina" in *Sex*, as in "honey poured from my 14-year-old gash and I wept."

GAULTIER, JEAN PAUL: *b. April 24, 1952.* Wildly imaginative bad boy of **fashion** and former assistant to Pierre Cardin, on his own from 1976. His **work** has consistently pushed boundaries and worked last **nerves** for 40 years, making him one of the most revered and influential designers in the **business**.

Madonna has long admired Gaultier, praising him in interviews as early as 1984, and posing in one of his tutu-like creations in *Harper's Bazaar* in 1988. Madonna had **Herb Ritts** communicate to Gaultier that she wanted to work with him, and wound up recruiting him and his **sexually-**charged fashions—**cone bras** protruding from pinstriped suits, gold lamé bustiers, etc.—to give her *Blond Ambition Word Tour* its visual bite. When Madonna met with Gaultier to brainstorm the tour, they huddled in a hotel suite in **NYC** and watched *Cabaret* (1970) for inspiration.

"She truly understands herself and always has something to say."
—JEAN-PAUL GAULTIER ON MADONNA (1992)

As the architect of some of Madonna's most famous costumes, Gaultier shared the June 1990 cover of French *Glamour* with her.

Most notoriously, Madonna headlined Gaultier's fashion show on September 24, 1992, in Los Angeles. Though Faye Dunaway strutted in Big Bird–esque thigh-high boots, **Mark Wahlberg** flaunted that third nipple, **Billy Idol** mooned the audience, Raquel Welch went seriously dominatrix, **Anthony Kiedis** left nothing to the imagination in his tight-tights and Dr. Ruth Westheimer jogged around dressed as a sort of black-rubbered sex nurse, it was Madonna who caught the most serious flak. She provided the show's finale, emerging with golden ringlets, garish makeup, a **gold tooth** and—after shucking her jacket—a high skirt that framed her bare breasts between crisscrossing suspenders. It was a transcendent moment in pop history, if reported with distaste at the time. She was fully equipped to nurse the entire crowd of 6,000 ... with *leftovers*. The show doubled as a benefit, raising $750,000

for **AIDS**. (Both Madonna and Gaultier have been extremely active in the cause; Gaultier lost his lover and business partner, Francis Menuge, to AIDS in 1990.)

The critical reaction to Madonna baring her breasts was swift and brutal. The media condemned her for her publicity-mongering as their cameras clicked, and—most disturbingly—insinuated that perhaps such provocative appearances were as much the problem behind AIDS as the solution.

Just for the record, nobody ever got AIDS from exposing or looking at breasts.

At that time, she said, "First and foremost, Gaultier has been a good friend to me. He has the perfect combination of compassion, vulnerability and mischievousness as a person and an artist. He's not afraid to take chances. I adore him."

In 1994, Madonna again walked for Gaultier, looking like a Liberty Head dollar coin (except in gold) and wheeling a puppy down the runway in a baby carriage.

Gaultier did some of the designs for Madonna's well-received *Confessions Tour* as well, demonstrating his versatility in creating equestrian dominatrix, Bedouin andgrogyne, as well as **disco** togs.

In 2012, Madonna sported Gaultier at her **Super Bowl** press conference, and when Madonna revived **"Vogue"** for her *MDNA Tour*, she did so in a revamp of Gaultier's **original** cone-bra look, this time an even pointier bustier that he designed to encase Madonna's breasts in a wasp-waisted shark cage.

GAUWLOOS, SALIM "SLAM": The strapping, darkly handsome Belgian **dancer** featured in the **"Vogue"** video, on Madonna's *Blond Ambition World Tour*, in *Truth or Dare* and as the most prominent boob-squeezer in the **MTV Video Music Awards** performance of "Vogue."

Gauwloos French-kissed fellow dancer **Gabriel Trupin** in *Truth or Dare* at Madonna's insistence, that Trupin later claimed, in a lawsuit, had outed him to his grandparents when it appeared in the film.

Though Gauwloos didn't sue Madonna as some of her other dancers did, he held a small grudge because she didn't remain close with him after *Blond Ambition* was over, making that clear on **Robin Leach**'s *Madonna Exposed*, a show on which he also debuted his song "Bring It."

"She's a very sensitive, sweet person and she's actually also very insecure, especially with other women around, because, I mean, we would have parties and there would never be beautiful women around," Slam said of Madonna in 1993.

Slam went on to **work** with many other pop stars and to become a noted ballet choreographer. He doesn't think too highly of today's chorus boys: "We were all classically trained. We were doing double tours, grand jetés and more. In America today, it's all about experience in hip-hop, especially when working with artists. There is nothing artistic about the dancing. It's all about shaking your butt, and I didn't feel it anymore."

MARIPOL

In 2015, he joined fellow Blond Ambition-era dancer Jose Gutierez (of **Jose & Luis**) to film a lively tribute to the 25th anniversary of "Vogue." He also appears in the film *Strike a Pose*.

> "I don't think I've ever seen anybody work that hard." -SLAM ON MADONNA (2008)

GAY: Madonna has a huge gay following. Like Judy Garland, **Marilyn Monroe**, **Barbra Streisand**, **Cher** and **Bette Midler** before her, Madonna has succeeded in capturing the hearts, minds and paychecks of gay men across the world.

Why do gay guys like Madonna so much? It's tempting to say, "Because she's *faaaaaaabulous*!" But there's more to it than that.

Like other gay icons, Madonna is campy, and **camp** is an important concept for gay men, a shared language of humorous disdain for the status quo and for one's lot in life. Also, she speaks directly to gay people as an audience. She's done so in her music (**"In This Life," "Veni Vidi Vici"**), in print (her 1991 interview with *The Advocate*, her 2005 *Attitude* interview) and on video (**"Justify My Love," "Erotica"** and **"American Pie,"** to name a few). Madonna has kissed women both in public and on film, encouraging speculation that she may be **bisexual** as a show of solidarity.

Perhaps most important to her gay **fans**, Madonna has always, in her very public private life, surrounded herself with openly gay men.

In short, Madonna is the first gay icon who made the conscious decision to be one, and who didn't do anything inorganic to her nature on the way to achieving that status.

In her **work**, Madonna's first reference to same-**sexuality** was the **"Open Your Heart"** video. The setting is a strip club, and in one of the booths watching Madonna are two beautiful sailors, their cheeks pressed together in bliss. Another booth features a lone butch woman, who had also been enjoying the girlie show. The video was extremely controversial, though its homosexual bits were less frequently cited than her sexualized character's friendship with an innocently smitten young boy.

There is an almost lesbian vibe in the gaze between Madonna and the black preacher/singer in her **"Like a Prayer"** video, which was one more reason to pay close attention to the **Sandra Bernhard**–fueled rumors of Madonna's bisexuality that were in full force at the time the video was released.

Her next use of homosexuality was far more explicit, depicting highly charged romantic embraces among men and among women—including her own passionate lesbian kiss—in the video for "Justify My Love." With *Sex* and its companion video, "Erotica," homosexuality could no longer be argued to be mere *chic* to Madonna; it became a full-fledged, fully integrated part of her work in the form of both political and prurient images (involving Madonna

directly) and in Madonna's erotic short stories, which were saturated with homosexual desire.

But as early as 1995, Madonna's bond with gay men was questioned by some in the LGBT community, spurred on by the perception that Madonna was merely using gay people for controversy and sales, as well as by short **memories** of all that she'd done for the community in the past. Outrageously, *The Advocate*, then under the direction of EIC Jeff Yarbrough, named Madonna its "Sissy of the Year," over inarguably awful baddies like Newt Gingrich and Charlton Heston, because she'd had the nerve to declare, "I'm not a lesbian." Writer Fred Goss reacted, "We hope this news won't come as too much of a surprise to **Ingrid Casares**, the Formerly Big M's gal pal–plus, who of course must not be a lesbian either. Wow. Sure had us fooled. So ... they're both fags, is that it?" The incendiary piece also trashed Ann Landers for using the term "sissies" as a pejorative, even though the **magazine** was doing the same thing.

Madonna's not a lesbian, though she has said that she has had sex with women. Biographer **Barbara Victor** begs to differ; she interviewed a woman she called "Kathy" for her 2001 **book** on Madonna. Kathy claimed to have been one of Madonna's best friends and also her lover from the ages of 15 to 21, describing their relationship as "a complete and total

M*n*M are "re-create-ional" clothing designers from Kenosha, Wisconsin. Matt's love for "M" can be traced back to the beginning of time (i.e., 1983). Mike wasn't shown the Ray of Light till 2005, but has been a devoted worshiper since. Matt and Mike's friendship began around the release of *Confessions on a Dance Floor*, and has seen them "Causing a Commotion" at multiple tour stops and other "M"-related events along the way, including the pictured "Golden Triangle" appearance during *The MDNA Tour*. It's not uncommon for the boyz to hold album-release parties in their M-inspired private club. Their Madonna fandom hit a new peak in 2014 when they met the "Queen of all Media" himself, Perez Hilton, at Hilton's Madonna-themed 36th birthday bash.

MEGA-FAN SPOTLIGHT:
MATT GALLEY & MIKE GIELAS (A.K.A. M*N*M)

"I might be responsible for as many gay marriages as I am for heterosexual divorces ..."–MADONNA (2015)

love affair." The anonymous woman said she visited Madonna in **New York** and that Madonna had sent her *The Hite Report* (1976) in 1987 as light reading about the fluidity of sexuality. When Kathy confessed her affair to her husband, he sought a **divorce**. Kathy's identity has not been revealed.

As the battle for gay rights heated up, Madonna was thought by some to have become less vocal about the struggle and was called out for it. In particular, many younger gay people, unaware of or unimpressed by her résu-gé, seem to resent Madonna's status as a gay sacred cow.

"... [T]he gays have kinda turned their back on her," Michelle Visage said on a 2015 episode of the Web series *Hey Qween!* "These young gays don't know what she did for the community and what she continues to do ... she still is there for the gays and the gay community. She did so much for HIV/**AIDS**. She has done *so, so* much for the gays. So much! And they forget. The young ones don't care. They don't see her—Helen Keller."

In 2015, *Refinery29* asked her what her younger fans should know about the past, and Madonna did not hesitate to tell the truth to people who in some cases were completely ignorant not only of her history, but of their own:

"It is important for them to realize that things that they take for granted weren't always as they are now. When I was coming up, the gay community was exceptionally marginalized ... There was a lot of discrimination and a lot of prejudice and a lot of craziness ... There was no way to keep people who were HIV positive alive, so I was growing up in a time where people I loved and artists that I admired were dying all around me. I think people take it for granted now that if you have HIV, you can live a **healthy** life. Or, if you're

. . . .

"IT'S TRUE I AM FASCINATED BY GAY CULTURE. THERE'S A VISCERAL THING THAT HAPPENS WHEN I GO TO GAY CLUBS. THE PLACE IS FILLED WITH MOVING, SWEATING BODIES THAT BECOME LIKE ONE ANIMAL. THERE'S SOMETHING VERY POWERFUL ABOUT THAT TO ME. I FEEL THEY'RE VERY MISUNDERSTOOD, AND SO AM I. I FEEL THEIR PERSECUTION, BUT ALSO THEIR SENSE OF HUMOR, AND THEIR WILLINGNESS TO DEAL WITH SEXUALITY IN AN UNCONVENTIONAL WAY IS REALLY INTERESTING TO ME. THEY ACCEPT THE MASCULINE SIDE OF MYSELF AS WELL AS THE FEMININE."–MADONNA (1991)

. . . .

"I WANT TO USE MY CELEBRITY AS A PLATFORM SO THAT A LOT OF THE PEOPLE WHO ARE PERSECUTED FOR THEIR LIFESTYLES WILL NOT BE SO IN THE FUTURE."–MADONNA (1991)

. . . .

"DON'T THEY KNOW I'M A GAY MAN TRAPPED IN A WOMAN'S BODY?"–MADONNA (1994)

. . . .

OPPOSITE: Madonna with gay bestie Martin Burgoyne at a *Vogue* shoot

gay, you can live an openly gay life. These things were not the norm when I was starting my career."

There is also the phenomenon of gay people resenting alleged social pressure to like Madonna, reacting by disliking her; this has more to do with a need to be seen as outside the norm and/or an ironically homophobic discomfort with anything "too gay" than it does with anything Madonna's said or done or sung.

One reason why Madonna may have become less vocal about gay issues after the '90s (she isn't big on labels, telling **Vanity Fair** in 2000, "I don't think you should be defined by your sexual preference") is that she felt it should be taken for granted where her heart was after decades of public statements on the subject. In a 2008 *Q* magazine piece, Pete Wentz asked Madonna how it felt to be the world's biggest non-gay gay icon, to which Madonna replied, "It feels great. If it's true. Why do I think that might be? Because since the very beginning of my career I've always promoted freedom of expression and embracing the idea of being different. Independence of thought; fighting any kind of oppression. And also: I'm a diva. I think 'queer nation' and 'diva' just go together."

Madonna did re-engage on the issue, speaking out against anti-gay bullying in 2010 in a chat with **Ellen DeGeneres**. Madonna said simply, "The gay community has been incredibly supportive of me. I wouldn't have a career if it weren't for the gay community ..." She's also spoken out on behalf of gay marriage ("Gay marriage would be legal everywhere and accepted," she said to *Us* when asked what she'd do as president) and placed herself in legal jeopardy by supporting gay rights while on tour in **Russia**, which has slid backward on gay

. . . .

"MADONNA IS THE RIGHT CHOICE FOR THIS MOVIE BECAUSE SHE, LIKE EVITA, IS ONE OF THE COMMON PEOPLE. MADONNA REPRESENTS ALL PEOPLE, NO MATTER WHAT THEIR FAMILY BACKGROUND, RACE OR SEXUAL PROCLIVITY."
–JORGE GUTIÉRREZ, AN ARGENTINEAN DESCRIBED BY *THE NEW YORK TIMES* AS "A TRANSVESTITE IN A GARISH LACE OUTFIT LIKE ONE THAT WAS ONCE THE SINGER'S TRADEMARK." (1996)

. . . .

"... THE ONLY THING I REALLY KNEW ABOUT HER WAS THAT SHE WAS THE ONE PERSON WHO COULD PROBABLY MAKE BOTH STRAIGHT WOMEN AND GAY MEN CHANGE THEIR MINDS ABOUT THEIR SEXUAL ORIENTATIONS."–BENJAMIN BRATT ON MADONNA (2000)

. . . .

"MY SHOW WAS BEING DAMNED BY THE [PUTIN] REGIME FOR BEING A 'GAY SHOW' AND FOR 'PROMOTING HOMOSEXUALITY.' ALL THE PEOPLE WORKING ON MY SHOW WERE TOLD THAT WE MAY BE ARRESTED."
–MADONNA ON HER *MDNA TOUR* (2014)

. . . .

rights at a breathtaking pace. Actions such as these should supersede phony controversies such as the one over Madonna referring to kale as "gay," as if she meant it negatively.

In 2013, Madonna appeared at the **GLAAD** Media **Awards** to bestow an honor upon her buddy **Anderson Cooper**, taking the opportunity to dress up as a **Boy Scout** as a protest against that organization's exclusion of gay individuals.

By 2015, the nine-lived UK gay mag *Attitude* was publishing the article, "*Attitude* Readers Answer the Question, 'What Does Madonna Mean to Gay Men?' ... and the response was the biggest they ever had. She seems to mean more than one thing to gay people, and to mean each one of those things a *lot*.

When thanked by a gay male *Pitchfork* writer for being "so supportive of my people," Madonna replied, "Your people? *My* people." And as a final word on the subject, in a 2013 Reddit .com Q&A, Madonna was asked if she'd be a top or a bottom if she were a gay man, to which she said: "I *am* a gay man."

G-A-Y (CLUB): *Formerly 157 Charing Cross Rd., London, England, UK. Now at Heaven, The Arches, Villiers St., London, England, UK.* Madonna performed at this long-running **gay** club on November 19, 2005, sporting a hot-pink leotard and matching glittery jacket. She dazzled the crowd with **"Hung Up," "Get Together," "I Love New York," "Let It Will Be," "Everybody"** and a piece of **"Jump."** Many **fans** had to sleep out overnight for entry.

GEFFEN, DAVID: *b. February 21, 1943.* Unbelievably successful out **gay** businessman who made his billions as the cofounder of Asylum Records, the founder of both Geffen and DGC Records, via his role as a successful actor's agent and as one of the triumvirate (along with Steven Spielberg and Jeffrey Katzenberg) behind DreamWorks SKG. A renaissance man, he **loves** some of the same things Madonna does: **art**, philanthropy and boys.

Madonna with beret and A-gay

According to Madonna's brother **Christopher Ciccone**, the mogul once proposed marriage to Madonna.

Madonna and Geffen have socialized countless times, including when Madonna attended Geffen's star-studded **birthday** party in 1991 on the arm of **Michael Jackson** and on November 7, 1991, when they went to her brother's art exhibition at Wessel + O'Connor Fine Art (580 Broadway, NY, NY) with **Alek Keshishian**.

Geffen wrote in *Interview* in 1992, "Madonna is the embodiment of the modern woman of legend. Instead of being stultified as an object, Madonna is a trailblazer who has confronted prejudice, smitten the obstacles of convention and distorted boundaries into challenges with the **power** of her will and inspiration. She is a **beauty** in **control** of her body, her image, her life and her art."

GERARDO: *b. April 16, 1965.* Ecuadorean two-hit wonder who—despite his boast that Madonna left an obscene message on his answering machine—had his 15 minutes in 1991 when Madonna summed him up with a caustic, "I'm not into **hair** extensions." He attended her 36th **birthday** party in **Miami** with his newly short haircut.

GERVAIS, RICKY: *b. June 25, 1961.* Once part of the teen-appeal New Wave duo Seona Dancing, Gervais became one of the world's most famous comic actors thanks to the phenomenon of the **original** British version of *The Office* (2001–2003) on **TV**. As a cocreator, continuing writer and director of the series, Gervais became an A-lister, and his success has translated to appearances in movies like the *Night at the Museum* series (2006–2014).

In 2005, Gervais reported that Madonna declared herself to be his biggest **fan**, to which he replied, "Who are you?" She laughed and claimed to be **Paris** Hilton. There was talk for a while that she would make an appearance on his series *Extras* (2005–2007), but nothing came to pass.

On the 2012 **Golden Globes** telecast, Gervais introduced Madonna by saying, "Our next presenter is the **Queen of Pop**. Not you, **Elton [John]**. Sit down. She's all woman. I'll give you some clues. She's always **'Vogue'**, she's a **'Material Girl'** and she's just **'Like a Virgin'**. [Coughs sarcastically] Please welcome Madonna."

Madonna emerged and said, "If I'm still just like a virgin, Ricky, then why don't you come over here and do something about it?" When the applause died down, she continued, "I haven't kissed a girl in a few years—on TV."

"GET OVER": Upbeat pop tune written by Madonna and **Stephen Bray** and demoed for inclusion on *The Immaculate Collection*, but that was shelved. It was later produced by Madonna and **Shep Pettibone** as the second single from male solo artist **Nick Scotti**. Scotti's first version is also found on the soundtrack of the **Demi Moore** flop *Nothing But Trouble* (1991). Madonna's **original** version has never **leaked** and remains **unreleased**, but her backing vocals appear on Scotti's track.

"GET TOGETHER" (SONG): *Release date: June 6, 2006. Billboard Hot 100 peak: NA.* As good a candidate as any for the title of "quintessential Madonna **dance** song" (earning a **Grammy** nomination for Best Dance Recording), this marriage of electronica and **disco** features a relaxed Madonna vocal, and lyrics that embrace the simplicity of connecting to—and via—music.

Madonna cowrote the deceptively sparse song with Anders Bagge, Peer Åström and **Stuart Price**, and produced it with Price. It became the third single from *Confessions on a Dance Floor* and wound up being performed in many venues, including on Michael Parkinson's show *Parkinson* in the UK, *Star Academy* in France, the *BBC Children In Need* 2005 telethon, at **G-A-Y**, at **KOKO** and at **Studio Coast** in Japan.

LAVINEL SAVU

On tour, "Get Together" was the second song performed on the ***Confessions Tour***. The single cover is a snapshot of Madonna with her *Confessions Tour* crew, including Price.

"GET TOGETHER" (VIDEO): *Director: Eugene Riecansky, 2006.* A clever workaround for creating a music video when your star isn't available, the clip for "Get Together" made use of Madonna's live performance of several songs at **KOKO** the year before, with all of the video stylized and animated by artist Nathaniel Howe for Logan Studios. Though the video is mainly just a visual feast, it does have a basic progression, starting with Madonna singing in primordial ooze and continuing until she's standing on a skyscraper.

The finished product is an achievement, and yet the video never really escapes the feeling that Madonna had better things to do than make a video ... tour rehearsals, for example.

"GHOSTTOWN" (SONG): *Release date: March 13, 2015. Billboard Hot 100 peak: NA.* This ***Rebel Heart*** track—written by Jason Evigan (who sings background vocals), Madonna, E. Kidd Bogart and **Sean Douglas**, and produced by Madonna, Billboard and Evigan—is easily one of the most popular on the entire album. It was one of the first six released to iTunes, became the album's second single and features a piercing vocal from Madonna.

Interestingly, all three of Madonna's cowriters on the song have famous fathers: Evigan's dad is the son of *B.J. and the Bear* (1978–1981) and *My Two Dads* (1987–1990) actor Greg Evigan, Douglas became Topic A thanks to his movie-actor dad Michael Keaton's heartfelt **Golden Globes** acceptance speech in 2014 and Bogart is the son of Casablanca Records founder Neil Bogart.

Madonna first performed "Ghosttown" live at a taping of *The Jonathan Ross Show*. It aired on ITV1 in the UK on March 14, 2015. Before that aired, she did a live broadcast of the song for *Le Grand Journal* in France and also performed it on *Che tempo che fa* in Italy. As part of "Madonna Week," she did her first US performance of the song on *The **Ellen DeGeneres** Show*, which aired March 19, 2015. Her final live performance of the song prior to her ***Rebel Heart Tour*** was an attention-grabbing pairing with **Taylor Swift** at the **iHeartRadio Music Awards** on March 29, 2015.

In spite of all the promo, the single became her fourth in a row to miss the ***Billboard*** Hot 100 in the US.

The song was sung as a bonus on her ***Rebel Heart Tour***.

"GHOSTTOWN" (VIDEO): *Director: Jonas Åkerlund, 2015.* On April 8, 2015, Madonna debuted her second ***Rebel Heart*** video, a romantalyptic vision in which Madonna—a veritable "Mad Maxine"—navigates a nuked world with fellow survivor Terrence Howard. The **Jonas Åkerlund**-directed video was supposed to premiere the day before on the app Meerkat, but all that premiered was an error page.

GHV2

① "Deeper and Deeper" 7" Edit (Madonna/Shep Pettibone/Tony Shimkin) –4:54, produced by Madonna/Shep Pettibone

② "Erotica" Radio Edit (Madonna/Shep Pettibone) –4:33, produced by Madonna/Shep Pettibone

③ "Human Nature" Radio Version (Madonna/ Dave "Jam" Hall/Shawn McKenzie/Kevin McKenzie/ Michael Deering)–4:31, produced by Madonna/ Dave "Jam" Hall

④ "Secret" Edit (Madonna/Dallas Austin) –4:30, produced by Madonna/Dallas Austin

⑤ "Don't Cry for Me Argentina" Radio Edit (Tim Rice/Andrew Lloyd Webber)–4:50, produced by Nigel Wright/Alan Parker/Andrew Lloyd Webber/David Caddick

⑥ "Bedtime Story" Edit (Nellee Hooper/Björk/ Marius DeVries)–4:07, produced by Nellee Hooper/Madonna

⑦ "The Power of Good-Bye" (Madonna/Rick Nowels) –4:11, produced by Madonna/William Orbit/ Patrick Leonard

⑧ "Beautiful Stranger" William Orbit Radio Edit (Madonna/William Orbit) –3:57, produced by Madonna/Willlliam Orbit

⑨ "Frozen" Edit (Madonna/Patrick Leonard) –5:09, produced by Madonna/William Orbit/ Patrick Leonard

⑩ "Take a Bow" Edit (Babyface/Madonna)–4:31, produced by Babyface/ Madonna

⑪ "Ray of Light" Radio Edit (Madonna/William Orbit/Clive Muldoon/ Dave Curtis/Christine Leach)–4:35, produced by Madonna/William Orbit

⑫ "Don't Tell Me" (Madonna/Mirwais/Joe Henry)–4:40, produced by Madonna/Mirwais

⑬ "What It Feels Like for a Girl" (Madonna/Guy Sigsworth) –4:44, produced by Madonna/Guy Sigsworth/ Mark "Spike" Stent

⑭ "Drowned World/ Substitute for Love" (Madonna/William Orbit/ Rod McKuen/Anita Kerr/ David Collins)–5:09, produced by Madonna/ William Orbit

⑮ "Music" (Madonna/Mirwais)–3:45, produced by Madonna/ Mirwais

Still, one forgot the botched roll-out upon first viewing—it was Madonna's finest video since **"Hung Up,"** featuring some of her best **acting**, a hot tango, her third hug of a **TV** in a video (after **"Take a Bow"** and **"Hollywood"**) and glimpses of personal photos of Madonna's mom and of **Lola** on the set of Mom's 2002 **Steven Klein** photo shoot for *W*. The video is a surprisingly moving meditation on ephemerality and the human condition when all bets are suddenly off. Madonna's character finds room in her heart to start over ... and room in her heart to give capes another try.

GHV2: *Release date: November 12, 2001. Billboard 200 peak: #7.* Standing for *Greatest Hits Volume 2*, Madonna's follow-up to ***The Immaculate Collection*** was not without its holy revelations, but it would be hard to compare the albums as equally sacred texts. This time, the songs were chosen from the years 1992 to 2001, an interesting pair of brackets considering the creative space she was in during those polar-opposite eras.

GHV2 was a Top 10 hit but did not offer as many smashes as *The Immaculate Collection*. For a slapdash collection released a month after **9/11**, it still did well, selling over 7 million copies worldwide to date.

Among promo collectibles, the remix album *GHV2 Remixed: The Best of 1991–2001* that was used to plug this is a highly desirable item for any music-lover's collection. Also fun is a promo-only single, "*GHV2* Megamix," which squeezes all of the hits into one sweaty workout.

GIFTS: Madonna said in 1990 that the best present she ever received was a handful of "sweaty diamonds and emeralds." She is known to lavish her close associates with gifts, taking the entire ***Blond Ambition World Tour*** troupe on shopping sprees across Europe. While doing ***Speed-the-Plow***, she gave floral arrangements to everyone involved in the show, and in 1992 gave director **Mary Lambert** a teeny-tiny black leather **motorcycle** jacket with a **crucifix** on the back as a baby gift.

GILROY, DAN: *b. June 24, 1959.* Dan Gilroy and his brother Ed (they'd once performed in an act called the Bil and Gil Show), formed the core of the **Breakfast Club**, the first band Madonna ever joined, initially on **drums**, later as a lead singer. A huge **Beatles** fan, Dan Gilroy coached Madonna on songwriting and also helped her keep warm for a year; he became her lover after meeting her at a May 1, 1979, party at the apartment of her ex, **Norris Burroughs**.

Madonna's first date with Gilroy was to the Cloisters (99 Margaret Corbin Dr., NY, NY), which features medieval **art**. Soon, she moved in with the Gilroys, who were living in a former yeshiva on 53rd Ave. in Queens.

"She'd have her hands in her jacket and looked like she just wanted to jump you. I used to be afraid of her," said neighbor Angie Giacomino, who **worked** at the Salumeria Italian Deli. She also said it seemed like Madonna was dating the whole neighborhood behind her boyfriend's back.

Monogamous or not, Madonna's relationship with Gilroy was instrumental in the genesis of her career. She said a few years later, "I got my boyfriend who was in a band to teach me how to play **guitar**, and then I started writing songs, and then the next thing you know it, I was wanting to be a singer."

Madonna experienced many firsts during her time with Gilroy: She wrote her first songs (still **unreleased**), sang her first duet (on his tune "Cold Wind") and gave her first street performance, dressed all in white in front of the Gulf and Western Building (formerly 15 Columbus Circle, NY, NY, now Trump International Hotel & Tower, 1 Central Park West, NY, NY). She also performed—off-camera—on *Unique New York*, a cable-access show, her first **TV** gig; this recording, in which Madonna plays a leek for percussion and uses an old toaster as a tambourine, has never surfaced.

—LARRY FLICK

"UNLIKE ITS PREDECESSOR … THIS COLLECTION ISN'T A NEARLY FLAWLESS COLLECTION OF JOYFUL, EXUBERANT POP MUSIC AT ITS FINEST. LEST WE FORGET, THERE WERE TIMES IN THE '90S WHEN IT SEEMED THAT MADONNA WAS LOSING IT—WHETHER THE 'IT' IN QUESTION WAS THE ABILITY TO PREDICT/CREATE THE NEXT TREND, HER CREATIVE DIRECTION, OR HER MIND."
—CHARLOTTE ROBINSON, *POP MATTERS* (2001)

"FOR THOSE WHO'VE ONLY RECENTLY DISCOVERED MADGE (ALL THOSE BILLBOARDS AND COLUMN INCHES JUST WEREN'T OBVIOUS ENOUGH BEFORE, PERHAPS), WHO'VE BOUGHT INTO HER *MUSIC* AND *RAY OF LIGHT* PHASE, THE LATTER HALF OF THIS ALBUM WILL BE NOVEL BUT NOWHERE NEAR AS IMMEDIATE AS WHAT THEY'RE USED TO."—MICHAEL HUBBARD, *MUSIC OMH* (2001)

"NOW, LIKE THE POPE, WE KNOW MADONNA IS FALLIBLE. YET SHE SEEMS AS IMMOVABLE A PART OF THE POP LANDSCAPE AS SHE DID IN 1990. IT'S A SHAME, THEN, THAT THIS ALBUM LACKS ANY NEW TRACKS TO SUGGEST WHERE SHE MIGHT GO NEXT …"—ALEX NEEDHAM, *NME* (2005)

They had a very domestic existence. Gilroy described her as "bratty" to the press in 1985, but qualified the statement: "Well, actually, she swings back and forth between being the bratty kid sister and being sweet and wonderful. She isn't dull, that's for sure … When we were together, she was in the housewife mode and would meet me at the door and give me a big kiss and then she'd have dinner ready … Leeks, steamed leeks. And she **loved popcorn**."

Madonna and Gilroy lost touch after she bolted to form **Emmy**, then went on to solo glory.

"I love people who are passionate about their stuff. She was excited and intense about working and preparing for whatever—yoga, running, music, dance. She would get on her drums and practice like crazy."
—DAN GILROY (2001)

GINSBERG, ALLEN: *June 3, 1926–April 5, 1997.* Legendary Beat poet most famous for his poem "Howl" (1956). When the first *Encyclopedia Madonnica* was being written, queries went out to countless personalities seeking one-word descriptions of Madonna. Most never replied, a few wrote back to beg off (Diane von Furstenberg, Helen Gurley Brown) and only **Michael Musto** replied correctly (he said "wily" back then). Ginsberg replied with a handwritten note, stating: "I had an intelligent conversation

ALEJANDRO MOGOLLO

with Madonna & **Warren Beatty** New Years (sic) Eve 1990 at Francesco Clemente's house, re: Eastern European economics & Western exploitation of that labor force. Earlier (a few years) introduced her to **William S. Burroughs** beside whom she sat & chatted for an evening after vernissage of his paintings at Tony Schafrazzi (sic) Gallery. —Allen Ginsberg, 5/23/94."

Ginsberg shot **black-and-white** images of Madonna and Beatty, which are housed, along with Ginsberg's photo archive, at the Thomas Fisher Rare **Book** Library (120 St. George St., Toronto, Ontario, Canada).

GIORGIADES, NICK: As a waiter at Uncle George's Greek Tavern (formerly 3319 Broadway, Astoria, NY), he claimed to the *New York Daily News* that at the end of 1994 (when Giorgiades was 21 or 22), a sexy **blonde** told him he looked like Adonis and asked him home with her. When he asked who she was, she said, "Don't you know who the **fuck** I am?" A male companion broke the news that she was Madonna. According to Giorgiades, they went out to eat on their first date and he "didn't waste the opportunity" on their second. He says they dated for three months, during which time Madonna called his workplace so much he had to quit, and their socializing at parties required him to pretend to be a friend of her brother's. He seemed happy to be rid of her but allowed, "When you're alone with her, she's very tender ... She can be a very loving person." And apparently a generous tipper—serve her well and sleep with her for 90 days.

"GIRL GONE WILD" (SONG): *Release date: March 2, 2012. Billboard Hot 100 peak: NA.* Second single from *MDNA*, written by Madonna, Jenson Vaughan, **Benny Benassi** and Alle Benassi, and produced by Madonna and the Benassis. It's a breakneck **dance** record that Madonna adapted from a demo featuring singer Rosette. The final song is remarkably similar to the demo, calling into question how much Madonna really invested in the track creatively.

Upon its release, "Girl Gone Wild" was greeted with a yawn. Although it's a fun club song in the mold of **"Celebration,"** many listeners seemed to be holding Madonna to a higher standard, expecting something more from her.

Madonna noted that when collaborating with the Benassis, she relied on Alle to communicate with Benny, who doesn't speak much English.

What's a Madonna song without a controversy, right? The track's title, a play on the lewd *Girls Gone Wild* series of DVDs by Joe Francis, attracted a lawsuit threat that never went anywhere, though she did change the **original** title of the song from "Girls Gone Wild" shortly before its release.

"Girl Gone Wild" provided a kick-ass kick-off number for *The MDNA Tour.*

"GIRL GONE WILD" (VIDEO): *Directors: Mert and Marcus, 2012.* **Fashion** photographers **Mert and Marcus**, who were in the process of becoming Madonna's new go-to shooters, were hired to create a **sexy**, edgy, **dance**-drenched music video for **"Girl Gone Wild."** They more than delivered, crafting a chic video that opens with Madonna—sporting a white-**blonde** mane—chanting the spoken-word intro to the song, and closes with a startling image of Madonna's eyeliner running down her face.

In-between, Madonna smokes and is **smokin'**, dancing her ass off alongside famous male models Brad Alphonso, Rob Evans, Jon Kortajarena, Sean O'Pry and Simon Nessman, as well as with genderfuck troupe Kazaky, instantly identifiable as the only lithe, muscled men in stilettos in any room.

The video manages to stuff almost all of Madonna's touchstone themes into a few short minutes: homosexuality (Kortajarena and Alphonse sensually share an apple), religion, dance, fashion, fun, **guns**, **nudity**, bondage ... even **vogueing**. The dancing sequnces are electrifying, especially camerawork that follows Madonna around a boxy room, in which she seems to defy gravity, reminiscent of Fred Astaire's *Royal Wedding* (1951) ceiling dance. The human pyramid she and her **orgy** of flesh create by video's end would not look out of place in a museum.

The song may be a guilty pleasure, somewhat phoned in, but the video is scandalously undervalued.

"Anyway, shitting's really big right now. Don't ask me why. Could be the stock market, I don't know."
—MADONNA AS "BOSS #3" IN *GIRL 6* (1996)

GIRL 6: *Director: Spike Lee. Release date: March 22, 1996.* Madonna has about three minutes of screen time in this poorly received erotic comedy from **Spike Lee** shot in April 1995. The film stars Theresa Randle, with appearances by Madonna associates **Debi Mazar** (longtime friend), **Naomi Campbell** (*Sex* participant) and **Peter Berg** (**sex** participant). In a fun, relaxed performance, she plays the skanky CEO of a phone-sex company, giving Randle's character an obscene **job** interview, later appearing in a direct-to-camera sequence in which she gives comical instructions (as **Prince**'s 1987 tune "Hot Thing" plays) on how to succeed in the **business** of getting guys off on the phone without really trying.

GIRLIE SHOW: LIVE DOWN UNDER, THE: HBO televised Madonna's *The Girlie Show World Tour* from Sydney, Australia, which **Maverick** packaged for home video under this title. Madonna made the entire experience on the road into her second **book**, *Madonna: The Girlie Show*, published by Callaway Editions in 1994.

GIRLIE SHOW WORLD TOUR, THE: *Show dates: September 25, 1993–December 19, 1993.* Madonna bashing was at an all-time peak in the last quarter of 1993. Rather than hide from the press, Madonna forged ahead with a limited world tour. How limited? Well, she skipped LA.

The Girlie Show World Tour, with direction and production design by **Christopher Ciccone**, musical direction by Jai Winding, stage direction by **Jeffrey Hornaday**, choreography by Alex Magno, Keith Young and Michelle Johnson, and costumes by **Dolce & Gabbana** and Rob Saduski, bravely **reinvented** Madonna as a one-woman song-and-**dance** *South Pacific* (1958) in a "Steve McQueen" haircut. It was a regular Barnum & Bailey three-(cock)ring circus. As sweet as ice cream and nearly as satisfying, *The Girlie Show World Tour* was Madonna's most entertaining concert, 90 minutes of sheer smile and bump and grind.

Not nearly as thematically complex as its predecessor, the ***Blond Ambition World Tour***, Madonna's fourth tour didn't need to be. What it lacked in depth it more than made up for with spectacle and eye **candy**.

She must've done something right: It sold out.

This tour was a spectacle about spectacle. It incorporated nearly every imaginable element of voyeurism: stardom, the circus, public **nudity**, **boxing**, strip shows, masks, the Golden Era of Hollywood, a **gay** disco (where everyone has an **eye** on everyone else) and its own grandiose setting, usually in an auditorium capable of servicing 50,000-plus watchers. It celebrated the pleasure in seeing, and in looking.

There were four sections to the show: an opening set of torrid performances known as *Dominatrix* that became progressively more amusing, ending with a happy ballad; *Studio 54*, a '70s **disco** set that began as a mindless party and ended with a moving representation of **AIDS**; an all-out Hollywood tribute set called *Weimar Cabaret* and an *Encore* that distilled the show's entire sensibility into two minimalist songs.

This concept concert started even before its star appeared onstage, Smokey Robinson's "Tears of a Clown" (1970) segueing into a circus aria as barkers offered the audience, "Peanuts, **popcorn**, cot-ton can-dy!" Never one to mince words, Madonna began her show with a topless dancer (future *Dancing with the Stars* judge **Carrie Ann Inaba**) performing a gravity-defying shimmy down a go-go pole. Once she had our attention, Madonna emerged from the floor as an SM "Robin" (Holy tit clamps, Batman!), sleek in a black-sequined bra and hotpants and that persona-obscuring/persona-projecting mask, standing heavily in enormous platform boots.

"My name is **Dita**," she began, reestablishing herself as Dita Parlo, the dominatrix who beat the world into submission in 1992 before the world burned the bed on her. Dita was back on top, crooning **"Erotica"** too aggressively for safe words to **work**. Behind her, in ingenious lightboxes far above the main stage, dancers enacted scenes of stylized violence and **sexuality**. A mute clown in royal blue made the first of its many appearances at this inopportune moment, like a child inadvertently stumbling upon the primal scene. There was no question that our sweet little clown liked to watch, a neat spin on the usual state of the world, since clowns themselves are usually the watchees.

Madonna transitioned smoothly into **"Fever,"** complete with copious molestation of her two primary male dancers. She presented a *The King and I* (1956) version of **"Vogue"** next, gaily flapping her hands above her head to approximate the fluttering synthesizer groove, wearing a black, beaded Dolce & Gabbana headdress. The first set was washed away by **"Rain."** When she appropriated a few lines from the oldie "Just My Imagination" (1971), the Motown girl was truly back home.

A breezy exposition of umbrella-bearing dancers escorted the audience to the next section.

The velocity increased in the second set, with Madonna—in disco-era **fashion** and a **blonde** 'fro—descending on a huge glitterball, inviting crowds to join her through **"Express Yourself"** and **"Deeper and Deeper"** in what resembled a gay club of the period. As she began a sincere plea for world tolerance in **"Why's It So Hard,"** she pitched unity by engaging in a sizzling mock **orgy**. AIDS smashed the party. Madonna delivered a stirring speech about the disease, begging for awareness. Her performance of **"In This Life,"** a song that on *Erotica* can sound trite, was a show-stopper.

The transition song was the controversial **"Beast Within"** mix of **"Justify My Love,"** brought to life (**death**?) by male dancers **acting** out a version of gay sex for dummies.

The third segment of the show was all fun and games. Madonna emerged transformed into **Marlene Dietrich**, crooning **"Like a Virgin"** in Dietrich's highly imitable **accent** in top hat and tails. She played a game of visual tag with the impish clown, who hid in a traveling trunk. The next number was more or less the same performance she'd given at the 1993 **MTV Video Music Awards: "Bye Bye Baby"** as a sex circus, with Madonna as barker and an all-girl stage that put the "gal" in gal pal.

"I'm Going Bananas," a short, **campy** Latin-kitsch song from *I'm Breathless: Music from and Inspired by the Film Dick Tracy*, was performed energetically, with Madonna in horizontal stripes and a bandanna, followed by one of her many live renditions of **"La Isla Bonita"** (perfect, since the tour traveled to Mexico and much of South America). Her **"Holiday"** (guess it was Memorial Day) was performed in military **drag,** the cast's severe coats fanning out into the US **flag.** The patriotism was almost surprising considering that *The Girlie Show World Tour* played only three American cities. It came complete with a James Brown–esque bit where Madonna kept falling and had to be literally dragged from the stage.

For her first encore, Madonna and her troupe slinked across the stage in exact replicas of the Cecil Beaton costumes from the "Ascot Gavotte" racing scene in *My Fair Lady* (1964), **lip-synching** along to "Justify My Love." That smoldering number was tempered by a dressed-down **"Everybody,"** a sweet, nostalgic way to end—with her very first single.

Madonna has never been more real onstage. She joked with the audience (different jokes at different performances!),

smiled warmly, shed real tears throughout her AIDS tribute and danced like a seasoned hoofer.

The show ignored most of Madonna's biggest '80s hits, but that's no criticism—as Madonna established with this tour, she is *not* a **nostalgia** act. The concert elevated Madonna's music to emotional anthems. If she could cook *this* up in a slump, there was no question that she was still going strong.

The critical reaction to the show was schizophrenic, with several British tabloids trashing it (thanks, **Piers Morgan**) despite uniformly positive **fan** reaction. In other venues, Madonna got mostly raves.

The tour was plagued by issues: Some venues forbade toplessness, so Inaba had to wear a halter sometimes; Madonna caused a traffic snafu by jogging in the streets of Toronto and was caught trading obscenities with a stockbroker at a hotel **gym**; Orthodox Jews protested Madonna's first-ever show in Israel; Madonna called reporters "sons of whores" at the birthplace of Christ in Jerusalem and infamously dodged a meeting with Mayor Teddy Kollek; let's not even talk about that flag flap (okay, we'll talk about it in the flag entry); and pious Mexican students burned Madonna posters because they were pissed the **fuck** off over Madonna's vulgarity. In Australia, Madonna was given a didgeridoo that she carried around, only to find out later it was for "men only."

The Sydney shows were crawling with **love**-starved bugs—it was mating season! The pests got ringside seats—you can see one crawling up her chest on the video of the tour.

I am girlie, hear me roar ...

FRANCESCO DE VINCENTIS

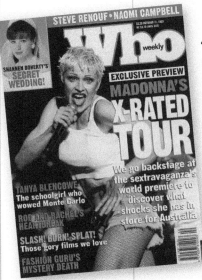

The tour required 1,500 costumes (including "Express Yourself" pants that got shorter and shorter each show; D&G were not thrilled about revising their work on the fly) for the cast and a 24-hour stage set-up time. The cast had rehearsed for 12 hours, six days a week for several weeks before their debut in front of 72,000 fans.

Madonna regulars included singers/dancers **Niki Haris** and **Donna De Lory**, *Blond Ambition World Tour* dancer **Carlton Wilborn** and Luca Tommassini, who would work with Madonna on **"Human Nature"** and in *Evita*. The tour's other unimpeachably on-point dancers were Ungela Brockman, Christopher Childers, Michael Gregory, Ruth Inchaustegui and Jill Nicklaus. They had beaten out, according to Madonna, "thousands of dancers and people who *think* they can dance."

The Girlie Show World Tour was recorded on November 19, 1993, and aired on HBO as *Madonna Live Down Under: The Girlie Show*. It was sold to the home-video market as **The Girlie Show: Live Down Under** and was nominated for a **Grammy** for Best Long Form Music Video. There was at one time a discussion to turn the show into a Las Vegas revue with Madonna as producer.

THE GIRLIE SHOW WORLD TOUR PERFORMANCES

September 25-26, 1993: London, England (Wembley Stadium)

September 28-29, October 1, 1993: Paris, France (Palais Omnisports de Paris-Bercy)

October 4, 1993: Tel Aviv, Israel (Hayarkon Park)

October 7, 1993: Istanbul, Turkey (İnönü Stadium)

October 11-12, 1993: Toronto, Canada (SkyDome)

October 14-15, October 17, 1993: New York, New York (Madison Square Garden)

October 19, 1993: Philadelphia, Pennsylvania (The Spectrum)

October 21, 1993: Auburn Hills, Michigan (The Palace of Auburn Hills)

October 23, 1993: Montreal, Canada (Olympic Stadium)

October 26, 1993: Bayamón, Puerto Rico (Juan Ramón Loubriel Stadium)

October 30-31, 1993: Buenos Aires, Argentina (River Plate Stadium)

November 3, 1993: São Paulo, Brazil (Estádio do Morumbi)

November 6, 1993: Rio de Janeiro, Brazil (Estádio do Maracanã)

November 10, November 12-13, 1993: Mexico City, Mexico (Autódromo Hermanos Rodríguez)

November 19, 1993: Sydney, Australia (Sydney Cricket Ground)

November 24, 1993: Brisbane, Australia (ANZ Stadium)

November 26-27, November 29, 1993: Melbourne, Australia (Melbourne Cricket Ground)

December 1, 1993: Adelaide, Australia (Adelaide Oval)

December 3-4, 1993: Sydney, Australia (Sydney Cricket Ground)

December 7-9, 1993: Fukuoka, Japan (Fukuoka Dome)

December 13-14, December 16-17, December 19, 1993: Tokyo, Japan (Tokyo Dome)

"THE TWO-HOUR EXTRAVAGANZA … WAS NOTABLE NOT ONLY AS A SHOWCASE FOR THE SUPERSTAR'S PRODIGIOUS TALENTS AS A SINGER AND DANCER, BUT ALSO FOR HER ABILITY TO ORCHESTRATE AND FILM AN APPROPRIATELY MAMMOTH PRODUCTION."
—*THE HOLLYWOOD REPORTER* (1993)

"THE ALL-SINGING, ALL-DANCING *GIRLIE SHOW* EVEN SOLVES THE MYSTERY OF WHAT MADONNA'S LATEST INCARNATION WILL BE: THE CAROL BURNETT OF HER GENERATION. GIVE THIS WOMAN HER OWN VARIETY HOUR!"
—PETER GALVIN, *THE ADVOCATE* (1993)

"THE FASCINATING THING ABOUT MADONNA IS THAT SHE IS ALL-REAL AND ALL-FAKE—IN OTHER WORDS, PURE SHOW BIZ … MADONNA, ONCE THE HARLOW HARLOT AND NOW A PERKY HARLEQUIN, IS THE GREATEST SHOW-OFF ON EARTH."
—RICHARD CORLISS, *TIME* (1993)

"THIS WAY LIES LAS VEGAS, WHERE MADONNA WOULD NEVER HAVE BEEN ENTIRELY OUT OF PLACE. THERE, SHE WOULDN'T BE BURDENED WITH THE EXPECTATIONS SHE HAS RAISED."
—JON PARELES, *THE NEW YORK TIMES* (1993)

"WHY DOES THE RHETORIC OF FIASCO AND DECLINE HOVER OVER THE PRODUCTION LIKE A VULTURE? FORGET THE NAYSAYERS—THE WISE THING TO DO IS TRY TO GET TICKETS. MADONNA MAY HAVE FAILED AT OTHER THINGS, BUT HER STAGE PRESENCE—HER FLUENT AND DARING DANCER'S IMAGINATION, HER GENIUS FOR ICONOGRAPHIC PLAYFULNESS, HER LIBERTINE EXPANSIVENESS—IS A WONDER OF OUR TIMES."—*THE NEW YORKER* (1993)

"I LOVED THE FACT THAT IT WAS SO THEATRICAL. I LOVE THE FACT, YOU KNOW, YOU CAN GO TO SOME SHOWS AND YOU CAN GO TO RAP AND SEE THEM SINGING AND DANCING ON THE STAGE, BUT I CAN DO THAT AT HOME, I CAN PUT THE CD ON AND DO THAT. BUT WHEN I GO TO A SHOW, I WANNA SEE, I WANNA BE ABLE TO USE ALL OF MY SENSES AND JUST BE IN A FANTASY WORLD."
—BRITNEY SPEARS, *TIME OUT LONDON* (2001)

"GIVE IT 2 ME" (SONG): *Release date: June 24, 2008. Billboard Hot 100 peak: #57.* The second single from *Hard Candy* was this club banger, written by Madonna and **Pharrell Williams** and produced by Madonna and the **Neptunes**. One of Madonna's most spirited latter-day singles, it failed to hit the Top 40 in the US but was nominated for a **Grammy** as Best **Dance** Recording.

Thematically, the song shares much with **"Don't Tell Me."**

There was never any doubt that "Give It 2 Me" would translate to the stage. Madonna told Ingrid Sischy, "It's very anthemic. I basically wrote it so I could have a great time doing it in a stadium." It was performed at her **Roseland** promo gig as well as being the finale on both legs of the *Sticky & Sweet Tour*.

For *The MDNA Tour*, Madonna used parts of "Give It 2 Me" in her performances of **"Girl Gone Wild"** and **"Celebration,"** and on November 13, 2012, she did a mash-up of the song with "Gangnam Style" (2012), joined by the latter song's performer, **Psy**.

"GIVE IT 2 ME" (VIDEO): *Directors: Tom Munro & Nathan Rissman, 2008.* Typical of some of Madonna's later-career music videos for songs other than lead singles, this lazy offering is simply a **Tom Munro** photo shoot (used for *Sticky & Sweet Tour* marketing) filmed by **Nathan Rissman**, during which Madonna improvises **dance** moves. She looks good, but there needs to be more than that in order for a video to have an impact. **Pharrell Williams** appears, too, in footage that was repurposed on tour. One of Madonna's worst efforts in the form she had dominated for 25 years, don't you think?

> "I used to really enjoy it. I used to enjoy doing video shoots. I don't have any patience for it anymore. I feel like I've done it all a billion, gazillion times."
>
> —MADONNA, *ROLLING STONE* (1997)

"GIVE ME ALL YOUR LUVIN'" FEAT. NICKI MINAJ AND M.I.A. (SONG): *Release date: February 3, 2012. Billboard Hot 100 peak: #10.* Madonna's lead single from *MDNA* marked her first collaboration with **Martin Solveig** (who coproduced and cowrote it with Madonna). It was written by Madonna, Solveig, **Nicki Minaj**, **M.I.A.** and Michael Tordjman, and features robust raps from Minaj and M.I.A.

Another of Madonna's notorious **leaks**, "Give Me All Your Love" (the earlier title) appeared on the Internet on November 8, 2011, three months prior to its release. The song was not well received in general, but upon release managed to squeak into the US Top 10 on a raft of publicity from its inclusion in Madonna's **Super Bowl** halftime show performance. It is one of several Madonna songs that mentions her name, including (in order of official release) the **Dance Mix Edit of "Angel," "4 Minutes," "Candy Shop," "I Don't Give A"** and **"Bitch I'm Madonna."**

Along with making it a part of pop history at the Super Bowl, Madonna performed the song winningly on her *MDNA Tour* in **drum**-majorette **drag**.

"GIVE ME ALL YOUR LUVIN'" FEAT. NICKI MINAJ AND M.I.A. (VIDEO): *Directors: MegaForce, 2012.* The team of Léo Berne, Charles Brisgand, Raphaël Rodriguez and Clément Gallet, known as MegaForce, gang-banged up for the direction of the first music video from Madonna's *MDNA* album. (Apparently, more and more, music videos need multiple directors in the same way simple pop ditties need multiple writers.) Unlike some of Madonna's post–**"Hung Up"** videos, "Give Me All Your Luvin'" makes for a better video than it did a song.

Playing off of Madonna's announced performance of the song at the **Super Bowl**, the video has an otherworldly **cheerleader** theme, opening with the song's guests **M.I.A.** and **Nicki Minaj** in stylized uniforms shaking their pom-poms for Madonna. Madonna emerges from a suburban home in a trench, pushing a baby carriage. The weather? 100% chance of golden showers. Spookily faceless football jocks crash into each other around her, intercut with scenes of similarly faceless cheerleaders. The surreal landscape conspires with the anonymous supporting players to give the video a lighthearted occult feel. Since "lighthearted" and "occult" don't often appear in sentences together, that at least means the video is off the beaten path.

Madonna is held aloft by the jocks, "walking" along a brick wall horizontally, performs against a similar brick backdrop and is then shot at by an unseen villain, requiring the players to take the bullets for her in scenes reminiscent of the *Batman!* **TV** series (1966–1968). By the time she's delivered to the presence of M.I.A. and Minaj in a club setting, all three are sporting "Breathless Mahoney" wigs.

A series of inscrutable, yet charged, images gives the feeling that the video is definitely about *something* ... but what? Whatever's going on, Madonna deemed it a success—the video ends with her triumphantly holding a player's helmet aloft while fireworks erupt and the legend, "Touchdown!" appears, "That's all folks!"–style.

It's a vibrant, hubristic completely unique video that presents Madonna as a siren and that perfectly set her up for the Super Bowl.

> "Fans can make you famous, a contract can make you rich, the press can make you a superstar, but only luv can make you a player."—"GIVE ME ALL YOUR LUVIN'" VIDEO (2012)

GLAAD: On April 21, 1991, Madonna became the first person to receive an Excellence in Media **Award** from GLAAD (formerly standing for the **Gay** & Lesbian Alliance Against Defamation, though the org's decision to expand to **bisexual** and transgender issues has led it to drop its acronymous standing), preceding Barbara Walters (1996), **Glenn Close** (2002), **Julianne Moore** (2004) and **Joy Behar** (2010), among others. The award, given by the media watchdog group, is intended to reward figures who have helped increase gay visibility through their **work.**

In 2013, Madonna playfully dressed as a **Boy Scout** when helping GLAAD honor **Anderson Cooper.**

GLEE: *Airdates: May 19, 2009–March 20, 2015.* This broadly drawn music-driven series became a cultural phenomenon in its first season, with its telegenic young cast of characters performing renditions of classic and contemporary songs.

On April 20, 2010, *Glee* aired its 15th episode, entitled "The **Power** of Madonna," written and directed by series creator Ryan Murphy. In the episode, which Madonna deemed "brilliant," some of her songs were heard as background music (**"Ray of Light," "Frozen"** and **"Justify My Love"**) while others were covered (**"Express Yourself," "Borderline"/"Open Your Heart," "Vogue," "Like a Virgin," "4 Minutes," "What It Feels Like for a Girl"** and **"Like a Prayer"**).

Stand-out performances included Jane Lynch's cover of "Vogue," accompanied by a **parody** of the **original** video (she won an Emmy for it), three storylines coming together (literally, in some cases) over "Like a Virgin" and the male cast members taking on "What It Feels Like for a Girl" in a **feminist** statement.

An EP called *Glee: The Music, The Power of Madonna* was released the same day the show aired, filled with full studio renditions of the songs performed, plus a bonus track of **"Burning Up"**; it went straight to #1 on the *Billboard* 200.

Glee's Madonna episode attracted 13.5 million viewers.

GMTV: *Airdates: January 1, 1993–September 3, 2010.* UK morning-show franchise that landed Madonna for a two-part sit-down in 2009 to promote *Celebration*. Adorable interviewer Ben Shephard gingerly teased game answers out of Madonna on various topics, including her feelings about **London**, the relatively new trend of achieving instant success via pop-music competition programs, parenting and her health.

Madonna also related that she'd had a good-natured **dance**-off with **Lady Gaga** at a **birthday** party for her manager: "... Lady Gaga was there and the DJ basically did a, sort of, we did a dance-off, sort of, so he would play one

of her songs and then he would play one of mine, and we, we both danced together in the middle and all of my dancers were, were around us, and we just took turns dancing to, and sh—I would dance to all of her songs and sing all the words and she did the same for me. It was really fun."

GOD: In 1992, Madonna said simply, "Everyone has their own God." Or goddess.

GOLD TOOTH: Madonna wore a $10,000 gold tooth—inscribed with a "D" for her persona **"Dita Parlo"**—fairly steadily from August through October 1992. The tooth (she actually had two, but didn't care for the "M" version) had to be fitted by a dentist each time she wore it, and removed by one each time she tired of it. The jack-o-lantern impression it lent her smile was highly effective in the **"Erotica"** video, but it got in the way of all the interviews she gave, causing a slight lisp. The tooth was a clear precursor to her **grills**.

GOLDEN GLOBES: Madonna has been nominated for seven Golden Globes, six for Best **Original** Song and one for Best Actress. The ones she lost were for the songs **"Who's That Girl"** in 1988, **"This Used to Be My Playground"** in 1993, **"I'll Remember"** in 1995, **"Beautiful Stranger"** in 2000 and **"Die Another Day"** in 2003.

On January 19, 1997, Madonna attended the 54th Golden Globe **Awards**, at which she received the Globe for Best Actress in a Motion Picture, Musical or Comedy, for her starring role in *Evita. Evita* also won Best Picture, Musical or Comedy (beating out *Everyone Says I* **Love** *You, Fargo, Jerry Maguire* and *The Birdcage*), and its **"You Must Love Me,"** as sung (but not written) by Madonna, won for Best Original Song.

To win the first and only major award for her **acting**, Madonna beat out **Glenn Close** (*101 Dalmatians*), Frances McDormand (*Fargo*), Debbie Reynolds (*Mother*) and **Barbra Streisand** (*The Mirror Has Two Faces*).

In spite of the presumption that Madonna would go on to receive an **Oscar** nomination, she was shut out, and the Oscar for Best Actress went to McDormand.

Nicole Kidman presented the Globe to Madonna, who was wearing a low-plunging **Dolce & Gabbana** gown that flaunted major post-**pregnancy** cleavage, and who had arrived with the **father** of her baby, **Carlos Leon.**

In her speech, Madonna became emotional, saying, "I have been so incredibly blessed this past year, and I have much to be thankful for." She thanked the film's director, **Alan Parker**, "for believing in me and for giving me this opportunity and for making such an exquisite film." She thanked **Antonio Banderas** and **Jonathan Pryce** and

Jimmy Nail from the film by name. She added a "**God bless you**" to producers Robert Stigwood and Andy Vajna, ending with thanks for **Andrew Lloyd Webber** and **Tim Rice** "for writing such beautiful music and inspiring us all."

Ever loyal to Dick Clark, Madonna gave him a radiant interview backstage, in which she referred to her award as her "other baby." Clark reminded her of her early appearance on *American Bandstand* in which she said she hoped she'd "rule the world." Madonna said her future plans were to "keep going as an artist, make more music, make more movies and have more children."

Madonna's next Globe win came in 2012, when she picked up her first **statue** for Best Original Song, for "**Masterpiece**" from her film *W.E.*, from presenters Adam Levine and **Jimmy Fallon**. It was a particularly sweet victory because the film had been largely savaged by critics, and **Elton John** had seethed on the carpet before the telecast that, "Madonna hasn't got a **fucking** chance." Including John's collaboration with Bernie Taupin "Hello Hello" (*Gnomeo & Juliet*), Madonna's vanquished competition was "The Keeper" (*Machine Gun Preacher*) by Chris Cornell, "Lay Your Head Down" (*Albert Nobbs*) by Brian Byrne and Glenn Close and "The Living Proof" (*The Help*) by Mary J. Blige, Thomas Newman, Harvey Mason Jr. and Damon Thomas.

The cameraman deserved his or her own award for which closeups were shown following Madonna's "Masterpiece" win, which included *Evita* costar Antonio Banderas, *Body of Evidence* costar **Julianne Moore** and, of course, the **bitchy** resting face of Mr. Elton John. Madonna's acceptance speech started to turn into the speech she may have given had *W.E.* been winning as Best Motion Picture, Drama, so the orchestra nudged her along.

GOLDFRAPP: Duo made up of Alison Goldfrapp (b. May 13, 1966) and Will Gregory (b. September 17, 1959), whose songs "Ooh La La" (2005), "Number 1" (2005), "A&E" (2008) and others have made them a prominent UK electronica force.

The band's "Lovely Head" (2000) appears in *Swept Away*, and Madonna was photographed carrying a copy of their CD *Supernature* (2005).

Madonna's *Confessions on Dance Floor* (particularly "**Like It Or Not**") was said to have been partly inspired by her admiration for Goldfrapp—Madonna has said that the first single she ever downloaded was the band's "Human" (2001)—but the feeling is *not* mutual. Alison Goldfrapp has said, "I don't like Madonna's music, but she's an amazing pop star. She's brilliant at borrowing other people's ideas. But I was starstruck when I met her. I couldn't get out of my chair to shake her hand. She has lifted ideas from us, but that doesn't bother me."

Apparently, it does. Alison Goldfrapp has clarified her disdain for Madonna and also **Kylie Minogue**, saying, "They're nothing but **dance**-floor divas. That's not what I aspire to be."

For a while, Madonna was derisively called "Oldfrapp" by the UK press, which Goldfrapp did complain about as **ageist**.

GOLF: She tried her hand at this, the dullest of all sports, in 1994, after receiving golf clubs as a Christmas present. Later, golfing made an appearance in the song "**I Love New York**," in which Madonna managed to insult both golfers and Texas simply by asking a question.

"**GONE**": Written by Madonna, Damian Le Gassick and Nik Young and produced by Madonna, **William Orbit** and Mark "Spike" Stent, "Gone" is a mournful ballad that serves as the last track on *Music*. The song was performed on most *Drowned World Tour* dates, occasionally swapped out for "**You'll See.**"

GOOD MORNING AMERICA: *Airdates: November 3, 1975–*. American morning talk show airing on ABC. Madonna has granted many exclusives to the show over the years, including an amusingly contentious 1991 sitdown with a smug Steve Fox to plug *Truth or Dare* ("... for every bit of strength I have, there's this much weakness ..."), another with Diane Sawyer in 2003 about *The English Roses* (Madonna uncharacteristically expressed **regret** over mistreating people in the past) and a 2013 interview with Elizabeth Vargas to promote her *MDNA Tour* Blu-ray that veered into parenting prattle ("My daughter just got an iPhone—she's 16. My son does not have a phone"). Portions of **Cynthia McFadden**'s classic "**reductive**" interview with Madonna for *Nightline* were also pimped out to the show, and *GMA* is where **Elton John** went to tell the **Super Bowl**–bound Madonna to "**lip-synch** good."

> "God, well, I mean, when I'm 50 years old, I have to be happy–A#1. And I mean, I don't know ... maybe I'll have children, so that would be good ..."–MADONNA ON GMA (1991)

GOOD MORNING BRITAIN: *Airdates: February 1, 1983– December 31, 1992.* British morning talk show on which Madonna appeared several times. During a 1989 appearance, Madonna said she didn't take **drugs** because "my imagination and my energy level is overdeveloped ... I don't wanna alter my state of mind." She admitted, "I've watched a lot of people kill themselves taking drugs, whether it's heroin or coke—ruin their careers, their lives, their families, their relationships."

A July 23, 1990, report on her *Blond Ambition World Tour* profiled **fans** stalking Madonna outside her **London** hotel and contained rehearsal and overseas footage from the show, a brief interview with her **sexy** former trainer **Rob Parr** and a casual coronation of her as the "Queen of Sleaze."

—OLIVIA NEWTON-JOHN

"GOODBYE TO INNOCENCE": Up-tempo tune originally recorded for *Erotica* whose beat was initially used for the recording of **"Fever."** Madonna and coproducer **Shep Pettibone** were so taken with the latter that they shelved "Goodbye to Innocence" until July 19, 1994, when it was released on **Sire**'s pro-choice compilation, *Just Say Roe*. A dub version gave birth to **"Up Down Suite."**

On the finished song—and often in conversation—Madonna mispronounces "anonymity" as if it were spelled "anonyminity."

GOODMAN, MARK: *b. October 11, 1952.* This handsome, curly-haired VJ was the first on **MTV** to interview Madonna, in May 1984. Madonna expressed admiration for Vivienne Westwood, claimed credit as the architect of her own look ("Do you think someone else could come up with this?") and showed off her graffiti-decorated leather jacket.

"GOODNIGHT AND THANK YOU": Song from the film *Evita* found on *Evita: The Complete Motion Picture Music Soundtrack* which sounds like a pretty Madonna/ **Antonio Banderas** duet but whose lyrics caustically delineate Eva's comfort with using men **sexually** to get what she wants. (Wait, is that wrong?)

GOOSE AND TOMTOM: *Director: David Rabe, 1986.* Written and directed by David Rabe, this **play** was staged as a workshop for four performances only at the Mitzi Newhouse Theater at Lincoln Center (150 W. 65th St., NY, NY) starting August 28, 1986. **Sean Penn** ("Tomtom") and Madonna ("Lorraine") starred in the show about a jewel thief and his moll, along with Barry Miller ("Goose"), Lorraine Bracco ("Lulu"), **Harvey Keitel** ("Bingo") and Jon Korkes ("The Man), with appearances by Jono Gero, Jason Kuschner and David Lawton as "Men." In the program, the place was described as "an apartment in the underworld," the time as "this was recently" and special thanks were offered to actors Brooke Adams, **Danny Aiello**, Ellen Barkin and **Christopher Walken**, as well as to designer **Norma Kamali**.

Madonna was said to have played her moll roll to the hilt, chewing and snapping bubblegum throughout her performance, as directed.

As it was a workshop, no media were allowed, but **Andy Warhol** was invited by Madonna's friend **Martin Burgoyne**, which gave the producers pause at first. He was let in and didn't write about it until his diaries were published posthumously, so that's basically the definition of his lips were sealed. He wrote:

"The best thing about the play was the costumes ... Madonna changes outfits all the time, from one beautiful one

to another one. And Sean Penn wore a **gun** holster and fuchsia socks and shoes. The play was like Charles Ludlam, abstract. Madonna was good when she wasn't trying to be Judy Holliday or **Marilyn [Monroe]**. She chewed gum through the whole two hours and I did, too. She was blowing bubbles and everything."

Media infiltrated anyway, and the reviews were withering; the play is now only infrequently staged.

The show may have been closed to the general public, but celebs were welcome to get a gander at Madonna's stage debut. Along with Warhol, **Warren Beatty**, **Cher**, **Tom Cruise**, Robert De Niro, Griffin Dunne, Melanie Griffith, **Keith Haring**, Kelly McGillis, John McEnroe & Tatum O'Neal, Liza Minnelli, Chris Penn, Eric Roberts, Julia Roberts and Martin Scorsese all saw it.

In 1994, Penn was preparing to direct a movie of *Goose and Tomtom*, but it never came to pass.

At any rate, the actual content of the show paled in comparison to the real-life drama of Penn's violent streak, which struck on opening night when he punched paparazzo Vinnie Zuffante and spat on Anthony Savignano, an attack that earned him probation.

> "[*Goose and Tomtom* is] ... an inarticulate and incomprehensible meditation on human grubbiness."-*THE WALL STREET JOURNAL* (1986)

GORE, TIPPER: *b. August 19, 1948.* Wife (they're still married, but separated) of former Democratic US Vice President Al Gore.

In the '80s, she cofounded the Parents **Music** Resource Center (PMRC) with Susan Baker, the wife of Republican Secretary of State James Baker. The PMRC was a conservative group that lobbied hard for mandatory rating labels on music after serial killer Richard "the Night Stalker" Ramirez was found to have been obsessed with rock group AC/DC, and after Gore heard her 11-year-old playing **Prince**'s "Darling Nikki" (1984). The PMRC also advocated banning "offensive" album covers and having lyrics printed on every album sleeve, and pressured record companies to drop raunchy acts. Madonna's **"Dress You Up"** appeared on the PMRC's, um, *diverse* "Filthy Fifteen" list of especially egregious affronts to decency.

The fact that the song is inoffensive points up that it's Madonna herself—not her music—that riles her uptight detractors. (In 1991, 64% of respondents in an *Entertainment Weekly* poll said they would not allow their children to see a Madonna concert.)

By 1986, Gore was praising Madonna for **"Papa Don't Preach."**

Though Madonna is actually in favor of voluntary record labeling (calling something naughty is the best way to make it appealing, no?), which Gore also supported, she never had any use for Miss Tipper Gore. When hypocritical Gore gushily greeted Madonna at the Washington, DC, premiere of *Dick Tracy*, she received total silence in return. Madonna later told **Liz Rosenberg,** "I think I'm going to throw up. I think I'm going to hurl some chunks."

Interestingly, the first presidential vote Madonna ever cast was for **Bill Clinton,** which helped elect Gore's husband as well.

GORILLAZ: Virtual, animated band put together in 1998 by Blur's Damon Albarn and *Tank Girl* designer Jamie Hewlett. Madonna kicked off the 48th Annual **Grammys** in 2006 with a performance that merged the 2-D Gorillaz apathetically performing their "Feel Good Inc." (2005) with a briefly 2-D Madonna, followed by a live performance by Madonna of **"Hung Up."**

Albarn later expressed some discontent with how the performance went down: "We opened the Grammys—on **television** it looked great, but we had an invisible film pulled across our stage, and you project onto that, and put smoke behind it—it's a Victorian technology, actually. So Madonna manages to come and gate-crash our idea, as people like Madonna do, because that's why they're so deep ... She gate-crashed our idea, so we couldn't play with any bass or any sound, because it would vibrate [the film], so it was really quiet ... [N]o one could hear us in this huge, great arena, and we were crestfallen at that moment. And I'm trying to get Bono to move, because his huge, great Stetson is obscuring my view. And then our song stops, and she appears on the other side of the stage, with her inflated-ABBA riff, at full volume, and the place just goes insane. And at [that] point, I just thought, 'You know what? Sometimes, just keep it simple.'"

"GRAFFITI HEART": A *Rebel Heart* Super Deluxe Edition track that equates **love,** pain and **art,** a clear, club-ready tribute to Madonna's time with the likes of **Keith Haring.** The song was written by Madonna, MoZella, Toby Gad and S1, with production by Madonna, Toby Gad, AFSHeeN and Josh Cumbee.

GRAHAM, MARTHA: *May 11, 1894–April 1, 1991.* This maverick choreographer and iconic modern dancer had a uniquely sensual, visually challenging style that shook the world of **dance** to its foundations. Her Martha Graham Dance Company (55 Bethune St., NY, NY) definitely has legs—it was founded in 1926 and is still (high-)kicking.

Madonna attended classes at Graham's **school** in 1978, recalling in *Harper's Bazaar* years later that she'd been determined to meet Graham but wound up running into her only once, after sneaking out of the class to pee:

"She stopped dead in her tracks to see who the violator was. I was paralyzed. She was part 'Norma Desmond' in

Sunset Boulevard. The rest of her was a cross between a Kabuki dancer and the **nun** I was obsessed with in the fifth grade, Sister Kathleen Thomas. In any case, I was overwhelmed, and all my plans to disarm her and win her over were swallowed up by my fear of a presence I'd never encountered before."

Graham merely looked her over and moved on.

A dozen years later, Madonna attended the opening night of Graham's 180th ballet, *Maple Leaf Rag* at City Center (130 W. 56th St., NY, NY) on October 2, 1990. Others in attendance were **Eartha Kitt,** Calvin Klein and **Kathleen Turner.** It turned out to be the evening of Graham's final onstage bows—she died six months later.

GRAHAM NORTON SHOW, THE: *Airdates: February 22, 2007–.* Hosted by the hysterically funny, quick-witted Irish comic and presenter Graham Norton, this comedic British talk show is known for its eclectic slate of guests, its racy humor and a directive for all involved to be open and un-PC in their remarks. It's a remarkably successful brew.

Madonna appeared on the show on January 11, 2012, first solo and then alongside her *W.E.* leads Andrea Riseborough and James D'Arcy. Clad in the royal color of purple, Madonna complained about the couch, spoke carefully of **Lady Gaga,** said she cherished anonymity whenever she could get a taste of it and plugged *MDNA.* She was presented with dolls in her likeness at which she turned her nose up and then grudgingly approved ("You kind of made me look like a Victoria's Secret model—thanks!"), though the creators would only part with one of the dolls.

Unfortunately, Norton (like **French and Saunders** and so many others before him) mistook **Garry Trudeau's**

Last laughs: Madonna with Martha Graham and Calvin Klein not long before Graham's death parody of an interview with Madonna for the real thing, wasting valuable time having D'Arcy and Riseborough act it out.

Later asked if Madonna had been a diva, Norton disappointed his questioner: "Actually she wasn't. She didn't make any demands. She came on, and within a few minutes she was on the floor on her hands and knees. She was on a charm offensive."

"She may not be God's gift to acting, but when it comes to being Madonna she can do it better than anyone else. She is so convinced she is special that we are all swept along by her tsunami of ambition and need."—GRAHAM NORTON (2014)

GRAMMYS: *Dates presented: 1959-.* The Grammy **Awards** are the American music industry's highest honor. Grammys are given in so many categories there's a chance this **book** will get one, and that you may get one for reading it. Dark **horse**, but a chance.

Wait, why are we talking about music? Because Madonna is a singer ... remember?

As a singer who has always pushed herself to be better, to explore different genres, to **work** with interesting people and who in over 30 years in the biz has become the most successful female singer of all time, Madonna has not been able to avoid accidentally winning a few Grammys and receiving some nominations. Yet as many categories as there are, it hasn't been easy. She doesn't have 20 like **Beyoncé** or 21 like **Kanye West**, but then again, **Diana Ross** has never won a competitive Grammy, so that tells you all you need to know about the validity of the honor.

Madonna has shown up at the Grammys even when she wasn't hoping to win a trophy or offering a new performance, most excitingly on February 8, 2004, when she took the stage in a ruffled pink dress, fishnets and shiny black boots, saying of **Sting**, "You cannot imagine what an honor it is for me to introduce the next performer. There isn't a person here, including me, who's not fallen in **love** with his music. And while he's done a great many things for the world, he will always have a special place in my heart for introducing me to my husband."

However, Madonna's most *important* night at the Grammys from the perspective of winning awards was February 24, 1999, when she picked up three awards, including the only major-category award she's ever won: Best Pop Album for *Ray of Light*, handed to her by Jerry Seinfeld and **Jennifer Lopez**. She accepted the award, saying, "This is such a surprise and I'm so honored," thanking all of her collaborators. At the same show, she was seen blowing kisses to **Luciano Pavarotti** when he sang, and she later surprised **Ricky Martin** in the press room—it was the night of Martin's crossover breakthrough performance of "The Cup of Life" (1998).

Madonna's own first-ever performance at the Grammys was that same evening, and it was ... a doozy. Inspired by the 1997 **book** *Memoirs of a Geisha*, Madonna opened

the show with a confidently sung but awkwardly staged (by **Christopher Ciccone**) **"Nothing Really Matters"**—Madonna, who would these days be condemned for **cultural appropriation** for her straight black **hair** and red John Broderick kimono, sang and **danced** on a teensy bridge while kooky characters from the music video struggled to move in straitjacket-like garments behind her. Yes, a shirtless dude did a little flaming-baton twirling, but it happened too late to save a total head-scratcher of a performance that fell flat. The excellent song wasn't a hit before the performance, and that didn't change after.

Fortunately, Madonna hasn't given up performing at the Grammys—she's done it several times since, usually with far more satisfying results.

Riding high on the success of *Music*, she performed the title track at the 43rd Annual Grammys on February 21, 2001. The performance was introduced by a snippet from the video for **"What It Feels Like for a Girl"** and a montage of many of Madonna's memorable musical moments playing behind her throughout the song. Madonna emerged from a limo (its license plate plugged hubby **Guy Ritchie**'s 2000 movie, *Snatch*) chauffeured by Lil Bow Wow, then just 13. (Apparently, no one thought twice about the optics.) In a skintight cropped leather jacket and black slacks, Madonna boogie-woogied on, against and near her ride, stripping off the jacket to reveal a black tank that read **"MATERIAL GIRL."** She was backed up by **Donna De Lory** and **Niki Haris**, all three of whom did 15 deep-squat pelvic thrusts in a row as the song—and Madonna **fans** across the country—climaxed.

Madonna entered into one of the oddest collaborations of her career on February 8, 2006, when her image was married with that of the virtual band **Gorillaz** to open the show. After the band blew through its "Feel Good Inc." (2005), Madonna's image appeared, interacting with them briefly before the flesh-and-blood **Queen of Pop** arrived in a corseted purple leotard to re-create her by then standard **"Hung Up"** performance.

Looking a bit worn out, on January 26, 2014, Madonna arrived to that year's ceremony with her son **David** in matching black Ralph Lauren tuxedoes to do the red carpet. Onstage, she joined **Macklemore**, Ryan Lewis, Queen Latifah and **Mary Lambert** for a mass same-sex **wedding** while the artists sang "Same Love" (2012). Madonna chimed in with bits of **"Open Your Heart"** and harmonized with Lambert ably, but much was made of her stage look: an all-white Colonel Sanders–esque suit. Still more focus went to the cane she hobbled in on; she was still recovering from an exercise injury.

On February 8, 2015, Madonna stole an otherwise stately Grammys show, first by appearing in a barely-there matador-inspired outfit (with veil) by Givenchy on the red carpet, where she mooned the paparazzi after vampily posing for them, and then with her stellar live performance of **"Living for Love."** Introduced by **Miley Cyrus** and **Nicki Minaj**, the segment began with imagery from the music video for the song and a spoken-word intro promising a love revolution. Madonna was revealed wearing a black bull-fighter's cape and the briefest possible, blood-red showgirl costume with matching jacket. She hustled through a tour-ready number, surrounded by a herd of hot male dancers sporting bull's horns, ending by being lifted heavenward, all made slightly tentative thanks to impossibly high heels … all the better to see those legs. How good Madonna had *looked* at 56 grabbed the initial attention in the resulting rave reviews, but a video purporting to offer her isolated vocals that stripped away the guide vocal she'd sung over led to further praise for how good she'd *sounded*.

```
MADONNA'S GRAMMY
NOMINATIONS & WINS

1986:
"Crazy for You"
(Best Pop Vocal
Performance, Female)

1987:
"Papa Don't Preach"
(Best Pop Vocal
Performance, Female)

1988:
"Who's That Girl"
(Best Song Written
Specifically for a Motion
Picture or Television)

1991:
"Oh Father"
(Best Music Video,
Short Form)

1992:
Blond Ambition
World Tour Live
(Best Music Video,
Long Form-WON)

1995:
"I'll Remember"
(Best Song Written
Specifically for
a Motion Picture
or Television),
The Girlie Show:
Live Down Under
(Best Music Video,
Long Form)

1996:
Bedtime Stories
(Best Pop Album)

1999:
Ray of Light
(Album of the Year;
Best Pop Album-WON),
"Ray of Light"
(Best Dance Recording-
WON; Best Short
Form Music Video-WON;
Record of the Year)
```

```
2000:
"Beautiful Stranger"
(Best Female Pop Vocal
Performance; Best Song
Written for a Motion
Picture, Television or
Other Visual Media-WON)

2001:
Music
(Best Pop Vocal Album),
"Music" (Best Female
Pop Vocal Performance,
Record of the Year)

2002:
"Don't Tell Me"
(Best Short Form
Music Video)

2004:
"Die Another Day"
(Best Dance Recording;
Best Short Form Music
Video)

2007:
Confessions on a
Dance Floor
(Best Electronic/
Dance Album-WON),
"Get Together"
(Best Dance Recording),
I'm Going to Tell
You a Secret
(Best Long Form
Music Video)

2008:
The Confessions Tour
(Best Long Form Music
Video-WON)

2009:
"4 Minutes"
(Best Pop Collaboration
with Vocals),
"Give It 2 Me"
(Best Dance Recording)

2010:
"Celebration"
(Best Dance Recording)
```

GRANDE, ARIANA: *b. June 26, 1993.* Pint-sized belter who has become a formidable pop princess since her 2013 album debut. Prior to her recording career, Grande became a **YouTube** sensation with her many vocally challenging covers, including a clever mash-up of **"Express Yourself"** with **Lady Gaga**'s **"Born This Way"** (2011).

Grande, a Madonna **fan**, told *V* **magazine**, "She is my idol as far as attitude. I just **love** how she stands up for what she believes in and surprises people by not eff-ing up when they want her to so badly. Madonna has always surprised people and she has always had her head on straight. Even when she pretends not to. When she shocks people and everything, there is always a method behind it."

In December 2014, Grande tweeted her excitement over the first part of Madonna's ***Rebel Heart*** release, to which Madonna replied, "You've been such a good girl this year I wanted to give you something special."

GRANDMOTHER: SEE: **Fortin, Elsie Mae.**

GRANDPARENTS: On her father's side, Madonna's grandparents were Gaetano (1901–1968) and Michelina **Ciccone** (1903–1968), who emigrated to Aliquippa, Pennsylvania, a suburb of Pittsburgh, from **Pacentro**, Italy. They had six children, the youngest of whom was **Silvio "Tony" Ciccone,** Madonna's oh **father.**

Madonna has no **memory** of her maternal grandfather, Willard Fortin (November 7, 1903–June 30, 1959), but her maternal **grandmother, Elsie Mae Fortin**, became a force in her life.

GRANT, HUGH: *b. September 9, 1960.* Dashing British actor from such films as *Maurice* (1987), *Four **Weddings** and a Funeral* (1994) and *About a Boy* (2002) with whom Madonna was reported to have been infatuated in 1994, sending him romantic faxes at all hours. It's been reported that they met for tea.

"I've never said anything as pompous as 'no comment' before, but—no comment," he replied to **Michael Musto**'s query on the subject. He did feign jealousy at hints that Madonna had moved on to Ethan Hawke, an example of Madonna's distressingly erratic taste in men.

Too bad! A Hugh Grant/Madonna **love** affair could have been so *Notting Hill* (1999).

In 2011, Madonna and Hugh were joined in the twisted mind of **Piers Morgan**—both were banned from his low-rated talk show for irritating him.

"Hugh Grant thinks he had it tough? That was nothing. Just imagine if *I'd* been arrested for hiring a *male* hustler. I'd be serving time, no doubt in my mind."-MADONNA (1996)

GRILLS: Madonna has sported grills off and on since 2013, **Instagram**ming that she was brushing them before booty popping. An early high-profile appearance with them was at the opening of her **Hard Candy Fitness Club** in Rome on August 21, 2013. The grills, which cannot be called flattering (and that doesn't seem to be the point), are often encrusted with 24 diamonds. When some **fans** complained that they were ugly and that she should ditch them, Madonna Instagrammed her advice, "The Grillz Are here to Stay! Don't like don't follow!" Bitch *sings* in them.

—MICHAEL AUSIELLO

Asked if she could manage to make out while wearing her grills, Madonna told a Reddit.com user, "yup it **works**."

The grills returned during her *Rebel Heart* promo, including for her **Howard Stern** interview and in the album's music videos.

GRINDR: Madonna did a promo for this **gay** hookup app, in which **fans** posted their faces in *Rebel Heart* mode for a chance to ask Madonna a few questions. (Presumably, "What are you looking for?" and "Are you a top?" among them.) Madonna said of the chat, "It's part of the modern world we live in. I think there are just as many assholes meeting the old-fashioned way as there are meeting in the new hookup culture."

GROI: A fave expression of Madonna's from 1985, meaning "get rid of it."

GROSSMANN, ANDRÉ: *b. April 15, 1955.* German photographer who specialized in shooting denizens of the downtown music scene. He met and photographed Madonna both at club appearances (Fresh 14, the **Celebrity Club**) and at her **East Village** apartment.

GRUBMAN, ALLEN: *b. 1942.* For many years, the man *Vanity Fair* has dubbed "the most **powerful** attorney" in the music biz was Madonna's entertainment lawyer. Grubman has represented many superstar clients, including **Michael Jackson, Bette Midler** and Bruce Springsteen, as well as Madonna's ex, **Jellybean Benitez.** So loyal was Madonna to Mr. Grubman that she attended his 1991 **wedding** reception (in a leopard-print coat) at the **New York** Public Library (Fifth Ave. at 42nd St., NY, NY) following Grubman's wedding to Deborah Haimoff.

As of 2015, an article listing Grubman's many high-profile clients does not mention Madonna. **Lady Gaga,** however, has joined the fold.

Guinness World Records: Living to tell is the best revenge!

GUCCIONE, BOB, JR.: *b. September 19, 1955.* Son and namesake of the *Penthouse* founder and the publisher of *Spin,* Guccione wrote a scathing editorial in 1992 arguing that "Madonna has overstayed her welcome. Not just in rock culture, or here in America, or even the Western Hemisphere. The planet ... She is not an important artist."

Madonna had appeared on three *Spin* covers at the time, including its premiere issue, and was asked by the **magazine** to write an article to coincide with the publication of *Sex,* but had declined. Perhaps Guccione didn't like the way she said no, or perhaps his diatribe was more principled.

After being invited to exit the planet by Guccione, Madonna appeared on three more *Spin* covers, counting a

15th-anniversary issue in 2000 that was a repeat of the cover they'd used in 1985.

Most interestingly, Madonna appeared on and in *Spin*'s January 1996 issue, a cover story consisting of a one-on-one interview by Guccione, who had suggested it, been denied and then been granted access after all. In that piece, he quizzed Madonna on everything from **sex** to **drugs** (she said ecstasy could make you "... walk up to Bob Dole and have a conversation and find something to like about him.") to religion to **race**. She also identified **"Live to Tell"** as her favorite song she'd ever written and **"Material Girl"** as her least favorite that she'd recorded.

She never appeared on the cover of *Spin* after 2000. It ceased printing in 2012, going all-digital.

"GUILTY BY ASSOCIATION": In 1995, Madonna teamed up with her brother-in-law **Joe Henry** for this touching duet, which appeared on the album *Sweet Relief II: Gravity of the Situation.* The song is a cover of a Vic Chesnutt tune, as are all the others on the album, which was created to raise cash for musicians in urgent need of health care. The album ignited interest in Chesnutt as a songwriter, bringing him more success than ever before. Chesnutt, a paraplegic since 1983, committed suicide in 2009.

Henry told the *New York* Post, "I agreed to do the song and then realized that it was about the albatross of someone else's celebrity. Vic wrote it about Michael Stipe and Michael sang backup vocals on Vic's version without knowing the song was about him. The **irony** of asking Madonna to sing the backing vocal with me was just too rich to resist."

GUINNESS WORLD RECORDS: In the 1988 edition of this book of world records, Madonna had already earned the distinction of being the world's most successful female singer of all time. By 2014, the authorities at Guinness had flatly declared her the world's "best-selling female artist," one who also managed to make—from June 2012 to June 2013—the "highest annual earnings ever for a female pop star, dwarfing those of record holder **Céline Dion** ..." And all the while, penniless bloggers **worked** feverishly on exciting new ways to prove that she was **irrelevant**.

Madonna was still setting records as of August 26, 2014, when the Fire Island Pines party "It's a Madge Madge Madge Madge World," themed to Madonna, racked up the most people simultaneously dressed as Madonna. In all, 440 people attended, including Mike Hisey, pictured in **drag** that salutes the *Confessions Tour.*

GUITAR: Madonna first picked up a Carlo Robelli acoustic guitar when she was a member of the **Breakfast Club** in 1979, tutored by her then-beau **Dan Gilroy**. She recalled in 1995, "As soon as Dan taught me a major chord progression, I was possessed by some spirit and became glued to my guitar and a rinky-dink tape recorder."

Once Madonna found success as a solo singer, she abandoned the guitar and other instruments she played until 2000, when husband **Guy Ritchie** bought her her first acoustic guitar in 20 years. Madonna earnestly began re-learning to play with the help of **Monte Pittman**. She debuted her skills during a chat with **David Letterman**, playing and singing **"Don't Tell Me."**

Madonna **worked** a guitar into her act for *Drowned World Tour* and has played it on tour ever since.

Madonna has played guitar on record, for example on **"Miles Away,"** but was double-tracked. She does not consider herself a guitar goddess, but she **loves** to play it and shows no signs of giving it up, going so far as to get credit for the rather light strumming of it on *MDNA*'s **"Falling Free."**

For her 2015 **iHeartRadio Music Awards** performance of **"Ghosttown,"** Madonna brought her acoustic guitar from home for **Taylor Swift** to play.

GUNS: In many ways, Madonna is a liberal, but there are aberrations. For starters, she has a fascination with guns. She learned to shoot while living in the English countryside, telling *Tatler* in 2005, "I was mad for shooting ... That all changed when a bird dropped in front of me that I'd shot. It wasn't dead. It got up and it was really suffering. Blood was gushing out of its mouth and it was struggling up this hill and I thought, 'Oh, **God**, I did that.'" She said she just couldn't shoot anymore. "I realized I had a kind of bloodlust and was manically shooting things and trying to kill as many things as possible."

Madonna seems to enjoy guns (like cigarettes) more as props, such as when she wore Chanel's revolver-heeled stilettoes in 2008—for effect.

Madonna's *MDNA Tour* made obsessive use of firearms, most shockingly in **"Revolver"** and in the Quentin Tarantino-inspired **"Gang Bang."** This artistic choice led to strong criticism as Madonna brought the tour to a Colorado venue 15 miles from the site of the Aurora movie-theater massacre three months earlier. The flap ignored the fact that the guns were a set part of the show as they are in countless stage **plays**, **TV** series and movies, all of which were also available in the vicinity of Aurora at the time.

Much to the consternation of some of her **fans**, Madonna—who's never met a cliché she didn't like—used a right-wing axiom in a 2013 *Good Morning America* interview when defending her *MDNA Tour*'s glamorized use of weaponry: "I mean, the thing is, guns don't kill people, people kill people. That whole first section of the show is like an action movie, and I was playing a super vixen who wanted revenge."

What's next, *"American Life—love* it or leave it"?

GUTHRIE, GWEN: *July 9, 1950–February 3, 1999.* Later famous for her sassy hit "Ain't Nothin' Goin' on But the Rent" and remake of "(They Long to Be) Close to You" (both 1986), Guthrie provided backing vocals on several songs from Madonna's debut album *Madonna*, including **"Borderline," "Burning Up"** and **"Everybody."** She died of **cancer** at 48.

GUTIEREZ (XTRAVAGANZA), JOSE: SEE: Jose & Luis.

GYM: The **fitness** freak once said, "If I had nothing to do, I would stay in the gym forever."

Oh ... that really was a gun in your pocket.

MATTHEW RETTENMUND

LAVINEL SAVU

HAIR: Hair color and style may seem like superficial aspects of who a person is, but for Madonna, they are signifiers. She feels more down-to-earth and centered as a brunette, more fabulous and playful as a **blonde** (she also thinks it looks better onstage). No word on how she feels as a redhead—maybe confused?

But also, as a creative force who is just shy of being classified as a performance artist, her hair is also part of her act. Thus, it tends to change from project to project in the same way Madonna's persona tends to change.

"With but a change of hair color ... she transmutes from blonde, aerobicized pop star into some pre-Raphaelite personification of spiritual **beauty**," Roy Wilkinson wrote in *NME* in 1989 of her *Like a Prayer* hair.

A classic example of the continuing changes to her 'do and of the challenge she presents to a lazy imagination came in anticipation of *The Girlie Show World Tour*. Asked what color her hair would be, her response was, "What hair?"

Respondents to a 1994 Neutrogena survey totally missed the point when they gave Madonna the Medusa Award for what they perceived to be her constant bad-hair days. Madonna doesn't have bad-hair days, she just sometimes has bad hairdos that only last a day.

The hair on her head isn't the only hair that gets Madonna in the news. When her **nudes** appeared in *Playboy* and *Penthouse*, most interesting was the underarm hair on that spindly baby goddess, the ultimate shock to Middle America. According to Tanis Rozelle, a former classmate of Madonna's, neither Madonna nor her sister **Melanie Ciccone** shaved their underarms in high **school**. She told biographer **J. Randy Taraborrelli**, "That was considered pretty weird. Both had thick tufts of hair growing out from underneath their armpits. It caused a minor controversy, but after a while people just accepted it."

In 2013, Madonna said, "I thought it was cooler not to shave my legs or under my arms. I mean, why did **God** give us hair there anyways?"

At one point, much was made by the foreign press about Madonna's bleached *facial* hair, pictured under such snappy headlines as "Hair's That Girl?" and "What's All the Fuzz About? (Being a Superstar Can Get You Down)."

> "It wouldn't surprise me if Madonna were a natural blonde who dyes her roots black."
>
> —ERIC SCHMUCKLER, *THE VILLAGE VOICE* (1984)

HAITI: Madonna participated in *Hope for Haiti Now: A Global Benefit for Earthquake Relief* in the wake of the island's catastrophic 2010 'quake. In November 2013, she joined her ex **Sean Penn** in the country to visit hospitals and lend support to the aid effort.

Penn said, "I don't know if I called her or if it was one time that we ran into each other but I said, 'Would you like to come down?' She said she would. She came down with her son **Rocco** and it was great to have them down there."

HALL, ARSENIO: SEE: *Arsenio Hall Show, The*.

HALL, DAVE "JAM": The record producer (married to comic Wanda Sykes before she came out as a lesbian) behind Mary J. Blige's massively influential *What's the 411?* (1992), he **worked** with Madonna on the *Bedtime Stories* tracks **"Human Nature," "I'd Rather Be Your Lover," "Inside of Me"** and **"Love Tried to Welcome Me,"** giving the album its R&B feel. Hall was suggested to Madonna by **Freddy DeMann**. Though their collaboration was fruitful, it was apparently not one of Madonna's favorites.

HANKS, TOM: *b. July 9, 1956*. After getting his start on the '80s cross-dressing sitcom *Bosom Buddies* (1980–1982) and in light movie fare like *Splash* (1984) and *Bachelor Party* (1984), Hanks became one of the most lauded actors of his generation, winning the **Oscar** as Best Actor in a Leading Role two years in a row for his performances in *Philadelphia* (1993) and *Forrest Gump* (1994).

Hanks costarred with Madonna in *A League of Their Own* at the **height** of his box-office supremacy and immediately prior to his graduation from bankable leading man to serious actor. His line, "There's no crying in baseball!" is one of the best-remembered movie quotes of the '90s.

At the time the movie was filming, Hanks said of Madonna's ability to throw a baseball, "In the early going, she has, yeah, her throwing tech was pretty much, it was a choreographed *step, step, kick, fling* kind of thing ... She's better now." Madonna joked, "I'm gonna kill Tom for saying that about me."

Hanks shared the March 1999 cover of *Esquire* with Madonna and other celebs to raise awareness of the ongoing **AIDS** crisis, has attended Madonna's hot-ticket Oscars party, was in the audience to watch her induction into the **Rock and Roll Hall of Fame** and huddled with her onstage during **Oprah Winfrey**'s final show.

"HANKY PANKY": *Release date: June 30, 1990. Billboard Hot 100 peak: #10*. The second and final single from *I'm Breathless: Music from and Inspired by the Film Dick Tracy* was this rip-roaring recommendation of light spanking that preceded the release of the novel *50 Shades of Grey* (2011) by over two decades.

The song was simultaneously a comment on "Breathless Mahoney's" status as a woman who thrives on abuse, and a saucy challenge to radio stations, some of which declined to play it. The lack of airplay kept "Hanky Panky" from rising above #10, but the single went gold anyway.

Madonna wrote and produced the song, which borders on being a novelty hit, with **Patrick Leonard**.

"Hanky Panky" was performed live on the *Blond Ambition World Tour*, the *Re-Invention World Tour* and as a bonus on the *Rebel Heart Tour*.

ALEJANDRO MOGOLLO

HARD CANDY: *Release date: April 19, 2008. Billboard 200 peak: #1.* Hyped as Madonna's foray into R&B—she had even toyed with an image of herself in **blackface** as the Black Madonna for the cover—and her second **dance**-oriented album in a row after *Confessions on a Dance Floor*, *Hard Candy* wound up being driven by her collaborations with hit-seeking missiles **Justin Timberlake**, **Timbaland** and **Pharrell Williams**.

Some **fans** and critics were skeptical of the organic nature of Madonna suddenly choosing to **work** with established, au courant **talents**—and to hand over so much production **control** to them—at this stage in her career.

"I felt more introspective because I was writing with Pharrell and Justin," she told *Dazed & Confused* in 2008. "On *Confessions*, which I wrote all the lyrics to, I wanted to stay away from anything serious, even though the word 'confession' implies seriousness. I just wanted to make a frivolous dance record, and with this one I had to dig deeper and go to a different place ... For me, it's a true collaboration, intellectually and artistically."

The album hit #1 and boasted a genuinely popular lead single, but is generally regarded as one of Madonna's weakest efforts; *Hard Candy* is deserving of a fresh listen, as it

contains quite a few well-crafted tunes. It also led to Madonna's most successful tour, her *Sticky & Sweet Tour*.

Who knew when **"Candy Shop"** oozed out months early via Internet **leak** that it wasn't a sneak peek at a future single, but a viral invitation to Madonna's next phase, as a guilt-free purveyor of guilty pleasures more closely resembling her first-album self than any other persona in her extensive inventory? When that song first began making the rounds, the reaction was mainly "underwhelmed." The chief complaint was that Madonna sounded awkward, too white and too old to pull off urban sass. A 49-year-old singing about the virtues of her Turkish delight? **Ageism**, the world's oldest repression. Madonna successfully reversed expectations with lead single **"4 Minutes,"** a bombastic hit that **candy**-coated those sourballs. Unwrapped, *Hard Candy* was revealed as a Halloween bag full of delicious goodies that ranged from favorite indulgences to new sensations and even an M-Dolla ... but absolutely no annoying pieces of fruit or bundles of pennies.

"Candy Shop," Madonna's fave track on the album, opens things up, having inspired both the title and the (queasily unfocused) **Steven Klein** album art. With a "You Should Be Dancing" (1976) command to "get up outta your seat" (not the last time you'll be asked to leave it) and a nod to **Prince**'s "I Would Die 4 U" (1984) sounding under the title verse, its hypnotic thump making it memorable against better judgment.

"4 Minutes" has been described as a "Timba-lake" song on which Madonna guests. The **original** leak that played on French radio did sound that way, but the final version—while remaining the most obvious stylistic departure for Madonna on the record—is the first hint that perhaps Madonna holds her own against/with her hired **guns**. Timbaland reserves a lengthy intro for his combo of beats and tics to get listeners marching to the beat of his own **drum** and Timberlake trades lines equally with his hostess, but Madonna sounds invigorated to be singing in a different way, one that leaves no room for her preferred hard "Rs."

"Give It 2 Me" is this album's **"Sorry,"** except having evolved to suit American radio (which rejected it anyway), taking on a more contemporary feel rooted in its eclectic combination of '80s pop—the throbbing opening similar to Matthew Wilder's "Break My Stride" (1983)—and a pleasantly jarring hip-hop interlude: "Get stupid! Get stupid! Get stupid! Don't stop it!" Compare that to Madonna's lofty, "Let's get unconscious, honey," from 1994's **"Bedtime Story."** Though "Give It 2 Me" missed the US Top 40 by a lot, it and some of Williams's other work on the album shares much with Robin Thicke's "Blurred Lines" (2013), another Williams joint. *Hard Candy* was a little ahead of its time.

"Heartbeat" is an overlooked morsel. Opening with what could be a fetal heartbeat and going on to define the life force of music from an almost childlike perspective, the song offers an abruptly softer Madonna both vocally and lyrically, but one who matures to a state of ecstasy with the revelation that dancin' makes her feel beautiful, which echoes **"Into the Groove."**

The **guitar** in the beginning of **"Miles Away"** recalls **"Don't Tell Me,"** and Madonna's vocal is lovely as she recounts "a fuzzy **dream**" from which she's just awoken. The first song on the record to touch on a personal issue outside of the freeing nature of dance, "Miles Away" is not angry like previous relationship songs (**"Till Death Do Us Part"** from *Like A Prayer*), even though its lyrics paint an unhappy moment between two people whose lives keep them geographically, and sometimes emotionally, distant. After all the worry that her collaborators would dominate Madonna, it's worth noting that Timbaland and Timberlake turned in this track, the album's most recognizable "mid-tempo Madonna" number, a successor to songs like **"The Power Of Good-Bye"** and **"Bad Girl,"** albeit also a direct descendant of Nelly Furtado's "All Good Things (Come to an End)" (2006).

Madonna's comfort with Timba-lake is clear on this song. "I just knew I wanted to collaborate with Pharrell and Justin. I needed to be inspired and thought, 'Well, who's making records I like?' So I went, 'I like that guy and I like that guy.' It's not like we hit it off right away. Writing is very intimate. You have to be vulnerable and it's hard to do that with strangers. I had ups and downs before everybody got comfortable, but I grew very fond of Pharrell and Justin," she told *Vanity Fair* in 2008.

Following a song about marital distance is, logically, **"She's Not Me."** Coming on strong—the "Bette Davis Eyes" (1981) opening could be a series of sampled **bitch**-slaps even if the music is a heavenly wash of '70s **disco** strings—"She's Not Me" brings out Madonna at her cattiest. This song would rip her **"Thief Of Hearts"** to shreds. Any woman competing with Madonna for a man should be prepared for a battle, as evidenced by this epic, layered song. Toward the middle, after a cold list of reasons why Madonna would win any man-battle, she says in a **voice** that could be a 20-year-old's, "I know I can do it better." Then out comes the **Donna Summer** whistle from "Bad Girls" (1979) and, eventually, Williams chimes in with a Sylvester falsetto that weirdly works. Wendy Melvoin from Wendy & Lisa is name-checked and contributes a riff.

"Incredible" is an exhausting, rockin' **Prince**-esque number, almost seeming to start mid-sentence, full of bluster and energy. Its content pairs it with "Miles Away" in that it's Madonna's call for a relationship intervention.

Out of nowhere, **"Beat Goes On"** appears, totally unrecognizable from a version that had previously leaked. With the pure, infectious fun of **"Holiday"** or "Into the Grove" and the call to arms of **"Express Yourself,"** Madonna and a spirited Williams sing of the need to hurry and "get up outta your seat" over a posh house beat and a twinkling sonic blanket of bells. Her "hey!" most prominently reminds one of Art Of Noise's "Close (To The Edit)" (1984). **Kanye West** smoothly inserts a cocky, devilish rap. Kanye's rap is slippery because it could almost be read as a cynical explanation for working with Madonna: "It's an impromptu 'I want you'" could refer to Madonna bumping

HARD CANDY

Standard Edition (1-12)

iTunes Store Pre-Order,
Japanese Edition (1-12, A)

Deluxe Edition
(1-12, B, C, D, A)

Limited Collector's
Edition Candy Box
(1-12, E, F)

Limited Edition LP
(1-12, G, H)

① "Candy Shop"
(Madonna/Pharrell
Williams)-4:16, produced
by the Neptunes/Madonna

② "4 Minutes"
feat. Justin Timberlake
and Timbaland
(Madonna/Timbaland/
Justin Timberlake/Danja)
-4:04, produced by
Timbaland/Justin Timberlake/Danja

③ "Give It 2 Me"
(Madonna/Pharrell
Williams)-4:48, produced
by the Neptunes/Madonna

④ "Heartbeat"
(Madonna/Pharrell
Williams)-4:04, produced
by the Neptunes/Madonna

⑤ "Miles Away"
(Madonna/Timbaland/
Justin Timberlake/Danja)
-4:49, produced by
Timbaland/Justin Timberlake/Danja

⑥ "She's Not Me"
(Madonna/Pharrell
Williams)-6:05, produced
by the Neptunes/Madonna

⑦ "Incredible"
(Madonna/Pharrell
Williams)-6:20, produced
by the Neptunes/Madonna

⑧ "Beat Goes On"
feat. Kanye West
(Madonna/Pharrell
Williams/Kanye West)
-4:27, produced by the
Neptunes/Madonna

⑨ "Dance 2night"
feat. Justin Timberlake
(Madonna/Timbaland/
Justin Timberlake/Hannon Lane)-5:03, produced
by Timbaland/Justin
Timberlake/Hannon Lane/
Demo Castellon

⑩ "Spanish Lesson"
(Madonna/Pharrell
Williams)-3:38, produced
by the Neptunes/Madonna

①① "Devil Wouldn't
Recognize You"
(Madonna/Timbaland/
Justin Timberlake/Danja/
Joe Henry)-5:09,
produced by Timbaland/
Justin Timberlake/Danja

①② "Voices"
(Madonna/Timbaland/
Justin Timberlake/Danja/
Hannon Lane)-3:40,
produced by Timbaland/
Justin Timberlake/Danja/
Hannon Lane

Ⓐ "Ring My Bell"
(Madonna/Pharrell
Williams)-3:54, produced
by the Neptunes/Madonna

Ⓑ "4 Minutes"
Peter Saves New York Edit
(Madonna/Timbaland/
Justin Timberlake/Danja)
-5:00, produced by Timbaland/Justin Timberlake/
Danja/Peter Rauhofer

Ⓒ "4 Minutes"
Junkie XL Remix Edit
(Madonna/Timbaland/
Justin Timberlake/Danja)
-4:38, produced by Timbaland/Justin Timberlake/Danja/Junkie XL

Ⓓ "Give It 2 Me"
Paul Oakenfold Edit
(Madonna/Pharrell
Williams)-4:59,
produced by the Neptunes/
Madonna/Paul Oakenfold

Ⓔ "4 Minutes"
Tracy Young House Edit
(Madonna/Timbaland/
Justin Timberlake/Danja)
-3:33, produced by
Timbaland/Justin Timberlake/Danja/Tracy Young

Ⓕ "4 Minutes"
Rebirth Remix Edit
(Madonna/Timbaland/
Justin Timberlake/Danja)
-3:42, produced by
Timbaland/Justin
Timberlake/Danja/
Demacio "Demo" Castellon

Ⓖ "4 Minutes"
Tracy Mixshow
(Madonna/Timbaland/Justin Timberlake/Danja)
-6:19, produced by
Timbaland/Justin Timberlake/Danja/Tracy Young

Ⓗ "4 Minutes"
Peter Saves New York
(Madonna/Timbaland/
Justin Timberlake/Danja)
-10:52, produced by Timbaland/Justin Timberlake/
Danja/Peter Rauhofer

Japanese flyer for
Madonna's "black
album"

into him while recording; "I used my celeb to get this one" is obvious; "What's left now?" could refer to Madonna trying the urban route; "I'm a professional, I admit that" sounds like a defense. And "**Fame** is a **drug**, wanna hit that? 'Cuz I know exactly where to get that—did you get that?" might apply to Madonna's fame or to Kanye's more current strain of it and her need to co-opt that to stay relevant.

"**Dance 2night**" is a slinky slow-grind that seems tailor-made for American radio, even if it lacks the pure-Madonna personality that emanates from some of Williams's contributions. Madonna's voice is again prominent, and yet goes through some unfamiliar exercises—her lower range is put to use, but she never stagnates into her overused "**Erotica**" intonation.

"**Spanish Lesson**" is an uninventive kind of song for both Madonna and Williams in that she's already had her

The *Hard Candy* era brought us together as a group, and we have enjoyed many M adventures since 2008. We have been fans since the '80s. We hail from all over the world, the epitome of "every nation." We tend to be a goofy bunch and we love to laugh, we like to get creative and we want to petition Merriam-Webster to add a new Madonna related phrase: "Madonnarhea," that delicate state between rapt excitement and extreme GI distress that is usually experienced during ticket pre-sales, also triggered heavily on the day of shows and usually during the procurement of any promo items (for the collectors in our group). Total lifetime M shows = 279 starting with the *Who's That Girl World Tour* ... Our respective mamas would not let us travel for *The Virgin Tour*. (We are actively practicing collective forgiveness for that.) Thanks to Madonna for all the great times, and here's to many more!

L TO R: STEVE FOSTER (BELFAST, NI), STEVEN YANY (WORCESTER, MA), RAVEN ROBLES (FLORIDA), GEORGE STANCHEV (BULGARIA/LONDON UK), KOSTA KALOGEROGIANNIS (NEW YORK), SAMMY TANNER (WASHINGTON, DC), HOWIE CHEN (NEW YORK), TRINA HISTON (DUBLIN, IRELAND/SAN FRANCISCO), JESÚS ROCA (LA CORUÑA SPAIN), AND MICHELE RUIZ (BROOKLYN, NY)

MEGA-FAN SPOTLIGHT: HARD CANDY CREW

"*CANDY* FINDS MADONNA DROPPING HER KABBALAH STRING ON THE DANCE FLOOR AND READOPTING AN AMERICAN ACCENT TO OFFER UP AN UNPRETENTIOUS, NONSTOP DANCE PART"
—CHRIS WILLMAN, *ENTERTAINMENT WEEKLY* (2008)

"MADONNA CAN STILL SCOFF AT WANNABES HALF HER AGE BECAUSE SHE'S STAYED SO FLEXIBLE WITH HER SOUND."—CARYN GANZ, *ROLLING STONE* (2008)

"... [P]ERHAPS THIS WINNING ALBUM'S GREATEST ACHIEVEMENT IS KEEPING CLASSIC MADONNA FANS HAPPY WHILE ENGAGING A YOUNGER AUDIENCE. IT'S BECOME FASHIONABLE TO SLAG OFF MADONNA FOR TURNING 50 THIS YEAR, BUT SHE PROVES ONCE AGAIN SHE WAS BUILT TO LAST."—KEO NOZARI, *NEXT* (2008)

slightly condescending Spanish **flirtation** ("**La Isla Bonita**"), but the actual execution is tarted up a lot with an urgency to Madonna's vocal that echoes "Incredible" but works much better here. Still, few fans like this song.

"**Devil Wouldn't Recognize You**" strongly resembles Timberlake's "Cry Me A River" (2002), even though Madonna had had the skeleton of this song for years prior to its inclusion on *Hard Candy*. The refrain is so edgy and deeply felt, and she allows the story to unfold as dramatically as the Eagles on "Hotel California" (1977). It's hard to make such a slow song so hummable and catchy, but that's what happens here. Michael Stipe once asked Madonna her favorite songs on *Hard Candy*; she chose "Candy Shop" and this one.

Rounding things out is "**Voices**," a jazzy, spooky song with an opening by Timberlake ("Who is the master ... and who is the slave?") that would have been at home at the very beginning of Queen's "Bohemian Rhapsody" (1975). The piano ends the song and ends the album with just a little touch of star quality.

Madonna seemed to be using *Confessions On A Dance Floor* to regroup from the (unfair) commercial and artistic failure of *American Life*; she did a whole record that could be danced to. But if *Confessions* was really *Concessions*, *Hard Candy* seems to have represented a genuine personal embrace of both melodic and beat-driven pop music, deeply felt themes and, simply, fun, but with her characteristic offerings of insight throughout.

Madonna told **John Norris** when he asked about why she collaborated with the artists she did on this record: "Because they're good and I like their shit."

Sometimes the simplest answer is probably the right one.

Hard Candy wound up selling over 4 million copies worldwide (with one major hit single), fewer than *American Life* (with no major hit), which was more a reflection of dwindling **album sales** in general than of dwindling interest in Madonna.

HARD CANDY FITNESS: In 2010, Madonna and her manager **Guy Oseary** partnered with 24 Hour Fitness CEO Mark Mastrov to launch **gyms** across the globe, their motto being "Harder is better." The centers have been rolled out in Australia, Canada, Chile, Germany, Italy and **Russia**, with Madonna making personal appearances at some of their launch events. She even did a full workout with some Toronto **fans** in 2014.

An affiliated series of **fitness** videos called *Addicted to Sweat* features Madonna's former trainer, **Nicole Winhoffer.**

HARING, KEITH: *May 4, 1958–February 16, 1990.* Young, instantly influential graffiti artist who helped revolutionize pop **art** in the '80s with his quirky radiant babies and **dogs**. His simplistic images addressed complex, sometimes taboo issues—**sexuality** and war in particular—in ways that were immediately accessible to any viewer. His push to make art universal led him to create many **works** on the **New York** subway system, pieces that today are worth hundreds of thousands of dollars.

Haring went from being arrested for defacing public property to being paid $20,000 per canvas while still in his early twenties.

Madonna hung around with the same crowd as Haring, becoming close friends with him. She told *Rolling Stone* in 2009, "I was introduced to Keith by a roommate, but I had already seen his work on the streets, subways and buildings. Then we started hanging out at **Danceteria** and Mudd Club [formerly 77 White St., NY, NY] and **The Roxy**. The Rock Steady crew was there. We'd **dance**, we'd watch breakdancing crews there and on the street."

On the occasion of Haring's first major retrospective at the Whitney (then 945 Madison Ave., NY, NY; now 99 Gansevoort St., NY, NY) on June 25, 1997, Madonna said, "Keith's work started in the street, and the first people who were interested in his art were the people who were interested in me. That is, the black and Hispanic community. We were two odd birds in the same environment, and we were drawn to the same world—and inspired by it ... Because we both became very commercial and started making lots of **money**, people eliminated us from the realm of being artists. When Keith and I were just beginning to soar, our contemporaries and peers showed all this hostility."

By all accounts, they were totally simpatico. She even slept on Haring's couch for a spell before finding success, which gave Haring—a libertine in his own right—an eyeful when it came to Madonna's sex life.

"Haring would get boys from Madonna," DJ Johnny Dynell said of their friendship.

Haring came out as HIV positive, using his status to spread the word about safer sex and about the importance of helping, not stigmatizing, people with **AIDS**. His harmless, cute, geeky face made for an effective **PSA**; it and he were impossible not to **love.**

Madonna's use of Haring's work includes her wearing of many items he hand painted, most spectacularly a hot-pink skirt and jacket for his May 16, 1984, **birthday** party at Paradise Garage (formerly 84 King St., NY, NY), at which she sang **"Dress You Up"** (six months prior to the song's release on *Like a Virgin*). She also wore a lime-green-and-black **Vivienne Westwood** skirt with Haring's designs in her **"Borderline"** video (and in more than one photo shoot) and a Haring leather jacket on *Solid Gold* and *Top of the Pops* in 1984 that Madonna has said she'd "never give up." Haring designed the cover for the *A Very Special Christmas* album, to which Madonna donated her rendition of **"Santa Baby."**

Madonna's **"Into the Groove"** performance on her *Sticky & Sweet Tour* was wholly inspired by Haring's work.

Their bond was so special that she was among the intimate group that gathered at an apartment party shortly before Haring's **death** from AIDS to say good-bye.

Today, Madonna owns a number of Haring **originals**, including four newspaper-based pieces that Haring and **Andy Warhol** collaborated on as **wedding** gifts when Madonna married **Sean Penn.**

"Even with his massive success, Keith still came out and said, 'I have AIDS, I'm gay.' He didn't worry if it was going to jeopardize his career, he just went with it. He gave all people courage to be strong and to stare death in the face."-MADONNA (1990)

HARIS, NIKI: *b. April 17, 1962.* Along with **Donna De Lory**, one of Madonna's two most well known backup singers. Haris **worked** with Madonna from the *Who's That Girl World Tour* (1987) through the *Drowned World Tour* (2001).

Haris's first meeting with Madonna sounds like every singer's **dream** audition. "They called me. It was a basic audition with about two hundred girls. I begged [Madonna] if I could go first, because I thought I wouldn't get the gig. She said that I could go first. Then basically she said, 'Everybody can go home, I found what I need ...'"

The tricky spelling of Haris's professional name came about when **Warner Bros.** misspelled her name on her first paycheck, kind of the Madonna-as-Ellis-Island **school** of nomenclature.

Haris was for years a fixture in Madonna's performances, including being on hand for the 1989 **MTV Video Music Awards** performance of **"Express Yourself"** (the first introduction of **vogueing** to Madonna's bag of tricks) and in the music videos for both **"Vogue"** and **"Music."** She was a potent screen presence in *Truth or Dare*, coming across as earthy and real.

Haris was never a pushover. For starters, she passed on appearing in Madonna's **"Like a Prayer"** video. "I have to pay attention to … what's, y'know, right for me," Haris explained. "No, it was not right for me to do that video, but not because she was dancing in church, because in my church we **dance** and we praise Him. But burning crosses does mean something to me and I couldn't dance in front of a burning cross because that means something to me as a black woman. So, but—it doesn't mean I'm against Madonna. It might be right for her. Go for it. She's gotta do what she's gotta do."

On Madonna's *Drowned World Tour*, Haris initially refused to style her **hair** into a Mohawk because she associated it with Aryan youth. "I fought her tooth and nail. It got really hairy for a while. She felt like I was fighting her, and how could I do this to her, and she thought I was her friend." Haris finally caved.

After battling through serious injuries and giving birth at age 41, Haris was replaced on Madonna's *Re-Invention World Tour* by **Siedah Garrett**. It is understood that the parting of ways—officially so she could spend more time with her child—was not 100% harmonious, even though Madonna threw Haris a **baby shower.** Haris commented negatively on the tour, dubbing it "regurgitation."

Still, by 2009, Haris viewed her Madonna years positively. "Maybe there was some drama, but I didn't buy into it. We were sisters for years. At the end of the day, really she is a gem and I'm so grateful."

Haris has gone on to a career as a successful jazz and dance-music artist. In 2015, she teamed up with De Lory to release a cover of **"Rain."**

HARPER'S BAZAAR: Venerable (this shit was launched in 1867) **fashion** magazine that has featured Madonna inside and on its cover many times, always memorably.

Perhaps Madonna's most bewitching appearance in *Bazaar*'s hallowed pages was its November 1984 issue, in a spread by **Francesco Scavullo** that featured shots of Madonna in black lace and a form-fitting, elasticized skirt by Comme des Garçons, her own boots and backwards-turned hat, a wild purple scarf with bronze bird clip, a snake bracelet and spooky **accessories** galore. The shoot was done to coincide with the release of *Like a Virgin.* Seen today, Scavullo's **work** makes one gasp at a lost vision of Madonna, the pagan goddess of lust and all things creepy-crawly.

For the May 1988 issue, Madonna's cover and layout, shot by Scavullo again, was to show off her demure brunette **look** while performing in *Speed-the-Plow.* Inside, she donned an unconventional straw hat with a big, juicy apple perched dead center like William Tell's son and a **Jean Paul Gaultier**–designed bodysuit that perfectly captured her playfulness. (The apple image made for a collectible cover, found only on the July 1988 Spanish-language edition.)

Her 1990 cover spread, shot by **Jean-Baptiste Mondino,** featured her as a metallic siren, cruising the country with her *Blond Ambition World Tour.*

Shooter Peter Lindbergh provided Madonna's May 1994 cover and layout, a series of translations of the spirit of **dance** owing much to Man Ray, which illustrated a short piece by Madonna describing her first encounter with **Martha Graham.**

In February 1999, Madonna covered the **magazine** as "Hatsumomo" from the 1997 novel *Memoirs of a Geisha,* shot by **Mario Testino.** Her obsession with geishas was nearly total that year.

By September 2003, Madonna was white again—*extremely* white, considering her cover was a blue-jeaned pose hyping her association with **Gap.**

The March 2006 issue featured a cover story shot by Sølve Sundsbø, presenting Madonna as a delicate, *Confessions on a Dance Floor* flower. As a bonus, the (now rare) subscriber's cover was a bold image showing three Madonnas posed together, electrifying in royal blue.

For *Bazaar*'s December 2011 issue, Madonna did something she doesn't do too often—she shared the cover. Madonna ceded valuable space to *W.E.* star Andrea Riseborough, posing protectively/possessively with her arm around the actor's neck.

Most recently, Madonna **flirted** with controversy, ignoring the scandal swirling around **Terry Richardson** by posing for him for the November 2013 issue of *Bazaar,* resulting in a genuinely arresting portfolio with medieval and Islamic overtones in which she showed off post-**Photoshop** cleavage—front 'n' **back.**

Along with these major appearances, Madonna has adorned the covers of the magazine's foreign editions. Perhaps the rarest two are the January 1987 German *Bazaar* featuring an Alberto Tolot cover and the May 1997 Russian *Harper's Bazaar* with a cover and spread by Mario Testino.

> "I was defiant. Hell-bent on surviving. On making it. But it was hard and it was lonely, and I had to dare myself every day to keep going."
> —MADONNA ON HER EARLY DAYS IN NYC, HARPER'S BAZAAR (2013)

HARRY, DEBBIE: *b. July 1, 1945.* Sultry, towheaded lead singer of the punk/rock/New Wave/**disco** group Blondie and, later, a solo act. Harry was a pioneer in incorporating **sexual** allure with brains in the music biz, wrote or cowrote many of the most famous songs with which she is associated and is universally acknowledged as a rock legend—as a part of Blondie, she was inducted into the **Rock and Roll Hall of Fame** in 2006.

Including hits like "Heart of Glass" (1979), "One Way or Another" (1979), "Call Me" (1980), "The Tide Is High" (1980) and "Rapture" (1981), Blondie's catalogue has aged almost as well as Harry.

Along with her rock cred, Harry acted on stage and in an eclectic assortment of films, including *Union City* (1980), *Downtown 81* (1981), *Videodrome* (1983), the ***Desperately Seeking Susan***-esque *Forever, Lulu* (1987), the John Waters classic *Hairspray* (1988) and *Heavy* (1995).

Harry is often cited as a precursor of Madonna, as if women evolve from one another. There is no doubt that Madonna was influenced by Debbie Harry, if only because Madonna herself has consistently cited Harry as an inspiration. But some critics, including downtown singer Bebe Buell, think Madonna ripped off Harry wholesale. Buell wrote on social media in 2015: "My personal Goddess has always been Debbie Harry who truly was/is **original** and has never, in my opinion, been given enough props from Madonna."

There are plenty of comparisons between Madonna and Harry as singers who acted and actors who rocked, but the actual content of their **work** has rarely overlapped in a substantial way, and their stage personae could not be more different. Harry in her prime had a somnambulant detachment that made her cool, untouchable. Madonna has always been a visceral performer, the kind of girl you could imagine beating you up or beating you off.

Of their musical output, Madonna's **"Thief of Hearts"** could be read as a bubblegum version of the earlier, more lethal Blondie single "Rip Her to Shreds" (1977) and Madonna's B-side delight **"Supernatural"** does seem to be an exploration of ghostly intercourse similar in content to "(I'm Always Touched by Your) Presence, Dear" (1977). Other than stretches like these, and a glancing similarity in style between early Blondie and Madonna's pre-**fame** rock demos, the artists' musical output diverges greatly. It would seem that Madonna's greatest debt to Harry is less creative than as an example of a woman in music expressing herself.

Harry has praised Madonna as "a great performer and a great **dancer**" with "determination and drive," and it's a miracle that she hasn't snapped after being asked her opinion on that subject in nearly every interview she's granted in the past 30 years. Harry has also called Madonna very "commercial" (a compliment ... she likes **money**!).

Harry's most candid assessment may be one she offered in 2011: "[Madonna] is so totally career-orientated and show biz–minded. I missed the boat on that one. If I had thought more, I would probably have been Madonna before she was ... She had some really great songs ... But she wasn't my favorite."

Harry has also shown up to several Madonna events, including the **New York** premiere of ***Truth or Dare*** and Madonna's 35th **birthday** party at **Castillo del Lago**, which she attended with **"Like a Prayer"** video director **Mary Lambert** (who directed Harry's "I Want That Man" in 1989).

Madonna has always sung Harry's praises. The first CD Madonna ever bought when vinyl started to die out was a Blondie greatest hits package.

In 2008, Harry was one of many music stars invited to ask Madonna a question for a *Q* **magazine** feature. She asked Madonna her motivation in life, to which Madonna replied, "The word 'no.'"

"In the very, very beginning, when I was just starting to write music and stuff, I, I was inspired by Debbie Harry because was very, she seemed very in charge of what she was doing and she, she also had a sort of ... wittiness about her and street smarts and, and I liked her. She was a role model."–MADONNA (1990)

"She has mentioned that I was important to her, and that's very satisfying. However, a check would be better!"–DEBORAH HARRY (1993)

HART, COREY: *b. May 31, 1962.* Canadian crooner and teen-mag heartthrob known for wearing his "Sunglasses at Night" (1984). In 1992, his *Attitude & Virtue* album contained the song "She's Everywhere," clearly inspired by Madonna. Sample lyrics: "Shocking **sexuality**/She's everywhere, creature of culture" and "Hear raptures playing on the radio/Now **New York** dilettantes are buying Ms. **Kahlo**."

"HAS TO BE": Japanese bonus track from ***Ray of Light*** that's as haunting and lonely as anything Madonna's ever recorded. It has a sound similar to Chris Isaak's "Wicked Game" (1989). It was included as the B-side of the **"Ray of Light"** single.

HATE: So much hate ... and it has plagued Madonna throughout her career. Hated for not having **talent** enough to warrant her success, for being **sexy** and embracing it, for being blunt, for not staying in touch with every person she ever met, for daring to speak with a long "A," for showing her body, for having political opinions, for lip-synching, for slagging off someone who was annoying her, for giving birth out of wedlock, for co-opting religious imagery, for aging, for having **plastic surgery**, for being a bad writer, for succeeding beyond anyone's wildest **dreams**, for wearing **grills**, for relying on **Photoshop**, for adopting a child from **Malawi** (twice!!!) and—ultimately—for being the Madonna she needs to be instead of the one other people want her to be.

Madonna has always been hated by more people than she's been **loved**, though she has had periods where enough people loved her that she's tasted incredible success. The hatred for Madonna has only intensified over the years; there was an (excruciatingly unfunny) *I Hate Madonna Handbook* and there are many sites devoted to taking the piss out of Madonna. Imagine spending so much time on something you don't like?

But as long as it doesn't lead to physical attacks, perhaps all the crankiness is for the best—if everyone loves you, you're **boring** as hell ... or successfully pretending to be.

–JUDITH REGAN

"What babies did she murder to warrant such press pleasure from her temporary popularity dip?"—LIZ SMITH (1993)

••
"I SEEM TO BE THE GIRL THEY HATE TO LOVE."
—MADONNA, *GRAFFITI* (1985)
••

"MORE VAMP THAN VAMPIRE, MADONNA HAS BEEN VILIFIED IN THE ROCK PRESS AS IF SHE WERE AN INVITATION TO A GANG BANG AND A THREAT TO THE NATION'S MORALS. THE ANTI-MADONNA DIATRIBES HAVE GONE BEYOND PROFESSIONAL CRITICISMS OF HER MUSIC, ACT, PERSONA; THEY'VE BECOME STABBINGLY PERSONAL. MADONNA BASHERS SEEM TO BE TRYING TO CARVE 'DIE, BITCH' IN HER HIGH-SCHOOL YEARBOOK. WHY ARE THEY ALL IN SUCH A RIGHTEOUS HUFF? NO ONE CONSIDERED TINA TURNER A THREAT TO THE REPUBLIC WHEN SHE MADE MOANING, THROATY LOVE TO THE MICROPHONE IN *GIMME SHELTER* [1970]. PRINCE DIDN'T EVEN CATCH AS MUCH GRIEF FOR FLOUNCING ABOUT LIKE A REGENCY-DANDY PIMP IN *PURPLE RAIN* [1984]. COULD IT BE THAT WHITE CRITICS *EXPECT* BLACK PERFORMERS TO BE LOOSE?"—JAMES WOLCOTT, *VANITY FAIR* (1985)
••

"MADONNA IS THE KIND OF WOMAN WHO COMES INTO YOUR ROOM AT 3 A.M. AND SUCKS YOUR LIFE OUT."—MILO MILES, *BOSTON PHOENIX* (1980S)
••

"WHAT ARE WE GOING TO DO ABOUT MADONNA? IS SHE LUCIFER'S REVENGE FOR JULIE ANDREWS? OR JUST NANCY REAGAN'S FREUDIAN FLIPSIDE IN DISGUISE?"

—DAVE HILL, *DESIGNER BOYS & MATERIAL GIRLS: MANUFACTURING THE '80S POP DREAM* (1986)
••

"IF SOMEONE BECOMES HUGELY SUCCESSFUL, THE PUBLIC BECOMES DISGUSTED WITH THEM AND BEGINS TO WISH THE STAR WOULD SLIP ON A BANANA PEEL."—MADONNA (1988)
••

"MADONNA IS AN AWFUL, UGLY, DULL PERSON WHO BY BEING COMPLETELY SHAMELESS, BLATANT AND CHEAP HAS BECOME SUCCESSFUL … IF SHE GOT A GUN AND BLEW HER OWN HEAD OFF I DOUBT IF ANYONE WOULD NOTICE."

—PINK FLOYD BASSIST ROGER WATERS (1992)
••

HAYES, DARREN: *b. May 8, 1972.* One half of the tremendously popular duo Savage Garden, Hayes, who has been solo since 2001, is an outspoken (and out) Madonna booster.

In 2007, Hayes covered **"Ray of Light"** sensationally for the **TV** show *Soundtrack of My Life*. Two years later, he offered up a faithful cover of Madonna's **"Dress You Up."** In 2012, he was tackling **"Like a Prayer"** on BBC Radio 2.

••
"I FELT THAT PEOPLE WERE BEING *UNBELIEVABLY* CRUEL TO ME FOR NO REASON, AND WHEN I LOST CONFIDENCE IN NOT [SIC] BEING ABLE TO FEEL LIKE THERE WAS A CERTAIN SORT OF, LIKE, LEVEL OF BEHAVIOR THAT I COULD DEPEND ON IN OTHER PEOPLE, A CERTAIN DECENCY. WHEN I LOST CONFIDENCE IN THAT, I BEGAN TO LOSE CONFIDENCE IN MYSELF, YES."—MADONNA (1999)
••

"THE INTERESTING THING, HOWEVER, IS HOW VITRIOLIC MUCH OF THIS ATTENTION IS, AND WHERE THAT VITRIOL IS COMING FROM. TAKE CAMILLE PAGLIA, FOR INSTANCE, WRITING IN SALON LAST WEEK OF THE 'HORRIFYING PAPARAZZI PIX OF MADONNA'S WAN FACE LOOKING AS RESCULPTED AS A PLASTIC DOLL,' AND OF THE 'BRASSY' COVER IMAGE FOR MADONNA'S LATEST CD, *HARD CANDY*, 'WITH THAT OSTENTATIOUSLY EXPOSED CROTCH AND HARD-BITTEN FACE LOLLING ITS TONGUE LIKE A DISSOLUTE OLD STREETWALKER … STILL HAMMERING AT SEX AS IF IT'S MADONNA'S LAST, DESPERATE SELLING POINT.' OR JULIE BURCHILL (NOT ONE, IT IS TRUE, TO BE RELIED ON FOR A CONSISTENT OR FAIR POINT OF VIEW), WHO BEGAN BY INVEIGHING AGAINST MADONNA'S 'VILE VEINY HANDS, THAT SAD STRINGY NECK—YUCK!' THEN PROCEEDED TO BRING UP THE CROTCH SHOTS IN MADONNA'S 1992 BOOK, *SEX*. 'VISIONS OF THAT GREASY MUFF, WHICH ONE COULD EASILY HAVE FRIED AN EGG ON WITHOUT BENEFIT OF OIL, HAUNT ME TILL THIS VERY DAY.' GERMAINE GREER, WRITING IN THE *SUN*, CALLED HER THE 'ELDERLY MOTHER OF LOURDES, NEARLY 12, ROCCO EIGHT, AND DAVID BANDA, NEARLY THREE.' SINCE WHEN DID ELDERLY MOTHER (OF A 12-YEAR-OLD, MEANING SHE WAS 38 WHEN SHE HAD LOURDES) BECOME A TERM OF INSULT? AT LEAST TWO OF THESE WOMEN WOULD CALL THEMSELVES FEMINISTS."

—AIDA EDEMARIAM, *THE GUARDIAN* (2008)
••

"I THINK MY BEHAVIOR AND MY LIFESTYLE THREATEN A LOT OF SOCIAL NORMS …"—MADONNA (2012)
••

In 2014, Hayes wrote a thoughtful piece for *Attitude* arguing why the world needed a brilliant new Madonna record, in which he pointed out that her best songs are anthems of "freedom, of escape and empowerment. Some might call them the soundtrack to coming out." His essay explained the allure of Madonna to **gay** men, but also stressed the one aspect of her existence that her critics try hardest to ignore: the potency and accomplishment of her music:

"I was 12 years old when *The Virgin Tour* was released on videocassette. When other boys in my **school** were sneaking off to watch boobs in *Porky's* or glimpses of **nip slips** in *Conan the Barbarian* [both 1982], I was sat glued in front of the telly trying to learn the choreography from 'Dress You Up.' I saw the sheer audacity in this woman who was teasing, nay, *demanding* the crowd beg for more. 'I said ... Do you want to hear some more!?' she screamed during an impossibly long pause in the middle of **'Holiday'**. And boy did I."

So did she come through with *Rebel Heart*? On December 23, 2014, Hayes tweeted: "The new @Madonna music. Wow. Modern, present, engaged, vital, adventurous, divisive. I missed this. Welcome **back** M."

HEALTHY: Madonna's vintage, midriff-baring tank top with the phrase "HEALTHY" across the chest and **"SWIMMER"** across the **back** became iconic via her **Ken Regan** shoot for *People*'s cover, all the more so because one of Regan's outtakes landed on the cover of *Penthouse*. She wore the same shirt on a Japanese show, lip-synching to **"Like a Virgin."**

Back in the day, Madonna gave the tank to manager **Freddy DeMann**'s daughter. In May 2014, the tank and a pair of shoes Madonna once wore were sold at **auction** by Julien's, realizing $15,000.

"HEARTBEAT": This *Hard Candy* track was cowritten by Madonna and **Pharrell Williams** and coproduced by Madonna and the **Neptunes**. The emotionally naked song was given a modern **dance**–driven, spare live performance on the first leg of the *Sticky & Sweet Tour* and was mashed up with **"Best Friend"** for an *MDNA Tour* interlude.

"HEARTBREAKCITY": Stirring breakup ballad from *Rebel Heart*, performed on the *Rebel Heart Tour*, that sounds highly personal (how many listeners can relate to having a **love** interest who was seeking "**fame** and fortune?"). It was written by Madonna, **Avicii**, Arash Pournouri, NoNoNo, Delilah, Michel Richard Flygare, Salem Al Fakir, Magnus Lidehäll and Vincent Pontare; it was produced by Madonna, Avicii, Fakir, Lidehäll, Pontare and Astma & Rocwell of NoNoNo.

HEERY, GARY: Australian photographer hired by Carin Goldberg to shoot the album cover of *Madonna.* He'd been in **NYC** for less than two years when he got the call for the **job**, which he executed in his Soho studio. Heery's **work** captured Madonna with maximum impact, blending '40s glamour lighting with punk immediacy. His entire shoot has since **leaked**; there wasn't one bad snap.

Madonna's jewelry from the Heery shoot has sold for astonishing amounts, including the coin bracelet (for $8,000) that she also wore on many other occasions.

She'd been instructed by Goldberg to arrive in her own clothes: "You've got your thing, just do it." She just did it, and so did Heery.

HEIGHT: Like a small–fry. Madonna, such an enormous personality, is actually a diminutive figure, all of 5'3.5." Aside from her "thin lips," her small stature is the one thing about her physicality that Madonna has consistently said she'd like to change.

"HELLO AND GOODBYE": A brief *Evita: The Complete Motion Picture Music Soundtrack* song in which Madonna's Evita, cold as ice, dismisses Perón's (**Jonathan Pryce**) mistress (Andrea Corr).

HELLO, SUCKERS!: Movie musical based on the colorful life of actor, chorine and entrepreneur Texas Guinan that Madonna was **working** on prior to abandoning and using some of its songs on her subsequent albums. Guinan, who inspired the *Chicago* character "Velma Kelly" that Madonna came close to playing in a 2002 film, was famous for the catchphrase, "Hello, suckers!"

Martin Scorsese had been mentioned as a possible producer if it had become a movie, and Madonna was said to have been writing a script based on the **book** *Texas Guinan: Queen of the Nightclubs* by **Louise** Berliner (University of Texas, 1993).

Speaking about the aborted musical with *Attitude*, Madonna confirmed, "I wrote the music with lots of different people—a lot of it with **Pat Leonard**, some with **Mirwais**, a few things by myself." When she couldn't decide what to do with it—movie? West End musical?—she wound up harvesting some of it for her *Confessions on a Dance Floor* ("How High," "Future Lovers") and *Hard Candy* ("**Devil Wouldn't Recognize You**") albums.

Several **unreleased** songs are confirmed to exist from the sessions, including a couple that truly deserve a proper release on a future career retrospective.

HELL'S KITCHEN: According to a letter Madonna sent to *A Certain Sacrifice* director Stephen Jon Lewicki, she was living in an undesirable apartment at 36th St. between 9th and 10th Aves. in this now highly desirable area of Manhattan just before departing for **Paris** to boogie with **Patrick Hernandez**. Madonna remembers the place as "really seedy," which was why she "kept being mistaken for a hooker." Yes ... that was why.

HENRY, CARESSE: *September 23, 1965–March 31, 2010.* Caresse Kristen Henry Norman was hired to be Madonna's personal assistant on July 29, 1992. A vivacious, bright, strong woman who was well liked by many with whom she **worked**, she had by 1996 been promoted to the position of Madonna's personal manager.

Henry made a positive impression with **fans** and enjoyed a tight bond with Madonna. She managed her during *Evita*, *Ray of Light* and *Music*, all incredible successes, but was also on duty during *American Life*, when Madonna's career was ruled "over" in the media.

Why Madonna's relationship with Henry soured is the source of conflicting speculation, but in November 2004, Henry was fired via fax by Madonna in a note that read: "I am writing to advise you that the engagement of you and Puddy, Inc. as my personal manager has ended and that you and your company may no longer hold yourself out as my manager, or take any further action on my behalf." **Liz Rosenberg** was designated as the publicist who would (and did) handle all public announcements, and their legal bond was formally dissolved by May 2005.

Henry, who had also worked with **Paula Abdul**, **Ricky Martin**, Jessica Simpson and Joss Stone, took her own life just under five years later via shotgun, a terrible shock to the people around her. Madonna sent flowers to her funeral but issued no statement.

What drove Henry to commit suicide at 44? Her sister, Yvette Dobbie, bluntly stated, "Madonna and **Kabbalah** have blood on their hands." Her contention was that Madonna's involvement with Kabbalah had driven a wedge between the star and her manager, and that being fired had sent her into a downward spiral. Others in Madonna's inner circle said that Henry had battled **drugs** and refused rehab, so Madonna had no choice but to fire her. It is known that Henry was romantically involved with one of Madonna's bodyguards, which was said to have caused tension.

Still, to lay Henry's suicide at Madonna's **feet** seems more a product of personal anguish than reason.

Henry was succeeded as Madonna's manager briefly by the duo of **Angela Becker** and **Guy Oseary**, before Oseary took over solo.

HENRY, JOE: b. December 2, 1960. Singer-songwriter and guitarist who is married to Madonna's sister, **Melanie Ciccone.**

Madonna greatly admires her brother-in-law as a musician, and has occasionally collaborated with him. The two sang a duet called **"Guilty by Association"** in 1995; Henry also cowrote Madonna's enduring hit **"Don't Tell Me,"** her single **"Jump"** and the album tracks **"Devil Wouldn't Recognize You"** and **"Falling Free."**

Henry said of Madonna in 2007, "I've known her since I was 15 and she was 17, longer than I've known my wife. We have had a great relationship, and part of that was because I never needed anything from her. I recognized that we were in two different occupations. Not to disparage one ounce of her musicality, I was always of the belief that her persona was her career. Whether she was making a movie or writing a song or punching a photographer, it was all pushing a persona forward, and that was the real body of **work**. I was never tempted to slip a song to her at Thanksgiving."

HEPBURN, KATHARINE: May 12, 1907-June 29, 2003. One of Old Hollywood's most independent and **original** actors. Her film *Bringing Up Baby* (1938) was a direct inspiration for **Who's That Girl**, and Hepburn is name-checked in **"Vogue."**

In 1993, Hepburn admitted to never having even *seen* Madonna (or **Kevin Costner** or Julia Roberts, for that matter). "The type of thing she does is not of a great deal of interest to me, but I should have seen her. I'm lazy." It must have slipped her mind that she'd actually seen Madonna in **Speed-the-Plow** on Broadway on about May 5, 1988.

Both **Liz Smith** and **Cynthia McFadden**, who have interviewed Madonna multiple times, were close friends of Hepburn's.

HERNANDEZ, PATRICK: b. April 6, 1949. French **disco** singer whose "Born to Be Alive" was one of the inescapable hits of 1979.

In the spring of 1979, Hernandez's producer Jean Vanloo and promoter Jean-Claude Pellerin came to the US to cast dancers for *The Patrick Hernandez Revue*, an international production they envisioned for their client. Madonna, who was auditioning for everything in **NYC** at the time, was among the hundreds of girls who showed up, looking very punk rock. She was asked to make up **dances** on the spot to music she'd never heard before.

Vanloo's wife told biographer **Barbara Victor**, "She was fantastic, and to this day, I'm convinced that with all her videos and stage shows, she holds **back**, because I never saw anyone with a better dance technique."

She had the dancing part down, but when asked to sing, Madonna … *refused!* She told them she was a dancer, not a singer. Having no choice, she went ahead and sang "Happy **Birthday**" and got the gig. She had aced the audition so hard that her new benefactors wanted to groom her for solo stardom, seeing her as a new Edith Piaf.

In May 1979, Madonna—teasingly called "Mademoiselle Bijoux" by her new boyfriend **Dan Gilroy** and pal Curtis Zale—arrived in **Paris**. Though she stayed a few months in a plush apartment owned by Pellerin and his wife (a 10-room pad that took up an entire floor on Rue de Courcelles), Madonna wound up bored as the revue failed to materialize, living off the producers but never getting a chance to show off her skills.

"I overdubbed vocals on already-recorded disco tracks, but basically it was pretty **boring**. As far as actual productive musical stuff I had nothing to show for the [time] I spent there," she told *Sounds* in 1983. "Eventually, I just got fed up."

An affair with Hernandez did nothing to stave off a bad feeling that she was on the wrong path and a song composed for her called "She's a Real Disco Queen" so rubbed her the wrong way that she never recorded it. Madonna quit and returned to NYC by July 1979.

The episode had given Madonna some life experiences, including a nearly fatal bout with pneumonia, a drive to Belgium for a meal (which came back to haunt her when she was wrongly sued for plagiarizing **"Frozen"** years later) and a quickie trip to Tunisia, her first visit to **Africa**.

It says a lot about Madonna's artistic drive that even though she'd been starving in NYC, she chose to go back there rather than be wined and dined ad nauseam in Paris.

Hernandez's people had lit a fire in Madonna; when she returned to NYC, she began writing songs and the rest is history.

In 1991, when Madonna was in France, she declined an offer to be on **TV** with Hernandez.

> "At the time I met Madonna in New York, she was running after the best opportunity, anything that paid her something to survive. And I'm a nice guy, I never exploited her. I only helped her." —PATRICK HERNANDEZ (2001)

HERNIA: Shortly after Madonna's **Grammys** performance in February 2006, she entered Cedars-Sinai Medical Center (8700 Beverly Blvd. LA, CA) for a hernia operation. If you're wondering how she got a hernia, check out the music video for **"Sorry."**

HEROES: Madonna's heroes, circa 1990, were **Spike Lee, Public Enemy,** Mikhail Gorbachev, **Mother** Teresa, Czech leader Vaclav Havel and **Martha Graham.** In 2015, she said the person she idolizes most is Paul Farmer, a doctor and activist who has **worked** wonders in **Haiti** and Rwanda.

"HE'S A MAN": The first song on *I'm Breathless: Music from and Inspired by the Film Dick Tracy,* written and produced by Madonna and **Patrick Leonard,** really holds up against that album's **Stephen Sondheim** compositions, and references a favorite motif (**guns**) in the context of a **flirty** period ditty.

"HEY YOU": *Release date: May 17, 2007. Billboard Hot 100 peak: NA.* Saccharine ballad Madonna wrote, and which became her first coproduction with **Pharrell Williams** to be heard when it was released to raise awareness of climate change in conjunction with the **Live Earth** concert and campaign. The single was made available for free via MSN and other platforms, and Madonna sang it at Live Earth. "Hey You" seems to have been spawned by the **unreleased** track "Keep the Trance."

"HIGH FLYING, ADORED": Stirring *Evita* duet between Madonna and **Antonio Banderas** found on *Evita: The Complete Motion Picture Music Soundtrack* that's one of Banderas's finest moments from the project. In the song, Evita coyly claims her rise to **power** was a matter of being in the right place at the right time, not a matter of the right man being in her at the right time.

"HISTORY": Recorded during the *Confessions on a Dance Floor* sessions, this tune didn't make the cut, but was used as the B-side of the single **"Jump."** The electronic

dance song with tribal **drums** warns against the tendency for history to repeat itself. Madonna's lead vocal doesn't kick in until after the 1:45 mark, whereupon she notes that "we" are not very generous toward people in need. The song is a remix of the earlier demo "History (Land of the Free)," which is superior (and far less repetitive) and yet remains **unreleased.**

HITLER, ADOLF: *April 20, 1889–April 30, 1945.* One of history's most reprehensible monsters, the Nazi leader and Saddam Hussein were both mentioned in the same breath as Madonna by Boston University president John R. Silber in 1991, in a speech that compared her message with theirs. *Huh?* Such a callous comparison is an extreme example of the overblown critical reception Madonna receives. Her next project might be X-rated or controversial or even *lame,* but it probably won't be a **death** camp.

HIV: SEE: **AIDS.**

H&M: Swedish retailer known for cute but inexpensive clothing for men, women and kids. On August 24, 2006, a series of print ads featuring Madonna (shot by Rankin) were unveiled to promote an affordable line of track suits ($29.90 for the top, $24.90 for the bottom ... why are tops always more valued?) as part of a deal in which H&M also clothed Madonna's entire 150-person *Confessions Tour* troupe, some of whom (including **Stuart Price**) appeared in ads with her.

Part two of the collaboration came on March 22, 2007, when H&M launched the M by Madonna line. This time around, Madonna was said to have designed every detail of its short-sleeved tops, kimonos, jersey dresses, blazers and pencil skirts. The new ad campaign, shot by **Steven Klein,** presented Madonna as a workplace dominatrix, and an accompanying TV **commercial** she directed with Dan Cadan (who had **worked** on four **Guy Ritchie** films including *Swept Away* and on Madonna's *I'm Going to Tell You a Secret,* and who had previously directed for H&M) was Madonna's directorial debut.

HOFFMAN, PHILIP SEYMOUR: *July 23, 1967–February 2, 2014.* One of the most respected stage and film actors of his time, Hoffman won the **Oscar** for *Capote* (2005) and was able to nimbly balance his appearances in artistically edgy films like *Boogie Nights* (1997), *Magnolia* (1999) and *A Most Wanted Man* (2014) with appearances in mainstream fare, most notably the *Hunger Games* series (2013–2015). Hoffman, a former heroin addict, had a relapse and was found dead in his bathroom.

Hoffman and John Ortiz, co-artistic directors of the LAByrinth Theater Company (155 Bank St., NY, NY), along with playwright Stephen Adly Guirgis, presented Madonna with the first Dave Hoghe **Award** for her financial support of the company. She helped bring *Jesus Hopped the A Train* to a legit **London** run.

In his intro of Madonna, Hoffman praised her for her "courage and longevity" and noted, "I found my libido when I was 15. There's nothing she won't do." Madonna thanked Hoffman for "providing me with such an undignified entrance!"

The benefit, on September 29, 2003, at the Daryl Roth Theatre (101 E. 15th St., NY, NY) attracted Kristen Johnston, Bebe Neuwirth, Ed Norton, Cynthia Rowley, Amy Sedaris, Justin Theroux, **Robin Williams** and Elijah Wood.

Upon hearing of Hoffman's **death** in 2014, Madonna tweeted: "Lost another Genius! What a tragedy. **Love** you P.S.H."

HOHNEN, JULIETTE: *b. circa 1965*. British **MTV** Europe on-air personality who married Steven Weber. (Weber suggested that Madonna and **Guy Ritchie** do *Swept Away*.)

Madonna became close with Hohnen after meeting her at a party in 1990, when Hohnen asked Madonna, who was pigging out at the buffet, "How can you eat so much and stay so thin?" The two became dancing buddies, even hitting the **AIDS** Dance-A-Thon in LA together. They attended the *Vanity Fair* party following the **Oscars** in 1997 as well as the 1998 premiere of the **Bruce Willis** movie *Mercury Rising*.

For the March 2000 cover of *Jane* **magazine**, Hohnen profiled Madonna, getting her to talk about her friendship with **Gwyneth Paltrow**, her desire to have another baby and her impending disaster flick *The Next Best Thing*.

"HOLD TIGHT": Sweeping *Rebel Heart* song with an incredible sense of optimism ("We're gonna be all right tonight"). It distinctly has the feel of a movie theme. The song was written by Madonna, **Diplo**, MoZella, Toby Gad, MNEK and Jr Blender; it was produced by Madonna.

"HOLIDAY": *Release date: September 7, 1983. Billboard Hot 100 peak: #16*. Madonna wasn't thrilled with her first album, *Madonna*, which was brilliantly produced by **Reggie Lucas** (hey, there's no accounting for taste), so she brought in her boyfriend **Jellybean Benitez** to do some remixing. Benitez also brought Madonna this song, written by Pure Energy's Curtis Hudson and Lisa Stevens, which had been rejected by Mary Wilson and Phyllis Hyman. Madonna **loved** it and immediately recorded it. It became the last completed song on the project, but would go on to become one of her most iconic hits.

"Holiday" was the first song Benitez produced and became Madonna's first Top 40 hit. "Madonna was going to happen whether I did it or somebody else did, but I'm sure 'Holiday' had a lot to do with it," Benitez told *Mixmag* in 2005.

When the song went Top 40, Madonna gave an interview to KTU in Boston, saying, "It's now Top 40 and hopefully it'll go Top 20; if it does, it's gonna open up a lot of doors for me. Um, it's done much better than we all hoped for, 'cause everyone kept saying, you know, 'This is another, y'know, **disco** record.' ... And my wish was that I would cross over with a real R&B record into the pop charts, and I did, so, that's, that was a real surprise and I'm really happy about it."

The song rose to #16 on the *Billboard* Hot 100. In the UK, it was released to great success three separate times.

Madonna lip-synched "Holiday" on *American Bandstand* (1984), *Di-Gei Musica* (Italy, 1983), *Discoring* (Italy, 1983), *Eurotops* (Germany, 1984), *Formula Ein* (Germany, 1984), *Hip-hop* (France, 1984), *Passeport pour la Forme* (France, 1984), *Solid Gold* (US, 1984), *Super Platine* (France, 1984), *Top of the Pops* (UK, 1984), *The Tube* (UK, 1984) and possibly others. Some of these performances, always with distinctive, aerobics-inspired choreography, were so elaborately filmed (check out the surreal *Les Enfants du Rock* performance on the beach in France, 1984) that the clips were later confused with lost or rejected official music videos for the song. In truth, "Holiday" was not granted a music video, unlike **"Burning Up"** before it and **"Lucky Star"** after.

In 1985, "Holiday" was on Madonna's *Live Aid* set list. Madonna has also performed this crowd-pleaser on many of her tours, rearranging it each time: *The Virgin Tour*, the *Who's That Girl World Tour*, the *Blond Ambition World Tour*, *The Girlie Show World Tour*, the *Drowned World Tour*, the *Re-Invention World Tour* and the 2009 leg of the *Sticky & Sweet Tour*. It was performed using classroom instruments by Madonna, **Jimmy Fallon** and the Roots on *The Tonight Show* in 2015, then became her *Rebel Heart Tour* encore. It was also the finale of her Melbourne *Tears of a Clown* performance.

"HOLLYWOOD" (SONG): *Release date: July 14, 2003. Billboard Hot 100 peak: NA*. The second *American Life* single continued the pattern of questioning American institutions, this time narrowing things down to the Hollywood lie of glamour and excess and easy living. Written and produced by Madonna and **Mirwais**, the song also—in a bravely self-defeating move—castigated radio for playing "the same song" and urged listeners to "change the channel." On a related note, "Hollywood" got next to no airplay, failing to chart on the *Billboard* Hot 100 (her first song to do so in 20 years, though not her last). It did become a big **dance** hit, but Madonna could sing a random person's **Twitter** feed and go to #1 on *that* chart.

The song was performed live on the *American Life* promo tour at Tower Records (formerly 1961 Broadway, NY, NY). More (in)famously, "Hollywood" is the song that Madonna sang—following a **"Like a Virgin"** intro—on the **MTV Video Music Awards**, when she kissed **Britney Spears** and **Christina Aguilera**. She also lip-synched it on *Top of the Pops*.

"Hollywood" was then mashed up with **"Into the Groove"** as part of Madonna's **Gap** ad campaign, resulting in **"Into the Hollywood Groove."** Even *that* failed to spark any interest in the punk-rock folk song about the empty glitz of the epicenter of the entertainment biz.

Madonna used the song as a dance interlude on her *Re-Invention World Tour*.

"HOLLYWOOD" (VIDEO): *Director: Jean-Baptiste Mondino, 2003.* When the video for Madonna's "Hollywood" debuted on **VH1** on June 23, 2003 (three weeks after it was shot from June 2–3 at Universal Studios), it was a big improvement over the edited version of **"American Life."** **Jean-Baptiste Mondino** shot Madonna as various women: **blonde**, brunette or redhead, take yer pick, decked out in glam and revealing period looks, dripping in jewelry that had belonged to the likes of Jean Harlow, Ginger Rogers and **Mae West**. The video had some echoes of Madonna's previous **work**—her blonde incarnation was reminiscent of her **"Express Yourself"** video character and images of Madonna hitchhiking, which appear on a **TV** screen, call to mind her **nude** hitching in *Sex.*

But the video's look was immediately identifiable for another reason: It was clearly an extended homage to the "sick and interesting" photography of **Guy Bourdin**, whose work Madonna had said in the past that she owned. Bourdin's son sued, claiming it was not merely an homage but theft; he apparently was not as bored as Madonna was with the concept of right and wrong. Madonna made things right, settling with him for somewhere in the neighborhood of half a million dollars.

It was all worth it for the opportunity to see Madonna receiving fake (?) Botox shots in the video—*that* was the sickest and most interesting part, and it didn't even come from Bourdin's estimable imagination.

"HOLY WATER": With 10 times the attitude of something like **"Queen's English,"** this clubby *Rebel Heart* song is polarizing for its blunt comparison of oral **sex** to worshiping **God**, for Madonna's angry little, **"Bitch**, get off my pole!"** and the declaration that, "Yeezus **loves** my **pussy** best!" (A **Kanye West** reference.) The titular liquid is, well, pussy juice. The song makes use of a **"Vogue"** sample as it encourages ladies to get what they deserve, making it a relative of **"Where Life Begins."**

This is the song **Prince** would write if he had a vagina and were still Prince. It was actually written by Madonna, Martin Kierszenbaum, **Natalia Kills**, Mike Dean, Kanye West and Tommy Brown, with production by Madonna, Dean, Charlie Heat and West.

Madonna characterized the song as humor in *Rolling Stone.* "But whenever I write about sex, I always do it tongue-in-cheek. That's the one thing that people misunderstand grossly about me. 'Holy Water' is obviously meant to be funny."

The song was given an R-rated performance on her *Rebel Heart Tour* that mixed nuns with stripper poles.

HONEYMOON: Mr. and Mrs. **Sean Penn** had a fabulous honeymoon at the Highlands Inn (now Hyatt Carmel Highlands, 120 Highlands Dr., Carmel, CA) in suite 429. They stayed for four days and nights. When they emerged for drinks at Clint Eastwood's Hog's Breath Inn (San Carlos St., Carmel, CA), the **paparazzi** saw to it that their **privacy**—and the honeymoon—was over.

Mr. and Mrs. **Guy Ritchie** honeymooned at **Sting** and Trudie Styler's 41-room Tudor mansion near Stonehenge, **England**.

HOOPER, NELLEE: *b. March 15, 1963.* British composer who **worked** with Madonna on her *Bedtime Stories.* He coproduced **"Survival"** with **Dallas Austin** and Madonna, coproduced **"Forbidden Love"** with **Babyface** and Madonna, did some remixing on **"Sanctuary"** and had both writing and producing credits on **"Inside of Me"** and **"Bedtime Story."**

HOPE FOR HAITI NOW: A GLOBAL BENEFIT FOR EARTHQUAKE RELIEF: Held on January 22, 2010, this telethon arranged by **George Clooney**, Wyclef Jean, Joel Gallen and **MTV** raised **money** for the victims of the devastating earthquake in **Haiti**. It was aired on the major networks and featured musical performances and appearances by dozens of stars, including **Beyoncé**, Mary J. Blige, **Anderson Cooper**, Leonardo DiCaprio, Jay Z, Alicia Keys, Robert Pattinson, Julia Roberts and Stevie Wonder.

Madonna appeared, backed by a choir, from **New York**, and sang a winning rendition of **"Like a Prayer,"** recovering smoothly after missing a lyric.

HOPPING GHOST: Chinese in origin, this little guy is the very same sort of puppet that stood up to **"Dita"** in the **"Erotica"** video and was rewarded with a glovejob. As harmless as these dolls should seem, they do emanate pure evil, no? The dolls represent dissatisfied revenants of Chinese legend that return from the dead in lethally odoriferous corpse-bodies, hopping in search of more psychically comfy graves. If they encounter you (they detect people by the smell of our breath) they will hop toward you until they have punctured your neck, leaving you to die in breathless agony. "Erotic, erotic ..." *Thud. Whoosh!*

HORNADAY, JEFFREY: *b. circa 1956.* Choreographer of *Flashdance* (1983), the movie version of *A Chorus Line* (1985) and, more recently, the choreographer and director of the Disney Channel **Original** Movie hit *Teen Beach Movie* (2013).

Blond, blue-**eyed** Hornaday tour-directed and choreographed Madonna's *Who's That Girl World Tour*, choreographed the film *Dick Tracy* and was stage director of *The Girlie Show World Tour*. Gossip linked him to Madonna romantically in 1989 immediately following her **divorce** from **Sean Penn**.

In 2013, Hornaday contrasted **working** with **Michael Jackson**, an organic force, with Madonna, whom he praised while describing as more calculated: "Madonna is, and I mean this in a good way, she's much more deliberate and **controlling**. So the first tour I did for her, I mean, every single movement she did on stage was evaluated and staged and really meticulously laid out, so it was repeatable every night and what she did was very precise ..."

"Blasphemy has truly never tasted sweeter."
—BRADLEY STERN ON "HOLY WATER," *MUUMUSE* (2015)

There was nothing holy about Madonna's *Rebel Heart Tour* performance of "Holy Water."

MATTHEW RETTENMUND

HORSES: On August 16, 2005—her 47th **birthday**—Madonna suffered the biggest injury of her life while riding her horse on her estate in the UK. She was thrown, cracking ribs, breaking her collarbone and hand. She'd only been riding for eight months.

"I wasn't galloping or even doing anything naughty. I was just riding a polo pony and I don't know how to ride polo ponies. It started playing polo with me!" she told *Tatler*.

Madonna has said the pain from that accident was the greatest she's ever felt. She also has blamed her children's former nanny and then stylist Shavawn for "making" her ride the horse. "It taught me to slow things down a bit. It was a great lesson, but I'm fine. I've never felt better," she said a month later.

At the September 11, 2005, debut of **Guy Ritchie**'s *Revolver* (for which she'd reportedly filmed a cameo as a female crime boss that was cut, a report that turned out to be mythological) at the Toronto Film Festival, she said of her accident, "I'm okay. A couple of Tylenol and a glass of wine and I feel great!"

On October 20, 2005, while promoting ***Confessions on a Dance Floor*** on *Late Show with David Letterman*, Madonna rode a horse outside the theater along 53rd St. to illustrate the old axiom about getting **back** on the horse.

Madonna's horse-riding accident directly inspired the equestrian theme of her June 2006 *W* **magazine** cover story by **Steven Klein**, and the first segment of her ***Confessions Tour***.

In 2008, Madonna said she had continued riding horses (especially her Irish draft horse Roller) because jumping her horse was one of the last wow-inducing things in her life. Her son **David** has also become a passionate rider.

On April 18, 2009, Madonna fell off a horse again, this time on Klein's Bridgehampton farm, and was treated for minor injuries at Luz Southampton Hospital. At first, the blame was placed on paparazzi, a claim that received considerable pushback.

HOSKINS, ROBERT DEWEY: Madonna's most serious stalker, this delusional drifter tried to gain entry to Madonna's **Castillo del Lego** mansion and paid dearly for it. He'd first tried to get in on April 7, 1995, returned on April 8 to threaten that he'd slit her throat from "ear to ear" and on May 29 was shot twice by Madonna's security detail as he tried to get in again. Hoskins had made it to within 40 feet of Madonna's front door.

Madonna was in **New York** at the time of the incident. #stalkerfail

Charges were filed, requiring Madonna to testify against Hoskins, something she resisted to the point where she was threatened with contempt. On January 3, 1996, Madonna testified against Hoskins, saying she had avoided testifying because he would get to see her up close, which had been his goal all along. Hoskins was found guilty of stalking, **assault** and making terrorist threats and was sentenced to 10 years.

"I'm very grateful justice has been served," Madonna said in a statement. "I hope this helps other victims of stalkers."

When Hoskins was released, he ran afoul of the law again, resulting in his incarceration at a mental-health facility, from which he escaped for several days in 2012 before being captured. Around this time, a storage unit belonging to Hoskins went into delinquency and its contents were **auctioned** off. They included fresh Madonna memorabilia, a creepy Pierrot mask, a bible and a bunch of knives.

Hoskins has also made threats against Halle Berry.

HOT MESS: Madonna and the camera have had a long **love** affair, but they *do* break up occasionally.

A bad snapshot of Madonna at the **Jean Paul Gaultier** show on January 25, 2006, led to false reports her face was falling apart, **Michael Jackson**–style.

One of Madonna's worst-ever candids was taken July 25, 2008, showing her looking gaunt and her cheeks unnaturally puffy. The shot is so bad **Liz Rosenberg** actually commented to *People*, "She's rehearsing eight hours a day for her tour. But I think the photographer got a bad shot of her, or she was about to hurl a spitball."

But the all-time worst shot is from August of 2009, and credited to Matrix/Flynet, showing Madonna's arms looking like something you'd find on a weightlifting mummy. Again, the image is so bad (and there's only one shot) that Rosenberg could not resist commenting, "Madonna's arms simply do not look that way ... The **muscles** are accentuated by the way the flash hit her."

Let's not even talk about unbecoming studio photo shoot **leaks**, except to wonder aloud if the password to **Steven Klein**'s network is "123."

Bottom line: Nobody looks good all the time—get over it.

HOUSTON, WHITNEY: *August 9, 1963–February 11, 2012.* Iconic '80s singer, movie actor and hapless reality-TV star whose meteoric rise to supremacy in the music biz rivaled Madonna's own. Houston racked up 11 #1 singles on the *Billboard* Hot 100, including an astonishing seven in a row (from 1985 to 1988). Her remake of Dolly Parton's "I Will Always **Love** You" (1992) from *The Bodyguard* (1992) is one of the most successful singles of all time. Later in her career, Houston lost much of her amazing vocal range and deteriorated before her public's very **eyes**, a victim of **drug** abuse and, some would argue, the pressure to live up to a public image that was not reflective of the flesh-and-blood human being she was. Under the influence of drugs, she drowned in a bathtub at the Beverly Hilton Hotel (9876 Wilshire Blvd., Beverly Hills, CA) during the festivities leading up to the **Grammys**. Her 21-year-old daughter with ex-husband **Bobby Brown**, Bobbi Kristina Brown, also had her final conscious moments in a bathtub, three years later.

In the '80s, Madonna and Houston were pitted against each other in the press because the media loves a catfight.

Houston was falsely quoted saying she'd kill her children if they looked like Madonna, so she went to the British **magazine** *Tatler* to clear the air in 1987, saying, "I have never said anything bad about Madonna. She is okay. She has her audience, I have mine."

Asked again about Madonna, Houston told ***Entertainment Tonight***, "Madonna is great, you know, because that girl sits down and she comes up with stuff that, you know, you have to look at it, and you go, 'Hmmmmm.' [Laughs] You know?"

Madonna good-naturedly joked about ***Bedtime Stories*** stalling at #3 while filming her **"Take a Bow"** video, "[W]hy can't I be #1? Why—Boyz II Men are always hogging the top position. Boyz II Men and that damn *Bodyguard* soundtrack—is that still in the charts? It's always on the charts." But Houston was ready with a comeback when asked about Madonna collaborating on "Take a Bow" with **Babyface**, who'd **worked** with Houston previously. "Before Madonna, it was Face and I. Okay? Do I have to say any more?"

Nope!

In 1995, Madonna said she'd had a Houston-based nightmare at the time **"You'll See"** was on the charts: "I **dreamt** that I opened up *Billboard* magazine and my song had dropped to #3 and Whitney Houston's had gone to #1 and then I went down to my **voice** teacher's, um, her studio where I take lessons and I walked in and she was humming Whitney Houston's song and I was devastated ... this is what I'm dreaming about!"

A **fan** at a Q&A trying to bash Madonna for wearing outrageous clothes (which would presumably be a bad influence on her future children), brought out a defensive side of Houston, who replied pointedly, "There are other things in life a little more important to, to be real with [my daughter] about. I mean, that's an image. I, I know Madonna, I've met her myself, and she doesn't wear those every day, you know?"

Through it all, it would seem Madonna and Whitney Houston had mutual respect, even if they weren't bosom buddies.

One of the last videos ever shot of Houston showed her dancing in her seat in a bar, thoroughly entertained by Madonna's **Super Bowl** performance. At one point, Houston chimed in with, "Go, Maddy! Go, Maddy! Go, Maddy!" A source at the scene said Houston "raved" about Madonna's performance and spent time reminiscing about battling her on the charts **back** in the day.

Less than one week later, Houston was gone.

"I have a lot of respect for Madonna, um, she works hard at what she does. And I think that anybody that, um, works as hard as Madonna does—or works as hard as I do—deserves everything that they get."
—WHITNEY HOUSTON (CIRCA 1988)

"HOW HIGH": Song written by Madonna, Christian Karlsson, Pontus Winnberg and Henrik Jonback that was produced by Madonna, Bloodshy & Avant and **Stuart Price**. The song appears on ***Confessions on a Dance Floor*** and questions the value of living life at full speed and the ultimate value of being creative.

HOWARD, FELIX: *b. January 14, 1973.* The little British boy who, in the **"Open Your Heart"** music video, simultaneously emulates and **crushes** on the glamorous stripper played by Madonna.

Howard's **mother** is a former model, which helped him make the cover of *The Face* **magazine**, and led to him meeting Madonna backstage at a **fashion** show in 1986. "She was really, really nice," he said at the time, but he cried his **eyes** out when his failure to get a **work** license mandated his replacement by **Chris Finch** on the ***Who's That Girl World Tour***.

He consoled himself for a time by hosting London's ***The Tube*** music show. Later in life, Howard appeared in Gus Van Sant's **book** *108 Portraits* (1993). Howard has cowritten hit songs for the Sugababes and Amy Winehouse and has worked in PR at EMI with artists like Lana Del Rey, Calvin Harris, **Martin Solveig** and Sam Sparrow.

Due to vitiligo, Howard's brown skin is now fair. He's a dad of two and easy to find on **Twitter** @felixhoward.

HOWSON, PETER: *b. March 27, 1958.* Scottish painter known for gut-wrenching depictions of **working**-class scenes. He was **England**'s official artist of the Bosnian Civil War (such a thing was needed?) and was later appointed an Officer of the Order of the British Empire, a prize he said in 2014 he would give **back** since he no longer felt British.

Madonna first met Howson around 1989 and is a **fan** of his work, some of which she owns. She has also sat for him. In 2002, he did a series of **nudes** based on Madonna that depicted her as a grotesque, golem-like, yet sinewy presence, one lying on her side and one in a carefree squat. He said at the time that his works, entitled *Madonna 2002* and ***Death and Madonna*** would probably leave her "flattered and pleased," as they were intended to show her as **powerful** and charismatic.

As for the reaction of her hubby **Guy Ritchie**, Howson mused, "I think he'll probably come and hit me."

"HUMAN NATURE" (SONG): *Release date: June 6, 1995. Billboard Hot 100 peak: #46.* Madonna had recently enjoyed the biggest hit of her career (how the???) with **"Take a Bow,"** then stumbled badly with **"Bedtime Story,"** considered a bit too out-there. It had failed to go Top 40, so this single from ***Bedtime Stories***—more urban, going with rather than against the trend at radio—was thought to be a good antidote. Rather than setting the word on fire, Madonna's feisty, self-referential "Human Nature" fizzled on the charts—her second single in a row to fail to go Top 40.

Apparently, people still weren't done hanging their shit on her.

A coproduction by Madonna and **Dave Hall**, the song was written by its producers as well as Shawn and Kevin McKenzie and Milo Deering, yet its lyrics were pure Madonna, daring the world to continue hating her for being a **sexual** person.

Over a hip-hop beat, Madonna seethes that she's not sorry and won't be anyone's **bitch**. She was directly addressing the drubbing she'd received during the *Sex* and *Erotica* era rather than letting bygones be bygones, and she paid for it.

In spite of the song's weak chart performance, it became a modern self-empowerment anthem and is probably the most familiar of all her non-hit tunes, thanks in part to Madonna's embrace of it in concert. She has performed it on her *Drowned World Tour*, *Sticky & Sweet Tour* and *MDNA Tour*, baring her breast in Istanbul and **Paris** while singing this song on the latter tour—she was just expressing herself and not repressing herself when she undressed herself.

"Human Nature" was trotted out again for **Coachella** in 2015, pre-emptively addressing the furor that erupted after she kissed **Drake** there.

"HUMAN NATURE" (VIDEO): *Director: Jean-Baptiste Mondino, 1995.* **God** bless **Jean-Baptiste Mondino**. One of Madonna's worst-performing singles was nonetheless given one of her best videos. Imaginatively choreographed (by **Jamie King**), inspired by the erotic **art** of Eric Stanton and simply staged, equal parts funny and sexy, "Human Nature" helps Madonna to flip the latex bird at her detractors, of which there were legions in 1995.

In cornrows and a latex bodysuit, Madonna's **dancers** slowly, forcefully open her legs while she whispers the song's opening lines, the troupe showing off how much art can happen in a simple rented chair. Every one of the song's pointed lines gets a corresponding movement, culminating with the production's most famous set piece, a series of boxes in which each performer (including Madonna) attempts to express himself or herself. Slinking outside the box, Madonna is shown bound to a chair and brandishing a riding crop, but it's done as a **parody** of her more literal *Sex* phase. Even her real-life pet **dog** Chiquita gets a spanky.

Toward the end, Madonna is violently tossed around within a series of ropes managed by the dancers. As the song winds down, we see Madonna alone in the same chair in which she first appeared, slamming her legs shut of her own volition to the sound effect of a slamming door. Seated, she stares us down, insisting, "Absolutely no **regrets**."

The final image is Madonna throwing punches.

If it's possible for one video to sum up Madonna's Madonna-ness, "Human Nature" is that video.

"HUNG UP" (SONG): *Release date: October 18, 2005. Billboard Hot 100 peak: #7.* For the lead single from *Confessions on a Dance Floor*, Madonna brought in the big **guns**: ABBA. The clever use of the hook from that band's "Gimme! Gimme! Gimme! (A Man After Midnight)" (1979) gave the song instant recognition and traded on **nostalgia** for the **disco** era, with the new parts of the song striking the perfect chord as a fresh **dance** groove for women (and men) who know exactly what they want.

The alchemy of ABBA + Madonna **worked**: "Hung Up" is one of the best-selling songs of all time, topping the charts in dozens of countries. Notably, airplay for the song was anemic in the US, where Madonna's age was cited as a factor. Even with meh airplay, "Hung Up" became a Top 10 hit and sold like crazy. Its use on a November 7, 2005, episode of *CSI: Miami* (2002–2012) didn't hurt a bit.

Madonna and **Stuart Price** were inspired by ABBA, Cerrone and Giorgio Moroder when creating *Confessions on a Dance Floor*. When Price came up with the idea of sampling "Gimme! Gimme! Gimme!," Madonna wrote the song in "about 10 minutes driving around in my car" and then had to worry about getting ABBA to sign off. She told *Attitude*, "I had to send my emissary to Stockholm with a letter and the record begging them and imploring them and telling them how much I worship their music; telling them it was an homage to them, which is all true. And they had to think about it, Benny and Björn; they didn't say yes right away. They could have said no. Thank **God** they didn't."

Madonna performed the song winningly on the **MTV Europe Music Awards** (Portugal), then again for the **BBC Children in Need** telethon (UK). She did several other high-profile **TV** performances: *Parkinson* (UK), *SMAPxSMAP* (Japan), *Star Academy* (France) and *Wetten, dass ...?* (Germany), and performed it at her promo gigs at **KOKO** and **G-A-Y** (UK) and **Studio Coast** (Japan). She opened the 2006 **Grammys** with the song and brought it to **Coachella** that same year.

The song was the heart of her *Confessions Tour*. In 2008, Madonna threw a heavy metal "Hung Up" onto her *Hard Candy* promo tour set list, and it was used in a rather off-putting way during her *MDNA Tour*—seeing Madonna getting brutally strung up surgically extracted all joy from the song. It was also one of the songs Madonna sang briefly at Coachella in 2015.

Considering it was released over 20 years into her career, "Hung Up" was something of a miracle in that it managed to forge a place among Madonna's best-ever singles.

"HUNG UP" (VIDEO): *Director: Johan Renck, 2005.* Madonna originally hired **David LaChapelle** to direct the music video for her comeback song **"Hung Up,"** wanting a documentary feel to match his film *Rize* (2005). They had creative differences (with LaChapelle bad-mouthing

ALEJANDRO MOGOLLO

Madonna ever after), leaving it to Johan Renck to capture what Madonna was going for: **disco** meets parkour.

In the same way that "Hung Up" became a surprisingly potent single decades into Madonna's career, so did the music video unexpectedly succeed at the hard task of living up to Madonna's reputation as a video visionary. Scenes of Madonna in her pink leotard, warming up her body in a lonely studio, stretching provocatively, twirling, practicing **dance** moves—strongly reminiscent of Karen Lynn Gorney in *Saturday Night Fever* (1977)—are intercut with scenes of her dancers succumbing to boogie fever in public places, including a diner, the subway system and a **back** alley, where a strutting Madonna dances in slow-mo with her young brood as the song's tone-setting alarm clock *tick-tock, tock-tock, tick-tock*s.

Images of Madonna literally humping her boom box are the stuff of pop culture legend. As a bonus, Madonna's pelvic-thrust deep squats, her tight bod and her ass renewed interest in admiring her form as an example of aging disgracefully well.

"I kind of liked that we didn't have time to overthink this and be too clever," director Johan Renck told *MTV News*. "I like being out on a limb and not knowing what we're doing and why. Just deal with it, the mayhem, you know?"

We know.

And speaking of limbs, amazingly, Madonna filmed the strenuous video not long after falling off her **horse** and seriously injuring herself.

HUTTON, TIMOTHY: *b. August 16, 1960.* Brat Pack actor who won the **Oscar** for his supporting performance in *Ordinary People* (1980), and who was a pal of ex–Mr. Madonna, **Sean Penn.**

Andy Warhol related a story, found in *The Andy Warhol Diaries* (1989), from the ***New York Post***'s Richard Johnson, who said the paper's newsroom had received a mysterious call from Hutton sometime prior to November 1986 saying, "Hello, this is Timothy Hutton. Did anyone there call me?" The answer was no, so Hutton then asked, "Well, did anyone call Madonna?" Again, no. Hutton was then informed that the number he was calling was the *New York Post*'s and was asked, "And since we've got you on the phone, what are you doing with Madonna?"

CLICK.

HYDRANGEAS: On September 1, 2011, Madonna appeared at a press conference at the **Venice Film Festival** to promote *W.E.* Seated at a long table with most of her cast, she was bum-rushed by a **"fan"** who approached her with a large bouquet of hydrangeas, telling her she was his

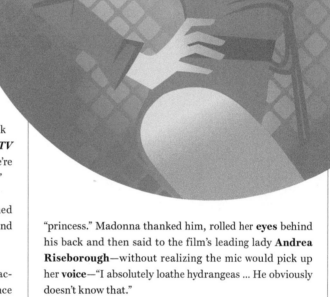

"princess." Madonna thanked him, rolled her **eyes** behind his back and then said to the film's leading lady **Andrea Riseborough**—without realizing the mic would pick up her **voice**—"I absolutely loathe hydrangeas … He obviously doesn't know that."

The incident became one of Madonna's first memes; her ungracious response (albeit not meant for public consumption) went viral. Less than two weeks later, Madonna released a video response to the floral flap, showing herself cradling hydrangeas in a silent film whose titles read: "You have no idea how many nights I have lost thinking how I hurt you. Words can not express how sorry I am. To think I may have caused you pain. My heart is going to burst with sadness. I need to know in time you may forgive me. If I could take **back** my words I would but I can't, so what am I left with? I'm left with the fact I still **hate** hydrangeas! And I will always hate them! It's a free country! So f**ck you I like roses!!"

Those who felt Madonna's accidental rudeness was unforgivable failed to pick up on the fact that the guy who gave Madonna the flowers did so as part of a stunt, hoping to embarrass her later when she in all likelihood had abandoned his **gift**. (She had, but lied and said her assistant had taken the flowers.) This fan was actually Ukrainian prankster Vitalii Sediuk, who became notorious for stealing a kiss from Will Smith, striking **Brad Pitt** at the *Maleficent* (2014) premiere, crawling under America Ferrera's skirt at **Cannes**, posing with his ass out alongside Ciara and trying to accept **Adele**'s **Grammy**.

The entire episode may have been ignited by a prank, but she wasn't joking around about her distaste for the glorified weeds. During a Reddit.com chat in 2013, Madonna was asked, "Where should I put these hydrangeas?" and replied, "up your ass."

A little "Hung Up" on herself

HYNDE, CHRISSIE: *b. September 7, 1951.* One of the most important female figures in rock music, and the lead singer of the Pretenders, whose singles like "Brass in Pocket" (1979) and "**Back** on the Chain Gang" (1982) helped define '80s music.

Madonna's former **Breakfast Club** band mate Gary Burke has said that while Madonna ate it up when people compared her to **Debbie Harry**, it was Hynde who was her favorite female artist. Her influence can be felt in some of Madonna's ***Drowned World Tour*** performances, and probably also every time Madonna defiantly lifts a **guitar** in concert.

Madonna has said that seeing Hynde perform back in the day was the only time she saw a woman on stage who made her think, "Yeah, she's awesome—she's got **balls**!"

"She's warm, thoughtful, dedicated, full of humor, intelligent, great-looking—and has a voice that reflects all of the above."
—CHRISSIE HYNDE ON MADONNA (1987)

MATTHEW RETTENMUND

RICHARD CORMAN

I AM BECAUSE WE ARE: *Director: Nathan Rissman. Release date: December 1, 2008.* Passionate about helping the people, in particular the children, of **Malawi**, Madonna decided to film her trips to the impoverished African nation, enlisting **Nathan Rissman**—who had previously been her gardener and babysitter—to direct. It's not like he had zero qualifications: He was her children's nanny's husband and had shown a facility for making entertaining QuickTime movies. Madonna's recognition of **talent** is amazingly democratic.

The film is a straightforward documentary that pulls no punches in painting Malawi as one of the most desperate places on earth. Audiences gasped when one boy's horror story of mutilation was revealed, and they may have been just as surprised to see a project associated with Madonna that wasn't about her (although she is seen with her adoptive son **David**, and her personal story of involvement with the country opens the film), and that wasn't "edgy" or livened up with gimmicks. For example, ***Truth Or Dare*** was the **original** scripted/unscripted reality show, and the **black-and-white** vs. color was a stylistic flourish. Here, while Madonna is shown mainly in black-and-white, it didn't seem so much a flourish as a necessity—her own story is not as compelling as the story of Malawi, as the story of our world.

Madonna chose her green-thumbed green director well; he plants seeds in the viewers' minds that later flower into hard-to-deny truths. The most insistent point made in the film is that the more modernized we become in the West, the less human we become. To some, this could come off as preachy or—buzzword of the millennium—elitist, a put-down of America. Madonna lumps herself in with those criticisms.

"It's funny, when you don't have a lot of distractions—which we have so many of in our western, privileged, modern world—um, you do have to ask yourself the hard questions and, and, um, and I think that's really why so many of the children that we met were so wise," Madonna said.

Madonna is not saying, "Be like me, for I am perfect," she's saying, "Can't we all do better?" This is enhanced by her narration of the film, during which she admits she's unsure how lasting her contributions to Malawi will be, "But it's a start."

The film contains interviews with Joyce Banda (a future foe), **Bill Clinton**, **Jeffrey Sachs**, Desmond Tutu and many Malawians struggling to cope.

I Am Because We Are does make one mistake, when it offers the Spirituality For Kids (**Success for Kids**) a lengthy, jarring plug toward the end. SFK is very much a part of Kabbalah—and this should have been fully disclosed in the film.

In the end, the film is a bracing document of man's inhumanity toward man—which comes in the form of direct action (a Malawian "cleansing" tradition that forces girls to have **sex** three times a day at first, and that invites HIV as

"a guest") as well as direct inaction (doing nothing once we know there is an issue).

At Tribeca, Madonna said at the top of the post-screening talkback, "... There are people suffering hardships and there is chaos and pain and suffering everywhere. And, uh, going to Malawi and, and witnessing these experiences made me understand that we are not only responsible for what's going on in Malawi and sub-Saharan Africa and the continent of Africa, but we are responsible for what's going on in our own backyard. And if you wanna change the world, then, then, just treat the person next to you with dignity and respect and that's a beginning."

I Am Because We Are became one of the best-received films with which Madonna has ever been associated. It had its world premiere on April 24, 2008, at the Tribeca Film Festival (Tribeca Performing Arts Center, 199 Chambers St., NY, NY) and also played at **Cannes** on May 21, a screening she attended in an off-message Chanel Couture dress with a 79-carat diamond necklace from Chopard.

> "You don't have to be rich to be good."
> —DESMOND TUTU, *I AM BECAUSE WE ARE* (2008)

> "The world's problems are our problems and *I Am Because We Are* reminds us of how interconnected we all are. It's a call to action and however you choose to act is based on what you take away with you from this documentary. It might not be enough, but it's a start."—PATRICK SAMUEL, *STATIC MASS EMPORIUM* (2009)

"I DESERVE IT": This Madonna/**Mirwais** collaboration from ***Music*** will probably never be performed again, considering its status as a Valentine from Madonna to her former husband, **Guy Ritchie**. Too bad, because the twangy, C&W ballad was a stunner on her ***Drowned World Tour***.

"I DON'T GIVE A": This acidic ***MDNA*** song launches with a vocal rap by Madonna that shares more than a little with the one in **"American Life,"** but its attitude—it's all about telling off any and every **hater** Madonna's ever had—is more freshly irritated than socially flustered. Its **Nicki Minaj** rap does the real dirty **work**, and Minaj returns at the end of the song to proclaim that there's only one queen, "... and that's Madonna, ***bitch***."

The song was performed by Madonna and her **guitar** as a straight-up rock song on her ***MDNA Tour***. Minaj appeared via the magic of video. As the number wrapped, amid music reminiscent of that from *The Omen* (1976), Madonna rose on an altar before her giant "MDNA"-emblazoned cross. Wham, bam, thank you, sacrificial lamb.

"I FUCKED UP": One of the Deluxe Bonus Edition tracks from ***MDNA***, this collaboration with **Martin Solveig** (plus

GREGORY PACE

Michael Tordjman, who also cowrote) is a **regret**-filled tune about the dissolution of a relationship. It is probably about **Guy Ritchie**, like most of the rest of that album.

"I KNOW IT": When Madonna was signed to her record deal and put together with **Reggie Lucas**, this was one of the songs she came with, rarin' to record. Though "I Know It" (written solely by Madonna and produced solely by Lucas—not often you see singular credits on pop songs anymore) was one of the only songs on the *Madonna* album not to become a single, it is a '60s girl-group confection with a cute-as-hell horn and a theme (a dude leaving Madonna?) any teenager could relate to, the breakup of a fiery romance. Gotta **love** the ad-libbed, "C'mon, baby!" at the end.

"I LOVE NEW YORK": Rocky filler from *Confessions on a Dance Floor* written and produced by Madonna and **Stuart Price** infamous for its Big Apple favoritism and arguably juvenile lyrics. Madonna has blown off criticism, asking if it were not okay for her to love **NYC** the best. She performed it live on her *Confessions* promo tour and on the *Confessions Tour*. The song's Demo Rock Version appears on the *I'm Going to Tell You a Secret* album.

"I SURRENDER DEAR": What the hell is Bing Crosby's first solo hit, from 1931, doing in a **book** about Madonna? Easy: She sang a duet of this song with Jennifer Grey in their film *Bloodhounds of Broadway*. The song, which cutely challenges the ladies' upper registers, is performed by the two in matching, silver-collared flapper costumes as Madonna's character makes **eyes** at her boyfriend, played by Randy Quaid. Essential line, by Grey: "I may seem proud/I may act **gay**/It's just a pose/I'm not that way," which **worked** well during Madonna's **Sandra Bernhard** period even if the **original** meaning of the line had nothing to do with the **Cubby Hole**.

"I WANT YOU" (SONG): Madonna covered this 1976 Marvin Gaye classic (written by Leon Ware and Arthur T-Boy Ross), with production by **Nellee Hooper**, along with Massive Attack, for the Gaye tribute album *Inner City Blues: The Music of Marvin Gaye*. Her trip–hop version aches with desire, earning it a spot on her *Something to Remember* collection. It was set to be a single, but Motown and **Warner Bros.** couldn't come to an agreement.

The Junior Vasquez remixes of this track are out of this world, but remain officially **unreleased**.

"I WANT YOU" (VIDEO): *Director: Earle Sebastian, 1995.* Madonna was so pleased with her cover of this Marvin Gaye tune that she insisted it be a single to promote *Something to Remember*. As a single, it required a video, so documentarian Earle Sebastian was hired and the concept chosen was the 1930 Dorothy Parker short story "A Telephone Call," and the Jean Cocteau **play** *The Human*

Voice (1930) adapted as the movie *L'Amore* (1948) starring Anna Magnani. To match the song's uncomplicated feel, the video, in **black-and-white**, follows Madonna in a negligée as she anxiously awaits a phone call from her lover. (Remember telephones with cords?) Madonna's **acting** and Sebastian's attention to detail (those false eyelashes drifting downward in a glass of water) made beautiful visual music together. The single never came to pass, but the video is an overlooked mini-masterpiece.

ICE-T: *b. February 16, 1958.* Now a successful **TV** actor playing a cop on *Law & Order: Special Victims Unit* (2000–), he was, ironically, the rapper whose incendiary song "Cop Killer" (1992) gave **Warner Bros.** major grief just before *Sex* came along to give the company even more grief.

"I like Madonna," he said in the '90s. "She's my idol. She performed in my club when she first started. She did **'Physical Attraction,'** pulled my shirt off and kissed me on the chest. Blew my mind. I **love** her, man. If she wants to do a 100-page **book** of herself butt-naked, licking **feet**, then do it, baby. That's what the **fuck** you're supposed to do."

Madonna attends the *I Am Because We Are* premiere in NYC as Jane Krakowski.

MATTHEW RETTENMUND

Madonna's "Iconic" *Rebel Heart Tour* opening was deemed offensive and omitted in Singapore.

"ICONIC" FEAT. CHANCE THE RAPPER AND MIKE TYSON: This soaring, single-ready *Rebel Heart* anthem encourages listeners to achieve greatness, making it quintessential Madonna-speak set to music. Her assurance that we are already superstars is reminiscent of **"Spotlight."** Featuring a stirring, surprisingly effective intro from **Mike Tyson** and an organic rap by Chance the Rapper, the song is possibly the most tuneful collection of egos ever assembled. It was written by Madonna, MoZella, Blood Diamonds, Chance the Rapper, DJ Dahi, S1 and Toby Gad, with production by Madonna, Gad, AFSHeeN and Josh Cumbee.

Madonna's *Rebel Heart Tour* opened with this song.

"I'D BE SURPRISINGLY GOOD FOR YOU": Madonna gets an appropriate laugh within a dramatic movie when she, as Evita, sings this duet with **Jonathan Pryce**, as her mark, blatantly selling herself as the best idea he's had all year. In *Evita*, they start out dancing vertically and end up, we presume, doing the same thing horizontally. It's found on *Evita: The Complete Motion Picture Music Soundtrack*.

"I'D RATHER BE YOUR LOVER": Featuring a rap by **Meshell Ndegeocello**, this steamy *Bedtime Stories* track, written and produced by Madonna and **Dave Hall** (sharing writing credits with the Isley Brothers and Christopher Jasper due to sampling) is most famous because its **original** version contained a wily rap by **Tupac Shakur** (he rhymed "media" with "greedier"). Madonna had, um, let's go with *dated* the rapper. Because of his notorious reputation and because the goal of *Bedtime Stories* was to deliver Madonna from notoriety, her **Maverick**-signed act Ndegeocello replaced him.

It seems likely the song would have made a popular single had it proceeded in its original form.

IDOL, BILLY: *b. November 30, 1955.* Pop rocker whose singles, like "Hot in the City" (1982), "White **Wedding**" (1982) and "Rebel Yell" (1984) made him an **MTV** staple.

Madonna told *Smash Hits* in 1987, "I was considering doing a song with Billy Idol, if you can believe it. That would have been good because we're both white and plastic and **blonde**."

"IF YOU FORGET ME": Madonna mesmerizingly reads this heart-wrenching poem by Nobel Prize–winning poet Pablo Neruda on the soundtrack of the 1994 film *Il Postino/The Postman*. The poem was written in 1952 by Neruda for his lover Matilde Urrutia before their marriage, but remained unpublished until it appeared in the 1963 **book** *The Captain's Verses*.

IHEARTRADIO MUSIC AWARDS: Madonna appeared on the second installment of this **awards** show launched by iheartmusic.com at the Shrine Auditorium (665 W. Jefferson Blvd., LA, CA) on March 29, 2015, introduced

—CARIN GOLDBERG

by **Mike Tyson**. Her performance of **"Ghosttown"** was a highlight of the evening, containing the night's biggest surprise: **Taylor Swift** accompanied her on the **guitar**. In a graceful performance, Madonna sang well, wore an oddly tasteful leather corset over a silk tank and a distressed, button-down vest, debuting stunning new long **hair** and softer makeup, her **grills** accentuating her famous **gap**. (They had a little black cross in the middle of them.) She returned later in a corseted Joan of Arc–inspired sheer, silver-chainmail dress by Alexander Wang, presenting Swift with the award for Song of the Year ["Shake It Off" (2014)]. "My favorite guitarist!" Madonna chirped as Swift, towering over her, accepted the honor.

Madonna continued to use projected footage of disasters behind her, including **9/11** imagery; surprisingly, no real objections were raised. The song went over well, leading to a brief peak at #1 on the *Billboard* + **Twitter** Real-time Chart—Trending 140.

"I'LL REMEMBER" (SONG): *Release date: March 8, 1994. Billboard Hot 100 peak: #2.* Madonna wrote this melodic mid-tempo song with **Patrick Leonard** and Richard Page and produced it with Leonard, offering it as the theme for her friend **Alek Keshishian**'s film *With Honors* (1994). As is often the case with the songs Madonna writes for the movies, she wrote it quickly and does not seem overly fond of it—she has never performed it live, even though it was a huge radio hit and helped her regain some luster after *Erotica* was painted as a disappointment. "I'll Remember" should have been nominated for an **Oscar** as Best **Original** Song, even if it was written for a weak film.

"I'LL REMEMBER" (VIDEO): *Director: Alek Keshishian, 1994.* The laziest gal in town! "I'll Remember" shares a bit in common with the video that directly preceded it, **"Rain."** We see the techies, behind the scenes at the recording studio and Madonna looking drop-dead in short black **hair**, emoting as she croons wistfully … but nobody's Japanese.

Another major difference between the videos is that in "I'll Remember," the hair is really Madonna's—in "Rain," she'd worn a wig. The cleverest bit is that Madonna (thanks to camera wizardry) watches herself **singing**. The voyeur Madonna is dressed in male **drag**, a man's suit coat and shirt, the **exhibitionist** Madonna in a clingy black gown; both stand before images of *With Honors*, the film for which the song is the **love** theme.

Madonna's going for the **Louise** Brooks **look** with her severe bangs and arch makeup, but when she stares into the camera at video's end, it's hard not to also think of Chita Rivera.

"ILLUMINATI": Madonna enlisted **Kanye West** (along with Mike Dean and Charlie Heat) to produce this shimmeringly gritty club track from her *Rebel Heart* album, thumbing her nose with it at conspiracy theories. "People often accuse me of being a member of the Illuminati," she told *Rolling Stone*, "but the thing is, I know who the real Illuminati are and I know where that word comes from." She thinks of it as a complimentary comparison to the bright minds from the Age of Enlightenment. Regardless of her intentions, it's one of the edgiest **dance** tracks she's ever sung. The song was written by Madonna, Toby Gad, Mike Dean, S1, MoZella, Kanye West and Tommy Brown.

"Vogue"-style, the song name-checks a number of **powerful** figures who have been rumored to be Illuminati (in order): Jay Z, **Beyoncé**, **Nicki Minaj**, Lil Wayne, **Oprah Winfrey**, **Barack Obama**, **the Pope**, **Rihanna**, **Queen Elizabeth**, Kanye West, **Lady Gaga**, Steve Jobs, Bill Gates, **Justin Bieber**, LeBron James and **Bill Clinton**.

The song made for an exciting, gravity-defying interlude on her **Rebel Heart Tour**.

"I'M A SINNER": Madonna wrote this laid-**back** song with **William Orbit** and Jean-Baptiste, and coproduced it with Orbit, the result being a not-so-distant cousin of their **"Beautiful Stranger"** collaboration. There is a naughty bliss to this song, in which Madonna embraces the fact that she's a bit of a bad girl, but does it with a mature flourish rather than with street-tough defensiveness.

The song was given an Indian-inspired airing on her **MDNA Tour**.

"I'M ADDICTED": This hard-driving EDM tune by Madonna and the Benassis (produced by them and the Demolition Crew) from **MDNA** is another good argument for why that album was drastically underrated. It's impossible not to move to this song, as was ably demonstrated by Madonna when she performed it with aggression and urgency on **The MDNA Tour**. Among all the non-single songs from *MDNA* that she brought to life on that tour, this one drew the most enthusiastic response.

Though Madonna had named the album on which it appears in such a way as to hint at the club **drug** MDMA, she denied endorsing the drug. However, in this album track, she explicitly compares **love** to MDMA, "... and that's okay." Somewhat distractingly, the song ends with a chant of "MDNA ... MDNA ... MDNA ..."—unnecessary since we all bought the album. Except for those of you who stole it.

I'M BREATHLESS: MUSIC FROM AND INSPIRED BY THE FILM DICK TRACY: *Release date: May 22, 1990. Billboard 200 peak: #2.* One of Madonna's most surprising musical curveballs was this sumptuously produced, impeccably authentic collection of '30s-style Broadway show tunes, all crafted faster than the speed of light between takes on **Dick Tracy** and launched to coincide with the film's release and the opening of her **Blond Ambition World Tour**.

The 1990 album was at the time Madonna's least successful full-length album of all-new material while still being an exceptionally well-reviewed #2 hit, eventually selling 7 million copies worldwide. It shed only two singles, the #1 hit **"Vogue,"** which relates to the rest of the songs on the album only thematically, and the #10 hit **"Hanky Panky,"** neither of them among the tunes written expressly for *Dick Tracy* by legendary composer **Stephen Sondheim**.

On *I'm Breathless*, Madonna stretches her vocals to encompass torch songs [**"He's a Man," "Sooner or Later (I Always Get My Man)"**], a chirpy slice of Mae Questel realness (**"Cry Baby"**), high comedy (**"I'm Going Bananas"**), romantic ballads (**"Something to Remember"**), dancehall ditties [**"Now I'm Following You (Part I)"**] and, as a concession to the market place, '90s club sounds [**"Now I'm Following You (Part II)," "Vogue"**]. For a woman whose critics often say she can't sing, she pulls off these diverse vocal demands with enthusiasm, style and aplomb.

Jack Nicholson said that when **Warren Beatty** played the track "Something to Remember" for some of his showbiz friends at a party with Madonna in attendance, "She stood there and accepted it all graciously ... this beautiful, unpredictable, amazing young woman with tears in her **eyes**, and I thought—Jesus! What a star."

I'm Breathless is a concept album. A soundtrack of sorts (though few of the songs are actually "from" *Dick Tracy)*, it manages to musically explore Madonna's screen persona from the film ("Breathless Mahoney") while simultaneously exploring the definitions of Madonna herself by presenting decidedly un-Madonna offerings. It answers the question, "What if Madonna were a legitimate **talent** and not just a product of hype?" with a resounding "Whaddaya mean 'if'???"

Most interesting is the album's flawless immersion in the musical sound of the Golden Age of Broadway (and Hollywood, for that matter), followed by its transition to a canny deconstruction of the style of that era. Most satisfying, even more so than hearing Madonna knock 'em dead on classy material her critics would never have believed her

She's addicted ... to chain mail.

MATTHEW RETTENMUND

capable of handling, is the finale: a commentary on all that has preceded it—both on *I'm Breathless* and in Madonna's entire career—with "Vogue."

The album is not as salacious as some of Madonna's **work**, "Hanky Panky" aside, but it does sample the movie's raunchiest lines ("You don't know if you wanna hit me or kiss me ... I get a lot of that," and "Dick—that's an interesting name."). Madonna would later admit that because the film was for Disney, she had to delete all references (well, *most*) to sodomy, intercourse or **masturbation**; where these themes originally fit is a mystery. Frankly, a '30s show tune on jerking off is not sorely missed.

Madonna's songwriting with **Patrick Leonard** is confident and assured. Try picking out the Stephen Sondheim numbers cold—it's difficult with gems like **"Back in Business"** on board. For the record, Sondheim penned the **Os-car**-winning "Sooner or Later (I Always Get My Man)," **"More"** (an upmarket version of **"Material Girl"** that could function as Madonna's theme song) and the album's only minor misstep, **"What Can You Lose,"** a somewhat simpering **love**-and-**regrets** ballad that finds tenor Mandy Patinkin scaling Everest with his mellifluous instrument (read: oversinging) and Madonna trying to play catch-up (read: undersinging). A bootlegged early version of this song featuring only Madonna's **voice** is catastrophic, so kudos to the final mix for its improvement.

Listen for Beatty's baritone on both parts of "Now I'm Following You," the second of which features him rapping, "10 million ... 20 million ... 30 million ..." and so on, mocking overblown estimates of *Dick Tracy's* final budget.

The downer of *I'm Breathless* is the cover **art**, an uninspired, unflattering mug shot of **Ciccone** Mahoney in black fur with Dick Beatty peering over her shoulder. It's the least beautiful of **Patrick Demarchelier's** shots of Madonna from the era: *I'm Lifeless*.

Other than one faulty song and faulty cover art, *I'm Breathless* is a compulsively listenable accomplishment, one that makes you long for Madonna in an all-singing, all-dancing Broadway extravaganza.

"I'M GOING BANANAS": Oh, loosen up, this Latin novelty number (with Yiddish thrown in for good measure) written by Michael Kernan and Andy Paley and produced by Madonna and **Patrick Leonard** is a giddy period hoot, one that livened up both *I'm Breathless: Music from and Inspired by the Film Dick Tracy* and, surprisingly, *The Girlie Show World Tour*—apparently, Madonna simply could not resist doing the song live at least once. It's the kind of song of which even Carmen Miranda might ask, "Too much?" And that's a good thing. Madonna's got plenty of songs with "anticipating" in them, she needs at least one with "non compos mentis."

I'M GOING TO TELL YOU A SECRET (ALBUM): *Release date: June 20, 2006. Billboard 200 peak: #33.* Madonna

I'M BREATHLESS:
MUSIC FROM
AND INSPIRED BY
THE FILM
DICK TRACY

① "He's a Man"
(Madonna/Patrick Leonard)
–4:41, produced by
Madonna/Patrick Leonard

② "Sooner or Later
(I Always Get My Man)"
(Stephen Sondheim)–3:18,
produced by Madonna/
Bill Bottrell

③ "Hanky Panky"
(Madonna/Patrick Leonard)
–3:57, produced by
Madonna/Patrick Leonard

④ "I'm Going Bananas"
(Michael Kernan/Andy
Paley)–1:41, produced by
Madonna/Patrick Leonard

⑤ "Cry Baby"
(Madonna/Patrick Leonard)
–4:04, produced by
Madonna/Patrick Leonard

⑥ "Something to Remember"
(Madonna/Patrick Leonard)
–5:03, produced by
Madonna/Patrick Leonard

⑦ "Back in Business"
(Madonna/Patrick Leonard)
–5:10, produced by
Madonna/Patrick Leonard

⑧ "More"
(Stephen Sondheim)–4:56,
produced by Madonna/
Bill Bottrell

⑨ "What Can You Lose"
duet with Mandy Patinkin
(Stephen Sondheim)
–2:08, produced by
Madonna/Bill Bottrell

⑩ "Now I'm Following You
(Part I)"
duet withWarren Beatty
(Andy Paley/Jeff Lass/
Ned Claflin/Jonathan
Paley)–1:35, produced by
Madonna/Patrick Leonard

⑪ "Now I'm Following You
(Part II)"
duet with Warren Beatty
(Andy Paley/Jeff Lass/
Ned Claflin/Jonathan
Paley)–3:18, produced by
Madonna/Patrick Leon-
ard/Kevin Gilbert

⑫ "Vogue"
(Madonna/Shep Pettibone)
–4:50, produced by
Madonna/Shep Pettibone/
Craig Kostich

"MADONNA'S LATEST MAY NOT BE FOR TOP 40 FANS, BUT THE MUSIC IS SOPHISTICATED POP, AS COMPELLING AS THE SCENES UNFOLDING IN A BROADWAY HIT. GOOD SHOW!"
—ANNE AYERS, *USA TODAY* (1990)

"*I'M BREATHLESS* IS AN ALBUM 10 TIMES MORE ACCOMPLISHED THAN ANY RECORD SHE HAS MADE BEFORE."—GREG SANDOW, *ENTERTAINMENT WEEKLY* (1990)

"NO OTHER POP STAR TODAY COULD—OR PROBABLY WOULD—MAKE AN ALBUM LIKE THIS, BUT THE THROBBING BEAT AND EMOTIONAL WALLOP OF 'VOGUE' MAKE THE REST OF *I'M BREATHLESS* SEEM ACADEMIC, A BRISK EXERCISE AS OPPOSED TO A SWEATY, CATHARTIC WORKOUT."—MARK COLEMAN, *ROLLING STONE* (1990)

"SHE HAS RECORDED PLENTY OF SPLENDID POP MUSIC BEFORE, ALONG WITH THE FLOUNCY DRIVEL, BUT THIS ALBUM IS MUSICALLY INTRIGUING, INTENSE AND A LOT OF FUN."
—*PEOPLE* (1990)

didn't release a live album until over 20 years into her career. When she did, she chose to release one from her **Re-Invention World Tour**, so that the tracks would be a mixture of old and new ... hell, even the old was new.

The album was a two-disc CD/DVD, the DVD containing her documentary of the same name, a sort of **Truth or Dare** update. All the tracks were live except for the bonus inclusion of the Demo Rock Version of **"I Love New York."**

Produced by Susan Applegate, it has sold fewer than 100,000 copies in the US but did get nominated for a **Grammy**.

I'M GOING TO TELL YOU A SECRET (MOVIE): *Director: Jonas Åkerlund. Release date: October 21, 2005.* It was like déjà vu all over again when Madonna decided to film the behind-the-scenes action surrounding her **Re-Invention World Tour**, with on-stage bits in color and off-stage bits in **black-and-white**. The film, shot by her video director **Jonas Åkerlund**, starts with the **X-STaTIC PRO-CeSS** exhibition and is heavy on **Kabbalah**, but does not scrimp on the live-performance aspect.

"I started off wanting to tell one story—which is what I always say to people about this film—and then I ended up telling several stories," Madonna said of the project.

I'm Going to Tell You a Secret had a premiere at AMC Loews Lincoln Square (1998 Broadway, NY, NY). In presenting the film in person to the select audience, Madonna spoke of how hard it was to edit it down from 350 hours to two. She quoted Jean-Paul Sartre: "If you look at the face of a man long enough, you'll see the face of humanity." But she also told the crowd to simmer down, listen and not disobey her. When someone asked if she were going to stay to watch the movie, she shouted, "Hell, yeah!"

Madonna also gave a speech on the film at Hunter College (695 Park Ave., NY, NY) as part of the program **MTV Presents mtvU Stand In**, an **MTV**-affiliated, college-based network. Students were surprised by Madonna's appearance, at which she noted, "To be totally honest, I think most people get into the entertainment **business** because ... there's something wrong with them."

I'm Going to Tell You a Secret aired on MTV on December 14, 2005, and did not get a theatrical release.

"Sometimes I was ecstatically happy and sometimes I was depressed. I seemed to be a bit more careless with people back in those days and not very nice. I don't miss being an idiot."-MADONNA, *I'M GOING TO TELL YOU A SECRET* (2005)

"Madonna has a documentary coming out ... They promise that in this one, they're going to show a side of Madonna that the public has not seen. Which I think means they're going to show clips from the movie *Swept Away*."-JIMMY KIMMEL (2005)

"I'M SO STUPID": Madonna sings about **dreams**, some of them fuzzy, an awful lot. Aren't any of them in focus? In this **American Life** track, a collaboration between Madonna and **Mirwais**, the song has a jarring start-stop quality and a dramatic first "I'm" that sounds like a swarm of mechanical mosquitos buzzing around your ear at space camp late one night. Once we get past that and the remarkably direct lyrics, Madonna's vocal has a rockin' punch to it that really tugs at your gut.

Also, never let it be said Madonna isn't self-deprecating, and that she does not from time to time hand her **haters** excellent song titles to use in their rants against her.

"I'm So Stupid" was rehearsed for the **Re-Invention World Tour**, but replaced. Madonna sang it at **Tears of a Clown** in Melbourne.

"IMAGINE": One of the most **powerful**, beloved and also controversial ("Imagine there's no heaven ...") pop songs of all time, written and performed by John Lennon, produced by Lennon, his wife **Yoko Ono** and future murderer Phil Spector. Madonna performed the 1971 song on her **Re-Invention World Tour** as well as on **Tsunami Aid: A Concert of Hope**.

IMMACULATE COLLECTION, THE (ALBUM): *Release date: November 9, 1990. Billboard 200 peak: #2.* The title is classic Madonna, a pun that hits her obsession with **Catholic** iconography while simultaneously referring to her position as a pop goddess. *The Immaculate Collection* was Madonna's first greatest hits album, and went on to become *the* greatest hits album—it lingered on the **Billboard** 200 for over two years and has sold over 30 million units worldwide, putting it in the Top 25 of all-time best-selling albums and making it the best-selling compilation by a solo artist.

The album, whose cover features not Madonna's famous face but a generic turquoise-and-gold design and logo, was set to bear a photo by **Herb Ritts** until Madonna yanked it. Madonna thought the photo—she had pointy black bangs and a bowler—made her look "like **Mike Tyson**." Still, **Warner Bros.**, preferred it to the racy, crotch-grabbing shot Madonna favored, so in the end a compromise was struck, resulting in the plain cover.

No matter. The double album's 17 songs are such perfect pop the cover is the last thing on your mind. Though many of her hits were sacrificed—**"Dress You Up," "Who's That Girl," "Causing a Commotion"** and **"Keep It Together"** come to mind—nothing seems out of place on this priceless disc.

Its two **original** tunes are among Madonna's best. In fact, it's disappointing that the radically bass-driven, overheated **"Justify My Love"** and **lyrically** and vocally daring **"Rescue Me"** originated on a best-of, but the former's controversial **video** gave this collection a major boost. It was the first record (and one of the last) engineered with **QSound**, which is definitely not a case of burying the lede.

Tongue firmly in cheek, Madonna dedicated the album to the **Pope** ... which was actually her **nickname** for her brother, **Christopher Ciccone**.

THE IMMACULATE COLLECTION

①
"Holiday"
(Curtis Hudson/Lisa Stevens)–4:04, produced by Jellybean Benitez

②
"Lucky Star"
(Madonna)–3:39, produced by Reggie Lucas

③
"Borderline"
(Reggie Lucas)–4:00, produced by Reggie Lucas

④
"Like a Virgin"
(Billy Steinberg/Tom Kelly)–3:11, produced by Nile Rodgers

⑤
"Material Girl"
(Peter Brown/Robert Rans)–3:53, produced by Nile Rodgers

⑥
"Crazy for You"
(John Bettis/Jon Lind) –3:45, produced by Jellybean Benitez

⑦
"Into the Groove"
(Madonna/Stephen Bray) –4:10, produced by Madonna/Stephen Bray/ Shep Pettibone

⑧
"Live to Tell"
(Madonna/Patrick Leonard) –5:19, produced by Madonna/Patrick Leonard

⑨
"Papa Don't Preach"
(Brian Eliot/additional lyrics by Madonna)–4:11, produced by Madonna/ Stephen Bray

⑩
"Open Your Heart"
(Madonna/Gardner Cole/ Peter Rafelson)–3:51, produced by Madonna/ Patrick Leonard

⑪
"La Isla Bonita"
(Madonna/Patrick Leonard/ Bruce Gaitsch)–3:48, produced by Madonna/ Patrick Leonard

⑫
"Like a Prayer"
(Madonna/Patrick Leonard) –5:51, produced by Madonna/Patrick Leonard/ Shep Pettibone

⑬
"Express Yourself"
(Madonna/Stephen Bray) –4:04, produced by Madonna/Stephen Bray/ Shep Pettibone

⑭
"Cherish"
(Madonna/Patrick Leonard) –3:52, produced by Madonna/Patrick Leonard

⑮
"Vogue"
(Madonna/Shep Pettibone) –5:18, produced by Madonna/Shep Pettibone/ Craig Kostich

⑯
"Justify My Love"
(Lenny Kravitz/Ingrid Chavez/additional lyrics by Madonna)–5:35, Lenny Kravitz/André Betts

⑰
"Rescue Me"
(Madonna/Shep Pettibone) –5:31, produced by Madonna/Shep Pettibone

IMMACULATE COLLECTION, THE (VIDEO COLLECTION): *Release date: November 13, 1990.* Madonna's first greatest videos compilation was released in conjunction with her first greatest hits album of the same name. Madonna's face was on the cover of this, unlike the album cover.

The collection included videos for: **"Lucky Star," "Borderline," "Like a Virgin," "Material Girl," "Papa Don't Preach," "Open Your Heart," "La Isla Bonita," "Like a Prayer," "Express Yourself," "Cherish," "Oh Father," "Vogue"** and also a video of Madonna's 1990 **MTV Video Music Awards** performance of "Vogue."

"IMPRESSIVE INSTANT": This Madonna/**Mirwais** whimsical **dance** song is the second track on *Music*, right after the title song. **"Music"** became a legendary part of her catalogue; "Impressive Instant," on the other hand, became that song in which Madonna says she wants to "… singy-singy-singy/Like a bird on a wingy-wingy-wingy." And yet

"SO THERE IT IS: GOOD SEX, BAD SEX, DOMINANCE, SUBMISSION, MONEY, RELIGION, RACE, IMAGE, REALITY, SLEAZE AND INNOCENCE. POP CULTURE COMES NO BETTER AND WE SHOULD BE GRATEFUL."

–RUSSELL BROWN, *SELECT* (1990)

"THE MOST EXCITING AND CULTURALLY RESONANT SINGLES COLLECTION OF THE LAST DECADE."–JIM FARBER, *NEW YORK DAILY NEWS* (1990)

"SEVENTEEN HITS, MORE THAN HALF OF THEM INDELIBLE CLASSICS: 'HOLIDAY' (EBULLIENT), 'LUCKY STAR' (BLESSED), 'LIKE A VIRGIN' (WICKED), 'PAPA DON'T PREACH' (IMMORAL), 'EXPRESS YOURSELF' (FEMINIST), 'MATERIAL GIRL' (DIALECTICAL), 'VOGUE' (EXPRESSIVE), 'OPEN YOUR HEART' (NAKED), 'JUSTIFY MY LOVE' (EROTICA), 'INTO THE GROOVE' (DISCO). STYLE-SWALLOWING OPPORTUNIST THOUGH SHE IS, EVERY ONE COULD HAVE BEEN CUT YESTERDAY … COULDN'T HAVE DONE IT WITHOUT MTV. TELL ME ABOUT IT. A+."–ROBERT CHRISTGAU (1990)

in 2000, **fans** seemed to have enough of a sense of humor to accept and appreciate the song without being too judgmental of its way with words. (Besides, it was the stuff of genius compared to the following track, **"Runaway Lover."**)

Mirwais said of the song, "The first song we **worked** on together was 'Impressive Instant'. It was the most complete of the demo tracks I sent her. It was an instrumental … But she said that she had an idea for lyrics. When we got to **London**, I asked her to sing it for me. I was surprised, of course, because it was new. But she improved my track! I was amazed. When you know your track well and it's finished, you're always afraid of what someone else can do to it. But I knew at the first listen that it was going to be cool."

Madonna performed "Impressive Instant" at both the **NYC** and London stops of her promo tour for *Music* and brought it to life, well, *impressively* on her *Drowned World Tour*, gas masks and all.

IN ARTIFICIAL LIGHT: *Director: Curt Royston. Filmed: 1981.* Madonna, as part of **Emmy**, appeared in this experimental short film by Curt Royston. Royston describes it as being about "a group of disparate characters." Everyone wrote their own dialogue, and each person is essentially playing a version of him- or herself. At one point, Madonna semi-raps a poem that's clearly influenced by "Rapture," Blondie's #1 hit from 1980. Two decades later, Royston told **VH1**, "She was enjoyable to watch because you knew you were getting the real person, and you weren't getting a veneer she'd put on."

Emmy performed early, **unreleased** songs (among them, "Hot House Flower") for the film, but the songs were not used in the final product. Madonna proudly listed it on her 1981 résumé.

IN BED WITH MADONNA: SEE: *Truth or Dare*.

IN THE REALM OF THE SENSES: *Director: Nagisa Ôshima. Release date: April 1, 1977.* The true story of an obsessive **sexual** relationship, this Japanese film ends with its female protagonist castrating her lover.

Madonna **loves** this **art** flick. She referred to it in *Sex* as an intensely erotic movie and also gave a copy of it to **Michael Jackson** to inspire ideas for their aborted collaboration on his song "In the Closet" (1991). He told her he liked the movie, but she later characterized his attitude toward this film and all her **books** of **nude** photographs as being that they were all "just **pornography.**"

"IN THIS LIFE": Madonna and **Shep Pettibone** collaboration from *Erotica* that became her first song to address **AIDS** (although the disease is not named), using the **deaths** of her friends **Martin Burgoyne** and **Christopher Flynn**. The ballad has a sincere vocal that is somewhat undercut by a spoken-word interjection over five minutes into the song that has an accidentally vampy air to it even though Madonna is very seriously pondering why people are so uncaring when it comes to tackling the AIDS crisis. Still, this thoughtful ballad is a welcome alternative facet for an album mostly about dancing and screwing. (Not that there's anything wrong with either.)

Madonna performed the song live on *The Girlie Show World Tour*, displaying her expanding range and **control**. She was angrily crying by the end of the song many of the nights she performed it.

> "This next song, this next song I wrote about two very dear friends of mine who died of AIDS. And though you don't know my friends, I'm sure that each and every one of you tonight knows someone, or will know someone, who is suffering from AIDS—the greatest tragedy of the 20th century. For all of you out there who understand what I'm talking about … don't give up."
> —MADONNA, THE GIRLIE SHOW WORLD TOUR (1993)

INABA, CARRIE ANN: *b. January 5, 1968.* She is the beautiful and opinionated female judge on the US **TV** hit *Dancing with the Stars* (2005–) ... but did you know she was also the **sexy**, shorthaired, G-stringed figure who slithered topless down a stripper pole at the beginning of *The Girlie Show World Tour*? Yes, Madonna allowed a woman 10 years younger and half-naked to be the first

visual impression of that tour. Inaba described the tour as "the pinnacle of my **dance** career," though lamented the requirement that she have her head shaved.

"INCREDIBLE": Ultra-positive, hard-to-keep-up-with song from *Hard Candy* that was written by Madonna and **Pharrell Williams**, and produced by Madonna and the **Neptunes**. It was identified as a standout track in some early reviews.

INFOMERCIAL: In an act of **Cher** madness, Diane von Furstenberg tapped Madonna to do an infomercial for a line of lingerie on Barry Diller's Q2 network. Von Furstenberg wound up marrying Diller in 2001, a union that has been described as a "merger." But Madonna's merger with the world of infomercials was called off; she got cold **feet**, as well as whatever else gets cold when one is wearing lingerie on **TV**.

"INSIDE OF ME": Girlishly inviting R&B/pop number that appears in the middle of *Bedtime Stories* and that involves the listener in an imaginary secret relationship with Madonna, one that exists only in our shared minds. For a song called "Inside of Me," there's no suggestiveness in the delivery; it's a lost-**love** song, one that's not full of rage—it's full of hope. Madonna wrote the song with **Dave Hall** and **Nellee Hooper**, and produced it with Hooper.

"INSIDE OUT": Gorgeous mid-tempo song from *Rebel Heart* that makes liberal use of **Catholic** imagery in expressing new **love**, and that references *Truth or Dare*. The song was written by Madonna, Jason Evigan, Sean Douglas, E. Kidd Bogart and Mike Dean, and produced by Madonna and Dean.

INSOMNIA: Madonna has suffered from sleeping issues for most of her life. She attributes it to the loss of her **mother**, saying sleep "has never been an easy thing for me." She is happy if she can get six hours of sleep.

INSTAGRAM: Madonna's is @Madonna. She has never been much of a **Twitter** girl, but visual junkie Madonna has embraced Instagram with zeal, posting personal photos, classic images of herself with some of her contemporaries and many **fan**-made photos. Madonna's use of fan-made images showing famous faces (Martin Luther King Jr., Nelson Mandela, **Bob Marley**) doctored to resemble her *Rebel Heart* album cover led to accusations of racial insensitivity. Declaring that one was abandoning Madonna forever because of her decision to make these posts was, in the warped minds of those who were outraged, the Selma of our time.

INTERSCOPE: In 2011, Madonna and **Live Nation** confirmed a three-album deal with this record company. *MDNA* and *Rebel Heart* were the first of the three.

"Don't look back, and don't think about what you're doing … just mix it up." —MADONNA, IN ARTIFICIAL LIGHT (1981)

"INTERVENTION": This folky **Mirwais** collaboration from *American Life* features a remarkably intimate vocal by Madonna; it sounds like she's singing it right in your ear, in marked contrast to some of Madonna's later-career records' habit of distorting and distancing her **voice**. Here, her voice is a supple instrument, her lyrics meditative. The song was performed live at the *Tears of a Clown* Melbourne show.

INTERVIEW: Founded in 1969 by **Andy Warhol**, this oversized chronicle of cool in **magazine** form made its name by having celebrities interview each other and by alternately focusing on personalities outside the mainstream, or on mainstream stars, but in an unconventional way. Known for its artful photography, *Interview* is the very definition of a prestige publication.

Madonna has appeared on the cover of *Interview* to promote her projects many times, and across all three of its incarnations—when it was Warhol's pet project, when it was run by the Brants with Ingrid Sischy as EIC and now that it's run by **Fabien Baron**.

Madonna first appeared on the December 1985 cover in the form of a Richard Bernstein illustration based on a **Herb Ritts** photograph. Inside, Madonna posed with hubby **Sean Penn** and was interviewed by character actor Harry Dean Stanton, a buddy of Penn's. "Now that I'm in **love**, all the songs I write ... I do for him ... (When I'm doing) anything that's creative, I think, 'Would (Sean) like it?'"

Four years later, Madonna—in a rare shoot that caught her short-lived **blonde**-streaked brunette **hair**—posed for Koto Bolofo for the May 1989 cover, submitting to questions from Becky Johnson. "People have certain notions about me, and it is time for a change," she asserted.

Perhaps Madonna's greatest *Interview* cover was her June 1990 crotch-grabbing pose by Herb Ritts. She was promoting her *Blond Ambition World Tour* and was in full brat mode, musing, "The idea that the first guy I ever slept with is married and has kids really breaks me up. I wonder if he still loves me. He probably does." **Glenn O'Brien**, an old **NYC** associate and the future editor of *Sex*, did the quizzing.

A partial cover in January 1992 was shared by "Madonna **Ciccone**," Chuck Close and Magic Johnson. Inside, photos of celebs from behind—they're facing the future ... get it?—included one of Madonna at an event.

Madonna came **back** to *Interview* for a June 1993 Ritts cover as a strawberry blonde to sell copies of *Erotica*. Her buddy Mike Myers did the honors, with Madonna suggesting to him that they do a remake of *Some Like It Hot* (1959), "... only with you and 'Garth' playing the Tony Curtis/Jack Lemmon parts. **Sharon Stone** should play the **Marilyn Monroe** part and I'm gonna play the bandleader. Only I want to change it slightly; I'm going to fire the **Marilyn** Monroe character for being unprofessional, and then we'll see what develops from there!"

For her *Music* era, Madonna posed for the March 2001 cover. Shot by **Jean-Baptiste Mondino** in brown leather pants and a holey patriotic shirt (with fox tails), the pose was defiant and offered "the ultimate interview by Ingrid Sischy" that didn't really live up to expectations.

Madonna's April 2008 cover, a **boxing**-themed, spread-legged, somewhat bedraggled look by **Steven Klein**, seemed to be an alternate take on her *Hard Candy* album cover. The piece inside was, again, by Sischy, and covered both Madonna's album and her interest in **Malawi**. "She spent several weeks **working** in the orphanages, particularly

Guess which was a promo poster and not an actual, printed cover ...

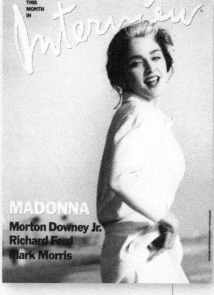

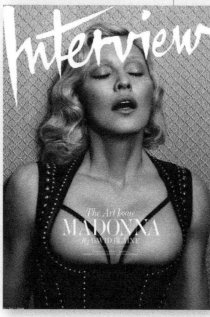

one with newborn children, and most of them were HIV positive," Madonna said, speaking of her daughter, **Lola**. "She so came into her own and was so responsible and stayed for eight hours every day and worked tirelessly. I thought, 'Why am I babying her so much? She's capable of so much more.' We don't let kids do anything. We think, 'Oh, they're kids—they can't take care of other kids; they can't do this; they can't do that.' And after you go to Africa, you drop all that silliness."

Changing things up, the magazine had **Mert and Marcus** shoot Madonna in throwback images ("Like a Virgin All Over Again") for May 2010, offering two variations of the cover for double the potential sales. The images were heralded as a return to photographic form for Madonna, and the Gus Van Sant interview was also a return to *Interview*'s roots as a magazine where celebs talk to celebs. In this case, filmmaker Van Sant was quizzing filmmaker Madonna about her work on *W.E.* In prepping to make the movie, she actually paced herself. "… I made *Filth and Wisdom* because I realized that I didn't really have a right to make a bigger film until I made a smaller film …"

Interview's most recent Madonna cover was its December 2014/January 2015 set of covers—three variants. Madonna, by Mert and Marcus, was seen in a flowered mask, bursting from a cleavage-baring garment and looking like a '40s starlet (except for the rubber top in which she was encased). The issue struck a nerve because inside, Madonna dared to bare her breasts at an age past which women are supposed to never be seen naked again. Magician David Blaine was the inquisitor, and it seemed a match made in heaven. As Madonna pointed out, "We're in the world of creating illusions and giving people the ability to **dream** and to be inspired or moved."

"INTO THE GROOVE" (SONG): One of Madonna's signature hits, this collaboration with **Stephen Bray** almost *didn't* become an '80s touchstone. Madonna's *Like a Virgin* album was all done, but she was filming *Desperately Seeking Susan* and still writing songs, so she brought a cassette of this track to the set. It was played during the scene set in **Danceteria** and **worked** so well the producers asked **Freddy DeMann** for the rights … but he had no clue what the song was. After some wangling with **Warner Bros.**, "Into the Groove" was used in *Susan* and became insanely popular when the movie was released. It was the B-side of Madonna's **"Angel"** 12" but was otherwise never a US single. Abroad, it was an easy #1.

Madonna originally wrote the song on her fire escape while gazing at a "gorgeous Puerto Rican boy" across the alley. Her intention was to give it to her old producer and lover **Mark Kamins**, who wanted it for an act he was working with named Cheyne. Once the song was locked into *Susan*, the other artist was Cheyne-outta-luck.

When Madonna re-recorded the song with Bray, she ad-libbed that enticing part about living out our fantasies there with her, a moment of inspiration that left her friend **Erika Belle**, a witness to the recording session, gobsmacked.

In 2005, **Stuart Price** told *Mixmag* of a conversation he'd had with Madonna about her early work. "She said, 'I used to hang around the DJs long enough to force them to make records for me,' so there's nothing changed there. When you hear her old records, there's no bullshit. On 'Into the Groove', if you solo the vocals, you can hear the cars going by outside in Manhattan."

"Into the Groove" did not appear on any of Madonna's US studio albums, but it was included on the European re-release of *Like a Virgin* abroad and was remixed for inclusion on *You Can Dance*. It later appeared on *The Immaculate Collection* and *Celebration*.

Madonna has performed the song live at *Live Aid*, and on *The Virgin Tour*, the *Who's That Girl World Tour*, the *Blond Ambition World Tour*, the *Re-Invention World Tour*, the *Sticky & Sweet Tour* and as part of a *Rebel Heart Tour* medley.

Even though Madonna has described the song as "dorky," she knows it's one of the most potent in her arsenal, and in 2003 brought it out to be mashed up with **"Hollywood"** to create **"Into the Hollywood Groove"** for her **Gap** campaign.

Madonna often calls this song "Get Into the Groove"; **Liz Rosenberg** calls it the national anthem.

If someone tells you they don't think "Into the Groove" is brilliant, they don't deserve another minute of your time, let alone **sex** with you … or with *anyone*.

"'Into the Groove' is as succinct and incontrovertible a paean to the new pop dance as can be …"-ANDREW HARRISON, SELECT (1985)

"If it were up to me, 'Only when I'm dancing can I feel this free' would be printed on Old Glory."-LOUIS VIRTEL, THE BACKLOT (2012)

"INTO THE GROOVE" (VIDEO): *Director: Susan Seidelman, 1985.* Though Madonna did not film a formal video for one of her biggest international hits, a clip of scenes from *Desperately Seeking Susan* with the song laid over them was serviced to **MTV** and went into heavy rotation. This kind of free advertising on MTV does not happen anymore. (Nor does MTV play music videos anymore, so it's okay.)

"INTO THE HOLLYWOOD GROOVE": Mash-up of **"Into the Groove"** and **"Hollywood"** that was used in **Gap** ads featuring Madonna and **Missy Elliott** in 2003. The song appeared on *Remixed & Revisited*.

—JOHN BLAIR

IQ: Madonna's is allegedly around 140, which would put her in the "extremely gifted" range, though there's no proof she has actually tested at this level.

IRONY: Madonna thinks "ironic" means "funny" or ... something. For example, during her **Rock and Roll Hall of Fame** speech, she noted that the first song she ever wrote was an **unreleased** tune called "Tell the Truth," paused and then added, "... ironically." If she meant to say she is liar, then the use **works**, but it seems more likely that she meant something more along the lines of, "funnily enough" or "appropriately."

When she caused jaws to drop during an *MDNA Tour* performance by saying that the US had a "black Muslim in the White House," she later explained she was being ironic. Again, there is no irony there. She was perhaps being facetious by mocking the fervently held belief by some that **Barack Obama** really is a black Muslim. But she wasn't being ironic.

This has to stop.

Madonna's **love** of the word "ironic" led to her rhyming it with "iconic" in the otherwise killer song **"Iconic"** from *Rebel Heart*. What's being iconic got to do with being ironic? Of course, Madonna would probably tell the author to suck her dictionary.

"She's funny. She does have an ironical sensibility, a wonderful Mae West scandalous sense of humor." -SUSAN SEIDELMAN, *THE VIDEO AGE* (1986)

IRRELEVANT: Much has been made of the argument over Madonna's relevance, an argument that by its very nature is self-defeating—people do not argue over the relevance of artists who are not relevant.

Blink. Blink.

Writing in January 2015, Austin Mutti-Mewse, author of the **book** *I Used to Be In Pictures* with his brother Howard Mutti-Mewse, recalled, "Twenty-odd years ago I asked the actress Patsy Ruth Miller, who was the lead in Lon Chaney's *Hunchback of Notre Dame* [1923], which Hollywood star she thought would continue to shine in decades to come. 'Easy,' she said, 'Madonna.' 'And why?' I asked. 'She'll always make sure she is relevant.'"

But what happens when a star remains relevant but is artificially put out to pasture? In February 2015, Madonna's lead single from *Rebel Heart*, **"Living for Love,"** was "banned" from airplay on the UK's Radio 1 station. It was actually played one time, on DJ Annie Mac's evening show. A whole one spin!

A supposed insider from Radio 1 claimed, "At the end of the day, it's all about relevance. It's natural that as an artist gets older their audience goes elsewhere and Radio 1 has to reflect that."

Radio 1 cannot be all things to all people, but had Madonna's audience really gone elsewhere? If anyone was moving, it seemed to be Radio 1 moving away from Madonna, as if inspired by *Logan's Run* (1976).

All Madonna wants to do is continue putting out music and performing, and continue having her output judged, enjoyed, dismissed, discussed—anything but arbitrarily ignored based on the year in which she was born.

"After years of seeing me get the shit kicked out of me ... I guess it's like if you keep spraying Raid on a cockroach and it won't die, after a while you just say, 'Oh, well, I'll let you live; there's your little space in the corner," Madonna told *Us* in 1997. She still wants that space, though no one really believes she'll be happy if it's in the corner, nor should she be.

The **ageism**-fueled argument over Madonna's relevance has, ironically, given her another frontier to conquer 30-plus years into her career, something new (even if it's the idea that she's old) to rebel against.

As for general relevance, let's put it this way: Madonna mooned the paparazzi at the **Grammys** in 2015 and it was a worldwide news story the next day. She's Argentina, and always will be.

Madonna has been writing the sequel to this book for decades.

"I love smart women and she is a very smart person." -ALAN PARKER ON MADONNA (1996)

THREE HUNDRED AND ONE THINGS A BRIGHT GIRL CAN DO

FRED SEIDMAN

© CURTIS KNAPP

"ISAAC": Moody Middle Eastern–tinged song from *Confessions on a Dance Floor* written and produced by Madonna and **Stuart Price** that gave the album its first controversy … before it was even out! A group of "naughty rabbis" (so termed by Madonna) complained bitterly that the song was about 16th-century mystic Yitzhak Luria, and therefore was a sacrilege. Madonna said it was actually named for the man who sings on it with her, Yitzhak Sinwani.

The song was performed as a duet with Sinwani on the *Confessions Tour.*

ISLAND: Madonna's first **magazine** cover was for the October 1983 issue of this downtown publication whose publisher—**Steve Neumann**—she was dating at the time. Right from the start Madonna knew the **power** of making classical images speak for you: She dramatically holds her face like the **famed** Greta Garbo pose by Edward Steichen on this nearly impossible-to-find collector's item that goes for $2,500 or more when it (rarely) appears on eBay.

The cover photo plus one inside were done by Curtis Knapp, with styling by **Maripol** (using her Maripolitan cross earrings and rubber bracelets and a Sherry Vigdor coat), **hair** by Shunji of Suga and makeup by Marci Makeup.

"To our photo session, it was Madonna who brought this wonderful youthful energy and brightness … It was seriously lovely and lively and it followed her everywhere," Knapp remembered years later. Though a chunk of his outtakes were published in an exquisite **book** [SEE: **bibliography (about Madonna)**], Knapp lost many of his negatives when a friend's basement flooded, discarded others because he didn't like them and lost still more when a producer in Tokyo failed to return some Knapp had sent.

Presciently, the *Island* story was entitled "Madonna: Virgin Pop" a full year before **"Like a Virgin"** kicked her up to superstardom. The writer, Neumann himself, notes that Madonna was born in "smelly" **Bay City**, claims her **father** is the one who decided she should be named after her **mother**, remarked upon her fondness for **popcorn** and asked, "Who could defuse her?"

The interview—further illustrated by a **Steven Meisel** photo (he's credited as "Steve Meisel") from Madonna's first-ever shoot with that master—begins with this scintillating exchange:

Island: Madonna.
Madonna: What?

In the Q&A, Madonna said her **fashion** sense could be explained by virtue of the fact that her clothes were "so worn out" more than intentionally distressed, owned up to her desire to achieve stardom and when asked if she wanted to make a lot of **money** or a lot of records said, "I want to make a lot of **love.**"

Madonna also lied in the piece, claiming never to have seen a penis by age 17, but hey, the time to start myth building is in your first cover story.

"I'm sincere to people who are sincere," she offered.

"I feel like when I meet people I can absorb their character and be them."—MADONNA, *ISLAND* (1983)

Original test Polaroid from the *Island* shoot, the final cover and invites to the pub party

"IT'S SO COOL": Written by Madonna, **Mirwais** and **Monte Pittman** and produced by Madonna and Paul Oakenfold, this track started life in 2002 as the **unreleased** "Cool Song." In 2009, it was finished and retitled, offered as a bonus track on the deluxe version of *Celebration*. The demo, which has **leaked**, is a beautiful acoustic number that comes off as a little preachy (it's even got a choir as Madonna takes you to church). The final song is a fun but generic **dance** version of the **original**, the choir having been sent home so Mama could dance in the mirror. In one early version of the song, six-year-old **Lola** was singing in the background.

Forever

–PEREZ HILTON

OLIVIU SAVU

JACKSON, JANET: *b. May 16, 1966*. Perhaps the second most iconic female pop star of the 1980s, Jackson was always compared to Madonna and to her own brother, **Michael Jackson**. Nonetheless, she forged an impressively successful career fueled by her devotion to rigidly orchestrated **dance** moves, a remarkably consistent sound and her fetishization of "**control**," which was nearly as potent as Madonna's for self-expression.

Jackson, eight years Madonna's junior, yet having been in show **business** far longer, often seemed influenced by the **Queen of Pop**, in particular her "**Love** Will Never Do (Without You)" video (1990), which boasted Madonna's go-to photographer **Herb Ritts** as its director. Songs like "That's the Way Love Goes" and "Throb" (both 1993) owed much to Madonna songs like "**Erotica**" (1992) and "**Vogue**" (1990), respectively. Her *Velvet Rope* (1997) album, with its SM vibe, was likened to *Sex* by **Kurt Loder** in an interview with Madonna.

In spite of their many comparables, Jackson has never been a Madonna **fan**.

In 1993, when Jackson was asked on video if her music were similar to Madonna's, she attempted to distinguish what she did from what Madonna did, saying, "I think that what I do has class to it."

Asked if it were true that she couldn't stand Madonna, Jackson went the "Thumper" route with *Vibe* **magazine** in its September 1994 issue: "How does my mom say it? If I don't have anything good to say, don't say anything at all ... **Hate** is a strong word. I never said 'hate'. But if I did hate her, I'd have valid reasons."

What could those valid reasons be? Well, in *Truth or Dare* (1991), Madonna is heard saying "bite your tongue!" when a dancer says something she's wearing is, "Very Janet Jackson/*Rhythm Nation*." Around the time that was filmed, Madonna had met with Michael Jackson and publicly criticized his style. According to Jermaine Jackson, Madonna may have privately criticized Janet to Michael.

Asked about Janet Jackson's contempt for her in 1994, Madonna told **MTV**, "What did I do? I have never met the woman, I don't know anyone she knows, um, I'm mystified. Maybe she'll tell me one day." She labeled Jackson's feelings for her as "transparent."

A moment when their feud had a chance to thaw came and went as Madonna eulogized Michael Jackson at the **MTV Video Music Awards**; the women never met that night, and Janet did not comment on Madonna's speech.

Madonna was perceived to be jabbing Janet in interviews leading up to her **Super Bowl** performance in 2012. Asked about Jackson's **nip slip**, Madonna told NY1's Neil Rosen, "You don't have to show nipples to be interesting. Or, and it doesn't necessarily mean you're cutting-edge if you do." Clearly, Madonna could not have been coming down hard on Janet for showing her nipples—she'd done it herself many times before and was about to do it many more times. It seemed more an assurance that she would

not do anything intentionally dirty during the show than a legit whack at Janet.

For her part, Janet feigned interest in Madonna's halftime performance before it happened, telling Mario Lopez, "It's cool. I think it'll be fun. I think it'll be exciting." She never commented on it after the fact.

JACKSON, LA TOYA: *b. May 29, 1956*. The bubbly sister of **Michael** and **Janet Jackson** whom Madonna offended in 1991 with speculation that her boobs were, like most of the rest of her, not **God**-given.

Madonna first made the call in a *Rolling Stone* interview, wherein she eagerly tore into a preview copy of Jackson's first *Playboy* spread. "She's had a boob job for sure," Madonna said, cattily remarking that the layout might actually land Jackson some **work**. She repeated the comment on national **TV** to **Arsenio Hall**, noting that she knew Jackson's breasts were fake because "somebody told me."

Jackson hurled the same accusation right **back** at the at-the-time surgically untouched (**collagen** doesn't count) Madonna.

By 2009, when parts of Madonna were no longer real either, the bad blood was gone, because after Madonna eulogized Jackson's brother on the **MTV Video Music Awards**, Jackson was appearing on *The View* and was led into an opportunity to get catty by **Joy Behar** ... but Jackson didn't bite. Instead, Jackson effusively praised Madonna's speech, saying, "I thought Madonna did a *fabulous job*—it was absolutely magnificent!—and I felt that she was trying to show the world, she was trying to show the world the parallels with the two of them. And, and I understood it. I have to be quite honest with you, that speech to me was so touching. I truly enjoyed every single word that she said. As a matter of fact, I didn't want it to end."

JACKSON, MICHAEL: *August 29, 1958-June 25, 2009*. So often, Madonna is compared to **Marilyn Monroe**. But an artist she more closely resembles is clearly Michael Jackson.

Jackson attained superstardom as the lead singer of his family act the Jackson 5 in the '60s and '70s, surpassed his success with his brothers as a **disco** and then pop artist in the '70s and '80s and, quite simply, became one of the most beloved, famous and ultimately controversial human beings to ever walk the face of the earth.

As a child and teen, Madonna's favorite music was bubblegum pop and Motown Top 40, so it's not surprising that once she had experimented with her budding musicality courtesy of her boyfriend's rock band the **Breakfast Club**, her solo **work** reverted to that sound—a sound typified by Jackson, an artist she has consistently praised.

As soon as she had a record deal, who did Madonna seek out to manage her but Jackson's (former) manager, **Freddy DeMann**. Little did she know that her own career and artistic output would one day rival Jackson's.

Madonna and Michael, merged

©NANCY BURSON & DAVID KRAMLICH. COURTESY JAYNE H. BAUM GALLERY.

There has been some direct artistic cross-pollination.

Madonna's **"Like a Virgin"** slinks along on a bass line that's a clever tweak of the one found in Jackson's "Billie Jean" (1983), a song she incorporated into *The Virgin Tour* performance of her own hit. The music track for **"La Isla Bonita,"** composed by **Patrick Leonard** (who was the *Victory Tour*'s musical director), was originally pitched to Jackson, who passed, giving Madonna one of her most familiar '80s hits. And who could miss Madonna's gender-flouting appropriation of Jackson's crotch-grab move, which livened up her **"Express Yourself"** video?

But if there was crossover, there was also a bit of professional rivalry.

When **MTV** named Madonna its Artist of the Decade for the '80s, Jackson was incensed, insisting they create an honor for him that sounded even more impressive: The Video Vanguard Artist of the Decade. Even the title "King of Pop" was bestowed upon Jackson by Jackson—not that anyone would ever argue he didn't deserve it. Speaking of titles, the one Jackson privately bestowed upon Madonna around this time was "heifer."

In 1991, Madonna and Jackson came close to collaborating musically. It started when Madonna called him up out of the blue to invite him out to eat at The Ivy (113 N. Robertson Blvd., LA, CA), then took him **back** to her place to watch a movie. She later recalled he held her hand in a friendly, non-romantic way. While talking, they discovered that each was dateless for the upcoming **Oscars**. Madonna popped the question and Jackson agreed to go.

They made a pop culture couple for the ages when they attended that ceremony together, she in Marilyn Monroe finery, he in his white, sequined jacket and enormous gold belt. It was one of the most surreal star outings of all time, and it captured the public's imagination.

After the Oscars, the glam, anime-like pair attended agent Swifty Lazar's famous party, where Madonna drifted away from Jackson, perching herself in the lap of her ex-beau **Warren Beatty**, leaving her date to seek sympathy from **Diana Ross**.

When it came to a professional collaboration, Madonna was skeptical. She told *The Advocate* that she'd laid down the law, saying, "Look, Michael, if you want to do something with me, you have to be willing to go all the way or

I'm not going to do it." He agreed, inviting her to work with him on his song "In the Closet" (1991). He hooked Madonna with the title alone, but the two didn't see **eye-to-eye** creatively, Madonna pushing for the video to feature her in male **drag** and him in female drag, the last thing on earth to which the allegedly closeted and clearly **sexually** confused superstar would ever agree. Prior to child sexual abuse allegations, Jackson's image was wholesome, even asexual, whereas Madonna's was the opposite.

Madonna further screwed up her chance to gain Jackson's trust and work with him by publicly telling *The Advocate* that she felt his image needed overhauling.

"I have this whole vision about Michael," she told the LGBT news **magazine**. "We're considering working on a song together. I would like to completely redo his whole image, give him a Caesar—you know, that really short haircut—and I want to get him out of those buckly boots and all that stuff. What I want him to do is go to **New York** and hang out for a week with the House of Xtravaganza. They could give him a new style. I've already asked **Jose & Luis** if they would do it. They're thrilled and ready. I said, 'Could you give this guy a makeover for me? Because I think that's really what he needs.'"

As for "In the Closet," the song wound up with a mystery vocalist often mistaken for Madonna, but the real Mystery Girl was Princess Stephanie of Monaco.

Madonna said she and Jackson hung out "a few more times" in 1991, then lost touch. Maybe the two had so little to do with each other in part because Jackson didn't particularly like Madonna.

In tapes made between August 2000 and April 2001 by his spiritual advisor Rabbi Shmuley Boteach, made public in 2009, Jackson said of his first meeting with Madonna, "Madonna laid the law down to me before we went out. [She said], 'I am not going to Disneyland, okay? That's out.' I said, 'I didn't ask to go to Disneyland.' She said, 'We are going to the restaurant. And afterwards, we are going to a strip bar.' I said, 'I am not going to a strip bar, where they cross dress. Guys who are girls,' I said. 'I am not going to there. If that's how it is, forget this whole thing.'"

Madonna zinged MJ's stilted, "And just think, nobody thought this would last," stage-kiss of his wife Lisa Marie Presley on the 1994 **MTV Video Music Awards** by showing up with **David Letterman** and saying, "And you thought we wouldn't last!"

In spite of their professional rivalry and the fact that they were rather different people making sometimes-similar music, Madonna always respected Jackson as an artist.

When Jackson suddenly died of acute **drug** intoxication and a heart attack in 2009, Madonna was bereft.

"I can't stop crying over the sad news," she said in a statement. "I have always admired Michael Jackson. The world has lost one of the greats, but his music will live forever! My heart goes out to his three children and other members of his family. **God** bless."

"… I think Michael Jackson is a very talented man, but I think he's gone past a certain point. He operates in a world that I don't want any part of. I don't want to cut myself off from the world. I don't want to alienate myself from humanity … Don't get me wrong, he's very talented, but I think he's killing himself."—MADONNA, *SEATTLE TIMES* (1992)

"It was hard for him to look into people's eyes."
—MADONNA ON MICHAEL JACKSON (2015)

She continued prostrating herself before a **talent** she deemed greater than, and inspirational of, her own. On the 2009 leg of her *Sticky & Sweet Tour,* Madonna added a medley of Jackson's songs, and video and **dance** tributes to Jackson.

At the 2009 MTV Video Music Awards, Madonna opened the show (in a L'Wren Scott trench and Chopard jewels) with a surprise six-minute eulogy for Jackson that stressed Jackson's lost humanity. "Yes, yes, Michael Jackson was a human being, but damn it, he was a king—long live the king."

JAGGER, MICK: *b. July 26, 1943.* Rock **god** who has fronted the Rolling Stones for over 50 years, had solo success and has acted in movies.

When Madonna was a newcomer, Jagger said her **work** was characterized by "a central dumbness." The two first met in 1984 via mutual acquaintance **Maripol**, and were later reintroduced after he'd made the slur against her. "I don't think he really felt that way when he said it," she told **Jane Pauley** in 1987. "I think he was feeling my threat."

In 1992, Jagger handed out as many as *20 cases* of *Sex* to his pals. After the **Oscars** in 1997, Jagger and Madonna were seated together at a party, photographed deep in discussion (or as deep into it as you can get with Tony Curtis horning in). Jagger attended the *Drowned World Tour* with his daughter, Georgia May Jagger, in 2001, saying they **"loved** it." By 2012, Georgia May had become the face of Madonna's **Material Girl** clothing line.

In 2014, Madonna offered condolences when Jagger's longtime girlfriend L'Wren Scott committed suicide. "This is a horrible and tragic loss. I'm so upset. I loved L'Wren's work and she was always so generous with me."

JAMES, MERCY: *b. January 22, 2006.* Born Chifundo James ("Mercy" is the English translation of her first name), she is the daughter Madonna adopted—with great difficulty—from **Malawi**.

Following an international outcry over Madonna and **Guy Ritchie**'s adoption of **David Banda**, it was somewhat surprising that she attempted to go **back** to the same poisoned well for a second child, but she felt a strong connection to the little girl she'd met at the Kondanani Children's Village. She pursued the adoption even after her separation from Ritchie became known.

Madonna's battle to adopt Mercy was grim from the beginning. Governmental official Penston Kilembe told the media, "We can't approve a child to go into a broken home because the **divorce** could be the result of the behavior of the party trying to adopt. Madonna should forget this one."

"I want to provide Mercy with a home, a loving family environment and the best education and health care possible," Madonna testified in court, and it appeared she would probably get her way once more. A pre-adoption party was held April 2, 2009, at which Mercy's uncle, Peter Baneti, was in attendance; he'd signed off on the adoption days before.

"Madonna is a fantastic and loving mother who cares deeply about her own children and children who may need additional help and support. I fully supported her decision to apply for this adoption, and I am saddened that her application has been rejected."-GUY RITCHIE (2009)

On April 3, 2009, Judge Esmie Chombo of Lilongwe's High Court issued a rebuke of Madonna in the form of a ruling, chastising her for failing to meet the country's residency requirement (minimum of 18 months in Malawi), and practically daring her to withdraw her millions in aid for the country's "so-called poor" children:

"By removing the very safeguard that is supposed to protect our children, the courts by their pronouncements could actually facilitate trafficking of children by some unscrupulous individuals who would take advantage of the weakness of the law of the land ... I have no doubt that all hope is not lost with the petitioner's noble and immediate ideas of investing in the improvement of more children's lives in Malawi. It is my prayer that [Mercy James] would be among the first children to benefit from that project. Having said all this then, at the end of the day I must decline to grant this application for the adoption of the infant [Mercy James]."

Madonna's lawyer Alan Chinula appealed, arguing that the laws in question were antiquated.

In another stunning blow to Madonna's quest, Mercy—always presumed to be an orphan—turned out to have a living **father**, one James Kambewa, whom the English tabloid *Mirror* helpfully located. Kambewa said, "I bear no grudge against Madonna. But I am Mercy's father and I want her to stay with me. **God** will take care of us."

Adding insult to injury, an ex-employee of Madonna's, apparently a chef with an ax (or at least a butcher's knife) to grind, told the media he was glad that Madonna had failed in her bid to adopt Mercy. Eric Ienco said, "She's hardly ever with her children." He went on to claim Madonna did **Pilates** the day David Banda arrived into her home rather than spending time with him.

A stunning 67% of *Now* (UK) readers were against Madonna's decision to adopt Mercy, based apparently on the lingering perception that Madonna was adopting for publicity, or on the discomfort society still has over white people adopting black children. (How many stale jokes have we heard about "collecting" children?)

But Madonna never gave up hope, and in the end, she prevailed. On June 12, 2009, the decision to deny the adoption was overruled by a higher court. Madonna told the media, "I am ecstatic. My family and I look forward to sharing our lives with her." Immediately thereafter, Mercy's alleged father dropped his bid for custody, asking that Madonna take care of Mercy and inform her who her father is.

On **Instagram**, Mercy mugs for paparazzi and indulges in a newfound taste for princessy **fashions**. Both she and her brother David have accompanied their **mother** to Malawi, including to the orphanage where Madonna met Mercy.

Mercy's blood family has retained no legal right to see her.

"... [I]f you're Mick Jagger, you're allowed to date a 25-year-old, but if you're me, you're a bitch/cunt/whore."–MADONNA (2015)

"JIMMY JIMMY": A Madonna/**Stephen Bray** collaboration that appears on *True Blue*. It's the aural equivalent of Josie Cotton, Toni Basil and Avril Lavigne having an unsatisfying three-way.

"JOAN OF ARC": A **fan**-favorite song from *Rebel Heart*, this tune is a rare insight into Madonna's reaction to the intense scrutiny and criticism she receives. Surprisingly, Madonna sings that while harsh words don't mean anything in the long run if she has **love**, she admits that she needs to "cry my **eyes** out" every once in a while. It was written by Madonna, MoZella, Toby Gad and S1, with production by Madonna and Gad, plus AFSHeeN and Josh Cumbee.

Her first-ever live performance of the song aired March 18, 2015, on *The Ellen DeGeneres Show*, and it was sung at *Tears of a Clown* in Melbourne.

Madonna has said that Joan of Arc, along with **Frida Kahlo**, is one of her personal muses.

JOBS: Madonna had a lot of odd jobs before gaining steady **work** as a tenured pop star, including working at Amy's (a Greek place), Arby's (not a Greek place), Burger King, Dunkin' Donuts (from which she was fired after one day for playing with the jelly-squirter), McDonald's, an ice cream parlor and—in high **school**—as a lifeguard.

As a **nude** life model for painters and photographers, she was paid about $10 an hour. "I kept saying, 'It's for **art**!'" she later explained.

Madonna worked at the **Russian Tea Room** in 1979 courtesy of a reference from **Pearl Lang**, and briefly at the Gossamer Wing dying silk fabric (BF **Dan Gilroy** was a partner in the company). Her first manager, **Camille Barbone**, once got her a job as a house cleaner, which, as you can imagine, proved Barbone had not missed her calling as a career counselor.

Madonna once applied to work at a reception hall called Terrace on the Park (52-11 111th St., Flushing, NY), but wouldn't sweep up ("I'm bound for something great"). She was hired, but didn't keep the gig as its elevator operator for long. According to a local, the elevator got "stuck" and when it was finally opened, Madonna and a waiter—with empty wine glasses—popped out.

JOHANSEN, DAVID: *b. January 9, 1950*. This **New York** Dolls front man and alter ego of Buster Poindexter was Madonna's **date** at **MTV**'s New Year's 1982 party. He is reported to have **loved** her stint opening for him at My **Father**'s Place (formerly 19 Bryant Ave., Roslyn, NY) that evening and introduced the newcomer to various movers and shakers.

JOHN, ELTON: *b. March 25, 1947*. One of the most accomplished singer-songwriters of the era, John has sold over 300 million records worldwide, has 54 Top 40 hits in the US, has won the **Grammy**, the **Tony** and the **Oscar**, was inducted into the **Rock and Roll Hall of Fame** and is one of the world's pre-eminent **AIDS** activists.

In the distant past, Madonna (who has said the second concert she ever attended was one by John) and John have socialized and enjoyed friendly relations.

Things began to go awry in 1997, when Madonna talked about the impact that **Princess Diana**'s **death** had had upon her and John excoriated her for it; he felt, apparently, a proprietary interest in his friend, the princess whom he had eulogized with one of the best-selling singles of all time, "Candle in the Wind 1997" (1997).

By April 27, 1998, all seemed to be forgiven; the two were on the bill of **Rock for the Rainforest**, a benefit to raise awareness and **money** to combat the destruction of the rainforest. At no less sacred a venue than Carnegie Hall (881 7th Ave., NY, NY), they shared a mic, singing their hearts out and dancing to an all-star rendition of that **Beatles** classic "Twist and Shout" (1963).

But John, who clearly sees himself as not only the superior artist but also a sort of legitimacy cop, has for the past decade disparaged Madonna in ways that reveal him to be bitter over her accomplishments, even though his own aren't too shabby.

In 2002, John pegged Madonna's **"Die Another Day"** as the worst Bond theme ever. Madonna told *W* at the time, "He said this about me? You feel that twinge. Then I snap out of it and think, 'Oh, who gives a shit?'"

At the 2004 Q **Awards** in **London**, Madonna—who was not present—was nominated but lost for Best Live Act. While accepting the Classic Songwriter Award, John—out of nowhere—sputtered, "Madonna, best fuckin' live act? **Fuck** off! Since when has lip-synching been live? Sorry about that, but I think everyone who lip-synchs in public on stage when you pay like 75 quid to see them should be shot. Thank you very much. That's me off her fuckin' Christmas card list, but do I give a toss? No. Thank you very much."

Continuing with the theme, John's advice for Madonna's **Super Bowl** performance was, "Make sure you lip-synch good," though this barb was at least in the context that he understood most people who took the gig had to lip-synch due to technical concerns.

When Madonna and John were both nominated in the Best **Original** Song category at the **Golden Globes** in 2012, John could not conceal his contempt for the idea that something she'd created could be seen as comparable to something he'd created. His fiancé (now husband) David Furnish vented on **Facebook** when Madonna's **"Masterpiece"** took the prize, writing, "Madonna. Best song???? Fuck off!!! Madonna winning Best Original Song truly shows how these awards have nothing to do with merit. Her acceptance speech was embarrassing in its narcissism." He brought his close friend **Lady Gaga** into the mix, as Madonna had recently commented on the similarity between 2011's "Born This Way" (a song John had hyped prior to its release as the ultimate **gay** anthem) and **"Express Yourself."**

Madonna killed Mr. and Mr. Elton John (if only!) with kindness, stating backstage at the Globes, "He's been known to get mad at me so I don't know. He's brilliant and I adore him so he'll win another award. I don't feel bad!"

When public opinion sided with Madonna—why would an artist of the stature of Elton John feel the need to be so nasty?—Furnish gutlessly pretended it had all been no biggie, Facebooking, "Wow! What a tempest in a teapot. My comments regarding The Golden Globes have been blown way out of proportion ... But I must say for the record that I do believe Madonna is a great artist, and that Elton and I wish her all the best for next week's premiere of the film **W.E.**"

The damage **control** was undone when John granted an August 2012 Australian interview, during which he spat of Madonna's **MDNA Tour**, "Her tour has been a disaster, and it couldn't happen to a bigger cunt," calling Madonna a "fucking fairground stripper" and then, revealing the real reason for his renewed loathing, confirmed that he felt she'd been "so horrible to Gaga." You know, Gaga, the artist John and Furnish barely knew when they saw fit to make her the godmother of their child.

Madonna dedicated one performance of "Masterpiece" on her **MDNA** Tour to John saying, "... I know he's a big **fan** of it, and he's a big fan of mine. And you know what? I forgive him. Gotta start somewhere." Examining video from the moment, it's clear Madonna was being sincere. If her push to forgive the undeserving likes of John can in any way be chalked up to **Kabbalah**, it might be time to consider est!

In 2013, John claimed he had finally buried the hatchet with Madonna. Spotting her at a restaurant in France, he sent her a private note expressing his embarrassment for their feud.

"[Madonna] came in, and I sent over a note. She was very gracious. I apologized profusely because what I said should never have appeared in public." (Hmmm, not that he didn't really mean it?)

Since it is highly unlikely that Elton John and David Furnish truly like Madonna, considering their candid remarks, it's hard to believe the truce will last.

As for the age-old argument about how gay men all too often embrace straight women as gay icons over actual gay people, consider this: Elton John hid behind **bisexuality** in the '70s, got married to a woman in the '80s and in 2008 criticized American gay activists for wanting marriage equality. "We're not married," he said of his union with Furnish. "Let's get that right. We have a civil partnership. What is wrong with Proposition 8 is that they went for marriage. Marriage is going to put a lot of people off ... I don't want to be married." He let everyone else fight for gay people to have the right to marry, then got married in December 2014 after all. As far as gay icons go, Madonna's got Elton John beat bi a mile.

As another insight into the irrationality of John's contempt for Madonna, consider this: John happily played his friend Rush Limbaugh's **wedding** (not to mention Sun City under apartheid, which is another conversation), claiming

that Limbaugh—who has derided gay rights to his millions of dittoheads for years—"sends me the loveliest emails."

And yet Madonna gets under his skin for not knowing her place? Vaginas really bring out the worst in some people.

JOHNSON, DON: b. December 15, 1949. By the time Don Johnson was circling Madonna in search of a duet partner, he'd been pretend-**raped** by for-real **bisexual** '50s **acting** idol Sal Mineo on stage in Fortune in Men's **Eyes** (1969), had enjoyed a semi-successful '70s acting career including the cult classic A Boy and His **Dog** (1975), had become passé, had experienced a **Joan Collins**–level comeback as the star of the **TV** series **Miami** Vice (1984–1989) and was in the midst of parlaying his sudden relevance into a little **Billboard**-choking pop-music potency.

Johnson, in the area shooting The Long Hot Summer (1985), sent Madonna flowers the night of her New Orleans **The Virgin Tour** show along with a card that read, "With major lust, Don Johnson." Not long after, over a meal at Helena's in 1986, he asked her to duet with him on an Otis Redding song. Instead, the two apparently collaborated by telephone on an **unreleased** tune, the existence of which Madonna confirmed in interviews in 1987.

What is it about men who've slept with Melanie Griffith that makes Madonna want to sing with them?

JOLIE, ANGELINA: b. June 4, 1975. SEE: **Pitt, Brad.**

JONATHAN ROSS SHOW, THE: Airdates: September 3, 2011–. Madonna made her first appearance on the ITV chatfest—representing her third sit-down with **Jonathan Ross** in the space of 23 years—in an episode airing March 14, 2015. The episode, like all of her Ross wun-ins, was noteworthy for the content of the interview: Madonna had only the night before been dragged off the stage at the **Brit Awards** in what she termed a "horror show" accident.

Vampy as hell in a black mesh dress, she performed her **Rebel Heart** tunes **"Living for Love"** (a remix) and **"Ghosttown"**; the former took two tries at the taping, while the latter took three due to her bobbling of the lyrics since it was her first time ever performing the song publicly.

Ross asked Madonna about rumors that she fell on stage purposefully for publicity. Madonna looked shocked then good-naturedly postulated that "the universe was trying to teach me a lesson, I don't know." She admitted she had some whiplash and "there was a man standing over me with a flashlight till about 3 a.m. making sure that I was still compos mentis."

Speaking at length about her fall, Madonna said, "I'm a creature of habit and I rehearse everything—everything, everything, everything—and I was thrown a wrench at the very beginning of my entrance. I was told to tie my cape and start much further **back** than we had rehearsed so because I had to walk so much further, everybody was worried that my cape was going to slide off because it's quite

–CHI CHI LARUE

heavy so they tied it really tight around my neck. So here I am marching in like a queen and I got to the top of the stairs and I pulled my silky string and it would not come undone and my two lovely Japanese **dancers** basically strangled me off the stage. I had a choice, I could either be strangled or fall with the cape and I fell."

Her remarks on the show were seemingly misread by Giorgio Armani, designer of her infamous cape, who tartly told the media, "Madonna is very difficult; I won't dare to say what I'd like to say ... The cape had a hook very easy to open, but she wanted a tie (or the other way around, I can't remember well). And then she didn't manage to untie it with her little hands."

We get it, Armani, it wasn't your fault.

Ross, as usual, got a **flirty** and playful side of Madonna on his program, spotlighting her resilience following her fall, not from grace, but just from one place to another.

JONES, GRACE: *b. May 19, 1948.* Jamaican singer and sometimes actor who is thought of as a downtown **original** thanks to her committed persona and avant-garde stage antics.

Though Jones is more clearly an inspiration for the likes of **Lady Gaga**, Madonna was a fan **back** in the day. The two were photographed together at **Private Eyes** video bar in 1984, both wearing sunglasses at night.

In 2011, Jones said without any apparent malice, "I don't mind, you know, Madonna used to come around and watch me ... but they're looking, they're searching for inspiration ..."

JOSE & LUIS: Jose Gutierez Xtravaganza and **Luis Camacho Xtravaganza** (b. April 3, 1970) are the out-and-proud **dancers** Madonna found at the House of Xtravaganza, the ones who taught her how to vogue. Madonna first saw the guys dancing at the Sound Factory (formerly 12 W. 21st St., NY, NY), then had them perform for her at a joint called Tracks before it opened for the night. The guys showed off their mad **vogueing** skills in her **"Vogue"** video, at the **MTV Video Music Awards** and on the *Blond*

... with Luis on her back

On Jose's shoulders ...

Ambition World Tour. In the latter, the boys are the ones sporting **cone bras** during that **"Like a Virgin"** sequence.

In 1992, Madonna said of the boys, "It's a highly dysfunctional but terribly rewarding relationship. They're a goldmine that needs to be explored. I think they should have their own talk show."

Gutierez also appeared in the controversial **"Justify My Love"** video as the undulating, hard-bodied connective tissue between soft-core scenes.

Madonna so adored the guys that she sang the chorus of their debut single, **"Queen's English,"** which had it been released 20 years later would have been a single from one of *RuPaul's* **Drag** *Race*-ers. Though it had been presumed that Jose & Luis would have an album release on **Maverick**, they wound up on **Sire**, their first three songs released on the compilation *New Faces*. Lost in the shuffle was what would have been Madonna's directorial debut—she had been mentioned as the director of a never-made video for their song "Groovin'."

Camacho has continued **working** as a choreographer (LuisCamacho.com). In 2005, he told **fan site** MadonnaTribe that when he first met Madonna, he was so uninformed about her work that he'd thought she was black: "All I knew was '**Holiday**' and '**Borderline**' and wasn't aware of her music videos." He wound up admiring Madonna after his time with her, praising her for "trying to broaden people's horizons with different cultures, for example dance, **fashion**, religion, **sexuality**."

Camacho's positive reaction to Madonna's **Super Bowl** performance was posted on **YouTube** in 2012. He liked the "Vogue" sequence best. Asked if the dancers at the Super Bowl had done it better than he had, he replied, "Well, we won't go *that* far, but ..." Gutierez was in the crowd at the September 22, 2010, launch of Madonna's **Material Girl** line at Macy's. Both appear in the film *Strike a Pose*.

©ARNAL/URLI/GARCIA/STILLS/RETNA

ALAN LIGHT

"I've never seen anyone give more shit to Madonna and get away with it than Jose & Luis."—LIZ ROSENBERG (1992)

JOY, ROBERT: *b. August 17, 1951.* Canadian actor who played "Jimmy" to Madonna's "Susan" in *Desperately Seeking Susan.* Since 1995, Joy's partner has been Henry Krieger, composer of the Broadway musicals *Dreamgirls* (1981) and *Side Show* (1997).

"JUMP" (SONG): *Release date: October 31, 2006. Billboard Hot 100 peak: NA.* This *Confessions on a Dance Floor* tune, written by Madonna, **Stuart Price** and **Joe Henry** and produced by Madonna and Price, became the album's fourth and final single. It's one of the album's best songs, a persuasive piece of **dance**-pop encouragement that harkens **back** to Madonna's self-help '80s output like **"Spotlight."**

"Jump" was on Madonna's **KOKO** and **G-A-Y** set lists and was given a robust live performance as part of her *Confessions Tour.*

"… [T]he song is a pulsing pop tune that has a positive, universal message about believing in yourself, not wasting time and taking a chance in life."—KEITH CAULFIELD, BILLBOARD (2006)

"JUMP" (VIDEO): *Director: Jonas Åkerlund, 2006.* With little time to make a proper video, Madonna enlisted go-to guy **Jonas Åkerlund** to bring to life one of the best songs—and the fourth single—from her massively successful *Confessions on a Dance Floor* album. Madonna wore a fetching (if unconvincing) asymmetrical platinum-bob wig for her studio performance, which consisted of dancing (including on her knees) in a confined setting stuffed with neon signs meant to evoke Tokyo, the city in which the video's parkour scenes were shot. It's a startlingly low-grade effort, a bit like canned Madonna, but is interesting for its hat tip to Japan, a country Madonna had visited for the first time in years to promote her album.

"JUST A DREAM": *Release date: March 9, 1993. Billboard Hot 100 peak: NA.* Madonna and **Patrick Leonard** co-wrote and coproduced a version of this perky track for inclusion on *Like a Prayer* before deciding it didn't fit. In 1993, Madonna gave the song to her friend and backup singer **Donna De Lory** for De Lory's self-titled debut album, complete with backing vocals (role reversal!). The song, a minor **dance** hit, has an E.G. Daily sound to it. Madonna's own version is still **unreleased.**

"JUSTIFY MY LOVE" (SONG): *Release date: November 6, 1990. Billboard Hot 100 peak: #1.* The song that curled Top 40 radio's toes and which foreshadowed Madonna's long-term commitment to explicitly politi-sexual **art** in the wake of an already suggestive career.

The song was initially credited to Lenny Kravitz with additional lyrics by Madonna, but **Prince** protégée Ingrid Chavez claimed the song was almost identical to her demo, which she'd written. "Lenny told me he was obsessed about getting it the same," she said at the time. Chavez had signed away credit in exchange for 25% of the royalties on the song. Kravitz explained that they'd initially agreed he would get the credit "for personal reasons." Chavez wound up receiving official credit.

Kravitz also caught flak when it was pointed out that the song's humming bass line was lifted from "Security of the First World" (1988) by **Public Enemy.** Kravitz denied intentionally sampling from the most notorious samplers in history, but his explanation was cringe-worthy: "I don't know which beat it is, actually. It's just one of those beats you find on the floor somewhere." It was alleged that Public Enemy had actually lifted the beat from James Brown's 1970 classic "Funky **Drummer**," an accusation their producer vehemently denied. No lawsuit ever happened regarding the music.

Craziest of all, can you believe the song was originally intended for **Paula Abdul**???

Contentious credits aside, Madonna's version of "Justify My Love" was an unqualified triumph. It sounded like nothing else on the airwaves at the time, and bears a rare truly erotic vocal from an artist whose songs are more often about **sex** than about being sexy. Madonna's direct come-on, delivered in a disembodied whisper, is riveting; her delivery even overcomes a silly lyric about riding trains cross-country.

Irish *Hot Press* **magazine** named it the #3 sexiest song of all time, and rightly so—listen to it with the lights off, but don't wear brand-new **underwear.**

"Justify My Love" was a ballistic #1, selling over a million copies and becoming one of Madonna's biggest hits, boosting sales of her greatest-hits collection (*The Immaculate Collection*), on which it originated.

The song generated a hilarious *Wayne's World* segment on *Saturday Night Live* featuring Madonna's participation, was performed on *The Girlie Show World Tour* and was remixed by **William Orbit** and used as a video interlude on *The MDNA Tour.* The song also inspired a mix known as **"The Beast Within"** that appeared on *The Girlie Show World Tour* and that preceded all the action on the *Re-Invention World Tour.*

"Justify My Love" was such a radical departure from mainstream pop music it also generated at least three answer songs: "Justify, Satisfy" (1990) from rapper D-Melo; "To My Donna" (1991) from Young Black Teenagers, who shared producers with Public Enemy; and "Al'l Justify Your Love" (1991) from Al B. Sure! (featuring K-Ci & JoJo as backup singers).

KEEP THE FAITH:
A LONG-AWAITED MESSAGE FROM
DESPERATELY SEEKING SUSAN'S
"JIMMY"

Robert Joy is one of those actors known for many different projects, but fans who recognize him sometimes don't know *exactly* who he is. That made him a perfect candidate for the 2012 documentary *That Guy ... Who Was in That Thing*, which profiled 16 successful, working actors whose famous faces are more famous than their names.

Though he's logged 168 episodes of *CSI: NY* as "Dr. Sid Hammerback" and has had memorable roles in the Louis Malle classic *Atlantic City* (1980) opposite Susan Sarandon and Burt Lancaster, in Milos Forman's *Ragtime* (1981) with James Cagney and Howard E. Rollins Jr., in some cult-classic horror films and on Broadway in the 2014 revival of *Side Show*, he's most famous to Madonna fans as her boyfriend "Jimmy" in *Desperately Seeking Susan*.

That's right: "Jimmy!"

Joy, who attended a February 2, 2015, screening of *Susan*, graciously spoke to *EM2O* in his Broadway dressing room between shows. He was only too happy to recall his experiences on the film and with Madonna.

EM2O: Thirty years after its release, how do you look back at *Desperately Seeking Susan*?

ROBERT JOY: I'm thrilled to be in *Desperately Seeking Susan*, because it's an iconic movie, it represents New York in such an interesting way. Now, looking back—we didn't think of it like this at the time—now, it's like a period piece. It captures bohemian New York.

EM2O: How did you hear about the role of Jimmy?

RJ: I must've heard about it through the casting person. I am a member of Ensemble Studio Theater on W. 52 St., and Billy Hopkins and Risa Bramon Garcia used to cast over there; they were part of that theater company and they kinda had just started. They had been casting the *Marathon of One-Act Plays* over there and stuff like that and were hired to cast this movie because people felt they were in touch with the New York acting community.

I remember auditioning and Risa and Billy casting me and I remember the callback because Madonna was at the callback. I didn't know who she was—nobody knew who she was, really, except we'd heard she had one record, she had one record that was on the brand-new MTV.

That was a very interesting callback because I felt that Madonna helped me get the part. We read that scene where we're reunited after a while and she just kinda draped herself around me. It must've seemed very much like there was chemistry there. [Laughs]

EM2O: That's not surprising to hear—you two have palpable chemistry in the movie.

RJ: I'd never played a role quite like that in a movie before. In movies, I'd played kinda crazy roles or outsider roles, and on stage I'd played a lot of innocent young men, so I'd done sorta both ends of the spectrum, but this was in the middle—a nice guy who was sort of an outsider, but he wasn't pathological or anything.

We started doing that first scene on that first day down in Battery Park, that was my first day on the movie—and there was no rehearsal. I was a theater actor, so there was no four weeks of rehearsal. You run through the lines once. We're going through the lines and I figure I'm the one who's put the ads in the paper for her and there she is so maybe it'll work if we're both puppy dogs and we're so playful with each other. So that was my first take in the very first rehearsal with Susan [Seidelman]. And Susan took me aside and she said, "Well, try something else. Try ... because Madonna is so cool in the scene, it might be better if you're kinda cool, too." It was partly her direction and partly this magnetic thing going on with Madonna.

Everyone knew it was Madonna's first movie, and you expect someone with their first movie to be a little scattered, like, 'Oh, I don't know what I'm doing!' She wasn't like that *at all*. And it's a great lesson about how to encounter a new situation. She seemed to be really grounded and relaxed and I don't know how to say this, but she found a place of comfort for herself and it created a kind of magnetism where my first take on the scene was in a funny way trying to take her out of her comfort zone.

EM2O: And you were basically meeting for one of the first times when filming that scene? What did you think when you first saw her?

RJ: We were—except for the callback. My memory of how she looked is how she looked on the first day of shooting. At the time, it was very stylish and hip in the old meaning of that word, you know what I mean? It was a style that none of my friends were wearing. She was a step ahead of all of us.

EM2O: You guys had such a big kiss, right on the first day.

RJ: Absolutely! She wasn't capital M Madonna then, but still she was obviously very attractive and charismatic and, you know, what kinda took the tension out of the scene is I approach her and she takes the gum out of her mouth and then kisses me. After the first scene, the cleanup was so extensive it made us laugh, because she had so much lipstick on and then when we did all the kissing, the two of us had faces that were colored by her lipstick.

EM2O: Any pre-discussion about how the kiss would go down?

RJ: Oh, no, no, no, no, we absolutely just did it. The story is clear. You read the script and in print it's very clear what's going on. That little conversation between there and the van is a good one, too, where she's wishing Jimmy wasn't going away.

We knew that Susan Seidelman had only ever done one indie film, so we all felt like we were part of an indie movie and very happy to be part of it ... the way the designer dressed us and the van and everything, it felt very much exotic. Whereas in *Smithereens* [1982], I think some of those people *were* part of that scene, most of us were actors. Annie Golden played the girl in the band and she had done a lot of singing and she was an Off-Broadway actor like I was, but we weren't necessarily a part of that punk scene at all, so we felt like we were invited into a world.

A lot of the people in the movie were from Ensemble ... I just ran into the magician from The Magic Club, Peter Maloney; he'd just come from seeing *The Illusionists* on Broadway. He's still studying magic.

EM2O: Were you expecting the film to become the box-office smash it became?

RJ: No. I didn't have *any* idea.

EM2O: What was the vibe on the set?

RJ: There was tension on the set. Susan Seidelman

Madonna embraces Joy

ANDY SCHWARTZ

had shot by the hip and she had people on the crew—which was very smart of [producers] Sarah Pillsbury and Midge Sanford—who had more experience than her. Her directorial style was very probing and if this is fair to say, kind of willing to be uncertain, and they weren't used to that, the crew. So her typical direction after a take would be, "So ... yeah ... let me think ... maybe if you ...? No, that was okay, let's move on." I found it great. She'd say we need to do it again and the DP or someone would say, "That's it, that's all the time we have, we gotta move on." There was that kind of a tension in the logistics. I felt that Susan was very much still in the underground world and other people were saying, "No, we're in limited-budget feature film world—you can't just ask us a favor to go past the time limit."

I think whatever aesthetic she came to the movie with, the success of the movie owes it to her.

EM2O: How did you find Madonna as an actress?

RJ: I think she was amazing for the reasons I said before. She could relax into this comfortable thing and be in front of the camera and that didn't bother her at all—there was no nervousness for a first-time actress in a central role. There was a gravity, like satellites around a planet and that's essential to why the movie works.

She was playful from the get-go, as you can tell in our scenes. She was a great acting partner.

She's a pro. She's got nothing, at least back then, she had nothing on her mind but her interests and getting the work done. She wasn't turning up late or anything like that.

EM2O: Tell me about The Magic Club.

RJ: It's where Malcolm X was shot. That was kinda hanging over us. It was exotic. You go in there in the light of day and realize Malcolm X was shot there, so there was a whole layer over it where we felt, "Wow, we're in this movie that has so much going on with it already," and then when we saw what Santo had done with it—we owe so much to Santo Loquasto for the look of the movie—it was so much fun with the waitresses going around with the Eiffel Towers on their heads.

I remember driving up to there—'cause we didn't have separate cars or anything—I'd get into a station wagon at my apartment and the station wagon would stop at W. 56th Street, where the Apple Health Club used to be, and we'd pick up Madonna there because she would've done a workout before the shoot, probably a night shoot, right? We were going up there from noon to midnight. All the way up, she'd be talking about songs on the radio and who produced that and, "I like this producer, I don't like that producer, I wanna work with this producer." So you felt her as a student of pop culture even then.

EM2O: Did you hear one of the *Susan* jackets sold at auction for a quarter-million dollars recently? [Editor's note: The jacket was re-auctioned for $87,500 in 2016 following problems with the initial sale.]

RJ: Get out of town ... wow. It is kind of amazing. It's such a tribute to the whole team. God, that's very impressive to hear that now. We really didn't know that we'd be making that kind of impression.

EM2O: When you burst into the window at the end is such a charming scene.

RJ: That's my favorite scene in the movie. It really was at the end of a shooting day and sometimes things just happen, you know. It wasn't that carefully blocked, so we said, "Let's see what we can capture," and we captured that and I think it was really fresh.

EM2O: What about the scene where Aidan clobbers you, and does a partial nude scene at the same time?

RJ: I remember working with Aidan on that. You know, he's a very diligent actor, so we rehearsed and rehearsed and rehearsed it. That was carefully worked out.

EM2O: The pinball-machine scene with Madonna feels very improvised.

RJ: Will Patton says, "Nice legs." I can't remember if that was improvised. I think it was. Will is, to this day, has the most interesting inner dialogue of any actor I know. He'll say unexpected things and have a perfectly felt out reason to say it. One of the film's strengths is that it was willing to be sexy and funny at the same time.

EM2O: There are almost too many moments in the film to ask about them all ...

RJ: Do you remember when the waitress in The Magic Club comes over to the people and she says to Laurie Metcalf, "This must be yours, rum and Tab?" She was my wife at the time, Mary Joy. Every small performance is a full performance.

EM2O: How did you like the movie when you finally saw it?

RJ: I remember seeing it for the first time and being blown away by how it came together. On the set, there was a sense of, "How is this going to work?" We'd get to the end of the day and be behind schedule and we'd be like, "Can we add this? Do we need to cut that?" It didn't feel *at all* like you were part of a juggernaut that *had to* go forward. It felt like we were part of something that was vulnerable with a lot of loose ends and would we all gather in the loose ends before we ran out of money?

I think the last scene I shot was in the movie theater eating popcorn, and I think that was emblematic of how we all felt. There's an accident with the movie in that scene, the film's melting—what's gonna happen?—then we'd laugh and eat the popcorn. And that was an improvised moment and she went with it.

EM2O: What do you think of Madonna now?

RJ: I'm impressed with Madonna. I remember when she came out with *Sex*. I thought that was an amazing book. I thought it was adventurous in all the right ways. She's saying, "Let's be freer than we thought we could be." And in a way, that's happening in *Desperately Seeking Susan*, too; it just so happened that I think Madonna's philosophy and attitude toward love dovetailed with the character of Susan. My daughter went to see Madonna on tour in Toronto and she was totally blown away. Whenever I see Madonna do anything, her rigor impresses me and her talent and that willingness to explore artistically. From the point of view of sexual politics, I love everything she does.

EM2O: On a separate note, I was also excited to see you on an episode of *Moonlighting* around that time.

RJ: Here's my Bruce Willis anecdote: A few years after *Susan*, I'm at the Oakwood School with my daughter in California at a parents' thing. Somebody who's a rep of Bruce Willis has his daughter there and he came up to me and said, "You don't know me, but I wanna tell you that Bruce Willis owes his career to you," or something stupid like that, and I said, "What are you talking about?" and he said, "Bruce Willis told me he really wanted that part you played in *Desperately Seeking Susan* and when he didn't get it, he said, 'Fuck this town, I'm going to LA!' ... and he got *Moonlighting*."

Madonna lightens the mood with a giggle.

"JUSTIFY MY LOVE" (VIDEO): *Director: Jean-Baptiste Mondino, 1990.* If the song was a naughty smash, the video was a pop cultural **sex** crime, so raunchy it was banned by **MTV**, even after the channel had promoted it as the capper of an all-Madonna weekend.

The channel objected not to one specific part of the video, but rather to its entire tone, taking a stand despite the **nudity** they had allowed in her **"Vogue"** video, the SM they had allowed in her **"Express Yourself"** video, and the steady stream of blatant sexism (Warrant's 1990 clip for "Cherry Pie") and violence (rap, anyone?—or how about a little heavy metal?) the channel regularly allowed. By telling the public "Justify My Love" was too sexy to be aired, MTV singlehandedly made the clip the hottest thing since Duran Duran's uncensored "Girls on Film" video (1981).

Displaying an intoxicatingly creepy, self-contained sexual netherworld, the **black-and-white** video was shot by **Jean-Baptiste Mondino** on and around November 9, 1990, on the sixth floor of Le Royal Monceau Raffles **Paris** hotel (37 av. Hoche, Paris, France).

"The whole idea was to lock ourselves into this hotel for three days and two nights. Without any rules," Mondino told *Rolling Stone* in 2015. "We rent the whole top floor of that hotel. You know usually when you do a shoot, you have timing ... So we didn't have none of this. This is the rooms that we were sleeping in, living in. Maybe 15 rooms. One room was [the] makeup room, one was the wardrobe. Nobody was allowed to go out. There were tables with food in it, and when people were starving, they were eating. There were no rules—we had **alcohol**, we could smoke."

In the finished piece, Madonna—looking like a hyper-**blonde**, hyper-**Marilyn Monroe** with severe makeup and newly **collagen**-swollen lips—is a lone woman, a sexual adventurer who mysteriously falls prey to the overheated atmosphere of a clinical hotel that houses the gamut of human sexuality ... or at least, every aspect of it that Middle America could even imagine at the time, even if it wasn't used to seeing such imaginings on **TV**.

Topless butch lesbians threaten from here, horny trans girls cuddle together there and real-life beau **Tony Ward** watches in awe as Madonna is straddled by and deep-kisses an androgynous woman (Amanda Cazalet). After the sexy time fades, Madonna streaks, laughing, from the hotel, invigorated by her experience. Never before or since have Madonna's musical and visual statements been so perfectly matched.

The video was inspired by the film ***The Night Porter***, so it was clearly always gonna be way over the head of the average MTV lunkhead. Still, what's deplorable is not that MTV rejected it, but the real reason why.

It wasn't the video's sexual nature, but rather the nature of its sex. Homosexuality was a longstanding taboo at milquetoast MTV (which didn't even play black artists initially) and there is no question that the reason the clip was sacked was Madonna's leisurely, undeniably hot same-sex kiss. Without that kiss, it seems likely MTV would've asked for the nipples to be scotched and then would've greenlit it. But we'll never know.

Once it was banned, Madonna sold "Justify My Love" as a VHS video single. It sold almost 800,000 copies at $9.98 a pop. So lucky her!

• •

"WHY IS IT THAT PEOPLE ARE WILLING TO GO TO A MOVIE AND WATCH SOMEONE GET BLOWN TO BITS FOR NO REASON AND NOBODY WANTS TO SEE TWO GIRLS KISSING OR TWO MEN SNUGGLING?"—MADONNA, *THE NEW YORK TIMES* (1990)

• •

"I DON'T THINK FOR ONE SECOND THAT MADONNA HAD ANY INTENTION OF GETTING THIS VIDEO ON MTV."—MTV MUCKY-MUCK MARSHALL COHEN (1990)

• •

"BY SUPPRESSING EROTIC DISSENT, MTV DOES ITS BEST TO SEE THAT THIS POWERFUL MEDIUM WILL NOT COMMUNICATE THE 'WRONG' IDEA ABOUT SEX. THAT MAY PACIFY THE PURITANS, BUT IT ALSO MAKES IT EASIER TO DENY WOMEN AND GAYS THEIR FULL HUMANITY—EASIER FOR THE METAL MASSES TO JUSTIFY THEIR HATE ... 'JUSTIFY MY LOVE' MAKES IT HARDER TO HURT PEOPLE ..."
—RICHARD GOLDSTEIN, *THE VILLAGE VOICE* (1990)

• •

"HONESTLY, I WAS SURPRISED THAT THAT VIDEO WAS *THAT* SHOCKING ... WE ARE HERE BECAUSE PEOPLE *FUCK*, SO, WE SHOULD BE PROUD OF THE FUCKING THING."
—JEAN-BAPTISTE MONDINO (2015)

• •

OLIVIU SAVU

K

KABBALAH: An ancient Jewish method of mystical interpretation of the Bible, the central text of which is the Zohar. Madonna is a devoted follower, specifically of the variety taught by the Kabbalah Centre, created in 1965 by the late Rabbi Philip S. Berg (real name: Feivel Gruberger). The Kabbalah Centre is a non-profit now run by Berg's widow Karen and their sons Yehuda and Michael Berg.

When lapsed **Catholic** Madonna's newfound spirituality became common knowledge (she'd first attended meetings while **pregnant** in 1996), critics scoffed, likening it to Scientology. "I may as well have announced that I've joined the Nazi party," Madonna said of the media reaction. "... I was accused of joining a cult. I was accused of being brainwashed. Of giving away all my **money** ... I was actually trying to become a better person."

Madonna's brand of Kabbalah cannot correctly be called a religion; it is rather a supplement to religious or spiritual beliefs.

"It is sort of like a manual for living. It has nothing to do with dogma. It is the mystical interpretation of the Old Testament," Madonna told the holy text *TV Guide* in 1998. "How has it changed me? It's helped me stand up and take responsibility for everything to do with me. To stop saying, 'You did this to me,' or 'They did this to me. It is their fault.'"

Madonna's Kabbalistic beliefs include a desire to tame (or destroy ...) the ego, a drive to create order out of chaos and the conviction that we invite negativity into our lives. In 2003, Madonna explained: "The core of Kabbalah is the same as Christianity, and that's to **love** your neighbor as you love yourself. The difference, at least for me, is that Kabbalah gives me the tools to apply that to my life. The soul of everyone is good. What's not good is the ego. And all the ego is is Satan trying to **control** you. Your **job** in life is trying to control the Satan in you." ("That's just Satan's game ..." she sings in **"Intervention,"** noting that the devil wants "to fool ya" in **"Devil Pray."**)

Madonna outwardly, proudly expresses her faith in much of her **work**, especially in her music and on tour (there are aspects of it in every tour since she began her studies); by regular visits to Kabbalah Centres in **New York** (155 E. 48th St., NY, NY), LA (1062 S. Robertson Blvd., LA, CA), **London** (12 Stratford Pl., London, England, UK) and other locations; and by wearing the talismanic red string associated with it around her wrist. She is said to carry a 22-volume commentary on the Zohar with her everywhere she travels.

Like Madonna, the Kabbalah Centre has seen its share of controversy—the organization was investigated for financial malfeasance and suffered bad press when its project with Madonna, **Raising Malawi**, was abandoned. A 2006 rumor that Madonna was leaving Kabbalah turned out to be wishful thinking or a **hoax**, depending on how you view the org. It has been alleged that she prefers to be surrounded by fellow Kabbalists, and she has (as by the sister of her late manager, **Caresse Henry**) been accused of forcing the practice on her team members. Her manager, **Guy Oseary**, attends services.

But far from seeming mired in a cult, Madonna acts like a woman empowered when it comes to her faith. Madonna explained her distaste for religious dogma in *Ladies' Home Journal* in 2005: "I don't reject the idea that Jesus Christ walked on this earth, and He was a divine being, and He had a very important message to bring to the world, but I reject the religious behavior of any religious organization that does not encourage you to ask questions and do your own exploration."

Kabbalah has seemed to give Madonna a center, has allowed her to accept failure and has made her a more serious person. Whether or not it's a huge scam would probably make for a lively debate at a Madonna Fan Convention.

> "I'm sort of searching for my own spirituality, so … but I think it kind of trivializes what I'm doing to say, y'know, 'the new spiritual Madonna.' I mean, what was I up until now, like, a heathen?" –MADONNA (1998)

KAHLO, FRIDA: *July 6, 1907–July 13, 1954.* The woman who once announced, "I was born a **bitch**" is considered by many to be the greatest Mexican painter of all time, ahead of her husband, Diego Rivera.

Much of Kahlo's **work** is self-portraiture, which portrays her as an enigmatic presence. And check out that single **eyebrow**! It puts Madonna's former fuzziness to shame. Madonna **loves** Kahlo's self-reflexive **art** and owns several of her best pieces, including *My Birth* (1932).

In 1990, Madonna began developing a film on the artist's life, which was to have starred Madonna herself, with a script by Jeremy Pikser, who would later write *Bulworth* (1998) with **Warren Beatty**. Kahlo was *too-too* trendy at the time, so several other entities were developing similar projects, one of which would have gone in front of the cameras were it not for Mexican-American outcry against the casting of Italian-American Laura San Giacomo as Kahlo.

Imagine how those complaining would have felt if Madonna had played her?

In 2002, Salma Hayek produced and starred in the film *Frida*, for which she received an **Oscar** nomination for Best Actress in a Leading Role. Perhaps still smarting from her inability to get a production off the ground, Madonna said she didn't like Hayek's film "at all," though did praise her for doing "a great **job**." Still, "The movie doesn't even scratch the surface of who she was and what she went through."

> "… [S]he was a freedom fighter and she lived a controversial life and was a survivor, so I admire her life story and art."
> –MADONNA, REDDIT.COM (2013)

RHONDA CORTE

KAMALI, NORMA: *b. June 27, 1945.* **Fashion** designer famous for her sleeping bag coats and as the woman who put Farrah Fawcett-Majors into that swimsuit ... you know the one.

Madonna modeled for this designer in 1981, according to **Camille Barbone.** When a string of rosary beads dangled below her waistline, Madonna said to Barbone, "See, Camille? Even **God** wants to get into my pants."

KAMEN, NICK: *b. April 15, 1962.* Many Brits remember a Levi's 501 jeans **commercial** from 1985 called "Laundrette" in which a heartthrob strolls into a Laundromat, strips to his **underwear** and sits patiently while his clothes are in the machine. That hunk was Kamen, a dark-featured, baby-faced model/singer whom Madonna took under her wing in 1986. She wrote, produced (with **Stephen Bray**) and provided prominent backing vocals to Kamen's first single, "Each Time You Break My Heart," which failed to launch him in the US but made him an overnight sensation in Europe. Madonna's own demo for the song, with her lead vocals, is available as a **leak** but remains **unreleased.** She also did backing vocals on "Tell Me" (1988), the lead single from his follow-up album *Us.* Madonna's frequent collaborator **Patrick Leonard** produced that album for Kamen.

Did they ever have an affair? Even her biographers stop short of saying yes, probably for a very good reason. Kamen told the British media he'd never had an affair with Madonna because, "It was so intense in the studio that seducing her never crossed my mind." A staged photo of Kamen and Madonna looking exhausted in the recording studio adorns the **back** cover of his "Each Time You Break My Heart" single.

Even if they only ever shared a label (**Sire Records**) and no bodily fluids, Kamen was and is a dreamboat, and possesses a strong, blue-**eyed** soul **voice.**

KAMINS, MARK: *April 13, 1955– February 14, 2013.* The man whose **jobs** as **Danceteria**'s hottest DJ and as a scouting **talent** for Island Records put him in a unique position to be able to "discover" Madonna. Madonna **flirted** with Kamins (and wound up dating him), which got him to listen to, then play for his club audience, her demo.

Kamins would later confess to Madonna biographer **Andrew Morton,** "I can't say I saw a star, but she had something special."

Kamins pitched Madonna to his Island boss Chris Blackwell, who allegedly rejected her on the grounds of body odor. (Nice.) But Kamins knew a good thing when it was right in front of (and under) him, so he pitched **Michael Rosenblatt** and **Seymour Stein** at **Sire Records,** with whom he had a good relationship via David Byrne of **Talking**

Heads. Stein liked what he heard. Madonna was signed to a $15,000, two-record deal, with her first two singles to be **"Ain't No Big Deal"** (later nixed) and **"Everybody."**

Kamins produced "Everybody," but due to his inexperience and friction with Madonna over it, he lost out to **Reggie Lucas** when it came to producing Madonna's debut album *Madonna.*

While it lasted, Madonna and Kamins had led a mutually beneficial existence together. In the mid-2000s, Kamins told *New York* magazine, "We had no **money** and we were sleeping on egg crates. She wasn't a homemaker. I bought some lingerie for her one **night, and she wasn't** interested. To Madonna, a boyfriend was secondary. She knew how to use her **sexuality** to manipulate men, everyone from promotion guys to radio programmers."

Kamins continued his career as a revered DJ. Sadly, he died of a heart attack while teaching in Guadalajara, Mexico. Madonna issued a statement: "I'm very sorry to hear about Mark's **death.** I haven't seen him for years but if it weren't for him, I might not have had a singing career. He was the first DJ to play my demos before I had a record deal. He believed in me before anyone else did. I owe him a lot. May he Rest in Peace."

mark kamins

KANE, BIG DADDY: *b. September 10, 1968.* Big-deal rapper of the '80s and '90s who made a surprise appearance with Madonna in *Sex* in a threesome with her and **Naomi Campbell.**

In 2014, Kane remembered he met Madonna when they (along with Color Me Badd) were dispatched by **Warner Bros.** to hospitals to cheer up sick kids. Kane was flattered when Madonna spent some of her time informing the kids who Kane was, singing a few bars of his hit "Ain't No Half-Steppin'" (1988). When he was sufficiently buttered up, Madonna asked Kane to be in *Sex.* When she emphasized that the photos would be **nude,** he agreed, saying, "Shit, even better—let's do it!"

Kane told *Ambrosia for Heads,* "... I remember the first day when we got there to, um, take, um, photos, I walked on the set and she just came runnin' through the hall, butt-ass naked, 'Hey, what's up! Yo, I'm glad you're here! Yo, let me tell you a funny story. I was just standin' outside in the middle of the highway, just like *this,* tryin' to hitchhike while they're snapping pictures of me. Nobody stopped. Can you believe that? **Fuckin'** *Madonna,* no cars stopped

—SUSAN MORABITO

for me!' And I'm just lookin' at her standin' butt-naked like, 'Wow, this woman is for *real*, like, this is, like, you know, like, this is, like, *not* a game to her ... She's a sweetheart. I have nothing but the utmost respect for her."

Though seeing Kane with Madonna and Campbell led to some sharp criticism of Madonna's use of the two as racial set pieces, seeing Kane naked was not unheard of—he had already revealed all but his prodigious digit in *Playgirl* the year before.

KEATON, DIANE: *b. January 5, 1946.* **Oscar**-winning lead actor in some of the most celebrated films of all time, including *The Godfather* (1972) and its sequels and a string of films with her ex, **Woody Allen.**

Keaton was the first actor meant to play "Susan" in *Desperately Seeking Susan*, when the character was conceived as a dried-flower child, and was also mentioned for the part of "Roberta."

She was the only **San Remo** resident to come to Madonna's defense in her effort to secure an apartment in that **NYC** co-op. Madonna bought Keaton's 1926, 7,000-square-foot, Spanish-style home in Beverly Hills in 2000 for $6.5 million, remarking how much she appreciated Keaton's renovation of the Wallace Neff–designed **home.**

 "KEEP IT TOGETHER": *Release date: January 30, 1990. Billboard Hot 100 peak: #8.* Written and produced by Madonna and **Stephen Bray**, the song is a heartfelt warning to always cherish your family. Madonna's fifth and final US single from *Like a Prayer* had the sound of Sly & the Family Stone's "Family Affair" (1971) but was remixed for Top 40 radio to echo the sound of R&B group Soul II Soul. (Madonna would **work** with the group's **Nellee Hooper** on *Bedtime* Stories a few years later.) The remix made Madonna's ode to the strength of family into a serviceable mid-tempo **dance** number.

Madonna has only performed the song live on her *Blond Ambition World Tour*, where it served as the finale.

"Family is really important to me, but strangely enough, family is not necessarily your blood. I mean, we are raised to think that, but, um, sometimes our family lets us down and we end up creating a new family for ourselves. And family is really people that you know you can rely on, people who, um, won't judge you, people who have your back, people you can trust, people who are loyal—that's family."—MADONNA (2015)

KEITEL, HARVEY: *b. May 13, 1939.* An actor's actor, the Brooklyn-born Keitel has under his belt a string of distinguished performance on stage and on screen. Some of his most memorable film appearances include *Mean Streets* (1973), *Taxi Driver* (1976), *Thelma & Louise* (1991), *Bad Lieutenant* (1992) and *Pulp Fiction* (1994).

Keitel is the person with whom Madonna has acted most frequently. He appeared with Madonna on stage in *Goose and Tomtom*, played "Eddie Israel" to her "Sarah Jennings" in *Dangerous Game* (for which he won the Golden Ciak for Best Actor at the **Venice Film Festival**) and the two shared a scene in Wayne Wang's *Blue in the Face.*

In 1992, Keitel was one of the toughs hilariously dissecting Madonna's music in the opening scene of *Reservoir Dogs* (1992). The following year, Keitel was the host of *Saturday Night Live* when Madonna was the musical guest.

KELLY, GENE: *August 23, 1912–February 2, 1996.* The broad-shouldered MGM **dance** legend came out of retirement to offer advice to Madonna and **Christopher Ciccone** as she rehearsed for *The Girlie Show World Tour* in 1993 in LA. Madonna's ex **Jimmy Albright** remembers that Madonna was in seventh heaven when Kelly compared her to **Marlene Dietrich**. Unfortunately, the octogenarian wrenched his leg while demonstrating a step and endured some painful moments for the rest of their meeting. His ideas were not incorporated into the final show.

KENNEDY, JOHN F., JR.: *November 25, 1960–July 16, 1999.* The Adonis-like son of slain US President John F. Kennedy had an affair with Madonna during her first separation from **Sean Penn** in 1987. They met at a party, chatted backstage after her *Who's That Girl World Tour* show at **Madison Square Garden**, then met up at a **fitness** salon (Plus One and/or Body Beautiful, depending on who's fibbing). Once they began seeing each other, they were extremely careful not to be detected, jogging and riding bikes together in Central Park and also on the beach near Hyannis Port (Kennedyville). Kennedy was concerned his **mother**, Jackie Onassis, would disapprove.

JFK Jr. screwed up the courage to introduce Madonna—who frequently mimicked **Marilyn Monroe**, the woman with whom his father had had such an indiscreet affair—to Onassis. Madonna and JFK Jr.'s mom had one meeting at Onassis's famous pad (1040 Fifth Ave., 15th Fl., NY, NY), where Madonna **ballsily** signed the guest register "Mrs. Sean Penn."

In 1988, when Madonna was starring in *Speed-the-Plow* on Broadway, Onassis attended the opening night performance. Privately, she told Christina Haag—whom she hoped might be the girl of her son's **dreams**—that the **play** was good but Madonna was terrible. "I think you should go. I think you should go next week—and have John take you. And go backstage!"

JFK Jr.'s biographer later said Madonna found him to be **sexy**, but a dud in bed, while he found her to be "a sexual dynamo." Madonna and JFK Jr. moved on, and she reconciled with Penn (for a while), who once confronted Kennedy at a party and demanded an apology for having slept with his wife. It was an awkward moment for which Madonna embarrassedly sent a funeral wreath to her ex-lover with the message, "In Deepest Sympathy."

In 1995, Madonna posed eating a (**candy**) goldfish for the premier issue of JFK Jr.'s political **magazine** *George*, illustrating a piece entitled "If I Were President." In it, she said she'd pay teachers more than stars; Rush Limbaugh, Jesse Helms and Bob Dole would be in labor camps; **Howard Stern** would be kicked out of the country while Roman Polanski would be allowed **back** in; and "the entire armed forces would come out of the closet."

A letter from Madonna to Kennedy later revealed that he had asked her to pose *as his **mother*** for the magazine. Madonna said her **eyebrows** weren't thick enough and, "I could never do her justice," but was game to try Eva Braun or Pamela Harriman.

Madonna and Kennedy were photographed together on June 28, 1997, in Las Vegas at the infamous **Mike Tyson/Evander Holyfield** match that resulted in Tyson **snacking** on his opponent's ear. It was probably the last time Madonna and her ex were in the same room. He died in a plane crash two years later, along with his wife and her sister.

KENTES, PETER: *b. 1950.* A **University of Michigan** classmate of Madonna's in **Christopher Flynn**'s ballet class, Kentes choreographed a "street scene" **dance** that he asked Madonna to bring to life. The dance was filmed and exists on the Internet and **in VH1**'s *Driven: Madonna*. Kentes also took a number of photos of Madonna in a revealingly brief, flowered onesie. His images often appear in "early-years" assessments of her. Kentes attended the first-ever **Madonnathon** in Detroit, **Michigan**, where he first debuted the '70s images, selling color Xeroxes of them to her **fans**.

KESHISHIAN, ALEK: *b. July 30, 1964.* Armenian-American writer and director who is a longtime Madonna associate.

For his Harvard senior project, Keshishian produced a rock-opera adaptation of the 1847 novel *Wuthering Heights* called *Trouble at the Linton Home*, featuring the music of Kate Bush to represent "Cathy Earnshaw" before her marriage to "Edgar Linton," then the music of Madonna to represent her after the **wedding**. He moved to LA, where he found **work** directing music videos for the likes of **Bobby Brown**, Edie Brickell & New Bohemians, **Elton John** and Vanessa Williams, as well as **commercials**. He met CAA agent Jane Berliner in 1989 through a former classmate, and when she got a load of a video of his *Wuthering Heights* piece, she introduced him and his work to Madonna herself.

Madonna and the aspiring director hit it off and she seemed eager to work with him, but it happened faster than either could have anticipated; she called him in March 1990—on only a few *days* notice—to shoot backstage footage of her *Blond Ambition World Tour*. The **original** director of the tour project, **David Fincher**,

hadn't worked out, so Madonna and Keshishian finalized an understanding of the parameters of what he would shoot over a meeting at the LA go-go bar the Body Shop (8250 Sunset Blvd., W. Hollywood, CA)—later the name of a *Rebel Heart* track.

Keshishian aggressively turned the assignment into the much more ambitious feature-film documentary *Truth or Dare*. He and his crew wore black as they filmed the goings-on behind the scenes of Madonna's grandest concert, producing a priceless piece of work for only $4 million. "I wanted the audience of *Truth or Dare* to feel the same emotional roller coaster I felt in getting to know her," he said at the time.

Keshishian pushed hard to make the film what it turned out to be. "I would constantly disobey her, to show she wasn't directing me. I was completely prepared to be fired. That's when you do your best work, when you're not scared of being fired. I wasn't so blinded by the idea of working with Madonna that I would do anything she asked," he said in 1991.

The two became good buddies and have since frequently socialized and sporadically worked together. He directed the music video for **"This Used to Be My Playground"** and they scouted strip clubs while Madonna was researching *Sex*. They even exchanged friendship rings—he gave her one with a cobra emblem, she gave him an antique with a huge precious stone.

Madonna contributed the song **"I'll Remember"** to the **Maverick** soundtrack of Keshishian's sophomore feature-film effort, *With Honors*; Keshishian directed the video.

"I've known Alek [Keshishian] for years, and we have a weird kind of brother-sister relationship. One minute we're hugging each other and crying on each other's shoulders, and the next minute we're slamming the door in each other's face and not speaking to each other for a month," she said in 2010.

Almost 20 years later, Madonna and Keshishian collaborated more closely than ever before on *W.E.*, a film she directed and which she cowrote with Keshishian. It was only his second writing credit, following the Brittany Murphy film *Love and Other Disasters* (2006).

KIEDIS, ANTHONY: *b. November 1, 1962.* Lead singer of the Red Hot Chili Peppers. It's been said that Kiedis and Madonna dated briefly in the '90s.

In 1990, when the band was asked about their infamous T-shirt of a woman pleasuring herself, Kiedis replied, "It's a drawing of Madonna **masturbating**, and she's **dreaming** of the Red Hot Chili Peppers. I think if she saw it, she'd want one; that's the type of girl she is. I mean, I don't think she's ever denied masturbating ..."

Regardless, Madonna and this fellow Michigander have crossed paths often. The Red Hot Chili Peppers were the musical guests on the **Roseanne Barr**-hosted episode of *Saturday Night Live* when Madonna appeared in a *Coffee Talk with Linda Richman* skit in 1992, they did a duet of

"You know more about my life than anybody. You've seen more of me than even Sean."—MADONNA TO ALEK KESHISHIAN (1990)

"I hate being called a pop star." —MADONNA ON LARRY KING LIVE (1999)

"The Lady Is a Tramp" (1937) in celebration of the 1,000th episode of *The Arsenio Hall Show* in 1993 and the two posed together at the 1995 **MTV Video Music Awards**.

In 2013, Kiedis worked with Madonna to choose her first **Art for Freedom** winner.

KIER, UDO: *b. October 14, 1944.* German film actor closely associated with **Andy Warhol**/Paul Morrissey's '70s horror flicks who has also **worked** with Rainer Werner Fassbinder and Lars von Trier. Interestingly, Madonna—a film buff—was not drawn to Kier in 1992 because of his cinematic past, but rather because of his then-recent appearance in **Gus Van Sant**'s *My Own Private Idaho* (1991).

Madonna recruited Kier to pose for **Steven Meisel** with her in *Sex*, in which Kier is seen dressed in leather, drinking urine (it was really champagne) from a woman's shoe, and as a tuxedoed man indulging in some **bisexual** carnal slumming at the **Gaiety** with Madonna, **Joey Stefano**, **Rocky Santiago** and others. In one image, Kier was directed to look up at Madonna, who stood over him in a short skirt … with no panties under it. He described the view as "very organized."

Because of his work in *Sex*, Kier is also seen in the music video for **"Erotica"** and in an **unreleased** documentary on the making of the **book** by **Fabien Baron**.

Madonna returned to the Kier well for her very next music video after "Erotica," **"Deeper and Deeper."** This time around, Kier's iconic scary-**sexiness** is mined much more directly—he opens the video shouting angrily in German, playing a Svengali to Madonna's **disco** dolly. He closes the video by heartlessly cutting the strings on her balloons, sending them into the sky. Madonna never metaphor she didn't like.

Kier hasn't been in touch with Madonna since, but not because of hard feelings: "As an actor, you never keep in contact with people if they're more important than yourself; they'll think you want something. And I don't need anything."

"I wouldn't have done [*Sex*] with anybody else in the world. A lot of people asked me why I did it, but I just said, 'Do you know how many people would be jealous when they see that book?' That's why I did it."-UDO KIER (2014)

KILLS, NATALIA: *b. August 15, 1986.* Singer-songwriter who, on the strength of eight singles and two albums was hired as a judge on *The X Factor* in New Zealand, then fired when she and her husband, Willy Moon, viciously berated a contestant. Madonna had **worked** with her on *Rebel Heart*, resulting in a credit for Kills on **"Holy Water."** Madonna told *Cosmopolitan* in 2015 of Kills that she **"loved** her from the minute she walked in the room."

KING, JAMIE: *b. circa 1972.* Fabulously **talented** (and **sexy**, don't forget sexy) choreographer and tour director who's worked with A-plus showbiz names like: **Michael**

Jackson, **Ricky Martin**, **Prince**, **Rihanna**, **Diana Ross** and **Britney Spears**.

King **danced** in and choreographed one of Madonna's most dance-oriented music videos, **"Human Nature,"** and went on to direct her *Drowned World Tour*, *Re-Invention World Tour*, *Confessions Tour*, her promo tour for *Hard Candy*, her *Sticky & Sweet Tour* and her **Super Bowl** halftime show. He served as creative producer of *The MDNA Tour*.

He is visible in Madonna's first **H&M** ad, along with the rest of her *Confessions Tour* principals, and appears in *I'm Going to Tell You a Secret*.

Madonna took out an ad to congratulate King on his success as a "billion-dollar tour director" which read: "To Jamie, The hardest working man in show **business**. It's an honor to work with you and I'm happy to see your efforts rewarded. Here's to our next tour! **Love**, Madonna."

KING, LARRY: *b. November 19, 1933.* American **TV** legend whose signature achievement was his *Larry King Live* show on CNN, which lasted from June 1985 until his departure on December 26, 2010. On the show, King, a folksy, distracted, nosy, friendly figure, was able to get priceless answers out of an array of celebrities. He was also famous for asking curveball questions both by design and by accident. He was an institution, while his successor—**Piers Morgan**—somewhat belonged in one.

King first interviewed Madonna on January 19, 1999. She had the straight black **hair** of her **"Nothing Really Matters"** era and was wearing the noisiest black jacket of all time. She spent the entire hour with King, seeming to like him, even though he immediately asked her about why she was named Madonna (an easy enough question to have figured out beforehand) and made her rehash well-known aspects of her career.

"Who are you? What are you?" he grilled her of her emphasis on singing over dancing over **acting**, making Madonna laugh, "I don't know!" Hilariously, when King asked Madonna if she wanted to be married again, she asked King what the point was of marriage. He was on wife #8 at the time.

On October 10, 2002, she visited him again, and sure enough, King immediately asked her about having one name. The **blonde**-again Madonna talked about promoting herself and about her battles with the paparazzi. She expressed that she was in the very "luxurious" place of being able to do whatever she pleased just for the experience, including her **work** on *Speed-the-Plow* and *Up for Grabs* as examples. Surprisingly, she said acting on stage, which she's rarely done, is preferable to making movies, which she's probably done a few too many times.

In 2010, **Lady Gaga** did a remote interview with King looking very much like Madonna during her *Erotica* era and was asked her thoughts on Madonna. She said, "I think Madonna's great. She's been a wonderful friend and very

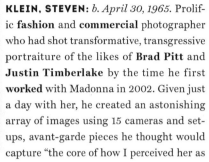

kind and supportive and, uh, amazing and she's, she's such an incredible woman." She went on to say that it's not her fault that she looks like Madonna, and to blame her mom (whose resemblance to Madonna had been pointed out by Little Monsters prior to the Hundred Years' Madonna/Gaga Stan Wars).

KITT, EARTHA: *January 17, 1927–December 25, 2008.* Growly, sultry singer with one of those **voices** one could ID from a single note. Kitt was a Broadway, film and **TV** [as one of the "Catwoman" actors on *Batman* (1966–1968)] star who used her **power** as a performer to become an unflinching activist against poverty and war and on behalf of **gay** rights. Look, she made Lady Bird Johnson *cry* in the White House—she was *not* timid.

Madonna, also not timid, was not Ms. Kitt's favor*rrr*ite performer. Madonna covered the Kitt hit **"Santa Baby"** on the *A Very Special Christmas* compilation—Kitt (not the song's writer) did not care for the version.

Queried by *Out* **magazine** in 2000 whether Madonna had ever asked Kitt what she thought about her cover of the song, Kitt replied, "She asked me, yes. I don't think she liked my answer. But she does what she does, and I do what I do. Whether people imitate me or not, there is never anything like the **original**."

"It's ter*rrr*ibly frustrating when—I call them the crotch-holders—make much more money than those of us making quality artwork."—EARTHA KITT ON MADONNA (1993)

KLEIN, STEVEN: *b. April 30, 1965.* Prolific **fashion** and **commercial** photographer who had shot transformative, transgressive portraiture of the likes of **Brad Pitt** and **Justin Timberlake** by the time he first **worked** with Madonna in 2002. Given just a day with her, he created an astonishing array of images using 15 cameras and set-ups, avant-garde pieces he thought would capture "the core of how I perceived her as a performance artist ..."

The images Klein shot that day were used in their first *W* **magazine** spread (April 2003's "Madonna Unbound") and also formed their collaborative multi-media exhibition ***X-STaTIC PRo=CeSS***.

"I think that project is the one that I'm most proud of," Klein said in 2014, after years of working with Madonna. "I find that was to me the most important piece of work about her that I've done."

That first shoot led to Klein providing video pieces for Madonna's ***Re-Invention World Tour***, ***Confessions Tour*** and ***Sticky & Sweet Tour***.

In the past decade and a half, Klein has become one of Madonna's go-to photographers (as well as a frequent companion). It would be rough to list every time they've worked together, but important shoots have included the mysteriously glam cover of August 2004 *Vogue Paris*, with its trippy, behind-the-scenes interior spread; the June 2006 equestrian-themed "Madonna Rides Again"

W magazine layout; their March 2009 "Blame It on Rio" Sylvia Miles-away spread for the same magazine; the 2007 **H&M** M by Madonna promo shots; the **cover** and marketing shoots for ***Confessions on a Dance Floor*** and ***Hard Candy***; the mamma mia 2010 **D&G** campaign; and the cover and interior shoot for the Bettie Page–themed *V* magazine summer 2014 issue with **Katy Perry**.

Klein also codirected Madonna's highly personal short film ***#secretprojectrevolution***.

Considering the length and thickness of their personal and professional associations, Klein has to be considered one of Madonna's Top 3 most important photographers, along with **Steven Meisel** and **Herb Ritts**. Some **fans** adore his work, others not so much. One aspect of his work that makes it easier to judge (and perhaps less special) is that countless outtakes from Klein's work with Madonna have **leaked**.

KMART: Unglamorous chain store founded in 1962. Madonna's **stepmother** shopped here for the fabric she used to make matching dresses for the **Ciccone** girls.

MATTHEW RETTENMUND

KAREN J. DOLAN

Klein at a 2013 Madonna event

BELOW: Madonna and Kitt conceal their distaste for one another.

KOKO: SEE: **Camden Palace.**

KONK: No Wave music group in whose 1982 video "Konk Party" Madonna and pal **Martin Burgoyne** appear as extras, dancing wildly, at 1:56 and 2:03. They were great **dancers**, but Madonna had to be told to rein herself in a bit—she and Burgoyne were camera hogging. Outtakes are visible on **YouTube.**

Ed Steinberg, who would later shoot Madonna's first official video, for **"Everybody,"** was the director of "Konk Party." Steinberg shot it "many months before" that debut video at a club called David's Loft (formerly 99 Prince St., NY, NY). Konk member Richard Edson later turned up in ***Desperately Seeking Susan***, trading lines with Madonna/"Susan" over a newspaper in the very first scene filmed for that movie.

KRISPY MARSHMALLOW TREATS: Madonna's generic version of a white-trash **snack** that happens to be one of the only dishes she can make. She is famous for whipping up a batch on the spur of the moment, and surprised everyone by passing some around at her 35th **birthday** party at **Castillo del Lago.**

In 1993, **Warner Bros.** Records released a promo recipe **book** that included Madonna's recipe for the sticky and sweet treats:

¼   C margarine
1   package (10 oz. or about 40) marshmallows, or 4C mini marshmallows
6   C cereal (you know which kind)
     vegetable **cooking** spray or waxed paper

(1) Melt margarine in large saucepan over low heat. Add marshmallows. Stir until melted. Remove.
(2) Add cereal. Mix well.
(3) Using spatula or wax paper, press evenly into 13"×9"×2" pan coated with spray or wax paper. Cut into squared when cool.

Serves 24

KULKENS, HERMAN: *circa 1918–?.* Amateur photographer in Ypsilanti, Michigan, who **worked** as a graphic illustrator for Chrysler. On "at least 10 occasions" in 1977, he paid Madonna $10 an hour to pose **nude** for him. Madonna was attending the **University of Michigan** at the time, meaning Kulkens was the second person to do a formal shoot with Madonna after **Linda Alaniz.** Due to uncertainty regarding the timing, he may have even been the first.

"... [S]he could really present herself," Kulkens said in 1985. "I knew sooner or later she'd get into the entertainment field."

As a surprise while Kulkens was on a bike trip, his wife, Susan, tried to sell the old Madonna images to *Playboy* and *Penthouse*, contacting both on May 31, 1985. This ultimately resulted in the publication of the images in

Ray (Kybartas) of Light

LAVINEL SAVU

various editions of *Penthouse* but only after a court battle; *Penthouse* had proceeded with publication after offering $25,000, but the Kulkenses claimed *Playboy* had doubled the offer and no deal had been reached.

While Kulkens was battling Guccione in court, he dredged up another set of Madonna nudes his brother had been holding, and announced he was going to sell them for $100,000. Apparently, all of the Kulkens images wound up with *Penthouse* once the legal wrangling was finished. Decades later, previously unseen images came to light when **original** chromes turned up as part of the publisher's estate.

In truth, the work by Kulkens—which included some images of Madonna nude with another woman—is ridiculous compared to that of Alaniz, **Lee Friedlander, Martin H.M. Schreiber** and **Bill Stone**, but it's important for how early it is on the Madonna timeline.

KYBARTAS, RAY: Celebrity personal trainer who **worked** with Madonna in the '90s. Madonna was so into the man's take on how to build a better body that she contributed an intro to his 1997 **book** *Fitness Is Religion: Keep the Faith.* In it, she said, "There are no rules. All you need is dedication."

Madonna met Kybartas via **Sean Penn**, whom he trained during the making of ***At Close Range*** (1986). He says he helped Madonna find her own trainer (**Rob Parr**), and when she was done with Parr, he began working with her directly, around 1989 (there is some overlap between Parr and Kybartas, probably due to murky **memories**). At any rate, Madonna thought highly of Kybartas, who asserts that he introduced her to **Carlos Leon**, presumably during a run in Central Park, which is where Madonna has always said she met the future father of her first child, **Lola.**

—MICKEY BOARDMAN

MATTHEW RETTENMUND

LA BOÎTE À QUESTIONS: *Airdates: 2008–.* French show (English: *The Question Box*) in which celebs are placed in a box and forced to answer random questions and perform acts to amuse the audience. Madonna, promoting ***Rebel Heart***, showed up in the box on March 3, 2015. She was asked if **Britney Spears** is a good kisser ("Hell to the yeah!") and what one should never say to her ("No!"). Madonna also happily demonstrated how to walk like a proper model, and in response to a request that she show why she is the queen of provocation, shyly and then aggressively felt up her crotch. It's France.

LA FARGO, JASON: *b. May 4, 1969.* Nineteen-year-old production assistant (and now DP) whom Madonna met while filming her **Pepsi** spot in 1989. According to *People*, they had a fling. That's better than having your **hair** catch on fire, which is what **Michael Jackson** got for doing a Pepsi ad. Sure, La Fargo was a little young for the 30-year-old Madonna, but she definitely enjoys the occasional taste of a new generation.

The affair came to light when La Fargo dumped his girlfriend, Stacey Gardner, and she went to the media. Gardner reported that Madonna had signed a T-shirt for La Fargo that said in Italian, "I want your body. Call me." When Gardner asked her boyfriend if he was dating Madonna, he replied, "If I was, I couldn't tell you."

Parsing her words, **Liz Rosenberg** denied that La Fargo was Madonna's "boyfriend." Ah, but did she get the body she wanted?

"LA ISLA BONITA" (SONG): *Release date: February 25, 1987. Billboard Hot 100 peak: #4.* Madonna called her fifth and final single from *True Blue* her tribute to "the **beauty** and mystery of Latin American people." In it, she sings (sometimes in Spanish) about the lost **love** from a romantic vacation.

The song was written by Bruce Gaitsch (apparently about a town in Belize) and offered to **Michael Jackson**, who rejected it. Gaitsch brought it to **Patrick Leonard**, who transformed and coproduced the song with Madonna. The new version owes much to the reality of being cooped up in a recording studio; Leonard told a **Warner Bros.** in-house publication of the song that it was inspired by the fact that, "The only place to eat near the recording studio was a Mexican restaurant."

Madonna has performed "La Isla Bonita" (too) many times. It's not that it isn't a great song, but it is surprising that with the depth of her catalogue, the song has been performed on most of her tours: ***Who's That Girl World Tour***, ***The Girlie Show World Tour***, the ***Drowned World Tour***, the ***Confessions Tour***, the ***Sticky & Sweet Tour*** and the ***Rebel Heart Tour***. She also performed it at **Live Earth**.

It's also been covered or sampled frequently, including by Alizée, Black Rob & **Jennifer Lopez**, Deetah and **Britney Spears**. David Hasselhoff covered the song on his German LP *David Hasselhoff Sings America*.

"LA ISLA BONITA" (VIDEO): *Director: Mary Lambert, 1987.* Director **Mary Lambert** elicited another fine video performance from Madonna in this precursor to **"Like a Prayer."** In the video, Madonna is first seen as a boyishly dressed, devout **Catholic** woman who seems to be confined to her apartment, haunted by the **memory** of a lost **love**. She is also seen as a colorful flamenco **dancer**, her freer self. By the end, the characters have merged and she is finally able to leave, to rejoin society. As in her later **"Who's That Girl"** video, Madonna ends by dancing in the street, this time doing so at the insistence of a band of stereotypical Latin street musicians and neighborhood types, who represent the concept of living in the moment.

"La Isla Bonita" is the least interesting of Mary Lambert's videos with Madonna, but for a video done to plug a fifth single from an album, it's got a solid concept and shows effort.

Watch for **Oscar**-winning actor Benicio del Toro smiling sheepishly in the background while Madonna dances like everybody's watching.

LABÈQUE SISTERS: Madonna adores the French concert pianists Katia (b. March 11, 1950) and Marielle (b. March 6, 1952) Labèque. She had a song (**"Freedom"**) on the rainforest-benefit album *Carnival*, which also had a piece by the sisters. In her ***I'm Going to Tell You a Secret*** documentary, Madonna takes her troupe from the ***Re-Invention World Tour*** to see the sisters play, believing they could use the exposure to classical music. The sisters introduced Madonna to their friends, the band Kalakan, which directly led to Kalakan's appearance on ***The MDNA Tour***.

LACHAPELLE, DAVID: *b. March 11, 1963.* Photographer known for his hyper-real tableaux. LaChapelle was the "It" photographer of the late '90s. One of his most famous images is that of lovers Bob and Rod Jackson-**Paris** dressed as sailors, kissing in a WWII-themed ad for Diesel from 1995. His celebrity portraiture includes dramatic **work** with Cameron Diaz, Leonardo DiCaprio, **Lady Gaga**, Amanda Lepore, **Courtney Love** and **Kanye West**, among many others.

In 1996, LaChapelle did a garish **commercial** and print ad for *MTV Raw* (2002–2003) that envisioned elderly versions of Courtney **Love** as "Baby Jane" and Madonna as "Blanche" from ***What Ever Happened to Baby Jane?*** Less than two years later, LaChapelle

MATTHEW RETTENMUND

did a widely circulated session with Madonna that drew heavily on Eastern faith for the July 9, 1998, cover of **Rolling Stone**, and a Maria Callas–inspired image of her to promote the 1999 **MTV Video Music Awards** of Madonna reaching for a note, an image that became the cover of the September 7, 1999, issue of *Daily Variety* and the September 11, 1999, issue of **Billboard**.

LaChapelle was set to direct the music video for **"Hung Up"** because she wanted a feel similar to his 2005 documentary *Rize*. The two fell out creatively, leading to LaChapelle being replaced. He told the Web host Yann that Madonna's bad behavior drove him to leave the project.

"We were in pre-production for the video 'Hung Up' ... I wanted all my life to do a Madonna video. And then when she was screaming at me on the phone, I just, I couldn't take it, like, honestly, I just was like, 'I'm gonna spend two weeks getting yelled at?' ... [W]e were doing the **job** and I just remember [that being] just, so mean ... And the shoots were always so stressful with her, when we did photo shoots and I thought, '**God**, I can't go through this. I just hung up the phone."

LaChapelle went on to say Madonna had taught him a lesson by pushing him to say no to a job for the first time in his life. He responded "not really" to the idea of whether he would consider working with her again.

"[She] looks one way in real life and another way in a photo. Her features just come together in front of a camera. I hardly did any retouching ..."–DAVID LACHAPELLE, *THE ADVOCATE* (1998)

LADY GAGA: *b. March 28, 1986.* Wrong **book**, **bitch**. (Kidding.)

In 2006, Stefani Germanotta, a **New York** singer-songwriter, **reinvented** herself (with the input of her producer Rob Fusari and a little help from an autocorrected text) as Lady Gaga, a reference to Queen's "Radio Ga Ga" (1984). The object was to transform the pop tunesmith into a pop star.

Gaga's initial out-there styling, out-sized personality and out-of-this-world **voice** made her seem like a cross between Yma Sumac, **Christina Aguilera** (who was accused of aping Gaga's style) and **Grace Jones**. Her **Warholian** record *The Fame* was released in 2008, followed by its sister EP *The Fame Monster*, delivering smash hits like "Just **Dance**" (2008), "Poker Face" (2008), "Bad Romance" (2009) and "Telephone" feat. **Beyoncé** (2010). Almost immediately, Gaga was embraced by the music industry, **working** with greats and receiving **MTV Video Music Awards** and **Grammys**.

Lady Gaga refers to her **fans** as "Little Monsters" and says she wants to be on their level, rejecting the title of queen. However, the media couldn't resist calling her a (the?) new **Queen of Pop**.

On May 1, 2009, Madonna took her daughter **Lola** to see Gaga play at NYC's Terminal (610 W. 56th St., NY,

She wasn't born *that* way ...

NY); also in the audience was **Cyndi Lauper**. It was like the old guard inspecting the new. Madonna would later tell **Graham Norton** that seeing Gaga's show left her impressed, "I thought she was really cool, and, and she did remind me of *me* **back** in the day. I **loved** her rawness and there was something fresh about her and **ballsy**, and when she spoke to the audience, she sounded like she had a similar sense of humor to me, quite ironic, and, um, and I liked her—I liked her. So I do think she's very **talented**."

Gaga said, "I was very humbled that Madonna came to the show ... I just thought it was kind that, uh, she would wanna come at all. And, uh, I didn't even know she knew who I was."

On September 14, 2009, both Madonna and Gaga were in attendance at the Marc Jacobs 2010 Spring **Fashion** Show at the State Armory (643 Park Ave., NY, NY 10065), where they happily posed together. A few weeks later, Madonna and Gaga participated in a painfully unfunny *Saturday Night Live* sketch that made fun of their supposed rivalry, dancing side by side and pretending to pull each other's **hair**, almost kissing.

By 2010, Gaga's **look** and style had gone from inspired chaos to a slightly more mainstream, if costumey, pop look. Music lovers (and especially Madonna stans) had noted that Gaga seemed, more and more, to be directly inspired by Madonna. Some of Gaga's looks most commonly referenced as owing much to Madonna include a leopard bodysuit with purple Haus of Gaga jacket that Gaga wore on tour that resembled Madonna's **"Hung Up"** look, another tour look that seemed to be a hat tip to Madonna's **Blond Ambition World Tour** ponytail, a champagne satin Marc Jacobs bustier that remarkably mimicked Madonna's *Blond Ambition* basque and an androgynous look for a 2010 sit-down with **Larry King** that called to mind Madonna's *Sex* era.

With the release of the video for "Alejandro" (with obvious references to Madonna's **"Express Yourself"** and **"Vogue"** music videos), **Ingrid Casares** tweeted to **Andy Cohen** on June 12, 2010, "as my friend Madonna says 'is that the video where she thinks she is me'?? ... weird!!"

It became fashionable to joke that Gaga was simply doing Madonna. Even Charo chimed in, praising Madonna and slamming Gaga: "I can tell you, to me, Lady Gaga is

"I don't know where San Pedro is."–MADONNA (2009)

Madonna with diarrhea. I don't like when somebody copies somebody and just adopt it. Like, their own idea."

Gaga was still very high on Madonna at this time. In an interview with Showstudio.com, a fan asked her what it was like having a personal relationship with Madonna, considering she'd been "such a big personal influence" and had known Gaga's idol Andy Warhol. Gaga replied, "Madonna is a wonderful, wonderful person, and she is so full of the most wonderful freedom and spirit and she's so kind and working with her has always been very exciting and very fun, and we have shared some wonderful, honest moments together. She comes to my shows, I ask her questions, she's given me advice."

The *wonderful* vibes quickly evaporated on February 11, 2011, when Lady Gaga's **gay** anthem "Born This Way" was released. Instantaneously and organically, "Express Yourself" became a trending topic on **Twitter** as pretty much everyone chimed in with the observation that Gaga's new song sounded like Madonna's classic. **Christopher Ciccone**, who rarely misses a chance to zing his sister, instead zinged Gaga, saying, "They should have noticed, somebody should have noticed that the songs are so remarkably alike. They should have pulled it or at least said, 'Change it.' ... And it's not like it's a direct copy, but it's more like that song than any other song I've ever heard before." He went on to compare Gaga to "my sister on crack."

Madonna's official **YouTube** channel—out of nowhere, or maybe out of *somewhere*—suddenly posted her performance of "Express Yourself" at the 1989 **MTV** Video Music **Awards**.

During a Valentine's Day 2011 stop at *The Tonight Show*, a jittery Gaga said of the comparisons, "Y'know, there is really no one that is a more adoring and loving Madonna fan than me; I am the hugest fan personally and professionally and ... well the good news is that I got an email from, uh, her people and, and her, uh, sending me their **love** and complete support on behalf of the single, and if the queen says it shall be, then it shall be."

Liz Rosenberg shot back, "I am not aware that Madonna sent Gaga an email. That's all I have to say on the matter."

Shortly thereafter, while accepting a Grammy for *The Fame Monster* as Best Pop Vocal Album, Gaga used her time onstage to bizarrely thank the late **Whitney Houston** for a song that did not even appear on that album. "I need to say thank you tonight to Whitney Houston. I wanted to thank Whitney, because when I wrote 'Born This Way,' I imagined she was singing it because I wasn't secure enough in myself to imagine I was a superstar. So, Whitney, I imagined you were singing 'Born This Way' when I wrote it."

At this point, the line in the sand was drawn. Gaga seemed to have been caught off-guard by the comparisons to Madonna's work and either fabricated the email or was misled by someone in her camp—she's never explained. Madonna seems to have been annoyed that Gaga didn't react by owning the similarities.

Time went by, so slowly.

In the January 30, 2012, issue of *Newsweek*, Madonna said her reaction to hearing "Born This Way" for the first time was, "'This is a wonderful way to redo my song.' I mean, I recognized the chord changes. I thought it was ... interesting."

That same month, Madonna was pinned down by **20/20**'s **Cynthia McFadden** on the topic of Gaga. In a piece that exists in longer (more measured, as aired on *20/20*) and shorter (more cutting, aired as a teaser on **Good Morning America**) forms, Madonna said of Gaga in the piece, "I certainly think she references me a lot in her work. Sometimes, I think it's amusing and flattering and well done. I can't really be annoyed by it or insulted by it because obviously I've influenced her ... She's she and I'm me."

In reference to the "Born This Way" song specifically, which Madonna again admitted she found to be "familiar," McFadden asked, "And that [familiarity] doesn't feel annoying?" Madonna said, "Um ... it feels ... uh ... reductive." When asked if that was good, Madonna purred, "Look it up," and regally sipped her tea. Clearly, she was not paying a compliment to Gaga, but the exchange was reported as if Madonna had called Gaga, in her entirety, reductive; the fact that Madonna said "it" feels reductive suggests that she was referring to Gaga's "Born This Way" absorption of "Express Yourself."

Unfortunately, she was not referring to the media's comparing of the two women, which is what could most properly be deemed reductive.

Gaga's surrogates went into attack mode, including vicious words against Madonna by **Elton John** and David Furnish, and this gem on Twitter from one of Gaga's producers, DJ White Shadow:

"And obviously: someone should take there old lady meds before they are allowed back in public, No **memories** having motherfucker." Called out for his bile, he added, "I obviously do not **hate** Madonna, or belittle her talent or achievements, however, if she thinks we stole a song from her she is wrong." He eventually admitted what he'd tweeted was "stupid shit" and said, "I love Madonna. I think Madonna's great."

When Madonna's **MDNA Tour** opened in Tel Aviv, Israel, on May 31, 2012, there was a Gaga-related surprise: While singing "Express Yourself," Madonna segued into a portion of "Born This Way"—and ended with a snippet of her own song **"She's Not Me."** The message was clear. Fans who assumed that the women—who share a record label—must have come to some understanding about the performance were mistaken; rather, Madonna, knowing she had a great copyright infringement case against Gaga, boldly performed "Born This Way" without permission on tour, and without credit.

At a June 8, 2012, concert, Gaga gave a rambling speech that indirectly swatted Madonna down while simultaneously blowing off all her critics.

On September 15, 2012, Madonna dedicated her performance of **"Masterpiece"** to Lady Gaga. "You wanna know something? I love her—I love her. I do love her. Imitation is the highest form of flattery. But one day, very soon, we're gonna be on stage together. You think I'm kidding?" At a St. Paul show a couple of months later, Madonna revealed she'd asked Gaga to duet with her on stage but said Gaga had declined.

The following year, Gaga told **Howard Stern**, "To me, honestly, I think she's more aggravated that I'm not upset that she doesn't like me. 'Cause I don't care that she doesn't like me." Asked by **Ellen DeGeneres** to sum up Gaga, Madonna paused dramatically and joked, "I know everybody's waiting on the edge of their seat ... I'm playing this one out ... good voice." She also complimented Gaga on her Rilke tattoo.

Gaga poked fun at the controversy on *SNL* late in 2013 by doing a **parody** of a music **commercial**, in which she sang "Born This Way" even though the legend below her read, "EXPRESS YOURSELF ...?"

The world's longest-running bitchfest continued in August 2014 when rumors swirled that Madonna had cut a nasty song about Gaga for her 2015 album *Rebel Heart*. The song, "Two Steps Behind Me," while **unreleased**, eventually **leaked in** full, and did, in fact, seem to be about Gaga. If it is not about Gaga, it's not believable that Madonna didn't think that would be the assumption.

Nonetheless, **Guy Oseary** tweeted of the tune "that song is NOT about gaga or anyone in particular." He followed it up by stating, "She has NO ill will towards Gaga. It's nonsense. She was listening to [Gaga's] **Tony Bennett** duet album last week and appreciating it." Madonna told *Rolling Stone* in 2015, "We live in a world where people like to pit women against each other. And this is why I love the idea of embracing females who are doing what I'm doing ... The only time I ever criticized Lady Gaga was when I felt like she blatantly ripped off one of my songs ... I do think she's a very talented singer and songwriter. It was just that one issue."

It was a shame that there was so much animus between Madonna and Gaga, and between at least some of their fans. Gaga's message is about love and acceptance, yet she had Little Monsters ripping Madonna a new asshole for being old and spreading **AIDS**. Madonna's the Queen of Pop; her legacy is safe from all comers, yet many Madonna fans saw Gaga as an undeserving, media-appointed successor, and used against Gaga some of the same slams used against Madonna in the '80s.

Madonna hinted at "a plan" she was **cooking** up in February 2015 to get people to "shut up about" their feud. On May 4, 2015, Madonna posed happily with Gaga and Katy Perry at the **Met Ball**. Her caption on Instagram? "Girls night out.......... Kissing the Ring........Finally!"

LADY MISS KIER: *b. August 5, 1963.* The ringleader of '90s **dance** group Deee-Lite (a rare club act that insisted on live tours over track dates), a **fashion** icon and an outspoken political activist, Kier has accused her old label mate Madonna of copying Deee-Lite's "Power of **Love**"

"… I CAN SEE MYSELF IN LADY GAGA. IN THE EARLY PART OF MY CAREER, FOR SURE … I CAN SEE THAT SHE'S GOT THAT 'IT' FACTOR."
—MADONNA (2009)

"I HAVE NO COMMENT ON HER OBSESSIONS RELATED TO ME, BECAUSE I DO NOT KNOW IF IT IS BASED ON SOMETHING PROFOUND OR SUPERFICIAL."—MADONNA ON LADY GAGA (2011)

"SHE SEEMS TO BORROW PRETTY HEAVILY, CLEARLY VISUALLY, AND SONICALLY, FROM MADONNA. WHICH IS PROBABLY SUPER SMART. I MEAN, WHY WOULDN'T YOU?"
—JOHN POLLY ON LADY GAGA, LOGO (2011)

"COME ON, GIRLS! DO YOU BELIEVE IN MADONNA? BECAUSE LADY GAGA HAS GOT SOMETHING TO SAY ABOUT 'EXPRESS YOURSELF,' AND SHE'S TURNED MADONNA'S FOURTH-BEST SINGLE OF 1989 INTO HER OWN INSTANT-CLASSIC CLUB ANTHEM, 'BORN THIS WAY.' EXCEPT IT'S ACTUALLY MUCH BETTER THAN 'EXPRESS YOURSELF,' BECAUSE IT'S FASTER, WITH GAGA CHANTING, 'DON'T BE A DRAG/JUST BE A QUEEN.'"
—ROB SHEFFIELD, *ROLLING STONE* (2011)

"I HONESTLY THINK THAT IF YOU'RE GOING TO TRY TO BE THE NEXT MADONNA, YOU NEED TO TIP THE HAT TO MADONNA. WHEN I FIRST HEARD THE SONG, I HEARD 'EXPRESS YOURSELF' MIXED WITH 'VOGUE.' I HEAR TWO OF THEM. I STILL THINK IT'S A GREAT SONG, BUT IT IS DEFINITELY INSPIRED BY MADONNA."
—E. KIDD BOGART ON "BORN THIS WAY" (2011)

"… I CAN SEE WHY SHE HAS A YOUNGER GAY FOLLOWING. I CAN SEE THAT THEY CONNECT TO HER KIND OF NOT FITTING INTO THE CONVENTIONAL NORM."
—MADONNA ON LADY GAGA, *THE ADVOCATE* (2012)

(1990) with her single release **"Rescue Me."** Both songs contain the lyric, "I believe in the **power** of love," but "Power of Love" also says to "open your heart"; pop songs are often about the same things.

In February of 2012, Kier commented on chatter that the Madonna/**Martin Solveig** composition **"Give Me All Your Luvin'"** sounded like João Brasil feat. Lovefoxxx's "L.O.V.E. Banana" (2011) by saying: "that is the exact same hook of the song (which is the only rememberable part of both songs) in the same key , same delivery. oops..she did it again. she'll probably pay them approx. 500,000$ in hush **money** to retain writers credit or probably already did. it's what she's always done. she's McDonna being herself."

She clearly has a *sic* mind.

Kier went on to call Madonna "thief," and has alleged on social media that Madonna "bit" the title for her ***Blond Ambition World Tour***—announced in November 1989—from a proposed **Debbie Harry** (a fellow **Sire** artist) album title. Harry's album, released under the title *Def, Dumb & Blonde*, dropped on October 16, 1989.

"LADY'S GOT POTENTIAL, THE": This rock 'n' roll, **guitar**-fueled song sung by **Antonio Banderas** from the movie *Evita* is found on ***Evita: The Compete Motion Picture Music Soundtrack***. It's about Evita's tendency for "knowing the right fella" in order "to be stellar."

LAGERFELD, KARL: *b. September 10, 1933*. The German designer who heads up Chanel, Fendi and the house that bears his name. An imposing presence with his white mane, sunglasses and no-BS collars, Lagerfeld has had sharp words for Madonna, and she has returned the favor.

They were okay in '95, when Lagerfeld and Claudia Schiffer presented Madonna with the **award** for Most Fashionable Artist 1995 at the **VH1 Fashion Awards**, which she accepted in a puke-green "Carol Brady" pantsuit.

But in 1997, when Madonna spoke at the **Met Ball** in honor of the late Gianni **Versace**, Lagerfeld sniffed, "But I was shocked by one thing: Madonna saying in her introduction of Donatella [Versace] that Donatella slips diamonds into her pocket. She can say, if she likes, that Donatella gives her diamonds, but to say she 'slips them into her pocket' makes it look like Donatella is buying friendship from some singer, no? This ruined my evening. And she looked like a housewife. Nothing. No style. This was over the borderline, huh? She'd better make a good record." Nudged to admit Madonna had meant well, Lagerfeld disagreed. "I'm not sure she meant well. She's a very rude person."

Speaking of rude, Lagerfeld stepped in it in 2012 when he criticized **Adele** for being overweight, comments that Madonna was quick to call "ridiculous."

In 2013, Madonna was said, by various observers, to be "morphing into" Lagerfeld thanks to some austere-collars-and-big-sunglasses combos. Thankfully, the process was never completed.

LAMBERT, MARY (DIRECTOR): *b. October 13, 1951*. Visionary music video director who has **worked** for some of the giants of '80s pop, including **Mariah Carey** & **Whitney Houston**, Sheila E., the Go-Go's, **Debbie Harry**, **Janet Jackson** and **Sting**.

Lambert is the force behind some of the strongest elements in Madonna's video canon: **"Borderline," "Like a Virgin," "Material Girl," "La Isla Bonita"** and **"Like a Prayer."**

After first working with Madonna, she directed the feature film *Siesta* (1987), which Madonna decided against starring in because of all the **nudity**. That was the difference between 1987 Madonna and 1992 Madonna.

Lambert tells *EM20* that she would "of course" work with Madonna again, if the opportunity arose.

"We had an amazing creative relationship and she is always looking to new inspiration, so it wound down in the late ['80s]. But it could easily become vital again." Pressed for further details of her days with Madonna, Lambert teases, "Someday I will write a memoir of my personal **memories**, so I have to save some of these anecdotes for that endeavor!"

LAMBERT, MARY (SINGER): *b. May 3, 1989*. The female **voice** featured on the landmark **gay**-rights hip-hop single "Same **Love**" (2012) with **Macklemore** and Ryan Lewis. Madonna harmonized with Lambert on the 2014 **Grammys** performance of that song.

"We spent a lot of time together!" Lambert later gushed to *Idolator*. "We had a lot of rehearsing to do, and we were just trying to figure out how to orchestrate the whole thing. I think the producers of the Grammys put it all together. They didn't tell me until the last minute because they knew I would tell everybody, because I don't know how to keep my mouth shut! ... We had four rehearsals together, and we really hit it off! I feel like we're not best friends, but if we were at the same house party and she had an extra beer, I would be the one she would give her extra beer to."

"LAMENT": Wrenching ballad found on ***Evita: The Complete Motion Picture Music Soundtrack*** on which Madonna sings Evita's final moments of life quite movingly. As she sings "... how soon the lights were gone," her character expires, leading to a funereal swell and a musical eulogy by Che (**Antonio Banderas**), as well as a creepy reprise of **"Rainbow High"** modified to address the fact that Evita's corpse was put on display after her **death**.

In the film, Madonna speak-sings the song rather than lip-synching. Her death scene is easily her finest sequence in the movie.

Madonna revisited "Lament" on her ***Re-Invention World Tour***, singing a **powerful** version in a prop electric chair as Hebrew letters flashed behind her.

LANG, K.D.: *b. November 2, 1961*. Androgynous, openly lesbian country/pop singer/songwriter with whom Madonna shared a casual friendship.

Way **back** when, lang and **Ciccone** complimented each other in the press (Madonna declared in 1989: "**Elvis** is alive ... and she's beautiful!"). Both were very good friends of one **Ingrid Casares,** who dated lang, and their paths also crossed at the 1991 **amfAR** benefit, where Madonna was given the **Award** of Courage and at which lang performed. Madonna socialized with lang at an **Oscars** after-party in 1998.

Madonna threw a bash for lang after her performance at **Radio City Music Hall** on August 25, 1992, at Remi (145 W. 53rd St., NY, NY). Madonna showed up with her **gold tooth**, but a press report at the time claimed she left in a huff before lang even arrived and that lang showed up, muttering, "We're having a lover's quarrel," to (provocatively) explain Madonna's absence.

David Munk, who **worked** at Time Warner, Inc., for Gerald Levin, has written on his blog *Stargayzing* that Madonna *was* at the extremely overcrowded party with lang and that she made an unkind remark to lang about the arrival of **Peggy Lee** in her wheelchair: "Oh, shit—where the **fuck** is *she* gonna go?"

In 2008, lang blew off her past association with Madonna: "… She never came on to me; that was a lot of publicity because we had the same publicist and it helped Madonna and it helped me. I don't think Madonna ever really liked me, to be honest. We're very different people."

> "She looks like Sean [Penn]. I met her and I thought, 'I could fall in love with her.'"
> —MADONNA ON MEETING K.D. LANG (1991)

LANG, PEARL: *May 29, 1921–February 24, 2009.* The former **Martha Graham** soloist was based in **New York** but visited the **University of Michigan**, Madonna's **school**, as an artist-in-residence in early 1978. Madonna performed a new Lang **work** set to Vivaldi, and would audition for Lang to get into the **American Dance Festival**, a six-week course at **Duke University**. Lang would later say that Madonna's hard work stood out among the 80 applicants, so she was chosen.

"She was young, and she was determined to do it right and *well*," Lang noted in a 2001 interview. "Many **dancers** can kick and exhibit acrobatic body **control**, but this is just run-of-the-mill, taken for granted. Madonna had the **power**, the intensity to go beyond mere physical performance into something far more exciting."

After completing her time at Duke, Madonna asked Lang if she needed any dancers in New York. Lang was skeptical, but Madonna reportedly told her, "Don't worry." In November 1978, Madonna showed up at one of Lang's classes in NYC at American Dance Center (formerly 229 E. 59th St., NY, NY). Lang was married to *Dr. No* (1962) actor Joseph Wiseman, but if she was married to "Dr. No," her student was apparently "Miss Yes."

Lang remembered on the VH1 show *Driven: Madonna*, "One day, she came in with a sweater cut from the neck [indicating **back**] all the way down to below the waist. *Cut.* And a safety pin about a foot long holding this garment together, but it was dripping off of *one's* shoulder. And I looked at her back and I thought to myself, 'She's gonna do something someday.'"

Madonna was cast in Lang's company's *I Never Saw Another Butterfly*, a Holocaust drama, impressing Lang as "an exceptional dancer" with her performance as a child starving in the Jewish ghetto. She also excelled in a production of *La Rosa en Flores*. Lang told Madonna biographer **Andrew Morton**, "I was fond of her for her arrogance, her hunger and her spunk."

But in spite of Madonna's skill and Lang's affection for her (she got Madonna a **job** checking coats at the **Russian Tea Room**) the two did butt heads and Madonna quit. In a 1984 cover story for ***Long Island's Nightlife***, Madonna remembered of her time with Lang, "It was interesting work. The style is very archaic, angular and dramatic. Painful, dark and guilt-ridden—very **Catholic**. I was always an outcast in my ballet classes, the freak. I didn't have long **hair** pulled back in a bun. Mine was short, and I used to dye it different colors."

LANGE, JESSICA: *b. April 20, 1949.* **Oscar**-winning actor who has also been acclaimed for her stage and **TV** work, especially on *American Horror Story* (2011–2015). Lange has long been one of Madonna's favorite actors. She personally congratulated Lange and Alec Baldwin backstage after a 1992 performance of *A Streetcar Named Desire* on Broadway.

LASERDISC: Pioneer Artists, which sponsored the ***Blond Ambition World Tour***, released a film of the concert exclusively on laserdisc to test the economic feasibility of the new format. "Madonna is the ideal artist to reach the new demographics that we are hoping to attract with the new, low-priced combination CD-and-laser players … the young, hip, 18-35 audience," Pioneer said at the time.

LAST TEMPTATION OF CHRIST, THE: *Director: Martin Scorsese. Release date: August 12, 1988.* In 1982, **Cis Corman** was helping to cast Martin Scorsese's follow-up to *The King of Comedy* (1983), which had featured Madonna's future friend **Sandra Bernhard**. The cast of *The Last Temptation of Christ* at that point included Aidan Quinn—Madonna's future ***Desperately Seeking Susan*** costar—as Jesus and Vanity as Mary Magdalene. Corman saw Madonna for Mary, **Mother** of Jesus (eventually played by Verna Bloom in the film, which wasn't released until 1988). While she didn't ultimately recommend her for the part, she was wowed by Madonna's **talent**.

LATE NIGHT WITH DAVID LETTERMAN: *Airdates: February 1, 1982–June 25, 1993.* Hosted by late-night master of snark David Letterman, this off-the-wall talk show had a cable-access quirkiness. It wasn't the same ol' scripted late-night banter that US audiences had come to expect from ***The Tonight Show***.

One of Letterman's favorite repeat guests was comic **Sandra Bernhard**. On Friday, July 1, 1988, Bernhard was set to appear to discuss her hit one-woman show *Without You I'm Nothing*, but an unscheduled visit by Madonna made for **TV** gold.

"We split each other's split ends."—MADONNA ON HER LEISURE-TIME ACTIVITIES WITH SANDRA BERNHARD (1988)

"She can't be stopped!"
—DAVID LETTERMAN ON MADONNA (1994)

Bernhard introduced Madonna, who came out to reveal that the women were in matching white T-shirts and jean shorts, kinda like a team uniform ... or a street gang, judging by their ensuing behavior. Letterman, visibly in awe of Madonna, charmingly stumbled over himself trying to win her favor, but she was a tough cookie, the pretty girl in **school** dangling her **power** over the nerd.

When Letterman asked Madonna if she enjoyed doing *Speed-the-Plow*, which was on Broadway at the time, she gave him a tight-lipped, "Mm-hm." Bernhard called her out immediately, shouting, "She **hates** it! She's miserable!" to which Madonna replied, "I am! I want out!" When Letterman attempted to get Madonna to explain her misery, she said, "I'm just effing with you," which was pretty raw talk for TV in the '80s.

"Let's talk about you two getting together—over my dead body!" Bernhard joked to Letterman, the beginning of their **flirtation** with the perception that Madonna and Bernhard were a **gay** couple. "We carouse ..." Madonna said of her nights out with Bernhard, claiming Letterman would need "a **sex**-change" to join them. Madonna was the one who claimed the two frequented the **Cubby Hole**, a lesbian bar; Letterman didn't pick up on this morsel, but the press did.

As the short (seven minutes and change) segment wound down, Madonna steered the conversation to unimagined places, leaving Letterman almost speechless with anticipation. "Sandra, I think we should just cut it right here," Madonna announced, as if she were about to come out of the closet. "I think, I think it's time to 'fess up and get real ..." Bernhard then piped up and claimed she'd slept with **Sean Penn**, but assured Madonna, "*You* were much better!"

Madonna cracked up, but continued. "David, you wanna know the truth? ... She doesn't give a damn about me. She **loves** Sean. She's been using me to get to Sean. I introduced her to Sean three years ago at **Warren Beatty**'s house ... and she has been in love with him ever since. It's true. She doesn't care about me. She's been using me."

The awkward sequence had been getting **nervous** laughs from the audience throughout, but Madonna did eventually land the biggest roar when she noted that she was attempting to humiliate Bernhard in front of "thousands" of people. Letterman, defending his show's reach, sniffed, "*Thousands* of people ..." leading Madonna to quip, "All right—a hundred!"

It's a wonder Letterman ever welcomed her **back**, and it's downright shocking that when she finally went on TV with him again—on the much more conventional *Late Show with David Letterman*—their exchange was even wilder and even less scripted.

LATE SHOW WITH DAVID LETTERMAN: *Airdates: August 30, 1993–May 20, 2015.* During Madonna's *Sex* era, she was the well-toned butt of many jokes, including lots of slut jokes from David Letterman. So it was a surprise when, on March 31, 1994, Madonna appeared on the new iteration of his late-night talk show, her first time being interviewed by Letterman since her bratty sit-down with **Sandra Bernhard** on *Late Night with David Letterman* six years previously. Her only current project to promote was a movie-soundtrack single, **"I'll Remember,"** which was never mentioned on the show.

On the April Fool's Eve show, Letterman introduced Madonna with an insult:

"Our first guest tonight is one of the biggest stars in the world. In the past 10 years, she has sold over 80 million albums, starred in countless films and slept with some of the biggest names in the entertainment industry."

Madonna walked out rocking a regal, serpentine look in a deep green velvet gown, she-means-**business** boots and center-parted black **hair**. She was also showing off her newly pierced nose. ("Yes, it hurt.") As Letterman hugged her, she stuffed a pair of her panties into his hands, then sat down and announced, "I'm only here 'cause there isn't a Knicks game—don't get excited."

Letterman tried to get Madonna to kiss a **fan** in the audience (she passed), but Madonna wanted to know, "Why are you so obsessed with my **sex** life?"

Letterman seemed to think that the appearance would be a scripted burying of the hatchet, but Madonna continued pushing it beyond his **control**, pronouncing Letterman to be "a sick **fuck**." She resisted his attempts to quiz her on other topics (and demonstrated her mistaken belief that "oxymoron" and "redundancy" mean the same thing). Was she high? She did bring up smoking **endo**. She must've been on something to think she would come out the winner by going against a seasoned comic.

Madonna's dreadfully unpleasant appearance didn't seek to entertain or to ingratiate. She seemed to be consciously doing everything possible to sabotage the segment. She ignored questions, swore, gave short answers, opened previously unapproved topics of conversation and insulted the host. She pointedly told Letterman he'd become uncool since their last encounter, criticizing him for kissing the asses of the big stars he had on the new show.

The rest of the appearance was excruciating, highly disturbing, legendary **TV**. Madonna—who was uncharacteristically giddy and witlessly vicious—called for break-all-the-rules questioning. She was rewarded with softballs like, "What's the next look?" Letterman clearly did not handle the situation assertively.

But though the ensuing media frenzy absurdly concentrated on the fact that Madonna, puffing on a cigar, used the word "fuck" 13 times, more shocking were her leaden wisecracks and her unhinged behavior. Letterman ended up completely flustered, the studio audience ended up completely annoyed and Madonna? Well, at least for an evening, she was completely insane.

Madonna's were the highest guest-generated ratings since Letterman's 1993 move to CBS, and her **gift** to him inspired a tradition of sorts: The very next evening, Charles Grodin gave him his boxers and Elvis Costello gave him a sock.

In a way, Madonna succeeded in dumping on Letterman, so she'd had her revenge. But she probably never anticipated the depth of the outrage her appearance would cause in the culture. Articles were written declaring her career over, and not just by unrepentant **haters**; this time, Madonna was condemned by just about everyone.

"The confidence and **power** that Letterman so effortlessly exudes these days are precisely the qualities that Madonna now lacks. Her once-exhilarating bravado and impudence have curdled into a sullen, crude rebelliousness," Ken Tucker wrote in *Entertainment Weekly*.

Liz Rosenberg painted the encounter in as positive a light as possible: "Madonna was extremely **nervous** and so cold she could barely talk ... I think it was nice that she wasn't in control for a change, not that Dave was in control, either ... Madonna isn't a seasoned TV performer, but she had fun, Dave had fun and Madonna has no **regrets**."

A couple of weeks later, Madonna faxed Letterman: "Happy fucking **birthday**."

The terrible twosome kissed and made up, appearing arm in arm at the 1994 **MTV Video Music Awards**, which washed away the aftertaste of their March run-in.

As badly as their encounter went, it didn't take long for her to visit the show again. For Valentine's Day 1995, Madonna—**back** to blonde, back on best behavior—showed up with flowers and **candy** for Letterman, who sputtered, "You look like a million bucks!" Madonna joked that she'd been encouraged to say "the bad word," but, "I'm a changed woman since I met you, and ... and I'm not gonna say 'fuck' anymore."

On December 28, 1998, Madonna popped in to help with a Top 10 list of what beautiful women like about David Letterman.

On November 3, 2000, Madonna returned to visit Letterman, who—playing with fire?—introduced her by saying, "In four days, Americans will go to the polls to elect

the father of our first guest's next baby." Lucky for him, Madonna was okay with the barb. Showing up to promote *Music* in a rootin' tootin' cowgirl suit, she sat for a proper interview, telling him, by way of explaining why she wouldn't be raunchy, "I have kids now." Their banter about married life was a world away from their 1994 encounter. They also chatted about Madonna's motherhood and her upcoming **Roseland Ballroom** show, and Madonna then gave a spine-tingling performance of **"Don't Tell Me"** alongside **Monte Pittman**. She admitted she was "incredibly nervous."

For her November 11, 2003, visit, Madonna did a short sketch with Letterman about his parenting skills in conjunction with the release of her **book** *Mr. Peabody's Apples*. [SEE: **bibliography** (**by Madonna**).] She came out in a conservative blouse and skirt and playfully sat one chair away from Letterman, who had a cold. She called him on a joke he'd made about her propensity for getting **pregnant** and brought him this time a hat instead of used panties.

On January 11, 2007, Madonna showed up to promote *Arthur and the Invisibles*. "I **love** underpants!" she joked when Letterman brought up the fact that **Britney Spears** and other starlets were being photographed with their lack of **underwear** on display. She suggested Letterman could give Spears the pair that Madonna had gifted him in 1994.

Madonna was back on September 30, 2009, to promote *Celebration*. She looked like Catherine Deneuve, and was carried in by members of the **New York** Rangers, bumping her head on entry. Right away, Letterman called her by the **nickname** "Madge," leading to her deciding out loud whether she liked the name or not. She also sorta admitted that she'd been high during their 1994 encounter. "I think I'd rather get run over by a train," she said in response to whether she might wanna get married again. But the big gag of the show was that haughty, macrobiotic Madonna had never eaten **NYC** pizza (gimme a break!), so she was taken downstairs, outside and into Angelo's Pizza (1697 Broadway, NY, NY). There, they ate **pizza** and washed it down with martinis.

There's no denying it: Watching the evolution of Madonna's TV relationship to David Letterman has been fucking fascinating.

"... [H]e knew I was going to come on and say the word 'fuck' a lot. I was doing it as a protest against censorship."-MADONNA (1994)

"It's such hypocrisy. The fact that everyone counted how many fucks I said—how small-minded is that? The way he introduced me was derogatory, so my whole thing was, 'Okay, if that's how you want to play it, you can not beat me at this game.'"

-MADONNA, *SPIN* (1996)

"Do you like me?"–DAVID LETTERMAN TO MADONNA (2009)

"LATIN CHANT": Chant found on *Evita: The Complete Motion Picture Music Soundtrack*. It follows the **death** of Evita.

LAUER, MATT: *b. December 30, 1957*. SEE: *Dateline NBC* and *Today*.

"LAUGH TO KEEP FROM CRYING": This **Chrissie Hynde**–inspired 1981 track was written by Madonna and produced by **Stephen Bray**. It was **unreleased** until 1997, when Bray made it commercially available on *Pre-Madonna*.

LAUPER, CYNDI: *b. June 22, 1953*. Singer-songwriter formerly of the rockabilly band Blue Angel who went solo and broke through in a huge way with her debut album *She's So Unusual* (1983), which spawned the iconic hit "Girls Just Want to Have Fun" and launched a Top 40 career that spanned the rest of the '80s. Over time, Lauper expanded to become a touring act, also **acting** in movies and on **TV** (winning an Emmy). In 2012, she had one of the greatest successes of her long career when she wrote the **Tony**-winning score for the Broadway musical *Kinky Boots*.

Early on, Madonna and Lauper had some visual similarities, including their outrageous second-hand outfits, but their music has always been quite different. Lauper's **work** is more informed by her rock past whereas Madonna's usually springs from her appreciation for Motown and **disco**.

Because of Lauper's sensational four-octave **voice** and earnest lyrics**,** Lauper was widely believed to be the female singer to watch for the rest of the '80s.

In its March 4, 1985, issue, *Newsweek* made a strong case that Lauper was the bigger **talent**, giving her the cover to illustrate its "Woman **Power**" story. *Billboard*'s Paul Grein said in 1985, "Cyndi Lauper will be around for a long time. Madonna will be out of **business** in six months. Her image has completely overshadowed her music." He was dead wrong about Madonna, even if he was absolutely right about Cyndi Lauper. The lesson should be: One's success was unrelated to the other's.

One example of direct crossover: Madonna's hit **"Open Your Heart"** began life as "Follow Your Heart," a demo rejected by Lauper and retooled for and by Madonna. Madonna and Lauper often competed on the charts, at one point having similarly-titled albums (*True Blue* and *True Colors*, respectively) and singles ("Open Your Heart" and "Change of Heart," respectively), but their careers otherwise diverged.

Lauper teased Madonna in 1987, saying, "When people say to me, 'Aren't you Cyndi Lauper?' I say, 'No, I'm Madonna, and watch out 'cause **Sean Penn** is gonna come at ya any second and beat the shit outta ya.'"

When Madonna was wrapping recording of *Erotica* in August 1992, Lauper was starting to record *Hat Full of Stars* across the street. Lauper hung out with Madonna's **fans** outside the studio, saying hi when Madonna walked past, which elicited a look of disbelief from Madonna and then a dismissive shake of the head. Lauper reportedly said something to the effect of, "Just as I remember her!" The only other reported direct confrontation between the women had been in 1984, when Madonna told friends that Lauper had been "mean" to her at the **MTV Video Music Awards**.

In 2014, Lauper spoke at length—and approvingly—about Madonna: "The media invented that rivalry. We really didn't even know each other. We had a lot of friends in common, but we never really even met except for a few quick times at **award** shows. We both came out at the same time, we both were very into **fashion**, we were both very opinionated and demanded to be heard, but our music wasn't and isn't similar. They don't compare men who have successful albums in the same year, do they?"

Lauper tweeted her praise of Madonna's **Super Bowl** shenanigans in 2012: "Just saw half time. Common [c'mon], visually OMG! And there is only one Madonna! Xx Cyn." In a hat tip to Lauper, Madonna's *MDNA* tune **"Girl Gone Wild"** contains the lyric, "Girls, they just wanna have some fun."

"I love her and think she's very inspirational … Her business sense is unbelievable, mine is not so good. My son would like me to be more like her."—CYNDI LAUPER ON MADONNA, *ATTITUDE* (2008)

LE BON, SIMON: *b. October 27, 1958*. The lead singer of Duran Duran told *Rolling Stone* in 1995 that his favorite Madonna incarnation was from 1985. "I actually liked her when she was a bit fatter. I liked that puffy fat that was on her. I found that very attractive." Le Bon is, of course, famous for dating and marrying zaftig women, *amiright?*

LE GRAND JOURNAL: *Airdates: August 30, 2004–*. Madonna appeared on this French news show on March 2, 2015. Continuing with the matador-inspired look from previous *Rebel Heart* promo performances, she was decked out in epaulets and a Spanish hat—no cape in sight!—climbing a flight of steps up a piano as she performed a remix of **"Living for Love."** Her **"Ghosttown"** performance was the first one of that song that made it to air. At the end of the show, Madonna curtsied demurely, received a kneeling kiss on the hand from the host, bowed and then saluted her audience.

Madonna met with a *Charlie Hebdo* survivor during the interview portion of her appearance.

LE PEN, MARINE: *b. August 5, 1968*. SEE: **"Nobody Knows Me."**

LEACH, ROBIN: *b. August 29, 1941*. The loud little man with the oft-mimicked **accent**, host of the series *Lifestyles of the Rich and Famous* (1984–1995) and lifelong pursuer of "champagne wishes and **caviar** dreams."

In March 1993, in the wake of Madonna's *Sex* and *Body of Evidence* media roasting, Leach hosted *Madonna Exposed*, a Fox **TV** special that was a live-from-the-Palladium (formerly 126 E. 14th St., NY, NY) attempt to smear her further.

"I was at Madonna's **book** party for the launch of her book. That party reminded me of pre-Nazi Germany. In came Madonna, dressed as Heidi. I kept thinking, 'Somebody is playing a joke on us,'" Leach said of his motivation to do the special.

Madonna Exposed took on a particularly aggressive tone after Madonna officially refused to cooperate and tried to persuade others to avoid participating. But after all, why would Madonna want anything to do with a wallow in her no good, very bad year?

"Tonight, you won't officially hear her sing or watch her **dance** because she banned us from airing any of her own videos," the show began—what a sell line! Leach castigated Madonna for trying to "**censor**" the show, going so far as to announce that Madonna's camp had been given a special phone number to call in and dispute anything said about her.

Cohosted by the late Eleanor Mondale (who seemed caught in a continuous state of "Huh?"), the show was fueled by tabloid clichés (she was called a "lurid lightning rod" and "libido torpedo") and gratuitous vaginal innuendos regarding Madonna's rumored **bisexuality** (talk about "snatching" girlfriends away, not "beating around the bush" and the tongue-twirler "cunning stunt").

The special actually wound up being a **fan**'s wet **dream**, featuring the first-ever playing of her Gotham demo, interviews with many of her early-years intimates, a performance by *Blond Ambition World Tour* dancer-turned-disher **Salim "Slam" Gauwloos** and lots of rare footage.

Leach attempted to milk some **hate** out of his guests, but even though these were the people so often pointed to as examples of Madonna's ruthlessness—**Camille Barbone** and **Mark Kamins** among them—no one had anything truly nasty to say.

After all his **work,** Leach had the profound embarrassment of having to announce that the show's call-in poll (to 1-900-89-MADONNA at $1.95 a crack) to the question, "Has Madonna gone too far?" ended with 79 percent of viewers saying that she had not!

Reminded of *Madonna Exposed* in 2011 by the author, Leach sighed, "Oh, *thaaat* ..."

LEAGUE OF THEIR OWN, A: *Director: Penny Marshall. Release date: July 1, 1992.* This richly nostalgic **feminist** baseball romp, directed by **Penny Marshall** and starring **Geena Davis, Tom Hanks,** Lori Petty, **Rosie O'Donnell** and Madonna, memorialized the nearly forgotten All-American Girls Professional Baseball League. The $40 million film was one of the biggest hits of summer '92— gallons of ink were spilled about the women's baseball league invented by chewing gum mogul Philip K. Wrigley

in 1943 and its place in the fabric of American history— knocking *Batman Returns* out of the top slot the week it debuted and going on to a lifetime US gross of $107,533,928 ($132,440,069 worldwide).

The story revolves around "Dottie Hinson" (Davis) and her kid sis "Kit Keller" (Petty), the latter of whom is constantly competing with her more **talented** sibling for recognition as a ballplayer. When Dottie is recruited to be the star player of the Rockford Peaches, Kit tags along as part of the deal, setting the women up for major sister drama. Anchored as it is by a Garbo-esque performance from Davis, the real charm of the film lies in its inspired game scenes, innocent period touches and the exhilarating female camaraderie among the cast members, especially when it rubs up against the macho grumpiness of manager "Jimmy Dugan" (Hanks).

Madonna played a tailor-made supporting role as "Mae Mordabito," the loosest member of the lady hardballers.

Marshall said, "When casting the part of 'All-the-Way' Mae, I thought, 'Maybe Madonna would be interested,' so she went to St. John's in **New York** and tried out for three hours. She was a real good sport." Luckily, Marshall never reconsidered casting Madonna when Debra Winger, who'd originally been hired to play Dottie, quit the movie over "stunt casting." Winger told Marshall of the decision to hire Madonna, "You're making an **Elvis** film!" Before Winger, Dottie had almost been played by **Demi Moore**, but by the time the film was going to shoot, she'd gotten **pregnant**.

Madonna as "Mae" in *A League of Their Own*, and (top) with Ann Cusack

Madonna doesn't like baseball. She once groused to **Harvey Weinstein** that it "has no relevance to the state of the world." So, to prepare for her role, she had to seek the expertise of relevant major-leaguers like **Jose Canseco**. She also endured batting practice at St. John's University (8000 Utopia Pkwy., Jamaica, NY) with acclaimed NCAA coach Joe Russo as part of the six months she spent learning to play baseball, suffering a bruised left hand (that's what the mitt's for, dear). Hanks said at the time of Madonna's baseball skills, "She throws like a girl but she can run like the wind."

Madonna also spent three weeks learning to jitterbug with Chicago dancer/choreographer Tony Savino and personally interviewed the woman on whom Mae was based.

"... [H]er name was Faye Dancer and she was a wild woman," Madonna said of the real-life Mae. "She's *still* a wild woman. The way she describes their games and their touring the country and stuff was just that every city was a party and she had six boyfriends in every town, and every night they snuck out." Dancer died at age 77 in 2002.

For all the **work** she had to put in to get ready for the role ("Madonna is the hardest-working human being I have ever seen in my life," observed coscreenwriter Lowell Ganz), and in spite of misgivings about her look (she called the Rockford Peaches uniform a "grotesque ... burlap sack"), Madonna came out smelling like a Pete Rose. Her comic timing, especially in her shared scenes with O'Donnell (with whom she became great buddies in real life), was on-point, she looked beautiful and she even got to do something she should've done a lot more of in the movies: **dance.** She jitterbugged her ass off with Eddie Mekka, best known as "Carmine Ragusa" from **TV**'s *Laverne & Shirley* (1976–1983).

One particularly affecting scene found Madonna's brassy character encouraging Ann Cusack's illiterate character "Shirley Baker" to read. Cusack reminisced about working with Madonna to the author: "She'd just come off her tour where she was in **control** of everything, so when she did this [movie], she has an incredible work ethic but ... she wasn't a ballplayer, she was a dancer, so she was learning how to do this." Of her touching scene with Madonna, Cusack says, "She was really lovely one-on-one—we spent the whole afternoon doing it—but there's the one-on-one persona and then there's the more-than-five-people [persona]."

Madonna even chalked up another #1 hit with the song **"This Used to be My Playground,"** which was included in the film but was not available on the soundtrack.

Hitting a homer with her *A League of Their Own* premiere party look

OLIVIA SAVU

OLIVIU SAVU

Madonna and O'Donnell bonded like a grilled cheese sandwich; Madonna and **Evansville,** Indiana, on the other hand, discovered a mutual loathing.

The filming was relatively uneventful, though a pregnant cow, a key player in the milking scenes, *did* cause a minor delay, and Madonna was doggedly pursued by the press for the duration of the on-location shoot in Chicago and other parts of the Midwest.

At the time of its release, *A League of Their Own* received strong reviews, but it was not a big **awards** contender; at the **Golden Globes,** Davis received a nomination for Best Performance by an Actress in a Motion Picture—Comedy/Musical, and Madonna and **Shep Pettibone** were nominated for Best **Original** Song—Motion Picture. But over time, the film's importance seems to have sunk in with critics.

At Chiller Theatre in New Jersey in October 2014, Tracy Reiner, a.k.a. "Betty Spaghetti" and the daughter of Marshall with **Rob Reiner,** said the film's importance snuck up on her.

"We weren't sure, but it was changing, like, the minds of all the coaches, and all the players—like, we got to play with the White Sox and with the Cubs—and it was messing with their heads a little bit." Years after its release, it became clear that the film had been a home run. "By the time we started doing [autograph] shows, [we had] veterans and P.E. teachers and **fathers** and crying women coming up and saying, 'Thank you, you made me feel important,' then it's a big deal."

In 2012, *A League of Their Own* was chosen to be preserved in the United States National Film Registry by the Library of Congress, an honor reserved for films that are deemed "culturally, historically or aesthetically significant."

"SHE'S OPINIONATED AND HEADSTRONG, SHE'S ALL THAT STUFF. SHE'S DETERMINED, SHE'S THERE FOR A REASON. WHAT THAT REASON IS, I DON'T KNOW. SHE WAS A PROFESSIONAL."-TOM HANKS ON MADONNA (1992)

"SHE WORKED SO HARD. SHE WOULD RUN EVERY MORNING, THEN SHE'D WORK OUT PLAYING BALL, THEN AT NIGHT SHE'D JITTERBUG … THERE WAS NO STAR-TRIPPING, NONE OF THAT."-PENNY MARSHALL ON MADONNA (1992)

"WHAT OTHER FILM COULD OFFER COMEDY, FEMINISM, THE NATIONAL PASTIME, PERIOD NOSTALGIA AND MADONNA SQUEEZING A LOUISVILLE SLUGGER?"-MIKE CLARK, *USA TODAY* (1992)

"MADONNA SEEMS NOTHING LIKE A VIRGIN ON THE FIELD, PLAYING WITH DEVIL-MAY-CARE GUSTO (WATCH FOR HER FACE-FIRST, DIRT-IN-HER-SKIRT SLIDE INTO THIRD)."
-MICHAEL J. BANDLER, *USA TODAY BASEBALL WEEKLY* (1992)

"NOT SINCE *DESPERATELY SEEKING SUSAN* HAS MADONNA HAD A ROLE THAT FITS HER PUBLIC PERSONALITY AS WELL AS 'MAE,' AN OPINIONATED, OPERATIONAL FIGHTER WHO'S NOT ABOUT TO PAY TOO MUCH ATTENTION TO TRAINING RULES WHEN IT COMES TO MEN. IT'S NOT A BIG ROLE, BUT IT IS CHOICE."
-VINCENT CANBY, *THE NEW YORK TIMES* (1992)

LEAKS: More than any other artist, Madonna has been plagued by unauthorized leaks of her music.

The first song to leak was **"Frozen"** in 1998, which happened in an analog way—it was played too early by a Singapore radio station, taped and uploaded to the Web.

By May 2000, when a grainy snippet of her forthcoming single **"Music"** leaked, the public was suspicious that it may have been intentional. "Oh, please!" Madonna said at the time, exasperated. "If I was going to leak my record, I would've put a better mix of it out there." In July 2000, six of the album's songs leaked.

At the time of the "Music" leak, Madonna wrote in her official **fan** magazine, *Icon,* "You may have heard bits and pieces of my new CD on the Internet. The music, unfortunately, was stolen and illegally played on various websites … I can't understand why people can't let me put it out when I'm good and ready."

In 2003, Madonna planted files online that posed as new music, but that contained her angrily asking, "What the *fuck* do you think *you're* doing?" Nonetheless, **"American**

Life" leaked, apparently in Poland, on March 23, 2003, so 4,000 paid copies of the song were sent to fans March 24, 2003, which led to the song hitting the Hot 100 Sales chart a week early.

By 2014, Madonna should've been used to her music leaking since all of her lead singles and numerous album tracks had leaked early since 1998. Still, nothing could have prepared her for what began on November 28, 2014, when demos of **"Rebel Heart"** and **"Wash All Over Me"**—two songs from *Rebel Heart*, an album she hadn't intended to release until April 2015—leaked in full. Entertainment outlets, ignoring the seriousness of the invasion, played and commented (favorably) on the songs, which led some to decide Madonna had done it for publicity, even though **Guy Oseary** tweeted that he wanted help in finding those who'd been responsible for the breach.

On December 4, 2014, Madonna posted an image of a smashed iPod and vented about being violated. When 13 tracks had leaked, she controversially termed the leaks to be "artistic **rape**."

Attempting to regain some **control**, on December 20, 2014, Madonna released six songs from *Rebel Heart* to iTunes and confirmed the album's title. She told *Billboard* the rest of the album would be handled in an "analog" way. "We're not on the Internet. Hard drives of music are hand-carried to people."

The leaks kept coming, including over 30 tracks, mostly demos that represented unfinished versions of her music, until the entire finished album leaked in February. The availability of the demos was a loss-loss for Madonna; they decreased the drive to pay for her music and they also gave fans an undeserved, backseat-producer perspective, an **excuse** to be able to compare and contrast early to finished versions of the song and decide, "I preferred the demos!"

Madonna was so incensed by the violation—which turned out to have originated when a hacker gained access to her personal computer, resulting in the release of family photos as well—that she spent 30 minutes Skyping with a fan who deals in stolen music in an effort to try to figure out what was going on. Israeli police and cyber crime unit Lahav 433 arrested 38-year-old Adi Lederman for hacking the accounts of people associated with Madonna as well as others. He denied the accusations, but on February 27, 2015, was indicted on four counts: computer trespassing, prohibited secret monitoring, copyright infringement and obstructing investigation. Lederman allegedly received only "tens" (**bitch**, please) to "thousands" for each item he sold to accomplices, which included files from the private cloud accounts of management employee Sara Zambreno, engineer Angie Teo and musical director Kevin Antunes. He also tapped into one of Oseary's email accounts.

Anyone still believing Madonna orchestrated the leaks has a fundamental misunderstanding of **business**, marketing and publicity. What Madonna *did* do was try to play the hand she was dealt.

Madonna later told a small cadre of **gay** media of the leaks, "First of all, it drove me insane—and made me feel an overwhelming sense of anxiety. It made me second-guess everything, because suddenly I thought, 'Oh, **God**, everyone's heard all these demos.' There were some demos that I actually liked the demo version of, and I thought, 'Well, they heard the demo, now they're going to be expecting other things.' Then they heard the next level of versions, and it kept making me think, 'Should I change it, or should I just leave it how it was?' I was second-guessing everything rather than having to just choose for myself and put it out as I would normally, as an artist ...'"

Going forward, it will be interesting to see how Madonna approaches new albums. Will she hype them on social media six to eight months in advance, encouraging intense interest? Or will she **back** off and try to be creative in secrecy, hoping to be able to surprise her market?

LECOMPTE, ANDY: Madonna's longtime **hair** stylist, including for **magazine** covers such as *Dazed & Confused* (April 2008), *Harper's Bazaar* (November 2013), *L'Uomo Vogue* (May/June 2014), *V* (Summer 2014) and *Interview* (December 2014/January 2015), and for the 2013 **Met Ball** and for the cover of *Rebel Heart*.

LEE, PEGGY: *May 26, 1920–January 21, 2002.* Icy-cool jazz vocalist and songwriter whose silky **voice** lit up classic songs like "I'm a Woman" (1962), "Big Spender" (1966) and "Is That All There Is?" (1969), and whose music and voice-over enriched Disney's *Lady and the Tramp* (1955).

Madonna, with bodyguard/lover **Jimmy Albright** in tow, took in Lee's show at the Hilton Hotel's Club 53 (1335 Ave. of the Americas, NY, NY) in 1992. Madonna had for Lee a bouquet of red roses and her big, **gold-toothed** smile. She greeted Lee, in a wheelchair, at a party for **k.d. lang**, with **Tony Bennett** also in attendance.

Immediately after their meeting, Madonna spontaneously covered Lee's signature song, **"Fever,"** after she began singing the words over the music track for a proposed song called **"Goodbye to Innocence."** A runner was sent for the actual lyrics and "Fever" made it onto Madonna's *Erotica*.

"I've heard the cut. It's wonderful. Hers is disco, mine is not."-PEGGY LEE ON MADONNA'S "FEVER" (1992)

LEE, SPIKE: Provocative, polarizing African-American auteur director of such diverse **movies** as *She's Gotta Have It* (1986), *Do the Right Thing* (1989), *Get on the Bus* (1996) and *Oldboy* (2013). Madonna attended the May 16, 1991, premiere of Lee's *Jungle Fever* while in **Cannes** promoting *Truth or Dare*, as well as his *Malcolm X* premiere at the **Ziegfeld Theatre** in **NYC** on November 16, 1992.

A radical thinker who's not above making cash (he's directed **commercials** for Nike), Lee shares a lot of common ground with Madonna and has always given Madonna's rebel-heart attitude high marks, eventually paying her the highest compliment any director can pay when he cast her as a phone-**sex** madam in his film *Girl 6* (1996).

"Marketing is something I'm very proud of. The only artist that does it better than me is Madonna. She's the champ."-SPIKE LEE (1992)

LEIBOVITZ, ANNIE: *b. October 2, 1949.* One of America's most famous portrait photographers, whose **work** has been prominent in *Rolling Stone*, in *Vanity Fair* and on album covers. In 2007, Leibovitz shot Madonna in a simple studio setting, **Photoshopping** her into poses with Djimon Hounsou and Maya Angelou, whom Madonna didn't meet, for two of *Vanity Fair*'s "**Africa** Issue" cover variations.

LENNOX, ANNIE: *b. December 25, 1954.* One half of the influential '80s British group Eurythmics, she was the startlingly androgynous lead singer with a flaming-**orange** crew cut and an out-of-nowhere '60s soul **voice**. With hits like "Sweet **Dreams** (Are Made of This)" (1983), "Here Comes the Rain Again" (1984) and "Would I Lie to You?" (1985), Eurythmics was a top act on both sides of the Atlantic. Lennox's solo career (from 1992 on) has been less successful, but has allowed for her to stretch into a multidimensional vocalist capable of delivering everything from standards to electronic pop.

In 2007, Madonna contributed to Lennox's song "**Sing**" from her album *Songs of Mass Destruction*. The song raised **money** for Treatment Action Campaign, an HIV/**AIDS** org. At that time, Lennox said that she invited various female artists to sing the chorus along with her (remotely), but was surprised when Madonna went the extra mile. "... Madonna sang the second verse as well ... [I]t was really cool of her. Look, I'll be as mercenary with this as I need to be. Madonna has a huge audience and her involvement will help to spread the word wider."

Now that she's 60, Lennox—who was quite provocative in her time—seems to have mellowed to the point of being a fuddy-duddy; she has criticized **Beyoncé** for using her **sexuality** on stage, and she has done the same when it comes to Madonna, more than once. When Madonna posed topless for *Interview*'s December 2014/January 2015 issue, Lennox said on the UK **TV** show *Loose Women*, "I *did* get things off occasionally, but not that ... not to *that* extent! ... Oh, **God**, you see, here's the ... here we go, here we go ... If it's down to me, if I have my comments, they go into the press and they start to be twisted and so, 'Annie Lennox is, you know, slates Madonna, da-da-da-da-da'—I don't think it's down to me. I mean ... I think already the verdict's probably out, would you not agree on that one? Probably, okay, what is, I think the question is, 'What is Madonna telling us?' Anybody know?" When it was sug-

gested Madonna's pose was an example of seeking attention, Lennox said, "Yes, I think it is."

However, Lennox stopped short of condemning Madonna, making sure to steer the conversation **back** to her in a positive way.

"And, you know, to give Madonna her due, she's just been to **Malawi** and *apparently* she's going to open up 300 hospitals, which I think is fantastic."

LENO, JAY: SEE *Tonight Show, The.*

LEON, CARLOS: *b. July 10, 1966.* Personal trainer (he was charging $100/hour **back** then) who Madonna met in September 1994 in Central Park. They struck up a relationship that resulted in Madonna's first child, **Lourdes Maria "Lola" Leon.**

Contrary to popular belief, Leon was *a* trainer, but not *Madonna's* trainer. "I was in **love** with him. A lot of people think I walked out on the street and looked at him and said, 'You're going to be my sperm donor.' I had a relationship with him for two years. We were together for three. And I am really insulted," Madonna told *TV Guide* in 1998.

When Madonna's **pregnancy** was announced by **Liz Smith**, a media feeding frenzy ensued. In 1996, conservative writer Jonathan Alter wrote a *Newsweek* open letter to Madonna urging her to get married, saying, "[W]hat's 'freedom' for the **rich** like you can spell disaster for the disadvantaged. When you're Madonna, you have to take account of your influence on them." Yeah, this was only four years after Dan Quayle's infamous attack on "Murphy Brown" for being a single mom.

Even Leon's parents were dragged into the fray, dogged by reporters for comment. "This is crazy, insane. We're just normal people. This is my son's life. We just want to live ours and we don't want to interfere," Carlos's mom, Maria, and dad, Armando, said.

The couple stayed together for three years, during which time Leon was a constant companion. He supported her throughout her stressful *Evita* period, including being with her at the **Golden Globes** when she won the only **award** for **acting** she is ever likely to receive. (She didn't thank him, and they were no longer a couple soon after.)

By all accounts, Madonna has maintained a friendly relationship with Leon. During her **divorce** from **Guy Ritchie**, Leon lent support to Madonna and spoke highly of her parenting.

Professionally, Leon has done a lot of TV and also appeared on Broadway in a liberal adaptation of *The Threepenny Opera* by Wallace Shawn with **Cyndi Lauper**, Alan Cumming and Ana Gasteyer. In 2008, Leon launched Leon Fitness. He helped to design the **fitness** center of the Crescent Club condo (41-17 Crescent St., Long Island City, NY).

On February 25, 2015, Leon had a son, Meeka Leon, with his wife, Betina Holte, giving Lola her first half-brother.

—GORGON CITY

GREGORY PACE

Madonna with her daughter at Macy's in 2010

LEON, LOURDES "LOLA" MARIA CICCONE: *October 14, 1996.* After Madonna playfully told *PrimeTime Live* in 1995 that she would place ads in *The Village Voice* and *The New York Times* asking for someone to **father** her first child, a dude named Eddie from Cincinnati placed an ad saying, "Give me 45 seconds and I'll give you 1.5 billion reasons to have a child with me." He was jizz kiddin'.

Following that kind of talk, in early April 1996, New York tabloids ran photos of Madonna leaving a Spring St. medical center, one of whose **businesses** was a gynecologist. So it wasn't exactly a shock when, on April 16, 1996, **Liz Smith** broke the news that Madonna was **pregnant** with her first child, by **Carlos Leon**. Madonna was reported to be "deliriously happy," but she was also in Budapest, Hungary, in the midst of making *Evita*. Committed to a physically challenging role, Madonna worried that her condition might jeopardize the production.

Madonna wrote, in a letter to her **fan** club, "... I'm adjusting to the idea of sharing my body with someone else, not to mention the idea of sharing the rest of my life with someone

else. I'm very excited about having a baby. I just wish October would get here already. I must learn patience!"

At 4:01 p.m. on October 14, 1996, Madonna produced a beautiful, **healthy**, 6 lb. 9 oz. baby girl at Good Samaritan Hospital (1225 Wilshire Blvd., LA, CA). She'd endured 12 hours of labor before opting for a C-section, joking as she was wheeled away, "Good-bye, everyone—I'm going to get my nose job now." She and Carlos Leon chose the name together.

Almost immediately, Madonna faced criticism for becoming an unwed mom. *Newsweek* and the *New York Post* slammed her for setting a bad example for teenagers. As Madonna would say to *USA Today* after she gave birth, "My having a child is not for public consumption. It's not a career move. It's not a performance to be judged and rated. Nor is my role as a **mother**."

Madonna immediately adjusted her priorities to satisfy the needs of her child, but she didn't exactly take it easy at **work**. In fact, after promoting the hell out of *Evita*, she was **back** with a new album, *Ray of Light*, a year later. One of the songs on the album was written about Lourdes, the spacy lullaby **"Little Star."** Madonna actually called her baby "Pumpkin" more than "Little Star" or, as the lyric goes, "Butterfly."

Speaking of names, Madonna quickly began calling Lourdes by the **nickname** "Lola," a name to which she'd been attached for years.

Lola changed Madonna in many ways. "I think [having Lourdes] made me face up to my more feminine side," Madonna said. "I had a much more masculine view of the world. Divide and conquer." At the time of her pregnancy, Madonna began studying **Kabbalah** as a way of making herself a better person and therefore a better mother. She's also cleaned house when it came to her associates.

"When I started seriously thinking about motherhood and taking care of a child, certain people that I found amusing and interesting didn't seem so terribly amusing and interesting. I did a lot of emotional housecleaning, and I wound up with a much smaller handful of friends," Madonna told *Redbook* in 1997.

Over the years, Lola has grown up before the **eyes** of Madonna's **fans**. Mostly, she had a smooth and not very public childhood. She was reportedly considered for a role in *Harry Potter and the Half-Blood Prince* (2009), but Madonna said no. In 2010, Lola teamed up with her mom to launch the **Material Girl** clothing line and did her first red carpet interviews to plug the venture alongside Mama at Macy's.

Lola attended Fiorello H. LaGuardia High **School** of Music & **Art** and Performing Arts (100 Amsterdam Ave., NY, NY), known as the *Fame* school, and appeared in several of its productions. Madonna attended *Grease* in 2013 to watch Lola as "Rizzo." Considering her choice of high school, the press often wondered if that meant she had Madonna's blessing to launch a show biz career. Madonna has said "as long as she takes what she does seriously," she is okay with whatever career path Lola chooses.

Speaking of the media, it was at her school that Lola met her first serious boyfriend, Timothée Chalamet from **TV**'s *Homeland* (2011–). Their relationship was covered in the media, though lightly.

As for her creative work with her mom, Lola appeared in ***I'm Going to Tell You a Secret***, played piano during **"Devil Wouldn't Recognize You"** on Madonna's final ***Sticky & Sweet Tour*** date and showed up in the fan version of the music video for **"Celebration,"** in which the 13-year-old gleefully lip-synched to the song while decked out in her mom's entire ***Like a Virgin*** album cover/**MTV Video Music Awards** dress, demonstrating more than just a little touch of star quality.

Lola has attended many of her mom's shows and gives her input on her mom's music (Madonna reported that her daughter was obsessed with **"Bitch I'm Madonna"**). But don't approach her for a picture or to get her **autograph**—she isn't interested.

In 2014, Lola started her college career at the school Madonna had attended in the late '70s, the **University of Michigan**. She is a stunning young woman, willful, direct and **talented** (her self-assured *Grease* vocal is on **You-Tube**), who seems well positioned to have a successful career and a public identity unique from her mother's.

> "If you listen to what she says, it instantly becomes a 'Madonna' record, no matter what producer she's working with."–PATRICK LEONARD (1986)

LEONARD, PATRICK: *b. 1955.* Songwriter and keyboardist who became one of Madonna's most important collaborators, a man with whom she's written and produced some of her most classic songs.

Leonard was the music director of ***The Virgin Tour*** and repeated his role for her ***Who's That Girl World Tour***. Their first song collaborations appeared on ***True Blue***, and what a great start they had: **"La Isla Bonita," "Live to Tell," "Love Makes the World Go Round," "Where's the Party"** (along with **Stephen Bray**) and **"White Heat"** were all cowritten by Madonna and Leonard, and Leonard also produced her #1 hit **"Open Your Heart."**

He continued **working** with her on her ***Who's That Girl: Original Motion Picture Soundtrack*** songs **"Who's That Girl"** and **"The Look of Love."**

Leonard had an even stronger role on what some would argue was Madonna's best album, ***Like a Prayer***, which featured his credit on **"Act of Contrition," "Cherish," "Dear Jessie," "Like a Prayer," "Oh Father," "Promise to Try," "Spanish Eyes"** and **"Till Death Do Us Part."** He was also behind the B-side **"Supernatural."**

Madonna said of her *Like a Prayer* sessions, "When Patrick and I wrote *Like a Prayer*'s 'Promise to Try', he started playing and I started singing. It was completely improvised, but he often has that effect on me and that's often how I work."

Leonard said of *Like a Prayer*, "I would just put the track, the chord changes, some kind of **drum** beat, bass line—something simple—and say, 'Here's the idea, here's what I have for the day.' She would listen, then we would talk a little bit. Oftentimes I'd say, 'Here's the verse, and here's the chorus,' and she'd say, 'No, it's the other way around, switch 'em.' So I'd switch 'em ... Then she would just start writing. She'd start writing lyrics and oftentimes there was an implied melody. She would start with that and deviate from it. Or if there was nothing but a chord change, she'd make up a melody. But a lot of the time in my writing there's a melody implied or I even have something in mind. But she certainly doesn't need that. She would write the lyrics in an hour, the same amount of time it took me to write the music. And then she'd sing it. We'd do some harmonies, she'd sing some harmony parts, and usually by three or four in the afternoon, she was gone."

He was a key part of Madonna's ***I'm Breathless: Music from and Inspired by the Film Dick Tracy*** as cocreator of **"Back in Business," "Cry Baby," "Hanky Panky," "He's a Man"** and **"Something to Remember."** As the cherry on top, he produced **"I'm Going Bananas," "Now I'm Following You (Part I)"** and **"Now I'm Following You (Part II)."**

Though Leonard had zero to do with ***Erotica*** or ***Bedtime Stories***, Madonna did go **back** to him for her single **"I'll Remember"** and worked with him on parts of ***Ray of Light***; he shared credits with her on lead single **"Frozen," "Nothing Really Matters," "Skin"** and **"Sky Fits Heaven,"** and he helped produce **"The Power of Good-Bye"** and **"To Have and Not to Hold."**

Madonna and Leonard have collaborated on other songs, including some **unreleased** material as well as songs that were recorded by other artists, such as **"Just a Dream"** and **"Possessive Love."** Leonard was one of the people with whom Madonna collaborated on her abandoned musical ***Hello, Suckers!***

Madonna's work with Leonard has tapered off over the years, but it's never felt like a hard out. As recently as 2008, he did the music score for her ***I Am Because We Are*** documentary. There is always hope held out that they will reunite; he is a thoughtful, sensitive composer whose work with Madonna is three-dimensional and timeless.

In 2015, Madonna told *MOJO* that Leonard "encouraged me as a songwriter. He encouraged me to dig deep and explore areas of my emotional life that I possibly hadn't really gotten into yet." Were they to team up again, perhaps he'd help her find still more to share.

"LET DOWN YOUR GUARD": Interesting song from the ***Bedtime Stories*** sessions that, more than any other song, unites the R&B and electronic halves of the album. Unfortunately, "Let Down Your Guard" didn't make the album. Instead, it became the B-side to **"Secret"** in the UK. The singsong ditty is very concerned with asking the listener to "come inside."

"Try to do everything in moderation. Try not to kill all your brain cells. And try to go to class."
—MADONNA'S ADVICE TO LOLA FOR COLLEGE (2015)

"LET IT WILL BE": Written by Madonna, **Mirwais** and **Stuart Price** and produced by Madonna and Price, a musical cautionary tale (**fame** = bad) from *Confessions on a Dance Floor*. Madonna performed the Paper Faces Remix of the song on her promo tour for the album and also on her *Confessions Tour*. It contains the essential line, "Just watch me burn!"

LETTERMAN, DAVID: SEE: *Late Night with David Letterman* and *Late Show with David Letterman*.

LIFECYCLE™: Stationary exercise bike that Madonna once described as one of her most **prized possessions**. One of these things was present at a major Madonna moment: **David Mamet** was riding his while considering whether to offer her *Speed-the-Plow*.

LIKE A PRAYER (ALBUM): *Release date: March 21, 1989. Billboard 200 peak: #1.* Madonna's fourth studio album, and the one that became her first across-the-board critical success. Unflinchingly personal lyrics, rich vocals and sophisticated instrumentation characterize the **work**, with Madonna cowriting and coproducing every track.

Madonna consciously crafted an album that would reflect her maturation as an artist and as a woman—she had just turned 30 when work began and was appearing in *Speed-the-Plow* on Broadway, a **job** she has described as physically and spiritually draining. Madonna's chemistry with **Patrick Leonard** on *True Blue* led her **back** to him, and she also turned to **Stephen Bray** once again for two tracks, both of which wound up as singles. For one song, Madonna collaborated with her ex-lover **Prince**, choosing to work with a fellow pop star for the first time, but choosing the one who was also the most serious musician of the era.

The album was recorded over the course of five months at D&D Recording (formerly 320 W. 37th. St., 4th Fl., NY, NY) and Ocean Way Recording (formerly 6050 Sunset Blvd., Hollywood, CA; now United Recording). The album's status as an expression of vulnerability, self-determination and a desire for real **love** is especially interesting considering Madonna finished it and then promptly asked for a **divorce** from her husband, **Sean Penn**, to whom her previous album had been dedicated. This time around, Madonna dedicated her album to her **mother**, a woman deeply committed to **Catholicism**, a theme that makes several appearances on the album and in its ensuing music videos.

"Most of the songs … are drawn from my life, factually speaking, but it's fictionalized, too," Madonna explained in

SENSATIONEN AUF CD · LP · MC von **wea**

1989. "Also, the overall emotional context of the album is drawn from what I was going through when I was growing up—and I'm still growing up."

Madonna has always had better reviews than most people remember, but if music critics and closet Madonna **fans** had been waiting for a good reason to *really* rave about her, *Like a Prayer* offered an admirable **excuse**. The album is even packaged to underscore the new, serious Madonna. For the first time, Madonna's face does not appear on the jacket. Instead, the cover is a tight close-up of her abdomen, her thumbs hooked into a pair of comfortable, partly undone jeans, fingers adorned with rings and sensuously intertwined with colorful beads. It's like a female take on the Rolling Stones' *Sticky Fingers* (1971).

On the back cover, Madonna leans toward the camera in a praying pose, her dark brown **hair** running to her shoulders. This imagery is a **powerful** statement from a woman for whom (created) **looks** are nearly everything. By appearing as a brunette, Madonna was officially back to her roots.

To add a bit of intimacy to the package, the album's inner sleeve was scented with patchouli oil, so that the consumer could smell Madonna's own favorite scent when listening to her music. (She now **hates** the smell.) There was also an **AIDS** fact sheet in every copy, the first time a pop artist had ever included AIDS information with a product.

Packaging alone does not guarantee respect or praise. But the music—not so much the radical departure some reviewers took it to be as a sobering and perfecting of Madonna's established brand of pop—is impressively sincere.

Album-opener **"Like a Prayer"** shows off Madonna's warmer, richer vocals and a soulful refrain provided by the Andraé Crouch Choir. From the moment it was heard, it was hailed as a turning point in Madonna's music. On the album, it functions as the pop equivalent of religious ecstasy, preparing the listener for a heavenly journey.

Second song **"Express Yourself"** became the **dance** song of the year and one of pop's most irresistible **feminist** anthems, opening with the indelible cry, "C'mon, girls! Do you believe in love?" It was and is the one song that most singularly sums up what Madonna is all about. You can't get Madonna if you don't get this song.

"Love Song," Madonna's duet with Prince, is one of the funkiest things Madonna's ever recorded, and has an uncharacteristically dissonant, leisurely feel. Parts of it come off as ad-libbed. The anti-love song "Love Song" is one of quite a few Madonna songs concerned with the slow passage of time.

"**Till Death Do Us Part**" follows, a vitriolic portrait of an abusive marriage that is obviously cribbed from her own marital nightmare. Its frenetic pace and Madonna's anguished pop vocal perfectly frame the intimate lyrics; hard to believe she and Penn wound up so friendly a few short decades later.

"**Promise To Try**" finishes side one of the **original** vinyl, a tearful remembrance of a **mother** who died young, another direct reflection of Madonna's real life.

Side two kicks off with "**Cherish**," a genuinely sweet ditty that returns the mood to hopeful. It's one of the simplest songs on the record, but has a dense production—as is often the case in Madonna's world, simplicity is usually the result of complex maneuvering.

"**Dear Jessie**" is a giddy, hallucinogenic extravaganza complete with pink elephants and lemonade that does the **Beatles** proud. "My feeling when we were making *Like a Prayer* is we pretty much knew that the whole world was gonna hear this record and we should make a great record," Patrick Leonard told *MOJO* in 2015. Done!

The Leonard collaboration "**Oh Father**" is a tortured ballad about an emotionally abusive **father** and the daughter who grows to understand—if never quite forgive—his behavior. Paired with "Promise To Try" and the following track, "**Keep It Together**," the song is yet another powerful rumination on family.

"**Spanish Eyes**," a ballad about the tragedy of a gang member's short life, marks Madonna's return to a Latin theme and contains spoken-word Spanish lyrics.

The final song on the album is a twisted and jarring chant called "**Act of Contrition**," whose music is looped from a backtracking of "Like a Prayer" and whose lyrics are a sort of ironic prayer that ends with Madonna finding that her reservations for a spot in heaven have been *misplaced*.

• •

"… [A]S CLOSE TO ART AS POP MUSIC GETS. *LIKE A PRAYER* IS PROOF NOT ONLY THAT MADONNA SHOULD BE TAKEN SERIOUSLY AS AN ARTIST, BUT THAT HERS IS ONE OF THE MOST COMPELLING VOICES OF THE '80S. AND IF YOU HAVE TROUBLE ACCEPTING THAT, MAYBE IT'S TIME FOR A LITTLE IMAGE ADJUSTMENT OF YOUR OWN." -J.D. CONSIDINE, *ROLLING STONE* (1989)

• •

"SHE SEEMS LIKE AN ABSOLUTE PRESENCE IN CULTURE. EVERYWHERE YOU LOOK, THERE'S EITHER MADONNA HERSELF OR A KIND OF ECHO OF HER, AND I THINK SHE'S USED THAT … YOU CAN CALL IT POWER, YOU CAN CALL IT REACH … TO CONTINUALLY MAKE INCREASINGLY EXTREME, RADICAL AND DISRUPTIVE AND CONFUSING STATEMENTS ABOUT EVERYTHING UNDER THE SUN: SEX, POLITICS, RACE, AUTONOMY-YOU NAME IT." -GREIL MARCUS (1990)

• •

It's not the kind of tune one finds oneself listening to over and over, but its echo of the album's first track makes it reminiscent of the repetition in a Broadway score. Should *Like a Prayer* be a Broadway show? It has all the elements of a strong theatrical statement.

Like a Prayer marked Madonna's third straight #1 album. It went on to sell over 15 million copies worldwide, as well as spawning several music videos that represent Madonna at her most engaged in the medium.

"LIKE A PRAYER" (SONG): *Release date: March 3, 1989. Billboard Hot 100 peak: #1.* This gospel-infused lead single from *Like a Prayer* (and #1 hit) paved the way for a critical reappraisal of the consummate singles artist of the '80s. The song is stylistically different from anything Madonna had sung before, the lyrics more universal and layered. It was the sound of a whole new Madonna, and its release was an event—it was first heard in the context of a **Pepsi** ad aired on the March 2, 1989, episode of *The Cosby Show* (1984–1992).

While danceable, "Like a Prayer" is a song more concerned with melody and with building to a crescendo via its stop-start structure and its feverishly romantic storyline. The song opens with Madonna's extremely vulnerable, little-girl vocals set off against the strains of a choir (led by Andraé Crouch, who passed away in 2015). She sings of a **love** so compelling it's practically a religious experience, and she delivers a performance on a par with previous highlights "**Live to Tell**" and "**Papa Don't Preach**."

The song's religious imagery was boldly interpreted by its controversial **video**, but "Like a Prayer" is a prime example of how Madonna's music endures even after the controversy surrounding it evaporates.

• •

"IN A CAREER FULL OF TRANSGRESSIVE MOMENTS, *LIKE A PRAYER* IS THE MOST TRANSGRESSIVE-AND THE MOST IRRESISTIBLE." -GAVIN EDWARDS, *ROLLING STONE* (2004)

• •

"ANY WOMAN MY AGE WHO CLAIMS TO HAVE NO EMOTIONAL CONNECTION TO *LIKE A PRAYER* IS A LIAR, NOT MY AGE AND QUITE POSSIBLY NOT A WOMAN. AND UNLIKE TOO MANY ALBUMS TO WHICH WOMEN ARE SUPPOSED TO HAVE EMOTIONAL CONNECTIONS, THIS ONE ISN'T MOPEY, SELF-INDULGENT, DIFFICULT OR WEIRD …" -HADLEY FREEMAN, *THE GUARDIAN* (2011)

• •

"THE ALBUM IS MADONNA'S *KÜNSTLERROMAN*- HER COMING OF AGE STORY, INTENSELY PERSONAL AND BOLD IN ITS LYRICS …" -BRIANA FASONE, *CATCH & RELEASE* (2014)

• •

As is befitting one of the best songs of her career, Madonna has performed the song live on many occasions. On tour, it was a part of the **Blond Ambition World Tour**, **Re-Invention World Tour**, **Sticky & Sweet Tour** and **The MDNA Tour**, and was a **Rebel Heart Tour** bonus. She also treated audiences to live versions during her **American Life** promo performances, at **Live 8** and on the **Hope for Haiti** telethon. She told *Cosmopolitan* in 2015 that "Like a Prayer" is her favorite song to perform live.

The song has been covered effectively many times, perhaps best by Jon Wesley Harding (1989), **Darren Hayes** (2012) and Pomplamoose (2015).

> "Only those who come to the music and lyrics with a grim determination to find prurience and blasphemy can miss—and then with considerable effort—the God hunger that animates them."-ANDREW M. GREELEY, *AMERICA* (1989)

> "… [A] pop-gospel workout that's as enigmatic as it is invigorating. It's 'Thriller' meets Catholic mysticism …"-KENNETH PARTRIDGE, *BILLBOARD* (2014)

"LIKE A PRAYER" (VIDEO): *Director: Mary Lambert, 1989.* One of the most controversial music videos of all time, **Mary Lambert** and Madonna's "Like a Prayer" doused America with accelerants (religion, **race**, **sex**) and lit a match (Madonna in a slip). It contains arresting images of Madonna defending a black man falsely accused of murder, kissing a black saint based on St. Martin de Porres (**Leon Robinson**), experiencing spontaneous stigmata and making her cleavage **dance** in front of a field.

Of burning crosses.

Director Lambert told *Rolling Stone* in 2015: "Using burning crosses to reference racism to religion. Why not a Black Jesus? Why can't you imagine kissing him? I wanted to speak about ecstasy and to show the relationship between sexual and religious ecstasy. I think that subconsciously a lot of people understood this and were either enthralled or outraged by it."

But listing the video's most shocking bits merely helps feed the confused readings it received at the time of its release. Called sacrilegious and profane by religious leaders and by Rev. Donald Wildmon of the American Family Association (based in Tupelo, Mississippi … wonder how they felt about **Elvis**'s pelvis?), the video actually embraces or at least appreciates **Catholicism** with the verve of a staging of The Passion **Play**, and makes an overt plea for racial tolerance.

Madonna's character in the video witnesses an **assault** and sees that the wrong man, a black man instead of the white perp, is arrested for the crime. With spiritual guidance that is naïvely portrayed as a romantic bond between Madonna and the saint/Jesus figure and which is reinforced by the video's setting in a church, she is able to

convince police to release the wrongly accused. The burning crosses, which offended some black groups, illustrate the racism the video was attacking; they are not mere adornments. Dancer **Niki Haris** refused to appear in the video because the crosses meant something to her, missing the point that they meant something in the context of the video as well … in fact, they meant the same thing.

Madonna's **original** storyline had her character and the accused being shot in the **back** by the KKK, but veteran Madonna director Lambert softened the content and stepped up some of the religious iconography.

The video was so controversial it sparked **Pepsi** to drop Madonna as a spokesperson. It was protested and banned briefly in Italy, drawing outraged criticism from the Vatican. It also proved Madonna was serious in her efforts to make important, thought-provoking, artful videos as opposed to fluffy filler.

> "THE MUSIC VIDEO IS UTTERLY HARMLESS, A PG-13 AT WORST, AND BY THE STANDARDS OF ROCK VIDEO, CHARMING AND CHASTE … THIS IS BLASPHEMY? ONLY FOR THE PRURIENT AND THE SICK WHO COME TO THE VIDEO DETERMINED TO READ THEIR OWN TWISTED SEXUAL HANG-UPS INTO IT."-ANDREW M. GREELEY, *AMERICA* (1989)

> "THERE WAS SOMETHING ABOUT MADONNA … SHE HAS THE ABILITY TO BE REALLY OPEN AND REALLY GIVE IT UP, WITHOUT GIVING IT AWAY. SOMEHOW SHE MANAGES TO KEEP HER MYSTERY AND HER SELF-RESPECT."-MARY LAMBERT (2008)

> "'LIKE A PRAYER' … ONLY HINTS AT THE RELATIONSHIP BETWEEN THE SACRED AND THE PROFANE. [ITS] MUSIC VIDEO, ON THE OTHER HAND, INSISTS ON IT."
> -BRIANA FASONE, *CATCH & RELEASE* (2014)

LIKE A VIRGIN (ALBUM): *Release date: November 12, 1984. Billboard 200 peak: #1.* Madonna's second LP, and the one that aggressively defined her image as a high-gloss bad girl.

With her debut album **Madonna** doing well, the newly minted diva was taken far more seriously by her record label when it came time to record her sophomore effort. She consciously wanted to produce something more English and "more techno." She was given the opportunity to **work** with **Nile Rodgers**, who had seen her perform and who said he had appreciated her star quality. Rodgers, famous for his work with Chic and hot for having had a huge pop success with **David Bowie**'s *Let's Dance* the year before, was seemingly tailor-made for Madonna's approval. Add to the mix that Rodgers had shown his grasp of the current pop scene via hits for Duran Duran and INXS. Pop success

ALEJANDRO MOGOLLO

LIKE A VIRGIN
(1-9)

2001 Remastered
Re-Release (1-11)

①
"Material Girl"
(Peter Brown/
Robert Rans)–4:00,
produced by
Nile Rodgers

②
"Angel"
(Madonna/Stephen
Bray)–3:56,
produced by Nile
Rodgers

③
"Like a Virgin"
(Tom Kelly/Billy
Steinberg)–3:38,
produced by
Nile Rodgers

④
"Over and Over"
(Madonna/Stephen
Bray)–4:12,
produced by Nile
Rodgers

⑤
"Love Don't Live
Here Anymore"
(Miles Gregory)
–4:47, produced
by Nile Rodgers

⑥
"Dress You Up"
(Andrea LaRusso/
Peggy Stanziale)
–4:01, produced
by Nile Rodgers

⑦
"Shoo-Bee-Doo"
(Madonna)–5:16,
produced by
Nile Rodgers

⑧
"Pretender"
(Madonna/Stephen
Bray)–4:30,
produced by Nile
Rodgers

⑨
"Stay"
(Madonna/Stephen
Bray)–4:07,
produced by Nile
Rodgers

①⓪
"Like a Virgin"
Extended
Dance Remix
(Tom Kelly/Billy
Steinberg)–6:08,
produced by
Nile Rodgers

①①
"Material Girl"
Extended
Dance Remix
(Peter Brown/Rob-
ert Rans)–6:07,
produced by
Nile Rodgers

was important to Madonna; in late 1983, she'd told a rock journalist that her second album would have a more "open feeling ... like Hall and Oates."

Madonna approved Rodgers without hesitation.

By all accounts, Madonna's work with Rodgers at the **Power** Station (now Avatar Studios, 441 W. 53rd St., NY, NY) in the spring of 1984 was a marriage of **creativity** and determination. The artists respected and understood each other, and both were present for every phase of the album's recording. Although she's thought of as having the world's biggest **ego**, Madonna took a step **back** with *Like a Virgin* and accepted three songs written by other people, and one remake, contributed four compositions with her favored collaborator **Stephen Bray** and wound up with only one solo-written track at a time when she could have pushed for more of her own stuff.

Madonna told *Rolling Stone* in 2009 that when she heard the demos for **"Like a Virgin"** and **"Material Girl,"** she liked them "because they were ironic and provocative at the same time, but also unlike me. I am not a materialistic person, and I certainly wasn't a virgin, and, by the way, how can you be *like* a virgin?"

When the record was ready for the world, Madonna said she felt that every song on it was like a different part of her personality.

Oddly and interestingly, the album opens with the arch sarcasm of "Material Girl," in which you're supposed to know she's making fun of the greedy '80s, but which could also be, and often was, embraced literally. It's one of Madonna's most dated hits at this point, but one whose title will follow her to the grave and beyond.

Next up, which is also odd placement, is the oh-gosh-I'm-in-**love** song **"Angel,"** an irresistibly swoony tune inspired by the concept of a girl literally falling in love with an angel.

The title track, one of Madonna's best-remembered hits, comes third, lighting a fire with its inverted "Billie Jean" (1982) bass line and genius presentation of a time-worn product (**sex**) presented in a daring new form ... the only time the word "virgin" was heard on the radio up until 1984 was around Christmastime.

"Over and Over" set the pace for Madonna's perceived ambition and drive, a persuasive bit of musical inspiration that can help bat away early-onset procrastination or just push you through your Jane Fonda workout.

The first side (remember, this was from the vinyl era, just after the dinosaurs died) of the album ends with a total curveball, Madonna's gut-wrenching cover of the Rose Royce hit **"Love Don't Live Here Anymore"** (1978). Rodgers has confirmed this was Madonna's first time singing with an orchestra, and reports that her breakdown at song's end—so reminiscent of **Michael Jackson**'s "She's Out of My Life" (1980)—was genuine.

One of the songs from an outside source and the last one finished for the album, **"Dress You Up,"** opens side two, offering a frothy, **fashion**-driven frolic that combines the propulsion of "Like a Virgin" with the manic energy of "Over and Over" in a perfect mix.

Madonna's sole and shared compositions finish out the record, starting with the simple, back-to-back, sonically similar pleasures of **"Shoo-Bee-Doo"** and **"Pretender."**

In 1984, Madonna said of the record, "On this one, I've chosen all the songs and I want them all to be hits—no filler! That's why I've done outside songs as well as six of my own—a lot of groups are stubborn about that, but I want every song to be really strong."

As if to prove it, the album ends with a track that could easily have been a hit single had it been released; **"Stay"** puts Madonna in the unusual position of begging a lover to stick around for more, and it doubles as an effective plea to her listeners to wait and see what she's got in store for us next.

Madonna has had several album covers that could be described as iconic, but perhaps none more so than *Like a Virgin*'s. Stylist and designer **Maripol** has called it a "bride of Satan" look, and it effectively communicates the conflicted views of what a **wedding** dress *traditionally* represents (virginity), and what—in this unlikely context—it *does* represent (sexual knowingness). She glares out directly at us, her breasts jutting from within the skintight bustier of a tarted-up wedding gown, **"BOY TOY"** belt buckle prominently cinched at her waist. **Steven Meisel**'s sepia-toned photography serves to make the shot all the more menacing. It's a sexual dare, not a tease.

Madonna's virgin-baiting dare was taken up by over 3.5 million US **fans** in its first 14 weeks of release, selling at a rate of 80,000 copies a day at its peak. Already completed months before her debut album had run out of steam, *Like a Virgin* shot to the top of the charts, alongside its #1 kick-off single of the same name. As of 2015, it is Madonna's best-selling studio album in the U.S., one of the best-selling albums by a woman (over 21 million worldwide) and one of the top sellers of the '80s.

Madonna dedicated the album to "the virgins of the world."

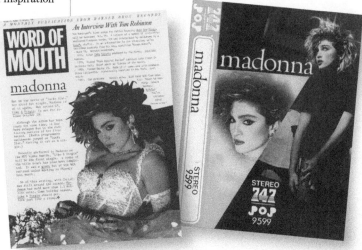

"THE SONGS ON THIS NEW ALBUM HAVE A LOT MORE OF A POP SOUND TO THEM. I USED SYNTHESIZERS A LOT MORE AND A LOT OF ELECTRONIC STUFF … NOT THAT I CONSIDER IT A 'TECHNO-POP' RECORD AT ALL. I JUST THINK IT'S MORE WIDE-OPEN AND ESTABLISHES ME MORE AS A POP ARTIST THAN AN R&B ARTIST."-MADONNA (1985)

"IN *LIKE A VIRGIN*, MADONNA'S NEW RECORD, BRILLIANTLY PRODUCED AND ARRANGED BY NILE RODGERS, SHE AND RODGERS REALIZE THAT SHE'S TURNED OUT TO BE A SPUNKY, BEAT-CONSCIOUS SEX KITTEN INSTEAD OF A DISCO PET … ANOTHER PART OF HER SUCCESS LIES IN HER PECULIAR CHARM—DESPITE HER PUNKINESS SHE DOESN'T REALLY SOUND LIKE A BAD GIRL AT ALL … IT SHOULD KEEP MADONNA DANCING ALL OVER THE AIRWAVES FOR A LONG TIME."-JAMES HUNTER, *RECORD* (1984)

"ALL TOO MANY DANCE-FLOOR DIVAS ARE NEVER HEARD OUTSIDE THE CLUBS—A FATE THAT MADONNA, LIKE DONNA SUMMER BEFORE HER, GUARDED AGAINST."-ALEX HENDERSON, *ALL MUSIC GUIDE: THE DEFINITIVE GUIDE TO POPULAR MUSIC-4TH EDITION* (2001)

"… *LIKE A VIRGIN* IS SOMETIMES THOUGHT OF AS MADONNA'S ARTISTIC COMING-OUT PARTY, THE MOMENT SHE SWAPPED FRIVOLOUS BUBBLEGUM FOR MORE THOUGHTFUL EXAMINATIONS OF FEMALE SEXUALITY … HOWEVER, FOR ALL ITS MERITS—AND IT HAS MANY—*LIKE A VIRGIN* ISN'T EXACTLY *THE FEMININE MYSTIQUE* SET TO MUSIC."
-KENNETH PARTRIDGE, *BILLBOARD* (2014)

"LIKE A VIRGIN" (SONG): *Release date: November 12, 1984. Billboard Hot 100 peak: #1.* The lead single from Madonna's sophomore album, *Like a Virgin*, was found by **Warner Bros.** exec Mo Ostin [father of Michael Ostin; SEE: **"Love Don't Live Here Anymore" (song)**] who thought Madonna would be right for the risqué song, which was written by Billy Steinberg and Tom Kelly. Madonna agreed, convincing her producer **Nile Rodgers** that it was massive. It was recorded and ready to be released in June 1984, the only problem being that *Madonna*, her first album, was still winding down.

When "Like a Virgin" was finally released in November 1984, it became one of the biggest hits of the year (only Wham!'s "Careless Whisper" bested it) and to this day is considered one of Madonna's Top 3 most successful songs by just about any measure. It hit #1 and held the pole position for six weeks.

Today, it's hard to remember just how shocking it was to hear the word "virgin" on the radio, much less on the boom boxes of Madonna's teen **fans**. The word "virgin" was rarely heard on **TV** (it was first uttered on *The Mary Tyler Moore Show* in 1970), and only came up in polite company when one was at church. "Like a Virgin" is not only allusive, it equates virginity with the pureness of true (but **sexual**) **love**.

As for live performances … hello? Madonna premiered "Like a Virgin" on the first **MTV Video Music Awards** telecast, bringing down the pop cultural house (if not the venue's audience) with an audacious roll on the stage and salacious fondling of her nether regions—way before this was precisely what was expected of her. She also provided a fun lip-synched version for *Top of the Pops* in the UK.

Though the **original** "Like a Virgin" is hopelessly 1984, Madonna has kept the song strangely current by reinventing it on many of her tours: a "Billie Jean" (1982) mash-up on *The Virgin Tour*, a farcical rendering on the *Who's That Girl World Tour*, an extremely effective Middle Eastern version (accompanied by simulated **masturbation**) on the *Blond Ambition World Tour*, a hilarious **Marlene Dietrich** send-up in *The Girlie Show World Tour* ["Like a Virgin" is to Madonna what "Falling in Love Again (Can't Help It)" (1930) was to Dietrich—the "inevitable one"], a sensual equestrian presentation (no, not bareback) in the *Confessions Tour*, a gut-wrenching waltz on *The MDNA Tour* and a solo cardio workout for the *Rebel Heart Tour*.

She revisited it briefly with a rusty performance during her *American Life* promo tour and on the 2003 **MTV** Video Music **Awards** as part of her **"Hollywood"** performance with **Britney Spears**, **Christina Aguilera** and **Missy Elliott**.

The song is more than just another '80s song. Witness the opening to *Reservoir Dogs* (1992) or the 2014 cover by Sister Cristina, a 26-year-old Italian **nun** who rose to **fame** on *The Voice* of Italy (2013–) and who sang a rather

THIS PAGE: Scarce 1984 promo calendar from Japan-photographer Curtis Knapp no longer has that original slide.

OPPOSITE PAGE: Rare WB in-house publication heralding the release of *Like a Virgin*, plus the Saudi Arabian album cover (retouched to introduce modesty).

literal version of the song to "bear witness to **God**'s **power** to move all things!"

Madonna confessed to hating "Like a Virgin" in 1998. Thankfully, she got over it.

P.S. The most bizarre Madonna-related lawsuit ever was filed against ABC-TV by Max Baer Jr., famous as "Jethro" on *The Beverly Hillbillies* (1962–1971). Baer claimed ABC had illegally threatened legal action against the songwriters behind "Like a Virgin" if the writers licensed the song's movie rights to Baer. Both ABC and Baer wanted to make a TV movie adaptation of the song. ABC's meddling cost them a reported $2 million decision in Baer's favor in 1991. Well, the first thing you know, old *Jethro*'s a millionaire.

"LIKE A VIRGIN" (VIDEO, 1984): *Director: Mary Lambert, 1984.* One of the reasons Madonna became Madonna is that she frequently married her best **work** with the best work of others. When she had a song as can't-fail as "Like a Virgin," she insisted on an expensive, imaginative video that would match it provocation for provocation—and she got it.

Shot on location in July 1984 in Venice, Italy, the video cost "$150,000? $175,000? ... It was way more than we'd ever spent on a video," according to **Warner Bros.** exec Jeff Ayeroff. It was filmed in three ruins.

"Like a Virgin" opens with a surreal nighttime cityscape, then dissolves to daytime scenes in which Madonna—at the **height** of her **"BOY TOY"** phase—walks through the historic city and **dances** into the cameras on a gondola. Her costar, a massive lion (named Charlie) walks and pants to the beat of the song (a shot seen only in a slightly different edit of the video from *The Immaculate Collection*), evoking the ferocity of Madonna's **sexuality**. The lion was supposed to stroll past Madonna on her right so they could lock glares, but instead it nuzzled her crotch when she wasn't expecting it. Their stare-down lasted three minutes, ending with the lion roaring at Madonna, who said, "[My] heart fell in my shoe."

Madonna told *Smash Hits*, via a self-penned remembrance of the shoot, that working with a lion was "one of the most dangerous experiences I've ever had. It had teeth and everything. The lion tamer said it wouldn't bite me—or at least it hadn't bitten anyone yet."

"It wasn't even a trained lion!" Lambert told *Rolling Stone* in 2015. "The local line producer made a deal with a guy from the circus. It was a circus lion! ... I thought she might be a goner."

Nonetheless, the video was filmed without harm to any animals or any pop stars.

Plumbing the virginal theme, Lambert has Madonna, in a custom-made white **wedding** dress, briskly removing white sheets from precious furniture as efficiently as a Casanova relieves young women of their hymens. In the end, a man in a lion mask literally sweeps Madonna off her **feet** and spirits her away in the night.

Mary Lambert tells *EM20* that the sexy wedding dress used in the video was a completely separate thought from the amazing **Maripol** creation on **Steven Meisel**'s album cover; she'd had no access to that image when arranging costumes for the video. "The wedding dress was designed by my brilliant costume designer."

The video was roasted by Dire Straits in its "**Money for Nothing**" video (1985), which features clips of a Madonna-ish woman in a video similar to "Like a Virgin" when they sing of a famous slut shoving her privates into the camera.

"LIKE A VIRGIN" (VIDEO, 1985): *Director: Daniel Kleinman, 1985.* Culled from the *Madonna: The Virgin Tour Live* home video release, this video featured Madonna's live *Virgin Tour* performance of "Like a Virgin" and got considerable airplay on **MTV**. This video was nominated for Best Choreography at the 1986 **MTV Video Music Awards**.

"LIKE A VIRGIN" (VIDEO, 1991): *Director: Alek Keshishian, 1991.* Scenes from Madonna's risqué *Blond Ambition World Tour* performance of "Like a Virgin" were cut into a new promo video in 1991 to help promote *Truth or Dare*. An interaction between Madonna and **Christopher Ciccone** kicks off the video from when Madonna was threatened with arrest in Toronto.

"LIKE IT OR NOT": The final song on Madonna's *Confessions on a Dance Floor*, written by Madonna, Bloodshy & Avant and Henrik Jonback and produced by Madonna and Bloodshy & Avant. Madonna **worked** with the latter after their huge success with **Britney Spears**. She performed the song on her *Confessions Tour*.

LIL BUCK: *b. May 25, 1988.* Model and **dancer** who was chosen to accompany Madonna on tour at the **Smirnoff Nightlife Exchange Project** at the **Roseland Ballroom** on November 12, 2011. Lil Buck (a.k.a. Charles Riley) became one of Madonna's *MDNA Tour* dancers, but became even more famous when Spike Jonze uploaded cell phone footage of one of his dance pieces with Yo-Yo Ma.

On November 5, 2014, Lil Buck was one of the honorees at *WSJ* **magazine**'s fourth annual Innovator **Awards** at the Museum of Modern **Art** (11 W. 53rd St., NY, NY). In her speech, Madonna told Buck, "You are more than a dancer. You are a poet." She also called him out for stopping by her house uninvited for dinner all the time and paused to reprimand an audience member for taking a picture of her while she was speaking.

"LITTLE STAR": Written by Madonna and **Rick Nowels**, and produced by Madonna and **Marius de Vries**, this blissful lullaby is the second to last track on *Ray of Light*, a sweet ode to Madonna's daughter **Lola** preceding the heavy, maternal meditation that is **"Mer Girl."** Madonna sang the song live only one time, a shimmering reading on *The Oprah Winfrey Show* in 1998.

LIVE AID: Enormous, bi-continental rock concert to benefit Ethiopia, organized by Bob Geldof and Midge Ure and staged simultaneously in Philadelphia's JFK Stadium (formerly S. Broad St., Philadelphia, PA) and London's **Wembley Stadium** on July 13, 1985. Madonna had missed the boat on "We Are the World" (1985), but she was gung-ho to participate in Live Aid.

Along with providing her international exposure just as she was exploding on the pop scene, Live Aid put Madonna in the midst of many of the music world's most popular and experienced acts. She shared a dressing area with, among others, Ashford and Simpson, with whom she nearly collaborated on an *Oliver Twist* reboot (for which there may be **unreleased** recordings) and was the talk of the Philadelphia show. Beach Boy Mike **Love**, whose band also shared the same dressing space, joked to the press, "We were looking for her clothes, but we hear she doesn't wear too much." Word of the **nude** photos Madonna had posed for a few years earlier had hit the newspapers, and were about to be splashed all over *Playboy* and *Penthouse*. Though Madonna is now seen as unflappable, at the time she was genuinely worried that her career had been torpedoed, so wasn't yet in a place where she could laugh it off.

Bette Midler was chosen to introduce Madonna. Backstage, Midler had to shout, "Hi, Madonna!" and struggle to get the young upstart's attention for a quick smile and handshake. Madonna was totally focused on every aspect of her set, as the at-home audience could see from the behind-the-scenes footage **MTV** was providing in real-time.

Midler, in a form-fitting number, sashayed out and greeted the crowd, "I want you to know that I have no idea why I was asked to introduce this next act, because you all know that I am the soul of good taste and decorum. However, we are thrilled—we are thrilled!—to be able to introduce to you today a woman whose name has been on everyone's lips for the last six months ... a woman who pulled herself up by her bra straps and who has been known to let them *down* occasionally. She's great, she's hot, she's a lot like a virgin ... she's Madonna!"

The two women are very different people and artists who were at very different places in 1985, so the introduction was probably more fun for Midler to say than for Madonna to hear. Madonna hadn't expected a crack about her nude photos to precede her appearance. Even if Midler probably felt it just a little joke from one raunchy babe about another, Madonna—about to hit the stage—thought it served to remind every viewer of the scandal she was bravely trying to weather. She soldiered through her performance. She's best when her **back**'s up against the wall, anyway.

Madonna gave a spirited and vocally confident performance of **"Holiday"** with her *Virgin Tour* backing **dancers** Elbee and Michael Perea, punctuating the song with a brief greeting to the audience: "I just wanna take this time to thank everybody for comin' here today. You know, there's a lot of major quote unquote stars here playin', but

you know it doesn't matter who you are, it's why you're here. And I'm glad you're here."

Next, she did an aggressive version of **"Into the Groove"**; if we had to prove our love to her, she also seemed to feel she had to prove she had musical chops.

After that sweaty workout of a song, Madonna—decked out in a heavy pastel paisley jacket, gold jewelry and a floral toreador pant—addressed the crowd, "So ... hot enough for you? I'm sympathizing with you by keeping my clothes on, okay? So don't feel bad." When the crowd booed the idea of a covered-up Madonna, she shot back, "No, I ain't takin' shit off today. You might hold it against me 10 years from now." She couldn't let Midler's intro be the final word on the photos.

Madonna then brought out the Thompson Twins and **Nile Rodgers** to help her sing **"Love Makes the World Go Round,"** a track that she not only had never performed live anywhere, it would not even be commercially available for another year, when it turned up on her *True Blue* album. Winded, her **voice** was weak by the time she got to this so-so song. One wonders if Madonna chose the song, with its message of not judging people, as another way of addressing her naked pictures.

When the Thompson Twins performed with Steve Stevens and Rodgers, Madonna joined them as a backup singer beating a tambourine on a cover of "Revolution" by the **Beatles** (1968).

The concerts were attended by about 172,000 people and were seen by a global audience of nearly 2 billion. The concerts and the ensuing products generated approximately $150 million in aid to Ethiopia, though there is plenty of doubt as to how much of that went directly to famine relief.

LIVE EARTH: Producer Kevin Wall and former US Vice President Al Gore created this international event, held July 7, 2007, to increase awareness of the global warming crisis via a series of concerts held in Antarctica; East Rutherford, New Jersey, US; Hamburg, Germany; Johannesburg, South **Africa**; London, **England**; Rio de Janeiro, Brazil; Rome, Italy; Shanghai, **China**; Sydney, Australia; Tokyo, Japan; and Washington, DC, US.

The event was controversial in that many of the acts could be pointed to as decidedly non-green (lots of jets are needed to fly you around when you're a touring artist), the commitment of some of the sponsors (Dow Chemical) was dubious and the event had no specific goals beyond raising awareness.

Madonna signed on, donating her previously **unreleased** song **"Hey You"** to the cause. The song was debuted on MSN.com on May 16, 2007, where the first million downloads were free. Madonna, in demure black, opened her live set with a pretty rendition of the song (backed by kids in **school** uniforms). Once the kids were safely away, she was encouraging the crowd to jump in her own inimitable way: "Okay, there's been a lot of talk about conserving energy tonight, but right now, I don't want anybody savin' up their energy. I want you all to give it up! If you wanna

—HOWARD BRAGMAN

save the planet, let me see you jumpin' up and down. Come on, motherfuckers!"

Madonna and her **dancers** offered up a straight performance of **"Ray of Light"** before she paused to thank Gore and Wall "for giving the world the wake-up call it so badly needs." Referencing a need for a "revolution"—soon to become a consistent theme for Madonna—she launched into a Gogol Bordello–fueled take on **"La Isla Bonita"** and finished with her most popular performance, another in a string of kittenish versions of her global smash **"Hung Up."** Discarding her skirt, Madonna's black Spandex pants left her looking like "Sandy" when she goes bad-girl in *Grease* (1978).

Though she was one of more than 100 performers spreading the message to 2 billion viewers, Madonna was one of the highlights of the event, proving herself to be the **charity**-concert MVP of all time.

Rumors that she went to Live Bloc's dressing room to say hi and wound up in a headlock proved to be made up.

LIVE 8: Charity concerts held across the globe on July 2 and July 6, 2005, at the same time as the G8 conference of 2005. The star-studded events were organized to help "Make Poverty History" by pushing for **African** debt relief. Founders Bob Geldof, Midge Ure and Ryan Jarman arranged the shows in Barrie, Ontario, Canada; Berlin, Germany; Chiba, Japan; Cornwall, **England**; Johannesburg, South Africa; London, England; Moscow, **Russia**; **Paris**, France; Philadelphia, Pennsylvania, US; and Rome, Italy.

Madonna, who had performed at **Live Aid** for Geldof 20 years earlier, had to be persuaded to lend her **talents** this time. She asked Geldof to explain exactly what he hoped to accomplish, and was impressed when he told her his specific goals.

Madonna, in great **voice** and resplendent in a white suit and "M" necklace, played an unaffected, rocked-up, three-song set that was generally regarded as among the highlights of all the performances. She owned the stage, rocking the Hyde Park venue while tearing through **"Like a Prayer"** (backed by the London Community Gospel Choir, also in white), **"Ray of Light"** and **"Music."** Madonna's rendition of "Like a Prayer" has to rank among her best live performances ever.

While her appearance was not without controversy ("Are you **fucking** ready, London?"), Madonna presented the most moving moment by appearing with Ethiopian student Birhan Woldu, who had been a starving child near **death** at the time of Live Aid. Woldu had selected Madonna to appear with because she was the only artist she'd ever heard of.

Rumors that Madonna had specifically asked that she and fellow performer **Mariah Carey** be kept apart were shot down by **Liz Rosenberg**.

Madonna **loved** her Live 8 experience ... as far as she knew. She said afterward, "I was so hyped up with adrenaline, I don't remember it actually happened. It's the biggest audience I've ever played to."

"Are you ready to change history?" Madonna had asked during her performance. Geldof has said he considers Live 8 to have been a success, but independent auditors have questioned how meaningful its contributions to African debt relief really were.

LIVE NATION: Madonna signed a 10-year, $120-million-dollar, 360 deal with this music-industry behemoth, giving it a stake in all aspects of her **work**. It is generally thought that Madonna's (and everyone's) declining album sales has led to the necessity of taking one's show on the road; working with Live Nation, first and foremost a touring organization, allows Madonna to be #1 in ticket sales even as demand for her music decreases. At the time of the deal, she summed it up in a more positive way herself, "For the first time in my career, the way that my music can reach my **fans** is unlimited."

Live Nation inked a three-album deal with **Interscope**.

"LIVE TO TELL" (SONG): *Release date: March 26, 1986. Billboard Hot 100 peak: #1.* One of Madonna's biggest musical risks was not singing about teaching you how to (fill in the blank), nor was it about the delicious taste of her **"Holy Water,"** it was releasing this spare, fatalistic, psychologically probing ballad at the **height** of her status as a teen idol. Written by **Patrick Leonard** as a song for a male to sing, he submitted it for use in the Craig Sheffer/Virginia Madsen movie *Fire with Fire* (1986). Rejected, it was rewritten by Madonna and coproduced by the two for inclusion on the soundtrack of her husband **Sean Penn**'s film *At Close Range* (1986), becoming the first Madonna/Leonard collaboration to hit the market. Despite reservations at Sire regarding leading with a ballad, the radically vulnerable song became a #1 single all around the world, preceding the June 30 release of Madonna's third studio album, *True Blue*.

Leonard, speaking in 2014, recalled of the song: "And when we finished it, the record company said, 'If she puts this out, her career is over—it will end.' It was seven minutes long, it stopped, it started, it was a ballad, it was harmonically completely unlike anything else on the radio, and she said, 'I'm sorry, I'm putting it out.' She believed in it, but she also believed in it because her and Sean Penn were going out together [sic] and he was doing a movie and it was the song from the movie, so she was gonna help her boyfriend."

Madonna has described the song in very personal terms. "'Live to Tell' was about my childhood, my father and my **stepmother**," she said in 2009. "But maybe not. It could be about something in an F. Scott Fitzgerald novel or a story that I heard once. It's true, but it's not necessarily autobiographical. I could say the same thing about **'La Isla Bonita.'**"

Madonna's look on the single—a **Herb Ritts** still from the music video—represented the public's first glimpse of her new, clean, classic image.

On her *Who's That Girl World Tour*, Madonna dedicated the song to her late friend **Martin Burgoyne**, who had passed away the previous November. Live, she turned the song into an aching **AIDS** metaphor, her hyperextended pauses creating enough dramatic tension to incite a frenzied crowd response. On her *Blond Ambition World Tour*, the song was blended with **"Oh Father"** to tease out its redemptive qualities.

Most famously, Madonna performed "Live to Tell" stretched out on a mirrored cross during her *Confessions Tour*. It stands as one of the most provocative performances Madonna has given, the artistic messaging of which outweighs empty shock value.

> "It changed the course of music in a weird way because suddenly this pop artist could do this thing with all this depth to it."
>
> —PATRICK LEONARD (2014)

Madonna goes black-and-white for Regis.

"LIVE TO TELL" (VIDEO): *Director: James Foley, 1986.* To go along with the vocal and lyrical quiet of the song, the video for Madonna's second big-hit ballad (after 1985's **"Crazy for You"**) was shot by director **James Foley** in December 1985 as a minimalist portrait of the new Madonna, who croons the haunting song while projecting herself as an enigma.

Shot with key lighting against a black backdrop, the video is filmed by a sweeping camera that catches its star sitting on a chair in a serenely simple, flowery frock, looking ultra-feminine with **blonde** ('40s-style) **hair** and makeup.

All dressed down and *everyplace* to go.

Foley cleverly inserts shots from the film in which the song appears—*At Close Range* (1986)—sometimes using images with similarly dark backgrounds, creating the effect that Madonna is part of the action.

Thanks to the use of these clips, "Live to Tell" became the first of two Madonna videos in which **Christopher Walken** appears, the second being **"Bad Girl."**

Madonna's look in her "Live to Tell" video was so striking it was somewhat surprising that relatively few images from the making of the video were released, especially because the onset photographer was **Herb Ritts**. In 2011, around 100 rare slides from the Ritts shoot were **auctioned** one by one on eBay, fetching in some cases over $200 each. Perhaps Madonna wanted to hold **back** on saturating the market with this look (which she rocked in her 1986 film *Shanghai Surprise*) because she knew she was going to chop her hair short and go for a similarly clean but distinctly modern, more youthful look with **"Papa Don't Preach."**

The image switch, the simple video and the moving song ushered Madonna on to even greater success.

LIVE WITH REGIS & KATHIE LEE: *Airdates: September 5, 1988–July 28, 2000.* One of Madonna's most winning **TV** interviews occurred on this massively popular morning show. Aired in two parts, on May 13 and 14, 1991, the Q&A found power-**blonde** Madonna in a black negligée on the patio of a 16th-floor suite at the Four Seasons Hotel Los Angeles at Beverly Hills (300 S. Doheny Dr., LA, CA) speaking with Regis Philbin one-on-one at dusk to promote *Truth or Dare*. The interview was shot in **black-and-white**, unprecedented for a daytime talk show since the days of J. Fred Muggs.

In the intro, when Philbin was throwing to his taped interview, his costar Kathie Lee Gifford exuded moralistic disdain for Madonna—good thing she was left in the studio.

When Philbin revealed he was wearing a shirt similar to one he'd bought **Warren Beatty**, Madonna teased, "Do you feel like a heel in that shirt?"—the first rumbling of her romantic breakup with her *Dick Tracy* director and the man who appeared to be so flummoxed by her goal in making *Truth or Dare*.

With Philbin, she talked about her discomfort with that errant earring during her **Oscars** performance, conversation topics with **Michael Jackson** ("we exchange powder puffs ... and compare bank accounts") and her feelings about **Marilyn Monroe** ("her **sexuality** was a big part of her and her persona and people were rather obsessive about that ... and I can relate to that").

When the subject of *Evita* came up, Madonna joked, "Yes, well, we're standing at a balcony—that's a good start." She acknowledged that *Evita* was a daring (and pricy) movie to make (it wouldn't start filming for another four years), but also said she wouldn't be involved in a "mediocre production." She described her *Shadows and Fog* director **Woody Allen** as "an elusive creature" who confused her with his silence.

For the second part of the interview, Madonna focused more on *Truth or Dare*, insisting that the movie was not just about herself, it was about the "unattractive," behind-the-scenes moments of being a celebrity. She acknowledged that she still hoped to please her **father** and admitted she'd get married again, "... if anyone's foolish enough to ask me." Toward the end, the two felt up each other's biceps.

Madonna's chemistry with Philbin is reminiscent of her chemistry with **Kurt Loder**; she does well in interviews with men who are not of her world, who are somewhat cowed by her cool and who play along with the male/female **flirtation** at which she excels.

LIVE! WITH REGIS & KELLY: *Airdates: February 5, 2001–November 18, 2011.* On February 21, 2003, *Live! With Regis & Kelly*'s cohost Kelly Ripa—a diehard Madonna **fan**—received a baby **gift** on the air from "Mrs. Ritchie, sometimes known as Madonna," announcing that she was looking forward to meeting her on April 23 of that year. Ripa, appropriately, lost her shit, soon gave birth and returned to the show at fighting **weight** to greet Madonna.

On April 23, 2003, Madonna made her first appearance on the show with mega-fan Ripa as cohost, and her first with Regis Philbin since 1991. Wearing a white cap and blouse and sitting with her legs perhaps a bit *too* far apart, Madonna was metaphorically rimmed on live **TV** by Ripa (not a criticism, we **love** rimming, Kelly!), who charmingly gushed to a brunette Madonna, "My entire life has been a series of your old looks." As usual, Madonna stiffened up a bit in the face of praise, but she did relax some, chatting about how much fun she'd had with **Megan Mullally** on *Will & Grace*, having tea with her future husband **Guy Ritchie** and whether or not she might want to have a third baby. "Are you just gonna ask me personal questions?" she wondered halfway through. They said they wouldn't but much time was devoted to when in the morning Madonna brushes her teeth. "Just to be a pillow on your bed!" Ripa squealed.

Overall, it was a pretty stilted appearance, even though Philbin walked away wearing Madonna's hat, but then again, Madonna was also under fire for her **"American Life"** video and it was early in the morning.

For Madonna's second appearance on this version of the show, November 11 of the same year, Madonna was infinitely more engaged and **back** to **blonde**. On board to promote the release of *Mr. Peabody's Apples* [SEE: **bibliography (by Madonna)**], Madonna put Ripa's mind to rest when Ripa expressed fear that she'd been too gushy the last time: "I like that," Madonna cooed. The appearance is also noteworthy for Madonna's comments on how her **MTV Video Music Awards** appearance that year went down. Of the **Britney Spears** kiss, she said, "We decided probably, like the day before that it would be funny for the groom to kiss both of her brides. Now, I did kiss **Christina Aguilera**, too, and nobody ever mentions that ... I'm here to tell you that I kissed two different girls. But anyway, let's talk about my **book**."

Most excitingly, Madonna was introduced to a starstruck **P!nk** at the end of her segment. Imagine the fireworks if they'd collaborated?

Madonna returned to the show on November 3, 2006, to promote *The English Roses: Too Good to Be True*. Ripa,

in a **black-and-white** outfit similar to Madonna's, offered to "take it off and burn it" if it offended her idol. Far from being offended, Madonna invited Ripa to audition to be one of her tour **dancers**, referring to Ripa's in-audience performance at her *Confessions Tour*. Madonna then offered to audition Philbin to be her son **David**'s godfather. She showed off pictures of David, whose adoption from **Malawi** had been such a trial.

Madonna was back January 11, 2007, chatting about *Arthur and the Invisibles* and again looking sophisticated in black. Ripa basically proposed marriage to Madonna this time around—an early supporter of marriage equality, one can only remain a single white female for so long. (To be fair, Ripa was already married to Mark Consuelos, but everyone is single when Madonna is around.)

Ripa has attended most of Madonna's concerts, usually multiple times. On October 11, 2008, she was handed the mic to sing **"Give It 2 Me"** along with Madonna during one of her *Sticky & Sweet Tour* performances at **Madison Square Garden**. "She gets better with age—she's perfect!" Ripa said of the show.

On a February 19, 2015, appearance on *Jimmy Kimmel Live*, Ripa admitted she was once invited to Madonna's **Oscars** party, at which she'd given Madonna a good whiff. "She smelled like gardenias, so I gave her a hug and I said, 'Mmm, you smell so good,' and she goes, 'Okay, that's ... that's all right.'"

Ripa is an honest-to-goddess fangirl in the media, and is often found with fellow true-blue fans **Andy Cohen** and **Anderson Cooper**.

"LIVING FOR LOVE" (SONG): *Release date: December 20, 2014. Billboard Hot 100 peak: NA.* The lead single from Madonna's 13th studio album, *Rebel Heart*, was rush-released two months early following a **leak** of dozens of in-progress demos. Written by MoZella, Madonna, **Diplo**, Toby Gad and Ariel Rechtshaid, it was produced by Madonna, Diplo and Rechtshaid.

The song was a total curveball from Madonna—there's nothing urban or Top 40 about it, it's a straight-up retro '90s house track that could have been recorded by **Cher**. Its coolness is supplanted by a sunny, feel-good, self-empowering vibe that lifts it up into anthemic status. It belongs in the same category as Madonna's **"Deeper and Deeper."**

"Living for **Love**' ended up being the 15th version of the song until it got perfect. There's that level of pride in the music," Diplo told *MOJO* in 2015 of the many previous takes of the song that pre-existed the final one released.

"Living for Love" was given an elaborate live performance at the **Grammys** on February 8, 2015, with a bullfighting theme. A variation performed at the **Brit Awards** resulted in a wardrobe malfunction that found Madonna flat on her ass (momentarily). She also performed it for **Jonathan Ross** in the UK, on *Le Grand Journal* in

France and on the March 17, 2015, episode of *The Ellen DeGeneres Show.* She performed a remix of the song on her *Rebel Heart Tour.*

> "[N]obody writes about having a broken heart and being hopeful and triumphant afterward. That was my challenge. I didn't want to be a victim."-MADONNA ON "LIVING FOR LOVE" (2015)

"LIVING FOR LOVE" (VIDEO): *Directors: J.A.C.K. (Julien Choquart and Camille Hirigoyen), 2015.* A return to form for Madonna after a string of uneven music videos, "Living for **Love**" finds her picking up her crown and putting it **back** on her head. The video, shot on a soundstage, features her in a series of Spanish-inspired bullfighter outfits, dancing in a circle of **dancers** with stylized horns. Surrounded, her dance moves seem to hold the beasts at bay. Created by Kuwait-based designer Shady Zeineldine, Madonna's bolero in the video is strongly reminiscent of the look from her *You Can Dance* album cover and **Mitsubishi** television **commercials.** When her **hair** comes down, it's reminiscent of her *Sticky & Sweet Tour.*

Fans were generally enthusiastic about the video, with its blood-red and sepia palette, intricate choreography and an out-of-nowhere **"Papa Don't Preach"** video allusion when Madonna step-dances across the screen. It ends with a Nietzsche quote ... but his name was misspelled in the **original** version released.

The video's premiere was a first: On February 5, 2015, Madonna became the first major artist to debut a music video exclusively on Snapchat's Snap Channel platform.

> "Man is the cruelest animal. At tragedies, bullfights and crucifixions he has so far felt best on earth; and when he invented hell for himself that was his very heaven."
> -FRIEDRICH NIETZSCHE QUOTE APPEARING AT THE END OF THE "LIVING FOR LOVE" VIDEO

LODER, KURT: *b. May 5, 1945.* Respected rock and movie critic and stone-faced **MTV** correspondent who was one of Madonna's most consistent boosters at the network in the '80s and '90s. Loder gushed over her *Blond Ambition World Tour,* even as Madonna playfully flipped him the bird on camera. His greatest hits with Madonna:

Loder's *Breakfast with Madonna* interview with Madonna in 1990 presented Madonna as a punchy (imagine her physical exhaustion at the time) ice queen at the time of her *Blond Ambition* debut in Japan. Loder, sounding **nervous** as hell, asked Madonna about her **Pepsi** brouhaha. "Well, I think that they were afraid of the controversy that the [**"Like a Prayer"**] video was gonna cause." Asked if Pepsi had said, "Well, we don't like black guys doing this with white girls, or, was there anything like that ...?" Madonna replied, "No, they would never be so *honest.* They

just said they didn't like it." She expressed surprise at Pepsi's reaction to a video about telling the truth, claiming she'd told Pepsi "everything" about her music video prior to its premiere. She also chalked up America's conversion into "'50s monsters" at the time to "fear of **AIDS.**"

Looking **back** on the interview, it's not her best. She's sleepy and irritated. It feels like an interview that would have been edited into sound bites but that MTV decided to run as a special with very few cuts. Nonetheless, it represents a rare glimpse of Madonna on the precipice of her most important tour.

The interview was such a hit that MTV assigned Loder to cover Madonna for **Truth or Dare** a year later. *Dinner with Madonna*, shot in **black-and-white**, opened with Madonna, in a black peignoir seated at a table and leaning with her cleavage toward the plate in front of her, saying coquettishly, "Thanks for coming over, Kurt. You're just in time for the ... *main course.*" Madonna discussed how the movie portrays her family, **Kevin Costner** and her **gay** dancers. This was also the interview in which Madonna grappled with the usefulness of outing, saying she understood the importance of coming out versus the **privacy** concerns. Loder, an Ayn Rand Libertarian, interjected his opinion on the issue—that the individual ultimately trumps the collective. Of the controversy surrounding the music used in **"Justify My Love,"** she said, "I challenge any rap artist to talk about **originality** because they all rip off tracks from everybody else—that is the essence of rap music."

It was a meaty interview with lots of information about Madonna's outlook on music and **art.**

Loder got an unusually playful interview out of Madonna during one of his most famous pieces on the pop star, *No Bull!: The Making of "Take a Bow"* in 1994. On the set of the video for what would become her most successful single, Madonna gave Loder a tour of the villa at which she was staying in Ronda, Spain. While **smoking**, Madonna showed off her wardrobe for the video (offering to lend Loder a red bra ... "It's your color!") while "feeling very Cindy Crawford right now." She also hilariously spoke about **Whitney Houston**'s domination of the music charts with *The Bodyguard* (1992) soundtrack. When Loder asked her if she liked Cuban men (knowing full well she was seeing **Carlos Leon**), Madonna admitted, "... Latin men do have their good points."

Loder was the guy interviewing Madonna after the 1995 **MTV Video Music Awards** when **Courtney Love** launched a compact at them and crashed the piece. Loder gets major points for having the stones to invite **Love** into the interview, when Madonna was clearly resistant.

Loder's final major piece with Madonna was his best: For MTV's *Ultra Sound*, he met up with Madonna during the making of *Ray of Light* and asked her characteristically serious questions about her most drastic musical transformation yet. Catching her in the recording studio and on the set of her **"Frozen"** video, Loder got Madonna to talk about her newfound self-examination and "joy of

—MICHAEL LERNER

Drama queen Madonna
is seen "Living for
Love" on her *Rebel
Heart Tour* ...

MATTHEW RETTENMUND

... before deciding
on a quick trip
to "La Isla Bonita."

MATTHEW RETTENMUND

"I listen to all of Madonna's music! It gets me going."—LINDSAY LOHAN (2007)

With her tour dancers, Steven Klein and La Lohan in 2013

living." She related how after giving birth, she "realized how blessed I was, and before I was just taking things for granted." Thanks to the intrepid Loder, we have footage of Madonna actually recording **"Skin"** (then called "Flirtation **Dance**," as seen on a lyric sheet) at Larrabee Studios (formerly 4162 Lankershim Blvd., Universal City, CA) and previewing **"Ray of Light"** and **"Candy Perfume Girl."** The piece also showed Madonna interacting with **William Orbit** and **Guy Oseary.**

Madonna summed up *Ray of Light* in this encounter as "drug music without **drugs**." and herself as "just a little bunny hopping along. Who was I? And why did people let me have my **hair** like that?"

If Loder's MTV interviews with Madonna are notable for his serious questions and Madonna's comfortable, articulate replies, it should be noted that his 1992 interview with her for *TV Guide* lost Madonna all of her **fans** in **Evansville**, Indiana, when she trashed the place in which she'd filmed *A League of Their Own.*

"... I mean, to show other dimensions, you have to sort of be willing to get down to the nitty-gritty ... undress, so to speak."
—MADONNA, DINNER WITH MADONNA (1991)

LOHAN, LINDSAY: *b. July 2, 1986.* Gifted child and teen actor in such movie hits as *The Parent Trap* (1998), the second best *Freaky Friday* ever made (2003) and *Mean Girls* (2004), who turned to music somewhat less successfully and then turned to substance abuse with a resounding thud.

Lohan is a longtime admirer of Madonna's. She was on hand at the premiere of *#secretprojectrevolution* in 2013, making a **Steven Klein** sandwich with Madonna for photographers. She wrote afterward, "Madonna is the ultimate icon. I had such an amazing time at her secretprojectrevolution party last night. I've always been a huge **fan** of her **art**, artistic passion and one-of-a-kind self-expression." TMZ wrote afterward that the women looked startlingly alike, which is good news if you're the fiftysomething and maybe less good news if you're the twentysomething.

In 2014, Lohan took on the role of "Karen" in a **London** production of *Speed-the-Plow*, which Madonna had originated in 1988.

"I wasn't alive when Madonna performed in *Speed-the-Plow* ... or was I? It was '86 [sic] so I would have been a year old." It was '88, dear, but who's counting?

LOLA: SEE: **Leon, Lourdes "Lola" Maria Ciccone.**

LOLLIPOP: Candy fiend that she is, some of Madonna's early poses for Deborah Feingold made famous use of one of these. Madonna used to be seen slurping lollipops while avidly watching **basketball** games, sucked the hell out of one in a shoot with **Dennis Rodman** for a *Vibe* cover that was killed and slurped on one all through her brief appearance at **Miami's** White Party at the Biltmore Hotel (1200 Anastasia Ave., Coral Gables, FL) in December 1992.

LONDON: SEE: **England.**

LONG, RUSSELL: *b. 1956.* Fifteen-year-old Madonna was involved with this cute boy from December 1973 to June 1974. She invited him to deflower her and lost her virginity to the 17-year-old, a jock who grew up to be a UPS driver. Little did she know he would sell all the intimate details to the British tabloids sixteen years later, going so far as to recount that she called him "baby" throughout and sighed, "Oh, honey," when he climaxed. Their first time was at Long's house with his parents out, but they also made good use of his "Passion Wagon," the blue 1966 Cadillac he drove.

Long confessed to biographer **Andrew Morton,** "I was so **nervous** I couldn't get her bra strap undone," and sweetly told biographer **J. Randy Taraborrelli** that he never would've forgotten Madonna, even if she hadn't become famous because, "She was one of a kind."

He was ungallant to kiss and tell, so let's hope he at *least* lived up to his surname.

"My father has this habit of giving old high school boyfriends of mine my phone number in New York. I could kill him. I get phone calls from these guys, 'Remember me? We went out in the tenth grade?' They want to visit me. They're strangers."—MADONNA (1985)

LONG ISLAND'S NIGHTLIFE: By fall 1984, Madonna had landed a partial cover of *Dance Music Authority* (December 10, 1982), her first full **magazine** cover on *Island* (October 1983) and a handful of covers in the UK, but one of her earliest cover stories was for the September 1984 issue of this **New York** mag. The cover was a unique shot by **Gary Heery** from her first album cover shoot, and the interview was conducted by Mitchell Kozuchowski, a freelancer who was **working** a "very, very low-level, menial position" at the brand-new music channel, **MTV.** This magazine is very rarely seen today. In 2008, one sold for in excess of $1,000. The author of this **book** wants your copy.

"LOOK OF LOVE, THE": *Release date: November 25, 1987. Billboard Hot 100 peak: NA.* A solid ballad cowritten and coproduced by Madonna and **Patrick Leonard** that appeared on the *Who's That Girl: Original Motion Picture Soundtrack*, "The Look of Love" was a Top 10 single outside the US. It should have been included on *Something to Remember* but was perhaps considered more mid-tempo than ballad. It's been said that the look of which Madonna sings was inspired by *Rear Window* (1954).

The song was performed on the *Who's That Girl World Tour*.

LOPEZ, JENNIFER: *b. July 24, 1969.* American superstar of Puerto Rican descent who began her career as a dancing Fly Girl on the *In Living Color* TV show (1990–1994), then broke through as an actor in the 1997 biopic *Selena* and as a recording artist with the 1999 debut album *On the 6*. Since then, Lopez has proved herself to be a box-office star and a force on the music charts, especially when paired with a rent-a-rapper. Her #1 hits are "If You Had My **Love**" (1999), "I'm Real" (2001), "Ain't It Funny" (2002) and "All I Have" (2003). Plus, she never fails to make a pop-cultural splash with her **beauty** and her booty.

In 1999, Lopez (and Jerry Seinfeld) handed Madonna her **Grammy** for Best Pop Album for *Ray of Light*. Lopez and **Mark McGrath** teamed up to hand Madonna her Best Video from a Film **MTV Video Music Award** for "Beautiful Stranger" that same year. Lopez kissed Madonna on both occasions, and Madonna must've liked it, because Lopez almost got some more sugar. On Madonna's **birthday** in 2003, Lopez was spotted at the **Queen of Pop**'s house at the same time as **Britney Spears**, one clue that Lopez—not Aguilera—had been one of Madonna's first choices for her **"Hollywood"** performance at the **MTV Video Music Awards**.

Madonna has spoken of how other singers at her shows can distract her because she realizes she is being studied. She told Ryan Seacrest in 2009 that Lopez gave her "super sharp looks" at a *Sticky & Sweet* gig, though she didn't seem to be complaining.

> "I remember being a little girl and watching Madonna jog in Central Park and thinking, 'Wow, she's, y'know, rich and famous and successful and an amazing performer and she's out there working— she doesn't need to be out there running, but that's what you have to do, you have to work hard.' Like, in my mind, like, just that little thing, just seeing that one picture inspired me."—JENNIFER LOPEZ (2014)

BURNING UP:
WHAT IT WAS LIKE INTERVIEWING MADONNA IN 1984

Like a lot of guys at the time, Mitchell Kozuchowski had a little crush on Madonna, thanks to her bedroom-or-anywhere-you-like eyes in her "Burning Up" video. Unlike a lot of guys at the time, his work as a music writer afforded him the chance to see Madonna performing at Danceteria and to interview her face-to-face, a meeting that led to her September 1984 *Long Island's Nightlife* cover story.

Over 30 years later, he gives *EM2O* an idea what Madonna was like before *Like a Virgin* took her to the fabled next level.

EM2O: What drove you to interview Madonna back then?

MITCHELL KOZUCHOWSKI: I just really liked her music; I really liked that first record.

I was working at MTV and the girl in the cubicle next to me was playing that [*Madonna*] cassette— I don't know if you remember that era, that's what we played—nonstop. I was like, "Who's the black girl that's singing?" and she was like, "She's a white girl." That's when I kind of got intrigued by her, so I went and saw her at Danceteria.

MTV played "Burning Up" ... I was kind of intrigued by a girl who rolls around on a highway in the middle of the night in a tight, clingy white dress.

EM2O: What was it like seeing Madonna play Danceteria?

MK: They'd have five, six acts a night. She had a couple of backup girls and would sing over a track. The sound system wasn't good there, but you could kinda look at her and say, "There's something there." Not that you thought she would've turned into the mega-pop star that she turned into.

She was already kind of a club favorite at that time. She was involved with Jellybean at that time, Mark Kamins was the DJ.

When I saw her, there seemed to be a little film of dirt on her. [Laughs] She wasn't well put together. She was just kind of a funky, East Village girl—she was like [approvingly] a dirty girl.

EM2O: How did you get the interview?

MK: I got the interview through *Long Island's Nightlife*. Her publicist Liz Rosenberg was very excited and told me Madonna was excited that it was going to be [a] cover story.

EM2O: Was it at the Warner Bros. offices? What was she like?

MK: Yes. Very nice. Very bright. She came dressed very funky. We chatted about books. Back then, you could smoke in waiting rooms and stuff, and I remember asking her if she wanted a cigarette and she said no, she had just quit. We also talked about our high schools because our high schools used to play each other; I was a basketball player, she was a cheerleader. She was telling me she grew up in Pontiac and her big quote was, "If Detroit took a shit, it would be Pontiac."

I do remember her trying to explain to me who Edith Piaf was. She talked about going to Paris with Patrick Hernandez and how they wanted to make her the next Edith Piaf and was explaining her to me, and I was like, "I'm very familiar with who Edith Piaf is, I don't need you to explain to me who Piaf is ..." But she was kind of fun, tongue-in-cheek on a lot of stuff.

I actually ended up re-selling the article to a porn magazine ... one of the lower-end ones. This guy turned me on to the editor there and said, "They'll pay you like 500 bucks for the article ..." and I think I told Liz and she said, "We don't care— sell it!"

EM2O: She talks about wanting to rule the world in your interview. Did that seem ridiculous at the time?

MK: I didn't think it was ridiculous! I thought it was very *ambitious*.

LOREN, SOPHIA: *b. September 20, 1934.* The quintessential iconic Italian actor, and the first person to win an **Oscar** for a non-English-language role, in 1961's *Two Women*. Madonna solicited a vintage gown worn by this living legend for her 1986 *Vanity Fair* spread. Two women with a great sense of style.

A Loren look-alike appeared in the unseen **"American Life"** video as an attendee of that video's gruesome **fashion** show.

LOS ANGELES RIOTS: Violence and looting that shook LA from April 29–May 4, 1992, following the acquittal of cops who had beaten a suspect named Rodney King after a high-speed chase.

It's not exactly an important take-away from that tumultuous event, but the bustier Madonna wore in her **"Open Your Heart"** video was looted from Frederick's of Hollywood Lingerie Museum (6608 Hollywood Blvd., LA, CA) during the riots. A $1,000 reward was offered for its return. Like the family cat accidentally abandoned on vacay, the bustier made its way **back**, and Mayor Tom Bradley declared December 1, 1992, "Frederick's of Hollywood Day."

LOS FELIZ: Madonna bought a $2.7 million-dollar Mediterranean-style, 5,000-square-foot mansion in this LA nabe in 1996, flipping it in 2000 for $4 million to Jenna Elfman.

LOST PROJECTS: For Madonna, a project is rarely a single piece of **work**. She is famous for launching multi-tiered projects whose pieces comment on, relate to, or negate each other. But despite her stick-to-itiveness, even Madonna embarks on projects that sink without a trace. Some of them are classic woulda/coulda/shoulda.

TV: Before she became a star, Madonna was turned down for roles in the **TV** series *Fame* and the movie *Footloose*. *Square Pegs* (1982–1983) was also allegedly "this close" to landing her for an appearance, according to series creator Anne Beatts. In 1985, she was collaborating with Ashford and Simpson to cowrite a big-budget urban musical called *Street Smart*, in which she would have starred and to which she was to contribute songs, some of which may exist and be **unreleased**.

Maverick misfires include a *Madonna: The Early Years* ABC-TV miniseries, (what was the point after **Madonna: Innocence Lost**?) and her proposed *Peep Show* HBO showcase for new **talent** from around the world. Both reportedly fell through when Madonna had differences of opinion with ABC and HBO (1994).

Television (cable or otherwise) has been risky in general for Madonna. In 1987, she was rumored to become the next *Dynasty* (1981–1989) **bitch**, but thankfully deemed such a career move to be a step down, and the series ended soon thereafter. More interestingly, Madonna was thinking of providing the **voice** of prim **Catholic** schoolgirl "Mary Elizabeth" for *The Simpsons* (1989–), but no agreement could be forged (1991).

In 2007, she came close to doing **Nip/Tuck**, an appearance that would no doubt have left everyone involved in stitches. It, too, never happened.

Even TV-to-film concepts are troublesome for Madonna; one that fell through was a brilliant idea in 1992 which had Madonna reinventing Anne Francis's sleek, curvy, Emmy-winning *Honey West* (1965–1966) on the big screen.

The only video-game-to-film project with which she's been associated was the PlayStation game *Parasite Eve*. She was reported to have bought the rights to the game, which had been adapted from the novel by Hideaki Sena. Though it had been made into a Japanese film in 1997, rumor had it Madonna planned to star in an English-language adaptation as a mind-**controlling** life form.

Movies: Starting around 1985, over a period of 18 months or so, Madonna backed out of *Ruthless People* (1986), was strongly considered for the title roles in a biopic of **bisexual** torch singer Libby Holman that was already a pet project of **Bette Midler**'s and for which Liza Minnelli had been considered, and also for *Blaze* (1989), which later became a Paul Newman–starrer. She said no to taking over Twiggy's role in the Broadway musical *My One and Only* (1983–1985) because it paid only $20,000 per week.

By 1987, despite the flop suey that was **Shanghai Surprise**, Madonna had set up a production studio, **Siren Films**, and still had the star **power** to be considered for a variety of films.

She was ready to sign on for *Angel Flight*, to costar **sexy** Jean-Hugues Anglade, but it never got off the ground. She was inked to star in the farce *Blind Date* (1987), but when producers signed **Bruce Willis** without giving her her contractual right to approve of the leading man (she'd wanted hubby **Sean Penn**), she backed out. The role went to Kim Basinger.

Madonna foolishly turned her nose up at 1989's *The Fabulous Baker Boys*, later a hit for Michelle Pfeiffer, whose script she admired despite the finished product's overabundance of "**boring** California people." (She apparently prefers boring Argentinians.) Madonna loved **Mary Lambert**'s *Siesta* (1987) script, but at the time couldn't "deal with all the **nudity**" required, so Ellen Barkin stepped into the plum role.

She was asked to play the Isabella Rossellini bit in David Lynch's *Wild at Heart* (1990) but has never been a Lynch **fan**, complaining that the nudity in his *Blue Velvet* (1986) was "only done to shock the audience" (!!!); wanted to star in *She's Da Lovely* (a screenplay by John Cassavetes) in 1988, with Sean Penn signed on to direct, but then Penn decided to direct *The Indian Runner* (1991) and Cassavetes died. Rude! Madonna was turned down by Francis Ford Coppola for the role that went to his daughter **Sofia Coppola** in *The Godfather Part III* (1990).

—TONY WARD

Things also didn't work out for the Sherilyn Fenn role in *Three of Hearts* (1993) and Gus Van Sant's fiasco, *Even Cowgirls Get the Blues* (1993), in which she would have had the opportunity to make time with Uma Thurman. After publicly grousing that **Tom Cruise**'s *Far and Away* (1992) bored her ("Sleeping!" was her one-word review to **Arsenio Hall**), Madonna was considered for a starring role opposite him in the 1993 remake of *The Three Musketeers*, but the mismatch became obvious and neither went on to make the film, which became a modest hit for producer Joe Roth, who infamously crossed Madonna regarding her interest in starring in *Angie* (1994).

Kim Basinger got Madonna's sloppy seconds again when Madonna stepped out of the amputee drama ***Boxing Helena*** (1993), but then Basinger stepped out and got sued; it cost her an arm and a leg.

Madonna campaigned to be *Tank Girl* (1995), but was outgunned by Emily Lloyd, who was unceremoniously replaced by ex–Rockford Peach Lori Petty.

In the casting-against-type department, Madonna was working on film projects that would have cast her as a **mother** who sacrifices everything for her children, and as an Auschwitz survivor opposite **Willem Dafoe** (both 1987ish), and was very interested in a Joel Schumacher screenplay featuring Madonna as a woman who learns her brother is **gay** when he announces he has **AIDS**. It would've been one of the first major Hollywood films on the subject. All concerned felt that the role called for a much older woman, and the studios were too AIDS-shy to forge ahead with the concept (1990).

Maybe out of gratitude, Schumacher wrote a female buddy movie about a wisecracking pair of policewomen called *Leda & Swan*. It came within weeks of going into production with Madonna and **Demi Moore**, stumbling when Moore got **pregnant**, never to regain momentum (1991).

There was talk of Madonna playing diva Maria Callas in a Ken Russell film, a film in which **Sophia Loren** had previously agreed to star. Imagine? More heartbreaking was the time she lost out to **Sharon Stone** for that **Oscar**-bait part in *Casino* (1995).

Losing ***Music of the Heart*** to Meryl Streep was a bitter pill to swallow. The world's tiniest violins really *were* playing just for Madonna.

Madonna has had several opportunities to remake famous and not-so-famous films from the past, and from abroad.

In 1985, it was reported that Madonna had been offered the lead in a remake of *And **God** Created Woman* (1956), but she did *Shanghai Surprise* instead. Madonna was proposed as the lead in a Goldwyn remake of the Barbara Stanwyck burlesque-performer-with-a-heart-of-gold classic *Ball of Fire* (1941), the role of "Tiger Lily" in an update of *Peter Pan* (which years later became Steven Spielberg's 1991 film *Hook*) and always wanted to remake **Marlene Dietrich**'s *The Blue Angel* (1930). A production of the latter with Robert De Niro in the Emil Jannings role was

proposed with direction by Alan Rudolph and with **Diane Keaton** as a producer, but when Dietrich herself snarled her disapproval, the subject was considered *dropped*.

As for American remakes of foreign flicks, Madonna was proposed as the female lead in a remake of the 1982 Israeli film *Dead End Street*, which would have costarred Sean Penn and been directed by his father, Leo Penn. One of Madonna's most interesting lost projects was a remake of the 1962 French film ***Cleo from 5 to 7***, and another French remake that was proposed and that vanished was of the 1983 film *I Married a Dead Man*. Miramax was interested in having Madonna remake the Swedish blockbuster *House of Angels* (1992), playing a glam singer who shows up in her small hometown to collect her family inheritance.

Since the late '80s and especially since the birth of Maverick (1992), Madonna has looked more and more at the possibility of film adaptations of **books**. She has considered starring in and/or producing adaptations of Lorrie Moore's novel *Anagrams* (1986); Erica Jong's racy, critically panned *Any Woman's Blues* (1999); James Baldwin's literary classic *Giovanni's Room* (1956); Kristin McCloy's briefly trendy *Velocity* (1988); Jeane Westin's sudsy '40s all-girl-band saga *Swing Sisters* (1991); and biographies of her idols **Martha Graham** and **Frida Kahlo** (both 1991).

Also up for consideration have been Michael Korda's *The Immortals*, which would have starred Madonna as **Marilyn Monroe**; even Madonna herself realized that "probably isn't a good idea'" (1992). She considered **Warhol** Superstar/**"Deeper and Deeper"** extra Holly Woodlawn's hilarious memoirs *A Low Life on High Heels*, as trans woman **Candy Darling** (1991), a real person she was allegedly

MEGA-FAN SPOTLIGHT:
VINCENT LONG

Growing up on a farm, in the middle of nowhere, in rural Ireland, I can honestly say that Madonna saved my life! I remember watching TV with my grandmother and the video for "Like a Virgin" came on. It was scandalous! All my family said what an abomination she was. Of course for me, I loved it! How could someone provoke such strong hate and love at the same time? From that moment it was love at first sight for me and continues to this day.

approached about playing in the later film *Factory Girl* (2006), too. She was also pitched for a favorable telling of the tale of junk-bond dealer Michael Milken, *Fall From Grace*, which Maverick wanted to **fashion** into a Ted Danson–starrer for TV (1992). Director Frank Pugliese met with Madonna in 1995 to discuss her starring in *Mob Girl*, the life story of mafia-adjacent Arlyn Brickman, with whom Madonna became friendly. "I had no idea who she was until the film came up," the director said of Madonna. The film never got made.

Screenwriter Adam Greenman [*Three of Hearts* (1993)] did a script for Madonna based on Joseph Koenig's *Little Odessa* (1989), about a **Russian** immigrant who gets swept up with expatriate spies. Greenman cleverly pitched it as "a story about a girl who is desperate to make it in America."

Also interesting was Madonna's possible involvement in an adaptation of Robert Plunkett's **Love** *Junkie* (1992), about a Bronxville hausfrau who ditches her hubby after becoming obsessed with the gay underground of '80s **NYC**, falls for a gay **porn** star and produces his directorial debut. The film was to have been coscripted by Plunkett and coproduced with Amy Robinson and Griffin Dunne, Madonna's straight man from **Who's That Girl**. The role resonated fortuitously with **Desperately Seeking Susan**, but it languished.

Madonna pursued *Bag of Toys: Sex, Scandal and the* **Death** *Mask Murder*, David France's 1992 nonfiction account of **art** dealer Andrew Crispo and the "death-mask slaying" of Eigil Dag Vesti, but her interest died unexpectedly.

· ·

Theater: Madonna was rumored, in 1998, to be prepping to star as "Maggie the Cat" in the classic 1955 Tennessee Williams **play** *Cat on a Hot Tin Roof* on **London**'s West End ... which ranks up there with some of the worst ideas anyone's ever had for Madonna, even though she has indeed jumped off many metaphorical roofs and landed uninjured.

· ·

Writing: Madonna has also failed to follow through on various writing projects, including a first novel she started in the early '80s (she could only complete "about 30 pages") and a screenplay of her early years she was to have cowritten in 1985.

The biggest writing project that got away has to be **Hello, Suckers!**, a proposed movie musical written by Madonna in which she would have starred.

· ·

Directing: Once Madonna effectively quit her **acting** career in the early 2000s, talk of new film projects has mostly, but not always, centered around directorial endeavors. She optioned Jennifer Belle's novel *Going Down* (1996), possibly to be her directorial debut, for six figures. It was about a drama student who prostituted herself for tuition. Madonna came hard for *Blade to the Heat*, a 1994 stage play about a gay Latino prizefighter in the '50s that scored at the Public Theater (425 Lafayette, NY, NY), where Madonna

saw and loved it. The boxing-centric production featured **Carlton Wilborn** in a key supporting role. Madonna summoned playwright Oliver Mayer to her Maverick office, where she stared him down and finally said, "I want to direct your play as a movie. Is that all right?" He replied, "Sure." Unfortunately, the film was never made.

Madonna did finally have a feature directorial debut (two, since she kinda stressed that **W.E.** was her first movie when **Filth and Wisdom** really was), so the question now is: What's next? We (probably) already know: In 2013, Madonna optioned *The Impossible Lives of Greta Wells*, a novel by Andrew Sean Greer about a woman living in the Village in 1985 whose gay male twin dies and whose lover dumps her. When she receives shock treatments as therapy to manage her depression, they allow her to travel **back** in time to 1918 and 1941, where she finds herself ... which is exactly what Madonna seems to be doing with the films she is seeking to direct, and which is probably to a large extent what she has been doing throughout her career, in every medium she has tackled.

· ·

LOUIS VUITTON: Madonna did a two-pronged 2008–2009 campaign for the **fashion** house, whose creative director Marc Jacobs told *WWD*, "I just blurted out, 'I think we should do Madonna.'"

She was first seen in a series of images for the fall/winter 2009 season in which she wore ridiculous bunny ears and was **Photoshopped** into oblivion, seemingly as a purposeful artistic statement (not just to cover up imperfections). She doubled down, wearing the bunny ears to the **Met Ball** and wound up looking pretty silly. When the unretouched images leaked, much was made of how bad Madonna looked "before."

The spring/summer 2009 portion of the campaign featured Madonna in a pub in a variety of tightly-fitted looks, including a green, ostrich-feather dress that looked way better in print than when Madonna wore it out (resembling a pimped-out emu). Madonna looked much better this time, even before retouching (as behind-the-scenes video shows), and one's gotta **love** any picture of Madonna holding a Louis V bag aloft with her spiked heel, which is just another perfectly good **excuse** for her to spread her legs.

Jacobs said, "... This is an iconic woman, this is a woman I love, this is a woman of talent, style, a woman I just really respect and I thought, 'Wow, I'd love to do this.'"

LOUISE: Madonna's middle name.

LOURDES: SEE: **Leon, Lourdes "Lola" Maria Ciccone**.

LOVE: Madonna has written songs about it for every one of her albums. So many of her songs *are* about love that in both **"Love Song"** and **"Bye Bye Baby,"** she has to remind listeners those two songs are *not*.

On a personal level, in 1991, she asserted that she'd never slept with anyone for whom she didn't have feelings of love. In early 1993, she cryptically confessed that she was in love, that it had been love at first sight, and that she felt the love would last forever. Only problem is, she wouldn't say who it was. Gossips speculated it could be **John Enos** or even her friend **Ingrid Casares**, but she was talking about **Jimmy Albright**.

She loved **Sean Penn** so much she married him, and called him the love of her life even after their **divorce**. She loved **Guy Ritchie** so much she changed her entire way of life for him.

Madonna was still quite fearful of the real thing circa 2001. "I mean, *duh*. Love is scary, isn't it? I'm not scared about commitment—that's nothing. I'm scared about love. Loving something—anything—intensely, there's major fear and awe. I guess if I were a highly evolved being, I'd say fear has nothing to do with it, but I don't think I've reached that level of consciousness yet."

As of 2014, Madonna's story is that she's living for love, and it's a story to which she's sticking.

LOVE, COURTNEY: *b. July 9, 1964.* This grungy lead singer of Hole and widow of Nirvana's Kurt Cobain was on Madonna's wish list of acts for her **Maverick** label, but it didn't **work** out; Madonna's interest in Hole was used by **Love** to **drum** up publicity and, ultimately, competitive offers, and she signed with another label. It was a very good thing Madonna didn't sign Hole, as Love's never really been Madonna's style, and for a period of time she and Madonna seemed to be ready to tear each other's throats out.

"She's a bad enemy to have. I don't want her to know anything about me, because she'll steal what she can. What I have is mine and she can't **fuckin'** have it. She's not going to be able to write lyrics like me, and even if she does get up onstage with a **guitar**, it's not going to last," the inappropriately named Love said. More specifically, in 1992 she predicted, "I don't care how vain and arrogant this sounds, but just watch ... In her next video, Madonna's going to have roots. She's going to have smeared eyeliner. And that's me ... She wants my image."

In 1995, Love, wasted again, tossed a compact at Madonna's head during an interview with **Kurt Loder** after the **MTV Video Music Awards**. Madonna, visibly unthrilled when Loder invited Love into the encounter, put up with the situation as well as could be expected. (Did the cameraman intentionally frame Love with the word "drugs" over her shoulder?) Love wound up at Madonna's **feet** as they compared shoes.

Before Madonna could escape, Love spontaneously told a juicy story about her late husband: "I went to *Truth or Dare* with Kurt and we were leavin' and he goes, 'Jesus, that's *you*.' When we were first going out." At this point, **Liz Rosenberg** swooped in and dragged Madonna away.

In 1996, **David LaChapelle** made his directorial debut via an ad for *MTV Raw* that imagined Madonna and Love as the key players in *What Ever Happened to Baby Jane?* (1962), probably directly inspired by the encounter.

That same year, in a circumstance few could have guessed **back** during their MTV match-up, both Madonna and Love were considered strong contenders to receive **Oscar** nominations as Best Actress in a Leading Role, Madonna for *Evita* and a scrubbed-up Love for *The People vs. Larry Flynt*. In the end, both rockstars-turned-actors were denied acknowledgment by the establishment.

Madonna called Love "supremely **talented**" when directly asked about her in 1996, and confirmed that Maverick had tried to sign her. Yet she still told *Spin*, "But I think that drugs have destroyed her brain, or they are slowly destroying her. I am fascinated by her, but the same way I am by somebody who's got Tourette's syndrome walking in Central Park."

Love responded via a rambling letter: "Dear Spin; Madonna wishes Id slag her. how can I insult wallpaper? Except to say, 'That wallpaper in your Guest Room kinda sucks & ignore it? Her **disco** sucks. Thats all. Finito. Im a Rock chick. Rock chicks dont like disco. Ok? In another publication she said that **Whitney [Houston]** and **Mariah [Carey]** have 'no point of view'. Fair Enough. But, what? She does? heh heh heh ... So me and P.J. and Liz and Elastica etc. are utterly too 'Angsty'? Oh Eat me!! I can't even recite a lyric of hers, shes a Disco singer. She's not a poet or a musician. Shes a Giant celebrity **Dancer**. What to Get the Girl who has Everything? Indie Credibility!! 'I want it NOW Daddy. Buy it for me'."

Madonna and Love—separated by a **Tina Turner**—went on to share the November 13, 1997, cover of *Rolling Stone*. Madonna and Courtney only fought over which music they would play (they settled on Tricky), and Madonna agreed with Kurt Loder in an MTV Q&A that Love had matured—"Oh, yeah. Definitely."

Love told **Howard Stern** in 1998 that she was friendly with Madonna, claiming she could count on Madonna for pep talks like, "Baby, when they write the **book** on the 20th century, there's gonna be two chapters—you and me." (Doubtful!) Yet in 2009, Love told all who would listen, "Madonna had better stay the h*ll away from **London** when I move here to live! There's no room for us both."

"LOVE DON'T LIVE HERE ANYMORE" (SONG): *Release date: March 19, 1996. Billboard Hot 100 peak: #78.* Madonna was proud of her vocal performance on this Miles Gregory **disco**-era classic that was originally recorded by Rose Royce in 1978. **Warner Bros.** exec Michael Ostin [son of Mo Ostin; SEE: **"Like a Virgin" (song)**] had suggested it to producer **Nile Rodgers**, who persuaded Madonna that it would be a great counterbalance to *Like a Virgin*'s bubblegum sound. It was released as a single in Japan only, until it was included on her

Something to Remember ballads compilation as remixed by David Reitzas and released in 1996.

Considering how much Madonna **loves** the song, it shouldn't have been so surprising that she brought it out of mothballs for her *Rebel Heart Tour.*

"LOVE DON'T LIVE HERE ANYMORE" (VIDEO): *Director: Jean-Baptiste Mondino, 1996.* In 1996, on the occasion of shooting a music video for this tune from 1984 to plug her *Something to Remember* package, Madonna noted that it is "one of my favorite songs." Therefore, she chose one of her favorite directors, **Jean-Baptiste Mondino**, to shoot it. She only had one day off from filming *Evita* in Argentina, so time was of the essence. On March 4, 1996, Madonna and Mondino teamed up and created a simple echo of her **"Like a Virgin"** video, shot in an empty ballroom with similarly wind-blown drapes and covered furniture. Madonna is seen in a long shot as the camera—all in one take—slowly approaches her. Finally, three quarters of the way through the video, the camera pounces on her as she emerges from behind a column, capturing her in a breathtakingly beautiful close-up. Definitely Madonna's least amazing lip-synch, but hey, it was all one take!

LOVE LETTER: In 1992, *Hard Copy* offered color copies of a **love** letter Madonna inscribed in a high **school** classmate's yearbook. She wrote it in purple ink because "purple is a sign of lustfulness," implored the object of her affections to think of her often, bemoaned the fact that they never had the chance to get together and urged, "Please don't get the wrong idea of me. I'm really a sincere person." An early example of her coquettish ways, the love letter probably earned "Mike, (**alias** Chomp)" a pretty penny.

Ex **Jimmy Albright** also apparently sold some of Madonna's love letters.

"LOVE MAKES THE WORLD GO ROUND": The last track on *True Blue* is this somewhat generic slice of calypso positivity, written and produced by Madonna and **Patrick Leonard**. She debuted the song on July 13, 1985, as the third song of her three-song set at **Live Aid**, almost a year before the release of *True Blue.*

"LOVE PROFUSION" (SONG): *Release date: December 8, 2003. Billboard Hot 100 peak: NA.* Warm, uplifting Madonna/**Mirwais** song from *American Life* that, somewhat surprisingly, became the fourth single from the album. Unsurprisingly, it was the third of the four songs to fail to hit the *Billboard* Hot 100—America had given up on the album, and a pretty number about feelings that run the gamut from bad to sad to good wasn't about to change it. Intentionally misheard lyric: "I got Jew under my skin."

The song was featured in an Estée Lauder campaign.

"LOVE PROFUSION" (VIDEO): *Director: Luc Besson, 2003.* Madonna had always wanted to **work** with **Luc Besson** after seeing *La Femme Nikita* (1990), and she got her wish when he agreed to do a music video for this song. Unfortunately, it's little ado about something; Madonna wears an *English Roses* promo-type flowery dress and walks purposefully—via green screen—through a variety of settings, including a city at night, a stretch of beach dotted by gigantic flowers and the very sky itself. In all, it feels like Besson was trying out ideas for *Arthur and the Invisibles*—the video is an attractive video postcard, and that's about it. We are a long way creatively from the earlier **"Vogue"** here, but happily, it turned out we were also a long way from the later **"Hung Up."** The video was identical to a Besson fragrance **commercial**, which financed this video. (Poor **"Nothing Fails"** didn't get a video because while nothing fails, everything costs.)

"LOVE SONG": The third song on *Like a Prayer*, this funky number is by Madonna and her ex, **Prince**, collaborated on from afar. Prince did the initial **work** on March 13, 1988, at Paisley Park Studios (7801 Audubon Rd., Chanhassen, MN), Madonna worked on it in LA later that year and Prince finished it off in November. The song sounds like a hate **fuck**, even if Madonna opens it murmuring

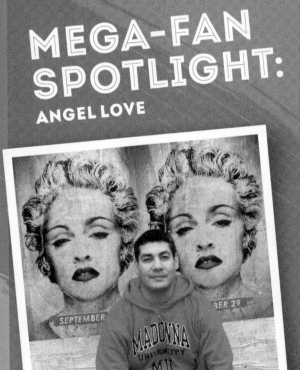

MEGA-FAN SPOTLIGHT: ANGEL LOVE

I started to become a Madonna fan when I first saw the *Blond Ambition World Tour* broadcast on HBO in 1990. It was during that show that I saw she was a serious performer and entertainer, and not just a typical pop star. Shortly after that, when the *Erotica/Sex* book era arrived, I became a mega-fan for life! Madonna has taught me to let go of my inhibitions and just have fun with my life. I owe a great deal of my happiness and good memories to her. It's through her that I've met other like-minded people who for over 20 years have been a permanent part of my family. We share the same passions and travel the same roads together. Life is so much better when you have great people by your side. And for that I say, "Thank you, Madonna, for bringing all of us together."

in French. Oddly, in spite of the star **power** involved, "**Love** Song" was not a single anywhere in the world.

"LOVE SPENT": Arguably *MDNA*'s finest moment, this eerily calm disparagement of a **money**-grubbing ex was written by Madonna, **William Orbit**, Jean-Baptiste, Priscilla Hamilton, Alain Whyte, Ryan Buendia and Michael McHenry (it took all those people to come up with that cringe-inducing Benjamin Franklin line?), and was produced by Madonna, Orbit and Free **School**. It took a lot of people to capture what ostensibly happened between two lovers, but the result doesn't feel overwritten or overproduced. Rather, it is a remarkably simple song that wouldn't have sounded out of place on *Like a Prayer*, yet does sound pretty lonely mired in *MDNA*. It's the kind of bitter song you can really savor, and it helps that there's a tiny synth hat tip to **"Hung Up"** in there.

Madonna shocked her **fans** by not performing it on *The MDNA Tour*, but fixed the situation by adding an acoustic version to her set list starting September 20, 2012.

"LOVE TRIED TO WELCOME ME": Poetic song from *Bedtime Stories* that was a collaboration between Madonna and **Dave Hall**. Its introspective lyrics foreshadowed the direction she'd be going in with *Ray of Light* a few years later. Madonna has said the song was inspired by a pole **dancer** who looked sad, so be grateful it wasn't called "Sad Pole Dancer."

"LOVE WON'T WAIT": Madonna wrote this song with **Shep Pettibone** during the early *Bedtime Stories* sessions before she changed direction and struck her Pettibone collaborations from that album. Years later, the song was given to Gary Barlow, a former (and future) Take That boy bander, who changed the gender perspective and made it his second #1 UK solo single in a row, after "Forever **Love**" (1996). Madonna's demo of the song is **unreleased**, but is available on **YouTube**.

LUCAS, REGGIE: *b. February 25, 1953.* Successful producer who was suggested by **Michael Rosenblatt** and approved by Madonna to produce her second single, **"Burning Up,"** on the strength of Lucas's **work** with singer Stephanie Mills, for which he'd won a **Grammy**. He wound up writing for and producing Madonna's first album, *Madonna*.

Prior to Madonna, Lucas had always coproduced (with James Mtume), working with R&B artists Phyllis Hyman, Lou Rawls and the Spinners. After Madonna, his solo production work was eclectic, encompassing artists as diverse as Rebbie Jackson and the Weather Girls. In 1993, he produced two songs on Madonna protégé **Nick Scotti**'s eponymous debut, including the Madonna-penned single **"Get Over."**

In 2013, Lucas recalled working with Madonna as a "pretty good experience," saying, "She wasn't the type of artist that you had to go and look for. She wanted to be successful." But after years of rumors about the making of *Madonna*, Lucas did allow that he had some **regrets** about how credit had been assigned, and about how he didn't work with Madonna after her debut in spite of its phenomenal success. "So this Madonna record was my first and worst introduction to the notion that you wouldn't have a linear continuation with someone who you've had success with. It totally blindsided me."

Madonna isn't fond of her first album. There's no accounting for taste.

"LUCKY STAR" (SONG): *Release date: September 8, 1983. Billboard Hot 100 peak: #4.* The next time a **hater** sneers that Madonna didn't write any of her hits, remind them that—as **Rosie O'Donnell** says—liars get **cancer**. Granted, she knocked off a nursery rhyme, but Madonna wrote the powder puff of pop perfection "Lucky Star" (produced by **Reggie Lucas** and then remixed by **Jellybean Benitez**) all by herself, and it's one of her most fondly remembered hits. When it was released as the fourth single from *Madonna*, it became her first Top 5 hit, and it spawned a classic video to boot.

Madonna has performed the song live at an unknown number of club dates prior to her first tour (for example, **The Metro Club**). On tour, Madonna performed "Lucky Star" on *The Virgin Tour*, the *Who's That Girl World Tour* and the *Confessions Tour*, where it was part of the finale. It was a **fan** request by Giulio Mazzoleni during the *Sticky & Sweet Tour* at **Madison Square Garden** and part of her *Rebel Heart Tour* medley.

"LUCKY STAR" (VIDEO): *Director: Arthur Pierson, 1983.* For a low-concept performance video, "Lucky Star" really hit it out of the ballpark. Director Arthur Pierson opened the video with a **black-and-white** shot of Madonna seductively lowering her sunglasses like a **disco** "Lolita," then cut to Madonna on a white background seeming to come to life as the music begins. Throughout the clip—featuring **Christopher Ciccone** and **Erika Belle** as **dancers**—Madonna's face, body and **fashion** are filmed in a fetishized way. Her **belly button** was immortalized, but so was her street urchin fashion sense. Kudos to Belle for the styling—it created a run on look-alike fashions. The video ends with the sunglasses sliding **back** up Madonna's face: The party's over.

LUPONE, PATTI: *b. April 21, 1949.* Broadway belter who originated the titular role in *Evita*, for which Madonna would later vie and win when it (finally) came time for a movie version.

While performing in *Anything Goes* in the Vivian Beaumont Theater at Lincoln Center (50 Lincoln Center Plaza, NY, NY), a hop, a skip and a jump away from Madonna's originally scheduled Mitzi Newhouse Theater (150 W. 65th

—TATIANA VON FURSTENBERG

GREGORY PACE

Madonna had a personal relationship with Jesus.

as a Carmen Dell'Orefice–esque ripe sexpot succumbing to her carnal urges in a Brazilian resort. "Blame It On Rio" was the name of the spread, and blame it on Rio if you must, but spread Madonna did. And who could blame her???

Madonna was spotted making out with Luz at the shoot's after-party while she was technically still Mrs. **Guy Ritchie**, though their **divorce** had been announced months earlier and was legally finalized the following month. Madonna and Luz were soon inseparable, and he bonded with her kids, even studying **Kabbalah** because of her.

Madonna took a lot of crap for being 50 and dating a 21-year-old. Sample unsolicited opinion from **Wendy Williams**: "He's not much of a conquest, either. Madonna has millions of dollars, and Jesus is a 20-something from another country who's said to be vapid and speak little English." (A comment that says little about Madonna and *lots* about Williams, and not just about her **ageism.**)

In July 2009, Luz filmed an appearance in Madonna's **"Celebration"** video as a DJ whom Madonna strips to the waist and kisses, becoming one of her real-life romantic partners to appear in one of her videos.

By summer 2010, the couple had broken up. Asked in December of that year how he was coping with the breakup, Luz replied, "Food, friends, music … and good sex."

LYPSINKA (JOHN EPPERSON): *b. April 24, 1955.* Epperson is an influential performance artist (so much more than a **drag** queen) whose shows consist of his female alter ego—the flame-haired, archly retro "Lypsinka," based on Broadway's Dolores Gray—lip-synching a series of exhaustively edited, expressively curated snippets from show tunes and too-bad-to-be-true **movies**, often punctuated by the sound of a ringing telephone.

Madonna was an investor in his first one-queen show in **LA**, *I Could Go on Lip-Synching!*

Epperson told *EM20* in November 2014, "Madonna sprinkled her fairy dust on me and it was very helpful. There were interactions. The first, she seemed excited, amused, cautious. The second, she was warmer, thoughtful, somewhat critical. There were others, but I was shy at all of them—my true nature more then than now. And she was giving off heat."

Epperson believes he rubbed off on Madonna.

"At the time we first met, I was onstage, wearing one glove with a bracelet over the glove. A few months later, she performed a song on the **Oscars** from the movie *Dick Tracy.* If I remember correctly, she wore one glove with a bracelet over it. And she punctuated the music with her arms and hands in a manner not dissimilar to what I do. I thought perhaps I had influenced her, just as so many other stars had influenced me."

A circa-1988 snapshot of Epperson alongside Madonna and her gal pal **Sandra Bernhard** appeared in his one-man show *John Epperson: Show Trash*, performed from November 11, 2014–January 3, 2015, at the Connelly Theater (220 E. 4th St., NY, NY).

St., NY, NY) debut in *Speed-the-Plow*, LuPone posted a satirical note to management, grumping that there wasn't enough room at the Center for *two* Sicilian divas. (Funny, Madonna's not Sicilian.)

LuPone wasn't joking later, though, when she publicly trashed the possibility of a Madonna-driven *Evita* film, and made cutting remarks about how the film looked based on some snippets she'd seen.

While prepping for the movie version of *Evita*, Madonna shared a **voice** coach with LuPone, and told her teacher she had nightmares of LuPone listening at the door.

LUZ, JESUS: *b. January 15, 1987.* Born during Madonna's *True Blue* era, Luz was making **love** to her during her *Hard Candy* era. Madonna met this boyishly **sexy** aspiring DJ at a **Steven Klein** *W* magazine shoot, in which she was styled

MATTHEW RETTENMUND

ALEJANDRO MOGOLLO

MACKLEMORE: *b. June 19, 1983.* Indie rapper famous for collaborations with Ryan Lewis, including "Can't Hold Us" feat. Ray Dalton (2011) and "Thrift Shop" feat. Wanz (2012).

In 2012, Macklemore, Lewis and **Mary Lambert** collaborated on the #11 hit "Same **Love**," a groundbreaking hip-hop song urging tolerance for LGBT people that opens with the admission, "When I was in the third grade, I thought that I was **gay** ..."

At the 2014 **Grammys** performance of "Same Love," Madonna and **Queen Latifah** joined the song's performers on stage for a mass **wedding**. Madonna threw in a little of her **"Open Your Heart"** for good measure.

Gay-rights media watchdogs GLAAD praised the performance, calling it "the latest in a long line of signs that our nation not only accepts, but celebrates the love and commitment of gay couples today."

MACZKO, SHARON: A high **school** classmate and friend of Madonna's, Maczko went on to become an accomplished artist. The two met in Mrs. Stenzel's 10th grade English class at Rochester Adams High School, where they were close enough for Madonna to give Maczko a Valentine's Day card (complete with intentionally crude, child-like signature), but fell out of touch. When the contents of Madonna's ex-assistant **Melissa Crow**'s storage unit were **auctioned** off in 2010, a 1988 letter from Maczko to Madonna, including a handwritten note from Madonna regarding an **art** exhibition in which Maczko was featured ("Mel—Please respond to this girl. Tell her I can't come to opening but will come to the show!"), was among the prizes.

MADISON SQUARE GARDEN: *4 Pennsylvania Plaza, NY, NY.* MSG, the iconic Midtown Manhattan arena, is a symbol of **New York** and a major stepping-stone in the world of entertainment.

Madonna first played MSG on June 10–11, 1985, immediately following three nights at **Radio City Music Hall**. The dates had been added due to popular demand after ticket sales for *The Virgin Tour* exploded. She has played the venue on all of her tours except for the *Blond Ambition World Tour*.

MADONNA (ALBUM): *Release date: July 27, 1983. Billboard 200 peak: #8.* Madonna's timelessly satisfying, self-titled debut album, dedicated to her **father**, may have launched her amazing career, but it was recorded in a hurry and on the cheap.

After struggling to survive in **New York** for four years, Madonna had landed a deal with **Sire Records** and done well with a 12" **dance** single that had been released before *Madonna* was assembled. Facing an April 1983 deadline, Madonna bypassed both **Stephen Bray**, with whom she'd created her demo, and **Mark Kamins**, who produced her club hit **"Everybody,"** in favor of **Reggie Lucas**, an established producer known for his R&B **work**. She was

probably looking not only for someone with an R&B track record, but for someone with a track record *at all*—Kamins did a great **job** on "Everybody," but by his own admission had to be told how to produce a record by **Arthur Baker**.

Lucas told *Rolling Stone* in 2013 that when **Warner Brothers** called him about possibly producing Madonna's first album, he was "the big score. It seems ridiculous in retrospect, but I was an established professional and she was a nobody. I met with her at a tiny little apartment she had in the Lower East Side. I thought she was vivacious and **sexy** and interesting, and had a lot of energy."

Working with Lucas at Sigma Sound Studios, Madonna wrote five of the songs—still finding time to play the "cowbelle" (sic)—and Lucas wrote two.

Lucas told *The Atlantic* in 2013, "When I came to the Madonna record, I came with two things. The first thing was I brought a lot of success and a solid background as a hit producer and songwriter within the R&B world, but it was also with the skill as a composer and rock and roll guitarist."

As the recording process neared an end, **"Ain't No Big Deal,"** which had always been intended to be an important part of the record, was jettisoned because Bray had sold it to another act. That left one slot for an eighth song.

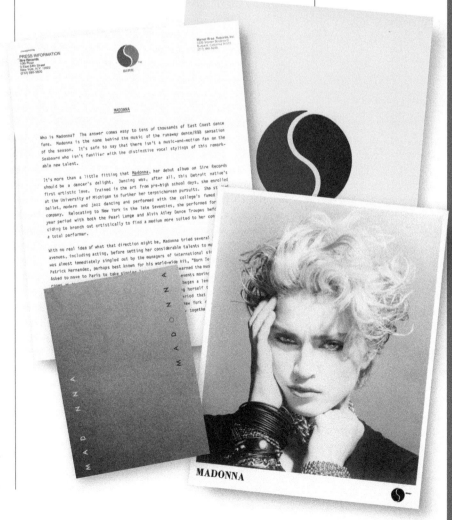

Madonna's first-ever press kit, complete with 8"x10", postcard, press release and custom Sire folder

MADONNA
(1–8)

2001 Remastered
Re-Release
(1–10)

①
"Lucky Star"
(Madonna)–5:37,
produced by
Reggie Lucas

②
"Borderline"
(Reggie Lucas)
–5:18, produced by
Reggie Lucas

③
"Burning Up"
(Madonna)–3:45,
produced by
Reggie Lucas

④
"I Know It"
(Madonna)–3:47,
produced by
Reggie Lucas

⑤
"Holiday"
(Curtis Hudson/
Lisa Stevens)
–6:08, produced by
Jellybean Benitez

⑥
"Think of Me"
(Madonna)–4:54,
produced by
Reggie Lucas

⑦
"Physical
Attraction"
(Reggie Lucas)
–6:39, produced by
Reggie Lucas

⑧
"Everybody"
(Madonna)–4:57,
produced by
Mark Kamins

⑨
"Burning Up"
12" Version
(Madonna)–5:59,
produced by Reggie
Lucas, remixed by
Jellybean Benitez

①⓪
"Lucky Star"
New Mix
(Madonna)–7:15,
produced by
Reggie Lucas, remixed
by Jellybean Benitez

Madonna was unhappy with how the songs had turned out, noting in the same year the album was released, "The musicians were all guys who are making a thousand dollars a day in the studio, so we couldn't rehearse much. Halfway through, we all started doubting each other." She was partly to blame; as a new artist, she was not afforded carte blanche, but she also took a trip while Lucas was working on it. "The songs on [*Madonna*] were pretty weak and I went to **England** during the recording so I wasn't around for a lot of it—I wasn't in **control**," she said in 1984.

The problem, from Madonna's point of view, was that Lucas didn't listen to her ideas and added too much instrumentation. After Lucas finished the project, Madonna asked her boyfriend **Jellybean Benitez** to remix some tracks. It was also Benitez who brought Madonna the last song to be added, her enduring hit **"Holiday,"** which took the place of "Ain't No Big Deal." Still, it was and is inarguably Lucas's album.

"… It's escapist … It's a form of entertainment. It's to make people forget their problems," Madonna told Boston's KTU of her music on the first album.

The packaging of the album prefigures a lot of later Madonna motifs. She has short-cropped, platinum **hair** on the front and **back** covers (1986's "new Madonna" was really just a throwback to this one), and stretches a chain roughly around her throat (baby **"Dita Parlo"**). Most importantly, Madonna's navel is prominent on the inner sleeve, and that **belly button** was the umbilical to a career built on the public's eventually conflicted fascination with her body.

Listening to *Madonna* is still a pleasure over 30 years after its release. The very first song on the record, **"Lucky Star,"** opens with an instantly iconic synth twinkling that perfectly matches the song's lyrical **flirtation** with the universally familiar nursery rhyme "Star Light, Star Bright." In the way modern rappers reference their own success on their first albums before they've even succeeded, presupposing it, "Lucky Star" can be read as an autobiographical explanation for Madonna's later meteoric rise. Madonna **loved** the song so much she had wanted to name the album after it, but the marketing people at Sire felt an eponymous album would better introduce the fledgling artist.

Another dazzlingly strong song follows, the Lucas-created **"Borderline."** As appealingly kittenish as Madonna sounds on the whole record, there is a nuanced sense of yearning in her vocal here brought out by the structure of this all-time pop classic.

From innocent to obscene: With **"Burning Up,"** Madonna bluntly tells the listener she's perfectly happy to go down on her knees or bend over backwards or, well, anything at all. Can't say we weren't warned. The first print run of the album had a unique arrangement of "Burning Up," different from the one on later pressings.

Next up is one of the album's two lesser-known Madonna songs, **"I Know It."** It's a girl-group shuffler with an impassioned vocal, a song overdue for rediscovery. It's also

a kind of song that Madonna does well—a sonic complaint from a woman scorned.

One of Madonna's least-known songs segues into one of her most famous, "Holiday," which feels oddly out of place in the middle of an album thanks to its obvious anthemic quality. It also sounds quite distinct from its seven brothers and sisters (*you* can assign the genders); it would have fit right in on her next album, *Like a Virgin*.

Another album track, **"Think of Me,"** displays a lot of Lucas's R&B roots, its title foreshadowing a major priority in Madonna's career. The bass line is funkier than anything else on the record. Hopefully the **guitar** and sax breaks toward the end were not against Madonna's wishes, because they give the album more musical depth.

If "Burning Up" takes the direct route on the subject of sex, **"Physical Attraction"** takes a far more seductive approach, presenting Madonna as an unrepentant, unrushed **fan** of casual sex. "Physical Attraction" also features one of Madonna's breathy spoken-word passages, a device she would employ effectively on numerous songs in the future. Though credited to Lucas, this song was first registered to Madonna; it's possible she wrote it and they arranged for Lucas to receive final credit for some reason.

The album closes with the song that started it all for Madonna, "Everybody." Its spoken-word intro echoes "Physical Attraction" nicely, and the song's call for individual expression via **dance** makes it a lesser "Holiday" and a more-than-worthy album-ender. Its generous 15-second fade gives the listener time to **regret** that *Madonna* is almost over.

The album cover is an iconic portrait of Madonna at her poutiest, cleverly shot by **Gary Heery** to squeeze all of her **accessories** into the tight shot. Designer Carin Goldberg recalled in *New York* **magazine** in 2015: "She came with a lot of bracelets on, and so I said, 'I think we ought to focus on the bracelets, let's really try to get that in the picture.' That was the one iconic thing about her outfit, besides the rag in her **hair**. I thought she needed even more, so the girlfriend of the photographer went into her jewelry box and took as many bracelets as she could find, to give it a bit more boom."

During the shoot, Madonna danced and sang to "Holiday" and gave the creative team no guff. "… Madonna was probably the easiest **job** I ever had—the most cooperation from a recording artist I think I ever had. She was a true professional, even at that young age," Goldberg noted.

Madonna took its time to bloom into a major hit, debuting at a lowly #190 on the ***Billboard* 200** on September 3, 1983, but clawing its way into the Top 40 and, over a year later, into the Top 10. In fact, *Madonna* had such a slow start in Europe that it was repackaged with a new cover and title in 1985 as *Madonna: The First Album*.

The album would go on to sell over 10 million copies worldwide. Not bad for a first-timer some male critics were openly branding a slut. (If chastity affected musical credibility, few of the greats, male or female, would have secured record deals.)

There are many firsts related to Madonna's first LP, among them her first Top 40 single ("Holiday"), her first Top 10 ("Borderline") and her first Top 5 ("Lucky Star"). So many hits led to a months-long delay in the release of *Like a Virgin*. In the end, *Madonna* spent 168 weeks on the *Billboard 200*, longer than any of her future albums ever would.

Madonna was one of the most auspicious debuts of the '80s, but it underwhelmed critics at the time. Why? Because it is a seamlessly sweet, lyrically coy, infectiously kinetic dance album that was released just a few years after some jack-offs decided "DISCO SUCKS." Moreover, *Madonna* is an unfashionably emo album for its era, filled with not just great grooves but loads of heart. It was always going to be devoured by teenagers and dismissed by critics.

If critics were unkind at first, they've now mostly forgotten their initial impressions, or outright changed their minds. *Madonna* is now regarded as a must-have for any pop collection. In 2013, *Entertainment Weekly* put only one Madonna album on its list of 100 Greatest Albums Ever—*Madonna*, at #43, right after AC/DC's *Back in Black* (1980) and just before **Michael Jackson**'s *Off the Wall* (1979).

. . . .

"WITHOUT OVERSTEPPING THE MODEST AMBITIONS OF MINIMAL FUNK, MADONNA ISSUES AN IRRESISTIBLE INVITATION TO THE DANCE."

—DON SHEWEY, *ROLLING STONE* (1983)

. . . .

"IN CASE YOU BOUGHT THE CON, DISCO NEVER DIED—JUST REVERTED TO THE CRAZIES WHO THOUGHT IT WAS WORTH LIVING FOR. THIS SHAMELESSLY ERSATZ BLONDE IS ONE OF THEM …"—ROBERT CHRISTGAU (1983)

. . . .

"THE FIRST ALBUM WAS REAL R&B. REAL DISCO—OR DANCE; I DON'T LIKE TO USE THAT WORD 'DISCO.' ALL THE TRACKS HAD A UNIFIED SOUND."—MADONNA (1985)

. . . .

"I MADE A GREAT RECORD, AND A LOT OF PEOPLE LIKED IT. IT SOLD A LOT OF COPIES AND LAUNCHED CAREERS AND CREATED OPPORTUNITIES FOR PEOPLE. AND THAT'S WHAT YOU WANT TO DO. THAT IS SUPPOSED TO BE THE OUTCOME OF YOUR GOOD WORK. I DON'T THINK IT CHANGED THE NATURE OF LIFE IN AMERICA OR ANYTHING LIKE THAT."

—REGGIE LUCAS (2013)

. . . .

"… *MADONNA* HERALDED SOMETHING MUCH BIGGER: THE ARRIVAL OF THE POP DIVA AS A SINGULAR FORCE WHO PUT PERSONALITY ABOVE ALL ELSE … LIKE ALL VISIONARY IDEAS, IT JUST TOOK A LITTLE WHILE FOR THE REST OF US TO CATCH UP."

—KYLE ANDERSON, *ENTERTAINMENT WEEKLY* (2013)

. . . .

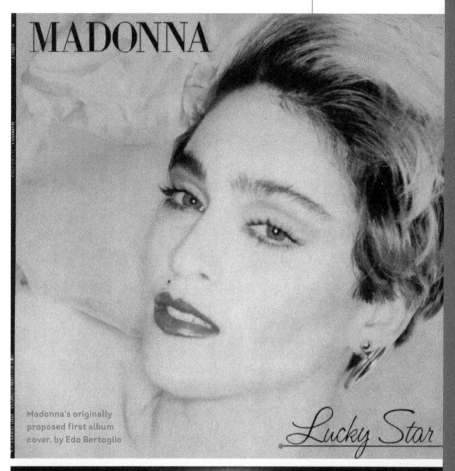

Madonna's originally proposed first album cover, by Edo Bertoglio

EVERYBODY IS A STAR:
AN ESSAY BY MADONNA'S CLASSMATE
& FRIEND SHARON MACZKO

Lady Stardust (Madonna)
2036 Oklahoma
Rochester, Mich.

In high school, Madonna was not only universally popular and extremely pretty, she was also self-assured in every way; essentially the complete polar opposite of me. And yet we became friends at age 15. It took only an obscure and odd, offhand remark from me to get her attention; we clicked and she befriended me. I absolutely adored her confident and cavalier attitude regarding life. It was enviable and I wanted so much to be like her.

There are many things I recall about my short relationship with Madonna. I knew that she was unique. And she was just so much fun to be around.

Most vividly, I recall the mannequin torso episode. Madonna, several other friends, and I were gathered at a table in Mrs. Cohoe's art class, where we had the liberty to work independently. A torso from a female store mannequin lay nearby, probably a leftover relic from a life drawing class. It was only the hollow shell of the front portion of the mannequin, but Madonna saw an opportunity. Picking up the torso,

she placed it on her chest over her blouse, tucked the bottom portion into the waist of her skirt, and buttoned her blazer below the breasts of the thing, so that the flesh colored chest was prominently displayed upon her, *Playboy*-style. We laughed so hard at her plaster X-rated image! The bell rang for the end of class, and I dared Madonna to walk out into the halls to her next class while still wearing the fake, exposed breasts. Without hesitation, she sashayed out into the halls with me trotting along behind her, hysterically laughing till I cried at the reactions of the other students walking toward us. It was hilarious! Then a teacher caught sight of her and yelled, "MADONNA!!!" And as he made his way toward her, I ran in the opposite direction.

Madonna sat next to me at a table with two other girls in a psychology class one afternoon, thumbing through a book she had carried in with her. I can't recall the exact title, but it was something akin to the *World Record of Sex Facts*. Reading from it, she enthusiastically informed our little group of an astounding

statistic: a lesbian whose tongue was so strong she could break a pencil in half with it. In response we all stared at her blankly, in complete naïveté regarding the importance of the matter at all.

Ironically, but not surprisingly since it was the early '70s, a huge stigma surrounded any hint of lesbianism or homosexuality in our high school. Displaying any trait at all that could be considered different resulted in cruel snickering, labeling and insults. Madonna had no inhibitions whatsoever, and because of her reputation, she was immune to any gossip; I, however, was not immune, and there were times her actions absolutely mortified me. Once, after applying fresh lipstick, she grabbed me by the neck and pretended to plant a giant kiss on my lips. My friends, standing behind Madonna, thought in horror that she had actually kissed me, and I had to explain that they were wrong. Another time she linked her arm in mine as we walked and talked, and I knew that something

even as minor as that was pushing the boundaries of tolerance for narrow-minded classmates.

Over the years, I've managed to salvage a few of the letters Madonna wrote to me while my family vacationed in California in the summer of 1973. She often borrowed a name from a David Bowie song to sign her letters with, and called me the same, as we both revered Bowie at the time. My parents dragged me along when they finally moved to California in 1975, just before my senior year in high school, and I lost contact with Madonna shortly thereafter.

Years later, but still at the onset of her career, Madonna was asked a question during a television interview regarding why she thought that Mick Jagger may have slighted her, and she took only a fraction of a second to respond, 'I think he felt my threat.'

I will never forget how my jaw dropped in awe of her boldness. It was inspiring!

Around that time, I felt Madonna's success had influenced and motivated me to overcome my inhibitions and exhibit my artwork publicly. I wrote what I view now as an embarrassingly maudlin letter to her via her agent at the time, inviting her to attend the opening reception of my first solo exhibition at a gallery in Los Angeles in 1988. Did she ever attend my opening? No. Melissa called and informed me that Madonna was unable to attend as she was in NYC at the time performing in a play.

If I had to sum up my impression of Madonna years ago when we were friends, I would simply say that she was a truly nice person with an enormous sense of humor.

–Sharon Maczko (2014)

Sharon, oh baby I'll gonna miss you out there in sunny california. but get ready cause I'll gonna come out & visit ya. just you wait. be a good girl & don't drink any tequila. love ya always Madonna

HI! HONEY BUNNY
—Be my Valentine

ARE YOU EXPERIENCED

TO MY LOVIE SHARON, KISSY KISSY HAPPY V.D. LOVE MADONNA

SHARON

MADONNA (VIDEO COLLECTION): *Release date: November 1984.* Released on VHS and **laserdisc**, this first music-video collection contains **"Burning Up," "Borderline," "Lucky Star"** and **"Like a Virgin."** The fact that **"Everybody"** is not included suggests Madonna doesn't consider it her true first video. It sold over 100,000 copies in the US, making it the best-selling music-video release of 1985.

MADONNA AND THE SKY: Managed by "Mark," a man whose surname is lost to history, this is the trio formed in 1980 by Madonna and fellow ex-**Breakfast Club** member (and, briefly, lover) Mike Monahan and Gary Burke. The group played publicly only one time, at an **NYC** club called Eighties, before Monahan quit. When Madonna's ex, **Stephen Bray**, arrived in NYC and joined the band, it would come to be known as **Emmy**.

MADONNA: INNOCENCE LOST: *Director: Bradford May. Air date: November 29, 1994.* In the 1990s, before Lifetime horned in on the action, Fox aired a slate of unapologetically cruddy **TV** biopics on a series of figures, including **Roseanne Barr**, Amy Fisher and, inevitably, Madonna.

Madonna: Innocence Lost was based on **Christopher Andersen**'s bio. It somehow managed to make unsympathetic source material into an even less sympathetic portrait of Madonna's early years in **NYC**. Cringe-inducing from beginning to end (that homemade **"True Blue"** video from the **MTV** contest was more professional), the flick imagines Madonna (Terumi Matthews) prostituting herself with a **Martin H.M. Schreiber** stand-in for dinner, failing miserably as a lousy **dancer** and being taken to **Paris** only to find out she was required to be a sort of all-singing, all-dancing hooker. Real people central to the Madonna story are left out or portrayed in ways that render them unrecognizable, the existence of her debut *Madonna* album is skipped and Madonna's very real embrace of her musicality is ignored in favor of painting her as a **fame**-hungry cipher.

Even with pros like Wendie Malick (who uses spiky **hair** to communicate **Camille Barbone**'s lesbianism) and Dean Stockwell (as Madonna's **father**), *Madonna: Innocence Lost* is not so innocently off the mark.

Matthews captures not one iota of Madonna's charisma, none of her brassy, street-smart persona. (She might have fared better in a biopic based on an older **Madonna**; she projects way too much refinement.) Oddly enough, even though she isn't exactly a dead ringer for Madonna, she played Madonna again in in ABC's *Bad as I Wanna Be: The **Dennis Rodman** Story* in 1998.

She's a pretty girl, I'll give ya that, but Matthews—who wound up with only nine TV and movie roles before apparently retiring in 2001—was more than two steps behind the superstar she was trying to embody.

MADONNA LIVE!–DROWNED WORLD TOUR 2001: The official title of the live broadcast of Madonna's *Drowned World Tour* on August 26, 2001, on HBO.

MADONNA LIVE: THE VIRGIN TOUR: *Director: Daniel Kleinman. Release date: November 13, 1985.* Recorded May 25 and 26, 1985, at Detroit's Cobo Arena (now Cobo Center, 1 Washington Blvd., Detroit, MI), Madonna's first concert video is notable for its sassy intro, a **black-and-white** clip of Madonna as a **blonde** bombshell—a marked contrast to the punky girl with dark roots who performs in the concert—reciting a myth-building summary of her rise to stardom that hammers home her early message that **"dreams come true."** The intro was shot by **James Foley**, the concert by Daniel Kleinman, later famous for creating many of the James Bond title sequences (including *Die Another Day*).

The home video was a huge success, and two of the live performances—**"Dress You Up"** and **"Like a Virgin"**—were serviced as music videos.

Missing from the only official record of Madonna's first tour are her performances of **"Angel," "Borderline"** and **"Burning Up."** Wouldn't you **love** to have those today?

The video contains: "Dress You Up," **"Holiday," "Into the Groove," "Everybody," "Gambler," "Lucky Star," "Crazy for You," "Over and Over,"** "Like a Virgin"/"Billie Jean" (1982) and **"Material Girl."**

MADONNA MONEY: In Madonna we trust? That's what Madonna **money** asks of us. Loads of the phony stuff—bearing Madonna's image—were printed up for *The Virgin Tour* and dumped on audiences at the end of **"Material Girl."** Her official **fan** club also used to mint its own Madonna money for use in buying merchandise from its catalogue.

MADONNA: ON STAGE & ON THE RECORD: *Director: Joe DeMaio. Air date: April 22, 2003.* Fairly incredible **MTV** special spotlighting Madonna's *American Life* material to coincide with that album's release. The special featured Madonna in a **black-and-white** striped top and jaunty cap.

For the very small in-studio audience, a brunette Madonna opened the show by performing **"American Life."**

It's Madonna's Material World—we're just living in it.

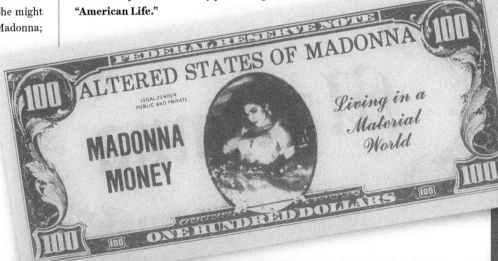

Host Carson Daly praised Madonna for her rapping, noting, "**Eminem** should look the F out!" Madonna laughed and said, "Well, you know, I was—I was born in Detroit first!" She also asserted that she hadn't performed in such a small setting in 20 years.

She used the special to explain why she'd pulled her "American Life" video: "Well, when I, when I first, uh, came up with the idea for the video, it was last November and there was talk of war, but war seemed very far away, so basically it was my, my last-ditch effort to kinda throw out the horrors of war, um, and the reality of war out there to people to try and … I don't know, galvanize people to become unified and do as much protesting as possible. But then the war started by the time I finished the video; it was kind of too late. And I didn't think people wanted to be inundated with, you know, war footage that we had used—stock war footage—in the video. I just thought, 'That's rubbing salt in the wounds.'" MTV did show scenes from the **unreleased** version.

Daley ran a lightning-round of questions from her **fans** in which Madonna praised the **book** *The Alchemist* (1988), picked **"Music"** as her favorite Madonna **dance** song and said making **"Justify My Love"** was the most fun she ever had on a video set.

The special included a feisty exchange with **John Norris** that had been pre-taped.

If you find this on **YouTube**, watch for **Andy Cohen** fanboying out behind Daly when Madonna breaks into the first-ever live version of **"Hollywood."** The other live numbers were **"Nothing Fails"** and **"Like a Prayer"** (she's definitely given better performances of this one since), with **"X-Static Process"** filmed as a Web bonus.

The special featured **Mirwais**, **Stuart Price** and **Monte Pittman**, among other Madonna regulars, including **tribute artist** Madiva, who was in attendance.

MADONNA QUEEN: An over-the-top Madonna **fan**, especially apropos for **gay** men, but it has become generic. If you find yourself calling hotels while Madonna's on tour to see if **Liz Rosenberg** is registered, buying one to save and one to keep of every product Madonna offers for sale and/or have recently started a Change.org petition to get "Ghosttown" played on the radio … **bitch**, you're a Madonna queen.

MADONNA RISING: *Producer: Carey Zeiser. Air date: April 12, 1998.* In the same way one can not live in Port-au-Prince without air conditioning, one can not be a Madonna **fan** and not have watched this shotgun trip down **memory** lane produced for **VH1** to promote *Ray of Light*. Hosted by **Rupert Everett**, the special followed/led Madonna **back** to some of the sites of her ascent in the early days of **NYC**, including an East Village apartment, **The Music Building** and the **Star Motel**. Filled with dead air and awkward moments, the special nonetheless strikes gold

occasionally, such as when Madonna is forced to interact with the people who've moved into her old spaces. Madonna's **accent** sounds 100% British in Everett's company. Hundred. Percent.

MADONNA SPEAKS: *Producer: Danielle Gelfand. Air date: April 3, 2003.* Hour-long special to promote Madonna's *American Life* album during which she was interviewed by her *Will & Grace* scene partner **Megan Mullally**. The backdrop for their talk had the words "**art**," "image," "motherhood," "music," "outspoken," "rebel," "religion," "strength" and "opinionated." Madonna, brunette and in a good mood, was open to Mullally's questions about their *Will & Grace* experience, her goals with her album and her early rebellion.

Mullally—underrated as an interviewer—got Madonna to speak on the problem with **fame** and maturing under scrutiny. "At the end of the day, everyone changes and everyone grows," Madonna said. "But if your changes and your growth are always documented and you always have to comment on them or explain them, and of course something you said and believed in a couple of years ago is gonna change—for a lot of people—but then, if you say *that*, they'll say, 'But you said *that* before!' and I'm constantly being held accountable for everything."

At the end of their talk, Mullally had Madonna agree to become a beautiful woman with wrinkles and gray **hair**. Conspicuously, no timetable was set.

MADONNA: THE NAME OF THE GAME: *Release date: 1993.* How low (budget) can you go before a film is really just a piece of tape with some stuff on it? This low! Yet if you're a **fan** of Madonna's, you might want to locate this delightfully shitty documentary, which splices together sound bites from **Warren Beatty**, **Martin Ciccone** and **Sean Penn**. Host **Mark Bego** has a tone to his **voice** so reminiscent of the John Waters narration of *Pink Flamingos* (1972) it sounds like he's ready to declare **Queerdonna** "the filthiest person alive!" at any moment.

The filmmakers and Brentwood Home Video probably made good **money** on this **back** in the day. **God** bless.

MADONNA: TRUTH OR DARE: SEE: *Truth or Dare*.

MADONNABILIA: Memorabilia that is Madonna in nature. Use it in a sentence? "Hey, Ma, where is all my Madonnabilia?" "I put it out at the curb like I told you I would if you didn't clean your room." Oh, you want it in a sentence that wouldn't have taken place in the '80s? Okay. "Hey, dude, where do you keep all your Madonnabilia?" "In protective plastic inside flood-proof boxes in storage, like any normal person."

Aside from all her regular film and record releases and tours, and all the ensuing promotional and commercial items available with each, there have been literally thousands of posters, stand-ups, nudie pens, T-shirts, concert programs, bicycle shorts, caps, sweatshirts, postcards, buttons, **magazine** covers, bandannas, patches, temporary tattoos, towels, **books**—you name it, she's sold it—that qualify as Madonnabilia.

Don't scoff at Madonnabilia! Today's crappy key chain is tomorrow's **artifact**.

MADONNATHON: You've heard of the far-out goings-on at Comic Con? Well, they're positively earthbound compared to the antics that went on at these Madonna-appreciation celebrations.

The first was staged in 1992 in Southfield, **Michigan**, the weekend of Madonna's **birthday**. About 1,500 **fans** converged to: buy **Madonnabilia** so fabulous it might have been offered up to a certain newborn in a manger along with frankincense and myrrh; to discuss their mutual heartache over the relative failure of **"Oh Father"** on the charts; to try to figure out what the hell to expect from her upcoming *Erotica* album; and to watch **tribute artists** of both sexes doing their thing. They also went simply to get together with like(a virgin)-minded people in an era before the Internet made it easy for freaks to meet.

The event sponsored a **"This Used to be My Playground"** bus tour of Madonna's childhood home, her **schools** and the site of her **first kiss**.

Another gathering around this time was LA's first Madonna expo, Justify My Life! (the same title as a fanzine). Held at the Hyatt Hotel on Sunset (formerly 8401 W. Sunset Blvd., W. Hollywood, CA), this show welcomed the authors of *The Madonna Connection* [SEE: **bibliography (about Madonna)**] and featured a Madonna museum. Attendance was way off from the first Madonnathon—what a difference the release of *Sex* makes!

Beginning in 2000, Nick Mendoros and Julio Perez began hosting annual Maddyfest conventions in **NYC** (even Madonna doesn't want to travel to Michigan), which closely followed the **original** Madonnathon model of merch, music and fan networking. The event was enhanced by the boys' classic fanzine, *All Access*.

Starting in 2003, Cathy Cervenka began running what she calls a Madonnathon Tribute Show, featuring over 20 performers interpreting Madonna's music, in NYC. For more info, check out **Facebook** @ Madonnathon.

The time is probably right for a proper Madonnathon comeback. Who's with me?

MAGAZINES: Madonna doesn't read 'em (haven't you listened to **"Nobody Knows Me"**?), she simply poses for them, and then only if it's for the cover.

Unlike any star since—and unlike only a precious few before—her, Madonna has made the act of being on the cover of a **magazine** into an **art** form. A gung-ho participant in creating a visual record of her **beauty**, her aesthetic,

her political and quasi-punk challenging of social norms and her status as a visual icon, Madonna has always taken her covers seriously, in some cases as seriously as other rockstars take music videos or even albums.

Basics take selfies; queens pose for magazine covers.

On the following two pages, then, a collection of some of Madonna's best, most interesting covers, presented to illustrate her ever-changing looks and her domination of the culture for the past 30+ years. But know this: It's a drop in the bucket.

MAGIQUE: *Formerly 1110 1st Ave., NY, NY.* Located at 1st Ave. and 61st St., Magique was a **disco** Madonna either played or was pitched to play for $2,000 in 1982. Around the same time, according to **original** notes obtained by *EM20*, the locations Madonna was being pitched to by her bookers [who'd been instructed to note that she was a "more significant music phenomenon than (A) **D. Harry**, (B) Go-Go's, (C) Joan Jett"] included: Bonds International Casino Nightclub (formerly 1526 Broadway, NY, NY), the **Celebrity Club**, Broadway International (formerly 461 W. 146th St., NY, NY), Club Zanzibar (formerly 400–430 Broad St., Newark, NJ), Copacabana (formerly 10 E. 60th St., NY, NY), Eclipse (formerly Queens Blvd, Queens, NY), The Palace (formerly U.S. Rte. 1 & 9, Elizabeth, NJ), Paradise Garage (formerly 84 King St., NY, NY), Red Parrot (formerly 617 W. 57th St., NY, NY), **Roseland**, The Saint (formerly 105 Second Ave., NY, NY), **Studio 54**, and Xenon (formerly 124 W. 43rd St., NY, NY).

MAILER, NORMAN: *January 31, 1923–November 10, 2007.* Ornery commentator whose conversation-topic **books**—among them *The Naked and the Dead* (1948), *Why Are We In Vietnam?* (1967) and *Tough Guys Don't Dance* (1984)—made him one of the most widely revered, reviled and read authors of the 20th century. Mailer also wrote the fictitious **Marilyn Monroe** memoir *Of Women and Their Elegance* (1980), marking him as being at least as obsessed with the icon as Madonna seems to be.

Mailer proclaimed Madonna to be our "greatest living female artist" in an August 1994 cover story for *Esquire's* "Women We Love" issue. Mailer's portrait with Madonna for the issue featured him in black tie and she in a deep green (**black-and-white** film) evening gown and matching **dog** collar.

Print ad for a "dance concert" featuring Madonna at the Red Parrot

ON THE COVER OF A MAGAZINE

"People always ask me why I chose Malawi. And I tell them I didn't. It chose me."—MADONNA (2008)

Mailer wrote hilariously of photographer **Wayne Maser**'s attempts to get a "stunt photo" of the famous pair, with Madonna on Mailer's lap, her breast exposed. But Mailer recoiled at the unceremoniously unsheathed breast, not out of modesty, but out of a wounded ego at its flaccid nipple! The lengthy essay/interview served to defend Madonna against the talons of the press during the backlash from her **David Letterman** appearance, but it was also a rare in-depth interview that allowed her to get real about her amazing resilience, to offer her thoughts on **condoms** and to cop to the fact that *Sex* was at least partially self-**censored**.

MALAWI: Southeast African nation of 16 million that is one of the world's poorest. Beginning in 2006, Madonna made a lifetime commitment to helping the people of Malawi to help themselves, which includes investment in her **Raising Malawi**, pledges to build **schools**, regular visits and the adoption of two of its orphans, **David** and **Mercy**, in spite of restrictive laws regarding foreign adoption.

When activist Victoria Keelan phoned Madonna to get her interested in Malawi, Madonna told her, "I don't even know where that is." Keelan hung up, hung up on her.

"Growing up in a privileged life, I took education for granted. But coming to Malawi has taught me a lot of things, and I have learned to appreciate what life gives," Madonna said in her well-reviewed documentary *I Am Because We Are*.

Madonna's visits to the country have been met with controversy, including an embarrassing war of words with former President Joyce Banda. Banda's sister, Anjimile Mtila-Oponyo, had **worked** with Madonna on Raising Malawi and *I Am Because We Are* until she was fired for suspected theft. After this time, a statement from Banda's office was released in which Madonna was described as "a musician who desperately thinks she must generate recognition by bullying state officials instead of playing decent music on the stage." Madonna shot **back** that she was "saddened" that Banda "has chosen to release lies about what we've accomplished, my intentions, how I personally conducted myself while visiting Malawi and other untruths." Banda was later said to be "incandescent with rage" that the inappropriate statement had been released, but there was no doubt that no **love** was lost between the two.

Banda's successor, President Peter Mutharika, has proved to be more Team Madonna than Banda ever was. In 2014, Mutharika met with Madonna, thanking her for returning with her adoptive children so that they may know their native land.

MALIBU: Madonna and **Sean Penn** lived in a $4-million Malibu beach house in Carbon Canyon (formerly 22271 Carbon Mesa Rd., Malibu, CA) as young marrieds. It was the site of their most loving moments, as well as the abusive times that led to their **divorce**. Madonna signed it over to Sean when they split, and he lived there with girlfriend Robin Wright and their children until it was burned to the ground in the brushfires of November 1993. Madonna was said to have offered Sean financial help in rebuilding.

While living there, Madonna often indulged in the Malibu eccentricity of wearing around her neck a tiny vial of soapy water with a little wand for blowing bubbles.

Madonna didn't choose Malibu—it chose her.

MAMET, DAVID: *b. November 30, 1947.* Intense playwright and film director known for **plays** including *Sexual Perversity in Chicago* (1974), *Glengarry Glen Ross* (1983) and *Oleanna* (1992), and for his film *House of Games* (1987).

In 1988, Mamet cast Madonna in the role of "Karen" in his new work *Speed- the-Plow*, ensuring the play's financial success for her entire run.

Madonna later described him as a misogynist; her meek, willingly exploited character certainly didn't do much for **feminism**. Of Madonna, Mamet said, "I think it's fairly evident she had a lot going for her in the audition. Does this mean I'm a big, fat whore? Maybe."

MA-MIXED MARRIAGE: When someone you're seeing thinks Madonna sucks.

MANILOW, BARRY: *b. June 17, 1943.* Composer, pianist and unlikely pop heartthrob behind some of the biggest easy-listening pop hits of the '70s, including #1 smashes "Mandy" (1974), "I Write the Songs" (1975) and "Looks Like We Made It" (1977),

The man who played the piano for **Bette Midler** during her **gay** bathhouse performances in the early '70s played for Madonna the night the American Foundation for **AIDS** Research (amfAR) honored her with its **Award** of Courage in 1991, just a few months after he attended the LA premiere of *Truth or Dare*.

In a Sirius XM interview with Jenny Hutt that aired on October 29, 2014, Manilow was asked what he thought of Madonna. He replied, "A genius."

MARILYN: *b. November 3, 1962.* Peter Robinson, dubbed Marilyn for his **Marilyn Monroe**-like **dreamy** eyes and perfectly arched brows, became a pop star in **England** with the Top 5 success of his single "Calling Your Name" (1983) from his cheekily titled album *Despite Straight Lines*. He'd been given the spotlight not in spite of but *because of* his cross-dressing and gender play—everyone was looking for the next **Boy George**, who was a compatriot of Marilyn's. Marilyn was romantically involved with **Gwen Stefani**'s ex-husband Gavin Rossdale at the time, a relationship that came to light thanks to George's autobiography and that has been confirmed by both parties.

Madonna was friendly with Marilyn **back** in the day; the two were photographed by Boy George backstage after one of *The Virgin Tour* dates at **Radio City Music Hall** as well as at a *Virgin Tour* after-party at Palladium (formerly 126 E. 14th St., NY, NY). At the latter, they enjoyed the musical stylings of go-go funk bands E.U., Redds and the Boys, Pump Blenders and Slug-Go, of whom Madonna exclaimed, "This is the baddest band in the land!"

In 2003, Marilyn recalled to *Attitude* the time he blew Madonna off accidentally when a friend called and said Madonna wanted to hang out with him. "I didn't believe him, so she came on the phone and was like, 'Hi, Marilyn, I really want to hang out with you.' I didn't believe it was her at first, so I said, 'Listen, **bitch**, if I drag my pretty arse all the way to Marble Arch and you ain't the real thing, I'll kick your ass!' Anyways, it turned out to be the real thing so Madonna, if you're reading this, sorry, we go way back and you know I know that you're fierce."

MARIPOL: US-based French designer/stylist responsible for Madonna's early ensembles avec rubber bracelets, neon, heavy **crucifixes** and mesh **hair** ties. In other words, the **"BOY TOY"** girl.

She operated a boutique called Maripolitan (formerly 59–65 Bleecker St., NY, NY), from which she sold all the components of the Madonna look, including some pieces she provided for *Desperately Seeking Susan*.

Maripol styled Madonna many times, including off-stage. Some important collaborations include Madonna's first international shoot (for a Japanese **magazine**), her first magazine cover (*Island*), the originally proposed album cover for *Madonna* and the album cover for *Like a Virgin*. She also styled Madonna for her appearance at the 1st Annual **MTV Video Music Awards**.

It was Maripol who first introduced Madonna to many downtown figures, including **Jean-Michel Basquiat**, **Andy Warhol** and **Deborah Harry**.

Maripol, noted for her **work** with Polaroids, has photographed Madonna more memorably than have most studio photographers. Hers are images that capture the period in ways that studio shoots rarely can.

She always knew her friend was a star-in-the-making, so when Maripol was working for **Fiorucci**, she insisted on hiring Madonna (over Jennifer Beals) to perform, jumping out of a big cake to celebrate the store's 15th **birthday**.

Madonna said of Maripol in 1985, "Whenever I do, um, y'know, photo sessions for, um, a magazine or, I'm doing, you know, video or **TV** or whatever, or even a live performance, Maripol comes and helps me with the whole stylization of it, helps me put my clothes together, gives me the

jewelry to wear, and she just has an **eye** for the whole, the whole *look* of everything."

In 1986, when Madonna streamlined her image, Maripolitan folded, but there was never acrimony between the two women; Maripol knows where all of the bodies are buried, but don't expect her to lead you to them.

The gracious Maripol remains friendly with Madonna to this day. In a rare TV interview in 1993 after the airing of **Robin Leach**'s *Madonna Exposed*, Maripol defended Madonna against bad press, flashing personal photos she'd taken of her young son with her. She has always spoken highly of Madonna's marketing genius, telling Yahoo! Music in 2013, "I think Madonna might have a multiple personality. I know you [think I am kidding], but I think it goes with the pain of losing your **mother** so young. Multiple personality, that's my theory. But that is really excellent for her career, because she decides to really change her look, so people will never get bored of her. It's a genius strategy."

Maripol still designs today; a 2010 collection of her work for Marc by Marc Jacobs showcased her signature textiles.

MARLEY, BOB: *February 6, 1945–May 11, 1981.* Jamaican reggae innovator whose image Madonna used on her **Instagram** as part of her posting of **fan**-made **art** themed to her *Rebel Heart* album release. Facing criticism for the move, Madonna apologized, but denied it was an issue of **race**.

Marley was actually the third artist Madonna ever saw in concert **back** in **Michigan**, on June 14, 1975. She has said her son **Rocco**, born 25 years after Marley's **death**, admires him greatly.

MARRIAGE REF, THE: *Airdates: 2010-2012.* US show airing on NBC that was produced by Jerry Seinfeld. The premise was that couples would tell the stories of their lightly rocky marriages via video while a panel of celebrities would offer humorous advice.

Twice-**divorced** Madonna taped an episode of the show on February 24, 2010, at CBS Studios (528 W. 57th St., NY, NY) that aired on March 11, 2010. Madonna's fellow A-list panelists were comic actor and writer Larry David and comedian **Ricky Gervais**. Madonna, looking like a million dollars in large bills, was remarkably at ease during the taping, getting along well with Gervais and David, who seemed quite taken with her.

More than relationship advice, Madonna focused on the bad interior design visible in the videos. She taunted David for being a misogynist by saying, "I don't **hate** men, I just hate you." She got the show's biggest laugh by noting that a man whose overbearing **mother**-in-law was ruining his marriage was **pussy**-whipped by "the wrong pussy!"

"How can Madonna give advice on *The Marriage Ref* if she can't even make it work with Gwyneth Paltrow?" –CHELSEA HANDLER (2010)

MATERIAL WITNESS:
MEETING MARIPOL

Maripol, the legendary mastermind behind Madonna's "BOY TOY" look, was more than just a stylist to Madonna–they were friends, with a sisterly connection. They were among the most prominent promulgators of the downtown aesthetic, and they are two of its most high-profile survivors.

Maripol didn't get rich from her proximity to Madonna, but her name still evokes awed respect in the world of fashion. She has published several books of her iconic Polaroid photography, including *Mes Polas*, 1977-1990 (1990), *Maripolarama* (2005) and *Maripol: Little Red Riding Hood* (2010).

At the time Maripol was beginning her career, her partner in love was photographer Edo Bertoglio. He shot Madonna for her first album cover, with styling by Maripol, but the cover

was rejected. Still, Maripol continued styling Madonna in the early years.

The women have drifted, but Maripol has enjoyed seeing Madonna's concerts and spending time with her whenever possible.

Speaking with her at her longtime studio on Broadway–a place where not only Madonna but Keith Haring, Jean-Michel Basquiat, Futura 2000 and countless others have spent time–was a highlight of the work that went into creating this book.

EM2O: What were your early years like, before you became a stylist?

MARIPOL: I would go, as a 16-year-old, every year in the summer to work in London. I was working as a waitress where I had all the

rockstars coming in. They wanted shrimp, "What's shrimp in French?" That's how I perfected my English.

My parents lived abroad and I was in boarding school, so I fended for myself. I would take the English Channel boat. I was paid £14 a week as a chambermaid, and I had a room and food. One time on my floor was Leonard Cohen–I was cleaning his room! I also met a rocker and traveled to Morocco with him; he was the son of Larry Adler, the harmonica music composer, and he had an African trading beads company. I started making jewelry with him.

EM2O: What was your very first job as a professional stylist?

M: I was the stylist and the model for a magazine that was kind of a division of *Penthouse*. But the pictures were not "pink" enough so they got denied. [Laughs] Thank God! Or they would have followed me all my life. But I have Polaroids ...

EM2O: What about your first time styling an artist?

M: I used to work with Moshe Brakha–great photographer from the LA scene; I did album covers for Hall & Oates, Blondie–*Parallel Lines* [1978] that Edo shot. Grace Jones was art directed by Jean-Paul Goude in the late '70s when he did that video "Jungle Fever" where everybody wears her facemask, there

are a hundred of them; I put rubber bracelets on their ankles, and I had invented the Slinky bracelet, which Grace wore in 1977–there are pictures of Grace Jones wearing it.

I was the art director for Fiorucci, and I also designed for them. They had an office in Hong Kong and they would fly me there, but I would stop in Tokyo first and I would come back with collections, the plastic square dresses included; always accessories ... bags, belts, jewelry.

EM2O: When you started styling, what inspired you?

M: Industrial items being repurposed, and I think it's natural for me. I came from a very stylish family–my paternal grandmother was really flamboyant, my mom was very elegant. I was raised with three brothers, and it was hard for me to get my femininity out. I have a memory of me at four years old taking my mom's clothes and raiding her closet and trying to walk with high heels.

Then I went to École nationale supérieure des Beaux-Arts, and to finance school, I'd do the flea market and I would sell vintage clothes that I dyed. I was never selling what the others were selling. I was really out-there. I would buy and sell 1940s.

EM2O: When did you become obsessed with taking Polaroids?

M: I got my first Polaroid in 1977. I came to America with Edo, and he gave me my first SX-70 Polaroid for Christmas. He was a

brilliant photographer, but man, just to see him schlepping–you had to bring your film to the lab, you had to correct the contact sheet, get it developed. And with a Polaroid, what did I have to do? Buy the packs of film.

EM2O: Do you remember the first time you met or saw Madonna?

M: Yes. I met Madonna at The Roxy, right when it was the beginning of this whole hip-hop/rap trend. It was a great mix of culture, local bands and New Wave coming from London. We saw bands like Bow Wow Wow. The party was produced by an English girl named Blue, who is an agent for rappers now. Malcolm McLaren was also involved.

Fab Five Freddy was doing a rap on stage and he asked me if I could find some cute girls. Of course, I see Madonna and I ask her, "Would you like to dance on stage?" She looked at me and I said, "Are you wearing a nice bra?" I wanted her to go on the stage without the top. As Madonna has said, she thought I was completely out of my mind. I knew who she was from "No Entiendes!" I had seen her perform "Everybody."

Not too long after, Martin [Burgoyne] called and said that he wanted me to meet Madonna because she needed an art director and that was for the first album cover. We staged the pictures and you know they were refused. This is when we stoked a friendship.

maripol

She's got style ... that's what all the material girls say.

RHONDA CORTE

"She was genuinely beautiful. I really loved when she had the big eyebrows." — Maripol

Madonna and Maripol at a shoot for a Japanese magazine in 1983

She came up here, to my loft. I started to decorate her like a Christmas tree. I was already making crosses; I was already doing the rubber bracelets. After that, we became inseparable. She really had this penchant for waking me up in the morning and saying, "Let's do things!"

EM2O: What was a typical hang with Madonna like—what would you do?

M: Dance rehearsal in her loft on Broome, going out at night to see DJs, planning shoots ...

EM2O: What was your first shoot with Madonna?

M: I organized a spread for a local magazine, *Island* which definitely was the first cover she had, but that wasn't the first shoot. The first shoot, with the band, was the Japanese magazine *Ryuko Tsushin*. [The photographer] was Kiri Teshigahara. We rented a mini-bus and went to Flushing Meadows and shot under the World's Fair Unisphere.

EM2O: What was the concept of the shoot?

M: Street! It was a New York background. The fuzzy sweater I took from Fiorucci, and the schoolboy belt and hat was from a Japanese postman uniform I had found in Tokyo.

EM2O: What was Madonna like during these early shoots?

M: Really nice and fun. We had a lot of selection of clothes and jewelry for *Island*.

EM2O: Do you remember where you shot the *Island* cover?

M: We shot in the East Village, probably in [photographer Curtis Knapp's] apartment.

EM2O: The pictures from that shoot that surprised me were the ones with her hair up.

M: Oh ... please. The makeup and the hair from that shoot were so '8Os.

EM2O: Did you attend the party celebrating the release of that issue of *Island*?

M: Yeah, at The Roxy, right?

EM2O: Yes. Did she perform?

M: I don't think so ... I don't remember. But then, in '83, I staged the party for the 15-year anniversary of Fiorucci. It was the 5O-year anniversary of *King Kong* [1933] and they had a huge rubber gorilla going around the Empire State Building and that gave me the idea. I found the company that did that and it cost me 7G ... half of my budget!
Madonna said, "I'm not jumping." The idea was to jump from the top of this cake structure inside the party. So *I* did it and I hurt myself. It could have killed her. [Laughs]
Then we went to Paris [in 1984], where she performed with DST and the New York City Breakers. Memorable night! Oliviero Toscani took pictures, which were published in *Donna* magazine, but the negatives were lost.

EM2O: Some exist.

M: Yes! They were taken at the Fiorucci Paris store opening party in an old pool called La Piscine. She was very beautiful ... but just to find that issue would be really hard. Her hair was all tied up!

Back in New York, for Keith Haring's birthday at Paradise Garage [formerly 84 King St., NY, NY], she was wearing two different outfits, one was Keith Haring painting pink on a leather skirt, and the other one was mine. Diana Ross was in the back and I had my big case of jewelry—we were all backstage—and she said, "I want some jewelry, too ..." so I gave her some.
Then, when she did the movie *Desperately Seeking Susan*, she said, "They want me to get dressed in these old rag-clothes, vintage ..." I said, "Madonna, you should just keep your look because you're a singer. You want to wear your own clothing." She listened to me.

EM2O: She was so downtown ... was it always a match made in heaven when she segued into the fashion world?

M: I think she was always really smart, with Liz Rosenberg doing her PR. All of a sudden, you're Madonna and you're on the top-charts and making the cover of *Life* and *Newsweek*, it's pretty obvious that the fashion world is gonna follow and there will be requests from *Vogue* and whatever. She was not going to do it unless she was getting the cover.

EM2O: When you moved on to style the *Like a Virgin* cover, where did you get that amazing wedding dress and how did you pull that all together?

M: I designed and sewed every single item—everything was handmade, and her bouquet was fresh. What happened is that the art director wanted her to be a Black Sabbath Virgin. We shot it at the St. Regis [2 E. 55th St., NY, NY], so we did the wedding look. I said, "Madonna, you have a song called 'Like a Virgin', why don't you play with that? Nobody's gonna believe that you're a virgin." [Laughs]
I guess she had the power to say something over Steven Meisel, and they okayed it. So the idea was still to have her be a little bit punky, the BOY TOY belt, the jewelry, the corset with the fishnet over, the special jewel for the hair.

EM2O: How did she and Meisel work together?

M: She loved him because she told me that he made her look beautiful. I don't know why she would say that because she *was* beautiful. She was genuinely beautiful. I really loved when she had the big eyebrows!

EM2O: Did you know when you had *the* cover shot for *Like a Virgin*?

M: I think I remember being with Liz and looking at everything and I knew that Madonna was gonna pick the best shots. And inside the sleeve, there is a different cover, the close-up in the mirror, and the one with the blue satin sheets, which I got for the shoot. That's part of being a stylist; you've got to have *everything* on the set.

—MARIPOL

MARIPOL

They had faces then.

EM2O: When Madonna performed at the MTV Video Music Awards in that same wedding dress, where did you see it? Were you in the audience or backstage or …?

M: I was backstage; I saw it from right behind the curtain!

EM2O: Do you think Madonna was confident that it had gone well?

M: No, her manager [Freddy DeMann] was worried. First of all, she had stage fright. It was unpleasant for her because it was really difficult to come out and do this in front of the whole Radio City audience—it was either break or make. And I think it was both at the same time. I think the industry tried to break her, because MTV filmed live under her skirt with that dress, which was not really closed in the back.

Everybody is like, "Who is this young girl singing 'Like a Virgin', rolling on the stage in a wedding dress?" Oooh. Then all the press ran after us.

EM2O: What were your friendships like with Keith Haring and Martin Burgoyne? Were you as close to the boys as you were to Madonna? Was she as tight with them as with you?

M: She was closer to Martin from the beginning; he designed her first single covers. They were great guys and great artists and every relationship is different. I remember she moved from the East Village and I had friends who were moving out of a beautiful loft on Broome, so she moved in.

Back in the day, it's not like now that we go to lunch and all that. I don't remember that we really

ate a lot back then. We were all very skinny!

And she went out with my friend Jean-Michel [Basquiat]. I was closer to him than I was with her when she was going out with him.

EM2O: What were they like as a couple?

M: Sweet. Didn't last long. Three months? And after that, when he was really big and depressed sometimes, he said, "I really miss her." He wanted to see her and stuff.

EM2O: I've heard Madonna remained very loyal to Martin and Keith when they became sick with AIDS.

M: I was pregnant up to *here* when we had the last dinner that we cooked at Keith's place. He was really happy Madonna was there, and not because she was "Madonna," it was because they were close. She was already really big; it was 1990. I wanted to do something and show him love. It was at his apartment right on LaGuardia Place. We had a beautiful dinner. It was just his close friends— Kenny Scharf and his wife Tereza Scharf; Francesco and Alba Clemente; Bruno Schmidt and Carmel Johnson Schmidt; Futura and CC McGurr; Madonna; and my husband Gigi and I. I gave birth maybe a few weeks after that.

Martin, Madonna got him an apartment and was very supportive. Those days were really awful. I mean … *all* of our friends were dying. Madonna was there when he closed his eyes.

EM2O: Did Madonna talk with you at all about Marilyn Monroe when you knew her, before "Material Girl," etc.?

M: Yeah, I think Marilyn was her hero. She was taking acting classes and one day we were riding [the subway] and she said, "You know how hard it is to be a singer and an actress?" and I said, "A lot of people do both. *You* can do it."

EM2O: Where did Madonna's pink wig come from? The one in your Polaroids?

M: I had them made for Fiorucci in bright colors when I was traveling in the Orient. They were beautifully done.

EM2O: It was so unusual for her.

M: She did an English TV show wearing it. They were better than the ones on 14th Street. And also, when she moved into her Broome Street loft, she said, "I threw out everything I had … except the stuff you gave me." I would go to Tokyo and bring her stuff back.

EM2O: Your clothes were also used in "Papa Don't Preach" and "Express Yourself."

M: The black bustier [in "Papa Don't Preach"] I gave to her. It was beautiful on her. And then the other one, I was doing a line called Aqua Girl in rubber that she wore in "Express Yourself."

EM2O: You'd seen Madonna with Jellybean Benitez and Jean-Michel Basquiat and many other boyfriends. What were Madonna and Warren like together?

M: I think he was very much attracted by her, but he might have become a little

bit too possessive, and I don't think she was the type of person who could be owned like that.

EM2O: What do you consider to be the best picture you ever took of Madonna?

M: They're all good! [Laughs] But I love the one where she's drinking and smoking because that's so *not* her. The lips are like a mirror inside—they're enlarged. And the pink wig is nice.

EM2O: When did you last shoot Madonna?

M: At the last concert [*MDNA World Tour*]. I don't do only Polaroids. Apart from that, she came here [to my studio] with Guy [Oseary] when my son was two years old. I'm not saying it's the last, but it's the last Polaroid. She wanted to show Guy what was her life before. And then there was a documentary with Rupert Everett for VH1 and I was on my way to Paris then and Liz says, "You know they're doing this thing for VH1 and there's no way we can do it without a visit to you." They interviewed me and I had a plane to catch and I told the girl, "Just leave and close the door behind." Am I trusting? [Laughs]

EM2O: You and Madonna were surrounded by drug abusers, but while you experimented, you and she were never too into that scene.

M: One time she said, "You know it's so hard … all my friends do drugs," and I said, "Madonna, it's so hard not to do it because everybody wants to give it to you, but if you wanna be great, you have to be straight." Quote me on that.

EM2O: I saw a picture of you, Steve Rubell, Debi Mazar, Keith Haring, Tom Cruise, Andy Warhol and Martin Burgoyne in a car at Madonna's wedding. What happened there???

M: [Laughs] That was so funny! At the wedding, first of all we fly there together— Steve Rubell, Keith, Martin, Andy, and Andy's right-hand man, Fred Hughes.

On the day of the wedding, we still don't know where it is. I'm driving with Liz and Seymour Stein and as soon as we got the address, we're driving to Malibu and we see the helicopters. We get there and it's a big nightmare because of the helicopters—you can't even hear when they say, "I do," and Madonna's hat and veil are not holding. Everybody's clothes are flying and Sean wrote in big letters on the beach, "FUCK YOU!" [Laughs]

I made her special earrings for her wedding— she wore it. It was pearls, two gold chains with a little cross and a little moon attached at the end.

I am sitting at Madonna and Sean's table, but it's half-empty. Andy and Keith were at another table. I told Madonna that I didn't have anyone next to my chair, so she goes to Sean and whispers in his ear and Sean comes back with Tom Cruise! [Laughs] During the whole dinner, we were talking. He was really cute and smart and polite.

So it's getting a bit worse with Steve Rubell, who is on Quaaludes, so we pick him up by the pieces and then we leave, and as we're going to our limo, Tom comes up to me and says, "Can I ask you a favor? Can you please hide me in your limo? The paparazzi are right outside, and they're gonna bug me." As we get in the limo, he is ducking, and we look like we're surprised because we were being flashed by cameras.

So then we're driving in the hills in Malibu and it's foggy. I am sitting on his knee and Andy is taking pictures. Finally, Tom said, "My car is parked here, can you tell the driver to stop?" So I tell the driver and Tom took off in the fog and Keith and Andy and Martin are like, 'Why did you let him go? Why didn't you take him to the hotel?" They were more starstruck than I was. I was the one who could be doing him and I couldn't care less. [Laughs]

EM2O: Madonna and Sean seem like they met too soon. They had a volatile relationship, but they're friendly again; does that surprise you?

M: No, I'm glad it happened. She took her son to Haiti with him after the earthquake. We all mature at some point in our lives.

EM2O: Can you walk me through your merchandising deal with Madonna?

M: I was selling a lot of jewelry with Fiorucci, and I had my own store, Maripolitan, my own gallery space. Madonna was at the opening. So we signed a merchandising deal, but by that time she was popular with the movie and the videos and everybody copied my rubber bracelets and other designs. So when I was ready with this whole packaging stuff, ready for the kids, it was too late. And then she married Sean and she changed her look and she had another image.

EM2O: What did it feel like seeing so many people copying you?

M: It felt awful. I remember I walked into this factory and this distributor wanted me to make a deal with him, but he said, "You know how many billions of those bracelets we sold?" But no one was doing rubber, just horrible plastic. I lost my company at the height of my company. That was the sad part, to have to close when you're successful.

EM2O: How would you describe your relationship with Madonna now?

M: Friendly—I miss her! I don't see her often. I would love to do something with her again.

The designer in 2015

MATTHEW RETTENMUND

MARSHALL, PENNY: *b. October 15, 1943.* A household name for her role as "Laverne DeFazio" on *Laverne & Shirley* (1976–1983), Marshall became a feature-film director with hits like *Big* (1988), *Awakenings* (1990) and *The Preacher's Wife* (1996).

Marshall spent a chunk of 1991 shooting *A League of Their Own* (1992), her movie about the 1940s all-female baseball league. She chose Madonna for a role at the expense of Debra Winger, who quit in protest. She has spoken highly of Madonna's performance and **work** ethic.

Marshall told Chelsea Handler in 2012 that there was one *tone* of contention: "She was in great shape, she just came with a trainer. I said, 'You've gotta stop—your arms shouldn't be this cut in 1943. They didn't work out that much, they were in the kitchen.'"

MARTIN, RICKY: *b. December 24, 1971.* First famous as a member in one iteration of Menudo, then later as an electrifying solo star with hits like "María" (1995), "Livin' La Vida Loca" (1999) and "She Bangs" (2000). In 2010, Martin confirmed longstanding rumors that he is **gay**, instantly making him one of the most famous people ever to come out.

Martin had been introduced to Madonna prior to his career-transforming performance of "The Cup of Life" (1998) at the 1999 **Grammys**, but it was at the **awards** show that Madonna was first spotted reaching out to Martin. His debut album was in the can, but the two quickly collaborated on the album track **"Be Careful with My Heart (Cuidado Con Mi Corazón)."**

Martin later told **Oprah Winfrey** that Madonna gave him some valuable advice, telling him to stop giving interviews because he had already established his identity; Martin, exhausted from overwork and overexposure, took her words to heart.

"She's always been extremely kind and very respectful."-RICKY MARTIN ON MADONNA (2015)

MARTINEZ, BOBBY: This extra-young graffiti artist was Madonna's teen lover in the early '80s. He appears with his arm slung over her shoulder, very boyfriend/girlfriend, in her 1984 *Ear Say* interview for British **TV** that was shot in **NYC**. She apparently carried on with him throughout her relationship with **Jellybean Benitez** and into at least her engagement to **Sean Penn**. Martinez blabbed to biographer **Christopher Andersen** in 1991 about Madonna's voracious **sexual** appetite at the time, including an **orgy** in Madonna's Jacuzzi involving men and women, in which he participated. Andersen also reported that Penn "stalked" Martinez in 1986 "with a **gun**."

MASER, WAYNE: The photographer who has taken some of Madonna's most daring and abrasive portraits of the '90s. Madonna gave us Madonna chomping a stogie, posing as Christ with a crown of thorns and that stunning *Esquire* '94 cover of Madonna in a leather bikini against a giant target.

MASSOT, ONDINE: *June 20, 1949–December 6, 2013.* **Christopher Ciccone**'s teacher, Massot formed a tight bond with Madonna. Massot remembered to *Hard Copy* their time together playing dress-up and mooning over Latin lovers. Madonna stayed in touch with Massot, sending her long letters after she left for **NYC**.

Massot said Madonna had mostly male friends, "**loved** getting men's attention" and called her college dorm the "Virgin Vault."

Massot allowed *Hard Copy* to highlight some of her personal letters because, "She has given me strength during my low points of my life, I would just think about what she went through." Massot said on camera to Madonna, whom she hoped would be watching, "I just want to say hi to you, that's all, and congratulate you in person." The women did not see each other again. Massot passed away after battling **cancer**.

"MASTERPIECE": *Release date: April 2, 2012. Billboard Hot 100 peak: NA.* Touching mid-tempo number written by Madonna, Julie Frost and Jimmy Harry and produced by Madonna, **William Orbit** and Harry, that was played over the end credits of *W.E.* and was included on *MDNA*.

MEGA-FAN SPOTLIGHT: SHAUN MARTZ

Whether I was begging my mom to request "Causing a Commotion" on our local Indiana pop station or finding myself mesmerized by the "Express Yourself" music video (I was five!), Madonna has always been tied to my life. Growing up gay in the Midwest wasn't always easy, but Madonna became the soundtrack of my experiences and gave me a little extra strength and resilience. I was, and continue to be, completely transfixed by her never-ending stream of style, attitude and reinvention. And the music has always been ace. I know Madonna has taught all of her fans a few lessons here and there, but one of her earliest is perhaps the one that resonates with me most to this day: "It's called a dance floor/And here's what it's for."

MATTHEW RETTENMUND

The song is about Wallis Simpson's **love** for an untouchable figure, the Duke of Windsor.

The song won a **Golden Globe** for Best **Original** Song, much to **Elton John**'s chagrin. It was ruled ineligible for **Oscar** consideration (songs must be a part of the films in which they appear, or the first song heard in the credits; "Masterpiece" was the second), much to *Madonna's* chagrin.

It was a winning component of Madonna's *MDNA Tour*.

MASTURBATION: Madonna mock-abused herself so unabashedly during her *Blond Ambition World Tour* performance of **"Like a Virgin"** that Toronto authorities threatened to arrest her. They backed down, and Madonna jerked all the way to the bank.

At the 11th Annual **MTV Video Music Awards,** Aerosmith's Steve Tyler was presented with the Best Video of the Year **award** by Madonna. Holding up his index and middle fingers, he queried his band mate, "Why do you suppose Madonna uses these two fingers to masturbate with?" The answer: "Because they're mine." Madonna giggled and retorted that that wouldn't be masturbating, it'd be **"sexual abuse."** They were just joshing and the audience ate it up.

MATERIAL GIRL (CLOTHING LINE): In a prime example of "if you can't beat 'em, join 'em," Madonna and her daughter **Lola** launched a teen **fashion** brand in 2010, calling it Material Girl. It's the perfect name, of course, but what about Madonna's contempt for that label? "Oh, please, that was like a hundred years ago—I'm so sick of being called the Material Girl," she pouted in 1998 ... quite rightly, since the press lazily calls her by that name in nearly every article published. But smart enough to realize it was a prefab brand, Madonna gave her blessing to its use while Lola **worked** on ideas with pro designers.

Material Girl was debuted at a pink-carpet event at Macy's (151 W. 34th St., NY, NY) on September 22, 2010. **Mother** and daughter met the press, then hosted a **dance** party inside the store, an event notable as the place where Madonna met her longtime boyfriend **Brahim Zaibat,** who was one of the dancers.

Welcoming the **fans** lucky enough to gain access, Madonna joked, "So, um, I guess I should just confess that I did all of this just as an **excuse** to go shopping."

The line has been a success, but led to a lawsuit by LA Triumph, which has held a registered trademark to "Material Girl" in the clothing category since 1997; the outcome of that suit is pending.

Material Girl has used a succession of famous young female faces as spokesmodels: George May Jagger (**Mick Jagger**'s daughter), Taylor Momsen, **Kelly Osbourne**, Rita Ora (of whom Madonna said, "What really drew us to her is the confidence she oozes through her music and her unique sense of style") and Zendaya. When Zendaya was selected, she summed up what must have been the feeling of the other young stars who'd preceded her: "Madonna knows who I am, that's all I need!"

Madonna has said, "A Material Girl is someone who's interested in fashion and interested in music and interested in fun and has a sense of humor—an adventurous human being."

"MATERIAL GIRL" (SONG): *Release date: November 30, 1984. Billboard Hot 100 peak: #2.* The second single from *Like a Virgin* launched a **nickname** that has followed Madonna in virtually every article written about her. The fact that she's gone from **rich** to *obscenely* rich doesn't help shake the image, which itself resonated sharply with the yuppie mentality so prevalent in the '80s.

The song was written by Peter Brown and Robert Rans, and was produced by **Nile Rodgers**. Its bass line is very similar to "Can You Feel It" by the Jacksons (1980).

The public reception of this song—though extra-positive—may be the earliest example of people not "getting" Madonna, as she has often complained; "Material Girl" is widely misinterpreted as an unabashed ode to wealth along the lines of Calloway's "I Wanna Be Rich" (1989). Quite the contrary; the song is a send-up of gold diggers.

True materialism is the absolute antithesis of Madonna. Madonna is about take-no-prisoners self-reliance, and material girls are about lazy dependence. The first clue that "Material Girl" isn't serious is Madonna's vocal, a forced chirp made even more hilarious by several excited hiccups.

In spite of the mixed signals people receive from the song and Madonna's dislike for it, it has become a staple of her tours, finding representation on *The Virgin Tour* (she threw out phony **Madonna money** at the end), the *Who's That Girl World Tour,* the *Blond Ambition World Tour* and the *Re-Invention World Tour*. Snippets were heard on *The MDNA Tour.* In 2010, Madonna repurposed the name for her clothing line. By 2015, she called it her least fave Madonna song, saying, "I never want to hear it again." So of course she performed it months later on her *Rebel Heart Tour.*

"Apparently, Madonna doesn't limit her financial affairs to old money." —JAMES HUNTER, RECORD (1985)

Dressing us up with her love at the Macy's Material Girl clothing line launch in 2010

ALEJANDRO MOGOLLO

"MATERIAL GIRL" (VIDEO): *Director: Mary Lambert, 1985.* The first video that proved Madonna was not just a sensation, but had the potential to be a star. "She is a star, George," as actor Keith Carradine, playing a Howard Hughes type, tells his gofer, played by Robert Wuhl, in a brief preamble to the video.

In "Material Girl," Madonna's turn as **Marilyn Monroe**—in a restaging of the "Diamonds are a Girl's Best Friend" sequence from the Howard Hawks film *Gentlemen Prefer **Blondes*** (1953)— is completely credible. In fact, Madonna's cool enough not only to play Monroe, but to *correct her* by showing that being a material girl is empty.

In the video—which was shot by **Mary Lambert** on January 11, 1985, after Jean-Paul Goude fell through—an enigmatic artist character, played by Carradine, obsesses over how to win the Madonna character's heart. He overhears that she is unimpressed by the 14 karat **gifts** bestowed upon her by other suitors while she tells a friend on the phone about one bauble, "Yeah, he thinks he can impress me by giving me expensive gifts. It's nice, though ... You want it?" Carradine eventually wins her over by taking her for a ride in a jalopy he buys off an old man, and by handing her a humble bouquet. In the end, we see them kissing beyond the truck's rain-streaked windshield. ("I **loved** that truck in the video," Carradine told *Empire*. "I would have liked to have kept it.")

This storyline is intercut with splashy performance sequences of Madonna reinventing the Monroe scene, which were choreographed by Kenny Ortega, who **worked** with **Michael Jackson** and later directed the *High **School** Musical* (2006–2008) movies for Disney.

The setting is so carefully evoked that the hot-pink gown Madonna wears was copied exactly from designer (Bill) Travilla's **original**, which led him to tell *People* **magazine**, "To paraphrase Madonna ... I've been knocked off for the very first time." But Madonna's character is very different from **Marilyn**'s, even before she decides that love trumps lucre. Madonna directs the fawning millionaires around her, taking charge in a way that the merely gold-digging Monroe character never could have—Madonna uses her animal magnetism not to dig gold, but to pick pockets!

"Material Girl" is about a lot more than greed. It's about independence and true love, two of the most consistently recurring themes in Madonna's work. The video is also about superstardom, which Madonna assumed as soon as it hit **MTV**. "Material Girl" earned Madonna her first *TV Guide* cover, illustrating an article on how to tell good videos (like this one) from bad.

If you find Madonna's playful interaction with the male **dancers** particularly charming, director Mary Lambert tells *EM20* it's with good reason: "Madonna loves working with her dancers and she always creates a family. She works them hard and expects perfection, but they adore her and she returns the love. She loves to dance and the joy spills over into the choreography and the personal relationships."

Speaking of dancers, **Taylor Swift**'s "Shake It Off" **MTV Video Music Awards** performance in 2014 was a hat tip to the "Material Girl" video; Lambert noted the similarity and humbly said she was "flattered."

"I have always been extremely interested in Marilyn Monroe—her life and persona. Madonna and I shared that fascination. I watched the dance sequence from *Gentlemen Prefer Blondes* about a million times with Kenny Ortega, who brilliantly reinterpreted it for the film. 'Material Girl' was my first collaboration with costume designer Marlene Stewart, who brilliantly reinterpreted the dress. If you have a very specific vision in mind, work with talented people, that's my advice."—MARY LAMBERT (2015)

MATERIAL GIRLS: *Director: Martha Coolidge. Release date: August 18, 2006.* This **Maverick** Films coproduction starring Hilary and Haylie Duff became one of the worst-reviewed films of all time, with a 4% rating from Rotten-Tomatoes.com. In the film, ditzy heiresses try to save the empire of their **father**, who is credited with "creating Madonna's first look. And then her second and third **looks**."

MAVERICK: In 1992, as part of a massive deal with **Warner Bros.**, Madonna earned her own record label, Maverick Records. It was not a vanity project. She became actively involved in scouting and signing new acts, which directly led to her **business** relationship and personal bond with upstart **Guy Oseary**, who would eventually become her manager.

Though Echobelly and Hole (ask **Courtney Love**) were the fish that got away, Maverick more than made up for it by signing **Alanis Morissette**, who has gone on to sell over 60 million albums, including over 30 million of her *Jagged Little Pill*. Other Maverick artists have included: Michelle Branch, Candlebox, the Deftones, Ebba Forsberg, Erasure, Jude Christodal, **Love** Spit Love, Lucy Nation, **Meshell Ndegeocello**, Neurotic Outsiders, **No Authority**, the Prodigy, Rule 62, the Rentals, Summercamp and UNV. The label released soundtracks to such films as *The **Wedding** Singer* (1998), *Austin Powers: The Spy Who Shagged Me* (1999) and *The Matrix* (1999).

In 2000, Maverick announced a Latin music division run by Bruno del Granado, a prominent music-biz figure who would go on to manage **Ricky Martin** for a decade.

Asked if she were looking for "another Madonna," Madonna's reply to **Jonathan Ross** in 1992 was, "I don't think that's possible." She spoke proudly of Maverick, including showing up at an August 1995 KISS-FM concert with her **dog** Chiquita to introduce UNV.

Maverick Pictures concerned itself with **TV** and movie ventures.

MAVERICK

MATTHEW RETTENMUND

Mazar attends an *MDNA Tour* Blu-ray event in 2013.

"I was always trying to pluck her eyebrows—they're caterpillars." -DEBI MAZAR (2013)

In 2003, Madonna was interviewed in her Maverick office in LA. She said, "I live down the street. I like having a company, I like coming here and spending time with my manager, **Caresse [Henry].**"

A lawsuit in 2004 led to Madonna's departure from the company. Currently, Maverick Records is an inactive part of Warner Bros. Records. However, Oseary is still CEO of the umbrella Maverick Entertainment; his business as the manager of Madonna, Alicia Keys, U2 and others is conducted under the Maverick brand.

MAZAR, DEBI: *b. August 13, 1964.* First a makeup artist ("Debi M."), scrupulously browed, Queens-born Mazar segued into **acting** with roles in **Spike Lee** films before gaining a foothold on **TV** in *Entourage* (2004–2011) and the **ageism** dramedy *Younger* (2015–).

Mazar is one of Madonna's oldest and dearest girlfriends, stretching **back** to their days as downtown scenesters. Mazar **worked** at **Fiorucci**, so knew **Maripol**, and she was a club regular, so it was only a matter of time before she'd bump into Madonna.

Of their very first encounter, Mazar recalled to *Madonna Rising* in 1998 that she asked, "So, like, what do you do?" and Madonna said haughtily, "I'm makin' a record." Mazar didn't believe her.

That encounter sounded a lot livelier when she recalled it in 2013:

"I was in **Danceteria**, working the elevator. She came into my elevator, and a great song was spinning and she goes, 'Hey, you wanna **dance**?' And I was like, 'Yeah!' And I parked the elevator, and we had a great dance together and then later on we danced some more. She wasn't, like, a big star yet. She was just a girl from Detroit who had a real raw **sexuality.** From there on we became pals and started dancing and hanging out. I was doing makeup then, and so I did her makeup for years. She was like, 'I'm gonna be a star one day,' and I was like, 'Great!'"

Along with painting Madonna's face from the time of the **"Everybody"** video right through the *Who's That Girl World Tour*, Mazar attended Madonna's **wedding** to **Sean Penn** (where she caught some of Steve Rubell's vomit on her dress) and appeared in the videos for **"Papa Don't Preach," "True Blue," "Justify My Love," "Deeper and Deeper"** and **"Music."**

In spite of their closeness, Mazar has not worked with Madonna in forever. "We're good friends, and not working together was the best thing we ever did. Two Leo women,

debi m.

Mazar in 1984 at Danceteria

one working for the other? Forget it!" she truth-joked in 1993. Even though she wasn't on the clock, she *did* give Rocco his first haircut.

Mazar is beloved by Madonna's **fans.** Seeing her alongside Madonna (done up in a leather bustier at the *Sex* launch party in 1992, hanging with her at the premiere of *Malcolm X* in 1992, supporting the Blu-ray release of Madonna's *MDNA World Tour* in 2013) makes Madonna's fans feel as good as the agelessly stunning Mazar looks.

MCARTHUR, ALEX: *b. March 6, 1957.* Lanky, **sexy** dude who played Madonna's Romeo in the underage-and-**pregnant** saga captured by the **"Papa Don't Preach"** video. He's the one her **father** warned her all about, and his baby blues certainly make a good case for teen pregnancy.

Madonna chose the former **Studio 54** bartender for the role after seeing him in the lesbian romance *Desert Hearts* (1985). McArthur has said, "I was in my garage **working** on my **motorcycle** when the phone rang. I answered the call and a **voice** said, 'Hi, this is Madonna, and I would like you to be in my next video.' She's sweet, yet very professional, and I was impressed with the fact that she knows exactly what she wants."

Madonna called her costar a "tremendously gifted yet unaffected actor."

MCCARTNEY, STELLA: *b. September 13, 1971.* The daughter of Paul McCartney and his late wife Linda, McCartney is a successful clothing designer who Madonna sought out when McCartney was still a college student. Becoming fast friends, they have hung out privately and publicly on many occasions.

McCartney, who is against the wearing of fur, has expressed anger over Madonna's continued wearing of the stuff. "I've been **working** on Madonna's honky ass for a very long time. Her thing is she won't wear anything she doesn't

RHONDA CORTE

eat. But the other day she was wearing this coat made from baby lambs that haven't even been born," she vented in 2001.

McCartney has dressed Madonna countless times, including designing her **wedding** gown, providing some costumes for the *Re-Invention World Tour* and lending Madonna her gorgeous dress for the 2011 **Met Ball** (a frock in which Madonna admitted to feeling "fat").

McCartney (in a **"Material Girl"** costume) and **Gwyneth Paltrow** (in a *Blond Ambition World Tour* bustier look) provided a videotaped intro to Madonna on the occasion of her induction into the **UK Music Hall of Fame**.

MCDEAN, CRAIG: *b. 1964.* British **fashion** photographer whose **commercial** work led to fashion and celebrity portraiture. McDean shot Madonna for her October 2002 *Vanity Fair* cover and did the packaging shoot for *American Life*. The image of Madonna on the cover of that album has been compared to Patty Hearst and Che Guevara.

MCFADDEN, CYNTHIA: *b. May 27, 1956.* Likeable **TV** journalist who has **worked** her way through various marquee media outlets, including *Entertainment Tonight* (2007–2010) and *Nightline* (2001–2014). She is a close friend of Madonna-lovin' journalist **Liz Smith**, and both were tight with screen legend **Katharine Hepburn**; McFadden wound up as one of Hepburn's executors.

Trusted by Madonna's camp to be fair, McFadden has been granted several sit-down interviews with Madonna, in 2004, 2005 and at **Cannes** in 2008. That last meeting only happened because Madonna jostled her schedule in order to accommodate McFadden's; that's how desirable she is as an interrogator.

Most famously, it was McFadden who skillfully teased the word **"reductive"** out of Madonna in a line of questioning about **Lady Gaga** in 2012.

MCGOVERN, ELIZABETH: *b. July 18, 1961.* The *Downton Abbey* (2010–) actor tsk-tsked Madonna's decision to pose topless at age 56 in 2014, telling the UK's *Daily Mail Weekend*, "It smacks of trying to be younger in an attempt to be **sexy**. That, to me, is the road to nowhere. There's something fantastic about being in your fifties and being sexy at that age, rather than trying to come across as a sexy 20-year-old."

Did we mention that, in 1985, **Sean Penn** broke off his two-year relationship with McGovern immediately before beginning his relationship with Madonna?

MCGRATH, MARK: *b. March 15, 1968.* The lead singer of '90s rock band Sugar Ray, noted for their hits "Fly" (1997) and "Every Morning" (1999). McGrath later became a co-host of the entertainment show *Extra* (2004–2008).

McGrath was reported to have had a fling with Madonna, but in 2014, he told **Wendy Williams** he'd merely met her at a party in 1999 and walked her to her car, giving her a kiss on the cheek. "So if that's sleeping with Madonna, I slept with Madonna." He admitted he perpetuated the rumor at the time.

Of course, his story doesn't cover the fact that they were photographed together more than once that year, nor does "a kiss on the cheek" really sum up just how in heat he looked in video footage outside that fateful party.

MCKENZIE, MICHAEL: *b. 1953.* Downtown artist, photographer and writer who shot Madonna in 1980 for a portfolio entitled *Androgyny* (she had short **hair** at that moment). McKenzie then created the **"Androgyny Cabaret,"** a show, and published the **books** *Lucky Star* (1985) and *Madonna: The Early Days* (1993). The latter is a reprint of the former with a previously unseen cover photo and collector's print of that image, entitled "Madonna in My Robe."

MCLAREN, MALCOLM: *January 22, 1946–April 8, 2010.* Avant-garde British artist who tried his hand at everything from **fashion** merchandising to pop music. As the manager of the **Sex** Pistols, he was the one who brought Johnny Rotten into the group.

In 1987, just a few years before Madonna's **"Vogue"** would follow McLaren's 1989 "Deep in Vogue" (with its early **William Orbit** production/remixing credit) into pop history as the first two songs about **vogueing**, he told *Tatler* of Madonna's initial impact, "The most wonderful thing was that **crucifix** that swung across her navel and the way you would see 10-year-old girls in **New York** and LA being sexually provocative in imitation of her. But the very best thing about her is that that is her real name."

MDNA: *Release date: March 23, 2012. Billboard 200 peak: #1.* In light of *Hard Candy*, considered by many to be Madonna's worst (okay, *least good*) album, some **fans** feared that Madonna was beginning to phone it in after so many years of musical supremacy. For every sign that she was still driving things (she seemed fully present on her *Sticky & Sweet Tour*), there would be other signs that she might be more interested in backing away from music. Who could blame her? Radio programmers had made it clear she was old news, and a chunk of her fan base is so jaded it seems to pre-reject anything she comes up with.

After her longest time between studio albums, Madonna returned and seemed semi-convincingly engaged on *MDNA*, an album that wins the title of her most divisive ever—some found it to be her best effort since the '90s, others found it scattered.

Madonna teamed up with EDM **gods** Alle & **Benny Benassi** and **Martin Solveig**, plus her old *Ray of Light* collaborator **William Orbit** ("We've **worked** on stuff for so many years that we kind of finish each other's sentences. He knows my taste and what I like ... Magic happens when we get into a recording studio together") on the schizophrenic album. It could fairly be called a **hot mess**, but hot messes are still, after all, *hot*.

—NADYA GINSBURG

Some of Madonna's critics like to call her "desperate," but her desperation is what made this album rock to the extent that it does, what made it push into new territory while still serving as a reinforcement of her 30-year-old brand. Madonna's desperation was and is a helpful desperation to be taken seriously, to have and to cause fun, to make people squirm, to provoke thought. In other words, Madonna demonstrated on *MDNA* that she'd never lost the artistic neediness that defines all creators and that almost invariably evaporates after so many creative cycles.

MDNA didn't have the introductory boldness of ***Madonna***, nor did it forge an entirely new sonic path as did *Ray of Light*, nor did it flaunt the impeccable consistency of ***Confessions on a Dance Floor***, but it radiated knowledge alongside an equal dose of unabashed hedonism.

"Girl Gone Wild" opens the album with a sarcastic act of contrition that sounds more defiant than despondent. It is a song perfect for a divorcée in her dirty thirties (or 53 in Madonna years). It also kicks off a dizzying series of self-referential lyrics and themes (especially those religious

ones) by managing to sound almost identical to **"Sorry"** and **"Celebration"** in patches. The lyric "girls, they just wanna have some fun" led some listeners to note a nod to **Cyndi Lauper**, but interestingly, Lauper changed the **original** dirty meaning of songwriter Robert Hazard's work to make her version a neo-**feminist** anthem. Madonna returned it to the brothel. Madonna, or the character "Madonna," throbs with recently unrepressed des-i-i-i-i-ire, a feeling that slams right into the listener over and over, like a Newton's cradle on a businessman's desk eternally passing energy.

"Gang Bang" starts with a flourish before immediately plunging into a relentless bass line. This song sounds spontaneous and exciting, but it was never going to win any **awards** for its sheer poetry. No matter. Giddy in its function as a techno-rant, the song uncoils with an intentionally humorous, dark intensity reminiscent of a Quentin Tarantino flick—hell hath no fury like a woman scorned, especially if the **bitch** has access to firearms. What should be a self-indulgent mess winds up being a far more convincing and fresher take on a previous song like **"Runaway Lover."** The singer's contempt is visceral, made all the spookier by the gravelly delivery and that long, eerie denouement filled with gleeful proclamations of hell-bound violence. This wild track is the best revenge song ever, reminding one of the songs on *1000 Fires* by Traci Lords (1995) and sounding like a song Divine should have sung.

After two songs devoted to abandon, rebellion and reactive retribution, **"I'm Addicted"** is an undisguised **love** song awash in a synth sensory overload. The beginning could be Yaz.

Calming down, the album gives up its first sweet treat in the form of **"Turn Up the Radio,"** which has all the sugar of **"Don't Stop"** but an anthemic quality that earned it its status as a single.

"Give Me All Your Luvin'" feat. Nicki Minaj and **M.I.A.**—Madonna's least adored lead single since **"American Life"**—makes so much more sense in the context of the album than it did as a first (and therefore implicitly best) single. It could be Madonna's ode to the '60s surfer sound, a far more Go-Go's or Toni Basil vibe than fans ever thought she'd embrace, and a continuation of the positivity begun by "Turn Up the Radio." Guests/cowriters **Nicki Minaj** and **M.I.A.** give it everything they've got.

"Some Girls" perfects the braggadocio of *Hard Candy*'s **"Candy Shop,"** brassily listing the types of girls Madonna is not ("Fake tits and a nasty mood" ... okay, then!) and asserting that, "I'm better than you ever **dreamed** of." The music is electrifying, sounds unlike any past Madonna songs and more than makes up for the pile of lyrical clichés that distracts, though never to the point of ruination, throughout. As for past works referenced, you don't get much more blatant than "like a virgin, sweet and clean" or "some girls are second best" (as in, don't go for them, baby).

Every album has filler, so say hello to **"Superstar,"** which features **Lola** on backing vocals (making it sort of like an

ALEJANDRO MOGOLLO

adolescent **"Little Star"**), a nonetheless pleasing and convincing romp that names real-life men to communicate its story: Marlon Brando, Abraham Lincoln, Michael Jordan, Al Capone, Julius Caesar, Bruce Lee, John Travolta and James Dean.

"I Don't Give A" is this album's **"Nobody Knows Me,"** an initially off-putting song with a quickly addictive rap and nakedly personal lyrics about all the hardest parts of being not only a single working mom but being Madonna.

"I'm a Sinner" soars, lyrically both light and engaging. Madonna's girlish vocal is lovely, as is the retro feel. Like "Girl Gone Wild," this tune plays on notions of sin and redemption. But unlike that brazen song, "I'm a Sinner" is about shrugging and accepting one's transgressive urges rather than shoving them down any throat that comes near.

"Love Spent" is one of the album's most special moments, an immediate addition to the very best Madonna's ever written or sung. It opens with a banjo and strings, like an affair between **"Don't Tell Me"** and **"Papa Don't Preach."** Leave it to half-billionaire Madonna to write a **love** song about **money**.

When *W.E.* was released, fans got a taste of **"Masterpiece."** The song comes closer to masterpiece status than did the film; it is a lilting, mid-tempo ballad featuring beautiful vocals and an earnest sense of love and loss, or if not loss, at least the fear of it.

As comfortably warm as "Masterpiece" is, it suffers being sandwiched between "Love Spent" and **"Falling Free,"** the latter of which sounds like Simon & Garfunkel and showcases Madonna's too-often underrated (sometimes by Madonna herself) **voice**.

The bonus tracks begin with **"Beautiful Killer,"** but it's a head-scratcher as to why Madonna didn't want this on the regular album. It's not only an earworm (with a faint echo of **"Die Another Day"**) but stylistically unique from the many club-friendly tracks that pave its way. A rollicking pop-rock song devoted to Alain Delon that manages to use Madonna's whisper to great effect in a way we're not used to experiencing.

"I Fucked Up" sounded like it might be painful to sit through based on its title alone, but it turned out to be a pretty, self-effacing admission of wrongdoing by a woman who notoriously has "absolutely no **regrets**."

"B-Day Song" may be unfairly maligned, but it seems to be a far more charming take on the sound explored out of nowhere on "Give Me All Your Luvin'," if nothing else. Gotta love that Madonna wrote a song about her **birthday** being a positive thing, knowing that critics would likely be trashing her for her age in reviews.

With **"Best Friend,"** Madonna offers another relationship post-mortem, but still manages to bring new observations to the table (before getting up and dancing on it), namely, themes about male/female **power**-sharing.

The "Give Me All Your Luvin'" Party Rock Remix is annoying and unnecessary; does it really count?

MDNA sold only about 2 million copies worldwide. Yet it spawned the massively successful *MDNA Tour* and it could

MDNA (1-12)

MDNA: Deluxe Bonus
Edition (1-17)

① **"Girl Gone Wild"**
(Madonna/Jenson
Vaughan/Alle Benassi/
Benny Benassi)—3:43,
produced by Madonna/Alle
Benassi/Benny Benassi

② **"Gang Bang"**
(Madonna/William Orbit/
Priscilla Renae/Keith
Harris/Jean-Baptiste/
Mika/Don Juan Demacio
"Demo" Casanova/Stephen
Kozmeniuk)—5:26, produced by Madonna/William
Orbit/The Demolition Crew

③ **"I'm Addicted"**
(Madonna/Alle Benassi/
Benny Benassi)—4:33,
produced by Madonna/Alle
Benassi/Benny Benassi/
The Demolition Crew

④ **"Turn Up the Radio"**
(Madonna/Martin Solveig/
Michael Tordjman/Jade
Williams)—3:46,
produced by Madonna/
Martin Solveig

⑤ **"Give Me All Your Luvin'"**
feat. Nicki Minaj
and M.I.A.
(Madonna/Martin Solveig/
Nicki Minaj/M.I.A./
Michael Tordjman)—3:22,
produced by Madonna/
Martin Solveig

⑥ **"Some Girls"**
(Madonna/William Orbit/
Klas Åhlund)—3:53,
produced by Madonna/William Orbit/ Klas Åhlund

⑦ **"Superstar"**
(Madonna/Hardy "Indigo"
Muanza/Michael
Malih)—3:55, produced by
Madonna/Hardy "Indiigo"
Muanza/Michael Malih

⑧ **"I Don't Give A"**
feat. Nicki Minaj
(Madonna/Martin Solveig/
Nicki Minaj/Julien
Jabre)—4:19, produced by
Madonna/Martin Solveig

⑨ **"I'm a Sinner"**
(Madonna/William Orbit/
Jean-Baptiste)—4:52,
produced by Madonna/
William Orbit

①⓪ **"Love Spent"**
(Madonna/William Orbit/
Jean-Baptiste/Priscilla
Renae/Alain Whyte/Ryan
Buendia/Michael McHenry)
—3:46, produced by
Madonna/William Orbit/
Free School

①① **"Masterpiece"**
(Madonna/Julie Frost/
Jimmy Harry)—3:59,
produced by Madonna/
William Orbit/Jimmy Harry

①② **"Falling Free"**
(Madonna/Laurie Mayer/
William Orbit/Joe Henry)
—5:13, produced by
Madonna/William Orbit

①③ **"Beautiful Killer"**
(Madonna/Martin Solveig/
Michael Tordjman)—3:49,
produced by Madonna/
Martin Solveig

①④ **"I Fucked Up"**
(Madonna/Martin Solveig/
Julien Jabre)—3:29,
produced by Madonna/
Martin Solveig

①⑤ **"B-Day Song"**
feat. M.I.A.
(Madonna/M.I.A./Martin
Solveig)—3:33,
produced by Madonna/
Martin Solveig

①⑥ **"Best Friend"**
(Madonna/Alle Benassi/
Benny Benassi)—3:20,
produced by Madonna/The
Demolition Crew/Benny
Benassi/Alle Benassi

①⑦ **"Give Me All Your Luvin'"**
Party Rock Remix feat.
LMFAO and Nicki Minaj
(Madonna/Martin Solveig/
Nicki Minaj/M.I.A./
Michael Tordjman)—4:02,
produced by Madonna/
Martin Solveig/LMFAO

fairly be said that it helped bring Madonna **back** into the ballpark of paying attention to detail, a trait fans missed on *Hard Candy*, and which she would display fully on her latter-day masterpiece, *Rebel Heart*. If Madonna was coming back around creatively (one of her collaborators, William Orbit, would disagree—he infamously vented online that Madonna was too busy with other **businesses**), promotionally she dramatically checked out: Aside from a few appearances, Madonna largely let the album sing for itself.

—CHARLES BUSCH

The album **art** was shot by **Mert and Marcus**, and was exquisitely tiled, recalling the work of Erwin Blumenfeld and giving Madonna's iconic visage a look at once tranquil and unbreakable. The album did the same for her, representing a record Madonna made to please herself and around which to build a live show; as all over the place as this album is, it doesn't feel like the woman whose name is on it second-guessed a moment.

"… MADONNA SHOWS THAT, AT 53, SHE IS STILL IN A LEAGUE OF HER OWN WHEN IT COMES TO PRODUCING EUPHORIC HIGHS ON THE DANCE FLOOR."-CHUCK ARNOLD, *PEOPLE* (2012)

"THERE'S SOMETHING REMARKABLE ABOUT MADONNA'S DECISION TO SHARE HER SUFFERING THE WAY SHE ONCE SHARED HER PLEASURE. HER MUSIC HAS ALWAYS BEEN ABOUT LIBERATION FROM OPPRESSION, BUT FOR THE FIRST TIME THE OPPRESSION IS INTERNAL: LOSS AND SADNESS. STARS—THEY REALLY ARE JUST LIKE US …"-JOE LEVY, *ROLLING STONE* (2012)

"LARGE CHUNKS OF *MDNA* ARE SHOCKINGLY BANAL, COMING ACROSS NOT SO MUCH AS BAD POP SONGS PER SE, BUT AS DRABLY COMPETENT TUNES BETTER SUITED TO D-LIST MADONNA WANNABES."-MATTHEW PERPETUA, *PITCHFORK* (2012)

"LOVE, LIKE CLUB ANTHEMS, PUBLIC OPINION AND LUCK, DOES CYCLE THROUGH YOUR SYSTEM LIKE A DRUG. WHATEVER MADONNA WAS ON HAS WORN OFF BY NOW, BUT A STAR THIS FEROCIOUSLY FOCUSED ON WHAT'S NEXT CAN ALWAYS POP ANOTHER."-CARYN GANZ, *SPIN* (2012)

"… [S]HE DOES HAVE THE AGGRESSIVE NICKI MINAJ GROWLING, 'THERE'S ONLY ONE QUEEN, AND THAT'S MADONNA, BITCH.' REGARDLESS OF THE ENDORSEMENT, IT MIGHT BEHOOVE HER TO START THINKING OF HER SUCCESSOR. THEN AGAIN, ELIZABETH I NEVER NAMED HERS, EITHER."-MICHAEL ROFFMAN, *TIME* (2012)

"ALL I'LL SAY IS THAT *MDNA* WAS A VERY, VERY DIFFERENT PROCESS IN ALL RESPECTS TO THAT WHICH WE'D EMPLOYED ON *RAY OF LIGHT*—FROM ARTISTICALLY TO TIME MANAGEMENT TO TECHNICAL APPROACH. I'LL LET YOU BE THE JUDGE OF THE RESULT, BUT IT WAS A VERY DIFFERENT BEAST TO *RAY OF LIGHT*."

-WILLIAM ORBIT, *OFFICIAL CHARTS* (2015)

MDNA TOUR, THE: *Show dates: May 31, 2012–December 22, 2012.* Increasingly, age is brought up a *lot* when discussing Madonna, but how about addressing it from a different angle: How many 54-year-old artists in 2012 were still pushing the envelope, growing and taking new risks in their **work** after being on top of their game for 30 years? Madonna, who was in a position to do and sing anything she wanted, did just that, with no regard for ruffling feathers. That is bad-ass. That was *The MDNA Tour*.

Madonna's darkest-ever tour, at times delving into a much more committed take on SM than her past **flirtations** with the topic, begrudgingly offered some classic hits of yesteryear while focusing on many tracks from *MDNA*. The **bitch** was not only out of order, she was apparently without a watch—Madonna routinely hit the stage two or more hours later than the advertised start time of 8PM, so that not only was the content challenging, just seeing the show became a feat of endurance as well.

While *The MDNA Tour* was a tour to be admired rather than clutched to the heart and **loved**, it was nonetheless an overwhelming piece of theater. It was intelligent, unpredictable (something hard for Madonna to do when she'd seemingly done *everything* already, some things more than once) and artful. Madonna seemed right at home.

Few artists have really attempted Madonna's touring template of a massive show broken into themed units, and no artist has matched her, but *The MDNA Tour*'s sections seemed less arbitrary than did some at her past shows. Rather, the show felt like one cohesive rumination on a relationship, and it's pretty hard not to imagine it was borne of Madonna's failed marriage to **Guy Ritchie**.

Whatever Guy did to her, judging from the mood of *The MDNA Tour*, the dude needs to be arrested—Madonna's stage persona communicated not just hurt feelings, but devastation, which made for a fascinating couple of hours. It can be hard to think of Madonna as vulnerable; that's due to the strength she emanates as a woman and as an artist. But even "Smaug," the dragon from Tolkien's *The Hobbit* (1937), had a chink in his armor, and Madonna's seems, over and over, to be love.

"It's a journey …," Madonna explained at the time *The MDNA Tour* was launching. "The first section of the show is like watching a movie, and then the second section of the show is like a Busby Berkeley musical, right? And then, the third section of the show is like a cabaret, very French, **fashion**, androgynous kind of **sexy**/erotic, right? Intimate. Then, the fourth show is just … celebration."

The MDNA Tour—and its first section, *Transgression*—opened with a prolonged religious chant called "Virgin Mary" by Basque group Kalakan. **Powered** by black-robed monks and an ominously swinging censer that was beyond spectacular, the opening left **fans** almost miserable with a desire for her to appear.

Especially as seen from the golden triangle, a VIP fan area **controlled** by Madonna's management, the opening really did a number on ticket-holders. If you had a Madonna tattoo, you were in. Otherwise, you needed to prove yourself worthy of being close enough to get splashed by Madonna's holy water.

Madonna's always good at ratcheting up anticipation, going so far as to write the word into many of her songs. Her eventual appearance from behind a scrim (***Who's That Girl World Tour***, anyone?), black-veiled, under a gold crown, sporting an automatic weapon, was just about orgasm-inducing.

Launching into a rousing **"Girl Gone Wild,"** Madonna showed off the fact that she would not be slowing down her dancing for the tour, even if it meant lip-synching the first proper song. In spite of challenging choreography, she maintained an alarmingly perfect look, right down to her pristine Hilary Duff updo. Dancing her ass off in heels, Madonna was supported by her male **dancers**, all sporting the same heels in the style of Kazaky, the dance troupe who had joined Madonna in her music video for the song.

"I force everyone to go outside their comfort zones," she said of her dancers in 2013. "So straight boys wear high heels. And **gay** boys have to, you know, man up! I think it's important for everybody to understand that they're playing characters when they come into my realm and that they're telling stories."

She then segued into **"Revolver,"** bringing the **gun**-filled *Celebration* tune to life with an all-girl pack of sharp shooters. Making use of her extensive catwalk, the star of the show was able to get up close and personal—it was point-blank Madonna. The song featured a larger-than-life Lil' Wayne projection duetting with the diva, and also led to controversy thanks to her repeated aiming of her stage firearms at the audience, which didn't go over well in areas that had recently suffered from gun violence.

"Gang Bang" wound up as one of the most cinematic bits Madonna had ever done on stage, an instant classic. The over-the-top theatricality more than made up for the harshness of seeing her pretend to blow people away. It's been said before, but the Tarantino vibe was hard to miss as Madonna scaled a wall in a stylized motel set using a cross that doubled as a mini-ladder. Climbing the metaphorical stairway to heaven while her lover gets ready for a trip to hell?

"Papa Don't Preach" appeared in a truncated but faithful version that was a welcome relief for casual fans not wild about hearing only music made from 2010 on.

It led into **"Hung Up"**—a joyous, bubbly dance tune **reinvented** as a cold, bondage-induced complaint. Seeing Madonna strung up by her terrorist-chic dancers hammered home the point of being restricted and controlled, but sacrificed the spirit of the **original** song in favor of continuing with the tour's themes. Madonna was put through her paces, trying her *foot* at ziplining, only to fall gracefully (and on purpose) and then be dragged across the stage in a fiery flourish.

"I Don't Give A" became the second song with a projected duet partner, this time **Nicki Minaj**. Madonna sang it just as it appeared on her album, strumming along with her **guitar**. It provided a hilarious moment—and levity was needed!—for Madonna to stare imperiously at her subjects when Minaj uttered the line, "There's only one queen, and that's Madonna … *bitch*." Madonna's false exit led to a reemergence on a pedestal, being lifted skyward toward a giant cross, bathed in red light. She seemed to be offering herself up to fate, the ultimate in not giving a [fill in the blank].

Madonna had done gas masks to perfection on her ***Drowned World Tour***, but they were welcomed **back** on a busy mix of **"Best Friend"** and **"Heartbeat."** This video interlude, primarily made up of images of grave markers, was upstaged by Madonna's hard-workin' dancers, who ignored the limits of their various joints and sockets. The final image on the screen? "Love is above all," paving the way for the second act, *Prophecy*.

In a tasteful majorette costume that nonetheless drew scads of criticism from the youth police (and even from fan **Kylie Minogue**), Madonna pranced out to **"Express Yourself,"** changing the mood entirely. The backdrops

Among other critics, Kylie didn't love Madonna's cheerleader getup.

MATTHEW RETTENMUND

MATTHEW RETTENMUND

were giddy pop-culture **artifacts** and hip clip **art** from days gone by. Ever the bad girl, Madonna slyly mashed up her hit with **Lady Gaga**'s "Born This Way" (2011), putting a fine point on her contention that Gaga had ripped her off. For the dullards in the audience who still weren't quite getting where she was coming from, she then segued into a couple of lines from **"She's Not Me."** The whole thing was a maneuver big on offense that drew cheers and wound down with a majestic levitating line march. Yay, team!

"**Give Me All Your Luvin'**" blasted in next, its bubble-gum pop quality continuing the feel-good air. Following it with the ebullient **"Turn Up the Radio"** was a note-perfect choice, and a sound way to keep the good times rolling. Most pleasantly surprising was **"Open Your Heart"**/"Sagarra Jo," a Basque-me-no-questions-I'll-tell-you-no-lies version of her #1 hit performed with Kalakan. The performance managed to pay homage to the original while still allowing Madonna to tinker with its form.

Madonna reserved this spot for a speech, which changed nightly. Sometimes she reiterated her support for **Pussy Riot**, sometimes she warned her fans not to get "fat and lazy" (not literally but ... y'know ... that, too) about rights or we'd find their "gay asses in jail"; sometimes she extolled the virtues of American democracy, freedom of speech and freedom of expression; and still others she tweaked **Elton John** or whomever else was annoying her at the time.

"**Masterpiece**" was the time to showcase her vocals. She consistently charmed with the vulnerable love song. It was recent and—relative to many items from her oeuvre—obscure, yet a crowd-pleaser. The ***Body of Evidence*** beret was a nice touch.

Following an interlude of a **"Justify My Love"** music video redo (when Gus Van Sant remade *Psycho* in 1998, it was a disaster—who knew remaking "Justify My Love" would be so killer?), Madonna emerged in one of her all-time greatest stage costumes, a stiff, skeletal version of Gaultier's **cone-bra** bustier. (Jeremy Scott and Alexander Wang also contributed costumes, all curated by **Arianne Phillips**.) Kicking off *Masculine/Feminine*, **"Vogue"** reprised, in part, her **Super Bowl** take on the hit (the music is identical), adding a RuPaul sashay and face-checking the icons in the song's rap via video. The art deco setting and Madonna's retro-chic dancers combined to give the presentation a timeless elegance. Short of bringing **Jose & Luis** out, Madonna truly did everything she could have to make this yet another show-stopping rendering of this song.

Somewhat surprisingly, Madonna revisited **"Candy Shop"** (a non-single already done on her *Sticky & Sweet Tour*), but the French café–take she offered, complete with a drinky-poo before starting, was far too delicious for one to object. Its blending with **"Erotica"** suggested the naughtiness inherent in indulging in treats both sugary and sexy. Her bump-and-grind with lover/dancer **Brahim Zaibat** left little doubt that her sugar was, indeed, quite raw, no doubt due to frequent visits to her secret garden.

THE MDNA TOUR SET LIST

① "Virgin Mary"/"Birjina Gaztetto Bat Zegoen" by Kalakan (2012)

② "Girl Gone Wild" (snippets of "Material Girl" and "Give It 2 Me")

③ "Revolver"

④ "Gang Bang"

⑤ "Papa Don't Preach"

⑥ "Hung Up" (snippets of "Girl Gone Wild")

⑦ "I Don't Give A"

⑧ "Best Friend"/"Heartbeat" video interlude

⑨ "Express Yourself"/"Born This Way" by Lady Gaga (2011)/"She's Not Me"

⑩ "Give Me All Your Luvin'"

⑪ "Radio Dial Static Medley" video interlude (snippets of "Holiday," "Into the Groove," "Lucky Star," "Like a Virgin," "4 Minutes," "Ray of Light" and 'Music")

⑫ "Turn Up the Radio"

⑬ "Open Your Heart"/"Sagarra Jo" by Kalakan (2012)

⑭ "Masterpiece"

⑮ "Justify My Love" video interlude

⑯ "Vogue"

⑰ "Erotic Candy Shop"–"Candy Shop"/"Erotica" [snippets of "Ashamed of Myself" by Kelley Polar (2005)]

⑱ "Human Nature"

⑲ "Like a Virgin Waltz"–"Like a Virgin"/"Evgeni's Waltz" by Abel Korzeniowski (2012)

⑳ "Love Spent"/"Like a Virgin Waltz"

㉑ "Nobody Knows Me" video interlude

㉒ "I'm Addicted"

㉓ "I'm a Sinner"/"Cyber-Raga"

㉔ "Like a Prayer" [snippets of "De Treville-n Azken Hitzak" by Kalakan (2012)]

㉕ "Celebration" (snippets of "Girl Gone Wild" and "Give It 2 Me")

MATTHEW RETTENMUND

MATTHEW RETTENMUND

THE MDNA TOUR PERFORMANCES

May 31, 2012:
Tel Aviv, Israel
(Ramat Gan Stadium)

June 3-4, 2012:
Abu Dhabi, UAE
(du Arena)

June 7, 2012:
Istanbul, Turkey
(Türk Telekom Arena)

June 12, 2012:
Rome, Italy
(Stadio Olimpico)

June 14, 2012:
Milan, Italy
(San Siro)

June 16, 2012:
Florence, Italy
(Stadio Artemio Franchi)

June 20-21, 2012:
Barcelona, Spain
(Palau Sant Jordi)

June 24, 2012:
Coimbra, Portugal
(Estádio Cidade de
Coimbra)

June 28 & June 30, 2012:
Berlin, Germany
(O₂ World)

July 2, 2012:
Copenhagen, Denmark
(Parken Stadium)

July 4, 2012:
Gothenburg, Sweden
(Ullevi)

July 7-8, 2012:
Amsterdam, The Nether-
lands (Ziggo Dome)

July 10, 2012:
Cologne, Germany
(Lanxess Arena)

July 12, 2012:
Brussels, Belgium
(Stade Roi Baudouin)

July 14, 2012:
Saint-Denis, France
(Stade de France)

July 17, 2012:
London, England, UK
(Hyde Park)

July 19, 2012:
Birmingham, England, UK
(National Indoor Arena)

July 21, 2012:
Edinburgh, Scotland, UK
(Murrayfield Stadium)

July 24, 2012:
Dublin, Ireland
(Aviva Stadium)

July 29, 2012:
Vienna, Austria
(Ernst-Happel-Stadion)

August 1, 2012:
Warsaw, Poland
(National Statium)

August 4, 2012:
Kiev, Ukraine
(Olympic Stadium)

August 7, 2012:
Moscow, Russia
(Olimpiyskiy)

August 9, 2012:
Saint Petersburg, Russia
(SKK Peterburgsky)

August 12, 2012:
Helsinki, Finland
(Helsinki Olympic Stadium)

August 15, 2012:
Bærum, Norway
(Telenor Arena)

August 18, 2012:
Zurich, Switzerland
(Letzigrund)

August 21, 2012:
Nice, France
(Stade Charles-Ehrmann)

August 28, 2012:
Philadelphia,
Pennsylvania, US
(Wells Fargo Center)

August 30, 2012:
Montreal, Canada
(Bell Centre)

September 1, 2012:
Quebec City, Canada
(Plains of Abraham)

September 4, 2012:
Boston, Massachusetts,
US (TD Garden)

September 6 &
September 8, 2012:
New York, New York, US
(Yankee Stadium)

September 10, 2012:
Ottawa, Canada
(Scotiabank Place)

September 12-13, 2012:
Toronto, Canada
(Air Canada Centre)

September 15, 2012:
Atlantic City, New Jer-
sey, US (Boardwalk Hall)

September 19 & 20, 2012:
Chicago, IL, US
(United Center)

September 23-24, 2012:
Washington DC, US
(Verizon Center)

September 29-30, 2012:
Vancouver, Canada
(Rogers Arena)

October 2-3, 2012:
Seattle, Washington, US
(KeyArena)

October 6-7, 2012:
San Jose, California, US
(HP Pavilion at San Jose)

October 10-11, 2012:
Los Angeles, California,
US (Staples Center)

October 13-14, 2012:
Las Vegas, Nevada, US
(MGM Grand Garden Arena)

October 16, 2012:
Phoenix, Arizona, US
(US Airways Center)

October 18, 2012:
Denver, Colorado, US
(Pepsi Center)

October 21, 2012:
Dallas, Texas, US
(American Airlines Center)

October 24-25, 2012:
Houston, Texas, US
(Toyota Center)

October 27, 2012:
New Orleans, Louisiana,
US (New Orleans Arena)

October 30, 2012:
Kansas City, Missouri, US
(Spirit Center)

November 1, 2012:
St. Louis, Missouri, US
(Scottrade Center)

November 3-4, 2012:
Saint Paul, Minnesota, US
(Xcel Energy Center)

November 6, 2012:
Pittsburgh,
Philadelphia, US
(Consol Energy Center)

November 8, 2012:
Detroit, Michigan, US
(Joe Louis Arena)

November 10, 2012:
Cleveland, Ohio, US
(Quicken Loans Arena)

November 12-13, 2012:
New York, New York, US
(Madison Square Garden)

November 15, 2012:
Charlotte,
North Carolina, US
(Time Warner Cable Arena)

November 17, 2012:
Atlanta, Georgia, US
(Philips Arena)

November 19-20, 2012:
Miami, Florida, US
(American Airlines Arena)

November 24-25, 2012:
Mexico City, Mexico
(Foro Sol)

November 28-29, 2012:
Medellin, Colombia
(Estadio Atansio Girardot)

December 2, 2012:
Rio de Janeiro, Brazil
(Parque dos Atletas)

December 4-5, 2012:
São Paulo, Brazil
(Estádio do Morumbi)

December 9, 2012:
Porto Alegre, Brazil
(Estádio Olímpico
Monumental)

December 13 &
December 15, 2012:
Buenos Aires, Argentina
(River Plate Stadium)

December 19, 2012:
Santiago, Chile
(Estadio Nacional)

December 22, 2012:
Córdoba, Argentina
(Estadio Mario
Alberto Kempes)

"Human Nature" was a somewhat winded rant in front of a wall of mirrors, that led to Madonna tearing off her shirt and (sometimes) removing her slacks, leaving her almost entirely exposed in a black, lacy undergarment.

Half-naked and with a slogan tramp-stamped across the small of her back (sometimes it was "Malala" for Pakistani activist Malala Yousafzai, sometimes it was "Obama" for you-know-who, sometimes she left it to an audience member to write something), Madonna then performed "Like a Virgin" as an angst-driven waltz (sung over "Evgeni's Waltz" from the soundtrack to *W.E.*). This performance will likely be the one for which the entire tour is most remembered, not only for the radical reinvention of a song she once said she'd never perform again, not only for Madonna's sensuality as she mounted the piano accompanying her, not only because she exposed her breast during performances in Turkey and France and not only because of the fact that she eventually demanded money be thrown at her from the crowd ... but because of all of those things. She later incorporated "Love Spent" into this piece.

The money Madonna raised from "tips" during this performance went to aid victims of Hurricane Sandy, and she was not shy about crawling around on all fours to grab every last dollar.

In a highly arresting "Nobody Knows Me" video interlude presenting Madonna as an array of world leaders and followers—including Sarah Palin, Trayvon Martin in a hoodie, the Pope and France's Marie Le Pen (complete with swastika)—Madonna gave space to several young people who'd committed suicide following bullying. (Permission was granted by their families.)

She recovered quickly for her final segment, *Redemption*, coming back with a breathless rendition of "I'm Addicted" in which she seemed to be a Joan of Arc action figure, followed by a feel-good "I'm a Sinner"/"Cyber-Raga" influenced by Indian motifs.

The MDNA Tour's ticket out of one's worries was probably its unabashedly joyous staging of "Like a Prayer," her dancers in church robes, a beaming Madonna in silver. As coolly modern as this song was on her *Sticky & Sweet Tour*, it was here more soulful (go Rocco, who jammed in the choir to this) and lighter, closer to the original. Madonna grinned from ear to ear while serving up this hard-earned cupcake. Some lucky fans were handed the mic and encouraged to sing along; pity any fools who forgot the words.

As a final dose of sugar to soften our overworked nerves, Madonna sent her fans away with a *Tron* (1982)-tastic "Celebration." The dancing, the colorful outfits on her dancers and the arrangement made the song—not much of a hit—into an incredible finale. Madonna looked about 20 years old, except for the fact that she had her 12-year-old son dancing directly in front of her. (Lola had helped out in wardrobe for part of the tour; perhaps David and Mercy will be future choreographers, directors or producers.)

"SHE'S MADONNA, AND NOBODY DOES THIS STUFF BETTER. NOT LADY GAGA, KATY PERRY, BRITNEY SPEARS, KE$HA, RIHANNA, CHRISTINA OR ANY OF THE OTHER GENERATIONS OF POP STARS WHO HAVE USED AS A MODEL MADONNA'S TIGHTLY CRAFTED CONCERTS/DANCE SHOWCASES/ ART PROJECTS/SPECTACLES."
—RANDALL ROBERTS, *LOS ANGELES TIMES* (2012)

"MADONNA'S SOLD-OUT CONCERT ... WAS A JAW-DROPPING SEQUENCE OF STUNNINGLY DESIGNED SET PIECES; INCLUDING AN AERIAL DRUM CORPS, A BATTALION OF DAZZLING DANCERS, AN EXPLOSIVELY BLOODY GANGSTER FANTASY AND A SURREAL SPIRITUAL VOYAGE. BUT THE TIRELESS WOMAN AT ITS CENTER, TAUT AND CONFIDENT AS EVER AT 54, WAS JUST AS RIVETING STRIPPED DOWN TO LINGERIE AND SINGING ALONE WITH A PIANIST."
—JORDAN LEVIN, *MIAMI.COM* (2012)

"... [I]S THE TRIGGER-HAPPY MOTEL SCENE REALLY GIVING WAY TO SOME CUBAN SANTERÍA AND TIGHTROPE-WALKING ZOMBIES? ARE THESE PRISON GUARDS BULLYING DANCERS IN ORANGE A NOD TO GUANTÁNAMO? AND, AFTER SO MANY YEARS WEARING ONE, IS MADONNA REALLY SINGING A SONG IN BASQUE? SHE IS."
—KITTY EMPIRE, *THE GUARDIAN* (2012)

The MDNA Tour, with its 200-body entourage—including 30 bodyguards, personal chefs, a yoga instructor, an acupuncturist and a dry cleaner—was the top-grossing tour of 2012, raking in $305 million. That qualified it as the tenth biggest tour of all time.

In the end, Madonna reflected of *The MDNA Tour*, "It almost killed me."

But that's the idea, to pull off something this grand and ballsy and still rely on that "almost."

MDNA WORLD TOUR (ALBUM): *Release date: September 6, 2013.* Double-disc CD, DVD, Blu-ray that captured *The MDNA Tour*. Recorded at a testy (she kept the audience waiting over three hours!) Miami performance, the DVD is peppered with snippets from other tour stops ... but good luck IDing which is from where. The video was granted a proper premiere on June 22, 2013, in NYC at the Paris Theater (4 W. 58th St., NY, NY) at which Madonna arrived in Marlene Dietrich finery.

Sadly, this release had major technical issues so severe that a recall of the Blu-ray in the US occurred. It was not a strong seller. At least the album and the DVD contain the whole show.

"Dancing in high heels? Not recommended."
—MADONNA ON *THE MDNA TOUR* (2012)

"ME AGAINST THE MUSIC" FEAT. MADONNA (SONG): *Release date: October 14, 2003. Billboard Hot 100 peak: #35.* **Britney Spears** single featuring Madonna that united the pop divas professionally for the first time on record.

After the commercial failure of *American Life*, Madonna did not sit out the rest of 2003. On the contrary, she dug in her high heels, **working** harder than ever to keep herself Topic A ... or at least Topic B.

With "Me Against the Music"—written by Britney Spears, Madonna, Christopher Alan "Tricky" Stewart, Thabiso "Tab" Nikhereanye, Penelope Magnet, Terius Nash and Gary O'Brien, and produced by Stewart and Magnet—Madonna put her **money** where her mouth was regarding her affection for Spears, allowing herself to be a featured artist (for the first time ever) on this Spears single, and even filming a music video.

Just two months earlier, Madonna had kissed Spears on the 2003 **MTV Video Music Awards**; returning to Spears so soon had the unintended effect of feeling anti-climactic, contributing to the song's weak performance on the charts. The two biggest female names in pop music and they barely cracked the Top 40. It was kinda like how **Whitney Houston** and Aretha Franklin could only attain the #41 slot with their 1989 duet "It Isn't, It Wasn't, It Ain't Never Gonna Be."

Following the folky sound of *American Life*, this collaboration seemed to be Madonna embracing pure pop again, but she has denied that it was a turning point for her. "Honestly, after I did that record I didn't think I should make this or make that. I just didn't think too much about it. I don't think about things as much as people think I do."

Madonna repaid Brit-Brit for the kiss with this song, but she's never shown up for any of its live performances; maybe Spears should have used more tongue?

"ME AGAINST THE MUSIC" FEAT. MADONNA (VIDEO): *Director: Paul Hunter, 2003.* Madonna may have been merely a featured artist on the **Britney Spears** song brought to life in this music video, but director Paul Hunter was smart enough to use the hell out of her in his **campy** mini-drama. A black-suited Spears, in the shiniest hat ever, was still dancing her butt off in those days, doing so in a stylized club setting while being watched by an imperious, white-suited Madonna, who seems to be some sort of club overlord.

The choreography of the video is a great record of each woman's signature moves—Britney jerks around impressively like an A-plus student in a hip-hop class, Madonna writhes on the floor and reverts to **yoga**. Madonna seems to steal the video at one point by rubbing her cane between her legs at just the right moment, which sucks up more attention than either her use of several businessmen as

dance props or her inexplicable glee at swinging in a totally-out-of-nowhere room filled with autumn leaves.

The video ends with Spears collaring Madonna and almost kissing her, a coy reference to their 2003 **MTV Video Music Awards** smooch. This time, Madonna cheats, escaping by disappearing into thin air.

MEASUREMENTS: On a Japanese talk show in 1985, a giggling group of adolescent girls asked Madonna her measurements. Shocked by their forwardness, she stammered that that information was top-secret, even as the cameraman zoomed in on her bustier.

MEDIOCRITY: Just to stave off any middle-of-the-road doldrums, Madonna kept a framed quote from Sir Arthur Conan Doyle on her desk at **Maverick**: "Mediocrity knows nothing higher than itself, but **talent** instantly recognizes genius." This vibed brilliantly with Madonna's observation in 1991, "My drive in life is from this horrible fear of being mediocre."

MEISEL, STEVEN: *b. circa 1953/1954.* Controversial **fashion** photographer who made the leap into fine **art** photography with Madonna in his first **book**, their collaboration *Sex*.

Meisel's association with Madonna stretches **back** to the dawn of her career. Though he didn't shoot her first album cover, he shot her first promo poster; the same image appeared as part of a January 1984 *Mademoiselle* magazine spread. One of his images from that shoot had appeared in *Island* in 1983, part of her first cover story.

Meisel shot Madonna's iconic *Like a Virgin* album cover, part of her 1995 **Versace** ad campaign, her 2009 **Louis Vuitton** ad campaign and cover stories for such magazines as *Rolling Stone* (1991), *Italian Vogue* (1991 and 1992), *Vanity Fair* (1991, 1992 and 2008) and *Vogue* (1996). He shot all the best *Truth or Dare* images as well.

It is a testament to the importance of Meisel's **work** with Madonna that no single image comes to mind when thinking about their creations. Rather, one unforgettable pose after another hovers in the mind's **eye**: Madonna as a pastel Lolita ... Madonna as **Marilyn Monroe**, hands on hips ... Madonna **smoking** in bed, fingering one nipple ... Madonna painting a poodle's toenails ... Madonna drinking from a glass clenched between her **feet** ... Madonna hitchhiking in the raw.

In some ways, Meisel is the Madonna of photography, an intensely creative co-opter of images whose work often reflects a preoccupation with brazen **sexuality** and harsh stylization. Of *Sex*, he said at the time, "After this, no one ever needs to do another book on erotica," with a bold confidence that surpassed even Madonna's own.

> "Steven, like me, likes to fuck with people ..."
> —MADONNA ON STEVEN MEISEL (1999)

MELDRUM, IAN "MOLLY": *b. January 29, 1943.* Colorful Australian pop critic and presenter of *Countdown* (1974–1997). With apologies to **deadmau5,** Madonna has seen Meldrum many times over the years, succumbing to the charms of his Stetson and his uncensored questions. They've become good media buddies; she has rarely seemed as at ease as in her chats with Meldrum.

On the December 16, 1984, episode of *Countdown*, Meldrum asked a flustered Madonna about **"Like a Virgin."** She replied, "Well, I was, um, laying in my bed one night and, well, Molly, I mean … it takes one to know one, doesn't it?" before laughing gleefully. Meldrum had been in town to interview Van Halen and took a chance on chatting with the relatively small-time solo singer just in case.

In 1985, Madonna—platinum **blonde** and sporting a white blouse with a strand of pearls—was interviewed at length in **NYC** by Meldrum, who asked her how she put together **The Virgin Tour**, at a time when most interviewers were avoiding asking any musical questions in favor of salacious subjects. She spoke about the **work** that went into putting together the tour and her favorite song at the time (**"Into the Groove,"** which she called "Get Into the Groove").

Meldrum's 1989 interview with Madonna for Super is an all-time classic. Blonde and in a white suit similar to her 1990 *Arsenio Hall Show* look, Madonna was filming *Dick Tracy* at the time and looked every inch the diva she was playing. The interview was conducted at her home during one of her **father's** visits, so at one point he came in to tell her she was just **dreaming** that she was a movie star and that she had to go do homework. It was the first time Madonna had ever done an interview with her dad, who gallantly said she'd never lied to him as a kid. She admitted she excelled in **school** as a child mainly to provoke the envy of her siblings and to gain her father's **love** … as well as for the 25 cents per A grade her father offered.

By the time of their 1991 meeting, Madonna was sporting "riveting red" **hair** in a beret, and was in the midst of shooting her happy **birthday** wishes for **MTV's** 10th anniversary. She told Meldrum she was about to go to **New York** to write her next album, which would of course turn out to be *Erotica*. When asked if she felt she was on the level of **Marilyn Monroe**, Madonna clarified with a wink, "That I'm a pop icon goddess? Yeah." Interestingly, when Meldrum asked her about touring, Madonna said, "Touring? Don't say that bad word." She even went so far as to say, "I would never do a tour like I did before again." A quarter-century later, touring was the major focus of her career.

In October 1993, Meldrum chatted with Madonna (in pixie cut and red-and-white-striped shirt) in **Paris** at the time of *The Girlie Show World Tour*. Madonna laughed at Meldrum's typically grasping questions regarding the *Sex* backlash.

Meldrum caught up with Madonna in November 2005 for an interview that ran on the morning show *Sunrise*. Continuing their decades-long **flirtation**, Madonna joked that **"Forbidden Love"** from *Confessions on a Dance Floor* was their song.

MEMORY: Madonna's earliest **memory** is of her **mother**, and of sleeping soundly between her parents in their bed.

Her second memory, quite the opposite, is of being four years old and knocking down a younger girl who was attempting to give her a dandelion.

MENJO'S: *928 W. McNichols Rd., Detroit, MI.* The first **gay** bar in which Madonna ever pranced, on the arm of mentor **Christopher Flynn.**

MENSTRUATION: Madonna first bled at age 10.

"MER GIRL": Probably the most uncomfortably personal song Madonna has ever written (with **William Orbit**, who coproduced it), "Mer Girl" is the epic finale of *Ray of Light*.

Beginning with one of Orbit's enigmatic synthesized noises (perhaps fairly described as a submerged-sounding telephone busy signal), the song is meandering and poetic, presented in a completely unique form from the rest of Madonna's musical output. The lyrics describe a girl's need to run away in order to find herself, culminating with a sort of living **death** in the belly of the earth that mirrors the cause of her desire to flee—the death of her **mother**. Madonna sings of smelling her mother's burning flesh, rotting bones and decay, spurring her to continue running, which is easy to interpret as a metaphor for everything Madonna does as an artist.

It is one of Madonna's greatest artistic achievements in her musical career.

"Mer Girl" was performed to mesmerized audiences on the *Drowned World Tour* in two halves, with **"Sky Fits Heaven"** in-between, and again at the Melbourne *Tears of a Clown* show.

MERCY: SEE: **James, Mercy.**

MERT AND MARCUS: *Both b. 1971.* Photography duo (Mert Alas and Marcus Piggott) that has, increasingly, become go-to shooters of Madonna. Among other assignments, they've photographed Madonna for her return-to-form *Interview* covers and features (2010 and 2014), and her *MDNA* and *Rebel Heart* album covers and campaigns. They also directed her **"Girl Gone Wild"** video.

"What the fuck is a Molly?"—MADONNA (1984)

TOP: Madonna and her special Guy (Oseary) at the Met Gala in 2011

BOTTOM: Channeling Brigitte Bardot at the same event in 2015

"MESSIAH": Aching **love** song from *Rebel Heart* and *Rebel Heart Tour* interlude that reaches **"Live to Tell"** heights with Madonna's emotional vocals. It was written by Madonna, **Avicii**, Arash Pournouri, Salem Al Fakir, Magnus Lidehäll and Vincent Pontare, and produced by Madonna, Avicii, Salem Al Fakir, Magnus Lidehäll, Vincent Pontare, with strings by *W.E.* soundtrack composer Abel Korzeniowski.

MET GALA: The Costume Institute Gala, held annually at the Metropolitan Museum of **Art** (1000 Fifth Ave., NY, NY), at which monies are raised to benefit the museum's Costume Institute. Each year, the benefit encourages wild self-expression via **fashion** around a central theme.

Madonna blew into the 1997 Met Ball in a Milky Way wrap in honor of the *Gianni Versace* retrospective. She was pictured with Donatella Versace and **Cher**, and also with both Kate Moss and **Elton John**.

In 2009, Madonna attended wearing thigh-high boots and a deep blue **Louis Vuitton** skirt with matching bunny ears. The show it was organized around was *The Model as Muse: Embodying Fashion*.

In 2011, she looked like 1930s Hollywood royalty in a blue **Stella McCartney** gown encrusted with Cartier diamonds. The gala celebrated *Alexander McQueen: Savage* **Beauty**.

On May 6, 2013, Madonna was deemed to have been one of the only attendees to correctly nail the *Punk: Chaos to Couture* theme, though she did it not in rags but in Givenchy Haute Couture by Riccardo Tisci—her shredded fishnet skirt, fishnet hose, thigh-highs, chains and tartan jacket looked damn good, as did her Bettie Page–banged brunette wig. She even flashed pink—her Casadei pumps. Madonna chatted up **Beyoncé**, Kim Kardashian, Frank Ocean (a man she has said she wishes she could turn straight) and **Katy Perry** at the event, but reportedly snubbed her onetime pal **Gwyneth Paltrow**. Paltrow later told *USA Today*, "I did not enjoy it at all. It was so un-fun."

On May 5, 2015, the gala became the site of the end of the feud between Madonna and **Lady Gaga**, and between Katy Perry and Lady Gaga and, well, everyone just got along great. Madonna and Perry showed up in matching Moschino (Madonna's said *Rebel Heart*, which promptly earned her comparisons to Macy Gray's shamelessly self-promoting "My New Album Drops Sept. 18, 2001" frock) and the ladies posed in a group hug with Gaga.

In honor of the *Manus x Machina: Fashion in an Age of Technology* theme of the May 2, 2016, gala, Madonna wore an outrageous sheer Givenchy number inspired by *Game of Thrones*. The media spanked her for the butt-baring outfit, prompting Madonna's retort that she was making a statement about gender equality.

METRO CLUB, THE: *Formerly 7–9 Lansdowne St., Boston, MA.* Madonna performed at this Boston club on December 4, 1983, belting out live versions of **"Physical Attraction," "Lucky Star," "Holiday"** and **"Burning Up."**

GREGORY PACE

M.I.A.: *b. July 18, 1975.* Artist and rapper whose "Paper Planes" single took her from the realm of the esoteric to the Top 40—briefly—in 2008.

Madonna collaborated with her on *MDNA* on the songs **"Give Me All Your Luvin'"** and **"B-Day Song,"** and invited her to perform with her at her **Super Bowl** halftime show. M.I.A. repaid Madonna—who was under tremendous pressure to deliver a family-friendly show—by flipping off the world on camera.

"I wasn't happy about it," Madonna told Ryan Seacrest.

M.I.A. apologized to Madonna for raining on her parade and Madonna—shocker!—accepted. (Could you really imagine Madonna holding a grudge over a gesture that in this day and age wouldn't shock a **nun**?)

> "People come up to me and say, 'Oh, my God, it's a thin line, you could either be Madonna or Johnny Rotten.' … I'm both, that's what it is."—M.I.A. (2013)

MIA MIND MUSIC: Production/promotion facility that hired Madonna, on the recommendation of the System's David Frank, in 1981 to provide backing vocals to songs by **Otto von Wernherr.** When Madonna hit it big, Mia Mind cashed in, licensing the von Wernherr songs, newly remixed to bring Madonna's vocals to the fore. This material is anything but vintage Madonna, a collection of jarring, tuneless compositions that are nonetheless curiosity pieces for Madonna **fans.**

Founder Steve Bentzel went on to pen the **"Papa Don't Preach"** spoof "Madonna Don't Preach," the **video** which featured von Wernherr performing as a priest hounded by **pregnant** teens in front of the Limelight (formerly 656 Ave. of the Americas, NY, NY).

Mia Mind also did individual **work** with Madonna at Evergreen Studios on the Upper West Side of Manhattan, and eventually licensed several Madonna performances— "Shine a Light," "Little Boy" (actual title: "Little Boy Lost"), "On the Ground" (actual title: "Safe Neighborhood"), "Time and Time Again" and "The Da-Da-Da-**Dance**"—written by "Daniel Giorlando," thought to be an **alias** either for **Dan Gilroy** or for Madonna herself. These songs appeared on 1992 vinyl releases in the UK. All of these Madonna songs lack her personal touch, but stand on their own as credible rock tunes with more aggressive vocals than she mustered for *Madonna.* They were withdrawn after Madonna's lawyers objected.

Before the various songs were yanked, Bentzel had high praise for Madonna: "I think we paid her less than union wages. I always found her nothing less than professional, and I've always felt that she's very **talented.** I never had a problem with her."

MIAMI: After doing an extensive *Sex* shoot in Miami Beach, Madonna spent almost $4.9 million for a sprawling, nine-bedroom, eight-and-a-half-bath, Spanish-style mansion at 3029 Brickell Ave. in Coconut Grove to add to her collection of part-time residences. The mansion overlooked Biscayne Bay, making it a scenic spot in which Madonna could burn through part of her dirty thirties.

When Madonna dumped the place in 1998 after having spent $700,000 in renovations, realtor Jeri Jenkins unloaded it for $7.5 million (in cash) to a boy band called the Burgundians who were backed by an unnamed investor ... which really does not sound shady *at all.* In 2000, the band—made up of Barbie K., Charlotte R., Chris A., Gene X and G.M.—gave a bizarre press performance in which it was said that they hoped to be inspired by Madonna's spirit, which is all very *Topper* (1937).

MICHIGAN: Madonna's home state. She now returns to visit her **father,** to see **Lola** at the **University of Michigan** and/or to perform racy concerts. She said of the state in 2005, "Now, Michigan's cool, but my whole life when I was growing up ... I kept saying, 'There's gotta be more to life than this and I don't want to be stuck here all my life.'" She left no room for doubt as to her feelings about her home state when asked by *Us* **magazine** in 2015 what she missed about growing up in Michigan: "Nothing at all."

> Madonna is a very hard-working and talented survivor of Detroit— as a survivor of Toledo, I admire her—
>
> Gloria Steinem

Gloria Steinem's hadwritten note for *EM2O* has praise for her Midwest sister.

MIDLER, BETTE: *b. December 1, 1945.* As a singer, Midler became the first to gain a **gay** following by performing directly to gay men in their milieu; she sang at the Continental Baths (formerly 2109 Broadway, NY, NY). Her **camp** humor and taste in show tunes, classic pop and contemporary rock endeared her to those audiences, who were passing up doing some guy's thing in order to watch her do *her* thing. Examples of those historically important performances have been, by the grace of **YouTube** (and much to Midler's discomfort), preserved for today's kids, who are so jaded that when new singers market themselves to LGBT people it's often considered patronizing.

The outrageous, loud, un-PC Midler crossed over in a big way with an establishment-friendly, **Oscar**-nominated role in the 1979 Janis Joplin–inspired film *The Rose,* the title song of which became one of her signature hits.

She cashed in by becoming the Minnie Mouse of the '80s, signing up for a string of Disney films, some better than others. When her film career tapered off, she refocused on her music, finding a niche in **nostalgia.**

WE HAVE GOT TO GET TOGETHER:
BEHIND THE SCENES AT MADONNA'S
1983 METRO CLUB PERFORMANCE

For nearly a decade on YouTube, watermarked clips of Madonna's 1983 performance at The Metro Club (formerly 7-9 Lansdowne St., Boston, MA) have teased fans with tantalizing snippets of what appeared to be a most unusual appearance.

According to Thomas De Pascale, it was like watching a shooting star.

De Pascale and longtime partner Michael O'Brien (who died in 1992) ran International Sounds in 1982, which booked acts in theaters in Boston and Worcester, Massachusetts. It then became Club New York Productions, and they, along with Yuki Watanabe and George DuBose, orchestrated evenings of New York performance art on special nights in various clubs on Lansdowne behind Fenway Park.

"We brought perform-ers we liked from New York, like the *Mermaids on Heroin* with Joey Arias, Man Parrish (introduced by a seven-foot alien dinosaur puppet) & Woman Parish featuring Adrian, Grandmaster Flash and Afrika Bambaataa and Bernard Zette's band Andronyx with Cha Cha Fernandez. We'd put them together with dance troupes like Yoshiko Chuma and the School of Hard Knocks, the NYC Breakers, the Danceteria Go-Go Corps de Ballet with Maurice under the direction of Brian Damage and Special Guest Mohawk by Audrey and breakdanc-ers the Ali Brothers (who were five and seven years old). Michael would talk with graffiti artists onstage and photographers could exhibit their work and talk about it. All of this on one night at one club. Locals were always welcome, too, like Sandy Dillon."

The performances were filmed from three camera angles (De Pascale was a film student) and edited at Nam June Paik's studios. They hoped to create a cable TV show, though it never materialized and the culturally important footage was never used. Madonna was the very last performer in the series.

Madonna was snagged for the gig when she performed at Danceteria in New York one night. De Pascale remembers, "At midnight on the roof, Madonna and two dancers performed two songs with flashlight props lighting up their faces. It was this really simple thing, but with the music and NYC in the background, that made it fantastic!"

This performance was captured by photogra-phers, including George DuBose, who'd already taken what would turn out to be historically significant images of Madonna's first solo showcase.

"There was some problem with the door being locked and people couldn't get downstairs, so there was a crowd by the door and Yuki was talking with Martin Burgoyne as George fixed the lock. Madonna came over and there were introductions and a brief explanation of what we were doing in Boston. She must have heard about it because people had already gone and come back with no problems. It must have felt like a tour because everybody wanted to go to Boston."

When everything was in place, Madonna was invited to perform on Sunday, December 4, 1983. "Michael told me that he had talked to Madonna or Christopher and they wanted to go home for Christmas with the money they made from the show; they were going to buy presents."

Madonna and Burgoyne were flown on a no-frills $49 Eastern Air Shuttle flight from NYC to Boston, while Christopher, Erika and Bags drove. De Pascale picked up Madonna and Burgoyne at the airport to escort them to their Holiday (Celebrate!) Inn in Kenmore Square.

"When I pulled up to Eastern, I saw two figures: Martin in shorts and a summer jacket in the middle of winter, and Madonna in this huge black cape/pashmina/parka Yohji Yamamoto coat-thing with no sleeves. Keith Haring had just had his first show at the Tony Shafrazi Gallery that week and I was wearing the 'Keith Haring World Tour 1983' painter's cap covered with Haring buttons from the gallery. We were getting into the limo and Madonna said, 'Where'd you get that hat???' She had some of the same buttons on her coat. I said, 'Where'd *you* get the buttons???' and she said, 'Keith's show.' I said 'I didn't see you there,' and Madonna said, 'No, *I* didn't see *you* there,' and we laughed. So I felt comfortable enough to ask for a pit stop."

De Pascale asked if they minded a quick stop at his home. "My house was in Charlestown, which was on the way to the Holiday Inn. There were no mobile phones then. I needed to make a call, so we stopped at my house on Soley Street."

Madonna and Burgoyne stayed in the car. "My mother beeped in on the other line and I told her I had to go because Madonna was outside and she said, 'Tell Madonna I said hi.' She didn't know who she was but she liked the name. When I got back in the limo I said, 'Oh, my mom said hi.' Madonna looked out the window at my house, at the top of Bunker Hill, and I asked her, 'Where does your mother live?' and she looked at me and said, 'She's dead.' That felt terrible. I said, 'Oh, my God, I'm sorry,' as we went down the hill. At the bottom of Soley Street was St. Mary's and as we turned and passed it I made the sign of the cross."

De Pascale took them through the North End, the Little Italy of Boston, which Martin said smelled of garlic before asking if they could stop at the 7-Eleven. "They both got out and Madonna got back in first so I asked what she got and she said, 'A snack.' We started talking about food and being vegetarian, when Martin comes out the door of the 7-Eleven and I looked at him in his Bermuda shorts and said to Madonna, 'Isn't he *freezing*?' and she said, 'No, he always dresses like that.'"

Once he dropped them off, he gave them a couple of hours to themselves before returning to pick them up for an interview at Kiss 108. Lisa Lipps and Diana Steele interviewed them, and the first thing Lipps asked was about Madonna's boyfriend Jelly-bean Benitez. "Madonna shrieked, 'Why is everyone asking me that?' Stare-down. Next question. Then

Madonna with De Pascale

she did some promos for Kiss 108, had a Fanta and then we left for rehearsal."

De Pascale reports that Madonna was in a great mood at the club. "We took some photos then talked about where the cameras would be set up. She had dark sweats with a *Vision Quest* logo across the front underneath the cape and when Michael asked her about the film she told a story about going to Barbra Streisand's house for dinner. Barbra asked her why she wore her hair the way she did. Madonna said back to her, 'Because I like it.' I thought it was awesome that she could be so comfortable around the real live Barbra Streisand to talk to her like that."

When he went back to pick up Madonna and Martin for the show, he brought two hand silkscreened promo posters he'd made of her first album cover, just to show her how the club would be decorated. "I knocked and Martin flung the door open and Madonna was standing there topless. He did it purposely and her and I both were shocked. 'SHUT THAT DOOR!' I heard Madonna scream. Martin said, 'It's only him.' She said, 'I DONT CARE WHO IT IS! SHUT THAT DOOR!' Then I stood out in the hallway for a while and knocked again. Martin answered and I said, 'Hey, I did these for promotion for the show and I was going to give them to Madonna; do you think she's really going to take them?' and Martin said, 'No, she going to throw them in the garbage as soon as you shut the door.' So I said, 'I'll be in the car.'" Madonna later said of the Warholian posters, "Oh, you beat Andy to it."

Madonna's Kiss 108 interview

THOMAS DE PASCALE

When they came downstairs to go to the club, Christopher had joined them. De Pascale introduced himself and while they were talking, Christopher blurted out, "Is this a *gay* club?" De Pascale didn't know what to think. "I didn't know exactly why he asked me that ... did a purse fall out of my mouth when I opened it? "I said, 'It's only gay on Sunday nights.' Madonna was smiling and I finally got the joke. I felt like a dope, so I said to him, 'That's the Fens over there, Chris. I mean, for on your way home." The Fenway was the gay cruising spot. Whether or not Mr. Ciccone availed himself of that information is lost to history.

Madonna got ready for the show. "Madonna had these perfectly beautiful lips lacquered the reddest red I'd ever seen and I made a comment about them. When she got out of the limo, she kissed my cheek and left the lipstick on my face. I wore it all night."

After a brief intro by O'Brien in a suit, Madonna, Erika and Bags strode to the stage, crouching in a spooning position with Madonna in the middle. As "Physical Attraction" began playing, they sprang to life, Madonna smiling warmly at the crowd, moving easily to

the music. The footage from the event is fetishistic, zooming in and lingering over every inch of her body: She was in an all-black outfit that included a hair tie, tight mesh tank with a looser black tank tied off at her waist, gazillions of Maripol rubber bracelets and other pieces of jewelry and a loose skirt riding low on her hips to reveal a sexy leotard underneath. She wore her favorite leather boots (in contrast to Belle, who was barefoot).

For the opening of the song, Madonna's effortless choreography was influenced by the aerobics craze. The song was sung live with only the backing vocals (including the whispered "you're confusing me" part) on tape. She sounded fantastic, singing the song in a higher key toward the end.

"I had originally wanted to connect the stage to this island in the middle of the club, but it was turning into something dangerous so we didn't do it," De Pascale says. "The camera people could've shot her from underneath—the only part of her we *didn't* shoot was the bottoms of her feet."

Finishing up, she coquettishly asked some audience members what they were doing with their fingers, making a sort of peace sign. "What does this mean? Does that mean

good? Does that mean somethin' dirty? No? It means luck? *Love!* Oh, thank you. I mean love, too."

"She was so accessible to the audience. They were mesmerized by her," De Pascale says, pointing out that she told one sexy South American guy, "I think I may have to kiss you."

For "Lucky Star," she swapped Bags out for Christopher and recreated the video's choreography. Again, she sang totally live with just some backing vocals on tape, a rare live performance of this song before her *Virgin Tour.*

Before her next song, Madonna tried some stage banter: "Thank you! Thank you very much ... Now this is the first time I've ever been here before and I can't see anything, but from the looks of everyone there are real people here and some very pretty ones. So, um, this is the moment you've been waiting for ..." She was referring to her performance of "Holiday" since that was, at the time, her biggest hit. Someone in the front was saying something to the effect of "what's up," and Madonna said, "All right, Bruce, this one's for you, 'cause you got what's up." She and her dancers got into formation and sprang into "Holiday."

The choreography for "Holiday" begins with a mini-wave between Madonna and her dancers before segueing into what would become familiar footwork for this number on her many lip-synched performances on foreign TV. She clearly had a blast with this song, tearing up the stage.

"All right, now listen. You're not gonna get away with it," she scolded the front row after, pointing out that they were supposed to sing "we have got to get together" during "Holiday," and making them sing it belatedly.

Before her "Burning Up" finale, Madonna announced, "Baby, variety is the spice of life." She went offstage, then her dancers (Christopher, Bags and Erika) kind of propelled her back out and onto the stage, where she literally crawled around—she really *would* do anything ... to entertain. When she screwed up, she paused to say, "Shit, I'm fuckin' up the words!" She added some unique vocal adlibs at the end, recovering nicely.

When her set was over, Madonna thanked the crowd and instantly turned off, walking off stage like she was browsing in a supermarket. She went upstairs, her troupe took a couple of pictures and had some champagne, then De Pascale made sure the limo was ready.

"On her way out the door, everybody was stopped," he says. "Nobody tried to touch her or say anything, they just wanted to look at her. They wanted to make sure they got an eyeful. She was so comfortable with that. There never was any faltering. Never any, 'I don't believe in myself ...' Never. She never got self-conscious."

The next day, De Pascale and O'Brien drove Madonna and her troupe to the local TV station, where

she did a very early (around 7 a.m.) interview with a news personality, a short piece that has never been seen on the Internet. Madonna, tired from the late night, started whining and O'Brien snapped at her, "Do you think I want to be here either?" Madonna got weepy, asking, "Why do you have to be so mean to me?"

"He liked to tell people he was the only person who could make Madonna cry. Everyone was just so tired!"

Madonna was off to the airport and back to NYC. She and Burgoyne thanked De Pascale for taking them around all day. Madonna asked him his mother's name and signed one of the Meisel promo posters for her first album to her: "To Nelda, What a wonderful mother. Love, Madonna."

"Then she looked at me and I was really happy she did that. My mother kept it in her office—she loved it."

And with that, the whirlwind club date was over.

"From what I understand, Madonna and Christopher *did* fly home to spend Christmas with their family," De Pascale remembers. "And when she arrived back in New York after Christmas, she'd become the most famous woman in the world." (Six months later, when O'Brien and De Pascale ran into Christopher in NYC, they asked him how it felt having the most famous person in the world for a sister. Christopher said Gorbachev was more famous, to which O'Brien said, "If Gorbachev was standing on *that* corner and Madonna was standing on *that* corner—who do you think people would run to?")

Madonna's Boston debut made a lasting impression on De Pascale. "I'll never forget the way that Madonna was. I had never experienced anything like that, but you could tell she had star quality. She was not like everybody else."

Behind the scenes at the Metro Club with a serious entrourage

©GEORGE-DUBOSE.COM

Metro Club rehearsal time!

Christopher Ciccone gathering notes ...

Madonna wows 'em at her first Boston gig.

Midler has tweaked Madonna often.

By the end of April and early May 1985, Midler had already incorporated Madonna into her stand-up comedy act. As immortalized on her album *Mud Will Be Flung Tonight!* (released at the end of 1985), Midler joked of Madonna's success in ***Desperately Seeking Susan***, "But now it's 'Move over, Meryl Streep, there's a new light on the cinematic horizon—Madonna!' No, this is not going to be so much mud-flinging as it's gonna be like a landfill. All right! 'Like a virgin/Touched for the very first time ...' For the very first time *today*. Oh, my **God**! Oh, pity the poor soul that has to rinse out that lingerie. The only thing that girl will ever do like a virgin is have a baby in a stable ... by an unknown father. Who *me*, jealous? Whaddaya mean? I'm a material girl, too. I've been on **MTV** ... *once*." (Thirty years later, Midler was slut-shaming **Britney Spears** and **Ariana Grande**.)

In introducing Madonna at **Live Aid** two months after that take-no-prisoners comedy album was recorded, Midler referenced Madonna's **nude** photo scandal. It was a **bitch** move, but also funny, and Midler kinda-sorta gave Madonna a bit of cover by pointing out her own lack of decorum, implying that she herself was in no position to judge Madonna's racy antics.

On a happier occasion, Midler was introduced to her #1 fan **Rosie O'Donnell** by Madonna at Spago (formerly 8795 Sunset Blvd., LA, CA) following the 1992 Oscars.

Midler spoke at length about her impression of Madonna as a performer after seeing her ***Blond Ambition World Tour***: "She does try [to be entertaining]. She really does ... She has spectacle, which I think is fabulous. She's sort of like the Lido de **Paris**, a one-woman Lido. I went to see her the last time she was out, and it was quite marvelous, but she doesn't talk. And I thought that was really too bad, because her crowd really wants her to speak. She doesn't go that extra step, which is to be enchanting. She doesn't care if they laugh or not. She doesn't care if they cry. She's not interested in moving them, and that, I think, is too bad, because she could. She can. She has that ability."

Midler's skepticism of Madonna as a **talent** shone through in 2003 following Madonna's **"Hollywood"** performance on the **MTV Video Music Awards**, during which she kissed **Britney Spears** and **Christina Aguilera**. Midler, who in spite of her gay cred was not even strongly in favor of gay marriage ("It's a real dilemma ...") yet, was also uncomfortable with lesbian kissing on **TV**. She said of the kiss that it was "tacky," specifying, "I thought it was cheesy because I thought—because there were—that's a show that little ones watch, you know, the little ones, the 7-year-olds, 8-year-olds."

The woman whose first opening act had been a **blowjob** and whose entire career could be evoked in a game of charades as a shake of one's rack was worried about children seeing ladies kiss on the lips?

Midler's later tweaks of Madonna were less political and more garden-variety catty: In 2008, Madonna posted a humorous clip showing herself vacuuming between takes of her **"Give It 2 Me"** video while dripping in gold jewelry. Midler posted a **parody** of the already intentionally campy video, in which she employs a heavy, phony British **accent**, mocking Madonna for being ostentatious.

She also tweeted of Madonna's **Super Bowl** halftime show, "Half time Madonna!! WORLD PEACE!??! Hilarious! But ditch the high heels next time!" a reference to Madonna's difficulty with one step in the performance. That same year, she decried the fact that the late **Donna Summer** was not in the **Rock and Roll Hall of Fame** (which truly was embarrassing) by tweeting, "Madonna is and Donna isn't." She clarified that she wasn't slamming "madge! love her."

Maybe it's a *tough* love, but Midler's digs at Madonna, while occasionally funny in a **Joan Rivers** way, have never been mitigated by a clear statement of respect for Madonna as a person or as an artist. It would seem, judging by the totality of her remarks, that Midler is of the opinion that Madonna is much ado about nothing, giving the impression that Midler perhaps resents that her own something never amounted to nearly as much as Madonna's nothing did.

MIKA: *b. August 18, 1983*. Inventive singer-songwriter who has found success with his offbeat pop hits "Grace Kelly" (2007), "Happy Ending" (2007) and "Popular Song" (2013), and who has become an A-list star in Italy thanks to his status as an *X Factor Italy* judge.

Mika has said he was shocked when he heard the song **"Gang Bang"** on *MDNA* because it was based on a song he'd been writing called "Bang Bang Boom" and he'd had no idea Madonna had altered it. **William Orbit** presented it to Madonna and the rest happened without any input from Mika.

"As far as I was concerned, it was just a song I was writing for myself. Madonna liked it and recorded her version and in the end she adapted it. I was never in the studio with Madonna. The song got changed countless times and in the end it was called 'Gang Bang'—probably because there were so many people who **worked** on it! It's kind of cool—it's my favorite thing off that ... record. It's kind of grown on me in a weird sort of way ... She certainly wasn't asking for my opinion. I don't think she was interested!"

 "MILES AWAY": *Release date: October 17, 2008. Billboard Hot 100 peak: NA.* Melancholic mid-tempo song from *Hard Candy* that became that album's third single. Written and produced by Madonna, **Timbaland**, **Justin Timberlake** and **Danja**, it was thought to be a long-distance **love** song dedicated to **Guy Ritchie**.

Madonna performed the song during her *Hard Candy* promo tour at the **Roseland Ballroom** in **NYC**, **Olympia Hall** and **Mote Park** in Maidstone, **England**, and on her

Sticky & Sweet Tour. At a Boston *Sticky & Sweet* stop, after it had become clear that she and Ritchie had just woken up from their fuzzy marriage, Madonna prefaced the performance by saying, "This song is for the emotionally retarded. You may know a few people that fall into that category—**God** knows I do."

A video was commissioned for this single; it appears on *Celebration: The Video Collection.*

"In 'Miles Away', I'm tapping into the global consciousness of people who have intimacy problems."-MADONNA (2008)

MILLER'S ICE CREAM PARLOR & DINER: *Formerly 536 S. Forest Ave., Ann Arbor, MI.* Ice cream parlor where Madonna and her roomie **Whitley Setrakian** worked in college. They were hired by a "big woman named Barb" who Setrakian recalled demanding that they both wear bras. The girls wound up subsisting on stolen soup and ice cream while they **worked** at the place, always careful not to jiggle too much.

MINAJ, NICKI: *b. December 8, 1982.* One of the most incredible musical success stories of the 2010s, Minaj is a singer, songwriter and rapper born in Trinidad and Tobago and brought up in **NYC.** She captured the attention of Top 40 radio with songs like "Your **Love**" (2010), "Super Bass" (2010), "Starships" (2012) and "Anaconda" (2014), and the imagination of the public with her more-is-more sense of style and down-and-dirty fights with **Mariah Carey** while the two were *American Idol* judges.

With just three studio albums under her belt, and thanks to countless featured spots on other artists' singles, Minaj had already tied Madonna and Dionne Warwick with 56 singles charted on the *Billboard* Hot 100.

Minaj collaborated with Madonna on *MDNA* and on *Rebel Heart.* On the former, Minaj contributed a killer rap to **"I Don't Give A"** and joined **M.I.A.** with Madonna on **"Give Me All Your Luvin',"** a collaboration that led to her appearance in Madonna's **Super Bowl** halftime show. On *Rebel Heart*, Minaj's rap gave **"Bitch I'm Madonna"** its bite. Madonna has confirmed that when she **works** with Minaj, it is a "total collaboration," not a phone-in effort by the guest rap artist du jour.

While filming the music video for "Give Me All Your Luvin'," Madonna led the production in a rousing chorus of "Happy **Birthday**" for Minaj, who was turning 29. At the end, Madonna gave Minaj a kiss on the lips. Minaj, overcome, said, "... I have to thank the queen, Madonna, for giving me this amazing opportunity. I love her so much and she's fierce and she didn't have to do this for me and M.I.A., but we love you—thank you so much!" She then made sure someone had gotten her kiss from Madonna on camera.

Minaj tweeted of the kiss, "OH MY f'ingggg Gahhhh!!!!! MADONNA jus kissed me!!!!! On the lips!!!!!! It felt soooooo good. Soooo soft!!!! *passes out* aahhhhh!!!!!!!!!"

"I like their independence, I like their spirit … they're cheeky and unique and they have individual voices and they're not conventional pop stars and I really admire them both."-MADONNA ON NICKI MINAJ AND M.I.A. (2012)

MINOGUE, KYLIE: *b. May 28, 1968.* Australian pop star and actor whose remarkable popularity began when she starred on the soap opera *Neighbours* (1986–1988). Using that as a platform, she launched a pop career with Stock Aitken Waterman bubblegum **music** on the PWL label. Her success was astronomical, immediate and long-lived, with classic singles like "I Should Be So Lucky" (1987), "Got to Be Certain" (1988) and "Better the Devil You Know" (1990). She **reinvented** herself as a more mature (but never too serious) artist beginning in 1994, and was well on her way to becoming a true icon, especially in her native Australia and in Europe. In the US, Minogue was, for the most part, a well-kept secret—to date she's only had seven *Billboard* Hot 100 hits.

In the early part of her career, Minogue seemed to be marketed as the non-thinking man's Madonna—she had fun music and was not about to venture into controversial territory. Even her answer to Madonna's *Sex,* a promo publication of risqué portraits, was tasteful rather than truly provocative.

As Minogue's post-pop princess career developed, she actually became a completely distinct entity from Madonna, both musically and personality-wise. She seems to have little of Madonna's defensive competitive drive, although that means she is also unlikely to present material much deeper than the prettiness of her many poses. It's a matter of impossible princesses vs. demanding queens.

Minogue is a dependable live singer but avoids dancing, preferring to present herself as the cherry on top of a visual sundae, making her tours spectacles to enjoy with no messages to unpack. Some **fans** have accused Madonna of copying Minogue, using examples both convincing and farfetched that seem to ultimately argue the point that there are only so many fabulous modes of presentation for divas.

Back when Madonna and Minogue were pitted against each other, Madonna broke the ice by wearing a Kylie Minogue tank for her 2000 **MTV Europe Music Awards** performance of **"Music"**—guess music really does bring the people together. Madonna said of the shirt, "Um, well, it's really my celebration of other girls in pop music, basically. I had to give a big up to **Britney [Spears]**, then I had to give a big up to Kylie … I think they're the cutest, so far, so stay tuned for the next T-shirt."

Ever since then, it's been mostly a lovefest between the two women, even if it would seem they've rarely met in person. Minogue has described their interactions as being

"I didn't know what to think ... I was, um, I was really chuffed!"
—KYLIE MINOGUE ON MADONNA WEARING A KYLIE T-SHIRT (2000)

limited to brief meetings (they were able to chat at the **Met Ball** in 2013) and some messages back and forth. One high-profile message from Madonna to Minogue came when Minogue was battling breast **cancer** in 2005. Madonna said at the time, "I think about her all the time. She's always in my prayers. I keep meaning to write her letters, but I don't know how to get in touch. Obviously there's a way to. I do wish her all the best. I think that she's a tough cookie and I think she's going to be all right."

In 2011, Minogue said definitively of her feelings, "I'm a massive Madonna fan ... How can you not love Madonna? ... I want her to do really, really well. As a fan, I want some great Madonna music." She did vote, "No, just no," when asked about Madonna's **MDNA Tour** majorette outfit on an episode of E!'s **Fashion Police** (2002–), on which the physically perfect **Joan Rivers** and Giuliana Rancic made **ageist** cracks about Madonna, but that same year, she also chose Madonna over **Lady Gaga** as to which artist has more **talent**.

For her part, Madonna has called Minogue "tremendously talented."

Minogue recorded the **unreleased** Madonna song "Alone Again," using it for a documentary, but it would seem a proper **Ciccone**/Minogue collaboration is long overdue. In 2014, Minogue said she would love to **work** with Madonna, but figured, "It's like maybe the world would stop mid orbit! ... I don't know if it would ever happen. Maybe it's something that will live in our imagination."

MIRWAIS: *b. October 23, 1960.* Swiss-born producer and songwriter Mirwais Ahmadzaï made a name for himself in the early '80s in punk and acoustic-rock groups Taxi Girl and Juliette et les Independents before his debut as a solo artist in 1990. By 1999, his single "**Disco** Science" had helped establish him as a hot commodity in electronic music, appearing on the soundtrack of **Guy Ritchie**'s 2000 film *Snatch.* From the first time she heard his **work**, Madonna was enthralled by the artistry of Mirwais.

"Madonna just picked up the phone and called me," Mirwais told *Mixmag* in 2000. "It's surprising to find myself working with the most famous artist in the world. But in the studio, you forget. She's a simple, normal, sociable person, with a really good sense of humor."

Madonna wound up inviting him to work with her on what became her massively successful *Music* album. He also became her prime collaborator on her massively *un*successful *American Life* album.

When Madonna and Mirwais click, they click bigtime—their song "**Music**" was potent enough for Madonna to notch a #1 hit on the *Billboard* Hot 100 in spite of being 42 years old; age is like programmer-repellent. Between that song and "**Don't Tell Me**," Mirwais helped Madonna achieve two of her greatest hits of all time.

From *Music*, Madonna and Mirwais cowrote and coproduced "Music," "**Impressive Instant**" (the first song they ever did together), "**I Deserve It**," "**Nobody's Perfect**," "Don't Tell

Me" and "**Paradise (Not for Me)**." Madonna would eventually perform every one of those songs live on various tours.

On *American Life*, Mirwais coproduced every song. He cowrote "**American Life**," "**Hollywood**," "**I'm So Stupid**," "**Love Profusion**," "**Nobody Knows Me**," "**Intervention**," "**Mother and Father**" and "**Die Another Day**."

By the time *Confessions on a Dance Floor* boogied around, Mirwais had only two songs on the record, "**Future Lovers**" and "**Let It Will Be**," though he also had the track "**Super Pop**" as a bonus download.

His *American Life*–era track "**It's So Cool**" was remixed and offered as a bonus track on *Celebration*.

Mirwais has performed live with Madonna on occasion, including during her *Music* and *American Life* promo appearances, and a **Paris** stop of the *Drowned World Tour*.

"He's so incredibly smart and visionary. I listen to his stuff and I think, 'This is the future of sound.'"—MADONNA ON MIRWAIS, BILLBOARD (2000)

MISPRONUNCIATIONS: Like much of the rest of the free world, Madonna consistently mispronounces mischievous as "mis-CHEE-vee-us" and tacks an "S" on "anyway." She has embarrassed herself by calling legendary French erotic writer Anaïs Nin "uh-NY-iss" in her best **Midwest** twang and, in a 1984 British telephone interview, referred to **director** Francis Ford Coppola as "kuh-POE-luh."

According to interviewer Andrew Neil, Madonna struggled to pronounce "totalitarian" (and asked if she were using "iconoclastic" correctly) during the course of their talk about *Sex* in 1992.

Nobody's perfect, especially those with no "anonyminity."

MISSHAPES, THE: An **NYC** creative collective (Geordon Nicol, Greg Krelenstein, Leigh Lezark) renowned for hosting parties fueled by an energizing '80s sensibility even as the rest of Manhattan seems to be hurrying toward homogenized boredom.

Immediately prior to her appearance at **The Roxy** on October 22, 2005, to promote *Confessions on a Dance Floor*, Madonna appeared at a Misshapes party at midnight at Luke and Leroy (formerly 21 7th Ave. S., NY, NY) in the West Village. The blog Brooklyn Vegan noted: "She walked right in through the front door. As soon as she came in the crowd went crazy. She went up to the DJ booth and said a little hello and then introduced her single. Pretended to a little DJing and then hung out while the at least 20-minute remix version of '**Hung Up**' played in the background!"

Madonna, in the DJ booth with **Stuart Price** and in a smokin'-hot **disco** dress, announced, "Okay, everybody, just calm down. I just want to hang out with you guys and listen to some really great music!"

Time spent at the place was brief due to the space, but Lenny Kravitz, **Guy Oseary** and **Liz Rosenberg** were there to cheer her on.

MITCHELL, JONI: *b. November 7, 1943.* Canadian artist who is one of her generation's ultimate singer-songwriters, and whose songs "Big Yellow Taxi" (1970), "You Turn Me On, I'm a Radio" (1972) and "Help Me" (1974) are '70s essentials.

Madonna has counted this singer's *Court and Spark* (1974) as an influential and favorite album, but Mitchell is not a **fan** of Madonna's. She told *Rolling Stone* in 1992 of Madonna "... [W]hat's the difference between her and a hard hooker, you know? Who's being exploited there? She's reveling in herself, too. But she can take it. I guess that's what it is. It's just being able to take it, you know ... Maybe that's where Madonna has the edge on us. Maybe she doesn't think it's horrible. I think it's degrading, humiliating—so does **Sinéad [O'Connor]**. Whereas Madonna's above being degraded or humiliated. She **flirts** with it. And perhaps that bravado is in some ways to be applauded, but at what cost to her soul, is my question."

In 1998, label mates Madonna and Mitchell were photographed looking convivial (with **Cher** and **k.d. lang**) at *Vanity Fair*'s annual **Oscars** party.

"... I think she's coming from a, uh, uh, different perspective," Madonna said of Mitchell in 2015. "... I grew up listening to her music and I was very inspired by the **art** that she made. I just think we, we live in a very different time and image is a really big part of, of, of our **work** and I don't think that **sexuality** was something that women were exploring or, or overtly, um, owning up to ... It's a question of taste."

"Americans have decided to be stupid and shallow since 1980. Madonna is like Nero; she marks the turning point."-JONI MITCHELL (2010)

MITCHELL, NANCY RYAN: Madonna's high **school** guidance counselor. She does *not*, as you might guess, wonder, "Where did I go wrong?!" Instead, she remembers Madonna as a gifted student who projected an extremely positive outlook, possessed an **IQ** that put her in "the top 10 percent of the range of intelligence" and, closer to graduation, a flamboyant **fashion** sense. She fondly remembers the time that **cheerleader** Madonna wore flesh-colored tights and **shocked** the entire **gymnasium** with a cartwheel. She helped Madonna apply for, and win, a **dance** scholarship to the **University of Michigan**.

MITCHELL, SASHA: *b. July 26, 1967.* Strapping male model/actor and star of the Paul Morrissey film *Spike of Bensonhurst (1988)* and the **TV** series *Step by Step* (1991–1996, 1998) with whom Madonna was purported to have had an affair. Whether she did or not, she styled him for over four hours for his profile in *Interview* magazine in 1987, which amounted to touches like removing his shirt and tearing his jeans artistically.

Madonna described Mitchell to a *Vogue* reporter with affectionate condescension as an eager downtown actor-type. An actor who's eager to go downtown can't be all bad.

MITSUBISHI: Japanese corporation whose stereophonic equipment Madonna endorsed in 1986 and 1987. As part of her $3 million deal, she made three **commercials**, including dancing and lip-synching to **"La Isla Bonita,"** and appeared in print ads wearing a leather jacket with silver studs forming the letter M.

An oversized poster **book** of *Who's That Girl World Tour* photos was given away with each purchase of a Mitsubishi stereo; Madonna/Mitsubishi phone cards were sold (flimsy, colorful cards which were punched with each use of a pay phone); and promo-only silk banners bearing unique photos of Madonna were used to attract young buyers.

No Japanese Christian groups threatened to boycott Mitsubishi for associating with Madonna.

MITZELFELD'S: *Formerly 401 Main St., Rochester Hills, MI.* Located opposite the **Rochester** School of Ballet, this **Michigan** department store was where Madonna **shoplifted** and hung out as a teenager.

MODOTTI, TINA: *August 16 or 17, 1896-January 5, 1942.* Italian photographer whose **work** has deeply inspired Madonna. Due to Madonna's donation—raised from the **auction** of her 1969 convertible Mercedes Benz 280 SE at Sotheby's (1334 York Ave., NY, NY) on June 10, 1995—the exhibition *Tina Modotti: Photographs* was successfully mounted at the Philadelphia Museum of **Art** (2600 Benjamin Franklin Pkwy., Philadelphia, PA) from September 16 to November 26, 1995, before traveling to Houston and then to San Francisco. It was the first retrospective of Modotti's work.

In order to help nudge the sale of her car, Madonna said she'd done "everything" in it ... including driving it in her **"Deeper and Deeper"** video. It brought $56,350.

Madonna's Japanese ads for Mitsubishi are characterized by their exquisite beauty.

Portion of a letter to pal Sharon Maczko illustrates Madonna's fandom for Joni Mitchell goes way back

Sounds like your having a better time than me! I went to see Billy Preston at Pine Knob and I'm also gonna see Joni Mitchell Todd Rundgren and Foghat! Far out ha! (It's better than nothing)

MONDINO, JEAN-BAPTISTE: *b. July 21, 1949.* French **fashion** and **commercial** photographer/director who brought to life Madonna's first truly **sexually** subversive music video (**"Open Your Heart"** video) and her celluloid bacchanalia, **"Justify My Love."**

Before Madonna, Mondino had shot music videos for mostly underground acts, including Taxi Girl, whose guitarist **Mirwais** would go on to become one of Madonna's most important collaborators. He gradually **worked** his way up to top pop acts, like Bryan Ferry and **Sting.**

Immediately after shooting "Open Your Heart," Mondino shot the incredibly stylish music video for "Each Time You Break My Heart" for Madonna protégé **Nick Kamen,** presenting him as a lone **Elvis Presley** figure singing in an all-but-empty club as young **Felix Howard** mimics his moves. Mondino cribbed from himself, drawing many ideas from his "Open Your Heart" video.

Mondino's work on "Justify My **Love**" was a cause célèbre, helping catapult Madonna to even greater **heights** when she already seemed to be the most famous woman alive. Her trust in him was total; he wanted to shoot, with no real script, a video involving her real-life lover **Tony Ward** and a cast of horny extras and she agreed, which led to one of her most self-assured, sexy and in-your-face visual statements.

His work on the **"Human Nature"** video correctly conjured a visual depiction of the censorious elements conspiring to put Madonna in a box.

Working with Mondino sporadically agreed with Madonna, as each collaboration seemed to be a unique statement, not derivative of the last. The one time they worked together **back** to back resulted in his least effective work for Madonna, the 1996 video for **"Love Don't Live Here Anymore."** Like Hitchcock's *Rope* (1948), which was noted for its extraordinarily long takes, this video is most remembered for being one agonizingly long take of Madonna performing at a distance and then up close while Mondino's voyeuristic camera closes in on her, gets a good look and departs.

In 2000, Mondino's **"Don't Tell Me"** video was one of Madonna's wittiest, visually, a sort of statement on the handy disposability of Madonna's embrace of the cowgirl image.

"Hollywood" marked their final collaboration so far, perhaps because it led to legal wrangling due to its use of imagery from the creative genius of **Guy Bourdin.** Or perhaps there is another Madonna/Mondino music video on the horizon.

Madonna has called him "my favorite director in the whole world."

MONEY: In 1984, Madonna said, "Before, I was just basically interested in my survival, like, what I was going to eat and what I was going to wear when it got cold outside and where I was going to live, but now I have to worry about who's ripping me off and is my accountant paying all my

"I'll do anything for money ... 'cuz money is my love."—MADONNA, *IN ARTIFICIAL LIGHT* (1981)

bills and is my lawyer making all those deals for me and, um, you know, **boring** and mundane things like that."

While she's always claimed to be anything but a material girl, it would seem that while Madonna is not driven simply by making money (if she were, she would have slid into touring with her greatest hits long ago), she does see money as a sign of **power** and success. It is tangible evidence that she's wanted, even adored.

"I mean, I'm happy that I've got money," she clarified in 1999. "I'm happy that I can buy beautiful **art** and travel to great places and buy expensive **gifts** for my friends. I'm incredibly lucky and blessed for all those things. But selling records is not what it's all about. It's about what you're saying to sell those records."

Still, if you're thinking Madonna finds the subject of money distasteful, she's not that girl. In 2008, telling *Dazed & Confused* **magazine** about her **dream** of doing little shows in opera houses, she explained the reason why it hasn't happened: "[W]ho makes money in opera houses?"

MONROE, MARILYN: *June 1, 1926–August 5, 1962.* Among Madonna's countless quotes related to Monroe, one stands out, "I'd like to leave the impression that **Marilyn** Monroe did, to be able to arouse so many different feelings in people." She's done that, but she's also left many impressions of Marilyn Monroe that arouse so many different feelings in people, from admiration to kinship to contempt.

Monroe started as an anonymous **nude** pinup girl with **dreams** of stardom, before achieving **fame** as a Hollywood actor with trademark-breathy, comic and occasionally dramatic roles in films like *All About Eve* (1950), *Niagara*

MATTHEW RETTENMUND

(1953), *Gentlemen Prefer Blondes* (1953), *How to Marry a Millionaire* (1953), *The Seven Year Itch* (1955), *Bus Stop* (1956), *Some Like It Hot* (1959) and *The Misfits* (1961). She was a **sex** siren first, a **blonde** bombshell who captured the world's imagination and stoked its repressed libido.

While notoriety had been Monroe's goal, it hadn't been her *only* goal; she soon tired of the single-minded sort of attention she drew, craving respect as an actor and a reputation as an intellect. Her personal ups and downs (those nudes surfaced, her marriages sank) fed the media frenzy, making her one of the cinema's most recognizable personalities. She died of a **drug** overdose, either accidentally or by her own hand (though her indiscreet affairs with two Kennedys spawned rumors of murder). Tragically, she'd finally become a symbol of more than just sex. One of the most famous women who ever lived, her image has been co-opted too many times to count.

Madonna has often expressed her interest in Monroe, both in interviews and by example, recreating many of her iconic, and even quite a few obscure, poses in photo shoots and in music videos.

Though there are comparisons to be drawn between Madonna and Marilyn, they are superficial in most regards: Blonde **hair**, a sexuality that the polite society of their times could never quite stomach, a tempestuous union with a hothead (Joe DiMaggio for Monroe, **Sean Penn** for Madonna), a desire to learn and to be good even as each woman's critics comfortably labeled them talentless sluts. But the women are wildly different in other regards. Madonna has some of **Marlene Dietrich**'s steely will, **Andy Warhol**'s artistic shamelessness, **Keith Haring**'s impish **creativity**, **Mae West**'s subtlety, **Martha Graham**'s avant-garde sense of movement, **Michael Jackson**'s gift for razzle-dazzle and **Cindy Sherman**'s obsession with the notion of self, but very little of Monroe's natural vulnerability.

In 1957, Monroe posed for Richard Avedon (one of the great photographers on whom Madonna missed out) done up as great beauties from the past: Lillian Russell, Theda Bara, Jean Harlow and Dietrich. In the images, she is consumed by the other women to the point that no casual observer would be able to pick out that it was Monroe in disguise. It was one of the very few occasions on which Monroe aped other personages. By contrast, Madonna's self-confidence has allowed her to ape countless other images, and she's never lost within them, but rather always looks like Madonna trying on an alternate reality. She is not consumed by the other image, but consumes it.

Monroe's image (and, to a lesser extent, Dietrich's), seems to have proven harder to immediately digest for Madonna, as she has returned to it many times, even after critics have expressed frustration at the lack of imagination. But that kind of criticism only applies if Madonna is trying to trick the viewer into thinking she is the originator of the Monroe poses. Instead, it would seem Madonna is purposefully using her appropriation of Monroe as a form

of communication with her audience. And what better icon to use than Monroe, whose face and figure and **fashion** are as common a part of our pop-cultural alphabet as the letter M is in that A to Z one?

Madonna's first use of Monroe in her **work** was a doozy, her 1985 **"Material Girl"** music video, directed by **Mary Lambert**. In it, the Jack Cole choreography and Travilla wardrobe from the "Diamonds Are a Girl's Best Friend" number in the Howard Hawks film *Gentlemen Prefer Blondes* (1953) were meticulously knocked off and reimagined (improved?) for the '80s. Never for a moment did one feel that Madonna was hoping no one would identify the source material. On the contrary, it was vital that viewers understood that the character Madonna was playing was the opposite of the material girl Monroe played in that great film.

Interestingly, Sean Penn first met Madonna on the set of this video, and took Madonna to visit Monroe's grave. Madonna later said, "Joe DiMaggio's rose was there. He really loved her."

In 1986, **Bruce Weber** shot Madonna for the first and last time, envisioning her as both Marilyn Monroe and James Dean, a clever understanding of Madonna's enthusiasm for and ability to embrace androgyny.

Madonna paid tribute to Monroe by name in her 1990 hit **"Vogue,"** listing her second after Greta Garbo and even finding room for DiMaggio when other legit Hollywood legends were shut out. (He rhymed with "Monroe.")

In November 1990, Madonna posed for longtime collaborator **Steven Meisel**, himself an unrepentant image junkie. The resulting spread for *Italian Vogue* (February 1991) was called "Madonna Come Marilyn," and while the poses were not directly inspired by Monroe, Madonna's lush glamour called her to mind more than ever. Meisel shot her again immediately for the cover and interior of *Vanity Fair*'s April 1991 issue. Here, Madonna seemed to fully embrace the comparisons between herself and Monroe that had followed her for the previous six or so years, recreating looks from Monroe's days as a model and from movies like *Bus Stop* (1956), as well as from Bert Stern's famous "Last Sitting" images of Monroe. (Madonna posed for Stern in 1985.)

The cover image of *Vanity Fair* worked so well that Madonna wore the entire get-up to the **Oscars** that year. With Michael Jackson as her date, she sang **"Sooner or Later (I Always Get My Man)"** and made the party scene looking like Monroe brought **back** from the dead.

Madonna has twice conjured Monroe on episodes of *Saturday Night Live*. As the host in 1985, Madonna played Monroe on the last night of her life in a terribly unfunny sketch meant to **parody** conspiracy theories about her **death**. Madonna was so far off the mark it was hard to watch. In 1993, though she was introduced as Madonna, she was styled as Monroe from the night in 1962 when she sang "Happy **Birthday**" to her secret lover, President Kennedy. Madonna made a better Marilyn this time, though still had trouble evoking Monroe's softness.

—STACEY Q

When Madonna was in France for *The Girlie Show World Tour*, Monroe's ex-lover, the actor Yves Montand, said wistfully of Madonna, "I wish I had known her 30 years ago." Not everyone has been impressed by her Monroe allusions. Ex-pal Sandra Bernhard said in 1994, "She thinks she's Marilyn Monroe; I guess she came back to get her **money**."

Other MM homages include Madonna's white, off-the-shoulder gown in her film *Who's That Girl*; her early-'90s embrace of Monroe's beloved designer Pucci; one of her **"Give It 2 Me"** video/photo shoot looks (OMG, the photographer's name is even **Tom Munro**); and some of her *Rebel Heart* packaging shots.

Madonna probably won't be done with Marilyn Monroe until we are.

"Some people will never take Madonna seriously—just as many never took Marilyn Monroe seriously. Novelty images—especially that of a sex symbol—are hard to erase."—ROBERT HILBURN, *LOS ANGELES TIMES* (1986)

"She's dead and I'm alive."
—MADONNA ON MARILYN MONROE COMPARISONS, *7 SUR 7* (1992)

MONTAUG, HAOUI: *March 6, 1952–June 7, 1991.* Poet, famous doorman at **Studio 54**, Palladium (126 E. 14th St., NY, NY) and **Danceteria**, and the promoter behind the **"No Entiendes!"** cabaret, at which Madonna performed her debut single **"Everybody."** The gig persuaded **Sire** to finance a cheap music video for the song—another Madonna first.

Montaug directed panel discussions at the **New Music Seminar**. He was so highly regarded that upon his **death** the organization created the Haoui Montaug New Music **Awards** in his name.

Montaug was one of Madonna's many friends to die of **AIDS**. When he lost the will to live in June 1991, he threw himself a farewell party in his apartment. Madonna is said to have made an "appearance" at the party via telephone. Surrounded by friends, Montaug swallowed what should have been a lethal dose of barbiturates. However, he woke up the next day and promptly took more pills ... this time, enough to kill him.

haoui montaug

A Polaroid of the connected, charismatic Montaug

MOORE, DEMI: *b. November 11, 1962.* Popular movie actor of the '80s and '90s who jumped from the soap *General Hospital* (1982–1983) to Brat Pack–laden films like *St. Elmo's Fire* (1985) and *About Last Night...* (1985) and on to major features like *Ghost* (1990) and *A Few Good Men* (1992).

Moore's **acting** talent has often been derided, but her choice of provocative material is **award**-worthy, such as with conversation pieces *Indecent **Proposal*** (1993) and *Striptease* (1996).

Madonna was long friendly with Moore, socializing with her at many events. They also very nearly made a female buddy movie about cops called *Leda & Swan* for director Joel Schumacher in 1991, but it was a **lost project** that never got off the ground.

Madonna and Moore cohosted private **Oscar** parties from 2006 until 2012 that attracted A-listers looking to have fun but *not* looking to be photographed while having it. When Moore and Ashton Kutcher **divorced**, it was speculated that Kutcher got Madonna (and manager **Guy Oseary**) in the settlement; Moore has not cohosted the party since.

MOORE, JULIANNE: *b. December 3, 1960.* One of the most acclaimed actors of the past 20 years, thanks to bold performances in films as diverse as *Short Cuts* (1993), *Safe* (1995), *Boogie Nights* (1997), *Far From Heaven*, *The Hours* (both 2002), *The Kids Are All Right* (2010) and her **Oscar**-winning turn in *Still Alice* (2014).

One of Moore's first movie roles was as "Sharon Dulaney," the wife of the lawyer (**Willem Dafoe**) who is defending **sexy** maybe-murderess "Rebecca Carlson" (Madonna) in *Body of Evidence*. As such, she was Madonna's character's **love** (lust) rival, and got to slap her face in a ladies' room during Carlson's trial. She also did a graphic sex scene with Dafoe, but at least she didn't have to do anything with candle wax.

In 2010, Moore graciously reminisced about the film with the author, laughing good-naturedly at its mention. The first thing she said was how "awful" her performance in the film had been, then she recalled that its director, Uli Edel, had been "so mean." She also said of her fellow actors, "Nobody would talk to me." She characterized Madonna as someone who seemed like she was going through a bad time during that period.

Moore said in 2015 of the experience, "I was actually super **nervous**; so, so nervous." Of the slap, she said, "It was a fake slap, but [Madonna] wasn't talking to me because she was being very method-y. I felt nervous and scared. I didn't want to hit her at all."

MOORE, MICHAEL: *b. April 23, 1954.* The most polarizing film director of all time, a liberal firebrand whose films on the auto industry, **guns**, President George W. Bush's failures and the healthcare establishment have carved out his niche as a dogged researcher and opinionated documentarian.

Madonna has much in common with Moore: Both were born in **Michigan**, both dropped out of the **University of Michigan** (Moore from the Flint location, Madonna from Ann Arbor) and both are driven by a belief that they are educating the masses.

Madonna's **Maverick** Pictures had a piece of one of Moore's least successful films, the comedy flick *Canadian*

RHONDA CORTE

Bacon (1995), which became the final movie starring John **Candy** to be released.

Madonna saw Moore's one-man show in **London** in 2003, calling it "revolutionary." She went on to say that seeing him speak led her to say, "Okay, I'm ready to go! I'm starting a revolution by myself!" Madonna's talk of revolution continues in her **work**.

On June 16, 2004, Moore attended Madonna's *Re-Invention Tour* at its **NYC** stop at **Madison Square Garden**, where she raved about his *Fahrenheit 9/11* (2004), urging her **fans** to see it: "I don't think I've ever cried so hard at a movie in my life." Moore had almost directed *I'm Going to Tell You a Secret*, filmed during the same tour, but though that never happened, Madonna's *I Am Because We Are* was screened at Moore's Traverse City Film Festival in Michigan on August 9, 2008. Upon attending to introduce her film, Madonna said, "There's something poetic about coming **back** to the place where I used to come for holidays—camping trips with my dad and **stepmother** and my very large family."

Moore said of Madonna, "She has such an incredible heart and such a generous spirit. She does so much out of the glare of the lights to make the world a better place."

"MORE": Objectively speaking, this song is one of the best things ever recorded. Less hyperbolically, it is further evidence that Madonna was perfectly cast in *Dick Tracy*, and that she was "more" than up to the film's musical demands.

Stephen Sondheim wrote this delicious ode to excess that treats materialism like oxygen and Madonna, who **worked** with a vocal coach to be able to hit his complicated notes, sounds comfy as hell demanding what's rightfully hers ... and *beyond*. The song's lyrical wit is matched by the gleam in Madonna's velvety vocal.

Produced by Madonna and Bill Bottrell, "More" is a definite highlight of *I'm Breathless: Music from and Inspired by the Film Dick Tracy*. Sadly, it did not receive a fraction of the attention paid to **"Sooner or Later (I Always Get My Man)"** or **"Vogue,"** two of the album's other priceless components. "More" has never been performed live, a situation which *EM20* calls on Madonna to change ... or does that sound too greedy?

MORGAN, PIERS: *b. March 30, 1965.* British "journalist" who made his name, such as it is, as the editor of right-wing reptile Rupert Murdoch's *News of the World*, a **job** he left when he broke a **privacy** law by publishing photos of **Princess Diana**'s brother's first wife leaving a clinic. He moved on to the *Daily Mirror*, where he continued to cause trouble (and generate sales) with his muckraking ways. He was fired for publishing faked images that purported to show Iraqi war prisoners being abused by British soldiers. He went on to be a judge on various reality shows, where his abrasive style made an impression, usually bad.

Surprisingly, Morgan was chosen to replace folksy **Larry King** on CNN in the US, where his profile was justifiably low. The show managed to last from January 17, 2011, until March 2014, but failed to capture King-sized ratings.

Before that show had even aired, Morgan made a big stink in the press, proclaiming that Madonna had been banned from appearing on it. It came off as wildly unprofessional, and his reasoning could not have been more juvenile.

"... Madonna and I, we've never really seen **eye**-to-eye. There was a bread roll throwing incident in **London** in the mid '90s; there was an incident at a hotel in the South of France, the **Cannes** Film Festival, involving a photographer and a bodyguard; there's been an incident involving a pub owner by her recently departed husband, **Guy Ritchie**, where my brother was the manager."

But Morgan claims the worst thing Madonna ever did to him was deny him a good story. "Madonna's publicist once said to me, 'Listen to me, Madonna is not **pregnant**,' when I was running a newspaper. And I said, 'Are you sure?' She said, 'Listen to me, Piers. Madonna is not pregnant.' The next day, they announced [the news] on a rival newspaper's website. There's a series of crimes."

But Morgan does not passively despise Madonna; he has used her **fame** to gain attention numerous times. When Madonna joined **Twitter** in 2012, Morgan tweeted to her, "Welcome to Twitter...-you're still banned from my show. **Love** Piers." **Guy Oseary** responded by making public an ass-kissing note asking Madonna to appear on Morgan's UK show, taped in LA, "where she would be welcome to promote her new film and forthcoming album release (and perform two numbers)." Morgan quickly clarified that she hadn't been banned from the UK show—but that she would be going forward.

Though Madonna's slights of Morgan would explain why he dislikes her, he has exposed the grotesque inner **workings** of his mind with some of his attacks on her. Though everyone knows Morgan's hatred is purely personal, his desperate grasping for a rationale usually hinges on Madonna's age and her **sexuality**.

"When I watched her in the days of **'Holiday,'** nothing was sexier. Watching Madonna at 52 going out with a 22-year-old called Jesus and stripping her clothes off, it's like, 'Please, it's over!'" he complained in 2011.

On an episode of *The Meredith Vieira Show* (2014-) in 2015, Morgan—whose contempt for women is so thorough that he often counts on them not to even have the spine to notice it—said, "I just find her, she's one of these people that, she seems to always want to shock and offend us, which is fine when you're, like, 22, if you're **Miley Cyrus** twerking. It's a little bit awkward when you're 58 or whatever she is now ... I don't wanna see you twerking, with great respect, Meredith." Vieira kept it light, but called him on his misogyny. When Morgan claimed to be equally embarrassed by **Mick Jagger**'s antics, she called him an **ageist**. Which he is, and proudly so.

A true tabloid click-whore, Morgan tweeted several times his glee when Madonna was brutally yanked off the stage at the **Brit Awards**, not even waiting to see if she'd been injured: "Dying on her ass. Literally." "Ambulance for Granny, please." "Hahahahahahahahahahaha," "Material Hurl" and more.

As outrageous as his gleeful tweets were, he—as the US editor-at-large of the UK-based *Daily Mail*—immediately wrote a shockingly barbaric and tone-deaf piece making light of Madonna's accident, and using it as another outlet for espousing his misogynistic views. The title? "Falling off the stage, Madonna, is **God**'s way of telling you you're too old to cavort like a hooker." (Because women who express their sexualities freely must be prostitutes ... which is okay if they're young. Follow?) The piece explained that Morgan had been a **fan** in 1987, but by 1993, when he wrote a widely published slam of ***The Girlie Show World Tour*** (the tour got raves in the US, another example of his Madonna Derangement Syndrome), he already found her to be "almost a **parody** of herself." The article attacked Madonna's artistry (fair game), then descended into mud-slinging about her spirituality, her love life and her parenting; as a **mother**, he branded her "negligent, dumb, self-obsessed and repulsive."

To see an adult and a presumed professional take such delight from a potentially serious stage accident because of perceived snubs from many years earlier was chilling. That lack of empathy is the mark of a true sociopath, for all his empty posturing on various liberal issues.

Considering his apparent bloodlust when it comes to Madonna, we can only cross our fingers that Madonna will bury him. Hopefully, alive.

> "Grotesque. Why would any woman want to look like a caveman? I'm serious. I don't want arms like that on my show … Long sleeves, maybe she can come on."—PIERS MORGAN ON MADONNA'S ARMS (2012)

MORISSETTE, ALANIS: *b. June 1, 1974.* Canadian rocker whose first incarnation as an entertainer was as a teeny-bopper. When she recorded a third album with producer Glen Ballard, she was shopped in the US and rejected by everyone ... except for Madonna's **Maverick** Records, courtesy of **Guy Oseary**. Just happy to have a release, Morissette wound up capturing the world's imagination with her incendiary single "You Oughta Know" (1995), a Top 10 hit that helped make the album, *Jagged Little Pill*, into the best-selling pop album of the '90s.

"... [W]e were just blown away by (A) her songwriting skills and (B) her **voice**, and then we met her and she was so young and yet she was so, um, mature for her age, and, so we knew right away that she was gonna do well," Madonna said of her in 1998.

At the time, Morissette said Madonna represented "another artist, going for it," but never appeared to be in Madonna's thrall.

Morissette publicly criticized Maverick when her album *Supposed Former Infatuation Junkie* (1998) didn't sell well, but Madonna met with her privately to persuade her to stick with Maverick, which she did. She and the label later parted ways, but only after Madonna had herself moved on.

When asked what Madonna had been like as a boss, Morissette said in 2012, "It was an interesting dynamic. It was kind of like **back** to the antiquated system of 80% record company and 20% artist. There was an inherent win-lose quality to that dynamic, so less a boss and more a pseudo-partnership, but it wasn't really a partnership because that's win-win or no deal, right? ... We met a couple of times and she was actually quite lovely with me ... early on." She may be referring to the fact that Madonna gave her platinum nail polish to celebrate the first million in sales of her album, and a Tiffany's bracelet several years later.

MORRISSEY: *b. May 22, 1959.* Brilliant lyricist and the front man of the Smiths, easily one of the most talented and artistically adventurous rock acts of the '80s, even if US teens didn't cede them (comparatively speaking) much ground during that decade's British invasion of the charts; they couldn't even crack the US ***Billboard*** Hot 100, not even with "This Charming Man" (1983), not even with "Girlfriend in a Coma" (1987). Single-wise, Morrissey's biggest dose of American crossover success was the #46 peak of "The More You Ignore Me, the Closer I Get" (1994), which is ironic, because there is no ignoring Morrissey, an outspoken, vitriolic campaigner on behalf of animal rights who has also waded into controversy by seeming to defend the purity of **England**, leading to numerous accusations—all denied—of racism.

He's so unpleasant that while he claims to be celibate, it may not be a matter of choice.

Morrissey has been attacking Madonna for many years, but perhaps the ugliest thing he said was at a PETA benefit on July 9, 2007: "I wouldn't be surprised if she made that **African** boy [**David Banda**] into a coat and wore him for 15 minutes, then threw it away." That's Madonna's son he was talking about, but since Morrissey has implied that animals are so special and important that eating meat is akin to pedophilia, perhaps that explains his lack of boundaries on the topic.

In 2015, he wrote a nasty essay slamming the 2015 **Brit Awards**, saying that Madonna was using the occasion to again promote "her frightening career."

Viva **hate**, baby.

> "Madonna reinforces everything absurd and offensive. Desperate womanhood. Madonna is closer to organized prostitution than anything else."—MORRISSEY (1997)

MORTON, ANDREW: *b. 1953.* Journalist and celebrity biographer (of **Princess Diana** and **Tom Cruise**, among others) who in 2001 published *Madonna*, a rather slim volume that treated its subject respectfully and broke little new ground. As *The Guardian*'s reviewer said, "... [I]n this 'unauthorized' exposé, the 'revelations' wash over the reader like a vast dirty **condom**-strewn tide, all the more ugly for their banality. Madonna has had lots of **sex**. She has had **abortions**. She has been known to be insecure, pestering her menfolk with telephone calls. Morton might as well have told us that 'Madonna has been known to menstruate', so routine, so feminine, so human, are all of these experiences." The **book** is worth a browse for Madonna **fans** if only for the early-years photos, which are pretty spectacular, including some by **Linda Alaniz**.

MOTE PARK: *Lower Rd., Maidstone, Kent, UK*. On May 10, 2008, Madonna brought her *Hard Candy* promo tour to this venue, where she performed **"Candy Shop," "Miles Away," "4 Minutes," "Hung Up," "Give It 2 Me"** and **"Music."** The latter classic she performed in a pair of vintage glasses with no lenses that she'd worn in the '80s and that daughter **Lola** had dug out of her archives.

MOTHER: SEE: **Ciccone, Madonna Fortin**.

"MOTHER AND FATHER": Song from *American Life* written and produced by Madonna and **Mirwais**. The song is characterized by a shrill tone to Madonna's **voice** that lends it a child-like quality, appropriate as it's a rumination about living a childhood bereft of her **mother**, and how her mother's **death** led her to lash out at her **father**.

Madonna performed the song live, accompanying herself on the **guitar**, as part of a *Dateline NBC* interview conducted by **Matt Lauer**, and the footage found its way to his daytime gig on *Today*. She also performed it on her *Re-Invention World Tour*.

MOTORCYCLE: As a wild young thing during her **Paris** years, Madonna described her favorite leisure-time activity as riding with Algerian and Vietnamese motorcycle toughs and swerving within inches of pedestrians, screaming epithets.

MTV: Music-television cable channel that launched August 1, 1981, as a 24-hour video station that set trends and revolutionized the music biz in the '80s and '90s, but that has become a purveyor of reality programming in recent years as **YouTube** and Vevo have taken its place.

Madonna was one of the first artists to build up a canon of provocative and artistic music videos (after Duran Duran), and from her earliest hit videos was a staple of MTV programming.

The network often ran weekends filled with Madonna videos, frequently world-premiered her new videos with great fanfare and, via correspondents like **Kurt Loder** and **John Norris**, was granted exclusive interviews with Madonna, though she candidly told Loder in one interview that she never had time to watch MTV.

In 1990, MTV backed out of its much-ballyhooed plan to debut her **"Justify My Love"** video after its **censors** deemed the clip too hot to handle, banning it entirely. MTV had similar issues with **"Erotica"** and **"What It Feels Like for a Girl."**

Madonna has made a habit of performing at the network's annual **MTV Video Music Awards**, having made a splash on the first one in 1984.

MTV EUROPE MUSIC AWARDS: The EMAs (1994–) have on occasion provided a good forum for Madonna to shake her ass and sell her latest songs.

On the November 12, 1998, telecast from Milan, Italy, Madonna offered a painfully wobbly rendition of **"The Power of Good-Bye,"** then picked up **awards** for Best Female (presented by Ronan Keating and **Dolce & Gabbana**) and Best Album (presented by Blur ad **Gorillaz** front man Damon Albarn and footballer Ronaldo) for *Ray of Light*.

On November 16, 2000, Madonna took the EMAs by storm in Stockholm, Sweden, clad in a **Kylie Minogue** shirt, singing **"Music"** in a stripped-down performance with backing from **Donna De Lory** and **Niki Haris** as images from throughout her career were projected behind her. Afterward, Kelis and Moby presented Madonna with the award for Best Female, which she won over **Jennifer Lopez**, **Janet Jackson**, Melanie C and **Britney Spears**, and which she accepted in a red cowgirl outfit. She thanked all the Europeans who had inspired her over the years. She also picked up a Best **Dance** award from actor Thora Birch.

Madonna's greatest EMAs moment was on November 3, 2005, when she brought **"Hung Up"** to life onstage in Lisbon, Portugal, the first live performance of the song. Clad in a purple Gucci jacket, YSL boots and leotard, she and her troupe were revealed from inside a giant **disco** ball, then stormed across the stage in an elaborately choreographed routine that made use of elements of the song's music video. A slow-mo dance break had the audience in the palm of her hand. Afterward, Robbie Williams raved about Madonna showing pop stars half her age how it's done.

"My heart was just pumping out of my chest!" she said after that performance.

Madonna has a total of 19 nominations and four wins in the EMAs.

MTV PRESENTS MTVU STAND IN: *Airdates: 2004–2008*. A broadcast of **MTV**'s mtvU network, played on hundreds of university campuses in the US, that featured Madonna in an episode taped October 18, 2005. In the midst of her *Confessions on a Dance Floor* promo, Madonna appeared at Hunter College (695 Park Ave., NY, NY) to chat about her documentary *I'm Going to Tell You a Secret*, with the film's director **Jonas Åkerlund** at her side.

"I'm your motherbrothersisterloverdaughterauntie-unclegrandmagrandpalittlebabyjesus."
—MADONNA TO MTV ON THE OCCASION OF ITS 10TH BIRTHDAY (1991)

Madonna's appearance was a total surprise to students, who had just watched a special screening of the documentary, and who were encouraged to participate in a Q&A with the filmmakers.

The main takeaway from Madonna's impromptu lesson? "You're either hungry and, and determined to make it no matter what, or you're, or you're *not*."

The episode was aired on November 7, 2005, on mtvU Über, the first MTV channel distributed via broadband.

MTV VIDEO MUSIC AWARDS: *Dates presented: 1984–.* Annual **awards** show staged by **MTV** in which musicians and their creative cohorts are handed awards ("Moonmen"— they're metallic representations of the network's **original** Neil Armstrong promo spot) for excellence in the field of music video. The idea that making music videos was an **art** form was almost laughable when the network aired its first awards in 1984, and the tongue-in-cheek nature was enhanced by its use of cohosts Dan Aykroyd and **Bette Midler.**

Since then, the entire Golden Age of Music Video has happened (past tense), and along with a handful of other artists, Madonna was a huge contributor to it.

Because Madonna is synonymous with great music videos and with MTV, she has a long history with this awards show, with her live appearances being far more interesting than which Moonmen actually got to go home with her.

If Madonna is an institution when it comes to this show, it is due in large part to her antics—and MTV's antics—on the very first telecast, on September 14, 1984: Madonna, previewing her single **"Like a Virgin,"** warbled the song from atop a frickin' **wedding** cake. Clambering down in her bustier wedding dress by **Maripol,** she stalked around the stage with increasing confidence, ultimately rolling around on the floor, exposing her panties and garter belt as MTV's cameras swooped in. In those days, MTV did not understand the **power** of audience reaction shots, so we have only an unblinking record of Madonna's moves, and they are still shocking over 30 years later—did she *really* hump her veil, making it seem to disappear between her legs? There are elements of punk and **porn** in that performance of a naughty bubblegum-pop song. Whatever the mixture, it was heady, and though her manager **Freddy DeMann** was angry with her, Madonna had just made herself more famous than she'd ever **dreamed** possible.

The audience applauded ... politely.

Madonna's most accomplished live performance at the VMAs was on September 6, 1989, when to the strains of **"Express Yourself"** her silhouette, projected onto a screen, **worked** a chair while backup singers **Niki Haris** and **Donna De Lory** got into position. Madonna emerged from behind the screen, walking down automatically lighting steps, "Billie Jean" (1982)–style. Her vocals on this song were powerful, even as she **danced** her ass off. It was a potent peek at what to expect when she returned to the road in 1990 for her *Blond Ambition World Tour.* Most importantly, this

performance (thank you, **Shep Pettibone** for the all-time classic remix) featured a lengthy dance break during which Madonna first demonstrated her newfound appreciation for **vogueing**. It simply does not get better than this.

Or does it?

As vocally thrilling as "Express Yourself" was, Madonna in some ways outdid herself the very next year, returning the following September 6 with a lip-synched staging of **"Vogue"** that nonetheless goes down in Ma-history as one of her most outstanding televised performances. Fresh off her tour, Madonna took the time to put together an **eye**-popping *Dangerous Liaisons* (1989)–like rendering of the song. Every member of her troupe paraded in 18th-century finery with Madonna, De Lory and Haris working some fancy **fans** with nail-biting precision, even cockily flipping them in mid-air and catching them to the beat. As classy as it was, the performance also relied on copious booby-grabbing. Madonna almost lost her steely composure when dancer Jose Gutierez (of **Jose & Luis**) stepped on her dress for a moment too long. The entire presentation was pop chutzpah at its fanciest.

Opening the show on September 2, 1993, Madonna did **"Bye Bye Baby,"** a lesbian-themed romp that was exactly what audiences would get if they were lucky enough to score tickets to her limited *Girlie Show World Tour.* Watch for **Carrie Ann Inaba**'s spread legs, a move that deserves a Bruno Tonioli–shouted, "10!"

For the September 10, 1998, show, Madonna's performance was a medley of the *Ray of Light* album track **"Shanti/Ashtangi"** and the album's title song. The chanting went over well, but when she switched to a rocked-up **"Ray of Light"** with Lenny Kravitz on **guitar**, Madonna— flashing her nipples through a sheer wifebeater—sounded terribly winded. It is considered one of her worst televised performances. Oh, well, she won a bunch of awards that night anyway. (She'd also told MTV not to proceed with its plan to invite Monica Lewinsky—and MTV obeyed.)

On August 28, 2003, Madonna gave her most controversial and probably best-remembered (perhaps even eclipsing her 1984 cakewalk) performance on the show— and it is so far her last. Preceded onto the stage by **Britney Spears** and **Christina Aguilera** in skimpy white wedding costumes reminiscent of Madonna's from '84 (the girls cooing "Like a Virgin"), Madonna was this time the groom, rising from the cake in a black suit and walking down it with considerably more sense of purpose than she had 19 years earlier. Singing a **"Hollywood"** remix, Madonna led the girls in a tango, felt up their merchandise and then erotically kissed them both on the lips before throwing it to **Missy Elliott** for a hot rap. The stunned reaction shot of Britney's ex **Justin Timberlake** alone was one of the most memorable images MTV has ever broadcast, and that includes that video "Fishheads" (1978) by Barnes & Barnes.

Along with performing, Madonna has also shown up to give and receive awards. On September 5, 1986, Madonna was the first recipient of the Video Vanguard Award, handed to her by Robert Palmer. An extremely jet-lagged Madonna accepted in her **"True Blue"** European video frock, saying, "I'm so tired right now, I don't know if I'm sleepin' or awake!"

On September 8, 1994, following her disastrous interview on *Late Show with David Letterman*, Madonna showed up to hand out Video of the Year to Aerosmith, first grabbing attention by appearing on Letterman's arm. "I'll, I'll be in the car ... watch your language," Letterman, playing "George" to her "Martha," said before departing.

The next year, on September 7, 1995, Madonna was **back**, looking groovy in Gucci. Introduced lamely with, "Attention, shoppers—Madonna!" by Dennis Miller, she walked out on to the stage like she owned MTV, saying, "Bob Dole is sorry he couldn't be here tonight to give the award away for the Best Rap Video, so I'll be speaking on his behalf. He's tied up in the Senate basement right now. Um, rap will not give in to government threats on **censorship**. Rap has proven itself a force to be reckoned with for male and female artists alike, leaving you ... so this leaves you with two choices: Either listen up, or get the **fuck** out of the way." The winner was Dr. Dre.

Madonna returned on the same telecast to accept Best Female Video for **"Take a Bow"** from **George Clooney**. She insisted on doing a little dance since she wasn't able to perform. This show was the one after which Madonna found herself in a sticky situation with **Kurt Loder** and **Courtney Love**.

On September 4, 1997, Madonna waltzed out onto the stage in a tie looking very much like a schoolmarm. She gave a short speech about the **death** of **Princess Diana**. She said, in part, "It's time for us to take responsibility for our own insatiable need to run after gossip and scandals and lies and rumors, to live vicariously through other people's misery." She claimed we are all connected, which reflected her recent embrace of **Kabbalah**. She went on to introduce a performance by Prodigy.

Madonna, a gorgeous redhead in black, won a huge ovation on September 9, 1999, when she won an award for Best Song from a Movie (for **"Beautiful Stranger"**). Everyone lost their shit, except for **Prince**, who was shown looking decidedly unmoved in the audience. She gave thanks to **Maverick Records** and her **fans**, among other deserving entities. Later, an array of **drag** Madonnas took to the stage, leading Madonna to inspect each one of them and to note, "All I have to say is that it takes a real man to fill my shoes! Give them all a big round of applause. Thank you." They disappeared, leaving Madonna to introduce Paul McCartney. "People like me need people like him to look up to," she said, calling him the kind of **talent** that comes along once a century. Their interaction as they announced Video of the Year was adorable. The winner? Lauryn Hill.

On September 13, 2009, Madonna opened the show with a lengthy eulogy of an artist she always admired, **Michael Jackson**. The King of Pop is dead, but the **Queen of Pop** is very much alive—why hasn't she been back?

MTV VIDEO MUSIC AWARDS NOMINATIONS & WINS

Here is how she's fared, and feel free to cluck your tongue at how rarely she's won a competitive MTV Video Music Award:

1984
Best New Artist ("Borderline")

1985
Best Art Direction, Best Choreography, Best Cinematography ("Like a Virgin"); Best Choreography, Best Female Video ("Material Girl")

1986
Video Vanguard Award-WON; Best Choreography ("Dress You Up"); Best Choreography ("Like a Virgin")

1987
Best Choreography, Best Art Direction, Best Female Video ("Open Your Heart"); Best Cinematography, Best Female Video-WON, Best Overall Performance ("Papa Don't Preach")

1989
Best Art Direction-WON, Best Cinematography-WON, Best Direction-WON, Best Editing, Best Female Video ("Express Yourself"); Video of the Year, Viewer's Choice-WON ("Like a Prayer")

1990
Best Art Direction, Best Choreography, Best Cinematography-WON, Best Dance Video, Best Direction-WON, Best Editing-WON, Best Female Video, Video of the Year, Viewer's Choice ("Vogue")

1991
Best Choreography, Best Female Video ("Like a Virgin"), Best Long Form Video-WON (*The Immaculate Collection*)

1992
Best Choreography, Best Dance Video, Best Female Video ("Holiday")

1993
Best Art Direction-WON, Best Cinematography-WON ("Rain")

1994
Best Video from a Film ("I'll Remember")

1995
Best Choreography, Best Dance Video ("Human Nature"); Best Art Direction, Best Female Video-WON ("Take a Bow")

1996
Best Cinematography ("You'll See")

1998
Best Special Effects-WON ("Frozen"), Best Choreography-WON, Best Cinematography, Best Dance Video, Best Direction-WON, Best Editing-WON, Best Female Video-WON, Breakthrough Video, Video of the Year-WON ("Ray of Light")

1999
Best Cinematography, Best Female Video, Best Video from a Film-WON ("Beautiful Stranger"); Best Special Effects ("Nothing Really Matters")

2000
Best Cinematography ("American Pie")

2001
Best Choreography, Best Female Video ("Don't Tell Me")

2003
Best Video from a Film ("Die Another Day")

2006
Best Choreography, Best Dance Video, Best Female Video, Best Pop Video, Video of the Year ("Hung Up")

2008
Best Dancing in a Video ("4 Minutes")

"Madonna may be a 'new' artist, but after two hit videos she's established herself as a success. Tonight she's here to share that success with us."–1ST ANNUAL MTV VIDEO MUSIC AWARDS PROGRAM (1984)

MTV VIDEO MUSIC AWARDS LATINOAMÉRICA:
Airdates: 2002-2009. **MTV**'s annual celebration of the best music videos of Latin America, later retitled Los Premios MTV Latinoamérica. In 2003, Madonna appeared on video to give a short introduction to the telecast, explaining the purpose of the **awards**. She gave the speech in Spanish (laughing at herself at one point), ending with, "Muchos besos—muah!"

MULLALLY, MEGAN: *b. November 12, 1958*. Comic actor best known for her over-the-top (and right on the **money**) Emmy-winning portrayal of "Karen Walker" on *Will & Grace* (1998–2006), and for later memorable appearances on *Parks and Recreation* (2010–2015) and *Happy Endings* (2011–2013).

When Madonna was pitched as a guest star on *Will & Grace* in 2003, she had never seen the show (**gay** gasp!), so was given DVDs by her manager, **Caresse Henry.** Madonna agreed to do the gig only because she **loved** Mullally.

Madonna was so taken with Mullally she also submitted to an on-camera interview by her for **VH1** called *Madonna Speaks*, an experience that in turn inspired Mullally to try being a talk show host on *The Megan Mullally Show* (2006–2007).

MUNRO, TOM: Fashion photographer and celebrity portraitist who has **worked** with Madonna quite often since 2008. He directed her music videos **"Give It 2 Me"** and **"Turn Up the Radio"** and tour backdrop videos for **"Die Another Day," "Human Nature"** and **"Justify My Love"** (*EM20* votes for the latter as his best contribution to the Madonna canon). His work decorates the *Sticky & Sweet Tour* program and was used to promote the concert that will wind up being the most successful tour of her career.

Munro has also shot Madonna for **magazine** cover spreads: *Harper's Bazaar* (December 2011) with *W.E.* star Andrea Riseborough and *L'Uomo Vogue* (May 2014), the latter of which was probably his most creative work with Madonna.

Like **Steven Klein,** Munro has had many unflattering outtakes from his shoots **leak.**

MUSCLES: By the time she was on her *Blond Ambition World Tour*, notice was being paid to Madonna's biceps. At the time it was usually complimentary. But a dozen years later, she was frequently described as mannish, an example of how discussions of Madonna are often discussions of other things entirely, in this case femininity vs. masculinity, and how these discussions can really flush out people's judgmental natures.

The most infamous **hot mess** pictures of Madonna seemed to enflame opinion more because of her muscular arms than for any other reason, and her appearance in *Swept Away* and on her *Sticky & Sweet Tour* was frequently cited as being too ripped.

One of the most reprehensible passages written about Madonna came in the form of a cutting "Tribute to Madonna's Current and Former Selves" for *The New York Times* in 2006. Ginia Bellafante, clearly vexed at Madonna's efforts to remain youthful, ripped her a new one for having the audacity to maintain a sinewy form, because even if it is attainable for Madonna, it isn't for others:

"... [H]ere again, her perfect musculature produces a kind of dissonance. Madonna doesn't have an altruist's body, she has a denier's. What you're tallying in your head when you watch her **dance** with the strength and agility of a 19-year-old are the number of hours she spends each day practicing Ashtanga **yoga,** running hills and bench-pressing the **weight** of a Regency table. You are tallying all the calories that Madonna is not eating."

There you have it—if you're muscular, you can't be truly altruistic. Bellafante, in documenting what she believes *we all* must be thinking when we watch Madonna perform proves only what is running through her own envious brain.

MUSIC (ALBUM): *Release date: September 19, 2000. Billboard 200 peak: #1.* Madonna's follow-up to *Ray of Light* extended her interest in electronic music, but shattered that previous record's pleasing consistency by offering listeners a wild ride of genre-busting **dance,** dippy pop and cerebral esoterica, a real stew of creative gestures, mostly successfully realized, and every one of them grand.

It was go big or go it-feels-like-home time for Madonna.

"I never want to repeat myself," Madonna told *Next* (something she'd said before). "The sound of my last album was very dense and layered, and the feeling was much more introspective. This time, both lyrically and sonically, I want to open things up." Open it up she did, with a little help from a man who would become one of her most important collaborators.

After hearing about **Mirwais** from **Guy Oseary,** Madonna was immediately attracted to his **work.** Like herself, Mirwais had been on the music scene (though in a decidedly more underground way) for 20 years, and his sound was similar to, but represented some kind of movement away from, *Ray of Light.* Madonna called him up and proposed they work together to see where things went. Their first encounter led to her recording the lush, spacy **"Paradise (Not for Me)"** which, perhaps due to their being about the same age (past 40), boldly (for a female pop artist) declared, "I can't remember/When I was young." The song was a winner, but their second match-up became one of her signature hits, **"Music,"** and they were off to the races; Mirwais wound up on more than half the songs.

"Everyone knows [Madonna] as a chameleon, or a businesswoman. I wanted to show her potential as a musician," Mirwais told *Interview* in 2001.

Their work together was hindered by his poor grasp of English. An interpreter helped, but one can't help but wonder if the language barrier helped create some of their songs' unusual poetry.

She also worked with a few other **voices,** as well as **William Orbit,** a holdover from *Ray of Light,* but his contributions wound up among the album's weakest, an example of how even the most creative of partners can use a break. (And can get **back** together at a later date to create magic again.) Orbit claimed he wasn't offended that Madonna worked with others following their success, "as long as she uses good people."

—JERRY MITCHELL

The album begins with the title track. In a kick to the **balls**, Madonna's unidentifiable voice is vocodered into a gender-neutral growl: "Hey, Mr. DJ ... put a record on ... I wanna dance with my baby." The song's beat is sick, a fruitier take on the "Jungle Boogie" (1973) trill that formed the basis of **"Erotica,"** and the musical structure chaotic, like the graffiti-sprayed walls of a Soho side street. The song's simple lyrics made it an instant anthem, and an easy #1 hit internationally. As cutting-a-rug-edge as the song was, there was still a lot of humor in it, and for once listeners understood and appreciated Madonna's winking delivery. As Madonna would later say, the song set the tone for the entire album.

Next up, Madonna's Mirwais concoction **"Impressive Instant"** is at least as risky as "Music," if not more, a creepy club song that again distorts Madonna's voice at every opportunity, and that ludicrously takes a left turn two minutes and 15 seconds in for a happily deranged Madonna to chirp, "I like to singy-singy-singy/Like a bird on a wingy-wingy-wingy." Even crazier, it totally works; the song is a **fan** fave. It's not a deep song, it's more like Madonna on mushrooms. But that's the idea. "Life would be such a **drag** if it was deep and probing all the time," she told *Billboard* of "Impressive Instant."

Things slow down considerably with the clunky Orbit collaboration **"Runaway Lover,"** with its more conventional narrative and awkward lyrics, but it's hard to complain too loudly when the song is still catchy.

Mirwais has said that the next track, **"I Deserve It,"** has Madonna's "dry" voice, meaning it isn't sweetened in any way. "The first time, she was afraid, honestly, of that. I think sometimes a lot of people are afraid of their own voice, you know?" She masks any fear well, instead sounding completely unconcerned, unadorned, vulnerable. It's an unselfconscious folky **love** song to her then-hubby **Guy Ritchie**. It's also the first hint of a decidedly country vein that runs through *Music*, whose cover and whose packaging **art** presents Madonna, in inspired shots by **Jean-Baptiste Mondino**, as a cowgirl. The synth effect two minutes in is like a cool-as-hell **reinvention** of *The NBC Mystery Movie* (1971–1977), in the best possible way.

Orbit, who had been so *on* with **"Beautiful Stranger"** in 1999 seemed to steer Madonna back to that sound with **"Amazing,"** a fairly generic soundalike. Madonna's description of it as an "I-love-you-but-**fuck**-you song" is rather more interesting than the song itself. "Amazing" is the only song on the album—even counting the bonus tracks—that Madonna has never performed live.

By contrast, Madonna's early-stages thrill at working with Mirwais expresses itself on **"Nobody's Perfect,"** an almost entirely vocodered (when she's not whispering) mid-tempo tune that sounds like a sad robot realizing it's not 100% human thanks to the fact that a flawed human invented it. This is the kind of song a Madonna fan will either dig or want to bury.

"I've been popular and unpopular, successful and unsuccessful, loved and loathed, and I know how meaningless it all is, therefore I feel free to take risks," Madonna told *Elle* in 2001, and a song like "Nobody's Perfect" is nothing if not a risk.

Just when things were getting maybe a bit too out-there, **"Don't Tell Me"** comes along, presenting itself as one of the most perfect Madonna's ever recorded. Inspired by "Stop," a rollickin' tune by Madonna's bro-in-law **Joe Henry**, it was adapted into a mature-sounding (as opposed to **"Human Nature"**'s defiant brattiness) refusal to play by the rules. The city girl goes country, but brings along the electronic trickery of Mirwais. That twang in her voice was no trick, though, and has been delivered beautifully live quite a few (but not enough) times.

Guy Sigsworth sent Madonna his demo for **"What It Feels Like for a Girl"** complete with its distinctive Charlotte Gainsbourg spoken-word intro/sample, and Madonna fell in love with it. And why not? It's a searing **feminist** screed that goes down as sweetly as a butterscotch **candy**. Madonna's vocals are left alone. It's a lovely expression of Madonna's long-held belief that women do not have it easy, even **rich** and famous ones.

ALEJANDRO MOGOLLO

One of the author's favorite Madonna songs, "Paradise (Not for Me)," reduces the proceedings to a crawl, and it is here that you must wonder how panicked **Warner Bros.** was regarding the prospect of Top 40 singles on this album. A melancholy rumination on aging and bad timing and missed chances, the song is a jewel in the **Queen of Pop**'s crown, but a dark and mysterious one about which gemologists might testily disagree. But as for Madonna letting French slip from her tongue? Magnifique.

"Most people think that someone like her has a big plan in mind, but we were like a young band. You work with a feeling. You do not have the charts or a video in mind," Mirwais told *Entertainment Weekly* of his work with Madonna. It shows on tracks like this, a devil-may-care attitude regarding chart potential; Madonna was still daring radio to keep up with her then.

The standard album ends with **"Gone,"** another country-style tune, one that reverberates with finality. "Nothin' equals nothin'," she sings with no need to explain.

Madonna's gimmicky but still easy-on-the-ears **"American Pie"** remake was available on overseas editions, but so was **"Cyber-Raga,"** an exciting Sanskrit song (now *there's* a phrase one rarely writes) done with Talvin Singh that revives the chanting style Madonna had embraced on **"Shanti/Ashtangi."** ("Cyber-Raga" was only available to Japanese and Australian customers or as the B-side of

MUSIC (1–10)

MUSIC European (1–11)

MUSIC Japanese & Australian (1–12)

① "Music" (Madonna/Mirwais)–3:44, produced by Madonna/Mirwais

② "Impressive Instant" (Madonna/Mirwais)–3:37, produced by Madonna/Mirwais

③ "Runaway Lover" (Madonna/William Orbit) –4:46, produced by Madonna/William Orbit

④ "I Deserve It" (Madonna/Mirwais)–4:23, produced by Madonna/Mirwais

⑤ "Amazing" (Madonna/William Orbit) –3:43, produced by Madonna/William Orbit

⑥ "Nobody's Perfect" (Madonna/Mirwais)–4:58, produced by Madonna/Mirwais

⑦ "Don't Tell Me" (Madonna/Mirwais/Joe Henry)–4:40, produced by Madonna/Mirwais

⑧ "What It Feels Like for a Girl" (Madonna/Guy Sigsworth) –4:43, produced by Madonna/Guy Sigsworth/ Mark "Spike" Stent

⑨ "Paradise (Not for Me)" (Madonna/Mirwais)–6:33, produced by Madonna/Mirwais

⑩ "Gone" (Madonna/Damian Le Gassick/Nik Young)–3:24, produced by Madonna/ William Orbit/Mark "Spike" Stent

⑪ "American Pie" (Don McLean)–4:33, produced by Madonna/ William Orbit

⑫ "Cyber-Raga" (Madonna/Talvin Singh) –5:33, produced by Madonna/Talvin Singh

"BECAUSE I'VE RECENTLY BEEN LIVING A RATHER LOW-KEY DOMESTIC LIFE, THERE'S A PART OF ME THAT SOMETIMES FEELS LIKE AN ANIMAL READY TO BE SPRUNG FROM A CAGE. I MISS PERFORMING AND DANCING AND BEING ON THE ROAD. SO PART OF THIS RECORD DEALS WITH THAT KIND OF ENERGY. THEN THERE IS ANOTHER PART THAT IS ABOUT LOVE, THE SIMPLEST AND MOST COMPLEX SUBJECT THAT THERE IS. PREVIOUSLY, I'VE ALWAYS MADE RECORDS ABOUT ONE OR ANOTHER OF THESE ASPECTS. THIS TIME I DID THEM BOTH."
—MADONNA, *MUSIC* PRESS RELEASE (2000)

"THE POP-SONG STRUCTURES ARE STABLE, BUT THEY'VE MOVED INTO A SONIC REALM WHERE ANYTHING CAN HAPPEN."
—JON PARELES, *THE NEW YORK TIMES* (2000)

"*MUSIC* ENGENDERS THAT PARTICULAR REACTION WITHOUT WHICH THE POP INDUSTRY AND THE FASHION SCENE WOULD STAGNATE AND DIE: 'GOD, THAT SOUNDS/LOOKS UGLY … SHE MUST KNOW SOMETHING!' TO QUOTE THE TITLE OF ANOTHER NEW MADONNA SONG, SHE HAS ONCE AGAIN CONJURED UP AN 'IMPRESSIVE INSTANT'. IT'S HARD TO THINK OF A MAINSTREAM ARTIST WHO WOULD TAKE AS MANY GLEEFUL RISKS AT THIS STAGE IN HER CAREER."—STEVEN DALY, *VANITY FAIR* (2000)

"NO POINT IN DWELLING ON THE DIRGEY STUFF, EXCEPT TO OBSERVE THAT MADONNA'S MORE FUN GOING LOCO THAN GOING NICO … MEANWHILE, SHOULD MADONNA DO ANYTHING REALLY DUBIOUS IN THE NEXT WHILE TO DRAW SOME ATTENTION TO HERSELF, PLEASE DISREGARD PARTS OF THIS REVIEW."
—PHIL DELLIO, *THE VILLAGE VOICE* (2000)

"Music," but it reappeared on *The MDNA Tour* during her **"I'm a Sinner"** performance.)

Music was an out-of-the-box (music used to come out of boxes … promise!) smash, selling 420,000 copies in its first week, Madonna's best first-week sales tally ever. Over time, it would go on to sell more than 15 million copies worldwide, pardner.

Madonna supported the album with a US promo gig at the **Roseland Ballroom**, her first live concert in almost seven years and her first following the birth of her son **Rocco**, and followed it up with another at the UK's **Brixton Academy**. The live gigs were said to prove that Madonna still had it, but in reality, *Music* had already made that point.

"MUSIC" (SONG): *Release date: August 21, 2000. Billboard Hot 100 peak: #1.* Madonna's last #1 single (so far!) was this game-changing, genre-thumping, trend-setting ode to **dance** that she wrote and produced with **Mirwais**. The lead single and title track from her #1 album *Music*, this brash and bumpin' song sounded like nothing else on the radio, and to this day it has a unique stop-start seductiveness.

The platinum single had its genesis when Madonna attended a **Sting** concert, his crowd giving her the idea for the quirky "Music" line about "the bourgeoisie and the rebel."

"Music" has gone on to become one of Madonna's most identifiable hits, one she has performed live many times, and one that *Entertainment Weekly* chose as the second-best single of 2000 after "Stan" by **Eminem**. According to *Billboard* magazine, "Music" is the ninth biggest hit of Madonna's career.

Madonna first performed the song live on November 5, 2000, at **Roseland Ballroom** as part of a promo tour for the album. She did it again at her **Brixton Academy** show a few weeks later. Other live performances include the 2000 **MTV Europe Music Awards**, the 43rd Annual **Grammys**, **Live 8**, her *Hard Candy* promo tour in 2008 and her **Super Bowl** halftime show. She lip-synched the song on *Top of the Pops*.

In concert, Madonna has included "Music" on the set lists of the *Drowned World Tour*, the *Re-Invention World Tour*, the *Confessions Tour*, the *Sticky & Sweet Tour* and the *Rebel Heart Tour*. On *The MDNA Tour*, the song popped up in a radio-themed interlude.

"Radio and listeners alike will be shocked, then mesmerized by this composition, showcasing yet another side of an artist who, after nearly 20 years, continues to be a true industry artisan and the by-the-book definition of 'evolutionary.'"—*BILLBOARD* (2000)

"MUSIC" (VIDEO): *Director: Jonas Åkerlund, 2000.* In April 2000, a **pregnant** Madonna was in need of a music video for her **dance** song **"Music,"** the lead single from her forthcoming album of the same name. Since she wouldn't be able to do any drop splits, she conceived of a humorous send-up of rap videos that would follow a "Puff Mommy" version of herself as she's party-limoed with her besties (**Niki Haris** and **Debi Mazar**), to a strip club. The video is tricked out with gold **accessories**, a split-screen effect and parts of the lyrics in '70s-style fonts.

On her decision to take her girlfriends to a titty bar, Madonna told the *New York Post*, "If you look at a lot of those [rap] videos, that's where they end up, in strip clubs. So, if I'm going to do a role reversal take on it, then I'm going to do it all the way."

Every aspect of the video was sketched out and developed, including funny banter between Madonna and her limo driver (in a genius bit of casting, **Sacha Baron Cohen**) and an animated sequence.

The director told *Rolling Stone* in 2015, "The treatment had dialogue and stuff like music videos usually didn't have **back** then. We wanted to have a comedian and Madonna was really good friends with **Chris Rock** and some of these other great comedians ... But I had just [discovered] Sacha Baron Cohen, the Ali G character, out of **London**. And I talked to her, 'Please, you got to check this guy out. He's awesome.' And nobody in America had heard of him. They actually ended up meeting, which was great because that kind of sold it right away."

The gold limo in the video was actually really busted inside, so the interior was shot in a sound stage. Happily, the studio (Charlie Chaplin Studios, a.k.a. Jim Henson Studios, 1416 N. La Brea Ave., Hollywood, CA) was right across from the venerable bikini bar Crazy Girls (1433 N. La Brea Ave., Hollywood, CA), in which the video's sleazetastic dance sequences were shot.

"Music" is a remarkably tongue-in-cheek offering following a slate of serious efforts from *Ray of Light*.

MUSIC BUILDING, THE: *584 Eighth Ave., NY, NY.* The storied W. 39th St. dump where Madonna hung out in her early days as a solo singer, a member of the **Breakfast Club** and a member of **Emmy**. The place is 12 stories tall, with 69 studios total, all chock-full of musicians engaged in various creative endeavors. Madonna lived here with **Stephen Bray** briefly, and it was here where she routinely bumped into bands like Nervus Rex, the **Dance** and the System.

"I thought they were all lazy," she told *Rolling Stone* in 1984. "I felt a lot of affection for them, but I thought that only a handful of people were going to get out of that building to any success."

Music Building manager Jack P. Lerner remembered Madonna almost two decades later as someone who wandered the building, singing and looking for partners ... *creative* partners, you sicko. "Well, there were a lot of cute boys in the building, I have to say ..." Madonna said in 1998, copping to making out on the roof. She would use a freight elevator since she usually had **drums** and other musical equipment. Her main studio was #604 (later #1205–#1207), which she could only afford because all the members of Emmy chipped in and then the band shared it with another band.

Talking about her time squatting there (which was against the rules), Madonna said she had to take a whore's bath (shut up) using a sink that only produced cold water. Perhaps the miserable conditions spurred her on, because she created some classic '80s pop tunes (or their forefathers) in this place. She would take most of her meals at a nearby donut dive.

"It was like a dormitory for freaks, basically." —MADONNA ON THE MUSIC BUILDING (1998)

(ANOTHER) OPEN LETTER TO MADONNA
BY MICHAEL MUSTO

In the early '80s, I shared a bill with Madonna at a downtown club called Chase Park (a converted Chase bank). I was the lead singer for a Motown group called the Must, and she and my band literally had equal billing. Well, we never got to sound check that night because she obsessively checked her mic from every angle (and those of her band, too) while we waited around to do our own check. And she was quite unknown at the time! But she took so long at it that the door of the club had to eventually open while she was still testing! I thought this was pretty bratty of her, and the pre-Madonna behavior, as it were, didn't stop there.

We went on first, and then were greeting friends in the shared dressing room. Madonna's manager, Camille [Barbone], came up to me and complained that Madonna was getting ready and I shouldn't be bringing friends in while she dressed! I told her a thing or two and said, "Look, we didn't even get to sound check, and now this? It's not my fault that we have a shared dressing room. Sorry, but we're greeting our friends." I thought it was pretty nervy of Madonna's camp, and especially bizarre since she later "made the world her gynecologist."

Some time later, "Everybody" started blaring out at every club you went to in NYC. I never saw Madge in her club dates, but I did hear that song all over the place—it should have been called "Everywhere"—and thought it was like dental work without anesthesia. Maybe my sour memory of her was fueling it, but I really couldn't stand that song! But while the feeling (or at least the hope) was that she'd go away, I did start enjoying her hits like "Holiday" and "Borderline" and "Into the Groove," and I appreciated her in *Desperately Seeking Susan*. (Who knew it would be the high watermark of her film appearances?)

With her crafty marketing, the woman was getting bigger and bigger, and soon enough, I had bought into the cult of Madonna, and recognized her as the greatest star of the new hot format—four-minute music videos, where you moved your mouth, but didn't speak. I also ended up praising her yay-gay actions—from gal-palling around with Sandra Bernhard to celebrating the vogueing community—and I wound up writing an *OutWeek* cover story about her status as a gay icon. I adored the way she continually re-invented herself by picking the best stylists and accompanists around, and I also loved her taste for scandal and knowing just how to whip it up so it can help your career rather than hinder it. And her concerts had become must-see events, where the socializing in the crowd was as delicious as the performance. But we never really interacted (though Liz Rosenberg has always been supernice).

At Madonna's *Sex* book party, I wore a Pope outfit, and wore as a necklace a picture of Sinéad O'Connor ripped up—pretty clever, no?—and Liz pointed me out to Madonna and said, "Look, Madonna, Michael Musto's dressed like the Pope." Madonna beatifically smiled, and I was thrilled. In the *New York Post* write-up of the event, they said I was one of the very few who dressed in the right spirit.

But I've liked keeping a distance from her—and I'm sure she has, too, lol—because it's better to cover her with some sense of mystery and detachment.

My recent letter to her wasn't criticizing her for aging—in fact, she's done trailblazing things for mature women and should be commended for that—but for acting like she always has to hop onto the young bandwagon to stay relevant. It's a sad reality that radio won't play people of a certain age, and she's realistically trying to circumvent that by duetting with teen idols, but sometimes I think she should maybe just do a Peggy Lee tribute album or something. (It would surely be #1 on iTunes, like Barbra's *Partners* and the Gaga/Tony Bennett duets.).

But who am I to say? After our initial horrible encounter, she's gone on to rule the world, while I've gone on to write about Madonna. So long live Madonna!

–Michael Musto, 2014

MUSIC OF THE HEART: *Director: Wes Craven. Release date: October 29, 1999.* Originally entitled *50 Violins*, this film about the life of charismatic East Harlem violin teacher Robert Guaspari-Tzavaras was set to star Madonna. Madonna met with Guaspari-Tzavaras and sang **"Frozen"** at a 1998 rainforest benefit and **"The Power of Good-Bye"** on VH1 with backing by the children in the teacher's violin program.

Madonna was replaced on the film at the last minute by Meryl Streep (from whom Madonna had snatched *Evita*) when Madonna and Craven had "creative differences."

Producer Marianne Maddalena said, in the **book** *Movie Moguls Speak: Interviews with Top Film Producers* (McFarland & Co., 2004):

"**Harvey Weinstein** really wanted Madonna. We didn't actually have a choice when it came to the casting of the lead role. So, we agreed and we **worked** with Madonna for a few months and in the end it was obvious it wasn't going to work with her. It came down to creative differences, with Madonna and Wes seeing the part differently. Then we parted ways with Madonna and shut down the movie after it was only two weeks into the filming." Madonna's violin classes (taken in May 1998) went to waste.

The film also stars Angela Bassett, Gloria Estefan (she had her last Top 40 hit with the film's title song, which was **Oscar**-nominated) and Madonna's old *Desperately Seeking Susan* costar Aidan Quinn. To date, it is Craven's only non-horror picture. It was not a success.

MUSTO, MICHAEL: *b. December 3, 1955.* The ultimate downtown gossip insider, Musto was for decades the influential "La Dolce Musto" columnist for **The Village Voice**, has published **books**, has appeared as a talking head (who never stops making sense) on **TV** and has performed on stage, sometimes in **drag**.

A close observer of Madonna from the beginning, he has heaped praise and scorn on her from time to time, affectionately sending up *Sex* with a **nude** image (tuck yeah!) shot by Catherine McGann on a New Jersey street shortly after that book came out.

In *NYQ* in 1992, he wrote, "Our greatest hero in the entertainment world continues to be an apparent heterosexual—Madonna, who seems to wield even more **power** to impact change than all our closeted queer icons and do-nothing politicians *combined* ... Her 'I'm not ashamed' approach to potential controversy has helped rub us in the faces of every household in America. Strike opposers."

In March 2014, Musto penned an open letter to Madonna for SceneMag.com, in which he took her to task for her tendency to "overly obsess on younger acts as a way to keep a fresh allure" about herself. His advice then? "Stop fearing the aging process and simply embrace it."

Musto in 1984

michael musto

RHONDA CORTE

MARIPOL

NAIL, JIMMY: *b. March 16, 1954.* British actor, writer and singer who hit #1 in the UK with the 1992 song "Ain't No Doubt." Nail played the important role of Magaldi in *Evita,* sharing scenes and a song with Madonna and crooning the pleasing **"On This Night of a Thousand Stars."**

NASTY GIRL, THE: *Director: Michael Verhoeven. Release date: March 1991.* Dramatic West German film about a woman who returns to her childhood home in Germany and forces the town to come to terms with its Nazi past.

Madonna saw the movie ("I saw it because it was two blocks from my house, and I liked the title"), **loved** it and on January 13, 1991, presented the 56th Annual **New York** Film Critics Circle **Award** to its director for Best Foreign Film.

To arrive at the ceremony quietly, Madonna used the trash elevator and slipped through the kitchen, showing up at Rockefeller Plaza's Pegasus Room (30 Rockefeller Plaza, NY, NY). She sported two inches of dark roots and a fetching black headband. Rex Reed introduced Madonna as "living proof that living right doesn't always pay off." He also referred to Kathy Bates's character in *Misery* (1990) as the "meanest **bitch** this side of the Rockies," to which Madonna quipped, "But I thought *I* was the meanest bitch this side of the Rockies!"

NC-17: Movie rating meaning "Not quite **porn**, but pretty close. Ages 17 and over."

Body of Evidence was slapped with an NC-17 prior to its release, and for a short time it looked as though MGM would release it intact, but MGM got cold **feet** and director Uli Edel snipped a few racy seconds. "I think there should be ratings for violence," Madonna snapped. "I just think the ratings are arbitrary in what they cut. I saw the NC-17 version and the R version, and it was ludicrous what was cut and what was acceptable." If you just gotta see the whole, raunchy thing, the "ludicrous" version was made available for purchase after its theatrical run.

Also, Billy Crystal referred to Madonna as "the NC-17 portion of our really big show" in his best Ed Sullivan **voice** on the 1991 **Oscars.**

NDEGEOCELLO, MESHELL: *b. August 29, 1968.* Acclaimed singer, songwriter and rapper who was one of the first artists signed to **Maverick.** Her arresting blend of hip-hop, rock, jazz and rap made her *Plantation Lullabies* debut one of the most critically acclaimed albums of 1993. She released five albums on the Maverick label through 2003.

Toward the beginning of her time on Maverick, Ndegeocello contributed the least obnoxious rap ever added to any Madonna song, for **"I'd Rather Be Your Lover"** on *Bedtime Stories.*

Madonna has explained her signing of Ndegeocello by calling her a "bad-ass," an incredible lyricist and an amazingly **talented** musician.

In 2012, Ndegeocello told BET of Madonna that she was "always grateful to her, she's, she gave me a chance to do this, what I'm doing with my life, so I'm always indebted." Madonna's bro-in-law **Joe Henry** has produced her **work** in the past.

NEPTUNES: Comprised of Chad Hugo (*b. February 24, 1974*) and **Pharrell Williams,** this premier hip-hop team produced seven of 12 songs on Madonna's so-called hip-hop album, *Hard Candy.* The songs include her favorite, **"Candy Shop,"** the single **"Give It 2 Me,"** the *Sticky & Sweet Tour* show-stopper **"She's Not Me"** and the critically appreciated album track **"Incredible."** They also did some **work** for *Rebel Heart* that remains **unreleased** [**"Back** That Up (Do It)," "Take a Day" and "Take It Back"].

NERVES: Always a confident performer on tour, Madonna has nonetheless succumbed to nerves on occasion.

She was trembling like a sapling in a hurricane onstage at the **Oscars** in 1991, stumbled over a chorus of **"Fever"** on **Arsenio Hall's** 1,000th-episode special and can become so tense during interviews that she offers terse, unilluminating answers or even turns the questions **back** on her interrogators.

Toward the end of *The Girlie Show World Tour,* Madonna joked with Japanese audiences that she was ready for a nervous breakdown. "Why not? I could do it. Judy Garland did. **Elvis** did."

In 2012, Madonna confessed to **Anderson Cooper** that she was rattled by the prospect of her upcoming **Super Bowl** performance. "Oh, my **God.** I'm so nervous. You have no idea."

NEUMANN, STEVE: Publisher of *Island* magazine (he gave Madonna her first full **magazine** cover) who began seeing Madonna at the time she was involved with **Jellybean Benitez.** Benitez allegedly forced his way into Neumann's apartment when he was with Madonna, which led to a hysterical argument. Neumann later claimed Madonna broke up with him because he had no **money** and no prospects.

"NEW ARGENTINA, A": A sung-through but intermittently conversational-style song that appears on *Evita: The Complete Motion Picture Music Soundtrack.* With music by **Andrew Lloyd Webber** and lyrics by **Tim Rice,** this song—a duet between Madonna and **Jonathan Pryce**—opens with the delicious sweet/salty moment when Madonna, singing as **power**-hungry Evita in her purest upper register, decries her hubby's enemies as "morons." It unfolds into a thrilling anthem backed by a singing mob. Think of it as the musical theater version of **"Everybody,"** where you get executed if you fail to **dance** and sing, get up and do your thing.

NEW MUSIC SEMINAR: Held from 1980–1995 (and resuscitated in 2009), this influential **NYC**-based conference consists of panels featuring music-industry movers and shakers. Madonna's friend **Haoui Montaug** ran the panels here until his **death** in 1991.

In July or August 1984, with her first Top 5 hit under her belt ("**Lucky Star**"), Madonna appeared on a panel with George Clinton, John Oates, Afrika Bambaataa, Fred Schneider, Lou Reed, Peter Wolf and James Brown.

Oates made an angry point that music videos were forcing musicians to become actors, eliciting applause from the audience. Madonna gave Oates a little adult education, reminding him, "Yeah, but, but, listen, when you perform onstage, you're **acting**. I mean, that's a performance ... I mean, if someone puts a camera on you, what's the difference?" She received louder applause.

She went on to say, "Videos might have a limited audience in one sense, but on the other hand, you could be reaching a lot of people that would never be able to come and see you live, so I think that they're definitely an advantage ... Kids today worship **television**, so I think it's a great way to reach them."

Thomas De Pascale, who attended, says Madonna was that year's biggest draw. "Everyone was there to see Madonna—there was a mad rush of people to her panel and everywhere she'd show up. She had the look and persona that attracted people, and she had fun with that **power**."

NEW YORK: Madonna always **dreamed** of moving to NYC, which she envisioned as "the center of the world." She said in 1984, "When I was five years old, I just woke up one day and I had this idea that I was gonna come to New York."

The city has been her adopted hometown since she first moved there in 1978; since 1985, she has continuously owned at least one dwelling in the city.

According to biographer **Andrew Morton**, Madonna first visited NYC in February 1977 on a 24-hour trip with her boyfriend Mark Dolengowski, who **worked** as a hairdresser in Ann Arbor, **Michigan**. The story goes that she arrived in the city, auditioned for an Alvin Ailey scholarship and turned right **back** around to head home that day. She won the scholarship, so spent the summer of '77 in NYC with friends on the **Upper East Side**. This account is dubious in that no other sources place Madonna in NYC in 1977. Perhaps the truth is that Dolengowski drove Madonna to NYC to audition in February of 1978; this would make more sense.

What's known for sure is that by summer 1978, Madonna had decided she was going to move to NYC full time at the expense of continuing her education. She dropped out of the **University of Michigan**, bought a one-way ticket to NYC and was driven to Detroit Metropolitan Wayne County Airport by her mentor **Christopher Flynn**. She landed at LaGuardia Airport.

Madonna has often told the story of her arrival in NYC. The way *she* remembers it, she arrived with just $35 in her pocket, telling the taxi driver to take her "to the middle

"From the minute I arrived in New York, it was, 'This is where I am, this is where I'm staying.' I *knew* I was going to suffer. I *knew* it was going to be hard. But I was not going back, and that's how it was, period."

—MADONNA (1998)

of everything," which wound up being Times Square. In Madonna's **memory**, her arrival in NYC that July was not only her first plane trip but her first time in the city. She recalls walking east on 42nd St. and then south on Lexington Ave. before bumping into a stranger at a flea market, a male **dancer** who allowed her to crash at his place. In this telling of the story, this is when Madonna auditioned for Alvin Ailey, but that is probably a reference to the fact that Madonna almost immediately left, via bus, to North Carolina to attend the **American Dance Festival**, which lasted until August of 1978.

"Coming to New York was the bravest thing I'd ever done," Madonna said in 1986. "My goal was to conquer the city, and I feel I have. I can't believe how frightened I was when I look back on it, but I was."

At the American Dance Festival, Madonna boldly petitioned **Pearl Lang** for a slot in her company back in NYC. Lang was dubious that Madonna could pull it off, but by that November, she'd showed up at Lang's studio, and her grueling time as a dancer began in earnest.

"I remember having bouts of the worst depression, especially when I first came here, where I just thought, '**God**, this city's so big, and there's so many people and I don't know anyone,'" she recalled in *Madonna Rising*. "And people were just rushing by me and shoving me around and I would just think, 'Will I ever have any friends?'"

In spite of that feeling, Madonna never considered going home. "Detroit is a more desolate, desperate place. At night, everyone locks themselves away," she melodramatically told *Flexipop* **magazine** in 1983. "There's always elements of danger in New York, but people are always out on the street. I don't feel scared there at all."

Madonna became a New Yorker for life, in spite of that stint she spent as a wife and mom in **England**, and in spite of her belief that the city has lost some of its star quality. In 2008, she told *Vanity Fair*, "[New York is] not the exciting place it used to be. It still has great energy; I still put my finger in the socket. But it doesn't feel alive, crackling with that synergy between the **art** world and music world and **fashion** world that was happening in the '80s. A lot of people died."

In 2015, New York's 1010 WINS profiled all the most iconic people in New York history. The Top 4 were all women: **Barbra Streisand**, Liza Minnelli, **Bette Midler** and Madonna. The list was rounded out by **Frank Sinatra**, Billy Joel, **Joan Rivers**, Robert De Niro, **Jerry Seinfeld** and **Woody Allen**.

—GEORGE DUBOSE

NEWSNIGHT: *Airdates: January 30, 1980-.* Weekday UK news show on BBC on which Madonna appeared on November 1, 2006, marking her first British sit-down following her successful adoption of son **David Banda**.

Madonna, sounding veddy British, told reporter Kirsty Wark right off the bat that the idea that she gets whatever she wants was an untrue, preconceived notion: "... I can assure you that I don't often have things my way." She was the picture of composure after the long battle to adopt, but spoke openly about the pain she felt at being branded a selfish celeb who was adopting to attain a trendy accessory.

Clearing up a common complaint, Madonna said she offered to support David in Malawi rather than adopting him, but David's father declined. Madonna said David had horrendous diaper rash and was suffering from pneumonia, and that his condition had declined rapidly. Madonna stressed that the adoption was not a case of special treatment and declared what was happening in **Malawi** "a state of emergency."

Wark wrote that she prepared for the interview by quizzing her 14-year-old son, a Madonna mega-**fan**. Werk!

NEWTON, HELMUT: *October 31, 1920–January 23, 2004.* **Fashion** shooter whose signature **work** was erotic, transgressive and starkly stylish. Already known for his fetishy, fine-**art** poses as well as his **magazine** work, it felt like something of a meeting of the dirty minds when Madonna finally posed for him for the April 1990 *Vanity Fair* cover story. On the cover, she sports a head filled with Shirley Temple curls and some awfully big knockers, offset by an impish grin. Some of his **black-and-white** work with Madonna calls to mind her 1986 *Vanity Fair* shoot with **Herb Ritts**, but the color images are pure Newton.

The two keepers are a shot of Madonna in a plastic raincoat and serious diamond necklace (and nothing else), and the *Cabaret* (1970)-inspired shot of her dancing on a bar, one breast bared like a cop flashing his badge.

NEWTON-JOHN, OLIVIA: *b. September 26, 1948.* One of the most beloved and successful female pop singers in history, "Sandy" in the movie mega-hit *Grease* (1978) and an example of how a **sexy** image-change can increase the public's interest.

Newton-John appears briefly in *Truth or Dare*, praising Madonna for her *Blond Ambition World Tour* performance. Also of note, **"Physical Attraction"** has definite echoes of Newton-John's 1980 smash "Physical."

In December 2014, Newton-John free-associated the words "liberated," "free" and "brave" for *EM20* in reference to Madonna.

NEXT BEST THING, THE: *Director: John Schlesinger. Release date: March 3, 2000.* After the success of **Ray of Light**, Madonna planned to go on tour, but was approached by longtime acquaintance **Rupert Everett** with the idea that they should star together in a film about the friendship between a **gay** man ("Robert"/Everett) and a straight woman ("Abbie"/Madonna) that is tested when they have a child together. Five years after the birth, the mother falls in **love** and wants to move, resulting in a bitter custody battle.

Madonna read the **original** script, entitled *The Red Curtain*, by Tom Ropelewski. It had been around a few years, and at separate points in time had had Richard Dreyfuss and Helen Hunt attached. She liked the script very much, but wanted the child to be the result of planned intercourse. Everett told her, "You're absolutely right. Of course we'd sleep together—why would you want to use a turkey baster? The audience would be walking out in droves."

Everett had his own reservations about the script, including finding his character too "flubby." A writer himself, Everett reportedly took a strong (and uncredited) hand with the script, as did future **Glee** show runner Ryan Murphy. Among the revised script's many "Rupertesque flourishes" was the idea that the assembled characters would sing the Don McLean song **"American Pie"** during a funeral scene, which led to Madonna recording the song for the soundtrack and releasing it as a single. Everett sings background vocals. Rumor has it that Madonna **hates** her version—don't wait for it to show up in concert.

The extent to which Everett tinkered with the script is perhaps insinuated by a 1998 note Madonna wrote to her **fan** club members, introducing the concept of *The Next Best Thing* by saying it was a romantic comedy Everett was writing.

The approved script attracted top **talent**. With Madonna and Everett as leads and **Oscar**-winning director John Schlesinger at the helm, Benjamin Bratt and Michael Vartan played Madonna's love interests (yes, two!), Josef Sommer (who'd done the *Bloodhounds of Broadway* narration) and Lynn Redgrave played Everett's parents and Neil Patrick Harris and Illeana Douglas were on board as friends.

It was not a harmonious shoot. Schlesinger clashed with Madonna, although he found her star quality to be a reserve he wished he could tap into for his movie. "She is indomitable. Whatever her failings as an actress, it's difficult for a director to ignore that attitude she has of, 'I am the center of the universe.' Madonna projects the kind of energy that makes a star," he told Madonna biographer **Barbara Victor**.

More ominously, Schlesinger described directing Madonna as an exercise in "confidence-building," conceding that she "came into her own by the end of the shoot." He called her performance very good, thoroughly researched and flexible in a *Genre* interview, yet in his private papers—bequeathed to the British Film Institute following his **death** in 2003—was a note in which he'd stated at the end of filming, when he was in the hospital with heart trouble, "I am **fucking** angry with [producer] Tom [Rosenberg] being influenced by Madonna ... I do not for one moment think that their behavior has not added to the reasons I have ended up here."

Yikes, how very Clark Gable/**Marilyn Monroe**/*The Misfits* (1961)!

Schlesinger was upset that Madonna's input on various scenes was being heeded, and resented even her respectful (as proven by a handwritten letter in the same archive) suggestions of types of music to be used in the film.

Schlesinger also claimed Madonna found a certain scene to be "too gay," writing, "I am outraged that Madonna is starting to express an opinion of what **works** and what doesn't and what is too gay when she wasn't even present at the previews. In any case, she is not the director; so far as I am concerned I want the scene to remain as it is."

For all the drama, Madonna was pleased with herself. Before the film had been shown anywhere, Madonna reported to her fan club members that she was "very happy" with her performance in the film, saying, "I've seen it 10 times already and I still cry at the end of it." She had previously told the same forum that Everett and Schlesinger had "taught me so much as an actress. I never cried and laughed so much in my life."

Everett praised Madonna's performance at the time, but later seemed to cop to her limitations. "Her main problem is that her 'Madonnaness' overpowered any **acting** talent she may have," he told Victor in 2001, after the film's failure.

The movie was given a splashy premiere in **NYC** with an after-party at Saci (135 W. 41st St., NY, NY) on February 29, 2000, ahead of its hotly anticipated March 3 release. The party attracted Madonna's buddy **Gwyneth Paltrow** and costar Bratt's lover Julia Roberts. Madonna was hiding her **Rocco** baby bump, but the bump took center stage at the film's **London** premiere in June.

The Next Best Thing flopped spectacularly. It had a decent #2 debut at the box office, making $5,870,387 in its opening week, but went on to make a mere $14,990,582 in the US, $10 million less than it had cost to make. Worldwide, the film made just about what it cost, but that was before factoring in marketing and distribution expenses.

The reviews were brutal, taking note of Madonna's stiffness, the distracting inclusion of aspects of her real life (why did Abbie have to be into **yoga**?) and an impossible-to-miss British **accent**.

Maybe "Abbie" should've had an **abortion** after all.

Everett was also attacked. "It blew my career out of the water and turned my pubic **hair** white overnight," he said in 2007.

There *were* some bright spots. First and foremost, who *can't* love the scene in which Madonna holds her breasts up, saying, "1989 ..." then lets them drop and finishes, "... 1999." Also, if "American Pie" seems kinda like a cheap thrill, Madonna's **"Time Stood Still"** on the soundtrack is a marvel, a gorgeous ballad worthy of rediscovery. Keep the kid, we want custody of that song.

As cruelly as Madonna was assessed, there is a **school** of thought that perhaps her acting was ... "underrated" isn't the right word. How about "overmaligned?" Everett, whose career was demonstrably torpedoed by the film, wrote in his memoir *Red Carpets and Other Banana Skins: An Autobiography* (Grand Central, 2007): "The vitriol engendered by Madonna's performance says as much about the resentment felt by a world of neurotic fans for its household **gods** as it does about her thespian skills. Acres of acting have been cheaper than hers and have yet been **awarded** Oscars and crowns."

••

"SOMETHING HAPPENS TO MADONNA WHEN SHE STOPS SINGING, DANCING AND POSING AND IS FORCED TO PLAY A SCREEN CHARACTER WHO SPEAKS IN PLAIN, EVERYDAY ENGLISH. THE EXTRAORDINARY DRIVE THAT MADE HER A WORLD-FAMOUS ENTERTAINER BECOMES STIFLED, AND THE PERSONALITY THAT WAFTS OFF THE SCREEN IS A CURT, COOL COOKIE WHO, EVEN IN MISTY-EYED MOMENTS, CONVEYS TRACES OF A SOUR SELF-ABSORPTION."

—STEPHEN HOLDEN, *THE NEW YORK TIMES* (2000)

••

"AFTER 15 FILMS, MADONNA HAS YET TO DECISIVELY DEMONSTRATE ACTING TALENT ... MADONNA IS AS FRUSTRATINGLY STIFF AS EVER HERE, BUT HER PERFORMANCE GROWS ON YOU."

—NICOLE KEETER, *TIME OUT NEW YORK* (2000)

••

"AN EMBARRASSMENT TO RIVAL HER 'RAY OF LIGHT' DEATH-YODEL AT THE MTV [VIDEO MUSIC AWARDS] TWO YEARS BACK, MADONNA'S PERFORMANCE HERE CONSISTS OF FEIGNING AN ENGLISH ACCENT FOR NO APPARENT REASON AND ONLY WHEN IT OCCURS TO HER TO DO SO."

—DENNIS LIM, *THE VILLAGE VOICE* (2000)

••

"YET IN A PART SANDRA BULLOCK OR JULIA ROBERTS COULD WELL SLEEPWALK THROUGH, MADONNA STILL LACKS THE ABILITY TO IMBUE A CHARACTER WITH THE SIMPLE CHARISMA THAT CONNECTS WITH CAMERA OR AUDIENCE."

—DENNIS HARVEY, *VARIETY* (2000)

••

"BUT WHEN [DIRECTOR JOHN SCHLESINGER] COMES IN FOR GAUZY CLOSE-UPS, MADONNA CAN BARELY MUSTER EVEN THE RUDIMENTS OF HUMAN EXPRESSION." —STEVE DALY, *ENTERTAINMENT WEEKLY* (2000)

••

"Madonna still cannot act."—SUSAN WLOSZCZYNA, *USA TODAY* (2000)

"I don't believe in gratuitous violence and I don't believe in degradation ..."—MADONNA, NIGHTLINE (1990)

NICKELODEON KIDS' CHOICE AWARDS: *Dates presented: April 18, 1988–.* The annual **awards** show hosted by American children's network Nickelodeon, honoring favorites in movies, music, **TV** and such colorful categories as Favorite Male Buttkicker and Most Addicting Game. Participants are in constant danger of being "slimed"— covered in green goo dumped on them from above and with no warning, wink-wink.

On April 4, 1998, Madonna attended the awards in LA, probably thanks to friend **Rosie O'Donnell**'s status as the host. With long **hair** showing waves from having been braided, Madonna took the stage with a kid named Blake. She admitted that she sometimes gets **nervous** and suggested the trick of imagining people in their **underwear** ... cut to a concessions salesman in his striped boxers.

Madonna and Blake presented the award for Best Movie to *Titanic* (1997).

NICKNAMES: Madonna's family called her "Nonni" or "Little Nonni" when she was little, a reference to the existence of "Big Madonna" (her **mother**) and "Little Madonna." Madonna was also apparently called "Squeeze" and "Mouth" by her family, while the first nickname she invented for herself, in junior high, was "Mudd."

When she was under contract to manager **Camille Barbone**, Madonna was sometimes called "Brat," but often called "**Emmy**," the latter of which became the name of her pre-solo, post-**Breakfast Club** band.

Hubby **Sean Penn** called her a variety of things, including "Daisy Cobb" and "Bud." Penn went along with Madonna's preference for the name "Kit Moresby" (from the 1949 novel *The Sheltering Sky* by Paul Bowles) to the extent that he allegedly tattooed the letters on the ends of his toes. The couple was wickedly called "S&M" by pals, and "the Poison Penns" by the press.

The press **loves** calling her the "**Material Girl**," a moniker she **hates**.

For many years as an adult, Madonna was called "Mo" by her close friends, especially **Rosie "Ro" O'Donnell**, but for the longest time, Madonna's intimates have merely called her "M," which is what she is most commonly called by friends to this day.

By the time she was married to **Guy Ritchie**, Madonna was allowing him to call her "Wiff," but also "Madge," which is now her most common public nickname, a name with which Madonna has a love/hate thing. It's a nickname that has completely superseded her previous professional nickname of "Maddy," and that has been associated with her from at least 1992, when **Jonathan Ross** casually used it in the introduction to their first interview. In 2009, Madonna said, "'Madge' is a press thing in **England**. I hear two versions of where it came from. One is that Madge is an English colloquialism, like a name that would suit a housewife, which is the opposite of who I am. The other is that it's short for 'majesty.' I like that one better."

Hint: When you are first introduced to Madonna, don't presume to call her M, and don't dare to call her Madge.

NIELSEN, BRIGITTE: *b. July 15, 1963.* Amazonian **blonde** pop culture figure. According to **Belinda Carlisle**, this former Mrs. **Sylvester Stallone** once tried to best Madonna in a **dance**-off at a club called Helena's in the Silver Lake section of LA. Carlisle recalled, "Even *I* wouldn't have the nerve to dance next to Madonna because she's such a great dancer ... It was the funniest thing. I had to hide my face because I was laughing so hard."

NIGHT PORTER, THE: *Director: Liliana Cavani. Release date: October 1, 1974.* Stylish SM-themed film to which both the "**Justify My Love**" video and *Sex* owe some of their visual sensibility. As early as 1984, way before Madonna went from tease to **sex** activist, she was raving to the British teenybopper **magazine** *Record*, "Oh, my **God**! ... What an incredible movie! ... Just like [Pier Paolo Pasolini's 1975 film] *Salò* ... absolutely sick! *The Night Porter* touches on a subject people don't like to talk about—that people are drawn to things that cause them pain. They *want* it."

NIGHTLINE: *Airdates: 1980–.* In one of her liveliest **TV** appearances, Madonna went head-to-head with host Forrest Sawyer on *Nightline*'s December 3, 1990, edition, discussing the **censorship** issues behind **MTV**'s banning of her "**Justify My Love**" video. She wore a severe, collared, black jacket suitable for a court appearance (which it kinda was), her **hair** tastefully upswept, and did her very best to defend her artistic integrity as well as champion the cause of less restrictive programming of erotic material.

Madonna's sincerity was obvious, but the via-satellite set-up made for a somewhat stilted exchange, one that was further hampered by her excessive reliance on "you know" and "okay?" in her otherwise carefully considered remarks. She scored points by contrasting the lack of public outrage over violence and degrading images of women with the uproar over her video, which she characterized as containing scenes of "... two consenting adults displaying affection for each other ..." and when she expressed disgust that network TV was still priggishly refusing to run **condom** ads even as the **AIDS** epidemic raged.

The most classic takeaway from this appearance has to be Madonna's assertion that one infamous scene in her "**Express Yourself**" video wasn't demeaning because, "I crawled under my own table, you know? There wasn't a man standing there making me do it."

Interestingly, Madonna also came out in favor of warning labels, whether on albums or on blocks of MTV's airtime.

The **money** shot of the program was toward the end, when Sawyer pointed out that losing MTV exposure had helped make her video into an even bigger moneymaker as a video single. Madonna just smiled and cracked, "Yeah— so lucky me."

Madonna's interviews with **Cynthia McFadden** were aired on *Nightline* in 2008 and 2012, but the show's format was completely changed to that of a soft-news format.

9/11: The September 11, 2001, terrorist attacks on **New York** and Washington, DC by al-Qaeda, which deeply affected many Americans and had an inestimable impact on US culture and world politics. The entertainment industry was at a loss for how to proceed and for guidance on when it would be appropriate to carry on with **business** as usual; *Vanity Fair* editor Graydon Carter famously declared, on September 18, 2001, "I think it's the end of the age of **irony**."

One of Madonna's final *Drowned World Tour* performances had been scheduled to take place on September 11, 2001, at the Staples Center (1111 S. Figueroa St., LA, CA), but was rescheduled for September 15, 2001, which became the final performance of the entire tour. In the tour's last three performances, Madonna spoke out about the tragedy to her shaken audiences. Her **dancer** Jull Weber told *MadonnaTribe*, "We weren't just continuing our tour, we were performing to celebrate joy and happiness, especially in that time of difficulty."

In 2005, Madonna entertained but seemed to reject 9/11 trutherism (the belief that the US government was complicit in the attacks or in covering up aspects of what really happened), telling *Rolling Stone*, "9/11 was too ambiguous. You couldn't prove how the government was somehow in on the deal." She went on to say that the damage from Hurricane Katrina was "worse in a lot of ways" than the aftermath of 9/11, and became an outspoken **fan** of **Michael Moore** and his documentary *Fahrenheit 9/11* (2004).

Madonna had a personal connection to 9/11—her business manager, thus far unnamed, was killed in the attacks. She told *The Sunday Times Magazine* in 2003, "... I was personally affected by it—but it's not about being a victim. It's not about saying, 'Oh, **God**, that's so horrible, we were hurt, we were attacked by those horrible people.'" Madonna's devotion to **Kabbalah** led her to opine that, "It's only a matter of time when people are negative, and the majority of people are, for us to open things up to an entity, for people like Osama bin Laden or **Hitler**. So the fact that they can do the evil deeds that they do, eventually that's our responsibility."

All of Madonna's live performances of **"Ghosttown"** during her *Rebel Heart* promo tour used video footage of the disintegrating World Trade Center towers projected on screens behind her—amidst stock footage of less iconic buildings crumbling—as a tableau for the song's post-apocalyptic theme.

NIP SLIPS: Like misbehaving chimps, Madonna's boobs have a tendency to demand attention, even when Madonna isn't revealing them on purpose.

It was "nips, ahoy!" during her **MTV Video Music Awards** rehearsals in 1984; an image exists showing both nipples plainly in view. Straps were added to the dress before airtime.

In her **"Material Girl"** video, when suspended upside down, we see way more breastage than was previously thought possible without glimpsing nipple, and when she arches her **back** in her **"Papa Don't Preach"** video, a nipple does pop into view, an occurrence that at the time could only be spotted after a master class on VHS pausing, and that is now a digital snap to see.

Madonna's breasts kept coming up for air while she rehearsed a musical number for *Dick Tracy*, so makeup artist John Caglione Jr. was asked to glue them into her gown. He respectfully declined, fearing he'd be blamed for defacing a "national treasure. I'll bet each one of those honeys is worth 6, maybe 7 million." He told *Ladies' Home Journal*. "It was like if the Museum of Natural History had asked us to watch the Star of India for the weekend."

They went flying during her 1991 **Oscars** rehearsal, too, so had to be taped into her Bob Mackie to avoid flashing over a billion viewers.

There aren't many more examples of accidental exposure because if you're seeing Madonna's nipples, it's usually because she wants you to.

NIP/TUCK: *Airdates: 2003-2010.* In 2007, Madonna agreed in principle to appear on the **TV** series; producer Ryan Murphy even told the cast to expect it. Word **leaked** that she would appear **nude**, a rumor that series star Julian McMahon told the press was false.

This foreign lobby card proves Madonna's character definitely made at least one good point.

On French TV, Madonna serves Twin Towers realness.

Madonna never did do the show, a particularly cutting **lost project**. Murphy probably felt like he had an inside track on getting Madonna—after all, he had done a rewrite on *The Next Best Thing*, although he was in turn rewritten. His *Next Best Thing* gig did lead to having a nice sit with Madonna in her apartment, during which she dished about her life.

NO AUTHORITY: Madonna's **Maverick** label signed the boy band No Authority in the '90s after they'd been signed to **Michael Jackson**'s MJJ Music. Efforts were made to capitalize on the success of Backstreet Boys and *NSYNC, but while the group invaded teen **magazines**, No Authority failed to hit the big-time. **Original** member Ricky Rebel (a.k.a. Ricky Godinez), now an emergent solo act, remembers meeting Madonna:

"[Rodney Jerkins] was **working** on our record in the same studio that [Madonna] was working on hers. He called me up and told me to get my butt to the studio 'right now!' I was walking down the hall and there she was in her office on the phone. I looked into the office and just saw my hero talking on the phone—angrily, I might add. I was spellbound. She immediately walked up to the door and slammed it in my face. I was even more in **love** with her after that."

Luckily, the encounter didn't end on that note.

"Later on, we saw that she was playing with **Lola** on my friend's truck, so I got up the nerve to walk up to her. She was embarrassed for playing on his truck with Lola. She immediately apologized and started a conversation with us. She asked about what it was like to be signed to Michael Jackson's label and how was the record coming along. She also introduced us to her producer **Shep Pettibone**. I knew exactly who he was. I was almost as honored to meet him as I was in meeting Madonna."

"NO ENTIENDES!": Eclectic cabaret series created by **Haoui Montaug** that included everything from fire-eaters to New Wave music. Originally called *I Dunno*, its name was changed to the Spanish for "I don't understand." It was hosted at international venues and became a huge gig for rising acts to **book**.

Back when Madonna was an opening act

"She was like a disco act backed by avant-garde dancers. I guess you could say Madonna was the first New Wave disco music."
—HAOUI MONTAUG (1985)

On December 16, 1982, Madonna opened for A Certain Ratio, a gig she got when her manager paid $100 to get her on the bill. She showed up with **Jellybean Benitez**, who brought a four-track tape machine.

Montaug took to the stage at **Danceteria** in top hat and tails and tried to get the unruly crowd to shout the word "everybody" in unison during his introduction of Madonna. In a tone that foreshadowed some of Madonna's own tough-**love** stage banter at future concerts, he told the assembled music lovers of their effort, "Well, *mediocre*, but better than really poor, anyway."

Madonna's **voice** was strong (an echo effect popped in mid-song, but prerecorded vocals only at the end) and her visuals for the performance were memorable—her entire troupe dressed in schoolboy outfits, complete with short pants and porkpie hats. Her dancers were **Bags Rilez**, **Erika Belle** and **Martin Burgoyne**, all of whose bodies seemed to have gotten the notion that their **feet** could make the motion.

Admission that night was a mere $5. Don't you wish you'd been there?

The crowd seemed to understand Madonna's 6:21 performance pretty well, giving her enthusiastic applause. "That's Madonna, that's 'Everybody' and you'll be hearing it a lot. Everybody liked it, I take it, yeah?" Montaug queried the venue's buzzed audience. "Well, it woke most of you up, anyway, and that's good news."

Martin Moscrop, the guitarist and trumpeter of A Certain Ratio, remembered in 2005 what Madonna was like at the gig: "You could sense she was going to be big—she was just bossing everyone around. It was very last-minute, and when she got there we were finishing the sound check. When you're the main band, you don't move any gear, the support has to fit in round it. But she started to move our gear to make room for her dancers. So we said in our Mancunian **accents**, 'Fook off.' We didn't move the gear."

"NOBODY KNOWS ME": Vocoder-happy song written and produced by Madonna and **Mirwais** that is found on *American Life*. The song trashes **TV** and other media, especially **magazines**, which helped ensure lots of press for the album when it was released.

Kidding aside, it's a scalding-cold smack down of a song, one Madonna brought to life on her *Re-Invention World Tour*. It became a memorable video interlude on *The MDNA Tour*, one in which Madonna's face morphs mesmerizingly into a slew of familiar figures. French right-winger Marine Le Pen threatened to bring suit against Madonna for depicting her with a swastika on her forehead and associating her with **Adolf Hitler**. In 2015, Madonna said on French TV that she'd like to have a drink with Le Pen to try to figure out where she's coming from; Le Pen immediately responded in the press, "I accept Madonna's invitation with pleasure. I appreciate people who have a good-faith approach."

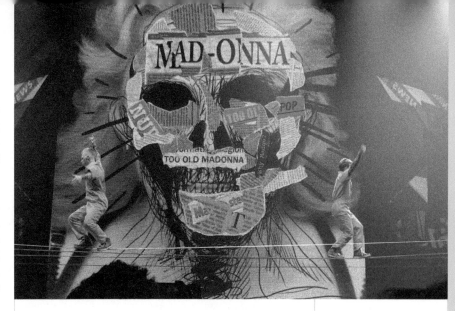

"NOBODY'S PERFECT": An even more vocoder-happy song than **"Nobody Knows Me,"** also written and produced by Madonna and **Mirwais**, from *Music*. This sad admission of one's limitations was performed on the *Drowned World Tour* and at *Tears of a Clown* in Melbourne.

NORRIS, JOHN: *b. March 20, 1959.* Popular **MTV** writer and on-air personality (1988–2008) who reported on Madonna countless times during his decades with the channel. Perhaps his two most noteworthy run-ins would include the time he talked to Madonna about the Iraq War, and the time he talked to her about something much more serious and controversial—her **age**.

On March 27, 2003, Madonna had a sit-down with Norris to discuss the **"American Life"** video, which she had edited down drastically in the face of damning criticism. He asked Madonna if she had conflicting feelings about the war as someone who is anti-war but who is also a proud American. Madonna said, "There were conflicting feelings in me, y'know, because, like, c'mon, like, Saddam is, like, a guy we just, like, wanna get rid of, right? No question about that. And there's parts of the video where you could almost feel, like, you know, when I'm carving 'protect me' into the wall, it's like I wanna go there and kick some ass, you know what I mean? And protect all those beautiful children and innocent families and people that've been tortured for years … Do I have the solution? No. Do I have all the answers? No."

In an interview on April 30, 2008, Norris asked Madonna about a past quote in which she said she couldn't imagine making pop music at 50. The 49-year-old mistakenly corrected him, saying she'd actually said she couldn't see herself "running around in limousines." **Liz Rosenberg** later put the kibosh on any negativity that various media outlets said arose from that exchange, saying, "Madonna adores John Norris."

NORTON, GRAHAM: *b. April 4, 1963.* SEE: *Graham Norton Show, The.*

NOSTALGIA: Judging from her professional comportment, Madonna has seemed at times to be one of the least nostalgic human beings alive, heaping scorn on her early, classic hits at every turn. She has expressed disinterest in resting on her laurels or reminiscing. Perhaps one reason is that her **memories** of her are not the same as *our* memories of her. "Sometimes, I see a picture of me and I really remember that moment—and it brings **back** memories, very specific memories. And other photographs that I see, I just think—who's that? I don't know that girl!" Madonna told *Dazed & Confused* in 2008. **Fans** think they know that girl, every one of her incarnations even.

But Madonna's war on nostalgia has thawed, beginning in 2015. With the release of *Rebel Heart*, her most self-referential **work**, it seemed Madonna was very much in the mood to take a bow, artistically, especially with a track like **"Veni Vidi Vici,"** in which she ticked off many of the components of her brilliant career.

She told *Rolling Stone*, "I don't think about my old stuff. I just move forward. I mean, it's funny, because when I work with people, they're referencing other things. **Diplo** kept wanting to play, like, the bass line for **'Vogue'** or something from **'La Isla Bonita'** over and over again. I'm like, 'Okay, let's move on.'" In spite of that statement, *Rebel Heart* would all but vanish if all of its nostalgic elements were surgically removed.

In press for the album, Madonna was even more open to discussing her past—and *the* past—with remarks about her early days in **New York**. The woman who has steadfastly professed a desire to move forward seems to be softening to the idea of looking (or at least peeking) back occasionally.

"Nobody Knows Me" tour interlude

"I make scrapbooks of anything that is dear to my heart. I have a scrapbook of making a movie, or of a relationship that I had. I put pictures in and write captions underneath."—MADONNA, WHO (1999)

"NOTHING FAILS": *Release date: October 26, 2003. Billboard Hot 100 peak: NA.* The third single from *American Life*, written by Madonna, Guy Sigsworth and Jem Griffiths, with production by Madonna, **Mirwais** and Mark "Spike" Stent. The song reminds one of **"Like a Prayer"** thanks to its choir, but failed to catch on in the US. Madonna performed it on her *American Life* promo tour and *Re-Invention World Tour*.

"NOTHING REALLY MATTERS" (SONG): *Release date: March 2, 1999. Billboard Hot 100 peak: #93.* One of the most conventional pop songs on *Ray of Light*, this song was written by Madonna and **Patrick Leonard** and produced by Madonna, **William Orbit** and **Marius de Vries**. It became the final single from the

WHY WOULD YOU WANT TO SAY SOMETHING IF IT'S OFF-CAMERA?: AN INTERVIEW WITH MTV'S JOHN NORRIS

John Norris spent 20 years at MTV, but by the first time he interviewed Madonna, he'd already met her on his own. With a unique perspective on the Madonna you see and the Madonna you don't see, he's still a fan, but don't expect him to stan for her—or anyone.

The longtime journalist and fashion plate plays "I'll Remember" with *EM2O* on his run-ins with Madonna, and speaks out on his perception of her today.

EM2O: You did some high-profile interviews with Madonna for MTV over the years—what sticks out to you about those encounters?

JOHN NORRIS: There's one clip from my interview with Madonna that I used in my reel. I remember it as a quick exchange [in 2008] where I asked, "Why did you choose to work with Justin Timberlake and Timbaland?" and her answer was something like, 'Well, they're great and I like their shit.' It was just like that; short and to the point.

EM2O: Madonna can do that in interviews—give short answers and turn things back on the questioner.

JN: Oh, she's the queen of that. The funny thing about my acquaintanceship with her over the years is that I kinda knew her in the '90s, but that was before I ever interviewed her for MTV; Kurt Loder did all the interviews with her up through *Ray of Light* or even *Music*. Did I interview her for *Music*? [Laughs] I did a red-carpet interview with her at the premiere of *Evita* in LA, but it was literally two questions on the carpet. So 1996 was the first time I'd ever spoken to her on camera. But I'd known her before that.

EM2O: How did you know her?

JN: Well, I had started at MTV around '88, and by like '90 I was filling in for Kurt—my nickname was "Substitute Newsboy" when Kurt wasn't around. So I'm at the opening-night party for *Truth or Dare* and I was just hanging out there feeling lucky to even be *at* the party. She was sitting up in this little round, semi-circular VIP area with Jose & Luis, and I'm stealing glances and stuff. Then she just screamed, "Hey! Hey!" She, like, waves me over. I was doing one of those things like, "Are you talking to me???" So I come over and she's like, "Hi ..." and she's got one of them on either side of her and says, "We just wanted to say hi. We think you're great on the air and we also wanted to say we love your clothes."

Even in that first year and a half, I'd already become known for taking early-'90s fashion risks. I'm telling you, I've still got a Manhattan Mini Storage unit filled with some really choice '90s outfits, many of which will never see anything other than the inside of a box. But she goes, "I really love your clothes," and I said, "Really? Because my boss thinks what I wear sometimes is kinda 'faggy.'" And she goes, "What??? Tell him he can kiss my faggy ass." [Laughs] I thought that was really awesome.

I didn't really sort of know her for a while, then I got to know her through Ingrid [Casares] when she was really BFFs with Ingrid a couple years later, and even talked to her a while about—I was at the MTV LA office—about coming to Maverick. She introduced me to Freddy [DeMann] and Guy [Oseary]. Nothing ever came of that and we became pals then. I can't remember how I met Ingrid, but it was through Ingrid that I became friendly with her.

My friends threw a big birthday party for me at a big club in New York in '93 or '94 and she actually came to that with Ingrid. Then I kinda lost touch with her in the late '90s and didn't interview her again until *American Life*.

EM2O: Was it odd to interview her once you'd known her?

JN: Not odd in a bad way, just she'd seen me socially—we'd been to dinner and she'd been to my party. It was just different than had I been meeting an artist for the first time.

EM2O: How was she as an interview subject?

JN: For sure challenging. The question about having known her prior and whether that affected the dynamic of the interview. Her vibe with Kurt was always very playfully confrontational. She's look for a way to get at him or come at him and he would laugh it off. It was this really entertaining sparring match, and I'm not really into that dynamic. It's just not something I'm comfortable with, and I'm especially not comfortable with a subject who wants to turn things back on me. It's not ... how shall I put this? ... I don't know, I've never really wanted to talk about myself. Which makes me a very strange fit in the world we live in now.

EM2O: When you interviewed her for *Hard Candy*, you brought up her '90s quote about not seeing herself performing at 50. What do you think about Madonna and ageism?

JN: I'm of two minds of that. I'm not that far off from her demographically and I can relate to being somebody who wants to stay current and stay in the moment. I mean, she's making records now and more power to her for *Rebel Heart* or for the last record, working with young, hot, current people because she's inspired by that and she vibes off of them and their energy and their creativity—that's great. The cynical counter to that is, "Oh, well, it's a vampire-like quality, sucking the energy out. I remain relevant by surrounding myself with the Disclosures and Nicki Minajs of the world." I get that point of view, but I have no reason to believe that she's not legitimately psyched to be working with those people.

I just ask myself sometimes, "Has William Orbit really lost any interest to you? Or Pat Leonard?" Sometimes I feel like it's a complete numbers game for her—if they're over 25, why bother?

EM2O: That's a hard theory to test because we'd have to come up with a middle-aged artist who is the latest and hottest thing.

JN: The only older artists that are hot are the very few like herself that have managed to remain that way.

I'd say 80% of my reaction to her in the last 10 years is, "More power to you for just doing what you do." There *is* part of me sometimes that when I see titles like "Bitch I'm Madonna" or "Unapologetic Bitch" I think, "Why so defensive?" I guess from my point of view is, who's coming after her? Who's suggesting she has to apologize in 2015, unless it's those ridiculous people saying, "You shouldn't be showing your boobs in *Interview*."

EM2O: Well, maybe it *is* about those people. Maybe her kids tell her about her critics.

JN: That must be weird, too, seeing nasty shit about your mom.

I refuse to take sides with the stans of the world. I've become, in the last couple of years ... somewhat close to Gaga and I think she's a, all my interactions with her, my conclusion is she's a sweet, warm, wonderful person, and yet I'm not gonna get drawn in by the Little Monsters taking me to be an ally. That's fine, they can see me as anything they want, I'm just not gonna be anti-anyone. The fact that, truly—it's not just those two, whether it's Taylor Swift, One Direction or the Beliebers—enough already with these wars.

I do get why, of all the current girls, why [Gaga] gets under the skins of Madonna fans the most.

EM2O: I think some people are waiting for them to just bury the hatchet to get it over with.

JN: Absolutely.

EM2O: How would you sum up your thoughts of Madonna the person and the artist, based on your interactions with her?

JN: This might sound crazy, but one of the things I have always loved about Madonna—and believe me, I am almost to a fault a disciplined person in my work, too—one of the things I noticed about her during my time around her is that she is incredibly punctual. I find that trait such a nice thing. We're talking about by the mid-'90s, she would make you wait as long as she wanted to. I love, love Mariah Carey, she's a sweet woman, but punctual, she is not. Madonna, socially or regarding business, she's extremely punctual and that is a measure of respect to the person you're dealing with.

And, I might add, extremely focused in conversation. I have interviewed so many people over the years and some of them are really big stars, and you will be talking to them and you can see their mind wandering. You can see them being distracted, particularly now—please, with phones—and in conversation, Madonna *so listens* to what you're saying. I find I've got actual friends, as opposed to an acquaintance, which is what she was of mine, who don't pay attention to me when I'm talking like Madonna would.

album, and the least successful in spite of being supported by a high-concept video. This Kabbalistic **dance** record was performed somewhat anti-climactically at the **Grammys**—and never again.

"NOTHING REALLY MATTERS" (VIDEO): *Director: Johan Renck, 1999.* Madonna's video for her final *Ray of Light* single bubbles with every bit as much energy as the others from the project, indicating the depth of her engagement in the entire era.

Filmed at the beginning of 1999, the music video for "Nothing Really Matters" was one of several items in Madonna's career that was inspired by the novel *Memoirs of a Geisha* (1997) by Arthur Golden (other examples being her **Grammys** performance of the song and a concurrent *Harper's Bazaar* magazine cover and layout). Madonna cast herself as a figure similar to the **book**'s villainous (but fabulous) "Hatsumomo."

Though the video was inspired by the historical novel, its vibe is breathtakingly avant-garde. Madonna, in geisha garb, cradles a plastic bag filled with fluid, and her Japanese extras spasm in eerie ways, as if the cast of a hard-to-explain nightmare. Madonna performs the song in a red kimono, dancing jerkily in a way that can only be likened to the moves displayed by "Elaine Benes" (Julia-Louis Dreyfus) on the famous *Seinfeld* (1989–1998) episode "The Little Kicks." The video is disturbing to watch, summoning images of involuntary confinement in a surreal asylum setting. Madonna's mood, at first serious, degenerates into frivolity ... or is it hysteria?

The video is a moment from Madonna's career that is usually cited by critics who accuse her of **cultural appropriation**.

"NOW I'M FOLLOWING YOU (PART I) & **"NOW I'M FOLLOWING YOU (PART II)":** Part I is a song by Andy Paley, Jeff Lass, Ned Claflin and Jonathan Paley, and produced by Madonna and **Patrick Leonard**, that's found on *I'm Breathless: Music from and Inspired by the Film Dick Tracy.* The leisurely soft-shoe number is a '30s pastiche that finds Madonna duetting with her lover (and co-star) **Warren Beatty.** Part II of the song is remixed (by the late Kevin Gilbert, who sadly died in 1996 of apparent autoerotic asphyxiation) as a sort of kitchen-sink, modernized version of Part 1. It includes dialogue from the film (sample: "Dick ... that's an interesting name ..."), Beatty droning about the film's production costs and an overall more contemporary bent, sampling **"Cry Baby"** and other tunes from the album.

The songs were performed on Madonna's *Blond Ambition World Tour* in a lip-synched number that caused many critics to cry foul. Though Madonna made no attempt to disguise that she was lip-synching, it was at the time unheard of to lip-synch at a live concert. Or at least to do so and *admit* it—Madonna specifically referred to the lip-synching in a skit that accompanied the presentation of the songs.

NOWELS, RICK: **Grammy**-winning songwriter and producer who **worked** with Madonna early in her *Ray of Light* sessions (April 1997), producing nine songs, most of them **unreleased**. "Madonna would show up at 3 p.m. and we would start from scratch. She would leave at 7 p.m. and we would have a finished song and demo with all her lead and background vocals recorded," he told *Idolator* in 2013.

Though she went in another direction, she did retain three songs that she cowrote with Nowels: the single **"The Power of Good-Bye," "Little Star"** and **"To Have and Not to Hold."**

In 2015, the Madonna/Nowels composition **"Beautiful Scars"** made the Super Deluxe Edition of *Rebel Heart.*

Nowels has high praise for Madonna's **talents**: "She is a brilliant pop melodist and lyricist. I was knocked out by the quality of the writing. The lyrics to 'The **Power** Of Good-Bye' are stunning. I **love** Madonna as an artist and a songwriter ... I know she grew up on **Joni Mitchell** and Motown, and to my ears she embodies the best of both worlds ... She doesn't get the credit she deserves as a writer."

NUDE: Director **Uli Edel** said it best (if not properly) when describing Madonna's **sex scenes** for *Body of Evidence:* "It was no problem for Madonna to pose without dresses."

By all accounts, Madonna has always been very comfortable with her body. As a kid, she and a pal named Carol went to church naked under their raincoats.

She became a skinny artist's model out of "desperation" during her early days in **New York**, posing for photographers who later capitalized by selling their photos to *Penthouse* and *Playboy* and by marketing posters and prints of their handiwork.

"When I modeled nude for **art** classes," Madonna said, for which she was paid all of $7–$10 an hour or $25–$30 per session, "I felt like I was being really feminine ... It was empowering for me to take my clothes off and then to put my clothing **back** on and go home and carry on with my day and not feel like I lost any dignity or self-esteem. It made me think of my body as a **work** of art."

"It was really good **money** and very flexible hours, which is why I chose to do it ... it's not because I enjoy taking my clothes off, or anything like that," she said in 1998.

She wasn't paid very well for the nudity she provided in her underground film debut *A Certain Sacrifice* either, but she later had the good sense to turn down a $1.2 million offer to pose nude for *High Society* **magazine**, which wound up running secondhand nudes under the headline: "MADONNA SHOWS YOU HER **PUSSY**!"

In a 1985 **fan** club mailing (originating from Like a Virgin, POB 77505, San Francisco, CA 94107-0505), Madonna was quoted as saying, "My body is something nice like my smile, so why not show it to people."

Though she showed plenty of skin (including some in a 1985 **fashion** layout in *Rolling Stone*, where her breasts are visible through a lacy top), she didn't allow herself to be

—MARK FISHER

NEW YORK POST | METRO TODAY'S RACING

MADONNA: 'I'M NOT ASHAMED'

Rock star shrugs off nudie pix furor STORY PAGE FOUR

REAGAN ON THE WARPATH

Blasts 'outlaw states run by misfits, looney tunes & squalid criminals...'

PREZ HITS BACK: PAGE 5

RAUNCHY STAR Madonna in action: No secrets, no shame.

A naked attempt to shame the new girl

photographed by any definition of "nude" again until she flashed a breast for **Helmut Newton** and *Vanity Fair* at Small's K.O. Bar (formerly 5547 Melrose Ave., Hollywood, CA) in 1990.

Soon after, Madonna appeared in a diaphanous garment in *Dick Tracy*, topless in *Truth or Dare*, nude in *Body of Evidence* and *Dangerous Game*, in various stages of undress for **Herb Ritts** and **Steven Meisel** shoots, and, of course, naked as a jaybird all through *Sex*, for which she rode a bicycle topless and hitchhiked naked on the streets of **Miami**. Just prior to the release of the **book**, Madonna appeared at a public event in a breast-baring garment by **Jean Paul Gaultier.**

For Madonna, nudity is not always for **sexual** titillation. The fact that Madonna made *Sex* proves as much; the real issue with that book was the incredible **power** behind the fact that so famous a woman—with so much to lose by posing nude—could strip, not for attention or praise or to turn men on, but because she felt like it. Nudity in the '90s and beyond is at least as much about power and liberation as it is about lust.

Madonna told *20/20* in 2004, "I did spend at least a decade taking my clothes off and being photographed" as an example of things she'd done in the past strictly for the sake of "turning over the apple cart." But it turned out she was not done overturning that particular cart after all. Madonna and nudity broke up for a while during her years with **Guy Ritchie**, but it didn't take.

In 2012, when Madonna showed her breast on stage during *The MDNA Tour* in both Istanbul and **Paris**, sure, she was proud to be in her fifties and still in possession of a nice rack, but she was also explicitly **protesting** the prevailing belief that women should be demure. She was saying that a nipple is just a nipple—why the fuss? As

recently as late 2014, she was posing topless for *Interview* and causing a commotion.

And Madonna did for asses what she'd done for nipples when, in 2015, she flashed her mostly bare butt to the event photographers at the **Grammys**, causing countless online meltdowns over her inappropriate behavior. Her response? "**Bitch**, this is what my ass looks like—show me what your ass looks like when you're 56. I take care of myself. I'm in good shape. I can show my ass when I'm 56, or 66—or 76."

At this point, Madonna is synonymous with nudity, so critics have reacted by claiming that her now-familiar nude body is devoid of sexuality or eroticism. If anything, her body has *transcended* the merely prurient. Madonna's so much a part of our daily culture that her nipples are like familiar coworkers, or like old friends we expect to see frequently and welcome warmly when we do.

"I was really naïve and I read *The Village Voice* and it said 'DANCERS WANTED' and I was a dancer at the time ... and I thought, 'God, a hundreds bucks a night! That's good money.' So I'd go to these agencies and these big, fat, disgusting, bald men would be in these offices and they'd say, 'Okay, take your clothes off.'"—MADONNA, *SEX* (1992)

NULLE PART AILLEURS: *Airdates: September 1987–June 2001.* French Canal+ **TV** talk show on which Madonna appeared on November 24, 2000, performing **"Don't Tell Me"** and **"Music."** Her rendition of the latter started with a French spoken-word introduction. **Mirwais** (who shouted nonsensically, "**England** forever!"), **Niki Haris** and **Donna De Lory** were in her troupe.

NUNS: In 1991, Madonna told *Rolling Stone*, "When I was growing up, I wanted to be a nun. I saw nuns as superstars."

"You know, there are many different ways to serve God, and Madonna is making many people aware of the Catholic Church and all its teachings who might not have been aware if she didn't exist." —DOLORES HART TO MADONNA BIOGRAPHER BARBARA VICTOR (2001)

NUREYEV, RUDOLF: *March 17, 1938–January 6, 1993.* One of the most acclaimed ballet and modern **dancers** of all time who defected from the Soviet Union to France in 1961. He remained a force into the '80s, and his striking face was often seen partying with the boldface names of the era.

Madonna, a dancer who sings, bought dance slippers, a costume and a Roman marble torso from the estate **auction** of this legend after he died of **AIDS** in 1993.

NYC: SEE **New York.**

GREGORY PACE

MATTHEW RETTENMUND

MATTHEW RETTENMUND

OAKLEY, TYLER: *b. March 22, 1989.* You-Tube star who has amassed a huge following since 2007 by speaking out on **gay** rights and pop culture. Because of his millions of followers, he has been afforded face time with Michelle **Obama**, and in 2014 was **awarded** the Out100 Readers' Choice Award by *Out* magazine. Oakley recreated a famous Truman Capote pose in *Out* in conjunction with the honor.

Unfortunately, perhaps because he was born as *Like a Prayer* was being released, Oakley does *not* get his fellow "shameless self-promoter" Madonna, posting negatively about her in stark contrast to his otherwise positive messages. He is a self-admitted **Lady Gaga** stan and, judging by a popular post he made comparing Madonna's and Gaga's reactions on *The Graham Norton Show* when each was presented with **fan**-made dolls, believes Madonna is ungracious. Madonna's fans like being acknowledged, but understand Madonna's playful hauteur. It's a shame such an effective **cheerleader** for gay rights does not appreciate Madonna's status as the same, decades before it was fashionable, and that such a connoisseur of pop culture seems unwilling to give Madonna her props as an artist because she rubs him the wrong way.

Going **back** to his Out100 pose, it should be noted that Capote, while brilliant and an icon in many ways, was not someone his peers would ever have deemed "nice."

Hopefully Oakley and other Gaga fans will warm to Madonna once the feud is over, because most of the *offensive* reactions on both sides seem to be *defensive*.

OBAMA, BARACK: *b. August 4, 1961.* The 44th POTUS and first person of African-American descent to hold the office. Obama, a Democrat, beat **Hillary Clinton** to the nomination and defeated Sen. John McCain (R-Arizona) and former Republican Massachusetts Gov. Mitt Romney in 2008 and 2012, respectively. Obama was from the get-go a major thorn in the sides of right-wingers, many of whom insisted he was a secret Muslim because his father—absent for all but the first two years of his life—had been a Muslim as a kid, although an atheist as an adult.

In 2008, Madonna was asked which (Democratic) presidential candidate would "make the least huge mistakes." She replied cryptically, "I'm excited about one of the candidates." As a follow-up, the interviewer goaded her with, "But you can't talk about him because the other one's husband is in your movie?" Hillary Clinton was running for the nomination against Obama, and her husband, former POTUS **Bill Clinton**, had appeared in Madonna's *I Am Because We Are*. Madonna said, "That's not nice. Um, I'm actually a big **fan** of the Clintons and Obama."

On her *Sticky & Sweet Tour*, Madonna was playing San Jose, California, on election night 2008. She took a moment to address the crowd, saying, "This is a historical evening. This ... is ... a motherfucking important evening.

RHONDA CORTE

And we are happy to be sharing it with each other." She also offered for sale a tour T-shirt with Obama's face on it.

Next election cycle, Madonna endorsed Obama on September 7, 2012, when she revealed an "OBAMA" tramp stamp on the small of her **back** during an *MDNA Tour* stop at Yankee Stadium (1 E. 161st St., Bronx, NY).

On another stop in Washington, DC on September 24, 2012, Madonna said to her captive audience, "So ... y'all better vote for **fuckin'** Obama, okay? For better or for worse—all right?—we have a black Muslim in the White House, okay? Now that is the shit. That's some amazing shit, that means there is hope in this country, and Obama is fighting for **gay** rights, so support the man, **God** damn it."

Criticized for referencing Obama as a Muslim, Madonna played the "ironic" card.

She got a few boos when she stumped for Obama at her October 27, 2012, *MDNA Tour* stop in New Orleans, telling the crowd, "I don't care who you vote for as long as you vote for Obama."

President Obama was one of the famous names listed in Madonna's **"Illuminati"** as *not* being a member of the titular, imaginary group of **power**-mad celebrities.

In 2015, Madonna told *Us* she was probably too "shocking" to receive an invite to the White House, noting it would help if she were "a little bit more demure ... or if I was just married to Jay Z." She finally met Obama at a taping of *The Tonight Show* in 2016, posting images of them backstage together on **Instagram**. The first, showing an "a little bit more demure" Madonna standing timidly before Mr. President, was captioned, "For Once I'm Speechless...........President Obama".

O'BRIEN, GLENN: *b. 1947.* Faultlessly stylish downtown writer who was an **Andy Warhol** Factory insider as well as the first editor of Warhol's *Interview*.

In 1992, he became the editor of *Sex*, a thankless task, to be sure. He missed a glaring its/it's error halfway through the **book** (page 53), but Madonna still thanked him for "teaching me how to spell." (Let's give him an "I" for "incomplete" grade on that one.)

O'Brien knew Madonna from at least 1983, when she attended a party at his home with **Jean-Michel Basquiat**. O'Brien was tight with Basquiat, and is the owner of many early **works** by the tragic artist.

After O'Brien left *Interview*, he continued contributing Q&As, among them one conducted with Madonna for her 1990 cover story. He was a cerebral, respectful and knowledgeable

glenn o'brien

O'Brien in 1984

inquisitor. One of his best quotes on Madonna involves her seeming enmity with the **Catholic** Church: "It's hard to have a religion based on dead **heroes** when you have live heroes around who are, y'know, taking away your customers."

O'CONNOR, SINÉAD: *b. December 8, 1966.* Cantankerous Irish diva whose aching vocals and bald head made her famous in 1990, and whose politically charged actions, such as refusing to allow the US national anthem to be played before one of her concerts, made her a reviled figure. She was so controversial even Madonna made withering comments about her, despite the fact that O'Connor once picked **"Live to Tell"** as one of the 10 best songs of 1986 for a teen **magazine**. (Madonna must not have been a subscriber, because she was quoted saying of O'Connor, "She's about as **sexy** as a Venetian blind," in 1989.)

On October 3, 1992, O'Connor was the musical guest on *Saturday Night Live* for the second time. She performed "Am I Not Your Girl?" and then for her second song, did an a cappella version of **Bob Marley**'s "War" (1976). At the end of the latter, after delivering the lines, "We have confidence in the victory of good over evil," she produced a photograph of **Pope John Paul II** and tore it to shreds, stating, "Fight the real enemy." O'Connor was condemned by many for her action, and was booed on stage at a Bob Dylan tribute 13 days later at **Madison Square Garden**.

Surprisingly, Madonna told the *Irish Times* of O'Connor, "I think there is a better way to present her ideas rather than ripping up an image that means a lot to other people. If she is against the Roman **Catholic** Church and she has a problem with them, I think she should talk about it."

No word on if Madonna was hanging on a **crucifix** while saying this.

As mild, if hypocritical, as this statement was, **Bob Guccione Jr.** of *Spin* said Madonna had "savaged" O'Connor to reclaim attention in the media. Yes, he is the same guy whose dad published *Penthouse*.

On January 16, 1993, Madonna was an *SNL* musical guest. After her performance of **"Bad Girl,"** she naughtily produced a photo of Joey Buttafuoco, a Long Island cad embroiled in a controversy about cheating on his wife with Lolita Amy Fisher, who later shot the wife in the head. In a belittling **parody**, Madonna repeated O'Connor's line: "Fight the real enemy."

One common denominator the divas share is Karl Geary, a former waiter at the music venue Sin-é (formerly 122 St. Mark's Pl., NY, NY) who was a great friend of O'Connor's and who appeared in Madonna's **"Erotica"** video and in *Sex*.

> "I love, adore and respect her. I feel a little sorry for her for all the analysis she goes through …"—SINÉAD O'CONNOR ON MADONNA (1992)

O'DONNELL, ROSIE: *b. March 21, 1962.* Stand-up comic, movie actor and—from 1996 until 2002—the hostess of the phenomenally popular daytime talk show *The Rosie O'Donnell Show*. O'Donnell came out as a lesbian in 2002 and has been associated with various causes, in particular championing the right for **gay** parents to adopt.

From 2006–2007, O'Donnell served as moderator on the long-running, all-female daytime talk show *The View* (1997–), but her tenure was marked by meltdowns and political spats. She left, only to return for the 2014–2015 season, during which O'Donnell had simmered down (a heart attack, which she suffered in 2012, can be calming), but not entirely. She left the show for a second time.

Madonna met the funny, forthright, self-conscious, tart-tongued O'Donnell when they costarred in *A League of Their Own* just a few weeks after O'Donnell saw *Truth or Dare* and had told a friend she would "never" meet Madonna. Their *League* costar Ann Cusack told *EM20*, "Rosie took [Madonna] under her wing and she really absorbed and learned from everybody around her, which was really great."

The women bonded over their similar childhoods. "My mom died when I was little, too," O'Donnell said to Madonna on the occasion of their very first meeting. Not only did they lose their **mothers**, both were the eldest girls in their families and were named for the mothers who died young.

Their director, **Penny Marshall**, said, in 2012, "I made them best friends, Ro and Mo—'cause it's too long to say their name—and so, I said, 'You teach, you keep food out of Rosie's mouth, and Rosie, you teach her how to play ball …'"

Madonna appeared with O'Donnell on *The Arsenio Hall Show* in 1992, attended the premiere of O'Donnell's films *Sleepless in Seattle* (1993) and *Wide Awake* (1998) and in that same year was persuaded by host O'Donnell to make a quick appearance on the **Nickelodeon Kids' Choice Awards**.

Madonna visited O'Donnell's talk show more than once.

For her first appearance on January 9, 1997, Madonna came out holding a baby, momentarily faking out the audience that she was showing off her daughter **Lola**. It was an imposter infant, but it was still adorable to see Madonna cuddle it and say, "Who's a baby punkin? You're just a baby

Butch/femme: Rosie O'Donnell mugs with Liza Minnelli

MATTHEW RETTENMUND

chicken!" The baby was Henry, the son of O'Donnell staffer Judy Gold, the well-known lesbian comedian. Madonna did speak a lot about Lola, including her ability to hold a conversation at three months of age and her **love** for Tickle Me Elmo. Madonna buried her face in embarrassment when shown a flashback video of her **"Like a Virgin"** performance on the **MTV Video Music Awards**. A running joke about whether O'Donnell's rival talk show hosts **hated** her was brought across the finish line when Sally Jessy Raphael called in to say she did *not* hate O'Donnell, but wanted her "to sing on key."

Madonna and O'Donnell sang a duet of the children's song "Three Little Fishies" (1939) and also a **parody** of **"Buenos Aires"** adapted to address unglamorous aspects of both women becoming new moms.

Madonna, three months **pregnant**, was **back** on February 4, 2000, to promote *The Next Best Thing*. The women immediately discussed O'Donnell's **weight** loss by remembering her previous diet (Dunkin Donuts, a sandwich from Blimpie, Domino's **pizza** ... and the list goes on), debated whether or not Madonna picks her nose and pinned down the genesis of *The Next Best Thing*. Best of all, Madonna addressed the burning issue of her **accent**. Costar Benjamin Bratt joined Madonna in the midst of the interview, flattering her by saying when he first met her, he was struck by how much prettier she was in person, how tiny she was and how buff her **muscles** were. The segment ended with a game called "Mo or Ro," in which audience members had to pick which descriptors applied to which of the famous ladies.

Madonna came back on March 13, 1998, to promote *Ray of Light*, helping O'Donnell to play "Mo or Ro" again and teaching her about henna tattoos. Most hilariously, Madonna tried to teach O'Donnell various **yoga** positions. Madonna later admitted she had secretly pulled her calf muscles thanks to her three-inch heels.

Over the years, O'Donnell has attended all of Madonna's tours (her photography adorns the cover and inlay of *Drowned World Tour 2001*), and Madonna was quick to defend O'Donnell in 2007 when **Donald Trump** was attacking her for being a "slob."

Madonna's friendship with O'Donnell is sweet and real and has lasted for almost 25 years.

"OH FATHER" (SONG): *Release date: October 24, 1989. Billboard Hot 100 peak: #20.* This dirgelike ballad, the fourth single from *Like a Prayer*, "only" made it to number 20 on *Billboard*, shattering Madonna's record-breaking string of Top 10 singles. Lesson learned: The fact that the word "**art**" appears in the word "charts" is a coincidence.

The song, written and produced by Madonna and **Patrick Leonard**, packs an uncommon emotional wallop, sung from the perspective of a woman trying to forgive her father for the **death** of her **mother**—something for which she now understands he was not responsible. It is possible that the song alludes to physical abuse, though that theme is much clearer in the music video. **David Fincher** persuaded Madonna to release it as a single (in the US, Canada and Japan; elsewhere abroad, **"Dear Jessie"** was the fourth single). It was also a *Something to Remember* single in parts of Europe.

Madonna performed the song live on her *Blond Ambition World Tour*.

"My favorite thing that we ever recorded, ever—or wrote—is 'Oh Father'."—PATRICK LEONARD (2014)

"OH FATHER" (VIDEO): *Director: David Fincher, 1989.* Highly cinematic, **black-and-white** video that references the classic Orson Welles film *Citizen Kane* (1941) with its winter-scene opening and use of deep-focus camera **work**. Madonna plays a woman coming to grips with the abuse she's suffered at the hands of her **father** in the aftermath of her **mother**'s **death**. The character is also shown as a young girl who squirms at the sight of her mother's corpse's sewn-together lips, and who eerily **dances** on her mother's grave.

"Oh Father" includes a scene in which Madonna's character is slapped by her lover, suggesting that abused children sometimes fall into abusive relationships as adults. That allusion is not made clear in the song, an example of how Madonna's **videos** are used less to illustrate than to reimagine her music. "Oh Father," intentionally or not, lends credence to reports that **Sean Penn** was violent with Madonna during their marriage.

It is without question one of Madonna's finest videos—future superstar movie director **David Fincher** really outdid himself—making its exclusion from *Celebration: The Video Collection* highly unusual.

"OH WHAT A CIRCUS": Expository number found on *Evita: The Complete Motion Picture Music Soundtrack*, on which **Antonio Banderas** sings. Banderas's Che sings cuttingly of Evita's legacy, "She did nothing for years."

OLYMPIA HALL: *28 Blvd. des Capucines, Paris, France.* L'Olympia Bruno Coquatrix, a.k.a. Olympia Hall, is a historical concert hall famous for its **eye**-popping façade and for the world-class singers who have graced its stage, Edith Piaf and **Marlene Dietrich** among them.

On May 6, 2008, Madonna brought her *Hard Candy* promo tour to the Olympia, performing **"Candy Shop," "Miles Away," "4 Minutes," "Hung Up," "Give It 2 Me"** and **"Music"** for an out-of-**control** crowd.

She also performed a highly unusual concert at the Olympia on July 26, 2012. On the one hand, it was a promo show to raise awareness for her ongoing *MDNA Tour*. On the other hand, tickets were not free. The fact that it was a mini concert was not well advertised, so **fans** arrived expecting a full show.

"Get the cream." —MADONNA'S ADVICE TO A MENOPAUSAL ROSIE O'DONNELL (2009)

"You mean, what does it feel like to be worshiped and adored? It feels great."–MADONNA, *OMNIBUS: BEHIND THE AMERICAN DREAM* (1990)

Madonna performed **"Turn Up the Radio," "Open Your Heart," "Vogue," "Candy** Shop" and **"Human Nature"** as heard on the tour (along with the video pieces "Radio Dial Static" and **"Justify My Love"** from the tour), then surprised with her first-ever performance of **"Beautiful Killer"** (set to the music of **"Die Another Day"**). Her final number was a cover of the Serge Gainsbourg/Jane Birkin classic "Je t'aime … moi non plus" (1969), hitting ze nail on ze head perhaps too much, non?

During the intimate concert, which was streamed live on **YouTube,** Madonna spoke at length about the "scary times" in which we live, touching on racism and intolerance, apparently in reference to her controversial use of far-right leader **Marine Le Pen**'s image with a swastika on her head in the **"Nobody Knows Me"** video interlude.

At the end of the show, a number of the 2,700 in the crowd nearly rioted, expressing contempt for the show's brevity even though she had received uproarious applause at the end of each number. Some tried to chalk it up to rabble-rousing right-wing extremists, but one shouted "Vive **Lady Gaga**!" so it was probably less political than just disgruntled consumers in a fit of pique.

Madonna revealed in 2015 that she'd actually been **working** to get Alain Delon to make a cameo appearance on stage with her during the show since he is name-checked in "Beautiful Killer." She told *Us* **magazine** that when he called her to decline, "I was shaking because I **love** him so much! I never met the dude and only knew him from movies. He was my ridiculous teenage **crush**."

OMNIBUS: BEHIND THE AMERICAN DREAM: *Producer: Nadia Haggar. Air date: December 7, 1990.* Incredibly thorough UK **TV** special that aired on BBC1, in which Madonna (lips filled with **collagen**) gives a lengthy, unguarded, **black-and-white** interview, complemented by commentary from pop culture critic Greil Marcus, *Los Angeles Times* reporter Kristine McKenna, writer **Glenn O'Brien,** *Vogue*'s André Leon Talley, former *Village Voice* nightlife chronicler **Michael Musto,** Professor Margo Johnson and more.

The show aired footage of US troops preparing to go to war in the Persian Gulf watching Madonna perform on the **MTV Video Music Awards.** It's striking to watch this now—red-blooded straight dudes gushing, "Madonna's very **sexy,** she has good music that's good to **dance** to!" and catcalling her. As Madonna's artistic statements became more extreme, it became very unusual for that crowd to cheer her on. Footage from inside **The Roxy** looks far more familiar, and scenes inside a Harvard classroom in which Madonna's appeal is being dissected seem less bizarre now than they did in 1990.

As far as her personal acquaintances, the special uses footage of Madonna's beloved high **school** teacher **Marilyn Fellows** and offers interviews with her brother **Christopher Ciccone** and her mentor **Christopher Flynn,** the

latter of whom said, "She so thoroughly enjoyed dancing that it just sprung out of her."

One of the best, most respectful and smartest profiles on Madonna to date.

"ON THE BALCONY OF THE CASA ROSADA 1 & 2": Two separate pieces, the first a short **Jonathan Pryce** speech from the film *Evita,* and the second a short "song" made up of a crowd's melodic chant and a fiery speech by Madonna as Evita. Both are found on *Evita: The Complete Motion Picture Music Soundtrack.*

"ON THIS NIGHT OF A THOUSAND STARS": Swoon-worthy tune sung solely by heartthrob Magaldi (**Jimmy Nail**) in *Evita.* Found on *Evita: The Complete Motion Picture Music Soundtrack.*

106 & PARK: *Airdates: September 11, 2000–December 19, 2014.* Madonna appeared on BET's video-countdown music show on May 1, 2008, toward the middle of its run to promote *Hard Candy.* Hosts Rocsi Diaz and Terrence J(enkins) welcomed "the one and only Madonna" to a flood of cheers. She entered looking like a pimp in a short Givenchy dress and draped in miles of gold chains and a fluffy black fur, and gave a subdued but genial interview on such topics as **Justin Timberlake,** parenting, **horses,** hip-hop and **Meshell Ndegeocello,** during which she had to be prompted to speak into her mic.

"ONE MORE CHANCE": *Release date: March 7, 1996. Billboard Hot 100 peak: NA.* One of three new songs included on *Something to Remember,* written and produced by Madonna and **David Foster.** The ballad shows off Madonna's pre-*Evita* vocal training. It was released outside the US as the album's second single, but was never a US single.

"A lot of artists, they want to be coproducers just because they can. [Madonna] wanted to be a coproducer, but she earned it. She really knows her way around a studio."–DAVID FOSTER (2005)

ONO, YOKO: *b. February 18, 1933.* John Lennon's controversial widow and executor of his estate, Ono is also an avant-garde multimedia artist, pacifist and musician who has enjoyed a string of #1 **dance** hits into her eighties thanks to clever remixes.

Ono threw a party in 1985 attended by **David Bowie,** Bob Dylan, **Andy Warhol** and Madonna. Ono asked that all guests remove their shoes, to which Madonna said that she'd feel more comfortable shirtless than shoeless. No kidding!

Ono was said to have appreciated Madonna's cover version of Lennon's **"Imagine."**

"OPEN YOUR HEART" (SONG): *Release date: November 10, 1986. Billboard Hot 100 peak: #1.* An enormous hit from Madonna's *True Blue* album in 1986, the song's success was doubly incredible since it was the fourth release from the album and the third to hit the top spot. A straightforward tale of a girl struggling to win the attention and affections of a self-involved guy, it's an example of Madonna singing about a simple situation and imbuing it with heartfelt emotion.

The song was originally written as "Follow Your Heart" by Gardner Cole and Peter Rafelson with **Cyndi Lauper** in mind. The songwriters sent the song to Madonna's manager **Freddy DeMann** along with two others. He liked it, so Cole had his girlfriend, **Donna De Lory** (who would go on to become Madonna's longest-running backup singer) demo it. Madonna liked the song but rewrote parts of it, hence her writing credit.

Madonna's vocals are comparable to those on **"Papa Don't Preach,"** full of pleading and infectious urgency.

The sleeve of the single represented a radical image change—a sultry photo of Madonna wearing a short black wig. It was taken during the filming of the music video that accompanied the song.

Madonna has performed the song live on her *Who's That Girl World Tour*, *Blond Ambition World Tour* and *MDNA Tour*. It was teased instrumentally on the *Drowned World Tour* and on the *Sticky & Sweet Tour*, and was a bonus on the *Rebel Heart Tour*. It was included briefly in her **Super Bowl** halftime show and was a memorable part of the **Grammys** in 2014.

"OPEN YOUR HEART" (VIDEO): *Director: Jean-Baptiste Mondino, 1986.* One of Madonna's best music videos was the first glimpse of how far she was willing to go to make jarring artistic statements using the media of pop music and music videos. The song is a cute **love**-angst number, but the video not only pushes the envelope, it addresses, **stamps** and mails it.

Madonna plays a white-**blonde** peep show stripper whose workplace is decorated by a gigantic **Tamara de Lempicka** cut-out. She is the object of a young boy's (**Felix Howard**) admiration. The boy falls in love with the apparent glamour of the stripper's life, caressing her image on a poster in front of the strip joint, and even mimicking how he imagines she would **dance** for the men inside.

Meanwhile, the stripper is performing in a gold-studded bustier (a precursor to the **cone bra**), strutting and dancing with a chair for a prop—a strong homage to **Marlene Dietrich**. Most shocking is the view we are afforded of the show's audience, ensconced in booths. Among others, we see a grinning cowboy, a pair of beautiful twin sailors who watch with hands clasped and heads pressed together and a butch lesbian. As her act comes to an end, there are shots clearly suggesting the viewers were **masturbating**.

For all the raunchy elements, the video, directed by French photographer **Jean-Baptiste Mondino**, is so stylized—almost animated—that it avoids feeling *too* prurient, which is precisely the point.

Mondino said in 2015: "[The set was built] from scratch. We found this place where we could actually build it. We just built the front of it and the little booth where the old man was inside. I guess it was my Hollywood period where I was in [a] Hollywood state of mind with my cranes, the building … We were very young and everything was possible, I guess. I like the fakeness of it."

When the stripper emerges from the theater, her **hair** is tousled and she looks like a little boy herself. She chastely kisses her young admirer, who had dozed while waiting for her to finish, and the two dance off together, playing like children, or like Charlie Chaplin's "Little Tramp" in *The Kid* (1921).

Though there were indignant whispers that the video pushed pedophilia, it's pretty clear that the boy-child is heroine-worshiping the stripper—coveting her feminine allure, even—a phase common in boys. That the stripper's real persona is that of an androgyne rather than a siren only underscores the false allure of the strip show and the artifice of performance as opposed to the genuine feelings of the boy. Just to blur the line between **acting** and real life, the stripper's name is "Madonna."

For her part, Madonna said "Open Your Heart," shot in Los Angeles's Echo Park, reminded her of her days on **New York**'s Lower East Side when she would try to overcome the **race** barrier and make friends with her young Latino neighbors. If you want to preserve the innocence of the video, try not to connect the dots between this **memory** and the story in *Sex* that begins, "Sex with the young can be fun …"

> "Extraordinarily provocative. In a brisk, haiku-like four minutes and 22 seconds, 'Open Your Heart' presents Madonna as every adolescent boy's wildest, sweetest fantasy. It's a tiny, comic, sexy classic."
> —VINCENT CANBY, *THE NEW YORK TIMES* (1987)

ORANGE: According to astrologer Daphne Weld Nichols in *Star* **magazine**, this is Madonna's color, corresponding with her number, two. Oranges "like to seek out as much **beauty** as possible in life, but are also materialistic and moody." Sorry, Madonna, but Mel Gibson is a fellow orange. Oy vey.

ORBIT, WILLIAM: *b. December 15, 1956.* English musician and producer noted for his inventive ambient albums in the *Strange Cargo* series (1987–).

After Orbit had remixed **"Justify My Love"** and **"I'll Remember,"** Madonna teamed up with him in 1997 at the suggestion of **Guy Oseary**, who had been in touch with him asking for material. "It just so happened I had a lot of tapes of half-formed ideas lying around, so when he

—BRAD GOOCH

asked me to send some stuff over I was happy to just knock off a DAT with miscellaneous bits on it." From that first contact, the duo would go on to create Madonna's most critically acclaimed album, 1998's *Ray of Light*. Of the 13 songs on the album, Orbit coproduced all but one ("**Little Star**") and had a hand in writing six of them ("**Drowned World/Substitute for Love**," "**Swim**," "**Ray of Light**," "**Candy Perfume Girl**," "**Shanti/Ashtangi**" and "**Mer Girl**"), among them two of the album's singles. He also **worked** on "**Has to Be**."

"I didn't reinvent her at all," Orbit said at the time of his work with Madonna on *Ray of Light*. "She's much, much more of a self-directed person than that. It was more that she produced me producing her."

Immediately following the album's enormous success, he and Madonna created "**Beautiful Stranger**," another in a long line of Madonna's songs for movies, in this case for *Austin Powers: The Spy Who Shagged Me* (1999). They coproduced Madonna's remake of "**American Pie**" and collaborated on the ballad "**Time Stood Still**," both for *The Next Best Thing* (2000), and worked on an **unreleased** song, part of which was used as the theme for the failed **TV** show *Wonderland* (2000).

"William had a very long leash, but I was firmly holding on to the end of it … I was the anchor, he was the waves, and the ship was our record."–MADONNA ON WILLIAM ORBIT AND *RAY OF LIGHT* (1998)

Madonna continued her collaboration with Orbit on *Music*, though to a lesser extent. Orbit cowrote "**Runaway Lover**" and "**Amazing**" and coproduced those songs as well as "**Gone**" and various unreleased outtakes.

Because of the artistic **heights** Madonna reached with Orbit, **fans** were excited when she teamed up with him again in 2012 for part of her *MDNA* album. The results were a mixed bag, with Orbit cowriting and coproducing "**Gang Bang**," "**Some Girls**," "**I'm a Sinner**," "**Love Spent**" and "**Falling Free**," and coproducing "**Masterpiece**."

Orbit was unhappy with the song selection and marketing of *MDNA*, and expressed his displeasure on **Facebook** in a self-described "screed" that read, in part:

"We were very pushed for time, due to a rather interesting and shall we just say, 'traditional' method of recording that the esteemed engineer Demo was partial to, and various pressing commitments that took up the artists limited time, such as perfume ranges and teen **fashion** contests and other such endeavours which are beyond my own limited understanding of pop star agendas.

"The recording sessions for the six songs I did were hugely enjoyable for all of us. M was on form and better than ever with her singing and writing and musicality, and was having a great time. We had songs lined up that were breathtaking. You'll hear some of them on Chris Brown's new album, and they are the best ones, Kreayshawn's (INCREDIBLE) new album, my own recently completed 'Strange Cargo' album. And some other surprising places. SNAPPED up by the artists concerned. Most of them, I believe, destined to become classics (let me know in a couple months wether you concur with that)…

"So basically, i'd lie down in the mud if she didn't want to get her shoes messed up (well, figuratively speaking, neither of us does a lot of Glastonbury mud tramping) it's hard to be an effective knight when your hands are bound. I will submit to wisdoms that are possibly beyond my comprehension and that will play out to glory in the fullness of time. And get **back** to my own fervent canvas, and speak no more of the matter."

He suggested that *MDNA* be repackaged.

When Orbit's comments upset Oseary, the two communicated and Orbit tweeted, "The MDNA comments. I should not have said them publicly. I see that and I **regret** that I said online. Not fair to M."

Though Orbit mocked Madonna's reaction to the **leak** of *Rebel Heart*, he had earlier tweeted of the album, "Sounds good." He was present at 2015's **Brit Awards**, but missed Madonna's accident because someone was speaking to him. In summing up the **awards**, Orbit noted of *Rebel Heart*, "imho, she's just made one heck of an album! :-)"

MEGA-FAN SPOTLIGHT: FRANK ORLIK

Because I have been a fan since 1982, Madonna's music has been the soundtrack of my life. She is someone who I admire and hold in the highest regard. The first time I fell in love with her was before I even saw what she looked like. It was at a roller-skating rink on Long Island called Good Skates. The DJ put on "Everybody" and immediately I needed to know who was singing. I went up to him and asked. He said it was a new artist called Madonna and he held up the 12" with pictures of NYC apartment buildings. That very afternoon, I went to the record store and purchased it. It was the start of my Madonna collection and also the beginning of my diehard fandom. There are other singers/bands that I enjoy, but there is only one Queen of Pop who will always hold the #1 spot in my heart. Madonna–who in 2012 signed my arm so I could get her autograph tattooed on me–has been and continues to be a constant inspiration in my life.

KEVIN MAZUR

ORGY: In *A Certain Sacrifice*, Madonna's character "Bruna" owns a pack of **sex** slaves, and in one climactic scene, they pleasure her from all angles as she writhes ecstatically on the floor. Much later, on *The Girlie Show World Tour*, after a piece depicting the joie de vivre of the club scene in the '70s, things wound down into an amazingly erotic, implied orgy, with male and female members of Madonna's troupe simulating a slow, sensual, mutual exploration of each other loose enough to seem unchoreographed. And as you may have seen, *Sex* has its share of group gropes.

All that said, Madonna has not expressed any special appreciation for group sex in her private life; she seems to get off on the attention of large groups, but usually while she's on a stage and the rest of us are just out of reach.

ORIGINALITY: The current concept of originality in pop music is ludicrous, not because *nothing* in pop is fresh or surprising, but because those who argue the hardest that this artist or that artist isn't original are usually **fans** of artists who are no more and no less original themselves.

The argument of originality used to center around an artist's musical choices, philosophy and overall visual presentation. It was the idea that an artist seemed to bring something new to the table, and to set or avoid trends more often than following them.

Increasingly, the argument of whether or not an artist is original has been commandeered by those who can only see music artists as a series of easily identifiable props, and hear them as a collection of studio noises that have been "ripped off" from other music artists that came before—sometimes *months* before.

Madonna was always criticized for being unoriginal. She was compared to **Pat Benatar** and **Chrissie Hynde**, then to **Debbie Harry** and **Marilyn Monroe**. She was rapped for referencing other artists in her **work** (**Tamara de Lempicka**, **Marlene Dietrich**, Horst P. Horst, the list is endless), with the underlying argument being that to be inspired, even directly, by *anything* that has come before is to be derivative. Entire websites have been created to track every time Madonna wears a frock similar to something one of the ABBA ladies wore.

"She is touched by everything and makes it hers. Not in the sense of copying, but in the sense of being a **fashion** chameleon. She chooses each heroine she wants to be," **Jean Paul Gaultier** told *Dazed & Confused* in 2008.

While detecting influences used to be exciting—you'll never see the music video for **"The Power of Good-Bye"** the same way again after comparing it to Joan Crawford's *Humoresque* (1946)—it has become petty to the point of tedium. The idea that anti-fans spend as much time on the objects of their derision as fans spend on their objects of admiration should be depressing.

The originality debate is empty because no pop artist is wholly original; it's an impossibility considering how diverse the definition of "pop" (or even "rock") music *seems*

Oriole Way:
Madonna doesn't
live here anymore.

to be, but is not. Countless artists are all creating music meant to hit a fairly small creative target, and have been doing so throughout the so-called rock era. There is overlap everywhere. It becomes very *A Beautiful Mind* (2001) once you allow yourself to see the connections. There should be joy in noticing them, not resentment.

Of course, pop's inherent unoriginality has to apply to Madonna, too, who is often held up by **haters** of **Lady Gaga** as not only an important influence who preceded Gaga (true), but as the person who invented bustiers, leotards, purple wigs and all manner of other fairly common stage props (false). Yes, Lady Gaga has taken things from Madonna's playbook, but neither Madonna nor any other pre-Gaga artist has clean hands. Actual rip-offs are going to be in the **eye** and ear of the beholder, but for the sake of one's sanity, liberal standards should be imposed.

Madonna freely admitted to *Aperture* (1999), "Every video I've ever done has been inspired by some painting or some work of **art**."

Ultimately, Madonna, while not wholly original, is nonetheless a *true original*. There is no other artist like her, even if her inspirational antecedents are clear.

"I changed my style a million times before I found myself, because like any other kind of artist, first you're inspired by things you listen to and you copy them." -MADONNA (1995)

ORIOLE WAY: Madonna lived for several years at 9045 Oriole Way in the Hollywood Hills. She bought it in 1989 for $2.9 milion from Macy's and Bloomingdale's bigshot Allen Questrom. The property, a gated three-bedroom built in 1968, had 13 rooms, 4,551 square feet and was described as very private. She took a loss, selling it in 1994 to **art** collector Daniel Melnick for $2 million, who later sold it for $3.2 million. After Madonna owned it, the place was owned by Leonardo DiCaprio, who rented it to, among others, his best bud Tobey Maguire.

While still living there, in December 1990, Madonna lost a lawsuit brought against her by her neighbor Donald Robinson. Though the judge scoffed at Robinson's claim of $1 million in damages resulting from Madonna's too-high **privacy** hedge, the judge (with the hard-to-believe name of Judge Sally **Disco**) did require Madonna to trim her bush and pay Robinson's attorney fees.

OSBOURNE, KELLY: b. October 27, 1984. Daughter of **Sharon Osbourne** and **Ozzy Osbourne**, this sassy Brit achieved notoriety as one of the stars of her family's pioneering (for better or worse) reality **TV** series *The Osbournes* (2002–2005). Growing up before the cameras from frumpy Goth teen to fashionista, she took third place on TV's *Dancing with the Stars* in 2009 and had a long run (2010–2015) on E!'s *Fashion Police*, on which she critiqued celebrities' outfits.

In 2002, Osbourne released her debut album, *Shut Up*. A self-professed Madonna **fan**, her very first single was a cover of Madonna's **"Papa Don't Preach,"** which was a #3 hit in the UK and which hit #74 on the *Billboard* Hot 100.

Osbourne's dad once sang on a song called "Shake Your Head (Let's Go to Bed)" that also featured Madonna's vocals, though the two were never in the studio together and that version remains **unreleased**.

Osbourne was selected by Madonna and **Lola** to be the face of their **Material Girl** clothing line in 2011, at which time Osbourne said, "I take so much of my style from Madonna in the '80s and I really admire how Lola dresses and that she stays true to herself." During her promotional activities, she went head to head with a skeptical **Piers Morgan**, sneering to him, "You just don't like her because you didn't get what you wanted." Morgan, who has given many different reasons for why he loathes Madonna tried to say Madonna was exploiting Lola with the fashion line; Osbourne, sitting next to the **mother** who put her on reality TV as a kid, shot him down.

She helped select her Material Girl replacement when her tenure was over: Georgia May Jagger.

In 2015, Osbourne quit her **job** at *Fashion Police* after her costar, Giuliana Rancic, made what was perceived as a racially insensitive remark when critiquing the dreads worn by TV personality Zendaya to the **Oscars**. Zendaya was a fellow Material Girl spokesmodel.

> "I wanted to be Madonna when I was little, have curly hairy and wear tons of bracelets and just, I loved her whole look and, I don't know, she was such an icon—and still is to me—growing up."—KELLY OSBOURNE (2011)

OSBOURNE, OZZY: *b. December 3, 1948.* SEE: **unreleased**.

OSBOURNE, SHARON: *b. October 9, 1952.* Manager and wife of **Ozzy Osbourne** who is responsible for maintaining his brand, reinvigorating it by masterminding the reality show *The Osbournes* (2002–2005). Osbourne has lived much of her life for the past 15 years in front of the cameras, whether as a talking head on entertainment-news shows, as the subject of celebrity interviews herself or as one of the panelists on the daytime chat show *The Talk* (2010–). Osbourne's health (she is a **cancer** survivor), appearance (she had lap band surgery, she speaks often about her **plastic surgery**) and family ups and downs (addictions, illnesses) have kept her interesting to viewers, as has her venomous wit.

Osbourne is *not* as big a **fan** of Madonna as is her daughter, **Kelly Osbourne**. In 2004, after Madonna made a smashing appearance in **Versace** on the **Grammys**, Osbourne cattily said, "I went into shock at Madonna's new head. See, she's got that Botox in her forehead. Oh, Madonna, I know what you've been doing. There's not one line on that bloody head." Unusually, Madonna denied she'd had Botox, via **Liz Rosenberg**.

The following year, Osbourne told *British GQ* of Madonna, "I would like to punch her. She is so full of shit. She's into **Kabbalah** one minute, she's a **Catholic** the next. She'll be a Hindu soon, no doubt." Soon after, she was quoted saying, "It's like dressing up with her. One day you're in fucking **gun** gear, then you're in horsing gear, then you dress like a **fucking** dyke, then you dress like a hooker, then you're in a flowery dress reading kids' poetry looking like a fucking librarian—then you're **back** looking like an old hooker again. You can't one day be in *Horse and Hound* **magazine** and the next in *Dyke Weekly* ... Writing those painful, silly **books** and reading them to your kids! If my mum came to me with a book like that I'd say, 'Fucking stick it up your arse.' Fucking *English Roses*. Bollocks."

Speaking with **Howard Stern**, Osbourne also had something to say about Madonna's adoption of **David Banda** in 2006: "Please give me a break. It's like getting a **Louis Vuitton** handbag. It is a crock of shit. If she wants to help the kid, she should have got the **father** a little trade going, a fruit stand or something like that, and built him a mud hut ... She bought a baby, for **God**'s sake."

In 2012, while interviewing celebrities at the **Golden Globes**, Osbourne had switched gears, saying in Madonna's presence, "I'm actually a bit speechless right now. Mrs. O is not often speechless, but I am speechless. Look at who I am stood with. I'm, like, all aquiver." Perhaps Madonna's hiring of Kelly as a **Material Girl** spokesperson in the interim helped change her mind?

By 2013, Osbourne was Team Madonna by default because **Lady Gaga** and Kelly were in a war of words over bullying and body image. When Gaga posted a public letter slamming Kelly and **Joan Rivers** for "pointing in the camera, laughing and making jokes about artists and celebrities as if we are zoo animals," Mama Osbourne fired back a missive to Gaga in which she noted that a large portion of Little Monsters had been "vile" not only to Kelly, but to **Adele**, **Rihanna** and ... Madonna.

Thank you, dear lady, for your concern, but you've said worse.

OSCARS: *Dates presented: May 16, 1929-.* Presented since 1929, the annual American **awards** ceremony honoring excellence in the film industry as decided by members of the Academy of Motion Picture Arts and Sciences.

Madonna's first run-in with the show was when she was asked to present the Oscar for Best Visual Effects in 1988, with clips from her **"Material Girl"** video to be used in the background. The reply producer Samuel Goldwyn Jr. got **back** was, "Madonna is not a singer, but she's an actress and will only give a Best **Acting** award." The quote is probably poorly remembered, but you get the idea. [The nominees were *Innerspace* (1987), which won, and *Predator* (1987).]

Madonna attended the Oscars in the flesh on March 25, 1991, sitting front and center at the Shrine Auditorium (665 W. Jefferson Blvd., LA, CA) with her surprise escort, **Michael Jackson.** The pair was dressed in white, Madonna in an extremely low-cut Bob Mackie gown and 20 million dollars' worth of borrowed Harry Winston diamonds. She was there to see how her hit, **Dick Tracy**, fared and to perform **Stephen Sondheim**'s nominated song, **"Sooner or Later (I Always Get My Man)."**

Introduced as "the **NC-17** portion of our really big show" by host Billy Crystal, Madonna emerged from a lift in the stage floor, slinkily removed a white glove and launched into the single best live vocal performance she's ever given, belting the tune in tandem with a 20-piece orchestra. Though Madonna's hand was visibly shaking and one of her earrings plopped down into her **hair**, the unexpected oomph to her **voice** combined with the visual impact of her white outfit against the pink setting made it one of the most exciting and well-received performances in the history of the show.

Midway through, she'd stopped the song to purr, "A girl can get awfully *awful* in this spotlight," and later directly referenced **Marilyn Monroe** by cooing, "Talk to me General Schwarzkopf, tell me all about it!," a take on Monroe's, "Talk to me Harry Winston, tell me all about it!" line from *Gentlemen Prefer **Blondes*** (1953). At song's end, she vamped offstage, shaking her ass at the audience, Gypsy Rose Lee–style. The votes had already been cast anyway; "Sooner or Later (I Always Get My Man)" won Best Original Song.

Madonna **nerves** could have been due to her appearance before the film establishment, of which she very much wanted to be a part, but she was also reacting to a warning at the start of her performance that her microphone was malfunctioning, and to **memories** of her breasts popping out at rehearsal. She was also singing live to an audience of more than a billion people.

Bruce Vilanch, one of the show's longtime writers, says Madonna's nerves were at least in part due to the fact that **Kevin Costner** was in the front row, and that she'd insulted him in **Truth or Dare**. The movie wasn't even out yet, so that seems unlikely. But when Madonna finished, Vilanch says she, "came off, threw herself into my arms, said, 'Thank **God** that's over,' and then walked away. I think she meant the song, but she could have meant being in my arms. I don't know. She picked the one person who didn't know what to do with Madonna when he had her in his arms."

Jeremy Irons apparently liked Madonna's performance—he kissed her when he won for Best Actor in *Reversal of Fortune* (1990). That's probably because at the time he was set (or so he thought) to play opposite Madonna in **Evita**.

Madonna did go on to play *Evita*, but it was five years later, and **Jonathan Pryce** had taken over for Irons. Her performance was outstanding, leading many to expect her to receive an Oscar nomination for Best Actress in a Leading Role. When she failed to get nominated, it was a bit of a surprise when it was announced that Madonna would still show up to the Shrine and sing the film's nominated song, **"You Must Love Me."** Crystal, again hosting, gave Madonna a respectful (if ultimately humorous) intro:

"Ladies and gentlemen, before I introduce Madonna, I wanna say one thing ... Even though she was not nominated and there was a lot of speculation that she was going to be, she accepted the invitation—actually, she called the show to say she wanted to sing and, uh, come here tonight, and I thought that was showing a great deal of class. So here she is ... to sing a song 'Don't Cry for Me Because I'll Get Back at You If It Takes Me the Rest of My Life' ... just joshin' ... please welcome, the one and only, Madonna."

The words had been a thinly veiled stab at **Barbra Streisand**, whose *The Mirror Has Two Faces* (1996) had been largely passed over, and who had decided not to sing the nominated song "I Finally Found Someone"; the telecast cut to a shot of Streisand pretending not to care in the audience before Madonna appeared on stage in a stunning beige and black brocade gown, her red **hair** pulled back from her face.

Madonna's tremulous, vulnerable take on the song led to many a **gay** Oscar party debate over whether she sounded pretty, or pretty weak.

The song won Oscars for **Andrew Lloyd Webber** and **Tim Rice**, who were presented their awards by Goldie Hawn, **Diane Keaton** and **Bette Midler** (she seemed to zing Madonna by noting all the songs had been "rendered in full-throated, ferociously committed performances"). Webber said, "We must say thanks to Madonna for coming tonight and singing the song so beautifully, and to Alan Parker for this wonderful movie."

After the show, Madonna changed into a deep blue suit with a loud floral pattern, gobs of makeup and a statement necklace whose statement seemed to be, "I can't believe this tiny thing can support me!" She attended the **Vanity Fair** party, where she was seen chatting with **Mick Jagger** and Tony Curtis, among others.

A year later, Madonna was on hand to present the award for Best Achievement in Music—Original Song to the composers of "My Heart Will Go On," James Horner and Will Jennings. Madonna's short laugh and exclamation, "What a shocker!" when announcing the winners has been misinterpreted as jealousy of Céline Dion (who wasn't nominated); it was more likely sarcasm over the idea that anything could beat that *Titanic* (1997) song.

—JANCEE DUNN

MATTHEW RETTENMUND

Madonna has never again attended the actual Oscars ceremony, but she has often been invoked in montages, popped up in a short film by host **David Letterman** and wound up hosting her own annual A-list after-party.

The short—aired on the March 27, 1995, show—was a gag in which Letterman showed fake audition tapes by stars who had tried out for his ignominious role in *Cabin Boy* (1994), each holding a stuffed monkey and reading Letterman's line from that film, "Would you like to buy a monkey?" The stars in the clip were Jack Lemmon, Martin Short, Steve Martin, Albert Brooks, Alec Baldwin, **Tom Hanks** and **Rosie O'Donnell** (Madonna's *A League of Their Own* costars), Madonna, Danny DeVito, Paul Newman, Michael Keaton, John Turturro (Madonna's *Desperately Seeking Susan* costar), Anthony Hopkins, Barry White and Michael Buffer. Buxom Madonna's version involved tears.

After that show, Madonna partied at Chasen's (formerly 9039 Beverly Blvd., W. Hollywood, CA) with Jodie Foster and Ellen Barkin, drank tequila, wore marabou, and also **worked** the room at the Beverly Wilshire, glad-handing John Travolta and holding Quentin Tarantino's Oscar.

After the March 23, 1998, show, Madonna posed with **Cher**, **k.d. lang** and **Joni Mitchell** at the *Vanity Fair* Oscars party in a Fred Leighton Gothic necklace.

She rubbed shoulders with Bob Dylan and **Chris Rock** at Sony's pre-Oscar party on March 21, 1999, then again with her brother **Christopher Ciccone** at *Vanity Fair*'s bash, where she was honored to meet bandleader Artie Shaw, then 88.

Madonna came bearing (and baring) cleavage in lavender **Versace** at the *Vanity Fair* party after the March 5, 2006, show. She was in good spirits, telling a reporter, "I'm happy for **George Clooney** and **Philip Seymour Hoffman**."

Guy Oseary

To celebrate the Oscars held February 25, 2007, Madonna wore a drop-dead black **Dolce & Gabbana** gown to the *Vanity Fair* Oscar party, posing like the old-time Hollywood star she never really got to be.

She had on a glittering black Christian Dior dress which went sheer on the bottom to flaunt her legs when she attended *Vanity Fair*'s post-party on February 22, 2009.

A straight-haired Madonna (in a barely-there Francesco Scognamiglio feathered dress paired with lace fishnets) and her daughter **Lola** (in an AllSaints Aztec mini) attended the *Vanity Fair* Oscar party ("I'm my mom's date!" Lola said) on March 7, 2010, igniting debates about whether she should start dressing her age.

Beginning with the 2008 ceremony, Madonna and **Demi Moore** hosted a post-Oscars party at **Guy Oseary**'s house, their first stab at what has become a tradition (minus Moore). **Sean Penn** was there, and **Lindsay Lohan** attended with her then-girlfriend Samantha Ronson. (Lohan was turned away in 2011.)

In the ensuing years, Madonna has always thrown the bash, which has become more and more of a must-attend. Famous faces who have sought refuge from the media in Madonna's presence have included Javier Bardem and Penélope Cruz, Orlando Bloom, Clooney, **Tom Cruise**, **Miley Cyrus**, Daniel Day Lewis, **Ellen DeGeneres** and Portia de Rossi, Cameron Diaz, Leonardo DiCaprio, Jamie Foxx, Ryan Gosling, Anne Hathaway, Salma Hayek, Katie Holmes, **Elton John** and David Furnish, Angelina Jolie and **Brad Pitt**, Mila Kunis and Ashton Kutcher, Jennifer Lawrence (who threw up on the porch in 2014), Jared Leto, Matthew McConaughey, Eva Mendes, Midler, Jack Nicholson, Lupita Nyong'o, **P!nk**, Jeremy Piven, Julia Roberts, Wesley Snipes, Meryl Streep, Channing Tatum, Travolta, Diane von Furstenberg and Forest Whitaker.

In 2015, Madonna had to skip her own Oscar party because she was rehearsing for the **Brit Awards** ... but the party went on without her, including revelers like **Beyoncé**, Sean Combs, Jimmy Iovine, Jagger, Adam Levine and Brett Ratner.

OSEARY, GUY: *b. October 3, 1972.* Madonna's wunderkind **business** partner started **working** for her **Maverick** Records when he was 19 years old. He was introduced to Madonna by **Freddy DeMann**, whose daughter Oseary was dating. Oseary quickly earned himself a reputation as an outstanding and precocious A&R guy. Dude brought Madonna **Alanis Morissette**, so it's not hard to see how he worked his way up through the ranks to become her manager in 2005.

Before then, Oseary had already had his hand in most of Madonna's businesses, including Maverick Pictures, extending his reach into the realm of film ... ever heard of the *Twilight* (2008–2012) movies?

Guy Oseary (on the right) has been with Madonna for over 20 years.

STEVEN CHRISTEN

Oseary is an accomplished multi-tasker; along with managing Madonna, he manages U2 and Alicia Keys and he is a partner in Untitled Entertainment, which offers management services (along with partners Jason Weinberg and Stephanie Simon) to actors Penélope Cruz, Jeremy Renner, **Alex Rodriguez** (maybe those rumors served a dual purpose?), Hilary Swank, Sofia Vergara, Naomi Watts and more.

Oseary is a business partner of Ashton Kutcher's; they run A-Grade Investments, which sinks **money** into startups like SoundCloud, Spotify and Uber.

The point is, Oseary is really smart and really **rich**. He's also helped enrich Madonna, by steering her through all of her most successful concert tours and locking her into business deals galore (**Truth or Dare by Madonna**, **Material Girl**, **Hard Candy Fitness**), some of which her **fans** seem to like and some of which her fans seem to think are diverting Madonna's attention from her creative side.

Oseary is a constant figure at Madonna events and concerts. Before shows, he is accessible in the pit, often photographing super fans and posing for photos himself. He has published two **books** of his own live shots of Madonna, *Madonna: Confessions* and *Madonna: Sticky & Sweet*. [SEE: **bibliography** (**about Madonna**).]

In his time with Madonna, Oseary has had to deal with many major issues, such as the unprecedented **leak** of almost all of her *Rebel Heart* demos. What's interesting about Oseary's approach is that he is often interacting with the public on social media, making him a sort of celebrity manager. He sometimes takes the bait when Madonna's being treated unfairly—he has gone after **Piers Morgan**, **Lady Gaga** fans and false rumors.

As an insight into Oseary's style, consider the fact that when Madonna's *Rebel Heart Tour* dates were announced, he put a sock on his arm and did an impromptu puppet show for Madonna to post on **Instagram** in which she demands of his hand, "Who are you?" only to be told, "**Bitch**, I'm a sock," a play on her song "**Bitch I'm Madonna**." Hard to imagine Freddy DeMann going along, or getting away, with something like this.

OUR LADY OF THE VISITATION CHURCH: *1106 State Street, Bay City, MI.* The site of Madonna's parents' July 2, 1955, **wedding**.

"OVER AND OVER": Criminally underused track from *Like a Virgin* that was written by Madonna and **Stephen Bray** and produced by **Nile Rodgers**. Its BPM frenzy, orgasmic interlude and inspirational quality rendered it absolutely single-worthy (it was released in Italy), but it remained album-bound.

Madonna has only performed "Over and Over" on her *Virgin Tour.* It was the only *Like a Virgin* track featured on *You Can Dance.*

RICHARD CORMAN

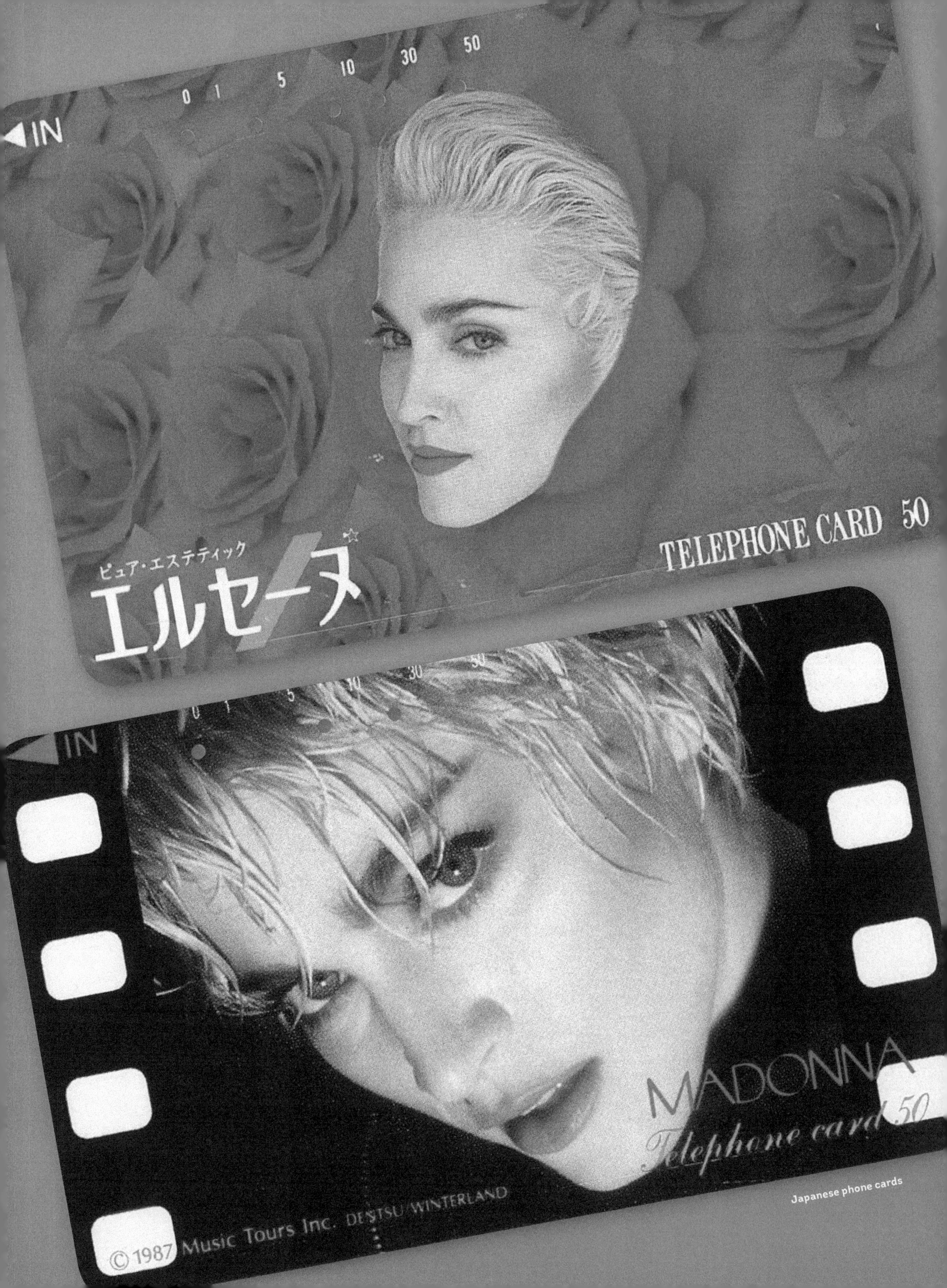
0 1 5 10 30 50
◀IN
TELEPHONE CARD 50
ピュア・エステティック
エルセーヌ
0 1 5 10 30 50
◀IN
MADONNA
Telephone card 50
©1987 Music Tours Inc. DENTSU/WINTERLAND
Japanese phone cards

PACENTRO: Italian village 60 miles NE of Rome on the Aterno Pescara River, where Madonna's paternal **grandparents** were born and raised, and where Madonna met with relatives who were complete strangers to her while she was in the vicinity for her ***Who's That Girl World Tour***.

A tabloid report quotes Madonna's relatives as saying, "That girl sings, **dances** and shows her thighs ... No Madonna, she! The devil is more like it!" Madonna's own great-aunt was said to seethe, "The girl is a singer, just a singer. In my times we didn't behave like that." However, the original video interview reveals Madonna's great-aunt, her **grandmother** Michelina's sister, saying in Italian, "I don't know Madonna in person, but I've seen her on **TV**. She sings, dances, but she moves too much. I'm pleased to have such a famous grandniece. She's so intelligent ... I'll watch the show on TV. I'm happy and wish her all the best." To Madonna she said, "I **love** you and like you—if you like, come visit me. I'll wait for you with all my heart."

Madonna donated $500,000 to the Red Cross when a 2009 earthquake devastated nearby L'Aquila.

PACIELLO, CHRIS: *b. September 7, 1971.* Nightclub impresario and former mob associate. In 1995, Paciello opened Club Liquid (formerly 1439 Washington Ave., Miami Beach, FL) with Madonna's close friend **Ingrid Casares** as his **business** partner. Madonna allegedly dated Paciello beginning around this time through his arrest for murder in 1999. He is also said to have dated Sofia Vergara and **Jennifer Lopez**.

Paciello got out of prison after serving six years (his status as an **FBI** informant earned him leniency) and continues to be in the business of running posh eateries and clubs.

PADELL, BERT: *b. 1931.* Highly esteemed financial advisor who handled Madonna's **business** affairs from 1983–98.

PAGLIA, CAMILLE: *b. April 2, 1947.* The Madonna of Academia is the author of such pop-culturally provocative **books** *Sexual Personae: Art and Decadence from Nefertiti to Emily Dickinson* (1990), *Sex, Art and American Culture: Essays* (1992) and *Vamps and Tramps: New* Essays (1994) and has been a Professor of Humanities at the University of the Arts in Philadelphia for over 30 years.

An intellectual whose writings are among the most consistently radical in her field, Paglia believes **feminism** has come to consist of Stepford Wives, that the animal sexuality of men is to be admired (she's written of "the wild, infectious delirium of gang **rape**") and that date rape is a joke ("We cannot legislate what happens on a date. **Sex** is a dangerous sport").

Paglia led the faction of academics who felt Madonna and her phenomenon were worthy of rigorous **analysis**. Paglia's December 14, 1990, essay in *The **New** York Times*, entitled "Madonna—Finally, a Real **Feminist**," established her bona fides as a student of Madonna. The piece was written in response to Madonna's appearance on ***Nightline,*** on which she defended her **"Justify My Love"** video. Paglia wrote, "The video is **pornographic**. It's decadent. And it's fabulous."

Paglia, who has made a career out of metaphorically leaving flaming sacks of shit on the porches of feminists, proclaimed: "Madonna is the true feminist. She exposes the puritanism and suffocating ideology of American feminism, which is stuck in an adolescent whining mode. Madonna has taught young women to be fully female and sexual while still exercising total **control** over their lives. She shows girls how to be attractive, sensual, energetic, ambitious, aggressive and funny—all at the same time."

Though she viewed Madonna as a polymorphously perverse goddess (and was among the few to write that Madonna never did anything *only* for publicity), her estimation of Madonna's wit and vision faded fast—Paglia trashed *Sex* in *Us* **magazine** in 1992 and has ever since written increasingly personal and damning observations about the woman with whom she formerly seemed to be infatuated.

Paglia has gone on to become Madonna's most vocal, least acknowledged concern troll, praising her faintly while criticizing her every move. Reacting to Madonna's **Mert and Marcus** images in ***Interview*** (December 2014/ January 2015), Paglia wrote, "I'm afraid I must agree with the online commentator at ***Billboard*** magazine who tartly declared: 'Those who find these ridiculous photos 'hot' are necrophiliac.' The muddy, slack-jawed cover image makes Madonna look as paralytically congealed and mummified as a Celtic bog body. What is shocking about these ugly photographs is not their tiny **nudity** but their **mediocrity** and monotony. Why is Madonna, a titanic pioneer of popular culture, tediously repeating formulas that she debuted a quarter-century ago and that have been exhausted by a host of imitators worldwide? She seems trapped by a past self and incapable of new ideas."

What's probably most infuriating to Paglia is that **back** in the '90s, Madonna refused to meet with her, and apparently did not take her seriously. Madonna joked that Paglia, an out lesbian, probably just wanted to sleep with her. Madonna seems to have wisely realized that Paglia overbilled her from the beginning: Paglia may have been exactly correct in her analysis of the effect of the Madonna Zeitgeist, but Madonna knew or at least sensed that she, as a *person*, could never live up to Paglia's imagination.

As far as the sharp turn against Madonna taken by Paglia and other female cultural critics, Aida Edemariam wrote in *The Guardian* in 2008, "Perhaps the answer lies in the hopes they had for her (and themselves) 20 years ago. In 1990, Paglia ... celebrated the snook Madonna was cocking at 'the puritanism and suffocating ideology of American feminism': Madonna, proclaimed Paglia, 'is the [real] future of feminism.' And now they feel betrayed by what that future held: **Catholicism** replaced by **Kabbalah**; one-night-stand babies by marriage and stately homes;

a vigorously pursued desire not to look old (by clinging to the in-your-face sexuality she pioneered)."

Paglia, like many other Madonna critics, seems to change her reasons for being discontented depending on the setting. She told **Joy Behar** in 2012 that Madonna's drive to "impose ideology in an artistic setting" via *The MDNA Tour* was "gimmicky" (ignoring that a huge percentage of all **art** carries with it references, implicit or explicit, to various ideologies). Most hilariously, she said Madonna should age gracefully, like **Marlene Dietrich** did. Dietrich was a legend, but one thing she did *not* do was age gracefully in the provincial way that Paglia surprisingly suggests. Dietrich would not have been Dietrich without her sheep injections, **nude** gowns reinforced with rubber contouring worthy of a Top 3 showing on *RuPaul's Drag Race* (2009–), wigs and lust for attention. Madonna would not be Madonna without her exposed nipples and ditties about **pussy** juice.

The fact is that Madonna could never have lived up to Paglia's ideals, as they're almost singular, nor can she live up to the diverse ideals of her many **fans**. Considering how Paglia survives in the media, it's also tempting to consider the idea that no matter what Madonna did, the amount of refracted attention Paglia would have received had she remained a **cheerleader** would not have been enough for her liking.

But Madonna herself probably figured out the most obvious reason why Paglia moved on from stanning for her. "I think I never paid her any mind, so she decided we didn't have anything in common after all," she said in 1997.

"Madonna and I are workaholics, okay? We are drug-free, okay? We are strong women who have projected our hallucinatory, pornographic visions to the world, okay? ... It's like she needs me to open up her life, I'm telling you. She needs help. Because all she ever sees are people in the performing arts. You know, there's no substance."—CAMILLE PAGLIA (1992)

"I've heard her say things under the guise of being adoring that make it very clear that she doesn't get me at all. Sometimes I think she's full of shit."—MADONNA ON CAMILLE PAGLIA (1992)

PALIN, SARAH: *b. February 11, 1964.* Former Governor of Alaska who was plucked from obscurity and thrust onto the national stage as the Hail Mary pick of Sen. John McCain (R-Arizona) to be his vice presidential running mate in 2008. Immediately upon her selection, Palin distinguished herself as a radical right-winger with a host of personal failings, not least of which were her comical unpreparedness for such a high office and knack for murdering the English language.

Madonna gunned for Palin while on her *Sticky & Sweet Tour.* On her October 2008 tour stops in **New York**, she noted of Palin that she'd like to "kick her ass" and also said to the crowd: "Thank you for coming to my party. You know who's not invited to my party? Sarah **Fucking** Palin! ... Sarah Palin has to go! Get this **bitch** out of here!" At the premiere of *Filth and Wisdom*, Madonna explained, "That's a metaphor. She's in the Republican Party, I'm in the Democratic Party."

Palin was, however, represented in Madonna's "**Nobody Knows Me**" video interlude on *The MDNA Tour*— parts of her face were superimposed over Madonna's after the line about how hard it is to find someone to admire.

PALTROW, GWYNETH: *b. September 27, 1972.* American leading lady who won the **Oscar** for her role in *Shakespeare in Love* (1998). Since then, her film career has been spotty at best, but her high-profile relationships with **Brad Pitt** and Ben Affleck, and her marriage to (and "conscious uncoupling" from) Coldplay's Chris Martin and her lifestyle brand Goop have kept her in the news. People seem to love her or **hate** her, making her an ideal bestie for Madonna. Unfortunately, that status didn't last.

After the publication of paparazzi images showing Paltrow and Pitt totally naked, Madonna phoned Paltrow out of the blue to offer her support. A close friendship ensued, with Paltrow fixing Madonna up on a date (from hell) with Viggo Mortensen and Madonna making herself available to give the younger woman advice.

Some found the match odd, seeing Paltrow as too vanilla for Madonna. Michael Vartan, who had acted with Paltrow in *The Pallbearer* (1996) and with Madonna in *The Next Best Thing* (2000), questioned the pairing for a different reason, saying in 2002, "That *absolutely* perplexes me ... I can't think of two more diametrically opposite people. My experience **working** with Gwyneth was absolutely wonderful; she was incredibly charming and sweet. Madonna, on the other hand, was a different experience. And I'll definitely leave it at that."

Paltrow told *In Touch*, "We're friends because she's a fantastically interesting woman, very **powerful** within. We are on similar paths in our lives—what we eat, our **yoga** and stuff like that. Anything I've been through, she's been through 10 times worse, 10 times more and 10 times longer. She gives me great advice about taking care of myself."

Madonna explained her appreciation for Paltrow to *Jane* in 2000: "She is sophisticated for her age. Both of her parents are in the **business** and I think that has allowed her to see a side of things, so she's not taking it too seriously. Mostly she just wants to know where I get my handbags." She gave Paltrow a diamond-encrusted apple brooch (her daughter's name is, famously, Apple) for her 33rd **birthday** in 2005.

The women socialized together for years (including attending a 2002 **Versace** show in the front row together with a starstruck Chelsea Clinton). On the occasion of Madonna's 50th in 2008, Paltrow said, "Madonna is, y'know, she's a dear friend of mine for like 10 years now and, um, she's always very ... she's a very inspiring woman. She has a lot of wisdom, and, uh, she's very strong, and she's very good with, you know, boundaries and, y'know, things that I ... I feel like I learn a lot from her. She's wonderful."

In spite of their long-term fondness for one another, Madonna and Paltrow seemed to consciously uncouple in 2009. Rumor had it that Paltrow felt mistreated so decided to cut Madonna out of her life, like the brown spot on an apple. They have not been photographed together since 2010.

In 2013, when asked by the press if she'd brag about her abs to Madonna, Paltrow joked that her abs were better than Madonna's. "Why, why rub it in? Let's face it ... Polaroid my abs and text them to her."

PANZERA, ANTHONY: Established artist who hosted Madonna in his 29th St. studio in **NYC** in 1979, where he sketched her **nude**. They got along, so she posed for him for a year, earning $10/hour for her **work**.

On *Driven: Madonna*, Panzera observed of Madonna, "She had this extraordinary way of looking different when she moved, changed the direction of her glance." Panzera completed a nude painting of Madonna, of whom he said, "There was always something very special about her **beauty** ... it's mostly in the **eyes**, I think."

Panzera inadvertently played a major role in Madonna's career by sending her to the photographer **Lee Friedlander**, whose nudes of her wound up being published in *Playboy* in 1985.

"PAPA DON'T PREACH" (SONG): *Release date: June 11, 1986. Billboard Hot 100 peak: #1.* Some of the strongest vocals Madonna ever recorded appear on her first politically controversial song, the second single and second #1 hit from *True Blue*. Written by Brian Elliot (with additional lyrics by Madonna, possibly just the, "Don't you stop lovin' me, daddy ..." bit) and produced by Madonna and **Stephen Bray**, this classic '80s song is sung from the perspective of a **pregnant** teenager pleading with her **father** to listen and offer rational advice regarding a jam she's in: She's preggers. Well, she probably is. The song does assert that the singer is "keepin' my baby," but it could be argued that the phrase is ambiguous enough that it may refer to a dad-unfriendly boyfriend. The music video, however, left no doubt that the girl Madonna was playing was in the family way.

Instead of tapping their toes to it, Planned Parenthood, the National Organization for Women and other **abortion**-rights groups blasted the song for seeming to reject abortion as an acceptable alternative, or for glamorizing teen pregnancy; "Papa Don't Preach" does no such thing.

Because Madonna sings it as a teenaged girl, the defiance and the shocking ignorance regarding how well things will **work** out are realistic. With this song, Madonna is not saying she believes things will always work out for pregnant teens—the teenager of the song is arguing with her father that *her* boyfriend and *her* situation will be different ... even though the listener has every reason to doubt both of her predictions.

From a **feminist** angle, the song is all about a woman's right to choose; in this case, the young woman has chosen to give birth.

Interestingly, a year after being named one of the PMRC's Filthy 15 thanks to **"Dress You Up,"** Madonna was praised by that organization's ringleader (**Tipper Gore**) for "Papa Don't Preach": "To me, the song speaks to a serious subject with a sense of urgency and sensitivity in both the lyrics and Madonna's rendition. It also speaks to the fact that there's got to be more support and more communication in families about this problem, and anything that fosters that I applaud."

"Papa Don't Preach" is one of Madonna's most lampooned songs. In 1986, its lyrics popped up on **Weird Al Yankovic**'s "Polka Party!" Though Madonna was not officially involved, in 1986 songwriter Elliot and his Elliot/Jacobsen Music Publishing Co. attempted to get an injunction against **Mia Mind Music** on the video and proposed single for the "Papa Don't Preach" **parody** "Madonna Don't Preach," citing copyright infringement, but backed down when Mia Mind threatened to subpoena Madonna herself. Another answer song—"Papa Wants the Best for You" by **Danny Aiello**—also made the rounds, also sliding by legally due to its status as a parody. Aiello posted the video on **YouTube** in 2013 then exercised his right to abort it, yanking it from view soon after.

Madonna has performed the song live on her *Who's That Girl World Tour*, *Blond Ambition World Tour*, *Re-Invention World Tour* and *MDNA Tour*.

"'Papa Don't Preach' is Madonna's finest three minutes, not merely because it addresses teen pregnancy, but because it suggests that a portion of the blame rests on parents' reluctance to discuss, not lecture about, sex."
—JOYCE MILLMAN, BOSTON PHOENIX (1986)

"PAPA DON'T PREACH" (VIDEO): *Director: James Foley, 1986.* Shot on Staten Island in **New York**, this illustration of one of Madonna's signature songs features some of her best silent **acting** in a video (eat your heart out, Lillian Gish). Then in her late twenties, she passes herself off as a **pregnant** teen, emoting to great effect as she bites the bullet and tells her **father** of her surprise pregnancy by a boyfriend he had told her not to hang out with. (Father doesn't always know best, but he might have mentioned the option of a diaphragm in the absence of abstinence.)

"It was a seductive message, one that resonated with a burgeoning feminist—oh, yeah, and millions of other girls and women."
—JESSICA VALENTI, *MADONNA & ME: WOMEN WRITERS ON THE QUEEN OF POP* (2012)

Candids that capture Madonna during her top-secret "Papa Don't Preach" video shoot

There's a lot going on in the video. Madonna's character is a cheesily attired in an "ITALIANS DO IT BETTER" T-shirt, and wearing a short, cute, pixie haircut; the father of her child (**Alex McArthur**) is a grease monkey with "Vinnie Barbarino" baby blues; her neighborhood is sketched with images of regular folks (look for **Erika Belle** and bestie **Debi Mazar** as two of the pregnant girl's friends) going about their **business**. This all creates a believably **working**-class setting. Before she tells her father, there is a striking shot of Madonna walking with determination—in time with the song's bass line—up the staircase to catch a train. Her journey is echoed by the camera panning out over the neighborhood. Every beat in this video adds to the dramatic tension—how will it end?

Interspersed with these scenes and successfully removing Madonna the singer from the character she's playing, are breathtaking shots of Madonna in a form-fitting black leotard and bustier, sporting **orange**-red lipstick. She performs with gusto, dancing archly and confidently (one of the steps would later be repeated in her 2015 **"Living for Love"** video). These scenes represented Madonna's first major new look after slimming down and blonding up. Becoming a cliché throughout her career, the concept of Madonna's expected **reinvention** every so often all started with this video.

It would be hard to overstate the cultural and artistic impact of the video. Its director—unlike many video directors of the '80s, who look **back** on their work as if it were all a lark—totally gets it. **James Foley**, who would direct Madonna in *Who's That Girl*, said in 2015: "I've made a bunch of films and videos and it's one of the five things that I've done that I feel unequivocally good about. The strongest thing I came away with was the value of creative freedom, and she used that in a very smart way. She's extremely focused and mature and had a work ethic. It was a good lesson to me: what to do with absolute creative **power**. She's respectful of people's **jobs** and sees herself where she fits into it very well. I always thought, 'Whenever I get total final cut on a movie, I will remember how she handled that freedom.'"

On a humorous note, Madonna had a **nip slip** during the filming, one that made it into the final video, right around the 1:38 mark. Back then, freeze-framing something taped on **TV** didn't give too much clarity, but it's as plain as day now when paused online. **Sandra Bernhard**

joked in 1987, "I give Madonna a hard time because I have a problem with 'Papa Don't Preach'. Not only does she tell young girls to have children, she tells them they can keep their girlish figures afterward."

"Papa Don't Preach" is one of the only music videos for which Madonna won Best Female Video at the **MTV Video Music Awards**.

"PARADISE (NOT FOR ME)": Second-to-last track on *Music,* written and produced by Madonna and **Mirwais**. This atmospheric number is one of the album's least formal pop songs, meandering for over six and a half minutes. It was the first song Madonna ever finished after she started **working** with Mirwais (he'd already completed most of it for another singer), and it appeared on his *Disco Science* (1999) album first.

Madonna included "Paradise (Not for Me)" in a geisha-themed video interlude on her *Drowned World Tour* and sang it live on her *Confessions Tour* and *Tears of a Clown* Melbourne gig.

PARIS: Madonna first visited Paris in 1979 as part of a revue being assembled for **disco** singer **Patrick Hernandez**. She fell in **love** with the place. "... [T]hat was the place that I sort of sat and, like, cooked on the stove and got it in my head what I wanted to do and planned everything," she said of this trip. When she returned from Paris, Madonna immediately began writing songs and the rest is l'histoire.

Paris is one of Madonna's favorite cities now, in spite of the rude reception it gave her at **Olympia Hall** in 2012, and in spite of her fear that France is becoming anti-Semitic and anti-immigrant.

In 2015, Madonna said of the country that it was feeling like "Nazi Germany" due to the rise of extremism. "France was once a country that accepted people of color, and was a place artists escaped to, whether it was Josephine Baker or Charlie Parker." Her first Parisian *Rebel Heart Tour* tickets sold out in five minutes—maybe she should insult every city before she arrives?

PARKER, SARAH JESSICA: *b. March 25, 1965.* An '80s actor who became a '90s icon of **sex** and style thanks to her starring role on HBO's *Sex and the City* (1998–2004).

Parker has sometimes been physically compared to Madonna, particularly when Madonna wore her **hair** long and with loose waves in the late '90s. Parker dressed in Madonna's **"BOY TOY"** look for a flashback scene in her film *Sex and the City 2* (2010). She was 45 playing 25, so it was all very *Evita*.

When Madonna turned 50 in 2008, Parker was asked to talk about her. She said, "She's just been incredibly inspiring and inspired and, um, smart and interesting and, uh, you know, done what suits her and what she's interested in doing, and I think as a result we become interested. So yeah, she's a very impressive person."

PARKINSON: *Airdates: June 19, 1971-*. After 20 years of being pursued to appear, Madonna gave a 2006 tell-all interview to preeminent British talk show host Michael Parkinson, the so-called "Charlie Rose of **England**," during her **Confessions on a Dance Floor** era. In the piece, she told Parkinson she fell for **Guy Ritchie** because, "I saw him with his shirt off playing tennis, and that was a big plus. And then I sat next to him at lunch and he was incredibly witty, which was another big plus. And finally I saw his first movie and I thought, '**God**, he is incredibly **talented**'—so those three things put together were a huge aphrodisiac."

Hilariously, Parkinson later revealed that Madonna had a girl following her around with a stick that had a cotton ball on the end—it was her **job** to hunt for boogers in-between takes.

PARLO, DITA: *September 4, 1906–December 13, 1971*. German **movie** star noted for her appearances in the French classics *L'Atlante* (1934) and *La Grande Illusion* (1937). She might've crossed over to the US, but her proposed big break, in an adaptation of Joseph Conrad's *Heart of Darkness* by Orson Welles, never materialized. *Heart of Darkness* would have been Welles's debut feature as a writer and as a director, but its length and themes turned off executives, so he abandoned his first-ever screenplay in favor of his second … *Citizen Kane* (1941).

In 1992, Madonna adapted Parlo's name for an apparently otherwise unrelated persona, a jaded dominatrix who was willing to give you lessons on how to **fuck**. The make-believe Parlo's gravelly **voice** is on display in Madonna's **"Erotica"** song and her raunchy lust letters to someone called "Johnny" are on display (alongside Madonna's hiney) in **Sex**.

PARODY: You know you're important when someone sees fit to parody you. Therefore, Madonna must be the most important woman in the world.

In response to **Truth or Dare**, **Julie Brown** came up with a hilarious spoof, *Medusa: Dare to Be Truthful* (1992), and *Musician* **magazine** proposed a **stamp** featuring Madonna fellating a bottle of Evian.

Sex provided more fertile ground for send-ups. Madonna's **Desperately Seeking Susan** costar Ann Magnuson parodied it before it was even published, appearing on and in *Paper* magazine **nude**, straddling a (fake) corpse whose toe tag is clearly visible. *Entertainment Weekly* had Anna Nicole Smith pose with Larry "Bud" Melman next to a phony page from the **book**, describing how as a little girl in confession, Madonna hadn't done anything naughty, so she invited the padre to tell her what badness she *could* be committing.

Old-time comic Jackie Mason started (but never finished) a send-up that would have featured him and two of his friends parading shirtless, Matt Groening's Akbar & Jeff cartoon characters offered a book of "grim and joyless

pseudo-sadomasochism" and **Saturday Night Live** imagined Charlton Heston reading the audio version of *Sex* with Al (*Screw* magazine) Goldstein describing the pictures.

More viciously, Diesel Jeans and Workwear designed an ad that offered a **sex** book designed to "turn any idiot into a star or make fading stars shine new again." After her 1994 **David Letterman** appearance, a restaurant called Dixie Que (formerly 2001 W. Fullerton Ave., Chicago, IL) commissioned a life-sized Madonna made out of … *ham*.

Aussie comic Gina Riley made fun of "bogans" (unsophisticated types) in a wildly popular **"Vogue"** parody (1990), **French and Saunders** tackled Madonna many times, and the 2010s have been graced by the exhaustingly thorough parodies of Madonna's looks, sound bites and actions perpetrated by **tribute artists**/karmic stalkers Charlie Hides and Nadya Ginsburg. Then there is **VH1**'s *"Madonna" Talks* series, videos using actual footage of Madonna with cruelly funny/funnily cruel words put into her mouth by Ginsburg.

Most of Madonna's actions are so different from the typical star's that they become the subject of proportionately grandiose discussion, praise and criticism. As long as Madonna matters, parodies—which contain elements of all three—will proliferate.

PARR, ROB: Celebrity personal trainer and former baseball player who has been in the biz of bullying bodies into better shape since 1983. Parr has **worked** with **Demi Moore**, Stevie Nicks, **Sharon Stone**, Naomi Watts and, of course, the ultimate fit celeb, Madonna. Parr and Madonna began working together in February 1987, just in time to whip her into shape for her **Who's That Girl World Tour**.

Parr was the first to train Madonna for two or three hours a day, a habit she never broke even after she moved on to other trainers. Madonna and Parr did cardio, an hour of running (sprints and cycling). He was often seen riding or running with her.

In 1990, Parr noted, "Madonna has the genetic potential to achieve what she has and she truly enjoys challenging herself. Not everyone can look like her, but with the right, intelligent workout, everyone can look better." That same year, **Liz Rosenberg** said, "All people want to know is about that body. How did that body happen? On the seventh day, **God** created Rob Parr."

Madonna worked with Parr until 1991.

"PARTIDO FEMINISTA": Track from *Evita: The Complete Motion Picture Music Soundtrack* as heard in *Evita*. The song is a fragment, consisting of a (female) crowd's chant, some speech from Madonna as Evita and a bit of singing from both **Antonio Banderas** as Che and a (male) crowd. The song is about Evita's desire to be veep of Argentina. If any DJ can remix this into something danceable, more **power** to him or her.

—JINKX MONSOON

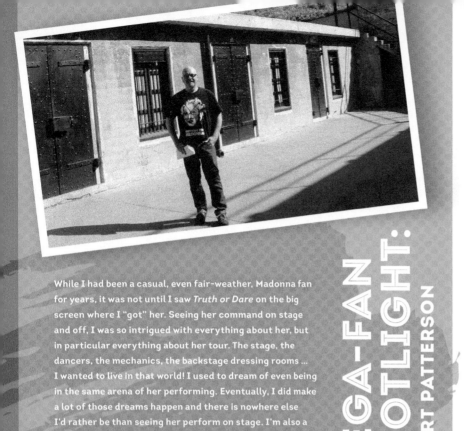

MEGA-FAN
SPOTLIGHT:
ROBERT PATTERSON

While I had been a casual, even fair-weather, Madonna fan for years, it was not until I saw *Truth or Dare* on the big screen where I "got" her. Seeing her command on stage and off, I was so intrigued with everything about her, but in particular everything about her tour. The stage, the dancers, the mechanics, the backstage dressing rooms ... I wanted to live in that world! I used to dream of even being in the same arena of her performing. Eventually, I did make a lot of those dreams happen and there is nowhere else I'd rather be than seeing her perform on stage. I'm also a fan of "set-jetting," and made it my mission to find locations from her videos and films. I'm most proud of finally finding and visiting the "Like a Prayer" exteriors, a true holy ground for any Madonna fan!

PARTITA DOPPIA: Italian **TV** show on which Madonna appeared in a segment that aired January 21, 1993. The show was **Fellini**-esque in its chaos. Madonna walked in wearing a beret and a smart brown suit, influenced by her starring role in ***Body of Evidence***. She was startled to find paparazzi *inside the studio*, exclaiming, "I've never seen paparazzi in a TV show." She smiled, sticking her tongue out at the shooters.

Madonna sat for an hour, giving the host a wide-ranging, feisty interview about the film, *Sex* and *Erotica* while the unruly crowd cheered as if they were at the circus.

Asked if she deliberately pursued scandal, Madonna said, "I don't think of it in terms of scandal, um ... I only think of, of expressing myself through music or singing or dancing or **acting** and it just so happens that my point of view often deals with eroticism, with **sexual** issues, which society is ashamed of. So they consider that everything I do is scandalous, but that's not what I'm trying to do."

She also spoke of her fears (being alone, being unloved, dying), which American actors she found sexy at the time (none!), her **fans** and her definition of vulgarity (ignorance, intolerance, sexism, homophobia, racism and violence).

Madonna, on a charm offensive, employed a little Italian, too.

> "I feel that I've achieved so much at this point in my life that if it were all to go away, I think I would be satisfied that I had the chance to do the things that I was able to do."
> —MADONNA, *PARTITA DOPPIA* (1993)

PATERSON, VINCENT: *b. May 4, 1959.* Famous choreographer and director who has been involved in most aspects of entertainment, especially concerts. He is known as the dude who **worked** with **Michael Jackson** (first) and Madonna at their arguable peaks, and also as the choreographer of (and an actor in) the **Björk** film *Dancer in the Dark* (2000).

Paterson choreographed Madonna's ***Blond Ambition World Tour***, the first show she did that gained her true artistic credibility, and that established her as a premier live entertainer, one with a penchant for not just singing and visuals, but for complicated, expressive, inventive **dance** gestures. He completely understood Madonna's desire to take risks in her **art**.

"Safe art is dull art; it's entertainment," he said at the time. "Madonna's an artist."

He also choreographed Madonna's **commercial** for **Pepsi** and her **"Express Yourself"** video and worked with her on her **MTV Video Music Awards** presentation of **"Vogue"** and her **Oscars** performance of **"Sooner or Later (I Always Get My Man),"** all platinum moments in Madonna's career. After a break, they were teamed up again when he choreographed **"Buenos Aires"** in *Evita*.

A Swedish doc on Paterson, *The Man Behind the Throne* (released March 9, 2013), effectively argues for Paterson's innovation, humility and his unusual lack of interest in taking credit and attaining personal notoriety. The film contains truly remarkable footage of Madonna rehearsing **"Keep It Together," "Like a Virgin"** and other numbers for her *Blond Ambition World Tour*.

Paterson's work with Madonna on that tour created the blueprint for the modern pop tour, and it is a scheme from which Madonna has never varied structurally. For this reason alone, he is one of her most important collaborators.

Pepsi ad director Joe Pytka broke it down like so in 2013: "There's a pre-Vincent Madonna and a post-Vincent Madonna, and the post-Vincent Madonna is a better performer than the pre-Vincent Madonna. She knows how to use her body much better ... Stick your butt out, honey."

> "She's the first person I've ever synthesized so completely with as an artist. She'll say something, and that will spark something in me. And I'll say something, and that will spark something in her."
> —VINCENT PATERSON, *SEVENTEEN* (1990)

PAULEY, JANE: *b. October 31, 1950.* Reserved NBC News correspondent who in 1987 interviewed Madonna on ***Today*** as part of the promo for the **"Who's That Girl"** song, video, album, tour and film. **Liz Rosenberg** later confessed that the interview came off like a meeting of ice maidens. Madonna never seemed more remote, looking untouchably beautiful, dead white and platinum-coiffed. She responded very guardedly to Pauley's generally skeptical, patronizing line of questioning. At the end of the three-part interview, Pauley's summary was the brittle one-liner, "A self-made woman."

Still, the interview is priceless for Madonna's foot-in-the-mouth branding of close-to-hometown **Bay City** as a "little smelly town in Northern **Michigan**." (The interview was telecast to coincide with her arrival in Michigan, where she apologized and reaffirmed her love for the place.)

The tensest moment came when Pauley implied that Madonna's success may have made her forget some of the "little people." Madonna asked Pauley if she herself still called and wrote and sent Christmas cards to everyone she'd met along the way. We never got her answer, but we also never got a Christmas card from Pauley that year.

The unedited, 40-plus-minute interview **leaked** on the Internet, and it's more frigid than "Marnie" from that Hitchcock movie (1964). Madonna, relieved when it was all over, announced, "The end!"

PAVAROTTI, LUCIANO: *October 12, 1935–September 6, 2007.* One of the most famous opera tenors of all time, known for the **beauty** of his **voice**, had a soft spot for pop stars—he sang with the likes of Bono and **Lionel Richie**, and he longed to sing with Madonna.

"Madonna has a very clear idea," he said in 2001. "She promised to come [to my hometown of Modena] if we sing together 'Caro Mio Bene' and I'm very interested. She told me in confidence. I have asked her, but she has been busy—first she makes the baby [**Rocco**] and then, I don't know."

Sadly, his **dream** went unfulfilled. It doesn't seem fair that Madonna made time for **Britney Spears** and **Avicii** and blew off Pavarotti, but then again, their vocal styles may not have gone together like pasta and sauce.

PENN, SEAN: *b. August 17, 1960.* She always gets her man, but she doesn't always *keep* him. Maybe she'll get him again someday?

Sean Penn is one of the finest actors of his generation. The son of actors Leo Penn and Eileen Ryan, he broke through quickly via roles in such '80s flicks as the intense *Taps* (1981) with **Tom Cruise**, the broadly funny *Fast Times at Ridgemont High* (1982) and dramas like *The Falcon and the Snowman* (1985). By the '90s, his choice of material had elevated to **Oscar** bait, like *Carlito's Way* (1993) and *Dead Man Walking* (1995). He has directed films and has twice won the Oscar for Best Actor in a Leading Role, for *Mystic River* (2003) and *Milk* (2008).

Madonna met Penn at his request on the set of her **"Material Girl"** video. It was the same day on which Madonna also first met **Elizabeth Taylor** and chicken entrepreneur Frank Perdue (just saying), but she focused on Penn. They visited **Marilyn Monroe**'s grave (fun couple!) and had a proper first **date** at **New York**'s **Private Eyes** club on February 13, 1985. He almost directed her **"Open Your Heart"** video, which ... would have been something. Penn also gets credit for introducing Madonna to two

people with whom she'd form important relationships: **Sandra Bernhard** and **Warren Beatty**.

After a whirlwind courtship, the couple became engaged in Nashville, Tennessee, while Penn was filming *At Close Range* (1986), the film for which Madonna wrote **"Live to Tell."** Madonna married Penn on her **birthday** in 1985, launching one of the stormiest pairings in Hollywood history. She enjoyed the spectacle of performance, he the quietude of being the lone wolf. Madonna was a liberal buttonpusher and early proponent of **gay** rights and **AIDS** awareness, Penn was—at least in his immature younger days—a homophobe. It was a pairing of a lover and a fighter. As the lover herself explained, "Opposites attract." She also referred to him as her hero and her best friend, and dedicated her *True Blue* album to him, dubbing him "the coolest guy in the universe."

They were so in sync that they made a movie together, the unmitigated disaster that became *Shanghai Surprise*. The exhausting shoot was a strain on their relationship, and the reviews—which threatened to sink their careers—were no picnic, either.

Outside of *Shanghai Surprise* photography, they only did one studio shoot together (for **Herb Ritts**, which appeared in *Interview* in December 1985), but were an irresistible mark for paparazzi, some of whom Penn brawled with. He slugged and spat on Anthony Savignano, and was sentenced to 60 days in jail in 1987 for beating up Jeffrie Klein, a Polaroid-wielding extra on his film *Colors* (1988). The latter incident was complicated by his arrest for charges of reckless driving under the influence in his '83 Chevy Impala. Penn served five days, filmed scenes of the film *Judgment in Berlin* (1988) in West Germany—a film directed by his **father**—then returned to serve 28 more days, getting the rest off for good behavior.

More disturbing to Madonna had been Penn's attack on her friend David Wolinski at Helena's in 1986, when Wolinski kissed Madonna hello. Penn's outburst cost him a $1,000 fine and probation, which he'd violated when he brawled with Klein.

By late 1987, the marriage was coming undone. For one thing, during a separation, Madonna had fooled around with **John F. Kennedy Jr.**, something Penn knew.

Penn showed up to spend Thanksgiving with Madonna after being absent for days, only to find she was spending it with her sister **Melanie Ciccone** in Brooklyn. Madonna filed for **divorce**. They made up, but she refiled at the tail end of 1988. The marriage had lasted about three and a half years.

"Most passionate people are headstrong," Madonna said in 1989 by way of offering a postmortem on their marriage. "We were two fires rubbing up against each other. It's exciting and difficult." Many years later, Penn reflected on his marriage, "I was not sober during most of that."

One of the last photos of Mr. and Mrs. Sean Penn. The two became close again more than 20 years later.

"So, I want to say, Sean, that I love you, from the moment that I laid eyes on you ... and I still love you, just the same."—MADONNA (2016)

Fueling predictions of a reunion someday was Madonna's frank admission of having feelings for Penn in a scene from *Truth or Dare*. When asked who the **love** of her life had been, she sighs wistfully and whispers, "Sean ... *Sean*." In a way, Madonna was kind of the first Jennifer Aniston. As she told *The Face* in 1994, "When Sean and I got divorced, I was forever reading stuff about how he seemed so much more happy. You know, how he'd finally found a virtuous woman."

After Madonna, Penn set up house with that virtuous woman, the actor **Robin Wright,** with whom he had two children ("**Thief of Hearts**" may be directed at her) and to whom he was married for more than a decade. He then dated **Naomi Campbell** and more recently got very serious with Charlize Theron.

At the **VH1 Fashion Awards** in 1995, Madonna approached the stage to accept an **award**, only to have the network spring Penn on her. A stunned Madonna kissed and hugged Penn, but scolded VH1, "That was really dirty." The following year, on January 10, 1996, it was reported that Madonna spent over 21 hours in a hotel room at the Carlyle (35 E. 76th St., NY, NY) with Penn, the rumor being that she was asking him to father a child for her. The rumor is all the more seductive in that 1996 *did* wind up being the year that she became **pregnant** and decided she was keeping her baby.

Over the years, Penn—ever volatile—did change his views on gay rights. He'd been uncomfortable around gay people when with Madonna (though he helped her get experimental AIDS meds for her dying friend **Martin Burgoyne**), but he won his second Oscar for portraying gay politician Harvey Milk. While on the set of that film in 2008, Penn texted Madonna after kissing **James Franco** in a scene, "I just [kissed] a guy. I thought of you. I don't know why." We do! And anyway, don't we all think of Madonna each time we kiss a guy?

Penn watched Madonna from the front row of *The MDNA Tour* on October 11, 2012. He was quoted as saying "Amazing! ... She's so hot!" On September 24, 2013, the former Poison Penns met up again at Madonna's *#secretproject-revolution* premiere, where they hugged warmly, chatted and briefly posed for pictures. In November of that year, Madonna and her son **Rocco** even made a surprise visit to **Haiti** at Penn's urging, which perhaps led to a psychologically rich photo of Rocco done up as Penn's classic *Fast Times* character "Spicoli" in 2014 that **Guy Ritchie** can't have found funny.

On January 9, 2016, Madonna was a surprise guest of Penn's at his 5th Annual Sean Penn & Friends Help Haiti Home Gala at Montage Hotel (225 N. Canon Dr., Beverly Hills, CA), where she spoke adoringly of Penn and his work with the impoverished country, singing "La Vie en rose" for the assembled donors.

Penn attended one NYC and one Vancouver performance of the *Rebel Heart Tour*, sparking rumors the exes were dating. Madonna told fans that "30 fuckin' years later," Penn wrote her a letter stating he finally appreciated her art. Madonna put the kibosh on any notion they were

"HE'S WILD ... HE'LL PROBABLY DIE YOUNG. I FEEL LIKE HE'S MY BROTHER OR SOMETHING." —MADONNA (1985)

"EVERY ONCE IN A WHILE I WAKE UP AND GO, 'MY GOD! I WAS MARRIED, AND HE WAS THE LOVE OF MY LIFE.' IT IS LIKE A DEATH TO DEAL WITH."—MADONNA ON DIVORCING SEAN PENN (1990)

"SEAN REALLY WANTED A WIFE, SOMEONE TO BE MORE NURTURING THAN I WAS PREPARED TO BE. I WAS FIGHTING THAT CONVENTIONAL IDEA OF HOW A WOMAN BEHAVES, AND I REALIZED IT WASN'T POSSIBLE FOR ME TO HAVE A RELATIONSHIP IF THE MAN ISN'T IN TOUCH WITH HIS FEMININE SIDE."—MADONNA (1991)

"I STILL LOVE HIM, BUT I HAVE TO BE REALISTIC: HE HAS HIS OWN FAMILY NOW. I DON'T THINK YOU COULD SPEND MANY YEARS OF YOUR LIFE WITH SOMEONE AND THEN, EVEN IF YOU'RE NOT TOGETHER, JUST STOP HAVING FEELINGS FOR THEM. I'LL PROBABLY LOVE HIM TILL I DIE–I'M AFRAID I GIVE AWAY MY HEART EASILY."—MADONNA (1991)

"THIS IS A FANTASTIC WOMAN, WHO I HAVE GREAT AFFECTION FOR—MADONNA ... SHE WAS A FIRE, YOU KNOW? IN HERSELF. APART FROM ALL THAT STUFF THAT CAME WITH IT. BUT IN A MARRIAGE? AT THAT TIME IN MY LIFE? AND, YOU KNOW, YOU WALK THROUGH THE FIRES YOU HAVE TO WALK THROUGH. AND I GUESS SHE PROBABLY WOULD HAVE DESCRIBED ME SIMILARLY. THE FIRES THAT WERE PUBLIC WERE ALL TRIVIAL."—SEAN PENN (2015)

a renewed item by calling Penn and Guy Ritchie "assholes" during the Miami stop of the same tour.

If your hunch is that the **Ciccone**/Penn story seems unfinished, you're not alone.

PENTHOUSE: *Publication dates: September 1969–.* Founded by the colorful, highly **sexed** player Bob Guccione, this men's **magazine**—the dirtier *Playboy*, if you will—shocked America (the rest of the world was used to **nudity**) in 1985 when it said that it would publish nude photos of Madonna taken by photographer **Bill Stone**. Guccione's announcement led to a race to press with bitter rival *Playboy*, which beat *Penthouse* to the newsstands with its own selection of nudes by **Lee Friedlander** and **Martin H.M. Schreiber**.

According to *American Photographer* (September 1985): "By pushing up its on-sale date by two weeks, Hugh Hefner's magazine beat Guccione's by days in some markets and by weeks in others."

Guccione claimed to have offered Madonna a million dollars to pose in the buff shortly before he went to press with the first nudes, as if she would be more comfortable showing off her current bod than allowing him to publish nudes from her past.

That's how Guccione was; Madonna later complained that he had snidely sent her volatile husband **Sean Penn** copies of a 1987 *Penthouse* follow-up issue featuring more nudes. Penn was in jail at the time.

With Stone's images inside, *Penthouse* chose an amazing **Ken Regan** shot that had been taken for *People* magazine earlier in the year. Her vintage tank in that image became so familiar to **fans** it was sold to the highest bidder in 2014 for a **healthy** sum. *Penthouse* printed 5.2 million copies of the issue, which sold out. Add in *Playboy*'s run and that means 10 million magazines were sold that summer thanks to Madonna's punani.

And yet with all the **money** spent, many copies of Madonna's *Penthouse* issue had upside-down page numbers and other mistakes; her images had been dropped in so last-minute, Guccione was lucky they'd made it in at all.

The history of *Penthouse* and Madonna's naked body went **back** to June 1985. The wife of **Herman Kulkens**, who knew Madonna in her days at the **University of Michigan**, sent 22 nude images of her to the magazine for consideration. A deal of some kind was struck, but when *Penthouse* went to publish, the Kulkenses sued for $2 million, saying it was not a binding agreement (they wanted to go with *Playboy*). The case was heard and Guccione said he settled by paying them $25,000 on June 21, 1985. Some of the images have since been published, including a silly one of Madonna with a cowgirl hat that (dis)graced the cover of the German edition of *Penthouse* in September 1987. Unused Kulkens images were discovered in Guccione's hoard when he died, and became a hot news item yet again in 2013; they were sold at **auction**.

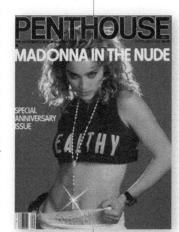

The legal wrangling held *Penthouse* up, allowing *Playboy* enough time to hit the newsstand first. In publishing, first is always best, though in this case, both publishers made out like bandits while Madonna made zero dollars ... directly. The ensuing press attention was, however, *priceless*.

"If you have such a lovely body, why not make the most of it? I was not the least bit appalled by her pictures in *Penthouse*. She never pretended to be Miss America."
—HELEN GURLEY BROWN (1985)

PEOPLE'S CHOICE AWARDS: *Dates presented: 1975–.* **Awards** show voted on by the public. Madonna has rarely been nominated, but she won Favorite Female Musical Performer on March 11, 1986. She gave a brief acceptance speech from the set of **Shanghai Surprise** in **London**: "Hi. I'm here on the set of my movie *Shanghai Surprise*, in-between takes, and I'm **working** very hard, so hard in fact that sometimes I forget that I make records, too. But this [award] is a very pleasant reminder. Thank you."

PEPSI: *Directed by Joe Pytka. Release date: March 2, 1989.* Though Madonna drank Diet Coke at the time and is now unlikely to ever drink another can of soda, she signed a lucrative $5 million deal to star in three Pepsi **commercials** in 1989. Pepsi was also to have sponsored a 1989 Madonna tour (that wound up never happening anyway).

"I do consider it a challenge to make a commercial that has some sort of artistic value," Madonna said of her deal.

The first commercial (and the only one ultimately produced) was teased for weeks on **TV** via a bizarre ad that first aired during the **Grammys** and showed an indigenous Australian and a "Crocodile Dundee" look-alike meeting up at an Outback bar to watch Madonna's Pepsi ad. The **voice**-over implored, "No matter where you are in the world, on March 2nd, get to a TV and watch Pepsi's two-minute Madonna commercial, featuring her latest release **'Like a Prayer'** for the very first time." The teaser used outtakes from the forthcoming video.

On March 2, 1989, during an episode of TV's #1 smash *The Cosby Show* (1984–1992), the commercial played, and 250 million people in 40 countries around the world watched, rapt, while they were sold a soft drink.

That commercial was a sweet fairy tale, showing Madonna watching a **black-and-white** (ouch!) home movie of her eighth **birthday** party. The young Madonna looked up from the screen to lock **eyes** with grown-up Madonna (who was sporting a **blonde** streak in her newly brunette **hair**), and the two traded places. For the rest of the

Madonna's '3Os vibe was loud and clear in the video she sent the People's Choice Awards in 1986.

Japanese ads that mingle Madonna's *Like a Prayer* album with Pepsi

commercial, the little girl wandered around in Madonna's full-color world (where she apparently kept posters of herself tacked to the wall) and the actual Madonna visited a variety of her early-years haunts: a **Catholic** school, a teen hang-out and that black church she must've attended as a kid.

At the end, when the kid discovered that her adult self has held on to a cherished childhood doll, the two switched places again and Madonna encouraged her younger self—and the world—to, "Go ahead ... make a wish."

The spot was precious, beautifully filmed and crackled with the choreography of **Vincent Paterson**, with whom Madonna was **working** for the first time. In point of fact, Madonna's deal with Pepsi was that she didn't have to be shown drinking their product and didn't have to **dance**; they would simply use her new single "Like a Prayer," which would give the song unprecedented exposure. Once Madonna saw Paterson working with all the backup dancers, the entire commercial changed; she wound up dancing strenuously, falling for Paterson's style.

When Madonna's actual music video for "Like a Prayer" was released the very next day, filled with burning crosses, a random occurrence of stigmata and interracial smooching, the American Family Association successfully pressured Pepsi to drop Madonna like a pop top. But due to her ironclad contract (and the fact that Madonna had told Pepsi all about her video in advance), she got to keep the millions she had been paid.

The commercial had aired only *twice*.

"Pepsi made the wrong conclusion. There is certainly no better time—and there may never be a better opportunity—for responsible advertisers to stand up to irresponsible boycotters. For starters, the spot in question is testimony to all that's good in advertising. It's a Mean Joe Greene for little

girls, a media must-see for impossible-to-reach teens. It's soft-sell imagery that hits hard, a hometown message that works around the globe," wrote Richard Morgan of *Adweek*.

On the set of her **"Vogue"** video a few months later, in footage leaked only 20 years after the fact, a topless Madonna filmed a tart, nine-second video in which she said, "I wear what I want, and I do what I want ... ask Pepsi." It is unknown if the spot was simply to have a laugh or was used to try to get a replacement sponsor for her tour, potentially Nike or **Reebok**.

Today, official products bearing Madonna's name and Pepsi's logo can go for big bucks due to their scarcity.

> "The story is definitely worthy of the attention of the proletariat."
>
> —THE REVOLUTIONARY WORKER ON PEPSIGATE (1989)

"PERÓN'S LATEST FLAME": Song from *Evita* found on *Evita: The Complete Motion Picture Music Soundtrack* in which **Antonio Banderas** and a chorus of jaded citizens mock this new girl Evita, not realizing the important role she is about to assume—or rather, demand. We all know who got the last laugh, even if she didn't laugh longest.

PERRY, KATY: *b. October 25, 1984.* One of the most successful solo singers of the 2010s, launched her career in Christian music in 2001. Bouncing from label to label, she landed at Capitol in 2007 where her *One of the Boys* album produced her first song to gain notoriety, the put-down record "Ur So **Gay**" (2008), and her breakthrough hit "I Kissed a Girl" (2008), a controversial tune about a chick experimenting with lesbianism. She followed that big success with a far bigger hit, the never-ending hit machine *Teenage Dream*, with its five #1 singles. A curvaceous **beauty**, she has continued to dominate the pop charts, charming **fans** with her propensity for playing dress-up and taking **hair** risks, her impact helped along by her relatively unadventurous agenda. Who's really offended by Katy Perry? (Well, except for her religious fundamentalist parents.)

Madonna was on the Katy Perry bandwagon very early on. In 2008, she said, "Well, I have a favorite song right now ... it's called 'ur so gay and you don't even like boys' ... have you heard it? You have to hear it. It's by an artist called Katy Perry. Oh, it's so good—check it out on iTunes." The DJs to whom she was speaking had no idea who Perry was.

Perry was surprised Madonna would praise a rival "female girl" singer, joking, "I would think that Madonna's more territorial than that. C'mon, honey!" But she was also blown away and intimidated by the spotlight shone on her by Madonna at a crucial phase in her career. "I **love** her music, but I'm still catching up on it because in the

She never touched the stuff.

Two of *V* magazine's collectible covers

household I grew up in, we didn't have many opportunities to listen to Madonna," she told *Star* sheepishly that same year, referencing her strict upbringing.

That upbringing was still bubbling under in 2010, when Perry picked a fight with **Lady Gaga**, tweeting of her "Alejandro" video, "Using blasphemy as entertainment is as cheap as a comedian telling a fart joke." By 2011, she was directly dogging Madonna, referring **back** to her *Confessions Tour* when saying, "For me, spirituality is something very important and I don't like it when people take it lightly. At times, I don't understand why there are artists who play that card, like when Madonna gets up on a cross to sing." One might think this would have disqualified Perry from Madonna's favor, but one would be wrong. Even Perry herself joked that Madonna would never give her her crown.

But Perry cited Madonna's *Truth or Dare* as the inspiration for her 2012 concert documentary *Katy Perry: Part of Me*, and by 2014, Madonna and Perry were fast friends. They teamed up to pose together for **Steven Klein** in Bettie Page-inspired dominatrix gear for the cover of *V* **magazine**'s summer 2014 issue. The bondage-lite session inspired Madonna to tell Perry her neck was sore from sucking on her heel. "I kept thinking, 'How many bacteria do you think there are on the heel of a shoe?' Then I thought, 'There's no point.' Do they have Purell mouthwash?"

Inside *V*, Madonna interviewed the younger star, which was much closer to a crown hand-off than Gaga ever got, speaking about **Kabbalah**, the vitality of touring and Perry's parents, who remain silently aghast at her **work**.

"Yeah, that's where I am with my dad, too," Madonna told Perry. "He's like, 'Do you have to simulate **masturbation** on the bed? ... 'Yes, Dad, I do.'" Perry replied, "I haven't gone that far yet, but maybe under your great mentorship I might reach that point."

Sisters really *are* doin' it for themselves.

Madonna has continued to be a strong influence on Perry. As part of her successful 2014 *Prismatic World Tour*, Perry performed **"Vogue"** in a medley with her own song, "International Smile" (2013). In 2015, Perry performed the **Super Bowl** halftime show, saying she had studied recent shows by **Beyoncé** and Madonna.

Perry doesn't seem to have quite as much influence over Madonna, who ignored Perry's nomination to do the ALS Ice Bucket Challenge.

"It's Madonna, and, y'know, this woman who, essentially every girl has her poster in their room their whole life and, y'know, you fall asleep looking at a poster of Madonna and you wake up looking at a poster of Madonna and then all of a sudden Madonna knows your first and last name and you're like, 'Holy crap!' y'know?"—KATY PERRY (2008)

PERRY, LUKE: *b. October 11, 1966.* Handsome star of **TV**'s *Beverly Hills 90210* (1990–1995, 1998–2000) who was Madonna's escort for the evening when the American Foundation for **AIDS** Research (amfAR) gave her its **Award** of Courage in 1991. Perry had the honor of handing the statuette to her and they gave each other a big kiss on the lips—it was no peck! (**Drake** might've tasted a little of it in 2015.)

Later, when asked about a possible Perry affair, Madonna sniffed that she didn't go out with people who posed with **guns** on **magazine** covers, referring to a *Vanity Fair* story featuring Perry cuddling up to a gun. By the time of her *MDNA Tour* era, her disaffection for guns had been cured.

PERSEVERANCE: Madonna is known as being fairly indestructible. By way of explanation, she said in 1984, "I went through a lot of pain when I was a very young girl and the only way to get through it was to tell myself that this was an education; this was a test for me. If I could get through this, then I would be rewarded in the end; when I'm older, I would get all the things I wanted."

PET SHOP BOYS: Duo made up of Neil Tennant (b. July 10, 1954) and Chris Lowe (b. October 4, 1959), the ultimate electronic maestros, who have been cranking out remarkably consistent pop jams since their first and still one of their biggest hits, "West End Girls" (1985). Amazingly, in spite of a slate of genre-defining classic songs, the Boys haven't hit the upper echelon of the **Billboard** Hot 100 in very close to 30 years, and their final Hot 100 song in the US was 1991's giddy mash-up of "Where the Streets Have No Name" by U2 (1987) and "Can't Take My **Eyes** Off You" by Frankie Valli (1967).

PSB have long been admirers of Madonna's **work**. Tennant, who was an editor at the teen-music **magazine** *Smash Hits* before becoming the kind of person he was assigned to write about, interviewed Madonna in the US on an October 1983 trip while he was helping to establish the magazine's US sister publication, *Star Hits*. He only met up with Madonna thanks to a flake-out by **A Flock of Seagulls**.

The Boys wrote their last #1 UK hit "Heart" with Madonna in mind, but decided it was too good to give away and were **nervous** she'd reject it anyway.

OLIVIU SAVU

"From the very start, I was a bad girl."
—MADONNA TO NEIL TENNANT (1983)

Tennant was on hand at the 2006 **Brit Awards** to hand Madonna her Best International Female Solo Artist **Award** (she beat **Björk**, **Mariah Carey**, Kelly Clarkson and **Missy Elliott**). When her name was called, Madonna strode to the podium as a **voice**-over snarkily noted, "Well, she turned down the Brits to play the **Grammys**, but we've forgiven her," and added that she was "nearly half a century old." Madonna listed some of her fave British artists in her acceptance speech, including PSB.

In 2006, the duo created the PSB Maxi Mix of Madonna's **"Sorry,"** adding lyrics sung by Tennant and using a brief sample from **Whitney Houston**'s "I Wanna **Dance** With Somebody (Who **Loves** Me)" (1987).

With Robbie Williams, PSB wrote the song "She's Madonna" for Williams's *Rudebox* album (2006). The song was inspired by words exchanged between Williams and Tania Strecker, a woman who had been dating **Guy Ritchie** but who was dumped because, as Ritchie said, "Look, you *know* I really love you, but she's *Madonna*." The song was a Top 20 hit in the UK in 2007, while "She's Tania Strecker" is a masterpiece waiting to be written.

In 2013, Tennant said, "Are the Rolling Stones still selling **sex** in their early seventies? I sort of think they are. Is Madonna still selling sex? I sort of think she is."

P.S. (B.): Who does a guy gotta blow to get a Madonna album produced by PSB?

PETE'S PLACE: Madonna told *Rolling Stone*'s Neil Strauss that she moved to **New York** in 1977 (not 1978, hmmm—there is some controversy about her actual arrival date) and that her first-ever club was Pete's Place. The way she remembers it, she felt so out of place she sat in the **back** and read a **book**. "The guys all had '40s suits on and porkpie hats. And the women were so glamorous. They all had red lipstick and black eyeliner and high heels ... I was like, 'Okay, I don't fit in. I'm not dressed appropriately. There's nothing cool about me. I'm going to go read a book.'"

PETTIBONE, SHEP: Record producer and songwriter who started as a remixer and DJ in the '80s, **working** with Cathy Dennis, **Janet Jackson** and Kim Wilde before his time with Madonna.

Pettibone's first official work for Madonna was on the 12" singles of her early hits **"True Blue"** and **"Causing a Commotion,"** on which he has credit for additional remixing. More prominently, he contributed substantially to her trendsetting remix album *You Can Dance*, on which he reimagined **"Into the Groove"** and **"Where's the Party"** in ways that gave the songs a whole new sound without overshadowing the originals.

Pettibone's remixing of Madonna was perfected during the *Like a Prayer* era, during which he crafted all-time classic versions of **"Like a Prayer"** and, perhaps his ultimate remix work with Madonna, **"Express Yourself."** What Madonna **fan** worth his or her salt isn't obsessively familiar with Pettibone's Non-Stop Express Mix of the latter?

Madonna and Shep Pettibone during the *Erotica* recording sessions

During this period, Madonna collaborated with Pettibone directly for the first time on a song meant to be a B-side for her excellent single **"Keep It Together,"** which Pettibone was remixing. When it was finished, her rattled-off **"Vogue"**—which she didn't see as having incredible potential—blew **Warner Bros.** away. It was pulled as a B-side and instead became the lead single from *I'm Breathless: Music from and Inspired by the Film Dick Tracy*. It would go on to become one of Madonna's top-selling, most-performed and most instantly recognizable hits.

Pettibone cowrote **"Rescue Me,"** one of the new cuts on her *Immaculate Collection*.

Following "Vogue" and "Rescue Me," Madonna had a #1 hit with Pettibone with their **"This Used to Be My Playground,"** the theme song from *A League of Their Own*.

After the amazing success Madonna had working with Pettibone, it was only natural that they would collaborate on a full album, which came to pass when they set to work on 1992's *Erotica*. The resulting album was a relative disappointment sales wise, coming at a time when Madonna's **sexual** provocations were working the public's last **nerve**. It was, however, critically acclaimed and is to this day a favorite Madonna album for many **fans** who resented how overlooked it was at the time.

On *Erotica*, Pettibone wound up with nine writing credits and 10 production credits out of 14 songs, working on **"Bad Girl," "Bye Bye Baby," "Deeper and Deeper," "Erotica," "Fever," "In This Life," "Rain," "Thief of Hearts," "Why's It So Hard"** and **"Words"**; in other words, he had a hand in every one of the album's singles, and only his contributions have ever been performed live.

Madonna began work on her next album with Pettibone, but then moved in a different direction. Though she abandoned most of their collaborations for *Bedtime Stories*, Pettibone did get a cowriting credit on that album's massive single **"Secret."**

Pettibone's work with Madonna has not been without its share of controversy; his boyfriend, personal assistant and collaborator **Tony Shimkin** felt "screwed" when it came to production credit, eventually receiving cowriting credits on most of Pettibone's work with Madonna (of whom Shimkin has always spoken respectfully). In 2012, Madonna and Pettibone were sued over "Vogue" when a company called VMG Salsoul claimed that "Vogue" illegally sampled horns and strings from a 1982 reworking of Salsoul Orchestra's 1977 song "Chicago Bus Stop (Ooh, I **Love** It)" called "Love Break." The contention was that VMG Salsoul had detected the sampling only recently, due to new technology (it is not audible to the naked ear). Shimkin had been hired by VMG Salsoul just prior to the filing of the suit, which gave it a decidedly personal twist. Oh, and the company's chief executive was Curt Frasca, who had also worked with Pettibone. Pettibone argued he owned part of "Love Break" anyway, that there was no sampling, that the sound in question was imperceptibly short and that the suit was without merit.

The suit was resolved in Pettibone and Madonna's favor, but it was a bitter, expensive battle, and one in which Pettibone reportedly felt abandoned by Madonna.

Regardless, Pettibone and Shimkin have helped to create many memorable Madonna musical moments.

Pettibone remains accessible on social media, where he has been known to sound off on Madonna's music from time to time (not a fan of "rent-a-rappers") and rightfully blow his own, non-sampled horn regarding his successes with her.

PHILBIN, REGIS: *b. August 25, 1931.* SEE: *Live with Regis & Kathie Lee* and *Live! with Regis & Kelly.*

PHILLIPS, ARIANNE: *b. December 26, 1963.* This film costumer and stylist has **worked** with Madonna since 1997 (on a *Rolling Stone* cover shoot), including on *Swept Away*, *W.E.* (for which she was **Oscar**-nominated) and all of Madonna's tours since her *Drowned World Tour*. (Those **"Frozen"** sleeves? Yep, hers.)

She told the site The Film Experience in 2012 that she and Madonna have matching communication styles and aesthetics. "I mean, 14 years in a world of freelance? That is a lifetime. We have definitely created a shorthand over the years and mutual understanding ... It's been an incredible journey, as you can imagine, to be there and watch her evolve and keep pushing herself. It's very inspiring."

PHOTOSHOP: Madonna broke up with the airbrush in favor of this newer model, a steady companion of hers (and of every public figure's) for years.

Madonna's gorge and a wiz at looking as different as humanly possible on a dime, but makeup and determination do not account for the totality of her changes.

For her May 1989 *Vogue* cover, Applied Graphics Technologies saw fit to eliminate Madonna's short-lived **blonde** streak, literally remove her legs and breasts, brighten the whites of her **eyes** and her teeth, darken her irises, spruce up her lipstick, round out her cheek, smooth away her early-onset crow's-feet and put her swimsuit strap on a crash diet.

Madonna flipped over *Glamour*'s decision in 1990 to change her **hair** from platinum to **orange** and her skin tone from vampiric to sun kissed, radically alter her eyes and bust and—most annoyingly—bleach her teeth and erase her famous **gap**. "Oh, my **God**, look what they did to my teeth! It looks like they glued them together, up and down and across." Madonna tried to stop the presses on the freaky cover, but it was too late.

Liz Rosenberg once admitted that every photo she received in her capacity as Madonna's publicist was subjected to the (now obsolete) Quantel Graphic Paintbox system, a rival and precursor to Adobe Photoshop so easy any **wannabe** could operate it.

Most of Madonna's classic images have benefited from subtle retouching, though **Steven Meisel** was particularly aggressive with his 1991 *Italian Vogue* shoot and **Jean-Baptiste Mondino**'s exquisite 1990 *Harper's Bazaar* cover feature is marred by an image in which one of Madonna's breasts seems to be attempting to storm off in search of a Russ Meyer flick for which to audition.

Over time, Madonna's image has been more and more radically altered in official photos, culminating with the painting-like offerings by **Mert and Marcus** that promoted her *MDNA* album, lovely **works** of **art** for which one wonders if Madonna even showed up.

Is it so bad that Madonna's image is frequently more the product of a computer program than of how she looks in the flesh? Nah. Every professional image put before us is retouched, and more importantly, these promotional images are works of art, not snapshots. What's art without a little **creativity**? (Answer: Unflattering.)

"PHYSICAL ATTRACTION": Sensual, underrated tune from the *Madonna* album, written and produced by **Reggie Lucas** (with some remixing by **Jellybean Benitez**), that was released along with **"Burning Up"** as a double-A single. The song was a US **dance** hit in spite of being so slow you could almost fall asleep to it (preferably after a sweaty session). It is a clear reference to **Olivia Newton-John**'s "Physical" (1980), though the songs have a totally different vibe.

Madonna is known to have performed the song sparingly, including live at **Uncle Sam's**, probably at **Escapes** and at **The Metro Club**.

Out of nowhere, Madonna led **fans** who'd crashed her sound check for an Amsterdam *MDNA Tour* date in a chorus of "Physical Attraction" 29 years after the last time she'd sung it, a hint that she hasn't forgotten the song after all.

PIANO: Though she doesn't play now, Madonna sulked through a year of tortuous piano lessons as a kid until her teacher made her quit because she kept ditching the lessons.

PIERCE, CHARLES: *July 14, 1926–May 31, 1999.* One of the most famous female impersonators who ever lived, Pierce effortlessly evoked Hollywood greats like Tallulah Bankhead, **Marlene Dietrich**, **Katharine Hepburn**, Gloria Swanson and **Mae West**, but the role he was born to play was Bette Davis. Pierce appeared on a precious few **TV** shows and in a few movies, but was most renowned as a cabaret act. He had real comedic **talent** and did his own singing, so thought of himself as more than a **drag** queen.

Pierce considered stars past the 1950s too **boring** to mimic, so apparently never did Madonna. However, an image of Pierce in drag as Davis's *What Ever Happened to Baby Jane?* character "Baby Jane Hudson" has been widely circulated on social media with the legend: "MADONNA: WORLD TOUR 2020" to poke fun at Madonna's age (SEE: **ageism**). Sadly, most of the people forwarding the image—old folks who don't own mirrors, young folks who don't own calendars—seem to believe the image is actually Davis, so ignorant are they not only of biology but also of pop culture history.

PILATES: Madonna immersed herself in Pilates in the early 2000s, then kicked it up a notch following her **horse**-riding accident. "I think it made me less muscular, believe it or not," she told *Harper's Bazaar* the following year. The exercise is immortalized in her **"American Life"** rap.

PILLSBURY, SARAH: Producer who teamed up with Midge Sanford in 1981 to form Sanford/Pillsbury Productions. Their first mutual project was *Desperately Seeking Susan*, a film whose hype combined with that of Madonna's first two albums to make 1985 the year of Madonna.

Sanford/Pillsbury went on to produce well-known films such as *River's Edge* (1986), *Eight Men Out* (1988), *Love Field* (1992) and *And the Band Played On* (1993), the latter of which won both women the Emmy.

PIMP MADONNA'S RIDE: *Air date: February 19, 2006.* British **TV** special, part of the series *Pimp My Ride*, in which Madonna enlisted the aid of host Tim Westwood to turn an ordinary white van into a tricked-out pimpmobile for her **"Sorry"** video. Madonna filmed a phone call to the host in which she said, "Come on, **MTV**—pimp my ride." In the end, Madonna entered the van, with its purple shag interior, and promptly pulled her leg over her head in appreciation.

PINK: *b. September 8, 1979.* Massively successful pop and R&B singer known for her **ballsy** lyrical content and her Flying Wallendas stage antics.

In 2000, at the very beginning of her career, P!nk landed a Fox Family Channel (RIP) concert special. Backstage, she hammed it up with a spirited cover of Madonna's **"Lucky Star,"** an honest expression of her appreciation for one of her idols.

In all the fuss over which new female artist can most correctly be called the next Madonna (answer: nobody), P!nk is often overlooked, perhaps because she's a bit older and a bit less likely to campaign for it, but her provocative songs, her devotion to her stage shows and her attitude should if nothing else secure her a spot in any conversation about how Madonna has influenced later generations of divas.

P!nk, somehow, has never **worked** with Madonna, but she was apparently one of Madonna's first choices—before **Britney Spears** and **Christina Aguilera**—to perform **"Hollywood"** with her in 2003. The missed opportunity was due strictly to geography, not to any misgivings about lesbian lip-locking.

"I was in Costa Rica. I couldn't be there for rehearsals," a bummed-out P!nk told *Access Hollywood* at the time. "I would kiss Madonna right now, right here." The following year, she said her **fandom** of Madonna was so complete that, "If Madonna came to me with her mouth open, I wouldn't know what to do!" Somehow, we think she would figure it out.

P!nk did get to meet Madonna that year, and the moment was captured on an episode of *Live! with Regis & Kelly*. She was brought out just before Madonna's interview ended (looking tense and excited) and got a big hug from Madonna.

PINK, ARIEL: *b. June 24, 1978.* Obscure EDM artist who in 2014 gave an interview with *Faster Louder* in which he confirmed he was **working** with Madonna on what would eventually come to be known as *Rebel Heart*. His caddish, unprofessional and egomaniacal comments included, "**Interscope** are calling me to help write Madonna's record. They need something edgy. They need songwriting. She can't just have her **Avicii**, her producers or whatever, come up with a new techno jam for her to gyrate to and pretend that she's 20 years old. They actually need songs. I'm partly responsible for that return-to-values thing." He said Madonna's musical career had been a downward slide from her *Madonna* album, and that *Ray of Light* "is not cool."

Guy Oseary immediately responded, saying, "[Madonna] and I have never heard of [Pink]. The label may have reached out but M has no interest in working with mermaids," a joke about Pink's Walt Disney–ready first name.

The artist Grimes savaged Pink's comments, tweeting, "Ariel Pink's delusional misogyny is emblematic of the kind of bullshit [every] woman in this industry faces daily."

PITT, BRAD: *b. December 18, 1963.* One of the biggest movie stars (and handsomest big-screen heartthrobs) of his generation, Pitt has parlayed a memorable eye **candy** role in *Thelma & Louise* (1991) into a career of increasingly lauded performances in films like *Seven* (1995), *12 Monkeys* (1995), *The Curious Case of Benjamin Button* (2008),

DOMENICO CROLLA

Inglourious Basterds (2009) and *The Tree of Life* (2011) with **Sean Penn**. He has begun producing films, in which he also often appears in smaller roles, such as the **Oscar**-winning *12 Years a Slave* (2013). He is equally famous for his broken relationship with Jennifer Aniston and his marriage to fellow star/filmmaker Angelina Jolie.

Pitt is friendly with Madonna, dating **back** to his **work** in **Guy Ritchie**'s *Snatch* (2000). He is closely associated with Madonna's greatest music video director, **David Fincher**, whose films with Pitt are among his most beloved.

Pitt and Jolie are often talked about in the same breath as Madonna thanks to their foreign adoptions. The press has often attempted to pit, as it were, Madonna against Jolie in this regard. A French interview in 2007 seemed to suggest Jolie was condemning Madonna for "illegally" adopting **David Banda** in **Malawi**, but Jolie clarified her remarks by saying, "The article contained many falsehoods. I said many positive things that were omitted. I feel we must focus on the present and I encourage everyone to be supportive so that every child can adjust nicely to their new home."

In 2013, Madonna answered Reddit.com questions, including one about **dreams**. She confessed a particular dream involved Pitt, saying, "Brad and I were living together, and there was a small blond child in the bed. Sorry, Angelina, it was only a dream!"

PITTMAN, MONTE: *b. November 19, 1975.* A familiar figure in Madonna's retinue, this kind, unassuming guitarist who can always be counted on for tour support is an accomplished songwriter. He met Madonna after giving **guitar** lessons to **Guy Ritchie**, then being employed to do the same for Madonna, who after many years was returning to the instrument in 2000. His very first performance with Madonna was on *Late Show with David Letterman*, during which he ably accompanied Madonna on an acoustic version of **"Don't Tell Me."** He has accompanied her on every tour from *Drowned World Tour* forward, appeared at her *On Stage & on the Record* and other promo stops, appeared in Madonna's **Live 8**, **Live Earth** and **Super Bowl** performances and is a constant figure alongside Madonna during live **TV** gigs, such as her 2015 *Che tempo che fa* performance of **"Devil Pray."**

Madonna has occasionally written with Pittman, with whom she has a playful chemistry, most importantly on the outstanding *American Life* track **"Easy Ride."** He also has credits on the songs **"Hey You"** and **"It's So Cool."**

PIZZA: In 2009, Madonna pretended she'd never had real **New York** pizza for a bit on *Late Show with David Letterman*, but nobody believed her former street urchin self had not gobbled up her share of slices before she became the healthiest woman alive.

Nowadays, it's worth knowing that Bella Napoli's (85 Kilmarnock Rd., Glasgow, Scotland) Chef Domenico Crolla is renowned for making pizzas with exact likenesses of celebrities on each pie—his replication of Madonna's 1990 *Glamour* cover pose, pictured, is said to be delicious and anything but cheesy.

PLASTIC SURGERY: There are countless rumors about what Madonna has and has not had done to her face and body. In the '90s, there were whispers that she'd had a nose job or two. If that happened, it or they was or were subtle. She defensively bragged about her perfect boobs in *Truth or Dare* when it was suggested they might not be real; they were, at the time. She copped to temporary **collagen** injections in her lips in 1990.

Because so much of what Madonna does has to do with her face and body, the specter of plastic surgery has haunted her since before she should've even been worrying about it. At age 38, she was asked about having a **face-lift**. She said, "Well, I've certainly thought about it: In terms of when the time comes, will I do it? Because it has nothing to do with personal vanity and everything to do with professional longevity. You're required to look a certain way. Period ... But if I ever do it, I want the guy who did Catherine Deneuve. My **God**, she looks incredible!" That was *sort of* a compliment.

Madonna bantered with **gay** writer Denis Ferrara in 2006 about her rejuvenation regimen, ultimately declaring, "I am not going to hold a press conference if I have plastic surgery." Her opinion on the matter is that she's not against plastic surgery, but is against *talking* about it.

Considering her status as a **sex** symbol, Madonna went a very long time before it became cool and commonplace to associate her with plastic surgery, but she is definitely associated with it now. Regardless of the probability that Madonna had been previously sneaking tweaks here and there, it was in early 2008 that the media seemed to decide collectively that Madonna had for sure had cosmetic **work** done on her face and that it was going to be brought up ad nauseam in articles forever after. In that year, just before appearing at her **charity** event for **UNICEF** at the UN, Madonna was pictured with bruising around her **eyes**. On the carpet in Berlin, her face was undeniably different—she had gone from an angular look to having plumper cheeks and more wide-open eyes. Within months, she was on the cover of *New York* **magazine** to illustrate its feature on "The New New Face," about how the women in Hollywood were all beginning to resemble each other thanks to plastic surgery trends.

Since then, images clearly show that the skin above Madonna's ears is tight, suggesting at minimum an upper face-lift; there are countless images of Madonna with unexplained bruises under her eyes and on her cheeks;

GOOD GOIN', STRANGERS:
THE BACKSTORY ON THE MAKING OF
DESPERATELY SEEKING SUSAN
FROM PRODUCER SARAH PILLSBURY

Neophyte feature-film producers Sarah Pillsbury and Midge Sanford had a problem—they were in love with a script for a feminist comedy, but they couldn't get it greenlit.

Pillsbury tells *EM2O*: "The only people who liked the script were women and gay men—that was it. And there weren't any of them who could actually say yes or no to a movie getting made."

Still, their devotion to the quirky script stayed alive. "We were always propelled by people saying they would wait out in the rain to see this movie."

After a few years and lots of development, the script found support at Orion, provided it could receive some sprucing up in the action department. Thanks to the insertion of The Magic Club, the comedy about a suburban housewife spying on a cool chick and getting drawn into her downtown drama was on its way to getting made—and the rest is herstory.

Pillsbury recalls to *EM2O* the madness behind their method and what it was like working with Madonna.

EM2O: What do you remember about first reading the script?

SARAH PILLSBURY: It was an original script by Leora Barish. She told me about it way back when at dinner when I was just becoming a producer. I'd done a short [*Board and Care* (1980)] that won an Academy Award, so had just gotten a big boost. I said, "I wanna see it when it's done!"—you never say no, right? Then

one morning, there it was on my doorstep. By then, I was partners with Midge Sanford who had worked a lot more with developing screenplays, so she was able to say, "This is really unique."

What we liked was that this was a woman who was not really conscious; it wasn't a big leap from the state she was in to amnesia. She's not happy and she doesn't know it. The fantasy propels her, which is true of a lot of people—they live vicariously. By losing herself, she finds herself. Interestingly enough, we made another movie with the exact same arc—*Love Field* [1992] with Michelle Pfeiffer, where her character is completely crazy about Jackie Kennedy. It's a great feminist comedy in so many ways, and it's also a metaphor for what happens when we go to the movies—we lose ourselves and live vicariously through others and we come out of the movies just a little bit different.

At that point, it didn't have any of the adventure in the middle of it with The Magic Club. It had the mystery with the jacket, but we hadn't even settled on what the MacGuffin was. Finally, after a few years, we heard about Susan Seidelman. We'd gone to a number of different directors before she'd even made *Smithereens* [1982]–Jonathan

Demme, Louis Malle and George Roy Hill were the first directors we went to. Then Hal Ashby. Jonathan Demme was interested, but he didn't want to make a development deal, he wanted to make a movie. But he liked it. Three years later, we *still* didn't have a director.

EM2O: How did you hook up with Susan Seidelman?

SP: I heard about Susan possibly from Midge's husband at the time who was a literary agent, and I still remember the big spread on her in *The New York Times*–Vincent Canby loved *Smithereens* and it had gone to Cannes. So we sent her the script and lo and behold she loved it. We asked her about casting and she said, "You know, I really didn't think about the cast because I kept thinking about a film called *Céline and Julie Go Boating* [1974]," and that was the film that had inspired Leora, so that was amazing.

But when we finally got first Warner Bros. interested, they felt there wasn't enough adventure. I won't go into detail about how it was developed there, but I think there was a stamp forger or something like that. So we went over to Orion and we kept going around in circles and I had to leave the meeting before the decision was made. I remember being on a ski trip. I arrived and found a place with a phone and Midge told me, "Before I tell you the idea, let me just tell you that everybody has agreed." So I said, "Okay, what's the idea?" She said, "The Magic Club." [Laughs]

I couldn't see it, but they could ... and it worked out great. Then we later came up with the idea of Nefertiti's earrings, which was so female-centric. At one point, there was a male executive *very briefly* involved in the development and he came in and had an idea about some guy who was involved with art insurance and breaking the case, and we just turned to him and said to him, "This is not a movie where a woman is saved by a man."

The original ending had the two of them going off on a trip with the guys wondering when they were gonna come back. We felt the important thing was that the women were in different places than they were in the beginning.

EM2O: Was developing the script a tumultuous process?

SP: There were differences of opinion about how long the amnesia should last and other differences and finally another writer came on from New York and he made some structural changes with Susan so Roberta comes out of the amnesia partway through the movie instead of at the very end, but in that rewrite it lost a lot of its charm and we hadn't really cracked the love interest for Roberta, the Aidan Quinn, so [writer] Craig [Bolotin] really developed that character.

Mark Blum and Laurie Metcalf, their characters are comic and silly and there's a lot of comic character in this. We had a wonderful meeting with Jim Brooks after we made the movie because he just loved the casting, particularly of Aidan Quinn and Robert Joy, because he

felt those were men only women would cast as love interests. Bob Joy was just so wonderful–goofy but real. Just terrific.

EM2O: The casting of the movie is flawless.

SP: Ellen Chenoweth was the first casting director we went to, but she said she wasn't available, but she mentioned Billy Hopkins and Risa Braman and it was interesting because I think I met one of them on the West Coast and Susan met the other on the East Coast and we both really liked them a lot and they did a genius job of getting the best indie people from independent films then, as well as so many great Off-Broadway people then, like Laurie Metcalf, who was a big hit in New York then in *Balm in Gilead* (1983).

EM2O: But Madonna wasn't from Risa and Billy, right?

SP: Madonna was entirely Susan's idea. I had never heard of her; neither had Midge. But even though we went through an extensive casting process, after we got the script in turn-around, we immediately were sending it out. I still have the letter where we were just saying that for casting we were thinking of, I think Rosanna Arquette and Jennifer Tilly, and Madonna–I wrote "the pop star Madonna" because she had "Lucky Star" and "Borderline" and she was making her way around New York with her boom box.

RICHARD CORMAN

The cast of *Susan* poses for *Vogue*.

EM2O: Were you confident about the casting of Madonna from the beginning?

SP: We were nervous about Madonna, even though her performance improved when she worked with Susan. Her screen test convinced us that she could pull it off, and there were some really strong actresses who we were leaning towards, but we were really very comfortable after seeing that screen test. She just really, she looked great, and I don't think she was styled at all. She just had that kind of sassy, bratty, sexy, Mae West-y thing, and was just a fantastic, fantastic contrast to Rosanna as Roberta, and Rosanna was just as perfect as she could possibly be.

I can't think of one person in the movie who wasn't perfect in the end ... and I didn't always think that while we were shooting!

EM2O: How was the character of Susan originally conceived?

SP: The funny thing is, I sort of thought of Madonna as the girl I had wanted to be, which was much more of the free spirit, the idea that you could be the girl who goes around the world with 10 cents in her pocket, never wondering where her next meal comes from. That character was in some ways more ethereal in my mind, and what Susan and Madonna brought to that character was to make her kind of naïve in her own way, not quite getting the world as being as dangerous a place as it is, and is therefore willing to take risks. She doesn't think anything of conning people almost, but it's more like, "C'mon, it'll be fun." She gets people to do things against their will and probably not in their best interest but you don't ever think it's that ... *wicked.*

I think one of the only bad things she does is jump out on the cab fare. She's definitely an anti-bourgeois character, and that was always a part of the original idea.

EM2O: Was Madonna easy to work with?

SP: Madonna was late one day, then she got an alarm clock and she wasn't late again. Susan worked with her a lot and made it comfortable and would change things a bit so it would feel more authentic for Madonna to say it. I think she's very authentic and really, really great in the role.

EM2O: When you finally saw a cut of the movie, did you think, "This is amazing!"?

SP: No. There's always something. It was our first movie and we'd imagined things differently and there were things we'd had problems with that stayed and things we liked that changed. But it really came together through the course of the editing and the music. I have to say that everyone on the film made compromises, but they were compromises where those who made compromises realized we weren't right in the first place. Susan made decisions and she was right and they worked.

One of the last things the director cut out was one of my favorite lines in the whole script, but when I saw the cut I didn't even notice.

EM2O: The film has such phenomenal music and a number of film clips. Wasn't that difficult, rights-wise?

SP: We did have a problem, surprisingly, with Marlo Thomas, who didn't want a scene from *That Girl* [1966-1971] in the movie– we couldn't get approval from her. When Susan's by the pool, she was going to be watching *That Girl.*

EM2O: What was the LA premiere like?

SP: I don't remember the premiere being a very big deal. It was in Century City–we were pissed off because you wanted your movie to premiere in Westwood. It went to Cannes after it opened.

EM2O: Madonna skipped the 25th-anniversary reunion for the film in NYC, which was a bummer. Do you think she doesn't appreciate the movie as much as we do?

SP: I have not seen Madonna in person in quite a while– well over 10 years–but every time I ever saw her after making the movie she was always forever grateful for the opportunity. I think that she absolutely knows that it was just a tremendous boost for our movie *and* tremendous synergy for her.

EM2O: How did "Into the Groove" make its way into the film?

SP: She came to the set when we were shooting the disco scene and she brought a tape of the song "Into the Groove" and I had not even heard *Like a Virgin* yet so I thought it was from *Like a Virgin.* So we used it and I called up Freddy DeMann and said, "Hey, we used this song and we could change it, but we really like it and it really works and we'd like to try to get the rights to use it in the movie." He said, "I don't know what you're talking about ... I've never heard that song."

Warners was reluctant to let us use the song even though they owned it. They were still trying to, when we were opening the movie, they were promoting *Like a Virgin* and here we were wanting to use a song that hadn't been properly recorded. Fortunately, our music supervisors Danny Goldberg and Tim Sexton were friendly with people at Warners and a wonderful guy there, Jeff Ayeroff, just said, "It's all good. It can't be bad. Just let them use the song." They wanted us to use "Material Girl" or "Holiday" and we just said, "No, we want 'Into the Groove.'"

What happened is Tim and Danny were also able to find a director and to get MTV to play what was really more of a trailer. We had only a little original footage, but it was so popular that DJs were playing "Into the Groove" on the radio by recording it off of MTV–I don't even know the technology they were using–and playing it on the radio. You can't even buy promotion like that.

EM2O: Do you have any souvenirs or props from the film?

SP: The only paraphernalia we have is a little button that has Madonna on it that we used for publicity. It was very funny–I was wearing it when we took the film to Cannes. Orion was reluctant to have someone go to Cannes because Susan Seidelman had gone previously [with *Smithereens*] and was part of the competition, and *Desperately Seeking Susan* wasn't picked for the competition. We were invited to the directors' fortnight.

We went over and it was the closing-night film and it was just *so* much fun because by then there'd been a number of press screenings and it had a lot of buzz. A friend of mine who was there remembers how exciting it was to get a ticket to go.

The movie went over really well, and when we walked out we were mobbed. I was wearing one of these buttons and this guy came up to me and he desperately wanted this button and I said, "I can't give it away," and he said, "Can I buy it?" and I said, "No, no," and then he took a picture of his daughter out of his wallet, she was three years old, and he said, "I'll trade you a picture of my daughter for it." I couldn't resist, so I traded the button for the picture of his daughter, which I carried around for years.

EM2O: What's your favorite line in the film?

SP: I'm always touched by a story about what a movie can do that you don't ever expect: In the movie, the ads go back and forth about "strangers," and at the end the women look at each other and speak to each other for the first time in the movie, kind of amazed. Madonna says, "Good goin', stranger." I heard a couple of years later that a woman a little older than me had been estranged from her twentysomething daughter and they were doing things together to build a bridge back and they went to see this movie and when it got to that point in the movie, the daughter gripped her mother's hand and they burst into tears. It was that line, "Good goin', stranger," and no one thought about what that meant.

ANDY SCHWARTZ

Never-before-seen image of Madonna on the *Desperately Seeking Susan* set holding little Nora, producer Sarah Pillsbury's infant daughter. This image became a holiday card for the movie's crew. The baby screened *Susan* when she was just two weeks old. Now, Nora Pillsbury Kletter is a writer. Check out her blog at Things I Wish I Knew Sooner on Tumblr.

"Whatever Madonna has had done—and I really don't know— she looks truly amazing."—LIZ ROSENBERG (2008)

and regardless of any actual surgeries she has or hasn't had, Madonna's face *does* change a lot, seeming to puff up and down with what is almost inarguably a regimen of fillers and Botox.

It's not wrong to notice when the face you've studied for 30 years changes. It's not wrong to have a personal affection for the various ways that Madonna's face can look. It probably *is* wrong to savage the woman for doing what almost 100% of people—men and women—in Hollywood are doing, punishing her because her face happens to be so much more familiar that she has less of a chance of getting away with changing it on the sly.

"That thing with the cheeks. Like Madonna … It doesn't make them look young. You end up looking like a freak," *natural* **beauty** Sofia Vergara uncharitably said in 2010. That same year, model Paulina Porizkova offered, "Madonna no longer looks like Madonna. What started as a sexy, well-shaped, somewhat **hairy** Italian girl has ended as a cool Nordic **blonde**."

The question is no longer whether Madonna indulges in cosmetic procedures, the question is: Does it matter? Does it make you lose interest in or respect for her? Is it more or less brave that instead of "fixing" her hands (somehow), Madonna has taken to wearing gloves for several years in order to avoid the gleeful attacks about how her hands were giving away her age?

Look, if you've ever been in your fifties, photographed daily, had half a billion dollars in the bank and have decided to do nothing more to combat aging than apply Oil of Olay, drink lots of water and get plenty of rest, then you can get on your high, unwrinkled **horse** and start judging Madonna for doing more.

Until then, while Madonna certainly does not look the way she would had she skipped all cosmetic intervention, she looks damn good. And more importantly, Madonna reserves the right to present herself to the world in any way she so desires, a prerogative we should all give ourselves.

PLAYBOY: *Publication dates: December 1953–.* The absolute definitive men's lifestyle **magazine**—and the first household-name titty mag—was founded by Hugh Hefner, a **pussy** hound who **dreamt** up a way to make loads of cash, be surrounded by beautiful and available women and help to invent the **sexual** revolution all at the same time.

Marilyn Monroe was on the magazine's first cover, and it sold approximately 54,000 copies. Madonna's issue sold out its 5.9 million copy run.

At the **height** of Madonna's initial burst of **fame** in 1985, with two hit albums, a string of hit singles and a hit movie

behind her, news broke that **nude** images she'd posed for years before were set to appear in the September issue of *Playboy* magazine hitting the street on July 10, 1985. *Penthouse* had lost a bidding war over the nudes *Playboy* had, but had in the meantime snapped up its own nudes. Second out of the gate, *Penthouse* sniffed that they'd seen and rejected the **black-and-whites** *Playboy* was using, which had been deemed "like scraping the bottom of the barrel." Those Gucciones always were jealous **bitches**.

Playboy's last stapled issue was, as its cover promised, definitely "a keeper," but not because there were so many **fans** of staples out there—the main attraction was a cover featuring a sultry **Herb Ritts** image of Madonna in full *Desperately Seeking Susan* gear, promising a nude spread inside.

Like **Marilyn** before her, Madonna had posed nude to make ends meet before her career started. Lucky for Madonna, she posed mostly for highly artistic (if 100% revealing) images, so that any impact more **pornographic** images may have caused was avoided. The *Playboy* nudes, shot by **art** photographers **Lee Friedlander** and **Martin H.M. Schreiber** in 1979, revealed Madonna's lithe **dancer's** body, perfect breasts and tendency toward the hirsute—women were not as likely to remove all their pubic **hair** back then, but Madonna's hairy armpits were definitely not the norm in 1985.

Madonna was said to have been rattled by the publication of these images, fearing even that she was about to lose her shiny and new career. Instead of freaking out, she sucked it up and appeared, as scheduled, on July 13, 1985, at **Live Aid**, where she commented obliquely—and defiantly—on the scandal.

By the numbers: Friedlander paid Madonna $25 for his session with her, Schreiber had paid her $30, and they were reportedly paid $500,000 between them by *Playboy*. An original, silver gelatin print of Madonna nude by Friedlander from the same time period sold at **auction** in 2009 for $37,500. **Love** doesn't make the world go 'round, **money** does. And perfect tits, don't forget perfect tits.

Over the years, Madonna has appeared on the cover of *Playboy*, its special editions and its foreign editions many times, most spectacularly the December 1986 of Japanese *Playboy* (a totally unique **Mitsubishi** promo shot).

> "In spite of all the hoopla, the fact is that all the pictures to date can only be called tasteful or, at best, artful. In reality, the imbroglio is just a tempest in a C-cup."–ANNE M. RUSSELL, *AMERICAN PHOTOGRAPHER* (SEPTEMBER 1985)

PLAYING THE FIELD: "The best thing about single life," Madonna told *Harper's Bazaar* in 1984, "is there's always someone else. And, besides, I wouldn't wish being Mr. Madonna on anybody!" In other words: *Next!*

PLAYS: Before *Goose and Tomtom*, *Speed-the-Plow* and *Up for Grabs*, Madonna was a stage star **back** at Rochester Adams High **School**. In the '70s, she had lead roles in **school** productions of *Cinderella* (1957), *Godspell* (1971), *The Wizard of Oz* (based on the 1939 film), *My Fair Lady* (1956) and *The Sound of Music* (1959)—OMG, **Lady Gaga** is such a copycat!

Madonna also appeared in more challenging fare like *Dark of the Moon* (1945) and *The Night Thoreau Spent in Jail* (1970).

> "I saw her in *Godspell*, and I remember that when the audience stood for the curtain call, she was crying. The sense of acceptance, I think now that this is what she most appreciated, most craved."–CLARA BONELL, MADONNA'S CLASSMATE, TO J. RANDY TARABORRELLI (2001)

PONTIAC: Madonna lived in this **Michigan** city (443 Thors St., Pontiac, MI) the first nine years of her life, before moving to **Rochester Hills**.

POP, IGGY: *b. April 21, 1947.* The wiry, usually shirtless punk rocker is a fellow Michigander whose influential punk band the Stooges helped play Madonna into the **Rock and Roll Hall of Fame** in 2008, at her invitation, performing covers of **"Burning Up"** and **"Ray of Light."** Madonna wanted the Stooges as a **protest** because the band had been nominated for the Hall themselves, but never made the grade. One year later, it was announced that the Stooges were being inducted.

The band's guitarist, Ron Asheton, later said, "The Stooges represent everything that's against what she is. I don't wish her ill. I don't **hate** her or anything. But I'd never ever heard of these songs until I had to listen to a tape and figure out what's going on with them ... I think she actually does like the band. She wouldn't have asked for us if she didn't. But she's also using us for **business** purposes." Asheton died of a heart attack at 60 less than a year later.

Interestingly, the Stooges' 2008 lineup included Mike Watt, who'd been a member of **Ciccone Youth**.

Pop had a little history with Madonna, having been selected to open for her in Dublin on her *Re-Invention World Tour*.

POPCORN: Madonna's favorite **snack**, which she claimed to eat all day long in the '80s.

In 1986, she said that the one thing she missed most about America while filming scenes for **Shanghai Surprise** in the Orient was cheese popcorn. In 1990, designer **Milena Canonero** said that in order to keep her attention while fitting her with her **Dick Tracy** wardrobe, she had to "hold on to her with popcorn and other goodies."

Madonna has also used popcorn to liven up meetings with industry executives. "I walk in there with my **orange** leggings and drop popcorn in my cleavage and then fish it out and eat it."

Original résumé, as printed on the back of a Fred Seidman head shot

POPE JOHN PAUL II: *May 18, 1920–April 2, 2005.* Karol Józef Wojtyła—John for short!—was considered the most pious being on earth by **Catholics** from October 16, 1978, until his **death.**

He was not one to keep his opinions of Madonna to himself. Though Madonna had said in 1989 that she was "convinced he has a sense of humor," the Pope proved her wrong, when his surrogates condemned her ***Blond Ambition World Tour.*** Madonna joked that, "If the Pope wants to see me, he can buy tickets like everybody else."

MADONNA'S FULL SPEECH IN ROME ON JULY 11, 1990, REGARDING *BLOND AMBITION*

••

"If anyone talks–*don't talk.* If you talk, I will stop speaking, all right? Allora. Ready?

"I'm an Italian-American, and I'm proud of it. Proud of being–[pauses in disgust at interruption] I want total silence or I will not speak. I'm an Italian-American and I'm proud of it. Proud of being an American because it is the country I grew up in, the country that gave me the opportunities to be who I am today, and a country that believes in freedom of speech and artistic expression. I am also proud of being an Italian because it is my father's heritage and because it is the reason that I am passionate about the things that I believe in.

"It is also the reason my blood boils when I am misunderstood or unfairly judged for my beliefs.

"I am aware that the Vatican and certain Catholic communities are accusing my show of being sinful and blasphemous, that they are trying to keep people from seeing it. Basta per favore! If you are su–if you are sure that I am a sinner, then let he who has not sinned cast the first stone. If you are not sure, then I beg of you–as righteous men and women of the Catholic Church, that worship a God who loves unconditionally–to see my show and then judge me.

"No, I must say it all.

"My show is not a conventional rock show, but a theatrical presentation of my music. And, like theater, it asks questions, provokes thoughts and takes you on an emotional journey, portraying good and bad, light and dark, joy and sorrow, redemption and salvation.

"I do not endorse a way of life, but describe one, and the audience is left to make its own decisions and judgments.

"This is what I consider freedom of speech, freedom of expression and freedom of thought. To prevent me from performing my show, you, the Catholic Church, are saying that you do not believe in these freedoms. If you do not believe in these freedoms–basta!–if you do not believe in these freedoms, you are imprisoning everyone's mind. When a mind is imprisoned, then our spirit–spiritual life dies. When the spirit dies, there is no reason to live.

"Every night before I go on stage, I say a prayer, not only that my show will go well, but that the audience will watch with an open heart and an open mind and see it as a celebration of love, life and humanity.

"Sono molto felice di essere qui."

••

Madonna's feud with the Pope (and you thought **Lady Gaga** was a **powerful** adversary?) culminated with her surreal speech directed at the Catholic hierarchy, throughout which she testily hushed noisy reporters.

The Pope wasn't too bothered by child **sex** abuse, but he sure drew the line at Madonna's **cone bra** and her fixation on religious iconography. He must've been right, because on April 27, 2014, the Church declared him a saint.

PORNOGRAPHY: Literally, prurient material with no redeeming social value. Popularly, anything mildly dirty that you might find on your first visit to the Internet but that is likely to incite obscenity charges in the US.

Madonna has often been labeled a pornographer (**Camille Paglia** meant it as a compliment) and *Sex* is, if not porn, porn-adjacent. Still, she said in 1992, "I have never **masturbated** to pictures of naked people."

In October 1990, erotic "extra" actor Mike Rick tried to **auction** a 1978 hardcore porn video, allegedly starring Madonna getting it on in the john with two guys and another woman. He wanted to start the bidding at over $50,000, but the tape's poor quality and the fact that the actor looked more like Chuck Connors scuttled plans for the auction.

Madonna's favorite blue material would include the **work** of George Bataille, Anne Rice and Marguerite Duras (1984's *The Lover* being Madonna's choice as the **sexiest** novel ever). She also adores the *Herotica* collections and Vladimir Nabokov's infamous ode to cradle-snatching, *Lolita* (1955).

"POSSESSIVE LOVE": *Release date: 1988. Billboard Hot 100 peak: NA.* **Marilyn** Martin single written by Madonna, **Patrick Leonard** and Jai Winding and produced by Leonard and Michael Verdick. The song was apparently written at Leonard's suggestion specifically for Martin, who later provided backing vocals for **"Cherish."** Martin recalled Madonna, during the recording of "Cherish," as "impressive, to say the least, very in charge." Madonna's original demo of "Possessive Love" remains **unreleased** and has yet to **leak.**

POWER: One of the hallmarks of Madonna's impact is her embodiment of power. "I **love** the fact that she is a woman who is fearless of her own power," Mink Stole said of Madonna in 1993.

Especially gripping to young women (and closet cases) in the mid-'80s was the notion that a woman, a physically *small* one at that, dressing and behaving independently, could catch the world's attention, make music and videos that dictated international popular culture and be in complete **control** of all aspects of her **art,** career and life. The fact that Madonna is a woman who has achieved power is behind readings that interpret her as necessarily **feminist.**

"When you deprive women of any notion of threat, it pretty much puts them **back** in the Victorian Age. All innocent, and without power, except the power of being good," Margaret Atwood wrote in 1993 of Madonna's popularity, likening her to the female outlaw "Zenia" of her **book**, *The Robber Bride*.

"Power is a great aphrodisiac, and I'm a very powerful person."—MADONNA (1991)

"POWER OF GOOD-BYE, THE" (SONG): *Release date: September 22, 1998. Billboard Hot 100 peak: #11.* Madonna's third US single from *Ray of Light* was this billowing ballad written by Madonna and **Rick Nowels** and produced by Madonna, **William Orbit** and **Patrick Leonard**. With a light Kabbalistic philosophy sprinkled in, the song laments the closing chapter of a relationship, but urges acceptance of all that comes.

Madonna has never performed the song on tour, but has performed it a number of times live, including on the **VH1 Fashion Awards** on October 23, 1998 (sounding pretty strong, looking like a beautiful witch); on *Wetten, das ...?* on November 7, 1998 (lip-synched); on TF1's *Sacrées Femmes* in France (gorgeous set, lip-synched); on **The MTV Europe Music Awards** on November 12, 1998 (sounding *awful*, on that high note in particular); on November 15, 1998, for the Swedish show *Sen kväll med Luuk* (in a totally see-through top and lip-synching ... nip-synching?); on *Top of the Pops* in the UK on November 20, 1998 (lip-synching); and on November 23, 1998 (live and sounding pretty damn good again)—introduced by Miguel Bosé—on an episode of *El séptimo de caballería* on RTVE in Spain.

"POWER OF GOOD-BYE, THE" (VIDEO): *Director: Matthew Rolston, 1998.* Madonna enlisted prominent celebrity portrait artist Matthew Rolston for her fourth video from *Ray of Light*, a coolly sensual presentation of id vs. ego that finds Madonna playing chess with about-to-be-TV-star Goran Višnjic in a set-up reminiscent of the film *The Thomas Crown Affair* (1968), dissolving into a passionate kiss with him and equally passionate parting. She then walks along the beach, apparently to commit suicide in the waves. The hyper-real beach scenes are straight out of the Joan Crawford film, *Humoresque* (1946).

Madonna's look for the video is unlike her look for any other—she wears long black tresses and a smoky **eye** and is shot through a blue gel that seems to imply submersion, and also depression.

In a making-of piece for the video for *Entertainment Tonight*, Madonna told correspondent Bob Goen, "There's more of a narrative story, a **love** story gone wrong ... We wanted to do something very dramatic, and since we're both very dramatic people, um, we just came up with a story, which I just think is really emotional."

Rolston said, "To **work** with Madonna is a privilege, and it's one that—it's a rare privilege—and one that I've really enjoyed. She's a great performer."

"PRAY FOR SPANISH EYES": The penultimate song on *Like a Prayer*, written and produced by Madonna and **Patrick Leonard**, this wrenching ballad about gang violence in the barrio was originally identified as "Spanish Eyes" but retitled for reprints of the album and as the B-side to the single release **"Oh Father."**

PREGNANT: For years, Madonna's only pregnancy news to share was that she *wasn't*. She even used her opening monologue when she hosted *Saturday Night Live* in 1985 to blow off rumors of that she had a bun in the oven.

The strongest phony rumors of "Madonna with child" came in June 1993, when photos of her in an Adidas dress showed a slight belly (now known by the dreadful phrase "baby bump") and the press went wild. False alarm.

Madonna used the **Liz Smith** column to announce that she was pregnant by **Carlos Leon** in 1996, and confirmed her pregnancy in 2000 via a joint statement with future husband **Guy Ritchie** that said, "We would be grateful if the media would kindly allow us some **privacy** at this special time and we thank you all for your good wishes." Yeah ... it didn't happen. Matt Lauer of *Today* had asked Madonna point-blank if she were pregnant on March 3, 2000, and Madonna had lied and said no; she wasn't ready to announce for a few more weeks. **Piers Morgan** was enraged by that announcement. Madonna's publicist **Liz Rosenberg** had told him the day before that her client was *not* pregnant, giving the scoop to his rival newspaper. Lauer got over it, Morgan most certainly did *not*.

Madonna reports that her pregnancy with **Lola** was easy until the last two weeks. She let herself eat whatever she wanted (but had no unusual cravings) and claimed, in 1996, that she had lost her relentless need to be in top physical shape. Obviously, that grew **back**. In September, her published "journal" of the event noted hemorrhoids and back pains. The pregnancy was tough enough that while she was going to give birth naturally while listening to the soundtrack from *The Moderns* (1988), the long-lasting labor convinced her otherwise.

Her pregnancy with **Rocco** was tough, too, and his birth complicated; Madonna swore that she would not get pregnant ever again and she stuck to her promise.

PRE-MADONNA: *Release date: June 10, 1997. Billboard 200 peak: NA.* Compilation of pre-**fame** recordings made by Madonna when she was first **working** with **Stephen Bray**, in the very early 1980s. Bray remixed them and released them under this title in the US and under the title *In the Beginning* (with a differently ordered track listing and missing the 1997 Extended Version of "Ain't No Big Deal") abroad. Madonna was *not* a **fan** of this venture.

PRE-MADONNA

① "Laugh to Keep from Crying" (Madonna)–3:50, produced by Stephen Bray

② "Crimes of Passion" (Madonna)–3:43, produced by Stephen Bray/ Tony Shepperd

③ "Ain't No Big Deal" 1997 Edit (Stephen Bray)– 4:00, Stephen Bray/ Tony Shepperd

④ "Everybody" 1997 Version (Madonna)–4:50, Stephen Bray/ Tony Shepperd

⑤ "Burning Up" (Madonna)–4:05, Stephen Bray

⑥ "Ain't No Big Deal" 1981 Version (Stephen Bray) –6:39, Stephen Bray

⑦ "Everybody" 1981 Version (Madonna)–4:49, Stephen Bray

⑧ "Stay" 1981 Version (Madonna)–4:21, Stephen Bray

⑨ "Don't You Know" (Madonna)–4:31, Stephen Bray

⑩ "Ain't No Big Deal" (1997 Extended Version)–6:39, Stephen Bray/ Tony Shepperd

PRESLEY, ELVIS: *January 8, 1935–August 16, 1977.* The undisputed King of Rock and Roll, a cute white dude from Tupelo, Mississippi, who popularized (and made semi-safe) black music for white audiences. His classic hits "Heartbreak Hotel" (1956), "Don't Be Cruel" (1956), "Hound **Dog**" (1956), "**Love** Me Tender" (1956), "All Shook Up" (1957) and dozens more—not to mention a reliably lucrative movie career—made him one of the most meaningful pop cultural figures of all time.

Madonna joked, "I love you, too, Elvis. Without Elvis, you are nothing," on the last night of her ***Blond Ambition World Tour*** in 1990 as a crew member in an Elvis shirt and carrying a gold Elvis bust (a good luck symbol from the tour) jumped off the stage at the end of the show.

Madonna and Presley are most often mentioned together every August 16—it's the anniversary of his **death**, and of her birth.

"PRETENDER": Easygoin' pop tune from *Like a Virgin* written by Madonna and **Stephen Bray** and produced by **Nile Rodgers**. The song, about a phony who breaks girls' hearts, presumably by cheating on them, has never been performed live. Interestingly, Madonna has admitted to being a serial **love** cheat herself in her younger years.

PRICE, STUART: *b. September 9, 1977.* British electronica guru whose '90s **work** as Jacques Lu Cont and Les Rhythmes Digitales in the '90s led to his work with producer **Mirwais**. Doing remixing with Mirwais on some *Music* songs led to his hiring as a tour guitarist, and then—suddenly—Madonna's musical director, a title he held for her ***Drowned World Tour***, ***Re-Invention World Tour*** and ***Confessions Tour***. Price, who got the call to join the *Drowned World Tour* from Mirwais at the very last second, inherited the musical director position when she fired his predecessor.

"I've always thought she's great to work with," Price said in 2002. "Good fun. Always a straight answer."

More good fun was had when Madonna cowrote "**X-Static Process**" with Price on *American Life*, a songwriting process she called a sort of "testing out the water." His most high-profile contribution to that era was his bombastic remix of "**Hollywood**," which was the version Madonna used on the **MTV Video Music Awards** when she played bridegroom to some former Mouseketeers.

Madonna collaborated with Price on what could be considered a comeback album, the nearly flawless ***Confessions on a Dance Floor***. Helping to craft her most consistent album since *Ray of Light*, Price had a writing credit on "Hung Up," "Get Together," "Sorry," "I Love New York," "Let It Will Be," "Forbidden Love," "Jump," "Isaac" and "Push." He produced all of the album's 12 songs, except for "Future Lovers" and "Like It or Not," though he had no writing or production credits on the era's two bonus tracks.

"I think she enjoys working with DJs because she recognizes the framework: a little songwriting naïveté mixed with a focus on the simple hook," Price reflected on his time on *Confessions* in 2015. "Madonna is all about making large, very digestible records. I think we were a good match musically."

Price remixed all of the *Confessions* singles plus "I Love **New York**" and "Let It Will Be," sometimes using his pseudonyms Thin White Duke, Man With **Guitar** and Paper Faces. He later remixed "**Miles Away.**"

Madonna told *Attitude* in 2005, on the occasion of the release of *Confessions on a **Dance** Floor*, "I'm very fond of him. I **love** his sensibility, I love his sense of humor, he has impeccable taste in music." Her fondness sparked rumors of an affair, with the British press camping out to spy on the pair whenever she paid him a visit at his one-bedroom apartment in Maida Vale, North West **London**.

Regardless of any romantic connection, during the *Confessions* era, Price was a near-constant figure in Madonna's posse, accompanying her on all her promo stops, including **Misshapes** and **The Roxy**.

Price was not a **fan** of the musical direction Madonna pursued with ***Hard Candy***, quitting the project and telling *Mixmag*, "This new record—Madonna wants to do an R&B record and it's a tough decision, but I don't think that's the right kind of record for her to make. I don't think I'm the right person to do it with her, either. She's worked with **Pharrell [Williams]** and **Timbaland** and I think Tim is great but Pharrell? I don't get it—he regurgitates the same crap again and again."

Regarding his apparently bad-blood break-up with Madonna, Price said, "You have to make the decision to stop being Madonna's music man and getting on with the rest of your life as well. For me, I'd rather have diversity and work with lots of people. Before I'd worked with Madonna, I'd already won **Grammys**. **William [Orbit]** and I aside, Madonna tends to take producers from obscurity and then they go **back** to obscurity. I'm one of the only people who have had things going on before and afterwards."

PRINCE: *June 7, 1958–April 21, 2016.* One of the defining forces of music of the '80s, a funk **god** as **talented** as he was offbeat. Always in character as an enigmatic enfant terrible, he launched his career in 1978 but hit his stride with his *1999* album, which offered radio-friendly singles like the title track (1982) and his opus "Little Red Corvette" (1983). Prince became a pop immortal with the release of his film *Purple Rain* (1984) and its soundtrack album, which offered **back**-to-back #1 hits. He continued to be a force throughout the '90s, and became a persnickety campaigner against the stranglehold record companies have over musicians during his contentious battles with **Warner Bros.** (Prince blamed some of the drama on label mate Madonna: "It was always about Madonna. She was getting paid, but at the same time we were selling more records and selling out concerts on multiple nights.") He has released his own material and gained a reputation as a litigious artist, threatening legal action against **YouTube**, eBay and other sites using his image and music. In spite of recording some beyond-suggestive music over the years, Prince became a devout Jehovah's Witness in 2001, inspiring darling Nikki to cancel all her **magazine** subscriptions.

Madonna was a big admirer of Prince's in the '80s and after meeting him backstage at the **American Music Awards** wound up dating the pint-sized pop star for two months in 1985. She attended one of his concerts just before embarking on *The Virgin Tour*, which definitely had a few Prince touches.

She would later describe him as reeking of lavender, like "Miss **Elizabeth Taylor**." Madonna told *Smash Hits* in 1987 that she could relate to Prince because he had "a chip on his shoulder, he's competitive, from the Midwest, a screwed-up home and he has something to prove."

Plans to cowrite a musical fizzled, but Prince visited Madonna after a performance of *Speed-the-Plow* and handed her some rough tapes of songs they'd recorded mostly via phone from opposite coasts. The result was **"Love Song,"** a funky little number on her *Like a Prayer* album, a disturbing and tense song with a pair of vocals that sometimes seems to be coming from the same mouth. The harmonizing is perfect and Madonna's performance is extremely embittered-sounding, complementing Prince's defiant apathy. Madonna played the keyboards herself, which she felt contributed to the song's appealing strangeness. They coproduced **"Act of Contrition,"** which Madonna sang and cowrote, and to which Prince lent some Jimi Hendrix–esque **guitar** work.

In 1990, a year after the phenomenal success of Prince's "Batdance" single from the *Batman* soundtrack, Madonna turned in a similarly meandering and catchy movie song, **"Now I'm Following You Part II."** She was directly inspired by Prince's song, sampling dialogue from *Dick Tracy* and using distorted vocals and instrumentation.

Madonna has attended Prince's concerts, and was photographed at his March 24, 1993, performance at **Radio City Music Hall**, where she chatted amiably with fellow spectator **Whitney Houston**. This in spite of the fact that Madonna only admires Prince's "older" stuff, which she considers "the real shit." She has said "When Doves Cry" (1984), as well as 1981's "Don't You Want Me" by the Human League, is among her favorite summer songs, a potent reminder of her early **NYC** years. Madonna loathes Prince's videos, which she branded "silly and cheap and below his ability."

Madonna has invoked Prince's name more than once as an excellent example of a sexist double standard: Prince was *man* who was doing virtually the same **sexually** explicit performing that Madonna was (and is) doing, and yet received little or no flak.

On July 9, 1999, Madonna and **Guy Oseary** sat with Prince and his wife Mayte, separated only by Donatella **Versace** at a dinner Versace held in Madonna's honor at

Johnny Depp's restaurant Le Man Ray (32 Rue Marbeuf, Paris, France), but otherwise, the two were on the outs for years. In 2007, at a **London** gig, Prince called out "I got so many hits, y'all can't handle me. I got more hits than Madonna's got kids."

Why the bad blood?

Maybe because Madonna had called Prince out in 1994 for refusing to eat during one of their long-ago dinner dates. "He was just sipping tea, very daintily. I have this theory about people who don't eat. They annoy me."

Based on her few encounters with Prince, Madonna described him as "very strange." Some may think that's the pot calling the kettle black, but in reality, Prince was strange and Madonna just does strange things.

Following her October 8, 2015, *Rebel Heart Tour* show, Madonna was among a handful of the lucky few who got to attend an intimate Prince set at Paisley Park, at which he sang, among other things, some of his recent work and his edgy hit "Sign o' the Times" (about the "skinny man who died of a big disease with a little name").

Following Prince's **death**, Madonna paid tribute to him at the **Billboard Music Awards** on May 22, 2016.

PRINCE CHARLES: SEE: **Charles, Prince of Wales.**

PRINCESS DIANA: SEE: **Diana, Princess of Wales.**

PRIVACY: Unlike the stars of the Golden Age of Hollywood, who hid shamelessly behind stainless-steel images and the **power** of their studios (until the less valuable ones were sold out to *Confidential* **magazine**), Madonna's private life is thoroughly vivisected by the press. Unlike many stars of today, who tremble at the appearance of any

GREGORY PACE

"Time to go visit the midget."—MADONNA TO A *PEOPLE* MAGAZINE REPORTER JUST BEFORE TAKING OFF FOR A MEETING WITH PRINCE (1985)

Don't you wish you'd attended Madonna's *Like a Virgin* release bash?

"I still have my sanity. I'm willing to sacrifice my private life if it will change people's point of view about life and the phobias they have."—MADONNA (1991)

invasion of their cherished privacy, Madonna moves about with an amazing degree of freedom in public despite the constant threat of being bogged down by clusters of **autograph** hounds and diehard **fans**.

Moreover, Madonna has been remarkably forthcoming about her personal history. She mentioned her **mother's** untimely **death** in her first interviews, has detailed her **first kiss,** first boyfriend and all of her personal opinions, has talked about such radically personal habits as picking her nose and, to **David Letterman,** peeing in the shower—the kinds of untidy realities that most non-stars wouldn't admit to their closest friends, much less announce to the planet. For Madonna, no matter how "private" the intricacies of her existence may seem, no amount of disclosure could ever reveal her true (or full) self.

She mined that vein to an extreme degree with *Truth or Dare*, about which she asserted that what's most revealing are the parts where she is *not* truthful. "Lies are telling," she claimed cryptically, leaving audiences and critics to paw through scenes of Madonna visiting and talking to her mother's grave, slurping soup completely sans makeup, flashing the camera while her **father** and **stepmother** await her patiently in the next room, fellating a bottle of Vichy water and being examined by a doctor. **Warren Beatty,** Madonna's reluctant costar, comments to the physician that Madonna doesn't see the point of existing off-camera, an oft-quoted observation that failed to see the **irony** in *Truth or Dare:* The star most devoured by the press was taking **control** of the situation, flaunting her unattractive attributes (as well as unguarded, appealing moments) in scenes that would leave her peers ripe for blackmail.

Madonna further tested the concept of privacy by publishing a **book** of written and visual erotica, *Sex,* which marked the first time a star published **sexually** explicit photos of herself. Madonna seemed to be saying, "I am public property right down to my short-and-curlies."

No wonder Kim Kardashian adores her.

And yet—with her overexposure, with the true invasions of her privacy, which include covert publication of personal medical documents, sneaky photos of her cavorting in the **nude** with **John Enos** and **Ingrid Casares,** illegal hacking of her computer, dissemination of private photos and publication of the contents of her **garbage,** as well as the self-invasions she has mounted in her **work**—Madonna is an enigma. We know nothing of the private Madonna because we only know what she's been willing to tell us.

One thing that helps: Madonna has all those around her sign privacy agreements, guaranteeing that the individual will not discuss his/her dealings with Madonna.

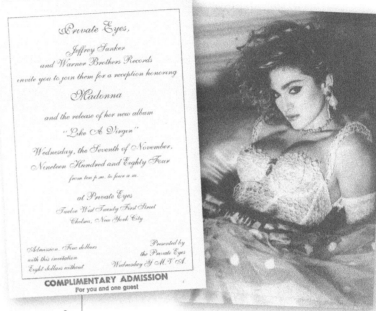

PRIVATE EYES: *Formerly 12 W. 21st, NY, NY.* Video club that Madonna frequented during her early days in **New York.** She was photographed there with **Jellybean Benitez** on July 17, 1984, and with **Grace Jones** that same year. On November 7, 1984, it was the site of the release party for *Like a Virgin.* It's where she had her first **date** with **Sean Penn** in 1985. Private **Eyes** was replaced by the Sound Factory, where Madonna first encountered **Jose & Luis.**

PRIZED POSSESSIONS: Madonna said in 1984 that her most prized possession was a photograph of her **mother** smiling and laughing when she was young.

A few years later, when asked what she'd rescue if her house were on fire, she said her Filofax, her **Frida Kahlo** painting and her **Lifecycle™.** One assumes her priorities have since shifted.

"PROMISE TO TRY": Affecting *Like a Prayer* ballad written and produced by Madonna and **Patrick Leonard** that directly addresses Madonna's feelings as a child when her **mother** passed away. The song is famous as the one played over images of Madonna visiting her mother's grave in *Truth or Dare.*

PROPOSAL: Madonna was never officially proposed to by **Sean Penn.** While she was jumping on the bed of their room at the "Something Inn" in Tennessee, she caught a look in his **eyes.** Reading his mind, she said, "Whatever you're thinking, I'll say yes to." They celebrated their engagement with jawbreakers from the 7-Eleven.

PROTEST: In spring 1989, over 200 high **school** students walked out of classes in Stamford, Connecticut, to protest the school library's decision to ban the ***Rolling Stone*** cover story that included photos of Madonna.

Pryce as Perón

PRYCE, JONATHAN: *b. June 1, 1947.* Madonna's Welsh *Evita* costar—he played Juan Perón and quipped that he had more suits than songs in the movie musical—said he grew to like Madonna a lot after getting past people's "preconceptions" about her. "She's a strong and dynamic force and I can only admire that."

PSA: Along with her involvement in **Rock the Vote**, Madonna had made a few other public service announcements.

In 1987, Madonna employed her "Nikki Finn" **voice** to implore holiday motorists, "Don't drive drunk!" in a radio spot.

The following year, the American Red Cross co-opted Madonna's "Material Girl" to seek some anti-materialist volunteers.

She next filmed a sobering **AIDS** PSA on December 1, 1988. Aimed at teens, "**Love** Won't Protect You" was done on behalf of Musicians For Life and the National AIDS Network. In the 30-second spot, a brunette Madonna said, "Many people think you can tell if someone has AIDS just by looking at them, but they're wrong. A person can have AIDS for a long time without showing any symptoms. So protect yourself. Not having **sex** is one way to avoid AIDS, staying away from people who shoot **drugs** is another. If you do have sex, use a **condom**—it may be the most important thing you ever do, because what you see may not be what you get. Help protect yourself against AIDS."

She also did a condom plug for Spanish radio in 1990, speaking Spanish. (Quick, what's the Spanish for, "Pass me the water-based lube"?)

Her funniest PSA was on behalf of Earth Summit, **MTV** and **VH1**, and was filmed in 1992 with crooner Seal. Made to raise awareness of global warming, Madonna, **blonde** and in a beret, **flirtatiously** cooed to her costar, "Seal ... I've got some globes you can warm." She ended with a little bathroom humor, urging viewers, "And tell President Bush to stop the gas."

PSY: *b. December 31, 1977.* Superstar Korean rapper (a.k.a. Park Jae-sang) whose "Gangnam Style" was one of the most ubiquitous hits of 2012, following the impact of its humorous, epic music video.

Psy joined Madonna on stage during *The MDNA Tour* for a mash-up of her song **"Give It 2 Me"** with "Gangnam Style." During the performance, Madonna rode Psy like a **horse** and put him away wet, flashed her red panties and straddled him when he dipped her in the end.

For some Madonna **fans**, this kind of association (with someone who in the US amounted to a novelty act) marked a low point in Madonna's career, a sign she was desperately trying to hitch her wagon to an of-the-moment sensation, to which it might be argued that Madonna was in the midst of an incredibly successful tour, has nothing to prove and ... can't a girl have a little fun every once in a while?

PUBLIC ENEMY: Influential hip-hop group whose albums *It Takes a Nation of Millions to Hold Us Back* (1988) and *Fear of a Black Planet* (1990) in particular set the standard for take-no-prisoners rap music that did not shy away from issues of **race**.

Madonna called them "my #1 favorite rap group" and listed them among her **heroes** as she defended herself against charges that she'd (via Lenny Kravitz) lifted the bass line from their "Security of the First World" (1988) for **"Justify My Love."** Public Enemy never sued, although it can't have endeared Madonna to them when she challenged any rapper to gripe about sampling, pointing out that rap is largely composed of found material refashioned into something new and fresh.

Who says Madonna has no sense of humor?

MATTHEW RETTENMUND

It was, however, noted in a *Vanity Fair* interview months earlier that one of the cassettes on display in Madonna's living room was the same Public Enemy album from which the bass line was supposedly lifted.

In 2015, when Madonna had her **Brit Awards** accident, Public Enemy's Chuck D tweeted: "Madonna has done thousands of flawless difficult performances thus easy to look at this rarity as news, good shes safe."

PURIM: Madonna enjoys the tradition of dressing up for this Jewish holiday that celebrates the deliverance of the Jews in the Persian Empire from certain **death**. Some of her most memorable costumes have included a **nun** (2005), a flapper (2007), Edith Piaf (2008) and her own daughter, **Lola** (2009).

Madonna loves her Pussy Riot best, and said so at this 2014 Amnesty International event in Brooklyn.

"PUSH": The penultimate song on *Confessions on a Dance Floor*, written and produced by Madonna and **Stuart Price**. It is one of the only tracks on the album that Madonna has never performed live.

PUSSY: Ever the unconventional example of **feminism**, Madonna's definition of pussy circa 1991 was "wimp."

PUSSY RIOT: Punk-protest group based in **Russia**, with a fluid membership of young women united in their **feminism** and in their disapproval of the Russian Orthodox Church and Russian President Vladimir Putin. When members performed at Cathedral of Christ the Savior (ulitsa Volkhonka, 15, Moscow, Russia) in 2012, three members were arrested, charged and convicted of inciting religious hatred. They were sentenced to two years.

Madonna and many other figures outside of Russia advocated on behalf of the imprisoned group. To show her support, Madonna stripped during her *MDNA Tour* on several occasions to reveal "**PUSSY** RIOT" or "FREE PUSSY RIOT" on her **back** or across the undersides of her arms.

On February 5, 2014, Madonna appeared in person at Amnesty International's Bringing Human Rights Home concert at Barclays Center (620 Atlantic Ave., Brooklyn, NY) to support the women. In her speech, she said:

"What I realized when I went to Russia and saw what was going on with Pussy Riot and this trial, and with the **gay** community, was how lucky I was and am to live in a country where I can speak my mind, where I can—yes—I know, America's not perfect, it's true, but I can speak my mind, I can criticize the government, I can speak out against religious fundamentalists, okay? And I don't have to fear being thrown in jail ... not yet, anyway. I do not take this freedom for granted and neither should you, okay? So the two members of Pussy Riot that I am about to introduce do not have this right in the country they come from, they do not share this freedom with me, so they must be commended for their courage and for their fearlessness. Yay. That would be a yay. You can do better than that. They must be commended!" Describing it as a privilege and an honor, she introduced two members of Pussy Riot (Maria Alyokhina and Nadezhda Tolokonnikova) to the crowd, who thanked Madonna for her support in their native tongue.

The women were immediately kicked out of Pussy Riot by the other members, who reaffirmed themselves as female separatists who do not agree with the fact that tickets were sold to the **charity** event. "We never accept **money** for our performances ... we only stage illegal performances in unexpected places."

The reaction wasn't too surprising; during an interview on Irish **TV**, the two women who Madonna introduced had earlier scoffed at her claim to be a fellow freedom fighter.

MARK DOCTROW

©GEORGE-DUBOSE.COM

QSOUND: Later renamed Q1, this 3D sound-processing algorithm was introduced on *The Immaculate Collection* and used on several dozen other 1990s albums by other artists, but never took off.

QUEEN ELIZABETH/QUEEN OF ENGLAND: SEE: **Elizabeth II, Queen.**

QUEEN OF POP: The title is a lifetime-and-beyond appointment, and it belongs to Madonna. Accept no arguments to the contrary. **Michael Jackson** is, of course, the King of Pop, and in the years leading up to his **death**, no one was arguing that he lose his title even though he'd had only one Top 10 hit in the US in a decade. Deeming him the King of Pop and Madonna the Queen of Pop does not mean they were the most or only **talented** people of their

This old thing?

respective genders to make pop music, nor does it mean either were the #1 top-selling or best artists every year of their careers. But it's ridiculous to argue that either has not earned their titles for their overall achievements, influence and impact.

In 2015, Madonna told *Rolling Stone*, "Well, I do think of myself as a queen, but I don't think I'm the only queen. There's room for other queens. We reign over different kingdoms."

"QUEEN'S ENGLISH": House of Xtravaganza **dancers** Jose Gutierez and Luis Camacho (**Jose & Luis**), Madonna's **"Vogue"**-ing partners on her *Blond Ambition World Tour*, cooked up this hilariously haughty dance single with Junior Vasquez and Merv de Peyer, enticing Madonna into singing the hook, "Queens that read are the best." The song is sometimes referred to as being **unreleased**, but it appeared on a compilation called *New Faces* and had a proper single release in 1993. A simple music video shows the guys hanging out in their neighborhood buying clothes, dancing and posing fiercely as a **Queen of England** stand-in lip-synchs Madonna's part.

QUEERDONNA: Literally one of the world's biggest Madonna **fans** of all time, 300-pound Greg Gostanian (a.k.a. Greg Tanian) turned his lifelong obsession into dual careers as a paparazzo—he made good **money** on shots he captured of Madonna—and as a Madonna **tribute artist**. Like a baby Divine, he was not shy, once claiming his act was "going over the edge [Madonna] doesn't dare go over."

In spite of wearing Madonna-inspired duds on stage, Gostanian identified as a guy. "I'm an actor and Queerdonna is my character." But he wasn't a **boring** guy, telling the original *EM*, "There are usually three types of **sexuality**: straight, **gay** or **bi**. I'm *tri*. I'm very open-minded."

Gostanian may have shared Madonna's outlook on sex, but one thing they did *not* share was a mutual affection. Things started well. He met her when he "cried [his] way in" to her *Who's That Girl* movie premiere in 1987, after which she sent him a T-shirt with the note, "Wear this shirt to bed at night—then tell everyone I slept with you!" But soon after, Madonna tired of being stalked by him, eventually demanding to know what he wanted one day outside her **Central Park West** apartment. Gostanian said all he wanted was a posed photo with her. She acquiesced, but another run-in occurred at the 1991 *Truth or Dare* premiere when Madonna noticed Gostanian (out of **drag**) was in attendance. **Joan Rivers** said on her show that Madonna had been angry to bump into Queerdonna, but he clarified, "If I'd been in costume, I would have stolen that show, I just know it. Every flashbulb in the place would have been on *me*."

Thanks to his penchant for going topless (he had a bigger cup size than his idol), Queerdonna's appearances at **New York**–area clubs were definitely flashbulb-bait.

MATTHEW RETTENMUND

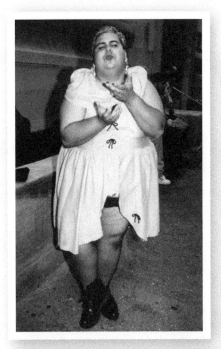

R.I.P.
QUEERDONNA!

UPPER LEFT BY LAVINEL SAVU. OTHERS COURTESY OF NICK MENDOROS.

"... Madonna's music said something to me: 'There's a lot to life, have fun, enjoy.'" —GREG GOSTANIAN A.K.A. QUEERDONNA (1991)

After doing well in his hometown, he got hired out across the country, most spectacularly at party promoter Chip Duckett's "Everything Old Is New York Again" bash at Ka-BOOM! (formerly 747 N. Green, Chicago, IL) on August 11, 1991, at which he lip-synched Madonna's hit **"Vogue"** and engaged in "tag-team spanking with a **nun**." He also made a memorable final appearance as Queerdonna at Maddyfest, held August 7, 1999, in NYC by All Access Fan Club, where he lip-synched **"Nothing Really Matters,"** **"Beautiful Stranger"** and **"Skin."** Having grown out of following Madonna everywhere, he told *The Richard Show*, "You've gotta be who you are in the end ... But what's next?"

Gostanian's **weight** had given him the opportunity to attract the attention he craved, but as it escalated, it also caused serious problems. At 468 pounds, he sued United Airlines for $400 million after the carrier's agents allegedly embarrassed him on a flight to San Francisco in a confrontation over his obesity. He claimed the run-in caused him to lose enthusiasm for his career and to gain another 85 pounds. Sadly, complications following gastric bypass surgery ended his life in September 2000. United reportedly settled with his family after his **death**.

Queerdonna can be glimpsed in the documentaries *Blast 'Em* and *Madonna: The Name of the Game*.

QUINN, TOMMY: This **NYC**-based studio musician said he dated Madonna **back** in 1984. Quinn told biographer **J. Randy Taraborrelli**, "Of course, she was brash and—oh, man!—she could be a royal **bitch**. But beneath it, if you really got to know her, she was a different kind of person, a very insecure girl." Quinn claims to have counseled Madonna on how to react to her **nude** photo scandal in 1985, remembering the episode as rattling her far more than she let on publicly.

RICHARD CORMAN

Parade

−DAVID FRANK

RACE: Before her face became one of the most recognizable on the planet, Madonna's early music led DJs and **fans** to believe she was black. This unusual confusion was an effective (if unintentional) bait-and-switch that earned Madonna a large black following, especially for her first two albums, which did well on the R&B (or, as they were then called, "black music") charts.

Madonna producer **Reggie Lucas** said in 2013, "If you can believe it, **Warner** Brothers had very limited interest in Madonna when she was first signed. You know what they thought? They said that Madonna is this new white artist that wants to sing black—so what they did was send her to the black radio stations when her first record came out, and that's how they promoted her at first. They just treated her as a black artist. I guess they kind of envisioned her as Teena Marie."

Madonna has always been organically attracted to black culture, possibly pining for the racially mixed neighborhood of her first home in **Pontiac**, or rebelling against the staid, repressed culture of all-white **Rochester Hills**. Like **Elvis Presley** before her, from the beginning, Madonna dealt with criticism that she was stealing a black sound.

"... [A]ll the black girls in my neighborhood had these **dances** in their yard where they had these little turntables with 45 records and they'd play all this Motown stuff and they would dance, just dance, all of them dancing together and none of the white kids I knew would ever do that ... I had to be beaten up so many times by these little black girls before they would accept me and finally one day they whipped me with a rubber hose till I was like, lying on the ground crying. And then they just stopped doing it all of a sudden and let me be their friend, part of their group," she told *Island* in 1983.

Her use of black sounds led to some criticism.

"It's not like I'm ripping them off," she said to *The Face* in its September 1983 issue. "Some of these new white producers are just scientists in a laboratory, making something they know all the little kids in the ghetto will want to buy. I'm at least sincere. I don't feel guilty about not being black."

Madonna's attraction to other racial perspectives pops up in early videos like **"Borderline"** and **"Lucky Star,"** which have an urban feel absent from some ensuing clips, at least until the racially-charged **"Like a Prayer"** video.

"Made to serve as supportive backdrop for Madonna's drama, black characters in 'Like a Prayer' remind me of those early Hollywood depictions of singing black slaves in the great plantation movies or those Shirley Temple films where Bojangles was trotted out to dance with Miss Shirley and spice up her act ... Madonna is a modern-day Shirley Temple," bell hooks infamously wrote in 1992.

Madonna's next formal comment on race was the song **"Vogue,"** which managed to deify the pristine images of white movie stars while celebrating the black, **gay** tradition of **vogueing**. Key lyric: "It doesn't matter if you're black or white," a sentiment she sold in the marketplace a year before her contemporary, **Michael Jackson**. The "Vogue"

video featured beautifully photographed black, Hispanic, Asian and white women and men who were not recruited to send a visual message, but who had been hired organically to accompany her on her *Blond Ambition World Tour*.

Madonna's **"Secret"** video is one of her most racially diverse, reflecting her bond with Hispanic culture. When obsessed with geishas, Madonna created her **"Nothing Really Matters"** video and posed for *Harper's Bazaar*.

Madonna's incorporation of black and other non-white sensibilities into her **work** is unmistakable. Her infrequent artistic comments on race are all the more gripping for her whiteness—white pop stars do not generally broach the subject.

Over time, Madonna's curiosity in the field of different cultures and races has become cynically chalked up to **cultural appropriation**, but there *are* other explanations, such as genuine kinship and appreciation.

There are some observers who have praised Madonna for working outside the box of her whiteness. J. Victoria Sanders wrote in *Madonna & Me: Women Writers on the Queen of Pop* (2012), "These days, the list of black women artists who have Madonna-esque elements is long: Lil' Kim, Eve, and **Nicki Minaj** are just a few who embody the essence of her swagger. As a white artist who was unafraid to express her affinity for black culture in time before it was cool, Madonna set the stage for a new generation of women—celebrities and regular folks alike—to express themselves outside of racial classifications."

Attempting to explain her outlook on race, Madonna told *Spin* (1996): "I've always in this naïve way identified with other minorities because I'm in a minority. You think that somehow unifies you in some philosophical way. But ultimately it doesn't." But she has controversially stated many times that gender, in her experience, trumps race. "... I've found that being a strong female is actually more frightening to the black men that I've dated. It took me a really long time to accept that."

"A white Deniece Williams we don't need."
—DAVE MARSH ON MADONNA (1985)

RADIO CITY MUSIC HALL: *1260 Ave. of the Americas, NY, NY.* Madonna first played this venerable Manhattan venue the night of the 1st Annual **MTV Video Music Awards**, where she made pop history by rolling around the stage in her **"Like a Virgin"** white **wedding** dress. On her own, she headlined here the following June for three nights in a row on *The Virgin Tour*. She barely had time to absorb it—she immediately went into a two-night stand at the even more important **Madison Square Garden**.

Madonna, at her most Miley in 1992

LAVINEL SAVU

She has only ever appeared at Radio City since 1985 at non-Madonna events. For example, it's the place where she fended off **Courtney Love**, kissed **Britney Spears** and eulogized **Michael Jackson**, all at **MTV** Video Music **Awards** ceremonies.

"RAIN" (SONG): *Release date: July 17, 1993. Billboard Hot 100 peak: #14.* Tranquil, Wilson Phillips–y ballad from *Erotica* that became the album's fourth and final US single release. A favorite among **fans,** the song received Top 10–status airplay but never rose above a respectable #14—sales during a peak period of Madonna overload failed to catch up to the song's radio-friendly quality. "Rain" is a simple **love** song (written and produced by Madonna and **Shep Pettibone**) with elegantly layered vocals and, on the album version, an inventive, overlapping vocal rap that makes it a standout production.

Madonna apparently wrote the song specifically for an **Alek Keshishian** musical version of the classic film *Wuthering Heights* (1939).

She has only performed the song live on *The Girlie Show World Tour*. It was included in a video interlude on her *Sticky & Sweet Tour*, in which it was mashed-up with the Eurythmics song "Here Comes the Rain Again" (1984).

"RAIN" (VIDEO): *Director: Mark Romanek, 1993.* Premiering on MTV on June 21, 1993, this visually lush, futuristic video was shot on **black-and-white** stock and hand-colored with appealingly icy blue tones, including memorable close-ups of Madonna (in a short black wig) singing into an old-fashioned mic, her **eyes** a brilliant sapphire.

The setting of the video is a sweeping, antiseptic studio full of Japanese technicians and enormous blow-ups of Madonna's face on curved screens. The conceit is that we are seeing behind the scenes of the actual filming, with multimedia artist Ryuichi Sakamoto posing as the director. **Famed** film directors Jean-Luc Godard and **Federico Fellini** had been approached to play the role before Sakamoto, but both had passed, though Fellini, who was ailing, took care to reply to Madonna personally.

It's a video masterpiece about **art** and artifice, and was Madonna's first of two videos (the other being **"Bedtime Story"**) directed by **Mark Romanek**. Romanek had expressed that he wanted to make a clip that was devoid of **nostalgia.** Instead, the video creates a modern enigma out of a woman who is no stranger to overexposure. He said he was inspired by a **Jean-Baptiste Mondino** commercial starring Catherine Deneuve.

In the video, Madonna is seen reclining on a riveted-aluminum chaise lounge, known as the Lockheed Lounge. Designed by Marc Newson, it was created in an edition of 10, there were four artist's proofs, one prototype and one earlier version. One example from the edition of 10 sold for over $2 million at **auction** in 2015.

The video won two **MTV Video Music Awards**, for Best Art Direction and Best Cinematography.

"RAINBOW HIGH": One of Madonna's best songs from *Evita*, found on *Evita: The Complete Motion Picture Music Soundtrack.* In the song, Madonna as Evita sings dictatorially of her determination to be shining like Illuminati for her tour of Europe. The song is dying to be done as a medley with **"Dress You Up,"** with its arch command by Evita to "Christian Dior me/From my head to my toes." This is the second song Madonna has sung in which Lauren Bacall was name-checked, the first being **"Vogue."**

"RAINBOW TOUR": Following the sartorial ecstasy of "Rainbow High" on *Evita: The Complete Motion Picture Music Soundtrack* is this massive come-down, a song sung by **Antonio Banderas**, Gary Brooker and Peter Polycarpou, in which Evita's successes and embarrassing stumbles on her troubled Rainbow Tour of Europe are recounted.

RAISING MALAWI: Madonna's non-profit org founded in 2006 to bring poverty relief to the orphans of **Malawi** through supporting community-based local groups. The **charity** has been dogged by problems, including criticism over its association with **Kabbalah** and the embarrassing collapse of a project to build a girls' academy. Madonna even attended a groundbreaking ceremony in Malawi on October 26, 2009. The academy was abandoned in a swirl of financial questions, culminating in the resignation of its proposed headmistress. Ever determined, Madonna came **back** with a new proposal in 2012, and by year's end, 10 **schools** had been built, a big success of the variety the cynical media tends to overlook.

Madonna cohosted with Gucci an event for the US Fund for **UNICEF** and Raising Malawi on February 6, 2008, at the United Nations, with such famous guests as Drew Barrymore, Orlando Bloom, Sean Combs, **Tom Cruise** and Katie Holmes, Kate Hudson, **Jennifer Lopez** and Marc Anthony, **Demi Moore** and Ashton Kutcher, **Rosie O'Donnell**, **Gwyneth Paltrow**, **Gwen Stefani** and many more.

Find out more about Raising Malawi at RaisingMalawi.org.

RAPE: Madonna has related that she was sexually **assaulted** in **NYC** in 1978. She told the story of her rape at knifepoint to a college confidante, photographer **Linda Alaniz**, at the time it happened. Though later misreported as a "date rape," Madonna was actually forced to perform oral **sex** by a stranger.

"The first year, I was … raped on the roof of a building I was dragged up to with a knife in my **back**," she told *Harper's Bazaar* in 2013. She elaborated on the nightmare to **Howard Stern:** "I was going to a **dance** class and the door was locked and I needed **money** for a pay phone. [This guy] gave it to me, he was a very friendly guy. I trusted everybody." He persuaded her to make the call from his apartment across the street instead, where she was assaulted. She never reported it to the police, saying that at 19, she already felt too violated. She has said she consciously decided not the let the rape make her feel like a victim.

In the '80s, rape came out of the closet as a common crime against women. One of the most explosive complicating factors of rape became the issue of "willingness," sometimes judged by the victim's apparel. Sexual availability, as first read from her provocative outfits, is a cornerstone of the Madonna myth. She popularized the street-urchin look—featuring visible bras, lace and heavy makeup. From then, Madonna has regularly appeared in sexually suggestive outfits and costumes: see-through negligées, form-fitting bodysuits, **cone bras,** the works.

Madonna has been perceived as, and called, a slut, and her influence on popular **fashion** often has been attacked for encouraging sexual promiscuity ... the undertone being that Madonna's sexy gear provokes the male sexual beast. (Overlooking the fact that the male sexual beast goes ape for anything with a heartbeat, regardless of something as superficial as *clothing*.) A reader's letter in the *New York Post* in 1992 accused Madonna of "bringing out the worst in men." Madonna's response to such criticism has always been a defiant reminder that everyone is free to dress as he or she pleases, although this is less a statement against blaming the victim than a steadfast urge for individual rights.

Rape has popped up only rarely in Madonna's **work.**

On film, Madonna's character in *A Certain Sacrifice* is savagely raped in the bathroom of a diner, temptress "Rebecca Carlson" is sodomized against her will (at first) in *Body of Evidence* and Madonna's "Sarah Jennings" is raped in *Dangerous Game*, scenes that Madonna plays with frightening realism.

There is a stunning **Herb Ritts** photograph of Madonna and **Tony Ward** in a 1991 issue of the Italian **magazine** *Moda* that portrays Madonna turning her head angrily away from Ward's firm sexual embrace. It suggests rape, or at least suggests the line between "Don't! Stop!" and "Don't stop!"

More shockingly, Madonna included a rape fantasy photo in *Sex*, appearing as a **Catholic** schoolgirl grinning broadly as two skinheads held her down and reached up her skirt. The photo was one of the most controversial in the **book.**

In *Truth or Dare*, where life and **art** were forcibly mixed, Madonna's chief makeup artist Sharon "Mama Makeup" Gault tells the backup singers that after a drunken night at a **disco** she woke up to find her anus bleeding, worrying that some men she'd met the night before had **drugged** and sodomized her. When Madonna is informed, the camera is there to capture her instant response: a guilty snicker, followed by fear that the makeup artist was singled out by the men because she was Madonna's employee; even Madonna is leery of the potentially negative **power** of her persona.

RAY OF LIGHT (1-13)

RAY OF LIGHT
Japan (1-14)

① "Drowned World/ Substitute for Love" (Madonna/William Orbit/ Rod McKuen/Anita Kerr/ David Collins)-5:09, produced by Madonna/ William Orbit

② "Swim" (Madonna/William Orbit) -5:00, produced by Madonna/William Orbit

③ "Ray of Light" (Madonna/William Orbit/ Clive Muldoon/Dave Curtiss/Christine Leach)-5:21, produced by Madonna/William Orbit

④ "Candy Perfume Girl" (Madonna/William Orbit/ Susannah Melvoin)-4:34, produced by Madonna/ William Orbit

⑤ "Skin" (Madonna/Patrick Leonard) -6:22, produced by Madonna/William Orbit/ Marius de Vries

⑥ "Nothing Really Matters" (Madonna/Patrick Leonard) -4:27, produced by Madonna/William Orbit/ Marius de Vries

⑦ "Sky Fits Heaven" (Madonna/Patrick Leonard) -4:48, produced by Madonna/William Orbit/ Patrick Leonard

⑧ "Shanti/Ashtangi" (Madonna/William Orbit) -4:29, produced by Madonna/William Orbit

⑨ "Frozen" (Madonna/Patrick Leonard) -6:12, produced by Madonna/William Orbit/ Patrick Leonard

⑩ "The Power of Good-Bye" (Madonna/Rick Nowels) -4:10, produced by Madonna/William Orbit/ Patrick Leonard

⑪ "To Have and Not to Hold" (Madonna/Rick Nowels) -5:23, produced by Madonna/William Orbit/ Patrick Leonard

⑫ "Little Star" (Madonna/Rick Nowels) -5:18, produced by Madonna/Marius de Vries

⑬ "Mer Girl" (Madonna/William Orbit) -5:32, produced by Madonna/William Orbit

⑭ "Has to Be" (Madonna/William Orbit/ Patrick Leonard)-5:15, produced by Madonna/ William Orbit

---

RAY OF LIGHT (ALBUM): *Release date: March 3, 1998. Billboard 200 peak: #2.* Following the soft performance of *Erotica* and having done a little damage **control** with *Bedtime Stories*, Madonna experienced a major rebranding when she starred in the film *Evita*. During this time, the public saw Madonna in new ways, and Madonna saw *herself* in new ways; not because of the film, but thanks to becoming a **mother** and to her study of **Kabbalah.**

"I don't consciously think, 'Oh, I have to change,'" she told *TV Hits* of where this rebirth took her music. "Hopefully, my music has always been a reflection of where I am, and where I am now is different from where I was when I made my last record."

In a more introspective headspace, she set out to create an album that would express her (new) self, and the market was eager to hear it—the timing couldn't have been better.

As sure as Madonna was that she wanted to say something different, she wasn't as sure how to get there. She approached Tricky, Goldie and Prodigy—none were interested.

"... Madonna has succeeded where all of her pop peers have failed: She's made not just street-smart disco, but smart pop."
—GREG KOT, *CHICAGO TRIBUNE* (1998)

"[I]f ever her future as the reigning queen of pop had been questioned, this album should squelch those thoughts for a long time to come."—JEFFREY L. NEWMAN, *HX* (1998)

She then **worked** with **Babyface**, **Rick Nowels** and **Patrick Leonard**, beginning in spring 1997, but she had reservations about all three; she never used her work with Babyface, although she did use several of the songs she wrote with the other two. But these sessions failed to suggest an overarching path for the new album. It wasn't until **Guy Oseary**, her future manager and then the **Maverick** CEO, suggested **William Orbit** that Madonna found her man. They were on the same page. She felt the sound was right, and she liked the idea of making electronica that had substantial lyrics.

Ultimately, Orbit coproduced all the tracks on the album (including a Japanese bonus track) except for one. He also had a writing credit on six of the tracks (seven, including **"Has to Be"**).

Recorded over four months (then considered a long stretch; who could've foreseen the never-ending *Rebel Heart* process?), *Ray of Light* emerged a thoughtful, emotionally deep, sonically adventurous and yet still consistent, even seamless, work of **art**.

It took her a while because "… I always had plans, because I'm the organized person in the group but oftentimes I'd get to the end of the day and we wouldn't really have accomplished much, but we'd get sort of, like, we'd get textures, we'd just get some *textures* for a song," Madonna said. "… I'm really super productive and I've gotta have something done every day and at the end of the day, I want to have a song written."

Orbit has described the sessions as leisurely and intimate, an assertion bolstered by **Kurt Loder**'s **MTV** studio visit, which showed few personnel and a centered Madonna.

The album begins with the **regretful**, creative-palate cleanser **"Drowned World/Substitute for Love,"** the first vocal heard being *not* Madonna's **voice**, but a sample of the words "you see" from the song "Why I Follow the Tigers" (1969) by the San Sebastian Strings, written by poet Rod McKuen. Against an eerily calm synth web, Madonna sings of trading **fame** for **love** (or vice versa?), effectively denouncing her past public persona and putting her **fans** on notice: The Material Girl was now the Earth Mother. Madonna's voice reflects her *Evita* vocal training.

Like the wide-open sea, **"Swim"** is expansive. Madonna's **"Secret"**-like humming is like an oceanic tide, but her deliberate vocal delivers startling lyrics about "children killing children." The song feels like a worry for one's self via a worry of the world at large. Madonna could've been speaking of this song when she told *The New York* Times of the album, "There are still a lot of people who are really uncomfortable with these topics, and they're going to go, 'We liked her better when she was hitchhiking naked in **Miami**. Where's the fun Madonna?'" News broke of the murder of Gianni **Versace** as Madonna was recording the song, but she pressed on, using it to inform her performance.

After two blissed-out sounding tracks, the album abruptly reannounces itself with its defining statement of purpose, the brainy **disco** song **"Ray of Light,"** which expresses Madonna's personal revolution with urgency that

slips into giddiness. Madonna's slide into opera-light scales and her atonal wail make the song a risk, and make its total success all the more joyous. It's a deliverance, this song.

Back to rock (with Orbit surprising himself by playing a mean **guitar**), **"Candy Perfume Girl"** has a slithering quality, playing with the slipperiness of pretty words like Madonna's licking them and sticking them together temporarily to hear how they sound. It ascends into a forest of guitar licks befitting a future **Rock and Roll Hall of Famer**.

The middle of the album is (with one break) a Patrick Leonard suite.

It's a testament to Madonna and Orbit's production that the first song cowritten with Leonard, **"Skin,"** fits right in with what's come before. With its Middle Eastern sweep and its nakedly desirous (not in a **sexual** way) lyrics, "Skin" is the album's most desperate plea, and its most lyrically vulnerable.

The album's most traditional pop song, **"Nothing Really Matters,"** is nonetheless a continuation of the album's embrace of the spiritual. It is also a pure Kabbalistic sentiment, to reject the import of everyday occurrences.

"Sky Fits Heaven" quickens the pace again, beginning with a throbbing bass line and electronic flourishes (did that comet almost hit me?) as Madonna sings pearls of wisdom that avoid cliché and instead offer a lyrically fresh perspective on how best to see one's life journey.

"Shanti/Ashtangi"—with its Bollywood "ah-ah-ah" and Madonna singing a **yoga** chant in Sanskrit—must rank as one of the most potentially esoteric things she ever recorded, yet in the same way yoga provides focus for so many people, the song has become a standout track for many. It's so hypnotic.

Unusually, the album's lead single is buried on the album, but as one of her finest creations, **"Frozen"** was bound to shine even as track #9. **Warner Bros.** was scared to **death** to release the song, which opens with panoramic gloom before dissolving into an Indian-inspired love song. In **"Open Your Heart,"** Madonna sang coyly of lock and key. Here, the key she refers to unlocks no double entendre; what you hear is what you get.

Following beautifully from that lesson about frozen hearts, the **Rick Nowels** suite of songs begins with **"The Power of Good-Bye,"** a sumptuous breakup song. It urges us to love our path, even when there is pain along the way.

Almost a reapproaching of the same theme, **"To Have and Not to Hold"** is another song about accepting inevitability.

"Little Star" is Madonna's female-empowerment lullaby for her daughter, **Lola**, a song that shimmers with pride in one's self as a mother and in one's offspring.

The album's final track (except in Japan) is the lurching, soul-baring **"Mer Girl,"** Madonna work that most directly addresses the loss of her mother.

The Japanese market received "Has to Be" as a bonus track. For once, the bonus was substantial. The Orbit cocreation seems to extend the album's thirst for knowledge (and thirst for imparting it), ruminating on the probability that there is a mate for every lonely soul out there. It is probably the most erotic touch on the album, and as such it sticks out—*Ray of Light* is Madonna at her least horny. Instead, she's sexually satiated, but hungry for truth.

Madonna said it best herself, to **Billboard**: "This record takes me back to where I started—in a club right in the middle of a **dance** floor. It's full circle, except I'm so different now. I've been transformed, and that's fully reflected in my music."

As Orbit said in 2015, the album is timeless: "I'm very proud of my work on that record—I think it still holds up today."

With help from "Frozen," a Top 2 smash, the album sold 371,000 in its opening frame and went on to sell over 16 million copies worldwide, held from #1 in the US only because of the *Titanic* soundtrack (1997) phenomenon.

Its cover was shot by **Mario Testino**.

Madonna actually changed the album's title five times, and came tantalizingly close to releasing a full remix album called **Veronica** *Electronica*.

••

"[WILLIAM] ORBIT DESERVES CREDIT FOR THE SHEER ARTISTRY OF SOUND ON THIS ALBUM. BUT THERE'S AN ART TO MADONNA'S VISION AS WELL. SHE'S AN INSPIRED NAVIGATOR AND CUTS A TANTALIZING PATH THROUGH HER NEWFOUND SPIRITUALISM, DANCE-CLUB ROOTS, AND ELECTRONIC SOUNDSCAPE."

–JOAN ANDERMAN, *BOSTON GLOBE* (1998)

••

"WHAT MAKES MADONNA'S RENEWED INTEREST IN THE POSITIVE FEEL SO REAL IS A BOTTOMLESS SADNESS THAT MAKES ITS PRESENCE KNOWN ON NEARLY EVERY CUT."

–BARRY WALTERS, *THE ADVOCATE* (1998)

••

"NOT ONLY IS *RAY OF LIGHT* AN OBJECT LESSON IN IMAGE RESUSCITATION, IT ALSO HAS THE POTENTIAL TO BE A LIFE-CHANGING RECORD."

–JONATHAN BERNSTEIN, *THE NEW YORK OBSERVER* (1998)

••

"SHE HASN'T REGAINED HER GENIUS FOR THE CRASS, LINEAR POP HOOK, AND THE '80S MADONNA OF HIGH-ENERGY BEATS AND WISE-ASS BRAVADO IS GONE FOREVER—THAT SHOW IS OVER, SAY GOOD-BYE. INSTEAD, *RAY OF LIGHT* SUMS UP THE BEST WE CAN EXPECT FROM MADONNA AT THIS LATE DATE: OVERLY ARTY, OCCASIONALLY CATCHY, CONFUSED, SECONDHAND, INFURIATING AND GREAT FUN IN SPITE OF HERSELF …"

–ROB SHEFFIELD, *ROLLING STONE* (1998)

••

"RAY OF LIGHT" (SONG): *Release date: May 6, 1998. Billboard Hot 100 peak: #5.* From the album **Ray of Light**, this quickly became one of Madonna's signature songs and a personal statement of freedom. "Ray of Light" rocks thanks to Madonna's unbridled howl toward the end. It's like scream therapy in a **disco**.

The song was created in an interesting way, starting life as a 1971 song called "Sepheryn" by the duo Curtiss Maldoon, then getting a modern rewrite by group member Clive Maldoon's niece, Christine Leach. Leach, a collaborator of **William Orbit**'s, let him bat it around with Madonna, which led to Madonna paring it way down and changing the song substantially—and for the better. The song's other original composer, Dave Curtiss, was suitably impressed by the new creation, and everyone got credit: Madonna and Orbit, Leach, her uncle Maldoon and Curtiss.

Madonna has performed "Ray of Light" live many times, including one of her best-ever live vocals and one of her worst.

The song's first live performance was heard (kinda … it was noisy) by only 2,000 people—she closed her exclusive set at **The Roxy** in 1998 with the song as the crowd of **fans** screamed their heads off.

Her first televised performance of "Ray of Light" was for *The* **Oprah Winfrey** *Show*, a simple take that Madonna sang live with reverb, perfectly capturing the tricky song and charmingly breaking into laughter during her shout of joy toward the end. When she tried it again at the **MTV Video Music Awards**, she got very winded and couldn't sustain almost any notes. Even a **sexy** assist from Lenny Kravitz couldn't distract from the train wreck. It's best forgotten.

She has included the song, which won the **Grammy** for Best **Dance** Recording, on her *Drowned World Tour*, *Confessions Tour* and *Sticky & Sweet Tour*. It had its largest audiences yet when she rocked it at both **Live 8** and **Live Earth**.

In 1999, "Ray of Light" became a rare Madonna song that was licensed for **commercial** use, specifically to advertise AT&T's Personal Network. **Pepsi** who? "The song is about communication and modern technology, so I think it's the perfect combination," Madonna said at the time. The song has continued speaking to the world as one of her most popular and meaningful **works**.

"The song is … about kind of being in wonderment of the world around you and seeing the world for the first time … looking at the world finally with your eyes open and seeing how big the universe is and seeing how small I am in the universe."-MADONNA (1998)

"RAY OF LIGHT" (VIDEO): *Director: Jonas Åkerlund, 1998.* One of Madonna's most critically acclaimed videos was her first with **Jonas Åkerlund**. In what became her longest-ever video shoot (she wasn't needed for most of it), "Ray of Light" was shot over the course of 14 days. The clip was made up of time-lapse scenes of a sun rising, people going about their day, the subway system, kids' playtime at a **school**, traffic and other daily events, with an artificially tanned Madonna (in head-to-toe denim) superimposed over them.

"We did a few tests in Stockholm with a film camera so I could show her the technique I was talking about," the director said, "and the test actually came out so good, that it ended up in the final video. So there's a lot of shots from Stockholm in there."

It sped up and slowed down the background footage and/or its star with a remarkably **eye**-capturing ebb and flow. **Music** fans watched it as intently as a cat watching the jerky movements of an insect.

Toward the end, Madonna **danced** rapturously on a lighted **disco** floor in her wifebeater, looking **sexy** as hell and freer than she'd ever looked on film.

Something about the video's unspoken message of the mad rush of our culture captivated a world hurtling toward the millennium; the video was such a hit it was sold as a video single and captured for Madonna her only **MTV Video Music Award** for Video of the Year and a **Grammy** for Best Short Form Music Video.

Åkerlund has acknowledged that the video was "a life-changing moment for me."

RAY OF LIGHT FOUNDATION: Org that supports Madonna's **Art for Freedom** initiative to encourage the creative addressing of human rights abuses. Guest curators choose an artist whose **work** is living up to the mission, and this foundation then cuts a check to the nonprofit of that artist's choice. It also supports other organizations worldwide to promote peace, education and human rights.

Find out more at RayofLight.org.

RAZZIES: Annual movie **awards** presentation, formally the Golden Raspberry Awards, dating back to 1981 that acknowledges the worst of the worst in film.

Madonna has received 16 nominations and has won nine Golden Razzies: Worst Actress for *Shanghai Surprise*, *Who's That Girl*, *Body of Evidence*, *The Next Best Thing* and *Swept Away*, Worst Supporting Actress for *Four Rooms* and *Die Another Day*, Worst Screen Couple for *Swept Away* and the once-in-a-lifetime Worst Actress of the Century award. For the latter, Madonna easily beat out Elizabeth Berkley, Bo Derek, Brooke Shields and Pia Zadora.

REAGAN, RONALD: *February 6, 1911–June 5, 2004.* Didja ever see *Being There* (1979)? Well, Reagan—a former "actor" and former Governor of California—was the president who was just kinda *there* during the first part of Madonna's career, the one we warned you all about, the one who couldn't bring himself to say "**AIDS**" for years. Reagan

was one of the stubborn, conservative papas whom Madonna urged not to preach—his image was projected on a massive screen to great effect during her *Who's That Girl World Tour* performance of **"Papa Don't Preach."**

As early as 1984, Madonna was making her ill will toward Reagan (and Republicans in general) known to the press, growling to the teen **magazine** *Star Hits*, "I don't think about him very much, but I think he's a pretty good actor. I think he's a puppet for all the people in [his] cabinet. I think everybody else makes the decisions and he's the guy that gets up there and hopefully doesn't get shot at."

Keep in mind, this was only a few years after Reagan had, in fact, been shot.

As for Reagan's wife, Nancy, Madonna chose to just say no. "Nancy? Give me a break."

REBEL HEART (ALBUM): *Release date: March 6, 2015. Billboard 200 peak: #2.* Madonna's thirteenth studio album took longer than Rome to build, but it was nearly destroyed by a series of **leaks** caused by an intrepid hacker in Israel. **Esther** was pissed, devastated and felt "artistically **raped**." This from a woman who had experienced actual rape.

Though the leak was not from studio techies or ego-driven collaborators with iPhones, instead coming from a hack into the cloud accounts of Madonna and her associates (Sara Zambreno, Angie Teo and Kevin Antunes), Madonna did tempt fate with *Rebel Heart* in several ways.

First, she began **work** on the album in February 2014, yet was already teasing collaborators and song titles within weeks. **Beyoncé** had just redefined the concept of the album release by dropping one with no advance notice, yet Madonna seemed to be broadcasting her intentions almost as soon as the ideas popped into her head.

Plus, stoking the interest of pop **fans** for such a long time—it wouldn't be released by **Interscope** for another *year*—created hype far too early for it to be of any use to the album, and probably made the thirst for leaks all the greater.

Madonna also worked with an incredible number of collaborators. A grand total of six people had songwriting or production credits on her entire debut album *Madonna*—it took about that to create just the *Rebel Heart* single **"Living for Love."** Madonna worked with a true vogue's gallery of hot producers, including **Diplo**, **Avicii** and **Kanye West**, plus entire camps of songwriters. Because of that, there were exponentially more people with knowledge of Madonna's creative movements in the song-making process than there ever had been before.

Just when fans were apoplectic for the new music, it happened: Demos of the songs **"Rebel Heart"** and **"Wash All Over Me"** leaked. The songs were widely played (and favorably reviewed) on entertainment programs in December 2014, a full four months before the album's proposed release. This threw a wrench into Madonna's plans.

Working with Avicii and his songwriters had helped Madonna decide that *Rebel Heart* would be a double album,

ALEJANDRO MOGOLLO

436 *REBEL HEART* (ALBUM)

one side dark ("rebel") and the other side light ("heart"). She abandoned that idea because as she second-guessed herself on what to do about the two leaks, more leaks came until over 30 were easily available on the Internet. In 72 hours, Madonna and her company of creative types finished and dumped six of the album's strongest tracks on iTunes in time for Christmas.

"I intended to think about things, choose things more slowly—the whole process," she told *The New York Times*. "Then I got forced into putting everything out …"

She decided she would alter the remaining demos—in the process unintentionally setting up her fans as undeserving backseat producers who had heard both versions of each song and who would feel entitled to dictate which was better—and would bump up the release to March 10.

She pulled the trigger on all the final versions of her songs after coming to the realization that "caring about what people think is the **death** of all artists, really."

As for the creative process leading up to the leaks, Madonna confirmed it had been brutal. In a *New York Times* interview, she confessed, "I didn't know exactly what I signed on for, so a simple process became a very complex process." She told *Pitchfork* she was a "schedule keeper trying to manage the comings and goings of crazy DJs who all have ADD."

West, for example, had asked to listen to Madonna's work and critique it, which led to his edits on some songs, and which led to them writing a song together that he wanted to use on his own future album.

Madonna seemed to be most in step with Diplo, whose musical sensibility set the album's tone. "It wasn't until I got about halfway through the album that I started thinking about sounds, and that's where Diplo came in," Madonna told *Pitchfork*. "He started adding these monster beats and punch-you-in-the-stomach bass sounds and 808s like you've never heard before, and that pushed me in a certain direction."

Diplo noticed while working with her that she was far from a passive pop star, telling *MOJO*, "It's like, she's already sold billions of records, and she's still treating this one as if it's her first record. But she is Madonna and she is really there to make music and that's the only thing she's there to do." He told her he didn't usually go into the studio with the major artists he worked with. She found this unfathomable because she lives in the studio while making her records.

"People are always saying, 'So he's the producer,' or 'Who produced it?' and I have to say, 'I did. I coproduced that with Diplo. I coproduced that with Kanye.' Whatever—everything is a coproduction," Madonna told *Out*. "I'm the one who stays in the studio throughout, from beginning to end—all of these people come and go."

Diplo went so far as to say, "I've worked harder on these songs than I've worked on *our* songs, and that's a lot of fucking work."

The hands-on, all-hands-on-tape-deck approach is one more artists should take, and it can be chalked up to one thing; as Madonna told **Rolling Stone**, "The world is

changing and what does it all come down to at the end of the day? It comes down to songs." She insisted the album needed to have nothing but killer songs that she felt confident she could perform in stripped-down versions live on stage if need be.

So did Madonna get her wish? *Rebel Heart*, in the form in which we have it, happened in a less than ideal way, but Madonna ended up with an album that has the **dance** DNA of *Madonna*, the prolapsed **Catholicism** of *Like a Prayer*, the icy sluttiness and tongue-in-ass-cheek humor of *Erotica*, the cohesive production of *Ray of Light*, the bonkers eclecticism of *Music* and the electro-folky wisdom of *American Life*. It's self-referential, not in a way that feels lazy, but in a way that feels clever and self-accepting. With *Rebel Heart*, Madonna demonstrates that she has nothing to prove, and instead just wants to make good music that speaks to, about and for her.

A total musical curveball, "Living for **Love**" opens the album with an unpretentious '90s house beat reminiscent of **"Rescue Me"** or even **"Vogue,"** giving longtime fans an instant Pettiboner. It's so fun-friendly it could pass for **Cher**, circa "Believe" (1998). Scuffing the song's shiny happiness, Madonna's vocal is raspy and world-weary; imbuing it with a higher purpose, a gospel-tinged backing vocal interrupting and enhancing the dance party. The song may be Madonna's most offensively unsuccessful single release, cold comfort for Diplo, whose production on it sparkles with the pride of a **job** well done.

With nary a transition, Madonna launches into chick-with-a-**guitar** mode, warning of the empty high of escaping via **drugs** on the country-tinged **"Devil Pray."** It has a faint echo of the traditional song "The House of the Rising Sun," most famously recorded by the Animals (1964). The perversely revivalist chorus can throw listeners not used to tapping their **feet** to words about sniffing glue, but that kind of offbeat lyric helps make the song the finger-in-a-light-socket barnstormer that it is. Avicii is the album's **Mirwais**.

Probably *Rebel Heart*'s finest moment is metaphorically dead on arrival: the post-apocalyptic love song **"Ghost-town,"** a sonic séance that resurrects **Karen Carpenter**'s **voice** and also Madonna's vulnerability cred. Just with her voice, she sketches an image of hope on the precipice of emptiness, of eternal life in the face of certain death. She told **Howard Stern** she thinks she'll never die, and a song like this almost makes you believe her. Songs do not exist in a vacuum; we can't possibly fairly compare a song released in 2015 to one we heard as teenagers in 1985 (or 1995, or 2005, depending on your age), but if they did, if every song Madonna ever sang had been released on the same day, a good case could be made for placing "Ghost-town" among her 10 best.

Ur so reggae: Another Diplo blast arrives in the form of the dancehall stomper **"Unapologetic Bitch."** Putting up her dub step dukes, Madonna womansplains to an ex exactly why he lost the good thing he had in her. The idea

"Rebel Heart is a long, passionate, self-referential meditation on losing love and finding purpose in chilling times."
—CARYN GANZ, *ROLLING STONE* (2015)

of Madonna singing a reggae song seemed scary before the song dropped, the effortless way in which she embraces the sound makes one hope she revisits it. **Debbie Harry** should cover this.

Madonna is criticized for being humorless, but she laughs in the face of the all-seeing **eyes** of those Internet whackjobs who insist she (and just about every famous person alive) is a member of the mysterious Illuminati. But as funny as it is that she wrote a song called **"Illuminati,"** the song itself, a coproduction with West, is a scorching party anthem made to fill a room of intersecting bodies. In the same way that Madonna openly singing about the secret sect makes conspiracy theorists look foolish, she also name-checks **Lady Gaga**, seeming to roll her eyes at the belief that they're feuding.

"Bitch I'm Madonna," featuring a tasty **Nicki Minaj** rap that feels like a perfecting of their work together, blows the album wide open. It's a song with a loose form that's overstuffed with effects, craftily disguised Madonna exhortations and huge **balls**. No surprise it was the most popular on iTunes of all Madonna's pre-release songs.

After that club-tastic journey, **"Hold Tight"** arrives to provide an anthemic and reassuring hug with the hip-shaking propulsion of a **Ricky Martin** World Cup song.

Madonna's not usually at her best when singing about how hard life as a semi-billionaire can be. But as specific to herself as **"Joan of Arc"** is (most of us are okay with having our picture taken), it doesn't come off as whiny so much as a concession that she is a human being. Her vocal is as pretty as her plea for mercy is understandable.

Hilariously, Madonna switches gears from fragile to indestructible with **"Iconic,"** by far her catchiest ode to self-expression since that one from 1989. With lyrics that refer obliquely to Muhammad Ali, it's only fitting that she allows old pal **Mike Tyson** to kick off the song with his inimitable trash talk. The only false note in the thrilling four and a half minutes is when she unimaginatively rhymes "iconic" with "ironic"; **irony** really has nothing to do with it. Madonna and Chance the Rapper's vocals fit like a (**boxing**) glove.

Madonna returns with the embittered **"HeartBreakCity,"** thought to be about her rocky split from boyfriend **Brahim Zaibat**. Even as she cops to hurt feelings, she spits out her contempt for a man who took more than he gave. For a woman who has no **regrets**, Madonna's rage in the song is so incandescent she curses the day they met.

Are you as turned on as I am? *More!* Madonna's anger switches gears to passion on **"Body Shop,"** a far less cloying metaphorical tune-up than **"Candy Shop"** was a metaphorical sweet-tooth indulgence. It's all in the delivery. Madonna's girlish chirp makes the song one sweet ride.

Start spreading the news: The first of *Rebel Heart*'s polarizing tracks (or the second, if **"Bitch** I'm Madonna" counts) is **"Holy Water,"** a **Natalia Kills** collaboration that frames eating Madonna's **pussy** as a religious experience. You won't concern yourself with the probability that holy

REBEL HEART:
Standard Edition (1-14)

REBEL HEART:
Deluxe Edition (1-19)

REBEL HEART:
Super Deluxe Edition
(1-25)

REBEL HEART:
Media Markt Standard
Edition (1-14 + A)

REBEL HEART:
Media Markt Deluxe
Edition (1-19 + A)

REBEL HEART:
Japanese Deluxe Edition
and Italian Media
World Edition (1-19 + B)

REBEL HEART:
Fnac Deluxe Edition
(1-19 + C, D)

① "Living for Love" (Madonna/Diplo/MoZella/Toby Gad/Ariel Rechtshaid)—3:38, produced by Madonna/Diplo/Ariel Rechtshaid

② "Devil Pray" (Madonna/Avicii/Arash Pournouri/Carl Falk/Rami/Savan Kotecha/DJ Dahi/Blood Diamonds)—4:05, produced by Madonna/Avicii/DJ Dahi/Blood Diamonds

③ "Ghosttown" (Madonna/Jason Evigan/Sean Douglas/E. Kidd Bogart)—4:08, produced by Madonna/Billboard/Jason Evigan

④ "Unapologetic Bitch" (Madonna/Diplo/Shelco Garcia/Bryan Orellana/MoZella/Toby Gad)—3:50, produced by Madonna/Shelco Garcia & Teenwolf/BV/Diplo/Ariel Rechtshaid

⑤ "Illuminati" (Madonna/Toby Gad/MoZella/S1/Mike Dean/Kanye West/TB)—3:43, produced by Madonna/Kanye West/Charlie Heat/Mike Dean

⑥ "Bitch I'm Madonna" feat. Nicki Minaj (Madonna/Diplo/Ariel Rechtshaid/MoZella/Toby Gad/Nicki Minaj/Sophie)—3:47, produced by Madonna/Diplo

⑦ "Hold Tight" (Madonna/Diplo/MoZella/Toby Gad/MNEK/Jr. Blender)—3:37, produced by Madonna

⑧ "Joan of Arc" (Madonna/Toby Gad/MoZella/S1)—4:01, produced by Madonna/Toby Gad/AFSHeeN/Josh Cumbee

⑨ "Iconic" feat. Chance the Rapper and Mike Tyson (Madonna/Toby Gad/MoZella/S1/Chance the Rapper/DJ Dahi/Blood Diamonds)—4:33, produced by Madonna/Toby Gad/AFSHeeN/Josh Cumbee

⑩ "HeartBreakCity" (Madonna/Avicii/Arash Pournouri/NoNoNo/Michel Flygare/Delilah/Salem Al Fakir/Magnus Lidehäll/Vincent Pontare)—3:33, produced by Madonna/Avicii/Salem Al Fakir/Magnus Lidehäll/Vincent Pontare/Astma & Rocwell

⑪ "Body Shop" (Madonna/Toby Gad/MoZella/S1/DJ Dahi/Blood Diamonds)—3:39, produced by Madonna/DJ Dahi/Blood Diamonds/Toby Gad

⑫ "Holy Water" (Madonna/Martin Kierszenbaum/Natalia Kills/Mike Dean/Kanye West/TB)—4:09, produced by Madonna/Mike Dean/Charlie Heat/Kanye West

⑬ "Inside Out" (Madonna/Jason Evigan/Sean Douglas/E. Kidd Bogart/Mike Dean)—4:23, produced by Madonna/Mike Dean

⑭ "Wash All Over Me" (Madonna/Avicii/Arash Pournouri/Salem Al Fakir/Magnus Lidehäll/Vincent Pontare/Mike Dean/Kanye West/TB)—4:00, produced by Madonna/Avicii/Mike Dean/Kanye West/Charlie Heat

⑮ "Best Night" (Madonna/Diplo/MoZella/Toby Gad/James Napes/Andrew Swanson)—3:33, produced by Madonna/Diplo

⑯ "Veni Vidi Vici" feat. Nas (Madonna/Diplo/Ariel Rechtshaid/MoZella/Toby Gad/Nas)—4:39, produced by Madonna/Diplo

⑰ "S.E.X." (Madonna/Toby Gad/MoZella/S1/Mike Dean/Kanye West/TB)—4:11, produced by Madonna/Kanye West/Charlie Heat/Mike Dean

⑱ "Messiah" (Madonna/Avicii/Arash Pournouri/Salem Al Fakir/Magnus Lidehäll/Vincent Pontare)—3:22, produced by Madonna/Avicii/Salem Al Fakir/Magnus Lidehäll/Vincent Pontare

⑲ "Rebel Heart" (Madonna/Avicii/Arash Pournouri/Salem Al Fakir/Magnus Lidehäll/Vincent Pontare)—3:21, produced by Madonna/Avicii/Salem Al Fakir/Magnus Lidehäll/Vincent Pontare

⑳ "Beautiful Scars" (Madonna/Rick Nowels/DJ Dahi/Blood Diamonds)—4:19, produced by Madonna/DJ Dahi/Blood Diamonds

㉑ "Borrowed Time" (Madonna/Avicii/Ash Pournouri/Carl Falk/Rami/Savan Kotecha/DJ Dahi/Blood Diamonds)—3:24, produced by Madonna/Avicii/Carl Falk/DJ Dahi/Blood Diamonds

㉒ "Addicted" (Madonna/Avicii/Ash Pournouri/Carl Falk/Rami/Savan Kotecha)—3:33, produced by Madonna/Avicii/Carl Falk

㉓ "Graffiti Heart" (Madonna/MoZella/Toby Gad/S1)—3:39, produced by Madonna/Toby Gad/AFSHeeN/Josh Cumbee

㉔ "Living for Love" Paulo & Jackinsky Full Vocal Mix (Madonna/Diplo/MoZella/Toby Gad/Ariel Rechtshaid)—7:14, produced by Madonna/Diplo/Ariel Rechtshaid

㉕ "Living for Love" Funk Generation & H3d Rush Dub (Madonna/Diplo/MoZella/Toby Gad/Ariel Rechtshaid)—6:07, produced by Madonna/Diplo/Ariel Rechtshaid

Ⓐ "Auto-Tune Baby" (Madonna/Diplo/Mike Dean/Kanye West/TB)—4:00, produced by Madonna/Kanye West/Mike Dean/Charlie Heat

Ⓑ "Living for Love" Dirty Pop Club Remix (Madonna/Diplo/MoZella/Toby Gad/Ariel Rechtshaid)—4:59, produced by Madonna/Diplo/Ariel Rechtshaid

Ⓒ "Living for Love" Thrill Remix (Madonna/Diplo/MoZella/Toby Gad/Ariel Rechtshaid)—5:11, produced by Madonna/Diplo/Ariel Rechtshaid

Ⓓ "Living for Love" Offer Nissim Living for Drama Remix (Madonna/Diplo/MoZella/Toby Gad/Ariel Rechtshaid)—7:12, produced by Madonna/Diplo/Ariel Rechtshaid

"*Rebel Heart*, like its creator, pushes through the pain and, more often than not, lands solidly and with great grace on its feet."—RANDALL ROBERTS, *LOS ANGELES TIMES* (2015)

water tastes no different than the stuff that gushes out of the tap; to linger on that would be labial libel. Madonna's most perfect **drag** offering ever, the song unashamedly offers up the lines, "Bitch, get off my pole!," "Kiss it better/Make it wetter" and "Bless yourself and genuflect"—and that's all before Madonna goes quiet and the throbbing song explodes in a brief sample from "Vogue." Madonna once said anyone who didn't like her favorite **Frida Kahlo** painting couldn't be her friend; if you don't see "Holy Water" as braggadocious brilliance, you can't be a friend of Dorothy.

"**Inside Out**" is about love and about **sex**. But don't forget that Madonna's a woman, so it's okay that it be about both. Actually, her gender gives the song a different dimension; if a man sang about loving you from the inside out, it could get real crass real fast. Madonna has said that she always writes about sex with humor, but there's nothing funny here; it's a song so sexy Barry White songs listen to it to get in the mood.

The regular edition of the album ends with "Wash All Over Me," a declaration that Madonna herself isn't sure what life's all about, but that she's going to accept it. This is a perfect example of a song whose message is married to its sound is married to its vocals. It feels like an end, but a beginning, which is good because anyone with the Deluxe or Super Deluxe edition is only halfway done with *Rebel Heart*.

"**Best Night**," with its snake-charmer horn in the background, is the sonic seductive sister of "Body Shop." For the first time ever, Madonna refers to herself in song by the **nickname** all her friends call her ("M"). She also sings a bit of "**Justify My Love**" for old times' sake.

Normally anti-**nostalgia**, Madonna wistfully reminds us—and herself—of her more than three decades in public life with "**Veni Vidi Vici**." She refers to "**Holiday**," her early years running with graffiti artists in NYC, "**Into the Groove**," her knack for being embroiled in scandals, "**Express Yourself**," "**Like a Virgin**," *Sex*, "**Borderline**," "Vogue," "Justify My Love," "**Like a Prayer**," her *Confessions Tour* performance of "**Live to Tell**," "**Open Your Heart**," "**The Power of Good-Bye**," "**Ray of Light**" and "**Music**." As if reminding us that she took her own advice from "Iconic," Madonna announces that she came, she saw, she conquered. Annoyingly, Nas is given an opportunity to tell his own career story via rap, and it pales in comparison. It's like he's crashing her edition of *This Is Your Life* (1952–1961).

Another of the album's polarizing songs, "**S.E.X.**," arrives, and you'll swear you smell poppers. Madonna touches on role-play, BDSM, barebacking, frottage, water sports and a host of other things, some of which you may not even associate with sex. She has said her intention with this song was to explore the impersonal nature of the new hook-up culture, and she succeeds. It's a clever, hot-cold song that could have emerged from the *Erotica* sessions, and as with that album's own sex ditties, it's, "Robotic, robotic ..."

"**Messiah**," one of the first titles Madonna teased on social media, winds up banished to the #18 position on the album and feels like a pleasant repetition of earlier tunes.

How the title track could not be included on the standard edition of the album is a mystery. Regardless, "Rebel Heart" is an instant Madonna classic, a sing-along about personal failings and potential. It's as nostalgic as "Veni Vidi Vici," yet universal. This feels like a song Madonna will sing live more than just on the tour that shares its name.

"**Beautiful Scars**" is a toe-tapping casting off of the fetish for perfection that infests our culture. Madonna has never underscored her dysfunctionality so disarmingly.

The album's only semi-preachy entry, the minor "**Borrowed Time**," only goes so far as urging that we live for the moment; no lines about students raping teachers.

If it's clear why "Borrowed Time" is a bonus track, it's absolutely inexplicable why "**Addicted**" is. With a rocky swagger, Madonna sounds like she did in **Emmy** 35 years earlier on the, well, *addictive* chorus. Her vocal hook is matched by the musical hook. While she would be well advised to stop singing about how attractive flames are to moths, the song is otherwise a revelation. "Addicted" should have been on the Standard Edition and would have been a fantastic single.

Unfortunately, the last non-remix on the album is the expendable "**Graffiti Heart**," too similar to several songs that came before. This is one that should have gotten away.

The Super Deluxe Edition ends with two "Living for Love" remixes, but the only other new song that's been released officially is "**Auto-Tune Baby**," available on the Media Markt Edition. Aside from an impossible-to-ignore, impossible-to-love crying baby in the beginning, it's otherwise a cunning, cooing "My Heart Belongs to Daddy" (1938) ... or maybe it's for the adult-baby crowd, since she forgot them on "S.E.X."?

Rebel Heart's cover, shot by **Mert and Marcus**, is up there with the covers of *Like a Virgin* and *True Blue* as her best. Calling to mind the **Steven Meisel** "She Does It This May" photo from the *Truth or Dare* teaser poster, Madonna's face looks shocked, wrapped up in an electrical cord. Pop will eat itself, but EDM will feast on *you*. Madonna said of the cord that it has layers of meaning. "On one hand, you could say it's an artist tied up in a bow, in a package. Another aspect is, it's the restriction, or, say, the resistance that all artists—real artists—have to go through and fight for. You're always fighting for something when you're an artist, to have your voice heard in a certain way without people tampering with it, **censoring** it, editing it. And it's getting harder and harder to have a pure voice."

Madonna's pure voice was stifled in part because of the *Rebel Heart* cover—when she reposted fan **art** of some of her idols wrapped in the same cords to show her affinity with them, it became the biggest **Instagram** faux pas ever; obligating Madonna to apologize. Her pure voice was further compromised by the leaks that preceded the album, which dictated her artistic choices.

But in the end, her pure voice is all over *Rebel Heart*, Madonna's first album that begins to sound like it's capturing her in totality as an artist and as a woman.

"HER NAME IS A METAPHOR FOR STRENGTH AND ENDURANCE … [*REBEL HEART*] PRESENTS A 56-YEAR-OLD WOMAN WHO, IN THE BEST POSSIBLE SENSE, SOUNDS HER AGE."

—JIM FARBER, *NEW YORK DAILY NEWS* (2015)

"THESE SONGS UNFOLD SLOWLY, BUILDING THROUGH FOREPLAY-LIKE INTROS BEFORE HOOKS ARE DISPLAYED OVER A SHIFTING SERIES OF TEXTURES, AS IF THE TRACKS WERE BEING REMIXED WHILE YOU'RE LISTENING TO THEM. IN A SHORT-ATTENTION-SPAN WORLD OF HITS THAT RELENTLESSLY SPOTLIGHT MINI-HOOK AFTER MINI-HOOK FOR CLUB DJS TO DROP IN A FEW BARS AT A TIME, THEY SEEM POSITIVELY LUXURIOUS AND DOWNRIGHT INTELLECTUAL."—JOE LEVY, *BILLBOARD* (2015)

"… [H]ER MOST CONSISTENT ALBUM IN A DECADE, AND ONE THAT RENDERS ANY HYPOTHETICAL 'BID FOR CONTINUED RELEVANCE' MOOT BY REMAINING PROUDLY SCATTERSHOT. IT'S AN ALBUM THAT PLACES MORE EMPHASIS ON MADONNA THE PERSON THAN MADONNA THE SONIC VISIONARY, AND IT BENEFITS AS A RESULT … IT'S THE REALEST, AND THE BEST, MADONNA HAS SOUNDED IN QUITE SOME TIME."

—JAMIESON COX, *TIME* (2015)

"AT THIS STAGE IN HER CAREER, IF MADONNA DOESN'T HAVE 'POP CHAMELEON' ON HER LINKEDIN PROFILE (AND WHAT A 'RÉSUMÉ' THAT WOULD BE), THEN *REBEL HEART* ALONE IS ENOUGH TO ENDORSE THAT TITLE … SOME OF HER MOST CAPTIVATING WORK IN YEARS."

—LEWIS CORNER, *DIGITAL SPY* (2015)

"ULTIMATELY, *REBEL HEART* FEELS LIKE A WASTED OPPORTUNITY. TRITE SELF-EMPOWERMENT ANTHEM 'ICONIC' INFORMS US THAT THERE'S ONLY TWO LETTERS DIFFERENCE BETWEEN ICON AND I CAN'T. SADLY, THERE ARE ALSO TWO LETTERS BETWEEN CLASS AND ASS."—GAVIN HAYNES, *NME* (2015)

"THE SOUND … IS … NOT SO MUCH RAW AS PURPOSEFULLY LEAN AND PIERCINGLY DIRECT, AS ARE THE LYRICS, WHICH MINE EMOTIONS FROM RIGHTEOUS ANGER AND PAIN TO RESOLUTE JOY."—ELYSA GARDNER, *USA TODAY* (2015)

"REBEL HEART" (SONG): The first song to leak from *Rebel Heart* in demo form was the title track, written by Madonna, **Avicii**, Magnus Lidehäll, Salem Al Fakir, Vincent Pontare and Arash Pournouri, and produced by Madonna, Avicii, Fakir, Lidehäll and Pontare. Though it received positive comments across the board, the leak vexed Madonna. Months later, the final version—sounding pretty close to the leak—became a stand-out from the record, a universal-sounding semi-apology for kneejerk rebellion, yet a declaration that everything was worth it and happiness is at hand. It's the very definition of excellent adult contemporary music. It provided a poignant sing-along moment on the tour of the same name.

REBEL HEART TOUR: *Show dates: September 9, 2015–March 20, 2016.* On March 2, 2015, Madonna's *Rebel Heart Tour* in support of her studio album ***Rebel Heart*** was announced, with tickets going on sale the following damn *day* in some areas for Madonna.com members, and going on sale to the general public beginning March 9, 2015.

Sales in the US were sluggish at first, though the first **Paris** date sold out in five minutes and dates were eventually added worldwide, including dates in some territories in which Madonna had never before performed live (Singapore, Taiwan, Thailand) and in Australia, which Madonna hadn't played in 23 years. She even played in exotic locales like Tulsa, Oklahoma, for the very first time.

Rebel Heart became almost like an antidote to the much more challenging ***MDNA Tour***, which preceded it; devoid of violence and heavy on sweet surprises from her **back** catalogue, it was a tour that pleased **fans** and critics and that at first generated relatively little outrage.

Not that some people didn't eventually find reasons to complain.

On May 21, 2015, after fans had already made expensive travel arrangements to attend the tour's scheduled opening in **Miami**, Madonna issued a statement that the tour would instead kick off on September 9 in Montreal. "As my fans already know, the show has to be perfect," she said. "Assembling all the elements will require more time than we realized. I apologize for any inconvenience this may cause my fans. I can promise you this show will be worth the wait. Can't wait to share it with all my Rebel Hearts out there."

Once the tour finally got around to debuting, it was the closest thing to an oldies tour we are ever likely to get from Madonna while still delivering live versions of her most current work and her trademark eye-popping visuals.

A specially filmed video intro featured an imprisoned Madonna bumping and grinding in her 1990 Oscars look and ruefully mocking a society that demands that women "show us your ass," her co-star a grumpy **Mike Tyson**. Madonna's dancers emerged as warriors of the Orient as she was lowered from the ceiling in a medieval cage. Dressed in a flowing red-and-black coat and heels that

An iconic "Iconic" opener

threatened to make her a six-footer, she seemed to lead her gold-gilt army up the show's long, phallic stage, a girlier Genghis Kahn.

Losing the angry-red top layer, Madonna kept a silky black kimono (with matching roots) and led the audience through a spirited, lip-synched rendition of **"Bitch I'm Madonna,"** surrounded by fans—of both the screaming and ornate Japanese variety.

The night's first throwback to the early days came next, a straightforward rock verson of **"Burning Up"** featuring our heroine rocking out on her trusty **guitar**.

Madonna's only truly controversy-worthy set piece followed, a row of stripper poles on which her female dancers performed in fetishized **nun** habits. Madonna, herself in just a small black corset with leather boots and a sheer skirt, looked a bit like a **sexed**-up Hester Prynne thanks to a paradoxically demure lace collar. Oh, she sang, too— **"Holy Water"** and **"Vogue"**—but isn't it more interesting that she did so while shimmying up a cross and taking it for a spin? The song ended with Madonna making her way to an elaborate Last Supper motif, featuring skin, sin and proclamations of how much Yeezus loves her **pussy**.

Winding up flat on her back on the ornate gold table, Madonna then cast off the iniquity, launching into a faithful, heartfelt rendition of **"Devil Pray."** Her sensual

interaction with a black priest called to mind themes from her **"Like a Prayer"** video and **_Blond Ambition Tour_**.

Thematically appropriate, a **"Messiah"** video interlude closed the show's religious excursion, giving way to perhaps its most purely enjoyable sequence. Looking cute on top of a vintage jalopy, Madonna sold the giddy innocence of **"Body Shop,"** whose double entendres are safe enough for a children's book.

Taking a break, Madonna sat on a pile of tires, surrounded by her '50s-garbed troupe, and shocked the hell out of the crowd with her 1986 hit **"True Blue,"** accompanying herself on the ukulele. It was a song she had not performed live since her **_Who's That Girl World Tour_** in 1987. At the Brooklyn performance of the song, **Debi Mazar**—who had appeared in the song's 1986 video—did all her original choreography and sang along from the audience.

If "True Blue" was a generous flashback to Madonna at her '80s best, **"Deeper and Deeper"** provided the same function for her naughty '90s. The performance came off well, but none of her clothes did—in marked contrast to most of her previous tours, the star remained covered from the neck down in a black suit and plaid blouse. The choreography for the song was straight out of **"Don't Tell Me,"** a tune that had been rumored to be an early set list, and that was later performed on the tour in select locations.

MATTHEW RETTENMUND

REBEL HEART TOUR
SET LIST
(OPENING NIGHT)

① "Revolution"
Video Intro
(snippets of "Iconic")

② "Iconic"

③ "Bitch I'm Madonna"

④ "Burning Up"

⑤ "Holy Water"/"Vogue"

⑥ "Devil Pray"

⑦ "Messiah"
Video Interlude

⑧ "Body Shop"

⑨ "True Blue"

⑩ "Deeper and Deeper"

⑪ "HeartBreakCity"/
"Love Don't Live Here
Anymore"

⑫ "Like a Virgin"
(snippets of "Justify
My Love"
and "Heartbeat")

⑬ "S.E.X."
Video Interlude
(snippets of
"Justify My Love")

⑭ "Living for Love"

⑮ "La Isla Bonita"

⑯ "Dress You Up"/
"Into the Groove"/
"Everybody"/
"Lucky Star" Medley

⑰ "Who's That Girl"

⑱ "Rebel Heart"

⑲ "Illuminati"
Video Interlude

⑳ "Music"
(snippets of "Give
It 2 Me")

㉑ "Candy Shop"

㉒ "Material Girl"

㉓ "La Vie en rose"

㉔ "Unapologetic Bitch"

㉕ "Holiday"

OTHER SONGS SUNG
AT SOME REBEL
HEART TOUR STOPS

"Beautiful Stranger"
(snippet)–Nashville

"Can't Get You
Out of My Head" (2001)
by Kylie Minogue
–Brisbane (one night)

"Crazy for You"
–Brisbane (one night),
Pasay City (one night),
Singapore

"Diamonds Are a Girl's
Best Friend" (snippet)
first sung by Carol
Channing (1949),
further popularized by
Marilyn Monroe (1953)
–Atlanta, Auckland
(one night), Bangkok,
London (one night),
Louisville, Mannheim,
Mexico City (one night),
Melbourne, Miami,
Paris, Puerto Rico,
Sydney, Tokyo, Tulsa

"Do-Re-Mi" (snippet)
first sung by
Mary Martin (1959),
further popularized by
Julie Andrews (1962)
–Brisbane (one night)

"Do You Know the Way
to San Jose?" (1968)
by Dionne Warwick
–San Jose

"Don't Cry for Me
Argentina"–Miami

"Don't Tell Me"
–Antwerp, Auckland
(one night), Barcelona
(one night), Nashville,
Prague (one night),
Tokyo (one night),
Tulsa, Turin

"Drowned World/
Substitute for Love"
–London (one night)

"Erotica" (snippet)
–Brisbane (one night)

"Fever"
–Cologne (one night),
Macau (one night),
Melbourne (one night),
St. Paul

"Frozen"
–Detroit, San Antonio,
San Diego, San Jose

"Ghosttown"
–Atlanta, Atlantic City,
Brooklyn, Chicago,
Edmonton (one night),
Glasgow, Herning, Las
Vegas, Mexico City (one
night), Philadelphia,
Prague (one night),
Quebec City, Toronto
(one night), Turin (one
night), Vancouver,
Zurich

"Hanky Panky"
–Brisbane (one night),
Sydney

"Happy Birthday to You"
(circa late 1800s)
–Miami (one night)

"Hung Up"–Tokyo

"Like a Prayer"
–Auckland (one night),
Barcelona (one night),
Berlin (one night),
Birmingham, Inglewood,
London (one night),
Louisville, Melbourne
(one night), Mexico
City (one night), Paris
(one night), Pasay City
(one night), Prague
(one night), Stock-
holm, Sydney, Turin
(one night)

"Mambo Italiano"
(snippet) by Rosemary
Clooney (1954)
–Turin (one night)

"Open Your Heart"
–Manchester

"Rebel Rebel" (1974)
by David Bowie
–Houston

"Redemption Song"
by Bob Marley & the
Wailers (1980)
–Paris (one night)

"Ring of Fire" (1963)
first sung by Anita
Carter, popularized
by Johnny Cash
–Nashville

"Secret"
–Amsterdam (one night),
Atlanta, Berlin
(one night), Cologne
(one night), Inglewood,
Las Vegas, Portland,
Prague (one night),
Turin (one night),
Vancouver

"Send in the Clowns"
(1973) by Stephen
Sondheim, first sung
by Glynis Johns
–Melbourne (one night)

"Spanish Lesson"
–Barcelona (snippet),
Miami, Puerto Rico

"Take a Bow"
–Bangkok, Brisbane
(one night), Hong Kong
(one night), Macau,
Melbourne (one night),
Sydney, Taipei,
Tokyo (one night)

"That's Amore"
(snippet) (1953)
by Dean Martin
–Turin (one night)

"Tu vuò fà l'americano"
(snippet) (1956)
by Renato Carosone
–Turin (one night)

"You Light Up My Life"
(snippet) sung by
Kasey Cisyk and Debby
Boone (both 1977)
–Pasay City (one night)

"Burning Up"
the guitar

Singing "Deeper
and Deeper," but
dancing like it's
"Don't Tell Me"

MATTHEW RETTENMUND

"Nobody fucks with the queen!"–MADONNA

Next, Madonna sang **"HeartBreakCity"** while she and a dancer adeptly made their way up and down an impressively massive, metal spiral staircase. Pouring all of her energy into the song, the crowd gave it back tenfold when she segued into a portion of **"Love Don't Live Here Anymore,"** a song no Madonna **fan** could ever have anticipated would be sung live. The performance ends with the massive staircase hoisted into the ceiling, tiny Madonna standing under it as if lifting it herself.

Some of her heaviest lifting yet came next, when the woman who at one point said she hated performing **"Like a Virgin"** brought that indelible hit back for one more outing. Skipping across the stage and flirtily opening her top to air out her cleavage, she sang the entire number without any props or dancers, just Madonna and her first #1 hit. And some deep squats.

"S.E.X." provided a racy video interlude *and* an excuse for Madonna's dancers to engage in some bed hopping before the star emerged in the infamous cape that had caused her such consternation at the **Brit Awards**. This time, the cape came off as expected, allowing her to serve a spot-on performance of a **"Living for Love"** remix in full matador mode, her dancers in skintight leather, minotaur horns and jeweled masks.

With her mic in her waistband, there was ample time for some HiNRG **vogueing** before a totally faithful return to **"La Isla Bonita,"** surely one of Madonna's favorites among her hits, considering how often she has performed it live.

Madonna's greatest concession to nostalgia had to be her indulgent, flamenco-spiked medley (a medley! Is this **Janet Jackson** or Madonna?) of **"Dress You Up," "Into the Groove," "Everybody"** and **"Lucky Star,"** some of her very earliest hits. Wearing a gaudy, Day of the Dead Mexican outfit Stevie Nicks no doubt looked for on QVC the next day, she seemed to be underscoring to fans, critics and future ticket-buyers that she is not above the tried and true. (She eventually all but discontinued the medley on later dates, perhaps having grown bored of it.)

One of the chattiest portions of this or any Madonna concert followed, with mama comfortably seated on a stool, telling stories, asking questions of the crowd and delivering up (early in the tour) **"Who's That Girl"** and **"Rebel Heart,"** back-to-back feel-good strummers, though this section did evolve into a bit of a surprise nightly, with **"Ghosttown,"** "Like a Prayer" and many other hits making appearances.

After the rest, the show ramped up again straight away with a Vegas-ready **"Illuminati"** interlude in which her dancers, looking like the little guy from Monopoly, ushered in a 1920s sequence while dipping nearly into the audience on flexible poles.

Doling out her #1 hit **"Music,"** Madonna appeared in one of her most fetching stage costumes of all time, a beaded flapper dress that rendered her a beautiful (Ruby) Keeler, gaily performing the Charleston with boogie-woogie urgency.

Madonna finished "HeartBreakCity" and "Love Don't Live Here Anymore" *strong.*

MATTHEW RETTENMUND

"Music" and its successor in the show, **"Candy Shop,"** are also noteworthy for their use of a Josephine Baker stand-in. Baker would certainly be a controversial show-girl from history with whom Madonna identifies. Another dancer also aped Charlie Chaplin, whose bowler hat she promptly nicked; Madonna bringing the early Hollywood genius into the mix called to mind Gloria Swanson's *Sun-set Boulevard* Chaplin impersonation.

Next up, she glittered against an art deco backdrop surrounded by handsome men in black tie, walking the aisle/catwalk in a sheer veil while singing a slowed-down

"Material Girl." At this juncture, Madonna would toss the bouquet to a lucky fan each night, usually after asking something like, "Who wants to get hitched?" and snapping, "Sucker!" to whomever took the bait.

She brought her uke out one more time for a respectful cover of Edith Piaf's "La Vie en rose" that brought thunder-ous applause in French-speaking areas and was the tour's clear vocal highlight; she sings the song so much better than she sings some of her own.

An awkward skit about **smoking** cigarettes—"I don't smoke ... but I do start fires!"—led to the main show's finale,

ALEJANDRO MOGOLLO

Madonna releases her maracas.

"Devil Pray"-ground

MATTHEW RETTENMUND

Madonna expands her horizons, continuing to sell her guitar skills and adding in the ukulele for good measure.

MATTHEW RETTENMUND

MATTHEW RETTENMUND

a crowd-pleasing **"Unapologetic Bitch"** that featured Madonna hitting a hands-on-hips pose that will probably survive as the most iconic image from the entire show. Most entertainingly, Madonna made a habit of dragging an honorary unapologetic **bitch** from the crowd each night to **dance** with her at song's end, usually gifting the lucky sap with a (real) banana. The bitches were sometimes random fans, but also included famous faces Amy Schumer (who opened for Madonna's three New York-area *Rebel Heart Tour* shows), **Anderson Cooper**, **Katy Perry**, **Ariana Grande**, Rita Ora, **Stella McCartney**, **Diplo** and even her daughter **Mercy**.

The show drew to a close with a peppy, Uncle Sam-dominated **"Holiday."**

One thing that makes it difficult to summarize Madonna's set list for this tour is the fact that—in the same way she did one audience-request song on her *Sticky & Sweet Tour*—she uncharacteristically loosened up on *Rebel Heart*, changing her set list in minor and sometimes major ways throughout the run. Just as Madonna giveth, so Madonna taketh away: She added songs, but at various times also deleted songs from the set list. For example, she quickly shortened her medley by one song ("Everybody"), dropped "Who's That Girl" in Philadelphia (and many other gigs thereafter) and, thanks to a disastrously late start in Manchester, lost a significant chunk of the entire show. Macau missed "HeartBreakCity"/"Love Don't Live Here Anymore" because the venue wasn't tall enough to accommodate the spiral-stair prop.

Most surprisingly, Madonna changed her show to placate censors in Singapore, dropping "Iconic," "Holy Water" and "Devil Pray," and eliminating all the pesky crosses.

Though Madonna started the majority of her *Rebel Heart Tour* shows at a reasonable hour (usually 9:20 p.m. to 10:00 p.m.), late starts in Europe, for some of the second U.S. leg and especially in Australia generated negative publicity, ludicrous accusations of drunkenness and pill-popping and even a public shaming from fellow performer Reba McEntire, whose **Instagram** was not amused to be kept waiting for hours.

Legit reviews were almost universally positive for the show, even if she would go on to earn a fraction of what she earned on her two previous, record-breaking outings.

Still, all in all, Madonna performed 82 shows (none canceled) to 800,000-plus people, earning $169.8 million.

There is almost no doubt that with each passing tour, Madonna is getting further and further away from feeling compelled to do another. While touring is where it's at financially, and while her success as a live act is the strongest argument for her relevance as a pop artist, Madonna has drifted a bit closer to the day when her tours might look a lot less like the most breathtaking Broadway musical you've ever seen and a lot more like Madonna in a nice dress in front of a mic.

With *Rebel Heart*, more than with any previous tour, Madonna proved that she could still deliver either/or.

"THIRTY SECONDS. THAT'S ALL IT TOOK FOR A SOLD-OUT CROWD … TO FORGIVE MADONNA FOR FINALLY GRACING US WITH HER PRESENCE AT 10:54 P.M. … WHAT MADONNA IS STILL ABLE TO ACCOMPLISH PHYSICALLY, AT 57, IS SIMPLY ASTOUNDING."

—MELISSA RUGGIERI, *THE ATLANTA JOURNAL-CONSTITUTION*

"YOU KNOW, WE ALL GO THROUGH CHALLENGING TIMES IN OUR LIVES, AND THAT INCLUDES ME … RIGHT NOW IS ONE OF THEM. SOMETIMES I THINK I CAN'T DO A SHOW, I DON'T HAVE THE ENERGY, I DON'T HAVE THE STRENGTH … BUT I COME OUT HERE TONIGHT AND SEE YOUR FACES, AND I LOOK INTO YOUR EYES, I SEE SO MUCH LOVE, AND YOU GIVE ME THE STRENGTH … I FEEL YOUR HEARTS BEATING WITH MINE."

—MADONNA ON STAGE IN MEXICO CITY, REFERENCING HER CUSTODY BATTLE OVER ROCCO

Madonna's never sounded better on her ballads.

"[I]N A SPARE-NO-EXPENSE THEATRICAL SPECTACLE THAT ARTFULLY FLOWED FROM SHOWSTOPPER TO SHOWSTOPPER, SHE PROVED ONCE AGAIN THAT SHE DOESN'T JUST CRAVE THE SPOTLIGHT—SHE OWNS IT."

—JORDAN ZIVITZ, *MONTREAL GAZETTE*

"HER SMILE IS GENUINE AND UNFORCED, RAMBLING[S] BETWEEN SONG MONOLOGUES SOUND SPONTANEOUS AND UNSCRIPTED AND HER PLEASURE IN PERFORMING IS UNDENIABLE AND INFECTIOUS … MADONNA DID NOT PUT A FOOT WRONG."—NEIL MCCORMICK, *TELEGRAPH* (UK)

"THERE ARE PEOPLE WHO HAVE NO RESPECT FOR HUMAN LIFE, AND THERE ARE PEOPLE THAT DO ATROCIOUS, DEGRADING AND UNFORGIVABLE THINGS TO HUMAN BEINGS. BUT WE WILL NEVER, EVER, EVER CHANGE THIS WORLD THAT WE LIVE IN IF WE DO NOT CHANGE OURSELVES. IF WE DO NOT CHANGE THE WAY WE TREAT ONE ANOTHER ON A DAILY BASIS. THE WAY WE CHANGE THE WORLD IS NOT TO ELECT ANOTHER PRESIDENT, NOT TO KILL A HUNDRED MORE PEOPLE. THE WAY WE CHANGE THE WORLD IS THAT WE CHANGE THE WAY WE TREAT ONE ANOTHER ON A DAILY BASIS, IN THE SIMPLEST WAYS. WE MUST START TREATING EVERY HUMAN BEING WITH DIGNITY AND RESPECT, AND THIS IS THE ONLY THING THAT WILL CHANGE THE WORLD."

—MADONNA ON STAGE IN STOCKHOLM, ADDRESSING THE PARIS MASSACRE

"FACTS: ITS GOOD TO HAVE THEM BEFORE YOU JUMP TO CONCLUSIONS! THE ENTIRE VIDEO FOR MY SHOW CRASHED AS I ARRIVED FOR SOUND CHECK. THE BACK UP FILE WAS CORRUPT. WE HAD NO CHOICE BUT TO REBOOT AND PRAY FOR A GOOD OUTCOME. THE VIDEO LIGHTS 75 % OF MY SHOW. WE CANT PLAY IN THE DARK. WE WERE REBOOTED AND READY BY 9:30 EVEN THOUGH WE PLANNED TO GO ION EARLIER. I HAD TO MAKE CUTS IN SHOW BEFORE SHOW STARTED. DRESS YOU UP WAS ONE OF THEM AND MY 3RD GUITAR SONG. THIS STILL BROUGHT US PAST THE 11:00 CURFEW! BUT WE WENT ON AND THE VENUE WAS KIND ENOUGH TO EXTEND TILL 111:39!! IT WAS THEIR CHOICE NOT MINE TO END THE SHOW!! ALWAYS WANT TO FINISH. SO WE ALL MISSED THE LAST 3 SONGS! AND I'M SORRY ABOUT THAT. AND I THANK ALL MY REBEL HEART FANS FOR UNDERSTANDING! WE DID OUR BEST! AND WE STILL HAD TO PAY A FINE! THAT'S LIFE."

—MADONNA ON INSTAGRAM IN RESPONSE TO HER MANCHESTER SHOW

MATTHEW RETTENMUND

MATTHEW RETTENMUND

Madonna,
still somewhat
like a virgin

REBEL HEART TOUR PERFORMANCES

September 9-10, 2015:
Montreal, Quebec, Canada
(Bell Centre)

September 12, 2015:
Washington, DC, US
(Verizon Center)

September 16-17, 2015:
New York, New York, US
(Madison Square Garden)

September 19, 2015:
Brooklyn, New York, US
(Barclays Center)

September 21, 2015:
Quebec City, Canada
(Centre Vidéotron Centre)

September 24, 2015:
Philadelphia, Pennsyl-
vania, US (Wells Fargo
Center)

September 26, 2015:
Boston, Massachusetts, US
(TD Garden)

September 28, 2015:
Chicago, Illinois, US
(United Center)

October 1, 2015:
Detroit, Michigan, US
(Joe Louis Arena)

October 3, 2015:
Atlantic City, New Jersey,
US (Boardwalk Hall)

October 5-6, 2015:
Toronto, Ontario, Canada
(Air Canada Centre)

October 8, 2015:
St. Paul, Minnesota, US
(Xcel Energy Center)

October 11-12, 2015:
Edmonton, Alberta,
Canada (Rexall Place)

October 14, 2015:
Vancouver, British
Columbia, Canada
(Rogers Arena)

October 17, 2015:
Portland, Oregon, US
(Moda Center)

October 19, 2015:
San Jose, California, US
(SAP Center)

October 22, 2015:
Glendale, Arizona, US
(Gila River Arena)

October 24, 2015:
Las Vegas, Nevada, US
(MGM Grand Garden Arena)

October 27, 2015:
Los Angeles, California,
US (The Forum)

October 29, 2015:
San Diego, California, US
(Valley View Casino
Center)

November 4-5, 2015:
Koln, Germany
(Lanxess Arena)

November 7-8, 2015:
Prague, Czech Republic
(O2 Arena)

November 10-11, 2015:
Berlin, Germany
(Mercedes-Benz Arena)

November 14, 2015:
Stockholm, Sweden
(Tele2 Arena)

November 16, 2015:
Herning, Denmark
(Jyske Bank Boxen)

November 19 & 21-22, 2015:
Turin, Italy
(Pala Alpitour)

November 24-25, 2015:
Barcelona, Spain
(Palau Sant Jordi)

November 28, 2015:
Antwerp, Belgium
(Sportpaleis)

December 1-2, 2015:
London, UK (O2 Arena)

December 5-6, 2015:
Amsterdam, Holland
(Ziggo Dome)

December 9-10, 2015:
Paris, France
(AccorHotels Arena)

December 12, 2015:
Zurich, Switzerland
(Hallenstadion)

December 14, 2015:
Manchester, UK
(Manchester Arena)

December 16, 2015:
Birmingham, UK
(Barclaycard Arena)

December 20, 2015:
Glasgow, Scotland
(The SSE Hydro)

January 6-7, 2016:
Mexico City, Mexico
(Palacio de los Deportes)

January 10, 2016:
San Antonio, Texas, US
(AT&T Center)

January 12, 2016:
Houston, Texas, US
(Toyota Centre)

January 14, 2016:
Tulsa, Oklahoma, US
(BOK Center)

January 16, 2016:
Louisville, Kentucky, US
(KFC Yum! Center)

January 18, 2016:
Nashville, Tennessee, US
(Bridgestone Arena)

January 20, 2016:
Atlanta, Georgia, US
(Philips Arena)

January 23-24, 2016:
Miami, Florida, US
(American Airlines Arena)

January 27-28, 2016:
San Juan, Puerto Rico
(Coliseo de Puerto Rico)

February 4 & 6, 2016:
Taipei, Taiwan
(Taipei Arena)

February 9-10, 2016:
Bangkok, Thailand
(IMPACT Arena)

February 13-14, 2016:
Tokyo, Japan
(Saitama Super Arena)

February 17-18, 2016:
Hong Kong, China
(AsiaWorld-Arena)

February 20-21, 2016:
Macau, China
(Studio City Event
Center)

February 24-25, 2016:
Pasay City, Philippines
(Mall of Asia Arena)

February 28, 2016:
Singapore, Singapore
(National Stadium)

March 5-6, 2016:
Auckland, New Zealand
(Vector Arena)

March 12-13, 2016:
Melbourne, Australia
(Rod Laver Arena)

March 16-17, 2016:
Brisbane, Australia
(Brisbane Entertainment
Centre)

March 19-20, 2016:
Sydney, Australia
(Allphones Arena)

RED KNAPP'S DAIRY BAR: *304 S. Main St., Rochester, MI.* The **Rochester Hills, Michigan,** hangout **famed** for its seasoned French fries and for the fact that Madonna went there all the time on dates with high **school** sweetheart **Russell Long.**

REDUCTIVE: SEE: **Lady Gaga.**

REEBOK: After **Pepsi** dumped the too-controversial Madonna, Nike briefly **flirted** with and then decided against the idea of employing her services. Finally, immediately before the premiere of her hitherto sponsorless *Blond Ambition World Tour*, it was reported that Madonna would endorse Reebok shoes, and vice versa. Talks never panned out, reportedly because of Madonna's refusal to actually *wear* the tennis shoes.

REGAN, KEN: *circa 1939–November 25, 2012.* The *People* **magazine** photographer who delivered dozens of original cover images for the entertainment magazine, including Madonna's first, on the March 11, 1985, issue. The image was a vixenish close-up of the newcomer in mid-pucker. She'd already become so famous that the only cover line needed was just: "MADONNA." That shoot, which happened at the Mondrian (8440 Sunset Blvd., W. Hollywood, CA), became iconic to Madonna's **fans** due to her vintage "HEALTHY" tank. One of the images graced *Penthouse* when her **nude** photos leaked.

In 2011, Regan recalled of his hotel shoot with Madonna: "I arrived at the Mondrian Hotel, I go up the elevator and this woman comes in; it looked like a lady of the evening, assuming the scene in LA. I was waiting for her to proposition me. It didn't happen. When Madonna came to my room later on, it was the hooker from the elevator!"

Regan had built a studio in the hotel's ballroom for the 4 p.m. shoot. He said Madonna arrived with no publicist or manager—totally alone. It didn't last long, but the results did, and they made him a mint. By Regan's estimation, he sold 24 covers. **Madonnabilia** collectors will attest to the fact that there were many more.

Madonna asked Regan to be the still photographer for her film *W.E.*, but he was unable to accept.

REGINA: *b. April 22, 1961.* Also known as Regina Richards and Regina Lee, the otherwise mononymous Regina is the singer of "Baby **Love**" (1986), a song even Madonna might mistake for being by Madonna. Madonna **hated** the soundalike song, which hit the Top 10, but Regina's take was, "Madonna's an individual, and I'm an individual. There's no way we *can't* be different."

Regina had a room in **The Music Building** where Madonna's band **Emmy** recorded their demo. According to **Stephen Bray,** who cowrote and produced "Baby Love," it was room 1002. Richards's husband ran Black Lion Music, which managed the publishing for Bray, so Regina always got a little piece of Madonna one way or another.

REGRETS: Madonna codified her take on regrets at the end of her **"Human Nature"** video, in which she says to the camera, "Absolutely no regrets." To ruminate over regrets would be to give her critics too much credit, and would keep Madonna from her favorite pastime—moving forward.

Clarifying her stance, she told *Good Housekeeping* in 2000, "Everybody has regrets, but mine are private ... They have nothing to do with my public life, my career."

Circa 2002, Madonna's ringtone was "Non, je ne regrette rien" (1960) by Édith Piaf.

REINCARNATION: In 1985, cat-**eyed** Madonna speculated on her past life as a feline: "I feel like in a past life I was a lion or a cat or something." She asserted her belief in reincarnation in 2015, saying our souls are energy, and are "eternal."

REINER, ROB: *b. March 6, 1947.* When the acclaimed director of *This is Spinal Tap* (1984), *The Princess Bride* (1987), *When Harry Met Sally* (1989) and *A Few Good Men* (1992) was introduced to Madonna by **Warren Beatty** in 1991, he gushed, "I never thought I'd meet Madonna!"—to which she replied, referring to his *All in the Family* (1971–1978) role, "I never thought I'd meet 'Meathead.'"

Almost immediately thereafter, she signed on to play ball with Reiner's ex, **Penny Marshall,** in *A League of Their Own.*

REINVENTION: Since 1986, Madonna has changed her **hair,** makeup, style—even her face and body. Madonna herself predicted that she would transform before our very **eyes** in a 1984 interview: "Every person is multi-faceted, and hopefully, the longer your career goes on the more you can get that out of you, but I, I couldn't begin to tell you what the world doesn't see in me right now. There's a million things."

As Melissa Maerz wrote so colorfully in 2015: "I **love** that Madonna always makes one thing clear: She didn't wake up like this. Ever. She built her image with her bare hands, out of **cone bras** and wigs and lipstick."

It has been a cliché since at least the '90s to say of Madonna that she "reinvents" herself with each project. "What she does is, she took a leaf from Detroit—the auto industry—which the auto industry forgot, and that is the annual model change," Steve Forbes said in 1993, when he was still called Malcolm Forbes Jr. Madonna's morphing appearance makes her hard to recognize in some incarnations. Comedian Elayne Boosler said in 1991, "I sat next to Madonna at a Laura Nyro concert and she was further from her stage persona than anyone I've ever seen. She looked so different it was unbelievable."

Even though she is the undisputed Queen of Reinvention, Madonna finds the term "reinvention" mildly offensive.

Regan's Madonna cover was one hot pucker.

Though she did it playfully, she razzed **gay** journalist Chris Azzopardi for using the word during a *W.E.* press roundtable. "Please don't throw those tired, old clichés at me," she groaned.

Madonna objects to the term partly because she's sick of being referred to in ways that are unimaginative (try calling her the **Material Girl** to her face), and partly because in the word "reinvention," she hears cynicism, judgment that perhaps her incarnations are not reflections of her true self but sales gimmicks.

However, in the same way that she has capitalized on the media's insistence on calling her the Material Girl by using it as the name of her teen **fashion** line, Madonna named the closest thing she's ever done to an oldies tour her *Re-Invention World Tour*.

If you can't beat 'em, reinvent 'em.

RE-INVENTION WORLD TOUR: *Show dates: May 24, 2004–September 14, 2004.* When *American Life* failed, it didn't seem likely that Madonna would go **back** out on the road anytime soon, especially considering there had been over seven years between *The Girlie Show World Tour* and her *Drowned World Tour*, and the latter had ended only a couple of years earlier. However, in the same way that Madonna answered the semi-rejection of *Erotica* with a tour, she answered the public's total rejection of *American Life* with her *Re-Invention World Tour*.

Though Madonna had recoiled during *On Stage & on the Record* when a **fan** suggested a "greatest hits tour," very few people were hankering for an *American Life Tour*, so a compromise was struck: Madonna, with director/choreographer **Jamie King** and with music director **Stuart Price**, conceived a show that would touch on *American Life* but that could be sold as an oldies outing, capitalizing on her reputation for **reinvention** by presenting her old hits in new arrangements.

As **Liz Smith**'s "man on the scene" Denis Ferrara wrote of the show in the *New York Post*, "She is giving her fans a taste of the past, washed with her refusal to compromise or to condescend. Or even to pretend for the sake of entertainment that she hasn't changed. She has changed. And she hopes you have too, or will."

After the resolutely current *Drowned World Tour*, audiences were attracted to the idea of a Madonna concert with more than a few hits on the set list, changed or not.

"People have always had this obsession with me, about my reinvention of myself. I just feel like I'm shedding layers. I'm slowly revealing who I am," Madonna had said in 1998. With the *Re-Invention World Tour*, she figured out a way to revisit some of those layers without feeling like a **nostalgia** peddler.

She not only changed, she changed into and out of some pretty amazing frocks, created by Chanel, Christian Lacroix, **Karl Lagerfeld**, **Stella McCartney** and **Arianne Phillips**.

Madonna's tour concept hit home, leading to a successful excursion, at the time her biggest and longest tour in over 20 years in the biz. The show mostly sold out, allowing nearly a million people to see Madonna in the flesh. It was reported that her tour crew consisted of 110 people and over 50 security personnel, and that the tour required 55 tons of equipment, a 40-ton stage and 25 cases of **Kabbalah** water at each stop.

Kicking things off in LA (a press-friendly strategy), Madonna's opening-night crowd was filled with celebrities (**Christina Aguilera**, Fran Drescher, **Debi Mazar** and David Spade among them), but she postponed her second show by a day due to a stomach flu.

Madonna started the show's *French Baroque/Marie Antoinette* section with an excruciatingly protracted **"Beast Within"** video introduction, teasing her audience with her recorded **voice** while scenes from her *X-STaT-IC Pro=CeSS* exhibition flashed on the screen. When it ended, the real show began, right after Madonna's words: "Behold: I am coming soon," were answered with "What are you lookin' at?"

"Just don't use that damn 're-invention' word."
—MADONNA, *INSTYLE* (2001)

RE-INVENTION WORLD TOUR SET LIST
1. "The Beast Within" Video Intro (snippets of "El Yom 'Ulliqa 'Ala Khashaba" by Nouhad Wadi Haddad)
2. "Vogue"
3. "Nobody Knows Me"
4. "Frozen"
5. "American Life"
6. "Express Yourself"
7. "Burning Up"
8. "Material Girl"
9. "Hollywood" Remix Video Interlude
10. "Hanky Panky"
11. "Deeper and Deeper"
12. "Die Another Day"
13. "Lament"
14. "Bedtime Story" Remix Dancer & Video Interlude
15. "Nothing Fails"
16. "Don't Tell Me" [some dates, snippets of "Bitter Sweet Symphony" by The Verve (1997)]
17. "Like a Prayer"
18. "Mother and Father" (snippets of "Intervention")
19. "Imagine" (1971) by John Lennon
20. "Into the Groove" (snippets of "Susan MacLeod" and "Into the Hollywood Groove")
21. "Papa Don't Preach" (snippets of "American Life")
22. "Crazy for You"
23. "Music" (snippets of "Into the Groove")
24. "Holiday" (snippets of "She Wants to Move" by N*E*R*D (2004)]

—COLMAN DEKAY

RE-INVENTION WORLD TOUR PERFORMANCES

May 24, May 26-27, 2004: Inglewood, California, US (The Forum)

May 29-30, 2004: Las Vegas, Nevada, US (MGM Grand Garden Arena)

June 2-3, 2004: Anaheim, California, US (Arrowhead Pond)

June 6, June 8-9, 2004: San Jose, California, US (HP Pavilion at San Jose)

June 13-14, 2004: Washington, DC, US (MCI Center)

June 16-17, June 20-21, June 23-24, 2004: New York, New York (US), Madison Square Garden

June 27-28, June 30, 2004: Worcester, Massachusetts, US (Worcester's Centrum Centre)

July 4-5, 2004: E. Rutherford, New Jersey, US (Continental Airlines Arena)

July 11-12, July 14-15, 2004: Chicago, Illinois, US (United Center)

July 18-19, July 21, 2004: Toronto, Ontario, Canada (Air Canada Centre)

July 24-25, 2004: Atlanta, Georgia, US (Philips Arena)

July 28-29, 2004: Sunrise, Florida, US (Office Depot Center)

August 1-2, 2004: Miami, Florida, US (American Airlines Arena)

August 14-15, 2004: Manchester, England, UK (Manchester Evening News Arena)

August 18-19, 2004: London, England, UK (Earls Court)

August 22-23, August 25-26, 2004: London, England, UK (Wembley Arena)

August 29, 2004: Slane, Ireland (Slane Castle)

September 1-2, September 4-5, 2004: Paris, France (Palais Omnisports de Paris-Bercy)

September 8-9, 2004: Arnhem, Netherlands (GelreDome)

September 13-14, 2004: Lisbon, Portugal (Pavilhão Atlântico)

"Vogue" began with the unforgettable image: Madonna stretched on all fours in a (lilac or gold, depending on your city) corset representing a cross between her 18th century look from the **MTV Video Music Awards** perf of the song and her classic **Gaultier** corsetry of yore, this time via Lacroix, sweetie. By the time the second "strike a pose" landed, the still-bendy Madonna had stretched into a wow-inducing headstand. *Yoga*, girl! The screens behind her screamed with video images by **Steven Klein**.

On **"Nobody Knows Me,"** Madonna made clever use of a conveyor belt to communicate the song's sense of being dragged backward while attempting to move on.

Don't remind **Elton John**, but the first fully live performance of the show, **"Frozen,"** found Madonna alone at a mic, emoting, hesitating in the phrasing to draw out the impact of the haunting chorus.

Flipping off everyone who'd made **"American Life"** her least successful lead single from one of her albums, she drafted the song to begin the show's *Military-Army* sequence. Even though she hadn't had to change her name or lose some **weight**, she *had* had to pull the original video for the song, which had been critical of going to war with Iraq. Even with that history, she did the song in a soldier's uniform, creating a remilitarized zone in which she seemed to be saying, "I told you so!" about the folly of war.

Still in her camo, she reinvented **"Express Yourself"** as an enthusiastic declaration of patriotism made at gunpoint—all of her **dancers** were heavily armed.

Having tried out her **guitar** on her previous tour, she brought it back out for a rock and roll take on **"Burning Up,"** snowy **TV** screens behind her reminiscent of the early days of **MTV**, when reception could be spotty. Who would ever have expected Madonna to perform this song again? Yet it's her close pal and future manager **Guy Oseary**'s favorite. A similarly rocky **"Material Girl"** worked just as well, bringing out the musicality of a song that for too long has floated in the realm of the novelty hit.

Ushering in the show's *Circus-Cabaret* sequence, the Stuart Price remix of **"Hollywood"** was used as a video interlude, during which Madonna's dancers literally played with fire, calling to mind an international sideshow.

Outta nowhere, Madonna brought back her lesser hit **"Hanky Panky."** In the same way that **"I'm Going Bananas"** seemed a surprising choice in *The Girlie Show World Tour*, "Hanky Panky" took up valuable time in the show that could've been filled with something more … essential. And yet, Madonna had a blast, giving it a three-ring of truth.

The most radical reinvention of the show arrived with her dramatically slowed-down **"Deeper and Deeper,"** which became a sensual torch song.

Madonna paid only lip service to **"Die Another Day,"** but did engage in a fetching **orgy**-tango with her cute male dancers.

Her sweet spot vocally came with her being strapped into an electric chair, from which she sang an anguished *Evita*'s **"Lament."** It had been her finest moment vocally in the film, and so it was on stage.

An *Acoustic* section was prefaced by a **"Bedtime Story"** video interlude, over which her dancers performed aerial acrobatics.

One of the very best songs on *American Life* was **"Nothing Fails,"** and Madonna did it justice as glam street singer. Strumming her guitar, she was only missing a tips jar.

"Don't Tell Me" is not the kind of song one wants to sing sitting down, so she got up and recreated the video's choreography.

Also a part of the *Acoustic* set, **"Like a Prayer"** got one of its most intimate airings. It has been done more explosively, but the song's quiet **power** has never been more adroitly communicated than on this tour.

Perhaps obscure album tracks like **"Mother and Father"**/**"Intervention"** could have been scheduled before, not after, one of her most beloved hits, but this mashup showed Madonna's **love** for the songs, and her vocals were outstanding.

Yoko Ono appreciated Madonna's inclusion of **"Imagine"** (1971) by John Lennon, but she may have been the only one. The sentiment is hard to knock, but it's a song no one really wants to hear covered by Madonna. The ad

for Madonna's Spirituality for Kids on the screen when she finished covering it was awkward.

Crowd-pleaser **"Into the Groove"** launched the *Scottish-Tribal* portion and was preceded by a bagpipes-only rendition of "Susan MacLeod," which introduced Madonna and her dancers in Scottish kilts. This marked Madonna's first video duet, with **Missy Elliott** helping to recreate her portion of **"Into the Hollywood Groove"** on the screen while Madonna did her thing live. **Guy Ritchie** loved this version of the song.

For shits and giggles, Madonna belted **"Papa Don't Preach"** and **"Crazy for You"** in either her "ITALIANS DO IT BETTER" or "KABBALISTS DO IT BETTER" T-shirt, depending on which date you attended.

"Music" and **"Holiday"** could be considered the show's double encore, and contained some of the night's most strenuous dance moves—both on stage and in the audience.

The show ended with the message, "Re-Invent Your Self," bringing to close a befuddling and bewitching mishmash of styles and songs.

The tour grossed $125 million, selling out all but one of its shows, none of which provided air conditioning because Madonna decided it messed up her voice. A behind-the-scenes look at the tour including its musical numbers was offered in the CD+DVD combo of *I'm Going to Tell You a Secret.*

"APPLAUSE RATTLED THE RAFTERS WHEN SHE THREW IN A BACK BEND AND HANDSTAND WORTHY OF OLYMPIC CONSIDERATION." -REBECCA LOUIE & LEO STANDORA, *NEW YORK DAILY NEWS* (2004)

"[M]EASURED IN VERVE, NERVE AND TECHNICAL WIZARDRY, IT'S HARD TO LEAVE THIS EPIC EXTRAVAGANZA FEELING ANYTHING LESS THAN AWE."-DAVID SEGAL, *WASHINGTON POST* (2004)

"WHILE THE LIGHTNING BOLT OF MUSICAL GREATNESS DIDN'T STRIKE THE STAGE DURING THE NEARLY TWO-HOUR CONCERT, MADONNA RAZZLE-DAZZLED HER WAY INTO THE HEARTS OF THE DEVOTED AUDIENCE WITH AN ENTERTAINING THEATRICAL REVUE THAT WAS ELABORATELY STAGED, COSTUMED AND CAST WITH A FULL DANCE TROUPE THAT INCLUDED ACROBATS AND EVEN A MOHAWKED SKATEBOARD BOY." -DAN AQUILANTE, *NEW YORK POST* (2004)

"MY HAIR WAS ON END. ANYBODY WHO TELLS YOU THE SHOW IS *TOO* POLITICAL OR *TOO* RELIGIOUS WAS AT THE CONCERT FOR ENTIRELY THE WRONG REASONS, AND PROBABLY HAS SOMETHING AGAINST MADONNA IN THE FIRST PLACE."-ANDY TOWLE, *TOWLEROAD* (2004)

REMIXED & REVISITED: *Release date: November 24, 2003. Billboard 200 peak: #115.* Madonna's final release under a long-term arrangement with the label she used to run, **Maverick**, was this hodgepodge, which offered remixes from her unpopular *American Life* album, the popular mash-up **"Into the Hollywood Groove"** from her **Gap** ads and also the stellar **Stuart Price** remix of **"Like a Virgin"/"Hollywood"** from her **MTV Video Music Awards** performance, with a nearly 10-year-old **unreleased** track to boot. It has sold approximately 150,000 copies in the US, and an uncertain (but unimpressive) number of copies internationally.

"Madonna's stocking stuffer *Remixed & Revisited* is an amusing collection of novelties—half a dozen new versions of old songs, plus a previously unreleased number, though it's little more than an 'oh by the way.'"-COMMERCIAL APPEAL (2003)

"REQUIEM FOR EVITA": Rocked-out, chant-infused overture for the late Evita, as heard in *Evita* and as found on *Evita: The Complete Motion Picture Music Soundtrack*. Madonna doesn't sing on the track, which was composed by John Mauceri.

"RESCUE ME": *Release date: February 26, 1991. Billboard Hot 100 peak: #9.* One of Madonna's most lyrically daring songs up to that point, "Rescue Me" had a wild ride in the charts; it was a radio hit with no single, so when it was finally put on sale it broke records by debuting at #15. Unfortunately, airplay had peaked, so it only went on to hit #9.

Written and produced by Madonna and **Shep Pettibone** (Pettibone's ex and ex-collaborator **Tony Shimkin** has asserted he cowrote it), "Rescue Me" was one of two new songs released on *The Immaculate Collection*, along with the #1 hit **"Justify My Love."** It is one of Madonna's most forgotten Top 10 hits, though **Lady Miss Kier** won't soon forget it.

In the song, Madonna sings that she feels she is a freak and that she wants to conquer the world despite her contempt for it. She also rasps (during the course of a lengthy whisper-chant) that she still believes there's hope in her search for a true soul mate. The songwriting was like nothing in Madonna's previous **work**, resembling her later work on *American Life*.

RESERVOIR DOGS: *Director: Quentin Tarantino. Release date: October 23, 1992.* Revered crime film noted for its ultra violence and gut-wrenching portrayal of the dishonor among a band of six thieves (including **Harvey Keitel**). At the opening of the film, the men are engaged in a heated debate over the true meaning of the song **"Like a Virgin."** Tarantino's character believes that the song is about a woman who **loves** big dicks so that each new experience hurts like the loss of virginity.

REMIXED & REVISITED

① "Nothing Fails" Nevins Mix (Madonna/Guy Sigsworth/Jem)-3:50, produced by Madonna/Mirwais/Mark "Spike" Stent/Jason Nevins/Vin Nigro/Joe "Magic"

② "Love Profusion" Headcleanr Rock Mix (Madonna/Mirwais) -3:16, produced by Madonna/Mirwais/Ray Carroll

③ "Nobody Knows Me" Mount Sims Old School Mix (Madonna/Mirwais) -4:44, produced by Madonna/Mirwais/Mount Sims

④ "American Life" Headcleanr Rock Mix (Madonna/Mirwais) -4:01, produced by Madonna/Mirwais/Ray Carroll

⑤ "Like a Virgin"/ "Hollywood" 2003 MTV Video Music Awards Performance feat. Britney Spears, Christina Aguilera and Missy Elliott (Billy Steinberg/Tom Kelly/Madonna/Mirwais)-5:34, produced by Nile Rodgers/Madonna/Mirwais/Stuart Price

⑥ "Into the Hollywood Groove" The Passengerz Mix feat. Missy Elliott (Madonna/Mirwais/Stephen Bray)-3:42, produced by Missy Elliott/Soul Diggaz/The Passengerz/Chad Griffin

⑦ "Your Honesty" (Madonna/Dallas Austin)-4:07, produced by Madonna/Dallas Austin/Daniel Abraham

KEVIN MAZER

"I always said I wanted to be famous. I never said I wanted to be rich."—MADONNA (1985)

RETTENMUND, MATTHEW: *b. December 25, 1968.* Bitch, I'm Matthew.

"REVOLVER" FEAT. LIL WAYNE: *Release date: December 14, 2009. Billboard Hot 100 peak: NA.* Written by Madonna, Lil Wayne, DJ Frank E, the Jackie Boyz and Brandon Kitchen and produced by Madonna and DJ Frank E, this **gun**-totin' tough-**love** song was on three new songs offered on her greatest hits package *Celebration*.

Madonna wasn't wild about the version found on the album, so that version is different from the single version. Producer David Guetta reported that Madonna preferred his "futuristic" remix to the **original**. Maybe she was on to something, as David Guetta's One Love Club Remix by Guetta and Afrojack won a **Grammy** for Best Remixed Recording, Non-Classical, an uncommon honor for a Madonna song.

The song is completely undistinguished in Madonna's canon, as was its perfunctory (if controversial) live rendition on *The MDNA Tour*, but it is noteworthy as the very last Madonna single ever released by **Warner Bros.**

RICE, TIM: *b. November 10, 1944.* British lyricist of the musical on which the 1996 film *Evita* was based. He has been **richly** rewarded for all of his collaborations with **Andrew Lloyd Webber**, receiving the **Golden Globe**, the **Grammy**, the **Tony** and, thanks in part to Madonna's high-profile performance of **"You Must Love Me,"** the **Oscar**.

Rice has been highly complimentary of Madonna's **acting** ("I thought it was very bad luck that she wasn't nominated for an Oscar") and singing in *Evita*. He has called her a "very **talented** artist" whose early **work** impressed him as timeless. Interestingly, he was rooting for Madonna to get the role of Evita over **Meryl Streep** and Michelle Pfeiffer.

"I think she's a fine artist and I was very keen for her to get the part, rather than some of the other ladies who would have been interesting but I don't think would have been right ..." he told **fan site** *MadonnaTribe* in 2005. "I would reckon she was by far the best because she just had the look, and there are obvious parallels to be made between Eva Perón and Madonna."

RICH: She certainly is. *Very*. In 1993, her estimated worth was $100 million, about half of **Oprah Winfrey**'s fortune at the time. By 2007, *Forbes* conservatively estimated the figure to be around $325 million, and upped it to $500 million max by 2013. In the past few years, Wealth-X estimated her net worth at $800 million and gossip columnist Rob Shuter—not a financial analyst—proclaimed her to be a full billionaire. It's highly unlikely Madonna is close to billionaire status. She's far more likely to be worth what *Forbes* said—around half that.

Regardless, as she enthused in 1992, "Having **money** is just the best thing in the world."

Though she's earned her money via her own hard **work**, Madonna's enormous wealth has actually become a bone of contention among her critics, who have argued that her riches have come between her and her street sensibility. Other critics simply use her wealth as a reason to resent her, and her most common **nickname** (you know the one) doesn't help matters.

Because Madonna has been an enormous success financially, because she rose to popularity in the "greed is good" decade of the '80s, because she has branched out into various non-creative **business** in the past decade and because her **controlling** nature has branded her a manipulator, Madonna's artistic ventures—though undeniably commercially-oriented—are frequently attributed only to her lust for more, more, more.

The criticism isn't valid; if Madonna only wanted to make big bucks, she could easily curtail some of her less commercial impulses (her abrasive humor, profane sensibility, affinity with **gay** culture, fascination with extreme sexuality) and churn out kinder, gentler pop music for far greater returns. If Madonna just wanted the money, all of her tours would be oldies revues.

More true is that in light of her middle-class background and impoverished years in **NYC** before making it big, Madonna feels that wealth grants her the freedom to do whatever she wants artistically, the **power** to help others and the leisure time that comes with not having to worry about things like homelessness and Dumpster diving.

GREGORY PACE

RICHARDS, NICKI: *b. March 24, 19–.* The second most famous Nicki (phonetically, anyway) to sing backup for Madonna, the always-positive belter has brightened Madonna's *Confessions Tour, Sticky & Sweet Tour* and *MDNA Tour* as well as at **Live Earth.** She has especially killed it on **"Like a Prayer."** She's a doll to **fans.**

Along with supporting Madonna, Richards has sung for and with a host of other A-list artists (**Mariah Carey, Michael Jackson, Bette Midler** and **Tina Turner** come to mind), releases her own albums and apparently knows the secret location to the Fountain of Youth considering she put out her first solo album in 1991. See NickiRichards.com.

RICHIE, LIONEL: *b. June 20, 1949.* As part of the Commodores, he sang on classic R&B singles like "Easy" (1977), "Brick House" (1977) and "Three Times a Lady" (1978). As a solo singer, he became one of the **voices** of the '80s with the #1 hits "Endless **Love**" with **Diana Ross** (1981), "All Night Long (All Night)" (1983), "Hello" (1984) and "Say You, Say Me" (1985), among many others.

Richie has long been friendly with Madonna, having been her neighbor at one time; she described their shared neighborhood as a "shithole."

In 2012, Madonna and Richie duked it out for a #1 album debut—she with *MDNA,* he with *Tuskegee*—and though hers made it to pole position, his was the stronger seller in the US over time. Madonna graciously sent Richie the tweet, "congrats on a successful record. To the other ritchie in my life …" He replied, "What's going on family? There is no one I would rather be on top with. Congratulations!! I am so happy for you."

Madonna's reply? "OK, but as long as I'm on top."

> "The beautiful part of where we were—we had shock value. But what came with shock value was hit after hit after hit. Madonna was outrageous—but she had a catalog of music that was unbelievable."
>
> —LIONEL RICHIE, *LONDON EVENING STANDARD* (2014)

RIHANNA: *b. February 20, 1988.* Barbadian bad girl whose meteoric rise to **fame** via a meeting with Def Jam prez Jay Z has been nearly unprecedented in terms of chart domination and album production. She has hit #1 with 11 songs, starting with "SOS" (2006), and with **Katy Perry** is a record-holder for the most #1 songs on *Billboard*'s Pop Songs radio airplay chart.

On September 9, 2008, Rihanna opened the **TV** special *Fashion Rocks* with a Josephine Baker–esque, lip-synched cover of **"Vogue"** surrounded by feathers, in a reference to the music video. (The rap was slightly changed with, "Rita Hayworth *give* good face …")

When Bravo's **Andy Cohen** asked her if she felt like "the black Madonna," Rihanna said, "There will never be another Madonna, like, that, that, just, like, just point-blank.

At this point, I am so good with being Rihanna and, like … like, I'm, I'm cool. Like, I'm, I'm okay. And Madonna's still the shit and she'll always be Madonna, like, she's the queen, like, she's awesome."

In 2012, **Ellen DeGeneres** asked Madonna to react to a list of female singers, one of whom was Rihanna. "Um, I like her …" Madonna replied.

RILEZ, BAGS: One of Madonna's early-'80s backup **dancers,** often along with her brother **Christopher Ciccone** and **Erika Belle,** on track dates.

"RING MY BELL": One of Madonna's most appealing bonus tracks, this collaboration with **Pharrell Williams** was the thirteenth track on *Hard Candy* if you bought the album as an iTunes Store pre-order, bought the iTunes Store Deluxe Edition or bought it in Japan. It is not related to the 1979 song of the same name by Anita Ward, and luckily, it sounds like nothing in Marvin Gaye's catalogue.

Madonna and Rihanna, in vogue in 2008

baqs rilez

He had Madonna's back.

RHONDA CORTE

RIPA, KELLY: *b. October 2, 1970.* SEE: *Live! with Regis & Kelly.*

RISSMAN, NATHAN: *b. February 9, 1972.* The guy who was Madonna's gardener (and who is the husband of **David**'s nanny, Shavawn Gordon) until his creative Quick-Time videos persuaded her to hire him to direct the documentary *I Am Because We Are.*

"He's a brilliant, lovely guy—one of those guys who came into my life and did every **job**. He was a runner, an intern, a gardener. He took care of my kids. He did everything, and he did it with humility," Madonna told *Interview* in 2008. So if Madonna hires you to do her hedges, bring your résumé and keep your head down and you, too, could have a career in the movies.

Rissman, whose **work** on *I Am Because We Are* was praised, was a director of the film made of Madonna's *Sticky & Sweet Tour* and second unit director on *W.E.*

The talented Mr. Rissman at his *I Am Because We Are* premiere

RITCHIE, GUY: *b. September 10, 1968.* While shooting her **"Drowned World/Substitute for Love"** music video, Madonna met her second husband in summer 1998 at a gathering at the Wiltshire estate of **Sting** and his wife, Trudie Styler. Madonna has said she was instantly attracted to the movie director, which isn't surprising—she has a soft spot for creative macho men (SEE: **Penn, Sean**).

At the time, Madonna was in a bad, on/off relationship with **Andy Bird**. She had a fling with Ritchie, but it developed into something more. Madonna dumped Bird (this Bird has flown?) and Ritchie dumped his own then-girlfriend (which made for the nifty Robbie Williams song, "She's Madonna," produced by **Pet Shop Boys**). The new couple vacationed in Italy in summer 1999 and they became a public item that fall.

Madonna, speaking to Miranda Sawyer for *The Face* early in her relationship with Ritchie, said of falling in **love** with him, "It only took me 40 years to get it right. Write that down."

Just over a year after they met, Madonna became **pregnant** with her second child, her first with Ritchie. She gave birth to **Rocco** in August 2000.

Ritchie was seen as the kind of bloke who liked to seem tough. At Madonna's *Music* release party at Catch One (4067 W. Pico Blvd., LA, CA), Ritchie got into a scuffle with security when he discovered he wasn't on the list, perhaps an ill omen of the **power** balance in their future marriage.

The couple wed on December 22, 2000, in a posh ceremony that made headlines. "I had to marry someone as tough as I am," she said of Ritchie in 2008.

Their marriage lasted just under eight years, during which time Madonna raised her children in **London** and the couple's Ashcombe House estate in Wiltshire, **England**. Madonna's transformation into "Mrs. Ritchie"—a faintly appalling appellation she wore across the **back** of her blazer at Ritchie's *Snatch* premiere—was one of her most discomfiting reinventions for **fans** used to seeing her as an independent spirit. She seemed to mellow a bit with Ritchie, even going so far as to present herself as a lady of the manor on the cover of *Vogue* (August 2005) … feeding chickens in the pictorial inside.

Madonna's brother, **Christopher Ciccone**, wrote that Ritchie was homophobic, accusing him of using anti-**gay** humor at the Ritchies' **wedding** reception. His allegations scarred Madonna's track record with her fans, some of whom decided that Madonna was betraying them by letting a homophobe run her world. Ciccone said he so disliked Ritchie that his toast to the couple was, "I would like to toast this happy moment. It happens only twice in a person's life … If anyone wants to **fuck** Guy, he will be in my room."

Asked what happened to his relationship with Madonna to make it deteriorate, **Ciccone** said, "Guy Ritchie pretty much happened to our relationship, for the most part."

During the course of their marriage, Ritchie participated in **Kabbalah** services and Madonna played wifey,

GREGORY PACE

GREGORY PACE

though she did manage to put out *Music,* ***American Life,*** ***Confessions on a Dance Floor,*** ***Hard Candy,*** toured three times (and a half!) and made quite a few appearances; if being with Ritchie changed Madonna, it was mostly perceptible in her more remote demeanor rather than in her creative output.

By 2006, there were rumors of discord in Madonna's marriage. She appeared at a **Gaultier** show on January 25, 2006, looking like she'd been crying, wearing no wedding ring. "Sometimes she wears it, sometimes she doesn't," **Liz Rosenberg** told Enquiring minds.

They had a tumultuous relationship, though both rather liked it while it lasted. Madonna likened herself to the Jackie Gleason character in *The Honeymooners* (1955–1956) with Guy as her "Alice." By 2008, Madonna wanted to send Alice to the moon.

The couple's final public appearance together was at Ritchie's **birthday** party in September 2008—tight smiles all around. Madonna wore exotic **eye** makeup and looked like a million bucks ... or maybe more like $76–$92 million bucks, depending on which amount you believe Ritchie took in their **divorce** settlement once their marriage was officially over in early 2009.

Madonna, often criticized as a **money**-grubber, hadn't insisted on a pre-nup, and only dickered with Ritchie for a couple of months on the amount he wanted in their split.

When their separation was announced, the couple said they couldn't handle living with "the pretense" any longer; they hadn't been intimate in more than a year, which makes Ritchie's compliments, paid to Madonna at her 50th birthday in August of the year they split, seem brittle. "She looks better now than she ever has done. I'm so proud. I love her so much."

A lady at 50 likes to hear that she looks good ("Her legs are Olympic standard. You won't find a fitter bird than her!" he'd also raved), but perhaps needs to know her man appreciates her for more than just her outer **beauty**.

The rage-filled *MDNA* was seen as Madonna's breakup album. Summarizing why her marriage failed in a poetic nutshell, Madonna sings in **"I Don't Give A,"** "I tried to be your wife/Diminished myself/And I swallowed my light."

> "I stepped into a soap opera, and I lived in it for quite a long period of my life. I'll probably be more eloquent on it 10 years from now … The experience was ultimately very positive … I enjoyed my first marriage. It's definitely not something I regret."—GUY RITCHIE (2011)

> "There was a time when I was less provocative—when I was married. My ex was not a fan of me kissing Britney Spears on stage."—MADONNA (2015)

The Ritchies step out in style.

RITCHIE, JOHN: Madonna's meddling former dad-in-law, the father of **Guy Ritchie**, was prone to blabbing to the media at inopportune moments. He called **Kabbalah** a "cult" and in 2006 sighed to *Closer*, "I hope that they still **love** each other, but to be honest, I just don't know that they do."

RITCHIE, ROCCO JOHN: *b. August 11, 2000.* Madonna, who'd been spending time in **England**, was determined to have her second child in the US. She told DJ Rick Dees, "Have you been to the hospitals in England?" calling them "old and Victorian." Hours later, suffering abdominal pains and bleeding due to a detached placenta, Madonna underwent an emergency C-section at Cedars Sinai (8700 Beverly Blvd., LA, CA). Rocco was kept at the hospital for several days and released August 16, Madonna's forty-second **birthday**.

"She is safe, as is little Rocco," **Liz Rosenberg** told reporters.

Madonna would later play down the drama surrounding the first of her children with Ritchie (she also adopted **David** with him), saying the situation hadn't been as dire as had been reported.

Rocco's godmother is Trudie Styler, the woman who introduced his parents, and his godfather is **Guy Oseary**. **Sting** sang "Ave Maria" at Rocco's (non-**Catholic**) baptism,

Now in his teens, Rocco is a constant figure at his mother's shows and events.

conducted by the Rev. Susan Brown. He was as well equipped materially as he was spiritually—upon his birth, he was **gifted** with a $45,000 romper by **Versace**.

It's been fun for **fans** to watch Rocco grow up around his mom. He was already showing off his moves at the final *Sticky & Sweet Tour* date in Tel Aviv and at Madonna's 2010 **Material Girl** clothing line launch, but he took his show on the road when he appeared as a featured **dancer** on the *MDNA Tour*.

On July 13, 2013, Rocco's Bar Mitzvah brought his **divorced** parents **back** together for a couple of days. He was also a strong presence at the *#secretprojectrevolution* premiere in **NYC**, where he posed for pictures with fans. He was a part of her **Elliott Smith** cover, coming out in a mask and helping Mom to her **feet** before revealing himself.

Joining **Instagram**, Rocco became a huge influence on his **mother**'s social media presence. She proudly shared images of him (and got into a heap of trouble when referring to him as **#disnigga**, for which she apologized) and his friends. Things went south when Madonna posted a backflip video of Rocco that seemed to show more of his teenage growth spurt than intended.

Rocco accompanied his mom on her *Rebel Heart Tour*, then left to live with his dad in England. This led to a bitter, high-profile custody battle.

RITTS, HERB: *August 13, 1952–December 26, 2002.* Influential celebrity portrait photographer of the '80s and '90s who got his start snapping **sexy** pics of his buddy Richard Gere at a gas station in the desert.

What Madonna has called her "incredibly long and fruitful **working** relationship" with Ritts qualifies him as, without question and with all due respect to **Steven Meisel**, the ultimate photographer of Madonna. It was Ritts who delivered unto us many of Madonna's most iconic images, whether it be the smoldering *Desperately Seeking Susan* poster and *Playboy* cover (shot the day they first met), the Hawaiian fantasy images for her first calendar and tour program (after which she swore she'd never work with him again), the dominantly submissive *True Blue* album cover (a refined replication of Ritts's own work on **Olivia Newton-John**'s 1981 *Physical* cover), her brunette ambition pics for *Like a Prayer* and *The Immaculate Collection*, many of her prettiest "Breathless Mahoney" poses and even some glamorous *Evita* shots, all of which left no doubt that Madonna was no second-rate queen getting kicks with a crown.

The first music video Ritts ever directed was Madonna's **"Cherish,"** which led to another dozen with artists like **Mariah Carey**, **Janet Jackson**, **Michael Jackson**, **Britney Spears** and **Tina Turner**.

Madonna trusted Ritts so much that he shot her in her **wedding** dress in 1985 and became the first person to take images of her with her baby, **Lola**, including a breastfeeding image that has, appropriately, **leaked**. He shot Madonna

MATTHEW RETTENMUND

©STEVE GRANITZ/RETNA. LTD.

casually as many times as he shot her formally, meaning there are thousands of unseen frames guarded by his estate. As Madonna said in *Aperture* in 1999, images of her at "parties, hanging out at my house, coming to visit me on the sets of movies" are the kinds of things that "will resurface someday, when I've been **reincarnated** as a camera lens."

Ritts, who Madonna thought of as a big brother, took images that looked naturalistically beautiful, rather than severe or overly **fashiony**. He excelled at shooting gorgeous men, including **Tony Ward**, whom he introduced to Madonna, leading to their steamy affair and Ward's appearance in the **"Justify My Love"** video and *Sex*.

Ritts wrote that the way to take a Ritts-style photo was to focus on the image, not on the technical aspects; allow yourself to make mistakes; start with **black-and-white**, which he saw as having a "fine-**art** quality"; and to use any camera handy. "It's not the camera, or having a ton of equipment. It's what you do with it that's important."

When Ritts, who lived with HIV for years, died of pneumonia at age 50, Madonna confirmed to *W* that she'd spent the last week of his life at his bedside. "That's what friends are for. He was a good egg. He didn't want people to know he was sick—he didn't want them to feel sorry for him. He just got on with his life. He was a very shy guy and didn't do the *fabulous* thing. Like a lot of other photographers who shall go unnamed."

On January 23, 2003, Madonna eulogized her friend at his memorial at Paramount Theatre (5555 Melrose Ave., Hollywood, CA). She recalled their first meeting, thinking he was "a real geek" who nonetheless "Herbified" her. Her explanation of being Herbified:

"He talks you into going to the beach. Then, he talks you into taking off your clothes. He talks you into dancing and frolicking in the sand like an idiot. He talks you into getting into the freezing cold ocean, and before you know it you have sunburn and you're freezing your ass off, um, and you're sure you've just made a huge fool out of yourself."

She recalled him as an innocent type who **hated** gossip, couldn't be paid to swear and **loved** to party and have fun.

"Just because we can't see Herb doesn't mean that he's not here. And just because that he's gone from our sight doesn't mean that he has ceased to exist. So today at this memorial, we're not here to say good-bye to Herb, but to renew our connection with him in a different way, in a way that is not hampered by the limitations of physicality, in a way that will

"We're on the same wavelength. She trusts me. And I try to come up with the best for her. She changes, I change. It's a true image that evolves."—HERB RITTS ON MADONNA (1989)

"Don't let the 'Beaver Cleaver' facade fool you He's a barracuda with a sweet countenance."—MADONNA (1985)

Madonna with Herb Ritts ... and a cigarette

never come to an end," she said at the service. She cried as she finished her speech when pointing out that (pre-digital) photography was about taking a negative and turning it into a positive, resolving to do so regarding Ritts's passing.

RIVERA, GERALDO: *b. July 4, 1943.* Shockmeister **TV** talk show host famous for occasionally inciting his guests to violence. Later became a Fox News regular and Iraq War correspondent.

Rivera's show *Geraldo* a.k.a. *The Geraldo Rivera Show* (1987–1998) hosted a segment on Madonna in 1991 that featured, along with cultural conservatives, Madonna intimates **Niki Haris**, **Jose & Luis**, Junior Vasquez and **Kurt Loder**. A phone call by Madonna punctuated the proceedings:

"Hi, Geraldo ... I just wanted to, I just wanted to say hi to Niki, Jo, Lu and Junior—it's Mommie Dearest, and I wanted you, I wanted you guys to know that I appreciate you giving all those emotionally, morally and intellectually repressed people a kick in the butt and, uh, and, I, I have—I don't know if you guys are gonna get around to playing Truth or Dare, but if you do, this is a dare for Kurt Loder: Kurt, I dare you to make out with Geraldo, and if you do, or Geraldo, if *you* do, I'll do any talk show you guys wanna do, all right? So, um, so go ahead—let's see which one of you guys are man enough."

Neither man accepted the dare, but Haris did engage in a feisty debate with a butch woman who argued that the black community was being used by **gays** to further their social agenda. Jose & Luis vogued and then did a makeover on Rivera that allowed the **exhibitionistic** host with the least to show some man-cleavage.

In 1994, Geraldo did a far less impressive follow-up show titled "Has the Goddess of Pop Fizzled?" stacked with pro-Madonna panelists, including the author of *EM20*.

FOR THE VERY FIRST TIME:
WHEN MADONNA MET HERB

One of the most famous Madonna shoots ever was her first with Herb Ritts, and it happened the first day they met.

Desperately Seeking Susan's publicist, Reid Rosefelt, was in charge of setting up a shoot with both Madonna and Rosanna Arquette in order to get images that could be used to market the film. Ann Lander of Orion decided on Herb Ritts. Rosefelt knew Ritts from his time at the PR firm PMK; back then, the firm's Michael Maslansky always had new clients shot by Ritts, who was a new shooter, maybe because Maslansky's wife, Marysa, ran Ritts's photo agency, Visages. (Luckily, Ritts was also talented.)

The shoot happened on a Saturday during the *Susan* shoot on the ladies' day off at Loft Associates

(now Studio 450, 450 W. 31st., NY, NY). Rosefelt had asked Madonna, "Can you come Saturday? I wanna do this shoot with this guy named Herb Ritts." Madonna replied, "Is he gay? Gay people take good pictures of me."

Check!

Rosefelt wrote on his personal blog: "Nowadays, photo shoots like these are a big deal, with limos for talent, and a gaggle of publicists and studio executives, but the only people from the movie were me and the wardrobe supervisor, Melissa Stanton (who brought the jackets, costumes and accessories), Herb's crew and Madonna and Rosanna, who cabbed over themselves."

Madonna arrived a little late, and was introduced to Ritts, who had brought along two assistants. Rosefelt does not recall an instant bond.

"I feel that she was so much in possession of her persona that it was just a day like any other," he tells *EM2O*. "She came in and did her thing. He told her, 'Go stand here against this curtain, stand like that,' but *she* was *her*."

Colin Booker, who did hair, makeup and styling for Ritts for "years and years and years and years," confirms to *EM2O* that the shoot was simple. "There wasn't a lot of people. It was kept very simple. It was basically the beginning of her career—she was still doing rags in her hair and crap. It didn't seem like a big deal to us." He thought Madonna was a pro. "She was really nice, open and pleasant, easygoing—she wasn't a diva, at all."

Madonna had arrived with some of her own

makeup done already, making Booker's job that much easier. "She was a hard worker. She was really into it. It was obvious to me that she was a hard-working girl who wanted to be something."

Rosefelt was familiar with Madonna the hard worker, but during the course of the afternoon, he saw a side of Madonna he'd never seen before and never saw again. "She got a call from Jelly[bean Benitez] and she was upset; her face just kinda fell and I immediately thought, 'Oh, my God, for the first time I'm seeing a human being and not a persona.' … It's the only time that mask ever broke and maybe that wasn't a mask, maybe the real Madonna is the person that everyone knows and maybe that was the moment that was unreal, but it seemed truthful to me."

One big surprise that happened was when *Vogue*'s André Leon Talley showed up to grab some photos of Madonna for the magazine. "I think it was Herb who set that up, 100%. He's not gonna just turn up in some random place," Rosefelt remembered. "He just *came*, and so then we had to call Freddy [DeMann] to ask if it was okay, but that's another testament to how Madonna was … Imagine if I went to any kind of photo shoot today, all the man-agement around people who would say, 'Are you nuts??? You need to come through us four weeks in advance!' I think I said, 'This is big.' So Madonna said, 'Let's just call Freddy and I'm done. No problem.' It was such a fucking different time."

The shoot lasted for several hours, and yet Rosefelt almost hadn't got-ten what he needed. Orion wasn't paying Ritts—the deal was, he would foot the bill for the shoot. Orion

would use the look they wanted for the movie, and Ritts would retain the rest (after the artists and their publicists made kills) to sell on his own. "I had to fight," Rosefelt said. "I mean, I think I had 10 minutes for those pictures that ended up on the cover of *Rolling Stone* and as the movie poster. It was the end of the day! I said, 'Herb, I really need you to do that shot of them in the costumes, the two of them.' We just went over to some spot. He got all the backgrounds of her and we just shot them against a wall."

Rocking a Keith Haring tube top, Madonna was the goddess the '80s required.

Original test Polaroid from Madonna's first shoot with Herb Ritts

©TREL BROCK

Those images are now among the most recognizable of Madonna, and have appeared on and in countless magazines.

Booker said the shoot didn't strike anyone on set as being as important as it seems today. "For us, it was another ad for a movie."

When it was all over, Madonna complained to Rosefelt that she had recently given up the subway and started having to cab everywhere, due to her rising profile.

Everyone went their separate ways, but the Ritts/Ciccone relationship continued because Ritts pursued Madonna. First, he made expensive prints from the shoot for her as a gift. "I remember her sharing with me some of Herb's earliest prints of her," *Susan*'s still photographer Andy Schwartz tells *EM2O*. "Gazing at her own stunning profile, she sighed, 'It takes my breath away.' I loved that she responded so candidly and viscerally to her own image."

Months later, when Madonna moved to LA, Ritts made a point of running into her and suggesting in his puppy-dog way that they work together again. She was charmed–and she knew a good thing when she saw it.

"Herb, I really need you to do that shot of them in the costumes, the two of them."

Underwear as headgear

An Audrey Hepburn look for Rosanna

©TREL BROCK

The only known image of Madonna with Herb Ritts on the day they met

Ritts contemplates his new muse.

"Is he gay? Gay people take good pictures of me." — Madonna

RIVERS, JOAN: *June 8, 1933–September 4, 2014.* Raspy-**voiced** comedy trailblazer, fashionista, businesswoman, reality-show star and talk-show veteran whose insult-comedy style made for many memorable Madonna-related wisecracks over the years, first about being a slut and later about being an old slut. Rivers definitely knew how to adapt her material to the times.

In 1986, Rivers devoted part of one of her legendary *Tonight Show* appearances to mocking Madonna's **wedding**. "Hairy! Hairy! I have never seen … she raised her arm, I thought **Tina Turner** was under there."

In one Madonna segment on *The Joan Rivers Show* in the early '90s, Rivers hosted Madonna **tribute artist** Viva **Sex**. On another, she dressed in *Desperately Seeking Susan*–wear and joked about suing "that **bitch**" after showing a fake **"Vogue"** video she claimed to have made before Madonna.

During her stand-up act in 2008, Rivers—whose act had gotten measurably more acidic in nature—got personal, asking why Madonna needed to leave the country to adopt an "ugly, skinny **African** baby" when there was one right here in the US: Nicole Richie.

Still, she sometimes had Madonna's **back**, tweeting in 2014, "**Lady Gaga** accused **Katy Perry** of stealing her idea. And Gaga knows she's right because she can remember stealing them from Madonna first."

For all her *talk* of Madonna, Rivers only *met* the woman who'd supplied her with so much material once in public. At the January 18, 1998, **Golden Globes**, Rivers was able to speak with Madonna on the red carpet, straightening Madonna's jewelry before noting, "You always look different, you know? It's wonderful. Your **hair** now, tonight, is right out of a Renaissance painting. I mean, you look absolutely like somebody could have painted you." After Madonna turned for her, she exclaimed, "Wonderful, absolutely wonderful." Then the interview turned to talk about **Lola**.

A less widely reported connection between Madonna and Rivers is via Rivers's daughter, Melissa, who signed with **Maverick** in late 1993 to helm a teen-oriented cable chat show called *Hangin' Out with Melissa Rivers* that never came to pass.

"She's got a great body … for her age, she's amazing. I love Madonna. What I find fascinating is that, um, uh, Lady Gaga, she keeps saying, 'Lady Gaga stole everything of mine.' Which I find—don't say that. You're *Madonna*. Shut up … How can you steal a rash? … You're *Madonna*, act like Madonna. Queen of the World, and Queen of the Jews."–JOAN RIVERS (2012)

RIVERSIDE DRIVE: In 1981, Madonna's manager **Camille Barbone** and Barbone's **business** partner **Adam Alter** recall finding her an apartment on the Upper West Side of **NYC** at Riverside Drive and W. 95th. It's unclear whether that exact location was misremembered, but it's known that Madonna soon after resided at 99th and Riverside (270 Riverside, #3B, NY, NY) when, in 1982, she first heard her single **"Everybody"** on the radio. She told *Rolling Stone* in 2009 her reaction was, "Oh, my **God**, that's me coming out of that box." Just because we all know you care (no judgment), her NYC phone number in 1982 was (212) 678-1155. *Don't call it.* It's an architecture firm today.

ROBINSON, LEON: *b. March 8, 1962.* Now known simply as Leon (you know, like … **Cher**), this actor played the dual role of a black man wrongly accused of murder and a smooch-worthy saint in the **"Like a Prayer"** video. Robinson later starred in the hit film *Cool Runnings* (1993), and has acted steadily since the early '80s. As a musician, he is front man and songwriter of the band Leon and the Peoples.

ROCCO: SEE: **Ritchie, Rocco John**.

ROCHESTER HILLS: Affluent **Michigan** city (the state used to have lots of those!) where Madonna moved in 1969. They lived at 2036 Oklahoma St., in a home the Ciccones had built. The hacienda was described as a two-story, chocolate-colored colonial with forest green shutters, a blue door and a ranch-style fence surrounding the grounds. Madonna lived there from sixth grade until she left for college. Her father sold the place in 2001 for $270,000. The property is a 2,600-square-foot colonial dwelling on 1.3 acres of land. The lot is described as pie-shaped, with over 300 feet on a **golf** course at the **back**.

In 2015, Madonna offended the citizens of the city during her **Howard Stern** interview when she noted it was a place where "basic, provincial-thinking people" lived. After telling the story of her **rape** the first year in **NYC**, Stern asked why she didn't just go home, to which Madonna replied, "Have you ever been to Rochester, Michigan?"

Madonna's childhood homestead, as it appears today

MARSENA FARRIS

ROCK, CHRIS: *b. February 7, 1965.* Taboo-tweaking comic whose edgy racial observations and cheerfully provocative delivery have propelled him from stand-up to movie stardom.

Rock and Madonna are friends. He's attended her tours and once said she was the wisest person he knows. This in spite of the fact that in 1992, Rock, then a *Saturday Night Live* cast member, did a *Weekend Update* riff on *Sex* in which he asked, "Who is your pimp? C'mon. Madonna puts the 'O' in 'ho'."

Rock said of Madonna on *The Oprah Winfrey Show* in 2003, "She's the smartest person I know, actually … [S]he could be 25 years old or she could be 500 years old—like, she's got that kind of knowledge."

Rock appeared in the **"Bitch I'm Madonna"** video.

ROCK AND ROLL HALL OF FAME: *1100 Rock and Roll Blvd., Cleveland, OH.* "They've called her everything from a creative cretin to a media whore (if not a literal one). So there must be scores of folks who consider it the greatest desecration to the Rock and Roll Hall of **Fame** yet that … its arbiters will usher into its heady ranks Miss 'How-Dare-She' herself: Madonna."

So wrote Jim Farber in the *New York Daily News* on the eve of Madonna's induction into the hallowed halls of the institution meant to honor rock innovators and legends. There had been a low but steady grumble about her worthiness for inclusion, but how could anyone seriously question her rock cred? She'd been in rock bands, had explored every style of music (including rock, most obviously on *Like a Prayer* and *Ray of Light*), had written or co-written many of the songs that had defined the previous 25 years and had enough attitude to choke a Johnny Rotten.

At the March 10, 2008, induction ceremony, held at the Waldorf-Astoria (301 Park Ave., NY, NY) and telecast live on **VH1** Classic, a career-retrospective video was played and Madonna's *Hard Candy* collaborator **Justin Timberlake** presented her to the crowd with a speech in which he reminded everyone that, "There is and will only ever be one Madonna," praising her for being "a singing, dancing, writing, promoting, achieving superstar who became the biggest name on the planet the old-fashioned way: She earned it."

Timberlake also related a story of how Madonna talked him into dropping his pants for a **B12** shot. She complimented him on his "nice top shelf."

Madonna, looking … *different* … in a see-through Chanel housedress and severely structured **hair** gave one of the longest speeches any honoree had ever delivered, one in which she did something her **haters** say she *never* does: She gave credit where credit was due. (There are others, but her most glaring omissions were: **Jellybean Benitez, Stephen Bray, Mark Kamins** and **Reggie Lucas**.)

Madonna had hand-selected fellow Michigander **Iggy Pop** to play her into the Hall. He rocked out with **"Burning Up"** and **"Ray of Light,"** which made for a rousing show.

Madonna has had only two more Top 10 hits in the US since her induction, which might mean she was on to something in the past, when she said that she hated career honors (and refused to write her memoirs) because going along with such things telegraphs that one has *done*, rather than telegraphing what one is *doing*.

Regardless, it was a richly deserved honor. Very few music artists, not only restricted to females, can honestly say their musical careers have not in some way been influenced by Madonna, the woman who's done it all and done it well.

Madonna's fellow inductees that evening were the Dave Clark Five, Leonard Cohen, John Mellencamp and the Ventures. It's a travesty that certain other artists have yet to be included, but the Hall's bizarre, political, sexist selection process should not be used to complain about the fact that at least one '80s lady rightly made it through the wilderness.

Rock chicks

GREGORY PACE

MADONNA'S ROCK AND ROLL HALL OF FAME SPEECH (2008) (yes … all of it)

....

I can't decide what I need to recover from: All my bad hairstyles in the previous video, or all of Justin [Timberlake]'s innuendos. Everything he said is basically true, but I didn't say, 'Drop 'em,' I said, 'Pull your pants down.' 'K? Just, just like to be accurate; as you know, I am a control freak.

I'm not sure my speech will be as entertaining, but I do mean it.

Um, it is a great honor to receive this award, and I'm grateful and appreciative for, for the acknowledgment that this implies. But there's something finite about an award, and I would like to reflect for a moment on the things in my life, on the things in my life, which have not been and continue to not be finite.

I have always been fortunate to have people around me who believed in me, starting with my ballet teacher, Christopher Flynn, in Detroit, Michigan, who told me, at the age of 14, that I was special, that I needed to believe in myself, that I needed to go out into the world and pursue my dreams. Those words meant everything to me because I can assure you, at the time I didn't feel special.

And then there was Dan Gilroy. He lived in an abandoned synagogue in Queens with his brother, Ed. They played in a band together. I was sick of being an out-of-work dancer, so he taught me how to play guitar. And every day when Dan and Ed would go to work on their day jobs, I would sneak down to the basement and I taught myself how to play the drums listening to Elvis Costello records and I practiced those four chords that Dan taught me over and over and over again. I wrote my first song in that synagogue. It was called, ironically, "Tell the Truth." I remember, I remember that moment so, so vividly, I remember the hairs standing up on the back of my arms, and I, and I, and I thought to myself, "Who just wrote that song? That wasn't me." I felt like I had been possessed by some magic. And luckily for me, I have been miraculously and continuously possessed by some kind of magic.

And even now, my manager, Guy Oseary, who's out there somewhere in the audience watching right now, says to me almost every day, "M, anything is possible. Just tell me what it is you want to achieve." And he really means it. Thirty-five years later, people are still encouraging me to believe in my dreams. What more could I ask for? There's a saying in the Talmud that for every blade of, that for every blade of grass, there's an angel that watches over it and whispers, "Grow, grow." And I can still hear those angels whispering.

And even the naysayers, the ones who said I was talentless, that I was chubby, that I couldn't sing, that I was a one-hit wonder—they helped me, too. They helped me because they made me question myself, repeatedly, and they pushed me to be better. And I am grateful for their resistance.

I know that I would not be here right now without all of it, without all of you. Because life, like art, is a collaboration, and I did not get here on my own, and why would I want to?

There's no way that I could ever imagined that my life would unfurl as it has. In one way, it feels like a series of suddenlys. One day I was a struggling dancer in Manhattan, and then suddenly I was teaching myself how to play the drums in a synagogue in Queens, and then suddenly I was in a band and I was doing gigs at CBGB's and Max's Kansas City, and, and then suddenly I met Seymour Stein hooked up to an IV drip in a hospital bed, and then suddenly I got signed to Sire Records, and then suddenly I was rolling around on the floor at the MTV Awards with my ass hanging out.

What nobody knows is that I lost one of my high heels and I dove to the ground to find it and suddenly it was a dance move. Yikes! And then I had to go backstage and look at my manager, who was white as a ghost, freaking out and telling me I had just ruined my career. What did he know?

Then, suddenly I was on the stage at Madison Square Garden, and I looked out into the audience and every girl was dressed like me. Freak me out! Anyways, suddenly, and suddenly and suddenly, that's one way of looking at it.

The other way of looking at it is that everything happened exactly at it was supposed to happen. That I worked with the amazing people I was supposed to work with, that I traveled to the amazing places that I was supposed to travel to, that I made the mistakes that I was supposed to make. That the universe would conspire to help me and guide me all the way up to this moment where I am standing in front of you. And finally I have the chance to say thank you to so many people.

First and foremost, I would like to thank my record company, Warner Bros., whom I have been signed to for my entire recording career. Not many people can say that. And then there's Michael Rosenblatt—I wish he was here tonight. He's the person that more or less discovered me in a nightclub in Manhattan. He told me w—, he was an A&R guy at Sire Records. I had no idea what an "A&R guy" was, but it sounded important.

So I jammed my demo tape into his hand, we both did a tab of ecstasy and then we danced the night away. That's the truth.

Um, which leads me to the next person I have to thank, and that is Seymour Stein, and I do think he's here tonight. Seymour, where are you? Somewhere? The legendary Seymour Stein. Yeah. Um, to know Seymour is to love Seymour. Yeah, who takes meetings with people when they're hooked up to IV drips in a hospital bed? 'K? I mean, I thought the guy was gonna die! But he asked me—he was wearing boxer shorts by the way, and a T-shirt, it was a little bit strange—he asked me to play my demo tape for him and I just happened to be carrying a boom box with me. So, yeah, so I played my music and he seemed to like it. And, um, anyways, Seymour's still alive and well, which is great news. Thank you, Seymour.

Does any of this sound strange? Hospitals, synagogues … ecstasy? I don't know … believe me, it just gets stranger.

Um, the next person I have to thank is Liz Rosenberg. I know she's also here somewhere. Yeah. Um, she's been, and still, um, still is, the head of publicity for my entire career. Now, does anybody understand the insanity of being my publicist for the last 25 years? Yup. Well, I think Liz was smoking a joint when I first met her. Yeah. Yeah. I walked into her office and she very politely stubbed it out in the ashtray. I don't think she thought I knew she was smoking a joint, but it was a little bit obvious. Anyway, um, we hit it off right away. She was my kind of girl—tough, irreverent and funny—and we've had a long and amazing, uh, chunk of time together. Oh, God. Um, after dealing with all the nutcases she's had to deal with and putting out all the fires that she's had to put out, it's kind of amazing that she's not shooting up heroin. I don't mean to grass everybody up and make it sound like everybody I hooked up with was, like, a drug addict or anything, but the fact of the matter is, the reality is, is that I ended up with a group of very responsible and hardworking people who gave me an enormous amount of love and support along with everyone else at my record company, and I don't have time to thank all of you, but thank you.

So then of course, I needed a manager, right? So, I asked myself, "Self, who is the most successful artist in the business today?" and Self answered, "Michael Jackson." So, off I went to LA, to find the man who managed Michael Jackson, to make him my manager. Cut to Freddy DeMann, another man I want to thank,

the ultimate mack daddy manager, slicked back hair, tan, smelling of expensive cologne, big desks, smoking a cigar … yep, he drove a Porsche. He gave me a ride back to my hotel in that Porsche. By the time we got there, he was my manager. And there was no monkey business, okay? He gave me … I'm just kidding. Um, see? He [Justin Timberlake] rubbed off on me. This speech was not meant to have a lot of sexual innuendos somehow. He's bringing sexy back. Okay? I'll get you, fucker! Okay, so, we had an amazing 15 years together, and I learned a lot from him, so thank you, Freddy DeMann.

It is while I was with Freddy that I met this incredibly cocky Israeli teenager named Guy Oseary. He was like Freddy's step-and-fetch-it boy. Yeah, he was always putting his two cents in, even when, and especially when, I didn't ask for it. He was the most ambitious, confident, idealistic, hungry-for-knowledge, obsessed-with-money 18-year-old I had ever met. He kept pestering me with his ideas. He never stopped scheming. He was relentless, and today, he is my manager. And I know that he would fly to the ends of the earth for me. So thank you, Guy.

And as you can see, everything kind of goes full circle here, doesn't it? Um, but what's a record without the music, right? That's right, motherfuckers! What's a record without Nile Rodgers, Pat Leonard, Babyface, Joe Henry, William Orbit, Mirwais Ahmadzaï, Stuart Price, Pharrell [Williams] and now Justin Timberlake and Timbaland? I feel so lucky to have been able to work with such amazing songwriters and producers. I can't underestimate how grateful I am for that.

I would also like to thank all of my fans, who have stuck by me through thick and thin. God knows, they have stuck by me. Yes. Now be quiet. Now, they've stuck by me through thick and thin, and God knows there's been a lot of thick. That's not an innuendo.

I'd also like to thank the Semtex Girls who are my soldiers, and I know they would walk through the fire with me. Thank you, ladies. To my, to my teachers, my friends and my family, I thank you all for facilitating this journey, which for me has only just begun, and for reminding me that I am only the manager of my talent, not the owner. I've gone on to do so many things in my life, from writing children's books, to designing clothes, to directing a film, but for me, it always does, and it always will, come back to the music. So thank you … very much.

Now, um, I would now like to, uh, introduce another ass-kicker from Michigan, Iggy Pop.

"I've never thought that Madonna's success was surprising or amazing or a fluke ..."—NILE RODGERS (1998)

ROCK FOR THE RAINFOREST: The ninth annual installment of **Sting**'s benefit for the salvation of the Brazilian rainforest was held April 27, 1998, at Carnegie Hall (881 Seventh Ave., NY, NY). Madonna performed a stirring rendition of **"Frozen"** (her only live vocal of the *Ray of Light* song until her *Drowned World Tour*) accompanied by the East Harlem Violin Project.

Later in the evening, Madonna did some three-part harmony with Roberta Flack and Wynonna Judd during "With a Little Help from My Friends" (1967), and she and **Elton John** danced together and did backing vocals on "Twist and Shout" (1961), both numbers featuring the entire lineup of stars, including Joe Cocker, Emmylou Harris, Billy Joel, Tsidii LeLoka-Lupindo, Sidney Poitier, Sting & Trudie Styler and James Taylor.

Jon Pareles of *The New York Times* recorded for posterity of the finale, "Madonna had topped her **Versace** dress with a cowboy hat, and she was showing all the sensitive songwriters around her how to do the Twist."

Emcee **Rosie O'Donnell** referred to Madonna as **Courtney Love**, and Madonna returned the favor by calling O'Donnell Kathy Bates.

At the May 13, 2010, edition of the same event, John returned to perform a medley of **"Material Girl"**/**"Like a Virgin"** surrounded by boys in Speedos.

ROCK THE VOTE: Organization founded in 1990 dedicated to getting young adults to exercise their right to vote. Rock the Vote employs the free services of rock stars and celebrities to make voter-awareness clips.

Madonna was an early booster. She lent a saucy **"Vogue"** musical and video **parody** called "Vote" to the very first Rock the Vote campaign, appearing in a red bra and panties and wrapped in the US **flag**. Framed by **Jose & Luis** in their denim cut-offs and too-tight Ts, Madonna changed the lyrics of her song to get across the point that freedom of speech is "as good as **sex.**" The clip was timely, coming after intense debates on the sacred nature of the US flag and on **censorship** in the aftermath of obscenity charges against the 2 Live Crew. Would she get away with this ad today? Unlikely.

Embarrassingly, Madonna was caught red-handed *not* voting—she wasn't even registered, and apparently, hadn't ever voted in her life.

Humbled—okay, not really—Madonna returned in 1992 to cut another **PSA** for the group. She'd finally registered to vote, and her **black-and-white** ad featured Madonna in a dressing room, having her **hair** and makeup done in advance of her first trip to the ballot box. The clip was ultra-**camp**, with Madonna joking about being 21 years old (she was only 34 and already thinking about **ageism**), complaining about having to listen to Kenny G while you're on hold with the Board of Elections, dissing **MTV** as being more **boring** than C-SPAN and knocking **Cher**'s wardrobe. One snippy remark that got snipped from the final cut was a jab at **Michael Jackson**'s silly **video** "Jam" (1992) with **basketballer** Michael Jordan. "Michael," she exclaimed, "white men can't jump!"

RODGERS, NILE: *b. September 19, 1952.* One of the founders of **disco** institution Chic, whose hits "Le Freak" (1978), "I Want Your **Love**" (1978) and "Good Times" (1978) are essentials of the era. He went on to become one of the music industry's most respected producers, **working** with everyone from Duran Duran to **David Bowie** to, in 2013 to great acclaim, Daft Punk.

Rodgers produced Madonna's second album, *Like a Virgin*. It remains her biggest-selling album in the US and is one of the foundational works of her entire career. Madonna had not enjoyed herself putting together *Madonna*, so with her next effort, she'd resolved to be there every step of the way, including throughout the final mixing.

When he was first introduced to Madonna, Rodgers found her to be interesting, but his opinion of her escalated the next time they met. "... I thought: This could be the most special person I've ever met in my *life*," he recalled in 2015. "She was brilliant and focused. After she played me demos she flat out told me: 'If you don't love these songs, we can't work together.'"

He loved them, and so they did. But it stopped at love; Rodgers recalled in 2013 that Madonna had said during their recording sessions, "Nile, do you think I'm **sexy**?" to which he replied, "Madonna, what kind of question is that? Of course! You're, like, one of the sexiest women I ever met." Madonna then burst out with, "Well, then why don't you wanna **fuck** me?!" When Rodgers told her it was because he was her producer so it wouldn't be a good idea, she replied, "Well, that didn't stop any of the other ones."

Madonna didn't get laid, but she did learn a lot from Rodgers. "He's a genius," she said right after they had finished recording. "We just have a really good chemistry and he understands my musicality. 'Cuz he's a trained musician and I'm not, really. I don't know musical terminology, he can just read my mind."

Within months of the album's release, Rodgers said, "Madonna is blatantly sexual and sensual, but not sleazy, not even a little bit. In my opinion, she's an excellent natural singer, a natural musician, a serious artist."

Rodgers learned from Madonna, too. He said she knew better than he which of their songs would be the bigger hit. "... I thought **'Material Girl'** was the best song to lead with. Madonna was convinced it was **'Like a Virgin'** ... She taught me that it was about being a girl, losing your virginity and how relevant a lyric like that would be. Sometimes there's an intellectual component to a record that can trump its primal component."

Not that Rodgers needed much schooling. Having a string of recent hits under his belt, he made a deal with **Warner Bros.** that if his work with Madonna could sell 5 million units, he would get major points. The label thought

he was crazy, as *Madonna* had yet to break a million. Now, *Like a Virgin* has sold over four times that amount, helping to enrich Rodgers substantially.

Madonna couldn't have been happier with how *Like a Virgin* turned out (Rodgers himself has liked other albums better, saying in 1995, "As a **fan**, it wouldn't be what I consider my favorite Madonna album compositionally"), but she's never worked with him again. Still, the two have traded compliments for one another through the years, and hugged and kissed when they were seated near each other at the **Grammys** in 2015.

"I'm always amazed at Madonna's incredible judgment when it comes to making pop records. She has the ability to try new things and always be right," Nile Rodgers said of Madonna in 1993. He was just continuing to express the same sound judgment he'd had right from the beginning that Madonna was way more **talented** than her critics, or even most of her *fans*, understood.

> "[Nile Rodgers] is passionate man. He lives life to the hilt. When you deal with people who are that way, you get good stuff and bad stuff, but it was really great working with him."
>
> —MADONNA, *STAR HITS* (1984)

RODMAN, DENNIS: *b. May 13, 1961.* Gargantuan **basketballer** known for his rebellious ways and perpetually changing **hair** color, who had some sort of limited fling with Madonna in 1994. The odd couple (with an almost two-foot **height** difference) made spectacles of themselves, exchanging signals and knowing glances at games and dodging *Hard Copy* cameras on Rodeo Drive.

Madonna and Rodman interviewed each other for a *Vibe* cover story that was pulled at the insistence of founder Quincy Jones, who felt readers might be annoyed by seeing a white person on the cover (she would have been the second white act in a row, following the **Beastie Boys**). The images of the two cavorting, shot by Melodie McDaniel, have **leaked**, and the interview is legendary for its rumored frankness and vulgarity.

Madonna was beyond unthrilled by Rodman's **book** *Bad as I Wanna Be* (1996), which painted Madonna as a **sex** machine dying to get impregnated. He also rated her in bed, writing, "She wasn't an acrobat. But she wasn't a dead fish, either." Madonna, in casting doubt on Rodman's chronicle of the events, has said he and she both know what really did and didn't happen between them.

RODRIGUEZ, ALEX: *b. July 27, 1975.* Some of Madonna's romantic conquests are fascinating men heavily involved in film, others are guys you can only imagine as pile-drivers in bed. A-Rod—one of the most famous pro baseball players ever, and not always in a positive way—would fall into that latter camp.

"She gives good soundtrack to life." That's my go-to phrase whenever I try to sum up the hold Madonna has had over me for her entire career. More than any other star, her music instantly signifies times and places and relationships from my life, from adolescent fantasy ("Like a Virgin") through my first serious adult relationship (*Sex*), to a personal and creative reawakening (hello, *Ray of Light*). Most people know me from one of the longest running movie sites on the Internet, *The Film Experience*. Despite her non-illustrious movie career, Madonna is permanently embedded in my cinephilia, too. I remember more details from the nights I first saw *Dick Tracy*, *Truth or Dare* and *Evita* than is humanly healthy. People have amusingly (and annoyingly) tried to write Madonna off since Day One, but she's always been the exact opposite of a flash-in-the-pan. How does she always resonate so far beyond the moment? By capturing it, amplifying it and twisting it to suit her own ever-shifting style and recurring favorite themes, then selling it all with incomparable showmanship. I hope she outlives me so that the music never stops.

A-Rod's wife Cynthia accused Madonna of carrying on an "affair of the heart" (if not of the private parts) with her husband in 2008. Madonna's hubby **Guy Ritchie** stood by her through the scandal (allegedly receiving as a thank-you from his wife a $25,000 vintage BMW **motorcycle** complete with sidecar, before the pair, like the A-Rods, **divorced**).

A-Rod and Madonna have always maintained that they were merely friends, but he certainly has a type, which is sinewy **blondes**—his wife, Cameron Diaz, wrestler Torrie Wilson—so the fact that he attended Madonna's *Sticky & Sweet Tour* does make one wonder if the friendship stayed at home plate or if he ever rounded any bases.

In 2009, A-Rod said of Madonna, "She's very smart and ... passionate. If there was ever any situation, she's a great ear to have, you know?" We know.

ROLE MODEL: Whether or not Madonna is a good role model for kids was for years a subject of debate, starting with her earliest incarnation as a bubbly **Boy Toy**, draped in layers of bright clothes and junk jewelry. Missing from the debate has been the idea that perhaps Madonna doesn't owe role-model status to the world, an argument that could be applied to any pop diva who's followed her.

Madonna never set out to be anyone's perfect heroine, and yet, whenever a person becomes a star, his or her life is expected to reflect society's rules of normalcy and morality, or the star is branded a "bad role model."

"I didn't realize ... that being famous was going to be such a responsibility, and that every thing I said or did was going to be scrutinized and that I was going to be such a role model, and that I had—you know what I mean?" Madonna said in 1990. "And so once that happens, then you start realizing that everything you say is really important ... I think you have to either take that responsibility and use it in a positive way or get out of the limelight."

Madonna is an *excellent* role model if your priorities are self-actualization, ambition, **creativity**, hard **work**, frankness and individuality; she is a bad role model if your priorities are adhering to the status quo, respecting religious dogma over all, maintaining one's chastity and behaving with a sense of modesty and decorum.

In the '90s, as her **fan** base aged, the debate of Madonna's influence on kids began to lose steam (though *Good Housekeeping* published an article on "How to Protect Your Children from Madonna"). Also, Madonna has made it clear that she has no problem allowing her products to be labeled with warning labels, and that she is not in **business** just to tickle the fancies of wee ones. "I'm not a child and all the things I do may not necessarily be for a child's consumption," she said in 1992.

Kurt Loder had said the year before, "I think she's very **talented**. I mean, I also think that she's a very good role model for young women. I mean, you can be in charge of your life—you can be in charge of your life, you can be entirely successful, you can express yourself in the way that you want and you can be sort of on the cutting edge of **art**—and I think what she does is art."

The funniest example of Madonna as role model is a paperback **book** for children from 1986 by Turman Publishing in Seattle. The book narrates Madonna's life story in a version as sanitized as possible for elementary-**school** kids, but it can't help offering vocab phrases like "ratholes" ("dark and dirty bars and clubs"), "amazingly attractive," "hung," "fishnet stockings," "completely alone," "ancient-looking" and "miles of buckwheat pancakes." The book offers enrichment activities for kids, which include writing a poem about Madonna and describing what they'd do if they could spend a whole day with her.

The author proposes spending it eating miles of buckwheat pancakes in fishnets.

As she's gotten older, Madonna's role-model status as a **mother** and as a woman of a certain age have each been questioned, leading to inane articles that have kept the Internet alive with activity if not with perception and sensible debate.

Amanda Platell, writing for the *Daily Mail*, said, "... I believe that for 25 years, Madonna, who has so cynically and assiduously promoted herself as a role model for independent, modern women, has, in fact, had a hugely detrimental effect on the values of those same women ... The greatest **irony** of Madonna is her very name, representing as it does one of the central icons of Christianity, the eternal mother. You'd have difficulty finding a more utterly selfish one."

The short answer as to Madonna's role-model status is that she may not be the role model of your **dreams** if you disagree with what she believes, but she is an admirable role model in that she's never been a person who doesn't care about her legacy or how it will affect others.

> "I am positive about life and promote the ideas of happiness and honesty. I know that a lot of people look up to me and copy me, so I'd certainly hate to be doing anything that might be harmful to anyone."—MADONNA (1988)

ROLLING STONE: *Publication dates: November 9, 1967–.* The rock and roll **magazine** of record, founded by Jann Wenner and Ralph J. Gleason in the '60s and still chugging along today as a biweekly with a strong Web presence and a continuing ability to drive pop-cultural and, increasingly, political narratives.

Along with *Interview* and *Vanity Fair*, *Rolling Stone* has long been one of Madonna's go-to publications for letting her public know what's on her creative mind, what she looks like right now and in what musical direction she intends to go. Along with the cover stories detailed below, Madonna has been inside the magazine countless times, and has appeared on a number of foreign editions.

Madonna's first appearance was on the November 22, 1984, edition. The cover, by one of her longtime photographers of choice, **Steven Meisel**, illustrates how Madonna's gaze is one of the secrets of her success as a subject; she **controls** the mood of most of her photographs with the greatest of ease, with the flick of an eyelash, or, as in this case, with her hardened, unblinking stare. Little did she realize that this choice image by Meisel would be used to enhance journalist Christopher Connelly's exceedingly cynical profile. It became a piece she would never fully live down, a story that broadcasted its intentions with that cover line: "MADONNA GOES ALL THE WAY." The article seemed to list every person Madonna had ever met and **worked** with, more than implying that she coldly used them to get what she wanted, and then discarded them. When commenting on her past association with **Stephen Bray**, Madonna said: "Looking **back**, I think that I probably did make him feel kind of bad, but I was really insensitive in those days. I was totally self-absorbed." To which Connelly added: "It wouldn't be the last time."

In spite of the magazine's sexist-feeling treatment of her, this also wouldn't be Madonna's last appearance on the cover, proving that if she didn't **love** that first profile, she still knew *Rolling Stone* was establishment—something she wanted to be part of, something she wanted to affect.

Madonna's May 9, 1985, cover was shared with her *Desperately Seeking Susan* costar **Rosanna Arquette**, in an image by **Herb Ritts**. Madonna doesn't always blend well in dual shoots, but her chemistry with Arquette was a perfect microcosm of their characters' relationship in the classic film: Madonna as **sex** bomb, Arquette as pretty but tentative doppelganger. The cover featured one of Madonna's patented put-your-jewelry-in-your-teeth poses, and the other two-shot inside presented the women in a retro floral motif. Madonna posed in Hawaii in a series of beach-**fashion** looks for Ritts, surrounded by a bevy of surfer **boy toys**. The feature detailed the making of their movie, including a candid admission from Arquette: "Madonna laughs off bad press, but I still get hurt."

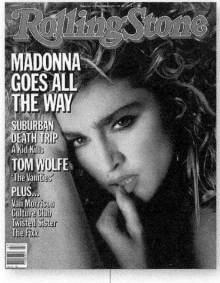

For the June 5, 1986, issue, Madonna was shot by Matthew Rolston. The first time she went through a radical image and look overhaul was in 1986, when the **"Papa Don't Preach"** video came out. Sure, the **"Live to Tell"** video threw some of us for a loop, but Madonna looked like she was playing a period character. In "Papa," it was like a whole new Madonna—slim, sleek, shorthaired, classic. *Rolling Stone* was the magazine that got to introduce us, photographically, to this new creature, who would be further rammed down our throats via the *True Blue* album cover by Ritts. For the magazine, Rolston was our "Henry Higgins," giving us a demure wallflower (welllll … she *was* up against a wall and she *did* have a flower in her cleavage on the cover) version of the woman who not long before had been caked with makeup and layers of flashy, trashy, downtown-chic glad rags. Inside, the images could not have been less like the Madonna of yesteryear: She posed as **Marlene Dietrich** in front of a mirror and as a circus ballerina next to a clown. In the Fred Schruers interview, Madonna articulated the difference between an actor and a singer: "When you're an actor, you do your work and you go home and people deal with what's up on the screen. When you're a singer … you're saying, 'This is me,' so people know you intimately." Interesting to keep in mind while listening to **"Gang Bang."**

Ritts got a second cover with Madonna for the September 10, 1987, issue. When she posed for this arresting shot (which is viewed most interestingly as a sort of follow-up to her *True Blue* album-cover pose), she was already a legend. *Rolling Stone*, which had smeared her in 1984, had nonetheless been following her slavishly ever since. The interview, conducted while Madonna was in Japan, compared her to the **Beatles**, and she tried to explain the mystery behind her own appeal to the Japanese: "I think I stand for a lot of things in their minds. You know, a lot of kinds of stereotypes, like the whole sex-goddess image and the **blonde** thing. But mainly I think they feel that most of my music is really, really positive, and I think that they appreciate that, particularly the women." Madonna's popularity in Japan has faded considerably over the years, but she enjoyed a

massive resurgence during her *Confessions on a Dance Floor* era.

The March 23, 1989, issue was another by Ritts. What a breath of fresh air it was when Madonna washed that blonde right out of her **hair** and presented herself as the brunette **Michigan** girl she'd been born as, and had always been underneath the glitz and the look-at-my-tits. Ritts perfectly captured Madonna's desire to be seen as a singer-songwriter, not just a provocateur. Of course, she almost immediately scandalized the world with her controversial **"Like a Prayer"** video, and then dyed her hair blonde again.

Speaking to Bill Zehme inside, Madonna earned some bitterness from **La Toya Jackson** by allowing herself to be quoted snarking about the latter's "major tit job." But she also commented on what turned out to be her crumbling marriage to **Sean Penn** by way of commenting on her song **"Till Death Do Us Part"**: "I wanted the song to be very shocking, and I think it was. It's about a dysfunctional relationship, a sadomasochistic relationship that can't end. Now that's where the truth stops, because I would never want to continue a terrible relationship forever and ever and ever until I die." And she didn't!

Ritts four-peated with the September 21, 1989, cover of the mag's summer "Rock & Roll Photo Album" issue. The image is a color portrait taken during the filming of the **"Cherish"** video.

Carrie Fisher interviewed Madonna for the June 13, 1991, cover (the second part of their endless and endlessly entertaining "Big-Time Girl Talk" piece appeared in the following ish), asking Madonna to name a star she likes. "Bette Davis. Oh, everybody I like is dead." Madonna confessed she was developing **Martha Graham** and **Frida Kahlo** films. The cover and inside portfolio, all racy shots with a '20s looks, were by Meisel.

After a huge gap in coverage, Madonna returned to the (partial) cover on November 13, 1997, in advance of *Ray of Light*, posing alongside former nemesis **Courtney Love** and **Tina Turner**, shot by Peggy Sirota for the "Women of Rock" issue. Apparently, Madonna and Love bickered over what music should play during their shoot while Turner went with the flow. Inside, Madonna was revealing her more maternal side: "Every since my daughter was born, I feel the fleetingness of time. And I don't want to waste it on getting the perfect lip color."

With *Ray of Light* setting the world on fire, Madonna was back for the July 9–July 23, 1998, cover, part of a visually gonzo **David LaChapelle** portfolio called "Indian Summer." *EM20* has always contended that Madonna looks like Kirstie Alley on this cover, and that LaChapelle—who seems to kinda detest Madonna now—was overrated.

—JOE JERVIS, JOE.MY.GOD.COM

SHARON SMITH

Madonna, caught at the Roseland, opening for New Edition

ROMANEK, MARK: *b. September 18, 1959.* Director of the Japanese-flavored **"Rain"** video who envisioned and executed its Japanese-influenced "clean, Zenned-out minimalism" in spite of almost turning down the **job** because he feared he wouldn't be able to deliver a video to such a romantic-seeming song.

Romanek has said his **work** on the video was "more collaborative" with Madonna than with other artists. "She would come into the editing room and look at a cut and she would say, 'You know, I think this would be better over here and this seems too slow here,' and we would go, 'She's right.' … She has a great sensitivity to filmmaking."

As exceptional as his work was on that clip, the best was yet to come; Romanek's **"Bedtime Story"** is Madonna at her weirdest, most ethereal and most enigmatic. If you're a huge **fan** of that one, don't miss his **book** *Mark Romanek: Music Video Stills* (Arena, 1999), which has an image of a sunflower-framed Madonna on the cover.

Romanek went on to direct the feature films *One Hour Photo* (2002), starring Robin **Williams**, and *Never Let Me Go* (2010), with Carey Mulligan, Keira Knightley and Andrew Garfield.

More currently he's the guy who directed **Taylor Swift**'s instantly iconic "Shake It Off" (2014).

ROSE, AXL: *b. February 6, 1962.* Skanky but worshiped lead singer of massive '80s and '90s rock band **Guns N' Roses**, whose body Madonna critiqued in 1991: "He doesn't have any muscle tone."

Rose attended Madonna's 48th **birthday** party in **London** in 2006 after her *Confessions Tour* gig, along with **Gwyneth Paltrow**, Kevin Spacey and many other luminaries … but Madonna left them at a bar called Loungelover (No. 1 Whitby St., London, England, UK) cooling their heels for over two hours.

ROSELAND BALLROOM: *Formerly 239 W. 52nd St., NY, NY.* Madonna performed or appeared several times at this classic, now defunct, **NYC** space.

Most importantly, on November 5, 2000, Madonna ended a seven-year live dry spell with a five-song, 25-minute set here to plug *Music*. The place was decorated in country & western chic, complete with haystacks, and Madonna herself had a black cowgirl hat (hey, those are for the bad guys!) and black, **"Britney Spears"**-bedazzled tank. She sang **"Impressive Instant," "Runaway Lover," "Don't Tell Me," "What It Feels Like for a Girl"** (dedicated to Spears) and **"Music"** to the 3,000 assembled **fans** (among them **Rosie O'Donnell**, **Gwyneth Paltrow** and **Rupert Everett**). She had given birth to **Rocco** just 11 weeks earlier, yet was already **back** in fighting shape. 'I'm happy to be onstage again!" she raved. "The last time I played Roseland was 18 years ago. I was the opening act for New Edition!" What a **Bobby Brown**-noser!

For the September 28, 2000, issue, a *Music*-era **Jean-Baptiste Mondino** shot of Madonna, the Urban Cowgirl, was used. She was knocked up with **Rocco** at the time (Rocc-ed up?), telling her inquisitor, "I get to the end of my day sometimes, and I think, 'Okay, I'm **pregnant**. I can't exercise. I can't wear cool clothes. I don't feel like dancing. And there's absolutely nothing remotely cool or cutting-edge about me right now.' I've become a domesticated cow."

Madonna's December 1, 2005, cover—her first by **Steven Klein**—was a sexy Ann-Margret homage. Inside, she complained about anti-**Kabbalah** forces, about her antipathy for W and about making *Confessions on a **Dance** Floor* with **Stuart Price**.

A vintage Ritts cover was used on the October 29, 2009, issue, in which Madonna reflected on her lengthy career. She thanked Stephen Bray for **"Into the Groove"** and admitted *Evita* was the greatest challenge of her entire career.

For the March 12, 2015, cover, a very *Truth or Dare*-looking **Mert and Marcus** pic fronted a feature called "Live to Tell" by Brian Hiatt in which Madonna revealed herself to be a spitfire as always. "Women my age have accepted they're not allowed to behave a certain way," she seethed, addressing the **ageism** that has plagued the latter part of her career. "I never followed rules. I'm not going to start now." She also sounded surprisingly backward-looking, **nostalgically** remembering of the '80s, "Life was different. **New York** was different. The music **business** was different. I miss the simplicity of it …"

No Madonna magazine collection is complete without all of her *Rolling Stone* covers.

The next time she played Roseland was in a sizzling promo show for ***Hard Candy*** on April 30, 2008. Fans stood in line overnight for free tickets, then nearly killed each other dancing to her run-through of **"Candy Shop,"** **"Miles Away," "4 Minutes"** (with duet partner **Justin Timberlake** on hand), **"Hung Up," "Give It 2 Me"** and **"Music."** One highlight was when she topped Timberlake from a standing position.

Her last appearance at the club was for a **Smirnoff Nightlife Exchange** event, at which she chose one **dancer** (**Lil Buck**) for her upcoming *MDNA Tour*.

After a series of sold-out **Lady Gaga** concerts, Roseland was gutted and razed beginning in August 2014 to make way for something of which NYC truly doesn't have enough: A 62-story condo tower.

> "... [Y]outhful, trim, decked out in glitter and studs, Madonna returned to her roots and sent us into the stratosphere at the same time."-BARBARA O'DAIR, *ROLLING STONE* (2000)

ROSENBERG, LIZ: How would you like to deal with pushy reporters disappointed that Madonna is not HIV positive? Or chat with **Pepsi** right after they screened the video for **"Like A Prayer"**? Or explain to a sobbing boy that yes, it's true, Madonna is so sick she's canceling the concert for which he's got *eighth-row seats?* Or have to reveal that Madonna never sent a "we cool" e-mail to **Lady Gaga** after hearing **"Born This Way"**?

Being Madonna's press agent entailed such ugly scenes on a daily basis.

Liz Beth Rosenberg Citron was Madonna's publicist from the beginning, when Madonna was in rags and rubber bracelets, years before she was a superstar worrying that something as trivial as a **nude**-photo scandal could destroy her career. (To which Rosenberg told Madonna, "This is not a big deal. We're not gonna let it be a big deal.")

Rosenberg recalled her first meeting with Madonna to Ingrid Sischy in 1998: "You felt her fearlessness, but she didn't have two cents. We used to give her cab **money**. She probably pocketed it all and took the train. She looked like a little doll with her stockings, and the schmatte, and the bow and the rubber bracelets. I **loved** the belief she had in herself."

She was the force behind all those hundreds of **magazine** covers, **TV** appearances, press blitzes and parties; she hand-selected all of the interviewers with whom Madonna's gone head-to-head, playing a huge part in the trajectory of Madonna's career and image.

Rosenberg was like a girl gone Oscar Wilde with her deliciously quotable responses to the press. Asked if Madonna smokes, Rosenberg once replied, "She doesn't smoke; she *sizzles.*" When **Elton John** called Madonna a "fairground stripper," Rosenberg serenely replied, "Elton John remains on her Christmas card list," displaying the **art** of dragging someone classily, so that it leaves marks on

them but doesn't soil your outfit. It's enough to make one wonder if some of Madonna's own wit trickled down from her publicist, or if Madonna's best comebacks in print were ghosted by Rosenberg entirely.

Though she has her favorite Madonna eras and songs and albums and lovers like any other **fan**, she has only once publicly said something unflattering about her most famous charge. In a 1992 ***Vanity Fair*** Madonna cover story, Rosenberg is quoted as saying that there was a "lot to **hate**" in *Sex.* But even *that* wasn't so much a criticism as a levelheaded statement of fact. Rosenberg went on to say, "I love when people really hate Madonna—Madonna does, too. She'd rather that than apathy."

Over the years, Rosenberg became well known to and loved by Madonna's fans, for a long time contributing answers to a column called "The Validator" in Madonna's official fanzine. She's notoriously shy, though, so don't bother asking her to pose for a picture with you or for her **autograph**—she will politely shut you down.

She did allow one major profile of herself, an October 1992 piece in *The **New York** Times.* In a photo to accompany the story, Rosenberg was pictured in her old 20th-floor office at 75 Rockefeller Plaza. Her lair looked like a fan's room just before Mom and Dad say, "Aren't you getting a little carried away?"—wall-to-wall **Madonnabilia**, including the **hair** salon seats used in the ***Blond Ambition World Tour*** performance of **"Material Girl."**

The Validator

In 1993, Rosenberg admitted she did most of the **work** herself: "It's a machine of one person ... People probably think that there are rooms with hundreds of people in it, strategizing about how to market Madonna's career. It doesn't really work that way. She's kind of a phenomenon unto herself ... It doesn't really take millions of phone calls of begging people to write about her, they just do it on their own."

Before leaving to form her own firm—Liz Rosenberg Media—she had become the first female senior vice president at **Warner Bros. Records**, working with Michael Bublé, **David Foster**, **k.d. lang**, Seal, Fleetwood Mac and Stevie Nicks, Charice, Van Halen, Rickie Lee Jones, Van Morrison, Katherine Jenkins and **Cher**. At the time of her departure from the company, Rosenberg said, "No one has had a more thrilling ride than I have had during my decades at Warner Bros. Records, where I grew up and learned my craft ... I was given the opportunity to work with the most **talented** artists in music history."

Only nine years younger than Rosenberg, Madonna nonetheless used to see her publicist as a **mother** figure. Rosenberg said, "She's just a regular girl to me with a lot of talent and a lot of brains and we have a lot of fun ... I'm just her mom." There has been other personal fall-out from Rosenberg's unique position as the mouthpiece for one

MATTHEW RETTENMUND

of the most outspoken women of the age—Rosenberg reports that her Aunt Pauline asked on her deathbed in 1988, "How's Madonna? Is the marriage gonna last?"

"Liz Rosenberg" is also the name of a middle-aged kvetcher Madonna brought to life on the *Saturday Night Live* sketch "Coffee Talk with Linda Richman," though Madonna's fake "Liz" didn't resemble her real one.

Rosenberg briefly left her position as Madonna's publicist in the wake of **9/11**, saying she could no longer "sustain the emotional commitment." When rumors arose that it was because Madonna had not reacted sensitively to the 9/11 attacks, Rosenberg wasn't having it. "That is so ridiculously not true at all," she insisted. "It's too insane." More likely true was Rosenberg's own account—the tragedy led her to momentarily question the importance of handling Madonna's press needs, which had become more about shielding her from the media than about building something from scratch. In June 2015, Liz retired, handing the reins to Brian Bumbery of BB Gun Press.

By all accounts (including in the personal experience of the author), Rosenberg is a nice lady; to do what she does for a living, she must also be a masochist.

ROSENBLATT, MICHAEL: This member of the **Warner Bros.** "kiddie corps" (young execs) was the dude who urged **Seymour Stein** to sign Madonna after he received her demo from **Mark Kamins**. In her 2008 **Rock and Roll Hall of Fame** induction speech, Madonna called him (not Kamins) the person who discovered her.

Kamins had already pitched Madonna to Rosenblatt when Rosenblatt first caught a glimpse of her. Rosenblatt told *Rolling Stone* in 2013, "A friend of mine had just signed a group called Wham! They were about to put out their first single, but before they put it out, my friend wanted them to see the **New York** club scene. So I was taking them to clubs on a Saturday night—I'm at the **Danceteria** second-floor bar with George Michael and Andrew Ridgeley, and I see this girl walk across the **dance** floor and up to the DJ booth to talk to Mark. I figured she had to be the girl with the demo. So I walked up and introduced myself as an A&R guy, and we started talking." According to Madonna, they danced and took ecstacy.

Madonna visited him on the following Monday and played her demo, which didn't bowl him over. " But this girl sitting in my office was just radiating star **power**."

Next, Rosenblatt had Madonna visit **Sire Records** honcho Stein in the hospital. Both Stein and Madonna's luck took turns for the better, and the rest is history.

Rosenblatt wound up marrying Madonna's roomie, **Janis Galloway**.

ROSIE O'DONNELL'S KIDS ARE PUNNY: *Director: Amy Schatz. Air date: December 6, 1998.* Madonna joined a host of other celeb **voices** (Gilbert Gottfried, John Leguizamo, Jackie Mason, Mary Tyler Moore) on this 30-minute animated HBO special branded to her close friend **Rosie O'Donnell**'s talk show. Madonna provides the voice-over for "The Camel **Dances**," about a camel that wants to be a dancer and is heckled and attacked by her peers. "Satisfaction will come to those who please themselves," Madonna says at the end of what could be her life story. The special was nominated for an **Emmy** for Outstanding Children's Program, and was released on VHS on August 1, 2000.

ROSS, DIANA: *b. March 26, 1944.* One of the most famous female singers (and a pretty damn good actor), this Supreme diva visited Madonna in the studio while the latter was slaving away on the making of *Like a Virgin*. Ross brought Madonna a bottle of champagne and raved that her *children* just *loved* Madonna's music. Madonna was jazzed that one of her idols had given her encouragement.

In a 1985 **TV** interview with Japan's *All Night Tokyo*, Madonna said, "Well, when I was growing up, all the Motown music I listened to—Diana Ross was a real big inspiration for me. And right now, I think probably **Michael Jackson** is the biggest inspiration for me."

Ross was also in attendance at **Keith Haring**'s 1984 **birthday** party at Paradise Garage (formerly 84 King St., NY, NY). She posed in a group shot with guitarist Jeff Beck, **Nile Rodgers**, Madonna and Madonna's then boyfriend **Jellybean Benitez**.

ROSS, JONATHAN: *b. November 17, 1960.* British **TV** presenter who isn't on speaking terms with the letter "R." Ross is famous for his shows *The Last Resort with Jonathan Ross* (1987–1988), *Friday Night with Jonathan Ross* and *The Jonathan Ross Show*, the latter two of which have hosted Madonna appearances.

But Ross's first run-in with Madonna was her best *Sex*-era interview, an hour-long special called *Jonathan Ross Presents … Erotica Madonna* (1992). In his intro to the riveting Q&A, Ross noted, "Perhaps the most remarkable thing about Madge is that people no longer seem to think about the fact that she's a **talented** singer or actress or live performer … Madonna is way above all that **boring**, song-and-dance talent stuff, she is the Napoleon of hype, the Attila the Hun of self-promotion, the Julius Caesar of mass marketing …" The interview took place in her **London** hotel, and found Madonna in a masculine suit, a polka-dotted tie and a beret. Asked how she'd changed since being in London and filming at *The Tube* nearly 10 years earlier, Madonna said, "I just know more about life, period, y'know?" and asserted that she'd never had any doubt that she was *not* just another flavor of the month.

Ross lobbed Madonna some softballs, but he also got her to talk about her songwriting process: "When I write music, I like to write them, like—in my mind, there's a little movie playing, and I always envision scenarios and characters and of course it's not always something that I've experienced but I always say it in the first person … so it seems like it's a personal thing." She rehashed why she never **worked** with **Michael Jackson** and advised Ross to wear less Thierry Mugler.

Ross was quite randy with Madonna, discussing eating out, **shrimping** and anal **sex** with boyish excitement.

> "She plays the game better than any other modern star. While others hide away from the glare, exciting us by remaining unavailable, unattainable, almost private, she seems to give more and more away each year." —JONATHAN ROSS ON MADONNA (1992)

ROVERSI, PAOLO: *b. 1947.* Madonna sat for this Italian **fashion** photographer in advance of *Bedtime Stories*. She adored one portrait so much she intended it as the album's cover, but **Warner Bros.** marketing did not care for it—it is a lovely image of Madonna with light makeup staring enigmatically at the camera from a guarded position in bed.

The only other images of Madonna by Roversi that have surfaced are the images used on the US cover of her **"Bedtime Story"** single (Madonna's hand holding a yellow flower) and a haunted shot (plus one outtake) of Madonna that was placed on an iridescent cover of her UK 12" for the same song.

ROXY, THE: *Formerly 515 W. 18th St, NY, NY.* One of **NYC**'s most fondly remembered places to get fondled and remember it, The Roxy was an expansive **disco** with a floor as big as your **dreams**—and size matters when you're dealing with music spun by DJs like Junior Vasquez and Frankie Knuckles, to name just two. The place started as a roller disco in 1978 and never lost its '70s vibe throughout its life as a club, when Roxy Saturdays (by John Blair Promotions) became the place to see and be seen for gay New Yorkers. It closed in March 2007.

Along with **Danceteria**, The Roxy holds a special place in Madonna's life and career. In 1984, Madonna told a journalist that whenever she wasn't **working**, she indulged in such "hedonistic pleasures" as dancing at The Roxy. Along with showing up there for fun, several events important to her career have taken place there.

In spring 1983 (and probably more than once), Madonna did a gig at The Roxy, performing **"Everybody," "Physical Attraction"** and some of her other early tunes. "All right, you get the message?" she snarled at the crowd as she finished a song. Not long after, on October 6, 1983, Madonna's *Island* magazine cover was toasted at a party at the club. Madonna attended with her boyfriend, the **magazine**'s publisher.

One of Madonna's most exciting live performances was also a near-total surprise. On February 7, 1998, tickets went on sale for the Ice Ball at The Roxy, to be held on Valentine's Day. As Madonna was about to release her album *Ray of Light*, rumors swirled that the "special surprise guest" referenced by the club would be Madonna. Adding credence to the rumor was the fact that only John Blair Roxy

NICK MENDOROS

A sneaked photo of Madonna's *Ray of Light* Roxy gig

cardholders (who were on the club promoter's mailing list) could buy tickets, and only two per card. Of the 2,000 available tickets, 1,500 were sold, 500 were held by **Warner Bros.** for VIPs and about 30 were sold at the door.

With an advertised start time of 9 p.m., doors to The Ice Ball were opened at 9:20 p.m., but only after attendees passed through a metal detector. Everyone was warned that there was strictly *no* photography; the outside brick wall of the club was littered with disposable cameras. Because of security and because it was before cellphone era, very few images of the evening exist, though along with some pro shots approved by Madonna's camp, a few images were sneaked via smuggled-in cameras (including one hidden in **Queerdonna**'s rolls of fat—werk!).

Fans rushed in and packed the stage, situated in the center of the far wall. The set was very junior high prom, decorated with metallic red strips and pale blue and green globes hanging overhead.

At 1:45 a.m., a hooded figure took the stage, unveiling herself slowly. It was Madonna, making her first club appearance in 15 years, dressed in a voluminous black gown similar to her **"Frozen"** video costume. The screams were so loud as to render her performance nearly inaudible.

"I'm glad you're screaming and all," she said between songs, "but I don't know about you, but I can't hear shit!" Still, she acknowledged that "it feels pretty **fucking** good" to be in an NYC club.

With William Orbit on the keyboard, Madonna sang **"Sky Fits Heaven," "Shanti/Ashtangi"** and **"Ray of Light"** over the roar of the crowd, accompanying herself on the air **guitar**. Party time! Excellent!

"Thanks for coming to my coming out party," she said when it was all over. "And if you're not out, you need to get out!" The largely **gay** crowd caught her drift.

Promoter John Blair tells *EM20* the setting-up of that appearance "happened very fast" and gives all credit to house DJ Victor Calderone.

Madonna never again performed a set at The Roxy, but she did make a similarly **powerful** appearance on October 22, 2005. In the middle of the night, after a quick stint at **Misshapes**, she arrived at The Roxy in full-on *Saturday Night Fever* (1977) mode, complete with her best dress in which to do "The Hustle" (1975). She wore $11,000 in diamonds *on her eyes* as well as mink eyelashes by Gina Brooke for Shu Uemura.

"You know I have a long history with The Roxy," she announced, "so I only thought it appropriate that I come here to share my new album with you and **dance**. It all started

here with 12 inches!" With that, she handed a vinyl record representing her new ***Confessions on a Dance Floor*** album to Peter Rauhofer in the DJ booth. He played **"Hung Up," "Sorry"** and **"I Love New York"** and Madonna danced for her subjects, eventually calling some of them up onto the stage to bump and grind with her. One of the boys she called up later remembered her asking him if he was having fun, and then instructing him and his friend to grind on her—one from the front and one from behind.

The late, great Rauhofer (who died of brain **cancer** in 2013) said the night was "one of the most intense events ever. A lot of excitement, mystery and drama—with the [bad] weather and masses lined up at the door. Everything played its part ... The moment she came out, it was like a bomb exploded."

That's what The Roxy was like—it was a place where oxygen and inhibitions were in short supply, but where anything seemed possible.

ROYAL BOX, THE: *Release date: December 1990.* Madonna's first proper box set was released in all territories and came with ***The Immaculate Collection*** (CD or cassette), glam **Herb Ritts** postcards and a poster of Madonna performing **"Vogue"** at the **MTV Video Music Awards.**

RUBAIYAT, THE: *Formerly at 102 S. First St., Ann Arbor, MI.* **Gay** restaurant and **disco** in the town in which Madonna went to college that was one of the premier places to get down and boogie-oogie-oogie in the late '70s. Madonna and pals like **Christopher Flynn** and **Whitley Setrakian** came here to **dance** their asses off.

RUBIO, PAULINA: *b. June 17, 1971.* Mexican multi-hyphenate who has become a cultural icon and is often called "the Latin Madonna." She rightfully dislikes that backhanded compliment, preferring to be known as *herself.*

But Rubio *is* a huge Madonna **fan**, listing the **Queen of Pop** and Celia Cruz as her all-time favorite singers.

During a 2013 ***Fashion*** *Police* (2002–) appearance, Rubio was asked by **Joan Rivers** to name her influences. Among them? "Obviously, I can not ignore Madonna. She is a warrior."

"RUNAWAY LOVER": Track from ***Music*** that was written and produced by Madonna and **William Orbit**. She has never performed it on tour, but did live versions at her **Roseland Ballroom** and **Brixton Academy** promo shows in 2000.

—KAREN FINLEY

RUSSIA: Madonna has taken two of her tours to this country, which under Vladimir Putin's iron fist has slid decisively backward on human rights, in particular **gay** rights. In advance of her arrival with *The MDNA Tour*, the government threatened Madonna with jail if she "promoted gay behavior." As Madonna told the crowd at an Amnesty International event, "Needless to say, I did not change one moment of my show. Eighty-seven of my **fans** were arrested for gay behavior—whatever that is."

She had spoken out during her concert, saying, "We are gay, we are straight, we are human beings ... I am here to say that the gay community and gay people, here and all around the world have the same rights, the same rights to be treated with dignity, with respect, with tolerance, with compassion, with **love**," voicing her support for **Pussy Riot**.

In spite of her defiance, the complaint filed against her was dismissed, as was a similar complaint filed against **Lady Gaga**.

For an example of the level of discourse at the uppermost reaches of the Russian government, consider the tweet of Deputy Prime Minister Dmitry Rogozin, who wrote (in Russian): "With age, every former s. tries to lecture everyone on morality. Especially during overseas tours." The letter used stands for either "slut" or "whore."

RUSSIAN TEA ROOM: *150 W. 57th St., NY, NY.* Madonna **worked** here for a short time in 1979 checking coats for $4.50/hour, a job **Pearl Lang** secured for her because she feared Madonna would have no other way to eat when she arrived in **NYC**.

"She was a frail girl, very thin," the tony establishment's manager Gregory Camillucci told Madonna biographer **J. Randy Taraborrelli** in 2001. "I often thought that the meals she had at the restaurant were probably the only meals she was eating. But she was upbeat, never rude, always on time ... I caught her staring at the customers. 'I watch **rich** people eating and drinking,' she explained,' so that when I can afford to, I can do it right.'"

Madonna's attire eventually proved incompatible with the exclusive restaurant—she told **Howard Stern** in 2015 that she was fired for wearing fishnets.

Madonna took her pro-gay attitudes to Russia on *The MDNA Tour.*

MATTHEW RETTENMUND

FRED SEIDMAN

SACHS, JEFFREY: *b. November 5, 1954.* Madonna has **worked** with this brilliant economist on two Millennium Village projects in **Malawi**. The idea is to spend approximately $1.5 million over the course of five years in order to help villages become self-sustaining. Madonna said of him in 2010, "He's an incredible human being."

SACRÉES FEMMES: French TF1 show on which Madonna appeared on November 11, 1998. Although her performances of **"The Power of Good-Bye"** and **"Drowned World/Substitute for Love"** were, per the show's requirements, lip-synched, each was performed on an imaginatively lighted stage that gave them visual depth, set off by a bewitchingly black-clad, black-haired Madonna.

The most surprising element of the show—and one that makes *Sacrées Femmes* one of Madonna's most incredible **TV** appearances—was when French **acting** great Jeanne Moreau, one of Madonna's cinematic **heroes**, was brought out for a meet-and-greet. Madonna, overjoyed, curtsied before her and clasped Moreau's hand as they spoke. "You are very beautiful," Moreau told Madonna, who thanked her and exclaimed, "You're my favorite actress in the whole world ... this is a great privilege." Madonna gushed of Moreau's screen image, "I think she's always been a modern woman ... and a combination of strength and vulnerability that's perfect." The two adorably applauded one another, Madonna resting her head on Moreau's shoulder.

The host then showed Madonna a video of her past looks, surprising her again, this time with special guest **Jean Paul Gaultier**. Madonna praised Gaultier's appreciation of the tradition of **fashion** as well as his unflinching urge to provoke discussions of politics and **sexual** identity. "We're going to get married!" Madonna exclaimed jokingly, but she followed up by saying he'd asked her every year. Gaultier got down on one knee and proposed yet again; Madonna wondered if he would design her **wedding** dress, which didn't sound like a hard "no."

With Madonna and Gaultier still in attendance, Patricia Kaas performed, then joined them on the couch, where Madonna perkily suggested that she and Kaas should sing the Serge Gainsbourg/Jane Birkin song "Je t'aime ... moi non plus" (1969) together. Madonna eventually sang the song at her 2012 **Olympia Hall** show.

SAN REMO: *145 Central Park West, NY, NY.* Co-op that dealt Madonna a stinging rejection in July 1985 when its members voted to disallow her from buying a $1.8 million apartment from producer Bill Gerber. The members of the San Remo were mostly older, but included future *Dick Tracy* costar Dustin Hoffman and singer Paul Simon.

The only board member to **back** her up was **Diane Keaton**.

"SANCTUARY": Written by Madonna, **Dallas Austin**, Anne Preven, Scott Cutler and with a Herbie Hancock "Watermelon Man" (1962) sample, this song (produced by Madonna and Austin and remixed by **Nellee Hooper**) is a spooky, contemplative tune that gives the impression of haunting need. It's one of the more celestial *Bedtime Stories* songs.

SANREMO MUSIC FESTIVAL: Madonna has appeared at the Festival della canzone italiana di Sanremo twice.

On February 22, 1995, she joined **Babyface** in lip-synching (a requirement) **"Take a Bow"** in the same stunning lavender gown she wore to the **Oscars** after-parties that year. The duo made a quick appearance for photographers.

A red-haired Madonna, looking radiant, lip-synched **"Frozen"** at the festival on February 24, 1998. She was interviewed backstage by Rai Uno, admitting that the title *Ray of Light* referred to a newfound happiness in her life.

"SANTA BABY": Madonna covered this 1953 holiday song, most famously sung by **Eartha Kitt**, in 1987 for the *A Very Special Christmas* album. It features one of Madonna's patented **accents**. Others who have covered this Yuletide scorcher include RuPaul, **Kylie Minogue** and **Ariana Grande**.

"SANTA EVITA": A children's choir sweetly sings this *Evita* piece, found on *Evita: The Complete Motion Picture Music Soundtrack*, which is conducted by John Mauceri.

SANTIAGO, ROCKY: Studly **New York** City male stripper who was featured prominently in *Sex*. Rocky's is the only penis seen in the **book** (and it's flaccid), in a scene full of naked men being ogled by a glammed-up Madonna at the **Gaiety**.

The story goes that Madonna saw Rocky **working** at a club called Tatou and recruited him for her book. She also could have seen him in the pages of *People*—the mag voted him one of the 50 Most Beautiful People in the World in 1990. She was said to have been quite taken with Santiago, who told friends he would star in *Angie* with her.

Rocky also performed at a small party Madonna threw in her apartment in 1992 around the time **Bill Clinton** was elected president, and Madonna bragged to reporters nosy about Rocky's finer points that he was a "registered Democrat."

ABOVE: Original "Santa Baby" sheet music

AT LEFT: Cuddling avec Moreau at *Sacrées Femmes*

Madonna sued Santiago for breaching a confidentiality agreement regarding *Sex*; the suit was later dropped. However, in 1995, Santiago shopped a book proposal called *Private Shows: Anatomy of the **Art** of Hustling*. Among other tidbits, the book claimed he was photographed making out with "a famous young actor whose **sexuality** has been in question."

SATURDAY NIGHT LIVE: *Airdates: October 11, 1975–.* Madonna has long been associated with the never-ending, weekly, late-night satirical **TV** sketch show, including one stint as a host, one as a musical guest and several one-off appearances as herself or in sketches.

Madonna called it the hardest thing she ever did when she hosted *SNL* on November 9, 1985. Fresh from her circus-like **wedding** to **Sean Penn**, she appeared in a navy

Triumphant after nailing her 1993 performance

parka, movie-star sunglasses and a fur-tail stole in her opening monologue, introducing footage sending up the ceremony, complete with faked scenes of descending news choppers, scaggy members of the bride's family and a publicity-shy Penn (played by 20-year-old Robert Downey Jr.). A **Cyndi Lauper** look-alike was identified as a cousin with whom Madonna "never got along, and I don't know why she came." In the footage, Don Novello as "Father Guido Sarducci" performed the nuptials.

Continuing with the theme of her **privacy**, Madonna closed her monologue with, "We have a great show tonight: We have Simple Minds, we have Penn & Teller, I am not **pregnant** and we will be right **back**."

Madonna performed in all the major skits:

For a *Who's Afraid of Virginia Woolf?* (1966) **parody** of the relationships of **Prince Charles** & **Princess Diana** and the First Couple of the US, Madonna was Di to Jon Lovitz's Charles, and Terry Sweeney debuted his hysterically crazed Nancy Reagan alongside Randy Quaid's note-perfect **Ronald Reagan**. Madonna, as a drunken Di, sang a bit of Lulu's "To Sir With Love" (1967), getting a big laugh when imploring Charles not to treat her like a thing. "You poor thing," he replied. Di was portrayed as such a pawn her husband knew she was pregnant before *she* did.

The most fascinating part of the show was an ahead-of-its-time piece that skewered HIV-shaming, likening the "paranoia … provoked by the tragic **AIDS** outbreak" to blacklisting in Hollywood in the '50s. A narrator warned: "**Gay** actors are forced back into the closet, leading double lives, wearing wedding bands, riding **motorcycles**—living in fear that they will fall victim to pinklisting." Madonna played soap opera diva "Melinda Zumont," a version of **Joan Collins**, tightening her neck **muscles** and nailing the **accent**. Sweeney arrived as her love interest, which bothered Melinda because they had a kissing scene and as she didn't know him, she feared he could be gay and therefore an AIDS carrier. The joke was that Sweeney played it flamboyantly gay while his character pathetically butched it up to keep the part.

Sweeney's character accidentally outed himself by shrieking when an overhead light plunged to the stage, but his admission led to everyone else on set coming out as gay, too. Feeling emboldened, Madonna's character confessed, "I'm an intravenous **drug** user." New problem: The gay guy wouldn't kiss one of *those*.

Quaid played their director, Jon Lovitz was a permissive **censor**, Joan Cusack was a makeup girl, Downey and Anthony Michael Hall (who had done short, on-air promos for the episode in which he ogled Madonna) played stagehands.

The sketch, mocking the tabloid freak-out over Rock Hudson—who'd died of AIDS five weeks before this episode aired—kissing Linda Evans on the February 6, 1985, episode of *Dynasty* (1981–1989), was a marvel at the time: An uncomfortably funny skit about AIDS that wasn't anti-gay. Madonna was on-point, albeit with some timing issues.

LAVINEL SAVU

Screen grabs from some of Madonna's *SNL* appearances

Though framed as a *Twilight Zone* (1959–1964) spoof called *The Limits of the Imagination*, a pre-taped sketch about "Nancy," a young woman who receives threatening calls on her **car** phone (remember those?) only to learn they're coming from under the hood, was actually a giggle-inducing parody of *When a Stranger Calls* (1979), with Madonna in the Carol Kane role. Quaid plays the show-within-a-show's announcer and a heroic cop, with Lovitz as the would-be psycho killer.

As **Marilyn Monroe** on the night of her **death**, Madonna truly stank, doing the **voice** all wrong; she even veered into her Diana and Joan Collins British accents. The gist of the sketch was that Monroe was murdered by the Kennedys. Quaid played JFK, Hall played RFK, Sweeney was Ted Kennedy, Downey cameoed as **Elvis Presley** and Cusack poured her heart into the throwaway character of an earnest maid. The joke was that the whole story was being presented by *National Inquirer* Theatre (hosted by Nora Dunn, with Lovitz as a reporter and the late Danitra Vance as a "journalist mentalist").

Madonna delightfully hammed it up as a Latina singer/**dancer** called "Marika" (before the real *Martika* burst onto the scene) on a spoof of a Spanish-language variety show called *El Spectaculare de Marika*. Marika performed a strangled medley of a-ha's "Take On Me" (1985) and "La Bamba" (1958), interacted with a talking duck ("El Pato Loco") and interviewed Quaid, who was playing real-life World Series baseball player Joaquín Andújar. Her full-throated performance of a gender-reversed "Three Times a Lady" (1978) parody was shockingly good, and her red dress was foreshadowing for her **"La Isla Bonita"** music video look. Downey played the silly show's **sexy** host, Sweeney and Hall her fey dancers and Lovitz was visible as a backup singer.

The experience of hosting *SNL* was good for Madonna, a welcome chance to try her hand at comedy and laugh at herself. In the audience were Jennifer Beals, **Cher** and Christopher Reeve.

Unfortunately, the 1985 season was considered a disaster for the show, which cleaned house and invited Madonna back to open the '86 season by reading a prepared statement: "It was all a **dream**, a horrible, horrible dream," spoofing the infamous "Bobby-in-the-shower" plot twist on *Dallas* (1978–1991).

On the May 11, 1991, episode of *SNL*, Madonna contributed one of her most memorable bits in a pre-taped "Wayne's World" sketch that found "Wayne" (Mike Myers) and "Garth" (Dana Carvey) freaking out over being in Madonna's bedroom and not feeling "worthy." When Wayne dared Madonna to make out with him, he glimpsed scenes from her **"Justify My Love"** video over her shoulder, including a **Prince** look-alike and Garth in a skintight bodysuit. Madonna really bombed in this one ... "NOT!" Flawless.

Madonna's most indelible *SNL* performance was on the February 22, 1992, show, hosted by **Roseanne Barr** and Tom Arnold, when she came on in an unannounced

"What kind of a name is Lady Gaga? It sounds like baby food."
—MADONNA, *SATURDAY NIGHT LIVE* (2009)

"Coffee Talk with Linda Richman" sketch as **"Liz Rosenberg"** (not that one!), so perfect as an overbearing Jewish lady that many viewers couldn't tell who it was under the curly wig, tacky *leathuh* suit and rose-tinted glasses. Host Barr played Rosenberg's gassy **mother** from Scottsdale, but more surprising was **Barbra Streisand**'s appearance at skit's end, which was a lot "like *buttah*."

Madonna returned to the show as a musical guest on January 16, 1993, to perform **"Fever"** and **"Bad Girl,"** which she did in a simple black halter blouse and flared pants. She wore the extra-long **hair** she'd been growing for her role in *Dangerous Game*, which she was about to start lensing with that week's host, **Harvey Keitel**. After her second performance, Madonna mock-defiantly raised a photo of Long Island cradle-robber Joey Buttafuoco and, lampooning **Sinéad O'Connor's** previous dissing of the **Pope,** exclaimed, "Fight the *real* enemy!" and tore it apart.

She opened that show in a hilarious skit as Marilyn Monroe singing "Happy **Birthday**" to **Bill Clinton** (Phil Hartman), ending by suggestively summoning not Bill but *Chelsea* to join her. She stumbled over the show's traditional intro, shouting, "Live from Sat—live from **New York**, it's *Saturday Night*!" Like all her TV appearances, that stint on *SNL* was a ratings blockbuster—its highest showing in a dozen years—with over 29 million viewers.

Madonna and **Lady Gaga** did an embarrassingly off-kilter "Deep House Dish" segment on October 3, 2009, in which the women poked fun at a rivalry that had yet to emerge between them. Skimpily and similarly styled, they engaged in a catfight, pulling each other's hair. Host Kenan Thompson (with no help from petrified sidekick Andy Samberg) tried to get them to kiss and make up, but they instead they kissed *him* ... with Samberg opportunistically joining in. Not even remotely amusing.

On December 12, 2013, Madonna made a puzzling appearance on a leadenly unfunny installment of "The Barry Gibb Talk Show" with **Jimmy Fallon** and **Justin Timberlake** as Barry and Robin Gibb in which the gag seemed to be that she was offering political insight that was actually

intelligent. She then "hypnotized" them with her **grills**. "She's tamed me like a wild **horse**," Barry groaned. "Well, she *is* Madonna," Robin concluded. *Thud*.

Hey, at least she had fun introducing a song by Timberlake with Fallon.

Though references to Madonna on the show are innumerable, it's worth noting that cast member Pamela Stephenson was the first person to portray Madonna, which she did on the November 3, 1984, episode, hosted by Michael McKean with Chaka Khan and the Folksmen as the musical guests. Stephenson played her hawking "Madonna Navel **Accessories**," a **"Lucky Star"** video reference. Molly Shannon showed up as Madonna on "Church Chat" on October 26, 1996, chatting about giving birth to **Lola**. (The father? "Satan!!!"). Popular cast member Kristen Wiig played a plasticized Madonna on April 4, 2009, angry that she was denied the right to adopt **Mercy James** from **Malawi** and in a heated baby-collecting competition with **Angelina Jolie**. Wiig repeated her Madonna on September 17, 2009; January 30, 2010; and February 11, 2012.

Madonna has also been played on the show by Joan Allen (November 14, 1998), Janeane Garofalo (December 3, 1994), Ana Gasteyer (February 15, 1997 and May 20, 2000) and Amy Poehler (May 3, 2003; January 17, 2004; and February 14, 2004).

• •

"HI, EVERYBODY! MY NAME'S MADONNA AND I'LL BE YOUR COMEDY LOVE-SLAVE FOR THE EVENING."-MADONNA, *SATURDAY NIGHT LIVE* (1985)

• •

"IF YOU SLIP ME THE TONGUE, I'LL KILL YOU."
-MADONNA TO MIKE MYERS
AHEAD OF THEIR "WAYNE'S WORLD" SKIT (1991)

• •

"SHE'S A TRAMP! EVERY WEEK WITH A DIFFERENT BOYFRIEND. AND THIS WEEK IN THE PAPER WITH NO CLOTHES ON. ECHHH! WHO NEEDS HER?"
-"LIZ ROSENBERG" ON MADONNA, *SATURDAY NIGHT LIVE* (1992)

• •

SATURDAY NIGHT ONLINE: Online radio show for which Madonna filmed a nearly 19-minute video of herself answering **fan**-submitted questions, which was released on May 2, 2015. In the video, Madonna ate **pizza** and drank wine in her palatial bathroom while touching on subjects such as her favorite music video to film (**"Justify My Love"**), a past album track she wished could've been a single (**"Falling Free"**), **Drake** ("I kissed a girl ... and I liked it") and her favorite *Rebel Heart* songs (**"Ghosttown"** and **"Bitch I'm Madonna"**). How-Old.net would have guessed Madonna's **age** at about 19 in this video. P.S. That probably isn't a mouse 9:55 into the video, but a reflected shadow from the piece of paper she had just tossed.

Giving good face on Saturday Night Online

SCAVULLO, FRANCESCO: *b. January 16, 1921.* Renowned **fashion** photographer who first shot Madonna in 1983. He was so impressed he exclaimed, "Baby **Dietrich**!"

Some of his most bewitching shots of the "vampy" and "**Marilyn Monroe**–like" Madonna—taken in May 1985 in Fort Lauderdale, Florida—while she was on *The Virgin Tour*, graced the May 27, 1985, cover of *Time* and the July 4, 1985, cover of *Hamptons* **magazine**. He went on to photograph Madonna for layouts in and covers of *Harper's Bazaar* and *Cosmopolitan*.

Scavullo never forgot his first impression of Madonna, saying in 1993, "It was magic. I mean, the camera loved her. I mean, the camera just wanted to keep taking pictures. Madonna just had a wonderful, beautiful look: She was fresh, she was young, she had a very independent way of dressing … She knows what's good."

SCHARF, KENNY: *b. 1958.* A major pop artist of the '80s and beyond who was a close friend and former roomie of **Keith Haring**. He was also pals with Madonna, **Maripol**, Klaus Nomi, **Andy Warhol** and other figures of the downtown renaissance.

Scharf attended Madonna's *Virgin Tour* and many other **NYC** appearances, including **Don't Bungle the Jungle**.

After seeing **Sean Penn** in *Milk* (2008), Madonna said, "Watching *Milk* was such a trip down **memory** lane for me. What the movie triggered for me was all my early days in New York and the scene that I came up in … with Andy Warhol and Keith Haring and **Jean-Michel Basquiat** and Kenny Scharf. It was just so alive with **art** and politics and this wonderful spirit."

SCHOOL: Madonna's **father** used to offer 50 cents to his children for every A they received in school. Since she was living in a material **Rochester Hills**, Madonna made sure to knock down almost straight As all through her primary education. As a child, she attended three different **Catholic** schools—St. Andrew Catholic School (1400 Inglewood Ave., Rochester, MI), St. Frederick's and the Sacred Heart Academy—before advancing to West Middle School (500 Old Perch Rd., Rochester, MI) in 1970.

Her school years had some highs, but she's never described them as idyllic. "I felt awkward and out of place at school," she told the *Sunday Times* in 2003. "No popular, not attractive, not special in any way."

She graduated with honors a half-semester early from Rochester Adams High School (2100 W. Tienken Rd., Rochester Hills, MI) in 1976. Her grade-point average, involvement in theater and outstanding skills earned her a scholarship to the **University of Michigan**, but she dropped out before earning a degree in order to head for **fame** and fortune in **New York**.

Two of Scavullo's most glam Madonna covers

During her 2013 Reddit Q&A, Madonna wrote "school is fun you get to learn"—not punctuation, apparently, but you know what she means.

SCHREIBER, MARTIN H.M.: *b. circa 1946.* Photographer who, on February 12, 1979, hired "Madonna Louise" to pose **nude** for him in his 22nd St. studio in **NYC**, when he was teaching a class called "Photographing the Nude" at The New **School** for Social Research (68 Fifth Ave., NY, NY). She earned $30 for 90 minutes, and Schreiber has said he wound up dating Madonna for a brief period.

When he saw Madonna on the cover of *Time* in 1985, it dawned on him that he'd known and photographed her. He called his lawyer, who it turned out was **working** on selling Madonna nudes for another client, **Lee Friedlander**. Schreiber used a different attorney, Stanley Nagler, who offered the images to *Penthouse* and then *Playboy*.

A half-million dollars later, nudes by Schreiber as well as Friedlander appeared in the September 1985 issue of *Playboy*. Madonna looks extra-sullen in Schreiber's images, some of which show a feline Madonna naked with Schreiber's cat. He published a **book** (and marketed posters) under the title *Madonna Nudes 1979*. For the May 2015 issue of *Playboy*, Schreiber's work returned in a feature entitled "Madonna: The Lost Nudes," a photo excerpt from his June 2015 book, *A Retrospective 1966-2014* (Duncan Meeder/Leica Store Lisse, Netherlands).

Madonna as a teenager, and her high school

JOSEPH A. LAWRENCE

Madonna hugs Nick Scotti at a *U* magazine launch party.

SCHWARTZ, ANDY: This **New York** still photographer has shot for dozens of memorable films, including *Fatal Attraction* (1987), *Wall Street* (1987), *Working Girl* (1988) and *When Harry Met Sally* (1989).

In 1984, Schwartz was hired as the still photographer on ***Desperately Seeking Susan***. His images of Madonna on the set and in action have been reproduced steadily ever since, including on **magazine** covers, in **books** and far and wide across the Internet.

Schwartz tells *EM20* that he shot 100% of the familiar images from the film, not counting the special shoot **Herb Ritts** did of Madonna and **Rosanna Arquette** on their day off. "In those days, there was only one still photographer allowed on set—no GoPros or iPhones."

Schwartz fondly remembers his **work** with Madonna. "Time spent photographing Madonna walking alone down Astor Place or dancing at **Danceteria** became defining turns in many careers. She'd sure never walk down 8th St. the same way."

He also recalls Madonna as a more than willing subject. "During *Desperately Seeking Susan*, Madonna **loved** being photographed and talking about images and photographers."

SCOTTI, NICK: *b. May 31, 1966.* **Sexy** Italian-American model-turned-singer whom Madonna took under her wing briefly in the early '90s.

As a teenager sneaking into the hot '80s club **The Fun House** (526 W. 26th St., NY, NY), Scotti met Madonna and was aware of her burgeoning **fame**, but the two were only formally introduced at **Herb Ritts**'s 1989 **birthday** party. By then, under the names Dominick Scotti and Nick Neal, he'd been a successful model in Europe and was looking to break into singing. He even took **voice** lessons from producer **Shep Pettibone**'s **mother**, Marie.

In 1992, Madonna let Scotti record **"Get Over,"** a song she'd written and recorded with **Stephen Bray** in 1990.

Scotti said it all happened very quickly. "Everyone was staring at her, and that's just something I could never do: gawk at celebrities. But we kind of caught each other's **eye** and started playing mind games with each other ... She asked for my tape ... It just so happened that the next day I was talking to her on the telephone, and she said, 'Oh, I just got a Federal Express.' So she put my tape on and had it blasting as we sat there on the telephone together. Two weeks later, we were recording a song ..."

Madonna's demo of "Get Over" remains **unreleased**. She produced the Scotti version with Pettibone, contributing prominent backing vocals. "Get Over" appeared in the **Demi Moore** film *Nothing But Trouble* (1991), was on its soundtrack and became Scotti's second single from his self-titled debut album (1993) on the **Warner** label Reprise.

Scotti told the author (for a December 1997 *Attitude* magazine cover story): "Whether or not I've shared intimacy with Madonna, she wouldn't have worked with me if

"When I first met him, I wanted him, but then when I heard his music, I wanted to work with him and you can't, you know … mix business with pleasure."—MADONNA ON NICK SCOTTI (1993)

she felt like I'd be an embarrassment. I'm really proud that I worked with her. But I wasn't Madonna's protégé."

Scotti never released another album, instead focusing on **acting**. He appeared on the soap opera *The Young and the Restless* (1973–) from 1996 to 1999 and had the title role in the **gay** romantic comedy *Kiss Me Guido* (1997), a feature film. He also hosted a lifestyle series called ***New York* Nick** (2004).

"SECRET" (SONG): *Release date: September 27, 1994. Billboard Hot 100 peak: #3.* Having been written off as "over" following a contentious run-in with **David Letterman**, and having underwhelmed the charts with her *Erotica* album, Madonna might have been forgiven for choosing a safe lead single from her ***Bedtime Stories*** album. On the contrary, she put out one of the most unexpected records of her career with "Secret," a quiet, folky, mid-tempo R&B number. It was a whole new side of Madonna, though the single's cover features a very familiar side: Madonna with her top down, revealing an opalescent brassiere to photographer **Patrick Demarchelier**.

Radio and the public approved: The single debuted at #30 on the ***Billboard* Hot 100**, her third-highest debut on that chart. "Secret" has become one of her most critically acclaimed singles, one she has performed on ***Wetten, das ...?*** (lip-synched), on the ***Drowned World Tour***, as a **fan** request on her ***Sticky and Sweet Tour*** and as a ***Rebel Heart Tour*** bonus. In a first for Madonna, she promoted the song with an audio message online.

LAVINEL SAVU

NICK MENDOROS

The song was written and produced by Madonna and **Dallas Austin**. Songwriting credit was also **awarded** to **Shep Pettibone**, after the fact, for his contributions.

> "Madonna's voice continues to grow, and it is put to excellent use over a haunting melody that is fleshed out with subtle, quasi-psychedelic guitar work."
>
> —LARRY FLICK ON "SECRET," BILLBOARD (1994)

"SECRET" (VIDEO): *Director: Melodie McDaniel, 1994.* **MTV** world-premiered this video to the first song from *Bedtime Stories* on October 4, 1994. Directed by Melodie McDaniel, who had done still photography on various Madonna projects previously, the video develops the song's unspecified secret into a very subtly orchestrated story of a Billie Holiday–esque singer's addiction to—and almost spiritual deliverance from—heroin. (Witness all the allusive rubbing of forearms.) Or is it just about her secret child?

Madonna's character is a **blonde** chanteuse in heavy **eye** makeup who's in immediate danger of catching a chest cold. She mixes her gritty glamour with an urban hipness: a pierced nose and **belly button**, a shimmering, clingy blouse and vintage high heels so clunky you're never sure that Madonna will actually make it up the stairs she's seen climbing. The supporting cast includes a **drag** queen, a prostitute, a pimp, a street tough who shows off his battle scar with pride and a variety of sketchy extras.

The singer performs in a jazz club, then appears to achieve some sort of salvation in the lap of an older, maternal woman, who symbolically baptizes her, splashing water on her forehead.

At video's end, the Madonna character finally does make it up those stairs (compare her climb to Madonna's deliberate strut in both the **"Papa Don't Preach"** and **"Like a Virgin"** videos), and to a joyous reunion with her family, a young Latin man (**sexy** model Richard Elms, not Jason Olive as many sources still report) and their son. "Secret" could almost serve as the sequel to the **"Borderline"** video, taking place 10 years after the events of that first scenario—it even has billiards!

Madonna grins exuberantly into the camera when it's all over, recalling the impulsive giggle in her **"Justify My Love"** clip.

Coming as it did on the heels of her widely-publicized interview with the British **magazine** *The Face*, in which Madonna reemphasized her desire for an old-fashioned family, the video seemed to indicate her interest in a partner and a child—and in happy endings—more strongly than ever.

The video was shot in Harlem from September 9–11, 1994, primarily at a club called Casablanca (formerly 308 Lenox Ave., NY, NY; later Bistro Chez Lucienne). The scenes of Madonna walking were shot on Lenox Ave.

Dan Rucks, better known as Dan-O-Rama, edited an official remix video, using the Junior's Luscious Club Edit mix by Junior Vasquez.

"SECRET GARDEN": Jazzy song written and produced by Madonna and **Andre Betts** that is the final track on *Erotica*. It's a garden in the same way that **"Body Shop"** is about automotive repair or **"Candy Shop"** is about sugar.

#SECRETPROJECTREVOLUTION: *Directors: Madonna and Steven Klein. Release date: September 24, 2013.* Arty, 17-minute, black-and-white short directed by Madonna and **Steven Klein** used as a kick-off for her **Art for Freedom** initiative.

Madonna and her tour **dancers** appear in high-glam mode in scenes that present Madonna as a sort of Mata Hari roughed up by police and imprisoned for her **art**. The film is "dedicated to those who have been persecuted, are being persecuted, or may be persecuted. For the color of their skin. Their religious beliefs. Their artistic expression. Their gender. Or their **sexual** preferences. Anyone whose human rights have been violated."

The movie was released, somewhat innovatively, on BitTorrent instead of via iTunes or Netflix. Criticized as making piracy easy, BitTorrent had begun **working** with

Filming her "Secret" video in Harlem

Remarkably accessible at her *#secretprojectrevolution* bash

MATTHEW RETTENMUND

"I'm a revolutionary and, yes, it's a burden." —MADONNA, *USA TODAY* (1991)

artists to release projects officially in order to monetize its vast network of users—it's been said BitTorrent is behind 20–40% of every day's Internet traffic.

The movie had a fabulous, messy premiere, of the variety that harkened **back** to Madonna's downtown **NYC** days, at the Gagosian Gallery (555 W. 24th St., NY, NY) on September 24, 2013, which was attended by art-world luminaries such as Chuck Close and **Cindy Sherman**, as well as celebs Marc Consuelos, **Anderson Cooper**, Perez Hilton, Donna Karan, Calvin Klein, **Lindsay Lohan**, Zac Posen and Zachary Quinto. **Liz Rosenberg** was, of course, on hand. **Sean Penn** made a quick appearance as well, which resulted in lots of press coverage.

At the event, a taped-off area attracted looky-loos. Unannounced, Madonna—wearing a shiny black trench—walked out and squatted at the **feet** of her adoring **fans**, checking out the perimeter of what would soon become her "stage." She looked up from her inspection, telling the spectators, "You guys are the front row. Don't let anyone **fuck** this up," indicating a stretch of white cloth that marked the end of the performance area. She left, then re-emerged, giving a 12-minute speech about her motivations for making the film, a work she called the most important thing she'd ever done outside of having children. When partygoers continued murmuring, she informed them, "Right now, I just wanna hear me."

She explained that the film was about wanting "to start a movement of people, of artists, who are not worried about winning popularity contests, who are not worried about approval, who are not worried about whether their ass looks good—although it is important to have a good-looking ass."

After the film played—with A-listers and fans seated on the gallery's cold floor to watch—dancers from Madonna's *MDNA Tour* performed a series of modern-dance routines, with outstanding contributions by Chaz Buzan and Marvin Gofin.

Madonna then performed a heartfelt cover of the **Elliott Smith** song "Between the Bars" (1997). A black-hooded figure that emerged at the end, helping her to stand, turned out to be her son, **Rocco**.

Madonna then spent the entire evening mingling with her guests, the most access fans had ever had, leading to clusters of people following her every move and photographing her from every angle. She eventually tired of it and left, but while it lasted, it was a fan's wet—and anything but fuzzy—**dream**.

To find out more, visit ArtforFreedom.com

SEDNAOUI, STÉPHANE: *b. February 27, 1963.* French photographer who directed the club-savvy music video for Madonna's **"Fever,"** a **dance** hit and non-US single. It remains Madonna's only music video in which she is—thanks to an assist from a short wig—a full-on redhead. The video is similar to Sednaoui's "Give It Away" (1991) by Red Hot Chili Peppers.

SEIDELMAN, SUSAN: *b. December 11, 1952.* Trailblazing director of such feature films as *Smithereens* (1982), *Making Mr. Right* (1987) and *She-Devil* (1989), she is best known as the director of ***Desperately Seeking Susan***.

Sarah Pillsbury and Midge Sanford approached Seidelman to direct *Susan* after several high-profile male directors had declined. Seidelman loved the material, and the producers loved the idea of a woman in the director's chair, considering the film's **feminist** underpinnings. Hiring her also made the film creatively a female clean sweep: Its studio exec, producers, director, writers and lead actors were all women.

Seidelman was the only person pushing for Madonna for the role of "Susan." She felt Madonna was a competent enough actor, but was especially insistent that she had the right kind of enigmatic, cool quality that the character and the film needed.

"She was **nervous** and vulnerable and not at all arrogant—sweet, but intelligent and verbal, with a sense of humor," Seidelman said in 1986 of Madonna on-set.

Seidelman rarely grants interviews on the topic of Madonna anymore, but she has appeared at many screenings of the film, proudly recalling her **work** on what wound up becoming one of the classics of the 1980s.

LEFT BY ANDY SCHWARTZ. RIGHT BY MATTHEW RETTENMUND.

Directed by Seidelman

Seidelman, Mark Blum, Rosanna Arquette and Aidan Quinn at a 25th-anniversary *Susan* screening

GREGORY PACE

SEINFELD, JESSICA: *b. September 12, 1971.* Philanthropist and cookbook author and wife of comedian Jerry Seinfeld. Madonna and Mrs. Seinfeld are friends and were for many years **NYC** neighbors. Madonna's kids have even trick-or-treated with Jessica and Jerry's. (Those kids have everything ... they expect free **candy**, too?)

The women have hung out on many occasions, including being spotted together at the **Met Ball** and the premiere of the film *Nine* (both 2009). Though tabloid rumors that same year claimed Jerry Seinfeld was not happy with Madonna's influence on his wife, Madonna appeared on his *The Marriage Ref* in 2010 and the Seinfelds attended Madonna's *W.E.* premiere in 2012.

SEN KVÄLL MED LUUK: *Airdates: 1996–2004.* Swedish talk show hosted by Kristian Luuk. Madonna appeared on the show on November 15, 1998, granting a short English interview.

She said her favorite music at the time was by Baxter and Lucy Nation (both **Maverick** acts), Air, Mono and Massive Attack. She denied having any of her own records in her collection: "I've heard enough of me." She joked that she didn't need to wear a mustache when going out in public because she was already growing one. The little sneak also said her favorite movie of the year was *Lock, Stock and Two Smoking Barrels*, though she didn't explain that it was written and directed by a man she'd recently met (**Guy Ritchie**), and with whom she was falling in **love**.

After the nerdtastic Q&A, Madonna performed a lip-synched version of **"The Power of Good-Bye."** She removed the black wrap she'd been wearing for the sit-down part of the appearance to reveal she was clad in a completely see-through top.

> "I can't live without my music."
> —MADONNA, *SEN KVÄLL MED LUUK* (1998)

SETRAKIAN, WHITLEY: *b. circa 1958.* Now known by her married name Whit Hill, this **dancer** and artist was Madonna's roommate during the time that they attended the **University of Michigan**. The girls shared a room at **University Towers**. Setrakian later wrote a memoir that was entitled *Not About Madonna* [SEE: **bibliography (about Madonna)**] in spite of the fact that it did touch on her friendship with the girl she once described as being "beautiful in a way that terrifies me."

Madonna was intimidating to Setrakian, sort of taking over their shared room. Setrakian has said that it was Madonna who "embarked on a campaign" to befriend her, eventually becoming physically affectionate and seducing her ... into **shoplifting**.

The young women became so close, dancing together suggestively at **The Blue Frogge**, that they were called lesbians by classmates. It was a development that—according to a letter made public by Setrakian—delighted Madonna. Setrakian recalled Madonna as being a sucker (wink-wink) for double entendres even **back** then.

On *Driven: Madonna*, Setrakian said, "She was fun to live with, once we got to know each other; she could be so sweet." Though Setrakian said she had seen unguarded moments and felt a closeness to Madonna, she also said she wouldn't be surprised if Madonna had then hung out with someone else and bad-mouthed Setrakian; loyalty was not a quality that stood out to her in early Madonna.

"Her passion was her *self*—the project of 'Madonna.'"

Setrakian's **book** is well written and anti-exploitative. She said of its publication, "I just wanted to take the celebrity 'I-Knew-Her-When' schlock and make something beautiful out of it. Like finding a piece of plastic on the beach and incorporating it into a mosaic." In spite of its higher aspirations, it's not devoid of juicy dish, relating a story about Madonna hitting on Al Pacino when Setrakian's father introduced the actor, a longtime buddy, to his daughter's friend. "That friend of your daughter's stuck her tongue in my ear!" Pacino later told Mr. Setrakian, never guessing he would one day appear in a movie (*Dick Tracy*) with the precocious **flirt**.

Whit Hill now lives in Nashville. She is a songwriter, and has recorded a song about Madonna called "Maddie."

Glowing in the presence of Jessica Seinfeld

—DEBORAH FEINGOLD

7 SUR 7: *Airdates: 1981-1997.* On October 11, 1992, at the **height** of her *Erotica* and *Sex* era, Madonna gave a 30-minute, wide-ranging sit-down interview to this French news show's Anne Sinclair. She was in braids and a plaid jacket and was sporting her **gold tooth**. Madonna declared **Paris** to be her "favorite city in the whole world—I truly mean that," discussed her ever-changing looks (she announced she was feeling "very Bavarian"), explained she felt unfairly attacked because "… many times when people criticize, are critiquing my **work**, they're *not* critiquing my work, they're critiquing my personality … Most people that write about me write about me in a very personal way …" and dipped her toe into the political arena. She concluded by teasing that if she ever ran for president, she'd have a huge advantage "because everyone already knows my past."

SEX: Madonna's image has always been sexual. "I think it's really important to exude sexuality on stage," she declared in 1983, "but I don't think I have to entice men. I don't think people have to be aroused sexually by what you wear. I get over that by way of being sexy just by the way I sing and move on stage." She's never been bashful about sex, saying in 1987 that sex is only dirty "when you don't take a bath."

The climax of Madonna's exploration of sex was even called *Sex*, a massive blueprint of the kinds of sex society considered fringe-worthy.

Madonna's own sex life has been the subject of considerable speculation. While it can be safely said she never had a shot of passing **Prince Charles**'s virginity test, she probably has not been as active as biographies hint or as public impressions presume. Madonna champions sexual exploration, but pulls **back** from suggesting wild, unrestrained hedonism and has implied that she's had only a handful of one-night stands.

"I would say I probably very rarely in my life had sex with someone that I didn't have real feelings of love for.

Because ultimately, I can only allow myself to be really intimate with someone if I really care for them."

As a little girl, Madonna was drawn to forbidden forms of play with her Barbies. "I dressed them up in sarongs and miniskirts and stuff. They were sexy, having sex all the time. I rubbed them and Ken together a lot. And they were **bitchy**, man. Barbie was *mean*." She has claimed that as a child, she witnessed a couple making **love** standing up in a church. She lost her **virginity** at 15, yet imaginatively told *Island* magazine in 1983 that she hadn't seen a penis by age 17. On a related note, later in the same piece, she said, "Fantasies are essential." She has said that her true sexual awakening didn't occur until 1988 (awkward for **Sean Penn** to hear).

In 1985, Madonna said her critics felt her lyrics were along the lines of, "Come on, baby, let's get *down* to it/Let's get in the bed and go right through it." They weren't … *then.*

Madonna's artistic concerns with sex and her second-nature **flirtatious** demeanor have made her the most famous sex icon of the past 35 years, even if she is more *about* sex than she is passively *sexy*. Madonna herself has as much as acknowledged this point, such as when *Vanity Fair* asked her in 1992, "Do you enjoy having sex?" and she replied, "That's like saying to a gynecologist, 'Do you enjoy having children?'"

On her album *Rebel Heart*, Madonna continued her long tradition of writing about sex, likening it to a tune-up on **"Body Shop,"** bragging about her delish vadge on **"Holy Water"** and referencing her infamous **book** with the similarly-titled **"S.E.X."**; even 1985-Madonna herself probably would've been shocked to learn she would be unapologetically singing about golden showers at age 56.

SEX (BOOK): *Release date: October 21, 1992. Sex* is Madonna at her most unnervingly best *and* worst, both a mythmaker building herself to new **heights** of **fame** and notoriety, and an icon/iconoclast, gleefully debasing all previous notions of celebrity. Shot at hip, seedy locales like the

"I DON'T THINK THAT I'M USING SEX TO SELL MYSELF. I THINK THAT I'M A VERY SEXUAL PERSON AND THAT COMES THROUGH IN MY PERFORMING, AND IF THAT'S WHAT GETS PEOPLE TO BUY MY RECORDS, THEN THAT'S FINE, BUT I DON'T THINK OF IT CONSCIOUSLY, 'WELL, I'M GOING TO BE SEXY TO GET PEOPLE INTERESTED IN ME.' IT'S THE WAY I AM. IT'S THE WAY I'VE ALWAYS BEEN." —MADONNA (1984)

"I'VE BEEN CALLED A TRAMP, A HARLOT, A SLUT AND THE KIND OF GIRL THAT ALWAYS ENDS UP IN THE BACK SEAT OF A CAR. IF PEOPLE CAN'T GET PAST THAT SUPERFICIAL LEVEL OF WHAT I'M ABOUT, FINE." —MADONNA (1985)

"I THINK SEXUALITY IS AT THE CORE OF EVERYONE'S BEING. EVERYBODY'S IN A DIFFERENT STATE OF DENYING IT." —MADONNA (1991)

"SO THERE YOU GO: LESS THAN MADONNA, MORE THAN PRINCESS DIANA … I HOPE." —ANDIE MACDOWELL'S CHARACTER ON HAVING 33 SEX PARTNERS, *FOUR WEDDINGS AND A FUNERAL* (1994)

"LOLA'S HORRIFIED BY ALL OF IT. AT THIS POINT, ROCCO DOESN'T CARE. IT JUST GOES OVER. HE'S LIKE, 'UGH, MOM. MOM'S BEING MOM.' THE OTHER LITTLE KIDS AREN'T TUNED INTO THAT FREQUENCY YET." —MADONNA ON HOW HER KIDS REACT TO HER SEXY LYRICS, *PEOPLE* (2015)

Hotel Chelsea (222 W. 23rd St., NY, NY), **gay** strip joints like the **Gaiety, sex** club The Vault (formerly 28 10th Ave., NY, NY) and in the streets of **Miami,** the **book** is Madonna's MAGNUM™ opus on all things erotic. Or it's Madonna self-destructively cashing in her hard-won artistic credibility in order to explode convention. Or it's Madonna thinking she's being transgressive while she is in fact being retrogressive.

Or it's all of those things.

Or none.

What *Sex* is for sure is a 128-page book (plus an eight-page comic book called *Dita in the Chelsea Girl* and a CD single with an **"Erotica"** mix called "Erotic") of images of Madonna photographed by **Steven Meisel,** edited down to 475 from 20,000. The book was designed by **Fabien Baron** and written by Madonna (edited by **Glenn O'Brien**), as narrated by the character "**Dita Parlo**." In Italian, "dita" means "fingers," which goes so well with the book's theme and with its desired effect on readers/viewers/fondlers.

The book that Madonna, in her introduction, claims to have made up, was nonetheless categorized as nonfiction.

Sex may have gotten its start as early as fall 1990, when, according to editor Judith Regan, she met with Madonna and **Freddy DeMann** while she **worked** for Simon & Schuster to pitch them an idea she had: *Madonna's Book of* **Erotica** *and Sexual Fantasies.* They never moved ahead with her, so imagine her surprise when Madonna announced she was publishing a book of erotica and sexual fantasies under the title *Sex.*

The text gets off to a good start with, "This book is about sex. Sex is not **love.** Love is not sex." As promised, the book is a stark, loveless portrayal of the kinkiest sex available over the counter. In fact, many of the bookstores that agreed to sell *Sex* would only offer the book *under* the counter.

Sex was a turning point in the public's perception of Madonna. Before the book, Madonna's sexy image was acceptable, fun, maybe a little racy, but generally accessible. The people morally outraged by her were squares who didn't believe in sex outside of marriage. But Madonna upped the ante here, portraying or hinting at SM, **bisexuality,** homosexuality, group sex, rough sex, anilingus and even a jokey hint at bestiality. (No, she does not have sex with a **dog** in the book.) For former admirers who felt the post-"**Justify My Love**" Madonna was too lesbian (is there such a thing as too lesbian?), *Sex* did nothing to appease them—Madonna cavorts with a couple of female skinheads. In short, post-*Sex,* even some of Madonna's self-proclaimed liberal **fans** felt she'd (get ready for one of the worst anti-Madonna clichés) gone too far.

In addition to the anonymous lesbians, Madonna makes implied love to Isabella Rossellini, rocker Tatiana von Furstenberg and pal **Ingrid Casares,** and toys with supermodel **Naomi Campbell,** sucking her toe like its an Everlasting Gobstopper.

During a *Weekend Update* rant on ***Saturday Night Live*** at the time, cast member **Chris Rock** joked, "The one good thing I gotta say about Madonna's book is that it's integrated. Y'know, Madonna's cool—I mean, she wants blacks and whites to come together."

Other star performers in the book include Clit Club (formerly 432 W. 14th St., NY, NY) impresaria Julie Tolentino, rappers **Big Daddy Kane** and **Vanilla Ice,** scion Daniel de la Falaise and dearly departed super bottom gay **porn** star **Joey Stefano,** whom Madonna knew as a former amour of mogul **David Geffen.**

When recruiting all of the above for her book, Madonna asked two questions: "Do you mind getting naked?" and "Would you mind kissing me?" They didn't and they didn't.

Madonna knew what she wanted to do with *Sex,* but it didn't come out exactly as she'd envisioned. It had initially been announced with the title *Erotica,* which later became the title of her concurrently released album, in an early **Warner** Books print ad. Even the book's final shape doesn't reflect Madonna's **original** vision—she wanted it to be oval, a publishing near-impossibility. The content is the result of Madonna's imagination as influenced by the reactions she received from her contributors, but Warner also had a say. She was expressly forbidden to include any scenes of sex with animals, children or religious objects, or any clear shots of actual penetration—a loose set of standards around which Madonna worked willingly. However, by her own admission, Warner *did* veto one image that Madonna wanted to include. Either her commitment to the image wasn't very strong in the first place, or her professionalism won out over her will.

The heavy hand of corporation led to the book's rushed release—Madonna wanted to work on it longer than she did, but Warner Bros. demanded a pre-Christmas release.

The publication of *Sex* was an expertly organized event, accomplished simultaneously in the US, **England,** France and Germany. A separate Japanese edition—minus pubic **hair**—was also created.

Its initial print run consumed 750,000 pounds of aluminum for the shiny covers, and as much Mohawk Superfine paper, a high-quality stock used to properly reflect all the nuances of the original photographs. The book was published on a specially designed, three-story printing press capable of 25,000 impressions per hour, or five times the amount of a typical press. This allowed all 1 million copies of the book's print run to be produced in a little over two weeks.

To protect the book's contents, *Sex* was manufactured with eight armed guards, representing an unprecedented amount of muscle used to keep some privates private. Though thousands of copies were stolen from the warehouse immediately prior to the book's on-sale date, its contents were, impressively, kept mostly a secret,

Prior to J.K. Rowling's *Harry Potter* (1997–2007), Madonna's nearly *Hairless Potter* did swift **business.** The book that nobody was sure would sell sold 150,000 copies in the US on its first day. It sold at the rate of 100 copies per hour in a single West Hollywood bookstore, and in fact

"Prurience is in the eye of the beholder."–MADONNA (1985)

ALEJANDRO MOGOLLO

outsold the entire Top 25-selling books at the time, *combined*. It completely sold out its US print run within two months, blasting Rush Limbaugh's *The Way Things Ought To Be* (1992) out of the #1 slot on the bestseller lists.

"One customer was really **nervous**," reported Barnes & Noble sales clerk Stacy Blease. "His hands were shaking when he gave me the **money**."

The book went on to sell 1.5 million copies worldwide (750,000 US), so 500,000 more were printed than had been announced after the demand became clear. Ever since the last copy was sold, the book has been at or toward the top of the list of the most requested out-of-print book titles.

Sex was published to considerable critical outcry. The book's original Japanese publisher, Kadokawa Shoten, dropped the book for which it had paid a million bucks, and fringe groups worked to ban it in France. The book was also unpopular among libertines, who found it desperate, unimaginative and crass.

As Fran Lloyd wrote in 1993's *Deconstructing Madonna*, "[T]he content and format of *Sex* places Madonna's work in the centre of the postmodern blurrings of the distinctions between high and low culture, often only predicated on context." That tension rended the book's reception, as well as its star's career, for years to come.

Library Journal declined to review the book, and in more than one instance, reviews refused to accept it as a "book" at all. The Mylar in which the book was sealed and its stainless-steel covers may have thrown critics, but such flashy packaging didn't make *Sex* any less of a book, but rather *more* than a book.

Sex received the most vicious, dismissive, damning reviews of the year. One recurring note in criticism of the book is money. Because the book was the first in a $5.5 million book deal with Time-Warner, and because its $49.95 price tag guaranteed a net profit in the neighborhood of $20 million, critics cynically cited profit as Madonna's only motive. Critics who held Madonna's capitalism against her ignored the fact that it is possible to make both **art** and bank.

One thing *Sex* was for sure: Singular. An announced paperback edition in 1993 was cancelled, and Madonna said there would "probably never" be a sequel to this "one time only" occurrence. Consider it the Halley's Comet of boner bait. Even though outtakes are viewable as **leaks** and hours of video footage filmed by Baron during the shoots is known to exist, Madonna has never hinted that any of it will be released. She said in 1998 that all the extra footage will "be unearthed after I die. It'll be playing at the Film Forum."

Judged on grounds of sheer impact, there is no competition. Judged on literary and photographic grounds, it is uneven in both capacities.

The writing is one aspect of the project that many critics either overlooked or discarded out of hand, but Madonna was actually most proud of her literary contribution to *Sex*. Though her style is unpolished, some of the passages

10

SMART THINGS SAID ABOUT *SEX*

1

"If your pornographic ideal is for no distracting interruptions to spoil your hand-eye coordination as you flog the duck, yes, it's pretty darn non-erotic. But look. Anyone who tells you that 100-plus pages of one of the world's best-known women cavorting in the nude with all sorts of other naked celebs and non-celebs can be *boring* is lying through his or her teeth."
—TOM CARSON, *LA WEEKLY* (1992)

2

"Let's face it—this book is review-proof."
—LAURENCE J. KIRSHBAUM, WARNER BOOKS (1992)

3

"Sexual fantasies require neither action nor guilt."
—HAROLD BLOOMFIELD, PSYCHIATRIST, *USA TODAY* (1992)

4

"*Sex* is like another comparably auspicious debut, *Moby Dick*. With 'My name is Dita,' we at last have a worthy successor to 'Call me Ishmael.'"
—HELEN EISENBACH, *QW* (1992)

5

"*The Times*'s belief that the only 'completely heterosexual' scenarios are those involving Madonna and Vanilla Ice … is only accurate if you don't believe male-female SM, sex with an older man, sex with a Botticellian younger man, biting a man's ass, shaving his pubic hair, sucking on his [sic] toe or sex with a man wearing makeup to be heterosexual."—MIM UDOVITCH, *THE VILLAGE VOICE* (1992)

6

"I've seen lots of pornography. This is not pornography. This book is about how sex is involved in the culture."
—KERIG POPE, *PLAYBOY* (1992)

7

"What other star has made herself so tantalizingly available while remaining so essentially remote?"
—VINCE ALETTI, *THE VILLAGE VOICE* (1992)

8

"By presenting the world with a range of sexual fantasies in which she poses successively as aggressor, victim, exhibitionist, housewife, gay and straight, Madonna is suggesting there is nothing essential about gender or sexuality—and by implication, identity. As a sexual object who is also subject—a woman who controls and determines the circulation of her image and her fantasies—Madonna takes us to the heart of contemporary fears about social disintegration."
—CATHARINE LUMBY (1993)

9

"My rebellion happened, instead of in my teens, when I was 30. I just wanted to go, 'Don't tell me what to do just 'cause I'm a girl. Don't tell me I can't be sexual and intelligent at the same time.' I'm proud of the way I acted because it set a precedent and gave women the freedom to be expressive. I'm happy to have been a pioneer."
—MADONNA (2000)

10

"While pop stars have ramped up the sex and kink factor since 1992, it's been in a carefully packaged, corporate-approved way. (Think Rihanna's bubble-gum hit 'S&M'). Any one of them might flash a tit, but RiRi, Nicki, Britney—and, yes, even Gaga—haven't claimed ownership of their sexuality the way Madonna did with this controversial tome."
—DAN AVERY, *QUEERTY* (2012)

①⓪ DUMB THINGS SAID ABOUT *SEX*

············ ① ············

"I never meant [*Sex*] to be the definitive statement on the most erotic fantasies ever made, and it's not meant to be taken so seriously. On the other hand, it is."–MADONNA (1992)

············ ② ············

"Of course, some of us actually like the opposite sex …"–CARYN JAMES, *THE NEW YORK TIMES* (1992)

············ ③ ············

"The only completely heterosexual scenes show Madonna with the white rapper Vanilla Ice."
–CARYN JAMES, *THE NEW YORK TIMES* (1992)

············ ④ ············

"Laughter is the enemy of lust."–PETE HAMILL, *NEW YORK DAILY NEWS* (1992)

············ ⑤ ············

"Pornography doesn't hold up to much serious analysis."–ROBERT HOFLER, *NEW YORK NEWSDAY* (1992)

············ ⑥ ············

"The taboo against pedophilia is no mere prejudice, and flirting with it, even sending it up, is neither worldly or clever. Unless you are Nabokov."
–VICKI GOLDBERG, *THE NEW YORK TIMES* (1992)

············ ⑦ ············

"It is … hard to stir up outrage when, for years, her albums and movies haven't seemed so much like products in themselves as deluxe keepsakes from the publicity campaigns that launch them."–PEOPLE (1992)

············ ⑧ ············

"That book's not art. I have to defend her right to do it, but I just thought it was embarrassing, tacky and unnecessary."
–SIR MIX-A-LOT (1992)

············ ⑨ ············

"In the case of Madonna, she's a megamillionaire and indeed at present is probably making so much money she herself doesn't have an accurate accounting of it. She has, therefore, no excuse whatever for deciding to become a public slut."–STEVE ALLEN, *JOURNAL OF POPULAR CULTURE* (1993)

············ ①⓪ ············

"I was so embarrassed and ashamed. It was a porno."
–VANILLA ICE (2011)

---

are memorable, creative and highly erotic. The introduction, though, is at once liberating and confused. The book is all "pretend," and yet she poses with real-life lover Vanilla Ice and later recounts incidents from the real Madonna's life on the Lower East Side.

The killer one-liners are the most **powerful** writing in the book: "I'll teach you how to **fuck**," also used on "Erotica," is an effective promise and a threat so audacious it's daunting, so confrontational it inevitably made many readers either shoot, or shoot her a mental, "Oh, yeah?" She dreamily writes, "My **pussy** is the temple of learning," a vastly underrated sentiment that is more **feminist** than a roomful of riot grrrls.

It's easy to be tough, but ridiculously brave to be sensitive, especially when you're big, bad Madonna and the critics have sharpened their pencils (which were used in those days) needle-fine.

Arguably her most erotic story is her sand-soaked lesbian fantasy, a funny, silly, sizzling piece that communicates real desire and a charming sense of spirited sensuality that should have characterized the whole book.

Elsewhere, the writing stumbles badly, notably in her unimaginative faux letters to "Johnny" from "Dita," and in page-long diatribes on how to seduce someone, how fat people are "overindulgent pigs" and a shockingly juvenile defense of **pornography** that polarizes erotica and humor, which, if it were true, would negate *Sex* entirely.

In 2004, even Madonna eventually admitted that while she was "looking for deeper meaning" with *Sex*, she "wasn't really offering an alternative." Not that she **regrets** it; when **Jonathan Ross** suggested she did during a 2015 taping, Madonna snapped, "I don't regret it at all. I never said that. I don't regret it. I love it. I paved the way."

The photography was slammed for being amateurish, but since **fashion** photographer Meisel's work is widely admired as fine art, much of the criticism can be attributed to his association with Madonna and with the unpopular premise of the book. In truth, a great number of the images crackle with desire, and many more are brilliantly stylized, if somewhat mechanical, realizations of sex.

The first image is a lovely silhouette reminiscent of Man Ray, or even of the girl-shadow one might find on a trucker's mud flap, and the disparity of these comparisons goes a long way toward explaining *Sex*'s merging of art and commerce, mystique and **exhibition**, elitism and solidarity.

The next photograph of Madonna is one of the book's strongest, a **masked** Madonna in a leather bikini, sucking the middle finger of one hand while simulating digital sex on herself with the other. No viewer familiar with Madonna prior to picking up the book could gaze on this without gasping at her audacity, though many viewers would later deny **shock** over this or any other image.

The photo of a woman with a switchblade at Madonna's crotch was singled out as the "scariest," despite the fact that all parties involved are laughing gaily, obviously just playing around. More impressive is a two-page spread in which Madonna and two women embrace tenderly; it makes excellent use of the book's spiral binding, splitting the photo at the metal seam, a reflection of the SM flavor of the women and of the book.

Madonna, bathed in white light, tugging on **Tony Ward**'s nipple ring with her teeth is another transcendent image, a supple composition that reflects their real-life intimacy. Other shots—Madonna snickering at her own gang-**rape**, pouring wax on a leather man, lying under a cross, sucking Campbell's toe—are too self-consciously naughty to evoke the longing this image evokes, or the lust evoked by a shot of Madonna chewing ass.

Many of the photos are soft and tender, but simply don't read as such because they are relegated to **Andy Warhol**-style repetitive background collages, robbed of any chance they might have had were they arranged more carefully.

The most effective images of all are of Madonna alone, and they stand as a testament to Madonna's **talent** for losing herself in the character of a given photograph—like **Cindy Sherman** in heat—more thoroughly than she has usually lost herself in a character on moving film. Thirty-two or 33 years old at the time of the image's creation, Madonna makes an utterly convincing adolescent in one photo, frankly exploring what appear to be newly sprouted breasts, and later, fingering herself over a mirror.

Meisel appropriates **Helmut Newton** in a series featuring Madonna as a glamorous socialite at a gay strip club, and also in an image taken in Miami, of Madonna arched over a ceramic fish—the sky, pool, ocean, fish and Madonna's flesh each a different and stimulating texture. It's so beautiful you forget to laugh at the joke that the fish is spurting water out between Madonna's thighs. (In 2008, Meisel reflected on his cocreation: "It allowed people to not be so afraid of sex, or, if anything, to simply talk about it … I think it helped people to not be so repressed.")

Ever allusive, one shot of Madonna hanging from a lift over the ocean suggests Leonardo da Vinci; Madonna's slippery beach persona could be Brigitte Bardot; and together, she and Vanilla Ice look more like Charlene Tilton and Brian Austin Green than the **Queen of Pop** and an unworthy knave.

The one image that lingers and that most perfectly captures Madonna's mission on earth is one of the last: Madonna is **nude**, her hair whipped up into a semi-bouffant, a cigarette clamped between her lips, an Azzedine Alaïa purse firmly in her grip, hitchhiking on the streets of Miami. The shot was impromptu, leaving motorists to fend for themselves. Like *Sex* itself, it's the most perfect representation of the exhibitionism and voyeurism inherent in stardom that you'll ever see.

Who is Madonna, to think *anyone* would want to see her in all these poses?

Who are we to deny that we do?

In the end, *Sex* is like sex: Sometimes brilliant, sometimes **boring**, but always worth the 50 bucks.

SEX (BOOK LAUNCH PARTY):

Publishers Weekly called it the "party of the century," but some of the attendees said the **book**-launch bash for *Sex* failed to live up to their expectations. What did they expect? To get laid?

Eight hundred of Madonna's nearest and dearest, all required to bear a photo ID, showed up at Industria Super-studio (775 Washington St., NY, NY) on October 15, 1992. Space-designer Anthony Ferraz offered 5,000 black roses intertwined in barbed wire as cheery party décor.

---

⑤

THINGS SAID ABOUT *SEX* THAT ARE SO BITCHILY FUNNY YOU CAN'T BE MAD

········ ① ········

"Artistic integrity? I'll believe it when she can spell it."
—PULITZER PRIZE WINNER ELLEN GOODMAN, *NEW YORK NEWSDAY* (1992)

········ ② ········

"*Sex* reveals the erotic imagination as daring as that of a middle-aged Westchester housewife out to shock the girls on bingo night …"
—DANIEL MENDELSOHN, *QW* (1992)

········ ③ ········

"*Sex* reminds me of a high-school yearbook for the School of the Performing Sex."
—BARBARA LIPPERT, *ADWEEK* (1992)

········ ④ ········

"… [S]he's simply undressed with no place to go."
—JOHN LELAND, *NEWSWEEK* (1992)

········ ⑤ ········

"… [E]veryone is being fucked, including those who think they are doing the fucking."
—MARGERY METZSTEIN, *DECONSTRUCTING MADONNA* (1993)

The bash featured: a single copy of the then still-top–secret *Sex* displayed in a sealed glass case at the entrance; **Warner** Books staffers dressed as priests to greet participants; blow-up **sex** dolls; a **bisexual** kissing booth; a Cleopatra impersonator dominating two submissive men; a guy in black leather hanging from the ceiling; live-action scenes of bondage and SM involving cat-o'-nine-tails; and a naked lady in a tub full of **popcorn**, who concealed any resentment she may have had over Madonna's love of having caramel on the stuff.

Most memorable was Madonna in one of her all-time least flatteringlooks, which nonetheless **worked** magnificently in context. She appeared at 10 p.m. (shouting "Vote for **Clinton**!" to the assembled media—it was an election year) in a traditional Bavarian dress that was a **gift** from a female German record-company executive, sporting Princess Leia dual buns, invisible **eyebrows**, about three miles of cleavage and a white stuffed lamb: Heidi Ho.

At a tattoo booth, a man who was having Madonna's face etched permanently on his buttocks mused, "You could get stuck with worse." When Madonna said she was flattered, he sassed, "You should be."

Though she did not strip as had been rumored she would, she did take off … promptly at midnight.

Presidential debates were broadcast on one **TV** amid a bank of screens flashing X-rated films and life-sized photos from the book. Madonna dictated the menu, which included, "Anything you can lick or suck." So, ice cream and **lollipops** galore.

No party is complete without a guest list, and some of the notables were: Ashford & Simpson, Tim Burton, **Naomi Campbell**, Rae Dawn Chong, **Willem Dafoe**, **Donna De Lory**, Amanda Donohoe, Griffin Dunne, Robert Evans, Pete Hamill, **Niki Haris**, Gregory Hines, **Billy Idol**, **Grace Jones**, **Jose & Luis**, **Alek Kes**hishian, **Udo Kier**, Lenny Kravitz, Irving "Swifty" Lazar, **Robin Leach**, **Spike Lee**, Jon Lovitz, Virginia Madsen, **Penny Marshall**, **Debi Mazar** (best-dressed!), Mary McFadden, **Steven Meisel**, Eric Nies, **Rosie O'Donnell**, Tatum O'Neal, **Liz Rosenberg**, David Lee Roth, **Francesco Scavullo**, Joel Schumacher, Christian Slater, Kevin Spacey, **Sharon Stone**, Jeanne Tripplehorn and **Vanilla Ice**.

The music was provided by star DJ Junior Vasquez.

—JESS GLYNNE

"S.E.X." (SONG): Oops, maybe she didn't know she couldn't talk about **sex** in 1994, but she could not believably plead ignorance for this 2015 **Rebel Heart** track, which harkens **back** to Madonna's bawdiest content from *Sex* and *Erotica*. Though her vocal is reminiscent of **"Bad Girl,"** there is absolutely no shame or **regret** as she offers to let her lover be her **father** and volunteers to play his nurse. This (rough) sex song lists quite a few arguably sexy things, including golden showers, Novocain, absinthe, raw meat, licorice whips and garter belts.

Madonna said of the outrageously S.E.X.-ually explicit song (written by Madonna, Toby Gad, Mike Dean, S1, **Kanye West**, TB and MoZella, and produced by Madonna, Charlie Heat, Kanye West and Mike Dean), "It's kind of a social commentary about the way everybody hooks up now and the lack of intimacy … [W]hen I do the sort of rap in the middle and I do the list, I made myself sound like I have a lisp. Go back and listen to it. It's meant to be ironic—even though there's some very handy items on that list."

The song made a raunchy **Rebel Heart Tour** interlude.

SEXTON, ANNE: *November 9, 1928–October 4, 1974.* Pulitzer Prize–winning word technician known for the extremely self-revelatory, confessional nature of her **poetry**. She suffered from depression, ultimately committing suicide by carbon monoxide inhalation.

Madonna and her sister **Melanie Ciccone** shared a bedroom and together became big **fans** of Sexton's **work**, in part because Sexton's work is **"death**-obsessed" and the girls were still dealing with the loss of their **mother**. Additionally, Sexton's mother had died of breast **cancer**, just like theirs had.

Madonna told *Pitchfork* in 2015 of the poet, "I worship her. She came up in a tough time, and she definitely wasn't encouraged to be a poet or to speak her mind or reveal anything personal. When I made **Truth or Dare**, I got so much shit from people for everything, for allowing cameras to follow me around all the time. Can you imagine, in this day and age?"

In 1991, Madonna ended her "X-rated" **Advocate** interview with a recitation of the Sexton poem "For John, Who Begs Me not to Inquire Further," but one that might have been even more appropriate is entitled "Madonna" and begins: "My mother died/unrocked, unrocked."

SHADOWS AND FOG: *Director: Woody Allen. Release date: March 20, 1992.* Expressionist film directed by **Woody Allen** that was based on his unproduced 1975 stage play *Death*. As with most Allen joints, the film boasts a cast that reads like an IMDb search: Allen himself, Kathy Bates, Philip Bosco, John Cusack, Mia Farrow, Jodie Foster, Fred Gwynne, **Robert Joy** (*Desperately Seeking Susan*), Julie Kavner, William H. Macy, Madonna, John Malkovich, Kate Nelligan, Donald Pleasence, James Rebhorn (soon to be in the **"Bad Girl"** video), John C. Reilly,

Wallace Shawn, Josef Sommer (***Bloodhounds of Broadway***), David Ogden Stiers and Lily Tomlin.

The film is about a meek bookkeeper (Allen) who becomes embroiled in the drama surrounding a town's serial strangler. The Kafka-esque goings-on are strangely pointless, yet the film has its esoteric entertainments here and there.

In the 85-minute experiment in improvisation, Madonna looks exotically enticing as high-wire artist "Marie," wearing a curly brunette wig and the kind of circus outfit she would later take to wearing to public events (**Grammys** 2015, anyone?). As the main squeeze of a sideshow strongman (Dennis Vestunis, in one of his only two movie roles), she has a few minutes' screen time—a frothy exchange with Malkovich.

The movie's **black-and-white** cinematography turns every scene into art-in-motion, but doesn't help make the proceedings as compelling as Allen clearly finds them. If ever a Madonna film could've been livened up by some of her songs on the soundtrack, this is it, and since the film features the music of Kurt Weill, that's saying a lot.

Madonna said making the movie "was like going to the psychiatrist—not necessarily fun, but certainly educational and enlightening."

Before the film's release, which was delayed from fall 1991 because its studio (Orion) was in Chapter Eleven bankruptcy, ***New York*** *Newsday* started the juicy rumor that Madonna's performance, in what she described as "a stupid little part," was so inept that Allen had cut her out of the film. Not so, said Allen, gallantly defending her in the press. "Not a frame of hers has been cut nor has that ever been contemplated. She's first-rate in the film." She is, and though her part wasn't cut, it wasn't big to begin with.

On March 5, 2013, Farrow tweeted a never-before-seen image of Madonna in costume on the set of *Shadows and Fog*, holding Allen and Farrow's toddler in her lap; their son grew up to be **TV** host Ronan Farrow.

"[*Shadows and Fog* is] unpredictable, with its own tone and rhythm, even though, like all of the director's work, it's a mixture of the sincere, the sardonic and the classically sappy."–VINCENT CANBY, *THE NEW YORK TIMES* (1992)

"Many of the actors, especially Madonna, Kate Nelligan and Fred Gwynne, are on so briefly they barely register. There's too little satire and too much best-of-Woody backpedaling. But the compassionate eloquence of the film is undeniable."

–PETER TRAVERS, *ROLLING STONE* (1992)

SHAKUR, TUPAC: *June 16, 1971–September 13, 1996.* A highly regarded rapper whose **work** dwells on his personal story, he was a top-selling artist in life and remains so in

death. Top songs "Dear Mama" (1995), "California Love" feat. Dr. Dre and Roger Troutman (1995) and "How Do U Want It" feat. K-Ci & JoJo (1995) and albums like *Me Against the World* (1995) and *All Eyez on Me* (1996) cemented him as a musical great.

Madonna dated Shakur, a fact that was fairly well known at the time but that seemed to shock the Internet when she confirmed it publicly in a conversation with **Howard Stern** in 2015. She mentioned it as a way of explaining her "gangsta" attitude toward the world in 1994 when she made a contemptuous visit to the *Late Show with David Letterman* that many had said would lead to the end of her career.

Madonna met Shakur on March 15, 1994, at the Soul Train **Awards**. Shakur escorted Rosie Perez to the show, but Perez revealed on *The View* in 2015 that they were just friends and Madonna wasn't shy in going after what she wanted. "Madonna comes over, she looks at me, she goes, 'Girl.' I go, 'I gotcha.'" When Perez told Shakur of Madonna's interest, he replied, "Hook that up." Perez had already revealed part of the story to **Wendy Williams** the year before.

The couple were only photographed together on one evening: Images exist of them at a Tribeca dinner party at Barocco (formerly 301 Church St., NY, NY) with **Ingrid Casares**, **Sting**, Gianni **Versace**, Raquel Welch and others.

Madonna's affair with Shakur was reported at the time by the tabloid *Globe*, which declared him to be "the perfect man" for Madonna because he was a "cop-shooting suspect." In the **book** *Like an Icon* by Lucy O'Brien (2007), Madonna's "friend" Alison Clarkson is quoted as saying Madonna was dumped by Shakur because "homegirls were saying to him, 'I can't believe you're going out with a white girl.'"

Shakur originally provided the rap for Madonna's **"I'd Rather Be Your Lover,"** but as she was attempting to present a softer side with her *Bedtime Stories* album, his work was scrapped in favor of a rap by **Meshell Ndegeocello**. The **original** version is **unreleased**, but has **leaked**.

On June 16, 2014 (what would've been Shakur's forty-third **birthday**), Madonna attended a preview of the musical *Holler If Ya Hear Me*, which used Shakur's music to tell a tragic Midwestern story.

SHANGHAI SURPRISE: *Director: Jim Goddard. Release date: August 29, 1986.* Surprise! This 1986 Madonna/**Sean Penn** vehicle is one of the worst movies of the '80s.

Adapted from the 1978 Tony Kenrick novel *Faraday's Flowers*, the plot has Madonna playing "Gloria Tatlock," an idealistic, repressed missionary **working** in Shanghai in the '30s who's helping to soothe the injured in the Japan-**China** War. She is in search of a large cache of opium, which she hopes to use as an anesthetic, and is forced to enlist the aid of a brassy American tie salesman (Penn). Enter the bad guys.

Madonna's look for the film was a drastic departure from her previous club kid wardrobe: a classic '30s 'do, prim, figure-obscuring missionary suits and refined makeup.

> "[J]UST BECAUSE SOMETHING TAKES UP TWO HOURS' WORTH OF SCREEN TIME AND OFFERS WELL-KNOWN PEOPLE THE CHANCE TO DRESS CLEVERLY AND TALK ABOUT STOLEN OPIUM AND JEWELS AND SECRETS OF THE ORIENT, IT ISN'T NECESSARILY A MOVIE. WE'D ALL BE BETTER OFF IF THAT WERE MORE WIDELY KNOWN."
> —JANET MASLIN, *THE NEW YORK TIMES* (1986)

> "SOME BAD FILMS BECOME KITSCHY-COOL WITH AGE, *SHANGHAI SURPRISE* CONTINUES TO ROT."
> —PAUL KATZ, *ENTERTAINMENT WEEKLY* (2007)

> "… [T]HIS TRUE-BLUE TURD IS DOWNRIGHT LOVABLE FOR CAPTURING EXACTLY A TIME IN 1986 WHEN TWO CELEBRITY SUPERNOVAS MARRIED, AGREED TO A 'VANITY' PROJECT WHERE MADONNA COULD EXERCISE HER DIETRICH FETISH (*SHANGHAI EXPRESS*, ANYONE?) AND AIRED THEIR STILTED CHEMISTRY FOR BOX-OFFICE RETURNS. IT IS AVANT-GARDE TABLOID DRAMA IN AN ERA WHERE *KEVIN AND BRITNEY: CHAOTIC* WOULD'VE SEEMED LIKE AN INDECIPHERABLE DYSTOPIA."
> —LOUIS VIRTEL, *MOVIELINE* (2011)

Lana Turner would've been proud. Actually, Lana Turner was alive and didn't express pride, so never mind.

Madonna's **acting** in the film is mechanical, deserving of mockery. Looking like a movie star didn't make her one; Madonna was all dressed down with no place to go.

The filming of the movie could not have been more of a disaster. Widely publicized differences between the Penns, producer George Harrison (for his Handmade Films) and director Jim Goddard (who would only make one more feature in his life after this) and Sean Penn's brawling with nosy photographers on the Hong Kong, Macao and **London** sets led to an almost unprecedented outpouring of antipathy for the Penns from the world press. Co-star Paul Freeman told biographer **Barbara Victor**, "There was a lot of sexist banter and innuendo going on when Madonna was around and which she didn't like at all and stamped on pretty firmly. I think Goddard was intimidated by both Sean and Madonna, and his general method of coping with that was with dirty jokes and put-downs. I was amazed by it, and I was amazed that Madonna never slagged him off or punched him." Goddard died in 2013.

Japanese *Shanghai Surprise* phone card

At one point, Penn held up filming for five hours when someone stole Polaroids of the couple taken for production purposes. He also threw his **weight** around to get well-liked publicist Chris Nixon fired when Nixon suggested that the Penns pose for photos to get the press off their **backs**.

Madonna gave a rare press conference before 75 reporters at London's ritzy Roof Gardens (99 Kensington High St., London, England, UK) to lay to rest the ugly rumors, appearing in **control** and on good terms with Harrison, whom most of the reporters forgot was doing his first press conference in a dozen years. Penn skipped the event.

Madonna would later say that when producer and co-writer John Kohn brought her the project, she decided to say yes only because of Harrison's involvement. Harrison rued the day she made that decision, saying, "We had the wrong script, the wrong director and the wrong stars." In 1991, Penn candidly confessed, "They offered me a lot of **money**. I just said, 'Fuck it, I'll do it.'"

Twenty years after the release of the film, Goddard directed a documentary called *I Love Shanghai Surprise*, a tongue-in-cheek tribute to the film featuring quotes from Melissa Rivers, Ted Casablanca and more, which was included along with the film's Special Edition DVD release. It was the last piece he directed.

A week after the film's premiere, ***Rolling Stone*** called it "Madonna's first flop" (how did they know there would be others?). The $15.5 million film ended up earning an anemic $2,315,683, garnered Madonna's first scorched-earth acting reviews and lives on in the Hollywood pantheon as an atrocity of (almost) unspeakable proportions.

"SHANTI/ASHTANGI": Incorporating a chant Madonna learned while getting into **yoga**, "Shanti/Ashtangi" is a ***Ray of Light*** track sung in Sanskrit. As influential as Madonna was and is, no other pop diva has chimed in with her own Sanskrit creation.

The song was written and produced by Madonna and **William Orbit**, but was adapted from the writings of Adi Shankara, taken from the Yoga Taravali, with additional text and translation by Vyass Houston and Eddie Stern.

The song, which is Madonna's buddy **Rosie O'Donnell**'s favorite from *Ray of Light*, has been given two live airings: Madonna sang it at her 1998 **Roxy** gig and on the **MTV Video Music Awards**, following it with a live rendition of **"Ray of Light."**

"SHE IS A DIAMOND": Song from *Evita* and found on ***Evita: The Complete Motion Picture Music Soundtrack*** that is solely performed by **Jonathan Pryce**. It summarizes Evita's appeal to the people of Argentina.

SHERMAN, CINDY: *b. January 19, 1954.* Photographer whose **work** mostly consists of images of herself embodying characters with the help of costumes and makeup. You wanna talk about the latest cool selfie *you* took? Is yours in a museum?

Madonna has long been a **fan** of Sherman's work; she told **Jonathan Ross** in 1992 that *Sex* was inspired, in part, by her.

The first **art** exhibit Madonna ever sponsored was *Cindy Sherman: The Complete Untitled Film Stills*, a showing of the only complete set of all 69 images in Sherman's influential 1970s series. The **original** series, shot between 1977 and 1980, shows Sherman as a **blonde** actress, re-enacting poses from movie **magazines**. The Madonna-backed exhibit took place June 26–September 2, 1997 at the Museum of Modern Art (11 W. 53rd St., NY, NY).

"I just always remember her talking about her work for years and what a fan she was," **Liz Rosenberg** told the ***New York*** Post of Madonna's decision to underwrite it.

Madonna met with Sherman for a private chat the week of June 16, 1997, at MoMA, introduced by Peter Galassi, the museum's chief curator of photography.

In 1998, Madonna said she loved Sherman's "chameleon-like persona—her transformation." Sherman was a guest at Madonna's *#secretprojectrevolution* premiere in 2013.

"SHE'S NOT ME": Scathingly defensive song from ***Hard Candy*** written by Madonna and **Pharrell Williams**, and produced by the **Neptunes** and Madonna. The song is sung from the perspective of a woman assessing her step-down replacement. Though never a single, it was performed live on the ***Sticky & Sweet Tour*** and again, in a medley with **"Express Yourself"** and **Lady Gaga**'s 2011 song "Born This Way," on *The MDNA Tour*. The latter performance was seen as Madonna's way of telling her critics and Gaga herself that Gaga was *not* the new Madonna.

SHIMIZU, JENNY: *b. June 16, 1967.* Japanese-American supermodel, dubbed a "lezbopunk bike-dyke" by the *Los Angeles Times* for being openly **gay** and for her fondness for tattoos, Harleys and **working** as a mechanic. She rose to **fame** in 1993 after being discovered riding on her **motorcycle** and appearing in Calvin Klein ads.

This unconventional model was once good buds with Madonna. Her attitudes toward **sex** sound vaguely familiar: "I'm all for sexual freedom: SM, bondage, dancing half-naked. I just think it's great."

Shimizu was reportedly on hand to escort Madonna home after her infamous appearance in 1994 on ***Late Show with David Letterman***.

In 2007, portions of a kiss-and-tell **book** by Shimizu were published in the *Daily Mail*. Shimizu allegedly confirmed a sexual relationship with Madonna, writing: "I was her secret 'booty call' available any time of the day or night for secret sex sessions." She also wrote of her intense affair with **Angelina Jolie**, which she apparently conducted at the same time she was seeing Madonna. Shimizu declined comment for *EM20*.

—LOUIS VIRTEL

SHIMKIN, TONY: Songwriter and producer who was musically and romantically partnered with **Shep Pettibone** from the time when Pettibone **worked** with Madonna on "**Vogue.**"

Shimkin was present for the creation of "Vogue" and played a large, initially underreported role in the *Erotica* sessions. At the time of the album's release, Shimkin had only a cowriting credit on "**Deeper and Deeper,**" due to an arrangement he had with Pettibone. He has since received cowriting credit on "**Bad Girl,**" "**Bye Bye Baby,**" "**Erotica,**" "**Thief of Hearts,**" "**Why's It So Hard**" and "**Words.**"

Shimkin has claimed he also cowrote "**Rescue Me**" and "**This Used to Be My Playground,**" though he has not been officially credited for any part of those works.

Shimkin hasn't worked with Madonna since the mid '90s, but is pragmatic about that fact, telling *MadonnaTribe* in 2012: "Once you work with Madonna, you never want to stop, but she is smart and is known for **reinventing** herself and keeping each record fresh, and sometimes that means changing who you collaborate with or who you use as a producer."

Shimkin's name came up in 2013 in relation to a major, ultimately unsuccessful lawsuit regarding "Vogue."

SHO-BAR: *750 E. Franklin St., Evansville, IN.* **Evansville**, Indiana, **gay** bar where Madonna partied to alleviate the stultifying boredom of small-town life while filming *A League of Their Own.* Though she refused to sign **autographs** (can you imagine how many hours it would take her to pass out Jill Hancocks to all the patrons of a gay bar?), she did impulsively spray-paint one across the outside wall.

SHOCK: Because she is unpredictable and so many of her projects push the envelope of what's considered permissible, Madonna has been unfairly branded a "shock artist." True, Madonna suddenly saying "**fuck**" 13 (who's counting?) times to **David Letterman** on live **TV**, Frenching a woman in a music video, peddling a **book** of naked pictures of herself, baring her breasts at a **fashion** show and instigating an on-stage intergenerational make-out sesh with **Drake** are all done for shock value, but Madonna rarely does anything *just* to shock. Rather, she uses shock to rouse people who need it and to invigorate those who are not shocked but who identify with her actions. After her Letterman fuckfest, Guy Trebay wrote, "The fact that Madonna may have contracted Tourette syndrome is hardly an occasion for a moral meltdown." He knew she had to take it there.

When she executes one of her stunts, Madonna is not attempting to shock *everyone*, just those whose shock threshold is embarrassingly low. The rest of us she'd much prefer to amaze.

> "The problem is that, thanks to herself, Madonna can't really shock us anymore, short of taking a dump onstage or receiving an abortion. ('Papa Don't Preach' could take on new overtones if the baby were dead.)"—MICHAEL MUSTO, *THE VILLAGE VOICE* (1993)

"SHOO-BEE-DOO": The only track on *Like a Virgin* 100% written by Madonna, this slow-jam was produced (like everything else on the record) solely by **Nile Rodgers.** Madonna has never performed it live, but really should. It's lush.

SHOPLIFTING: Not just grapes … Madonna frequently shoplifted **candy**, **magazines** and sundries as a teenager from **Rochester Hills** establishments like **Mitzelfeld's** and the D&C dime store (now Rojo Mexican Bistro, 401 Main St., Rochester Hills, MI). She introduced her college roommate **Whitley Setrakian** to the fine **art** of sticky fingers.

SHRIMPING: Erotic toe-sucking. "The **feet** are very sensitive—as long as they are clean," Madonna instructed in 1992. "All your nerve endings are in your feet, I found out from a reflexologist."

Madonna shrimps **Naomi Campbell** in a photo from *Sex* that was also used as the **back** cover for her *Erotica* album. That same photo was used on a picture disc (a collectible album with an image directly on the vinyl) in **England**, but was recalled out of sensitivity to royal Sarah Ferguson, who was embroiled in the Great Shrimping Scandal of 1992, caught by paparazzi being shrimped by a man not her husband. Legend has it that only 138 copies of that disc survived destruction, though that number is likely quite a bit higher. Still, because of its rumored scarcity and its status as contraband, it has sold for thousands of dollars … and has also been widely counterfeited.

"SIDEWALK TALK": *Release date: October 21, 1984. Billboard Hot 100: #18.* Madonna wrote this bubbly song about the propensity of street urchins to gossip—a document of her life in downtown **NYC** in the early '80s—and gave it to her producer boyfriend **Jellybean Benitez** for his debut EP *Wotupski!?!* (1984). Benitez—the artist to whom the song is solely credited—hired Catherine Buchanan to sing the vocals, with Madonna providing backing vocals, and released it as a single. Madonna's **original** demo remains **unreleased**. Madonna regulars **Stephen Bray** and **Fred Zarr** play on the song.

SINATRA, FRANK: *December 12, 1915–May 14, 1998.* One of the first teen idols, Sinatra was a big-band singer who became the lust object of legions of bobbysoxers in the 1940s, crooning standards and **original** compositions by songwriters of the day. He went on to reinvent himself as an **Oscar**-winning actor before settling into a lucrative touring career that ended with a few lines sung for a **TV** special on November 19, 1995, his final public singing. Renowned for his vocal stylings, his political activities (as a Democrat, then as a Republican), his many affairs and his alleged mob connections, Sinatra was one of the most important stars of the 20th century.

Madonna met the so-called "Chairman of the Board" on September 18, 1992, backstage at the Greek Theatre (2700 N. Vermont Ave., LA, CA) after his dual concert with Shirley MacLaine.

When Madonna met Sinatra, she posed for a photo with him that shows both Italian-American music greats grinning exuberantly, tangled in a bear hug. Madonna was offered a spot on Sinatra's 1993 *Duets* album, but turned it down because it would have consisted of her recording a vocal that would be married to his pre-existing performance, and she preferred the idea of a true collaboration.

SIRE RECORDS: A part of **Warner Bros.**, Sire was the first record label to sign Madonna. She remained associated with Sire, in conjunction with her own **Maverick** label, for many years. And why not? Sire and its boss, **Seymour Stein**, served her well. In the process, the label earned an estimated low figure of a half billion dollars from Madonna's recordings during just the first 10 years of her career.

Madonna announced in 2007 that she was ending her 25-year association with Warner Bros. in favor of a 360 deal with **Live Nation**.

SIREN FILMS: Before **Maverick**, Madonna formed this film development company in January 1987. Though Siren never produced a single film, it landed a five-picture deal with Columbia Pictures. Madonna said in 1989, "Do you know what a siren is? It's a woman who lures men to their **deaths**."

***60 MINUTES II**: Airdates: January 13, 1999–September 2, 2005*. The comparatively short-lived Wednesday edition of the **TV** news show featured an interview with Madonna by Charlie Rose on May 19, 1999. In it, Madonna joked that while her priorities in life had been "... me, me, me, me, me, me, me, me, me, me" before she gave birth, they had changed to "I, me, me, me, me, *her* ..." once **Lola** arrived. She was also quizzed about her religious beliefs, confirming that her daughter was baptized **Catholic**. Madonna

Bringing disco back to Japan in 2005

went on to say that religion is "about realizing that all paths lead to **God** in the end ... **Love** is the most important thing" and refused to acknowledge any **regrets** in her life.

More hilariously, outtakes revealed Madonna petulantly complaining about the chair she was in, the position of the camera and the lighting, calling to mind a more jocular version of **Barbra Streisand**'s infamous *60 Minutes* sit-down with Mike Wallace (1991).

SIZE QUEEN: Contrary to popular belief, Madonna has gone on record saying that penis size "doesn't matter" to her, casting doubt on rumors that she once led a cartoonishly well-endowed man around by his schlong at size-queen-infested penthouse **sex** club Club Nine (formerly West 50s, NY, NY) in the '90s.

"SKIN": Sensory-overload fifth track on *Ray of Light*, written by Madonna and **Patrick Leonard**, and produced by Madonna, **William Orbit** and **Marius de Vries**. The song, a good example of how to use the aural to suggest the tactile, has a decidedly Indian flavor. Less than 10 years earlier, she was singing about kissing in **Paris**, and here she is urgently asking to be kissed as she *dies*.

"SKY FITS HEAVEN": Hard-driving seventh track on *Ray of* Light written by Madonna and **Patrick Leonard**, and produced by them and **William Orbit**. Rarely has a Madonna tune sought profundity more feverishly and achieved it so gracefully. The song beautifully captures her spiritual journey at the time.

Madonna performed the song for the first time at her **Roxy** gig in 1998, and again on her *Drowned World Tour*.

SLUTCO: Brilliant name of Madonna's now inactive video production company, which was dissolved into **Maverick** in 1992.

***SMAPXSMAP**: Airdates: April 15, 1996-*. Madonna's final stop on her *Confessions on a Dance Floor* promo tour was a December 19, 2005, appearance on this Japanese **TV** show. She performed a version of her standard live take on "Hung Up," thrusting from within a lightly constructed mini podium and burning up the glittering **dance**-floor stage in a red jacket. **Daniel "Cloud" Campos** was wearing his best outfit—no shirt.

Madonna gamely sat for bizarre interview, during which a buffoonish character in a gold-sequined kimino and an earnest host quizzed her on her artistic intentions. The clown then mimicked her performing style on **"Like a Virgin," "Vogue"** and "Hung Up."

Somehow, they got her to return on January 16, 2006, for a completely whacky **cooking** parody. A guy in Madonna **drag** was just one more ingredient in the mix. It was hilarious to watch Madonna doing something so completely out of her comfort zone.

MATTHEW RETTENMUND

SMIRNOFF NIGHTLIFE EXCHANGE PROJECT: On November 12, 2011, Madonna showed up to the **Roseland Ballroom** to choose one future tour **dancer** ... and wound up dancing with boyfriend **Brahim Zaibat** and all comers until well past 2 a.m. Rocking fishnets and short-shorts that revealed an ass any 20-year-old would kill for, Madonna was in rare form.

The winning dancer was **Lil Buck**, who became one of her *MDNA Tour* dancers.

Because the event was in advance of her *MDNA* album release, it was a special treat that the DJ was **Martin Solveig**, who had **worked** with Madonna on her leaked single **"Give Me All Your Luvin'."** He did get Madonna to chant the song's chorus briefly, but otherwise, the music was mostly non-Madonna (save for **"Hung Up"**), giving **fans** a chance to see Madonna do the **gay** boogie to things like titanic remixes of **Adele**'s "Rolling in the Deep" (2010) and **Benny Benassi**'s "Satisfaction" (2002).

SMIT, ANGIE: A striking brunette friend of Madonna's from her early **NYC** days, Smit met Madonna in **dance** class and wound up in the **Breakfast Club** with her, **Dan Gilroy** and Ed Gilroy. Smit also costarred in *A Certain Sacrifice*, playing Madonna's **sex** slave.

SMITH, ELLIOTT: *August 6, 1969–October 21, 2003.* Singer-songwriter admired for his ethereal music and brutally honest lyrics, which tackled his battle with depression and alcoholism. He died as the result of a stabbing that could have been suicide or murder.

Madonna chose Smith's "Between the Bars" (1997) as the song released between 1986 and 2006 that she most wished she'd written. She performed it live at her *#secretprojectrevolution* premiere and her *Tears of a Clown* Melbourne one-off.

SMITH, LIZ: *b. February 2, 1923.* There aren't many people who can be described as good gossips who could also be described as national treasures, but Smith fits both bills. With a writing career that has spanned seven decades and as the author of one of the most widely read columns in history, the so-called Grand Dame of Dish is to celebrity news what Madonna is to provocation. And she's **bisexual** to boot.

From the very beginning, Smith—whose self-titled column was in the *New York Daily News*, then *Newsday* and later the *New York Post* before going digital at wowOwow.com—has been Madonna's most vehement defender in the media. Smith's clever writing always raises valid points toward a favorable reading of Madonna, though her respect for Madonna grants her the leeway to assess the icon critically at times. Case in point: During Madonna's *Rebel Heart* scandal on **Instagram** in 2014, Smith wrote, "Egomaniac? Let's say she has a **healthy** dose of ego, mixed with a sense of victimization. This makes her exactly like all big stars."

Deliciously, the normally positive gossip girl often tweaks other commentators when their condemnation reaches ridiculous **heights**. When **Elton John** threw a hissy fit over Madonna's alleged mistreatment of **Lady Gaga** and the poor taste she showed in beating him out for a **Golden Globe**, Smith wasn't having it:

Watching dancers compete at her Smirnoff event

Stooping to conquer just before she performed Elliott Smith's signature tune

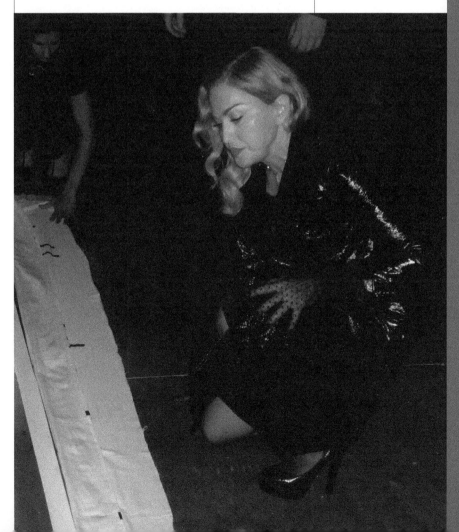

"You're fed up with her? Nonsense. Millions of fans are still panting."—LIZ SMITH ON MADONNA (1992)

"Elton has had a bee in his bonnet about Madonna for years. At various times he has criticized her singing, dancing, her right to be a star, even. She has rarely responded. In this case, however, it is Elton who appears to be 'desperate.'"

Madonna so adores Smith and her equally gifted aide-de-camp Denis Ferrara (a massive **Elizabeth Taylor** fan, this **talented**, witty scribe knows a great **bitch**-goddess when he sees one) that she granted Smith the April 14, 1996, exclusive to announce that she was **pregnant** with her first child. Both Smith and Ferrara have interviewed Madonna, Smith for *Good Housekeeping* and Ferrara for *Cosmopolitan* and *Out*.

When asked to provide a single word to describe Madonna for this **book**, Ms. Smith's full response was, "Impossible. Certainly for us, who have written so much about her. Forget one word. I have two. Iconic, which she is. And ironic, which she insists is the explanation for everything she does. (Uhhh … NOT.) She is the only real star since the rise of **Barbra Streisand**. And I don't mean that ironically."

SMITH, PATTI: *b. December 30, 1946.* Iconic singer-songwriter and artist who was a close friend of photographer Robert Mapplethorpe's. Her visual sensibility was often punk, but her **work** has a folk influence, as on her most famous tune, "Because the Night" (1978), cowritten with Bruce Springsteen.

Smith was a huge **fan** of Madonna's *W.E.*, attending two **New York** screenings including the premiere. Madonna name-checked Smith in her 2012 *Advocate* interview, noting, "Reading Patti Smith's **book** *Just Kids* really helped me." She was referring to using the 2010 book to help her remember her own early days in NYC. She has referenced it since, including in an **Instagram** post featuring a photo of Madonna with **Jean-Michel Basquiat**.

SMITH, SAM: *b. May 19, 1992.* English singer whose *In the Lonely Hour* album and singles "Stay With Me" and "I'm Not the Only One" made him the hot act of 2014.

Via his **Twitter** (@samsmithworld), the out artist enthused, "Up until a month ago, I wasn't a @madonna **fan**. All of a sudden I have become OBSESSED. Everything she's done is gold. So inspiring." It's worth noting that Smith has collaborated with **Nile Rodgers**.

SMOKING: In 1985, Madonna said, "When I'm recording and people light up I say, 'Put that cigarette out RIGHT THIS MINUTE!' It's so rude!" While friends have always said Madonna was the most clean-living club kid of all time, she *was* spotted smoking socially and has frequently used cigarettes as props in photos (by Matthew Rolston, **Steven Meisel**, **Herb Ritts**, **Patrick Demarchelier** and **Mert and Marcus**) and music videos.

She even took to smoking a cigar to rattle **David Letterman**.

But while Mama can smoke on her own terms, she detests it when others try to smoke on theirs. At *The MDNA Tour*

sound check in Chile, Madonna halted the proceedings when the atmosphere got too hazy. "If you smoke, I'm not doing a show. You don't care about me, I don't care about you."

SNACKS: Madonna indulged in caramel corn, Fiddle Faddle, peanut brittle and licorice whips while filming *Evita*, courtesy of **Freddy DeMann**. When on her macrobiotic diet, she has described toast as a treat, but is known to indulge in French fries.

SNATCH BATCH: A takeoff on the "Rat Pack" moniker from the '60s used for **Frank Sinatra** and his cronies, the "Snatch Batch" is the off-color name devised for Madonna, **Sandra Bernhard**, Jennifer Grey and their female comrades. The Batch was born in 1988, while Madonna was on Broadway, and gradually dissolved as Grey drifted from the group and Madonna and Bernhard fell in loathe.

"I'm a brat for sure, but I don't travel in a pack."—MADONNA (1990)

SOLID GOLD: *Airdates: September 13, 1980–July 23, 1988.* Cheese-tastic, **dance**-oriented music series that counted down the week's hottest hits with the help of its scantily clad *Solid Gold* dancers.

On January 14, 1984, the same day Madonna made her official national **TV** debut on *American Bandstand*, she was introduced on *Solid Gold* by host **Marilyn** McCoo, performing a spirited, lip-synched version of **"Holiday."** To Madonna's annoyance, she had to perform in front of the show's dancers, not her own.

Her second appearance became one of her strangest US gigs—introduced by hosts Rick Dees and David Hasselhoff as one of the industry's "Cinderella stories," Madonna lip-synched **"Like a Virgin"** in a long pink wig and **Keith Haring**-style leather jacket. The performance was filmed mostly in long shots and ended with Madonna sinking into a fog caused by what must've been all the dry ice the local dry ice store had in stock.

SOLVEIG, MARTIN: *b. September 22, 1978.* French electro DJ, songwriter and producer who achieved pop immortality with his hit song "Hello" with Dragonette (2010).

In 2011, Solveig collaborated with Madonna on **"Give Me All Your Luvin'," "Turn Up the Radio," "I Don't Give A," "Beautiful Killer," "I Fucked Up"** and **"B-Day Song"** for *MDNA*. Two of the songs became singles, and four were performed on *The MDNA Tour* or at Madonna's **Olympia Hall** show.

"She said I was the sweetest producer she'd ever worked with. Probably too sweet."—MARTIN SOLVEIG, MOJO (2015)

Solveig told *Billboard* of his **work** with Madonna, "It's given me a bit more maturity and experience in the process of collaboration with an artist of that level ... Before this, I was very, very inexperienced in collaborating with that kind of artist. I realized I was in some ways a little naïve."

He reported that Madonna was very hands-on, unlike other artists he'd worked with, both creatively and personally—she made him quit **smoking**.

"SOME GIRLS": Attitude-heavy track on the *MDNA* album written and produced by Madonna, **William Orbit** and Klas Åhlund. Madonna **bitch**-tastically sings about girls with "fake tits and a nasty mood," contrasting them with the ones who are "**Like a virgin**—sweet and pure."

SOMERVILLE, JIMMY: *b. June 22, 1961.* The **original** Bronski Beat lead singer and prolific queer musician had this to say when asked by *EM20* about Madonna in November 2014: "Ummm ... Incredible as a kind of, what can I say? She had her finger on the button ... she was a wise, a very smart woman. But I've still, I've never understood her as a singer."

SOMETHING TO REMEMBER (ALBUM): *Release date: November 3, 1995. Billboard 200 peak: #6.* Madonna's second hits compilation, which was initially going to be called *Sacred Ballads*, focused on her often-overlooked **talents** as a balladeer. Madonna signed off on the project as a way to remind people that she could sing (without scaring children or old people) ahead of her **work** on *Evita*, a film that was going to require audiences to believe she could pull it off before they would spring for tickets. She also liked the timing, coming soon after her longest-running #1 hit of all time, the ballad **"Take a Bow."**

Only two of the songs on *Something to Remember* had previously appeared on *The Immaculate Collection*; her hits **"This Used to Be My Playground"** and **"I'll Remember"** had not been available on a Madonna album until here.

Best of all, the album offers three new songs—her cover of Marvin Gaye's **"I Want You"** and the **David Foster** collaborations **"You'll See"** and **"One More Chance."** "I Want You" was scheduled to be a single and music video was shot, but **Warner Bros.** and Motown couldn't come to an agreement. Instead, "You'll See" was released, going Top 10, followed by the revamped **"Love Don't Live Here Anymore,"** which tanked. **"Oh Father"** and "One More Chance" were moderately successful non-US singles.

Something to Remember has sold over 10 million copies worldwide.

"SOMETHING TO REMEMBER" (SONG): Madonna/ **Patrick Leonard** song that appeared on *I'm Breathless: Music from and Inspired by the Film Dick Tracy*, and that was later the title of, and appeared on, Madonna's first ballads collection, ***Something to Remember***. Musically, it's a world-weary slice of canned jazz, and vocally Madonna strains for some of the notes, but it shows off genuinely

SOMETHING TO REMEMBER
(1-14)

SOMETHING TO REMEMBER
Japanese Edition
(1-14, A)

SOMETHING TO REMEMBER
Latin American Edition
(1-14, B)

① "I Want You" with Massive Attack 7" (Leon Ware/T-Boy Ross) –6:23, produced by Nellee Hooper

② "I'll Remember" (Patrick Leonard/Madonna/Richard Page) –4:22, produced by Madonna/Patrick Leonard

③ "Take a Bow" (Babyface/Madonna) –5:21, produced by Madonna/Babyface

④ "You'll See" (Madonna/David Foster) –4:38, produced by Madonna/David Foster

⑤ "Crazy for You" (John Bettis/Jon Lind) –4:02, produced by Jellybean Benitez

⑥ "This Used to Be My Playground" (Madonna/Shep Pettibone) –5:08, produced by Madonna/Shep Pettibone

⑦ "Live to Tell" (Madonna/Patrick Leonard) –5:51, produced by Madonna/Patrick Leonard

⑧ "Love Don't Live Here Anymore" Remix (Miles Gregory) –4:53, produced by Nile Rodgers/David Reitzas

⑨ "Something to Remember" (Madonna/Patrick Leonard) –5:02, produced by Madonna/Patrick Leonard

⑩ "Forbidden Love" (Babyface/Madonna) –4:08, produced by Nellee Hooper/Madonna

⑪ "One More Chance" (Madonna/David Foster) –4:27, produced by Madonna/David Foster

⑫ "Rain" (Madonna/Shep Pettibone) –5:24, produced by Madonna/Shep Pettibone

⑬ "Oh Father" (Madonna/Patrick Leonard) –4:57, produced by Madonna/Patrick Leonard

⑭ "I Want You" Orchestral with Massive Attack (Leon Ware/T-Boy Ross) –6:04, produced by Nellee Hooper

Ⓐ "La Isla Bonita" (Madonna/Patrick Leonard/Bruce Gaitsch) –4:02, produced by Madonna/Patrick Leonard

Ⓑ "Verás" Spanish "You'll See" (Madonna/David Foster/Paz Martinez) –4:21, produced by Madonna/David Foster

"COULD IT BE THAT EVERYBODY WAS WRONG ABOUT MADONNA?" –J.D. CONSIDINE, *BALTIMORE SUN* (1995)

"THROUGHOUT THE ALBUM, MADONNA PROVES THAT SHE'S A TERRIFIC SINGER WHOSE VOICE HAS IMPROVED OVER THE YEARS. NOT ONE OF THE TRACKS IS SECOND-RATE, AND THE BEST SONGS ON *SOMETHING TO REMEMBER* RANK AMONG THE BEST POP MUSIC OF THE '80S AND '90S." –STEPHEN THOMAS ERLEWINE, *ALLMUSIC.COM* (1995)

touching lyrics that one would not be wrong to apply to her relationship with her mentor **Christopher Flynn**.

SONDHEIM, STEPHEN: *b. March 22, 1930.* The most famous American composer of his time, he's famous for his way with words and complicated melodies. Among his signature **works** are the lyrics for *West Side Story* (1957) and *Gypsy* (1959), plus *Follies* (1971), *Sweeney Todd* (1979) and *Into the Woods* (1987).

Sondheim, who had written a song for **Warren Beatty**'s film *Reds* (1981), was enlisted to write five **original** songs for Beatty's *Dick Tracy*, in which Madonna starred as "Breathless Mahoney." Madonna sang three of them. Though Madonna herself was not sure she had the chops, once she wrapped her vocal cords around **"What Can You Lose,"** **"More"** and **"Sooner or Later (I Always Get My Man),"** the style inspired her to create a similar-vibed album, *I'm Breathless: Music from and Inspired by the Film Dick Tracy*. (Sondheim's other two songs on the soundtrack are "Live Alone and Like It" and **"Back** in **Business,"** the latter of which should not be confused with the Madonna track of the same name.) Her performance of "Sooner or Later (I Always Get My Man)" wowed 'em at the **Oscars**, where Sondheim was announced as the winner of the **statue** for Best Original Song by Gregory Hines and Ann-Margret, who accepted it on his behalf since he did not attend. Madonna was right there in the front row and could've accepted for him ... but perhaps he realized he might never receive his Oscar if Madonna got her mitts on it.

Sondheim was pleased with Madonna's renditions of his songs. He also quoted her in 2010 as having told him that some artists have a bad case of "important-itis," meaning they want to be important more than they want to simply create.

"SOONER OR LATER (I ALWAYS GET MY MAN)": Written by **Stephen Sondheim** and produced by Madonna with Bill Bottrell, the song became the best-known from the film *Dick Tracy* thanks to Sondheim's saucy lyrics and Madonna's sultry performance of it.

She was intimidated by having to learn to sing songs by Sondheim. She said at the time, "When I first heard them, I just said, 'I can't sing those kind of songs.'" But while taking **voice** coaching and **working** with Sondheim, she came to embrace the style. "... [I]t was a great learning experience because Stephen was very, very, um, helpful and generous and he gave me a lot of encouragement."

Which is saying a lot because Sondheim in 2015 was one of the only people in the world to turn up his nose at **Lady Gaga**'s Julie Andrews **Oscar** tribute.

Speaking of Oscars, "Sooner or Later (I Always Get My Man)" was nominated for and won the Oscar for Best **Original** Song. Madonna's dynamic performance of it live on the telecast is arguably her best live **TV** performance of all time.

Madonna has also sung the song on tour, during the *Dick Tracy* sequence on her *Blond Ambition World Tour*.

"SORRY" (SONG): *Release date: February 7, 2006. Billboard Hot 100 peak: #58.* Madonna's second single from *Confessions on a Dance Floor* was another big hit in Europe and elsewhere, but flopped in her native country, where it failed to hit the Top 40. It was nonetheless a major (#1) **dance** hit.

The song was written and produced by Madonna and **Stuart Price**. It opens with Madonna expressing **regret** in different languages before launching into what is surely one of her best club bangers. It's an unyielding number, one Madonna herself has termed her "ultimate scorned-lover song."

The single **art** was unusual in that it was the first time Madonna used a **fan** image. Marcin Kokowski had attended her **G-A-Y** show in **London** and taken great photos, which were put on display on his friend's Mad-Eyes **fan site**. Madonna's people saw the images and loved them. One was chosen for use as the "Sorry" art, after being reworked (it was brightened, her **hair** was tinted **orange** and some wrinkles went bye-bye, baby) by Giovanni Bianco.

The song has only been performed live on her *Confessions Tour*.

"SORRY" (VIDEO): *Director: Jamie King, 2006.* Madonna's choreographer **Jamie King** took the reins for this sort of sequel to the action in the **"Hung Up"** video. (Think of how **"Take a Bow"** begat **"You'll See."**) The same Madonna from that previous video is seen riding around **London** in a van with her female **dancers**—chicks before dicks!—picking up various guys and having them perform for the girls' amusement. There's a bodybuilder, hood rats, a little street dancer, a fat guy, a nerd—but no **porn** star; that was just a rumor.

The frisky ladies head to a Thunderdome-esque cage fight, where Madonna casually wraps a leg behind her head, apparently just 'cuz she can, before they all end up at a '70s-style roller rink.

Choreographer Fred Tallaksen spent three weeks teaching Madonna to skate for the video, a **job** he got overnight after e-mailing a video he'd made of dancers skating to the song.

He told *The Advocate*, "She'd shut everyone else out. We'd get a bunch of Red Bull, put on one of her mix tapes, and skate for hours and hours with no breaks." They had such great chemistry that Madonna put him in the video—he's the guy who executes that through-the-legs maneuver.

Madonna looks so at-home on skates in the final product that one wishes the whole video happened on wheels.

SOUND OF CHANGE LIVE, THE: Madonna was a speaker at this June 1, 2013, concert in Twickenham, **England**, which was held to improve education, health and justice for women and girls internationally by raising **money** for the Chime for Change (ChimeforChange.org) **charity**, founded by Frida Giannini (Gucci's creative director), Salma Hayek and **Beyoncé**.

She was dressed like a cat burglar, all in black, but it was Madonna's puffy face that garnered the headlines when news outlets might have instead focused on her message. She spoke eloquently for about 10 minutes on "what happens when we educate girls." She introduced filmmaker Sharmeen Obaid Chinoy but did not perform; she left the performing to Iggy Azalea, Beyoncé, Mary J. Blige, Florence + the Machine, Ellie Goulding, John Legend, **Jennifer Lopez**, Rita Ora (a future **Material Girl** clothing line spokesperson), Laura Pausini and **Timbaland**.

Backstage, she gave a brief interview to Savannah Guthrie, in which she said, "When this event came up ... it seemed like a perfect fit and, um, a perfect opportunity for me to **voice** my opinion and my enthusiasm and my passion about educating girls around the world."

"SPANISH LESSON": *Hard Candy* song written by Madonna and **Pharrell Williams** and produced by the Neptunes and Madonna. The song may well be the fans' least favorite on the album, but it was performed on her *Sticky & Sweet Tour* and as a *Rebel Heart Tour bonus* nonetheless.

SPARKS: Extremely eclectic rock duo consisting of Ron Mael (b. August 12, 1945) and Russell Mael (b. October 5, 1948). They had a run of success in the UK, most notably with "This Town Ain't Big Enough for Both of Us" (1974), but their greatest US hit was the #49 single "Cool Places" (1984), a duet with Go-Go's member Jane Wiedlin.

Sparks recorded a haunting song called "Madonna," which was on their album *Interior Design* (1988). The song, which they also recorded in French, German and Spanish, is a narrative about a man who gets picked up by Madonna in her limo and goes **back** to her penthouse, where she uses him for a one-night stand and then kicks him to the curb in the morning following a continental breakfast. With a simple chorus, the song seems to comment on society's obsession with **fame.**

SPEARS, BRITNEY: *b. December 2, 1981.* It's tempting to make the entire entry begin and end with, "It's Britney, **bitch**!"

The southern sexpot from Kentwood, Louisiana, was introduced to America by Jive Records as the girl next door in 1998, but her video for "... Baby One More Time" left no doubt as to that girl's game: Tease her male elders while **acting** as if she had *no* clue why they were drooling. Spears became one of the most potent female teen idols of all time seemingly overnight, thanks to her unapologetically sugary (like Swedish fish) pop tunes and her soap operatic relationship with fellow *The All-New Mickey Mouse Club* (1989–1996) alum **Justin Timberlake**; both had been on the revival of the Disney series from 1993 to 1995. Beloved singles like "(You Drive Me) Crazy" (1999), "Oops! ... I Did It Again" (2000), "I'm a Slave 4 U" (2001), "Toxic" (2004), "Womanizer" (2008) and "I Wanna Go" (2011), and the relatable haplessness of her meltdown, during which she shaved her head and performed a memorably sluggish "live" rendition of her single "Gimme More" (2007), have combined to make Spears a true icon of her era.

Spears was often seen as a potential successor to Madonna. This talk came at the right time—a **Kabbalah**-fied Madonna, then a new mommy, was seemingly easing into the idea that she would not be **Queen of Pop** forever, graciously wearing a tank with Spears's name on it during her comeback gig at the **Roseland** in 2000. She said she had made Britney her "talisman" during her *Music* promo in **NYC**. "I became obsessed with wearing [Britney] T-shirts. I slept in them, as well. It was like I felt it would bring me luck. And it did."

Spears told *In Touch* about discovering that Madonna had worn her name on her chest: "I've listened to Madonna since I was a kid. So one day, I'm looking through this **magazine** and I see Madonna wearing a T-shirt with my name on it and I go, 'What?' I was proud and honored."

In a 2001 *Time Out London* Q&A, Spears said she was a big **fan** of Madonna's "ever since I was a little girl" and that "she's the person that I've really looked up to." She said **"Borderline"** was the first Madonna song she remembers obsessing over, and **"Vogue"** and **"Like a Prayer"** were her all-time faves.

While Spears was always written about as an "It" girl, she never truly dominated the singles charts in the way later aspirants (**Nicki Minaj**, **Katy Perry**, **Rihanna**, **Taylor Swift**) would. In 2003, after a string of not-so-hot chart performances, Spears teamed up with rival **Christina Aguilera** and Madonna, herself reeling from the commercial failure of *American Life*, for a much-ballyhooed same-sex kiss during a performance at the **MTV Video Music Awards**.

The performance began with Spears singing **"Like a Virgin"** from atop a **wedding** cake, Aguilera coming in from the side to join her, each in wedding dresses, a reference to Madonna's performance of the song at the show's first installment in 1984. Madonna then appeared, this time dressed as a top-hatted groom in a Louis Verdad cashmere suit, singing a remix of **"Hollywood."** She descended, engaging the women in a sensual tango, removing Aguilera's garter, and then kissed both women on the lips right before a lively **Missy Elliott** rap break.

It brought down the house. Attendees Jason Biggs, Jack Black, Fred Durst, Rocco DiSpirito, Carmen Electra, **Jimmy Fallon**, **Kelly Osbourne**, the cast of *Queer Eye for the Straight Guy* (2003–2007) and **Chris Rock** seemed to dig it, while Mary J. Blige looked shocked, Snoop Dogg giggled and Avril Lavigne looked aggressively unimpressed.

The kiss was a watershed pop-culture moment. Madonna has said it was sort of a passing of the torch, though many commentators—each thinking he or she to be the clever one to have **dreamt** it up—have said that Madonna seemed to metaphorically suck the life out of Spears via their liplock, citing the rocky road Spears traveled soon after. The kiss has inspired **works** of **art**, including a bar code–like silkscreen by Mr. Brainwash entitled *Freedom Kiss* (edition of 15, 2008) and his similar *Line Kiss* (edition of 50, 2009), as well as a wicked take by Saint Hoax that shows Madonna kissing Snow White.

Spears's manager Larry Rudolph recalled in *Billboard* in 2014 that most of the performance had been rehearsed

"... I was a Spice Girl once."–MADONNA (1998)

into the ground. "Madonna had been very, very, very rigid about the rehearsals. She was telling Britney and I every day, 'Be here tomorrow at 10 o'clock.' She would never address me by name, she would just say, 'You, make sure Britney's here tomorrow at 10 o'clock.' And I would say, 'Okay.' You don't want to upset her." And yet, the kiss(es) never happened until the performance itself.

"... [W]e never actually, like, really did it in rehearsal but, um, when we got on stage she was like, 'Let's just see what happens.' I was like, 'Okay,' and then we did it ... It was cool," Spears said of the way in which the kiss was blocked out in advance.

Spears, who like her family is reportedly a conservative, told the press that her mom was cool with the kiss. "She liked it! And my dad, weirdly enough, he thought it was fine, too. I mean, come on ... it's Madonna." Spears later said that both Madonna and Colin Farrell (a fling of hers) were excellent kissers. She also said, "I didn't know it was gonna be that long and everything ... I've never kissed a woman before," before adding that she wouldn't kiss a woman again ... except for maybe Madonna.

Madonna's husband, **Guy Ritchie**, was "not a fan" of the kiss, but her daughter **Lola** was actually a flower girl in the performance. This decision came home to roost a few years later, as Madonna told *Out* in 2006: "[Lola] is really obsessed with who is *gay*. And she even asked, 'Mom, you know they say you are gay?' And I'm like, 'Oh, do they Why?' And she says, 'Because you kissed Britney Spears.' And I said, 'No, it just means I kissed Britney Spears. I am the mommy pop star and she is the baby pop star. And I am kissing her and passing my energy on to her.'"

There was a bit of a backlash regarding Madonna's age, something that wouldn't have come up if she were Steven Tyler kissing a hot babe. Madonna's *Goose and Tomtom* costar Lorraine Bracco sniped, "I wouldn't want Madonna kissing my daughters." Duran Duran's **Simon Le Bon** said, "It worried me when Britney snogged Madonna. It looked a bit fake. It screamed, 'We're in this for the **money**.'" Kim Cattrall praised them as women, but felt they were "too heterosexual" to pull it off.

The kiss felt 'round the world revived interest in the women, though their subsequent duet **"Me Against the Music"** was only a minor hit.

In general, Madonna has seemed to take on a maternal interest in Spears. "I see a little bit of myself in her when I first started out and she's a sweet girl," she said the year of their collaborations. An alternate reading would be that Madonna saw no real threat in Spears, so extending a hand of celebrity friendship offered no risk.

Spears has continued to express herself as a Madonna fan. On January 24, 2004, she appeared at the NRJ Video Music **Awards** (in France, y'all!) to present a career-achievement award to "my special friend Madonna." Following her tumultuous 2007, a somewhat recovered Spears came out on stage to support Madonna at her

November 6, 2008, *Sticky & Sweet Tour* stop in LA during **"Human Nature,"** a song featuring imagery of Spears recreating a viral video of a man trapped in an elevator.

"I had the great pleasure to perform with her. She is one of the best artists I have ever met in my life ..."-BRITNEY SPEARS ON MADONNA (2004)

SPEED-THE-PLOW: *Director: Gregory Mosher. Performance dates: April 9, 1988–May 1, 1988 (previews; originally scheduled for March 29); May 3, 1988–December 31, 1988.* Tense, abrasive, anti-Hollywood **play** written by **David Mamet** that became Madonna's Broadway debut. Film director Mike Nichols had told Madonna about the role, and she immediately "pursued it like a motherfucker," calling up Mamet to request an audition. She had already written him a **fan** letter after seeing his feature-film debut as a director, *House of Games* (1987). Mamet granted Madonna a reading, at which he recalled being "blown away." When Elizabeth Perkins removed herself from consideration for the part, Mamet and director Gregory Mosher confidently chose Madonna, saying, "It's scary how much **talent** she has."

Madonna originated the role of "Karen," a seemingly naïve, principled young office temp who attempts to convince a conniving producer of the validity of a film adaptation of a brainy **book** called *The Bridge, or Radiation and the Half-Life of Society—A Study of Decay*. The movie mogul "Bobby Gould" (rumored to be based on Paramount big-shot Ned Tanen), played by Joseph Mantegna, had already made a bet with his colleague "Charlie Fox" (Ron Silver) that he would be able to bed Karen, a bet he won.

The play reveals that Karen is no better than the sleazy producers, having been a manipulative participant in the events the entire time. Still, Mamet referred to Karen as a "latter-day Joan of Arc." Interpretations aside, Madonna **hated** the grueling performance schedule and came to feel beaten down by playing the part over and over, but was toughened by the rigorous experience, both in playing a character so unlike herself, and in receiving malicious reviews for her efforts.

She had been drawn to the role because she saw Karen as "a sympathetic, misunderstood heroine who speaks the truth at any risk."

The play was a phenomenal success. It was nominated for **Tonys** for Best Play, Best Direction of a Play and Best Performance by a Leading Actor in a Play, the latter of which Silver (who died of **cancer** in 2009) won. It had originally been slated to have its run at the Mitzi E. Newhouse Theater at Lincoln Center (150 W. 65th St., NY, NY), but explosive ticket sales bumped it over to the Royale (now the Bernard B. Jacobs Theatre, 242 W. 45th St., NY, NY). Madonna's performances sold out. After her final performance, on August 28, 1988, sales dropped 60 percent. Audiences should have reconsidered—Madonna's then-unknown

"I KNOW WHAT IT IS TO BE BAD; I'VE BEEN BAD."-MADONNA AS "KAREN," *SPEED-THE-PLOW* (1988)

"I JUST WANNA BE GOOD—THAT'S ALL." -MADONNA AS "MADONNA," *SPEED-THE-PLOW* AFTER-PARTY (1988)

"HER INEPTITUDE IS SCANDALOUSLY THOROUGH. SHE MOVES AS IF OPERATED BY A REMOTE CONTROL UNIT SEVERAL CITIES AWAY." -DENNIS CUNNINGHAM, WCBS-TV (1988)

"IT'S A RELIEF TO REPORT THAT THIS ROCK STAR'S PERFORMANCE IS SAFELY REMOVED FROM HER HOLLYWOOD PERSONA. MADONNA SERVES MR. MAMET'S PLAY MUCH AS SHE DID … *DESPERATELY SEEKING SUSAN*, WITH INTELLIGENT, SCRUPULOUSLY DISCIPLINED COMIC ACTING."-FRANK RICH, *THE NEW YORK TIMES* (1988)

"NO, SHE CAN'T ACT." -*NEW YORK DAILY NEWS* HEADLINE (1988)

"MADONNA, NOT YET AN ACCOMPLISHED ACTRESS BUT A STEADY PERFORMER IN THE MAMET STYLE, CONVINCINGLY SHOWS THE STEELY CONVICTION BENEATH HER PROTESTATIONS OF BEING 'ONLY A TEMPORARY.'" -RICHARD CHRISTIANSEN, *CHICAGO SUN-TIMES* (1988)

"THOUGH SHE LOOKS TERRIFIC, SHE RECITES HER LINES PROSAICALLY AND WITHOUT MUCH CHARACTER. SHE ATTEMPTS TO STRETCH A TALENT SHE DOESN'T SEEM TO HAVE DEVELOPED."-DAVID PATRICK STEARNS, *USA TODAY* (1988)

replacement was future **Oscar** nominee Felicity Huffman, who decades later revealed she'd been excited to find one of Madonna's thongs had been left behind … until she realized it didn't fit her.

In spite of the hoopla surrounding the biggest star in the world appearing on such a small stage, only two unscripted incidents marred the run of the play. Once, a crazed **wannabe** leapt onstage to meet Madonna, only to be escorted off by Mantegna. The other incident was of Madonna's doing, though still beyond her **control.** While reading from *The Bridge*, she suddenly developed a case of the giggles.

Brooke Shields, who had seen the play in previews, said, "She really challenged herself, and I think she should be proud." Opening night was attended by the likes of Jennifer Beals, Candice Bergen & Louis Malle, **Sandra Bernhard**, **Christopher Ciccone**, Cathy Lee Crosby, Jennifer Grey,

Billy Joel & Christie Brinkley, **Debi Mazar**, John McEnroe & Tatum O'Neal, Jackie Onassis (whose son **JFK Jr.** had been trysting with Madonna) and **Christopher Walken**. At the after-party, Madonna jubilantly proclaimed her first night to have been "like really good **sex!**"

It has been said that **Katharine Hepburn** caught Madonna's performance during her run as well.

One non-star who saw the show and loved it was a Vietnam veteran who sent Madonna a medal praising her courage in tackling Broadway. Some critics **awarded** her medals, too, but most reviewed her so aggressively that she became an instant candidate for the Purple Heart.

Random side notes: Both Mamet and Silver were lifelong Democrats who cited **9/11** as a motivation for switching political allegiances to the GOP. **Lindsay Lohan** recreated the role of "Karen" in a production on **London's** West End in 2014.

The play's title is a variation on a vague quote from George Chapman's 1607 play *Bussy D'Ambois*: "Speed his plow." More germane to the play is the Chapman quote: "So our lives in acts exemplary, not only win ourselves good names, but doth to others give matter for virtuous deeds, by which we live."

SPICE GIRLS: The record-breaking pop phenomenon from the UK, a girl group with five members **nicknamed** by the teen press as "Scary," "Baby," "Ginger," "Sporty" and "Posh." A marketer's **dream**, they ruled the world for several years in the '90s, cheekily flaunting their grasp of their catchphrase "girl **power**."

Madonna took her toddler **Lourdes** to see the group at one of their **Madison Square Garden** concerts in **NYC** in 1998. She said at the time, "I believe in girl power. I like Posh Spice the best."

SPITTING IMAGE: *Airdates: February 26, 1984–February 18, 1996.* British puppet show, known for its take-no-prisoners humor and celebrity-bashing. In 1990, the show licensed trading cards, one of which was a garish likeness of Madonna that likened her to **pizza**: "Italian, hot 'n' spicy and … not deep."

"SPOTLIGHT": *Release date: April 25, 1988. Billboard Hot 100 peak: NA.* **Stephen Bray** produced this effervescent song written by Madonna, Bray and Curtis Hudson. Stylistically, the song shares a lot with **"Holiday,"** which also had Hudson on its writing team. It was recorded during the *True Blue* sessions but didn't get a release in the US until it was included on *You Can Dance*, remixed by **Jellybean Benitez**. "Spotlight" was released as a single from the album only in Japan, where it became a moderate hit and was used in Madonna's **Mitsubishi** ads.

STALLONE, SYLVESTER: *b. July 6, 1946.* Actor, writer and director known for his slurred delivery and preening appearance who permanently injected himself into the culture via the film series *Rocky* (1976–2015) and *First Blood* (1982–2008).

When Madonna lived in **Miami Beach**, "Sly" was her neighbor. She even attended his housewarming party, but was ticked off when he was about to sell his place to Orient-Express Hotels, which meant she'd be living next door to a *lot* of activity. Madonna reportedly sent **Ingrid Casares** to tell him of her concern, but he said, "If Madonna wants to fight me on this, she can try."

She tried, and Stallone was knocked out by the results: He was barred from selling to the hotel. Both Madonna and Stallone had sold and moved on by 2000.

Gambia gave her stamps, yet she adopted from Malawi?

STAMPS: In 1989, Grenada became the first country in the world to slap Madonna on a stamp, featuring her in a live pose from her **Who's That Girl World Tour.** The tiny Caribbean island of St. Vincent issued a set of nine $1 Madonna stamps in 1991, paintings of mostly early poses with one then-current **Blond Ambition World Tour** pose thrown in for good measure. Since then, other countries have also honored/exploited Madonna with a stamp, including a series from the **African** nation of Gambia in 1992.

STAR: Director: *Guy Ritchie. Release date: June 2001.* A short film presented by Anonymous Content as one of eight in a series of creative **commercials** for BMW called *The Hire.* The short was written by **Guy Ritchie** and Joe Sweet and directed by Ritchie. The film starred Madonna (uncredited) in the title role of a legendary pop star with the manners of a fishwife.

"The first thing you notice physically about this lady is her **eyes**. Bright, blue eyes … The next thing you notice is her hands. Strong, **powerful**, yet feminine hands. But the real heart-stopper this woman has in her galaxy of **talents** is her **voice**—her billion-dollar voice," Clive Owen, playing her driver, says in a voice-over.

Vocal prowess aside, she abuses everyone in her sight, including her meek manager (Michael Beattie) and especially Owen, getting much more than she bargained for in the process. The star eggs him on until he decides to get even by speeding so dangerously that she's tossed around the interior of the car like a rag doll, and gets deposited onto a red carpet having peed her pants.

The short was strikingly similar to the official music video for **"What It Feels Like for a Girl,"** shot by Ritchie a few months earlier. Also worth noting, Ritchie never photographed his wife flatteringly. Ever.

STAR ACADEMY: *Airdates: 2001–2008; 2012–2013.* French edition of the talent-search show *Operación Triunfo* on which Madonna appeared on November 11, 2005, performing **"Hung Up"** and **"Get Together"** in a shimmery, silvery dress.

STAR MOTEL: *Now the Manhattan West Hotel, 303 W. 30th St., NY, NY.* Madonna lived on the third floor of this dump for several months around 1981, before the **business** relocated across the street and renamed itself the Star Hotel, and eventually became the rather snazzy Riff Hotel (300 W. 30th St., NY, NY). Madonna only ever set foot in the Star Hotel/Riff in 1998, while filming **Madonna Rising.**

As part of Madonna's deal with Gotham Records, manager **Camille Barbone** set her up in what biographer **Andrew Morton** described as "a shabby, one-room apartment" at the motel for $65 a month

Madonna later remembered that she almost always ate at a nearby deli, usually salted peanuts and yogurt, or cheese **popcorn** and cranberry juice—and that was it for the entire day. She spent time with the "very nice" Spanish landlady, Charito Viera, and her "really cute" son, but the rest of her stay was less positive.

"I shared a bathroom with two fat Colombians and then, uh, this Irish, old Irish [man] who'd just been released from an insane asylum. He would just be wailing all night long. It was quite scary, I have to say. I used to have to come down and sort of shove bums out of the way to get out my door."

It was broken into almost immediately, making her feel unsafe and leading her to "cry and cry" during her time there. Hey, it was a step up from squatting in **The Music Building**.

"It was like a flophouse. I shared a bathroom in the hallway. These two guys used to sleep with the doors open. I think they were **drug** dealers. I realized that I put myself into some pretty harrowing, potentially dangerous situations. I'm not saying I didn't feel despair. But I never doubted that I was going to achieve my goals," she told *TV Guide* in 1998.

Madonna did what Judge Judy always recommends: She *moved!*

STATUE: In 1987, a bronze, thirteen-foot-tall likeness of Madonna in her *Who's That Girl World Tour* bustier was commissioned to stand in the hometown of her **grandparents, Pacentro,** Italy. The statue was designed by an artist named Walter Pugni, and included a suitcase in Madonna's grasp, meant to represent the 20,000 emigrants who had made their way from Pacentro to the United States. The statue was removed after parish priest Don Giuseppe Lepore denounced it as a sacrilege. That's all it takes sometimes.

The statue's whereabouts today are unknown.

"STAY": The final track on Madonna's *Like a Virgin* is this girl-group **reinvention** that makes great use of a sort of thunderclap percussive element. Madonna's vocal is outta **control** on it, in the good way. The woman ventures into scat on this!

The song was written by Madonna and **Stephen Bray** in 1981 (versions now called "Stay 81" and **"Don't You Know"**) but radically rewritten for *Like a Virgin*, for which it was produced by **Nile Rodgers**. The equally magical 1981 version appears on *Pre-Madonna*.

STEA, KEVIN: *b. October 17, 1969.* After appearing in the music video for **"Vogue,"** Stea became widely known as one of Madonna's *Blond Ambition World Tour* dancers. He shares a sweet kiss with his boss in the film *Truth or Dare*, filmed **back** at a time when Stea, now openly **gay,** described himself as "straightish."

Stea, **Oliver Crumes** and **Gabriel Trupin** sued over their appearance in the movie. Stea was the spokesman for the group, telling *Entertainment Tonight* they decided to sue because, they alleged, they had never signed up for all the behind-the-scenes footage to be used commercially in *Truth or Dare*. The suit was withdrawn and settled for an undisclosed amount in October 1994.

Stea has a strong presence in entertainment and on social media to this day. He admitted in a **YouTube** video decades later that **Carlton Wilborn** had been his least fave fellow **dancer** on *Blond Ambition* ... and yet is now one of his great friends. He appears in the doc *Strike a Pose*.

He has also related that his fondest **memory** of **working** with Madonna is the time he, Trupin and Madonna drove around Rome late at night touring the ruins and soaking in the ancient city's atmosphere ... accompanied by bodyguards with machine **guns**. Would he work with Madonna again? "Yes, absolutely ... I actually really miss her."

Stea has danced with/for numerous other household names: **Cher, Janet Jackson, Michael Jackson, Ricky Martin, Britney Spears** and countless others. He has modeled, had a part in the notorious **camp** classic *Showgirls* and is now a silver fox putting his **creativity** to good use in the one-man band project That Rogue Romeo.

STEARNS, JEFF: The good-natured "world's fastest grocery bag boy," from Shenandoah, Iowa, who in 1994 lost his big chance to perform on *Late Show with David Letterman* when Madonna commandeered his scheduled segment.

He didn't mind, because in the green room she pulled him into a corner to keep warm in the freezing studio. It was all a **flirtation**—it had to be, since his **pregnant** wife Connie was tapping her foot nearby—but Stearns *did* find Madonna to be exceptionally charming. "She was great backstage," he beamed. "She was terrific. Very nice."

STEFANI, GWEN: *b. October 3, 1969.* Stylish lead singer of No Doubt whose solo career has spawned hits like **"Rich Girl"** feat. Eve (2004), "Hollaback Girl" (2005) and "The Sweet Escape" feat. Akon (2006), a **fashion** empire and many comparisons to Madonna, chiefly because of their similar bottle-**blonde** looks.

In 2005, Madonna was asked if she felt Stefani had taken a few moves out of her playbook. "She ripped me off. We **work** with a lot of the same people, she married a Brit, she's got long **hair**, and she likes fashion," Madonna joked. "But I don't mind. I think she's very sweet and **talented**."

Rather than escalating things to the feud level, Stefani's take on the similarities was to say, "Show me one girl my age who was not influenced by her."

In fact, Stefani has professed nothing but respect for Madonna: "Watching how she's kept people interested after all this time, growing older in front of people and still being **sexy**—obviously I really admire her."

Stefani and her then husband, Gavin Rossdale, have socialized with Madonna several times. She attended Madonna's 2000 *Music* launch party and was photographed air-kissing her predecessor at an **Oscars** after-party in 2009.

STEFANO, JOEY: *January 1, 1968–November 26, 1994.* **Porn** star (born Nicholas Iacona Jr.) who for his **work** in the late '80s and early '90s is known as one of the industry's most famous bottoms of all time. He wasn't **gay** for pay, he was gay for play, and got paid.

Stefano appeared in *Sex*, Madonna's bend-me-over-the-coffee-table **book**, in the scenes shot in **NYC**'s the **Gaiety**. By default, he is also (barely) visible in the music video for **"Erotica,"** but contrary to what other sources say is not in **"Deeper and Deeper."**

STEIN, SEYMOUR: *b. April 18, 1942.* **Sire Records** cofounder and chairman responsible for signing Madonna, after she was paraded before him by **Michael Rosenblatt** while Stein was recuperating at Lenox Hill Hospital (100 E. 77th St., NY, NY). He was among the first with the vision that Madonna could become "the next **Marilyn Monroe**," or even, he mused cautiously, another **Barbra Streisand**. He approved her to receive a $5,000 advance (plus royalties and $1,000 for every approved song she wrote).

Stein had been responsible for signing Talking Heads and the Pretenders, two acts who had been hugely inspirational to a young Madonna.

Stein recalled that he could tell Madonna was determined to get signed when she entered his hotel room: "She couldn't have cared, at that point, if I was laying in a coffin, as long as my hand was out and I could, y'know, sign."

Madonna has confirmed the mythic-sounding encounter. "It's true; I did walk in there with, like, a big boom box and my demo tape and my big, like, rag tied on my head," she said in 1998.

He was formerly married to Linda S. Stein, a successful music manager and real estate broker, who **worked** with Madonna separately from her husband. Stein's ex-wife was murdered by a former personal assistant in a shocking case in 2007. Her killer was sentenced to 25 years to life.

Seymour Stein appeared in the **"Deeper and Deeper"** video as a music mogul. He was among the first people chosen by Atlantic Records founder Ahmet Ertegun to help establish the **Rock and Roll Hall of Fame**, of which both Madonna and Stein himself are now esteemed members.

STEINBERG, ED: Founder of RockAmerica, a music video subscription service for DJs that was the first-ever company to offer videos to clubs in the pre-**MTV** era, Steinberg was the director of Madonna's first official music video, the performance clip **"Everybody."** He told **Andrew Morton** in 2001 of **working** with Madonna that she's "very clear about what she wants, but at the same time she accepts the creative input of other people. That is one reason why she is so successful—she is not a total egotist."

Steinberg was familiar with Madonna when he was hired to direct "Everybody," having dealt with her as an attention-seeking extra in a 1982 **Konk** video. He has said he was the one who introduced Madonna to tragic artist **Jean-Michel Basquiat**, at a club called Lucky Strike (formerly 9th St. & Third Ave., 2nd Fl., NY, NY).

Steinberg tells *EM20* his association with Madonna might have been even greater, but when he proposed hiring her for a spring break gig in Daytona Beach, Florida, the **powers**-that-be "nixed it—$2,500 [was too] expensive for what they thought was a track act!!"

> "… [O]nce you get to know her, she's extremely sexual, very alluring, very strong, yet you want to be close to her, you want to touch her."
> —ED STEINBERG ON MADONNA (1993)

STEPMOTHER: SEE: **Ciccone, Joan Gustafson**.

STERN, HOWARD: *b. January 12, 1954.* The self-proclaimed "King of All Media," this pioneering **shock** jock dominated talk radio with his WXRK show, which ran from 1985 until 2005. Via a mega-bucks deal, he has been heard exclusively on Sirius XM ever since. Stern's earlier persona was resolutely offensively, abrasive, narcissistic and willing to do anything for a cheap laugh, including scatological humor, smallest penis contests and strippers. More recently, he has mellowed considerably.

Stern has had harsh words for Madonna many times over the years. On his May 11, 1991, episode of the **TV** series *The Howard Stern Show* (1990–1993), he donned **drag** to lampoon Madonna in her **"Justify My Love"** video, poking fun at her envelope-pushing by commanding two male **sex** slaves to kiss each other and burn their genitals (the latter of which was a sight gag—no junk was hurt during the filming of this production). He also sent his minions to harass her at her *Truth or Dare* premiere.

Madonna's only retaliation was to ignore Stern, though she did write in **John F. Kennedy**'s *George* magazine that if she were president, she'd have Stern deported.

Stern's daughter Emily, then 22, played Madonna in the Off-Broadway comedy *Kabbalah* in 2006, sporting a **cone bra** but also going **nude** for 10 minutes. Stern reportedly objected because producers used her status as his daughter to sell tickets.

As recently as late 2014, Stern was spending time on his show lecturing Madonna on not exposing her breasts.

It was a whole new Stern when Madonna agreed to sit with him on March 11, 2015. Stern hyped the appearance by raving about Madonna's longevity and social impact and artistry. He also praised her album *Rebel Heart*, which he compared to *Ray of Light* ("Ghosttown" is his favorite track).

During the course of their 84-minute live talk, Madonna—who for some reason wore diamond **grills**, causing a small lisp—sounded sexy (she was sick, her **voice** reminiscent of her raspier *Blond Ambition World Tour* moments in *Truth or Dare*) and spoke freely as Stern grilled her on her lovers (she talked about **Jean-Michel Basquiat, Tupac Shakur, Warren Beatty, Sean Penn** and **Guy Ritchie**), her early days in **NYC**, the loss of her **mother** (she revealed that her **stepmother** had been **pregnant** by another man after **working** for the **Ciccone** family and before marrying Madonna's **father**???), her kinship with **Michael Jackson**, her **Super Bowl** stage fright, her take on **drugs** and her **Brit Awards** accident.

The interview broke some new ground, in some cases by accident. Stern seemed cowed by Madonna for a large part of it, loosening up as the two felt each other out. At the end, Madonna said she'd waited so long to come on the show because she thought he didn't like her. She likes him now—the show was considered a huge pop-cultural powwow.

STEWART, MARLENE: *b. August 25, 1949.* **Talented** designer and stylist who **worked** with Madonna from 1985 to 1990, making her responsible for *The Virgin Tour*, the *Who's That Girl World Tour* and Madonna's looks for "Material Girl," "Open Your Heart" (those tassels!), "Like a Prayer," "Express Yourself" and "Vogue." She even designed Madonna's (first) **wedding** gown, which featured a black bowler cap as the "something old." The gown sold for over $80,000 at **auction** in 2014, with funds going to help **Sean Penn**'s **charity** work in **Haiti**. "We wanted a '50s feeling, something Grace Kelly might have worn," Stewart said of the dress at the time she created it.

Madonna wore many of Stewart's designs offstage, including the blue floral summer dress she preened in before the press on the opening night of *Speed-the-Plow*, a look she repeated in a shoot for her 1989 official calendar.

Stewart was on track to design the costumes for the *Blond Ambition World Tour* in 1990, but was bumped from the assignment by **Jean Paul Gaultier** with his expressionistic fantasy gear. Although Stewart's "Holiday" look was used in the show, Madonna's move from Stewart to Gaultier marked her move into the world of brand-name designers, evidenced by her preoccupation with high **fashion** and the seasonal shows in **Paris** and Milan.

Right after she stopped working with Madonna, Stewart became an in-demand costumer for movies.

> "I hate this costume, Marlene!"
> —MADONNA COMPLAINING TO MARLENE STEWART OF HER POP ART CHARM-BRACELET JACKET FROM THE *WHO'S THAT GIRL WORLD TOUR* (1987)

STEWART, MICHAEL: *Circa 1958–September 28, 1983.* Graffiti artist Madonna hung out with, especially in 1982 when he appeared briefly in her "Everybody" video. A black man, he was arrested by three white Transit Police officers in September 1983 at the 14th St. and First Ave. **NYC** subway station for scribbling on the subway. He allegedly resisted arrest and his legs were taped together. Thirty-two minutes after he was arrested, he was delivered by the officers to the hospital, suffering from injuries consistent with an all-over beating. He later died of his injuries. The officers were indicted but were not convicted due to lack of evidence.

***STICKY & SWEET TOUR* (ALBUM):** *Release date: March 26, 2010. Billboard 200 peak: #10.* Madonna's third live album contains tracks from her record-breaking, globe-trotting *Sticky & Sweet Tour*. The album extended Madonna's run of Top 10 albums, but overall has probably sold fewer than 150,000 units worldwide.

***STICKY & SWEET TOUR* (TOUR):** *Show dates: August 23, 2008–September 2, 2009.* Codirected by **Nathan Rissman** and Nick Wickham, Madonna's *Sticky & Sweet Tour* was her longest and most successful tour, yet also her least critically praised since the '80s.

With 3,500 different wardrobe elements by 36 designers (**Tom Ford**, Yves Saint Laurent, **Stella McCartney** and Miu Miu, under the direction of **Arianne Phillips**) for Madonna and her troupe, $1.9 million in Swarovski crystals, 100 pairs of kneepads, 30 wardrobe trunks, 69 **guitars** and 653 rehearsal hours, there was no denying its enormity. Its reliance on *Hard Candy* songs was not an enticement so much as was seeing Madonna in action.

The most serious accident of any Madonna tour occurred on July 16, 2009, when two **workers** (Charles Criscenzo and Charles Prow) died and eight more were injured after the stage they were erecting collapsed. The July 19 Marseille stop was cancelled. Madonna visited some of the injured as well as the dead men's families and spoke in their **memory** from the stage in Italy. Madonna said of the terrible tragedy, "I feel so devastated to be in any way associated with anyone suffering."

As with all of Madonna's concerts since her *Blond Ambition World Tour*, the show was separated into sections, this time *Pimp*, *Old School*, *Gypsy* and *Rave*.

Pimp and the show itself began with as much fanfare as everyone had come to expect from Madonna. This time, instead of a typically drawn-out opening, she emerged from behind a revolving panel. The element of pomp came from the massive throne supporting her toned booty as she sang along to herself on "Candy Shop."

Next up was "Beat Goes On," the second *Hard Candy* song in a row. It should have been the song of that summer. Instead, thanks to indifference from radio programmers, it was just another song she may or may not ever perform again. Madonna had a blast with it, the first of many that found her showering the audience on her left with an inordinate amount of attention, and the first to make use of projections featuring absent collaborators—the visual ghost of **Kanye West** rapping. Shimmying down the catwalk and **back**, she returned in a white limo, at her most beautiful in her barely-there, nearly-**Cher** outfit, elongated by leather boots and capped off with a festive top hat that would become this tour's most enduring **fashion** statement.

Following was yet another live rendition of the non-hit "Human Nature," performed simply by a guitar-strumming

STICKY & SWEET TOUR
SET LIST 2008

① "The Sweet Machine"
Video Intro
[snippets of "Manipu-
lated Living" by Michael
Andrews (2002), "4 Min-
utes," "Human Nature"
and "Give It 2 Me"]

② "Candy Shop"
(snippets of "4 Minutes"
and "Beat Goes On")

③ "Beat Goes On"
[snippets of "And the
Beat Goes On" by The
Whispers (1980)]

④ "Human Nature"
(snippets of "Gimme More"
by Britney Spears (2007)
and "What You Need" by
Main Source (1993)]

⑤ "Vogue"
(snippets of "4 Minutes"
and "Give It 2 Me")

⑥ "Die Another Day"
Remix Video Interlude
[snippets of *Mortal
Kombat: The Album* by The
Immortals (1994), "Do
You Wanna Get Funky" by
C+C Music Factory (1994),
"Planet Rock" by Africa
Bambaataa & the Soulsonic
Force (1982) and "Look-
ing for the Perfect Beat"
by Afrika Bambaataa & the
Soulsonic Force (1983)]

⑦ "Into the Groove"
[snippets of "Back in
the Day" by Christina
Aguilera (2006), "Toop
Toop" by Cassius (2006),
"Body Work" by Hot Streak
(1984), "Jump," "Apache"
by the Sugarhill Gang
(1981), "It's Like That"
by Run-D.M.C. (1983) and
"Double Dutch Bus" by
Frankie Smith (1981)]

⑧ "Heartbeat"

⑨ "Borderline"

⑩ "She's Not Me"

⑪ "Music"
[snippets of "Put Your
Hands Up 4 Detroit" by DJ
Fedde le Grand (2006),
"Last Night a D.J. Saved
My Life" by Indeep (1982)
and "Heartbeat"]

⑫ "Rain"
Remix, Video Interlude
[snippets of "Here Comes
the Rain Again" by
Eurythmics (1984) and
"4 Minutes"]

⑬ "Devil Wouldn't
Recognize You"

⑭ "Spanish Lesson"

⑮ "Miles Away"

⑯ "La Isla Bonita"
[snippets of "Lela Pala
Tute" by Gogol Bordello
(2006)]

⑰ "Doli Doli"
by Kolpakov Trio [snip-
pets of "Me Darava"
by Kolpakov Trio (2006)]

⑱ "You Must Love Me"

⑲ "Get Stupid"
Video Interlude
(snippets of "Beat Goes
On," "Give It 2 Me,"
"4 Minutes" and "Voices")

⑳ "4 Minutes"

㉑ "Like a Prayer"
[snippets of "Feels Like
Home" by Meck (2007)]

㉒ "Ray of Light"

㉓ "Hung Up"
[snippets of "A New
Level" by Pantera (1992)
and "4 Minutes"]

㉔ "Give It 2 Me"
[snippets of "Fired Up!"
Club 69 Mix by Funky
Green Dogs (1996) and
"Give It 2 Me" Jody Den
Broeder Remix]

STICKY & SWEET TOUR
SET LIST 2009

1-7 Same as 2008

⑧ "Holiday"
[snippets of "Celebra-
tion," "Everybody,"
"Jam" by Michael Jackson
(1991), "2000 Watts" by
Michael Jackson (2001),
"Billie Jean" by Michael
Jackson (1983),
"Another Part of Me" by
Michael Jackson (1988)
and "Wanna Be Startin'
Somethin'" by Michael
Jackson (1983)]

⑨ "Dress You Up"
[snippets of "My Sharona"
by the Knack (1979),
"God Save the Queen" by
The Sex Pistols (1977)
and "Mickey" by Toni
Basil (1982)]

10-21 Same as 2008

㉒ "Frozen"
[snippets of "I'm
Not Alone" by Calvin
Harris (2009) and
"Open Your Heart"]

㉓ "Ray of Light"

24 Same as 2008

Madonna, her **voice** a tuneless snarl. **Britney Spears** was on the screen mimicking a then-famous viral video of a man trapped in an elevator for days. What did this touch mean? Probably just that it was a famous singer referencing a famous video. In Madonna's best tours, there's a lot of rich, contrasting imagery, there are competing messages, mysterious symbols and different ways to interpret what she and her creative team had in mind. For *Sticky & Sweet*, the cerebral Madonna was absent. Nothing *meant* anything. It was just a fun show with dancing. "Human Nature" could have been a try-out for Madonna's eventual Vegas residency. (Don't sneer, you *know* you'll go.)

The section ended with an inventive update of **"Vogue"** that leaned heavily on **"4 Minutes."** The choreography was exciting and fresh and her **dancers** in hyper-erotic **nude**-illusion bodysuits ensured that the ladies in the audience who brought their boyfriends/husbands would be giving the stage their full attention for at *least* four minutes.

"Die Another Day" came next, a lengthy, **boxing**-themed video interlude in which Madonna debuted severe bangs like '40s Barbara Stanwyck at her most film-noir fuckable, or like a not-yet Joan of Arc.

"Into the Groove" kicked off *Old School*, allowing Madonna to have fun with the kind of abandon one has when one locks their door where no one else can see—not to mention she jump-roped with the precision of a 12-year-old. Her rich history with **Keith Haring** became a subway-themed backdrop.

"Heartbeat" was one of the best-integrated tunes, merging what was happening live with what was happening on the screens.

Thrilling **fans**, Madonna revived her Top 10 hit **"Borderline,"** albeit in a rocked-out version. If your choice is getting the song **reinvented** or not at all, take reinvented.

For **"She's Not Me,"** Madonna revived her, "But I'm Madonna! I'm Madonna!" routine, positioning four look-alikes representing **"Open Your Heart," "Like a Virgin," "Material Girl"** and **"Express Yourself"** on a satellite stage and confronting each with aggression and eventual dismemberment (for Madonna, removal of costume constitutes removal of limbs). Finally, once she'd debased them completely, she gave them a kiss. It ended with a frenzied freak-out reminiscent of **"Let It Will Be"** from her *Confessions Tour*.

Speaking of which, no rendition of **"Music"** could ever top the one she'd rolled out on her *Confessions Tour*, but almost any attempt would be better than the weak try offered on *Sticky & Sweet*. It wasn't incompetent, nor insubstantial, and there was an allusion to subways and graffiti that suggested the downtown scene from whence Madonna had sprung, but it wasn't enough to jazz up an amazing song that had nonetheless been presented far better.

The most off-brand video interlude Madonna's ever offered, **"Rain"** with a dash of "Here Comes the Rain Again" by Eurythmics (1984) provided a buffer before the next section. It was an absurd animation showing a featureless

MATTHEW RETTENMUND

figure reacting to an otherworldly garden setting, reminiscent of her **"Love Profusion"** music video but executed with the technological prowess of her **"Dear Jessie"** music video.

In a massive cage and cloaked like a monk, Madonna performed **"Devil Wouldn't Recognize You"** to usher in *Gypsy*, making her clearly visible for part of the song and not for another part of it, depending on its lighting.

Oddly, the much-maligned **"Spanish Lesson"** was one of the songs that had the most life in it. Madonna loves her Spanish dances and was overdue for a heavily Latin-themed segment. Instead, she eased into gypsy territory, which also suited her.

Her best use of the guitar, by then a staple of any Madonna concert, was **"Miles Away,"** a beautiful song she's always able to deliver plainly and simply. She dedicated it to the emotional cripples of the world.

"La Isla Bonita" mashed up with "Lela Pala Tute" was a riot, not least of all for Madonna, who had a ball on it. The following folk song "Doli Doli," which Madonna watched while downing shots (great audience interaction, by the way) was also fun, fun, fun, yet off the beaten path.

The vocal highlight of the show was on **"You Must Love Me."** When that song first came out, it felt like tacked-on

Oscar-bait (it won!) for *Evita*, but hearing it a dozen years later was more **nostalgic** and stirring for some fans than hearing an older tune.

One of her best video interludes, "Get Stupid," found a gorgeous Madonna preaching over a series of images of great and not-so-great leaders. It was a surprisingly effective political snapshot that resulted in boos for John McCain and cheers for **Barack Obama**.

Rave began Madonna's most recent big hit, "4 Minutes." As fun as the use of spinning panels was for her promo show at the **Roseland Ballroom**, the major difference there was the presence of **Justin Timberlake**. Seeing Madonna do the same thing—grinding against a video of Timberlake—reminded one of teenyboppers kissing posters on their walls. Thrust your crotch into the camera and you'll have my respect, but grind it on an absent idol and I think some dignity is lost.

The chilly house arrangement of **"Like a Prayer"** took it from quasi-spiritual into a full-on club record, the reinvention more than satisfying. Madonna's robust performance, the strobe lighting and a dramatic conclusion made it one of her most memorable renditions of the signature tune.

STICKY & SWEET TOUR PERFORMANCES

August 23, 2008: Cardiff, Wales, UK (Millennium Stadium)

August 26, 2008: Nice, France (Stade Charles-Ehrmann)

August 28, 2008: Berlin, Germany (Olympiastadion)

August 30, 2008: Zürich, Switzerland (Militärflugplatz Dübendorf)

September 2, 2008: Amsterdam, The Netherlands (Amsterdam Arena)

September 4, 2008: Düsseldorf, Germany (LTU Arena)

September 6, 2008: Rome, Italy (Stadio Olimpico)

September 9, 2008: Frankfurt, Germany (Commerzback-Arena)

September 11, 2008: London, England, UK (Wembley Stadium)

September 14, 2008: Lisbon, Portugal (Parque da Bela Vista)

September 16, 2008: Seville, Spain (Estadio Olímpico de Sevilla)

September 18, 2008: Valencia, Spain (Circuito Ricardo Tormo Cheste)

September 20-21, 2008: Saint-Denis, France (Stade de France)

September 23, 2008: Vienna, Austria (Danube Island)

September 25, 2008: Budva, Montenegro (Jaz Beach)

September 27, 2008: Athens, Greece (Olympic Stadium)

October 4, 2008: East Rutherford, New Jersey, US (Izod Center)

October 6-7, October 11-12, 2008: New York, New York US (Madison Square Garden)

October 15-16, 2008: Boston, Massachusetts, US (TD Banknorth Garden)

October 18-19, 2008: Toronto, Canada (Air Canada Centre)

October 22-23, 2008: Montreal, Canada (Bell Centre)

October 26-27, 2008: Chicago, Illinois, US (United Center)

October 30, 2008: Vancouver, Canada (BC Place Stadium)

November 1-2, 2008: Oakland, California, US (Oracle Arena)

November 4, 2008: San Diego, California, US (Petco Park)

November 6, 2008: Los Angeles, California, US (Dodger Stadium)

November 8-9, 2008: Las Vegas, Nevada, US (MGM Grand Garden Arena)

November 11-12, 2008: Denver, Colorado, US (Pepsi Center)

November 16, 2008: Houston, Texas, US (Minute Maid Park)

November 18, 2008: Detroit, Michigan, US (Ford Field)

November 20, 2008: Philadelphia, Pennsylvania, US (Wachovia Center)

November 22, 2008: Atlantic City, New Jersey, US (Boardwalk Hall)

November 24, 2008: Atlanta, Georgia, US (Philips Arena)

November 26, 2008: Miami Gardens, Florida, US (Dolphin Stadium)

November 29-30, 2008: Mexico City, Mexico, US (Foro Sol)

December 4-5, December 7-8, 2008: Buenos Aires, Argentina (River Plate Stadium)

December 10-11, 2008: Santiago, Chile (Estadio Nacional de Chile)

December 14-15, 2008: Rio de Janeiro, Brazil (Estádio do Maracanã)

December 18, December 20-21, 2008: São Paulo, Brazil (Estádio do Morumbi)

July 4-5, 2009: London, England, UK (The O₂ Arena)

July 7, 2009: Manchester, England, UK (Manchester Evening News Arena)

July 9, 2009: Paris, France (Palais Omnisports de Paris-Bercy)

July 11, 2009: Werchter, Belgium (Werchter Festival Park)

July 14, 2009: Milan, Italy (San Siro)

July 16, 2009: Udine, Italy (Stadio Friuli)

July 21, 2009: Barcelona, Spain (Estadi Olímpic Lluís Companys)

July 23, 2009: Madrid, Spain (Vincente Calderón Stadium)

July 25, 2009: Zaragoza, Spain (Recinto de la Feria de Zaragoza)

July 28, July 30, 2009: Oslo, Norway (Valle Hovin)

August 2, 2009: Saint Petersburg, Russia (Palace Square)

August 4, 2009: Tallinn, Estonia (Tallinn Song Festival Grounds)

August 6, 2009: Helsinki, Finland (Jätkäsaari)

August 8-9, 2009: Gothenburg, Sweden (Ullevi Stadium)

August 11, 2009: Copenhagen, Denmark (Parken Stadium)

August 13, 2009: Prague, Czech Republic (Chodov Natural Amphitheater)

August 15, 2009: Warsaw, Poland (Bemowo Airport)

August 18, 2009: Munich, Germany (Olympic Stadium)

August 22, 2009: Budapest, Hungary (Kincsem Park)

August 24, 2009: Belgrade, Serbia (Ušce Park)

August 26, 2009: Bucharest, Romania (Parc Izvor)

August 29, 2009: Sofia, Bulgaria (Vasil Levski National Stadium)

September 1-2, 2009: Tel Aviv, Israel (Hayarkon Park)

"Ray of Light" was given a standard presentation, paling in comparison to the spectacle of "Like a Prayer."

A metal version of **"Hung Up"** robbed that song of all that made it so delicious. Fortunately, even before that, Madonna announced she would take requests. She usually settled on "Express Yourself" or "Like A Virgin," but she went along with a variety of oldies, including "Open Your Heart."

The closing song was **"Give It 2 Me,"** a dance-floor stomper that American radio ignored. It became a similar finale to the *Confessions Tour* sign-off version of "Hung Up."

The whole flawed show wrapped with "Game Over" flashing on the screen, just like how on the **Re-Invention World Tour** the words "Re-Invent Yourself" flashed … just like how on the *Confessions Tour* … you get the picture.

Madonna at half-strength is still Madonna, making her twice as interesting and satisfying as her nearest rivals.

The tour became the highest grossing by any solo artist, grossing $408 million. (She has since been surpassed only by Roger Waters, leaving her as the female record holder.) The *Sticky & Sweet Tour* is one of the Top 5 highest-grossing tours of all time.

• •

"WELL, THERE'S ONE THING YOU CAN'T DOWNLOAD AND THAT'S A LIVE PERFORMANCE. AND I KNOW HOW TO PUT ON A SHOW, AND ENJOY PERFORMING, AND I'LL ALWAYS HAVE THAT."

—MADONNA, *VANITY FAIR* (2008)

• •

"*STICKY & SWEET* COULD BE DESCRIBED AS ART DECO MEETS KEITH HARING MEETS BOXING MEETS DRUID MEETS GOD KNOWS WHAT ELSE. MADONNA'S GIFT AS A STYLE VULTURE REMAINS UNSURPASSED, AND THE PASTICHE SOMEHOW MADE SENSE, EVEN WHEN DANCERS IN SILVER HELMETS SLID AROUND LIKE LIZARDS DURING 'RAY OF LIGHT.'"—JASON GAY, *ROLLING STONE* (2008)

• •

"TIME MEANS BEAT AND RHYTHM, AND IT MEANS THE POP HISTORY ENCAPSULATED IN THE HITS MADONNA HAS BEEN MAKING SINCE 1982. IT ALSO MEANS THE AGING THAT SHE DEFIES WITH WORKOUTS, IMAGE MAKEOVERS AND WHAT LOOKS LIKE PLASTIC SURGERY. AT 50, MADONNA CAN NO LONGER BE SEEN AS A CLUBLAND INGÉNUE, A HOLLYWOOD GLAMOUR QUEEN, AN ICONOCLAST REJECTING A ROMAN CATHOLIC UPBRINGING OR A KINKY PROVOCATEUR, AND SHE WON'T BE ANY KIND OF DOWAGER YET. TIME HAS BROUGHT OUT HER CORE: CAREERIST AMBITION AND A COMBATIVE TENACITY. HAS THERE EVER BEEN A COLDER POP SEX SYMBOL?"

—JON PARELES, *THE NEW YORK TIMES* (2008)

• •

STICKY & SWEET TOUR (VIDEO): *Release date: March 26, 2010.* The DVD and Blu-ray record of Madonna's *Sticky & Sweet Tour* contains not only her full show, but also includes the Argentina-only performances of **"Don't Cry for Me Argentina"** and **"Like a Virgin."** The Blu-ray hit #1 on the **Billboard** Top Music Videos chart.

STILLER, BEN: *b. November 30, 1965.* Comedy actor, director, producer and writer famous for his tightly-wound everyman characters, memorably in *There's Something About Mary* (1998), *Zoolander* (2001) and the *Night at the Museum* series (2006–).

In 1998, Stiller hosted the **MTV Video Music Awards**, at which Madonna performed. In advance of the show, Madonna did a short promo in which she bumps into Stiller at the **gym** and mentions having dinner reservations at Spago (formerly 8795 Sunset Blvd., LA, CA), leading him to believe she's asked him on a date. When he shows up, he sees Madonna already has an escort (**Guy Oseary**); she was really asking him to babysit for **Lola**. The clip closes with Stiller furtively sipping the extra breast milk Madonna left in the fridge.

STING: *b. October 2, 1951.* One of rock's most enduring singer-songwriters, first as the **sexily** brooding lead singer of New Wave band the Police and later as a multi-instrumentalist solo artist. With the Police, he began charting in 1978, and was a part of their enduring classics "Roxanne" (1979), "Message in a Bottle" (1979), "Don't Stand So Close to Me" (1980), the #1 smash "Every Breath You Take" (1983) and many more. As a solo act, he broke through with "If You Love Somebody Set Them Free" (1985) and made big impressions with the Cold War peace song "Russians" (1985), the jazzy "We'll Be Together" (1987) and his most recent US *Billboard* Hot 100 hit on which he is the main artist, "Desert Rose" with Cheb Mami (2000).

Madonna has been very friendly with Sting and his wife Trudie Styler for 20 years. Madonna seems to be friendlier with Styler; she's admitted to being intimidated by Sting, whom she acknowledges is a genius as a musician, describing times chatting with Styler while Sting was in another room playing instruments Madonna had never seen before.

She met future husband, **Guy Ritchie**, at Sting and Styler's home in 1998.

Madonna appeared at Sting's **Rock for the Rainforest** benefit in 1998, and gave Sting his *GQ* Man of the Year **award** at **Radio City Music Hall** on October 21, 1998. In her speech, she noted she'd once stayed at his house and had slept in every bed, joking, "Unfortunately, Sting wasn't in any of them."

In 2004, Madonna introduced Sting's performance at the **Grammys**: "You cannot imagine what an honor it is for me to introduce the next performer. There isn't a person here, including me, who's not fallen in **love** with his music. And while he's done a great many things for the world, he

"As for ambition, she makes Streisand look squishy." —LIZ SMITH ON MADONNA (1988)

will always have a special place in my heart for introducing me to my husband."

Forget about Ritchie! Sting's biggest contribution to Madonna was the fact that she became inspired to write "**Music**" after attending one of his concerts.

STONE, BILL: *b. circa 1913–?.* One of several photographers who shot Madonna **nude** in the late 1970s, Stone jokingly described himself as "108 with the mentality of a 12-year-old" **back** in 1985, when he was in his seventies.

Stone encountered Madonna in **NYC** in 1978, after she'd stripped for **Herman Kulkens** in **Michigan** but before she'd stripped for **Lee Friedlander** and **Martin H.M. Schreiber**. In June 1985, a young friend of Stone's saw his Madonna images and freaked out, insisting he get in touch with *Penthouse* publisher Bob Guccione Sr. He did so, and sold them to the **magazine** for considerably less than what *Playboy* had just paid Friedlander and Schreiber; Stone claimed he lost $4,000 to $5,000 on the deal because he had to make copper sulfate prints, but Guccione claimed he'd paid him more than the $50,000 that he'd previously paid Tom Chiapel for his scandalous "lesbian" nudes of Miss America Vanessa Williams.

A 1978 toned gelatin silver print of Madonna by Stone with notations in the margin was estimated at $2,000–$3,000 in a 2014 Sotheby's **auction**; its hammer price with a buyer's premium was $20,000.

STONE, SHARON: *b. March 10, 1958.* Stunning **blonde** actor in movies since 1980 whose big break was as Arnold Schwarzenegger's phony, nearly lethal wife in *Total Recall* (1990). By starring in 1992's box-office bonanza *Basic Instinct* as a murderous lesbian with many secrets but no panties, she became a star and **sex** symbol overnight.

Madonna and Stone were pitted against each other in the press in the 1990s, mainly because both were blonde and willing to open their legs on camera to prove a point. Their only legit moment of rivalry was over *Casino* (1995); Madonna campaigned for the part of "Ginger McKenna" (to add to her collection of ridiculously named women she's played in the movies, no doubt) and later admitted it was a disappointment when she was Scorsese's second choice. Stone was **Oscar**-nominated for the role.

Madonna's ***Body of Evidence*** was a thinly veiled stab at replicating *Basic Instinct*, a pretty bad and—as it turned out—singularly successful movie in the first place.

In 1995, Stone zinged Madonna in an *Esquire* interview when she was told Madonna wanted to kiss her. "Not in this lifetime," she replied. "Because I'm the only one she hasn't done it to."

During the making of *Evita*, Madonna said she had **dreamed** that Stone invited her to her house, dressed to the nines, and then **Courtney Love** had pounded on the door, saying she had a **gun**. Madonna opened the door, and Love said she was just kidding.

On May 21, 2008, Madonna and Stone posed happily together, Stone with her arm around Madonna, on the red carpet at the premiere of Steven Soderbergh's epic film *Che* (2008) at Cannes.

The following evening, Madonna (in coral **Stella McCartney**), Stone (in leopard-print Cavalli), **Harvey Weinstein**, Michelle Yeo, Michel Litvak, Carine Roitfeld, Caroline Gruosi-Scheufele and Kenneth Cole chaired the amfAR Cinema Against **AIDS** gala, joined by Mary J. Blige, Georgina Chapman, Diddy, Joshua Jackson, Milla Jovovich, Rose McGowan, Petra Nemcova, Natalie Portman, Cliff Richard, Joely Richardson, Victoria Silvstedt, Christian Slater, Kristen Scott Thomas, Donatella **Versace**, Dita von Teese and many more. At the event, held at Le Moulin de Mougins (1028 Ave. Notre Dame De Vie, Mougins, France), Madonna **auctioned** off a one-of-a-kind Chanel alligator bag personally designed by **Karl Lagerfeld** with 334 diamonds on it, into which she transferred personal items from her own purse (Shu Uemura blotting papers, a lip gloss and a magnifying mirror—no jewelry, **bitch**). A short clip of Madonna's *I Am Because We Are* was shown during the evening.

Madonna gave heartfelt thanks to Stone at the amfAR event: "… I know how hard it is, what you do, and I truly admire you and I don't say this about many, many people, but you're a hard act to follow. So thank you, Sharon." She also spoke about losing three people that she loved dearly within the space of one year to AIDS: "… I was freaked out and outraged … and I watched people that I loved shake people's hands and then see them wipe their hands on the side of their pants." She also recalled having to tell people in 1991 that she was not HIV positive, a situation she found "absurd."

It took a few years, but Madonna wound up getting that kiss from Stone when they greeted each other onstage. The serious nature of the event seemed to erase any past bad blood anyway.

"… Like Sharon and I were discussing earlier, before the evening began, you know you're doing the right thing if everyone is against you …"—MADONNA, CINEMA AGAINST AIDS GALA (2008)

STREISAND, BARBRA: *b. April 24, 1942.* One of the—if not *the*—iconic performers of the 20th century, this singer, actor and director is one of the few women to whom Madonna can realistically be compared in terms of record sales, artistry and international impact.

Streisand has charted with albums and singles in each of the past six decades. Among her most *buttah*-like hits are "People" (1964), "Stoney End" (1970) and the #1 hits "The Way We Were (1973),"Evergreen (**Love** Theme from *A Star Is Born*)" (1976), "You Don't Bring Me Flowers" with Neil Diamond (1978), "No More Tears (Enough Is Enough)" with Donna Summer (1979) and "Woman in Love" (1980). She got her start in theater, became a **TV** and recording star, made an impact in the movies from her very first appearance [she won the **Oscar** for *Funny Girl* (1968)] and went on to become a director of the films *Yentl* (1983), *The Prince of Tides* (1991) and *The Mirror Has Two Faces* (1996). She remains a sporadic but reliable concert draw.

There are many parallels between Madonna and Streisand, if one sets aside Streisand's once-in-a-lifetime **voice**: Each woman is self-made, has an unwavering personal artistic vision, is known for perfectionism bordering on obsession, wants things their way (end of discussion), is annoyingly exacting about being properly lit for interviews and insists on tackling creative challenges outside the boxes in which their audiences have placed them. Both are liberal firebrands and outspoken, often considered direct to the point of bitchiness and feel persecuted for being women in a man's world (Hollywood and ... beyond). They're both a li'l crazy, but a lot **talented**, and a chunk of their success is surely due to each of their own neuroses and how they've spun them into **art**.

Madonna's first encounter with Streisand was reportedly in 1983, when they had Chinese together with Streisand's lover man Jon Peters. Peters wanted to discuss Madonna's role in his film ***Vision Quest***, while Madonna wanted to discuss herself and to pick Streisand's brain. Streisand thought highly of Madonna's star potential, yet later said she'd been put off that Madonna ordered a "whole fish! When I go out with people, I don't order lobster or steak. I think maybe they can't afford it or something."

Madonna and Streisand thought enough of each other that the former visited the latter on the set of *Nuts*, a film Streisand produced and in which she starred, in early 1987. They posed for a photo together, which Streisand shared on **Facebook** in December 2014.

In a 1987 interview, Madonna refused to choose music over movies, saying she wanted to have her cake and eat it, too. "Gee, look at Barbra Streisand—she does both, consistently."

Ciccone and Streisand appeared on ***Saturday Night Live*** together in 1993, **back** when a surprise appearance (by both Streisand and Madonna) was genuinely a surprise. In 1996, Madonna said the most recent album she'd bought was the soundtrack to *Funny Girl*.

The following year, Streisand refused to sing at the **Oscars** while Madonna agreed, even though both had been snubbed by the Academy in different ways. Host Billy Crystal thumbed his nose at Streisand by underscoring Madonna's graciousness in showing up to perform. This may have been picking at a scab Crystal wasn't aware existed, as it was reported that Streisand had not thought Madonna worthy of starring in ***Evita*** (a movie for which Streisand herself, when younger, had been considered) and had attempted to persuade **Andrew Lloyd Webber** to go with someone else.

By 1998, when **Kurt Loder** asked Madonna to choose between Streisand or Celine Dion, Madonna went with ... Dion.

STUDIO COAST: *2-2-10 Shinkiba, Koto, Tokyo, Japan.* On December 7, 2005, Madonna played this Tokyo venue as part of her club tour to promote ***Confessions on a Dance Floor***. It was her first-ever club gig in Japan. The set list consisted of **"Hung Up," "Get Together," "I Love New York," "Let It Will Be"** and **"Everybody."**

STRIKE A POSE: *Directors: Ester Gould & Reijer Zwaan. Release date: 2016.* A documentary about a documentary? This film features interviews and flashback footage of all of the surviving **Blond Ambition World Tour** dancers—**Oliver Crumes, Salim "Slam" Gauwloos, Jose & Luis, Kevin Stea** and **Carlton Wilborn**. The project documents how the young men's lives changed when Madonna tapped them to **dance** on her tour, and when **Alek Keshishian's** behind-the-scenes tour footage of them became a huge part of ***Truth or Dare***.

Zwaan told *Loverboy* Magazine of the film, which debuted at the Berlin International Film Festival on Monday, February 15, 2015, "For some reason, I think [Madonna] still cares about these guys. Obviously, many people pass through her life, but I do think that that particular era of the *Blond Ambition Tour* and *Truth or Dare* must have been special for her, too. I can imagine she will be touched by the stories of the dancers whom she has known so well and who were there with her."

The film's debut was greeted with an extended standing O.

STUDIO 54: *Formerly 254 W. 54th St., NY, NY.* Anything-goes, anything-to-get-in **NYC** disco founded in 1977 by Steve Rubell and Ian Schrager, who were not long after tossed into prison for tax evasion. The wild goings-on included open drug use and sex in the corners. The guest list included glitterati like **Andy Warhol, Elizabeth Taylor,** Liza Minnelli, **Debbie Harry,** Bianca Jagger, **Grace Jones** and *everyone* else who was *anyone* else. It operated as Studio 54 under various regimes until 1986.

An occasional addition to the fabled club's sweaty **dance** floor, Madonna's most important association with Studio 54 was headlining **Fiorucci's** 15th anniversary there on May 19, 1983, a gig that led **Freddy DeMann** to sign her as a client. She also performed there on June 4 that same year, hyping her single **"Holiday."** Following her performance, the song was added to New York radio station Z100's playlist. It went on to become her first Top 40 hit.

SUCCESS FOR KIDS: Madonna's **Kabbalah**-driven **charity** founded in 2001. It's meant to provide children fun and inspiring ways to explore their faith, even if that kind of thing always winds up sounding like a pre-K version of a cult.

Madonna donated $671,000 to the org between 2001 and 2011, and during her ***Re-Invention World Tour***, when it was still known as Spirituality for Kids, flashed its website on a screen following her performance of **"Imagine."**

In 2011, reports circulated that the charity was being investigated by the **FBI** for financial malfeasance, but **Liz Rosenberg** swatted down those rumors.

—STEVE KMETKO

That same year, the Kabbalah Centre suspended the group's US operations in **schools** (separation of church and state, anyone?), but announced it would continue its **work** overseas.

SUNRISE: *Airdates: January 17, 1991-.* Journalist **Molly Meldrum** conducted an interview with Madonna when she was in Japan in November 2005 that appeared in two parts on this popular Australian morning show. Meldrum reminded her of their first chat over 20 years earlier and told her that when he was at the **MTV Video Music Awards** in 1984, he was seated with **Tina Turner**, who said of Madonna's legendary **"Like a Virgin"** performance, "What on earth is that woman doing?"

Meldrum asked Madonna directly about personal attacks she'd endured from **Elton John** and **Sharon Osbourne**, which Madonna graciously chalked up to people having a bad day. She discussed her **horse**-riding accident, recalled having to persuade ABBA to let her sample their song in **"Hung Up"** and discussed the difficulty of touring Australia, something she wouldn't do for another 10-plus years.

SUNSET BOULEVARD: *Director: Billy Wilder. Release date: August 10, 1950.* SEE: **Webber, Andrew Lloyd** and ***What Ever Happened to Baby Jane?***

SUPER BOWL: Joining a host of artists before her (**Janet Jackson**, **Michael Jackson** and **Diana Ross**, among many others), Madonna performed the Super Bowl XLVI halftime show on February 5, 2012. Who even remembers who was playing at Lucas Oil Stadium (500 S. Capitol Ave., Indianapolis, IN) that day? Okay, a lot of people do. But for Madonna **fans**, it was more about Madonna tackling one of the greatest challenges of her career than about football.

The timing of the show was fortuitous—it allowed Madonna to promote her current single **"Give Me All Your Luvin'"** and her *MDNA* album as well as her forthcoming *MDNA Tour*. She knew a lot was riding on it.

"First of all, it's the Super Bowl. The Super Bowl is kind of like the holiest of holy in America," Madonna said. "I'm going to come in halfway between the church experience and I'm going to have to deliver a sermon that's going to have to be very impactful ... I have to put on the greatest show on earth in the middle of the greatest show on earth."

Her set opened with her as a sort of ancient Egyptian queen, carried by a bevy of shirtless muscle men (local volunteers). To the strains of **"Vogue,"** Madonna rose from her perch on a gold-and-black throne to throw some human-hieroglyphic vogue moves before stepping onto her hastily-built stage to kick the thing into *thigh* gear. With in-stage screens shimmering from one image to another (including the faces of some of the song's name-checked icons), Madonna strutted with remote, regal supremacy.

The next, warmer, segment found Madonna letting go some with **"Music,"** but making a rare misstep, failing to step up onto a bleacher row fluidly. She recovered in time to engage in some nifty assisted cartwheels before a toga-wearing **dancer** (Sketchy Andy Lewis) did some mind-blowing slacklining.

LMFAO were on hand to interject their "Party Rock Anthem" (2011) and **"Sexy** and I Know It" (2011) into the proceedings, which allowed Madonna to appeal to teens, and also gave her a chance to dance her ass off—in way-too-high heels, it must be noted. She goofily made **muscles** and did pushups, brushing off any lingering stiffness from "Vogue" and showing the sense of humor she's so often accused of not having.

Stripped to a slightly less cumbersome outfit, Madonna led the stage in the cheerful, cheer-infused "Give Me All Your Luvin'" with help from **Nicki Minaj** and **M.I.A.** Breaking Madonna's promise to deliver a clean show, M.I.A spontaneously gave the camera the finger, for which she was later fined $16.6 million (a confidential settlement was reached; she apologized, including to Madonna, but rest assured that M.I.A. didn't pay that amount). The marching band accompanying the song was led by Cee-Lo Green, who joined in on a medley with brief elements of **"Open Your Heart"** and **"Express Yourself"** before they closed the show with **"Like a Prayer."**

Madonna's dramatic exit—sucked downward beneath the stage in a puff of smoke—was the moment when she could finally breathe a sigh of relief: The show had gone well. She has admitted that she went to her dressing room, lay down on the floor and cried in relief.

There's no crying in baseball, but no one ever said anything about football.

'WORLD PEACE" was spelled out via lights, a stirring ending for what had been a truly engaging and inspiring visual performance. (The entire thing, every note—yes, including "Like a Prayer"—had been lip-synched due to the complexity of the performance and the reality of it being a tightly choreographed, live number.)

These 12 minutes were among the most-watched of Madonna's entire career. Hers became the highest-rated halftime show in history (114 million viewers—more than watched the game!), clearly spurring interest in her upcoming tour. She received almost unanimous praise for her performance, which was done with input from Cirque du Soleil and her trusty collaborator **Jamie King**.

A slew of famous names rushed to social media to gush that Madonna had nailed it, including **Paula Abdul**, Kirstie Alley, Marc Anthony, Alec Baldwin, Kelly Bensimon, Giovanni Bianco, Drew Carey, **Andy Cohen**, Carson Daly, Snoop Dogg, Fred Durst, Eliza Dushku, Bethenny Frankel, Goldie Hawn, Nicky Hilton, **Paris** Hilton, Kris Jenner, Kim Kardashian, Kourtney Kardashian, Adam Lambert, **Cyndi Lauper**, Eva Longoria, Heidi Montag, **Michael Moore**, **Kelly Osbourne**, **Sharon Osbourne**, **Katy Perry**, **P!nk**, Denise Richards, **Kelly Ripa**, RuPaul (his "Shante U Stay" was a clever way to acknowledge and absolve her lip-synching), Ryan Seacrest, **Jessica Seinfeld**, Serena Williams, Patrick Wolf and Tracy Young.

"SUPER POP": Written and produced by Madonna and **Mirwais**, this **disco**-influenced display of hubris features Madonna encouraging listeners to aim sky-high in life. In communicating this message, she name-drops Muhammad Ali (by his previous name, Cassius Clay), Marlon Brando (her second song in which he appears, after **"Vogue"**), Martin Luther King Jr., **Frida Kahlo** and Isaac Newton, as well as choosing the Lemon Drop as the gold standard of drinks. The song was available as a bonus download to **fan** club members who bought *Confessions on a Dance Floor*.

SUPERCUTS: National hairstyling chain that in 1990 introduced a 'do inspired by Madonna's look in *Dick Tracy*, the "Breathless Bob."

"SUPERNATURAL": This Madonna/**Patrick Leonard** ghostly **love** song, reminiscent of Blondie's "(I'm Always Touched by Your) Presence, Dear" (1977), originally appeared as the B-side of the **"Cherish"** single in 1989. Almost three years later, its **Original** Arms House Mix was donated to *Red Hot + Dance*, a compilation whose proceeds benefited the **AIDS** org amfAR.

"SUPERSTAR": Singsong, underwritten track from *MDNA* written and produced by Madonna, Hardy "Indiigo" Muanza and Michael Malih. The song is one of at least three in which Madonna references Marlon Brando (along with **"Vogue"** and **"Super Pop,"** the latter of which feels like a not-so-distant cousin of this tune). Incidentally, Madonna used to coo over the "Brando body" of short-term boyfriend **Norris Burroughs**.

"SURVIVAL": Blissful opening track of *Bedtime Stories* that seemed to represent Madonna taking the musical high road in response to critics of her antics from 1992–1994. Written by Madonna and **Dallas Austin**, the song was produced by its writers plus **Nellee Hooper**. Along with **"Candy Shop,"** it's one of two songs to appear as the first track on one of Madonna's studio albums never have been released as singles.

SWEPT AWAY: *Director: Guy Ritchie. Release date: October 11, 2002.* **Guy Ritchie**'s remake of the 1974 Italian film of the same name—for which Linda Wertmüller became the first woman nominated for an **Oscar** for Best Directing—was an idea so bad that Madonna and her husband kept contradicting each other as to where it originated. "I was watching [the **original**] *Swept Away* on **TV** and the wife and I happened to be sitting on the bed together. I wasn't paying attention to it. It seemed a bit **camp** to me. But then about 40 minutes into it—I was cutting my toenails by then or something—I suddenly got it and I loved it," Ritchie told *Movieline* prior to the film's release. But Madonna wasn't having it, asserting that it was the actor Steven Weber who'd suggested it.

Like the original, the film is about a **rich** monstress, here named "Amber" (Madonna), who gets marooned on an island with a sailor, "Giuseppe" (Adriano Giannini), whose **sexual** subjugation of her puts her in her place and fulfills her as a human being. The film features Elizabeth Banks and Jeanne Tripplehorn as Amber's buddies and Bruce Greenwood as her Big Pharma–**working** exec hubby. Probably its most **fan**-appeasing scene is a bizarre sequence in which Madonna, in a yellow dress, attempts to give Rita Hayworth a run for her **money** in a wild **dance** sequence, all done while lip-synching Della Reese's cover of the Rosemary Clooney classic "Come On-a My House" (1951).

Madonna's **acting** in the film is wooden and she looks extremely gaunt; she shot the movie immediately after her grueling *Drowned World Tour*. It's odd that Ritchie didn't make sure she looked her best, but he certainly didn't. She chose the over-the-top role because, "For me to play the girl next door is a big leap for people."

Giannini is great eye **candy**, his casting another oddball aspect of the film because he is the son of acting legend Giancarlo Giannini, who played the sailor in the original film, yet Madonna has claimed that Ritchie didn't know who Giannini's dad was, just picking his face out of a pile of résumés. When they realized who he was, Ritchie still cast him because while he knew it was weird, he was convinced he was the best actor for the part.

Giannini told *Us* the year the film was released, "The sex scenes were difficult, and at first, I was like, 'Oh, my **God** I have to do this with Madonna!' But once we started shooting, she made me feel at ease. I hear that Guy was **nervous**, but we were laughing!"

So were audiences and critics.

Ice princess in *Swept Away*

"A film that never asked to be made ..." —MICHAEL ATKINSON, *THE VILLAGE VOICE* (2002)

"WHILE NOT THE UNMITIGATED DISASTER EARLY WORD PREDICTED, MADONNA'S LATEST FILM CONFIRMS THAT WHEN IT COMES TO HAVING A MOVIE CAREER, THE MATERIAL GIRL HAS YET TO FIND THE RIGHT MATERIAL. I'M BETTING SHE NEVER WILL. TO BE BLUNT, MADONNA SIMPLY ISN'T A MOVIE STAR …"-*PEOPLE* (2002)

"GUY RITCHIE DIRECTS HIS WIFE—THAT WOULD BE MADONNA—IN A MOVIE THAT CASTS HER AS A 24/7 ICE-COLD BITCH WHO WARMS UP ONLY AFTER A REAL MAN SLAPS, KICKS AND THEN SEXUALLY SUBJUGATES HER: KISS MY FEET. SUCK MY DICK. CALL ME MASTER … LET THE MARRIAGE COUNSELORS WEIGH IN."
—PETER TRAVERS, *ROLLING STONE* (2002)

Madonna believes *Swept Away* is good work (and there are *some* viewers who swear it's unfairly maligned). She chalks up the skin-flaying reviews it received to critics enjoying writing nasty things. Schadenfreude, analyze this! Her favorite scenes are the ones where she gets spaghetti poured on her head, where she performs the Della Reese number, where the castaways play charades and where she's being chased. She feels the remake wound up being "more redeeming" than the original.

Regardless, Madonna was never again a leading lady in a feature film. But she may just be readying herself for her close-up.

The film was modestly budgeted at $10 million, but made a total of $598,645 … worldwide.

SWIFT, TAYLOR: *b. December 13, 1989.* Massively popular hitmaker whose *Billboard* successes already rivaled Madonna's by the time she was the age Madonna was when she had her very first hit.

In 2015, Madonna told Australia's Richard Wilkins, "I like Taylor Swift. She writes so many catchy pop songs. Can't get them out of my head." Swift's tweeted reply? "Thanks now I'm dead" and "#HOW AM I SUPPOSED TO DEAL WITH THIS #BE COOL TAYLOR STOP BEING EMBARRASSING."

At the **Grammys** in 2015, Swift said on the red carpet she wouldn't say hi to Madonna because it mattered too much to her, expressing fear. But the two did say hi, and posed for a photo that Swift posted on social media. She tweeted "Madonna is now a person I've met. #TheGrammys"

The Madonna/Swift lovefest came to a head on March 29, 2015, when Madonna performed **"Ghosttown"** at the **iHeartRadio Music Awards** with Taylor Swift accompanying her on the **guitar**. The performance

"FOR THE FIRST TIME SINCE *DESPERATELY SEEKING SUSAN*, MADONNA DOESN'T SUCK AS AN ACTRESS. IN A MOVIE CAREER THAT IS BY NOW NEARLY AS BENIGHTED AS THAT OF LINDA BLAIR OR MARIA MONTEZ, SHE COMES THROUGH WITH A PERFORMANCE IN WHICH HER LINE READINGS DON'T CLATTER LIKE BROKEN PLATES, AND SHE LOOKS AT LEAST HALF AS RELAXED AS SHE DOES ON STAGE …"
—OWEN GLEIBERMAN, *ENTERTAINMENT WEEKLY* (2002)

"WATCHING [MADONNA] SHRIEK, POUT AND SNARL HER WAY THROUGH [GUY RITCHIE'S] ILL-ADVISED AND DISASTROUS REMAKE OF THE 1974 LINA WERTMÜLLER FILM *SWEPT AWAY* HAS PRETTY MUCH DRIVEN A SPIKE THROUGH THE COFFIN LID OF THE PUBLICITY-BESOTTED HUSBAND-AND-WIFE TEAM'S FUTURE PLANS TO BECOME THE NEXT ORSON WELLES AND RITA HAYWORTH."-REX REED, *NEW YORK OBSERVER* (2002)

"… IT'S ONE THING TO SAY YOU DON'T LIKE A MOVIE. OKAY, FINE—DON'T LIKE THE MOVIE. BUT THEY WEREN'T REALLY CRITICIZING THE MOVIE … IT WAS, LIKE, PERSONAL VENDETTAS."-MADONNA (2003)

was very well received (*Time* called it "the most memorable moment" of the show). Swift would later tweeted of her excitement "*ugly cries forever*"

At the end of the evening, Madonna also gave Swift her **award** for Song of the Year for "Shake It Off."

"SWIM": The second song on *Ray of Light*, written and produced by Madonna and **William Orbit**. A rhythmic, spiritually sophisticated, poetic **work**.

SWIMMING: By the mid-'80s, Madonna's preferred workout was swimming 100 laps every day.

SYLBERT, RICHARD: *April 16, 1928–March 23, 2002.* *Dick Tracy's* set designer, he also created an entire fantasy bedroom for Madonna, full of **Herb Ritts** and **Steven Meisel** portraits and primary colors. The masterpiece was one room at the Metropolitan Home Showhouse (115 E. 79th St., NY, NY) in a benefit for Design Industries Foundation Fighting **AIDS** (DIFFA) in 1991.

Sylbert had earlier done the production design for the **"Open Your Heart"** video.

GREGORY PACE

RICHARD SE

"TAKE A BOW" (SONG): *Release date: October 28, 1994. Billboard Hot 100 peak: #1.* Madonna and **Babyface** wrote, produced and performed this sentimental ballad with a show-biz theme and a Japanese flavor. A sort of marriage between "Sukiyaki" by Kyu Sakamoto (1961) and "Superstar" by the Carpenters (1971), it was the second single from ***Bedtime Stories***, becoming Madonna's longest-running #1 single when it clung to pole position for seven weeks thanks in part to Babyface's radio-friendliness at the time.

Madonna sang the song at the 1995 **American Music Awards** and lip-synced it with Babyface at the **Sanremo Music Festival** in 1995, wearing the same lavender dress she wore the night of the **Oscars**. She didn't perform the song again until it emerged as a ***Rebel Heart Tour*** bonus. The song was a welcome addition to her Melbourne ***Tears of a Clown*** gig.

"TAKE A BOW" (VIDEO): *Director: Michael Haussman, 1994.* One of Madonna's signature music videos, "Take a Bow" is a narrative piece that presents her as a lady of mystery conducting an affair with a famous Spanish bullfighter, played by real-life torero Emilio Muñoz. The viewer sees the couple dressing (separately) for his big fight, which was filmed in a bullring in Antequera, Spain. Their star-crossed affair is compared to his battle with the bull—and both end badly.

Madonna was in peak form as a glamorous girlfriend, whether rocking a veil, a **John Galliano** suit or luxuriating in her bra 'n' panties in bed, ogling her lover boy on **TV**.

The styling, by Lori Goldstein, made the video a virtual audition for ***Evita***.

The video was filmed in Ronda, Spain, a region Madonna recommended when she finished **working** there, but not the "very dangerous sport" of bullfighting. PETA was unhappy that the video contained actual scenes of bulls killed in action, though no bulls were harmed specifically for the sake of the video.

Director Michael Haussman recalled, "It was such a fiery topic that we had to have to have the police in my office in **London** opening our mail because a lot of animal rights groups send letter bombs to scientists and things. The producer had a rose taped to his door and it said, 'Hasta la vista, baby!' All kinds of really scary shit."

The making of the video was chronicled by **MTV** for *No Bull! The Making of 'Take a Bow,'* a special in which Madonna famously, jokingly whined about not hitting #1 thanks to Boyz II Men and "that damned *Bodyguard* soundtrack."

The video for **"You'll See"** was filmed as a sequel to "Take a Bow."

TALENT: One of Madonna's most misunderstood and misapplied quotes of all time is the one where she said, in ***Truth or Dare***, "I know I'm not the best singer and not the best **dancer**, but I'm not interested in that. I'm interested in pushing people's buttons, and being provocative and political." This quote is often interpreted to mean that Madonna thinks she's a bad singer and dancer and is only about **shock** value. Nope. She was simply being humble and acknowledging that she is no **Whitney Houston** vocally and that **Michael Jackson** could dance her off the stage ... that doesn't mean she wouldn't call herself a great singer and dancer, just not *the best.*

"What I was trying to say is that it's not a question of being the best at anything, it's a question of what is special about me and what is it that I have to say," she clarified on the French show ***7 sur 7*** in 1992 ... but nobody remembers that quote because people have a talent for hearing what they believe.

More indicative of how Madonna views her talent is this quote from 1983, one of the first things to she told **J. Randy Taraborrelli:** "People don't know how good I am yet."

One measure of her talent is Madonna's desire to write most of her own stuff. She said in a 1983 radio interview, "I write, I'd say, three-quarters of my own material ... Other people give me stuff—I don't have anything against that—but I think it's also good to nurture my own creative talents so I can develop, you know, my own singing style. I think you develop yourself better as a singer when you write your own material."

Another measure of her talent is her **voice**, which in spite of being looked down upon for its limited range, is one of the most distinctive in pop.

"I remember when I did ***Like a Virgin*** with Madonna, everyone around her and around me was ... saying that she didn't have a great voice," **Nile Rodgers** recalled in 2015. "I said, 'So you're saying that **art** is based on the quality of your voice and not other great nuances?' ... Madonna at that time may have been one of the greatest storytellers I had ever met."

Madonna isn't to everybody's liking, but anyone arguing that she isn't talented is a potential Flat Earth Society recruit.

TARABORRELLI, J. RANDY: Celebrity biographer most famous for his **Diana Ross** tome *Call Her Miss Ross* (1989) and ***Michael Jackson: The Magic and the Madness*** (1991). Taraborrelli appeared on **Robin Leach**'s *Madonna Exposed* **TV** special in 1993 to speak about his upcoming biography, then entitled *Shock Value.* Taraborrelli's Madonna bio was finally released in 2001 as *Madonna: An Intimate Biography.*

"I thought, in beginning the **book**, that Madonna was pretty much an open book to all of her, her **fans**, and I discovered that really she is an open chapter of an otherwise very closed book ... I'm fascinated by this lady," he said in 1993.

TAYLOR, ELIZABETH: *February 27, 1932–March 23, 2011.* The so-called "last movie star," a violet-**eyed** child actor who grew up in films, giving her audience a strong sense of ownership over her professional and personal choices. A two-time **Oscar** winner, she was married to seven men eight times and was one of the first and loudest celebs to speak up for people with **AIDS**. Her name synonymous with serious jewelry and the finer things in life, her final act was as a businesswoman, marketing her luxury brand via a personal fragrance line.

Taylor, along with **David Geffen** and Bob and **Harvey Weinstein**, were honorary cochairs of the May 8, 1991, **NYC** premiere of Madonna's *Truth or Dare*, to benefit amfAR, a group cofounded by Taylor. Taylor was unable to attend in person.

On December 10, 1991, Madonna was given the **Award** of Courage by amfAR, an event Taylor had to skip due to a bout of flu. She sent a note declaring Madonna "a heroine and a symbol of our times."

Madonna was one of many stars who appeared on the **TV** special *Happy* **Birthday** *Elizabeth: A Celebration of Life* on February 24, 1997. She wore her **hair** strawberry **blonde**, mid-length and with bangs, and a powder blue coat dress, emerging to give a speech about Taylor that the birthday girl listened to from the front row with her crony **Michael Jackson**. "When I was a little girl," Madonna read, "I wanted to be as beautiful as Elizabeth Taylor. I wanted to ride **horses** with my long, lustrous hair trailing behind me. I wanted to swing on a swing set with a velvet dress on. I wanted violet eyes and translucent skin. I wanted a 16-inch waistline, and I wanted Montgomery Clift, Paul Newman, James Dean and Rock Hudson to put their arms around it." She went on to wax **nostalgic** about the first time she saw Taylor in *A Place in the Sun* (1951) and to sing Taylor's praises for being a tireless AIDS advocate. Taylor was moved as she sprang from the audience to kiss and hug Madonna.

When the screen legend was recovering from surgery to remove a brain tumor soon after the taping, Madonna sent her a fruit basket along with the note: "There will never be another Elizabeth Taylor. You are my idol. Get well." This led to a light friendship, with Madonna visiting Taylor in Bel Air.

When Taylor died, Madonna's statement read: "I am so sorry to hear that this great legend has passed. I admired and respected her not only as an actress but for her amazing and inspiring **work** as an AIDS activist. She was one of a kind."

Tears of a Clown-ing around

TEARS OF A CLOWN: Performed at the Forum Melbourne (*Flinders St. & Russel St., Melbourne, Victoria, Australia*) on March 10, 2016, *Tears of a Clown* was announced as a one-off, comedy-fueled club gig that would serve as a gift to an audience of 1,500 during Madonna's **Rebel Heart Tour** swing through Australia.

It wound up being one of the best gigs Madonna has ever played, a fantasy for hardcore **fans** and perhaps a great insight into how she will eventually, inevitably segue from aerobic stadium-stomping to girl-with-guitar glory.

Arriving hours late (so, right on time!) Madonna took the stage dressed as a clown whose idol is Zandra Rhodes, nimbly zipping around on a tiny trike. Toppling over—without a cape in sight—the show finally began. It was immediately clear Madonna wasn't going the Amy Schumer route with her clown theme, but more the Jerry Lewis route. Lewis infamously shot and never released a clown Holocaust movie, and while Madonna's clown was far less serious, it was also a far cry from the impish icon who flitted about her *Girlie Show World Tour*. Think of it as *The Day the Clown Sang*.

The show opened with a cover, followed by **"Drowned World/Substitute for Love,"** one of her lesser chart hits, and yet it turned out to be one of only four singles performed out of 15 songs.

Madonna mined her maligned *American Life* record for a third of her set, offered her moving cover of **Elliott Smith**'s "Behind the Bars," surprised with a sensitive take on **Stephen Sondheim**'s 1973 tune "Send in the Clowns" from the musical *A Little Night Music* and still managed to sing favorites like **"Borderline"** and **"Take a Bow."**

Between the musical bars, our hostess talked about falling at the **Brit Awards**, her relationship with **Sean Penn**, her devotion to son **Rocco** (over whom she was embroiled in a fierce custody battle with **Guy Ritchie**) and even her **father**'s vineyard.

At the end of the show, Madonna had clearly exorcised some demons by performing the type of show she has probably always wanted to perform, and yet could never get herself to choose over the fun of bigger venues, more eyes and more catcalls. It was an artistic zenith for Madonna as a stage performer, and fans can only hope it was a sign of things to come.

Famous faces at the venue included **Kylie Minogue** and Dawn French of **French and Saunders**.

TELEVISION: SEE: **TV**.

"TELL THE TRUTH": Madonna remembers her first-ever song, written in 1978, as being this simple ditty, written under the tutelage of **Dan Gilroy**. In 1995, she told *ASCAP Playback*'s Jim Bessman, "I recorded it on tape and played it **back** and I was so proud, I called my **father** and made him listen to it on the phone. I probably sounded like shit, but he said, 'That's very nice!'" She also mentioned it in her **Rock and Roll Hall of Fame** speech. It remains officially **unreleased**.

RICHARD SE

RICHARD SE

The press must've been high to suggest that Madonna was drunk.

"ONE THING I'M GOING TO DO TONIGHT WHICH I'VE NEVER DONE BEFORE ONSTAGE IS DRINK."-MADONNA

"*TEARS OF A CLOWN* HAD A DELIGHTFUL, RAW, CASUAL AND CANDID AURA TO IT, UNLIKE THE REGIMENTED FEEL OF MOST OF HER WORLD TOURS … SOME RAG PAPERS HAVE BEEN SAYING SHE WAS A BOOZING MESS ONSTAGE. NO, SHE WASN'T. MADONNA NEVER DRINKS WHILE ON TOUR OR WHEN SHE'S PERFORMING. SHE ONLY (SHOCKER ALERT!) ACTS LIKE SHE'S DRINKING DURING THE SHOW."

-MARGUERITA TAN, *MUSINGS ON THE M49*

"GOOD THINGS COME TO THOSE WHO WAIT … FOR THE QUEEN OF SELF-CONTROL, IT WAS AN OPEN, AT TIMES EVEN VULNERABLE INSIGHT INTO HER PERSONA."

-DEBBIE CUTHBERTSON, *SYDNEY MORNING HERALD*

"I WANT TO MAKE A DISCLAIMER: IF ANYONE THINKS THEY CAME HERE TO SEE A FINISHED, FINAL SHOW, THERE'S THE DOOR."-MADONNA

"LIKE A THIRD GIN? MADONNA STUNS FANS IN BIZARRE, BOOZY MELTDOWN OVER SON."-*THE SUN*

"I'M NOT REALLY SURE WHAT I THOUGHT OF IT? IT WAS QUITE DEEP AND EMOTIONAL AND NOT THE MADONNA I'VE SEEN BEFORE!"

-CHYKA KEEBAUGH, *THE REAL HOUSEWIVES OF MELBOURNE*

"I PROBABLY COULD HAVE ENJOYED MYSELF A LITTLE BIT MORE ON THIS TOUR IF HE HADN'T DISAPPEARED SO SUDDENLY, AND ALSO IF I KNEW WHEN I WOULD SEE HIM AGAIN. I WANT TO DEDICATE ['INTERVENTION'] TO HIM, TO ROCCO."-MADONNA

"WOW"-DAWN FRENCH

TESTINO, MARIO: *b. October 30, 1954.* Madonna told Vince Aletti in 1998 that Testino is "the kind of guy who will photograph you, and if he doesn't like the way you're standing or something, he'll kick you." This prolific **fashion** shooter became one of Madonna's favorites after he shot her in *Evita*-wear for *Vanity Fair*'s November 1996 cover. She loved his **work**, hiring him to shoot her *Ray of Light* album cover, an assignment that resulted in an iconic image, but that almost resulted in far less; this is where that kicking came in.

Testino recalled to the UK newspaper the *Telegraph*: "At 2 p.m. she said, 'Okay, I'm tired. We're done.' And I said,

'But I don't have the pictures yet.' She said, 'You're working for me and I say we're done.' I said, 'No, we carry on.' The picture she used on the cover came after that. She didn't intimidate me, you see. I thought, 'I have to push my luck here,' so I started *kicking* her like *this*, with my foot.' … 'She was, like, 'Hey, what are you doing?' And I was, like, 'Move here, move here,' and suddenly this created an *intimacy*. When these people come across someone who treats them as an equal, it puts them at their ease."

Testino shot Madonna again for *Vanity Fair*, and also for **Versace**, the latter of which resulted in images she used as promo shots and the cover of *Something to Remember*.

Fearless

—ANGIE MARTINEZ

RICHARD SE

"THIEF OF HEARTS": Track on *Erotica* written by Madonna, **Shep Pettibone** and **Tony Shimkin**, and produced by Madonna and Pettibone. The song is a **bitchy** put-down to a woman who has stolen the singer's man. Speculation is that the song's "Susie ho-maker" was Robin Wright, with whom Madonna's ex-husband **Sean Penn** was involved.

"THINK OF ME": Plucky song from the *Madonna* album written by Madonna and produced by **Reggie Lucas**. It's a simple ditty about a bad boyfriend who made the unforgivable mistake of standing Madonna up.

"THIS USED TO BE MY PLAYGROUND" (SONG): *Release date: June 16, 1992. Billboard Hot 100 peak: #1.* Timeless, mournful ballad that served as the theme for *A League of Their Own*, though it did not appear on the soundtrack, but only on an Olympics collection called *Barcelona Gold* (1992) and, later, on *Something to Remember.*

Madonna herself tends to view her movie music as "assignment **work**" that she dashes off quickly and with minimal emotional investment, but the ballad—however marred by a few clichés on the shortness of life and the importance of living and learning—became a #1 hit for its honest delivery and aching sense of loneliness, **regret** and **nostalgia** for friendship lost.

"Chalk up another hit with no errors for Madonna," Edna Gundersen wrote in *USA Today.* "'This Used to Be My Playground' is a desperately sad ballad that oozes vulnerability and exhibits none of the singer's legendary toughness."

Written and produced by Madonna and **Shep Pettibone**, the song was the last completed from their *Erotica* sessions, but preceded that album's release by several months. The song was nominated for a **Golden Globe** for Best **Original** Song.

"THIS USED TO BE MY PLAYGROUND" (VIDEO): *Director: Alek Keshishian, 1992.* Most videos of movie themes are straight performance pieces featuring haphazard clips from the film in question. This one avoids that trap. It's a stylish rendering featuring a pair of hands slowly flipping pages in an old-fashioned photo album. The photos are moving images of Madonna in a black beret on a pew-like seat, roaming in hand-colored shots of grassy fields, lying in bed with a crisscrossing shadow on her face and writing on pages in a café.

Though simple, the imagery cleverly depicts the act of introspection. At the end, the man who has been looking **back** at his scrapbook of Madonna lays his head down, sealing the video with the perfect bit of sadness to resonate with Madonna's ennui.

Boy George has saucily referred to this clip as "This Used to Be My Video" because director **Alek Keshishian**'s treatment is nearly identical to the 1987 video by George for his song "To Be Reborn."

TIDAL: Streaming music service launched by Jay Z in 2015. Madonna appeared in **commercials** for the service, along with fellow musical luminaries Jason Aldean, Arcade Fire (via Skype), **Beyoncé**, Daft Punk, Calvin Harris, Alicia Keys (via Skype), Chris Martin, **Nicki Minaj**, **Rihanna**, Usher (via Skype), **Kanye West** and Jack White.

At the March 30, 2015, launch event for TIDAL at Skylight at Moynihan Station (360 W. 33rd St., NY, NY), Madonna appeared live with several others. At the event, it was revealed that in addition to most of the artists in the teaser video, TIDAL's stakeholders include J. Cole and **deadmau5**.

Madonna threw one of her legs up on a table while ceremonially signing on for the project at the event, a gesture that became an Internet meme. After an awkwardly missed handshake, she made a point of hugging deadmau5, who'd ripped her a new one in 2012 for joking about **drugs**.

"TILL DEATH DO US PART": One of the most personal songs Madonna has ever recorded, this track helped define *Like a Prayer* as a **work** of substance. Written and produced by Madonna and **Patrick Leonard**, it's a jaded song about a violent relationship that needs to come to an end, clearly a document of Madonna's "mad marriage" to **Sean Penn**.

TIMBALAND: *b. March 10, 1972.* Rapper and producer best known for bringing "SexyBack" (2006) with **Justin Timberlake**. Timbaland cowrote and coproduced several songs on *Hard Candy*: the international hit **"4 Minutes"** (on which he was also a featured artist), **"Dance 2night,"** **"Devil Wouldn't Recognize You," "Miles Away"** and **"Voices."** His **work** on the album was not as extensive as the work of **Pharrell Williams**, but Madonna has called him the project's "silent godfather."

Timbaland started the trend of collaborators on Madonna projects who talk up their involvement far in advance of the project's release. In April 2007, Timbaland teased *Hard Candy* by saying, "It's kinda like **'Holiday'** with an R&B groove." Which it kinda wasn't, but okay. He also said of his boss, "Madonna's a funky lady—she's up for everything."

TIMBERLAKE, JUSTIN: *b. January 31, 1981.* One-time *All-New Mickey Mouse Club* player (from 1993–1995) who became the heartthrob lead singer of the boy band *NSYNC, screwed **Britney Spears** (who still publicly claimed to be a virgin, but luckily that kind of double life didn't affect her mental well-being) and wound up one of the most successful cross-over artists of the era, singing blue-**eyed** soul and dazzling **fans** with his comic timing on *Saturday Night Live*.

Madonna and Timberlake first intersected when she performed with his ex on the **MTV Video Music Awards**. The camera caught some Timberlake side-eye early in the performance, then cut to his nonplused reaction after Madonna and Spears kissed, thus almost completely skipping Madonna kissing **Christina Aguilera**.

Timberlake and his longtime collaborator **Timbaland** teamed with Madonna on *Hard Candy.* Timberlake cowrote and coproduced **"4 Minutes," "Dance 2night," "Devil Wouldn't Recognize You," "Miles Away"** and **"Voices,"** and was a featured artist with Madonna on "4 Minutes" and "Dance 2night." He also sang with her on "Across the Sky," which remains **unreleased.**

Timberlake described himself as Timbaland and **Ciccone**'s creative go-between on the project. "I mean, we literally were in the corner, like, y'know, with her notebook and everything. It's a very intimate experience," he said in a dual interview with Madonna conducted by **MTV**'s **John Norris.**

Though some fans felt "4 Minutes" was an example of Madonna giving up too much creative **control** in search of relevance (unusually, she wasn't a coproducer on the track), it was her last massive radio hit. Timberlake appears in the song's music video and dynamically performed it with Madonna live at her **Roseland Ballroom** gig to promote *Hard Candy,* leading to media sniping that Madonna was too old to be dry-humping her 22-years-younger duet partner. He repeated the performance on November 6, 2008, in LA during her *Sticky & Sweet Tour.*

On her only *106 & Park* appearance, Madonna called Timberlake a "smooth operator." She thinks very highly of his songwriting skills and seems to like him as a person, too, asking him to be the artist who welcomed her into the **Rock and Roll Hall of Fame** and showing up at his request for an *SNL* spot in 2013.

In 2014, Timberlake made waves when he wished Madonna a happy **birthday** on **Twitter** with the message, "A HAPPIEST of Bdays to my **mother** chucking ninja ..."—the word "ninja" being a stealth way to say "nigga" without saying it. This, not long after Madonna's **#disnigga** controversy.

"TIME STOOD STILL": Compelling, emotionally rich ballad written and produced by Madonna and **William Orbit** that appears on the soundtrack of *The Next Best Thing* (it includes the phrase "the next best thing" in its lyrics.) One of Madonna's best non-singles.

"TO HAVE AND NOT TO HOLD": This *Ray of Light* track was written by Madonna and **Rick Nowels** and produced by Madonna, **William Orbit** and **Patrick Leonard**. It was one of the earliest songs from her **work** on the album to make the cut. It's one of three Madonna songs to use the cliché "like a moth to a flame," along with **"Turn Up the Radio"** and **"Addicted."**

TODAY: *Airdates: January 14, 1952–.* US **TV**'s longest-running morning program, an NBC staple. Madonna has appeared on the show many times, among them her 1987 interview with **Jane Pauley** in which **Bay City** took it on the chin.

On January 15, 1993, Bryant Gumbel quizzed Madonna about *Body of Evidence*, stumping her by asking why people find her so fascinating. She said she'd gone home to

Michigan for Christmas 1992, spending it on an air mattress. She refused to speculate what she might be doing in 15 years, but said retirement was out of the question.

In 1996, Gumbel rode her hard about lionizing Eva Perón in an interview about *Evita,* eliciting the **money** quote: "Well, I think you can do good things for people and have high ideals and be incredibly moral and still like to buy a lot of shoes."

In 2000, Madonna gave her first of several interviews to **Matt Lauer**, with whom she has a playful, **flirty** chemistry. She admitted she'd changed her *The Next Best Thing* character from a **swimming** instructor to a **yoga** instructor to avoid the chlorine. She would later also speak with him for *Dateline NBC.*

A two-part interview on the show in 2007 with Meredith Vieira was to plug *Arthur and the Invisibles.* It was Madonna's first time ever doing the show live, due to the earliness of the hour. "Why are they up so early?" Madonna asked of the **fans** waving to her outside the windows. Being sleepy was becoming—Madonna was teetering on giddiness and quite loose, defending **Rosie O'Donnell**, reminiscing about **"Burning Up"** and about her kiss with **Britney Spears**. She even (reluctantly) went outside to greet the crowd. As she left the studio, she cooed, "Hi, Matt Lauer ..." to her usual interrogator, then was ambushed by an excited fan, who turned out to be Cybill Shepherd.

On April 25, 2008, Madonna told Ann Curry, "Well, I had to look good next to somebody who's half my age," when asked about her suspiciously youthful appearance in her **"4 Minutes"** video with **Justin Timberlake.**

She chatted with Savannah Guthrie backstage at **The Sound of Change Live.**

In a prerecorded interview with her old *TRL* buddy Carson Daly, Madonna appeared on the March 9 and March 10, 2015, episodes of *Today.* Madonna confessed on the show that the **leak** of *Rebel Heart* led to the release of items she "had no intention of ever finishing. They're like scribbles on a pad ... It's unspeakably embarrassing." She said her children **loved** all the **Diplo** songs and that **Lola** had banned her from showing up to any **University of Michigan** games.

TONIGHT SHOW, THE: *Airdates: September 27, 1954–.* A **blonde** Madonna made her talk show debut on *The Tonight Show Starring Johnny Carson* on June 9, 1987, as part of her *Who's That Girl World Tour* and *Who's That Girl* movie blitz. She showed up in what she called a "kinda **sexy**" black bustier and loose pants, wore her **hair** short and immaculately coiffed and charmed the pants off of Carson and his viewers with her timidity, humble take on her **fame**, gentle defense of hubby **Sean Penn** and the admission that she **loves** to **flirt**. The funniest moment was Carson's deadpan expression when Madonna hypothesized that an irksome studio fly was probably attracted to the mousse in his hair.

"I don't normally fall in love with 10-year-olds."
—MADONNA ON *ARTHUR AND THE INVISIBLES, TODAY* (2007)

Madonna sketch and original *Tonight Show* (2015) designs, by Scooter LaForge

Carson seemed bewitched with the winking Tinker Bell before him. "I figured if I'm gonna present myself as a virgin to anyone it should be you," she quipped, referring to her status as a first-timer on talk-**TV**.

Madonna returned to the show—rechristened *The Tonight Show with Jay Leno*—for a surprise 1994 appearance, joking with Carson's successor and presenting herself as virginal once again in the aftermath of her unpopular *Late Show with David Letterman* appearance. She was in a conservative black suit and had her brunette hair highlighted blonde with exaggerated curls.

Referencing her disastrous Letterman contretemps, Madonna began by saying to Leno, "Can I just say that it's so nice to have a real gentleman in **New York** City?"

Madonna admitted her dad loves Celine Dion, said she wanted to play "the flying rug in *Beauty and the Beast*" on Broadway and cracked that she collects hair barrettes, two of which she **gifted** to Leno—an echo of her stunt of giving her panties to Letterman. She was played off by "Ain't She Sweet" (1927).

A threat to say "the F word, over and over ..." was hollow.

Madonna returned on November 26, 2003, to promote her career as a children's **book** author. She gamely handed Leno a framed illustration from her book and a baseball jersey, also chatting about her **father**'s vineyard. "He forced me to **work** behind the wine-tasting bar," she revealed, claiming to put her mouth under the faucet in his distillery.

On January 30, 2012, Madonna appeared as a director on *The Tonight Show*, plugging her film *W.E.* to Leno. For this appearance, Madonna had filmed a promo in which Leno is called out for having **"Lucky Star"** and **"Vogue"** as his ringtones.

For her first appearance on the show since **Jimmy Fallon** took over, Madonna appeared on April 9, 2015, sitting for a relaxed interview (she talked about kissing one of the **Beastie Boys** in '85, how great New York used to be and the fact that her children urge her not to be "basic"). A pre-taped acoustic performance of **"Holiday"** using classroom instruments became a hit online, and her elaborate, semi-live performance of **"Bitch I'm Madonna"** was arguably her greatest of the *Rebel Heart* era.

For the latter, Madonna and her troupe (decked out in Christopher Lee Sauvé and Scooter LaForge finery) began a lip-synched, pre-taped portion of the song from backstage, dancing out and onto the main stage. Madonna tore up the theater with youthful **dance** moves, rubbing a guy's face in her crotch (he was a plant) and gyrating on Fallon's desk. The number was shot twice when Madonna slightly stumbled on the first try.

On June 9, 2016, Madonna made an out-of-nowhere appearance on the show, singing a stripped-down version of

"Borderline" with the Roots. Rocking a chic menswear look, she lay down on the stage at the end, spooning with Fallon, who she urged to literally push her over the borderline (he didn't get it). The straightforward performance drew raves.

TONYS: *Dates presented: 1947–.* The Tony Awards are the ultimate honor of the American theater. Madonna made her debut as a Tony presenter on June 5, 1988, at the Minskoff Theatre (1515 Broadway, NY, NY) before an audience of 28 million viewers. She appeared in a Rachel London form-fitting black gown studded with enormous pink roses, her **hair** dark brown and pulled **back**.

When London heard Madonna would be appearing on the Tonys the following evening, she brazened her way past security where Madonna was appearing in *Speed-the-Plow*, confronting her in her dressing room with the frock in question. "This is the dress you should wear tomorrow," she said confidently, and so Madonna did, along with an $835 floral bolero jacket.

On the telecast, Madonna struggled with a short mic and a cue-card crisis, joking in-between her remarks, "I ... I know this is bad for my posture," and "I'm being punished for not coming to rehearsal today," a wisecrack that got a howl out of audience member Glenda Jackson.

> "I started this organization that rehabilitates rappers and basketball players, and there's just so much work to be done." —MADONNA, *THE TONIGHT SHOW* (1994)

Madonna was on hand to give a special **award** to the founders of South Coast Repertory (655 Town Center Dr., Costa Mesa, CA). She misspoke during her speech, saying that they had launched the company as "two men" before correcting herself to say "two young men." Sensing the audience was with her, she then devilishly added, "Now they're old men ..." to big laffs.

Madonna's *Speed-the-Plow* costars Joe Mantegna and Ron Silver performed a scene from the **play** on the show, and Silver walked away with a Best Performance by a Featured Actor in a Play Tony that evening (as presented to him by **Kathleen Turner** and Richard Chamberlain), thanking Madonna, "a very, very classy lady and a professional."

The host that year was Angela Lansbury, who posed for a picture with Madonna backstage.

TOP OF THE POPS: *Airdates: January 1, 1964–July 30, 2006.* Weekly British countdown show on the BBC. This was the place to be seen (and heard) if you were hoping to make a dent in the British charts.

The show typically used tracks, so Madonna never did a live vocal in her appearances, lip-synching every time.

Her debut on the show was on January 26, 1984, with **"Holiday"** (the song was #29 at the time), wearing a sheer skirt and gaudy tank, backed up by **Christopher Ciccone** and **Erika Belle**. The performance represents one of her most spirited of the song.

She returned on December 13, 1984 (performing in a **New York** studio), with **"Like a Virgin"** (#5 that week), brought to life in a pink wig and to-die-for **Keith Haring** leather jacket (which she stripped off). She did no other performances in the UK until her *Who's That Girl World Tour*.

Madonna's only **"You'll See"** (#11 at the time) track performance was November 2, 1995, on *Top of the Pops*. Looking stunning with honey-blonde **hair**, blue **eye** shadow and a black tee, she mimed the song simply.

She returned for the November 20, 1998, episode with **"The Power of Good-Bye,"** all in black and geishaed-out.

She didn't perform **"Beautiful Stranger"** (which was #2), but she did appear in a taped sequence to introduce the video in May 1999.

Madonna's most elaborate performance had to be of **"Don't Tell Me"** (too new to have charted yet) on November 25, 2000. In full leather-cowgirl regalia, she and her troupe even imported haystacks on which to sit and around which to **dance**.

Madonna killed it with **"Music"** (#22 for the year). Think: Confetti! The episode aired on Christmas Day 2000.

Her final appearance on the show was to faux-warble **"Hollywood,"** promoting the fact that *American Life* was then #2 on the charts. In a sequined half-jacket and black slacks, a raven-haired Madonna danced in parts as provocatively as she had almost 20 years earlier on the same program.

TRESSY: Madonna has cited this vintage '60s and '70s doll—a Barbie **wannabe** whose **hair** grew when you pushed a button in the small of her **back**—as the inspiration for her *Blond Ambition World Tour* ponytail.

TRIBUTE ARTISTS: In the last edition of this **book**, there was an entry devoted to "impersonators." Well, that word is like "maid," "waitress" and "stewardess"—tired, and retired. Now, we celebrate tribute artists, people who have, as amateurs or pros, become renowned for their uncanny takes on Madonna's greatest looks. Here are some essential examples ... some of whom almost do Madonna better than Madonna does Madonna. (Don't forget to check out the legend of **Queerdonna**, too.)

· ·

Chris America: *ChrisAmerica.com*. The other Miss America has been portraying Madonna professionally since March 1984. As a singing-telegram girl, she was offered a gig as the up-and-coming pop singer while in college. "I had not even *heard* of Madonna yet, but suddenly I was constantly being stopped on the street. People were reacting to me wherever I'd go," she tells *EM20*. She kicked it up a notch by posing, Madonna-and-child-style, for the satirical cover of *Esquire*'s December 1991 issue ... but it was no joke that most people who saw the issue thought she was the real Madonna. At the time, Madonna said that America was a "great representation." She's shared **TV** time with **Oprah Winfrey**, been photographed by **Francesco Scavullo**, performed for **Jean Paul Gaultier**, entertained at the White House and was for years a headliner at **NYC**'s annual **Madonnathon**. America has won multiple **awards** and appears in the documentaries *Just About Famous* (2015) and *MAD for Madonna* (2015). If you haven't had the pleasure of seeing her show yet, you'll be crazy for her—she sings live, making her a feast for the ears as well as the **eyes**. She's currently **working** on a touring show that will recreate iconic moments of Madonna's career.

· ·

Samantha-Donna Ciccone: *SamanthaDonnaCiccone @ Facebook*. The fabulous Samuel Telfair shares not only Madonna's visage but her altruism—all proceeds from his semi-pro Madonna career go to LGBT youth shelters or the Matthew Shepard Foundation (MatthewShepard .org). Known as "that guy in high **school** who was in **love** with Madonna," he combined his **art**-school background as a painter and costumer to create Samantha-Donna **Ciccone** in 2005. He takes his work seriously, saying, "If you perform as the Queen, you can't half-ass it, right?" Along with the **money** he raises for charities, Telfair says, "The true thrill of performing is the ability to remind people how incredible Madonna has been for decades, and to bring **back** and perform some of the more meaningful and challenging classics for the hardcore Madonna **fans** in the audience."

—ANDY SCHWARTZ

UPPER LEFT, CLOCKWISE:
Venus D Lite, Samantha-Donna Ciccone,
Lorelei Prince, Chris America,
Denise Bella Vlasis and Nadya Ginsburg.

Venus D Lite: *VenusDliteFans @ Facebook.* Adam Daniel Guerra used Madonna's music to help him through his teen years, but he never knew he would wind up recreating her signature looks until his boyfriend encouraged him to do it—at 17—for "Madonna Night" at the popular club TigerHeat (1735 Vine St., Hollywood, CA). Out of nowhere, Guerra found the courage to dress as Madonna and do **"Vogue"** for the screaming crowd ... and he hasn't looked back. Going by the name Venus D Lite, he's won SoCal's *Drag Idol* competition four times, appeared on TV with Ricki Lake, has had parts in movies and for years was a star attraction at The DreamGirls Revue (Rage, 8911 Santa Monica Blvd, W. Hollywood, CA). D Lite has received amazing exposure on TV, first as a contestant on *RuPaul's Drag Race* (2009–) in 2011, then on a 2015 episode of TLC's *My Strange Addiction* (2010–), on which he admitted spending $175,000 to look like his idol. Even though he said he would give up on Madonna, he made a comeback, performing in March 2015 on *The Doctors* (2008–). "No matter if you are straight, **gay**, a drag queen or whatever obstacles come your way, if you believe in yourself anything is possible and you can rule the world," Venus D Lite *and* Adam Daniel Guerra tell *EM20.*

Nadya Ginsburg: *NadyaGinsburg @ YouTube.* Nobody does Madonna's **voice** like Ginsburg, who has mastered the **Queen of Pop**'s quavery over-enunciation to the point that it's hard to hear the real Madonna speaking without thinking of this fake one. She isn't a tribute artist in the literal sense, but a comedian and actor who channels Madonna in order to make fun of the cult of personality and all of its worshipers. Therefore, though she is a self-professed fan of Madonna, she will do anything for a laugh; she whips her heroine back and forth, skewering Madonna in her ever-evolving one-woman stage and **You-Tube** show *Madonnalogues* and (voice only) on *Madonna Dearest* for **VH1.** In 2015, she made headlines when she accused Madonna of ripping off her material (jokes about dating younger men) on ***The Tonight Show.*** Ginsburg does other stars as well, including lethally funny send-ups of **Cher** and Winona Ryder.

Charlie Hides: *CharlieHidesTV.com.* Like Ginsburg, Hides isn't a tribute artist so much as an in-character assassin ... but it's all done with a poison-lashed wink. His videos contain, hands-down, the most elaborately conceived and executed Madonna knock-off looks, often thrown together on a schedule that should make him a candidate for Madonna's dresser. (She may already have a restraining order in place.) His spoofs of Madonna sometimes don't sit well with her fans, like the time he did a **parody** of **"Living for Love"** called "Wearing My Gloves," in which he referred to Madonna's "man hands," suggesting that the only way to fix them is amputation. He plays a wide variety of other stars, including **Justin Bieber**, Cher,

AMERICA BY MICHAEL CAIRNS. CICCONE BY VEGA VASHTIARY. GINSBURG BY GABRIEL GOLDBERG. MADIVA BY MATTHEW RETTENMUND. ALL OTHERS COURTESY OF THE ARTISTS.

UPPER LEFT, CLOCKWISE:
Gisele Rahimi, Viva Sex, Charlie Hides,
Marla, Melissa Totten and Madiva.

Miley Cyrus, Lana Del Rey, **Lady Gaga**, **Katy Perry**, Joan Rivers and an **original** character named Laquisha Jonz (in **blackface**, something even Madonna has not dared to do publicly yet).

Madiva: *ChrisSavastano @ Facebook*. Chris Savastano, as Madiva, has not only caught the eye of many longtime Madonna fans, she's caught the eye of Madonna herself. In 2003, Madonna told **John Norris** that Madiva was "amazing" and "resourceful," marveling at her ability to recreate all of her *Drowned World Tour* looks. Madiva was in the audience for *On Stage & on the Record*, where Madonna could only say, "Four stars for ingenuity!"

Marla: *ManuelDesgrugillers @ Facebook*. Belgian Manuel Desgrugillers got into the Madonna groove back in 1994, inspired by the *Bedtime Stories* period. He's done many of Madonna's greatest looks, but perhaps most brilliantly the **"Hung Up"** leotard and *The MDNA Tour* costume for "Vogue" by Jean Paul Gaultier. "For me, being Madonna is much more than a look-alike costume," he tells *EM20*. "It's all about the attitude." You can catch Marla at Chez Maman (Rue des Grands Carmes 7, Brussels, Belgium).

Lorelei Prince: *Lorelei-Prince-as-Madonna @ Facebook*. This stunner looks so much like Madonna she misses **Lola** now that she's at college! Not really, but she definitely has that early Madonna look. Unfortunately, Prince does *not* consider herself a tribute artist; she only (rarely) does the Madonna thing, and always as an actor. Her Madonna-related claim to **fame** is as the star of *Physical Attraction* (2015), a short written and directed by Guy Guido about a suburban kid and his girlfriend who venture into Manhattan in search of his obsession, an up-and-coming singer named (you know who).

Gisele Rahimi: *GiselleRahimi @ Facebook*. Rahimi fell into being Madonna after a career as a model and actor. Whenever she auditioned, she ran into a small problem: "No matter what I did, all anyone could see was Madonna's face, which led me to do look-alike work." Rahimi looks so much like Madonna she doesn't have to work too hard to get into character; in fact, she says she has to wear sunglasses so no one will approach her and ask for an **autograph** in spite of the 25-year age difference. Her daughter even looks like Lola ... now *that's* dedication.

Viva Sex: *VivaCullen @ Facebook*. Viva Sex a.k.a. Viva Cullen a.k.a. Julian Nieves was the very first male Madonna look-alike to attain national notoriety, doing her from 1983 onward. Viva livened up a 1991 episode of *The Joan Rivers Show* (1989–1993) with same-sex grinding (courtesy of dancing boy Wes) to lip-synched renditions of **"Justify My Love"** and "Vogue." She also brought her "Vogue" to *The Tonight Show* and *Into the Night with Rick Dees* (1990). On the latter, Viva was presented *as* Madonna,

fooling much of the audience until he doffed his top to reveal his flat chest. Dees did a gay-panic routine in response. Viva's specialty is doing the **Blond Ambition World Tour** ponytail look to perfection, but she's easily slipped into all of Madonna's greatest guises.

Melissa Totten: *MelissaTotten.com*. Totten started impersonating Madonna in 1990 on a dare from a professor. For the last three credits of her degree in advertising copywriting, her independent study challenge was to market herself as a Madonna tribute artist. "I was heavily teased in high school for my resemblance," she tells *EM20*. "I went to an audition for a small show that was rolling through Chicago, strictly as part of my school project. The audition happened to be held in the same building I lived in, so it was a matter of slapping on some lipstick and getting in the elevator. I took it as a glaring sign from the universe, put everything in storage and spent the next six months on a cruise ship." She's since performed in more than 30 countries in front of more than 1 million people. Among her favorite **memories** are fundraising for life-saving surgeries for children in Istanbul, performing for **Live Nation** VIP ticket-holders in **London** and offending the president of Thailand ("Oops") "I have tried through the years to stop performing, but interesting and challenging opportunities keep showing up, and that is what life is about. I've never met Madonna, but if I did, I would say: 'Thank you. For everything.'"

Denise Bella Vlasis: *TributeProductions.com*. The Madonna-lovin' world has been catching glimpses of Vlasis as their icon since 1985, and she's been doubling as Madonna—and getting double-takes as Madonna—steadily ever since. She hit the big-time with her appearance as "Shoshanna" in **Sandra Bernhard**'s movie *Without You I'm Nothing* (1990), and Vlasis appeared in (and styled, and choreographed) that "I'm Madonna!" **MTV** ad in 2000. She was hired to entertain **Christina Aguilera** in Hawaii, performed for Seal (who told her, "That was **fucking** Madonna!" afterward) and worked as Madonna's *Drowned World Tour* stand-in. She's also done a shoot with **Udo Kier** and was featured in the *A Day in the Life* book series. Yes, she *has* met Madonna, which means Madonna has, in fact, met her match!

TRL: *Airdates: September 14, 1998–November 16, 2008.* The **American Bandstand** of the 2000s, **MTV**'s weekday video countdown show—formally known as *Total Request Live*—hosted by Carson Daly and then Damien Fahey, providing music artists invaluable exposure for their video creations and their pop personae.

The show was more the stomping grounds of *NSYNC and **Britney Spears**, but Madonna showed up in person for the first time on March 1, 2000 (to plug *The Next Best Thing*), was interviewed by Daly and fielded **fan** questions as curated by Dave Holmes in Times Square. She phoned in to hype up her **"Music"** video premiere later that year.

In 2003, she received a hug and kiss from 50 Cent on the show, giving a shout-out to their home state of **Michigan**.

Madonna returned only one more time to the show, on October 17, 2005, chatting with Fahey about **Confessions on a Dance Floor**.

TRUDEAU, GARRY: *b. July 21, 1948.* Popular cartoonist behind the long-running *Doonesbury* (1970–) strip.

A satirical piece Trudeau authored for *Time* in 1996 entitled "I Am a Tip-Top Starlet" was written to **parody** what a Hungarian Madonna interview might sound like once (badly) translated. In it, the interviewer refers to *Sex* as her *Slut book*, and asks if Madonna is "a bold hussy-woman that feasts on men who are tops." The interview has made the rounds so widely that its status as a joke is often lost—famously, **French and Saunders** talked about it on the radio as if it were real, it was referred to as a real interview in at least one high-profile Madonna bio and it also fooled **Graham Norton**.

TRUE BLUE (ALBUM): *Release date: June 30, 1986. Billboard 200 peak: #1.* Madonna's third studio album proved she was able to relay her initial success into something broader, a demonstrable, global, lasting following.

Perhaps realizing that she should not relinquish too much authorship of her own success, Madonna this time cowrote (or in one case provided additional lyrics) as well as coproduced every one of the album's nine songs. She **worked** with two producers: **Stephen Bray** and **Patrick Leonard**.

In a joint interview conducted for **Warner Bros.** marketing purposes in 1986, Leonard and Bray were effusive about working with Madonna.

"Madonna approached each of us individually and told us that her plan for this album was to cowrite and coproduce one half of the record with each of us. Of course, that sounded great to us. We wrote songs and came up with new material as we went along. It was easy to do things this way because Madonna is really down-to-earth."

Leonard went on to say, "Making a record can be very difficult, but this one wasn't at all. It was fun and easy because Madonna is such a pleasant person to be around."

The three worked together well, but it wasn't all fun and games. Madonna's collaborators noted that they were on a mandatory "Madonna Diet," which consisted of not eating until the day's recording was done—as late as 9 p.m.

According to a Warner Bros. in-house publication, *True Blue* was previewed to the label's employees in Burbank on May 19, 1986, hosted by Lenny Waronker "with a radiant Madonna in attendance." Madonna told the assembled unwashed masses of executives that she considered it her "first record" because of how involved she was.

The hard work and Madonna's relentless focus paid off with the album that bore her largest number of massive pop hits on a single record.

In stark contrast to Madonna's increasingly all-encompassing **control** behind the scenes was the submissive sleeve, a colorized **Herb Ritts** portrait of Madonna's profile originally shot in **black-and-white**, her neck exposed. Along with *Like a Virgin*, it is one of her most famous album covers, and ranks as one of the most instantly recognizable sleeves of all time.

The first song on the album was its second single, **"Papa Don't Preach,"** a surprisingly political yet daringly relatable tune about a **pregnant** teen.

"Open Your Heart" follows, the second song in a row to contain Madonna singing with a newfound urgency and emotion. It's a beseeching **love** song. The listener can't help feeling Madonna is urging us just as surely as she's urging her imaginary lover.

With no let-up in sight, **"White Heat,"** a highly visual story of a rocky relationship, sizzles down the pike. As soon as it's heard, it's seen—it was no surprise that it featured prominently on her next tour.

Side one (if you remember vinyl) ends with an unbeatable wallop, the **powerfully** undulating ballad **"Live to Tell,"** which had been a #1 hit even before the album's release and which doubled as a movie theme. The song is a complete 180; Madonna sings mournfully, her true vocal range on full display, about secrets and lies. As much potent fun as the first four tracks just were, "Live to Tell" almost erases them.

Side two begins with one of Madonna's most beloved album tracks, the frothy, good-time anthem **"Where's the Party,"** which took Bray, Leonard *and* **Ciccone** to pound it into shape. Madonna's carefree laughter echoes in the song, and we're back on track for big fun.

It's strange to think about this now, but Madonna was often associated with a girl-group sound on her first two records. Her ultimate embrace of that style comes next, on the title track. **"True Blue"** is to the Crystals what *I'm Breathless: Music from and Inspired by the Film Dick Tracy* is to Tin Pan Alley.

"La Isla Bonita" seems like a slightly cheesy Latin-pop song, yet it fits the album's unrepentant lovey-dovey vibe and has gone on to become one of her most-performed tracks in concert.

True Blue is not usually ranked among Madonna's very best albums, perhaps because it ends less memorably than it begins, with the slight **"Jimmy Jimmy,"** a self-indulgent Shangri-Las homage that pales in comparison to "True Blue," and **"Love Makes the World Go Round",** a kid-gloves protest song so by-the-numbers earnest it even only *kinda* worked at **Live Aid**. Still, the album may well survive as her most fondly remembered for its vibrant, carefully crafted pop magic and its summer launch; summer has a way of burning music into your consciousness.

True Blue hit #1 in 28 countries (an achievement that **Guinness World Records** at the time called "totally unprecedented") as diverse as Austria, Brazil, Ireland, Israel, New Zealand and, of course, the good old U S of A. It produced five Top 5 hits, three of which went to #1 in her home

TRUE BLUE
① "Papa Don't Preach" (Brian Elliot/Madonna) –4:29, produced by Madonna/Stephen Bray

② "Open Your Heart" (Madonna/Gardner Cole/ Peter Rafelson)–4:13, produced by Madonna/ Patrick Leonard

③ "White Heat" (Madonna/Patrick Leonard) –4:40, produced by Madonna/Patrick Leonard

④ "Live to Tell" (Madonna/Patrick Leonard) –5:51, produced by Madonna/Patrick Leonard

⑤ "Where's the Party" (Madonna/Stephen Bray/ Patrick Leonard)–4:21, produced by Madonna/Patrick Leonard/Stephen Bray

⑥ "True Blue" (Madonna/Stephen Bray) –4:18, produced by Madonna/Stephen Bray

⑦ "La Isla Bonita" (Madonna/Patrick Leonard/ Bruce Gaitsch)–4:02, produced by Madonna/ Patrick Leonard

⑧ "Jimmy Jimmy" (Madonna/Stephen Bray) –3:55, produced by Madonna/Stephen Bray

⑨ "Love Makes the World Go Round" (Madonna/Patrick Leonard) –4:31, produced by Madonna/Patrick Leonard

2001 Remastered Re-Release Bonus Tracks

⑩ "True Blue" The Color Mix (Madonna/Stephen Bray) –6:40, produced by Madonna/Stephen Bray, remixed by Shep Pettibone

⑪ "La Isla Bonita" Extended Remix (Madonna/Patrick Leonard/ Bruce Gaitsch)–5:27, produced by Madonna/ Patrick Leonard, remixed by Chris Lord-Alge

Japanese ad for Madonna's biggest-selling studio album

"THE SONGS ARE SHREWDLY CRAFTED TEENAGE AND PRETEENAGE DITTIES THAT REVEAL MADONNA'S UNFAILING COMMERCIAL INSTINCTS. AND HER SINGING, WHICH HAS BEEN HARSHLY CRITICIZED AS A THIN IMITATION OF THE '60S GIRL-GROUP SOUND, HAS STRENGTHENED."
-STEPHEN HOLDEN, *THE NEW YORK TIMES* (1986)

"MADONNA'S STURDY, DEPENDABLE, LOVABLE NEW ALBUM REMAINS FAITHFUL TO HER PAST WHILE SHAMELESSLY RISING ABOVE IT. *TRUE BLUE* MAY GENERATE FEWER SALES AND LESS ATTENTION THAN *LIKE A VIRGIN*, BUT IT SETS HER UP AS AN ARTIST FOR THE LONG RUN. AND LIKE EVERY OTHER BRAINY MOVE FROM THIS BEST OF ALL POSSIBLE POP MADONNAS, IT SOUNDS AS IF IT COMES FROM THE HEART."
-DAVITT SIGERSON, *ROLLING STONE* (1986)

"*TRUE BLUE* IS MADONNA'S *RUBBER SOUL*, AS A CRITICAL MOMENT WHEN SHE DROPS THE VEIL OF SOMNAMBULISM AND REVEALS TRADE TRICKS AND SECRET FANTASIES."-*LA WEEKLY* (1989)

"*TRUE BLUE* INCLUDES SOME OF MADONNA'S GREATEST, MOST INFLUENTIAL HITS … BUT IT'S ALSO HOME TO SOME OF HER BIGGEST CLUNKERS."-SAL CINQUEMANI, *SLANT* (2003)

Alejandro Mogollo

Because you're an insane **fan**, it's important to know that novelist John Updike called the song "catchy" in *Esquire* in 1987.

Madonna performed "True Blue" live on her *Who's That Girl World Tour*, then not again until her *Rebel Heart Tour*. It was blessed with not one but two music videos—a fan-made version chosen after an **MTV** promotion that was aired in the US, and a studio video for the rest of the world.

"TRUE BLUE" (VIDEO, NON-US): *Director: James Foley, 1986.* A knock-out with her mink **eyebrows**, red lips, blue **eye** shadow and **flirty** party skirt over a black bustier and black Capri pant, Madonna shot this no-frills video with her buddy **James Foley.** Through various minimalist settings (a diner, a park, Madonna's own T-bird), Madonna and her girls (including **Erika Belle** and **Debi Mazar**) cutely frolic through modified '50s sock-hop moves. Much is made of a hanky **dance**, after which Madonna drops hers, a cute visual trick that leaves the viewer wanting to pick it up, either to chivalrously return it to her, or to stash the **artifact** in a safety-deposit box. Though this version of the video was obviously an afterthought for Madonna, it looks snazzy and is preferable to the American one, if only because Madonna is actually *in* it.

"TRUE BLUE" (VIDEO, US): *Directors: Angel Gracia and Cliff Guest, 1986.* **MTV** sponsored a "Make My Video" competition for Madonna's third release off *True Blue*. Madonna promoted it with a snappy, "Go ahead—make my video!" ad, delivered with extra sass. "C'mon … I dare ya! C'mon!" she continued in her best **Cyndi Lauper** voice.

MTV picked five finalists so viewers could select the overall winner. A daylong airing of some of the best—and *weirdest*—entries was capped off with the unveiling of the winner, a well-crafted, sepia-toned, poodle-skirted, Romeo-and-Juliet-they-never-felt-this-way-I-bet affair by Angel Gracia and Cliff Guest that went into heavy rotation.

Madonna showed up in person at the MTV studios (1515 Broadway, NY, NY) in October 1986 to hand the winners a $25,000 check, which turned out to be a great investment on their part—they'd shot their creation for under $1,000.

For non-US audiences, Madonna did a studio video with director **James Foley.**

Gracia continued directing, his main claim to **fame** being the Mexican comedy feature *From Prada to Nada* (2011). Guest became Geffen's in-house music video director, putting him on a collision course with **Cher.** He directed the low-budget slasher flick *The Disturbance* (1990).

country. Though *True Blue* sold fewer copies than *Like a Virgin* in the US, worldwide it is Madonna's #1 best-selling studio album, with over 25 million in sales.

The **love**-soaked album is dedicated to **Sean Penn**, "… my husband, the coolest guy in the universe."

"TRUE BLUE" (SONG): *Release date: September 29, 1986. Billboard Hot 100 peak: #3.* Sweet girl-group tune that features Madonna at her chirpiest and most **flirtatious**, beginning with a pert call-out (echoed in the later **"Express Yourself"**), to which she offers her own coy rejoinder along with a bossy command to "listen!" "True Blue"—written and produced by Madonna and **Stephen Bray**—is the song that best illustrates *True Blue*'s, and Madonna's own, dedication to **Sean Penn.** The singer's lyrical vow of chastity is utterly convincing, especially in light of the honesty of her admission to having had other **lovers**, an odd note in such an unabashed valentine.

TRUMP, DONALD: *b. June 14, 1946.* Smug, poorly coiffed wheeler-dealer with a penchant for women who don't dare assert anything beyond their **beauty**. Trump has kept himself in the media since the '80s via **divorces**, **business** deals, ignorant **Twitter** comments, celebrity feuds, management of the Miss Universe brand, his **TV** series *The Apprentice* (2004–) and a xenophobia-charged presidential run.

Madonna had comp tickets to the **Mike Tyson** title fight in 1988 at the invitation of "The Donald," but blew any favor she had with him by telling an interviewer, "He's a wimp. Oh, don't print that. I want tickets to the next Tyson fight." Reasserting his manhood (two years later), Trump said of *Sex*, "Not great. I don't think you'll be impressed. If Madonna were in this room, she'd be the least attractive woman here." Since he was in a crowd of old biddies at the time, flattery got him everywhere.

Madonna defended her pal **Rosie O'Donnell** when Trump branded O'Donnell a "pig" in 2007. Trump trashed Madonna in 2008 over her lack of a pre-nup in her failed marriage to **Guy Ritchie**, telling *Life & Style* **magazine**, "I always thought she was smart—until now." Unable to resist a good opportunity to use Madonna's name for attention, Trump tweeted in October 2012, "Many people walked out on Madonna's concert when she told them to vote for **Obama**. Years ago I walked out because the concert was terrible!"

Trump is fond of branding people losers, but regardless of what battles he wins in life, all the evidence points to the fact that he's nothing more than a **rich** loser himself.

TRUPIN, GABRIEL: *September 19, 1969–December 15, 1995.* "Vogue" video and *Blond Ambition World Tour* dancer who was one of Madonna's favorites. Trupin is shown kissing fellow dancer **Salim "Slam" Gauwloos** in *Truth or Dare*, a scene Trupin later claimed he'd been promised would never be shown.

"It's been a real struggle, it's been a lot of ups and downs, a lot of, um, even crank calls. From that to just … it's been kind of a nightmare," he said of the experience of allegedly being outed by the movie.

Kevin Stea answered a question on **YouTube** in 2011 about Trupin's **death**, saying that he'd been closest to Trupin on the tour. He remembered calling Trupin from Italy after a **job** he was on only to be told by his **mother**, "He's not here and he won't ever be here again." Trupin had died of **AIDS** two hours earlier.

Trupin's greatest concern about being shown as a **gay** man in *Truth or Dare* was what his **grandparents** would think. All four of his grandparents wound up surviving him.

Trupin was one of the *Blond Ambition* dancers to sue Madonna over his appearance in the film. It was settled the year before he died.

TRUTH OR DARE: *Director: Alek Keshishian. Release date: May 10, 1991.* Madonna's critical acclaim and popularity in the realm of film merged and—so far—peaked, with the release of this inventive, engaging combination of all the best elements of a tour movie with the voyeuristic thrill of a convenience-store surveillance tape.

Truth or Dare was the world's first reality show, and it's still the best.

Madonna's first concept for the film was as a documentary of what she knew would be her most extravagant and important tour, *Blond Ambition World Tour*. She'd lined up **David Fincher** to direct, but when he pulled out at the last minute, she indulged in one of those eccentric decisions that superstars sometimes make: She called a smalltime video director whose college thesis she'd liked and offered *him* the **job**. **Alek Keshishian**, a self-professed Madonna **fan**, flew to Japan to start shooting on a week's notice.

Over the course of the shoot, Keshishian realized from dailies that this was no mere *Rattle and Hum* (1988), but a unique peek inside the truly private moments of a truly public woman's existence. Keshishian had footage of Madonna without makeup, behaving like a spoiled brat, flashing her breasts, calling her brother crazy, calling her lover **Warren Beatty** a "**pussy**" man before a roomful of people, fellating a water bottle … the **works**.

He also had the quiet moments: Madonna chatting tiredly with her best girlfriend **Sandra Bernhard**, worrying over Beatty's lack of attention to her, succumbing to a throat ailment, mothering her **gay** dancers.

When Madonna got a load of Keshishian's work and realized how deliciously iconoclastic it was, she bit, giving him carte blanche to continue, despite the fact that the icon in question was herself. Or maybe *because* of it. At one point in the film, Madonna remarks that her screaming fans want her no matter what.

Perhaps *Truth or Dare* was meant to test that desire.

Truth or Dare, in its stylish frankness, was nearly unprecedented. Forget about comparisons to Dylan concert movies—that's not what this film's about anyway. This film is about Madonna, about the life of the world's most famous and controversial woman. It's not about the road, or about music. It's about **fame** and its corrupting influence on public perception. Its existence proves why Madonna is a bigger, or at least greater, star than any of her peers.

Parts of the film left some viewers cold: Madonna visiting her **mother**'s grave in **Michigan** for the first time since she was a child is a stagey-seeming scene that Keshishian maintains was completely unrehearsed. Its inclusion enraged **Christopher Ciccone**, who wrote in his tell-all memoir, "I am horrified at the lengths my sister is prepared to go to promote herself

Truth or Dare home video teaser

and her career. I fear she no longer has any boundaries, any limits. To Madonna, nothing is sacred anymore." She also famously disses **Kevin Costner**, who stops backstage after a show to proclaim it "neat." Madonna's reaction, and the only sane response, is to stick her fingers down her throat to mimic vomiting. (She apologized for this decades later.)

Her crass rejection of Costner is a juicy metaphor for Madonna's self-fueled outcast status as an actor, a status she reiterates toward the end of the film, when she and her **dancers** sneer to the camera that they don't want to be accepted by Hollywood.

Does the film stop at nothing? Well, even Madonna has limits. She refused Keshishian access to any **business** meetings, and also refused to allow her frail **grandmother** to be photographed. "You just can't!" she decreed, afraid the cameras would startle her.

Shot alternately in grainy **black-and-white** (for the behind-the-scenes moments) and super-vivid color (the concert sequences), the film ingeniously juxtaposes the flawless choreography and nonstop fun of the performance part of Madonna's life with her less-than-perfect reality: In real life on the tour, Madonna's makeup person was sexually **assaulted**, a random event that left most of the players indifferent or confused; the gay dancers and the lone straight dancer clashed angrily behind the scenes; and **sex** siren Madonna couldn't win the affections of Spain's handsomest leading man (**Antonio Banderas**) simply because he was married at the time.

Through all this fascinating chaos, the tour remains perfect and immutable, so uniform that the performance sequences are sneakily interchanged throughout. When Madonna is threatened with arrest for indecency in Toronto, and manager **Freddy DeMann** bets a cop that she'll go out of her way to make her performance of **"Like a Virgin"** all the raunchier, the audience can't help but feel that the ensuing performance *does* seem really out-there. But she sports the curly **hair** she only reverted to later, when the tour swept through Europe, a tell that the footage wasn't from Toronto at all.

Madonna's most emotional outbursts occur due to technical snafus that threaten to mar the concert's perfection. When testing a sound system early in the film, her demeanor is take-no-prisoners. The most **shocking** moment in the film is the clip of **"Keep It Together"** with chunks of Madonna's vocals lost to electrical malfunctioning.

Much was made of the gay content of the film. Madonna herself expressed pride in riling America with her depiction of sexuality, a good example of how Madonna doesn't often shock only for the sake of shocking, but does so in order to scare out some prejudices that she feels shouldn't be allowed to comfortably exist.

Her attempt is praiseworthy, but the gay men in the film are allotted so little screen time that they're almost indiscernible from each other. We never get to see the kind of personal awakening that we see happening with homophobic **Oliver Crumes**—in a scene where he visits with his **father** after years of estrangement.

The much-ballyhooed gay kiss—Madonna's favorite scene—is supposed to be liberating, but the way it emerges, as a *dare*, colors it as a freakish act. In execution, the kiss is too scary for homophobes to warm up to, and too straight-directed to be a truly proud moment for gay audiences. It's more grenade than parade, and received "ugh"-ly reactions in movie theaters across the US. Still, not every aspect of fighting for gay rights can be diplomatic, and it stands as a defiant representation of male desire. (The kiss may have been directed, but passionless it was *not*.)

"I **love** that people will go home and talk of it. I live for things like that," she said.

Much more effective are the later scenes of Madonna in bed with her dancers (hence the film's non-US title, *In Bed With Madonna*), in which her charm and her empathy with them goes a long way toward humanizing a star as well her gay troupe.

Truth or Dare is a masterfully executed piece of film that lives up to its name as half truth, half dare. The fun is in trying to figure out the "or" ... which is which? It's hilarious, can't-take-your-**eyes**-off-it reportage that preserves Madonna for all time, warts and all, and it is without question among the most important things Madonna has ever done in her career.

The film was distributed by Miramax, marking Madonna's first collaboration with the Brothers **Weinstein**. It was controversial from the start. The word "**masturbation**" earned its trailer an R rating.

Miramax hosted a screening of *Truth or Dare* at the Tribeca Film Center (375 Greenwich St., NY, NY) for an audience composed of 150 self-proclaimed Madonna-**haters** in order to gauge the film's appeal to a broad audience. They knew they had a hit when 65% admitted they liked the movie, and liked Madonna more after seeing it.

Critics were won over by Madonna's candor, giving the pic near-universal raves, though retrospective analyses have grown more pointed, arguing that the film's reality is itself constructed for the camera. Madonna has the last word: "Even a lie is telling."

MATTHEW RETTENMUND

Madonna launched the film triumphantly at **Cannes**, and appeared at two different premieres in the US. The May 6, 1991, LA premiere was in benefit of **AIDS** Project Los Angeles and AIDS Action Foundation. It was held at the Cinerama Dome (6360 Sunset Blvd., Hollywood, CA) with an after-party at Arena (6655 Santa Monica Blvd., Hollywood, CA). Madonna wore her hair brunette, long and straight, with almost Goth eyeliner. The Arena party was so overheated that guest Marlee Matlin's signer read Madonna's lips for the press: "It's so **fucking** hot!"

Besides Matlin, other guests included **Rosanna Arquette**, **Sandra Bernhard**, Valerie Bertinelli ("I would kill to have just one of her **balls**, and then I'd be happy!") & Eddie Van Halen, Lara Flynn Boyle, Christopher **Ciccone**, **Melanie Ciccone**, **Paula Ciccone**, **David Geffen**, **Gerardo**, Kid 'n' Play, **k.d. lang**, **Barry Manilow**, Matthew Modine (*Vision Quest*), **Herb Ritts**, Steven Seagal, Alan Thicke, **Vanilla Ice** and Wendy & Lisa.

• •

"IT'S KIND OF LIKE FELLINI MEETS *THE BOYS IN THE BAND*. IT'S ALSO A POLITICAL FILM. IT BRINGS OUT ALL THE FAMILY SECRETS THAT EVERYBODY WANTS TO KEEP IN THE CLOSET."–MADONNA ON *TRUTH OR DARE* (1991)

• •

"IT'S LIKE BEING IN PSYCHOANALYSIS AND LETTING THE WHOLE WORLD WATCH."

–ALEK KESHISHIAN ON *TRUTH OR DARE* (1991)

• •

"UNLIKE MOST ROCK DOCUMENTARIES, THE REAL HEART OF THIS FILM IS BACKSTAGE, AND THE ONSTAGE MUSICAL SEGMENTS, WHILE EFFECTIVELY PRODUCED, SEEM OBLIGATORY—THEY'RE NOT THE REASON SHE WANTED TO MAKE THIS FILM."

–ROGER EBERT, *CHICAGO SUN-TIMES* (1991)

• •

"AS SHE DISEMBOWELS HERSELF IN DESPERATE AND SPECTACULAR SPLATTER, WE CANNOT EVEN MUSTER, MUCH LESS JUSTIFY, OUR LOVE TO PUT AN END TO THIS SUICIDAL PSYCHOSIS."–FENTON BAILEY, *PAPER* (1991)

• •

"FOR THE FIRST TIME ON FILM, THE BITCH GODDESS DESCENDS FROM HER PEDESTAL TO LAUGH AT HER NARCISSISM. SHE BARES HER NIPPLES AND HER SOUL. SHE WANTS TO BE LIKED … *TRUTH OR DARE* IS AT ITS RAUNCHY BEST WHEN MADONNA IS KICKING ASS INSTEAD OF KISSING IT."

–PETER TRAVERS, *ROLLING STONE* (1991)

• •

Elizabeth Taylor, David Geffen and Bob and Harvey Weinstein were honorary cochairs of the May 8, 1991, **NYC** premiere. This event was to benefit amfAR, a group cofounded by Taylor, who was unable to attend. The evening began with a 5:30 p.m. reception at Laura Belle (formerly 120 W. 43rd St., NY, NY) and an 8 p.m. screening at the **Ziegfeld**, with an after-party at the Shelter (formerly 157 Hudson St., NY, NY). Madonna wore what resembled a sparkling one-piece bathing suit and sported glamorous, Evita-like hair. The celebrities at that launch included Carol Alt, Corbin Bernsen, Sandra Bernhard, **Naomi Campbell**, **Debbie Harry**, Lauren Hutton, Beverly Johnson, Dr. Mathilde Krim, **Steven Meisel**, Mike Myers, Billy Norwich, Ron Perelman, Susan Sarandon & Tim Robbins ("It was much more than just 'neat,' that's for sure," Sarandon quipped to **Kurt Loder**), Arnold Scaasi, Ron Silver (*Speed-the-Plow*), **Liz Smith** and Keenen Ivory Wayans Sr.

Fans and a significant portion of the general public flocked to see the movie, making it the most financially successful documentary of all time (it is now #15), bringing in $15,012,935 at the box office domestically and almost as much from the rest of the world (the film was made on a $4 million budget). A bootlegged version was reported to be available in New York with a $10,000 price tag. This version was said to contain Madonna's private phone calls to Beatty and a reference to **Sean Penn** as an ex-husband who sucks. The surviving *Blond Ambition* dancers from *Truth or Dare* all participated in the 2016 documentary *Strike a Pose*.

TRUTH OR DARE BY MADONNA (FOOTWEAR): On August 1, 2012, Madonna launched this line of footwear with longtime stylist **Arianne Phillips**. Prices on an initial selection of 32 pairs of shoes and boots ranged from $89 to $349.

TRUTH OR DARE BY MADONNA (FRAGRANCE): The first item sold in Madonna's lifestyle brand was this cologne, launched in April 2012 by Coty Prestige. The fragrance was officially launched on April 12, 2012, at Macy's (151 W. 34th St., NY, NY). Madonna walked a red carpet and then, inside a massive tent, answered questions submitted by **fans** after announcing, "Wearing perfume and smelling good has been a big part of my life." She signed one fan's arm so he could get it tattooed later; she never realized he had **Lady Gaga**'s signature on the other arm.

Coming out smelling like a tuberose at her Truth or Dare fragrance Macy's launch

WHERE'S MY IDOL?:
AN INTERVIEW WITH *TRUTH OR DARE*'S
MOIRA MCPHARLIN MESSANA

Truth or Dare has so many oh-no-she-didn't (before that phrase was invented) moments, it would be impossible to pick just one to savor. But one diva-tastic scene actually introduced viewers to the person who comes off the most real, unguarded and sincere in the film– Madonna's childhood friend, Moira McPharlin.

Waiting to ask Madonna to be the godmother of her unborn child, McPharlin is granted a breezy meeting with the star, who on top of having very little time to spare was preserving her voice in advance of one of her many *Blond Ambition World Tour* stops. It's a groaner of a moment, one in which Madonna has an opportunity to be gracious but instead comes off as emotionally unavailable. We can't help but laugh when McPharlin mumbles, as Madonna takes off, "Little shit!"

Flash forward 25 years since *Truth or Dare* was filmed, and Moira McPharlin Messana is a hairstylist in North Carolina. Like everyone who does hair, she gives good dish. Some of her answers to *EM2O*'s questions are daring, but *all* have the ring of truth.

EM2O: How much of your encounter with Madonna in Truth or Dare do we not see?

MOIRA MCPHARLIN MESSANA: It was definitely sliced and diced ... although the part with Madonna and I was pretty much what happened. I think Alek Keshishian was the one that was responsible. He was a manipulator.

EM2O: Kurt Loder wondered aloud in an interview with Madonna if you might be "devastated" by what she said about your shared childhood experiences. Did you feel devastated when you saw the film? How do you view it now?

MMM: I wasn't devastated, but I got a call from my in-laws complaining that they saw a commercial for *Entertainment Tonight* and they wanted to know what was going on. So I called Madonna to ask. She told me I needed to see the whole thing and she flew my husband, myself and my new baby to New York for the premiere. We stayed at the Mayflower [15 Central Park W., NY, NY]. She flew us first class.

During the film, I cried during the part when she was at her mom's graveside. You see, her mom was a very good friend of my mom's. My mom was pregnant with my sister when her mom died. We had moved to Dearborn for a short time, and shortly after her mom died my sister was born. She was named after Madonna's mom: Madonna.

EM2O: In the movie, you ask Madonna to bless your unborn child and to wish for you to have a girl. Did you?

MMM: I always wanted to have a girl and name her Madonna. After three boys, I found out I was pregnant again–and it was a girl! I had my Madonna. I just always loved the name ... my friend, my sister and my mom's friend [Madonna's mother], who was the kindest and sweetest surrogate mom also to me during her short life on earth.

So yes, I had my Madonna, my girl; she's quite beautiful, just turned 24, put herself totally through college because her dad left me after 25 years of marriage when she was a senior in high school. An extremely determined "Madonna" decided no matter what, she was going to college. She graduated in four years with a communications degree. She's still searching for exactly what she wants to do. Very talented and smart.

EM2O: Madonna had different memories about your childhood encounters. Do you think she was showing off/making things up?

MMM: We did have different memories of our childhood because she lost her mother, I did not ... Also, those answers were the result of Alek who creatively manipulated the answers from both of us!

EM2O: Did your Truth or Dare encounter make you think less of Madonna?

MMM: Madonna was totally like family, just like any of her siblings would be to me. You accept unconditionally the good and bad no matter what.

EM2O: You made Madonna promise to stay in touch in the movie. Did she?

MMM: The last time I actually saw Madonna was at the premiere of *Truth or Dare*. We spoke at the after-party at some club. I was living in North Carolina then, and since she never played in North Carolina until her last concert in 2012, I normally never asked for tickets for any of her shows. But if I did or if I ever needed anything, I always knew I could go to her.

EM2O: Have you kept up with Madonna's career? Ever seen her in concert?

MMM: In 2001, right before 9/11, I asked for tickets to Madonna's show in Atlanta and my daughter, Madonna, who was 10, and I went to the show in Atlanta. I don't know if anyone knew who we were ... no one said anything. We flew under the radar. We did not talk to Madonna then.

After that, my son was injured and I gave up many things to take care of him; in 2001, my youngest son, Nicholas, who was 13, was hit by a drunk in a hit-and-run. He was left with a traumatic brain injury to his frontal lobe; it changed our lives forever and we still have many tough issues. Someone in my community somehow let Madonna know, and she sent a check. I was disappointed that it was not a call, but understand.

According to Coty, the fragrance is comprised of "narcotic florals." Madonna herself has said the scent was inspired by her mom, who she remembers smelling like tuberose. A second fragrance, Truth or Dare by Madonna: Naked, was launched in December 2012.

TSUNAMI AID: A CONCERT OF HOPE: A benefit held on January 15, 2005, and spearheaded by **George Clooney** to raise **money** for the victims of the 2004 tsunami. The telethon included performances or appearances by Eric Clapton, Sheryl Crow, **Elton John**, **Brad Pitt**, Roger Waters and many more. Madonna performed **"Imagine"** by John Lennon (1971).

TUBE, THE: *Airdates: November 5, 1982–April 26, 1987.* British music-based **TV** show hosted by Jools Holland and Paula Yates, among others. Madonna's January 27, 1984, Hacienda (formerly Whitworth St. W., Manchester, England, UK) performance was filmed for the show. She lip-synched to **"Everybody," "Burning Up"** and **"Holiday"** with backup dancing by **Erika Belle** and **Christopher Ciccone**. Years later, Madonna ran into the Hacienda manager Tony Wilson, who told her she'd played his club. Madonna's cold reply? "My **memory** seems to have wiped that."

Even if Madonna's forgotten it, it survives as an early record of Madonna's showmanship and charisma even without elaborate props, costumes or live singing.

"TURN UP THE RADIO" (SONG): *Release date: August 3, 2012. Billboard Hot 100 peak: NA.* Produced by Madonna and **Martin Solveig**, and written by both of them, Michael Tordjman and Jade Williams, think of this *MDNA* track and international single as the radio-air-kissing anti-"**Hollywood**." Ironically, even as Madonna was urging her listeners to turn up the radio, radio was continuing its nasty habit of turning down the opportunity to play any new Madonna tune.

A **dance** hit, the song was performed live on *The MDNA Tour*.

"TURN UP THE RADIO" (VIDEO): *Director: Tom Munro, 2012.* Shot in Florence, Italy, June 18–19, 2012, this fun-loving video was shot by **fashion** photographer **Tom Munro** while Madonna was on her *MDNA Tour*. It's a pure party video, showing cock-tease Madonna with teased **hair** riding around Italy in a convertible in her revealing Balmain wardrobe, picking up fellow revelers and performers along the way.

"**Vogue**," it ain't, but it is an interesting companion piece to "**Drowned World/Substitute for Love**," the latter being a glum take on **fame** whereas "Turn Up the Radio" seems to suggest that being pursued by paparazzi doesn't have to be **Diana**-serious all the time.

TURNBERRY ISLE: Resort in **Miami** where Madonna and **Sean Penn** rekindled the romance after a brief separation in 1987, immediately before he left to serve prison time and Madonna was about to appear at **Madison Square Garden** in **New York** to perform a *Who's That Girl World Tour* show for **AIDS**.

TURNER, KATHLEEN: *b. June 19, 1954.* Smoky-**voiced** '80s and '90s movie star who Madonna went to see in the Broadway **play** *Indiscretions* in 1995. It had been reported that when **Barbra Streisand** attended, she'd ducked out without seeing the end, so Turner asked of Madonna's attendance, "Did she stay for the whole thing?" She had.

TURNER, TINA: *b. November 26, 1939.* Rock, pop and soul legend famous for burning up the '60s with legs up to *there*, teaching **Mick Jagger** how to **dance**, leaving her abusive husband Ike and having a surprising musical comeback at age 44.

Madonna and her manager, **Camille Barbone**, watched a Tina Turner gig in 1981 at The Ritz (formerly 119 E. 11th St., NY, NY) in **NYC**, an indication of the rock and roll direction in which Barbone wanted Madonna to go.

Madonna met Turner at **Live Aid**, where she posed for the July 29, 1985, *People* **magazine** cover with her, Bob Dylan, Mick Jagger, **Keith Richards**, Ron Wood and Hall & Oates. She also posed with Turner and **Courtney Love**

for the November 13, 1997, cover of *Rolling Stone*, representing the magazine's "Women of Rock" issue.

Turner said of the *Rolling Stone* shoot before it came out: "I, y'know, I've watched these two ladies often, and I've wondered what it would be like—actually, Madonna and I have been photographed together before—but, with three of us, the energy of the three of us ... I'm very excited about it!" So, yeah.

TURN-ONS: Like any good *Playboy* bunny, Madonna wouldn't be caught dead without some turn-ons. In a man, she's turned on by intelligence, confidence, humor, artistic passion; she also expects him to like antiques, write her lots of letters and smell good. She also prefers a man who can pay his own rent. But it's not a deal-breaker.

TV: She has famously said she grew up without it and doesn't watch the "poison box," but she did used to sneak behind her parents' **backs** to watch shows like *Dark Shadows* (1966–1971), *The Monkees* (1966–1968) and *The Partridge Family* (1970–1974).

In 1998, Madonna admitted she does watch things she thinks are milestones, like when **Ellen DeGeneres**'s character came out as a lesbian.

Madonna told *Elle* in 2005, "My information doesn't come from television. I'm informed by **art**, **books**, old films, photography." I guess that definitely softens the blow of events like **9/11**. She clarified in 2006 that she gets her world-at-large info from "friends, coworkers and people that I trust and respect."

This may be one reason why Madonna's **work** has very few (if any) classic TV references, in spite of its many nods to classic music and film. One rather misses an "Alice the housekeeper" **Steven Klein** photo shoot.

By 2015, Madonna's anti-TV outlook was softening ... she admitted to loving *The Fall* (2013–) because Gillian Anderson is "so good" and *True Detective* (2014–).

"TV is mesmerizing, you know? It's very powerful, television—very, very powerful—and it's kind of scary to me. I probably could get very addicted to TV."—MADONNA (1991)

12 YEARS A SLAVE: *Director: Steve McQueen. Release date: November 8, 2013.* Madonna attended the October 8, 2013, **New York** Film Festival premiere of this Steve McQueen–directed film, which would go on to win the Best Picture **Oscar**.

That evening, Salon writer Charles Taylor reposted on his **Facebook** page an irate item from a former NYU student of his who claimed to have been at the screening, seated behind actors Jason Ritter and Michael K. Williams, **fashion** diva J. Alexander and a "mysterious **blonde** in black lace gloves." The blonde had been rudely texting throughout the early part of the film, until a female audience member tapped her and told her to stop. The offender reportedly "hissed" (the *New York Post* used the phrase "shot **back**," Gawker changed it to "snarled," *Indiewire* went with a "yell," the *Los Angeles Times* upped it to "shouted"), "It's for **business** ... *enslaver*!"

The rest of the story goes that once the film ended and the blonde departed, Alexander wondered aloud who that girl had been. Ritter turned to the people behind him and, picking up the discarded ticket envelope at the blonde's seat, expressed surprise at the fact that it bore the notation: "2 screening tix MADONNA."

The story was picked up (without attribution) by the *Post*'s "Page Six" and went viral, with pretty much everyone's reaction being that Madonna was, as the **original** Facebook spy had concluded, "The worst person in America." Haters gon' **hate**.

As ironic as it would be for Madonna to offhandedly call someone an enslaver during a *12 Years a Slave* screening, is it not at least as ironic that while watching the horrors of slavery unfold on the big screen, this film **fan** couldn't think of anything worse than texting during a movie? (Yes, it's bothersome, but being sold sucks, too.)

None of the famous-ish names dropped in the story has ever commented on the incident. Another question mark: Could Ritter, Williams and Alexander *really* have been sitting next to Madonna without realizing it?

What is known for sure: Madonna was at the screening and adored the movie, returning to hear McQueen's remarks after having ducked out when it ended. She later posed for pictures with McQueen.

Sensing an opportunity to self-promote, CEO Tim League of the Alamo Drafthouse (drafthouse.com) announced via **Twitter** that Madonna was persona non grata at his chain of theaters: "Until she apologizes to movie fans, Madonna is banned from watching movies @drafthouse." League later said his decree had been "an offhand joke," but that, "... I don't think it really affects her life that much" and that it was "more of a means to get the issue out there, that it is rude to text during movies."

Madonna now has a reputation for being bad in movies *and* in movie *theaters*.

P.S. Madonna attended the April 18, 2015, evening performance of the hot Off-Broadway show *Hamilton*, and allegedly texted during the show, much to creator/star Lin-Manuel Miranda's chagrin. When he appeared on stage after the show to ask for Broadway Cares/Equity Fights **AIDS** donations, he noted that someone in the audience had deep pockets and should donate lots ... someone who was texting a lot. He then tweeted: "Tonight was the first time I asked stage management NOT to allow a celebrity (who was texting all through Act 2) backstage #noselfieforyou." He quickly deleted the tweet. Madonna denied she'd been texting during the show, and asserted she'd been invited backstage four times.

Honestly, people can be so *rudeist* in their complaints about Madonna ...

20/20: *Airdates: June 6, 1978-.* Soft-news **TV** series on which **Cynthia McFadden** interviewed Madonna on June 18, 2004, to promote her ***Re-Invention World Tour*** and her children's **books**. Relaxed and girlish, Madonna talked about choosing **Esther** as her Hebrew name, provided a dismissive post-mortem on *Sex* and had many Kabbalistic things to say about conquering ego ("I want to be more liberated from my ego, less concerned with what people think of me") and trying to avoid being a part of the chaos of the world.

She said, "Once you enter the popularity sweepstakes, which you do when you become famous, whether you're a singer or an actress or a model or a journalist, a TV journalist, whatever, y'know, you enter the world of, y'know, 'How'm I doin'? How'm I doin'? How's my rating? How's my ... y'know ... How do I look? Where am I in the '50 Most Beautiful People,' y'know, poll?'"

TWITTER: Madonna is on Twitter @madonna, but it's really just a supplement for her **Instagram** account.

TYSON, MIKE: *b. June 30, 1966.* **Boxing** champ who was allegedly abusive toward his wife, **TV** actor Robin Givens, and who was convicted of **rape** in the '90s. Nonetheless, he continued to be the definitive boxer of his generation and a pop culture figure with a one-man show and a memorable appearance in the movie *The Hangover* (2009). A 1995 TV movie about his life was directed by Uli Edel, who had directed ***Body of Evidence***.

Madonna and **Sean Penn** were friendly with Tyson and Givens in the '80s. They double-dated to a screening of *Pee-wee's Big Adventure* in 1985. "Me and Sean fell asleep in the movie," Tyson told Jimmy Kimmel in 2015, copping to being slightly drunk. When Kimmel asked Penn about the date, Penn replied, "That's true."

Madonna and Penn were there for the 91-second bout in which Tyson knocked out Michael Spinks at the Atlantic City Convention Hall (now Boardwalk Hall, 2301 Boardwalk, Atlantic City, NJ) on June 27, 1988.

Madonna, who bumped into old flame **John F. Kennedy Jr.** while there, was in attendance on June 28, 1997, at the MGM Grand Garden Arena (3799 Las Vegas Blvd. S., Las Vegas, NV) when Tyson fought Evander Holyfield. Tyson infamously bit off a hunk of Holyfield's ear.

In 2014, Madonna invited Tyson to record a trash-talking intro at the beginning of her **Rebel Heart** track **"Iconic."** Tyson told TMZ he would do more music "only if Madonna asked me for another song." She hasn't yet, but she did get him to introduce her at the **iHeartRadio Music Awards**.

GREGORY PACE

MATTHEW RETTENMUND

UK MUSIC HALL OF FAME: On November 11, 2004, Madonna was among the first to be inducted into the UK **Music** Hall of **Fame**, along with **Elvis Presley**, the **Beatles**, **Bob Marley**, Cliff Richard, the Rolling Stones, Queen, **Michael Jackson**, Robbie Williams and U2. Madonna was inducted by Tracey Emin and Radio 1 DJ Jo Whiley, saying of the honor, "I am so grateful to the people who have stuck their neck out for me and taken the slaps. I've taken many slaps and I don't **regret** a thing." Best girlfriends (at the time) **Stella McCartney** and **Gwyneth Paltrow** did a video **parody** in which Paltrow dressed up in *Blond Ambition World Tour* gear and McCartney donned "**Material Girl**" pink. "She's made it okay to be **sexual** as a woman," Paltrow testified.

ULTRA MUSIC FESTIVAL: On March 24, 2012, Madonna appeared at this electronic music festival, walking out onstage and introducing **Avicii**. She teased, "How many people in this crowd have seen Molly?" referencing the club **drug** MDMA, for which her *MDNA* album was playfully named.

Almost immediately, EDM producer deadmau5 slammed Madonna for glamorizing drugs: "seriously, i giveth not a fucking single **FUCK** for slating on madonna for reaching an entirely NEW level of idiocy … i can appriciate her meteoric career, and all good deeds done, but WHAT THE FUCK WAS THAT? That's your big contribution to EDM? That's your big message to ultra attendies? hipsterspeak for looking for drugs? fuck off you fucking IDIOT. fuck."

Madonna tweeted the mouse-branded deadmau5 a classic **Herb Ritts** image of herself in Minnie ears with the word balloon: "From one mouse to another, I don't support drug use and I never have. I was referring to the song called 'Have You Seen Molly' written by my friend Cedric Gervais who I almost **worked** with on my album."

The two buried the hatchet, with Madonna suggesting he call her in the future to solve their differences privately.

As for the rest of the appearance, Avicii debuted his "**Girl Gone Wild**" UMF Mix live on stage as Madonna **danced** like a teenager at his side. Avicii later said of Madonna, "She was super sweet and super professional and everything went really smoothly." Avicii didn't see the big deal about the molly reference; he told *Access Hollywood*, "I didn't take it that seriously … Honestly, I just didn't really care."

> "I can honestly say that a DJ saved my life."
> —MADONNA AT THE ULTRA MUSIC FESTIVAL (2012)

"UNAPOLOGETIC BITCH": A successful excursion into a reggae sound from *Rebel Heart* written by MoZella, Madonna, **Diplo**, Toby Gad, Bryan Orellana and Shelco Garcia, and produced by Madonna, Shelco Garcia & Teenwolf, BV, Diplo and Rechtshaid. The song sounds like absolutely nothing else in Madonna's catalogue, nor does it sound like the rest of the songs on *Rebel Heart*, but its status as a coarse dressing-down of a **love** interest fits nicely with one of the album's overall themes, best described as, "**Fuck** you, **bitch**."

The song closed the main set of the *Rebel Heart Tour*. Madonna brought **fans** and celebs onstage as nightly "unapologetic bitches."

UNCLE SAM'S: *Formerly 2965 Hempstead Tpke., Levittown, NY.* Madonna performed a set of four songs at this Long Island club on September 24, 1983, after having recorded a short **commercial** to advertise her appearance. The club's owner, Nick Paccione, told a **NYC** news station in the '90s, "That night was more exciting than any other night that we've had a [sic] entertainer perform here." A low-quality, yet priceless, 25-minute video on **YouTube** captures Madonna's full set at the club with **Erika Belle**, **Christopher Ciccone** and **Bags Rilez** as her **dancers**: "**Physical Attraction**" (one of the only club-date performances of this one available), "**Everybody**," "**Holiday**" and "**Burning Up**." Cover charge was $5.

The club's owners were convicted of arson for burning Uncle Sam's down in 1994 to collect the insurance.

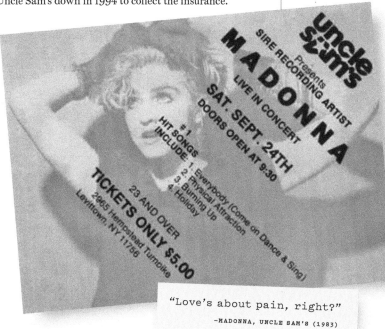

> "Love's about pain, right?"
> —MADONNA, UNCLE SAM'S (1983)

UNDERWEAR: Madonna has said that she wore "colorful, **sexy** underwear" as a schoolgirl. "I'd hang upside down on the bars in the **gym** just so they could see my undies." She told *Spin* in 1985 that one thing she'd never wear in public was "just sexy underpants," a vow she has obviously broken. Many, *many* times.

Since those days, Madonna has **reinvented** the term, routinely donning men's boxer shorts, bras, girdles, garter belts and bustiers as *outer*wear, making unmentionables eminently mentionable.

In concert, **fans** have sometimes thrown *their* undergear at Madonna. "Stop throwing your underpants up here," she told **London** at a *Who's That Girl World Tour* performance. "First of all, they're not my **size**."

UNICEF: Madonna attended Gucci's November 19, 2008, bash for this **charity** wearing an instantly infamous **Louis Vuitton** green dress that looked like AstroTurf.

UNIVERSITY OF MICHIGAN: On a **dance** scholarship, Madonna spent a year and a half at this prestigious **Michigan** college. She studied in Gay Delang's technique class ("She was lean. She had a nice edge to her **muscles**. She was hungry. Great appetite") and with **Christopher Flynn** and got good grades, but chucked it all to move to **New York** in search of **fame** and glory.

In 2014, Madonna's first child, **Lola**, started her college career in the same place. Madonna and Lola were spotted dining at Café Felix (204 S. Main St., Ann Arbor, MI) in August 2014.

Madonna said of Lola's departure for **school**, "It's hard letting them go out into the world, but when she left home to go to college I was a mess … I've come to terms with it but yes, I miss her and she's a part of me. It was like losing my arm."

UNIVERSITY TOWERS: *536 S. Forest Ave., Ann Arbor, MI.* High-rise where Madonna roomed with **Whitley Setrakian** and two dudes while attending the **University of Michigan**. They lived in #1001.

UNRELEASED: Aside from all her commercially or promotionally available music, Madonna's discography would not be complete without some mention of the tunes that got away … or, at least, the ones that somehow escaped an *official* release. This entry will attempt to summarize most of the songs Madonna is known, or is reasonably thought, to have written and/or recorded, but which remain unreleased. Many have **leaked** and are available on **YouTube**, others are confirmed to exist but are unheard and still others could be mere rumors.

We are not going to list songs that are early versions of released tracks—though there are many examples of demos wildly different from the songs to which they led, such as "Infinity," which became **"Give It 2 Me."**

....

1979 Dan and Ed Gilroy tapes: The bros of the **Breakfast Club** made extremely brief excerpts of these historic home recordings available to Madonna biographer **Andrew Morton** to share on *The Daily Beast* in 2008. The songs, all collaborations with Madonna's songwriting input, were "Born to Be a **Dancer**" (like an off-key **Chrissie Hynde** number), an early take on **"Over and Over," "Tell the Truth"** (sweet ballad) and "I Got Trouble (Roll Over It)" (funky little rocker). The brothers confirmed that another song—still unheard—exists called "Trouble"; Madonna remembers "Tell the Truth" as being the first song she ever wrote, while Ed Gilroy says it was "Trouble." The recordings also capture goof-off bits of conversation about such pressing issues as

—SARAH PILLSBURY

picking one's nose vs. scratching one's butt. Priceless stuff, all in all.

....

1979 pre-Emmy recruitment solo cassette: Madonna's earliest known actual demo was discovered in 2009 and detailed in the UK **magazine** *Record Collector*. It contained "All My Love," "No Running in the City," "Hear Me" (early version of "Shine a Light," a catchy '80s rock track), "Safe Neighborhood" (hard-driving rock tune that surfaced on a bootleg picture disc as "On the Ground" years later), "Simon Says" (loping **guitar** track with dying-goose vocal), "Love Express" (rockabilly-flavored), "Little Boy Lost" (like a slower "Safe Neighborhood," with a strong B-52s sound), three separate instrumental tracks and two versions of a nameless song. All were sung by Madonna, who accompanied herself on guitar. The tape was sold at **auction** on November 21, 2009, with a pre-sale estimate of $1,000–$2,000, selling for $6,000.

....

1979 Patrick Hernandez–era solo cassette: The sale of the above 1979 tape inspired Stella Monfort, who had been a dancer in the **Patrick Hernandez** Revue at the time Madonna was brought to **Paris**, to offer her own Madonna demo for sale. This (fabulously **orange**-colored) cassette was simply labeled "Madonna" and contained four tracks: early versions of "Shine a Light," "Safe Neighborhood" and "Little Boy Lost" and a fourth, unidentified song. Monfort sold it as a "buy it now" for $6,000 on eBay.

....

1980 Emmy studio demo: "(I Like) Love for Tender" (Madonna's **Elvis Presley** imitation on the verses amps up the rockabilly vibe), "No Time for Love" (mid-tempo rock tune), "Bells Ringing" (mature melodic rock with a guitar lick that predicts Van Halen's 1982 "Pretty Woman" remake) and "Drowning" (one of the closest to her eventual solo style, with a dodgy vocal) are the unreleased songs from this batch.

....

1980 Emmy live tracks: Recorded from gigs, these songs have leaked online: "Best Girl" (messy punk track) and "Nobody's Fool" (meandering and guitar-driven).

....

1980 Emmy mystery tracks: Photographer **George DuBose**'s images of **Emmy** performing live have confirmed the existence (via set list) of the songs "Prisoner," "Head Over Heels," "Get Away" and "Call on Me"; there's no evidence any were recorded, but all were played live in 1980 and/or 1981.

....

1980 Shamrock tape: This reel-to-reel, so named for the brand of tape used, is in private hands following an auction. It contained "Tell the Truth" (see above), "Hothouse Flower" (loud, angsty rock song), "Simon Says" (see above), "I Got Trouble (Roll Over It)" (see above), "Oh Oh the Sky Is Blue" (unheard), "Nobody Wants to Be Alone (Once I Thought I Was Good)" (unheard) and "Well Well" (unheard).

GREGORY PACE

1981 Gotham demo: "I Want You" (breezy, pop tune with an echo of Kirsty MacColl's 1979 "They Don't Know"), "Love on the Run" (reggae-infused ditty that starts out with a Village People flourish), "Get Up" (one of Madonna's best early tracks, this complaint song has a strong, driving vocal) and "High Society" (languid social-issue song sounds like something from the first, pre-**fame** Eurythmics album, except for Madonna's **voice**) are songs that Madonna's manager **Camille Barbone** guided her in recording. Two rejects, "Remembering Your Touch" (leak exists in terrible quality but has a highly infectious chorus) and "Are You Ready for It" (Madonna sounds like she has a cold in this otherwise catchy tune) were cut at the same time. All of these songs have an underwritten, repetitive quality, especially in their choruses.

1982 confirmed recordings: Madonna definitely recorded with the group Spinal Root Gang a song called "We Live in a House" (Joshua Braun/**Janis Galloway**); snippets were played on *All About Madonna*. Around the same time, an A&R guy from ZE Records (which had signed the Breakfast Club) pointed Madonna to a **job** singing the female lead vocal on the delightfully nutty Was (Not Was) track "Shake Your Head (Let's Go to Bed)" for their *Born to Laugh at Tornadoes* album. Ozzy Osbourne had done the male lead vocal first, and Madonna's voice was to have been added in, forming a sort of duet. Don Was later said, "We brought her up and she sang really well, but I've always imagined the vocalists as extensions of ourselves, and I couldn't relate to female vocals being our voice." **Sire Records** balked anyway, and the song was released without Madonna. She didn't want her voice used when it was remixed for release in the early '90s, so Kim Basinger filled in, but Madonna's **original** vocal has leaked.

Early '80s rumored tracks: Madonna apparently wrote songs called "Afterglo," "Cherish" (not that one), "Girl with Stars in Her **Eyes**," "Rock Your Body" and "Swing With Me," as is evidenced by handwritten lyrics that were auctioned in 2011. There is no proof that these songs were ever recorded.

1983 debunked track: A hot song called "Lies In Your Eyes" from 1983 that purports to have Madonna's vocals on it was actually recorded by a group called I-Level. They *did* want Madonna to record it, going so far as to send the demo to Madonna and her collaborator **Stephen Bray**, but Bray is certain Madonna never recorded it. Its appearance on various bootlegs has confused **fans** for years.

1984 TV theme: One 1984 mystery is that of the song "Writer's Block," which is listed in a songwriting database as a collaboration between Madonna and Rick Warren for the **TV** series *Cover Up* (OMG ... Madonna and Jon-Erik Hexum in the same thought!). There was an episode of

the series with this exact title that aired on November 24, 1984, a month after Hexum's **death.**

1984 *Vision Quest* track: Along with the classics **"Gambler"** and **"Crazy for You,"** Madonna cowrote and recorded the song "Warning Signs" for the movie ***Vision Quest***. "Warning Signs" was listed on an early flyer for the soundtrack, but never actually appeared on the soundtrack or in the movie. Collaborator Stephen Bray remembers it as a "good little synth track," and it is accounted for in the Library of Congress. Madonna told interviewer Rick Sky, "I sing three songs on the soundtrack." Sample lyrics: "Warning/I see danger up ahead/I can see it in your eyes/And it's really no surprise/Because I can see your warning signs."

1984 debunked track: In '84, **Mark Kamins** told writer **Mark Bego:** "I'm producing a girl for Island Records, and Madonna wrote a song for me. Her name's Cheyne. Her first single will be out in a couple of weeks. The song that Madonna wrote will be her second single. She's wild. It's called 'Call Me Mr. Telephone.'" It seems as if something was lost in *transcription*, because while Madonna did, indeed, write a song that was originally intended to be for Cheyne, that song—**Into the Groove**—was probably the proposed second single, because "Call Me Mr. Telephone" was *not* written by Madonna, but by Toni C. It became a big dance hit, but not as big as "Into the Groove," a song Madonna happened to play for her ***Desperately Seeking Susan*** director and producers, leading her to yank it **back** from Cheyne. Cheyne apparently recorded "Into the Groove," a version that's never been heard. "Call Me Mr. Telephone" sounds nothing like Madonna's **work** at the time but includes a tight little rap. The music video reveals Cheyne to have been a cute candidate for a black version of Madonna, who herself was a white version of artists like Cheyne. (The music video features images of several '80s stars—**Cyndi Lauper**, **Billy Idol**, David Lee Roth, Sade ... but pointedly, no Madonna.)

1984 *Desperately Seeking Susan* title theme: Speaking of *Desperately Seeking Susan*, Madonna and Bray wrote a title song for the film that has never been heard or confirmed to actually exist. Rumors that it was rejected by the film's producers are apparently not true; the producers tell *EM20* they don't recall hearing it, and that other songs under consideration to be used in the movie were **"Holiday"** and **"Material Girl."** (Another title song was written by the brother of casting director Risa Bramon, Michael Bramon; this, too, remains unheard.)

1984/1985 rumored tracks: Madonna claimed authorship of an unspecified song for a French act called Nathalie in 1985, which could be any number of near-anonymous tunes on Nat's one-and-only album. Or not. Madonna implied in an interview with Bego that she was writing a song for the soundtrack of the film *Fast Forward* (1985), but she was

credited with none on the released album. There is allegedly an unheard title song that may be Madonna's handiwork.
It's a dance movie, so it seems logical that she would've
been pursued to write for it, and her boyfriend **Jellybean
Benitez** did, in fact, work on it. But the most likely scenario
is that this is an erroneous report/attribution.

Another soundtrack for which Madonna was reported
to have written a song or songs was a rock-opera remake of
Oliver Twist, which never got made. The most intriguing
aspect of this is the fact that her collaborators were Ashford
& Simpson (Madonna's publicist is a huge fan of the husband-and-wife duo; Nick Ashford passed away in 2011). It is
unlikely that this film, with a working title of *Street Smart*,
is related to the 1988 Disney release *Oliver & Company*.

• •

***True Blue* era:** In 1986, Madonna and Bray cowrote tracks
called "Working My Fingers to the Bone" (said to sound
like a Jacksons song) and "Pipeline" that were left off of
True Blue. EM20 supposes that if fans had been able to
hear leaked demos back then, people would have been crying bloody murder that these tracks were left off the album
while crap like **"Open Your Heart"** made the cut?

Madonna also collaborated on two or three songs with
Fred Zarr that were not finished. Teen-mag rumors that
Madonna had a song on the soundtrack of the **David Bow-
ie** movie *Labyrinth* (1986) went nowhere.

• •

1986: Madonna's demo of "Each Time You Break My Heart"
has leaked, but was never released; it's a fantastic version of
a song officially recorded and released by **Nick Kamen**.

• •

1987 rumors: Madonna was quoted as saying she'd written
a song for Bryan Ferry for his album *Bête Noire* (1987), but
it has never surfaced and can't be confirmed. Perhaps she
used it herself and we're just not privy to which of her hits
could have instead gone on to be a Bryan Ferry miss?

An odd coupling that doesn't sound all that promising
is a tune called "Love Over the Phone" or "Love Over the
Telephone," which Madonna wrote—wait for it—over the
phone with **Don Johnson**. Copyright disputes kept the
song under wraps, but Madonna confirmed it was written
and it is rumored to have been recorded.

Around this time, Madonna and Stephen Bray recorded a
song called "I Want You" (different from her early-years song
and from her later Marvin Gaye cover of the same name).

• •

***Like a Prayer* era:** The *Like a Prayer* sessions in 1988
yielded several mystery titles, including the well-established,
never heard "Love Attack" (Madonna/Stephen Bray) and
a safe-sex ballad called "First Is a Kiss" (Madonna/Ste-
phen Bray). "Good-Bye My Forever Friend"/"Good-Bye
Forever My Friend" is another rumored title, possibly related to "First Is a Kiss," and "Angels With Dirty Faces" was
confirmed by guitarist/**"La Isla Bonita"** cowriter Bruce
Gaitsch as existing on a rehearsal tape from this period.

Prince wrote a song called "By Alien Means" for this
album, described by PrinceVault.com as "alternating between a slow, wistful melody and a monotonous vamp" and
as tackling the issue of suicide. Madonna almost certainly
never recorded it.

• •

***I'm Breathless: Music from and Inspired by the Film
Dick Tracy* era:** Madonna's collaborator Patrick Leonard
wrote a song called **"Dick Tracy"** with Madonna that has
not been heard, nor has the same-titled "Dick Tracy" written by Danny Elfman and sung by Madonna materialized.

"Dog House" (Madonna/Patrick Leonard) was reported to be in *Dick Tracy* by **Billboard**, but it's possible the
song changed to the point where the credits changed—
"You're In the Doghouse Now" (Andy Paley) appears on the
soundtrack in a recording by Brenda Lee. "To Love You"
(Madonna/Andy Paley) is another outtake fans expect to
hear sooner or later.

• •

***Erotica* era:** The red-hot "Shame" (Madonna/**Shep Pet-
tibone/Tony Shimkin**) from 1991, cut for *Erotica*, is a
fan-fave leak for the ages.

More titles from the *Erotica* period that did not get
released (maybe a three-disc **Rebel Heart** Super-Duper
Deluxe Edition could correct that oversight?) are the unheard "Show and Tell" and the theorized early **"Erotica"**
take "Love Hurts" (Madonna/Junior Vasquez). Two leaks
of unreleased tunes are the cheery house track "You Are
the One" (Madonna/Shep Pettibone/Tony Shimkin) and
"Dear **Father**" (Madonna/**Andre Betts**/Mic Murphy), the
latter of which is a fairly standard mid-tempo song.

• •

***A League of Their Own* soundtrack:** "Jitterbug" (Madon-
na/Shep Pettibone/Tony Shimkin) may be little more than
a fragment; it seems to be generic house music with Madonna speaking over it in the studio. Its existence has been
confirmed by Shimkin, who described it as being a song
abandoned due to lack of time.

• •

***Bedtime Stories* era:** "Bring It" (Madonna/Shep Pet-
tibone), "Goodtime" (Madonna/Shep Pettibone) and
"Tongue Tied" (Madonna/Shep Pettibone) are three unheard songs Madonna was working on with Shep Pettibone before she decided to go in a different direction with
this album. Another, "Something's Coming Over Me," was
the beginning of what became **"Secret."** There is also another **Babyface** track floating around.

A song called "Right on Time" (Madonna/**Dallas Austin**) is thought to have been recorded, but may have been a
variation on a song that made the final album.

• •

***Something to Remember* era:** The leak "I Can't Forget"
(Madonna/**David Foster**) is a beautiful ballad that was
later recorded as "Come Closer" by Tilt and that was recorded by Angelica Di Castro in 2011.

The tantalizing snippet of a song heard in the 1995 Japanese Takara **commercial** is from an unknown, unreleased piece.

••

Ray of Light era: Madonna's greatest album gave us some of her greatest rejects: "Revenge" (Madonna/**Rick Nowels**/Greg Fitzgerald), "Gone, Gone, Gone" (Madonna/Rick Nowels/Greg Fitzgerald) and "Like a Flower" (Madonna/Rick Nowels/Greg Fitzgerald), are beautiful-sounding, polished leaks. "Like a Flower" was recorded by Laura Pausini in 2004. Lyrically, "Revenge" is a dizzying barrage of clichés.

"Be Careful" (Madonna/Patrick Leonard) from this phase may just be her **Ricky Martin** duet, but "Regfresando" with Leonard is in the Warner-Chappell database and seems likely to be an unheard (and misspelled, try "Regresando") song. Madonna also apparently worked with Babyface on as many as four unreleased tracks for the album, with two rumored titles being "Don't Love a Stranger" and "Forever One."

••

Music era: "Alone Again" (Madonna/Rick Nowels) is the most famous unreleased song from this era because though Madonna's demo hasn't been heard, it was recorded by **Kylie Minogue** and released in her *White Diamond* (2007) documentary.

"Arioso" (Madonna/**William Orbit**), a genteel complaint song about being judged, leaked in December 2014. It had previously been the source of the brief theme used for the controversial, short-lived TV series *Wonderland* in 1999.

Madonna's faithful cover of ABBA's "Like an Angel Passing Through My Room," produced with Orbit, is this writer's pick for one of the technically unreleased (but leaked) songs most deserving of an official release. It's been easily findable on **YouTube** since 2008. Her ABBA itch was eventually scratched with **"Hung Up."**

"Liquid Love" (Madonna/William Orbit) lived up to its name and leaked. Recorded in 1999, Madonna never released this lovely William Orbit collaboration because it gave her the "wrong-tingles" at the time. Perhaps the song's unsubtle semen allusion made her gaggy? It's got a beautiful vocal and could be compared favorably to some of the tracks included on the final version of *Music*. Orbit repurposed much of the music for his song "Bubble Universe" (2006).

"Mysore Smile" (William Orbit) is probably an embryonic form of **"Cyber-Raga,"** but it's never leaked. "Run" (William Orbit): Guitars 'n' spaceship noises characterize this bubbly number, which leaked to the Internet. It has a similar message as **"Don't Tell Me."**

"Little Girl"/"La Petite Jeune Fille"/"Dear Pumpkin" are rather distinct versions of the same song, with the more up-tempo version sounding like **"Runaway Lover."**

Madonna/**Mirwais** compositions for the album that didn't make the cut include "Eagle's Wings," "Just Another," "Mechanical," "No Choice," "One," "Remember Me" and "When the Light Fades." All were mentioned in the media, but none has ever been confirmed, nor leaked.

Madonna collaborated with Sasha and William Orbit and confirmed some material was "in the vault." These songs may have been *Music* cast-offs, and are said to include "All the Way Down," "Heartbeat," "Painted Picture," "Relief on Demand," "Room for Squares" and "Take Away."

Finally, Madonna allegedly recorded three songs with the fusion band Zap Mama.

••

American Life era: Madonna and Mirwais recorded a song at the same time as **"Die Another Day"** called "Can't You See My Mind." Considering the nature of the lyrics of "Die Another Day," it sounds like she really had brain on the brain at the time.

The leaked songs "The Game," "Miss You" and "Set the Right" (Madonna/Mirwais) are respectable acoustic tracks very much in the *American Life* mold. They all compare favorably to a few of the songs that made the album. "React," a fourth song from the era, has never been heard.

••

Movie musicals era: Madonna was working on a movie musical called *Hello, Suckers!* with Patrick Leonard and Mirwais, among others, and also with director Luc Besson (**"Love Profusion"** video, *Arthur and the Invisibles*) on a separate film project. Neither came to pass, but quite a bit of the music was repurposed on *Confessions on a Dance Floor* and *Hard Candy*, though it was created in 2004, in some cases while Madonna was on her *Re-Invention World Tour*.

"I'm in Love with Love" (Madonna/**Monte Pittman**) is a leaked pop/rock tune that still sounds very *American Life*. Around the 1:31 mark it takes on a sound reminiscent of the *Desperately Seeking Susan* score.

"Curtain," **"How High,"** "If You Go Away", "Is This Love (Bon D'Accord)" and "Boum" were songs apparently intended for *Hello, Suckers!* Of the lot, the first two were repurposed. "Is This Love" and "Boum" were not used in any other form, and both are pretty damn solid. "If You Go Away" is a dazzling, melodramatic redo of Jacques Brel's "Ne me quitte pas" (1959).

••

Confessions on a Dance Floor era: There are some shockingly different early versions of **"Get Together"** and the B-side track **"History"** out there, as well as "Keep the Trance," a bizarrely different take on what eventually became the treacly **"Hey You."** As for completely unreleased/unrepurposed songs, there are very few because Madonna was using a lot of material from her no-go movie musicals.

One of Madonna's best unreleased tracks is "Triggering" (Madonna/Mirwais), an edgy **disco** track that's crying out for an official release or **reinvention** (resuscitation?) on tour. It's even got a "Rapper's Delight" rap break and a lot of talk about being "on the street," which would make for a great mash-up with **"Sidewalk Talk."**

Hard Candy era: "Across the Sky" (Madonna/**Justin Timberlake/Danja/Timbaland**) is as good as any song included on the final *Hard Candy* album, a danceable ode to righteous indignation. "Animal" (Madonna/Justin Timberlake/Danja/Timbaland) is less distinguished ... sounds like something Rockwell would have pounced on in 1983. "Pala Tute" (often wrongly called "Latte" ... get over that **"American Life"** rap!), was eventually used, in part, in Madonna's "La Isla Bonita" performances at **Live Earth** and on her *Sticky & Sweet Tour.*

"The Beat Is So Crazy" (Madonna/Eve/**Pharrell Williams**) is a song that finds Madonna singing the choruses while Eve handles the rest. It's completely forgettable, and as such, Madonna and Eve both forgot to include it on their albums.

Celebration and *MDNA* era: There don't seem to be any major unreleased songs from these eras that are known, just lots of very different early demos and a couple of tracks that were eventually released in some form.

Rebel Heart era: Hard to believe anything wasn't used when the album has over 20 songs, but there are many demos that didn't make the cut and that may never be released officially, although most are easy to find online. They include: "Alone With You" (defensive plea not to be criticized), "Back That Up (Do It)" "Eye Wide Open," "Freedom," "Heaven," **"God** Is Love," "La Isla Bonita" (Dubplate), "Never Let You Go," "Nothing Lasts Forever," "Queen" (originally called "God Save the Queen," it was written and produced by Madonna/The-**Dream**/Mike Dean, and has a tribal urgency to it as it touches on the world's fixation on conspiracy theories and dystopian fantasies),"Revolution," "Score" (juvenile **basketball**-as-sex ditty), "Take a Day" (feat. Pharrell Williams, it has a '60s sitcom–theme sound), "Take It Back," "Tragic Girl" (timeless and vulnerable ballad), "Trust No **Bitch**" (Question: How many songs with the word "bitch" in the title can exist from one era? Answer: Three! This one was written by Madonna/Martin Kierszenbaum/**Natalia Kills** and produced by Madonna/DJ Dahi/Blood Diamonds) and "Two Steps Behind Me" (shockingly underdeveloped anti-copycat song that could only be about **Lady Gaga**, though that reading was denied by **Guy Oseary**).

"UP DOWN SUITE": This B-side to the 12" maxi of **"Rain"** is a 12:17 club fantasia of epic distortions—it's essentially a hypnotic, long-winded dub created from the (at that point) **unreleased** song **"Goodbye to Innocence,"** which itself was discarded during the *Erotica* sessions when Madonna sang the lyrics to **"Fever"** over it, leading to "Fever" making the album in its stead. Lyrically, "Up Down Suite" uses the first verse from "Goodbye to Innocence," but is otherwise just Madonna chanting, "Up-up-up, down/Up-up-up,

down" and "oh" (and for some reason the "oh" gets louder briefly, at the 10:20 mark). You wouldn't guess it from this description, but it's actually the shit.

UP FOR GRABS: *Director: Laurence Boswell. Performance dates: May 9–May 22 (previews); May 23–July 13, 2002.* Madonna acted in a **play** for only the third time during her professional career when she appeared in a 10-week run of this 2001 play by David Williamson on **London**'s West End.

Once Madonna was announced to appear at the 700-seat Wyndhams Theatre (Charing Cross Road, London, England, UK), it sold out in 10 days. She earned £10,000 per week to play "Loren" (it had been "Simone" in the **original** version, but Madonna apparently didn't dig the name), a neophyte **art** dealer desperately attempting to sell a Brett Whitely painting for a cool $2 million during the dot com boom in 1990 in order to establish herself as a player in the market.

The play was directed by Laurence Boswell, who a decade later admitted that **working** with Madonna had been nightmarish. "If there's a way you could redefine and rebirth the word 'stress,' it would be that. It was utterly, utterly stressful. As soon as it started, my life disappeared," he told *The Telegraph* in 2010. "She has people in London, she has people in **New York**, she has people in Los Angeles. She is constantly firing out questions, worries, anxieties. From the minute I signed up, 24 hours a day, seven days a week, I was answering questions about the show and her involvement and how it would happen for her. So in the simplest terms, you're lifted into Madonna-land, which is ... incredibly intense."

By virtue of the fact that Madonna was the play's main attraction, and because it was a relatively new work, Madonna had an inordinate amount of **power**. The playwright said in 2010, "I was there for the first week of rehearsals in London ... It was fascinating to see how she operated. She was very aware of her power and exercised it and demanded rewrites that she assumed would suit her character. I either did them or the play didn't go on. I think the Australian version of the play was probably better."

Madonna's dressing-room door read "JUDI **FUCKING** DENCH."

Fans and press mobbed the theater for a glimpse of its star, "Madonna Ritchie," making it the spectacle of the season.

On Madonna's opening night, she received a standing ovation simply for showing up. Her appropriately manic performance went down well with audiences (early on, her **nerves** were noted) but was mostly written off, though not as savagely as past stage performance, by critics.

The author was in the front row, and while he would never attempt to defend Madonna's **acting** in *Body of Evidence* or *Swept Away*, would argue that she gave an interestingly vulnerable, confidently unconfident, relaxed and engaging lead performance. Particularly effective was her final defiant speech, ending with, "... I'll start again."

—DENNIS HENSLEY

©GEORGE-DUBOSE.COM

Madonna in "shy" mode (1981)

"MADONNA IS OFTEN FUNNY, AND SOMETIMES VULNERABLE AND TOUCHING. SHE LOOKS TERRIFIC, COMES OVER AS A FAR MORE APPEALING PERSONALITY THAN I EXPECTED, AND IS A DAB HAND AT COMICALLY KINKY SEX SCENES."–CHARLES SPENCER, *THE TELEGRAPH* (2002)

"A BETTER SCRIPT MIGHT HAVE TRULY EMBARRASSED A STAR WHOSE SPEAKING VOICE BETRAYS A TIMIDITY AND INEXPERIENCE FURTHER EXPOSED BY THE PREDOMINANTLY AMERICAN SUPPORTING CAST (THOUGH ON THE FIRST NIGHT, AT LEAST, MADONNA SOUNDED FAR STRONGER AFTER THE INTERMISSION)."

–MATT WOLF, *VARIETY* (2002)

A writer for the *Evening Standard* had come away "loving the dame" after the first performance, while the *Times of London* sniffed, "Great play, shame about Madonna."

At least Madonna's mom-in-law, Conservative Association chair Shireen Ritchie, liked it: "I really enjoyed the evening. There wasn't anything that was actually overt on stage."

"MADONNA IS NOT POSITIVELY BAD: JUST TECHNICALLY AWKWARD … THE DESIGN IS ELEGANT, FUNCTIONAL AND, IN ITS PROJECTED IMPRINTS OF NEW YORK, BEAUTIFUL. IT MAKES UP FOR THE NON-EVENT OF MADONNA'S PERFORMANCE WHICH, IRONICALLY, IN A PLAY ABOUT THE EXCESS VALUATION OF ART, SIMPLY CAPITALIZES ON HER EXISTING FAME."

–MICHAEL BILLINGTON, *THE GUARDIAN* (2002)

UPPER EAST SIDE: In 2009, Madonna paid $32 million (and pays $30,000 in taxes, quarterly) for a 12,000-square foot, red-brick Georgian townhouse at 152 E. 81st St., NY, NY. The triple-wide (57' across) place was extensively renovated, including gaining a level for a **gym**. With 13 bedrooms, 14 baths, a 19'×21' kitchen, a 38'×22' drawing room, a wine cellar, an elevator, a wood-paneled dining room, three pantries and nine fireplaces, the place's pièce de résistance is its 3,000 square-foot garden, the largest enclosed garden space in **NYC**.

The housekeeper who **worked** for the home's previous inhabitant (who lived there into her nineties) was quoted as saying, "Whoever lives in this house is going to be happy."

U.S. BLUES: *Formerly 1353 Old Northern Blvd., Roslyn, NY.* Also known as Uncle Sam's Blues, and not to be confused with Levittown's **Uncle Sam's**, this Long Island bar was open from 1978 to 1982. Madonna played here with the **Breakfast Club**, and it was here that she appeared solo (with backing band) after being guided by **Camille Barbone** in October 1981 (possibly consecutive shows on October 16 and 17).

Photographer **George DuBose**, who captured astounding pro images of Madonna at the club (which are for sale at RockPaperPhoto.com) remembers, "I was contacted by John Phillips, the bouncer at Hurrah's, who was sidelining as a radio promotions man and shopping Madonna's first demo to radio stations in **NYC**. He put me together with Camille of Empire Management, Madonna's manager. Camille asked me to go to Uncle Sam's Blues, a club in Roslyn, Long Island, and photograph just the singer, who was fronting a band … Onstage at U.S. Blues, I found this **sexy** young woman, wearing barely concealing costumes of chamois skin and foxtails. She was oozing sexuality, but seemed shy or unsure of herself. Nevertheless, she put on quite a performance."

GREGORY PACE

MATTHEW RETTENMUND

VAN LAMSWEERDE, INEZ & MATADIN, VINOODH: *b. September 25, 1963 & September 29, 1961, respectively.* Dutch **fashion** photographers and artists whose **work** makes use of extensive digital retouching, addressing issues of **sexuality** and gender. In 2013, they directed **Lady Gaga**'s gonzo "Applause" music video.

The duo shot Madonna for the April 1998 *Spin* cover, the **magazine**'s thirteenth anniversary. Madonna gazes regally from the cover, her chin tilted upward, her **eyes** locked with the viewer. Madonna looks very natural and austere in the shoot, with a sort of Judy Collins vibe. One of the images, an intentionally blurred, overlapping diptych, was chosen as the single cover of **"The Power of Good-Bye."**

VANILLA ICE: *b. October 31, 1967.* Everyone was shocked to see the has-been white rapper featured so prominently in cooler-than-cool Madonna's *Sex*. Rumors that Ice and Madonna were having an affair had been swirling since they went to see the movie *Frankie and Johnny* (1991) while they were on location in **Evansville** shooting *Cool as Ice* (1991) and *A League of Their Own* (1992), respectively. Ice was also by Madonna's side when she accepted a British *Smash Hits* **Award** on video.

He looked terrific in *Sex*, but as with **Justin Bieber**'s Calvin Klein fiasco in 2015, he was a bit passé for the room. Madonna said that he reminded her of, gulp, *Elvis Presley*.

Ice later 'fessed up to the relationship, detailing their "eight-month" fling.

"She would freak out, do weird, crazy things out of the blue. She would call me at strange hours, 'Are you in bed with another girl?' At six in the morning, I'm like, 'I'm **fucking** sleeping. All alone!'" He later said Madonna is "10 different people in one," and that he split when the relationship got too **serious**.

The straw that broke pre-**Eminem**'s **back** was the **book**. "I broke up with her after she printed [*Sex*] because I was hurt to be an unwitting part of this slutty package. We were in a relationship, yet it looked like she was screwing all these other people …"

> "She's got a great body for her age."
> —VANILLA ICE ON MADONNA (1994)

VANITY FAIR: Published since 1983, this high-gloss American **magazine** is self-consciously classy, yet affords the same sort of juicy dish that tabloids provide, (usually) with the cooperation of the celebrities. Madonna has been thoroughly documented in its pages via in-depth cover stories, the photo shoots from which are among her most iconic.

Along with all of the following **original** covers, images of Madonna have graced foreign editions.

On the December 1986 cover, Madonna looked like 18th century French royalty in a stunning image by **Herb Ritts**. The cover line, "Lady Madonna: A Change of Face," really summed it all up. Inside, Ritts captured Madonna in a sultry pictorial shot in **black-and-white** and tinted sepia and blue. Michael Gross's profile, "Classic Madonna," extracted delish quotes from Madonna, including regarding her first of many (many, many) transformations: "I wanted to change my clothes. You wait for things to cool off. You wait for your image not to be plastered up everywhere. It goes in cycles. If you've got a product, you promote it."

In April 1990, it was time to crank up the "White Heat" in a piece by Kevin Sessums. Sessums got Madonna to express herself while **Helmut Newton**—in his only shoot with Madonna—got her to undress herself; she bared a breast for the first time since becoming famous. Sessums bonded with Madonna over the loss of her **mother** at an early age. Madonna said, "I thought something horrible was going to happen to me when I turned 30. I kept thinking like this is it, my time is up." Would she die young like **Marilyn Monroe** had?

In April 1991, Lynn Hirschberg profiled Madonna as "The Misfit," a clear reference to Monroe (maybe the culture almost *wants* her to pull a Monroe, to fulfill some weird pop cultural destiny?), in a piece illustrated with all-time classic **Steven Meisel** portraits inspired by Monroe poses. The cover line, "Who Can Justify Her Love?" is a question for which we're still awaiting a reasonable reply.

Madonna's October 1992 cover was one of her most controversial for any magazine, a pose by Meisel in which she is styled to look like a young girl—a Lolita, to be more specific. Inside, the images play with an underage vibe, the edge taken off by a pastel, gauzy focus. At least one of the images—in which Madonna's bare breasts are framed by her wide-open cardigan, is a near-exact replication of an old *Playboy* pose. Maureen Orth did the editorial duties this time, in a piece entitled "Madonna in Wonderland." Madonna was still in full-on *Sex* mode, teasing, "I have a lot of fantasies about women, but I'm mostly fulfilled by being with a man." Meisel hubristically declared, "I don't think anyone else needs to do a photo essay on erotica—*Sex* is it."

Madonna had her mojo **back** by the time of the November 1996 cover story. The cover promised "The Madonna Diaries," and the inside delivered just that—extensive personal notes Madonna had taken during the filming of *Evita* and, as luck would have it, around the time when

"I've been provoking people since I was a little girl."
—MADONNA, *VANITY FAIR* (1986)

she first learned she was **pregnant**. The piece was extremely intimate, and the austere Evita looks as shot by **Mario Testino** so pleased Madonna that Testino became preferred photographer, shooting her next album cover (*Ray of Light*).

In a rare non-cover appearance, Madonna unsentimentally brushed off her *Evita* image with wasp-waisted, **art** deco showgirl shots by Ritts that were photographed on January 31, 1997, and that were contained inside the magazine's "Hollywood Issue" (April 1997). She was designated "The Icon" and listed as "actress, singer, diarist, madre."

Madonna's "Mother & Child" cover line for March 1998 promised exactly what the interior spread by Testino delivered—two beatific images of Madonna with her first child, **Lola**. Ingrid Sischy—who has profiled Madonna more times than any other writer—plumbed such topics as *Ray of Light*, Madonna as mother and even got Madonna to admit that *Sex* was "my own personal rebellion against my **father**." Reading the piece, it was hard to imagine Madonna would ever be racy again.

Madonna shared a cover with Rupert Everett in March 2000.

Probably Madonna's least resonant cover came in advance of her least impactful era. On the cover of the October 2002 issue, Madonna, shot by **Craig McDean**, appears in a sort of '40s WAC–meets–leather look. Inside, the '30s/'40s styling continues, but it's in pursuit of a somewhat well-played (and disconnected from her upcoming *American Life* album) **Marlene Dietrich** vibe. The article is even called, unimaginatively, "Madonna Marlene." Madonna was laying the groundwork for her next, more mature offerings, denying she felt competitive with younger artists. "I'm still going to write the music I want to write. I can't pretend I'm 18 years old."

For the mag's special **Africa** issue, guest-edited by Bono, Madonna and a host of other noteworthy figures posed for **Annie Leibovitz** on a series of July 2007 covers. Madonna had never posed for Leibovitz before, but the results were less than amazing—simple portraits on a red backdrop that Leibovitz **Photoshopped** to make it look as though Madonna were posing, on one, with Djimon Hounsou and, on another, whispering into Maya Angelou's ear.

Madonna's last (so far) cover for the mag came in May 2008, to promote *Hard Candy*. Madonna was, somewhat counterintuitively, chosen to cover the mag's "Green Issue," and was posed against a plaster mold of the world conceived by style director Michael Roberts, and shot by Meisel. The poses are Photoshopped grotesquely, while unretouched **leaks** to the Web are quite lovely. Rich Cohen's piece boorishly asked, "Madonna made her fortune selling **sex**—what will she sell when the thought of sex with

Madonna seems like a fetish?" She was 49 years old at the time.

We know why she hasn't posed for the magazine since.

"VENI VIDI VICI" FEAT. NAS: With an assist from Nas, Madonna quasi-raps about her entire career over a creeping beat on this *Rebel Heart* song. The song was written by Madonna, Toby Gad, **Diplo**, Ariel Rechtshaid, MoZella and Nas, with production by Madonna and Diplo.

"I don't like to dwell in the past," she has said of this song, "but it seemed like the right time to do so. After three decades, one has to look **back**."

Madonna said Nas was "incredibly gracious" when she asked him to collaborate on the song. "He just turned up one day all by himself—no bodyguards, no assistants, nothing—and listened to the track before saying, 'Yes, I'm in. I'll do it.' And now we're friends and I really like him."

VENICE FILM FESTIVAL: *Dates presented: 1932–.* Prestigious international film fest held annually in Venice. Madonna returned to the scene of her **"Like a Virgin"** video for the 68th edition of the festival (held August 31–September 10, 2011) to present, out of competition, her second directorial effort, *W.E.*

On September 1, 2011, at a press conference with Madonna and her cast, Madonna was given a bunch of **hydrangeas** by a "**fan**," leading to a hot-mic video that made her seem like an imperious **bitch**. That evening, she presented *W.E.*, appearing on the carpet in a playful, vibrant Vionnet dress decorated with butterflies. The next night, Madonna handed the inaugural Gucci **Award** for Women in Cinema to Jessica Chastain.

Unfortunately, Madonna's dress was some of the only good news out of Venice—her film received a drubbing from the critics.

"I can't think of a better example of a … intelligent, creative, dynamic woman than Madonna."—JESSICA CHASTAIN IN VENICE (2011)

VERONICA: Madonna's **Catholic** confirmation name. Madonna chose it because Veronica wiped the face of Jesus on his way to Calvary, which she found "very dramatic."

VERSACE: Italian **fashion** house founded by designer Gianni Versace (December 2, 1946–July 15, 1997) in 1978 with which Madonna has had close ties, thanks to her friendship with both Versace and his sister, Donatella Versace (b. May 2, 1955), who took over for him when he was murdered.

> "Others worry about marketing or what people will think, but Madonna doesn't care. She's herself. And best of all, she's daring." —DONATELLA VERSACE (2003)

In December 1994, Madonna posed for **Steven Meisel** as part of her first stint as the face of Versace, images that included a take on *Snow White* (Madonna lying on a flight of stairs, a once-bitten apple at hand) and wildly funny poses lunching with a **dog** and doing another's nails. The high **camp** was replaced by glamour-goddess sophistication in the ensuing shots she did for **Mario Testino** in Milan in summer 1995.

Donatella met Madonna in **Miami** for the first time and was surprised how vulnerable and yet direct she seemed. "The word 'icon' is overused, but in the case of Madonna I believe it has some meaning. She has become an icon because she has been able to constantly re-invent herself—always remaining contemporary. She is the symbol of a modern woman."

On Donatella's decision, Madonna was again chosen as the face of the brand in 2005 and was shot by Testino in jeans (does Madonna own jeans?) and a series of colorful looks fit for a (**business**) queen. "She is an innovator, a groundbreaker and the best in her field," Donatella proclaimed. "She relates to women of all ages, and she's got extraordinary personal style.

For the spring/summer 2015 campaign, Donatella Versace personally chose Madonna to replace **Lady Gaga** (nothing personal, somebody had to) as the face of Versace again, this time posing for **Mert and Marcus**. Donatella said, "Madonna says it best herself: She is unapologetic. She is her own woman, a **role model** who shows other women how we can do what we want, and get what we want, and do so for all of our lives, with no compromise."

Madonna said, "It's always exciting to be dressed head-to-toe in Versace and experience first-hand Donatella's vivid imagination and passion that she has created for this collection."

Madonna's body looked so bangin' in this latest Versace campaign that people talked about the excessive **Photoshop**, to which Donatella replied that the images were not retouched. Presumably, she meant Madonna's body didn't need to be slimmed.

Madonna's affection for the Versaces seems to be genuine, and goes beyond business. In *Time*, Madonna fondly related a story of the time she stayed in his Lake Como villa after shooting her second Versace campaign. She brought along her friend Marjorie Gross, who was dying of **cancer**. It was a wonderful **gift** for her friend, and Madonna never forgot the kindness the Versaces extended to them both.

"I slept in Gianni Versace's bed. Of course, he wasn't in it at the time, but I couldn't help feeling that I was soaking up some of his aura … I kept wanting to leap out of the bed and do things: write poetry, smell the gardenias and jasmine that surrounded the house, gaze out my window at the magnificent lake and press my face onto the cool marble of any number of naked-men **statues** that filled his bedrooms."

VH1: MTV's sister network that launched January 1, 1985, geared to a slightly more mature audience. Madonna was massive on VH1 in the '90s.

Interestingly, she managed to provoke controversy in 1993 via VH1 without even trying. The network bought space on **New York** City buses and at bus stops for ads featuring an image of Madonna from the **"Like a Prayer"** video juxtaposed with an image of Mary, **Mother** of **God,** and the tag line: "VH1: The difference between you and your parents."

Catholic groups denounced the ad as blasphemous and seemed to blame Madonna (the newer, **sexier** one), as if she'd been behind it herself. This has more than a little to do with the **power** of her "**control** freak" image.

VH1 FASHION AWARDS: *Dates presented: 1995–2002.* Madonna appeared at this ceremony on December 3, 1995, showing off three different looks and picking up **awards** for Most Fashionable Artist and Viewer's Choice. VH1 surprised her by having her ex **Sean Penn** pop up on stage to hand her her award.

On October 23, 1998, Madonna appeared at the slightly rebranded VH1/*Vogue* **Fashion** Awards at **Madison Square Garden**. She performed **"The Power of Good-Bye"** and won awards for Most Fashionable Artist, Most Stylish Music Artist and The **Versace** Award. She again appeared in multiple outfits.

VICODIN: When she broke her collarbone in 2005, the **drugs**-aversive Madonna tried this **powerful** painkiller because, "It was the most painful thing that happened to me in my life." This was after she'd given birth. *Twice.* Vicodin made her crazy, cranky and, "I just chewed the entire inside of my mouth." She was also offered Demerol, Xanax, Valium, and Oxycontin but was too afraid to try them. Morphine received a thumbs-up from Madge, a **nickname** you should only call her once she is wasted on it.

VICTOR, BARBARA: Journalist who wrote a biography of Madonna called *Goddess: Inside Madonna* that came out in 2001. The **book** was infamous for asserting that Madonna had had 11 **abortions** and trapped **Guy Ritchie** into marrying her by becoming **pregnant**. Madonna was so pissed off at this book that she did something she rarely does regarding bios—she had her publicist dismiss it on the record. Any book (including this one) on a person's life is going to have honest mistakes, but Victor's has so many right from the start that it's distracting. She also has some dubious-sounding sources. (How did she find the total stranger with whom Madonna crashed for two weeks when she first came to **NYC**, and how was his identity verified?) Yet, Victor *was* somehow able to secure interviews with Madonna's **father**, **grandmother** and some of her siblings.

—DON SHEWEY

VIDEO COLLECTION 93:99, THE: *Release date: November 2, 1999.* The video component of Madonna's *GHV2* contains her videos from 1993 until 1999, including: **"Bad Girl," "Fever," "Rain," "Secret," "Take a Bow," "Bedtime Story," "Human Nature," "Love Don't Live Here Anymore," "Frozen," "Ray of Light," "Drowned World/ Substitute for Love," "The Power of Good-Bye," "Nothing Really Matters"** and **"Beautiful Stranger."**

VIEW, THE: *Airdates: August 11, 1997-.* All-female talk show created by Barbara Walters and Bill Geddie. The show addresses all the news of the day, especially issues germane to the female experience, and frequently dissolves into shouting matches.

Madonna has often been rhetorically spanked by the hostesses over her various foibles, but she still taped an interview on the show on June 8, 2005, to discuss her children's **book** with Walters, **Joy Behar**, Star Jones and Elisabeth Hasselbeck.

This appearance became Madonna's only interview with the legendary Walters, who asked her for her thoughts on marriage. Madonna said true **love** isn't based on romance, it's the "... ability to love each other unconditionally."

VILLAGE VOICE, THE: *Publication dates: 1955-.* Madonna has a history with this **NYC** arts tabloid, which remains the country's best-known alternative newspaper. This was the paper she consulted, in her early days in the city, when looking for **jobs** (including **nude** modeling gigs) and when looking for a place to stay.

Madonna appeared in the "Getting & Spending: Things to Buy" column in the August 10–18, 1981, edition, illustrating the Linda Dyett article about chunky jewelry. A brunette Madonna posed for Fred Seidman. Her image, another by Seidman, appeared in the same column, this time written by **Michael Musto**, on March 2, 1982—Madonna was shown reading *101 Uses for a Dead Cat* (1981) by Simon Bond and *Three Hundred and One Things a Bright Girl Can Do* (1911) by Jean Stewart.

VIRGIN TOUR, THE: *Show dates: April 10–June 11, 1985.* Though she'd been borderline homeless only a few years earlier, Madonna was more than ready to show the world what she was capable of when the opportunity arose for her first tour. She knew exactly what she wanted, and she got it, auditioning musicians and **dancers** on both coasts. When it turned out that most of the people she wanted were based in LA, that became her tour HQ, where she assembled her creative war room and set about **working** with choreographer Brad Jeffries and musical director **Patrick Leonard** to serve up a show with sass, class and rocky versions of her string of big hits. Leonard, fresh off of the Jacksons' *Victory Tour,* would go on to become one of Madonna's most important collaborators, so she'd chosen particularly well with him.

ITINERARY

4/10-12-13	Seattle, WA	Paramount
4/15-16	Portland, OR	Schnitzer
4/19-20	San Diego, CA	Open Air Theater
4/21	Orange County, CA	Pacific Amphitheater
4/23	San Francisco, CA	Civic Auditorium
4/26-27-28	Los Angeles, CA	Universal Amphitheater
4/30	Tempe, AZ	ASU Activity Center
5/3	Dallas, TX	Civic Center
5/4	Houston, TX	Hofheinz Pavilion
5/5	Austin, TX	Frank Irwin Center
5/7	New Orleans, LA	Lakefront Arena
5/9	Tampa, FL	Sun Dome
5/10	Orlando, FL	Orange County Civic Center
5/11	Miami, FL	Sportatorium
5/14	Atlanta, GA	Omni
5/16	Cleveland, OH	Public Hall
5/17	Cincinnati, OH	Gardens
5/18	Chicago, IL	Pavilion
5/21	St. Paul, MN	Civic Center
5/23	Toronto, ON	Maple Leaf Gardens
5/25	Detroit, MI	Cobo Hall
5/28	Pittsburgh, PA	Civic Center
5/29	Philadelphia, PA	Spectrum
5/30	Hampton, VA	Coliseum
6/1	Washington, DC	Maryweather Post
6/2	Worcester, MA	Centrum
6/3	New Haven, CT	Coliseum
6/6-7-8	New York, NY	Music Hall
6/10-11	New York, NY	Madison Square Garden

VIRGIN TOUR SOLD OUT

The Virgin Tour itinerary and letter sent to fans by an early version of Madonna's fan club

The troupe rehearsed for several weeks in North Hollywood before switching to Hollywood Center Studios (1040 N. Las Palmas Ave., Hollywood, CA).

Even if the show had sucked, it would've been successful—it sold out all over after it was announced on March 15, 1985. In **NYC**, Madonnamania was in full swing as 17,672 tickets sold out for her show at **Radio City Music Hall** in 34 minutes flat, a new record, quickly following suit in the other cities she invaded.

Madonna's aptly named first full-scale tour was so hot that manager **Freddy DeMann**—who'd booked the relatively unknown **Beastie Boys** as her opening act—had to hustle to bump up the bookings from the small venues he'd originally scheduled. She was even able to pack them into **Madison Square Garden** for her final two shows.

Bill Lanphier, who played bass **guitar**/synth bass, told *MadonnaTribe* decades later that the first-night reception at the historic Paramount Theatre (901 Pine St., Seattle, WA) was, "Like nothing I'd ever been a part of. The **fans** went berserk. We could do no wrong." By the time they hit San Francisco, tour shirts sold at a rate of one every six seconds. (Due to its relatively brief itinerary, official *Virgin Tour* merch is hard to find these days.)

The tour's **look** was "Vegas urchin," with an array of changes in and out of brocade jackets, a faux **wedding** gown with "fun fur," **crucifixes** and peace symbols at every turn. Most prominent was her bare midriff, exposing the famous **belly button** that was getting so much press, and the tendency for her lacy bra to peek out from beneath a lavender halter with each shake and shimmy.

Madonna tore through her shows with the zeal of a new kid on the block, exuberantly proposing to her audiences—"Will you marry me?"—seducing them with her enthusiasm and with what had already become an impressive list of solid-gold hits.

"Dress You Up" made for a killer opening, establishing what is still some of Madonna's most imitated choreography and spawning a live music video that hit **MTV** in time to help the song go Top 5. At song's end, Madonna cleverly dressed herself down, removing her jacket by **Marlene Stewart**. Stewart had been hired instead of Madonna's pal **Maripol**, who nonetheless provided **accessories** and who told Madonna bluntly that the look was too similar to **Prince's**.

On **"Holiday,"** Madonna and her adorable dancers Elbee Johnson and Michael Pera danced their asses off in a preview of their **Live Aid** performance of the hit.

"Into the Groove" allowed for a great shout-out to the audience ("Now I know you're mine ... Dallas!") and featured Madonna tossing up and catching (usually) a tambourine.

"Everybody" may have been her most performed song by the time the tour rolled around, but Madonna totally **reinvented** the dance moves, seemingly asking for a little more Fosse.

She used **"Angel"** to get closer to the audience, but became a sort of go-go dancer for the fast-paced **"Gambler,"**

shaking her moneymaker in a new black outfit, barely able to maintain the pace and still sing. No guide vocals or Auto-Tuning in those days, folks, just scrupulous breathing.

She presented a shortened-but-still-sweet **"Borderline,"** and then **"Lucky Star"** in an uncomplicated way that echoed her music video.

On **"Crazy for You,"** Madonna delivered a large part of the song on her knees, crawling toward the lucky sumbitches in the front row. Her **voice** was up to the challenge of her first #1 ballad, sending the crowd into a frenzy.

"Who here has **dreams**?" Madonna asked ahead of the encouraging **"Over and Over,"** illustrated with '60s dance moves.

When she sang "I'm on fire!" in **"Burning Up,"** Madonna threw one of her dancers to the stage, bringing to life an implied three-way.

"Like a Virgin" was easy enough; all she had to do was wear a modified wedding gown and dance in a way that would

Original UK ad for "Gambler"

Madonna
GAMBLER

The New Single

Not Available On Any Other Madonna Album

Bet you can't wait till next week for it!

ALEJANDRO MOGOLLO

"She did things on that stage I never did with my husband!"
–"SOPHIA PETRILLO," *THE GOLDEN GIRLS* (1985)

remind her crowds of that **MTV Video Music Awards** performance. As a surprise, she threw in a big dose of **Michael Jackson**'s "Billie Jean" (1982). This became another live video for MTV.

She ended her first show in a fun fur stole, sending the kids home to the strains of **"Material Girl."** "Do you think I'm a material girl?" she asked. "Well, you're wrong!" She threw specially made **Madonna money** at the audience, finishing with a recording of a paternal voice demanding that she get home immediately. "Well, I'm not leaving without my fur!" her recorded reply pouted, and Madonna ran **back** out to the spotlight to retrieve it, the image she left her fans with after 70 minutes' worth of screaming their heads off.

THE VIRGIN TOUR PERFORMANCES

April 10,
April 12-13, 1985:
Seattle, Washington, US
(Paramount Theatre)

April 15-16, 1985:
Portland, Oregon, US
(Arlene Schnitzer
Concert Hall)

April 19-20, 1985:
San Diego, California, US
(SDSU Open Air Theatre)

April 21, 1985:
Costa Mesa, California, US
(Pacific Amphitheatre)

April 23, 1985:
San Francisco, California,
US (San Francisco Civic
Auditorium)

April 26-28, 1985:
Los Angeles, California, US
(Universal Amphitheatre)

April 30, 1985:
Tempe, Arizona, US
(ASU Activity Center)

May 3, 1985:
Dallas, Texas, US
(Dallas Convention Center)

May 4, 1985:
Houston, Texas, US
(Hofheinz Pavilion)

May 5, 1985:
Austin, Texas, US
(Frank Erwin Center)

May 7, 1985:
New Orleans, Louisiana, US
(UNO Lakefont Arena)

May 9, 1985:
Tampa, Florida, US
(USF Sun Dome)

May 10, 1985:
Orlando, Florida, US
(Orange County
Convention Center)

May 11, 1985:
Pembroke Pines, Florida, US
(Hollywood Sportatorium)

May 14, 1985:
Atlanta, Georgia, US
(The Omni)

May 16, 1985:
Cleveland, Ohio, US
(Public Auditorium)

May 17, 1985:
Cincinnati, Ohio, US
(Cincinnati Gardens)

May 18, May 20, 1985:
Chicago, Illinois, US
(UIC Pavilion)

May 21, 1985:
Saint Paul, Minnesota,
US (Saint Paul
Civic Center)

May 23, 1985:
Toronto, Canada
(Maple Leaf Gardens)

May 25-26, 1985:
Detroit, Michigan, US
(Cobo Arena)

May 28, 1985:
Pittsburgh, Pennsylvania,
US (Pittsburgh Civic Arena)

May 29, 1985:
Philadelphia, Pennsylvania,
US (The Spectrum)

May 30, 1985:
Hampton, Virginia, US
(Hampton Coliseum)

June 1, 1985:
Columbia, South Carolina,
US (Merriweather Post
Pavilion)

June 2, 1985:
Worcester, Massachusetts,
US (Worcester Centrum)

June 3, 1985:
New Haven, Connecticut,
US (New Haven Coliseum)

June 6-7, 1985:
New York, New York, US
(Radio City Music Hall)

June 10-11, 1985:
New York, New York, US
(Madison Square Garden)

> "YOU GOTTA HAVE A GREAT BEGINNING AND A GREAT MIDDLE AND THE BEST ENDING SO THAT THEY DON'T FORGET YOU WHEN THEY LEAVE."
> –MADONNA TO MOLLY MELDRUM (1985)

> "MADONNA … SIMPLY DIDN'T SING VERY WELL. HER INTONATION WAS ATROCIOUS; SHE SANG SHARP AND SHE SANG FLAT, AND THE COMBINATION OF HER UNSURE PITCH AND THIN, QUAVERY VOCAL TIMBRE MADE THE HELD NOTES AT THE END OF HER PHRASES SOUND LIKE THEY WERE CRAWLING OFF SOMEWHERE TO DIE … AND ONE HOPES THAT THE NEXT TIME SHE PERFORMS HERE, SHE WILL HAVE LEARNED NOT TO TOSS TAMBOURINES INTO THE AIR UNLESS SHE'S GOING TO BE ABLE TO CATCH THEM."
> –ROBERT PALMER, *THE NEW YORK TIMES* (1985)

> "[F]OR THE MOST PART, MADONNA'S SINGING WAS LIKE A SOUNDTRACK TO A MORE VISCERAL DISPLAY OF HERSELF, HER PERSONA, HER NONSTOP DANCING AND HER SURPRISINGLY EXPLICIT SEXUAL DARE, WHICH INCLUDED A VISUAL CLIMAX–SO TO SPEAK–TO EVERY SONG."
> –*VARIETY* (1985)

> "I IGNORED THE CRITICS BECAUSE I KNEW DEEP DOWN IN MY HEART THAT IT WAS GOOD AND … I WILL ALWAYS WILL MEET UP WITH A CERTAIN AMOUNT OF CONTROVERSY, A CERTAIN AMOUNT OF OPPOSITION TO WHAT I'M DOING."
> –MADONNA (1985)

> "PERHAPS EVERY GENERATION NEEDS REMINDING THAT ROCK AND SEX ARE SOMETIMES INDISTINGUISHABLE. AT THE MOMENT, MADONNA'S THE APOSTLE OF THE BODY GOSPEL, AND, AS HER SHOW MAKES APPARENT, IT'S HARD TO RECALL A MORE FETCHING ZEALOT."
> –PAUL EVANS, *RECORD* (1985)

COURTESY OF WILL MORGAN

The concert endeared Madonna to all her fans, many of whom were Madonna **wannabes** arriving in full **Boy Toy** regalia, threatening to make her a walking, talking *Rocky Horror Picture Show* (1975). Her performance was scrutinized cynically by rock critics, many of whom openly admitted in the text of their lukewarm-to-pukewarm reviews their inability to accept **sexuality** as part of artistic entertainment.

"What Madonna is really about is sex ..." Michael Goldberg huffed in his **Rolling Stone** recap of her Seattle debut, polarizing that aspect from the loftier aspects of music and dance, but missing the point that personality—often sexually charged—is on an equal par when it comes to any live performance.

The Virgin Tour was considered a guilty pleasure at best for the critics who praised it, but it has since attained a mythic status as containing Madonna's most accessible image and her most audience-friendly set list. She's become a much stronger performer since then, improving her voice, her dancing skills and her stage presence, even if she's never been so huggable. The tour grossed about $5 million, or just about what you'd expect to pay for restricted-view seats at a Madonna concert nowadays.

The tour was filmed and was packaged for home video as *Madonna Live: The Virgin Tour*.

VISION QUEST: *Director: Harold Becker. Release date: February 15, 1985.* Madonna's first post-**fame** film appearance was in this romance starring Matthew Modine as a high **school** athlete who falls in **love** with sultry older woman Linda Fiorentino. This is one film role in which Madonna *was* playing herself, a hot singer performing two songs in a club.

In *Vision Quest*, Madonna debuted her first hit ballad, **"Crazy for You"** and the mile-a-minute **dance** track **"Gambler."** Originally, she was to have sung another song; the **Stephen Bray** collaboration "Warning Signs" was listed on early promo material for the film but remains **unreleased**.

Her part was small, but Madonna made the most of it, connecting strongly and with magnetic confidence. Madonna shot *Vision Quest* in November 1983 on location in Spokane, Washington. The film wound up being a disappointment for producer Jon Peters, but it did manage $12,993,175 at the box office. In deference to Madonna-mania, it was released as *Crazy for You* in parts of Europe.

Photographer **Richard Corman**, who had already shot Madonna in her apartment, shot her performance stills, images that perfectly captured the image your mind calls up if someone says to you, "Madonna 1985."

RICHARD CORMAN

THEY HAD STYLE, THEY HAD GRACE:
STARS OF "VOGUE"

The centerpiece of Madonna's "Vogue" is her vocal rap immortalizing 16 famous faces representative of the type of glamour the song celebrates.

Herewith, all 16 stars of "Vogue," listed in order of appearance and with the order in which they died (#) and birth/death dates noted. Almost none of the stars commented on their inclusion in the song; to be fair, #1–#7 were all dead before it came out (the "Bette Davis—we love you!" line was clearly in reference to Davis's 1989 death). Garbo died three weeks after the song's release so probably never heard it.

The only "Vogue" star Madonna is known to have met was Gene Kelly, who almost worked with her on her *Girlie Show World Tour*.

#8 GRETA GARBO
(September 18, 1905–
April 15, 1990)

#3 MARILYN MONROE
(June 1, 1926–
August 5, 1962)

#9 MARLENE DIETRICH
(December 27, 1901–
May 6, 1992)

#13 JOE DIMAGGIO
(November 25, 1914–
March 8, 1999)

#15 MARLON BRANDO
(April 3, 1924–
July 1, 2004)

#2 JAMES DEAN
(February 8, 1931–
September 30, 1955)

#4 GRACE KELLY
(November 12, 1929–
September 14, 1982)

#1 JEAN HARLOW
(March 3, 1911–
June 7, 1937)

#12 GENE KELLY
(August 23, 1912–
February 2, 1996)

#6 FRED ASTAIRE
(May 10, 1899–
June 22, 1987)

#10 GINGER ROGERS
(July 16, 1911–
April 25, 1995)

#5 RITA HAYWORTH
(October 17, 1918–
May 14, 1987)

#16 LAUREN BACALL
(September 16, 1924–
August 12, 2014)

#14 KATHARINE HEPBURN
(May 12, 1907–
June 29, 2003)

#11 LANA TURNER
(February 8, 1921–
June 29, 1995)

#7 BETTE DAVIS
(April 5, 1908–
October 6, 1989)

"VOGUE" (SONG): *Release date: March 20, 1990. Billboard Hot 100 peak: #1.* Written by Madonna and **Shep Pettibone** and produced by Madonna, Pettibone and **Warner Bros. dance**-music exec Craig Kostich, "Vogue" is one of Madonna's biggest hits, inspired by the ballroom **vogueing** that Madonna witnessed in **gay** clubs in the late '80s.

Warren Beatty, Madonna's *Dick Tracy* director (and dick-delivery system) was looking for a pop song to help plug the movie and Warner Bros. was looking for a fresh B-side to help sell the *Like a Prayer* single **"Keep It Together."** Madonna had started **working** with remixer Pettibone, who whipped up the music. She wrote the lyrics on a flight, they recorded it and—as Pettibone's collaborator **Tony Shimkin** has said—it was clear that magic was being made in the studio.

Saved from B-side oblivion, "Vogue" became the lead single from *I'm Breathless: Music from and Inspired by the Film Dick Tracy* and sparked a dance craze. It's almost as hard to get through a **wedding** reception without hearing "Vogue" as it is to get through one without hearing Kool & the Gang's "Celebration" (1980).

The song reverentially provides the background on which the listener is invited to strut his or her stuff, listing celebrities of the past famous for giving good face. Madonna's lyrics baptize the dance floor as a place where no boundaries exist, where rebirth is possible, where a new life based on gesticulation can replace motionless and emotionless reality and anyone can become, if only for the duration of a song—or of one's stamina—a "superstar." Because of this and because it is so concerned with appearances, vogueing holds special appeal to its gay black and Latino pioneers, who know from experience that how you look sometimes defines who you are perceived to be. This was a message that resonated with Madonna, a woman often pigeonholed by how she looks.

Madonna has performed "Vogue" many times, including on her *Blond Ambition World Tour, Girlie Show World Tour, Re-Invention World Tour, Sticky & Sweet Tour* (mashed up with **"4 Minutes"**), *MDNA Tour* and *Rebel Heart Tour* (as part of **"Holy Water"**). She knocked it outta the park with the song at the **MTV Video Music Awards**, at the following night's **AIDS** Project Los Angeles performance at the Wiltern (3790 Wilshire Blvd., LA, CA) and made it a centerpiece of her **Super Bowl** halftime show.

"VOGUE" (VIDEO): *Director: David Fincher, 1990.* One of Madonna's most popular videos, a glamorous attitude-workout shot in **black-and-white** that presents Madonna in poses inspired by **Marilyn Monroe**, **Marlene Dietrich**, Bette Davis and **Veronica** Lake,

ALEJANDRO MOGOLLO

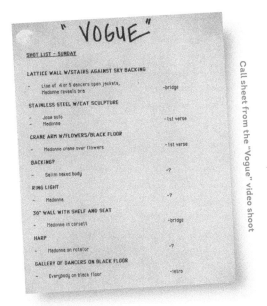

and, perhaps most thrillingly, bringing to life photographer Horst P. Horst's famous *Mainbocher Corset* photograph (1939) with a **sexy** wriggle.

"You can't fault her for taste," Horst's manager Richard Tardiff said at the time. "But the video should have been called 'Homage to Horst'. We just wish we could have **worked** something out beforehand—like doing an **original** photograph of her in the **nude**."

The video is directed with ruthless simplicity by **David Fincher**. His **memory** of how it came about mirrors that of the creation of the song: It was a quickie.

Fincher told *The Guardian*, "I had kinda talked Madonna into releasing **'Oh Father'** as a single and we did this video and we were very happy with the video and nobody ever saw it because the song wasn't a hit, so she came **back** to me and said, 'You screwed me up. You wanted to make this video for the song and no one liked the song and I went to bat for you and now I have to make a video by Tuesday.' And I said, 'What's the song called?' And she said, 'Vogue.'"

"Vogue" contains Madonna's most vigorous video dancing since **"Lucky Star."** She cuts a rug amid mirrors, feathers and her beautiful dancers and backup singers (including **Niki Haris** and **Donna De Lory**), who are photographed as if they were household names in their own right; all of them became **gay**-household names once they joined Madonna on her ***Blond Ambition World Tour***.

"It was one of those things where the DP, Pascal Lebegue—who's brilliant—literally showed up off the plane with his light meter and it was semi-pre-lit and he walked in and said, 'This, this, this, this,' and we shot the video for like 16 hours and we were done, that was it, she got on the plane and went on her world tour," Fincher said.

Madonna has never looked more gorgeous, nor has her form been better utilized. "Vogue" is widely accepted as Madonna's best music video.

"VOGUE" BOYS: In 2011, lifelong Madonna **fan** Robert E. Jeffrey a.k.a. Angelo de Vries (RobertJeffrey.blogspot.com) posted a video of himself as a kid that was shot in the summer of 1991 at Hampton Beach Casino (169 Ocean Blvd., Hampton Beach, NH) lip-synching to **"Vogue."** In front of a blue-screened cityscape, he shook his ass and recreated Madonna's moves from the video with utter

"Vogue" is surely Madonna's ultimate visual statement.

abandon. There is something not only cute but empowering about seeing this kid expressing himself so unselfconsciously. His video deservedly became a viral sensation. Thus, Vogue Boy #1 was born.

In 2012, Vogue Boy #2, Shaun Sperling (ShaunSperling.blogspot.com) posted a strikingly similar video, shot at his Madonna-themed March 14, 1992 bar mitzvah in the grand ballroom of the Hyatt Deerfield (1750 Lake Cook Rd., Deerfield, IL). In the video, the shameless Oy toy does Madonna's moves in spite of wearing his dress clothes and a tie. It was shot on the day he became a man, but had he become a woman instead, she surely would've been **blonde**. Sperling rode his 15 minutes hard and put them away wet, doing press, getting invited to see Madonna appear on *The **Ellen DeGeneres** Show* (he was originally going to be a guest but wound up in the audience, interacting with Madonna from afar) and getting to sing a verse of **"Like a Prayer"** into Madonna's mic at her Chicago *MDNA Tour* stop.

Between them, these "Vogue" Boys have demonstrated that when it comes to loving and dancing like Madonna, it makes no difference if you're a boy or a girl.

VOGUEING: Hilariously ostentatious form of **dance** that emerged in the '80s ballroom **drag** scene in Harlem. The dancer mimics—and makes broader—the haughty movements of a wealthy woman, with a major dose of catwalk swish. Madonna, an avoid club-goer, first took note of the phenomenon on a night out at the **gay** club Sound Factory (formerly 12 W. 21st St., NY, NY) with her friend **Debi Mazar**. She was smitten, and almost immediately incorporated vogueing into her act, debuting some moves in her 1989 **MTV Video Music Awards** performance of **"Express Yourself."**

A year after pop cultural gadfly **Malcolm McLaren** released his own vogueing single, "Deep in Vogue," Madonna offered her tribute to the **art** form with the 1990 single **"Vogue."** It quickly became one of her signature hits, and has been a staple of her career as a live performer.

Madonna has been criticized for "stealing" vogueing, but such arguments of **cultural appropriation** fail to take into account the fact that Madonna has always acknowledged the origins of the dance—and, breaking news, Madonna didn't invent **disco**, either, but that doesn't mean she's stealing it every time she sings some.

Kurt Cobain, while otherwise casting aspersions on Madonna's musical sincerity in 1992, told **MTV**, "... I respect Madonna for the things that she has introduced, because she has introduced some subversive things and it has nothing to do with **sex**, as far as I'm concerned. I'm talkin' about, like, the, um, introduction to the vogue dance, which originated in the gay clubs ..."

VOICE: Madonna's true claim to **fame** is her singing career, despite having a voice that was never as technically strong as the voices of peers like **Mariah Carey** or **Whitney Houston**. That her voice is fragile and wears out easily (compare her vocals at the first and last stops on any given tour) is certain. That she is, as some critics (and lots of people who've figured out how to tweet) allege, a lousy singer, is *not*.

Madonna may not have the range of some singers, but her voice makes up in sincerity for what it lacks in note-by-note perfection. Madonna-**haters** can't understand how her admirers can find her voice appealing, but it's a lovely pop instrument with more personality than most opera divas can muster.

"I think she has the perfect pop voice," singer Joan Armatrading said in 1986, giving Madonna a little **love** and affection. But Billy Joel razzed her while using some throat spray before a 2014 concert, announcing, "I saw Madonna use this once ... it didn't help her much."

Regardless of any other trappings, Madonna's voice is always laced with immediacy and emotion. She imbues even her most pedestrian lyrics with a sense of purpose, as she does with the simple romantic ballad, **"La Isla Bonita,"** which was one of her biggest international hits, partially because she emotes the longing that the straightforward lyrics specify.

"Madonna may not be remembered in the annals of pop music history for having the greatest singing voice ever to grace a recording," biographer **J. Randy Taraborrelli** wrote in 2001. "That voice, however, will most certainly be noted for its emotional quality. In her own way, Madonna sold **'Open Your Heart'** as convincingly as Aretha Franklin sold 'Respect' [1967]; as heartfelt as **Barbra Streisand** rendered 'A House is Not a Home' [1971]."

In 2009, Madonna identified **working** the **Andrew Lloyd Webber** and **Tim Rice** material from *Evita* as her greatest challenge. "It's a whole different singing sensibility." In order to embrace that sensibility, Madonna—already a phenomenally successful singer—humbly took months of vocal lessons. The result was a significant change; she was able to access new parts of her voice. Madonna's new range was evident on the new songs on *Something to Remember*, on *Evita: The Complete Motion Picture Music Soundtrack* and on every album going forward, particularly *Ray of Light*.

Even after Madonna's voice improved, it's still often asserted that it's weak or that she "always" lip-synchs. In 2015, when Madonna's **Grammy** vocals on **"Living for Love"** were isolated, the video went viral—not because she sounded awful, but because she sounded pretty on-point. With Houston's voice lost to **drugs** before her untimely **death** and Carey's own deteriorating range, somehow, the girl who started out with the least voice looks to be ending up with the most.

"VOICES": The haunting, Queen-like final song on *Hard Candy*, written by Madonna/**Timbaland/Justin Timberlake/Danja** and Hannon Lane, and produced by all of the same artists, minus Madonna.

—KIESZA

"MADONNA DOES AT LEAST PROVE THE EXISTENCE OF A VOICE. LIKE EVELYN KING, OR EARLY DIANA ROSS, IT HAS A FRAILTY AND GIRLIE SWEETNESS TO COMPENSATE FOR WHAT IT LACKS IN GUTS: CROSSOVER POTENTIAL TO THE MAX."-JAMES TRUMAN, *THE FACE* (1983)

"MADONNA IS AN ARTIST WITH ONE OF THE MOST LUSCIOUS VOICES I HAVE EVER HEARD—SOFT, POWERFUL AND VERY APPEALING … REGGIE LUCAS HAS PROVIDED AN IDEAL MEDIUM IN WHICH MADONNA WILL BE MOST RECOGNIZED AS A TRUST ARTIST AND ENTERTAINER."
—DAVE PEASLEE ON "BURNING UP"/"PHYSICAL ATTRACTION," *DANCE MUSIC REPORT* (1983)

"IN TRUTH, SHE IS AN INDIFFERENT SINGER, BUT HER VOICE HAS THE WHISPERED ASSURANCE OF ONE OF THOSE PHONE-FOR-SEX GIRLS."
—*TIME* (1985)

"HER SOUND IS HER OWN; HER VOLUPTUOUS VOICE, SOMETIMES SUGARY AND HIGH, SOMETIMES STEAMY AND LOW, DELIVERS A VITALITY, A *HUMANNESS*, THAT'S MORE BEWITCHING THAN ANY OF HER GLAMOUR-GIRL POSES AND MORE LUMINOUS THAN HER FAME. MANY OF HER ORIGINAL LYRICS MAY BE LITTLE MORE THAN ROMANTIC CLICHÉS, BUT LIKE GIRL-GROUP DIVAS RONNIE SPECTOR, DARLENE LOVE, AND MARY WEISS (THE SHANGRI-LAS), MADONNA USES HER WHOLEHEARTED SINGING TO ENRICH HER WORDS."
—JOYCE MILLMAN, *BOSTON PHOENIX* (1986)

"I'VE HEARD THE TALK ABOUT HOW MADONNA CAN'T SING, AND I CAN TELL YOU THAT'S BULL. SHE'S A NATURAL, INTUITIVE SINGER WITH GREAT INTONATION, AND SHE PUTS ACROSS A VULNERABLE QUALITY THAT YOU CAN'T COPY, AND I KNOW BECAUSE I'VE HEARD PEOPLE TRY."
—PATRICK LEONARD (1987)

"HERS IS ONE OF THE MOST COMPELLING VOICES OF THE '80S."—*ROLLING STONE* (1989)

"I'M NOT A GREAT LOVER OF MADONNA'S VOICE. SHE'S DONE VERY WELL WITH WHAT SHE'S GOT AND I'M SURE MY VOICE TURNS HER RIGHT OFF, BUT SHE'S NOT MY FAVORITE SINGER."
—ROD STEWART (2006)

VON UNWERTH, ELLEN: *b. 1954.* **Fashion** photographer whose **sexy** work dominated *Vogue* in the '90s and who shot *those* Guess Jeans ads starring Claudia Schiffer. She was slated to direct the **"Bad Girl"** video after Tim Burton backed out, but her schedule didn't permit, and bad boy **David Fincher** took over.

Von Unwerth shot Madonna exclusively for *Vogue Paris*'s October 1993 issue to promote *The Girlie Show World Tour*, rendering her in stark **black-and-white** with heavily kohled **eyes**. She shot Madonna a second time for four different covers of the May 2015 *Cosmopolitan*, showing Madonna in full sex-kitten (and *Playboy* bunny) mode.

VON WERNHERR, OTTO: Mysterious German avant-garde singer who was involved with Madonna's pre-**fame** film *A Certain Sacrifice*, appeared in the cult film *Liquid Sky* (1982), was a veteran of episodes of the daytime soap *The Edge of Night* (1956–1984) and—most famously —is the alien-sounding **voice** on a series of records featuring bizarrely edited vocals by Madonna. Madonna was paid to do some backing vocals for von Wernherr in 1981, and they were later remixed into oddball punk **dance** songs and licensed all over the world by **Mia Mind Music** as singles.

The songs von Wernherr released (he was sued but prevailed) were "Cosmic Climb," "Dance to the Beat," "Get Down," "Give It To Me" (not *that* one), "Let's Go Dancing," "Life Is a **Bitch** (And Then You Die)," "Oh My!!!," "On the Street," "Shake," "Time to Dance," "We Are the **Gods**" and "Wild Dancing."

Von Wernherr, who also performed the **parody** song "Madonna Don't Preach" and appeared in the video, disappeared with his wife and child into Europe in the late '80s after suffering from a serious illness. Any information on where he ended up has thus far eluded Madonna scholars.

"Of course I tried to pick her up–she would stand against a telephone pole and smile at me–but it was only out of animal habit."—OTTO VON WERNHERR ON MADONNA (1986)

FABIO DIENA

WAHLBERG, MARK: *b. June 5, 1971.* Impossibly well-built Boston rapper, famous for his shirtlessness and the playful wink of his peekaboo **underwear**, he hit it big with his Funky Bunch and their "Good Vibrations" single in 1991, and even bigger as a Calvin Klein model along with waif Kate Moss from 1992 till the end of 1993.

Who could have guessed he would achieve even more success as one of Hollywood's biggest actors and producers, starring in movies both amazing (*Boogie Nights* in 1997) and amazingly popular (*Ted* in 2012)? He produced *Entourage* (2004–2011), not to mention the **Oscar**-nominated *The Fighter* (2010).

But **back** to his Marky Mark incarnation, because that's when Madonna first noticed him. In 1991, she said, "I turn the TV on and there's a boy in his underwear—for 20 minutes. I thought *I* was bad. He's *very* cute. He's adorable. What else can he do?"

Wahlberg allegedly said after meeting her in 1992, "I always thought she was at least 'cute.' When I met her, she looked like **fucking** 'Beetlejuice.'"

Which brings us to 1993, when Wahlberg reportedly sparred with Madonna at a **birthday** party for **Alek Keshishian** thrown by Gerry and Angela Janklow Harrington. The story, depending on whom you believe, is either that Wahlberg, fresh from making public amends for the minority-bashing he indulged in as a teen (something that would tarnish his image decades later), called **Guy Oseary** a "homo," decked him, exchanged obscenities with Madonna, and was ejected from the party; or that Madonna, still smarting from his slam, deliberately provoked a brawl that got him ejected from the party and earned him grief from his **gay** following.

That Wahlberg defended righteous dancehall rapper Shabba Ranks for his belief that gays should be "crucified" does not help his cause, but Wahlberg has since denied being homophobic, whether sincerely or cynically. Madonna didn't comment on the brouhaha, but Wahlberg told *The Advocate* in 1994 that what happened was he saw her at the party and said, "What's up, Madonna?" to which she replied, "Don't fucking say hi to me. You know what the fuck you fucking did. You dissed me. You're a fucking asshole, a fucking fake ... I'm going to get somebody to kick your ass." Years later, his story changed. He whined that he'd almost missed out on his role in the 1994 film *Renaissance Man* because, "I got into a fight at a party in LA with three guys and broke a guy's nose. It was a few of Madonna's people, so she called the fucking cops on me. Told everybody this bullshit story that I was doing shit that I wasn't. [**Penny Marshall**, the producer] called me saying, 'What the fuck did you do?', but then she was like, 'Fuck that, I'm giving you the part anyway.'"

"I mean, honestly, I had a lot of respect for her. I think she's very talented. She's very smart. She does a lot of good. As much as she promotes wild sex, she does a lot for AIDS research ..."—MARKY MARK ON MADONNA, *THE ADVOCATE* (1994)

You decide. The lady ... or the rapper?

Hostess Janklow Harrington quipped at the time, "Thank **God** that happened—it was such a bad party!"

WAINWRIGHT, RUFUS: *b. July 22, 1973.* Snobbish singer-songwriter who recreated—live—Judy Garland's Carnegie Hall concert album from 1961 and wrote an opera, among other things that make him better than you, dear.

He's no Madonna **fan**, telling *Attitude* in 2007, "I consider her to be the end of the idea of Western Culture as a viable response to humanity. There are a few great tracks in there and she was the most incredible model ever, for photographs ... But culture-wise and the mindset that she spawned is completely toxic. It's horrible. I can't even come up with words to describe that mindset, it's so repulsive to me."

In 2012, he dissed **Lady Gaga's music**, and compared her unfavorably to Madonna because Gaga's shtick is "you're like me" whereas Madonna was "you'll *never* be like me."

"WAITING": An *Erotica* track cowritten and coproduced by Madonna and **Andre Betts** that's all about anticipating (without using the actual word, which is a staple of Madonna song lyrics). The song was reworked into another track that also appears on the album, **"Did You Do It?"** feat. Mark Goodman and Dave Murphy, and remixed with alternate vocals as the B-side of **"Rain."**

WALKEN, CHRISTOPHER: *b. March 31, 1943.* Towering, terrifying actor known for the kinds of roles about which casting directors could only say, "Get me Christopher Walken."

Walken appears in the **"Live to Tell"** video, and starred opposite Madonna in her video for **"Bad Girl"** as her character's guardian angel ... of **death**. He told **Jonathan Ross** how it came about: "Well, I, I, I had known Madonna for a long time, from, uh, when she was married, married to **Sean Penn**. I had been **working** with, uh, uh, with him right before they were married." He said of Madonna, "I like her very much."

Walken attended Madonna's **wedding** to Penn, and saw her in *Speed-the-Plow*.

"WALTZ FOR EVA AND CHE": Vocally **taxing** duet between Madonna and **Antonio Banderas** from *Evita* found on *Evita: The Complete Motion Picture Music Soundtrack* that was brought to life on screen via a physically demanding waltz, a major challenge for a **pregnant** Madonna. This became her first—but not her most famous—song with the word "bourgeoisie" in its lyrics.

WANNABE: In 1985, when **"Like a Virgin"** went nuclear, a spate of teenage girls (and, at home in the **privacy** of their rooms, not a few teenage boys) began dressing and **acting** like Madonna, copying her revealing clothes, mesh gloves, sunglasses and streaked, tousled **hair**. These were the

"I'd like to see every teenage girl in America dressed up like me. Why not?"—MADONNA (1985)

Madonna wannabes. Though their numbers and fervor have diminished through the years along with Madonna's growing movement toward adult themes, wannabes persist to this day.

The first known use of the word was in 1981, so its association with Madonna occurred very shortly after it came to be. In 1990, the word was added to *Webster's Dictionary*.

WARD, SELA: *b. July 11, 1956*. Striking **TV** actor known for *Sisters* (1991–1996).

Madonna bought a $12 million, 16,500-square-foot French chateau–style home in Beverly Hills from Ward in 2003, selling it 10 years later for $20 million.

WARD, TONY: *b. June 10, 1963*. Madonna's onetime boyfriend is now one of the most famous male models of all time.

Ward got his start posing **nude** for Jim French and others under the names "Franco Kier" and "Tony Troy." He was intrigued by the interest his naked body generated, recalling an elderly photographer "shaking" when he disrobed. Ward has said, "The first person who ever told me I was beautiful was a man ..."

A **gay** man (**Christopher Flynn**) was the first person to tell Madonna she was beautiful, too.

Ward **worked** as a model for the likes of Greg Gorman, **Bruce Weber** and **Steven Meisel**, and starred in Bruce LaBruce's **Warholian** feature film *Hustler White* (1996). He was a featured interview subject in *Sex Life in LA*, a 2000 documentary about "young men who earn their livings with their bodies."

In the late '80s, Ward became a favorite subject of Madonna's preferred photographer **Herb Ritts**. Ward knew Ritts worked with her and pushed for an introduction, but Ritts "kinda didn't rush into that." Ritts hired Ward to portray one of the mermen in Madonna's **"Cherish"** video, but the two did not interact during filming.

They're real ... and they're spectacular!

Ward, you were a little hard on the Beaver last night ... Madonna and Tony at an AIDS event

Instead, Ward has said he bumped into Madonna organically at Ritts's studio. "I've always been in **love** with her, I've always had a very strong, **powerful** feeling for that woman, not exactly knowing why because I was not a **fan** of her music—I just loved her."

Once Ward had made Madonna's acquaintance, he had a more famous encounter with her months later in August 1990 at a joint **birthday** party for Ritts and Madonna. "I was completely **fucked** up on **drugs** and alcohol ... I hear this, this *voice* ... she wanted to introduce me to **Alek Keshishian**; she wanted to hook him up because she thought I was gay. Before I knew it, [Madonna and I] were kissing and **acting** like children, really." The rumors are true—Madonna really *did* boldly put out a cigarette on Ward's **back**, and she really *did* say she thought she could balance a drink on his ass.

Four days after the Ritts party, on August 21, 1990, Ward got married, something he neglected to let Madonna know. It was a marriage of convenience to Greek national Amalia Papadimos, a photographer, and was a development he managed to keep secret throughout most of his time with Madonna.

Nonetheless, for many fans, Ward seemed to be Madonna's perfect mate: His unorthodox, edgy look was an admittedly fine complement to Madonna's, and his adventurousness in front of a camera was in a league of its own compared to ex-hubby **Sean Penn**'s stick-in-the-mud attitudes.

When the tabloids gleefully reported that nudes of Ward had once appeared in the gay (gasp!) **porn** mag *In Touch for Men* (#101, March/April 1985), Madonna shrugged it off, mirroring her response when her own early-years nudes had found their way into *Playboy* and *Penthouse*. The credits for Ward's shoot were: "Photographed by Blue Leader. Camera by Canon, sweatpants by Big 5, socks by Calvin Klein, linens by Vera, carpet by Dynasty, scent by Old Spice, body by **God**, financial partner? New **England** Life, of course." So who supplied the saucy ankle bracelet? Some of the same photos, along with fresh outtakes, were reprinted in *In Touch for Men* (#168, February 1991) under the title "**Boy Toy**."

And yes, one *could* feasibly balance a drink on his ass.

Ward and Madonna were a very public couple at events like the **AIDS** Project Los Angeles benefit on September 7, 1990, at which Madonna performed **"Vogue,"** and the premiere of *GoodFellas* at the MoMA (11 W. 53rd St., NY, NY) on September 18, 1990. On October 19, 1990, the jet-setting lovers were photographed by Ritts in a series of impromptu images taken backstage at a **Jean Paul Gaultier** show. Three weeks later, Ward joined Madonna in **Paris**, where he became her most prominent costar in her sizzling **"Justify My Love"** video. Madonna was widely reported to have terminated a problem **pregnancy** by Ward on

ALAN LIGHT

December 14, 1990, at Cedars-Sinai Medical Center (8700 Beverly Blvd., LA, CA).

A tempestuous pair, they broke up in February 1991 when Madonna discovered Ward's marriage. She bemoaned single life in May 1991 while at **Cannes**, got back together with Ward the same month and attended the Love Ball II gala to benefit DIFFA (the Design Industries Foundation Fighting AIDS) on May 22, 1991, at the **Roseland Ballroom**. Their last public appearances as a couple were the August 7, 1991, LA premiere of *Paris Is Burning* (1991) and Madonna's birthday that same year.

Madonna later called Ward to pose for *Sex* in early 1992.

WARHOL, ANDY: *August 6, 1928–February 22, 1987.* Pop **art** pioneer famous for his hyperliteral interpretations of ordinary objects, like Campbell's soup cans, as well as his confoundingly plotless, absorbing/banal films. Warhol was sort of the aesthetic overlord of the downtown **New York** scene from the '60s until his **death** following routine surgery.

Madonna was acquainted with Warhol, who was close friends and a collaborator with **Keith Haring** and **Jean-Michel Basquiat**. Warhol served as a celebrity judge at a chaotic Madonna look-alike contest at Macy's on June 6, 1985, saw Madonna perform in *Goose and Tomtom* and photographed her from time to time, albeit sparingly (at her *Like a Virgin* album-release party on November 7, 1984, with **Jellybean Benitez**; also, going incognito in a brunette bob on November 17, 1984). His only finished Madonna art pieces outside of snapshots are tabloid covers with news of Madonna's **nude** photos that he painted in conjunction with Haring.

Madonna has recalled hanging out with Warhol in combos including **Martin Burgoyne**, Haring and **Basquiat**. Madonna was closer to each of them than she was to Warhol, who she says "didn't talk that much."

In his infamous, posthumously published diaries, Warhol praised Madonna's *Virgin Tour* and commented on her favorably quite a few times. Had he lived, it's impossible to believe that Warhol wouldn't have eventually immortalized Madonna as he did **Marilyn Monroe**. *The Andy Warhol Diaries*, edited by Pat Hackett (Warner **Books**, 1989), is chock-full of Madonna references, but there's no index. Take note of pages: 574, 599, 613, 616, 632, 637, 648, 649, 655, 665, 667, 669, 670, 671, 674, 675, 687, 693, 698, 706, 718, 728, 750, 754, 755, 756, 762, 765, 772, 773, 778 and 779.

> "... Madonna really knows how to do her makeup in that great Hollywood way."
> —ANDY WARHOL (1985)

WARNER BROS. RECORDS: Mega-corporation that is the parent company of **Sire Records**, the first label to sign Madonna. **Maverick** was also under the Warner umbrella. Beginning with Madonna's rise in the '80s, Warner's fortunes became increasingly dependent on the girl's material. It was said that as Madonna went, so went Warner Bros.

In 2007, Madonna went—she signed a massive deal with **Live Nation** for all music-related **business**, sublicensing to **Interscope** for album distribution.

"WASH ALL OVER ME": This *Rebel Heart* song has the dubious distinction of being one of the first two tracks to **leak**. Artistically, it features Madonna's most vulnerable vocal in ages. The song was written by Mike Dean, Magnus Lidehäll, **Avicii**, Arash Pournouri, Salem Al Fakir, Vincent Pontare, **Kanye West**, TB and Madonna, and produced by Madonna, West, Dean and Charlie Heat.

WAX, RUBY: *b. April 19, 1953.* Brassy comedian born in the US who lives in the UK, where she has for 30 years played an exaggerated version of a loud-mouthed American. In the '90s, she hosted a series of *Ruby Wax Meets* interview specials.

On October 23, 1994, the BBC presented the special *Ruby Wax Meets Madonna*, in which Madonna—promoting *Bedtime Stories*—huddled in a hotel bed with Wax.

Madonna was a high-maintenance subject, but seemed to have fun, cracking herself up while telling Wax to always keep her chin up on camera ("You never wanna get a **Shelley Winters** thing happening ...") and then bossing the cameramen like she was Miss **Barbra Streisand**.

One line of questioning that touched a nerve was when Wax encouraged Madonna to let go of her vanity and Madonna wanted to know, "Can't I be funny and pretty?" Wax declared it impossible. She also **worked** up the courage to ask Madonna about **Warren Beatty**, whose brain Madonna readily admitted to having picked.

"I was just shitting myself with **nerves**, looking for some topic to talk about ... she's more famous that I'll ever **dream** of, and talented," Wax told *Attitude* in 2002. "I was a **fan** then. I don't know now ... **God** knows what she's like as a person, I never cracked it. I couldn't. It was really uncomfortable. Not because of her, but because there were 30 people standing there three feet out of shot, watching and laughing every time she opened her mouth."

WAZOO: Clothing manufacturer behind Madonna by Wazoo, a line that in 1985 offered French terry cowl neck tops (probably made from spare washcloths) with matching skirts, suspender dresses, a brocade waiter's jacket, fitted cotton pants, bras as outerwear, and **BOY TOY** belts for under $40 to teenage girls. A breathless *Bop* **magazine** editorial at the time pointed out that "Madonna personally helped the designers create her very unique look down to every last detail." The magazine also praised the line's see-through lace skirts "for a sheer and ultra-**sexy** look!"

W.E.: *Director: Madonna. Release date: February 3, 2012.* Though she had directed *Filth and Wisdom* a few years prior, Madonna seemed to offer *W.E.* (which she pronounces "we") as her feature directorial debut.

—SCOOTER LAFORGE

Directing from a script she cowrote with longtime friend and collaborator **Alek Keshishian** (***Truth or Dare***), Madonna uses the film to tell the historical story of the romance between Wallis Simpson (Andrea Riseborough) and King Edward VIII (James D'Arcy), simultaneously telling the make-believe **love** story between modern-day Simpson fangirl "Wally Winthrop" (Abbie Cornish) and museum guard "Evgeni" (Oscar Isaac), set around the 1998 **auction** of the Duke and Duchess's belongings at Sotheby's. A woman famous for looking forward made a movie set entirely in the past.

Madonna wrote *W.E.* over two and a half years, ignoring her music. She brought in Keshishian because, "I quite like the idea of collaborating in general. Not only is it lonely to do things on your own creatively, it's also kind of arrogant. I guess some people are brilliant enough to be brilliant on their own and never doubt anything and come up with fabulous things. But I think it's good to get into arguments with people and have them say, 'That sucks' or 'You're crazy' or 'That's cheesy' or 'What do you think of this?'" she told ***Interview*** in 2010.

The film was first put before a test group—with no credits or advance info given—on June 13, 2011, at the AMC Loews Lincoln Square (1998 Broadway, NY, NY). The recruited audience watched the film, filled out typical two-page surveys littered with questions about which parts of the movie were slow, which performances **worked** and what types of films they normally enjoy. In the surveys, *W.E.* was implicitly compared to: *Babel* (2006), *Blue Valentine* (2010), *The Duchess* (2008), *The Illusionist* (2006), *Jane Eyre* (2011), *The King's Speech* (2010), *Marie Antoinette* (2006), *A Mighty Heart* (2007), *The Queen* (2006), *The Reader* (2008), *Revolutionary Road* (2008) and *Water for Elephants* (2011).

Madonna and **Harvey Weinstein**, whose company was distributing *W.E.*, snuck into the **back** of the screening to listen to viewers' responses to the film, which were mixed but generally positive. When, toward the end, one audience member said he'd been attracted to the film because of its director, the others expressed confusion and were told that Madonna was the auteur. The response to the film changed almost instantly. Madonna left, while Weinstein moved up to within two rows of the test group.

When the film premiered, the reviews were mostly dismissive, questioning Madonna's motives in romanticizing a couple of (alleged) Nazi sympathizers. Guess that made Madonna a Nazi sympathizer sympathizer? Another criticism was that the film was obsessed with style, though its few positive reviews gave Madonna credit for its look.

W.E. is not a masterstroke, but like many of Madonna's projects, it was unfairly brutalized.

Madonna uses the modern and historical halves of her film to comment on each other, creating a surprisingly old-fashioned "woman's picture," as they were called in the '30s and '40s. Madonna knows how to make a scene, but

here she also demonstrates her ability to create a mise-en-scène, the modern part of the film looking **dream**-like, while the historical part has a crisp **beauty** enhanced by **award**-worthy **Arianne Phillips** costumes. The entire thing is uplifted at every turn by Abel Korzeniowski's out-of-*this*-world and into-*that*-world score.

If only Madonna and Keshishian had produced a tighter script, and if only Cornish had been on her game, *W.E.* might have been a triumph instead of an interesting but ultimately flawed effort.

A major shortcoming of *W.E.* is that Wally's story is clearly weaker than Wallis's, leaving the film lop-sided. The latter is incredibly rich, touching on key events from her first marriage all the way through a scene at the Duke's deathbed—literally providing a "twist" ending with Wallis dancing for her duke—while the former is numbingly simple and frustratingly flat. Overall, the sleepwalking Cornish seems simultaneously out of her depth and dragged down by the one-dimensional script.

In 2010, Madonna told Gus Van Sant the film wasn't really about the Duke and Duchess of Windsor. "It's really about this other woman's spiritual journey, and the Duchess is kind of her spiritual guide."

The Duke and Duchess segment, the only part of the film anyone remembers, is far more satisfying. Madonna got to know more about Simpson once she moved to **England**, "Like Wallis Simpson, I felt like an outsider. I thought, 'Life is so different here, and I'm used to being a **New Yorker**, and I have to learn how to drive on the other side of the road.' Suddenly, I found myself living out in an English country house and trying to find my way in this world, so I decided to really take it on and do research and find out about English history and learn about the royal family."

Madonna has said she didn't want to do a straight biopic, but the evidence shows she could have pulled off a great one. Riseborough is far prettier than the real Mrs. Simpson but a close enough double, and she's got the Duchess's mannerisms down pat without venturing into mimicry. D'Arcy is slightly modelly and wooden. Still, the two of them have good chemistry, not just good clothes and breeding.

The film's two most memorable scenes are a party at which the Duke and Duchess anachronistically cut loose to a **Sex** Pistols tune, and an interaction between Wally and Wallis in which Wallis sharply turns on Wally and snaps, "Get a life!"

What Madonna **fan** hasn't needed to hear *that* at some point?

The bottom line: *W.E.* is an uneven but respectable film that makes an impression, a film of which Madonna can and should be proud, and that most audiences would find entertaining on some level.

The film was first premiered, out of competition, at the **Venice Film Festival** on September 1, 2011. The film's North American premiere was on September 12, 2011, at the Toronto International Film Festival. Madonna gave

—MICHAEL MUSTO

GREGORY PACE

"W.E. is an elegant, ambitious and relentlessly monotonous film." —ROGER EBERT, *ROGEREBERT.COM* (2012)

a short, warm speech thanking Canada and reminiscing about the time she was almost arrested while in Toronto on her ***Blond Ambition World Tour***. Rumors swirled that she'd insisted the fest's volunteers turn their backs when she passed them; **Liz Rosenberg** issued a statement denying it.

The US premiere on January 23, 2012, at the **Ziegfeld** found Madonna wearing a suitably empress-ive Marchesa gown. She did a full red carpet sweep and then spoke passionately, emotionally before the film screened, saying it is, in part, about "having the courage to know when it's not love." Tears welled in Madonna's **eyes** when she ended her speech by thanking her **mother**.

Budgeted at nearly $30 million, *W.E.* took in a mere $583,455 in the US and another $284,984 overseas.

"IS MAKING A FILM RE-INVENTING MYSELF? I DON'T THINK SO. I'M JUST TELLING STORIES WITH DIFFERENT CLOTHES ON."
—MADONNA, *THE ADVOCATE* (2012)

"THE MOVIE IS A FOLLY, A DESULTORY VANITY PROJECT FOR ITS DIRECTOR AND COWRITER. BUT FOR THOSE VERY REASONS, *W.E.*, BY WORLD-RENOWNED PERSONAGE AND LESSER-KNOWN FILMMAKER MADONNA, IS NOT WITHOUT TWISTED INTEREST."
—LISA SCHWARZBAUM, *ENTERTAINMENT WEEKLY* (2012)

"… [I]T'S DESIGNER VIAGRA."
—BAZ BAMIGBOYE, *DAILY MAIL* (2011)

"*W.E.* DOES HAVE ITS SHARE OF POTENTIAL CAMP MOMENTS, AS WHEN THE FEMALE DOUBLES (WASN'T THIS WHAT *DESPERATELY SEEKING SUSAN* WAS ABOUT?), WALLY AND WALLIS, CROSS TIME AND MEET EACH OTHER IN THE SAME SPACE SO ONE CAN OFFER THE OTHER EXISTENTIAL ADVICE … YET MADONNA HANDLES THIS FILM LIKE A MASTERFUL AESTHETICIAN."
—DIEGO COSTA, *SLANT* (2011)

WEBER, BRUCE: *b. March 29, 1946.* He's the fashion photographer whose fetishization of the male form in the early '80s ushered in a new **commercial**, erotic appreciation of men's bodies, most iconically with his image of Olympic star Tom Hintnaus in tightie whities for Calvin Klein.

For the December 1986 issue of *Life* **magazine**, Weber shot Madonna with all of her siblings in **New York**'s Little Italy. The rest of the **black-and-white** shoot had a distinctly retro feel, with Madonna in poses inspired by **Marilyn Monroe** and James Dean, reading an Alfred Hitchcock biography, kissing a mirror and **flirting** with boys on the street. Incredible alternate takes appeared in the Italian magazine *Lei* (February 1987).

Madonna used an image from the sessions as the cover of her ***Who's That Girl World Tour*** program (it was also sold as a poster). A dress from the shoot was offered at **auction** with an estimate of $40,000–$50,000 in 2012, but went unsold.

WEBBER, ANDREW LLOYD: *b. March 22, 1948.* British composer of some of the most widely seen musicals ever staged, including *Jesus Christ Superstar* (1970), *Evita* (1976), *Cats* (1981) and *The Phantom of the Opera* (1986).

When Oliver Stone was set to make the film version of Webber's *Evita*, Webber was turned off because Madonna asked for script approval and **ballsily** suggested she might wanna futz with his score.

Nonetheless, Madonna and the relatively unknown **Antonio Banderas** were on hand on February 25, 1991, at a Los Angeles Music Centre (1135 N. Grand Ave., LA, CA) benefactors' dinner, at which she presented Webber with a lifetime achievement **award**. She was wearing one of the dresses she'd worn when posing for *Vanity Fair* (April 1991). This appearance was one many saw as a way to cement in the public's mind that she was going to star in the movie version of *Evita*. The deal fell apart at the time, but Webber was supportive of Alan Parker's eventual choice of Madonna.

"I always thought Madonna was a very, very intelligent idea … She plays Madonna, really," he told Barbara Walters in 1996.

Webber **worked** with Madonna on her interpretation, including in the recording studio. Webber warmly thanked her for singing **"You Must Love Me"** when he and **Tim Rice** won the Best **Original** Song **Oscar**.

Webber said in 2011 that he had another **job** for Madonna. "I bet you this never, ever happens, but you know who would make a great 'Norma Desmond' on screen? Madonna … she's the right age."

Webber's musical version of *Sunset Boulevard* (1950) had starred **Glenn Close** on Broadway, and while it didn't become one of his biggest hits, it has been talked about for the big screen ever since it opened in 1993. It's a daunting job, considering the original film on which the musical is based is considered one of the greatest ever made. Then there's the little problem that if Madonna were to do it, the media would immediately announce she was playing herself, a crazy old lady who doesn't realize she's passé.

"I've not got through to her. She hasn't taken my call this time," Webber said in 2011. If Andrew Lloyd Webber calls, she's not here.

WEBSTER HALL: *125 E. 11th St., NY, NY.* Night club in a building protected as a historic landmark, which is basically the only way to ensure cool structures in **NYC** aren't bulldozed to make way for condos.

Madonna's most famous affiliation with Webster Hall happened on March 18, 1995: She threw a pajama party to promote *Bedtime Stories*, appearing on stage in powder-blue PJs on a bed to read to her audience of 2,000 (radio contest winners) from the **book** *Miss Spider's Tea Party* by David Kirk (1994). Madonna wasn't thrilled with her loud, unruly guests, surveying the crowd and grousing, "So it's New York City, and this is the best you could get?" People kept interrupting her while she read, leading her to stop reading and demand total silence.

Once the interminable reading part was over, Madonna changed into a cheap, off-the-rack nightgown (no bra) and **danced** her ass *off* and her boobs *out*. Junior Vasquez DJed.

Backstage, Madonna told **Liz Smith** that she was officially going to be doing the movie version of *Evita* and that a planned tour to support her album was therefore impossible. "I've waited years for this role, and I have to pour every ounce of concentration into it. I *love* touring, and I very much want to go out with this album. But I can't—I'd be going straight from months on the road into filming; I'd be exhausted and strained. It wouldn't be in the best interests of the movie for me to be at any less than the peak of my energy."

WEDDING: Madonna's first one was from hell.

When she decided to marry **Sean Penn** in 1985, the couple tried to keep the ceremony shrouded in secrecy, the unintended side effect being that it was all the more attractive to paparazzi. The invitations alerted guests to the date (August 16, 1985) and time (6 p.m.) of the nuptials, but warned that the exact location would not be given out until the last minute.

When guests were guided to Penn family friend Dan Unger's $6 million Point Dume **Malibu** mansion (6970 Wildlife Rd., Malibu, CA), they told waiting press there was no wedding, just a party. The exceptions, **Andy Warhol** and **Keith Haring,** paused to flaunt their joint **gift**, paintings of the **New York** tabloid front pages blaring the news of Madonna's **nude**-photo scandal. Madonna was most displeased—but she got over it.

Her wedding vows were drowned out by fiercely beating helicopters whose occupants snapped distant photo after distant photo. Leave it to the **paparazzi** to find a way to crash a wedding, and leave it to Penn to find a way to welcome them warmly: with a giant "**FUCK** YOU" spelled out in footprints on the beach.

Photog Kip Rano had actually donned camouflage and secreted himself in the shrubbery from 1:30 a.m. on, only to be booted out by Penn personally.

Penn wore a $695 double-breasted **Versace** tux while Madonna was resplendent in a $10,000 off-white **Marlene Stewart** gown with a 10-foot formal train, a pink sash studded with rosebuds and jewels and a jaunty black bowler cap. (The ensemble sold for $81,250 at a 2014 **auction**.) **Herb Ritts** was the official wedding photographer, and a portrait of the bride-to-be in his 1992 **book**, *Notorious*, shows a face of Madonna we've never seen: She's radiant with **nerves**, excitement and **love**.

There were 220 guests at the wedding, including **Rosanna Arquette**, Tai Babilonia, **Martin Burgoyne**, **Cher** & Josh Donen, **Candy** Clark, **Tom Cruise**, John Daly, Emilio Estevez, **Carrie Fisher**, **David Geffen**, **Timothy Hutton**, **Diane Keaton**, **David Letterman**, Rob Lowe, **Debi Mazar**, Steve Rubell, Martin Sheen, Eric Stoltz, **Christopher Walken** and **Andy** Warhol.

Madonna's sister **Paula Ciccone** was her maid of honor, and fought tooth and nail to catch the bridal bouquet. Gossip swirled that she had a meltdown in the bathroom about how everything happening for Madonna should have been happening for her. Hopefully, that's made up. Penn's actor brother Chris Penn (who passed away in 2006) caught the garter. Penn's best man was his best friend, director **James Foley**.

The reception afterward featured mostly swing and jazz records, including Bing Crosby, Ella Fitzgerald and Cole Porter. Vangelis's "Chariots of Fire" (1981) boomed when the couple kissed, and a Sarah Vaughan record was used for the bride and groom's first **dance**.

The menu was fit for a king—and a queen—including lots of Madonna's beloved **caviar**, curried oysters, lobster ravioli, rack of lamb, swordfish and Pinot Noir wine.

Madonna was ecstatic over Penn's gift of a coral pink convertible '57 Thunderbird. She sold it at **auction** after their **divorce**.

When Madonna got married for the second time—to **Guy Ritchie**—she made it almost impossible for information about the nuptials to leak. She chose Skibo Castle (west of Dornoch in the Highland county of Sutherland, Scotland) for its position amidst 7,500 acres of rolling hills, which provided seclusion and security. She booked all 51 bedrooms for five nights, and informed guests they would all be expected to stay on the grounds the whole time (or not come at all), save for a brief trip to **Rocco's** baptism.

Madonna mandated no **TV**, radio or phones, though Calum Fraser, a.k.a. Spud the Piper, provided roving bagpipe entertainment.

Madonna on her *Rebel Heart Tour*: "Getting married? Suckers!"

The ceremony was held on December 22, 2000, at 6:30 p.m. **Lola** led the procession, sprinkling the way with red rose petals. Madonna's betrothed wore full Highland dress with antique diamond cufflinks. (Rocco had a diaper under his kilt.)

Madonna's maid of honor, **Stella McCartney**, designed her strapless ivory silk gown with a long train, antique veil, pearls and diamond bracelets. Madonna's Edwardian tiara bore 767 diamonds, 80 karats total, on loan from Asprey & Gerrard of **London**. Bracelets were by Adler of London. A 37-karat, 2.5" diamond cross she wore had been designed for her specifically by Harry Winston.

When Madonna appeared, the crowd gasped at the impact of the dress and tiara.

The couple was married by a rare female minister in charge of a cathedral, Church of Scotland Rev. Susan Brown, who also baptized Rocco.

Guests included **Ingrid Casares**, **Rupert Everett**, Jason Flemyng, **Jean Paul Gaultier,** Vinnie Jones, **Alek Keshishian**, **Debi Mazar** (one of the few non-family members present at both of Madonna's weddings), **Gwyneth Paltrow**, Jason Statham, **Sting** & Trudie Styler, Matthew Vaughn (one of Ritchie's two best men, the other being London club owner Piers Adam) and Donatella **Versace**.

The wedding cost $1.5 million, or just about $526 per day that the couple remained married. By 2009, Madonna was single and more than ready to mingle.

After the ceremony, guests drank Beaujolais and champagne and ate langoustines, salmon, mussels, Aberdeen angus beef, roasted potatoes, red cabbage and a caramelized profiterole cake baked by a London chef. The great **Luciano Pavarotti** sent a telegram of congratulations and DJ Tracy Young did the music.

Though Madonna has said two of the happiest days in her life were the days she got married, don't hold your breath waiting for her to have a third.

"Although there will be times that your moods may falter, and you'll question each other's actions, the faith and love that you share will help to show that your inconsistency is only for the moment." —JUDGE JOHN J. MERRICK, MARRYING MADONNA AND SEAN PENN (1985)

WEIGHT: Madonna's weight has gone up and down over the years—compare the softness of her *Bedtime Stories* body to the ruthlessly taut figure she cut during her *Confessions Tour* (during which time she was married to a man she said preferred his women lean).

It would seem that unlike most of us, whose bodies change against our will, Madonna changes her body at will. Her micromanagement of her weight is probably the result of her days as a **dancer**, when most people who knew her described her as wafer thin, and when she would survive on **candy** and air.

"I'm not going to get off this ride, stay home and get fat. I've got work to do, children to raise, a husband to please and a world to save." —MADONNA ON TURNING 50 AND SETTLING DOWN, *LIFE & STYLE* (2008)

Is Madonna fat-phobic? She defended **Adele** against **Karl Lagerfeld**'s unkind remarks, but she *did* pen this rather unpleasant passage in *Sex*:

"I had **sex** with someone who wasn't grossly obese but he was pretty overweight. It was the first and the last time ... If I see someone who's not necessarily conventionally beautiful, I can still be attracted based on their intellect or whatever. But fat is a big problem for me. It sets off something in my head that says 'overindulgent pig.'"

That "something" in her head might be the ghost of **Christopher Flynn**.

WEINSTEIN, HARVEY: *b. March 19, 1952.* Colorful film producer who cofounded Miramax (with less colorful brother Bob Weinstein, b. October 18, 1954) and who is now a cochair (again, with Bob) of The Weinstein Company.

Madonna has a long history with the Weinsteins. Miramax distributed *Truth or Dare* with great success, and after that, Madonna appeared in the Miramax releases *Blue in the Face* and *Four Rooms* and provided a **voice** for the Weinstein Company animated film *Arthur and the Invisibles*.

According to Reid Rosefelt, the publicist on *Desperately Seeking Susan*, Madonna and Harvey Weinstein are birds (of prey) of a feather. "They're the same kind of people ... how many people in the world have the mental makeup of Madonna? Not many. And Harvey Weinstein is her equal."

The Weinsteins' biggest gamble on Madonna came when they bought the rights to distribute *W.E.*, which didn't turn out as well for them as *Truth or Dare* had.

"Of all the movies this year that have gotten a bad shake from the critics, this is the one," Harvey Weinstein said when *W.E.* failed at the B.O. "I think they see the personality behind the film ... I wanted to take the adventure with her. She did a damn good **job** ... So, if it wasn't Madonna, if it was Joe Smith, this movie would be getting three stars and about the director we would be saying, 'Wow, this is a talent to watch and a movie you should see.' Of course, Madonna's line is, 'I don't want to be Joe Smith.'"

WEMBLEY STADIUM: *Formerly Wembley, London, England.* Famed **London** performance venue in service from 1923 to 2000 that was demolished in 2003 and replaced by a younger model. **Ageist** Brits.

In 1987, appearing there with her *Who's That Girl World Tour*, Madonna became the first woman in history to top the bill at the 70,000-seater. She performed at the **original** stadium a total of nine times, including *Blond Ambition World Tour* and *The Girlie Show World Tour* gigs.

WEST, KANYE: *b. June 8, 1977.* Rapper and record producer who's reviewed as a genius and yet *still* believes himself to be underrated. West has over 20 **Grammys**, is married to one of the most famous women in the world (you know which one) and has kidnapped the media's attention many times over, whether for stating, "George Bush doesn't care about black people" (2005), crashing **Taylor Swift**'s 2009 **MTV Video Music Awards** acceptance speech in order to assert that **Beyoncé** should've won or halting his concert until an attendee stood up and **danced** ... even though the concert-goer was wheelchair-bound.

Madonna first **worked** with West on the underrated track **"Beat Goes On"** from *Hard Candy*, to which West (a cowriter) contributed a spiffy rap. He filmed a video of himself delivering the rap, which was shown during Madonna's live performance of the song on her *Sticky & Sweet Tour*.

Madonna called West in when she was working on *Rebel Heart*. He wanted to hear her music and offer his opinions, and wound up with credits on four songs, including **"Illuminati"** (in which he is name-checked). Their work together was rushed; Madonna admitted she had to finish one song they created from scratch in four hours because Kanye had to catch a plane. The song was finished, then he kept it for his own album.

"He's a brilliant madman. He can't help himself," Madonna said of West in 2015. "Like, he doesn't have the same filters other people have ... I don't always agree with the things he says or does—I don't always like his music, even. But he's a beautiful mess. I **love** him."

> "Kanye is the black Madonna ... we're comrades in the envelope-pushing genre."
>
> —MADONNA, *NEW YORK DAILY NEWS* (2015)

WEST, MAE: *August 17, 1893–November 22, 1980.* Iconic **sex** bomb, actor, playwright and stage performer whose early movies so scandalized the US in the '30s that Hollywood was pressured into self-regulating via the restrictive Hays Code. She was known for her trademark innuendo, slow swagger and for clinging to her glamour-puss appearance until her **death** at age 87.

West is one of most shocking omissions from Madonna's **"Vogue"** rap (along with Joan Crawford). Now, West—who was a self-made woman, great wit and major **fan** of young bodybuilders—is often conjured as an insult against Madonna, meant to imply that Madonna refuses to accept her age.

Madonna was once compared to West in a more complimentary way. In 1993, historian Carl Anthony noted comparisons between the women as self-marketers and self-appointed sex educators, writing, "It may be easier and more amusing to think of West and Madonna as celebrities than as sociological figures, but it is a glib assumption neither has been flattered by. As West put it, 'In my long and colorful career, one thing stands out. I have been misunderstood.' Or, as Madonna told *Vanity Fair* last autumn, 'I think I've been terribly misunderstood because sex is the subject matter I so often deal with.'"

By the way, West's most notorious creation, in 1926, was a raunchy Broadway **play** entitled simply *Sex*. It was a huge financial hit but caused outrage. Sound familiar?

W. 37TH ST.: Madonna lived in a shithole of a loft on this then-unfashionable street in 1980–81. Despite reports that it was barely livable, it was likely a space and location for which most **New Yorkers** would kill today.

WETTEN, DASS ...?: *Airdates: February 14, 1981–December 13, 2014.* Meaning "wanna bet?" this **TV** show was an institution in Germany, Austria and Switzerland, offering live appearances (but canned vocals) from the top acts of the day. It was held in various venues around the country.

Madonna's first appearance (on this show or one featuring one of its hosts) was a video message: A bratty Madonna (her **hair** still styled from her **Helmut Newton** photo shoot) ate **popcorn** and referenced her upcoming *Blond Ambition World Tour*, introducing **Oliver Crumes**. This video was the world's first glimpse of what to expect from that tour.

At Ravensburg on February 18, 1995, Madonna's lip-synched performance of **"Take a Bow"** was especially odd since **Babyface** wasn't available, so another guy was recruited to mouth his part alongside her. (Oh, that sounded very X-rated.) That same show's performance of **"Secret,"** sans Babyface **wannabe**, allowed Madonna's unique look to be absorbed without distraction: A flowing **blonde** wig and latex top gave her a **Gwen Stefani** vibe. While being interviewed by host Thomas Gottschalk, she was sketched by an artist and signed the artwork with a big kiss.

On February 28, 1998, in a Gothic black vinyl dress and the pre-Raphaelite hair typical of that era, Madonna (with **William Orbit** miming on keyboards and percussion) offered a high-drama **"Frozen"** in a telecast from Duisburg. In an interview with Gottschalk, Madonna spoke less than

"I believe in censorship; I made a fortune out of it."

—MAE WEST (ATTRIBUTED)

Blonde venus on *Wetten, Dass ...?* (1995)

—ESAI MORALES

he did, although she was feisty when asked if she'd heard of the **Spice Girls**. "Am I living under a rock? ... I was the **original** Spice Girl."

She came right **back** on November 7, 1998, her hair dyed black, to lip-synch **"The Power of Good-Bye"** in Linz, then made a bet with Gottschalk that he couldn't do a bendy **yoga** pose of her choosing. He couldn't. Backstage, she met the #1 Madonna **fan** in Holland, who showed Madonna her CD and the **art** she'd created. The card read, "Your **mother** and my **father** are already in heaven ..." and you can imagine the rest. It's always interesting watching Madonna's discomfort at being openly fawned over considering her reputation as a person who craves attention.

Madonna brought her hit **"Don't Tell Me"** to the show in Freiburg on November 11, 2000. She **danced** with abandon, clearly into the song.

On November 5, 2005, from Mannheim, Madonna lip-synched **"Hung Up"** in a boss silver jacket and matching boots, stripping down to a white leotard. She accepted a bouquet of non-**hydrangeas** from Gottschalk, and thanked him by easily tossing a leg on his shoulder, a standard **Ciccone** form of thanks. She admitted her shoulder was still "a little bit hurt" following her **horse**-riding accident.

Madonna never made another appearance on the show, which lost its mojo when a young man attempting a stunt on the live broadcast injured himself so badly he became a quadriplegic. Gottschalk left the show, the new host failed to catch on and it was cancelled in 2014.

"WHAT CAN YOU LOSE": This duet with Mandy Patinkin appears on *I'm Breathless: Music from and Inspired by the Film Dick Tracy*. It was written by **Stephen Sondheim** for the movie in which both Madonna and Patinkin appear, and was produced by Madonna and Bill Bottrell.

In the film, Madonna and Patinkin perform the song side by side at a piano while a heart-tugging montage is shown. It precedes one of Madonna's best scenes in the film, in which she pleads with "Tracy" (**Warren Beatty**) to admit he wants her.

WHAT EVER HAPPENED TO BABY JANE?: *Directed by Robert Aldrich. Release date: October 31, 1962.* If you've never seen this classic film, honey, put the **book** down—there's more to life than Madonna! Not much more. But still.

Robert Aldrich's delicious portrait of reclusive Hollywood star "Blanche Hudson" (Joan Crawford) and her maniacally jealous sis, former Vaudeville child star "Baby Jane Hudson" (Bette Davis), is equal parts thriller and cautionary tale. Though it has undeniable elements of **camp** (every word out of the mouth of Davis's **talent**-free daughter B.D. Hyman), the movie is more a documentary *about* camp.

For many years, Madonna has been compared in a derogatory, **ageism**-powered way to Davis's character in the film.

MTV may have gotten the ball rolling with **TV** and print ads directed by **David LaChapelle** in 1996 that cast Madonna and **Courtney Love** look-alikes in the *Baby Jane* roles, though Madonna was in the Blanche role that time around. **Liz Rosenberg** told MTV that when she showed Madonna (in Budapest shooting *Evita*) the ad, she "was laughing hysterically."

Good humor aside, **fuck** anyone who compares Madonna in her fifties to characters/caricatures like Baby Jane or "Norma Desmond" from *Sunset Boulevard* (1950). Such insulting comparisons reveal a shallow understanding of the films and of Madonna. Baby Jane's story was that she never had **beauty** or talent or success as an adult, which could not be said of Madonna by any serious person. Norma Desmond was at least a character who'd had beauty *and* talent *and* success, albeit one who failed to realize her time had passed. Madonna in her fifties remains an attractive and, more importantly, an intellectually engaged artist. She knows her age is a stumbling block, but refuses to go away; that's the kind of refusal to accept reality that should be inspirational rather than grounds for institutionalization.

Madonna occasionally reveals that flaw that every famous person possesses—a detachment from everyday normalcy that leads to self-absorbed pontification. But she's not delusional, nor is she no longer famous, both of which made Desmond who she was in that film. No one is asking, "Who was Madonna?"

Madonna *is* big ... and even the videos haven't gotten small.

It's not Madonna who is deluded about who she is and what she has to offer; it's her detractors who are suffering from a derangement brought on by the fact that Madonna, whom they're welcome to find annoying or shallow or amoral, is still a force. She's more current than any other pop star of her age ever (you should pardon the expression) has been. And she's not done yet.

But just for the sake of OMG!!!, Madonna is older than Bette Davis (April 5, 1908–October 6, 1989) or Gloria Swanson (March 27, 1899–April 4, 1983) were when they played Baby Jane and Norma Desmond, respectively. She's also older than Rue McClanahan (February 21, 1934–June 3, 2010) was when *The Golden Girls* (1985–1992) first aired and is older than **Joan Collins** (b. May 23, 1933) throughout the entire run of *Dynasty* (1981–1989).

"WHAT IT FEELS LIKE FOR A GIRL" (SONG): *Release date: April 17, 2001. Billboard Hot 100 peak: #23.* The third single from *Music*, this poetic rumination on **feminism** was written by Madonna, Guy Sigsworth and David Torn, and produced by Madonna, Sigsworth and Mark "Spike" Stent. It begins with a spoken-word passage by Charlotte Gainsbourg from the film *The Cement Garden* (1993). (Madonna would sing a song by Gainsbourg's father, Serge, at **Olympia Hall** in **Paris** in 2012.)

The song was performed live at her 2000 **Roseland** and **Brixton Academy** promo shows, as well as in a Spanish version called "Lo Que Siente La Mujer" on her ***Drowned World Tour***. A remix was also used as a video interlude on that tour.

The song was positively reviewed by critics. *Variety* noted: "[*Music*]'s shining moment is 'What It Feels Like for a Girl,' a worldly commentary on womanhood that should give the **Britney Spears/Christina Aguilera** generation of teenage female listeners a little food for thought."

"WHAT IT FEELS LIKE FOR A GIRL" (VIDEO): *Director: Guy Ritchie, 2001.* Madonna's hubby **Guy Ritchie** directed her in this incongruous (one might even go so far as to say *ironic*) video take on Madonna's easy-listening song about girl **power**. Using the Above & Beyond trance remix of the song, the video follows Madonna as a lady psychopath (her hotel room is 666 once that pesky 9 flips) who picks up an elderly woman from a rest home and tools around with her in her hot rod, ramming a car filled with men, tasering a guy at an ATM to rob him, then baiting a couple of cops into a high-speed chase. Madonna and her aged sidekick then steal a car, blow up a gas station and crash into a pole in a sort of suicide mission. It's **feminism** of the Valerie Solanas variety.

For the third time (after **"Justify My Love"** and **"Erotica"**), **MTV** restricted the video; in this case, the station aired it on March 20, 2001 at 11:30 p.m. and then effectively banned it. It was marketed as a video single.

Why ask macho Ritchie to direct a song about the feminine mystique? Madonna asked him which song on her album he most responded to, and he chose this one.

"WHERE LIFE BEGINS": Hot song Madonna wrote and produced with **"Justify My Love"** veteran **Andre Betts** for *Erotica*. The lyrics make plain that this is Madonna's first pro-oral **sex** song, 23 years before she would liken the act to a religious experience on **"Holy Water."** Pervy **Jonathan Ross**'s reaction to the message of "Where Life Begins" was to tell Madonna, "Author! Author!"

The tune makes use of the Kentucky Fried Chicken slogan "finger-lickin' good" and name-drops that chain's founder, Col. (Harland) Sanders, who had gone to heaven (or to hell, if **God** is a chicken) in 1980.

"WHERE'S THE PARTY": Written and produced by Madonna, **Stephen Bray** and **Patrick Leonard**, this unapologetic party anthem from *True Blue* was, surprisingly, passed over for release as a single. It was performed on both her ***Who's That Girl World Tour*** and ***Blond Ambition World Tour***. It was also included on ***You Can Dance***, for which it was remixed by **Shep Pettibone**.

"WHITE HEAT": Song written and produced by Madonna and **Patrick Leonard** that appears on ***True Blue***. The song begins with a slightly edited quote sampled from the 1949 gangster flick *White Heat*. James Cagney, as "Arthur 'Cody' Jarrett" says, "A copper? How do ya like that, boys ... a copper! [Laughs] And we went for it. *I* went for it. Treated him like a kid brother. And I was gonna split 50/50 with a copper. [Laughs] Maybe they're waitin' to pin a medal on him." Edmond O'Brien as "Hank Fallon/Vic Pardo" urges, "C'mon, get up. Get your hands up," to which Cagney replies, "Yeah, that's it, a nice gold medal for the copper. Only maybe he's gonna get it sooner than he thinks."

The song is a fairly typical '80s stomper about a boyfriend who's underestimating Madonna's desire to wear the pants in the relationship. And no, she's *not* just happy to see him—that really *is* a **gun** in her pants.

"White Heat" has a great rock vocal by Madonna. It was performed live only on her ***Who's That Girl World Tour*** before going away for a long time.

"WHOLE LOTTA LOVE": *Release date: November 7, 1969.* Madonna preferred to blast rock tunes like this Led Zeppelin standard while the **sex** scenes were being filmed for ***Body of Evidence***.

WHO'S THAT GIRL (MOVIE): *Director: James Foley. Release date: August 7, 1987.* Madonna's third starring role in a feature film became her second big bomb in a row. Though not nearly as bad as reviewers suggested at the time, *Who's That Girl* is a misguided attempt at a modern screwball comedy that sank without a trace at the box office, dying a quiet **death** amid the hype and critical raves for her world tour and song of the same name.

As is common in the Madonna film canon, she **worked** with some very **talented** people who had participated in, and would go on to participate in, far better projects: The film was directed by her close pal **James Foley**, whose next two movies were *After Dark, My Sweet* (1990) and *Glengarry Glen Ross* (1992); its cinematographer, Jan de Bont, would go on to direct *Speed* (1994) and *Twister* (1996); and **Oscar**-winning actor Sir John Mills was lured into participating.

The movie is like a souped-up take on the previous year's Melanie Griffith dud *Something Wild*, which did only marginally better at the B.O., though the films were conceived and created independently of one another.

Madonna is recently sprung convict "Nikki Finn" (a play on the phrase "Mickey Finn," a drink laced with **drugs** used to knock someone out) who is freed after spending time in jail for a crime she didn't commit. Uptight "Louden Trott" (Griffin Dunne) is forced by his crooked boss and future father-in-law "Mr. Worthington" (veteran actor John McMartin) to escort Nikki to the bus station to be sure she returns to Philadelphia so she won't expose his wrongdoing. It wouldn't be a screwball comedy without

complications, and this film's got 'em, including an antsy cougar and a disastrous **wedding** party made worse by Nikki's uncouth demeanor.

Madonna saw Nikki as "sweet and she's smart and … street-smart … She's resourceful and she's funny, and I think I'm funny." She chose the role in spite of many other offers: "I could have done others, but I liked my character in this one."

Madonna is quite good in *Who's That Girl*, exhibiting no sign of her characteristic stiffness on film. Her mistake is that she employs an annoying **accent** that's a cross between Brooklyn and a bullhorn, and it all but destroys her obvious screen presence and comedic delivery. She's clearly drawing on Judy Holliday for inspiration, but she doesn't modulate it.

Haviland Morris as Louden's veddy cultured fiancée "Wendy" is a delight; watching her **rich**-brat it up at her "bed-and-kitchen shower" as Madonna's Nikki pretends to be Louden's cousin from Atlanta is hysterical to this day, as is clocking Wendy's catlike interest in muscleman "Buck."

Madonna—and many of her **fans**—always liked this movie and couldn't understand why it was so badly

• •

"'WHO'S THAT GIRL?' ISN'T REALLY THE QUESTION. 'WHAT THE HELL HAPPENED?' IS."

—MIKE CLARK, *USA TODAY* (1987)

• •

"IN THE SECOND HALF OF THE FILM, WHEN SHE'S ALLOWED TO PLAY AT HER OWN INSINUATING PACE, MADONNA AT LAST EMERGES AND IS A DELIGHT … IN MADONNA, HOLLYWOOD HAS A POTENT, POCKET-SIZED SEX BOMB. SO FAR, THOUGH, ALL IT DOES IS TICK."

—VINCENT CANBY, *THE NEW YORK TIMES* (1987)

• •

"… MADONNA TURNS IN A CUNNINGLY DIZZYING, OFTEN AFFECTING PORTRAYAL …"

—FRED SCHRUERS, *ROLLING STONE* (1987)

• •

"I PROMISE I'LL SAY HAIL MARYS UNTIL MADONNA HAS A HIT MOVIE."

—"DOROTHY ZBORNAK," *THE GOLDEN GIRLS* (1987)

• •

received in the US. Her guess was that it was lost in the shuffle of her tour, but it is also pedestrian, if harmless and sporadically enjoyable, fare. It was apparently a blast to make, though; Coati Mundi, who acted in the film and contributed a song to the *Who's That Girl Original Motion Picture Soundtrack*, said, "Remember the old days when you used to have **sex** without a condom on a Sunday morning? That's how great it was."

The film was launched at the National Theatre (now *Good Morning America* street-view studios, 1500 Broadway, NY, NY) in Times Square, which boasted one of the largest marquees in Manhattan. Madonna's appearance drew an unruly crowd of 10,000. That was the good news. The bad news, in contrast, was that the opening-day *paying* audience at the **Ziegfeld** a few blocks away boasted only 60 takers.

Though it only grossed $7,305,209 in the US, the film made another $2,548,205 overseas, where Madonna received the favorable notices she lacked in her home country. It was unusual in those days for a film to hit the home video market soon after release, but *Who's That Girl* arrived just three months after its ignominious bow.

"WHO'S THAT GIRL" (SONG): *Release date: June 30, 1987. Billboard Hot 100 peak: #1.* Madonna the singer was unstoppable in the summer of '87, so she racked up another #1 smash with this laid-**back**, almost lazily haunting song that she wrote and produced with **Patrick Leonard**. It was the theme to the film *Who's That Girl*, an unfortunate example of how Madonna the actor was usually very stoppable indeed.

The title was often seized by the media as a good **excuse** to psychoanalyze Madonna and to remark on her enigmatic presence in light of her overexposure. It seems to have faded as a go-to title for articles about Madonna, while **"Material Girl"** has only strengthened over time, like a mighty oak. Or **cancer**.

"Who's That Girl" became Madonna's second song to contain Spanish lyrics, after **"La Isla Bonita."** Though she views it as a lesser work (it was performed live only on her *Who's That Girl World Tour* and part of her *Rebel Heart Tour*, and was left off *The Immaculate Collection*), it was nominated for a **Grammy** and a **Golden Globe**.

"*Desperately Seeking an Audience.*"–*US* (1987)

ALEJANDRO MOGOLLO

LOUDEN, WHO IS THIS WOMAN?: A QUICK Q&A WITH *WHO'S THAT GIRL*'S "WENDY WORTHINGTON"

These days, Haviland Morris acts only whenever her successful career as a real estate agent in NYC allows it. She was "Caroline Mulford" in the ultimate '80s movie *Sixteen Candles* (1984) and, more importantly to us, she was overbred princess "Wendy Worthington" in *Who's That Girl*.

Here, Morris opens her heart a little about working on the movie and her impressions of Madonna.

EM2O: What were your thoughts about *Who's That Girl* being a Madonna movie when you were offered the role?

HAVILAND MORRIS: I don't think I really had any. Had she been in any movies other than *Desperately Seeking Susan* by then …?

I remember at the first read-through of the script thinking that she was so much tinier than I had expected and had the most beautiful skin.

EM2O: How was Madonna to work with?

HM: Fun! Smart! Lively!

EM2O: Did Madonna's increasing fame make shooting difficult?

HM: Yes, she was a big pop star at the time so shooting on the street was difficult because the fans would stand behind the barricades, shouting, "Madonna! Madonna!"

EM2O: What was it like filming the wedding scene on that huge estate?

HM: That was a lovely house. Perfect for Wendy.

EM2O: Do you have any favorite lines from the movie?

HM: People do occasionally quote my line to Buck, "Is it possible for you to be any dumber." [Buck's reply: "I-I don't see how."] Tragic that he died so young. [Muscular James Dietz, who played Buck,

died of Wolf-Parkinson-White syndrome on April 22, 1987.]

EM2O: What was your favorite thing–and what was your least favorite thing–about making *Who's That Girl*?

HM: I loved Wendy Worthington. My favorite thing was just getting to play ridiculous her every day for a few weeks.

My least favorite thing was that I absolutely loved the script, thought it was hilarious and great, and then as the movie started to come together, it just *didn't*, really, and it became clear that it was likely going to be a huge disappointment.

EM2O: Do you have any mementos from the movie, like props, wardrobe or photos?

HM: Yes, I have pictures and Wendy's watch!

"WHO'S THAT GIRL" (VIDEO): *Director: Peter Rosenthal, 1987.* A truly bizarre, makeshift effort to make a movie-plugging video that stands alone, "Who's That Girl" gives us a subdued Madonna dressed like a little boy, porkpie hat perched on her moussed-up brown **hair**. She possesses a **Michael Jackson**-like Pied Piper quality, attracting the attention of two kids (one of whom is *Who's That Girl World Tour* dancer **Chris Finch**) and a Latin hottie who **dance** with her adoringly while she watches or triggers scenes from the *Who's That Girl* film. A malformed subplot finds her wandering into a Tarot card reading that results in the discovery of some kind of crystal. And then everybody dances. Um … and then it ends.

WHO'S THAT GIRL: LIVE IN JAPAN: The first commercially available video of Madonna's *Who's That Girl World Tour* was filmed on June 22, 1987, at Korakuen Stadium in Tokyo, Japan, and sold exclusively in the Japanese market. It contained the entire show. The concert was later made more widely available with *Ciao Italia: Live from Italy*.

WHO'S THAT GIRL ORIGINAL MOTION PICTURE SOUNDTRACK: *Release date: July 21, 1987. Billboard 200 peak: #7.* For her third major film, Madonna had the pleasure of putting together the soundtrack, though she had to choose from her **Sire Records** label mates. The fruit of her labor is this so-so collection whose highlights are Madonna's own songs (she's not stupid!) including the title ballad, the **dance** tune **"Causing a Commotion,"** the sweeping ballad **"The Look of Love"** and the throwaway ditty **"Can't Stop."** In-between are some space-filler songs by acts unlikely to distract from Madonna's spotlight.

The album jacket is her worst, a garish close-up of Madonna sporting bleached, super-teased **hair** and harsh makeup. Thanks to the crop of the photo, her neck looks unnaturally extra-wide. The image was also used as the movie poster in spite of the existence of possibly hundreds of better images from the film.

Nonetheless, on the strength of its two Top 2 singles, the album sold a million copies domestically and 6 million worldwide, meaning it has outsold *Erotica* (though it's a close race there), *American Life* and all of her studio albums after *Confessions on a Dance Floor*.

WHO'S THAT GIRL ORIGINAL MOTION PICTURE SOUNDTRACK

① "Who's That Girl" by Madonna (Madonna/Patrick Leonard) –3:58, produced by Madonna/Patrick Leonard

② "Causing a Commotion" by Madonna (Madonna/Stephen Bray) –4:20, produced by Madonna/Stephen Bray

③ "The Look of Love" by Madonna (Madonna/Patrick Leonard) –4:03, produced by Madonna/Patrick Leonard

④ "24 Hours" by Duncan Faure (Mary Kessler/Joey Wilson) –3:38, produced by Stephen Bray

⑤ "Step by Step" by Club Nouveau (Jay King/Denzil Foster/Thomas McElroy/David Agent)–4:43, produced by Jay King/Denzil Foster/Thomas McElroy/David Agent

⑥ "Turn It Up" by Michael Davidson (Michael Davidson/Frederic Mercier)–3:56, produced by Stock, Aitken & Waterman

⑦ "The Best Thing Ever" by Scritti Politti (Green Gartside/David Garnson)–3:51, produced by Green Gartside, David Gamson, John "Tokes" Potoker

⑧ "Can't Stop" by Madonna (Madonna/Stephen Bray) –4:45, produced by Madonna/Stephen Bray

⑨ "El Coco Loco (So So Bad)" by Coati Mundi –6:22, produced by Hubert Eaves III

WHO'S THAT GIRL WORLD TOUR: *Show dates: June 14, 1987–September 6, 1987.* The tour responsible for launching Madonna's reputation as the world's premier live entertainer, thanks to tweaks in her presentation and her James Brown physicality. For her second tour, and her first world tour,

Madonna incorporated multimedia components, including gigantic video screens, to go along with her already heavy choreography and maturing music. The show wasn't yet up to the theatrical level of her future *Blond Ambition World Tour*, but it was well on its way and is deserving of reappraisal.

This time around, Madonna hired Broadway choreographer **Jeffrey Hornaday** as her tour director, which injected lots of razzle-dazzle into the presentation of her songs. She hired **Marlene Stewart** to do costumes, and collaborator **Patrick Leonard** was music director as well as playing keyboards.

The show opened with **Chris Finch** dashing out to look around, finally expressing elation when Madonna's silhouette appeared on a scrim. Her **dancers** Angel Ferreira (in matador gear) and Shabba Doo (in a gold suit like one Madonna would later wear) executed some nimble moves on either side of the scrim, which had turned into a **Tamara de Lempicka** painting from the "**Open Your Heart**" video. Madonna emerged as her stripper character from that video, complete with gold-tasseled bustier. Her body was transformed from the video—she was now lean and toned. The performance was straightforward after the tease, just Madonna and her mic, ending with a cute side-by-side dance-off with Finch.

A Vegasy, sped-up "**Lucky Star**" followed, punctuated by aerobics-level dance moves. There was a **nervous**, youthful energy to Madonna's dancing in this concert, as if she were trying to cram in all the moves she'd ever learned.

Throwing on a prom dress over the bustier led to a faithful rendition of "**True Blue.**" In the background, concertgoers could clearly see backup singers **Niki Haris** and **Donna De Lory**, who would **work** with Madonna for decades, as well as Debra Parsons, filling out her girl group fantasy. Shabba Doo was on hand to be "Danny" to Madonna's "Sandy."

Things were kicked up a notch as Madonna slipped on a leather jacket and her screens reflected the image of a cathedral. She delivered a spirited "**Papa Don't Preach,**" one of her best vocals of the show. With images on the screen showing conflicting imagery—the earth from space, Martin Luther King Jr., the **Statue** of Liberty, Vietnam War protests, JFK, Nixon, Bobby Kennedy's assassination, the detonation of the A-bomb—Madonna lay still, acquiescing to a **guitar** solo. The message could have been that men weren't doing such a great **job** of running the world. It did, after all, end with **Ronald Reagan**'s face smiling out from the White House. The choreography, dominated by Madonna stamping her **feet**, cleverly evoked a young girl having a tantrum. The final message that flashed? "SAFE

SEX." She was talking about the kind that keeps you safe from both parenthood and **AIDS**.

Up next was Madonna's only live performance of "**White Heat,**" her gangster song. Shabba Doo was **back** in his gold suit, as was Madonna in hers—from social consciousness to Hollywood escapism. Madonna's raspy, tour-tired **voice** was perfectly suited for singing the song live.

"**Causing a Commotion**" was simply presented, allowing Madonna to lose her jacket and perform some funky-white-girl air guitar.

The forgotten *Who's That Girl* movie ballad "**The Look of Love**" was next, a chance for Madonna to catch her breath.

Changing inside a prop telephone booth, she emerged in a clown-like outfit whose skirt called to mind **Cyndi Lauper**. The function of the goofy ensemble (complete with **underwear** that had "KISS" printed on the ass) was to allow Madonna to show off her ability to laugh at herself while performing a medley of "**Dress You Up,**" "**Material Girl**" (she trotted out her Queens **accent** for the latter) and "**Like a Virgin.**" All three songs were somewhat thrown away, spiked with a bit of "I Can't Help Myself (Sugar Pie Honey Bunch)" (1965) by the Four Tops. Madonna seemed to already be impatient with those hits from her *Like a Virgin* album, and was giving them to the audience in a way that she found tolerable—with humor.

In a black boa and sunglasses, pursued by paparazzi, she then tore through "**Where's the Party.**" Hey, paparazzi *are* Madonna's Monday through Friday.

Slowing things down, she gave an emotionally draining "**Live to Tell**" performance, drawing out the dramatic pauses to drive the audience crazy. Somewhat oddly, the image on the screen was a blown up image of Madonna's own face.

Her rendition of "**Into the Groove**" incorporated a remix, leading to her recreating the stuttered "c'c'c'c'c'c'c'c'c'c'c'c'cmon" live. Dancing with Finch, she wore a leather jacket adorned with an **Andy Warhol** soup can, one of Stewart's most inspired creations for the show.

Leaving the stage briefly, she returned in a red Spanish-themed skirt over a red one-piece for "**La Isla Bonita,**" which would go on to be one of her most performed live songs. It wasn't much of a leap from that to the similarly arranged "**Who's That Girl**" which, by contrast, she never performed again.

For "**Holiday,**" she stripped off the skirt and rocked out in red pants, her sweaty **hair** now slicked back like a boy. One of her greatest songs, it's reliably one of her best closers, making for a pleasantly draining conclusion.

MADONNA OFFICIAL TOUR MERCHANDISE

The tour was not without its bumps. In Japan, a thousand troops had to restrain a crowd of 25,000 **fans** seeking to greet Madonna at the airport. When severe storms forced the cancellation of her first shows, despondent fans nearly rioted, and Madonna was confronted with out-of-**control** teenagers soaking themselves in the rain outside the stadium. Promoters had no choice but to refund $7 million to ticket-buyers.

The rain followed her to North America. When the US portion of the tour kicked off in **Miami** (ticket price: 20 bucks!) before 70,000 people (a record for a female artist in that city), De Lory slipped and fell on the stage's treadmill during "Causing a Commotion." With all **eyes** on her, Madonna covered, chirping, "It's slippery up here!"

Madonna had plenty of triumphs on the tour, including her **Madison Square Garden** performance, which

· ·

WHO'S THAT GIRL WORLD TOUR PERFORMANCES

June 14-15, 1987: Osaka, Japan (Osaka Stadium)	July 26, 1987: Irving, Texas, US (Texas Stadium)
June 20-22, 1987: Tokyo, Japan (Korakuen Stadium)	July 29, 1987: Saint Paul, Minnesota, US (Saint Paul Civic Center)
June 27, 1987: Miami, Florida, US (Orange Bowl)	July 31, 1987: Chicago, Illinois, US (Soldier Field)
June 29, 1987: Atlanta, Georgia, US (The Omni)	August 2, 1987: East Troy, Wisconsin, US (Alpine Valley Music Theatre)
July 2, 1987: Washington, DC, US (Robert F. Kennedy Memorial Stadium)	August 4-5, 1987: Richfield, Ohio, US (Richfield Coliseum)
July 4, 1987: Toronto, Ontario, Canada (CNE Stadium)	August 7, 1987: Pontiac, Michigan, US (Pontiac Silverdome)
July 6-7, 1987: Montreal, Quebec, Canada (Montreal Forum)	August 9, 1987: East Rutherford, New Jersey, US (Giant Stadium)
July 9, 1987: Foxborough, Massachusetts, US (Sullivan Stadium)	August 15, 1987: Leeds, England, UK (Roundhay Park)
July 11, 1987: Philadelphia, Pennsylvania, US (Veterans Stadium)'	August 18-20, 1987: London, England, UK (Wembley Stadium)
July 13, 1987: New York, New York, US (Madison Square Garden)	August 22, 1987: Frankfurt, West Germany (Waldstadion)
July 15, 1987: Seattle, Washington, US (Kingdome)	August 25-26, 1987: Rotterdam, Netherlands (Feijenoord Stadion)
July 18, 1987: Anaheim, California, US (Anaheim Stadium)	August 29, 1987: Paris, France (Parc de Sceaux)
July 20-21, 1987: Mountain View, California, US (Shoreline Amphitheatre)	August 31, 1987: Nice, France (Stade de l'Ouest)
July 24, 1987: Houston, Texas, US (Astrodome)	September 4, 1987: Turin, Italy (Stadio Comunale)
	September 6, 1987: Florence, Italy (Stadio Comunale)

· ·

> "IT WAS AN ENDURANCE TEST, AND MADONNA CAME THROUGH IT WITH APLOMB … AS SHALLOW, KITSCHY, POP ENTERTAINMENT—NO BIG MESSAGES, NO REVELATIONS, FAMILIAR SOUNDS AND IMAGES, PLENTY OF CATCHY TUNES— THE SHOW WAS EASY TO ENJOY."
>
> —JON PARELES, *THE NEW YORK TIMES* (1987)

· ·

> "AFTER MADONNA TOLD THE CROWD SHE WAS GOING TO DANCE HER DERRIERE OFF FOR US, OR WORDS TO THAT EFFECT, SHE LAUNCHED INTO A BRAND-NEW SONG CALLED 'CAUSING A COMMOTION.' SHE PROCEEDED TO SHOW SOLDIER FIELD A FEW MOVES THAT WOULD GAIN WALTER PAYTON SOME YARDAGE, WHILE PUTTING A WHOLE NEW TWIST ON THE TERM 'BACKFIELD IN MOTION.'"—DON MCLEESE, *CHICAGO SUN-TIMES* (1987)

· ·

> "MADONNA'S VOICE SHOWED A STRONG RANGE ON SUCH BALLADS AS 'LIVE TO TELL' … AS A DANCER, MADONNA IS SUPREME ON STAGE … AND SHE WORKED THE CROWD EXPERTLY."
>
> —SCOTT A. ZAMOST AND ELIZABETH SNEAD, *FORT LAUDERDALE NEWS & SUN-SENTINEL* (1987)

· ·

was an **AIDS** benefit for amfAR (ticket price: $25–$100). She dedicated "Live to Tell" to her late friend **Martin Burgoyne**. The commercial success of the tour was overwhelming: She sold 150,000 tickets for her Japanese shows at $45 each, and her first two shows at **Wembley Stadium** in **London** (144,000 tickets) sold out in 18 hours, nine minutes. She still holds the record for the largest audience in the history of France (130,000). All told, she took in over $23 million on the tour.

The tour was preserved for home video with *Ciao Italia: Live from Italy*, and broadcast live in Italy to an audience of 14 million.

"WHY'S IT SO HARD": Madonna's first foray into a reggae sound, this *Erotica* track was written by Madonna, **Shep Pettibone** and **Tony Shimkin**, and produced by Madonna and Pettibone. It resides with songs like **"Love Makes the World Go Round," "American Life"** and **"Hey You"** as among Madonna's most explicitly socially conscious **work**. It was given an earnest airing on her *Girlie Show World Tour*.

Also, like most of Madonna's songs that are questions, its official title annoyingly has no question mark.

WILBORN, CARLTON: *b. May 29, 1964.* Wilborn has **danced** with **Paula Abdul**, **Janet Jackson** and **Whitney Houston**; appeared in **Sandra Bernhard**'s *Without You I'm Nothing* (1990); starred in the film *Grief* (1993), directed by the late Richard Glatzer, who codirected **Julianne Moore** to an **Oscar** in *Still Alice* (2014); and was a big part of Madonna's **"Vogue"** video, *Blond Ambition World Tour* and *The Girlie Show World Tour*.

Most importantly, he's the guy with the big, "**fucking blue**" dick from *Truth or Dare*. Or, if you're less sensationalist, Wilborn is the dancer who introduced his cool **mother** to Madonna in that film. Either way, he makes a big impression in the movie.

Wilborn has said when Madonna was interested in hiring him for *Blond Ambition*, she invited him and some of the other prospective dancers to an underground place in LA called Club Louie. They all partied that night, then hung out while Madonna attended a hip-hop dance class in the morning, which was where she offered him a spot on his tour—if he cut his **hair**. He cut it.

Wilborn recalled in 2013 how he wound up being the only *Blond Ambition* dancer asked **back** for *The Girlie Show World Tour*:

"I got a call from Madonna. She initially said, 'I'm in **New York**, and I'm about to go back on the road. I can't find anyone in LA.' That was literally the premise—she needed to find dancers in LA. I got the info from her, and hung up. Ten minutes later, she called back: 'I'm so sorry; I didn't even think to ask you. Are you interested in going back out?' I said yes. For that tour, I actually choreographed and ran the auditions."

Wilborn is close to Madonna's heart; in 1995, when he was down on his luck, she allowed him to live at **Castillo del Lago** for months. In 2016, he appeared in the film *Strike a Pose*.

WILL & GRACE: Airdates: *1998–2006*. Groundbreaking NBC sitcom about a **gay** male lawyer (Eric McCormack) and his straight female friend (Debra Messing), an interior designer. An appearance on the show became a must for all gay icons: **Sandra Bernhard**, **Cher**, **Elton John** and many others showed up to play.

On the April 24, 2003, 40-minute episode entitled "Dolls and Dolls," Madonna played ditzy office **worker** "Liz," sharing most of her screen time with **Megan Mullally** as flamboyant "Karen Walker." Madonna only agreed to the part after viewing tapes of the show and falling for Mullally's comic timing. "I said, 'Okay, but I want my scenes to be with her. She just cracks me up."

Madonna, brunette for her *American Life* era, wore an unconvincing long **blonde** wig for the part,

When the show was taped, Mullally had to announce to the live studio audience to keep it down because its reaction to Madonna was so over-the-top. "Try not to applaud when we do the take ..." but Madonna interjected, "But whenever I'm funny, applaud."

The standout scenes were arguably in a bar, where Liz and Karen engaged in some accidental lesbian action before brawling. When Karen damaged Liz's blouse, Liz's

reaction was classic: "You ripped it! This is everybody's favorite top on me!"

Madonna enjoyed the experience, expressing how much fun it was to play someone "who's just a little bit of a loser."

Though Madonna and Mullally were friendly following the appearance, she seemed to offend others on the show. Cocreator Max Mutchnick—an outspoken essayist—accused Madonna of pretending not to remember people's names on set in order to make herself feel important. "That might be impressive for some development executive who's happy to be in the room with her. But it doesn't fly here." Specifically, Madonna—known to avoid **TV**—had to ask series star McCormack his name. "It's easy, just check the opening credits of the other 120 of these that we've done," he told her. Now, which of the two sounds like more of the diva in that case? Madonna must've known she'd goofed and must've cared: "... [S]he sent me the most expensive thing of roses I've ever seen, and a card from her saying, 'Eric, thank you so much. I'm gonna have your name tattooed on my arm, if **Guy [Ritchie]** will let me."

The episode had a whopping audience of 17.7 million. Madonna received mixed reviews; one thing that mars some of her **acting** performances and was prominent here is a tendency to say her lines with her **eyes** closed. There was, therefore, no Emmy nomination for what is to date her final acting gig, not counting **voice** work, inconsequential *Saturday Night Live* appearances or whatever she was doing in *#secretprojectrevolution* (not exactly acting, not exactly playing herself).

WILLIAMS, PHARRELL: *b. April 5, 1973*. N*E*R*D singer and prolific record producer/songwriter with whom Madonna collaborated on *Hard Candy*. At the time, Williams seemed a passé choice, though **"Give It 2 Me,"** one of his contributions, became an international hit. The song, which bears a passing resemblance to the 2013 Williams song did for Robin Thicke, "Blurred Lines" (which infamously bears something more than a passing resemblance to a Marvin Gaye tune), tanked in the US, while "Blurred Lines" became one of the biggest-selling singles of all time. Madonna was both late and early in her choice of Williams as a production partner.

She told *Dazed & Confused* **magazine** in 2008, "I think Pharrell is a natural musician. I like his inventiveness—he would grab my acoustic **guitar**, which he couldn't play, but start playing percussion on it. He would find bottles and start playing them with spoons. He is very inventive in the studio, he's not precious and I like his lo-fi approach to making music."

On *Hard Candy*, Williams has writing and production credits on **"Beat Goes On," "Candy Shop,"** "Give It 2 Me," **"Heartbeat," "Incredible," "She's Not Me"** and **"Spanish Lesson."** He appeared via video with Madonna on her *Sticky & Sweet Tour*, and performed live with Madonna at the tour's **Madison Square Garden** stop.

Their *Rebel Heart* collaborations remain **unreleased.**

—BRUCE LABRUCE

WILLIAMS, ROBIN: *July 21, 1951–August 11, 2014.* One-of-a-kind comedian and actor famous for his '70s space-alien **TV** character "Mork" and his performances in films like *Good Morning, Vietnam* (1987), *Dead Poets Society* (1989), *Mrs. Doubtfire* (1993) and *Good Will Hunting* (1997), the latter of which was Madonna's favorite film of 1997.

In 1986, Madonna attended Williams's comedy show at the Metropolitan Opera House (30 Lincoln Center Plaza, NY, NY), later saying she was particularly amused by his impression of **Sylvester Stallone** as Hamlet: "To be, or *what*?"

Ten years later, in the film *The Birdcage* (1996), directed by Mike Nichols, Williams played flamboyant "Armand," who instructs a young, dumb and full of questions **dancer** on how to react to female impersonator "Albert" (Nathan Lane). In character, Williams tells and shows the dancer how to "do an eclectic celebration of a dance. You do Fosse-Fosse-Fosse, you do **Martha Graham**-Martha Graham-Martha Graham, or Twyla-Twyla-Twyla, or Michael Kidd-Michael Kidd-Michael Kidd-Michael Kidd, or Madonna-Madonna-Madonna—but you keep it all inside." With the mention of each legendary figure's name, Williams demonstrates his or her most famous moves hilariously, ending with Madonna's from **"Vogue."**

WILLIAMS, WENDY: *b. July 18, 1964.* Schlock jock known for her bluntly expressed, freely offered opinions on *everything*, especially her cutting words regarding public figures like Diddy, **Whitney Houston**, Will Smith and Bruce Jenner ("Belinda, shame on you!"). She has a regular column in the weekly tabloid *Life & Style*, and (since 2008) hosts the daytime talk show *The Wendy Williams Show*.

Williams has expressed disdain for Madonna on a regular basis, often mixing her negative comments with feigned respect, in the same way an online troll will say things like, "I used to be the biggest Democrat in the world ..." in order to give phony credibility to his follow-up statement, "... but I think **Obama** is a **gay** socialist."

In 2013, in response to an innocuous photo of her cleavage that Madonna posted on **Instagram**, Williams wrote, "When I saw the photos of Madonna's sweaty breasts on Instagram, I was saddened. I've always thought of her as a **powerful**, strong woman, but this latest move just seemed desperate. I know that her music isn't that popular anymore and that she hasn't been in a movie in a while, but she doesn't need to show her boobs all over the Internet to get attention."

On a 2014 show, Williams blubbered about how her own 13-year-old son no longer liked her (kid's got taste) as a way to comment on Madonna's use of **#disnigga** in reference to **Rocco** on Instagram, saying first that Madonna was lucky that Rocco liked her ... but then saying Madonna needed sit her "old, wrinkled ass" down. Her rant included the assertion that Madonna is "stupid."

By the end of the year, Williams was reporting on Madonna's topless *Interview* photos, saying, "I think she looks terrific, **haters**."

When *Rebel Heart's* first six songs were released, Williams dragged the project, saying the cover **art** was meant to look bondage-y, and that, "At this point in Madonna's life, nobody even cares anymore." She also made sure to throw in an "I like Madonna" for good measure.

Anti-**fans** like Williams and **Roger Friedman** seem to be expressing their superiority when they claim to respect Madonna and then trash her in highly personal ways; they want to seem above fandom, and also to come off as cooler than the person/phenomenon they're bashing. Unfortunately, they materially benefit from their passion for aggression because, as much as they would like to say otherwise, Madonna is still a touchstone—their outlets get maximum play whenever she's mentioned, even more so when they dare to belittle someone bigger than they could ever hope to be.

Wallowing in negativity sells: Williams as of late 2014 was experiencing her highest **TV** ratings ever. It would be fascinating to see her interview Madonna, but you're more likely to see Hedda Hopper interview Madonna.

WILLIS, BRUCE: *b. March 19, 1955.* Rascally leading man most famous for the *Die Hard* film series (1988–), he was once married to Madonna cohort **Demi Moore**.

Before his first claim to **fame** as one half of the **TV** show *Moonlighting* (1985–1989), he tended bar under the moniker "Bruno." In fact, he did the honors at the wrap party for ***Desperately Seeking Susan*** at the club Kamikaze (formerly 531 W. 19th St., NY, NY) in December 1984. Those must've been tough drinks to serve, considering Willis had auditioned for the movie and been passed over. When Willis was signed as the male lead in the film *Blind Date* (1987), Madonna—who had been attached as the female lead—bailed.

WINFREY, OPRAH: *b. January 29, 1954.* The most successful talk-show host of all time, an **Oscar**-nominated actor and a philanthropist known for helping those in need as well as those in need of, "... a car!!! Everybody gets a car!!!"

In ***Truth or Dare***, Madonna said out of nowhere that she had no interest in living in Chicago thanks to its conservatism, "beside for the fact that Oprah Winfrey lives here."

She had changed her mind by the time of Madonna's first appearance on *The Oprah Winfrey Show*, which aired on December 13, 1996. Winfrey started by announcing that Madonna had never done a **TV** interview that was longer than 12 minutes (um, no), then brought out Madonna for her first interview since giving birth to **Lola**. In high *Evita* mode, Madonna looked like a visiting dignitary in a cornflower blue suit, her strawberry **blonde** hair pulled aside with a barrette. Madonna got big **love** from the audience, which applauded Winfrey's statement that she couldn't imagine anyone but Madonna as Evita. Madonna emotionally remembered thinking of her **mother** while filming Evita's deathbed scene.

MATTHEW RETTENMUND

A totally different Madonna made her second appearance on *The Oprah Winfrey Show* on May 29, 1998, giving Winfrey a totally relaxed interview about posing with Lola for *Vanity Fair*, Lola's favorite words ("pretty!" and "gorgeous!"), her addiction to clothes, her size in clothing ("anywhere from four to … four and a half—just kidding!"), how **yoga** "changes the molecular structure of your body" and her spiritual rebirth as reflected on *Ray of Light*. It was a winning appearance, and came with two of her finest live performances: **"Ray of Light"** and **"Little Star."** Madonna also took questions from the audience.

She was **back** on the September 16, 2003, episode of the show, coming out and dancing to **"Into the Hollywood Groove"** with Winfrey and some **Gap** dancers before sitting for an interview that recapped her **MTV Video Music Awards** appearance with **Britney Spears**, *The English Roses*, *Swept Away*, a body-bending *W* **magazine** pose for **Steven Klein** and lots about **Kabbalah**. A letter from a young woman was read, in which she revealed that Madonna had called terminal **cancer** patient Kerri Yascheshyn throughout her illness to cheer her up. Madonna tearfully greeted the writer of the letter and the deceased girl's family members.

Madonna's final appearance on Winfrey's regular show was on October 25, 2006, in an interview conducted via satellite from **London** in which she spoke for the first time about her adoption of **David Banda**. She couldn't have found a more sympathetic interviewer; as she described her decision to adopt a child from a Third World country, Winfrey said firmly, "… **God** bless you for that."

Along with Halle Berry, **Beyoncé**, **Tom Cruise** & Katie Holmes, Dakota Fanning, Aretha Franklin, Patti LaBelle, Queen Latifah, Diane Sawyer, Jerry Seinfeld, Will Smith & Jada Pinkett Smith, Usher, Stevie Wonder and many more, Madonna appeared on the May 25, 2011, special finale of *The Oprah Winfrey Show*. Introduced by her *A League of Their Own* costar **Tom Hanks** as a "hardworking mother of four," Madonna looked demure in a retro '40s dress. She spoke warmly of her admiration for Winfrey, crediting her with inspiring her own continuing **work** in **Malawi**. Madonna also vowed to "never give up—never!" thanks to Winfrey's example.

Madonna praised Winfrey for "… her unflagging spirit, her strength, the fact that she's earned everything that she has, her compassion … she has a lot of tenacity, she's courageous, she makes people think, she's provocative—but in a nice way …"

Madonna and Winfrey's kinship seems genuine, two women with very concrete ideas of how to live and how *we* should live, who have endured compliments and criticism and seem to increasingly know how to direct the energy inherent in their unfaltering **fame**.

> "I think it's a part of our culture to make ourselves feel better by putting other people down."–MADONNA, *THE OPRAH WINFREY SHOW* (1998)

Lola and Nicole in 2011

WINHOFFER, NICOLE: Madonna's personal trainer, who succeeded **Tracy Anderson**. They met when Winhoffer trained *Sticky & Sweet Tour* dancers. Winhoffer is credited with helping Madonna transform her cut body from a lean machine into a more voluptuous form.

Winhoffer told *New York* **magazine** that training Madonna was a challenge because her body is already so strong. "For her to feel an exercise, I have to put her in these really odd positions to even make a butt lift work. We'll be hanging from the ceiling, dangling from ropes, or on ballet bars. Because she's been working out for so long, it's always a challenge to put her body in a pose that she has never done before."

The women cofounded **Hard Candy Fitness**, with Winhoffer appearing in the accompanying DVD series *Addicted to Sweat*. They stopped working together in 2014. In 2016, Madonna slut-shamed Winhoffer (without naming her) at a gig in the Philippines, claiming, "Once I had a Filipino [sic] trainer, this beautiful, beautiful girl. She was gorgeous and very talented as a trainer. She **fucked** my boyfriend, so I fired her."

WINTERS, SHELLEY: *August 18, 1920–January 14, 2006.* The two-time **Oscar**-winning method actor, known for her wild youth, faulty **memory**, indiscreet memoirs, close friendship with **Marilyn Monroe** and late-in-life, braying supporting performances, bragged to *Vanity Fair* (September 1989) that Madonna had once offered her $100,000 to coach her during *Shanghai Surprise*. "I read the script and told her it was dreck, but she did it anyway." Winters also said she'd put Madonna in touch with **acting** coach **Marilyn** Fried, who coached her "every day" for *Speed-the-Plow* and that Madonna wanted to play Winters in a **TV** movie. Of the last proposition, Winters said, "Fine by me. Madonna is very smart. Very shrewd. She's called the most famous woman in the world now."

Madonna wrote a letter to the **magazine** that was published in its November 1989 issue, asserting that while she'd been "an admirer of Shelley Winters as an actress for many years, I (a) have never met her; (b) have never offered her any sum of **money** to coach me on a project; (c) was introduced to acting coach Marilyn Fried by Lee Grant

> "I think that if you learn self-respect, you don't need to be taught about men."–MADONNA, *THE OPRAH WINFREY SHOW* (1996)

when I did *Desperately Seeking Susan*; (d) have never expressed interest in portraying her in the TV movie based on her life; (e) must have been out of the room when she was preparing me for my role in *Speed-the-Plow*."

Madonna later took Winters' name in vain during her **Ruby Wax** interview.

In spite of the bad blood, Winters appeared in one of Madonna's all-time **favorite movies**, *A Place in the Sun* (1951). It really is too bad Winters didn't learn to **swim** until *The Poseidon Adventure* (1972).

WIRETAPPING: Madonna bugged her phone calls with **Warren Beatty** for inclusion in *Truth or Dare*, but had to edit them out of the final cut when Warren asked her to. "There were some phone conversations I thought were really moving and touching and revealing ..." But, in the end, "... it wasn't fair, plus it's a federal offense."

WOGAN, TERRY: *August 3, 1938–January 31, 2016.* Lauded Irish presenter whose show *Wake Up to Wogan* (1993–2009) was an institution in the UK.

Madonna granted Wogan an interview on a *Truth or Dare* press day at **Cannes** in May 1991. She wore an olive satin dress, her **hair** a tribute to Marlo Thomas's in *That Girl* (1966–1971). Madonna admitted to Wogan that some people are afraid of her. "... I'm very confrontational ... I think it's hard for people to hide from me when they meet me." She also drew a distinction between **fame** and **power**, the latter of which she said she prefers: "I don't think you would find a human being on this earth that wasn't interested in power."

Their interview covered a multitude of topics (**Michael Jackson**, **Sean Penn**), but when Madonna did Wogan's *BBC Children in Need* cause, Wogan complained that she acted as if she had no idea who he was. It's hard to believe she didn't remember the shirt Wogan had worn for their meeting—it wasn't just loud, it was deafening!

WOLF, NAOMI: *b. November 12, 1962.* Third-wave **feminist** and author of the 1991 **book** *The Beauty Myth* who has praised Madonna for how she wields her **power**.

In a 1994 *Esquire* poll of 1,000 women aged 18–24, 58.9% said they'd rather be Madonna than Wolf, but those results should reflect that 74.1% of the women polled weren't familiar with Clarissa Pinkola Estés, Susan Faludi, **Camille Paglia**, Susan Powter or Phyllis Schlafly, so "Naomi Wolf" as an answer probably translated into "anyone but Madonna."

Wolf interviewed Madonna for a December 2011 *Harper's Bazaar* cover story. Wolf wrote in the piece, "At 53 years old, I find, Madonna is scrappy, really smart and young in the way that people who have had a childhood trauma—she lost her **mother** when she was five years old—often seem to be."

WONG, GWEN: *b. August 12, 1942.* For one memorable shot of a topless Madonna grabbing her argyle-socked foot from *Vanity Fair* (October 1992), it's clear shooter **Steven Meisel** was copying a Mario Casilli/Gene Trindl centerfold of this busty Filipina-American *Playboy* Playmate from April 1967.

"WORDS": Written by Madonna, **Shep Pettibone** and **Tony Shimkin**, and produced by Madonna and Pettibone, this track from *Erotica* coulda-would-shoulda been a single, though it definitely has a defensive air about it. The clicking typewriter sound might as well be a rare tape recording of the mating call of a dodo bird—the two are about equally recognizable to today's listeners. It's a deliciously insightful song that shows maturity in its lyrics and its composition.

WORK: In a 1994 sidebar, *Us* **magazine** used a pie chart to represent what portion of Madonna's **fame** was due to her work (as opposed to scandal, just being famous, **sex**/romance, charitable endeavors, or hanging with other celebs). She scored an impressive 41% in the work category, as opposed to **Michael Jackson**'s puny 10%, and Julia Roberts's anemic 19%.

If anything, Madonna is now considered an even harder worker. Her detractors can call her almost anything, but never has she been slurred as "lazy."

MEGA-FAN SPOTLIGHT: DARREN WOOD

Where do I start? As a young boy in the dark countryside of Devon, UK, Madonna was my only shining light. Decades on, I can feel and touch the memory of the "La Isla Bonita" picture disc on my wall. To me, it was always about escape, and that's what the Queen's music does. I still go there in times of trouble. Enjoy the picture of me with my beautiful blond ambition boyfriend in Barcelona for *The MDNA Tour*.

LAVINEL SAVU

X: The **original** working title of *Sex* before **Spike Lee**'s *Malcolm X* (1992) laid claim to the twenty-fourth letter of the alphabet for 1992. That's why there's an "X" die-cut into the **book**'s back cover.

***X-STATIC PRO≈CESS* (EXHIBITION):** Bold, avant-garde exhibition staged by **Steven Klein** and Madonna at Deitch Projects (18 Wooster St., NY, NY) from March 28–May 3, 2003. Coinciding with a mind-boggling 44-page spread in *W* **magazine**'s April 2003 issue, the show one-upped Klein's expectations-shattering **work** with David Beckham, **Brad Pitt** and **Justin Timberlake**, showing Madonna in images representing her as a contortionist, **dancer** and otherworldly goddess. The images were created in the space of one 10-hour day in August 2002, then the installation was constructed by Ada Toll and Giusepe Lignano of LOT/EK Architecture. The show made use of photography, sound and video, including jerky images of Madonna that were haunting to behold.

The show featured a burning **wedding** dress, photographs as large as 8'×26' and images of snarling **dogs**. Madonna transformed into a gothic entity on all fours when not propped up in inscrutable, gem-encrusted masks and gowns.

Klein has refused to interpret the enigmatic photos, saying, "I see this as a platform to bring Madonna's ideas to life—or to **death**."

The title comes from the dissatisfaction Madonna expressed with the end result of the creative process. Klein said, "She started talking about how the final product is always disappointing, how sometimes the perfected performance no longer has the energy that the process originally had."

Lest we forget, the images were originally going to be for a conventional **fashion** spread in *W*, so the brands used were YSL Rive Gauche (leather boots), Prada (tap pants), **D&G** (silk corset) and Lacroix Couture.

The exhibition was memorialized in an elaborate and damn expensive **book** (limited to 1,000 copies) on very thin paper that came in a unique sleeve. The first 50 copies were signed and numbered by Madonna and Klein. Some **fans** who were shut out of Madonna's Tower Records *American Life* promo performance in 2003 were mailed free copies of the book as a make-good. It changes hands for $1,500+ these days.

"X-STATIC PROCESS" (SONG): Written by Madonna and **Stuart Price** and produced by Madonna and **Mirwais**, this intimate ballad from *American Life* is ingeniously constructed as a sort of ballad between Madonna and Madonna. It has a stunning vocal performance by Madonna (both of them!) that would have made it a worthy single choice. It has been performed for *Madonna On Stage & on the Record*, at *American Life* promo gigs in **NYC** and **London** and at *Tears of a Clown* in Melbourne.

An X-rated moment is born on the *Rebel Heart Tour*.

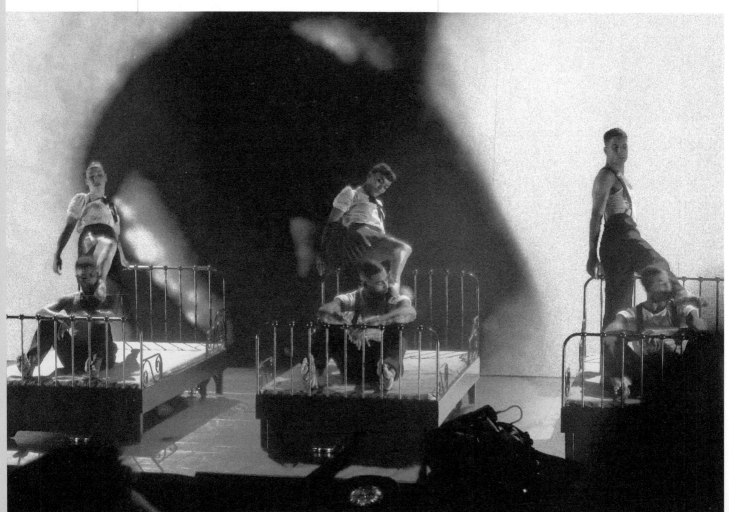

MATTHEW RETTENMUND

YANKOVIC, WEIRD AL: *b. October 23, 1959.* Parodist and songwriter who made a (big) name for himself beginning in the '80s by lampooning popular songs, most successfully **Michael Jackson**'s "Beat It" (1983) as the gourmand-bashing ditty "Eat It" (1984) and Chamillionaire and Krayzie Bone's "Ridin'" (2006) as the send-up "White & Nerdy" (2006).

On June 4, 1985, Yankovic released his spoof of Madonna's **"Like a Virgin,"** entitled "Like a Surgeon," about a quack who somehow made it through the wilderness of medical **school**. The single cover features a Madonna **tribute artist** in scrubs. The look-alike makes a brief appearance in the music video, which is filled with cartoonish gore, Yankovic's characteristically broad humor and send-ups of Madonna's **dance** moves in both her "Like a Virgin" and **"Lucky Star"** videos.

"Like a Surgeon" hit #47 on the *Billboard* Hot 100, making it Yankovic's fifth most successful novelty pop hit of all time.

Madonna allegedly spawned the **parody** by casually wondering aloud how long it would take for "Like a Virgin" to become "Like a Surgeon" at the hands of Yankovic. A shared acquaintance mentioned her remark and the deal was sealed.

In 2013, Yankovic told the author Madonna had been "cool" with "Like a Surgeon," but qualified his comment: "She didn't actually *write* that song ... but she *was* cool with it."

For his *Al TV* series (1984–2006), Yankovic at least twice (1985 and 1996) did phony interviews with Madonna by editing her real answers from other interviews with hilariously self-aggrandizing questions on his end.

YOGA: After Madonna's C-section giving birth to **Lola**, she couldn't go **back** to her usual strenuous workouts. She turned to Ashtanga yoga. In 1998, she told Barry Walters, "When I first started, I couldn't do any of the poses. I used to call the balancing positions the 'humiliation positions.' I just kept falling and falling." But she got there, and would eventually credit yoga for changing her life. Or at least helping make for a stunning *Re-Invention World Tour* moment.

Madonna moved away from yoga following her **horse**-riding accident, focusing instead more on Pilates, but by 2015 she'd drifted back. She told *Rolling Stone*, "But you know, yoga is a preparation for **death**."

YOU CAN DANCE: *Release date: November 17, 1987. Billboard 200 peak: #14.* Rather than releasing a greatest-hits album, Madonna's first compilation was a groundbreaking remix album of some of her best **dance** hits segued into one long grind, made available just in time for Christmas 1987. The concept caught on, and soon artists like **Paula Abdul** and Jody Watley were following suit.

You Can Dance bore remixes by **Jellybean Benitez**, Bruce Forest and Frank Heller, Steve Thompson and Michael Barbiero, and **Shep Pettibone**, who would become Madonna's right-handjob man on her **sexed**-up *Erotica* album.

The only **original** song on the album is the spritely **"Spotlight."** That song was to have been a single release, but fears that it wouldn't be a major hit (it had previously failed to make it onto *True Blue*) scrapped those plans.

The lack of a proper single didn't hurt the energetic, innovative album, which easily went platinum. It has sold 5 million copies worldwide, making it the second-best-selling remix album ever, after **Michael Jackson**'s 1997 *Blood on the Dance Floor: HIStory in the Mix* (with 6 million).

The orgiastic liner notes by Brian Chin make an excellent connection between Madonna and dancing, from club DJs to dancers to the music itself.

On the jacket (by **Herb Ritts**), Madonna appears in a bolero outfit against a flaming red backdrop. The photos were done simultaneously with her taping of a **commercial** for **Mitsubishi** that aired exclusively in Japan.

A promo-only CD and matching vinyl record featuring single edits of all the tracks on the album are highly sought after collectibles, as are three 12" vinyl promo-only singles featuring mixes and dubs of the album's songs.

Note: *You Can Dance* was intended for a much earlier release, but was bumped due to the *Who's That Girl: Original Motion Picture Soundtrack*, as evidenced by the fact that the former's catalogue number precedes the latter's.

"YOU LOOK MARVELOUS": *Release date: 1985. Billboard Hot 100 peak: #58.* Novelty hit by Billy Crystal in character as "Fernando" (inspired by the late Hollywood actor Fernando Lamas) in which his backup singers ask him if a series of famous women look marvelous, ending with Madonna, of whom the character exclaims: "Her **belly button** is absolutely marvelous!"

"YOU MUST LOVE ME" (SONG): *Release date: October 27, 1996. Billboard Hot 100 peak: #18.* Flexing her pop muscle, Madonna made a Top 20 hit out of this downer of a ballad, written specifically for the film version of *Evita* by **original** songwriters **Andrew Lloyd Webber** and **Tim Rice**. (The song is routinely performed in new revivals of the stage version.) The creation of the song was to give the movie a chance for a Best Original Song **Oscar** nomination, which happened; it also won in that category.

Entertainment Weekly wrote: "'You Must **Love** Me' is a sweet nothing ... Let's just hope the sly, frisky Madonna comes **back** to us someday."

In the song (which Madonna has possessively called "my song"), Madonna as Evita sings yearningly of her desire to be loved and accepted. In the film, it's sung when Evita has taken ill and is being cared for by her husband, including being carried up the stairs to what will become her deathbed. Flashbacks to happier times are recalled in montage.

"You Must Love Me" was performed at the Oscars in 1997 and on the *Sticky & Sweet Tour*.

YOU CAN DANCE

① "Spotlight" (Madonna/Stephen Bray/Curtis Hudson)–6:23, produced by Stephen Bray/Jellybean Benitez

② "Holiday" (Curtis Hudson/Lisa Stevens)–6:32, produced by Jellybean Benitez

③ "Everybody" (Madonna)–6:43, produced by Mark Kamins/Bruce Forest/Frank Heller

④ "Physical Attraction" (Reggie Lucas)–6:20, produced by Reggie Lucas

⑤ "Over and Over" (Madonna/Stephen Bray)–7:11, produced by Madonna/Stephen Bray/Shep Pettibone

⑥ "Into the Grove" (Madonna/Stephen Bray)–8:26, produced by Madonna/Stephen Bray/Shep Pettibone

⑦ "Where's the Party" (Madonna/Stephen Bray/Patrick Leonard)–7:16, produced by Madonna/Patrick Leonard/Stephen Bray/Shep Pettibone

"(I guess she never bothered to record 'You Must Impregnate Me' and 'You Must Nominate Me.') But … Madonna doesn't so much snarl the song—and the whole score—as take a plaintive approach that aims to humanize Evita. She's tasteful!"—MICHAEL MUSTO, *THE VILLAGE VOICE* (1996)

"YOU MUST LOVE ME" (VIDEO): *Director: Alan Parker, 1996*. Filmed on August 31, 1996, when Madonna was still great with child, the video finds her standing at a piano (which conceals her **pregnancy**), emoting all **Barbra Streisand**-like. Shots of Madonna's heartfelt performance are intercut with scenes from *Evita*, the film in which the song appears and for which the song was written.

"YOU'LL SEE" (SONG): *Release date: October 30, 1995. Billboard Hot 100 peak: #6.* Written and produced by Madonna and **David Foster** for inclusion on *Something to Remember*, this **power** ballad seemed to be explicitly about not only reminding a man that she will survive without him, but about reminding the world that Madonna was more than **sexy** shenanigans.

"Verás," a Spanish version written by Paz Martinez, was released in Spanish-language markets.

Madonna lip-synched the song on the UK show *Top of the Pops* and performed it totally live on select US dates of her *Drowned World Tour*.

"YOLO" doesn't apply to Madonna, who has lived several times since this 1983 *Island* portrait was taken.

"YOU'LL SEE" (VIDEO): *Director: Michael Haussman, 1995.* Madonna's first "part two" video, "You'll See" picks up where **"Take a Bow"** left off, following a ladylike Madonna on her journey away from her ex, the same bullfighter (Emilio Muñoz) from that previous, massively successful video. She is shown on a park bench, leaving by train and ultimately jetting away from his bad vibes. Auburn-haired Madonna's Lori Goldstein–styled look for the video and the scenes on the train falsely suggest it is a period piece.

"YOUR HONESTY": Funky, delicate *Bedtime Stories* track that was left off that album in 1994 (there was probably a bit too much overlap with the feel-good shuffle of **"Don't Stop"**) but that was officially released on *Remixed & Revisited* almost a decade later. Written by Madonna and **Dallas Austin**, the song was produced by the songwriters and Daniel Abraham.

"YOUR LITTLE BODY'S SLOWLY BREAKING DOWN": Brief song from *Evita: The Complete Motion Picture Music Soundtrack* in which Juan tells it like it is to Evita, pointing out her decline. Madonna's vocal performance here is stellar, filled with defiance and vulnerability. It ends with a haunting **"Another Suitcase in Another Hall"** reprise.

YOUTUBE: You will find Madonna at YouTube.com/Madonna. She joined on Halloween 2005. At press time, Madonna had around 500,000 subscribers and 400 million views.

©CURTIS KNAPP

GREGORY PACE

ZAIBAT, BRAHIM: *b. September 6, 1986.* Madonna met this extremely hot (let's be honest) **dancer** on September 22, 2010, at the launch of her **Material Girl** clothing line at Macy's in **NYC**. He had just turned 24. What else do you need to know, that he was well read?

In 2010, Zaibat's mom Patricia Vidal gave an unfortunate interview to the tabloid press, noting, "Madonna was already a big star when I was a schoolgirl, let alone when Brahim was growing up. The whole situation is very strange." Zaibat said Madonna was just a woman like any other, refusing to accept why their relationship was a big deal.

Zaibat, a Muslim, attended **Kabbalah** services with Madonna and her kids, though there is no indication that he was circumcised for her, as **Guy Ritchie** reportedly was.

He is an excellent dancer and performed in *The MDNA Tour*, most memorably in the steamy **"Candy Shop"**/**"Erotica"** performance, during which the couple felt each other up and usually kissed. He was also a prominent figure on that tour's **"Vogue."**

By December 2013, the couple had split. Three years ain't half bad for a relationship routinely lampooned in the media as a fling designed to stave off old age. Sample comment by **Joan Rivers** in 2013: "The reports that Madonna is engaged to her 25-year-old [sic] boyfriend are false. She isn't marrying him, she's adopting him!"

Madonna's *Rebel Heart* songs **"Unapologetic Bitch"** and **"HeartBreakCity"** have been rumored to be about Zaibat; Madonna is not one of those "we can still be friends" girls.

> "She was just a woman almost like the others. An exceptional artist and world-famous, of course, but a woman first. I was just happy to meet her. But not particularly stressed!"
> —BRAHIM ZAIBAT, *OK!* (2012)

ZARR, FRED: *b. 1955.* A friend of **Arthur Baker**'s, Zarr—a synthesizer genius who also plays the **piano** and **drums**—was suggested by Baker to **Mark Kamins** when Kamins was producing Madonna's **"Everybody."** Zarr wound up playing on every one of the songs on *Madonna*, even though Kamins produced nothing after "Everybody."

Zarr later became a producer in his own right. He also cowrote the 1983 **Eartha Kitt** song "Where Is My Man" and has **worked** with artists as diverse as **Whitney Houston**, Tommy Page, **Regina** and **Tina Turner**.

ZIEGFELD THEATRE: *Formerly 141 W. 54th St., NY, NY.* Legendary, old-**school** movie theater at which several Madonna films have had their **New York** premieres.

Who's That Girl bombed here, but *Truth or Dare* fared much better, raising big bucks for **AIDS** (amfAR). When *A League of Their Own* world-premiered at the Ziegfeld, it attracted the entire cast (minus **Geena Davis**), plus Cindy Crawford, Sonia Braga, Robert De Niro, David Lee Roth, Charles Grodin, James L. Brooks, Nicole Miller and Lauren Hutton. For *Body of Evidence*, Madonna spoke before the screening, saying "I don't think I have to introduce myself, unless some of you don't recognize me with my clothes on," thanked the crowd for coming, then took off ahead of the widely-reported jeers that followed. Madonna's January 23, 2012, *W.E.* premiere found **Patti Smith** watching the movie again (she's a big **fan** of the flick) and was highlighted by Madonna emotionally addressing the audience in ruffled Marchesa.

> "Finally, I would like to thank my mother. Because really, this story is … the journey of a female soul and my mother gave me life, so thank you. And enjoy the film."
> —MADONNA, INTRODUCING *W.E.* AT THE ZIEGFELD (2012)

ZITS: Madonna breaks out easily—"I have adult acne," she has said. When asked why he shot so much **black-and-white** footage for *Truth or Dare*, director **Alek Keshishian** replied, "Because it covered her zits better than color—no kidding."

Zaibat strikes a pose.

MATTHEW RETTENMUND

MATTHEW RETTENMUND

—ED STEINBERG

Unstop

US ALBUMS DISCOGRAPHY

Madonna (1983)

Like a Virgin (1984)

True Blue (1986)

Like a Prayer (1989)

Erotica (1992)

Bedtime Stories (1994)

Ray of Light (1998)

Music (2000)

American Life (2003)

Confessions on a Dance Floor (2005)

Hard Candy (2008)

MDNA (2012)

Rebel Heart (2015)

US SOUNDTRACK ALBUMS DISCOGRAPHY

Who's That Girl: Original Motion Picture Soundtrack (1987)

I'm Breathless: Music from and Inspired by the Film Dick Tracy (1990)

Evita: The Complete Motion Picture Music Soundtrack (1996)

US COMPILATION ALBUMS DISCOGRAPHY

You Can Dance (1987)

The Immaculate Collection (1990)

Something to Remember (1995)

GHV2 (2001)

Remixed & Revisited (2003)

Celebration (2009)

US LIVE ALBUMS DISCOGRAPHY

I'm Going to Tell You a Secret (2006)

The Confessions Tour (2007)

Sticky & Sweet Tour (2010)

MDNA World Tour (2013)

US SINGLES DISCOGRAPHY

"Single" (Year of Release)
Billboard Hot 100 Peak,
Version Pictured in *EM20*

"Everybody" (1982) NA,
US 12" single

"Burning Up"/"Physical Attraction"
(1983) NA, Spanish 12" single

"Holiday" (1983) #16,
UK 12" train-sleeve single

"Lucky Star" (1984) #4, UK single

"Borderline" (1984) #10,
Australian 12" single

"Like a Virgin" (1984) #1,
US 12" promo single

"Material Girl" (1984) #2, UK single

"Crazy for You" (1985) #1,
Japanese promo single

"Angel" (1985) #5, Japanese single

"Dress You Up" (1985) #5, US 12"

"Live to Tell" (1986) #1, US single

"Papa Don't Preach" (1986) #1,
US CD video single

"True Blue" (1986) #3,
Japanese single

"Open Your Heart" (1986) #1,
US single

"La Isla Bonita" (1987) #4,
ad for UK single

"Who's That Girl" (1987) #1,
US single

"Causing a Commotion" (1987) #2,
US single

"Like a Prayer" (1989) #1,
US 12" single

"Express Yourself" (1989) #2,
UK limited edition zipper bag single

"Cherish" (1989) #2,
Hong Kong 12" promo single

"Oh Father" (1989) #20, UK single

"Keep It Together" (1989) #8,
US single

"Vogue" (1990) #1, US single

"Hanky Panky" (1990) #10,
US 12" single

"Justify My Love" (1990) #1,
US single

"Rescue Me" (1991) #9,
UK 12" poster-sleeve single

"This Used to Be My Playground"
(1992) #1, US single

"Erotica" (1992) #3, US single

"Deeper and Deeper" (1992) #7,
US single

"Bad Girl" (1993) #36, US single

"Rain" (1993) #14, US single

"I'll Remember" (1994) #2, UK single

"Secret" (1994) #3, US single

"Take a Bow" (1994) #1, US single

"Bedtime Story" (1995) #42,
US single

"Human Nature" (1995) #46,
UK 12" single

"You'll See" (1995) #6, US single

"Love Don't Live Here Anymore"
(1996) #78, US single

"You Must Love Me" (1996) #18,
US single

"Don't Cry for Me Argentina" (1996) #8,
US single

"Frozen" (1998) #2, US single

"Ray of Light" (1998) #5, US single

"The Power of Good-Bye" (1998) #11,
US single

"Nothing Really Matters" (1999) #93,
US single

"Beautiful Stranger" (1999) #19,
US single

"American Pie" (2000) #29,
US single

"Music" (2000) #1, US single

"Don't Tell Me" (2000) #4,
US 12" single

"What It Feels Like for a Girl" (2001) #23—US single

"Die Another Day" (2002) #8, US single

"American Life" (2003) #37, US single

"Hollywood" (2003) NA, global single

"Me Against the Music" by Britney Spears feat. Madonna (2003) #35, US single

"Nothing Fails" (2003) NA, UK single

"Love Profusion" (2003) NA, US single

"Hung Up" (2005) #7, global single

"Sorry" (2006) #58, global single

"Get Together" (2006) NA, global single

"Jump" (2006) NA, global single

"Hey You" (2007) NA, global single

"4 Minutes" feat. Justin Timberlake and Timbaland (2008) #3, global single

"Give It 2 Me" (2008) #57, global single

"Miles Away" (2008) NA, global single

"Celebration" (2009) #71, global single

"Revolver" feat. Lil Wayne (2009) NA, UK single

"Give Me All Your Luvin'" feat. Nicki Minaj and M.I.A. (2012) #10, global single

"Girl Gone Wild" (2012) NA, global single

"Turn Up the Radio" (2012) NA, global single

"Living for Love" (2014) NA, global single

"Ghosttown" (2015) NA, global single

"Bitch I'm Madonna" (2015) NA, global single

NON-US SINGLE COVERS USED IN *EM2O*

"Over and Over" (1985), Italian single

"Gambler" (1985), UK poster-sleeve single

"Into the Groove" (1985), UK 12" single

"The Look of Love" (1987), French single

"Spotlight" (1988), Spanish promo single

"Dear Jessie" (1989), UK single

"Fever" (1993), UK 12" single

"Rain" (1993), UK single

"Bye Bye Baby" (1993), German single

"One More Chance" (1996), UK single

"Another Suitcase in Another Hall" (1997), UK single

"Drowned World/Substitute for Love" (1998), UK single

VIDEOGRAPHY & DIRECTORS

"Everybody" (1982) Ed Steinberg

"Burning Up" (1983) Steve Barron

"Borderline" (1984) Mary Lambert

"Lucky Star" (1984) Arthur Pierson

"Like a Virgin" (1984) Mary Lambert

"Material Girl" (1985) Mary Lambert

"Crazy for You" (1985) Harold Becker—film clips only

"Into the Groove" (1985) Susan Seidelman—film clips only

"Gambler" (1985) Harold Becker—film clips only

"Dress You Up" (1985) Danny Kleinman—live performance

"Live to Tell" (1986) James Foley

"Papa Don't Preach" (1986) James Foley

"True Blue" US (1986) Ángel Gracia and Cliff Guest—does not feature Madonna

"True Blue" non-US (1986) James Foley

"Open Your Heart" (1986) Jean-Baptiste Mondino

"La Isla Bonita" (1987) Mary Lambert

"Who's That Girl" (1987) Peter Rosenthal

"Like a Prayer" (1989) Mary Lambert

"Express Yourself" (1989) David Fincher

"Cherish" (1989) Herb Ritts

"Dear Jessie" (1989) Derek Hayes—animated, does not feature Madonna

"Oh Father" (1989) David Fincher

"Vogue" (1990) David Fincher

"Justify My Love" (1990) Jean-Baptiste Mondino

"This Used to Be My Playground" (1992) Alek Keshishian

"Erotica" (1992) Fabien Baron

"Deeper and Deeper" (1992) Bobby Woods

"Bad Girl" (1993) David Fincher

"Fever" (1993) Stéphane Sednaoui

"Rain" (1993) Mark Romanek

"I'll Remember" (1994) Alek Keshishian

"Secret" (1994) Melodie McDaniel

"Take a Bow" (1994) Michael Haussman

"Bedtime Story" (1995) Mark Romanek

"Human Nature" (1995) Jean-Baptiste Mondino

"I Want You" feat. Massive Attack (1995) Earle Sebastian

"You'll See" (1995) Michael Haussman

"Love Don't Live Here Anymore" (1996) Jean-Baptiste Mondino

"You Must Love Me" (1996)
Alan Parker

"Don't Cry for Me Argentina" (1996)
Alan Parker—film clips only

"Another Suitcase in Another Hall"
(1996) Alan Parker—film clips only

"Frozen" (1998) Chris Cunningham

"Ray of Light" (1998)
Jonas Åkerlund

"Drowned World/Substitute for Love"
(1998) Walter Stern

"The Power of Good-Bye" (1998)
Matthew Rolston

"Nothing Really Matters" (1999)
Johan Renck

"Beautiful Stranger" (1999)
Brett Ratner

"American Pie" (2000) Philip Stolzl

"Music" (2000) Jonas Åkerlund

"Don't Tell Me" (2000)
Jean-Baptiste Mondino

"What It Feels Like for a Girl" (2001)
Guy Ritchie

"Die Another Day" (2002) Traktor

"American Life" (2003)
Jonas Åkerlund

"Hollywood" (2003)
Jean-Baptiste Mondino

"Me Against the Music" Britney
Spears feat. Madonna (2003)
Paul Hunter

"Love Profusion" (2003) Luc Besson

"Hung Up" (2005) Johan Renck

"Sorry" (2006) Jamie King

"Get Together" (2006) Logan

"Jump" (2006) Jonas Åkerlund

"4 Minutes" feat. Justin Timberlake
and Timbaland (2008)
Jonas & François

"Give It 2 Me" (2008) Tom Munro
and Nathan Rissman

"Miles Away" (2008)
Nathan Rissman

"Celebration" (2009) Jonas Åkerlund

"Give Me All Your Luvin'" feat. Nicki
Minaj and M.I.A. (2012) Megaforce

"Girl Gone Wild" (2012)
Mert and Marcus

"Turn Up the Radio" (2012)
Tom Munro

"Living for Love" (2015) J.A.C.K.

"Ghosttown" (2015) Jonas Åkerlund

"Bitch I'm Madonna" feat. Nicki
Minaj (2015) Jonas Åkerlund

FILMOGRAPHY

The Egg Film (1974)—short; self

A Certain Sacrifice (released 1985)

Vision Quest (1985)

Desperately Seeking Susan (1985)

Saturday Night Live (1985)—TV

Shanghai Surprise (1986)

Who's That Girl (1987)

Bloodhounds of Broadway (1989)

Dick Tracy (1990)

Truth or Dare (1991)—
self; executive producer

Shadows and Fog (1991)

A League of Their Own (1992)

Saturday Night Live (1992)—TV

Body of Evidence (1993)

Dangerous Game (1993)

Blue in the Face (1995)

Four Rooms (1995)

Girl 6 (1996)

Evita (1996)

The Next Best Thing (2000)

Swept Away (2002)

Die Another Day (2002)

Will & Grace (2003)—TV

I'm Going to Tell You a Secret (2005)
—self; executive producer

Arthur and the Invisibles (2006)—
voice

Filth and Wisdom (2008)—
writer, director, executive producer

I Am Because We Are (2008)—
narrator, writer, executive producer

W.E. (2011)—
cowriter, director, producer

#secretprojectrevolution (2013)—
short; writer, codirector, producer

Additional appearances as self,
including non-character
appearances on *Saturday Night Live*
and elsewhere, not noted here.

BIBLIOGRAPHY (ABOUT MADONNA)

A not-very-selective list of books
about Madonna:

Cherish: Madonna, Like an Icon,
David Foy. Ivy Press, trade paper,
UK, 2013. (978-1908005670)

*Complete Guide to the Music of
Madonna, The*, Rikki Rooksby.
Omnibus, trade paper, UK, 1998.
(0-7119-6311-8)

Deconstructing Madonna, Fran Lloyd
(editor). B.T. Batsford Ltd., trade
paper, UK, 1993. (0-7134-7402-5)

*Designer Boys & Material Girls:
Manufacturing the '80s Pop Dream*,
Dave Hill. Blandford Press, UK,
1986. (0-7137-1857-9)

Desperately Seeking Madonna,
Adam Sexton (editor). Delta, trade
paper, 1993. (0-385-30688-1)

Encyclopedia Madonnica, Matthew
Rettenmund. St. Martin's Press,
trade paper, 1995. (0-312-11782-5)

*From Mae to Madonna: Women
Entertainers in Twentieth-Century
America*, June Sochen. The University
Press of Kentucky, cloth, 1999.
(0-8131-2112-4)

Goddess: Inside Madonna, Barbara
Victor. Cliff Street/HarperCollins,
cloth, 2001. (0-06-019930-X)

GREGORY PACE

LAVINEL SAVU

Guilty Pleasures: Feminist Camp from Mae West to Madonna, Pamela Robertson. Duke University Press, trade paper, 1996. (0-8223-1748-6)

Holiday with Madonna, Gordon Matthews & Julian Messner. Simon & Schuster, cloth and trade paper, 1985. (cloth: 0-671-60375-2; paper 0-685-10385-4)

I Dream of Madonna: Women's Dreams of the Goddess of Pop, Kay Turner (editor). HarperCollins San Francisco, cloth, 1993. (0-00-255257-4)

The I Hate Madonna Handbook, Ilene Rosenzweig. St. Martin's Press, trade paper, 1994. (0-312-10481-2)

The I Hate Madonna Jokebook, Joey West. Pinnacle, mass paper, 1993. (1-55817-798-1)

Lady Madonna, Guy et Daniele Abitan. Editions Encre, trade paper, France, 1986. (2-86418-290-4)

Life with My Sister Madonna, Christopher Ciccone with Wendy Leigh. Simon Spotlight/Simon & Schuster, cloth, 2008. (978-1-4165-8762-0)

Madonna, Elena Baroncini. Forte Editore, cloth, Italy, 1987. (No ISBN)

Madonna, Henning Behrens. V.I.P. Music/Paul Zsolnay Verlag, trade paper, Germany, 1994. (3-552-05137-6)

Madonna, Christine Blake. Omnibus, trade paper, UK, 1985. (0-7119-0745-5)

Madonna, Anne Bleuzen. K&B, cloth, France, 2005. (2-915-95703-7)

Madonna, Marie Cahill. Gallery Books, cloth, 1991. (0-8317-5705-1)

Madonna, Theresa Celsi. Ariel, cloth, 1993. (978-0836230437)

Madonna, Nicole Claro. Chelsea House Publishers, trade paper, 1994. (0-7910-2355-9)

Madonna, Daryl Easlea. Sterling Publishing, cloth, 2010. (978-1435125445)

Madonna, Keith Elliot Greenberg. Lerner, cloth, 1986. (0-8225-1606-3)

Madonna, Philip Kamin. Robus, trade paper, UK, 1985. (978-0881884043)

Madonna, Andy Koopmans. Cengage Learning/Lucent, trade paper, 2003. (978-1590181386)

Madonna, Michelle Morgan. Robinson, trade paper, 2015. (978-0762456215)

Madonna, Andrew Morton. Michael O'Mara Books, cloth, UK, 2001. (978-1854798886)

Madonna, Betty Shapiro. Edizioni Blues Brothers, trade paper, Italy, 1989. (No ISBN)

Madonna, Caroline Sullivan. Carlton Books Ltd., cloth, UK, 2014. (978-1780975634)

Madonna, Jill C. Wheeler. Abdo, trade paper, 2002. (978-1577657682)

Madonna!, Mark Bego. Pinnacle, mass paper, 1985. (0-523-42576-7)

Madonna: Bawdy & Soul, Karlene Faith. University of Toronto Press, cloth & trade paper, Canada, 1997. (cloth: 0-8020-4208-2, trade paper: 0-8020-8063-4)

Madonna: A Biography, Mary Cross. Greenwood Biographies, cloth, 2007. (978-0313338113)

Madonna: The Biography, Robert Matthew-Walker. Sidgwick & Jackson, cloth, UK, 1989. (0-283-9905-9)

Madonna: Blonde Ambition, Mark Bego. Harmony Press, trade paper, 1992. (0-517-58242-2)

Madonna: The Book, Norman King. William Morrow, cloth, 1991. (0-688-10389-8)

Madonna & Child: A Maternally Hip Baby Book, Cathy Crimmins. Dove, cloth, 1996. (0-7871-1259-3)

Madonna Companion, The: Two Decades of Commentary, Allan Metz & Carol Benson. Schirmer Books, trade paper, 1999. (0-02-864972-9)

Madonna Confessions, Guy Oseary. powerHouse, cloth, 2008. (978-1-57687-481-3)

Madonna Connection, The: Representational Politics, Subcultural Identities & Cultural Theory, Cathy Schwichtenberg (editor). Westview, cloth and trade paper, 1992. (cloth: 0-8133-1396-1; trade paper: 0-8133-1397-X)

Madonna: The Eighties, Madonna: The Nineties & Madonna: The Millenium, Frédéric Gillotteau. Editions Nemo Media, cloth, France, 2009, 2009 & 2010, respectively. (978-2-918230-00-7, 978-2-918230-04-5, & 978-2-918-230-12-0, respectively)

Madonna: Entertainer, Hal Marcovitz. Chelsea House, trade paper, 2010. (978-1604138597)

Madonna Exposed: Desperately Seeking Superstardom, Jessica Jayne. Platinum Publishing, digital, 2012. (B0086SCUB0)

Madonna: Express Yourself, Carol Gnojewski. Enslow, trade paper, 2007. (978-0766024427)

Madonna: Fighting Her Fade, Michael Essany. Sports Entertainment Publishing, digital, 2012. (B008RADCZ0)

Madonna: Her Complete Story, David James. Signet, trade paper, 1991. (0-451-82240-4)

Madonna Illustrated, Tim Riley. Hyperion, trade paper, 1992. (1-56282-983-1)

Madonna: The Illustrated Biography, Debbi Voller. Omnibus, trade paper, UK, 1988. (0-7119-1466-4)

Madonna: The Illustrated Biography, Marie Clayton. Transatlantic Press, cloth, UK, 2010. (978-1907176197)

Madonna In Art, Mem Mehmet. Pop Art Books, cloth, UK, 2004. (1-904957-00-5)

Madonna In Her Own Words, Mick St. Michael (editor). Omnibus, trade paper, UK, 1990. (0-7119-2139-3)

—AMANDA LEPORE

Madonna In Quotes, Ann Child (editor). Babylon Books, trade paper, UK, 1985. (9780907188315)

Madonna: Inspirations, Essential Works. Andrews McMeel, cloth, 2005. (978-0740754562)

Madonna: An Intimate Biography, J. Randy Taraborrelli. Simon & Schuster, cloth, 2001. (9780743227093)

Madonna: l'itinéraire d'une légende, Caroline Lafarge. Perles De Vie, cloth, 2010. (1-978-2-7466-2651-5)

Madonna: Like an Icon, Lucy O'Brien. HarperEntertainment, cloth, 2007. (0060898968)

Madonna Live!, Susan Black. Omnibus, trade paper, UK, 1987. (0-7119-1376-5)

Madonna: Lucky Star, Michael McKenzie. Contemporary, trade paper, 1985. (0-8902-5233-3) Updated as *Madonna: The Early Years Collector's Edition*, Michael McKenzie. Worldwide Televideo Enterprises, trade paper, 1993. (0-9638519-3-4)

Madonna Megastar: Photographien 1988—1993, Camille Paglia (essay) & Daniel Dreier (captions). Schirmer/Mosel, cloth, Germany, 1994. (9783888144981)

Madonna & Me: Women Writers on the Queen of Pop, Laura Barcella (editor). Soft Skull Press, trade paper, 2012. (978-1-59376-429-6)

Madonna Nudes 1979, Martin Hugo Maximilian Schreiber. Taschen, trade paper, 1990. (3-89450-083-2)

Madonna: NYC83, Richard Corman. Damiani, cloth, 2013. (978-88-6208-288-4)

Madonna: Portrait of a Material Girl, Rebecca Gulick. Courage Books, cloth, 1993. (1-56138-236-1)

Madonna as Postmodern Myth: How One Star's Self-Construction Rewrites Sex, Gender, Hollywood and the American Dream, Georges-Claude Guilbert. McFarland & Co., trade paper, 2002. (978-0786414086)

Madonna Revealed: The Uncut Biography, Douglas Thompson. (Birch Lane Press, trade paper 1991. (1-55971-099-9)

Madonna on Stage, Frédéric Gillotteau. Editions Why Not, cloth, 2008. (978-2-916611-06-8

Madonna: The Rolling Stone Files, Editors of *Rolling Stone*. Hyperion, trade paper, 1997. (0-7868-8154-2)

Madonna Scrapbook, The, Lee Randall. Citadel, trade paper, 1992. (0-8065-1297-0)

Madonna: The Scrapbook, Frédéric Gillotteau. Editions Nemo Media, trade paper, France, 2010. (978-2-918230-24-3)

Madonna: Séduction, Catherine et Michel Rouchon. Editions Michel Rouchon, trade paper, France, 1994. (2-950-4821-9-8)

Madonna Speaks, Bruce Nash, Allan Zullo & Mike Fleiss (editors). Expression Press, trade paper, 1993. (0-941263-83-5)

Madonna Special, John Kercher. Grandreams, cloth, UK, 1986. (0-86227-371-4)

Madonna Special, Jayne Lanigan. Grandreams, cloth, UK, 1987. (0-86227-485-0)

Madonna Special, Jayne Lanigan. Grandreams, cloth, UK, 1988. (0-86227-599-7)

Madonna Special, Kesta Desmond. Grandreams, cloth, UK, 1990. (0-862277-797-3)

Madonna Special, John Kercher. Grandreams, cloth, UK, 1992. (0-86227-956-9)

Madonna: The Spirit and the Flesh, Various. Signet/New American Library, trade paper, 1985. (0-71162-00495)

Madonna: Sticky & Sweet, Guy Oseary. powerhouse, cloth, 2010. (978-1576875322)

Madonna Style, Carol Clerk. Omnibus, trade paper, UK, 2002. (978-0711988743)

Madonna: The Style Book, Debbi Voller. Omnibus, trade paper, UK, 1992. (0-7119-7511-6)

Madonna Superstar Photographien, Karl Lagerfeld. Schirmer/Mosel, trade paper, Germany, 1988. (978-3888142789)

Madonna Ultiography, Kevin Parrish. Self-published, trade paper, 1992/1994/1997. (No ISBNs)

Madonna Unauthorized, Christopher Andersen. Simon & Schuster, cloth, 1991. (0-671-73532-2)

Madonnarama: Essays on Sex and Popular Culture, Lisa Frank & Paul Smith (editors). Cleis, trade paper, 1993. (9-39416-719)

Mammoth Book of Madonna, The, Michelle Morgan (editor). Running Press, trade paper, 2015. (978-0762456215)

My Madonna: An Intimate Friendship with the Blue Eyed Girl on Her Arrival in New York, Norris W. Burroughs. Whimsy Literary Agency, LLC, digital, 2012. (B009QUMAE4)

No. 7 Madonna 2004, Julien D'Ys. Colette.fr, trade paper, 2005. Limited edition of 3,000. (No ISBN)

Not About Madonna: My Little Pre-Icon Roommate and Other Memoirs, Whit Hill. Heliotrope Books, trade paper, 2011. (978-0983294009)

Portrait of Madonna, A, Curtis Knapp. Editions Nemo Media, trade paper, France, 2011. Limited edition of 600. (782-9-18230-28-1)

Reinvención, Germán Weissi, Alejandro Parrilla & Laura Mazzini. Reinvencion.com.ar, trade paper, Argentina, 2013. Limited edition of 100. (No ISBN)

The Sexiest Jokes About Madonna, "Cardinal Syn." Shapolsky Publishers, mass paper, 1994. (1-56171-074-1)

GREGORY PACE

Sticky & Sweet Tour European Memories, Frédéric Gillotteau. Editions Nemo Media, trade paper, France, 2008. (No ISBN)

Unruly Catholics from Dante to Madonna: Faith, Heresy, and Politics in Cultural Studies, Marc DiPaolo (editor). Scarecrow Press, cloth, 2013. (978-0810888517)

Who's That Girl?: The Ultimate Madonna Trivia Book, Michael Craig. iUniverse, trade paper, 2001. (978-0595210145)

BIBLIOGRAPHY (BY MADONNA)
A list of books credited to Madonna as author:

American Dreams (The English Roses #11), Madonna. Puffin, cloth, 2009. (978-0142411285)

Being Binah (The English Roses #6), Madonna. Puffin, cloth, 2008. (978-0142410950)

Big-Sister Blues (The English Roses #5), Madonna. Puffin, cloth, 2008. (978-0142410936)

Catch the Bouquet! (The English Roses #12), Madonna. Puffin, cloth, 2009. (978-0142411292)

English Roses, The, Madonna. Callaway, cloth, 2003. (0670036781)

The English Roses: Too Good to Be True, Madonna. Callaway, cloth, 2006. (B001D8ZYKO)

Friends for Life! (The English Roses #1), Madonna. Puffin, cloth, 2007. (978-0142411148)

Goodbye, Grace? (The English Roses #2), Madonna. Puffin, cloth, 2007. (978-0142408834)

Hooray for the Holidays (The English Roses #7), Madonna. Puffin, cloth, 2008. (978-0142411247)

Lotsa de Casha, Madonna. Callaway, cloth, 2005. (978-0670058884)

Madonna: The Girlie Show, Madonna (preface). Callaway/Boy Toy, cloth, 1994. (0-935112-22-7)

Mr. Peabody's Apples, Madonna. Callaway, cloth, 2003. (978-067-58839)

New Girl, The (The English Roses #3), Madonna. Puffin, cloth, 2007. (978-0142408841)

Perfect Pair, A (The English Roses #8), Madonna. Puffin, cloth, 2008. (978-0142411254)

Ready, Set, Vote! (The English Roses #10), Madonna. Puffin, cloth, 2009. (978-0142411278)

Rose By Any Other Name, A (The English Roses #4), Madonna. Puffin, cloth, 2007. (978-0142408858)

Runway Rose (The English Roses #9), Madonna. Puffin, cloth, 2009. (978-0142411261)

Sex, Madonna. Warner Books, metal, 1992. (0-446-51732-1)

Tom Munro, Tom Munro & Madonna (introduction). Damiani, cloth, 2010. (978-8862081252)

Yakov and the Seven Thieves, Madonna. Callaway, cloth, 2004. (978-0670058877)

It's ENCYCLOPEDIA MADONNICA *bitch!*

Hold on to the past: "Madonna" reads the last edition of this book with its Richard Corman cover.

ALEJANDRO MOGOLLO

Lightning Source UK Ltd.
Milton Keynes UK
UKHW052004030619

343791UK00005B/126/P